FIRST CANADIAN EDITION

SOCIOLOGY IN OUR TIMES

FIRST CANADIAN EDITION

DIANA KENDALL
Austin Community College

JANE LOTHIAN MURRAY
University of Manitoba

RICK LINDEN
University of Manitoba

an International Thomson Publishing company

Toronto • Albany • Bonn • Boston • Cincinnati • Detroit • London
Madrid • Melbourne • Mexico City • New York • Pacific Grove
Paris • San Francisco • Singapore • Tokyo • Washington

I(T)P™
International Thomson Publishing
The ITP logo is a trademark under licence

Published in 1997 by
I(T)P Nelson
A division of Thomson Canada Limited
1120 Birchmount Road
Scarborough, Ontario M1K 5G4

Visit our Web site at **http://www.nelson.com/nelson.html**

Canadian Cataloguing in Publication Data

Kendall, Diana Elizabeth
Sociology in our times

1st Canadian ed.
Includes bibliographical references and index.
ISBN 0-17-605629-7

1. Sociology. I. Murray, Jane, 1960-
II. Linden, Rick. III. Title.

HM51.K46 1996 301 C96-990100-3

Publisher and Team Leader: Michael Young

Acquisitions Editor: Charlotte Forbes

Production Editor: Tracy Bordian

Project Editor: Evan Turner

Production Coordinator: Brad Horning

Editorial and Marketing Assistant: Mike Thompson

Art Director: Sylvia Vander Schee

Cover Design: Sylvia Vander Schee

Cover Illustration: Paul Watson

Composition: Zenaida Diores

1 2 3 4 (VH) 00 99 98 97

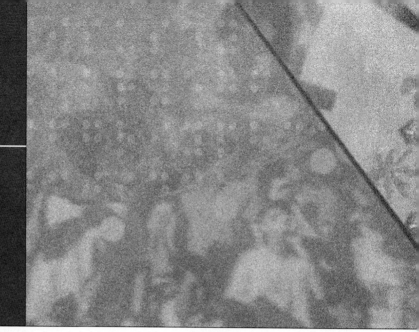

BRIEF CONTENTS

DETAILED CONTENTS

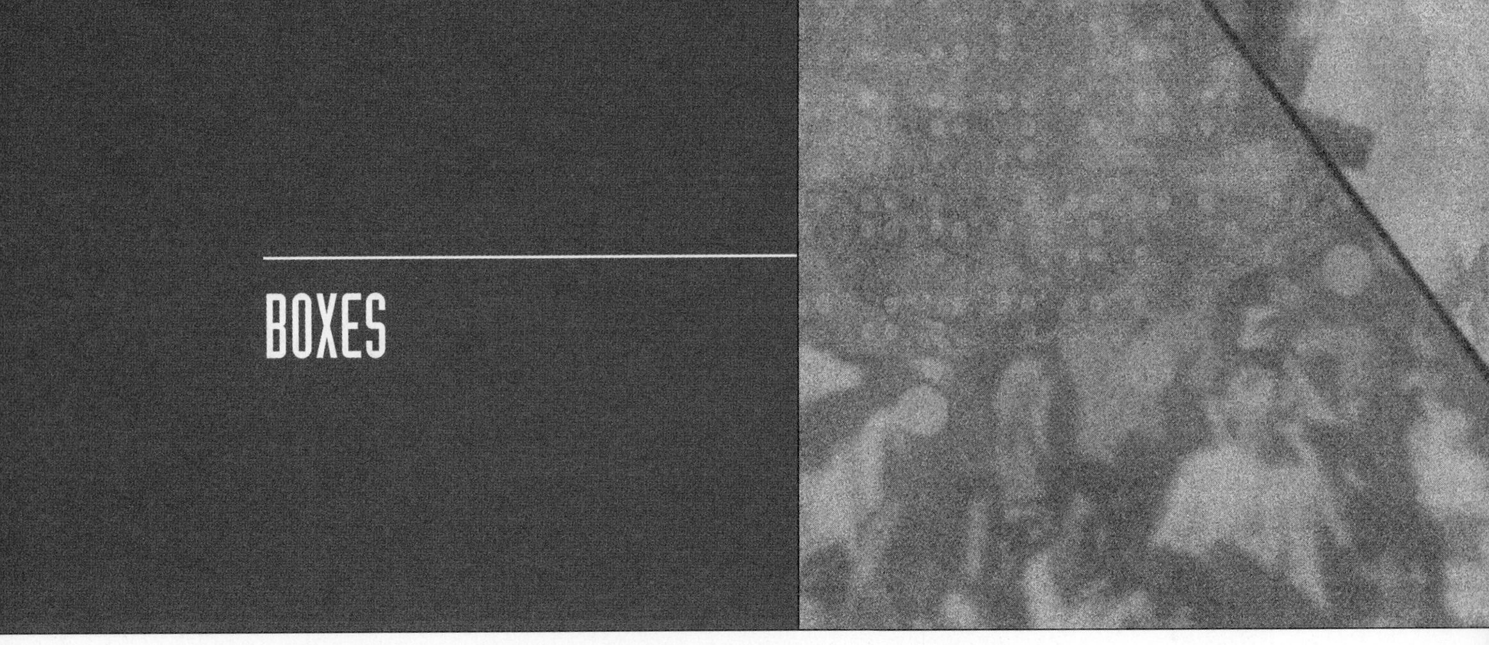

BOXES

SOCIOLOGY AND EVERYDAY LIFE

SOCIOLOGY AND MEDIA

BOXES

SOCIOLOGY AND LAW

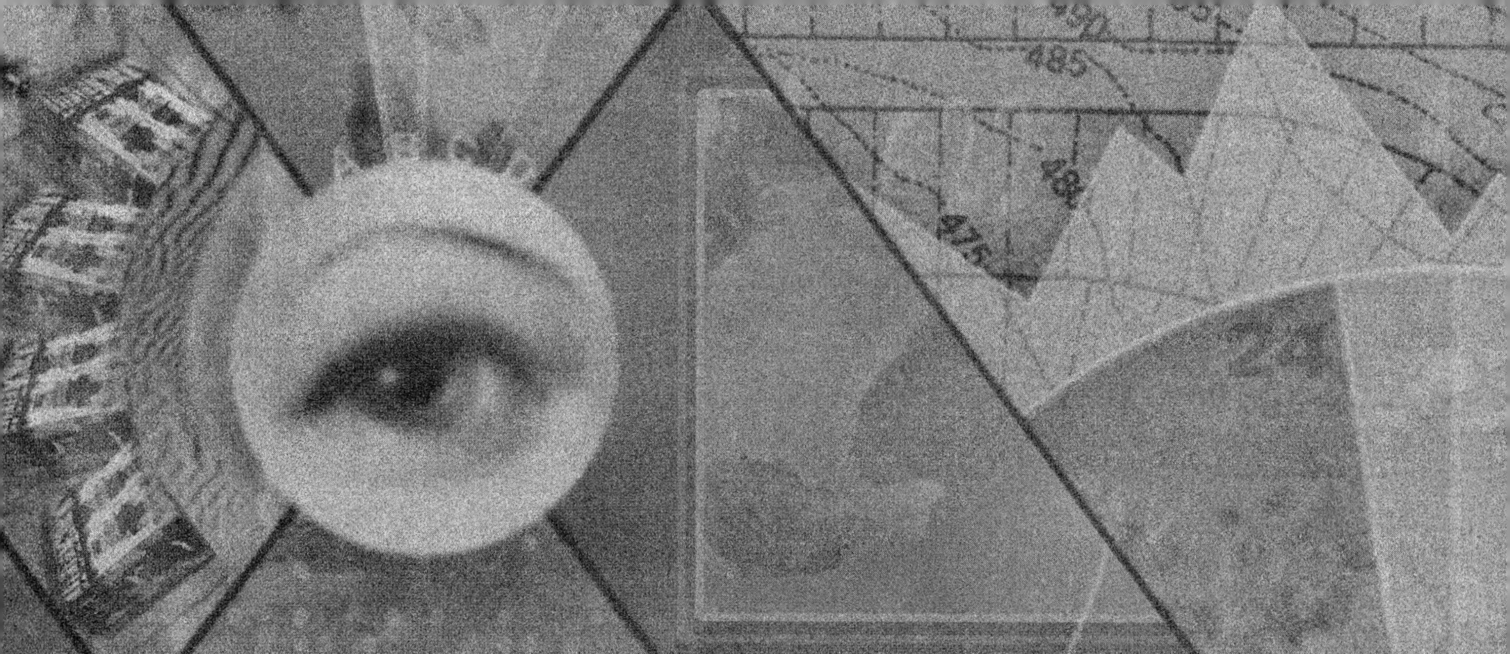

SOCIOLOGY IN GLOBAL PERSPECTIVE

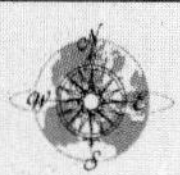

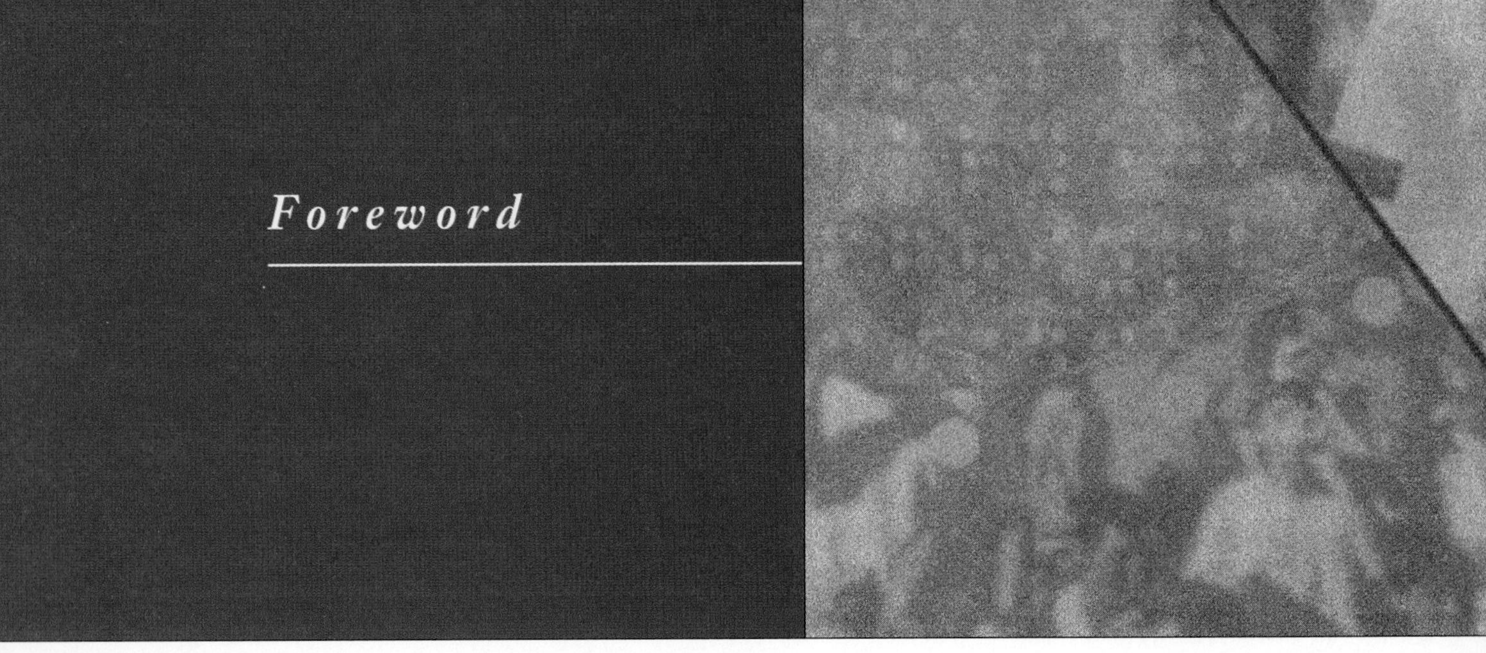

Foreword

As sociology professors, we have a unique passion for passing on the sociological perspective to our students. We are excited when we see students make connections between personal troubles and public issues. We delight in telling students about the first sociology course we took and how we became interested in becoming sociologists. When we watch television, go to movies, or surf the Internet, we look for relevant ideas and examples we can use in class. We spend hours examining textbooks, looking for the right book for our students. And, for many of us, therein lies the problem! The texts we review seem virtually interchangeable. We cannot find a book that captures students' imaginations, enhances our course, and speaks in an authentic way to the diversity of students in our class.

Why is finding such a book so difficult? In a recent review in *Contemporary Sociology*, Jodi O'Brien (1995:307) provides this answer: Many sociology textbooks have become so obscure and irrelevant that they are now the subject of jokes about meaningless education. This observation, confirmed by other instructors, explains why I spent three years writing *Sociology In Our Times:* I do not want students to see sociology as irrelevant or boring when the sociological perspective has so much to contribute to a better understanding of the complex world in which we live. As a student in one of my classes stated, "sociology opened up new compartments in my mind."

To those students: Welcome to *Sociology In Our Times!* This book has been written with you—the student—in mind. I enjoy interacting with students in my introductory sociology classes, and I now look forward to your questions and comments about sociology and this text. I hope you will find sociology as fascinating as I did when I took my first courst in sociology. After majoring in another field, I enrolled in Introduction to Sociology because it met the social science requirement for my degree. Once in sociology, I began to explore all aspects of social life. I saw that sociology helps all of us gain a better understanding of ourselves and others. I became aware that our behaviour is largely shaped by the groups to which we belong and the society in which we live. Sociology helped me to look beyond my personal experiences and gain insights into the larger world order. Little did I know that taking introductory sociology would change my career plans! I eventually pursued my master's and Ph.D. in sociology and have taught numerous sociology courses at various colleges and universities.

Although we will part company at the end of this book, I hope you will choose to pursue additional studies in sociology by taking other courses. If you wish to comment on different sections of *Sociology In Our Times*, I welcome (and will respond to) your messages.

Diana Kendall
Austin Community College
1212 Rio Grande
Austin, TX 78701
Internet address: dkendall@austin.cc.tx.us.edu

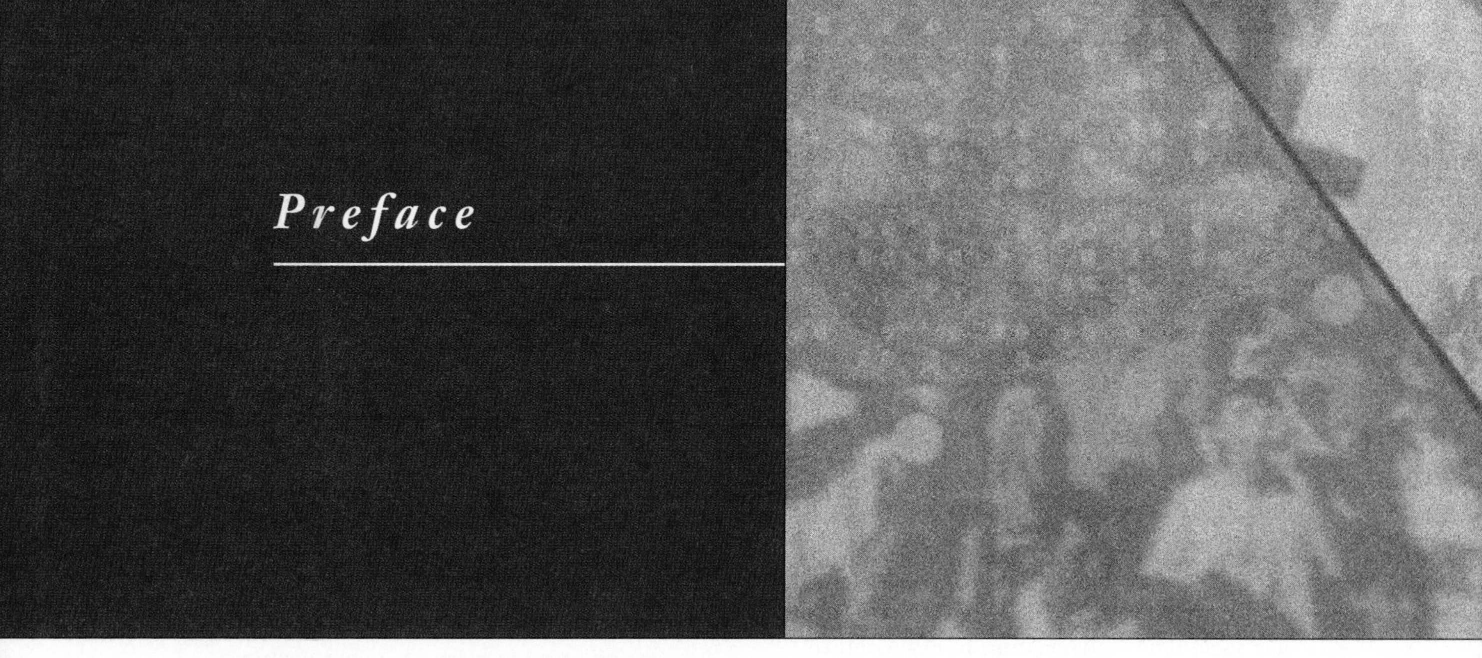

Preface

Sociology In Our Times is designed to be a cutting-edge book that highlights the relevance of sociology for students. It does this in at least two ways: by including a diversity of theory, research, and lived experiences that accurately mirror the diversity in society itself; and by showing students that sociology involves important questions and issues that they confront both personally and vicariously (for example, through the media). This text speaks to a wide variety of students and captures their interest by taking into account the concerns and perspectives of its intended audience.

Sociology In Our Times is unique in its relevance and its use and application of diversity. Throughout the book, timely everyday examples and illustrations have been systematically incorporated to reflect the tremendous range of diverse experiences that constitute life in Canada and around the world. The research used in this text includes the best work of classical and established contemporary sociologists, but it also introduces students to newer perspectives that bring us into areas unexamined in other texts. Instead of simply giving the appearance of inclusion, *Sociology In Our Times* weaves an inclusive treatment of *all* people into the examination of sociology. At the same time, the writing style remains both accessible and engaging for students. Not only are concepts and theories presented in a straightforward and understandable way, but the wealth of concrete examples and lived experiences makes the relevance of sociological theory and research abundantly clear.

DISTINCTIVE FEATURES

The following special features are specifically designed to reflect the themes of relevance and diversity in *Sociology In Our Times*, as well as to support student learning.

LIVED EXPERIENCES

Authentic first-person accounts are used as opening vignettes and throughout each chapter to create interest and give concrete meaning to the topics being discussed. Lived experiences including racism, child poverty, environmental activism, sexual harassment, disability, and sexual assault provide opportunities for students to examine social life beyond their own experiences and to examine class, ethnicity, gender, and age from diverse perspectives. An unusually wide range of diverse experiences—both positive and negative—is systematically incorporated to expose students to a multiplicity of viewpoints. These lived experiences were selected for their ability to speak to students, to assist them in learning concepts and theories, and to determine how they can be applied to other situations.

DISTINCTIVE BOXES

Each chapter contains four boxes: Sociology and Everyday Life, Sociology and Law, Sociology and Media, and Sociology in Global Perspective. The themes and content of these boxes were selected to expand students' depth of knowledge and to give them the opportunity to apply their sociological imagination in new contexts.

- *Sociology and Everyday Life*. This box, located near the start of each chapter, is a brief quiz that relates the sociological perspective to the pressing social issues presented in the opening vignette. (Answers are given on a subsequent page.) Is sexual assault a personal trouble or a social issue? Does increasing cultural diversity lead to an increasing incidence of hate crimes and racism? Are the rich getting richer and the poor getting poorer? Topics such as these will pique the interest of students.
- *Sociology and Law*. Based on the latest legal research, this box encourages students to think critically about the many ties between sociology and law. Topics such as child abuse, assisted suicide, social welfare, and social activism, and equal justice under the law encourage students to apply the sociological imagination to contemporary issues and provide a springboard for discussion.
- *Sociology and Media*. Like most people in our society, students get much of their information about the social world from the media. A significant benefit of a sociology course is encouragement to think critically about such information. Focusing on various types of media depictions—including television news, daytime talk shows, television commercials and magazine advertisements, cartoons, movies, and mainstream and alternative presses—Sociology and Media boxes provide an overview of sociological topics as seen through the "eye" of the media. Topics range from "Racism in the Media" and an analysis of cartoon depictions of labour unions to "The Electronic Church and the Internet" and news coverage of diverse topics such as homeless and disabled persons.
- *Sociology in Global Perspective*. In our interconnected world, the sociological imagination must extend beyond national borders. The global implications of each chapter's topics are explored in these boxes. Topics include rape in wartime, poverty among women and children in Brazil, the international problems of pollution, organized crime in Japan, homelessness in Japan and France, and the politics of disability in China.

SOCIOLOGY IN THE TWENTY-FIRST CENTURY

In addition to highlighting the contemporary relevance of sociology, students are encouraged to consider the sociological perspective as it might be in the future. The concluding section of Chapters 3–17 looks ahead to the next century and suggests how our social lives may look in the years to come. Environmental issues, homelessness, technology, population, deviance and crime, and the economy and work are among the topics discussed.

LEARNING AIDS

Several features are included in this book to promote students' mastery of sociological concepts and terminology.

- *Chapter Outlines*. A concise outline at the beginning of each chapter gives students an overview of major topics and a convenient aid for review.
- *Questions and Issues*. After the opening lived experience in each chapter, a series of introductory questions invites students to think

about the major topics discussed in the chapter.

- *Integrated Running Glossary.* Major concepts and key terms are concisely defined and highlighted in bold print within the text flow to avoid disrupting students' reading. These concepts and terms are also listed at the end of the chapters and in the glossary at the back of the book.
- *End-of-Chapter Study Aids.* The *Chapter Review* provides a concise summary of key points and theoretical perspectives, along with a list of *Key Terms*. *Questions for Analysis and Understanding* and *Questions for Critical Thinking* encourage students to assess their knowledge of the chapter and apply insights they have gained to other issues. The *Suggested Readings* list describes recent publications related to the chapter. This list also is a good source for book review suggestions.

ORGANIZATION AND CONTENT

Sociology In Our Times is divided into five parts.

Part I, "Studying Society," focuses on the sociological perspective and sociological research methods. After introducing students to the sociological imagination in Chapter 1, the development of sociological thinking and the major perspectives used by sociologists in analyzing compelling social issues are presented. Chapter 2, on sociological research, provides a thorough description of both quantitative and qualitative methods. Beginning with Emile Durkheim's study, research on suicide is used to show students how sociologists do research. Experiments, surveys, secondary analysis of data, and field research—including observation, case studies, ethnography, and unstructured interviews—are described to give students a balanced perspective on the diversity of methods used by contemporary scholars.

Part II focuses on "The Nature of Social Life." In Chapter 3, culture is spotlighted as either a stabilizing force or a force that can generate discord, conflict, and even violence in societies. Cultural diversity and hate crimes are discussed as a contemporary cultural issue. Chapter 4 looks at positive and negative aspects of socialization and presents an innovative analysis of gender socialization. Chapter 5 examines social structure and social interaction in detail, using homelessness as a sustained example of the dynamic interplay of structure and interaction in society. Unique to this chapter are discussions of the sociology of emotions and of personal space as viewed through the lenses of race, class, gender, and age. Chapter 6 analyzes groups and organizations, including innovative forms of social organization and ways in which organizational structures may differentially impact people based on race, class, gender, age, and disability. Chapter 7 examines diverse perspectives on deviance, crime, and the criminal justice system.

In Part III, we examine "Social Differences and Social Inequality," looking at issues of class, race/ethnicity, gender, age, and disability. Chapter 8 addresses social stratification and class, including systems of stratification, major perspectives on the Canadian class system, and the causes and consequences of inequality and poverty. Chapter 9 extends the discussion to race and ethnicity, focusing on the issue of racism. A thorough analysis of prejudice, discrimination, theoretical perspectives, and the experiences of racial and ethnic groups is presented, along with global racial and ethnic issues in the twenty-first century. Chapter 10 examines sex and gender with special emphasis on gender stratification in historical perspective. Linkages between gender socialization and contemporary gender inequality are described and illustrated by lived experiences and perspectives on body image. Chapter 11 provides a cutting-edge analysis of aging and disability, including theoretical perspectives and inequalities related to each. Lived experiences deal with the realities of these issues but also show how older persons and persons with a disability resist discrimination and seek to live with dignity and autonomy.

Part IV, "Social Institutions," makes students more aware of the importance of social institutions and shows how problems in one have a significant impact on others. Chapter 12 delves into the economy and work, examining contemporary economic systems, the social organization of work, unemployment, and worker resistance and activism. Chapter 13 discusses the intertwining nature of politics and government. Political systems are examined in global perspective, and politics and government in Canada are analyzed with attention to governmental bureaucracy and the role of political parties. The issues of Quebec separatism and Aboriginal self-government are recurring themes in the chapter. Families and intimate relationships are explored in Chapter 14, and education and religion are presented in Chapter 15.

Part V shifts students' focus to "Social Dynamics and Social Change." Chapter 16 examines population and urbanization, looking at demography, population growth in global context, and the process and consequences of urbanization. Special attention is given to gender and city life and issues concerning immigration. Chapter 17 ends the textbook with a discussion of collective behaviour and social change. Environmental activism is used as a sustained example to help students grasp the importance of collective behaviour and social movements in producing social change. The concluding section on the twenty-first century takes a final look at the physical environment, population, technology, social institutions, and change.

INSTRUCTOR'S SUPPORT MATERIAL

Ancillary materials that enhance teaching and learning are an important feature of a textbook, and the supplements offered with *Sociology In Our Times* ensure that the themes of diversity, inclusiveness, and contemporary issues are consistent with the text. These pieces work together as an effective and integrated teaching package.

INSTRUCTOR'S RESOURCE MANUAL

The Instructor's Resource Manual provides lecture outlines, chapter summaries, and teaching tips, as well as a list of further print and video resources. In addition, guest speaker suggestions, student learning objectives, student projects, and essay questions are included. Instructors wishing to insert their own examples and references can download chapter outlines from the Internet or they may request them from ITP Nelson in ASCII format.

COMPUTER TEST BANK

ITP Nelson has created an outstanding Test Bank with 2000 multiple-choice and true–false items. Each question is categorized as testing conceptual understanding, concept application, or factual knowledge, and a page reference is provided for each answer. It is available in either Windows or Macintosh versions to facilitate the creation of your own tests.

POWERPOINT PRESENTATION SOFTWARE

PowerPoint presentation software is available to assist instructors in managing lectures. ITP Nelson has reproduced chapter objectives, key definitions, and a brief overview of the important concepts in a PowerPoint format. Instructors will also have the ability to add, delete, or modify the slides according to their individual requirements.

VIDEOS

ITP Nelson offers a videotape featuring 180 minutes of 10–15-minute excerpts compiled from the CTV Television Network archives that correspond to each chapter of the book. The segments were chosen to amplify the concepts of each chapter and provide further examples of the sociology of everyday life. A guide to the videos offering a synopsis of each segment, suggestions for introducing the videos and discussion questions, and test questions is included in the Instructor's Resource Manual.

INTERACTIVE WEB SITE

Students and instructors can access *Sociology In Our Times* on the Internet by visiting the ITP Nelson sociology Web site at

http://sociology.nelson.com

ACKNOWLEDGMENTS

Sociology In Our Times, First Canadian Edition, would not have been possible without the insightful critiques of these colleagues who have reviewed some or all of this book: Bonnie Haaland (Qwantlen University College); Dr. Terry L. Hill (Lakehead University); Patti Gouthro (St. Mary's University); Sandra Kirby (University of Winnipeg); and Harry W. Rosenbaum (University of Winnipeg).

We would like to acknowledge the efforts of the many individuals at ITP Nelson responsible for the development and production of the first Canadian edition of *Sociology In Our Times*. Among them, Charlotte Forbes, Acquisitions Editor, for convincing us to take on this project; Evan Turner, Project Editor, for ensuring that once we started this project we never stopped; and Tracy Bordian, Senior Production Editor, whose attention to detail helped to ensure that the final product reflected the efforts of all involved. Your good humour, energy, creativity, and professionalism were greatly appreciated. Thanks also to our research assistant Joanne Minaker for all her assistance in the early stages of this project. Finally, we would like to express our thanks to our families who tolerated the frequent absences required to complete this book under a challenging deadline. Four-year-old Drew Murray best expressed the sentiments of everyone involved with this project. When he was told that Mommy had completed the book, he threw his arms up and shouted, "Three cheers! Hip hip hooray!"

The first Canadian edition of *Sociology In Our Times* is dedicated to our spouses, Craig and Olive.

Jane Lothian Murray and *Rick Linden*
University of Manitoba

Part One

STUDYING SOCIETY

Chapter 1

THE SOCIOLOGICAL PERSPECTIVE

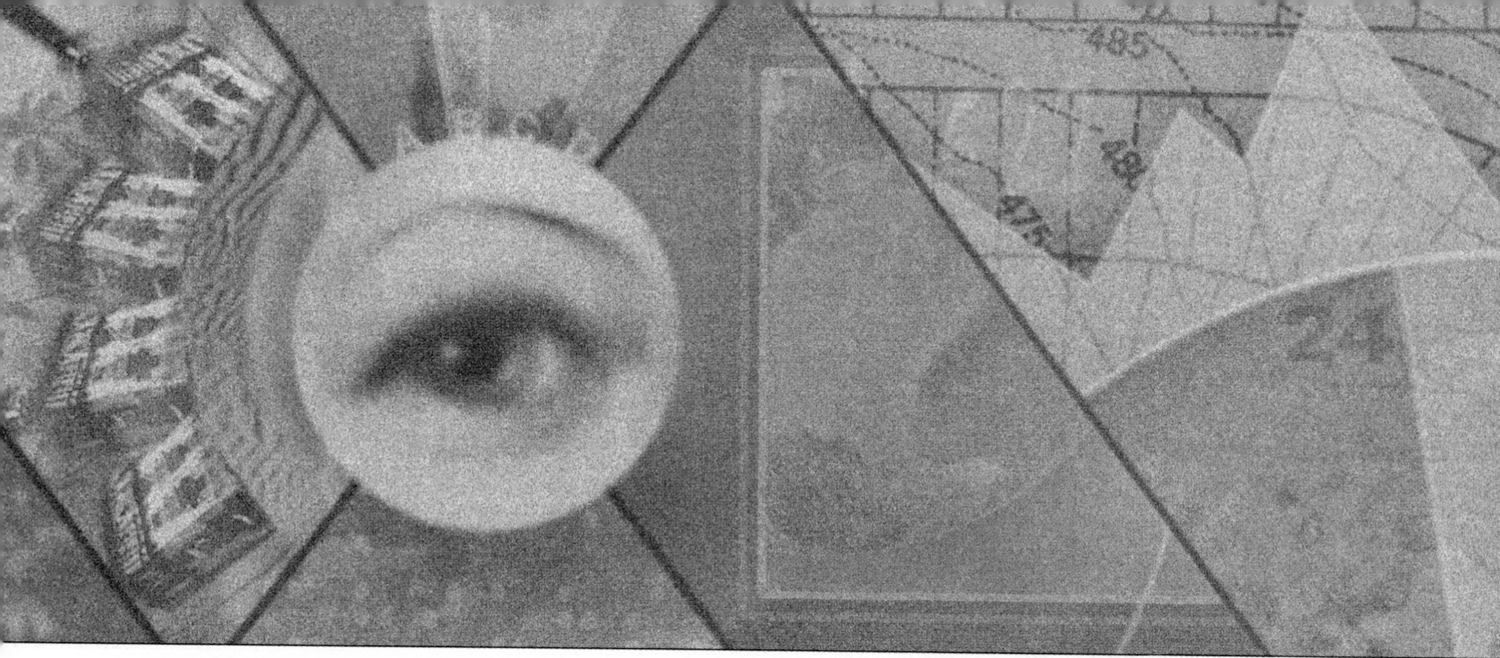

> The ground has shifted, the dialogue is new. The words "rape" and "sexual assault" have come out of the closet. For the first time, men and women in office corridors, night-clubs and classrooms are talking openly about the difference between date rape and consensual sex, about when dirty jokes are appropriate and when no means no. (Nemeth et al., 1992:42)

The following account of a young woman's experience highlights the fact that people may have different views on charged subjects such as rape or sexual assault:

> She met him in a Vancouver bar. He was a friend of a friend. They arranged to go out for dinner, but dropped by her apartment first. There, says the woman, who asked to remain anonymous, it happened: "I said no and pushed him away. He thought, 'I'm going for it,' and he went for it. And by then it was too late. I couldn't get away. It just happened so fast and I was scared to death." Later, she says, fear turned to anger and she decided to press sexual assault charges.
>
> "Everybody I knew said, 'Don't put yourself through this hell.' But I said I don't care, I didn't do anything wrong. And this guy has to pay." A year later, a judge acquitted the man of sexual assault, saying that his accuser may have given the impression that she was consenting to sex. "I could not believe what I was hearing," she says. (Nemeth et al., 1992:42)

In your opinion, was this young woman a victim of sexual assault? Who should define what sexual assault is? Given who we are, what we know, and what we believe, our individual answers to these questions may vary. In this chapter, sexual assault is used as an example of a problem that sociologists examine. It definitely *is* a problem, not only for victims but for the larger society.

Although both men and women may be sexually assaulted, women especially are affected by the fear that the threat of sexual assault engenders in them. For example, the threat of sexual assault makes nighttime a frightening time for women—in the privacy of their own homes as well as in public. The threat of sexual assault reduces women's ability to enjoy nature and solitude. The threat of sexual assault also can have a significant economic impact on women, who may feel compelled to live in secure neighbourhoods, to provide themselves with safe transportation, to

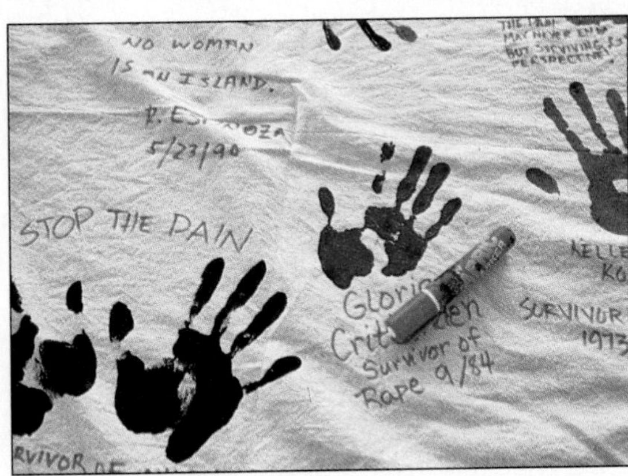

These handprints and messages on a "Survivor's Wall" at a Rally Against Rape point to the larger social context in which sexual assault occurs.

purchase a virtual arsenal of security devices and systems (for example, pepper spray, mace, alarms for body, house, and car), and to take courses in self-defence. At the same time, women's job opportunities may be limited by safety concerns: time of day they feel they can work, types of positions they safely can take, and problems associated with travelling alone. The threat of sexual assault may make women more dependent on others, make time alone less possible, limit their dress and behaviour options, and inhibit eye contact and communication with other people (Beneke, 1982, quoted in Minas, 1993).

People in va ious occupations may have different perspectives on sexual assault. A journalist may wonder whether a sexual assault is "newsworthy." Is either the victim or the accused well known? Is the victim quite young or very old? Is there some unique aspect to the crime, such as the victim asking the assailant to wear a condom? Did the assault occur at an unusual time or location? Was the sexual assault unusually brutal?

A physician might assess the nature and extent of the physical injuries. A psychiatrist might evaluate the mental states of the victim and the offender. A social worker might consider the appropriate counselling for the victim.

Law enforcement officers would want to determine the legal "facts" of the case and ascertain whether charges should be laid. They would attempt to determine whether sexual assault (nonconsensual sexual activity) had occurred. (As discussed in Box 1.1, the issue of consent is central to the legal definition of sexual assault.) The police might attempt to determine whether the rape arose from the social interaction between friends or acquaintances—what is known as *acquaintance* or *date rape*—or whether the rapist and victim were strangers. The lawyer for the accused might look for ways to build the best defence for the client. The crown attorney may want to reduce the charges to relieve crowded courts.

What, then, is the sociologist's perspective on the problem of sexual assault? The sociological perspective is a point of view that helps us understand human behaviour in the larger social context in which it occurs. Accordingly, sociologists would focus on the social environment in which rape occurs, seeking explanations by analyzing *why* and *under what circumstances* that behaviour takes place. Using existing sociological theories and methods of inquiry, sociologists would sort out probable answers from unlikely ones in their search for recurring patterns of social behaviour (see Wilson and Selvin, 1980).

There are over 25,000 sociologists in North America, and not all of them would apply the same theory or methods to study the issue of sexual assault. Some sociologists would be most interested in the demographic profiles of the victims and the offenders: their age, marital status, occupation, and any one of hundreds of other statistical categories. Others might seek to document the factors that contribute to societal breakdown and result in high incidences of sexual assault. Still others might attempt to frame sexual assault in terms of sexual terrorism. Sociologists constantly debate issues such as sexual assault, asking what its causes and effects are and what should be done to prevent it. Both the sociological study and the related debate help society articulate and deal with a multitude of such problems.

BOX 1.1 SOCIOLOGY AND LAW

The Issue of Consent

As a result of 1983 changes to the Criminal Code, the offences of rape and indecent assault no longer exist in Canadian law. These offences were replaced with sexual assault, sexual assault with a weapon, and aggravated sexual assault. Furthermore, the law is no longer gender specific (i.e., both women and men can be victims or assailants in cases of sexual assault), and married men can no longer avoid prosecution for sexually assaulting their wives.

Sexual assault cases have one key element—the presence or absence of the victim's consent. The original sexual assault legislation retained the "honest but mistaken" defence. This defence had its origins in a 1980 case (*R. v. Pappajohn*) in which the Supreme Court decided that a person accused of sexual assault could claim as a defence that he honestly believed that the woman had consented. As a result, the honest-but-mistaken defence was used to obtain acquittals in cases involving passive, sick, or unconscious victims. If the accused had mistakenly believed that a woman's resistance or failure to offer sufficient physical resistance was an attempt to pretend to be coy, salvage her reputation, or play hard to get, he could be acquitted. The issue of consent was vague and ambiguous and involved the word of the victim against the word of the accused.

Not until 1992 was the issue of consent clearly defined in law. The law now states that a woman cannot be considered to be consenting to sexual activity if someone else consents for her, if she is drunk or high on drugs so that her judgment is impaired, if she complies by reason of a person's position of trust or authority over her, or if she indicates by words or conduct that she does not consent, or has withdrawn her consent.

Clearly, the 1992 changes to the Criminal Code provided limits to the honest-but-mistaken defence. The onus is now on the accused to ensure that consent (and not just lack of active resistance) is present. The accused can no longer claim that, due to his own drunkenness, recklessness, or wilful blindness, he mistakenly believed the victim was consenting. In other words, to simply indicate that the accused thought the victim was consenting is no longer a viable defence.

Are these changes in the law reflected in changing attitudes toward sexual assault and date rape? Have these legal changes dispelled any rape myths? Research on date rape seems to show that many individuals have yet to understand that "No means no." Is legal reform, therefore, enough? What do you think?

Sources: DeKeseredy and Hinch, 1991; Johnson, 1996.

QUESTIONS AND ISSUES

What is the sociological imagination?

How do you form a sociological perspective on issues such as sexual assault?

Why were early thinkers concerned with social order and stability?

Why were later social thinkers concerned with change?

What are the assumptions behind each of the contemporary theoretical perspectives?

PUTTING SOCIAL LIFE INTO PERSPECTIVE

***Sociology* is the systematic study of human society and social interaction.** It is a *systematic* study because sociologists apply both theoretical perspectives and research methods (or orderly approaches) to examinations of social behaviour. Sociologists study human societies and their social interactions in order to develop theories of how human behaviour is shaped by group life and how, in turn, group life is affected by individuals.

Events around the world affect us all. These demonstrators outside the Chinese consulate in Toronto were protesting the massacre in 1989 at Tiananmen Square in China.

WHY STUDY SOCIOLOGY?

Sociology helps us gain a better understanding of ourselves and our social world. It enables us to see how behaviour is largely shaped by the groups to which we belong and the society in which we live.

Most of us take our social world for granted and view our lives in very personal terms. Because of our culture's emphasis on individualism, we often do not consider the complex connections between our own lives and the larger, recurring patterns of the society and world in which we live. Sociology helps us look beyond our personal experiences and gain insights into society and the larger world order. A ***society*** **is a large social grouping that shares the same geographical territory and is subject to the same political authority and dominant cultural expectations,** such as Canada, the United States, or Mexico. Examining the world order helps us understand that each of us is affected by ***global interdependence*—a relationship in which the lives of all people are closely intertwined and any one nation's problems are part of a larger global problem.**

Individuals can make use of sociology on a more personal level. Sociology enables us to move beyond established ways of thinking, thus allowing us to gain new insights into ourselves and to develop a greater awareness of the connection between our own "world" and that of other people. According to sociologist Peter Berger (1963:23), sociological inquiry helps us see that "things are not what they seem." Sociology provides new ways of approaching problems and making decisions in everyday life. Sociology promotes understanding and tolerance by enabling each of us to look beyond our personal experiences.

SOCIOLOGY AND COMMON SENSE Many of us rely on intuition or common sense gained from personal experience to help us understand our daily lives and other people's behaviour. ***Commonsense knowledge*** **guides ordinary conduct in everyday life.** We often rely on common sense—or "what everybody knows"—to answer key ques-

BOX 1.2 SOCIOLOGY AND EVERYDAY LIFE

How Much Do You Know About Sexual Assault?

TRUE	FALSE	
T	F	1. Most sexual assaults are committed by strangers.
T	F	2. In some cases, a woman who is sexually assaulted deserves it, especially if she agreed to go to the man's house or ride in his car.
T	F	3. Women who don't fight back haven't been sexually assaulted.
T	F	4. If a weapon—such as a gun or knife—isn't used, the woman hasn't been sexually assaulted.
T	F	5. A woman who asks a sexual assailant to wear a condom is consenting to have sex with him.
T	F	6. It's not really sexual assault if the victim has been sexually active with other men.
T	F	7. If a woman lets a man buy her dinner or pay for a movie or drinks, she *owes* him sex.
T	F	8. A woman who engages in necking or heavy petting with a man has consented to have intercourse with him.
T	F	9. Many women lie about being sexually assaulted, especially if the man breaks up the relationship.
T	F	10. Married women cannot be sexually assaulted by their husbands.

Answers on page 8

tions about behaviour: Why do people behave the way they do? Who makes the rules? Why do some people break rules and why do others follow them?

Many commonsense notions actually are myths. A *myth* is a popular but false notion that may be used, either intentionally or unintentionally, to perpetuate certain beliefs or "theories" even in the light of conclusive evidence to the contrary. Before reading on, take the quiz in Box 1.2, which lists a number of statements about sexual assault.

There are a number of "rape myths" in our society. The research has indicated that these myths are part of some university students' commonsense knowledge. For example, one survey found that many young men found it "acceptable for a man to force a girl to have intercourse when she initially consents and then changes her mind, or when she has sexually excited him" (Gabor, 1994). Commonsense notions, which often, like this one, are *untrue*, still have wide acceptance.

Many myths are passed on as common sense from one generation to the next. To illustrate, a recent survey of 2,092 high-achieving high-school students found that both male and female students viewed certain actions as demonstrating that "a woman is willing to continue sexual activities even though she says no." As shown in Figure 1.1, 42 percent of the male students and 39 percent of the female students thought a woman is willing to

BOX 1.2

Answers to the Sociology Quiz on Sexual Assault

TRUE	FALSE	Each of the ten statements regarding sexual assault is false. Although many of these ideas are supported by "common sense" notions, they have been contradicted by social science research.
T	F	1. *False.* In reality, most women are sexually assaulted by men they know—acquaintance or date rape—not by strangers. In one study of university and college students, over 80 percent of the sexual assault victims knew their attacker.
T	F	2. *False.* No one, male or female, deserves to be sexually assaulted. A person has not given consent to have sex simply by being in someone's house or car. This is a "victim-blaming" strategy.
T	F	3. *False.* It is irrelevant whether a woman fights back or not—she has been sexually assaulted when she has been forced to have sex against her will. Under some circumstances, fighting back might endanger the victim's life.
T	F	4. *False.* It is sexual assault whether the perpetrator uses a weapon, his fists, verbal threats, drugs or alcohol, physical isolation, the woman's own diminished physical or mental state, or simply his superior weight to overcome the woman.
T	F	5. *False.* Even when a woman asks her attacker to wear a condom to protect her from AIDS, she has been sexually assaulted when she is forced to have sex against her will.
T	F	6. *False.* The victim's previous sexual activity has no bearing on whether she has consented to sexual activity with another person.
T	F	7. *False.* No one owes sex as a payment to anyone else.
T	F	8. *False.* Everyone has the right to say no to sexual intercourse, regardless of what has preceded it, and to have that "no" respected.
T	F	9. *False.* Very few women lie about being sexually assaulted. Many do not report sexual assaults at all because they fear their attacker will come back, they think that no one will believe them, they do not want to be embarrassed and ridiculed in the court system, and they believe nothing can be done about it.
T	F	10. *False.* In 1983 the law was broadened to allow prosecution of men who sexually assaulted their wives. Under the previous law there was a "spousal exemption" for sexual assault.

Sources: Based on Warshaw, 1988; Russell, 1990; Bridges, 1991; DeKeseredy and Hinch, 1991; and Johnson, 1996.

continue sexual activities if "she continues to be affectionate and passionate." Even more disturbing are the results from a survey conducted at York University in Toronto. Almost one-third of the male students interviewed agreed with the statement "Many times a woman will pretend she doesn't want to have intercourse because she doesn't want to seem loose, but she's really hoping

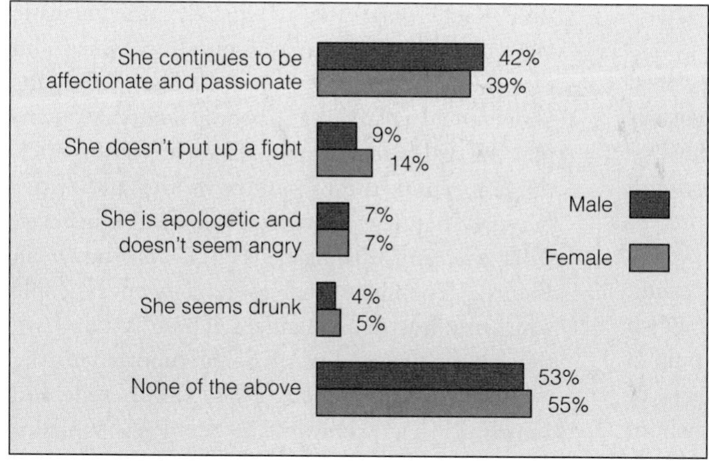

FIGURE 1.1

Teen Responses to Questions About Sexual Violence and Sexual Assault

Percentages of students who believe the statement listed means that a woman is willing to continue sexual activity even though she says no.

Source: Adapted from Cox News Service report, 1993.

the man will force her" (Gabor, 1994:106). Even though these surveys have limitations, they tend to demonstrate that many people still subscribe to the myth that women *cause* sexual assault. As sociological research has found, however, sexual assault is a crime of *violence* directed against women, not a crime of *sexual passion* or *seduction.*

SOCIOLOGY VERSUS "POP" SOCIOLOGY The media provide more information than we possibly can use on all aspects of social life. Television talk show hosts and news anchors, journalists for magazines and newspapers, and authors of the many books in print all provide us with information about family life, sexual assault, homelessness, AIDS, violence, and thousands of related sociological topics. With all of this information readily available, why should we study sociology? What can we learn that is better than relying on common sense or information from an alleged expert on a talk show?

The answer is that sociologists strive to use scientific standards, not popular myths or hearsay, in studying society and social interaction. They use systematic research techniques and are accountable to the scientific community for their methods and the presentation of their findings. While some sociologists argue that sociology must be completely ***objective*—free from distorting subjective (personal or emotional) bias**—others do not think that total objectivity is an attainable or desirable goal when studying human behaviour. This issue will be discussed in Chapter 2 ("Sociological Research Methods").

The "pop" sociology of the mass media is quite different from the intellectual and academic discipline of sociology. The mass media tend to look at singular events in isolation—as individual and often bizarre occurrences. It is impossible, however, to study human behaviour in one hour on television or by reading an article in a magazine; much more is involved in studying society and social interaction. Sociologists attempt to discover patterns or commonalities in human behaviour. For example, when they study violent crimes such as sexual assault, they look for recurring patterns of behaviour even though *individual* offenders usually commit the acts and *individual* victims suffer as a result of these actions.

Consequently, sociologists seek out the multiple causes and effects of sexual assault or other social issues. They analyze the impact of the problem not only from the standpoint of sexual assault victims or perpetrators but also from the standpoint of the effects of such behaviour on all people (for example, fear of crime and demands for "law and order").

THE SOCIOLOGICAL IMAGINATION

Sociologist C. Wright Mills (1959) described sociological reasoning as the ***sociological imagination*—the ability to see the relationship between individual experiences and the larger society.** This awareness enables us to understand the link between our personal experiences and the social contexts in which they occur. The sociological imagination helps us distinguish between personal troubles and social (or public) issues. *Personal troubles* are private problems of individuals and the networks of people with whom they associate regularly. As a result, those problems must be solved by individuals within their immediate social settings. For example, one person being unemployed may be a personal trouble. *Public issues* are matters beyond an individual's own control that are caused by problems at the societal level. Widespread unemployment as a result of economic changes such as plant closings is an example of a public issue. The sociological imagination helps us place seemingly personal troubles, such as being the victim of sexual assault or losing one's job, into a larger social context, where we can distinguish whether and how personal troubles may be related to public issues.

SEXUAL ASSAULT AS A PERSONAL TROUBLE Many of our individual experiences may be largely beyond our own control. They are determined by society as a whole—by its historical development and its organization. In everyday life, we do not define personal experiences in these terms. If a woman is sexually assaulted, many people—sometimes including the victim—consider it to be her personal problem, as well as perhaps being her fault, because "she *asked for it.*"

Let us consider the case of Rachel, who was sexually assaulted in a dormitory room. Describing the attack afterwards, she stated: "I just wanted to block it out. I felt ashamed because it happened. I just felt dirty, violated. I thought it was my fault. It wasn't like he did something to me, it was like I let him do something to me, so I felt very bad about myself" (Warshaw, 1988:30). In this situation, Rachel expressed a typically individualistic view that her problem was purely personal and that she caused it. Due to socially accepted myths about sexual assault, many people ignore or downplay the reality of acquaintance rape. Victims often do not report these assaults to the authorities because they fear that they will not be believed (Maguire and Flanagan, 1991). As shown in Figure 1.2, most sexual assaults involve people who are at least acquaintances. These assaults have the lowest probability of being reported to the police (Gunn & Minch, 1988; DeKeseredy and Hinch, 1991). According to the 1993 Violence Against Women Survey, only 6 percent of all sexual assaults were reported to the police (Johnson, 1996). Many of these victims do not report the offence, the survey found, because they believe they will be blamed by others for having caused the sexual assault (Martin, 1992).

SEXUAL ASSAULT AS A PUBLIC ISSUE We can use the sociological imagination to look at the problem of sexual assault as a public issue—a societal problem. Despite widespread underreporting, over 31,000 incidents of sexual assault were reported in 1994—this accounts for approximately 10 percent of all violent crime in Canada (Statistics Canada, 1994). Between 1984 and 1993, the rate of sexual assault reports increased by 205 percent (Johnson, 1996). As the rate of reported sexual assault increases, more people are becoming aware that sexual assault is a public issue, not merely a personal problem for each of the victims, and that no *private solutions* exist for this societal problem (Brownmiller, 1975).

Some social scientists stress that North America has a "rape-supportive" belief system. For example, men typically are encouraged to be more aggressive and physically assertive than women. Moreover, women often are considered to be "asking for it" if they wear a short skirt or go out alone at night. These culturally transmitted assumptions about women, men, sexuality, and violence may result in many sexual assault victims being victimized twice. They are victimized first by the actual rape and then a second time by

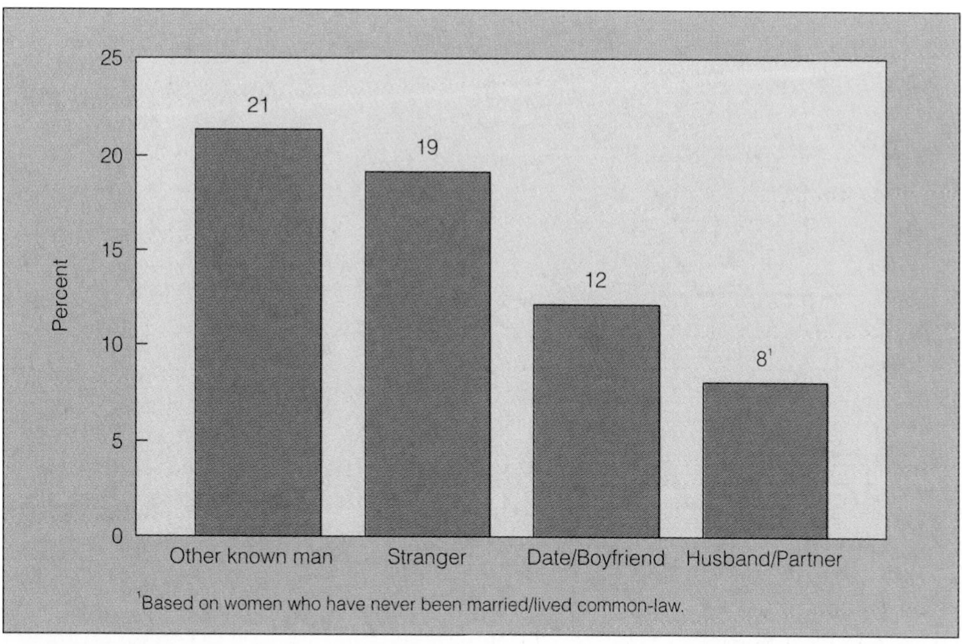

FIGURE 1.2

Relationship of Perpetrator to Victim in Cases of Sexual Assault, 1993

Reproduced by authority of the Minister of Industry, 1996, Statistics Canada, from Violence Against Women survey, 1993.

family, friends, or personnel in the criminal justice system who believe sexual assault victims are responsible in some way for their own victimization (Madigan and Gamble, 1991). In fact, research indicates that there are women whom police consider "open territory victims" or "women who can't be raped." Included in this category are prostitutes, alcoholics, drug users, women on welfare, and unemployed women (DeKeseredy and Hinch, 1991:67). False assumptions about sexual assault provide a social context for potential offenders in which sexual assault not only is possible but goes largely undetected or is ignored.

DEVELOPING A "PERSONAL" SOCIOLOGICAL IMAGINATION To develop your own sociological imagination, you must understand how acts such as sexual assault are, in part, a product of society and not merely *personal* problems (see Figure 1.3). The sociological imagination requires us to recognize the connection between individual experience and the social world or as C.W. Mills described it "to grasp the interplay of man and society, of biography, and history, of self and world" (1959:3). Box 1.3 puts the problem of rape into a global perspective.

Although we can use existing sociological theory and research as the foundation for sociological thinking, we must reach beyond past work to develop a more comprehensive approach for the future. As we approach the twenty-first century, we face important challenges in a rapidly changing nation and world—individually and collectively. For example, new social issues have emerged as a result of recent political transformations in Eastern Europe. The former Soviet Union and Yugoslavia have fragmented along

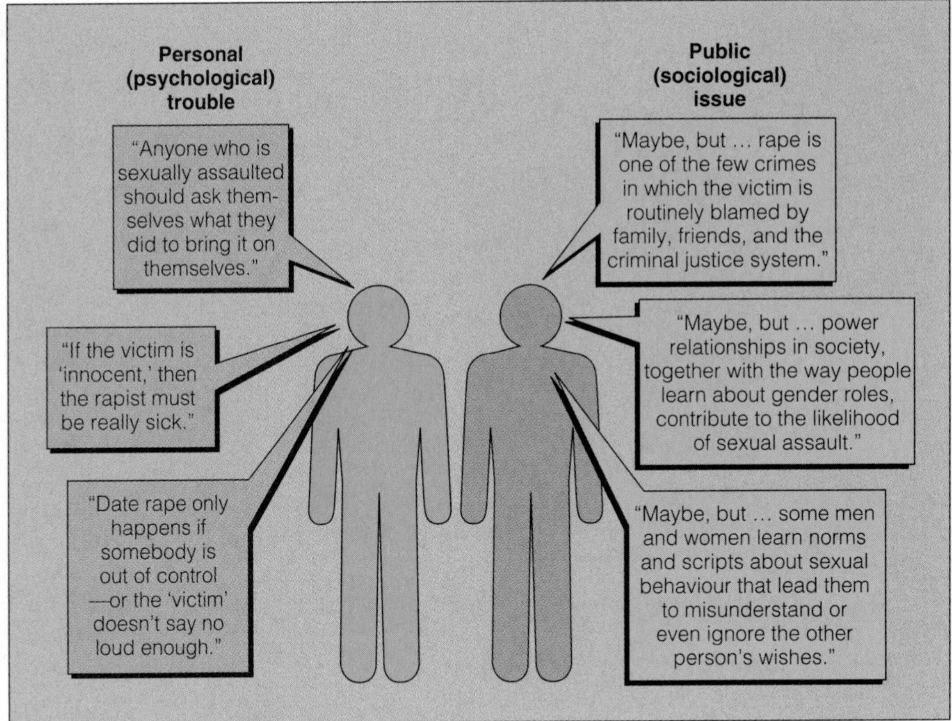

FIGURE 1.3

Two Perspectives on Sexual Assault

The sociological imagination makes it possible for us to see pressing social issues such as sexual assault in their societal context, not just as personal problems.

ethnic lines; at the same time, Western Europe is moving toward unification. The world's population is increasing by almost 94 million people per year, and most of this growth is occurring in the world's less-developed nations (see Chapter 16).

Canada, whose future is intertwined with that of the rest of the world, is itself experiencing dramatic population changes that will have long-term effects. The majority of women and men in this country are in the paid labour force. Women's participation in the labour force has led to a reduction in the number of children in Canadian families (see Chapter 14). Couples are choosing to delay childbearing and are having fewer children. Because of these very low birth rates, our population is aging; by the year 2036 approximately 25 percent of Canadians will be over the age of 65 (see Chapter 11). Also, if current trends in immigration continue, Canada will become even more ethnically diverse (see Chapter 9). Can you use your sociological imagination to predict how these *social* changes will affect your *personal* life?

Including the experiences of all people is of vital importance in analyzing personal troubles, public issues, and social policies for the future. Whatever your race/ethnicity, class, sex, or age, are you able to include in your thinking the perspectives of people with quite dissimilar in experiences and points of view? Before answering this question, a few definitions are in order. ***Race* is a term used by many people to specify groups of people distinguished by physical**

BOX 1.3 SOCIOLOGY IN GLOBAL PERSPECTIVE

Rape in Wartime

Bosnia-Herzegovina—February 12, 1993

> *I was raped by three Serb soldiers and assaulted by a fourth. He forced his arm inside my vagina and then he made me lick the blood from his fingers ... again, again, and again.—Sixty-year-old Muslim woman*
>
> *I would rather we had all been killed. The Serbian policy of driving us from our homes has worked ... we will never go back.—Husband of the woman* (CNN, *1993)*

Thousands of refugees in the former nation of Yugoslavia told similar horror stories about the massive scale of rape in Bosnia that was part of a deliberate Serbian policy to build a Greater Serbia through "ethnic cleansing"—the driving out of non-Serbs. The United Nations High Commission for Refugees reported finding evidence that "rape [was] part of a pattern of abuse, usually perpetrated with the conscious intention of demoralizing and terrorizing communities, driving [Bosnians] from their homes and demonstrating the power of the invading forces" (Drozdiak, 1993). Women from different towns in Bosnia reported that Serbs had set up "rape camps" in their towns, abducted the younger women, and repeatedly raped them with the deliberate intention of making them pregnant. Children as well as women were being raped. Although it is impossible to know how many Bosnian women have been raped, one report estimated that over 300 babies have been abandoned by women raped during this ethnic war and another 2,000 women were reported to be pregnant as a result of rape (*Austin American-Statesman*, 1993). Even worse, in the brutal conflict in Bosnia, rape has not been just a by-product of war but an actual *weapon*.

Under the international rules of war, rape is outlawed as a criminal act; however, rape persists as a common act of war (Brownmiller, 1975). Mass rape is one of the most heinous of war-related crimes. Many women and particularly children have died during or after rape, while surviving victims have suffered humiliation, lifelong psychological scars, and, often, the presence of unwanted and unloved children. Can the sociological imagination help us understand brutality such as this?

Sources: Lewis, 1993; and Morrow, 1993.

characteristics such as skin colour; in fact, there are no "pure" racial types, and the concept of race is considered by most sociologists to be a myth. ***Ethnicity*** **refers to the cultural heritage or identity of a group and is based on factors such as language or country of origin.** ***Class*** **is the relative location of a person or group within a larger society,** based on wealth, power, prestige, or other valued resources. ***Sex*** **refers to the biological and anatomical differences between females and males.** By contrast, ***gender*** **refers to the meanings, beliefs, and practices associated with sex differences,** referred to as *femininity* and *masculinity* (Scott, 1986:1054).

In our sociological imaginations, we must include the experiences of people in all nations: those that are similar to Canada and those that are not. As we seek to uncover similarities and differences in the experiences of diverse categories of people, we are not making value judgments—better or worse, right or wrong—about different groups. Instead, we are attempting to develop a holistic view of how people, as a result of gender, race or ethnicity, age, or class, encounter different opportunities and constraints and how they respond to their relative circumstances.

Developing a "personal" sociological imagination may be the first step in producing societal change. We are more likely to demand social change when we see that our problems are "larger than ourselves"; in other words, we begin to develop a group consciousness. ***Group conscious-***

This opening ceremony of Expo 1986 in Vancouver reflects the increasing diversity of the Canadian population—and the need to take all people's experiences into account as we confront public issues.

***ness* is an awareness that an individual's problems are shared by others who are similarly situated in regard to race, ethnicity, gender, class, or age.** In this context, individual problems are issues—public matters that may require social and not necessarily individual changes. At the same time, individuals begin to see that collective action will be necessary to produce the social change they need. As a result of developing this group consciousness, we start to understand the sociological perspective and to see ways to apply the sociological imagination to our own lives.

In forming your own sociological imagination and in seeing the possibilities for sociology in the twenty-first century, it will be helpful to understand the development of the discipline, beginning about one hundred years ago.

THE DEVELOPMENT OF SOCIOLOGICAL THINKING

Throughout history, social philosophers and religious authorities have made countless observations about human behaviour. However, these early thinkers primarily stated what they thought society *ought* to be like, rather than describing how society actually *was*. The idea of observing how people lived, to find out what they thought, and doing so in a systematic manner that could be verified, did not take hold until the nineteenth century. In light of the sweeping political and economic changes in the late eighteenth and early nineteenth centuries, people realized that some of the answers given by philosophers and theologians to some very pressing questions no longer seemed as relevant. Many of these questions concerned the social upheaval brought about by industrialization and urbanization that occurred first in Britain, then in Western Europe, and later in Canada and the United States.

***Industrialization* is the process by which societies are transformed from dependence on agriculture and handmade products to an emphasis on manufacturing and related industries.** This process occurred first during the Industrial Revolution in Britain between 1760 and 1850 and soon was repeated throughout Western Europe. By the mid-nineteenth century, industrialization was well under way in North America. Massive economic, technological, and social changes occurred as machine technology and the

Early in the twentieth century, sights like this 14-year-old girl working in a factory caught the attention of social thinkers and brought demands for protective child labour laws.

factory system shifted the economic base of these nations from agriculture to manufacturing. A new social class of industrialists emerged in textiles, iron smelting, and related industries. Many people who had laboured on the land were forced to leave their tightly knit rural communities and sacrifice well-defined social relationships to seek employment as factory workers in the emerging cities, which became the centres of industrial work.

***Urbanization* is the process by which an increasing proportion of a population lives in cities rather than in rural areas.** Although cities existed long before the Industrial Revolution, the development of the factory system led to a rapid increase in both the number of cities and the size of their populations. People from very diverse backgrounds worked together in the same factory. At the same time, many people shifted from being *producers* to being *consumers*. For example, families living in the cities had to buy food with their wages because they no longer could grow their own crops to consume or to barter for other resources. Similarly, people had to pay rent for their lodging because they no longer could exchange their services for shelter.

These living and working conditions led to the development of new social problems: inadequate housing, crowding, unsanitary conditions, poverty, pollution, and crime. Wages were so low that entire families—including very young children—were forced to work, often under hazardous conditions and with no job security. As these conditions became more visible, a new breed of social thinkers turned its attention to trying to understand why and how society was changing.

EARLY THINKERS: A CONCERN WITH SOCIAL ORDER AND STABILITY

At the same time as urban problems were growing worse, natural scientists had been using reason, or rational thinking, to discover the laws of physics and the movement of the planets. Social thinkers started to believe that, by applying the methods developed by the natural sciences, they might discover the laws of human behaviour and apply these laws to solve social problems. Historically, the time was ripe for such thoughts because the Age of Enlightenment (a period that followed the "dark ages" and was characterized by reliance on scientific analysis) had produced a belief in reason and humanity's ability to perfect itself. Early social thinkers—such as Auguste Comte, Harriet Martineau, Herbert Spencer, and Emile Durkheim—were interested in analyzing social order and stability, and many of their ideas had a dramatic influence on modern sociology.

AUGUSTE COMTE The French philosopher Auguste Comte (1798–1857) coined the term *sociology* from the Latin *socius* (social, being with others) and the Greek *logos* (study of) to describe a new science that would engage in the study of society. Even though he never actually conducted sociological research, Comte is considered by some to be the "founder of sociology." Comte's theory that societies contain *social statics* (forces for social

Auguste Comte

Harriet Martineau

order and stability) and *social dynamics* (forces for conflict and change) continues to be used, although not in these exact terms, in contemporary sociology.

Drawing heavily on the ideas of his mentor, Count Henri de Saint-Simon, Comte stressed that the methods of the natural sciences should be applied to the objective study of society. While Saint-Simon's primary interest in studying society was social reform, Comte sought to unlock the secrets of society so that intellectuals like himself could become the new secular (as contrasted with religious) "high priests" of society (Nisbet, 1979).

Comte's philosophy became known as ***positivism*—a belief that the world can best be understood through scientific inquiry.** Comte believed that objective, bias-free knowledge was attainable only through the use of science rather than religion. Scientific knowledge, however, was "relative knowledge," not absolute and final. Comte's positivism had two dimensions: (1) methodological—the application of scientific knowledge to both physical and social phenomena—and (2) social and political—the use of such knowledge to predict the likely results of different policies so that the best one could be chosen. For Comte, the best policies involved order and authority. He envisioned that a new consensus would emerge on social issues and that the new science of sociology would play a significant part in the reorganization of society (Jary and Jary, 1991:374).

The ideas of Saint-Simon and Comte regarding the objective, scientific study of society are deeply embedded in the discipline of sociology. However, a number of contemporary sociologists argue that overemphasis on the "natural science model" has been detrimental to sociology (see Vaughan, Sjoberg, and Reynolds, 1993). Still others state that sociology, while claiming to be "scientific" and "objective," has focused on the experiences of a privileged few, to the exclusion by class, gender, race, ethnicity, and age of all others (see Harding, 1986; Collins, 1990; Andersen and Collins, 1992). As we study early thinkers like Saint-Simon and Comte, we must realize that they probably were unaware of the many biases of the "worlds" within which they themselves operated (Lee, 1986).

HARRIET MARTINEAU Comte's works were made more accessible for a wide variety of scholars through the efforts of British sociologist Harriet Martineau (1802–1876). Until recently, Martineau received no recognition in the field of sociology, partly because she was a woman in a male-dominated discipline and society. Not only did she translate and condense Comte's work, but she also was an active sociologist in her own right. Martineau studied the social customs of Britain and the United States and analyzed the consequences of industrialization and capitalism. In *Society in America* (1962/1837), she examined religion, politics, child rearing, slavery, and immigration in the United States, paying special attention to social distinctions based on class, race, and gender. Her works explore the status of women, children, and "sufferers" (persons who are considered to be criminal, mentally ill, handicapped, poor, or alcoholic).

Although Martineau did not believe that she should criticize Comte's ideas publicly, historians have documented that she strongly disagreed with several of his ideas. For example, even though she agreed with Comte that science could facilitate the growth of knowledge and a new social order, Martineau disagreed with his advocacy of a secular religion with sociologists as high priests and Comte himself as "pope." She also strongly disapproved of his early proclamation that sociology would prove that women were physically, emotionally, and intellectually inferior to men (Hoecker-Drysdale, 1992).

HERBERT SPENCER British social theorist Herbert Spencer (1820–1903) used an evolutionary perspective to explain social order and social change. He believed that society, like a biological organism, has various interdependent parts (such as the family, the economy, and the government), which work to ensure the stability and survival of the entire society. According to Spencer, societies developed through a process of "struggle" (for existence) and "fitness" (for survival), which he referred to as the "survival of the fittest." Because this phrase often is attributed to Charles Darwin, Spencer's view of society is known as ***social Darwinism*—the belief that those species of animals, including human beings, best adapted to their environment survive and prosper, while those poorly adapted die out.** Spencer equated this process of *natural selection* with progress, because only the "fittest" members of society would succeed. As a result of these ideas, he strongly opposed attempts at social reform that might interfere with the natural selection process and, thus, damage society by favouring its least worthy members.

Although Spencer contributed many useful concepts and terms, many of his ideas had serious flaws. For one thing, societies are not the same as biological systems; people are able to create and transform the environment in which they live. Moreover, the notion of the survival of the fittest easily can be used to justify class, racial-ethnic, and gender inequalities and to rationalize the lack of action to eliminate harmful practices that contribute to such inequalities. Not surprisingly, Spencer's "hands-off" view was applauded by wealthy industrialists of his day. John D. Rockefeller, who gained monopolistic control of much of the U.S. oil industry early in the twentieth century, maintained that the growth of giant businesses was merely the "survival of the fittest" (Feagin and Feagin, 1994).

Social Darwinism served as a rationalization for some people's assertion of the superiority of the white race. After the Civil War in the United States, it was used to justify the repression and neglect of African Americans as well as the policies that resulted in the annihilation of native American populations. Although some social reformers spoke out against these justifications, "scientific" racism continued to exist (Turner, Singleton, and Musick, 1984). In both positive and negative ways, many of Spencer's ideas and concepts have been deeply embedded in social policies for over a century.

EMILE DURKHEIM French sociologist Emile Durkheim (1858–1917) disagreed with many of Spencer's views. Durkheim stressed that people are the

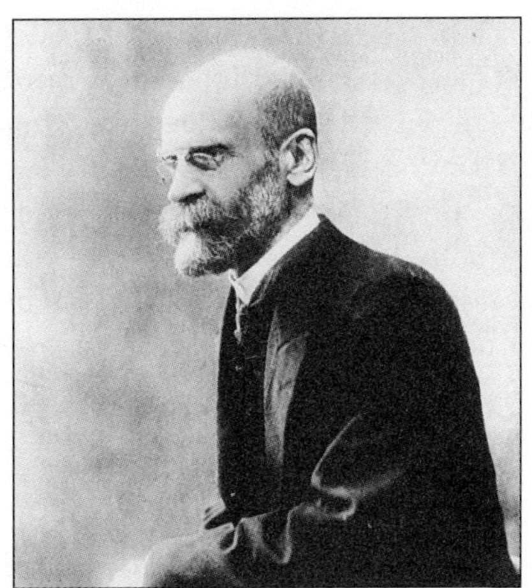

Emile Durkheim

product of their social environment and that behaviour cannot be understood fully in terms of *individual* biological and psychological traits. He believed that the limits of human potential are *socially*, not *biologically*, based.

In his work *The Rules of Sociological Method* (1964/1895) Durkheim set forth one of his most important contributions to sociology: the idea that societies are built on social facts. ***Social facts* are patterned ways of acting, thinking, and feeling that exist *outside* any one individual** but that exert social control over each person. Durkheim believed that social facts must be explained by other social facts—by reference to the social structure rather than to individual attributes.

Durkheim was concerned with social order and social stability because he lived during the period of rapid social changes in Europe resulting from industrialization and urbanization. His recurring question was, How do societies manage to hold together? In *The Division of Labor in Society* (1933/1893), Durkheim concluded that preindustrial societies were held together by strong traditions and by members' shared moral beliefs and values. As societies industrialized, the more specialized economic activity became the basis of the social bond because people became interdependent.

Durkheim observed that rapid social change and a more specialized division of labour produce *strains* in society. These strains lead to a breakdown in traditional organization, values, and authority and to a dramatic increase in ***anomie*—a condition in which social control becomes ineffective as a result of the loss of shared values and of a sense of purpose in society.** According to Durkheim, anomie is most likely to occur during a period of rapid social change. In *Suicide* (1964b/1897), he explored the relationship between anomic social conditions and suicide, as we will see in Chapter 2 ("Sociological Research Methods").

Durkheim exhibited many of the prevalent biases of his era against women. The popular view was that men's tastes, aspirations, and humour were "almost entirely the product of society," while women's were less socialized and "more directly influenced by anatomy [a woman's body]" (Durkheim, 1964b/1897). It is ironic that Durkheim did not extend his belief in the importance of social facts to the entire human population. However, Durkheim's contributions to sociology are so significant that he has been referred to as "*the* crucial figure in the development of sociology as an academic discipline [and as] one of the deepest roots of the sociological imagination" (Tiryakian, 1978:187).

DIFFERING VIEWS ON THE STATUS QUO: STABILITY VERSUS CHANGE

Together with Karl Marx, Max Weber, and Georg Simmel, Durkheim established the course for modern sociology. We will look first at Marx's and Weber's divergent thoughts about conflict and social change in societies and then at Georg Simmel's microlevel analysis of society.

KARL MARX German economist and philosopher Karl Marx (1818–1883) often is regarded as one of the most profound sociological thinkers; his theories combine ideas derived from philosophy, history, and the social sciences. Central to his view

Karl Marx

was the belief that society should not just be studied but should also be changed, because the *status quo* (the existing state of society) was resulting in the oppression of most of the population by a small group of wealthy people.

In sharp contrast to Durkheim's focus on the stability of society, Marx stressed that history is a continuous clash between conflicting ideas and forces. He believed that conflict—especially class conflict—is necessary in order to produce social change and a better society. For Marx, the most important changes were economic. He concluded that the capitalist economic system was responsible for the overwhelming poverty that he observed in London at the beginning of the Industrial Revolution (Marx and Engels, 1967/1848).

In the Marxian framework, ***class conflict* is the struggle between the capitalist class and the working class.** The capitalist class, or ***bourgeoisie*, is comprised of those who own and control the means of production. *Means of production* refers to the tools, land, factories, and money for investment that form the economic basis of a society. The working class, or *proletariat*, is composed of those who must sell their labour because they have no other means to earn a livelihood.** From Marx's viewpoint, the capitalist class controls and exploits the masses of struggling workers by paying less than the value of their labour. This exploitation results in workers' ***alienation*—a feeling of powerlessness and estrangement from other people and from oneself.** Marx predicted that the working class would become aware of its exploitation, overthrow the capitalists, and establish a free and classless society, as discussed in Chapter 8 ("Social Stratification and Class").

How do race, gender, class, and age affect a person's life? Marx emphasized that gender differences between men and women (as well as racial-ethnic differences) in power and social position primarily reflect *class* divisions. He noted that gender and class divisions were not present in the earliest forms of human society. The power of men over women first developed when class divisions appeared. Women came to be a form of "private property" owned by men through the institution of marriage. He emphasized that women would become free from this bondage only when class divisions were overcome. Some scholars have criticized this notion, arguing that it does not fully reflect the nature of men's and women's power relations (see Hartmann, 1981). Others have disagreed with the notion that racial-ethnic inequalities and racism in general derive only from the forces of capitalism and will disappear after the class struggle has been won (Martin and Cohen, 1980).

Marx's social and economic analyses have inspired heated debates among generations of social scientists. Although his evaluation of capitalism and his theories on the process of social change have been criticized, many of his ideas form the foundation of contemporary conflict theory.

MAX WEBER German social scientist Max Weber (pronounced VAY-ber) (1864–1920) also was concerned about the changes brought about by

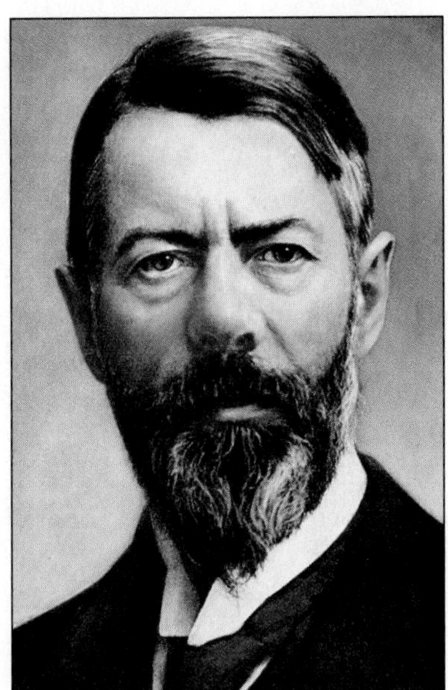

Max Weber

the Industrial Revolution. Although he disagreed with Marx's idea that economics is *the* central force in social change, Weber acknowledged that economic interests are important in shaping human action. Even so, he thought that economic systems were heavily influenced by other factors in a society. As we will see in Chapter 15 ("Education and Religion"), one of Weber's most important works, *The Protestant Ethic and the Spirit of Capitalism* (1976/1904–05), evaluated the role of the Protestant Reformation in producing a social climate in which capitalism could exist and flourish.

Unlike many early analysts, who believed that values could not be separated from the research process, Weber emphasized that sociology should be *value free*—that is, research should be conducted in a scientific manner and should exclude the researcher's own personal values and economic interests (Turner, Beeghley, and Powers, 1995:192). However, Weber realized that social behaviour cannot be analyzed by the objective criteria that we use to measure such things as temperature or weight. Although he recognized that sociologists cannot be totally value free, Weber stressed that they should employ *verstehen* (German for "understanding" or "insight") to gain the ability to see the world as others see it. In contemporary sociology, Weber's idea is incorporated into the concept of the sociological imagination (discussed earlier in this chapter).

Weber also was concerned that large-scale organizations (bureaucracies) were becoming increasingly oriented toward routine administration and a specialized division of labour, which he believed were destructive to human vitality and freedom. As we will see in Chapter 6 ("Groups and Organizations"), Weber's work on bureaucracy has had a far-reaching impact.

Weber made significant contributions to modern sociology by emphasizing the goal of value- free inquiry and the necessity of understanding how others see the world. He also was more aware of women's issues than many of the scholars of his day. Perhaps his awareness at least partially resulted from the fact that his wife, Marianne Weber, was an important figure in the women's movement in Germany in the early twentieth century (Roth, 1988).

GEORG SIMMEL German sociologist Georg Simmel (pronounced ZIM-mel) (1858–1918) had an important influence on sociology despite the fact that he was excluded from high academic positions because of his Jewish heritage. Unlike Comte, Durkheim, Marx, and Weber—who focused on macrolevel analyses of society—Simmel primarily explored smaller social units. He thought that society is best seen as a web of patterned interactions among people. The main purpose of sociology, according to Simmel, should be to examine these interaction processes within groups. For example, he analyzed how social interactions vary depending on the size of the social group (Simmel, 1950). He concluded that interaction patterns differed between a *dyad*, a social group with two members, and a *triad*, a social group with three members. He developed *formal sociology*, an approach that focuses attention on the universal

According to sociologist Georg Simmel, society is a web of patterned interactions among people. If we focus on the behaviour of individuals in isolation (for instance, the couple in the foreground of this photograph), we may miss the underlying forms that make up the "geometry of social life."

recurring social forms that underlie the varying content of social interaction. Simmel referred to these forms as the "geometry of social life." He also distinguished between *forms* of social interaction (such as cooperation or conflict) and the *content* of social interaction in different contexts (for example, between leaders and followers).

Like the other social thinkers of his day, Simmel analyzed the impact of industrialization and urbanization on people's lives. He concluded that class conflict was becoming more pronounced in modern industrial societies. He also linked the increase in individualism, as opposed to concern for the group, to the fact that people now had many cross-cutting "social spheres"—membership in a number of organizations and voluntary associations—rather than having the singular community ties of the past. Finally, Simmel assessed the costs of "progress" on the upper-class city dweller, who, he believed, had to develop certain techniques to survive the overwhelming stimulation of the city. Simmel's ultimate concern was to protect the autonomy of the individual in society.

Although Simmel is less well known than Durkheim, Marx, and Weber, his contributions to sociology are significant. He wrote more than thirty books and numerous essays, and his works influenced the sociologists of the Chicago School, which we will examine in the next section.

THE DEVELOPMENT OF SOCIOLOGY IN NORTH AMERICA

From Western Europe, sociology spread in the 1890s to the United States, and in the early 1900s to Canada. It thrived in both countries as a result of the intellectual climate and the rapid rate of social change.

IN THE UNITED STATES The first department of sociology in the United States was established at the University of Chicago in 1892. Albion Small (1854–1926), its founder and first chairman, started the *American Journal of Sociology*. The male sociologists who were at the University of Chicago from the 1920s to the 1940s became known as the "Chicago School" (Faris, 1967). Robert E. Park (1864–1944), an original member of the Chicago School, assisted in the development of the sociology of urban life (see Chapter 16).

George Herbert Mead (1863–1931), a sociologist and social psychologist, became one of the best-known members of the Chicago School and the founder of the symbolic interaction perspective, which is discussed later in this chapter. Chapter 4 ("Socialization") provides a detailed look at his theory that individual behaviour is the product of social interactions with other people. The University of Chicago continues to be an important centre for sociological research and instruction.

In the early years, women were welcomed to sociology departments such as the University of Chicago's. However, as the departments became more established, a number of its male members became disenchanted with their own earlier radical ideas, including feminism. When many of the women were unable to gain more than a temporary foothold in academic sociology, they sought employment in the emerging field of social work. This change marked the beginning of a dual system of sex-segregated labour, whereby sociology became male-dominated and social work became female-dominated. While the men were engaged in teaching and research, the women became active in establishing and running settlement houses for newly arrived immigrants and the poor (Deegan, 1988).

Jane Addams (1860–1935) is one of the best known of these sociologists because she founded Hull House, one of the most famous settlement houses, in an impoverished area of Chicago. She advocated that the world needed women's special moral sensitivities to "purify" politics (Donovan, 1992/1985). Although Addams was awarded a Nobel Peace Prize for her contributions to the field of social work and her assistance to the underprivileged, her sociological work was not acknowledged until recently.

W.E.B. Du Bois

The second department of sociology in the United States was founded by W.E.B. Du Bois (1868–1963) at Atlanta University. Sociology, according to Du Bois, must be scientific and have one goal—"the discovery of truth"—that, in turn, should be used to reform society (Du Bois, 1967/1899).

His classic work, *The Philadelphia Negro: A Social Study* (1967/1899), was based on his research into Philadelphia's African American community and stressed the strengths and weaknesses of a community wrestling with overwhelming social problems.

Over the years, Du Bois became frustrated with the lack of progress in race relations and helped found the National Association for the Advancement of Colored People (NAACP). He later became a revolutionary Marxist and emigrated to Ghana at the age of 93, where he died two years later (Baltzell, 1967; Green and Driver, 1978).

Despite the fact that he was the first African American to receive a doctorate from Harvard University and had produced many scholarly articles and books, he never was offered a position at

Harold A. Innis

a major (translated "white") university, which would have given him access to research facilities (Green and Driver, 1978:41–47).

IN CANADA The first sociology department in Canada was established in 1925 at McGill University in Montreal. The faculty consisted of Carl A. Dawson and Everett Hughes. Dawson modelled the McGill sociology department after the University of Chicago's, at which he was trained. Although other Canadian universities offered sociology courses through other departments, particularly history and economics, McGill had the only independent sociology department until the early 1960s, at which time there were only fifty sociologists teaching in Canada (Denton and Hunter, 1995).

The University of Toronto, although equally influential in the field, had a very different approach to sociology than McGill. Sociology courses were taught as part of the department of political economy and did not form an independent department until 1963. Modelled on British sociology, the sociology taught at the University of Toronto focused on how issues of political and economic history affected Canadian society. In 1930, economic historian Harold A. Innis wrote *The Fur Trade*, in which he introduced what is referred to as the *staples thesis*, which maintains that the Canadian economy has been based on the extraction and export of raw materials. S.D. Clark further developed this theory in his 1942 book *The Social Development of Canada*, where he discussed the historical factors that make Canada a unique society. The works of these scholars laid the groundwork for the *political economy perspective*, which is central to Canadian sociology today.

By the late 1960s, sociology departments had been established across the country. The first Canadian sociology journal, *the Canadian Review of Sociology and Anthropology*, appeared in 1964. In 1966, the Canadian Sociology and Anthropology Association was established with only 189 founding members. Today, there are more than a thousand trained sociologists in Canada.

The 1970s was a period of "Canadianization" of sociology in Canada. Prior to this time, Canadian sociology departments had tended to hire sociologists trained in the United States and to use American textbooks. During the 1970s, pressure was put on universities to hire sociologists trained in Canada. As a result, graduate programs across Canada were developed and expanded. A unique sociology was developed that focused on Canadian issues such as regionalism, ethnic relations, multiculturalism, and national identity, as well as issues common to all societies such as social inequalities created by social class, ethnic origin, or gender. Canadian works such as John Porter's 1965 book *The Vertical Mosaic* and Patricia Marchak's *Ideological Perspectives on Canadian Society*, published in 1975, became landmarks in Canadian sociology.

Sociology in Canada today represents our country's bicultural nature, with its two sociological orientations—French-Canadian and English-Canadian (Denton and Hunter, 1995). Francophone sociologists, influenced largely by European sociologists, tend to focus on large-scale social factors such as economic trends, trade union movements, and relations between church and state (Spencer, 1993). Francophone sociologists have traditionally paid more attention to the abstract or theoretical aspects of their research than their Anglophone counterparts who tend to place more emphasis on research techniques and methods (Spencer, 1993).

CONTEMPORARY THEORETICAL PERSPECTIVES

Given the many and varied ideas and trends that influenced the development of sociology, how do contemporary sociologists view society? Some see it as basically a stable and ongoing entity; others view it in terms of many groups competing for scarce resources; still others describe it as based on the everyday, routine interactions among individuals. Each of these views represents a method of examining the same phenomena. Each is based on general ideas as to how social life is organized and represents an effort to link specific observations in a meaningful way. Each utilizes ***theory*****—a set of logically interrelated statements that attempts to describe, explain, and (occasionally) predict social events.** Each theory helps interpret reality in a distinct way by providing a framework in which observations may be logically ordered. Sociologists refer to this theoretical framework as a ***perspective*****—an overall approach to or viewpoint on some subject.** Three major theoretical perspectives have emerged in sociology: the functionalist, conflict, and interactionist perspectives (see Figure 1.4). These perspectives will be used throughout this book to show you how sociologists try to understand many of the issues affecting Canadian society.

FUNCTIONALIST PERSPECTIVES

Also known as *functionalism* and *structural functionalism*, ***functionalist perspectives*** **are based on the assumption that society is a stable, orderly system.** This stable system is characterized by ***societal consensus*** **whereby the majority of members share a common set of values, beliefs, and behavioural expectations.** According to this perspective, a society is composed of interrelated parts, each of which serves a function and (ideally) contributes to the overall stability of the society. Since this approach was influenced by Comte, Spencer, and Durkheim, who often drew on the work of natural scientists, early functionalists compared society to a living, evolving organism. Societies develop social structures, or institutions, that persist because they play a part in helping society survive. These institutions include the family, education, government, religion, and the economy. If anything adverse happens to one of these institutions or parts, all other parts are affected and the system no longer functions properly. As Durkheim noted, rapid social change and a more specialized division of labour produce *strains* in society that lead to a breakdown in these traditional institutions.

TALCOTT PARSONS AND ROBERT MERTON Talcott Parsons (1902–1979), a founder of the sociology department at Harvard University, was perhaps the most influential contemporary advocate of the functionalist perspective. He stressed that all societies must make provisions for meeting social needs in order to survive. Parsons sought to identify major functions such as the integration of the various parts of society into a whole, the achievement of goals, an incentive to work and cooperate, and adjustment to the environment (Parsons, 1951; Parsons and Shils, 1951).

In a functional analysis of the U.S. family in the 1950s, Parsons (1955) suggested that a division of labour (distinct, specialized functions) between husband and wife is essential for family stability and social order. The husband/father performs the *instrumental tasks*, which involve leadership and decision-making responsibilities in the home and employment outside the home to support the family. The wife/mother is responsible for the *expressive tasks*, including housework, caring for the children, and providing emotional support for the entire family. Parsons believed that other institutions, including school, church, and government, must function to assist the family and that all institutions must work together to preserve

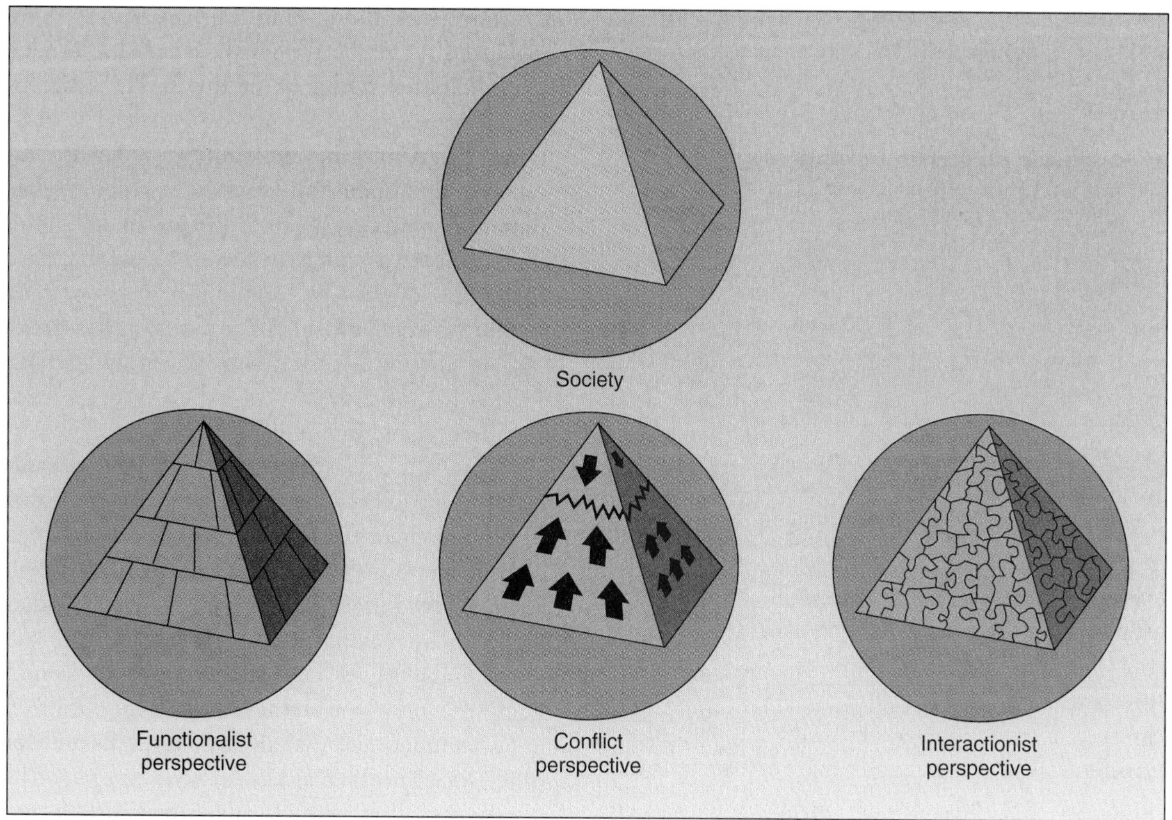

FIGURE 1.4

Three Views of Society

Is society built on consensus or conflict? How do the individual parts add up to the sum total of society? Just as astronomers get very different views of a planet depending on which bands of light they filter out, sociologists using different theoretical filters get different views of society.

the system over time (Parsons, 1955). Although Parsons' analysis has been criticized for its conservative bias, his work still influences sociological thinking about gender roles and the family.

Functionalism was refined further by one of Parsons' students, Robert K. Merton (b. 1910), who distinguished between manifest and latent functions of social institutions. ***Manifest functions* are intended and/or overtly recognized by the participants in a social unit.** In contrast, ***latent functions* are unintended functions that are hidden and remain unacknowledged by participants.** For example, a manifest function of education is the transmission of knowledge and skills from one generation to the next; a latent function is the establishment of social relations and networks. Merton noted that all features of a social system may not be functional at all times; ***dysfunctions* are the undesirable consequences of any element of a society.** A dysfunction of education can be the perpetuation of gender, racial, and class inequalities. Such dysfunctions may threaten the capacity of a society to adapt and survive (Merton, 1968).

Between 1945 and 1960, the functional perspective flourished in sociology; however, social strife during the 1960s exposed the limita-

M.P. Roseanne Skoke took a public stand against rights for same sex couples. Contemporary debates over "family values" reflect the significance of family in society. For functionalists such as Talcott Parsons, families serve important functions that other social institutions can't perform.

tions of this perspective. Critics questioned Parsons's rigid differentiation of gender roles and his assumption that the public sphere belonged to men and the private sphere to women. The functional perspective also was criticized for its tendency to legitimize the status quo without effectively examining conflict and social change. Recently, functionalism has experienced a resurgence and now is referred to by some as "neofunctionalism" (see Alexander, 1985).

APPLYING A FUNCTIONAL PERSPECTIVE TO RAPE How might functionalists analyze the problem of sexual assault, which we examined at the beginning of this chapter? Although a number of possible functionalist explanations exist, we will look briefly at only one. Most functionalists emphasize the importance of shared moral values and strong social bonds to a society. When rapid social change or other disruptive conditions occur, moral values may erode, people may become more uncertain about how to act, and so crime rates—including that of sexual assault—may increase.

Industrialization and urbanization have produced rapid social change, which has eroded the traditional functions of the family, religious organizations, schools, and other social institutions. As a result, these institutions today are less effective in establishing bonds between people than they were in the past. For instance, higher rates of sexual assault may occur in areas that have high rates of divorce, high rates of geographic mobility (people moving in or out of a given area), and/or high rates of tourism (Baron and Straus, 1989).

What would functionalists do about the problem of sexual assault? Families, religious organizations, and schools need to foster higher levels of shared values and morality that encourage respect for others. The criminal justice system needs to get tough on sexual assailants and other criminals by making sure that justice is "sure and swift" and that the punishment "fits the crime." In other words, society needs "law and order."

This functionalist analysis of sexual assault (or other social problems) has been criticized for its assumption that shared values and beliefs are equally beneficial for everyone. However, if a society values men more than women or ties being a "man" to sexual aggression, these values may contribute to the victimization of women and children. Likewise, the law-and-order solution to crime may have inherent class, race, gender, and age biases, as discussed in Chapter 7 ("Deviance and Crime").

Proponents of functionalism point out that this perspective demonstrates the importance of social bonds for the stability of society and the well-being of individuals. If, for example, there is no shared sense of community, people cannot feel safe on the streets or in their own homes.

CONFLICT PERSPECTIVES

According to ***conflict perspectives*, groups in society are engaged in a continuous power struggle for control of scarce resources.** Conflict theory sharply contrasts with functionalist approaches, which see society as based primarily on consensus. Conflict may take the form of politics, litigation, negotiations, or family discussions about financial matters. Simmel, Marx, and Weber contributed significantly to this perspective by focusing on the inevitability of clashes between social groups. Today, advocates of the conflict perspective view social life as a continuous power struggle among competing social groups.

MAX WEBER AND C. WRIGHT MILLS As previously discussed, Marx focused on the exploitation and oppression of the proletariat (the workers) by the bourgeoisie (the owners or capitalist class). Weber recognized the importance of economic conditions in producing inequality and conflict in society but added *power* and *prestige* as other sources of inequality. Weber (1968/1922) defined power as the ability of a person within a social relationship to carry out his or her own will despite resistance from others. Prestige ("status group" to Weber) is a positive or negative social estimation of honour (Weber, 1968/1922).

Other theorists have looked at conflict among many groups and interests (such as employers and employees) as a part of everyday life in any society. Ralf Dahrendorf (1959), for example, observed that conflict is inherent in *all* authority relationships, not just that between the capitalist class and the working class. To Dahrendorf, *power* is the critical variable in explaining human behaviour. People in positions of authority benefit from the conformity of others; those who are forced to conform feel resentment and demonstrate resistance, much as a child may resent parental authority. The advantaged group that possesses authority attempts to preserve the status quo—the existing set of social arrangements—and may use coercion to do so.

C. Wright Mills (1916–1962), a key figure in the development of contemporary conflict theory, encouraged sociologists to get involved in social reform. He contended that value-free sociology was impossible because social scientists must make value-related choices—including the topics they investigate and the theoretical approaches they adopt. In his own work, Mills examined the distribution of wealth and power in the United States. He encouraged others to look beneath everyday events in order to observe the major resource and power inequalities that exist in society. He believed that the most important decisions in the United States are made largely behind the scenes by the ***power elite*—a small clique composed of the top corporate, political, and military officials.** Mills's power elite theory is discussed in Chapter 13 ("Politics and Government").

The conflict perspective is not one unified theory but rather encompasses several branches. One branch includes feminist perspectives, which focus on gender issues (Feagin and Feagin, 1994). A second branch focuses on racial–ethnic inequalities and the continued exploitation of members of some racial–ethnic groups. A third branch is the neo-Marxist approach, which views struggle between the classes as inevitable and as a prime source of social change.

FEMINIST APPROACHES Feminist approaches (or "feminism") direct attention to the importance of gender as an element of social structure. In Canada, feminist sociologists including Dorothy Smith (1987) and Margrit Eichler (1988), have developed a perspective based on women's experience that uses gender as a framework for analysis. Feminism is not one single unified approach. Rather, there are different approaches among feminist writers, namely the liberal, radical, and socialist strains (discussed in Chapter 10, "Sex and Gender"). All of these approaches share the belief that "women and men are equal and should be equally valued as well as have equal rights" (Basow, 1992). According to feminists (including many men as well as women), we live in a *patriarchy*, "a sex/gender system in which men dominate women, and that which is considered masculine is more highly valued that that which is considered feminine" (Renzetti and Curran, 1995:3). Feminist perspectives assume that gender roles are socially created, rather than determined by one's biological inheritance, and that change is essential in order for people to achieve their human potential without limits based on gender. Feminism assumes that society reinforces social expectations through social learning: what we learn is a social product of the political and economic structure of the society in which we live (Renzetti and Curran, 1995). Feminists argue that women's subordination can end only after the patriarchal system becomes obsolete.

APPLYING CONFLICT PERSPECTIVES TO SEXUAL ASSAULT How might advocates of the various conflict approaches explain sexual assault in Canada?

Patriarchy and Sexual Assault A feminist perspective on sexual assault and other types of violence against women suggests that such acts are means of reinforcing patriarchy (Dobash and Dobash, 1992). In patriarchal societies men are socialized to believe that they are superior to women and that they have the right to control and dominate females with whom they are intimate (DeKeseredy, 1988; DeKeseredy and Kelly, 1993a and 1993b). Within patriarchal systems, the sexual marketplace is characterized by unequal bargaining power, making transactions between men and women potentially coercive in nature. Gender stratification is reinforced by powerful physical, psychological, and social mechanisms of control, including force or threat of force. As industrialization and technology have eroded the traditional underpinnings of male privilege, violence has become an increasingly important tool in keeping women "in their place" (MacLeod, 1987; Harris, 1991). Rape and physical brutality continue to be used as a means for men to degrade women who challenge their sense of superiority and to express rage against society in general.

DeKeseredy and Kelly (1993a) conducted an exhaustive study of date rape in Canadian colleges and universities. Data were collected from a representative sample survey of 1835 female students and 1307 male students. DeKeseredy and Kelly (1993a) tested the contention that men who hold patriarchal beliefs have higher rates of violence against intimate female partners than men who hold more egalitarian beliefs. Table 1.1 outlines the four statements used to measure patriarchal beliefs and for each gives the percentage of male respondents who adhered to them.

DeKeseredy and Kelly (1993a) found that although most students did not report attitudes supportive of male dominance in intimate relationships, those male students who had these attitudes and beliefs were the most likely to sexually assault their dating partner.

Racial Oppression and Sexual Assault Conflict theorists who focus on racial–ethnic inequalities emphasize that sexual assault cannot be studied without reference to the racism in which the history of sexual assault is embedded (Collins, 1990; Scully, 1990). For example, in the United States, the rape of African American women by white men virtually was institutionalized during the antebellum South, and the alleged rape of white women was used as a postslavery justification to lynch African American men (Davis, 1981). Before the U.S. Civil War, rape laws were explicitly racist in many states. For example, capital punishment was mandated in Georgia if an African American man was convicted of the sexual assault or attempted sexual assault of a white woman, while the penalty for white men convicted of sexually assaulting African American women was a fine, prison, or both (LaFree, 1989).

Consistent with this differential treatment, 89 percent of the men executed for rape in the United States since 1930 have been African Americans. African American men charged with raping white women continue to be treated more harshly in the criminal justice system than those charged with raping African American women (LaFree, 1980, 1989). While an estimated 80 percent of all rapes and attempted rapes are intraracial (white on white and black on black), the myth persists that most rapes are interracial (between races) (Herman, 1989; Scully, 1990).

Few systematic studies exist pertaining to the victimization of visible minority women in Canada.

TABLE 1.1

Patriarchal Beliefs Among Male Students, 1993

	Agree/Strongly Agree
1. A man has the right to decide whether or not his wife/partner should work outside the home.	6.1%
2. A man has the right to decide whether or not his wife/partner should go out in the evening with her friends.	9.5%
3. Sometimes it is important for a man to show his wife/partner that he is the head of the house.	18.1%
4. A man has the right to have sex with his wife/partner when he wants, even though she may not want to.	2.4%

Source: DeKeseredy and Kelly, 1993a:33. Reprinted by permission.

Class Oppression and Sexual Assault The problem of sexual assault and other crimes of violence is part of a larger system in which sexism and racism are reinforced by an overarching class system that benefits the powerful at the expense of the powerless. Exploitation of people of colour and the poor creates a sense of hopelessness, frustration, and hostility, and such feelings may boil over into violent acts such as sexual assault. However, sexual assault occurs within all social classes in Canada.

Laws pertaining to sexual assault in capitalist countries historically have had a class bias. These laws were framed for the protection of *upper-class white males*, who feared that their wives or daughters might be assaulted. Since women historically were viewed as the sexual "property" of men, marital (or wife) rape was not considered to be a crime in Canada. The 1983 amendment to the Criminal Code has made sexual assault within marriage illegal (DeKeseredy and Hinch, 1991). The sexual assault of working-class women and women of colour was generally of little concern to the courts (Davis, 1981).

The various conflict approaches help clarify the connections between social arrangements in society and problems such as violence and sexual assault. However, these perspectives have been criticized for giving little attention to social stability and shared values. Critics contend that conflict perspectives have lost at least some claim to scientific objectivity. Advocates of conflict perspectives respond that all social approaches have inherent biases, as will be discussed in Chapter 2 ("Sociological Research Methods").

INTERACTIONIST PERSPECTIVES

Both the conflict and the functional perspectives have been criticized for focusing primarily on macrolevel analysis. A ***macrolevel analysis*** **examines whole societies, large-scale social structures, and social systems** instead of looking at important social dynamics in individuals' lives. Our final perspective, interactionism, fills this void by examining people's day-to-day interactions and their behaviour in groups. Thus, interactionist approaches are based on a ***microlevel analysis*,** **which focuses on small groups rather than large-scale social structures.**

According to ***interactionist perspectives*,** **society is the sum of the interactions of individuals**

and groups. This approach focuses on how people act toward one another and how they make sense of those interactions. George Herbert Mead, the original force behind this perspective, emphasized that the ability to communicate in symbols is the key feature distinguishing humans from other animals. Although there are a number of loosely linked interactionist approaches, symbolic interaction is the most widely used.

SYMBOLIC INTERACTION For *symbolic interactionists*, people create and change their social worlds through the use of mutually understood symbols. **A *symbol* is anything that meaningfully represents something else.** Examples of symbols include signs, gestures, written language, and shared values. Symbolic interaction occurs when people communicate through the use of symbols; for example, a gift of food—a cake or a casserole—to a newcomer in a neighbourhood is a symbol of welcome and friendship.

Some interactionists focus on people's behaviour while others focus on the ways in which people impose their shared meanings on others. From this perspective, each person's interpretation or definition of a given situation becomes a *subjective reality* from that person's viewpoint. Individuals generally assume that their subjective reality is the same as that of others; however, this may be incorrect. Subjective reality is acquired and shared through agreed-upon symbols, especially language. If a person shouts, "Fire!" in a crowded movie theatre, for example, that language produces the same response (attempting to escape) in all of those who hear and understand it. When people in a group do not share the same meaning for a given symbol, however, confusion results; for example, people who did not know the meaning of the word *fire* would not know what the commotion was about. How people *interpret* the messages they receive and the situations they encounter becomes their subjective reality and may strongly influence their behaviour. Two branches of this approach, dramaturgical analysis and ethnomethodology, are discussed in Chapter 5 ("Social Structure and Interaction in Everyday Life").

APPLYING INTERACTIONIST PERSPECTIVES TO SEXUAL ASSAULT How might the interactionist perspective analyze sexual assault? As previously discussed, this perspective focuses on the microlevel of society and stresses that human behaviour is learned through social interaction with other people. The basis for understanding the interactionist perspective of sexual assault is the recognition that people interact on the basis of *shared meanings*. As long as the meanings of our actions and behaviours are shared, relationships are relatively free of conflict. However, as DeKeseredy and Hinch comment, "It is when meanings are not shared, or when actions are interpreted differently by the participants that problems arise" (1991:79).

Social Learning and Sexual Assault The roots of the physical abuse of women—including sexual assault—lie in macrolevel societal beliefs about appropriate gender roles. In patriarchal systems, men are taught in a microlevel setting (such as the family or a peer group) that they should be aggressive and dominant; women are taught to be dependent and passive. The mass media constantly reinforce these beliefs by bombarding people with images of sexual violence, as discussed in Box 1.4. A great deal of this violence is against women. According to social learning theory, repetitive exposure to violence can influence some individuals to model that behaviour (Johnson, 1996).

The language that people use may condone or even encourage sexual assault and other violent behaviour. Some men are taught to see sex as something that men do *to* women. Use of words such as *screw* in everyday conversation may signify both sexual intercourse and "doing someone in." Language also can indicate that a person deserves to have something happen to them. For example, the term *cocktease* is often used to describe women viewed as flirtatious or seductive. However, that usage may encourage a man to believe that a woman is "leading him on" and therefore that it's okay to force her to have sex with him.

Most sports, as well as "men's" activities such as hunting and "boy's" war toys, contribute to

BOX 1.4 SOCIOLOGY AND MEDIA

Rape in Prime-Time

Rape is a crime ideally suited to television: It is violent, its sexual nature can be emphasized, and it can be presented as the act of a mentally unbalanced person. Indeed, rape has been depicted extensively on television for the past thirty years. Unfortunately, storylines on prime-time dramas in the 1990s continue to perpetuate such rape myths as the victim was "asking" for it, "wanted" it, is "lying" about it, or was "not hurt." These myths reinforce the notion that women, not men, are responsible for rape. They also suggest that rape is an act of sex, not violence.

Newspapers and television news programs tend to focus attention on the bizarre and unusual in their coverage of rape. The case of Joey Buttafuoco, an auto body mechanic who served a six-month sentence for the statutory rape of Amy Fisher, a 16-year-old girl, was one such situation. The case gained notoriety because Fisher was sentenced to five to fifteen years in prison for the nonfatal shooting of Buttafuoco's wife on the front steps of the Buttafuoco residence. In investigating that shooting, the police uncovered the evidence that resulted in Buttafuoco being arrested for statutory rape.

Not only did Amy Fisher "sell" her story to a tabloid news show, but Joey Buttafuoco attained celebrity status as a result of his crime. When he was released from prison, a tabloid news show paid him a reported $500,000 for an exclusive interview. In addition, fifteen camera crews from television stations and tabloid news programs recorded the events as he left jail and proceeded to a "welcome home" party with several hundred guests, where he announced that he hoped to have a career in Hollywood.

Joey Buttafuoco was inundated by reporters and photographers after he was convicted in the rape of Amy Fisher.

The Buttafuoco-Fisher story is but one example of the increasingly blurred line between rape as "news" and rape as "entertainment."

What do you think is "news"? What is "entertainment"? Is the line between the two getting blurred?

Sources: Based on Faludi, 1991; Lichter, Lichter, and Rothman, 1991; Brinson, 1992; and Marks, 1994.

males' learning to value competition and violence. From a male perspective, sexual violence may be seen as a display of "real masculinity." Women, on the other hand, often are taught to be cooperative and "feminine." They are "educated for romance" and led to believe that some "Prince Charming will sweep them off their feet" (Dowling, 1981; Holland and Eisenhart, 1990).

Different Definitions of the Situation How does our definition of a situation affect how we act? To interact with others, we define the situation according to our own subjective reality. This applies to sexual assault just as it does to other types of conduct. For example, recent studies that analyze date rape on university campuses concluded that the organizational structure and

CONCEPT TABLE 1.A

The Major Theoretical Perspectives

Perspective	Analysis Level	Nature of Society	Application to Sexual Assault
Functionalist	Macrolevel	Society is composed of interrelated parts that work together to maintain stability within society. This stability is threatened by dysfunctional acts and institutions.	High rates of sexual assault result from disorganization in society and the erosion of social institutions that traditionally have functioned to control behaviour.
Conflict	Macrolevel	Society is characterized by social inequality; social life is a struggle for scarce resources. Social arrangements benefit some groups at the expense of others.	High rates of sexual assault result from class, race, and/or gender oppression; the concept of women as "property" to be violated is central to the act of sexual assault.
Interactionist	Microlevel	Society is the sum of the interactions of people and groups. Behaviour is learned in interaction with other people; how people define a situation becomes the foundation for how they behave.	High rates of sexual assault result from learned behaviour that encourages or condones it, including portrayals of such behaviour by the media.

membership in some male peer support groups may encourage sexual violence (Luffman, 1996). DeKeseredy (1988), for example, found that male peers may perpetuate and maintain victimization of female university students. Male peers provide what DeKeseredy refers to as "vocabularies of adjustment," which help men to alter their subjective interpretations of assaultive behaviours. As a result, abusers may experience physical and psychological well-being following a date rape rather than guilt, remorse, or depression. A recent incident at Queen's University demonstrates the potential effects of male peer support: after the student council launched a "No means no" campaign to address the sexual assault of women, students in one of the male residences responded with signs bearing slogans of their own, including "No means more beer," "No means tie me up," and "No means kick her in the teeth" (Comack, 1996:144).

When sexual conquest is defined as the ultimate goal, women are viewed as the objects of that conquest. Language reinforces the acceptability of violence against women. Consider this sign in the yard of a fraternity house at a major university: "Roses are red, orchids R black, I like my date, when she's on her back" (Moss, 1990). However, what a man may define as "seduction," a woman may define as rape, as this conversation among fraternity brothers suggests:

> "Sometimes, a woman has to resist your advances to show how sincere she is. And so, sometimes you've gotta help them along. You know she means no the first time, but the third time she could say no all night and you know she doesn't mean it."
>
> "Yeah, no always means no at the moment, but there might be other ways of ... "
>
> "Working a yes out?"
>
> "Yeah!"
>
> "Get her out on the dance floor, give her some drinks, talk to her for a while."
>
> "Agree to something, sign the papers ... "
>
> "And give her some more drinks!"
>
> "Ply her with alcohol." [Laughter] (Sanday, 1990:113)

In this microlevel interaction, the fraternity brothers have created their own social reality through their interaction. Clearly, their perspective differs from that of many women and men who have spoken out against sexual assault and are actively combating violence against women. Certainly, not all fraternities condone aggressive sexual behaviour. However, organizations such as these may unintentionally reinforce the linkage between masculinity and sexual aggression. They also reflect the ways in which social learning, language usage, and the social construction of reality can shape the manner in which men interact with women, and vice versa (Sanday, 1990; Copenhaver and Grauerholz, 1991; Kalof and Cargill, 1991).

As this interactionist analysis of sexual assault makes clear, social learning is important in how we define ourselves and our relationship to others. Because interactionist perspectives focus on the microlevel of society, they help us see how individuals interact in their daily lives and interpret their experiences. However, this approach also is limited in that it basically ignores the larger social context in which behaviour takes place. If we focus primarily on the individual and small-group context of behaviour, we may overlook important macrolevel societal forces that are beyond the control of individuals, such as the effects of socially imposed definitions of race-ethnicity, gender, class, and age on people's lives.

Each of the three sociological perspectives we have examined involves different assumptions. Consequently, each leads us to ask different questions and to view the world somewhat differently. Different aspects of reality are the focus of each approach. While functionalism emphasizes social cohesion and order, conflict approaches focus primarily on social tension and change. In contrast, interactionism primarily examines people's interactions and shared meanings in everyday life. Concept Table 1.A reviews the three major perspectives. Throughout this book, we will be using these perspectives as lenses through which to view our social world. Each approach also will be helpful in developing your own sociological imagination for the twenty-first century.

CHAPTER REVIEW

Sociology is the systematic study of human society and social interaction. As we explore sociology, we begin to understand how individual behaviour is largely shaped by the groups to which we belong and the society in which we live. Sociology also makes us aware of global interdependence.

- The sociological perspective enables us to examine individual behaviour and group interactions to find explanations for recurring patterns of social behavior. We study sociology to understand how human behavior is shaped by group life and, in turn, how group life is affected by individuals. Our culture tends to emphasize individualism, and sociology pushes us to consider more complex connections between our personal lives and the larger world.
- According to C. Wright Mills, the sociological imagination helps us understand how seemingly personal troubles, such as sexual assault victimization, actually are related to larger social forces. It requires us to include many points of view and diverse experiences in our own thinking.
- Industrialization and urbanization increased rapidly in the late eighteenth century, and social thinkers began to examine the consequences of these powerful forces.
- Auguste Comte coined the term *sociology* and argued that this new discipline should apply the objective research methods of the natural sciences to the study of society. Harriet Martineau examined social customs and analyzed specific consequences of industrialization and capitalism. According to Herbert Spencer's evolutionary perspective, society—like a biological organism—is composed of interdependent parts that must work together to ensure the stability and survival of the entire society.
- The ideas of Emile Durkheim, Karl Marx, and Georg Simmel helped lead the way to contemporary sociology. Durkheim argued that societies are built on social facts, that rapid social change produces strains in society, and that the loss of shared values and purpose can lead to a condition of anomie. Marx stressed that within society there is a continuous clash between the owners of the means of production and the workers who have no choice but to sell their labour to others. According to Weber, it is necessary to acknowledge the meanings that individuals attach to their own actions. Simmel explored small social groups and argued that society was best seen as a web of patterned interactions among people.
- From its origins in Europe, sociology spread to Canada in the 1920s. The first sociology department was located at McGill University in Montreal.
- Three contemporary sociological perspectives incorporate much of the earlier social thinking. Functionalist perspectives assume that society is a stable, orderly system characterized by societal consensus; however, this perspective has been criticized for overlooking the importance of change in societies. By contrast, conflict perspectives argue that society is a continuous power struggle among competing groups, often based on class, race, ethnicity, or gender. Critics of conflict theory note that it minimizes the importance of social stability and shared values in society.
- Interactionist perspectives focus on how people make sense of their everyday social interactions, which are made possible by the use of mutually understood symbols. However, this approach focuses on the microlevel of society and tends to ignore the larger macrolevel social context.

KEY TERMS

anomie **18**
alienation **19**
bourgeoisie **19**
class **13**
class conflict **19**
commonsense knowledge **6**
conflict perspectives **26**
dysfunctions **25**
ethnicity **13**
functionalist perspectives **24**
gender **13**
global interdependence **6**
group consciousness **13**
industrialization **14**
interactionist perspectives **29**
latent functions **25**
macrolevel analysis **29**
manifest functions **25**
means of production **19**
microlevel analysis **29**
objective **9**
perspective **24**
positivism **16**
power elite **27**
proletariat **19**
race **12**
sex **13**
social Darwinism **17**
social facts **18**
societal consensus **24**
society **6**
sociological imagination **10**
sociology **5**
symbol **30**
theory **24**
urbanization **15**

QUESTIONS FOR ANALYSIS AND UNDERSTANDING

1. How does the sociological imagination help us understand that "things are not what they seem" (Berger, 1963:23)?
2. How did the process of industrialization contribute to the development of the field of sociology?
3. How does conflict produce social change?
4. According to the functionalist perspective, what would happen to society if one of its institutions—say, the educational system—were to break down?
5. How are symbols a part of the interactionist perspective?

QUESTIONS FOR CRITICAL THINKING

1. What does C. Wright Mills mean when he says the sociological imagination helps us "to grasp history and biography and the relations between the two within society" (Mills, 1959:6)?
2. As a sociologist, how would you remain objective and yet see the world as others see it? Would you make subjective decisions when trying to understand the perspectives of others?
3. Early social thinkers were concerned about stability in times of rapid change. In our more global world, is stability still a primary goal? Or is

constant conflict important for the well-being of all humans? Use the conflict and functionalist perspectives to support your analysis.

4. Some people think that a woman's willingness to wear revealing clothing is sexually provocative. How would you find out whether a woman's clothing is a factor in sexual assault? If sexual assault is an act of violence rather than of sexual passion toward women, then is the way a woman looks or dresses a factor in sexual assault?

SUGGESTED READINGS

These two classics describe sociological thinking and implementation of the sociological imagination:

Peter L. Berger. *Invitation to Sociology: A Humanistic Perspective*. New York: Anchor, 1963.

C. Wright Mills. *The Sociological Imagination*. New York: Oxford University Press, 1959.

The following books examine various aspects of sociological theory in more depth:

Randall Collins. *Four Sociological Traditions*. New York: Oxford University Press, 1994.

George Ritzer. *Sociological Theory* (3rd ed.). New York: Knopf, 1992.

Dorothy Smith. *The Everyday World as Problematic: A Feminist Sociology*. Toronto: University of Toronto Press, 1987.

These excellent books discuss the contributions of early women sociologists:

Mary Jo Deegan. *Jane Addams and the Men of the Chicago School, 1892–1918*. New Brunswick, N.J.: Transaction, 1988.

Susan Hoecker-Drysdale. *Harriet Martineau: First Woman Sociologist*. Oxford: Berg, 1992.

To find out about career possibilities in sociology, contact the Canadian Sociology and Anthropology Association, Concordia University, 1455 Boul. de Maisonneuve Ouest, Montreal, Quebec M3G 1M8. Ask for the publication *Opportunities in Sociology*.

To find out more about the problem of sexual assault, see:

Walter S. DeKeseredy and Ronald Hinch. *Woman Abuse: Sociological Perspectives*. Toronto: Thompson Educational Publishing, 1991.

Holly Johnson. *Dangerous Domains: Violence Against Women in Canada*. Scarborough, Ont.: Nelson Canada, 1996.

Robin Warshaw. *I Never Called It Rape*. New York: Harper & Row, 1988.

Chapter 2

SOCIOLOGICAL RESEARCH METHODS

Why Is Sociological Research Necessary?

Common Sense and Sociological Research

Sociology and Scientific Evidence

The Theory and Research Cycle

The Sociological Research Process

Selecting and Defining the Research Problem

Reviewing Previous Research

Formulating the Hypothesis (If Applicable)

Developing the Research Design

Collecting the Data

Analyzing the Data

Drawing Conclusions and Reporting the Findings

A Qualitative Approach to Research

Research Methods for Collecting Data

Experiments

Surveys

Secondary Analysis of Existing Data

Field Research

Feminist Research Methods

Multiple Methods of Social Research

Ethical Issues in Sociological Research

The Zellner Research

The Humphreys Research

The Scarce Research

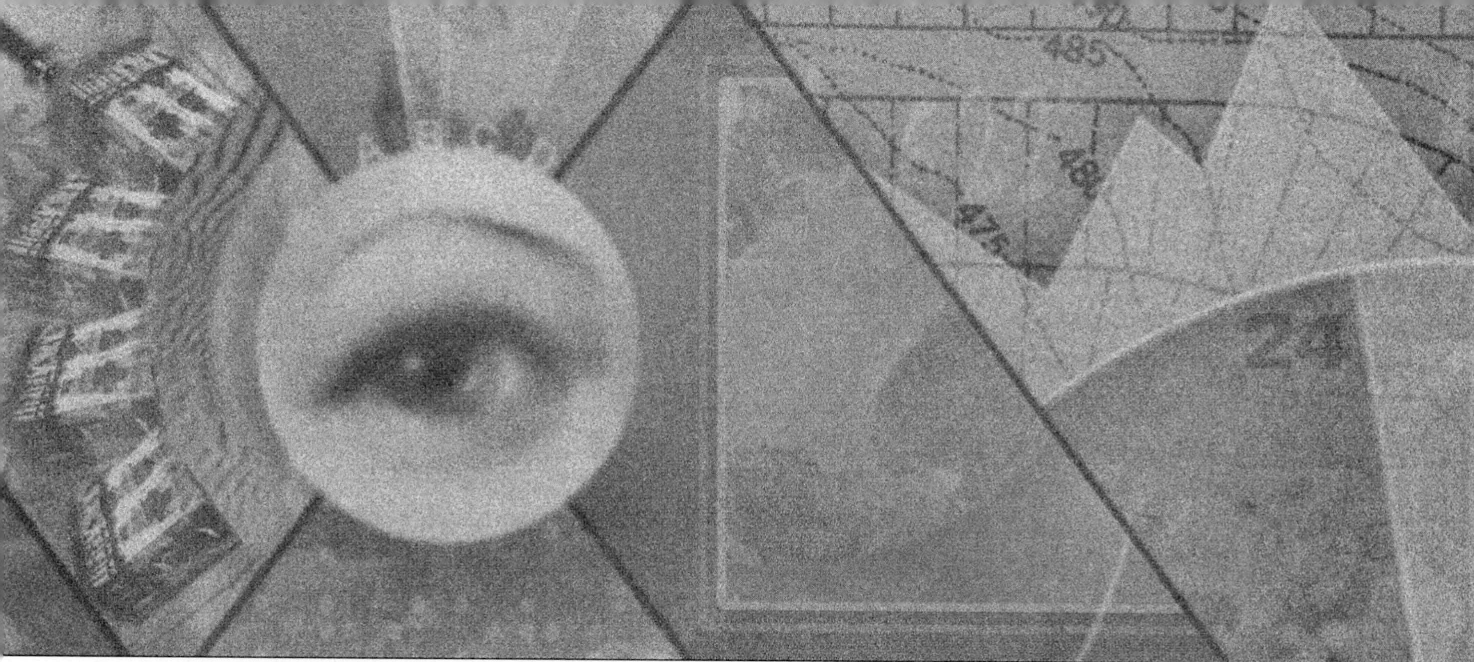

How do sociologists determine what to study? How do they go about conducting research with human subjects? What factors determine the appropriate method to use in their research? These are all questions pertaining to the process of "doing research"—questions that will be addressed in this chapter. Conducting sociological research is an interesting, exciting, and, at times, depressing and difficult process. Why? Because sociological research is directed at understanding human social interaction and solving problems in our social world. Sociological research offers the challenge of going as a "stranger" into a familiar world. In her book, *A Poison Stronger Than Love: The Destruction of an Ojibwa Community*, author Anastasia Shkilnyk discusses the reality of this challenge. Like many social scientists, her research evolved out of her real life experiences:

> My destination was a small Indian reserve called Grassy Narrows, about 1,200 miles northwest of Toronto, my hometown, and 120 miles east of Winnipeg. I did not know at the time, and could never have foreseen, that it would be my destiny to live in this village for two and a half years in order to bear witness to an awesome human tragedy. (1985:1)

Shortly after her arrival in Grassy Narrows, Shkilnyk learned of the high incidence of violent death and suicide. In 1977–78, twenty-six persons between eleven and nineteen had tried to take their own lives. This number represented almost one-fifth of the entire population of this age group. Furthermore, the incidence of violent death was a recent phenomenon at Grassy Narrows. What had happened to make Grassy Narrows "the place where sudden death from violence is most likely?" (1985:3). Why would children attempt to commit suicide? Shkilnyk's research was the result of trying to answer these questions. She

explains how she went about this arduous task and the inspiration that gave her the drive to complete her research:

I committed the next year to a search for more information on how the assault on the Indian people had been delivered. On the basis of data gleaned from public records and archives, additional interviews, and my own extensive collection of field notes, diaries, and transcripts, I wrote a dissertation on the origins of breakdown in community life. This book emerged from that document. It was inspired by the desire to make the story known to a wider public because, to date, the Grassy Narrows people have not been compensated for the personal and communal losses they have suffered. (1985:5)

As this narrative reveals, Shkilnyk did not just decide at random to research the incidence of suicide on a Native reserve. Rather, she was compelled to find answers to the human destruction and suffering that she witnessed while living in Grassy Narrows. In this case, it took years of work, with data obtained from a number of different sources, to develop an understanding of the lives of the Ojibwa living in this community. Sociologist Ian Robertson describes the process of doing research:

> Research in sociology is really a form of systemic detective work—it poses the same early puzzles and suspicions, the same moments of inspired guessing and routine sifting though the evidence, the same disappointments over false leads and facts that do not fit and perhaps, the same triumph when the pieces finally fall into place and the answer emerges. Research in sociology is where the real action takes place. (1977:29)

In this chapter, we will see how sociological research methods are used to answer complex questions, and we will address some of the difficulties in studying human behaviour.

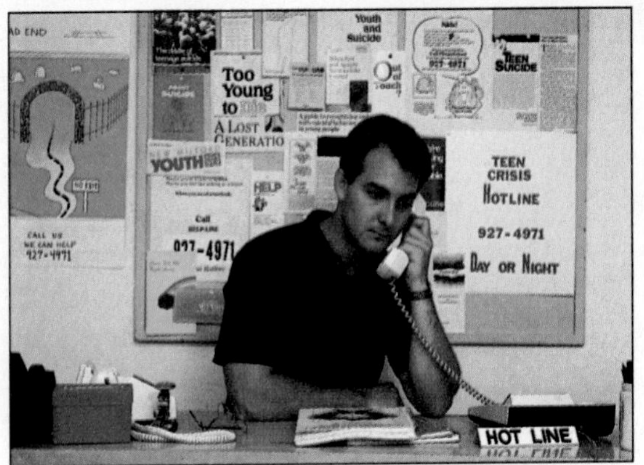

Can a suicide crisis centre prevent a person from committing suicide? People who understand factors that contribute to suicide may be able to better counsel those who call for help.

QUESTIONS AND ISSUES

How does social research add to our knowledge of human societies?

What is the relationship between theory and research?

What are the main steps of the sociological research process?

Why is it important to have different research methods?

What has research contributed to our understanding of suicide?

Why is a code of ethics for sociological research necessary?

WHY IS SOCIOLOGICAL RESEARCH NECESSARY?

Sociologists obtain their knowledge of human behaviour through research, which results in a body of information that helps us move beyond guesswork and common sense in understanding

BOX 2.1 SOCIOLOGY AND EVERYDAY LIFE

How Much Do You Know About Suicide?

TRUE	FALSE	
T	F	1. For people thinking of suicide, it is difficult, if not impossible, to see the bright side of life.
T	F	2. People who talk about suicide don't do it.
T	F	3. Once people contemplate or attempt suicide, they must be considered suicidal for the rest of their lives.
T	F	4. In Canada, suicide occurs on an average of one every two hours.
T	F	5. Accidents and injuries sustained by teenagers and young adults may indicate suicidal inclinations.
T	F	6. Alcohol and drugs are outlets for anger and thus reduce the risk of suicide.
T	F	7. Older men have higher rates of both attempted and completed suicide than older women.
T	F	8. Children don't know enough to be able to intentionally kill themselves.
T	F	9. Suicide rates for native Canadians are the highest in Canada.
T	F	10. Suicidal people are fully intent on dying.

Answers on page 42

society. In Chapter 1, we looked at commonsense ideas about sexual assault and noted that these beliefs often are incorrect. The sociological perspective incorporates theory and research to arrive at a more accurate understanding of the "hows" and "whys" of human social interaction. Once we have an informed perspective about social issues, such as who commits suicide and why, we are in a better position to find solutions and make changes. Social research, then, is a key part of sociology.

COMMON SENSE AND SOCIOLOGICAL RESEARCH

Most of us have common sense ideas about suicide. Common sense, for example, may tell us that people who threaten suicide will not commit suicide. Sociological research indicates that this assumption frequently is incorrect: people who threaten to kill themselves often are sending messages to others and may indeed attempt suicide. Common sense also may tell us that suicide is caused by despair or depression. However, research suggests that suicide sometimes is also used as a means of lashing out at friends and relatives because of real or imagined wrongs. Before reading on, take the quiz in Box 2.1, which lists a number of common sense notions about suicide.

Historically, the common sense view of suicide was that it was a sin, a crime, and a mental illness (Evans and Farberow, 1988). Emile Durkheim

BOX 2.1

Answers to the Sociology Quiz on Suicide

TRUE	FALSE	
T	F	1. *True.* To people thinking of suicide, an acknowledgment that there is a bright side only confirms and conveys the message that they have failed; otherwise, they, too, could have a bright side of life. Being told that "things will look better tomorrow" only causes a depressed person to feel more isolated and alone.
T	**F**	2. *False.* Some people who talk about suicide do kill themselves. Warning signals of possible suicide attempts include talk of suicide, the desire not to exist anymore, despair, and hopelessness.
T	**F**	3. *False.* Most people think of suicide for only a limited amount of time. When the crisis is over and the problems leading to suicidal thoughts are resolved, people usually cease to think of suicide as an option. However, if in the future problems arise with which the individual cannot cope, suicide may once again be an option.
T	F	4. *True.* A suicide occurs an average of every two hours in Canada; however, the rate of suicide differs with respect to the sex, race/ethnicity, and age of the individual. For example, men kill themselves more than three times as often as do women.
T	F	5. *True.* Accidents, injuries, and other types of life-threatening behaviour may be signs that a person is on a course of self-destruction. One study concluded that the incidence of suicide was twelve times higher among adolescents and young adults who previously had been hospitalized because of an injury.
T	**F**	6. *False.* Excessive use of alcohol or drugs may enhance a person's feelings of anger and frustration, making suicide a greater possibility. This risk appears to be especially high for men who abuse alcohol or drugs.
T	F	7. *True.* In Canada, as in other countries, suicide rates are highest among men over the age of 70. One theory of why this is true asserts that older women may have a more flexible and diverse coping style than older men.
T	**F**	8. *False.* Children do know how to intentionally hurt or kill themselves. They may learn the means and methods from television, movies, and other people. However, the Division of Health Statistics of Statistics Canada (the agency responsible for compiling suicide statistics) does not recognize suicides under the age of 10; they are classified as accidents, despite evidence that young children have taken their own lives.
T	F	9. *True.* The rate of suicide among native people in Canada for all age groups is 2 to 3 times higher than the rate among non-native people. It is 5 to 6 times higher among native youth than non-native youth.
T	**F**	10. *False.* Suicidal people often have an ambivalence about dying—they want to live and to die at the same time. They want to end the pain or problems they are experiencing, but they also wish that something or someone would remove the pain or problem so that life can continue.

Sources: Based on Levy and Deykin, 1989; Patros and Shamoo, 1989; Wickett, 1989; Leenaars, 1991; Health Statistics, Statistics Canada, 1994; and Royal Commission on Aboriginal Peoples, 1995.

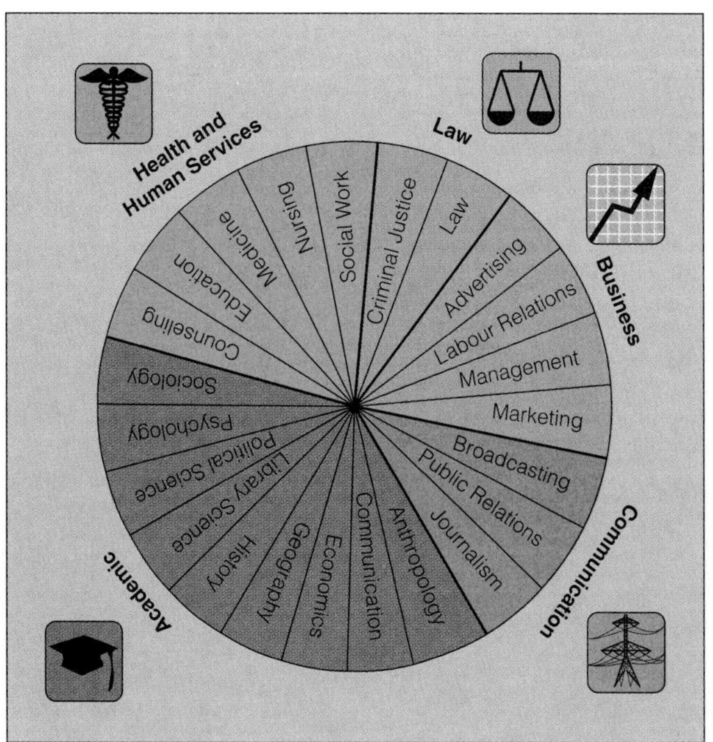

FIGURE 2.1

Fields that Use Social Science Research

In many careers, including jobs in academia, business, communication, health and human services, and law, the ability to analyze social science research is an important asset.

Source: Based on Katzer, Cook, and Crouch, 1991.

refused to accept these explanations. In what is probably the first sociological study to use scientific research methods, Durkheim did not view suicide as an isolated act that could be understood only by studying individual personalities or inherited tendencies; instead he related suicide to the issue of cohesiveness (or lack of cohesiveness) in society. In *Suicide* (1964b/1897), Durkheim documented his contention that a high suicide rate was symptomatic of large-scale societal problems. In the process, he developed an approach to research that influences researchers to this day. As we discuss sociological research, we will focus on the problem of suicide to demonstrate the research process.

Since much of sociology deals with everyday life, we might think that common sense, our own personal experiences, and the media are the best sources of information. However, our personal experiences are subjective, and much of the information provided by the media comes from sources seeking support for a particular point of view. The content of the media also is influenced by the continual need for audience ratings.

We need to be able to evaluate the information we receive. The quantity of information available has grown dramatically as a result of the information explosion brought about by the computer and telecommunications. For example, in 1993, people around the world watched as a fifty-one-day standoff between law enforcement officials and members of a religious cult ended in a fiery mass suicide. Box 2.2 discusses the widespread publicity given to both the standoff and its dramatic conclusion.

SOCIOLOGY AND SCIENTIFIC EVIDENCE

In taking this course, you will be studying social science research and may be asked to write research reports or read and evaluate journal articles. If you attend graduate or professional school in fields that use sociological research, you will be expected to evaluate existing research and perhaps do your own. Figure 2.1 shows some of the fields in which the ability to analyze social

BOX 2.2 SOCIOLOGY AND MEDIA

Televising a Mass Suicide

On February 28, 1993, more than one hundred federal agents arrived at the compound occupied by the Branch Davidian cult in Waco, Texas, to serve search and arrest warrants for illegal weapons. A forty-five-minute gun battle ensued, during which four federal agents and at least one cult member were killed. During the fifty-one-day standoff that followed between David Koresh (the self-proclaimed messiah of his cult of fundamentalist Christians) and federal agents, a few cult members and children were released sporadically; however, the others refused to surrender. The media set up a press encampment near the compound. Mobile homes soon appeared, complete with artificial grass, folding lawn chairs, and mail boxes.

Approximately seven weeks later, federal agents notified the cult they were going to use tear gas to evacuate the compound if the members did not surrender peacefully. When no one surrendered, agents proceeded to ram the building with an armoured vehicle and inject tear gas; cult members shot rounds of ammunition at the vehicle. Between 7:00 A.M. and noon, armoured vehicles continued to ram holes in the building and inject tear gas. Shortly after 12:00 noon, what may have been a mass suicide occurred when Koresh and his followers allegedly set a series of fires that engulfed the compound in minutes.

The blaze that destroyed the cult's headquarters was a television spectacular. The story that had begun seven weeks before had been languishing, and the initial pictures of federal agents being gunned down as they attempted to penetrate the compound gradually were replaced by less intriguing footage.

Once a "grabber" of a story makes it onto television, it loses some of its reality and assumes the aspect of soap opera or made-for-television drama. The confrontation in Waco had audience-holding elements that have been depicted in a television special: a cult, fueled by religion (or sex or drugs) and run by a self-proclaimed prophet or simply a control freak, had for some reason brought down the wrath of the federal government, which evidently did not know what it faced.

On the final day of the standoff, CNN and other media representatives broadcast live at various times during the day, filling the screen with pictures of an orange inferno—the burning compound that the FBI hours earlier had rammed with military vehicles and bombarded with tear gas in hopes of flushing out cult leader Koresh and his followers. "The fire went through [the compound] like kindling," ABC's Charles Murphy reported. "In about 10, 15 minutes it was done" (Rosenberg, 1993:A3).

Local stations were scrambling to interview surviving cult members and their relatives, and cult experts were "weighing in." Later, as the image of the flames engulfing the structure reappeared on the evening news, the drama took on a kind of show-business inevitability. It is hard to ignore such a story. If, as the authorities insist, the Branch

research is important. Hopefully, you will find that social research is relevant to the practical, everyday concerns of the real world.

Sociology often involves *debunking*—the unmasking of fallacies (false or mistaken ideas or opinions) in the everyday and official interpretations of society (Mills, 1959). Since problems such as sexual assault and suicide involve threats to existing societal values, we cannot analyze the problems without acknowledging the values involved.

Based on your own beliefs, do you think that suicide and/or assisting suicide should be legal? How should society deal with these issues? We often answer questions like this by using either the normative approach or the empirical approach. The ***normative approach*** **uses religion, customs, habits, traditions, and law to answer important questions**. It is based on strong beliefs about what is right and wrong, and what ought to be in society. Issues such as assisted suicide (see Box 2.3)

BOX 2.2 SOCIOLOGY AND MEDIA

Continued

Davidians set their own fires, that was, of course, a horror. Yet, in a grim way, it made for satisfying television. The expectation of some such spectacle had been in many viewers' minds for weeks.

Was it inevitable that the Branch Davidians would die in what may have been a mass suicide? Or did the constant media attention contribute to that end, causing law enforcement officials to feel compelled to end the standoff and encouraging Koresh to choose the martyr's fiery death for himself and his followers rather than surrender? Do the media just present the news, or do they sometimes contribute to it?

The media often provide us with answers that are based on and that reinforce popular assumptions. Sociologists, on the other hand, attempt to provide systematic examinations of phenomena such as mass suicides or homicides using scientific criteria.

Sources: Based on Church, 1993; Goodman, 1993; Rosenberg, 1993; and Verhovek, 1993.

The international media's attention was riveted on the standoff between members of the Branch Davidian cult and federal agents from the U.S. Bureau of Alcohol, Tobacco, and Firearms. Did the constant and intense media attention affect the outcome?

often are answered by the normative approach. From a legal standpoint, the consequences of assisting in another person's suicide may be severe.

While these issues are immediate and profound, contemporary sociologists, for the most part, discourage the use of the normative approach in their field and advocate use of the empirical approach. The ***empirical approach*** **attempts to answer questions through systematic collection and analysis of data.** This approach is referred to as the "scientific method" and is based on the assumption that knowledge is best gained by direct, systematic observation. Sociologists, then, adhere to two basic scientific standards: (1) "scientific beliefs must be supported by good evidence or information" and (2) "beliefs must be open to debate and criticism, and alternative interpretations must be considered" (Cancian, 1992:631).

Sociologists typically use two types of empirical studies: descriptive and explanatory. ***Descriptive studies*** **attempt to describe social reality or provide facts about some group, practice, or event.** Studies of this type are designed to find out what is happening to whom, where, and when. For example, a descriptive study of suicide might attempt to determine the number of people who recently contemplated suicide. Well-known descriptive studies include the reports on the Canadian Census and the Uniform Crime Reports; however, even these "objective" studies have certain biases, as discussed in this chapter and in Chapter 7 ("Deviance and Crime"). By contrast, ***explanatory studies*** **attempt to explain cause-and-effect relationships and to provide information on why certain events do or do not occur.** In an explanatory study of suicide, we

BOX 2.3 SOCIOLOGY AND LAW

Assisting Suicide

In a recent Gallup poll, over 75 percent of people surveyed agreed with the statement "When a person has an incurable disease that causes great suffering, competent doctors should be allowed to end the patient's life through mercy killing" (Wood, 1994). Another recent study—this one conducted by the Manitoba Association of Rights and Liberties—found that although prohibited by law from doing so, many physicians are participating in physician-assisted suicides (Searles, 1995).

Under common law (the legal system developed in England and adopted in Canada), suicide was a crime. This legal view of suicide as a serious crime may have been influenced by a number of considerations: religious (life was sacred), moral (suicide was wrong), practical (society needed the benefit of the person's labours), and political (the offender's property was forfeited to the government, as was true with other serious crimes, such as treason and murder). It was also an offence to "aid and abet" suicide—to counsel someone to commit suicide or to help the person end his or her own life. Thus, the government was "reimbursed" for its loss of the individual, through both financial and other penalties imposed on the perpetrator and any "accomplices."

In legal terms, suicide consists of voluntary and intentional destruction of one's own life by someone old enough to know what he or she is doing. In Canada, suicide is no longer a crime; the courts have done away with the property forfeiture aspect of the penalty (thus, the state does not gain by prosecution), and the person who committed suicide is not around to punish.

That leaves two other crimes: attempted suicide and assisting suicide. In 1972, attempted suicide was removed from the provisions of the Criminal Code. The then Minister of Justice explained: "We have removed the offence of attempted suicide … on the philosophy that this is not a matter which requires a legal remedy; that it has its roots and its solution in sciences outside of the law and that certainly deterrence under the legal system is unnecessary" (Health Canada, 1994:77). Counselling or assisting suicide remains a criminal act in Canada, punishable by a maximum of fourteen years' imprisonment.

Medical science has progressed to the point where people can be kept alive by machines long after there is any realistic expectation that they will ever again function independently. In such cases, friends and relatives frequently have sought legal authorization to allow the patient to die "in peace and dignity." As will be discussed in Chapter 11 ("Aging and Disability"), the cost of maintaining life at this point is high when one considers the unlikely chance that the individual will again function outside of the hospital. For those (and other related) reasons, many individuals have chosen to have a *living will*, which is written in advance and which directs that they not be kept alive past the point when life—without the support of medical technology—is no longer possible. To some people, a living will is still a form of suicide: the individual is directing that life end before the last point at which it can be maintained. In Canada, a person who turns off the life-sustaining treatment under

The controversy over assisted suicide in Canada usually is linked with the name Sue Rodriguez, who battled all the way to the Supreme Court in an attempt to have physician-assisted suicide decriminalized.

BOX 2.3 SOCIOLOGY AND LAW

Continued

the authority of a living will is *not* committing an offence.

Still to be resolved, however, is the issue of assisting people who have a terminal illness and who want to end their own (and perhaps their family's or friends') agony over an apparently irreversible physical deterioration—and the pain that may accompany it. Should it be up to the courts or the legislatures to decide this issue? This question was recently pursued all the way to the Supreme Court of Canada by Sue Rodriguez, a 42-year-old woman suffering from Lou Gehrig's disease (a degenerative fatal disease in which the muscles weaken until eating and breathing are no longer possible). Rodriguez requested the legal right to have the assistance of a physician in ending her life. She was told that it is illegal for anyone to assist in a suicide, even if the person wanting to die is too disabled to commit suicide on her or his own. In 1993, in a narrow decision, the Supreme Court declined Rodriguez's challenge and upheld the law prohibiting assisted suicide.

Does a person have a right to die if they are physically healthy? Does society have the right to say that such a person does not have that right? If a person has the right to terminate her or his own life, should that person be able to get advice and assistance regarding that decision—just as the person does for any other legal action? If the answer is yes, then does a person have the right to at least request (and does someone else have the right to provide) assistance in committing suicide? If the answer is yes, then there are further questions, such as: When should that assistance be made available? Should a perfectly healthy (in a physical sense) person have that right? Should a minor or a person who simply has suffered a temporary setback have it? These are the types of questions sociologists, lawyers, legislatures, courts, and the general public must continue to try to answer. What do you think?

Sources: Based on Humphrey, 1993; Lester and Tallmer, 1993; Health Canada, 1994; and Searles, 1995).

might ask, Why do Native people in Canada have such high suicide rates? or Why do more women than men engage in nonfatal suicidal behaviour? Seeking answers to questions such as these is why sociologists engage in the research process.

THE THEORY AND RESEARCH CYCLE

The relationship between theory and research has been referred to as a continuous cycle, as shown in Figure 2.2 (Wallace, 1971). As we saw in Chapter 1, a theory is a set of logically interrelated statements that attempts to describe, explain, and (occasionally) predict social events. A theory attempts to explain why something is the way it is. Research is the process of systematically collecting information for the purposes of testing an existing theory or generating a new one. The theory-and-research cycle consists of deductive and inductive approaches. In the ***deductive approach*, the researcher begins with a theory and uses research to test the theory**. This approach proceeds as follows: (1) theories generate hypotheses; (2) hypotheses lead to observations (data gathering); (3) observations lead to the formation of generalizations; and (4) generalizations are used to support the theory, to suggest modifications to it, or to refute it. To illustrate, if we use the deductive method to answer the question, Why do people commit suicide?, we start by formulating a theory about the "causes" of suicide and then test our theory by collecting and analyzing data (for example, vital statistics on suicides or surveys to determine whether adult church members view suicide differently from nonmembers).

In the ***inductive approach*****, the researcher collects information or data (facts or evidence) and then generates theories from the analysis of that data.** Under the inductive approach, we would proceed as follows: (1) specific observations suggest generalizations; (2) generalizations produce a tentative theory; (3) the theory is tested through the formation of hypotheses; and (4) hypotheses may provide suggestions for additional observations. Using the inductive approach to study suicide, we might start by simultaneously collecting and analyzing data related to suicidal behaviour and then generate a theory (see Glaser and Strauss, 1967; Reinharz, 1992). In fact, researchers rarely, if ever, begin with either just a theory or data. Inductive theorists need at least rudimentary theories in order to guide their data collection, and deductive theorists must refer constantly to the real world as they develop their theories. Researchers may break into the cycle at different points depending on what they want to know and what information is available. Theory gives meaning to research; research helps support theory.

Research helps us question assumptions we may have about suicide and other social problems. A healthy scepticism (a feature of science) is important in research because it keeps us open to the possibility of alternative explanations. Some degree of scepticism is built into each step of the research process. With that in mind, let's explore the steps in the sociological research process.

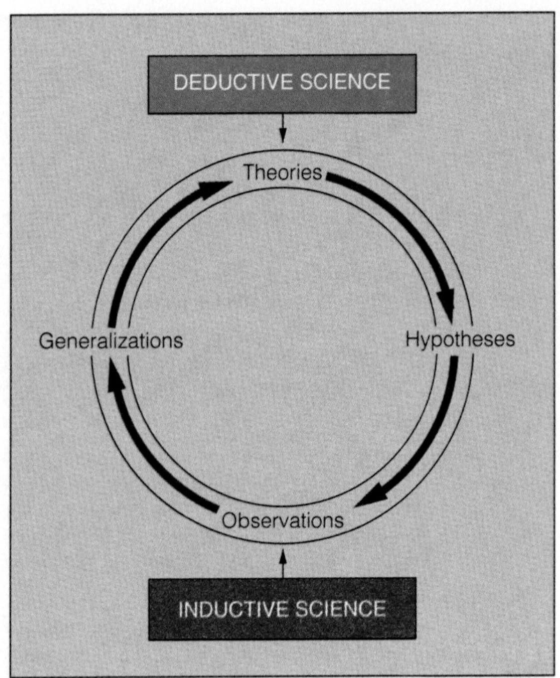

FIGURE 2.2

The Theory and Research Cycle

The theory and research cycle can be compared to a relay race; although all participants do not necessarily start or stop at the same point, they share a common goal: to examine all levels of social life.

Source: Adapted from Walter Wallace, *The Logic of Science in Sociology*, New York: Aldine de Gruyer, 1971.

THE SOCIOLOGICAL RESEARCH PROCESS

Suppose you were going to do some sociological research. How would you go about conducting your study? The procedure outlined here provides the guidelines for sociological research. As revealed in Figure 2.3, the order of these steps may vary depending on the type of research you are doing.

SELECTING AND DEFINING THE RESEARCH PROBLEM

The first step is to select a topic to research. Sometimes, a specific experience such as knowing someone who committed suicide can trigger interest in a topic. Anastasia Shkilnyk selected her topic when she became aware that suicides were reaching epidemic proportions in

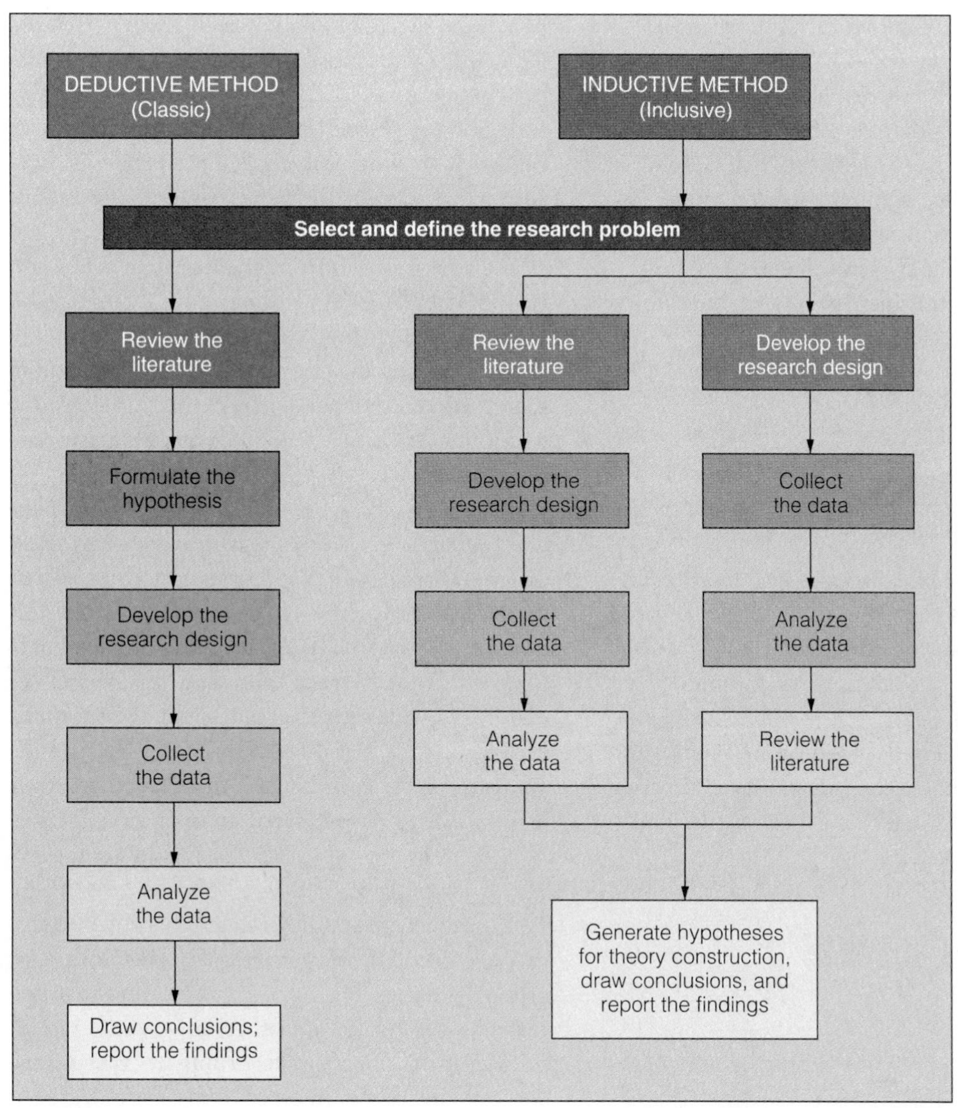

FIGURE 2.3

Steps in Sociological Research

Grassy Narrows. You might select topics to fill gaps or challenge misconceptions in existing research or to test a specific theory (Babbie, 1992). Sociologist Lesley Harman describes how she selected homeless women as the topic of her research:

> Something important began while I was teaching a course in sociology of deviance at York University, during the final year of my Ph.D program. I was giving a lecture on homelessness and one student asked, "What's all this about 'bag ladies'? I've never seen one and I don't think we have any in Toronto." I suggested that the fact that she lived, worked, shopped and studied in North York might have something to do with her perceptions, and that she might have a

> change of heart if she ventured downtown. The next week she could hardly wait to announce to the class that she had "seen one," confirming that I was right and that "there really are such things as 'bag ladies'." My interest in the cultural production of homeless women grew, and came to encompass a concern for the experience of homelessness among this increasingly visible category of women. (Harman, 1989:1)

Once a topic is selected, you must ask yourself, What do I want to know about this topic?

REVIEWING PREVIOUS RESEARCH

Once you have defined your research problem, you need to review the literature (relevant books and scholarly articles). Knowledge of the existing literature is essential for a number of reasons. It helps to refine the research problem, provides possible theoretical approaches, indicates which aspects of the research topic have already been examined and where the gaps are, and identifies mistakes to avoid.

FORMULATING THE HYPOTHESIS (IF APPLICABLE)

After reviewing previous research, you may formulate a ***hypothesis*—a statement of the relationship between two or more concepts**. Concepts are the abstract elements representing some aspect of the world in simplified form (such as "social integration" or "loneliness"). As you formulate your hypothesis about suicide, you may need to convert concepts to variables. A ***variable* is any concept with measurable traits or characteristics that can change or vary from one person, time, situation, or society to another**. Variables are the observable and/or measurable counterparts of concepts. For example, "suicide" is a concept; the "rate of suicide" is a variable.

Now you are ready to answer two important questions: What are the essential variables? and What are the relations between them? (Hoover, 1992:48). The most fundamental relationship in a hypothesis is between a dependent variable and one or more independent variables (see Figure 2.4). The ***independent variable* is presumed to cause or determine a dependent variable.** Sociologists often use age, sex, race, and ethnicity as independent variables. The ***dependent variable* is assumed to depend on or be caused by the independent variable(s)** (Babbie, 1992). Durkheim used the degree of social integration in society as the independent variable to determine its influence on the dependent variable, the rate of suicide.

Whether a variable is dependent or independent depends on the context in which it is used. To use variables in the contemporary research process, sociologists create operational definitions. An ***operational definition* is an explanation of an abstract concept in terms of observable features that are specific enough to measure the variable.** Suppose, for example, your goal is to earn an "A" in this course. Your professor may have created an operational definition by defining an "A" as "having an exam average of 90 percent or above" (Babbie, 1992:G6).

Durkheim's hypothesis stated that suicide rates vary according to strength of social integration, or group solidarity. His hypothesis asserted that two variables are related in a specific way: the rate of suicide varies *inversely* according to the degree of social integration. In other words, a low degree of social integration may "cause" or "be related to" a high rate of suicide.

Events such as suicide are too complex to be caused by any one variable. Therefore, they must be explained in terms of *multiple causation*—that is, an event occurs as a result of many factors operating in combination. What *does* cause suicide? Social scientists cite multiple causes, including rapid social change, economic conditions, hopeless poverty, and lack of religiosity (the degree to which an individual or group feels committed to a particular system of religious beliefs). Usually, no one factor will cause a person to commit suicide. For example, poverty alone typically does

FIGURE 2.4

Hypothesized Relationships Between Variables

A causal hypothesis connects one or more independent (causal) variables with a dependent (affected) variable. The diagram illustrates three hypotheses about the causes of suicide. To test these hypotheses, social scientists would need to operationalize the variables (define them in measurable terms) and then investigate whether the data support the proposed explanation.

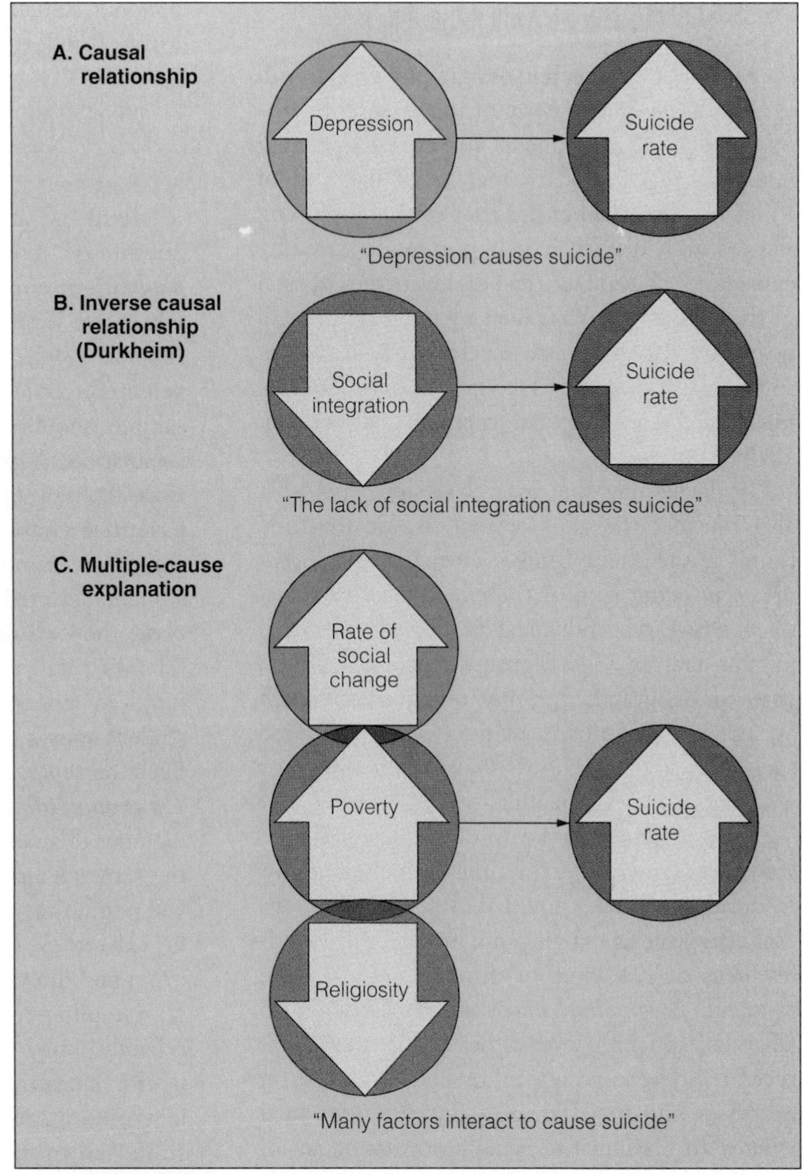

not cause people to kill themselves—only a small proportion of poor people take their own lives. Rather, other factors must combine with a factor such as poverty to cause a person to commit suicide. Sociologists cannot produce an equation (such as poverty + homelessness = suicide) to predict a social occurrence.

Not all social research makes use of hypotheses. If you plan to conduct an explanatory study (showing a cause-and-effect relationship), you likely will want to formulate one or more hypotheses to test theories. If you plan to conduct a descriptive study, however, you will be less likely to do so, since you may want only to describe social reality or provide facts.

DEVELOPING THE RESEARCH DESIGN

During the research design phase, you will decide on one or more of the research methods—including experiments, survey research, field research, and secondary analysis of data, all of which are described in this chapter. In developing the research design, it is important to carefully consider the advantages and disadvantages of each of these methods. Your final research results will be no better than the data on which they are based, so the researcher must take great care in collecting and recording information (Robertson, 1977:43).

In developing the research design, you must also consider the units of analysis and the time frame of the study. *Units of analysis* are the *what* or *whom* being studied (Babbie, 1992). In social science research, individuals are the most typical unit of analysis. Social groups (such as families, cities, or geographic regions), organizations (such as clubs, labour unions, or political parties), and social artifacts (such as books, paintings, or weddings) also may be units of analysis.

After determining the unit of analysis for your study, you must select a time frame for study. *Cross-sectional studies* are based on observations that take place at a single point in time; these studies focus on behaviour or responses at a specific moment. *Longitudinal studies* are concerned with what is happening over a period of time or at several different points in time; they focus on processes and social change. Some longitudinal studies are designed to examine the same set of people each time, while others look at trends within a general population. Longitudinal studies have produced important information about suicide that could not have been obtained in a cross-sectional study. For example, researchers have found that, when an unusually large *cohort* (a group of people who share some demographic characteristic—in this case, age) of adolescents exists, their suicide rate increases. Longitudinal studies have followed such cohorts to determine if increased competition for jobs, admission to certain universities, and academic and athletic honours contribute to increased rates of suicide within a cohort (see Hollinger, 1990).

COLLECTING THE DATA

Your next step is to collect the data. You must decide what population will be observed or questioned, and carefully select a sample. The ***population*** **consists of those persons about whom we want to be able to draw conclusions** (Babbie, 1992). A ***sample*** **is the people who are selected from the population to be studied**; the sample should accurately represent the larger population. A ***representative sample*** **is a selection from a larger population that has the essential characteristics of the total population**. For example, if you have to interview five students selected haphazardly from your sociology class, they would not be representative of your school's total student body. By contrast, if five hundred students were selected from the total student body by a random sample, they would very likely be representative of your school's students. A ***random sample*** **is chosen by chance**: every member of an entire population being studied has the same chance of being selected. For example, you might draw a sample of the total student body by placing all the students' names in a rotating drum and drawing names from it.

Sampling errors, subjectivity, and validity and reliability may be problems in research. ***Validity*** **is the extent to which a study or research instrument accurately measures what it is supposed to measure**. A recurring issue in studies that analyze the relationship between religious beliefs and suicide is whether "church membership" is an accurate indicator of a person's religious beliefs. One person may be very religious yet not belong to a specific church; another person may be a member of a church yet not hold very deep religious beliefs. Religion can be viewed not only in terms of specific behaviours, such as frequency of attendance at services, but also as a set of values, beliefs, or attitudes, thus making measurement an important issue (see Breault, 1986). ***Reliability*** **is the extent to which a study**

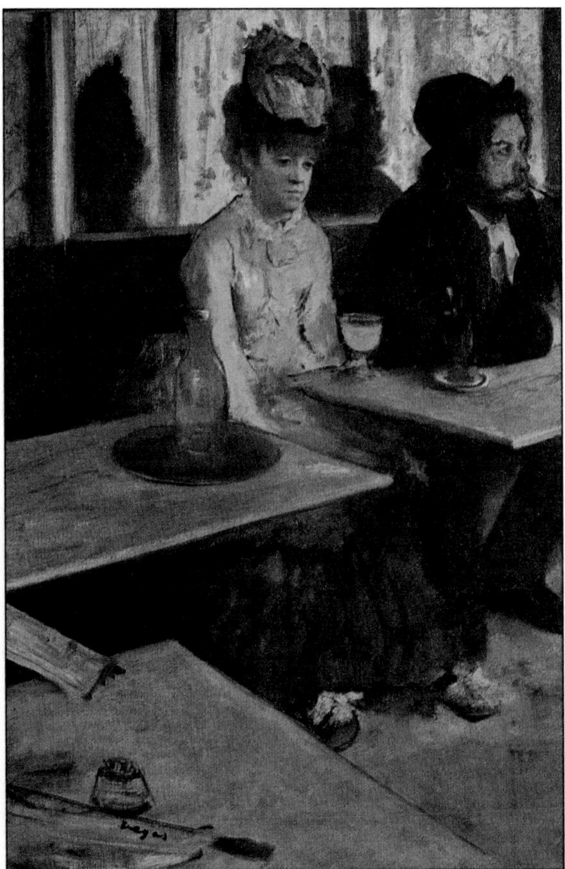

From Emile Durkheim's day to the present, people are more likely to kill themselves when their ties to others are very weak—as shown by two lonely people at L'Absinthe in Paris during Durkheim's time—or when ties are very strong—as shown by the 1994 mass suicide in Cheiry, Switzerland, where forty-eight members of a Canadian-based cult allegedly committed suicide.

or research instrument yields consistent results when applied to different individuals at one time or to the same individual over time. Sociologists have found that different interviewers get different answers from the people being interviewed. For example, how might interviews with college students who have contemplated suicide be influenced by the interviewers themselves?

Researchers using a qualitative approach typically are less concerned about scientific sampling techniques and statistical measures of reliability and validity. They are more concerned with creating a collaborative effort in which the participant is interested in investing the time necessary for the project. Collaborative problem formulation minimizes the possibility of misleading or deceiving participants, because they are involved at all stages of the research process.

ANALYZING THE DATA

Once you have collected your data, they must be analyzed. *Analysis* is the process through which data are organized so that comparisons can be made and conclusions drawn. For example Box 2.4 addresses suicide rates in different countries. The data is organized in such a way that international comparisons can be made. Sociologists use

BOX 2.4 SOCIOLOGY IN GLOBAL PERSPECTIVE

A Look at International Trends in Suicide

Researchers have difficulty making global comparisons regarding certain kinds of behaviour. Suicide is no exception. Frequently, suicide is discussed in Canada as if the patterns for this country are typical of all countries; however, this assumption generally is invalid.

In Canada, the two most discussed trends in suicide are the increasing suicide rate with age and the rising adolescent suicide rate among young men. How do these trends compare with other nations? Worldwide, there are three basic patterns in the variation of suicide rates:

1. an incline where the suicide rate increases regularly with age;
2. the two-peak model, where the suicide rate increases slightly in young adulthood and increases dramatically in old age;
3. one that peaks in middle age and has an inverted U-shaped curve.

Table 1 lists some countries that generally meet each of these criteria. Note that the trends for men and women are different within a number of the countries.

As Table 1 shows, several countries have suicide rates that rise with age for both sexes. In Austria and France, the peak in old age is particularly striking. For example, in Austria, the suicide rate for men aged 75 and older in 1989 was 96.0 per 100,000; in France, it was 109.0 per 100,000. In 1989 Japan had one of the highest rates of suicide for women aged 75 and older—51.6 per 100,000. Among developed nations, the second pattern—a slight peak in young adulthood and a major peak in old age—primarily describes male suicide patterns. Other nations have peak suicide rates in the middle-aged years. In Canada, the peak suicide rate for men is at age 75 and older, while 45 to 54 is the peak age range for women.

What reasons can you think of that might cause the differences discussed here? How would you analyze the data and what conclusions might you draw on the basis of these international comparisons of suicide data?

Sources: Lester, 1992; and Health Statistics, Statistics Canada, 1994.

In Japan, the suicide rate peaks for both men and women at age 75 and over. By contrast, in France the peak suicide rate for men is 75 and over, but the peak rate for women occurs between 45 and 54 years of age. Do these patterns provide us with insights about the intertwining of attitudes regarding gender and aging in these societies?

BOX 2.4 SOCIOLOGY IN GLOBAL PERSPECTIVE

Continued

TABLE 1

Global Trends in Suicide

Pattern	Country	
	Males	**Females**
1. Rate increases regularly with age	Austria France Italy Japan West Germany	Austria Italy Japan West Germany
2. Rate peaks twice: once in young adulthood (ages 15–24, 25–34, or 35–44) and once in old age	Australia Canada England and Wales Netherlands United States	
3. Rate peaks in middle age (ages 45–54 or 55–64)	Denmark Poland Sweden	Australia Canada France Netherlands Poland Sweden United States

many techniques to analyze data. The process for each type of research method is discussed later in this chapter. Data analysis requires considerable skill as the data do not automatically suggest a particular interpretation. The same facts can often be interpreted in several different ways. Therefore, the researcher has to evaluate each of these possibilities with as much objectivity as possible (Robertson, 1977).

DRAWING CONCLUSIONS AND REPORTING THE FINDINGS

After analyzing the data, your first step in drawing conclusions is to return to your hypothesis or research objective to clarify how the data relate both to the hypothesis and to the larger issues being addressed. At this stage, you note the limitations of the study, such as problems with the sample, the influence of variables over which you had no control, or variables that your study was unable to measure.

Reporting the findings is the final stage. The report generally includes a review of each step taken in the research process in order to make the study available for ***replication*—the repetition of the investigation in substantially the same way that it originally was conducted.** Social scientists generally present their findings in papers at professional meetings and publish them in technical journals and books.

A QUALITATIVE APPROACH TO RESEARCH

We have traced the steps in the "conventional" research process (based on deduction and quantitative research). How would the research process differ with an alternative approach based on induction and qualitative research? First, researchers following a qualitative approach may not always do an extensive literature search before beginning their investigating, but rather may wait until later to avoid having preset ideas or biases about what they should find. Researchers pursuing a qualitative approach may engage in problem formulation instead of creating a hypothesis. The researcher may clarify the research question by thinking about the following: What is a significant issue? Why do I want to study this? or What do I want to discover? The researcher may also attempt to formulate questions of concern and interest to the "subjects" at this time (Reinharz, 1992:176). In a qualitative approach, the next step is to collect and analyze data to assess the validity of the tentative hypotheses. Data gathering is the foundation of the research. Researchers pursuing a qualitative approach tend to gather data in natural settings, such as where the person lives or works, rather than in a laboratory or other research setting. In this environment, the researcher can play a background rather than a foreground role. Data collection and analysis frequently occur concurrently, and the analysis draws heavily on the language of the persons studied, not the researcher.

RESEARCH METHODS FOR COLLECTING DATA

How do sociologists know which research method to use? Are some approaches better than others? Which method is best for a particular problem? ***Research methods* are strategies or techniques for systematically conducting research.** Not all sociologists conduct research in the same manner. Some researchers primarily engage in quantitative research while others engage in qualitative research. With ***quantitative research*, the goal is scientific objectivity, and the focus is on data that can be measured numerically.** Quantitative research typically emphasizes complex statistical techniques.

With ***qualitative research*, interpretive description (words) rather than statistics (numbers) is used to analyze underlying meanings and patterns of social relationships.** A study of suicidal behaviour based on suicide notes is an example of qualitative research.

Research designs are tailored to the specific problem being investigated and the focus of the researcher. Both quantitative and qualitative research contribute to our knowledge of society and human social interaction. Qualitative researchers frequently attempt to study the social world from the point of view of the people they are studying, relying on interpretive methods such as observational studies or interviews. Quantitative researchers generally use experiments, surveys, and analyses of existing statistical data. We will now look at these research methods.

EXPERIMENTS

An ***experiment* is a carefully designed situation in which the researcher studies the impact of certain variables on subjects' attitudes or behaviour.** Experiments are designed to create "real-life" situations, ideally under controlled circumstances, in which the influence of different variables can be modified and measured.

TYPES OF EXPERIMENTS Conventional experiments require that subjects be divided into two groups: an experimental group and a control group. The ***experimental group* contains the subjects who are exposed to an independent variable** (the experimental condition) to study its effect on them. The ***control group* contains the subjects who are not exposed to the independent variable.** The members of the two groups

Natural disasters such as this flood in Piedmont, Italy, may be "living laboratories" for sociologists.

are matched for similar characteristics or randomly assigned to each group so that comparisons may be made between the groups. In the simplest experimental design, subjects are (1) pretested (measured in terms of the dependent variable in the hypothesis); (2) exposed to a stimulus representing an independent variable; and (3) post-tested (remeasured) in terms of the dependent variable. The experimental and control groups then are compared to see if they differ in relation to the dependent variable, and the hypothesis about the relationship of the two variables is confirmed or rejected.

In a *laboratory experiment*, subjects are studied in a closed setting so researchers can maintain as much control as possible over the research. For example, if you wanted to examine the influence of the media on attitudes regarding suicide, you might decide to use a laboratory experiment. Sociologist Arturo Biblarz and colleagues (1991) designed a laboratory study to investigate the effects of viewing films containing suicidal acts or other types of violence on attitudes toward suicide. He showed movies to subjects and assessed the extent to which the films affected the subjects' perceptions about suicide.

Not all experiments occur in laboratory settings. *Natural experiments* are real-life occurrences such as floods and other disasters that provide researchers with "living laboratories." Sociologist Kai Erikson (1976) studied the consequences of a deadly 1972 flood in Buffalo Creek, West Virginia, and found that extensive disruption of community ties occurred. Natural experiments cannot be replicated because it is impossible to recreate the exact conditions, nor would we want to do so.

DEMONSTRATING CAUSE-AND-EFFECT RELATIONSHIPS Researchers may use experiments when they want to demonstrate that a cause-and-effect relationship exists between variables. In order to show that a change in one variable causes a change in another, these three conditions must be fulfilled:

1. *You must show that a correlation exists between the two variables.* ***Correlation*** **exists when two variables are associated more frequently than could be expected by chance** (Hoover, 1992). Suppose, for example, that you wanted to test the hypothesis

that the availability of a crisis intervention centre with a twenty-four-hour counselling "hot line" on your campus causes a change in students' attitudes toward suicide. To demonstrate correlation, you would need to show that the students had different attitudes toward committing suicide depending on whether they had any experience with the crisis intervention centre (see Figure 2.5).

2. *You must ensure that the independent variable preceded the dependent variable.* In this case, if differences in students' attitudes toward suicide were evident before some students were exposed to the intervention centre, then exposure to the centre could not be the cause of these differences.
3. *You must make sure that any change in the dependent variable was not due to an extraneous variable*—one outside of the stated hypothesis. For example, if some of the students receive counselling from off-campus psychiatrists, any change in attitude they experience could be due to this third variable and not to the hot line.

The Far Side Cartoon by Gary Larson is reprinted by permission of Chronicle Features, San Francisco, CA. All rights reserved.

STRENGTHS AND WEAKNESSES OF EXPERIMENTS The major advantage of the controlled experiment is the researcher's control over the environment and the ability to isolate the experimental variable. Since many experiments require relatively little time and money and can be conducted with limited numbers of subjects, it is possible for researchers to replicate an experiment several times by using different groups of subjects. Replication strengthens claims about the validity and generalizability of the original research findings (Babbie, 1992).

Perhaps the greatest limitation of experiments is that they are artificial. Social processes that occur in a laboratory setting often do not occur in the same way in real-life settings. Social scientists frequently rely on volunteers or captive audiences such as students. As a result, the subjects of most experiments may not be representative of a larger population, and the findings cannot be generalized to other groups.

Experiments have several other limitations. First, the rigid control and manipulation of variables demanded by experiments do not allow for a more communal approach to data gathering. Second, biases can influence each of the stages in an experiment, and research subjects may become the objects of sex/class/race biases. Third, the unnatural characteristics of laboratory experiments and of group competition in such settings have a negative effect on subjects (Reinharz, 1992).

Researchers acknowledge that experiments have the additional problem of *reactivity*—the tendency of subjects to change their behaviour in response to the researcher or to the fact that they know they are being studied. This problem is known as the Hawthorne effect. The ***Hawthorne effect*** **refers to changes in the subject's behaviour caused by the researcher's presence or by the subject's awareness of being studied.** A

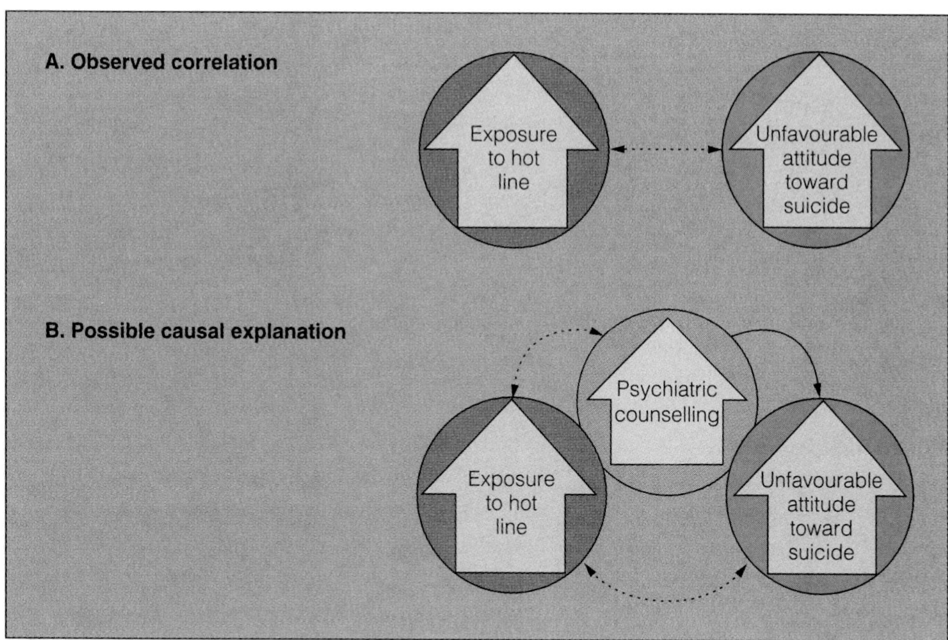

FIGURE 2.5

Correlation versus Causation

A study might find that exposure to a suicide hot line is associated (correlated) with a change in attitude toward suicide. But if some of the students who were exposed to the hot line also received psychiatric counselling, the counselling may be the "hidden" cause of the observed change in attitude. In general, correlations alone do not prove causation.

classic study in the late 1920s by social psychologist Elton Mayo used a series of experiments to determine how to enhance worker productivity and morale at Western Electric's Hawthorne plant. To identify variables that might increase worker productivity, Mayo separated a group of women (the experimental group) from the other workers and then systematically varied factors in that group's work environment while closely observing them. Meanwhile, the working conditions of the other workers (the control group) were not changed. The researchers tested a number of hypotheses, including one stating that an increase in the amount of lighting would raise the worker's productivity. Much to the researchers' surprise, the level of productivity rose not only when the lighting was brightened but also when it was dimmed.

Indeed, all of the changes increased productivity. The researchers concluded that the subjects were trying to please them because of the interest being shown in them (Roethlisberger and Dickson, 1939). Since then, the Hawthorne effect has been used to describe a change in the behaviour of subjects because they realize they are being studied. Other aspects of this study are discussed in Chapter 6 ("Groups and Organizations").

SURVEYS

A *survey* is a poll in which the researcher gathers facts or attempts to determine the relationship between facts. Researchers frequently select a representative sample (a small group of respondents) from a larger population (the total group of people) to answer questions about their attitudes, opinions, or behaviour. ***Respondents*** **are persons who provide data for analysis through interviews or questionnaires.** The Gallup and Angus Reid polls are among the most widely known large-scale surveys; however, government agencies such as Statistics Canada conduct a variety of surveys as well. Unlike many polls that use various methods of gaining a representative sample of the larger population, the census attempts to gain information from all persons in Canada. Surveys are the most widely used research method in the social sciences because they make it possible to study things that are not directly observable—such as peoples' attitudes and beliefs—and to describe a population too large to observe directly (Babbie, 1992).

TYPES OF SURVEYS Survey data are collected by using self-administered questionnaires, personal interviews, and/or telephone surveys. A ***questionnaire*** **is a printed research instrument containing a series of items to which subjects respond.** Items are often in the form of statements with which the respondent is asked to "agree" or "disagree." Questionnaires may be administered by interviewers in face-to-face encounters or by telephone, but the most commonly used technique is the *self-administered questionnaire*. The questionnaires typically are mailed or delivered to the respondents' homes; however, they also may be administered to groups of respondents gathered at the same place at the same time. Antoon Leenaars and George Domino (1993), for example, utilized a Suicide Opinion Questionnaire (SOQ) to measure differences in attitudes toward suicide in two cities: Windsor, Ontario, and Los Angeles, California. This self-administered questionnaire was completed by 103 subjects in each city, matched in terms of gender, age, ethnic origin, and occupational status. The Suicide Opinion Scale included 100 attitudinal statements to which the subject was to indicate agreement ranging from strongly agree to strongly disagree. The attitudinal questions included statements such as "A suicide is essentially a 'cry for help'"; "The most frequent message in suicide notes is of loneliness"; "People do not have the right to take their own lives" (Leenaars and Domino, 1993). In this study, researchers found significant differences between the Windsor and Los Angeles respondents in terms of their attitudes toward suicide. The Canadian respondents were more likely to view suicide as an indication of mental illness or a cry for help. The Canadian respondents also indicated stronger agreement with the statement "If someone wants to commit suicide, it is their business, and we should not interfere" (Leenaars and Domino, 1993:259). Leenaars and Domino suggest that these differences in attitudes may explain, in part, why Canada's rate of suicide is higher than it is in the United States.

Self-administered questionnaires have certain strengths. They are relatively simple and inexpensive to administer, they allow for rapid data collection and analysis, and they permit respondents to remain anonymous (an important consideration when the questions are of a personal nature). A major disadvantage is the low response rate. Mailed surveys sometimes have a response rate as low as 10 percent—and a 50 percent response rate is considered by some to be minimally adequate (Babbie, 1992). The response rate usually is somewhat higher if the survey is handed out to a group that is asked to fill it out on the spot.

Survey data also may be collected by interviews. An ***interview*** **is a data collection encounter in which an interviewer asks the respondent questions and records the answers.** Survey research often uses *structured interviews*, in which the interviewer asks questions from a standardized questionnaire. Structured interviews tend to produce uniform or replicable data that can be elicited time after time by different interviews.

Interviews have specific advantages. They usually are more effective in dealing with complicated issues and provide an opportunity for face-to-face communication between the interviewer and respondent. When open-ended questions are used, the researcher may gain new perspectives. The major disadvantage of interviews is the cost and time involved in conducting them.

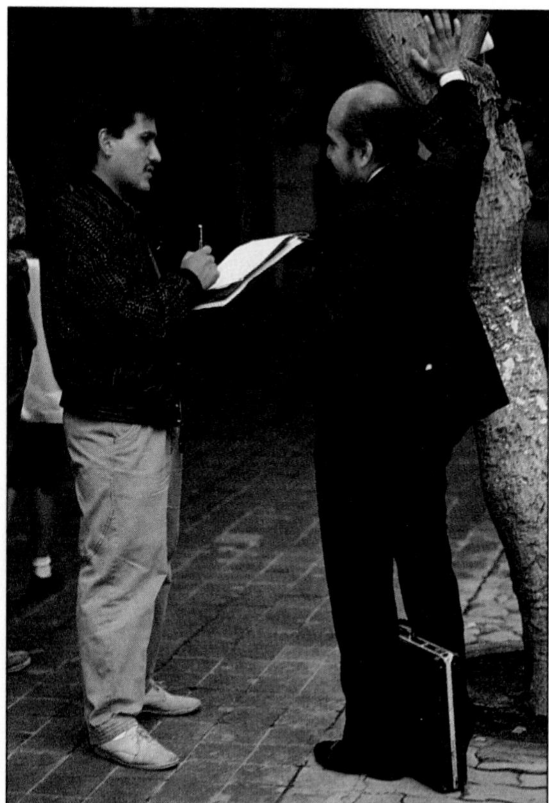

Conducting surveys or polls is an international means of gathering data. This investigator is conducting his research in Mexico City.

Questionnaires may also be administered by *telephone surveys*, which are becoming an increasingly popular way to collect data for a number of reasons. Telephone surveys save time and money compared to self-administered questionnaires or face-to-face interviews. Some respondents may be more honest than when they are facing an interviewer. Telephone surveys also give greater control over data collection and provide greater personal safety for respondents and researchers than do personal encounters.

In *computer-assisted telephone interviewing*, the interviewer uses a computer to dial random telephone numbers, reads the questions shown on the video monitor to the respondent, and then types the responses into the computer terminal. Telephone answering machines, caller identification systems, and voice mail have made this type of survey more difficult since some people now are less accessible to researchers.

SAMPLING CONSIDERATIONS Survey research has certain built-in sampling considerations. Researchers begin by identifying the population they want to study. They then determine what constitutes a representative sample of the entire population being studied. Use of probability sampling methods makes it possible to estimate the amount of *sampling error*—the extent to which the sample does not represent the population as a whole—that should be expected in a particular sample. Next, researchers decide how to avoid conscious and unconscious sampling biases in their study. In order for survey research to produce findings that can be accurately generalized to larger populations, it must give proportionate attention to the opinions and perceptions of *all* people (see Eichler and Lapointe, 1985; Eichler, 1988b). Suppose, for example, you wanted to determine how many students on your campus *thought* about committing suicide each year. A survey in which people at your university were asked to answer a series of questions would be an appropriate method. To generalize your findings to all Canadian university students, you would have to select a sample that was representative of this larger population.

QUESTIONNAIRE CONSTRUCTION The quality of the questionnaire is central to the success of survey research. The more specific a survey question is, the more likely respondents are to interpret the question in the same way and the more easily comparable their answers will be. Questionnaires may vary in length and complexity, but in a specific study, each questionnaire must be identical in wording and in the order of items. Questions generally are pretested for reliability and validity, and they should be worded so that they are easily understood.

Most survey research relies on *closed-ended questions*, in which the respondent is asked to answer from a list of alternate responses (for example, multiple-choice questions). These responses are fairly easy to measure and compare; however, closed-ended questions sometimes fail to increase our insights into the respondents' real feelings, attitudes, and beliefs because they are forced to choose from predetermined answers that may not accurately reflect their true thoughts. By contrast, open-ended questions provide respondents with the opportunity to reply to a question in their own words (for example, "Please describe your views on assisted suicide for terminally ill patients"). This type of question allows more flexibility in the respondent's answer, but it also makes it more difficult to measure and compare answers. Both kinds of questions should be free from biases implying that one sex, class, or age serves as the standard against which all others are measured (Eichler, 1988; Reinharz, 1992).

STRENGTHS AND WEAKNESSES OF SURVEYS Survey research has several important strengths. First, it is useful in describing the characteristics of a large population without having to interview each person in that population. Second, survey research enables the researcher to search for causes and effects and to assess the relative importance of a number of variables. In recent years, computer technology has enhanced our ability to do *multivariate analysis*—research involving more than two independent variables. For example, to assess the influence of religion on suicidal behaviour among French Canadians, a researcher might look at the effects of age, sex, income level, and other variables all at once to determine which of these independent variables influences suicide the most or least and how influential each variable is relative to the others. Third, survey research can be useful in analyzing social change or documenting the existence of a social problem. Contemporary scholars have used survey research to provide information about problems—such as racial discrimination, sexual harassment, and sex-based inequality in employment—by documenting the fact that they are more widespread than previously thought (Reinharz, 1992).

Survey research also has several weaknesses. One is that the use of standardized questions tends to force respondents into categories in which they may or may not belong. Another weakness concerns validity. People's opinions on issues seldom take the form of a standard response ranging from "strongly agree" to "strongly disagree." Moreover, as in other types of research, people may be less than truthful, especially on emotionally charged issues such as suicide, thus making reliance on self-reported attitudes problematic.

Some scholars also have criticized the way survey data sometimes are used. The data collected are not always "hard facts" as some researchers claim. For example, survey statistics may over- or underestimate the extent of a problem and work against some categories of people more than others, as shown in Table 2.1.

SECONDARY ANALYSIS OF EXISTING DATA

In ***secondary analysis*****, researchers use existing material and analyze data originally collected by others**. Existing data sources include public records, official reports of organizations or government agencies, and surveys conducted by researchers in universities and private corporations. Research data gathered from studies is available in data banks, such as the Inter-University Consortium for Political and Social Research, and the York University Institute for Behavioural Research. Many Canadian university libraries have recently joined the Data Liberation Initiative, which gives members of the university community access to a wide variety of databases. Other sources of data for secondary analysis are books, magazines, newspapers, radio and television programs, and personal documents. Secondary analysis is referred to as *unobtrusive research* because it includes a variety of nonreactive research techniques—that is, techniques that have no impact on the people being studied. In Durkheim's study of suicide, for example, his analysis of existing statistics on suicide did noth-

TABLE 2.1

Statistics: What We Know (and Don't Know)

	Topic		
	Homelessness in Canada	**Gay Men in Canada**	**Suicide in Canada**
Research Finding	Over 100,000 people in this country are homeless.	At least 1 percent of Canadian men are exclusively homosexual.	At least 3709 Canadians committed suicide in 1992.
Possible Problem	Does that badly underestimate the total number of homeless people?	Does this underestimate the gay population? Is the actual figure higher?	Are suicide rates recorded in the official death certificates?
Explanation	The homeless are difficult to count. They may avoid interviews with census takers. The 1996 census was the first attempt to count the number of homeless in Canada. However, these numbers will not be released by Statistics Canada.	As one analyst noted, many people lie about their sexuality; people often are hesitant to report their sexual orientation. This may result in estimates being too low; however, gay rights organizations may overstate percentages to gain political clout.	Suicides for children under 10 are not recorded in Canada. Accidental deaths may in fact be suicides.

ing to increase or decrease the number of people who *actually* committed suicide.

ANALYZING EXISTING STATISTICS Secondary analysis may involve obtaining *raw data* collected by other researchers and undertaking a statistical analysis of the data, or it may involve the use of other researchers' existing statistical analyses. In the analysis of existing statistics, the unit of analysis often is *not* the individual. Most existing statistics are *aggregated*: they describe a group. Durkheim wanted to determine whether Protestants or Catholics were more likely to commit suicide; however, none of the available records indicated the religion of those who committed suicide. Although Durkheim suggested that Protestants were more likely to commit suicide than Catholics, it was impossible for him to determine the suicide rates from the existing data.

In a contemporary study of suicide, K.D. Breault (1986) analyzed secondary data collected by government agencies to test Durkheim's hypothesis that religion and social integration provide protection from suicide. Using suicide as the dependent variable and church membership, divorce, unemployment, and female labour force participation as several of his independent variables, Breault performed a series of sophisticated statistical analyses and concluded that the data supported Durkheim's views on social integration and his theory of egoistic suicide. He also found support for Durkheim's proposition that Protestants are more likely to commit suicide than Catholics.

ANALYZING CONTENT ***Content analysis*** **is the systematic examination of cultural artifacts or various forms of communication to extract thematic data and draw conclusions about social life.** *Cultural artifacts* are products of individual activity, social organizations, technology, and cultural patterns (Reinharz, 1992:147). Among the materials studied are *written records*, such as diaries, love letters, poems, books, and graffiti; and *narratives and visual texts*, such as movies, television shows, advertisements, and greeting cards. Also studied are *material culture*, such as music, art, and even garbage; and behavioural residues, such as patterns of wear and tear on the floor in front of various exhibits at art museums to determine what exhibits are the most popular (see Webb, 1966; Reinharz, 1992). Martineau noted that more could be learned about a society in a day by studying "things" than by talking with individuals for a year (Martineau, 1988/1838:73). Researchers may look for regular patterns, such as frequency of suicide as a topic on television talk shows. They also may examine subject matter to determine how it has been handled, such as how the mass media handle "celebrity" suicides. Systematic coding and objective recording of data according to some conceptual framework are essential in content analysis.

In a recent study, sociologists Myra Ferree and Elaine Hall (1990) examined the 5413 illustrations (including photographs, drawings, and cartoons) in thirty-three introductory sociology textbooks published in the United States between 1982 and 1988. The individuals in each illustration were coded for race and sex, location in or outside the United States, and placement in one of twenty-six chapters (such as race, gender, economy, politics, and family). From their content analysis, Ferree and Hall concluded that women were not represented in the illustrations in numbers proportionate to their distribution in the population. They were particularly invisible in the chapters on politics and the economy. Although individual people of colour were shown in numerically fair proportions, they were conceptualized as essentially different and given distinctive visual roles in the text. For example, African Americans often were included to show racial integration in the United States, while Asians, Hispanics, and other racial–ethnic groups largely were depicted as living in other countries, where they provided a "comparative" perspective on the United States (Ferree and Hall, 1990:528). What do you think the results would be of a content analysis of Canadian sociology textbooks? Would the results be similar? How would visible minorities be represented?

How might a social scientist use content analysis to study why people commit suicide? Suicide notes and diaries are useful forms of cultural artifacts. Suicide notes have been subjected to extensive analysis for a number of years because they are "ultrapersonal documents" that are not solicited by others and frequently are written just before the person's death (Leenaars, 1988:34).

What patterns can be observed from content analysis of suicide notes? Many notes provide new levels of meaning regarding the individuality of the person who committed or attempted suicide. Suicide notes and diaries often reveal that people committing suicide consider their death as a "passing on to another world" or simply "escaping this world." Some notes indicate that people may want to get revenge and make other people feel guilty or responsible for their suicide: "Now you'll be sorry for what you did" or "It's all your fault!" Thus, suicide notes may be a valuable starting point for finding patterns of suicidal behaviour and determining the characteristics of people who are most likely to commit suicide (Leenaars, 1992).

STRENGTHS AND WEAKNESSES OF SECONDARY ANALYSIS One strength of secondary analysis is that data are readily available and are often inexpensive to obtain. Another is that, because the researcher often does not collect the data personally, the chances of bias may be reduced. In addition, the use of existing sources makes it possible to analyze longitudinal data to provide a historical context within which to locate original research. However, secondary analysis has inherent problems. For one thing, the data may be incomplete, inauthentic, or inaccurate. For another, the various data from which content analysis is done may not be strictly comparable with one another (Reinharz, 1992), and *coding* these data—or sorting, categorizing, and organizing the data into conceptual categories (Babbie, 1992)—may be difficult. Finally, as Durkheim found in his study of suicide records (that did not include religious affiliation), secondary data are often collected for administrative purposes, so the categories may not reflect variables of interest to the researcher.

FIELD RESEARCH

Field research is the study of social life in its natural setting: observing and interviewing people where they live, work, and play. Some kinds of behaviour can be studied best by "being there"; a fuller understanding can be developed through observations, face-to-face discussions, and participation in events. Researchers use these methods to generate *qualitative* data: observations that are best described verbally rather than numerically. Although field research is less structured and more flexible than the other methods we have discussed, it also places many demands on the researcher. To engage in field research, sociologists must select the method or combination of methods that will best reveal what they want to know. For example, they must decide how to approach the target group, whether to identify themselves as researchers, and whether to participate in the events they are observing.

OBSERVATION Sociologists who are interested in observing social interaction as it occurs may use either complete observation or participant observation. In ***complete observation*, the researcher systematically observes a social process but does not take part in it**. Observational research can take place just about anywhere. For example, sociologists David Karp and William Yoels (1976) became interested in why many students do not participate in discussions in university classrooms. Observers sat in on various classes and took notes that included the average number of students who participated, the number of times they talked during one class session, and the sex of the instructor and of the students who talked in class. From their observational data, Karp and Yoels found that, on average, a very small number of students are responsible for the majority of all discussion that occurs in class on any given day.

Suppose you wanted to study your own class to identify the "talkers" and the "silent ones." You would need to develop a game plan before you started to observe. A game plan typically is guided by a research question, such as, "Why don't more university students participate in class discussion?" Subjects in observation studies may not realize that they are being studied, especially if the researcher remains unobtrusive. Observations help us view behaviour as it is taking place; however, it provides limited opportunities to learn why people do certain things. One way for researchers to remain unobtrusive is through ***participant observation*—collecting systematic observations while being part of the activities of the group they are studying**. Participant observation generates more "inside" information than simply asking questions or observing from the outside. As sociologist William Whyte noted in his classic participant observation study of a Boston low-income neighbourhood: "As I sat and listened, I learned the answers to questions I would not have had the sense to ask" (1955:303).

Clearly, a participant observation study of individuals who are in the process of committing suicide is out of the question. However, important insights still may be gained by using this method. For instance, research can be conducted on how certain deaths are (or are not) classified as suicides. Sociologist Steve Taylor (1982) designed a study of coroners (medical examiners) to learn more about their rulings of "suicide" and to analyze what, if any, effect these rulings have on the accuracy of "official" suicide statistics. Taylor engaged in participant observation at a coroner's office over

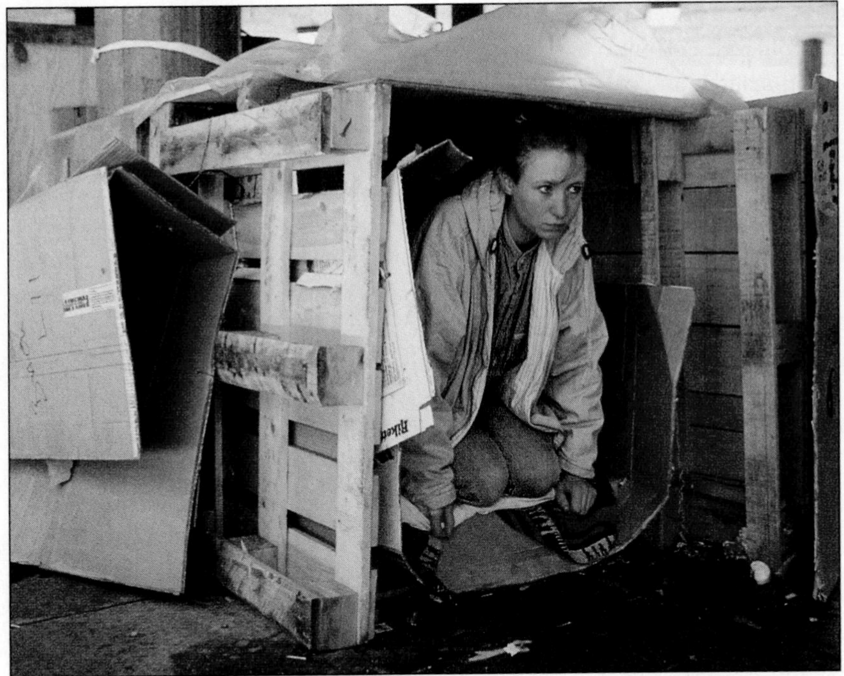

Case studies of homeless persons have added to our insights on the causes and consequences of this major social concern. Women often are the "invisible homeless."

a six-month period. He followed a number of cases from the initial report of death through the various stages of investigation to the inquest (hearing) and the verdict. In addition to reading reports, he found it important to "be around," listen to the discussion of particular cases, and ask the coroners questions. Taylor concluded that intuition and guesswork play a much larger part in coroners' decisions than they are willing to acknowledge.

CASE STUDIES Most participant observation research takes the form of a *case study*, an in-depth, multifaceted investigation of a single event, person, or social grouping (Feagin, Orum, and Sjoberg, 1991). Case studies often involve more than one method of research, such as participant observation, unstructured or in-depth interviews, and life histories.

How do social scientists decide to do case studies? Initially, some researchers have only a general idea of what they wish to investigate. In other cases, they literally "back into" the research. They may find themselves in proximity to interesting people or situations. For example, anthropologist Elliot Liebow "backed into" his study of single, homeless women living in emergency shelters by becoming a volunteer at a shelter. As he got to know the women, Liebow became fascinated with their lives and survival strategies. Prior to Liebow's research, most studies of the homeless focused primarily on men. These studies typically asked questions like, "How many homeless are there?" and "What proportion of the homeless are chronically mentally ill?" By contrast, Liebow wanted to know more about the homeless women themselves, wondering such things as, "What are they carrying in those [shopping] bags?" (Coughlin, 1993:A8). Liebow spent the next four years engaged in participant observation research that culminated in his book *Tell Them Who I Am* (1993).

In participant observation studies, the researcher must decide whether to let people know they are being studied. After Liebow decided that he would like to take notes on informal conversations and conduct interviews with the women, he asked the shelter director and the women for permission and told them that he would like to write about them. Liebow's findings are discussed in Chapter 5 ("Social Structure and Interaction in Everyday Life"). While some social scientists gain permission from their subjects, others fear that people will refuse to participate or will change their behaviour if they know they are being observed. On the one hand, researchers who do not obtain consent from their subjects may be acting unethically. On the other hand, when subjects know they are being observed, they risk succumbing to the Hawthorne effect (discussed earlier in this chapter).

The next step is to gain the trust of participants. Liebow had previous experience in blending with individuals he wanted to observe when he gained the trust of young lower-class African American men who talked and passed time on an inner-city street corner in Washington, D.C., in the 1960s. The result was his classic study *Tally's Corner* (1967), in which he described how he (as a 37-year-old white anthropology graduate student) played pool and drank beer with his subjects. While interacting with the men, Liebow gathered a large volume of data that led him to conclude that his subjects had created their own "society" after being unable to find a place in the existing one. Liebow found "insiders" to help him gain the trust of other participants in his research. In a participant observation study, you may wish to identify possible informants—individuals who introduce you to others, give suggestions about how to "get around" in the natural setting, and provide you with essential insider information on what you are observing. Informants are especially useful in the community study/ethnography.

ETHNOGRAPHY An ***ethnography*** **is a detailed study of the life and activities of a group of people by researchers who may live with that group over a period of years** (Feagin, Orum, and Sjoberg, 1991). Although this approach is similar in some ways to participant observation, these studies typically take place over much longer periods of time. For example, researcher Anastasia Shkilnyk (1985) lived in an Ojibwa community in Grassy Narrows, in northwestern Ontario, for several years. As a result, she was able to describe the destruction and human suffering brought about by mercury contamination and by the relocation of the residents of Grassy Narrows to a new reserve.

In another classic study (referred to earlier in this chapter), *Street Corner Society*, sociologist William F. Whyte (1988/1943) conducted long-term participant observation studies in Boston's low-income Italian neighbourhoods. Whereas "outsiders" generally regarded these neighbourhoods as disorganized slums with high crime rates, Whyte found the residents to be hard-working people who tried to take care of one another.

UNSTRUCTURED INTERVIEWS An ***unstructured interview*** **is an extended, open-ended interaction between an interviewer and an interviewee.** The interviewer has a general plan of inquiry but not a specific set of questions that must be asked, as is often the case with surveys. Unstructured interviews are essentially conversations in which interviewers establish the general direction by asking open-ended questions, to which interviewees may respond flexibly. Interviewers have the ability to "shift gears" and pursue specific topics raised by interviewees, because answers to one question are used to suggest the next question or new areas of inquiry.

Lesley Harman's (1989) study of homeless women in Ontario is an example of research that used in-depth interviews to examine the challenges homeless women face to survive in a domesticated culture. Many perplexing questions arise in deciding how to conduct unstructured interviews. Harman identified some of them as: "The dilemmas of how much closeness to develop with my subjects, how much to reveal about my own life, how much to ask about their previous lives, and how much to believe, plagued me everyday" (1989:43).

Even in unstructured interviews, researchers must prepare a few general or "lead-in" questions to get the interview started. Following the interviewee's initial responses, the interviewer may wish to ask additional questions on the same topic, probe for more information (by using questions such as, "In what ways?" or "Anything else?"), or introduce a new line of inquiry. At all points in the interview, *careful listening* is essential. It provides the opportunity to introduce new questions as the interview proceeds while simultaneously keeping the interview focused on the research topic. It also enables the interviewer to envision interviewees' experiences and to glean multiple levels of meaning.

The Interview and Sampling Process Before conducting in-depth interviews, researchers must make a number of decisions, including how the people to be interviewed will be selected. Respondents for unstructured interviews often are chosen by "snowball sampling." In *snowball sampling*, the researcher interviews a few individuals who possess a certain characteristic; these interviewees are then asked to supply the names of others with the same characteristic. The process continues until the sample has "snowballed" into an acceptable size and no new information of any significance is being gained.

Researchers must make other key decisions. Will people be interviewed more than once? If so, how long will the interviews be? Is there a specific number and order of questions to be asked or a certain order to be followed? Will the interviewees have an opportunity to question the interviewer? Where will the interview take place? How will information be recorded? Who should do the interviewing? Who should be present at the interview? (Reinharz, 1992:22). Unstructured, open-ended interviews do not mean that the researcher simply walks into a room, has a conversation with someone, and the research is complete. Planning and advance preparation are essential. Similarly, the follow-up, analysis of data, and write-up of the study must be carefully designed and carried out.

Interviews and Theory Construction In-depth interviews, along with participant observation and case studies, frequently are used to develop theories through observation. The term *grounded theory* was developed by sociologists Barney Glaser and Anselm Strauss (1967) to describe this inductive method of theory construction. Researchers who use grounded theory collect and analyze data simultaneously. For example, after in-depth interviews with 106 suicide attempters, researchers in one study concluded that half of the individuals who attempted suicide wanted both to live and to die at the time of their attempt. From these unstructured interviews, it became obvious that ambivalence led about half of "serious" suicidal attempters to "literally gamble with death" (Kovacs and Beck, 1977, quoted in Taylor, 1982:144). After asking their initial unstructured questions of the interviewees, Kovacs and Taylor decided to widen the research question from, "Why do people kill themselves?" to the broader question, "Why do people engage in acts of self damage which may result in death?" In other words, uncertainty of outcome is a common feature of most suicidal acts. In previous studies, researchers had simply assumed that in "dangerous attempts" the individual really wanted to die while in "moderate" attempts the person was ambivalent (Taylor, 1982:160).

STRENGTHS AND WEAKNESSES OF FIELD RESEARCH Participant observation research, case studies, ethnography, and unstructured interviews provide opportunities for researchers to view from the inside what may not be obvious to an outside observer. They are useful when attitudes and behaviours can be understood best within their natural setting or when the researcher wants to study social processes and change over a period of time. They provide a wealth of information about the reactions of people and give us an opportunity to generate theories from the data collected (Whyte, 1989).

Social scientists who believe that quantitative research methods (such as survey research) provide the most scientific and accurate means of measuring attitudes, beliefs, and behaviour often are critical of data obtained through field research. They argue that what is learned from a specific group or community cannot be generalized to a larger population. They also suggest that the data collected in natural settings are descriptive and do not lend themselves to precise measurement. Researchers who want to determine cause and effect or to test a theory emphasize that it is impossible to demonstrate such relationships from participant observation studies.

Some scholars argue that the weakness in case studies is in *how* this method has been used, not in the method itself. Sociologists historically have used case studies to document the experiences of dominant group members in society and to focus on "mainstream" organizations. For example, in studies of medical schools in the 1950s and 1960s, researchers excluded the four to five women in each class from their data, thus making women "invisible" in medical education (for example, see Becker et al., 1961; Freidson, 1970).

Through unstructured interviews, researchers gain access to "people's ideas, thoughts, and memories in their own words rather than in the words of the researcher" (Reinharz, 1992:19). Research of this type is important for the study of race, ethnicity, and gender because it lets people who previously have had no "voice" describe their experiences and provides researchers with an opportunity to explore people's views of reality. Again, however, quantitative researchers are critical of unstructured interviews, because there typically is no comparability in the wording of questions from one interviewee to another. Also, the number of respondents in such studies is small, thus making it impossible to generalize to a larger population.

FEMINIST RESEARCH METHODS

During the past two decades, feminist social scientists have focused a critical eye on traditional sociological research, as well as on the research methodologies and findings of other disciplines. Margrit Eichler (1988) has identified several limitations in research that relate to gender, including androcentricity (which means approaching an issue from a male perspective or viewing women only in terms of how they relate to men); sexist language or concepts; research methods that are biased in favour of men (for example, in sampling techniques or questionnaire design); and research results that overgeneralize (which means that results that focus on members of one sex are used to support conclusions about both sexes).

Most writers on feminist research issues agree that there is no one method that can be termed *the* feminist methodology. However, qualitative methods and, in particular in-depth interviews, tend to be associated with feminist research. Although feminist research may involve the same basic methods for collecting data as other research, the way in which feminists use these methods is very different. First, women's experiences are important and, to understand them, women's lives need to be addressed in their own terms (Edwards, 1993). Feminist research is woman centred, that is, "it puts women at the center of research that is nonalienating, nonexploitive, and potentially emancipating" (Sculley, 1990:2–3). Second, the goal of feminist research is to provide explanations of women's lives that are useful to them in terms of improving their situations. It is important, therefore, to ensure that women's experiences are not objectified or treated as merely "research data." In fact, feminist sociologist Dorothy Smith (1987) suggests that "giving voice" to disadvantaged and marginalized groups in society is a primary goal of sociology. Finally, feminist research methods challenge the traditional role of the researcher as a detached, "value-free," objective observer. Rather, the researcher is seen as central to the research process and her feelings and experiences should be analyzed as an integral part of the research process (Edwards, 1993; Kirby and McKenna, 1989).

MULTIPLE METHODS OF SOCIAL RESEARCH

What is the best method for studying a particular topic? How can we get accurate answers to questions about suicide and other important social concerns? Summary Table 2.A compares the various social research methods. There is no one best research method because of the "complexity of social reality and the limitations of all research methodologies" (Snow and Anderson, 1991:158).

Many sociologists believe that it is best to combine multiple methods in a given study. *Triangulation* is the use of multiple approaches in a single study (Denzin, 1989). Triangulation refers not only to research methods but also to multiple data sources, investigators, and theoretical perspectives in a study. Multiple data sources include persons, situations, contexts, and time (Snow and Anderson, 1991). For example, David Snow and Leon Anderson's study of unattached homeless men and women used as their primary data sources "the homeless themselves and the array of settings, agency personnel, business proprietors, city officials, and neighborhood activities relevant to the routines of the homeless" (1991a:158). Snow and Anderson gained a detailed portrait of the homeless and their experiences and institutional contacts by tracking over seven hundred homeless individuals through a network of seven institutions with which they had varying degrees of contact.

The study also tracked a number of the individuals over a period of time and used a variety of methods, including "participant observation and informal, conversational interviewing with the homeless; participant and nonparticipant observation, coupled with formal and informal interviewing in street agencies and settings; and a systematic survey of agency records" (Snow and Anderson, 1991:158–169). This study is discussed in depth in Chapter 5 ("Social Structure and Interaction in Everyday Life").

Multiple methods and approaches provide a wider scope of information and enhance our understanding of critical issues. Many researchers also use multiple methods to validate or refine one type of data by use of another type. Multiple methods allow for the greatest range of exploration of subjects of importance to groups that historically have been excluded from the research process (see Reinharz, 1992; Ristock and Pennell, 1996).

ETHICAL ISSUES IN SOCIOLOGICAL RESEARCH

The study of people ("human subjects") raises vital questions about ethical concerns in sociological research. Because of past abuses, researchers are now required by a professional code of ethics to weigh the societal benefits of research against the potential physical and emotional costs to participants. Researchers are required to obtain written "informed consent" statements from the persons they study. However, these guidelines produced many new questions, such as, What constitutes "informed consent"? What constitutes harm to a person? How do researchers protect the identity and confidentiality of their sources?

The Canadian Sociology and Anthropology Association has outlined the basic standards sociologists must follow in conducting research. Social research often involves intrusions into people's lives—surveys, interviews, field observations, and participation in experiments all involve personally valuable commodities: time, energy, and privacy. Participation in research must be voluntary. No one should be enticed, coerced, or forced to participate. Reseachers must not harm the research subjects in any way—physically, psychologically, or personally. For example, the researcher must be careful not to reveal information that would embarrass the participants, or damage their personal relationships. Reseachers must respect the rights of research subjects to anonymity and confidentiality.

A respondent is *anonymous* when the researcher cannot identify a given response with a given respondent. Anonymity is often extremely important in terms of obtaining information on "deviant" or illegal activities. For example, in a study on physician-assisted suicides conducted by the Manitoba Association of Rights and Liberties (Searles, 1995) ensuring the anonymity of the physicians responding to the survey was crucial because the doctors were being asked about their

SUMMARY TABLE 2.A

Strengths and Weaknesses of Social Research Methods

Research Method	Strengths	Weaknesses
Experiments Laboratory Field Natural	Control over research Ability to isolate experimental factors Relatively little time and money required Replication possible, except for natural experiments	Artificial by nature Frequent reliance on volunteers or captive audiences Ethical questions of deception Problem of reactivity
Survey Research Questionnaire Interview Telephone survey	Useful in describing features of a large population without interviewing everyone Relatively large samples possible Multivariate analysis possible	Potentially forced answers Respondent untruthfulness on emotional issues Data that are not always "hard facts" presented as such in statistical analyses
Secondary Analysis of Existing Data Existing statistics Content analysis	Data often readily available, inexpensive to collect Longitudinal and comparative studies possible Replication possible	Difficulty in determining accuracy of some of the data Failure of data gathered by others to meet goals of current research Questions of privacy when using diaries, other personal documents
Field Research Observation Participant observation Case study Ethnography	Opportunity to gain insider's view Useful for studying attitudes and behaviour in natural settings Longitudinal/comparative studies possible Documentation of important social problems of excluded groups possible	Problems in generalizing results to a larger population Nonprecise data measurements Inability to demonstrate cause/effect relationships or test theories
Unstructured interviews	Access to people's ideas in their words Forum for previously excluded groups	Difficult to make comparisons because of lack of structure Not representative sample

participation in illegal acts (see Box 2.3, "Assisting Suicide").

Maintaining *confidentiality* means that the researcher is able to identify a given person's responses with that person but essentially promises not to do so. Whether the researcher should reveal his or her identity is also a difficult issue. In some cases, it is useful to identify yourself as a researcher to obtain cooperation from respondents. However, there are other instances when revealing your identity can affect the content and quality of your research. Deception should not be used where another methodology would accomplish the same research objectives. Furthermore, it is not acceptable to use deception to obtain informed consent. For example, not informing a research subject of potential risk or harm constitutes deception. Finally, researchers have an obligation to report all of their research findings in full, including unexpected or negative findings and limitations of the research.

Sociologists are committed to adhering to these ethical considerations and to protecting research participants; however, many ethical issues arise that cannot be resolved easily. Ethics in sociological research is a difficult and often ambiguous topic. However, ethical issues cannot be ignored by researchers, whether they are sociology professors, graduate students conducting investigations for their dissertations, or undergraduates conducting a class research project. Sociologists have a burden of "self-reflection"—of seeking to understand the role they play in contemporary social processes while at the same time assessing how these social processes affect their findings (Gouldner, 1970).

How honest do researchers have to be with potential participants? Let's look at a specific case in point. Where does the "right to know" end and the "right to privacy" begin in this situation?

THE ZELLNER RESEARCH

Sociologist William Zellner (1978, in Schaefer and Lamm, 1992) sought to interview the family, friends, and acquaintances of persons killed in single-car crashes that he thought might have been "autocides." Zellner wondered, Are some automobile "accidents" actually suicides? Did the individual wish to protect other people and perhaps make it easier for them to collect insurance benefits that might not be paid in suicide cases? By interviewing people who knew the victims, Zellner hoped to obtain information that would help determine if the deaths were accidental or intentional. To recruit respondents, he suggested that their participation in his study might reduce the number of accidents in the future; however, he did not mention that he suspected autocide. In each interview, he asked if the deceased had recently talked about suicide or about themselves in a negative manner.

From the data he collected, Zellner concluded that at least 12 percent of the fatal single-occupant crashes were suicides. He also learned that in a number of the crashes, other people (innocent bystanders) were killed or critically injured. Was Zellner's research unethical because he misrepresented the reasons for his study? Does the right to know outweigh the right to privacy in this situation? Other important questions also are raised in the process of social scientific investigation. Consider, for example, the following two cases.

THE HUMPHREYS RESEARCH

Laud Humphreys (1970), then a sociology graduate student, decided to study homosexuality for his doctoral dissertation. His research focused on homosexual acts between strangers meeting in "tearooms," public restrooms in parks. He did not ask permission of his subjects, nor did he inform them that they were being studied. Instead, he took advantage of the typical tearoom encounter, which involved three men: two who engaged in homosexual acts, and a third who kept a lookout for police and other unwelcome strangers. To conduct his study, Humphreys showed up at public restrooms that were known to be tearooms and offered to be the lookout. Then he systematically recorded details of the encounters that took place.

Humphreys was interested in the fact that the tearoom participants seemed to live "normal" lives apart from these encounters, and he decided to learn more about their everyday lives. To determine who they were, he wrote down their car license numbers and tracked down their names and addresses. Later, he arranged for these men to be included in a medical survey so that he could go out and interview them personally. He wore different disguises and drove a different car so that they would not recognize him. From these interviews, he collected personal information and determined that most of the men were married and lived very conventional lives.

Humphreys probably would not have gained access to these subjects if he had identified himself as a researcher; nevertheless, the fact that he did not do so produced widespread criticism from sociologists and journalists. The police became very interested in his notes, but he refused to turn any information over to the authorities. His award-winning study, *Tearoom Trade* (1970), dispelled many myths about homosexual behaviour; however, the controversy surrounding his study has never been resolved. Do you think Humphrey's research was ethical? Would these men willingly have agreed to participate in Humphrey's research if he had identified himself as a researcher? What psychological harm might have come to these married men if people, outside of those involved in the encounters, knew about their homosexual behaviour? Ethical issues continue to arise in sociological research. A recent case involved a different sort of question from the Humphreys case.

THE SCARCE RESEARCH

Rik Scarce, another sociology graduate student, was jailed for over five months in 1993 because he refused to testify before a grand jury investigating break-ins at university laboratories by animal-rights activists. Scarce wrote *Ecowarriors: Understanding the Radical Environmental Movement* in 1990 based on data gathered from activists in the environmental movement. Investigators believed that a person who had been house-sitting for Scarce had been involved in a 1991 raid on a university laboratory that resulted in $150,000 in damage and the release of twenty-three animals. The prosecutor in the grand jury investigation claimed that he wanted to ask Scarce questions about this missing house sitter, not about his research. The judge ruled that the "government had a clear need for the information, and that no blanket privilege protected academics, or even journalists, from testifying" (Monaghan, 1993:A10). Scarce said that he was taking his stand because he refused to breach guarantees of confidentiality he made to his subjects. He also was "concerned that activists within the environmental movement may refuse to speak to me if I testify." He noted that social scientists "would be less willing to go out and do research which in some instances does require of us that we grant promises of confidentiality" (Monaghan, 1993:A10). Based on the *Code of Ethics*, many sociologists supported Scarce's stand (Monaghan, 1993). However, some scholars have stated that social scientists should not be granted an exemption from testifying if they have information relevant to possible crimes (see Comarow, 1993:A44).

In this chapter, we have looked at the research process and the methods used to pursue sociological knowledge. We also have critiqued many of the existing approaches and suggested alternate ways of pursuing research. The important thing to realize is that research is the "life blood" of sociology. Without research, sociologists would be unable to test existing theories and develop new ones. Research takes us beyond common sense and provides opportunities for us to use our sociological imagination to generate new knowledge. For example, as we have seen in this chapter, suicide cannot be explained by common sense or a few isolated variables. In answering questions such as, "Why do people commit suicide?" we have to take into account many aspects of personal choice and social structure that are related to one another in extremely complex ways. Research can help us unravel the complexities of social life if sociologists observe, talk to, and interact with people in real-life situations (Feagin, Orum, and Sjoberg, 1991).

Our challenge today is to understand how to determine what is useful for enhancing our knowledge, to find new ways to integrate knowledge and action, and to encourage the inclusion of all people in the research process. This inclusion would be on two levels: (1) as *active* participants in research, to give "voice" to previously excluded people's experiences, and (2) as researchers, to help fill some of the gaps in our existing knowledge on how the research process is shaped by gender, race, class, and sexual orientation of the researcher and by the broader social and cultural context (Cancian, 1992).

CHAPTER REVIEW

Social research is part of the sociological imagination. Research on human behaviour and social interaction leads to a more accurate understanding of society. Sociological research provides a factual and objective counterpoint to common sense knowledge and ill-informed sources of information. Emile Durkheim, in one of the first studies to use scientific methods to analyze society, found that a lack of social cohesiveness contributed to suicide. Through his research, he refocused attention on the societal problems, rather than the individual tendencies, that lead to suicide.

- Sociological research is based on an empirical approach that answers questions through a direct, systematic collection and analysis of data. Sociologists generally use two types of empirical studies. Descriptive studies attempt to describe social reality or provide facts. Explanatory studies attempt to explain cause-and-effect relationships and the reasons certain events do or do not occur.
- Theory and research form a continuous cycle that encompasses both deductive and inductive approaches. With the deductive approach, the researcher begins with a theory and then collects and analyzes research to test it. With the inductive approach, the researcher collects and analyzes data and then generates a theory based on that analysis.
- Many sociologists engage in quantitative research, which focuses on data that can be measured numerically (comparing rates of suicide, for example). Other research may be more qualitative, based on interpretive description rather than statistics (such as field research in a suicide prevention clinic). Sociologists tailor their research to the specific problem under study and their own particular focus.
- A conventional research process based on deduction and the quantitative approach has these key steps: (1) selecting and defining the research problem, (2) reviewing previous research, (3) formulating the hypothesis, which involves constructing variables, (4) developing the research design, (5) collecting and analyzing the data, and (6) drawing conclusions and reporting the findings.

- A researcher taking the qualitative approach might (1) formulate the problem to be studied instead of creating a hypothesis, (2) collect and analyze the data, and (3) report the results.
- Research methods are systematic techniques for conducting research. Through experiments, researchers study the impact of certain variables on their subjects. Surveys are polls used to gather facts about people's attitudes, opinions, or behaviours; a representative sample of respondents provides data through questionnaires or interviews. In secondary analysis, researchers analyze existing data, such as a government census, or cultural artifacts, such as a diary.
- In field research, sociologists study social life in its natural setting. Participant and complete observation, case studies, unstructured interviews, and ethnography are methods of observing attitudes, behaviour, and social interactions in the field. Field research often emphasizes qualitative data that is more open to interpretation by the researcher.
- Many sociologists use multiple methods, or triangulation, to study a particular issue. Multiple methods can provide a wider scope of data and points of view.
- Studying people—with or without their permission—prompts ethical questions about potential physical and psychological risks.

KEY TERMS

complete observation **65**
content analysis **64**
control group **56**
correlation **57**
deductive approach **47**
dependent variable **50**
descriptive studies **45**
empirical approach **45**
ethnography **67**
experiment **56**
experimental group **56**
explanatory studies **45**
Hawthorne effect **58**
hypothesis **50**
independent variable **50**
inductive approach **48**
interview **60**
normative approach **44**
operational definition **50**
participant observation **65**
population **52**
qualitative research **56**
quantitative research **56**
questionnaire **60**
random sample **52**
reliability **52**
replication **55**
representative sample **52**
research methods **56**
respondents **60**
sample **52**
secondary analysis **62**
survey **59**
unstructured interview **67**
validity **52**
variable **50**

QUESTIONS FOR ANALYSIS AND UNDERSTANDING

1. What are the limitations of a normative approach to social issues? What are the limitations of an empirical approach?
2. How is it possible to conduct sociological research without a theory?
3. What purpose does replication serve?

QUESTIONS FOR CRITICAL THINKING

1. The agency that funds the local suicide clinic has asked you to study the clinic's effectiveness in preventing suicide. What would you need to measure? What can you measure? What research method(s) would provide the best data for analysis?
2. Together with a group of students, perform a content analysis on the photographs in your textbooks. First, determine whether to sample texts from various fields of study or just one field. Try to follow the steps in the sociological research process.
3. You have been assigned a research study that examines possible discrimination against men in child custody cases. What will be the population(s) you will study? How will you sample the population(s)? How will you account for sex, race, age, income level, and other characteristics in your population(s)?

SUGGESTED READINGS

The following books provide in-depth information about research methods:

Earl Babbie. *The Practice of Social Research* (6th ed.). Belmont, Cal.: Wadsworth, 1992.

Therese L. Baker. *Doing Social Research* (2nd ed.). New York: McGraw-Hill, 1994.

Margrit Eichler. *Nonsexist Research Methods: A Practical Guide.* Boston: Allen & Unwin, 1988.

Sandra Kirby and Kate McKenna. *Experience Research Social Change: Methods from the Margins.* Toronto: Garamond, 1989.

Shulamit Reinharz. *Feminist Methods in Social Research.* New York: Oxford University Press, 1992. (Provides excellent information and examples of qualitative research using methods such as oral histories, content analysis, case studies, action research, and multiple-method research.)

Janice L. Ristock and Joan Pennell. *Research as Empowerment: Feminist Links, Postmodern Interruptions.* Don Mills, Ont.: Oxford University Press, 1996.

To find out more about writing a sociology term paper or report, see:

Richard Floyd. *Success in the Social Sciences: Writing and Research for Canadian Students.* Toronto: Harcourt Brace, 1995.

Margot Northey. *Making Sense: A Student's Guide to Research, Writing and Style.* Don Mills, Ont.: Oxford University Press, 1993. (Takes the reader from the initial steps of choosing a topic to doing research and writing the final paper. Describes the types of social science literature and makes suggestions about writing a research paper and preparing an oral presentation.)

Journals that present findings from sociological research include:

Canadian Journal of Sociology

Canadian Review of Sociology and Anthropology

Canadian Social Trends

Social Problems

Journals that focus on sociological research methods include:

Qualitative Sociology

Social Science Research

Sociological Methods and Research

To find out more about suicide:

Derek Humphrey. *Lawful Exit: The Limits of Freedom for Help in Dying*. Junction City, Ore.: Norris Lane Press, 1993.

David Lester. *Understanding Suicide: A Case Study Approach*. New York: Nova Science Publishers, 1993.

David Lester and Margot Tallmer (eds.). *Now I Lay Me Down: Suicide in the Elderly.* Philadelphia: Charles Press, 1994.

Part Two

THE NATURE OF SOCIAL LIFE

Chapter 3

CULTURE

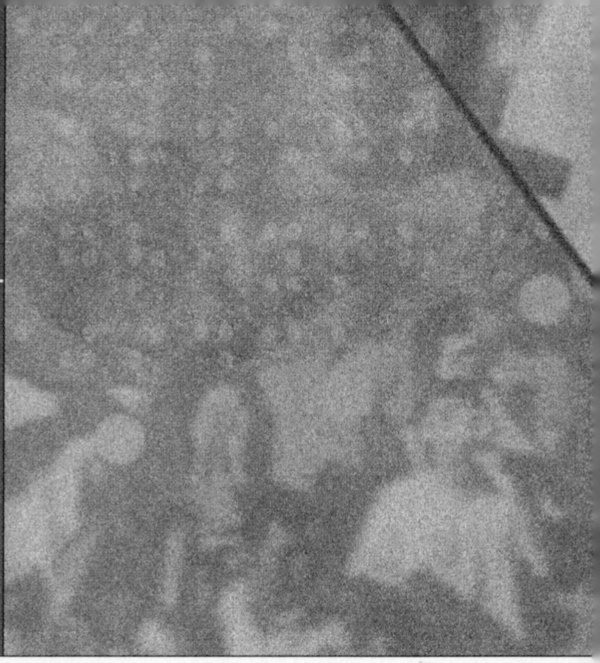

Culture and Society

The Importance of Culture

Material and Nonmaterial Culture

Cultural Universals

Components of Culture

Symbols

Language

Language Diversity in Canada

Values

Norms

Popular Culture

Popular versus High Culture

Divergent Perspectives on Popular Culture

Cultural Change and Diversity

Cultural Change

Cultural Diversity

Canadian Culture

Culture Shock

Ethnocentrism

Cultural Relativism

Sociological Analysis of Culture

A Functionalist Perspective

A Conflict Perspective

An Interactionist Perspective

Cultural Patterns for the Twenty-First Century

Culture and Technology

A Global Culture?

A young woman was going about her daily activities in her Toronto apartment block when she was attacked because of her ethnic origin. Her description of what happened provides insight on being a victim of hate crime:

> I was riding up the elevator from the apartment's laundry room with a basket of clothes in my arms when I was confronted by three boys. None of them could have been over 12. They began taunting me and calling me names. I immediately reprimanded them and asked them to mind their manners, but they continued unabashed. I got off on my floor. As the elevator doors were about to close, one of them lunged forward and spat on me. A split-second later I stood there alone in the corridor, helpless, my hands full, the elevator gone, filled with impotent rage and shame as tears began to smart my eyes. A few days later, a voice screamed out, "Hey you paki! Everybody hates a paki!"... From the corner of my eye I could see two young boys in the distance ... Was he the one who had shouted? Why was this little boy so full of hate for me? He was just a child, he probably attended the same school as my children. And yet he dared to assault me so loudly in front of everyone. It felt as though his action was sanctioned by public sentiment. (McKague, 1991:12)

Was this hate crime an isolated incident? Or is there a relationship between cultural beliefs and values in Canada and attacks on people because of their ethnicity, gender, sexual orientation, or religion? Hate and intolerance, like love and compassion, may be embedded in the cultural fabric of a society.

The following three excerpts are from accounts of recent incidents reported by the news media:

> Four youths, described by police as neo-Nazi skinheads, were charged with first degree murder yesterday in the stalking and killing of a gay man in a Montreal park on Sunday.
>
> Civil rights and gay leaders expressed profound shock and horror ...
>
> "This is a very grave crime," said Alain Dufour, leader of the World Anti-Fascist League, a national anti-racism group. "This is murder with ideological underpinning ..."
>
> The body of engineer Yves Lalonde, 51, was found near a path in Angrignon Park, a popular meeting place for gay men, on Monday morning. He had been savagely beaten and robbed of $92.00. (Picard, 1992)

> Four men have been arrested and are facing murder charges in the beating death of Gordon Kuhtey. Police believe all four suspects were involved in a neo-Nazi skinhead group known as the Northern Hammerskins ... Kuhtey was taking an early morning walk along the Assiniboine River near the Osborne Street Bridge [an area frequented by gay men] when he was attacked by four men ... He was then thrown into the river and stoned. The killing was witnessed by residents of nearby apartment blocks who heard the man's screams for help. The police treated the case as a hate crime from the beginning but took five years to piece together enough evidence to lay charges against the four men. (Owen, 1996a)

> Seven Montreal-area synagogues were defaced with swastikas and a Nazi slogan. The attacks, which appeared to be orchestrated, were described as the worst acts of anti-Semitic vandalism in Quebec in nearly three years. (Peritz, 1993)

***Culture* is the knowledge, language, values, customs, and material objects that are passed from person to person and from one generation to the next in a human group or society.** As previously defined, a *society* is a large social grouping that occupies the same geographic territory and is subject to the same political authority and dominant cultural expectations. While a society is comprised of people, a culture is comprised of ideas, behaviour, and material possessions. Society and culture are interdependent; neither could exist without the other.

Culture can be an enormously stabilizing force for a society, and it can provide a sense of continuity. However, culture also can be a force that generates discord, conflict, and even violence. How people view culture is intricately related to their location in society with regard to their ethnicity, class, sex, and age. From one perspective, Canadian culture does not condone or tolerate *hate crimes*—attacks against people because of their religion, colour, disability, sexual orientation, ethnic origin, or ancestry. For example, the police in some cities, including Ottawa, Toronto, and Montreal, have recently set up special units to investigate hate-motivated crimes (Gilmour, 1994). From another perspective, however, hatred and intolerance may be the downside of some "positive" cultural values—such as individualism, competition, and materialism—found in Canadian society. Just as attitudes of love and tolerance may be embedded in societal values and teachings, beliefs that reinforce acts of hatred and intolerance may also be embedded in culture.

In this chapter, we examine society and culture, with special attention to the components of culture and the relationship between cultural change and diversity. We also analyze culture from functionalist, conflict, and interactionist perspectives. Before reading on, test your knowledge of the relationship between culture and hate crimes by answering the questions in Box 3.1.

QUESTIONS AND ISSUES

What part does culture play in shaping individuals and groups?

What are the essential components of culture?

To what degree are we shaped by popular culture?

How do subcultures and countercultures reflect diversity within a society?

How do the various sociological perspectives view culture?

CULTURE AND SOCIETY

Understanding how culture affects our lives helps us develop a sociological imagination. When we meet someone from a culture vastly different from our own, or when we travel in another country, it may be easier to perceive the enormous influence of culture in people's lives.

BOX 3.1 SOCIOLOGY AND EVERYDAY LIFE

How Much Do You Know About Culture and Hate Crimes?

TRUE	FALSE	
T	F	1. In recent years, the number of reported attacks in Canada against persons because of their race, religion, sexual orientation, or ethnic origin has increased.
T	F	2. The Ku Klux Klan and other hate groups such as White Aryan Resistance and the "hard-core" skinheads exclusively target racial minorities as their victims.
T	F	3. Most victims of hate crimes do not report the incident to the police.
T	F	4. The majority of hate crimes recorded by police are directed against gays or lesbians.
T	F	5. The incidence of anti-Semitic activity has risen in recent years.
T	F	6. Some people are born with hatred for people who are different from themselves.
T	F	7. As the rate of immigration to Canada has increased rapidly in recent years, anti-immigrant feelings also have risen.
T	F	8. The Criminal Code of Canada has a provision to increase the penalty for a crime when it is hate-motivated.
T	F	9. It is illegal to be a member of a racist organization.
T	F	10. Hate crimes are often excessively brutal and more likely to entail personal violence.

Answers on page 84

However, when we turn our sociological lens on our own society, it is more difficult to examine culture because we take our own way of life for granted.

THE IMPORTANCE OF CULTURE

How important is culture in determining how people think and act on a daily basis? Simply stated, culture is essential for our individual survival and our communication with other people. We rely on culture because we are not born with the information we need to survive. We do not know how to take care of ourselves, how to behave, how to dress, what to eat, which gods to worship, or how to make or spend money. We must learn about culture through interaction, observation, and imitation in order to participate as members of the group (Samovar and Porter, 1991a). Sharing a common culture with others simplifies day-to-day interactions. However, as our society becomes more diverse, and

BOX 3.1

Answers to Sociology Quiz on Culture and Hate Crimes

TRUE	FALSE	
T	F	1. *True.* The number of reported hate, or bias, crimes has increased in recent years. Although such incidents are seriously underreported in Canada, more comprehensive reports may be available if the proposed Bias Incidents Statistics Act (Bill C–455) is passed.
T	**F**	2. *False.* Hate groups such as the KKK and the skinheads also target gay men, lesbians, minority religious group members, and individuals believed to be recent immigrants.
T	F	3. *True.* Most hate crimes are never reported to the police. Reasons for not reporting them include fear of reprisal; feelings that the justice system may not perceive the offences as serious; and, in the case of hate crimes against gays and lesbians, fear of stigmatization on the basis of homophobia.
T	**F**	4. *False.* Of all hate crime incidents recorded by the police in 1994, 61 percent were directed against racial minorities, 23 percent against religious minorities, 11 percent against gays or lesbians, and 5 percent against ethnic minorities. However, police statistics are likely to seriously underestimate the extent of hate crimes against the gay community in Canada.
T	F	5. *True.* According to the League for Human Rights, the number of reported anti-Semitic incidents increased by 50 percent between 1992 and 1994.
T	**F**	6. *False.* Sociologists agree that hatred and violence are "learned" attitudes and behaviours, not genetic by-products. Factors such as the availability of guns, economic inequality, and a violence-saturated culture are not rooted in human biology.
T	F	7. *True.* Polls show that high rates of immigration, combined with the tightening economy, are related to an increase in anti-immigrant sentiment.
T	**F**	8. *False.* However, Bill C–41, the Sentencing Reform Bill, if approved, will create a statutory aggravating factor, according to which, harsher penalties for crimes motivated by hate will be required.
T	**F**	9. *False.* As provided for in the Charter of Rights and Freedoms, individuals have the right to belong to any organization they choose to join.
T	F	10. *True.* Hate crimes typically are excessively brutal because the force used is more than would be necessary to subdue victims, make them comply, disarm them, or take their material possessions.

Sources: Based on Levin and McDevitt, 1993; Gilmour, 1994; and Roberts, 1995.

communication among members of international cultures more frequent, the need to appreciate diversity and to understand how people in other cultures view their world has also increased (Samovar and Porter, 1991b:65).

Just as culture is essential for individuals, it also is fundamental for the survival of societies. Culture has been described as "the common denominator that makes the actions of individuals intelligible to the group" (Haviland, 1993:30). Some system of rule making and enforcing necessarily exists in all societies. What would happen, for example, if *all* rules and laws in Canada suddenly disappeared? At a basic level, we need rules in order to navigate our bicycles and cars through traffic. At a more abstract level, we need laws to establish and protect our rights.

In order to survive, societies need rules about civility and tolerance toward others. We are not born knowing how to express kindness or hatred toward others, although some people may say, "Well, that's just human nature," when explaining someone's behaviour. Such a statement is built on the assumption that what we do as human beings is determined by *nature* (our biological and genetic makeup) rather than *nurture* (our social environment)—that is, that our behaviour is instinctive. An *instinct* is an unlearned, biologically determined behaviour pattern common to all members of a species that predictably occurs whenever certain environmental conditions exist. For example, spiders do not learn to build webs. They build webs because of instincts that are triggered by basic biological needs such as protection and reproduction.

Humans do not have instincts. What we most often think of as instinctive behaviour can be attributed to reflexes and drives. A *reflex* is an unlearned, biologically determined involuntary response to some physical stimulus (such as a sneeze after breathing some pepper through the nose or the blinking of an eye when a speck of dust gets in it). *Drives* are unlearned, biologically determined impulses common to all members of a species that satisfy needs such as sleep, food, water, or sexual gratification. Reflexes and drives do not determine how people will behave in human societies; even the expression of these biological characteristics is channelled by culture. For example, we may be taught that the "appropriate" way to sneeze (an involuntary response) is to use a tissue or turn our head away from others (a learned response). Similarly, we may learn to sleep on mats or in beds. Most contemporary sociologists agree that culture and social learning, not nature, account for virtually all of our behaviour patterns.

Since humans cannot rely on instincts in order to survive, culture is a "tool kit" for survival. According to sociologist Ann Swidler (1986:273), culture is a "tool kit of symbols, stories, rituals, and world views, which people may use in varying configurations to solve different kinds of problems." The tools we choose will vary according to our own personality and the situations we face. We are not puppets on a string; we make choices from among the items in our own "tool box."

MATERIAL AND NONMATERIAL CULTURE

Our cultural tool box is divided into two major parts: *material* and *nonmaterial* culture (Ogburn, 1966/1922). ***Material culture* consists of the physical or tangible creations that members of a society make, use, and share.** Initially, items of material culture begin as raw materials or resources such as ore, trees, and oil. Through technology, these raw materials are transformed into usable items (ranging from books and computers to guns and bombs). Sociologists define ***technology* as the knowledge, techniques, and tools that make it possible for people to transform resources into usable forms, and the knowledge and skills required to use them after they are developed.** From this standpoint, technology is both concrete and abstract. For example, technology includes a pair of scissors and the knowledge and skill necessary to make them from iron, carbon, and chromium (Westrum, 1991). At the most basic level, material culture is important because it is our buffer

Shelter is a universal type of material culture, but it comes in a wide variety of shapes and forms. What might some of the reasons be for the similarities and differences you see in these cross-cultural examples?

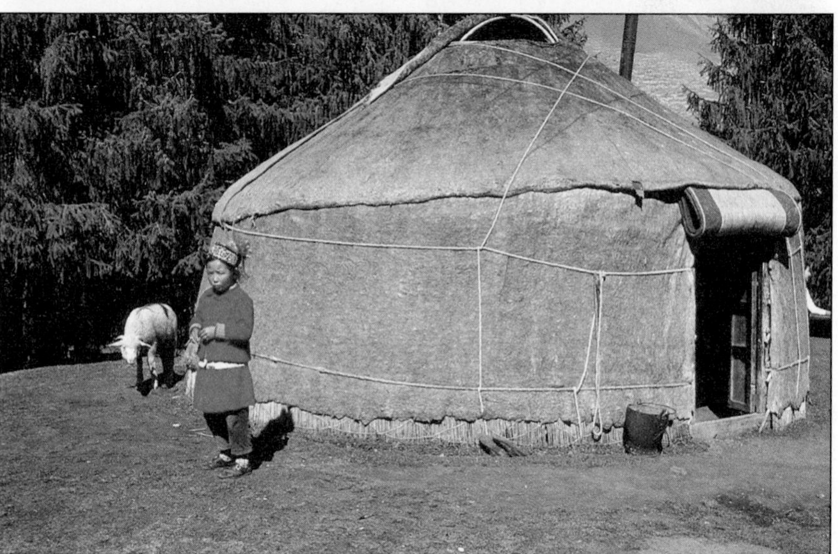

against the environment. For example, we create shelter to protect ourselves from the weather and to provide ourselves with privacy. Beyond the survival level, we make, use, and share objects that are interesting and important to us. Why are you wearing the particular clothes you have on today? Perhaps you're communicating something about yourself, such as where you attend school, what kind of music you like, or where you went on vacation.

Nonmaterial culture **consists of the abstract or intangible human creations of society that influence people's behaviour.** Language, beliefs, values, rules of behaviour, family patterns, and political systems are examples of nonmaterial culture. A central component of nonmaterial culture is *beliefs*—the mental acceptance or conviction that certain things are true or real. Beliefs may be based on tradition, faith, experience, scientific research, or some combination of these. Faith

The customs and rituals associated with weddings are one example of nonmaterial culture. What can you infer about beliefs and attitudes concerning marriage in the societies represented by these photographs?

in a supreme being, that education is the key to success, and that smoking causes cancer are examples of beliefs. We also have beliefs in items of material culture. For example, most students believe that computers are the key to technological advancement and progress.

Cultural beliefs are reflected in the material objects we make and use. For example, in the United States, some people own guns because of a long-enduring cultural belief that guns represent a source of power over or protection from others. As a young person stated, "If you have a gun, you have power. That's just the way it is. Guns are just a part of growing up these days" (Hull, 1993:21). To this individual, a sawed-off shotgun (an item of material culture) meant having "power" and being "grown up" (nonmaterial cultural beliefs). Many American citizens consider owning a gun to be a constitutional right; however, widespread ownership of guns tends to produce more deadly violence in a society. In the United States, for example, one of every four deaths among teenagers is the result of gunshots (Hull, 1993:22). Sociologist Joe R. Feagin (1986:275) has suggested that "there is a long tradition in the United States that legitimates violence as the way to solve problems, be they personal or national." Just as the use of guns in the United States is influenced by the predominant beliefs and expectations in the society, so, too, are all other items of the material culture.

CULTURAL UNIVERSALS

Because all humans face the same basic needs (such as food, clothing, and shelter), we engage in similar activities that contribute to our survival. Anthropologist George Murdock (1945:124) compiled a list of over seventy ***cultural universals*****—customs and practices that occur across all societies.** His categories included appearance (such as bodily adornment and hairstyles), activities (such as sports, dancing, games, joking, and visiting), social institutions (such as family, law, and religion), and customary practices (such as cooking, folklore, gift giving, and hospitality). While these general customs and practices may be present in all cultures, their specific forms vary from one group to another and from one time to another within the same group. For example, while telling jokes may be a universal practice, what is considered a joke in one society may be an insult in another.

How do sociologists view cultural universals? In terms of their functions, cultural universals are useful because they ensure the smooth and continual operation of society (Radcliffe-Brown, 1952). A society must meet basic human needs by providing food, shelter, and some degree of safety for its members so that they will survive. Children and other new members (such as immigrants) must be taught the ways of the group. A society also must settle disputes and deal with people's emotions. All the while, the self-interest of individuals must be balanced with the needs of society as a whole. Cultural universals help to fulfil these important functions of society.

From another perspective, however, cultural universals are not the result of functional necessity; these practices may have been *imposed* by members of one society on members of another. Similar customs and practices do not necessarily constitute cultural universals. They may be an indication that a conquering nation used its power to enforce certain types of behaviour on those who were defeated (Sargent, 1987). Sociologists might ask questions such as, "Who determines the dominant cultural patterns?" For example, although religion is a cultural universal, traditional religious practices of indigenous peoples (those who first live in an area) often have been repressed and even stamped out by subsequent settlers or conquerors who hold political and economic power over them.

COMPONENTS OF CULTURE

Even though the specifics of individual cultures vary widely, all cultures have four common nonmaterial cultural components: symbols, language, values, and norms. These components contribute to both harmony and conflict in a society.

SYMBOLS

As defined in Chapter 1, a symbol is anything that meaningfully represents something else. Culture could not exist without symbols because there would be no shared meanings among people. Symbols can simultaneously produce loyalty and animosity, and love and hate. They help us communicate ideas such as love or patriotism because they express abstract concepts with visible objects.

For example, flags can stand for patriotism, nationalism, school spirit, or religious beliefs held by members of a group or society. They also can be a source of discord and strife among people, as evidenced by recent controversies over the Canadian flag. In 1996, a retired Canadian couple, vacationing in a Florida trailer park, decided to fly the Canadian flag on their trailer. Their neighbours, patriotic Americans, objected so strenuously that the Canadians were forced to take their flag down. One of the neighbours even claimed (mistakenly) that it was against the law to fly a foreign flag on American soil. In 1992, a U.S. marine inadvertently held the Canadian flag upside down during the singing of "O Canada" at a World Series game. Although baseball administrators immedi-

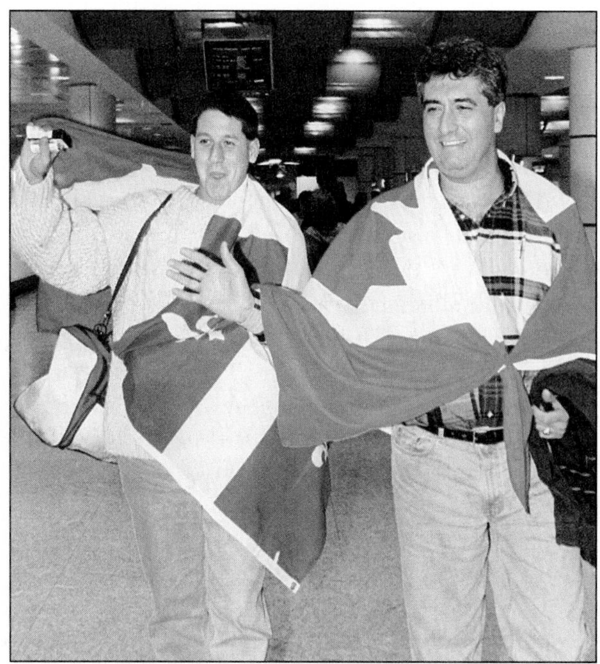

Symbols are powerful sources of communication. What messages do these two pictures communicate to you?

ately apologized, Canadians were outraged and insulted by the improper display of our national symbol. This incident had a happy ending for some enterprising individuals who did a booming business at the next World Series game, selling ... you guessed it—upside-down American flags.

Symbols can stand for love (a heart on a valentine), peace (a dove), or hate (a Nazi swastika), just as words can be used to convey these meanings. Symbols also can transmit other types of ideas. A siren is a symbol that denotes an emergency situation and sends the message to clear the way immediately. Gestures also are a symbolic form of communication—a movement of the head, body, or hands can express our ideas or feelings to others. For example, in Canada, pointing toward your chest with your thumb or finger is a symbol for "me." We are also all aware of how useful our middle finger can be in communicating messages to inconsiderate drivers.

Symbols affect our thoughts about gender. The colour of clothing, for example, has different symbolic meaning for females and males. In a study of baby clothing, sociologist Madeline Shakin and her associates (1985) found that 90 percent of the infants they observed were dressed in colours indicating their sex. Most boys were dressed in blue or red while most girls were dressed in pink or yellow. The colour of the clothing sends implicit messages about how the child should be treated. If a female infant is wearing a pink dress, the message is, "I'm a girl. Say that I'm pretty, not that I'm handsome." Such messages about gender have long-term effects on individual and societal perceptions about how women and men should think and act.

Symbols also may affect our beliefs about race and ethnicity. Although black and white are not truly colours at all, the symbolic meanings associated with these labels permeate society and affect everyone. English-language scholar Alison Lurie (1981:184) suggests that it is incorrect to speak of "whites" and "blacks." She notes that "pinkish-tan persons ... have designated themselves the 'White race' while affixing the term 'Black' [to people] whose skin is some shade of brown or gold." The result of this "semantic sleight of hand" has been the association of pinkish-tan skin with virtue and cleanliness, and "brown or golden skin with evil, dirt and danger" (Lurie, 1981:184).

LANGUAGE

Language **is a set of symbols that express ideas and enable people to think and communicate with one another.** Verbal (spoken) and nonverbal (written or gestured) language help us describe reality. One of our most important human attributes is the ability to use language to share our experiences, feelings, and knowledge with others. Language can create visual images in our head, such as "the kittens look like little cotton balls" (Samovar and Porter, 1991a). Language also allows people to distinguish themselves from outsiders and maintain group boundaries and solidarity (Farb, 1973).

Language is not solely a human characteristic. Other animals use sounds, gestures, touch, and smell to communicate with one another, but they use signals with fixed meanings that are limited to the immediate situation (the present) and cannot encompass past or future situations. For example, chimpanzees can use elements of Standard American Sign Language and manipulate physical objects to make "sentences," but they are not physically endowed with the vocal apparatus needed to form the consonants required for verbal language. As a result, nonhuman animals cannot transmit the more complex aspects of culture to their offspring. Humans have a unique ability to manipulate symbols to express abstract concepts and rules and thus to create and transmit culture from one generation to the next.

LANGUAGE AND SOCIAL REALITY One key issue in sociology is whether language *creates* or simply *communicates* reality. For example, consider the terms used by organizations involved in the abortion debate: pro-life and pro-choice. Do such terms create or simply express a reality? Anthropological linguists Edward Sapir and Benjamin Whorf have suggested that language not only expresses our thoughts and perceptions but also influences our perception of reality. According to the ***Sapir-Whorf hypothesis*****, language shapes the view of reality of its speakers** (Whorf, 1956; Sapir, 1961). If people are able to think only through language, language must precede thought.

If language shapes the reality we perceive and experience, some aspects of the world are viewed as important and others are virtually neglected because people know the world only in terms of the vocabulary and grammar of their own language. For example, the Eskimo language has more than twenty words associated with snow, so that people can make subtle distinctions regarding different types of snowfalls. English speakers in North America perceive time as something that can be kept, saved, lost, or wasted; therefore, "being on time" or "not wasting time" are important. Many English words divide time into units (years, months, weeks, days, hours, minutes, seconds, and milliseconds) and into the past, present, and future (yesterday, today, and tomorrow) (Samovar and Porter, 1991a). By contrast, according to Sapir and Whorf, the Hopi language does not contain past, present, and future tenses of verbs, or nouns for times, days, or years (Carroll, 1956); however, scholars recently have argued that this assertion is incorrect (see Edgerton, 1992).

If language does create reality, are we trapped by our language? Many social scientists agree that the Sapir-Whorf hypothesis overstates the relationship between language and our thoughts and behaviour patterns. While acknowledging that language has many subtle meanings and that the words used by people reflect their central concerns, most sociologists contend that language may *influence* our behaviour and interpretation of social reality but does not *determine* it.

LANGUAGE AND GENDER What is the relationship between language and gender? What cultural assumptions about women and men does language reflect? Scholars have suggested several ways in which language and gender are intertwined:

- The English language ignores women by using the masculine form to refer to human beings in general (Basow, 1992). For example, the word *man* is used generically in words like *chairman* and *mankind*, which allegedly include both men and women. However, *man* can mean either "all human beings" or "a male human being" (Miller and Swift, 1993:71).
- Use of the pronouns *he* and *she* affects our thinking about gender. Pronouns show the gender of the person we *expect* to be in a particular occupation. For instance, nurses, secretaries, and schoolteachers usually are referred to as *she*, while doctors, engineers, electricians, and presidents are referred to as *he* (Baron, 1986).
- Words have positive connotations when relating to male power, prestige, and leadership; when related to women, they carry negative overtones of weakness, inferiority, and immaturity (Epstein, 1988:224). Table 3.1 shows how gender-based language reflects the traditional acceptance of men and women in certain positions, implying that the jobs are different when filled by women rather than men.
- A language-based predisposition to think about women in sexual terms reinforces the notion that women are sexual objects. Women often are described by terms such as *fox*, *broad*, *bitch*, *babe*, or *doll*, which ascribe childlike or even petlike characteristics to them. By contrast, men have performance pressures placed on them by being defined in terms of their sexual prowess, such as *dude*, *stud*, and *hunk* (Baker, 1993).

Gender in language has been debated and studied extensively in recent years, and greater awareness and some changes have been the result. For example, the desire of many women to have *Ms.* (rather than *Miss* or *Mrs.*, which indicated their marital status) precede their names has received a degree of acceptance in public life and the media (Tannen, 1995). Many organizations and publications have established guidelines for the use of nonsexist language and have changed titles such as *chairman* to *chair* or *chairperson*. "Men Working" signs in many areas have been replaced with ones that say "People Working" (Epstein, 1988:227). Some occupations have been given "genderless" titles, such as *firefighter* and *flight attendant* (Maggio, 1988). Yet many people resist change, arguing the English language is being ruined (Epstein, 1988).

Unlike English, in which nouns can be feminine, masculine, and sometimes neuter, the aboriginal language Ojibwa is not preoccupied with gender and divides nouns into two classes—the animate and inanimate. In addition, only one pronoun is used for *he* or *she*. To develop a more inclusive and equitable society, many scholars suggest that a more inclusive language is needed (see Basow, 1992). Perhaps we need to look to our First Nations languages for examples of how to create a more gender-inclusive English language.

LANGUAGE, RACE, AND ETHNICITY Language may create and reinforce our perceptions about race and ethnicity by transmitting preconceived ideas about the superiority of one category of people over another. Let's look at a few images conveyed by words in the English language in regard to race/ethnicity.

- Words may have more than one meaning and create and reinforce negative images.

TABLE 3.1

Language and Gender

Male Term	Female Term	Neutral Term
teacher	teacher	teacher
chairman	chairwoman	chair, chairperson
policeman	policewoman	police officer
fireman	lady fireman	firefighter
airline steward	airline stewardess	flight attendant
race car driver	woman race car driver	race car driver
wrestler	lady/woman wrestler	wrestler
professor	female/woman professor	professor
doctor	lady/woman doctor	doctor
bachelor	spinster/old maid	single person
male prostitute	prostitute	prostitute
male nurse	nurse	nurse
welfare recipient	welfare mother	welfare recipient
worker/employee	working mother	worker/employee
janitor/maintenance man	maid/cleaning lady	custodial attendant

Sources: Adapted from Korsmeyer, 1981:122; and Miller and Swift, 1991.

Terms such as *blackhearted* (malevolent) and expressions such as "a black mark" (a detrimental fact) and "Chinaman's chance of success" (unlikely to succeed) give the words *black* and *Chinaman* negative associations and derogatory imagery. By contrast, expressions such as "That's white of you" and "The good guys wear white hats" reinforce positive associations with the colour white.

- Overtly derogatory terms such as *nigger, kike, gook, honkey, chink, squaw, savage,* and other racial/ethnic slurs have been "popularized" in movies, music, comic routines, and so on. Such derogatory terms often are used in conjunction with physical threats against persons.
- Words frequently are used to create or reinforce perceptions about a group. For example, native peoples have been referred to as "savages" and described as "primitive," while blacks have been described as "uncivilized," "cannibalistic," and "pagan."
- The "voice" of verbs may minimize or incorrectly identify the activities or achievements of members of various minority groups. For example, use of the passive voice in the statement "African Americans *were given* the right to vote" ignores how African Americans *fought* for that right. Active-voice verbs also may inaccurately attribute achievements to people or groups. Some historians argue that cultural bias is shown by the very notion

that "Columbus discovered America"—given that America already was inhabited by people who later became known as native Americans (see Stannard, 1992; Takaki, 1993).

- Adjectives that typically have positive connotations can have entirely different meanings when used in certain contexts. Regarding employment, someone may say that a person of colour is "qualified" for a position when it is taken for granted that whites in the same position *are* qualified (see Moore, 1992).

In addition to these concerns about the English language, problems also arise when more than one language is involved.

LANGUAGE DIVERSITY IN CANADA

In 1969 the federal government passed the Official Languages Act, making both French and English official languages. In doing so, Canada officially became a bilingual society. However, this action by no means resolved the very complex issues regarding language in our society. Canada is a linguistically diverse society consisting of aboriginal languages, French and English, and heritage languages. Language has been referred to as the keystone to culture. In other words, language is the chief vehicle for understanding and experiencing one's culture (McVey and Kalbach, 1995). Canada's two charter language groups are often referred to as "two solitudes" (Hiller,1995). How is it possible to have a unified country when groups of people within a society cannot talk to each other? According to a recent census, 67 percent of Canadians speak English only, another 15 percent speak French only, and slightly more than 16 percent are bilingual. Only 1 percent, or 378,000 Canadians, indicated they lacked the skills to converse in either French or English (McVey and Kalbach, 1995). Although French-versus-English language issues have been a significant source of conflict, bilingualism remains a distinct component of Canadian culture. As one Canadian said to the Citizen's Forum on Canada's Future, a commission that toured Canada in the early 1990s and that was set up to enable Canadians to discuss the country's political future:

> Most people I talk to do not want a divided country. Nor do they deny the right of Québécois to preserve their language and culture ... having two languages doesn't split up the country, it *makes* it. Without Quebec and their French language I would feel lost as a Canadian. (1991:55)

Although it may be easy for members of the English-speaking majority to display such acceptance and tolerance of bilingualism, francophones are concerned that this policy is not enough to save their culture. As a French community in the middle of a predominantly English-speaking country, Québécois feel that their language and culture are threatened, and this feeling tends to provoke a defensive reaction. Efforts to protect French language and culture have resulted in some exclusionary policies. For example, in 1988, then premier Robert Bourassa's provincial government passed Bill 178, whereby the exterior signs on stores, restaurants, and offices had to be only in French; English would not be tolerated (Dryden, 1995). As the following incident demonstrates, this law has increased the tension between our two charter linguistic groups:

> I went to meet some friends at a downtown bar ... As I arrived, a solemn middle-aged man was taking photographs of the blackboard mounted on the outside steps. He was intent on a notice scrawled in chalk on the board: Today's Special—Ploughman's Lunch. This notice happened to be a blatant violation of Quebec's Bill 178 ... and the photographer was one of a number of self-appointed vigilantes who ... dutifully search the downtown streets for English language or bilingual commercial signs ... They photograph the evidence and then lodge an official complaint with the Commission de Protection de la Langue Française. Woody was lucky. A chalkboard sign could be erased. (Richler, 1992:1)

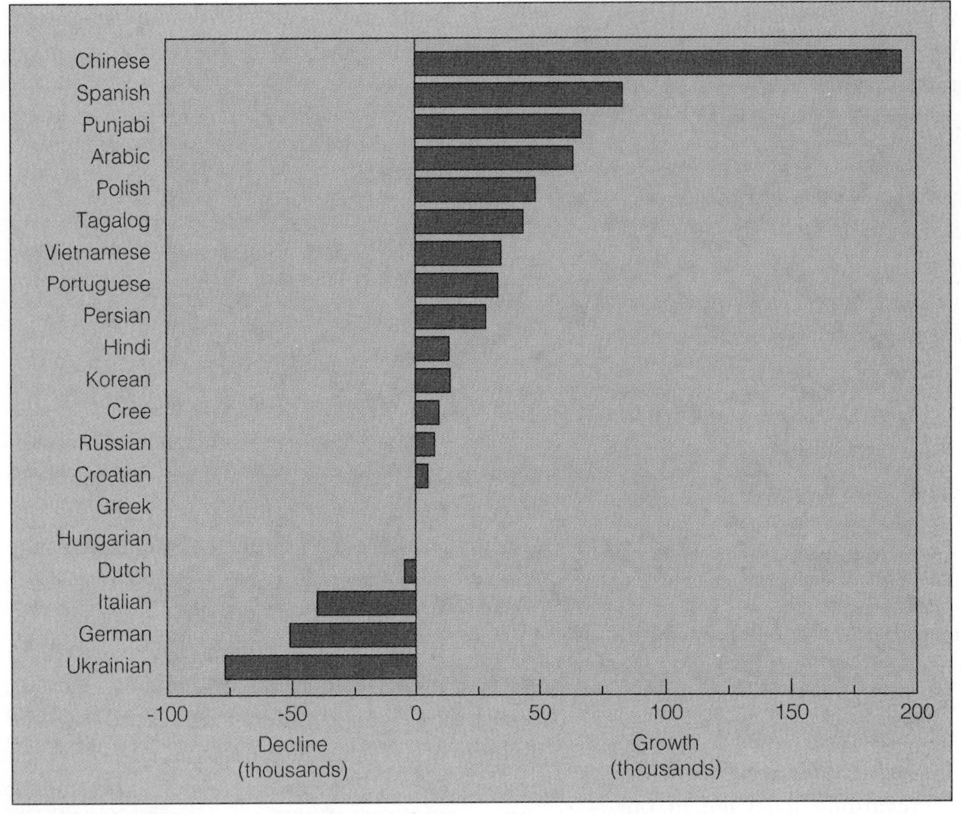

FIGURE 3.1

Change in Size of the Twenty Largest Heritage Language Groups, Canada, 1986–1991[a]

[a]Includes single and multiple responses to the mother-tongue question.

Source: Statistics Canada, *The Daily*, Cat. no. 11-001E, September 15, 1992, p. 3. Reproduced by authority of the Minister of Industry, 1994.

Aboriginal and heritage language groups are also adamant about maintaining their languages. But only three of the fifty-three aboriginal languages in Canada are in a healthy state, and many are near extinction (Fleras and Elliott, 1992). Aboriginal identity, language, and culture are all interconnected. For example, some aboriginal stories can only be passed on in their native languages. Therefore, loss of the language will have a direct effect on the cultural survival of aboriginal peoples in Canada. According to Eli Taylor, a Dakota-Sioux from Manitoba:

> Our native language embodies a value system about how we ought to live and relate to each other ... Now if you destroy our language, you not only break down these relationships, but you also destroy other aspects of our Indian way of life and culture, especially those that describe man's connection with nature, the Great Spirit, the order of things. Without our language, we will cease to exist as a separate people. (Fleras and Elliott, 1992:151)

Aboriginal leaders have taken steps to retain their language through the introduction of aboriginal language courses in schools and universities.

The term *heritage language groups* refers to those groups whose language is not English, French, or aboriginal. In recent decades Canada has experienced a number of significant changes in the composition of its heritage languages. For example, the number of speakers of Asian languages has increased sharply (McVey and Kalbach, 1995). Figure 3.1 lists the change in size of heritage language groups spoken in Canada.

How does the introduction of all of these different languages affect Canadian culture? From the functionalist perspective, a shared language is essential to a common culture; language is a stabilizing force in society and is an important means of cultural transmission. Through language, children learn about their cultural heritage and develop a sense of personal identity in relation to their group. Functionalists would therefore view language diversity as potentially detrimental to Canadian culture.

Conflict theorists view language as a source of power and social control; it perpetuates inequalities between people and between groups because words are used (intentionally or not) to "keep people in their place." For example, derogatory messages such as the rap lyrics "Beat that bitch with a bat" on T-shirts may devalue women and desensitize people toward violence (Gleman, 1993). As linguist Deborah Tannen (1993:B5) has suggested, "The devastating group hatreds that result in so much suffering in our own country and around the world are related in origin to the small intolerances in our everyday conversations—our readiness to attribute good intentions to ourselves and bad intentions to others." Furthermore, different languages themselves are associated with inequalities. Consider this aboriginal language instructor's comments on the lure of the English language, "It's to do with the perception of power. People associate English with prestige and power. We don't have movies in [native language], we don't have hardcover books ... or neon signs in our language" (Martin, 1996:A8). Language, then, is a reflection of our feelings and values.

VALUES

***Values* are collective ideas about what is right or wrong, good or bad, and desirable or undesirable in a particular culture** (Williams, 1970:27). Values do not dictate which behaviours are appropriate and which ones are not, but they provide us with the criteria by which we evaluate people, objects, and events. Values typically come in pairs of positive and negative values, such as being brave or cowardly, hardworking or lazy. Since we use values to justify our behaviour, we tend to defend them staunchly (Kluckhohn, 1961).

CORE CANADIAN VALUES Do we have shared values in Canada? Sociologists disagree about the extent to which all people in this country share a core set of values. Functionalists tend to believe that shared values are essential for societies and have conducted most of the research on core values. Between November 1990 and July 1991, approximately 400,000 Canadians participated in the above-mentioned Citizen's Forum on Canada's Future. The participants focused a great deal on what it meant to be Canadian. In doing so, they discovered a distinct Canadian identity and set of core Canadian values. Some of these values were expressed as purely Canadian traits whereas others were expressed in a comparative sense, in terms of how we differ from our American neighbours. The following list summarizes the core values that emerged most strongly from participants in all regions of Canada:

1. *Equality and fairness in a democratic society.* Equality and fairness were not seen as mutually exclusive values. As one respondent indicated: "My hope for the future of Canada is for ... a country where people feel comfortable with one another, are tolerant and understanding with one another, and where each person recognizes they have the same opportunities, responsibilities and privileges" (1991:37).
2. *Consultation and dialogue.* Canadians view themselves as people who settle their differences peaceably and in a consultative rather than confrontational manner. The view was widely held that Canadians must work together to solve their problems and remedy

the apparent lack of understanding between different groups, regions, and provinces.

3. *Accommodation and tolerance.* The forum participants recognized the existence of different groups in Canadian society and their need to sustain their own culture while attaching themselves to the country's society, values, and institutions.
4. *Support for diversity.* This diversity has a number of facets, including linguistic, regional, ethnic, and cultural differences. Again, the respondents spoke of the difficulty of achieving a balance between a multicultural Canada and a secure sense of a Canadian identity. One Ontario participant said, "Ethnic and cultural diversity is an attractive embroidery on our national fabric, but ... if we really want a country, we must be Canadians first" (1991:41).
5. *Compassion and generosity.* Forum participants deeply valued Canada's compassion and generosity as exemplified in our universal and extensive social services, health-care and pension systems, immigration policies, and commitment to regional economic equalization.
6. *Canada's natural beauty.* Canada's unspoiled natural beauty was identified as very important. The forum also recognized that this may be threatened by inadequate attention to environmental protection issues.
7. *Canada's world image: Commitment to freedom, peace, and nonviolent change.* Canada's role as a nonviolent, international peacekeeper was summed up in one respondent's comments: "Canada should not try to be a world power like the U.S.A. We should be the same kind of nation that we have always been, a peaceful and quiet nation" (1991:44).

As you can see from this list, some core values may contradict others.

VALUE CONTRADICTIONS All societies have value contradictions. ***Value contradictions* are values that conflict with one another or are mutually exclusive** (achieving one makes it difficult, if not impossible, to achieve another). For example, core values of morality and humanitarianism may conflict with values of individual achievement and success. In the 1990s, for example, humanitarian values reflected in welfare and other government aid programs have come into conflict with values emphasizing hard work and personal achievement. Similarly, despite the fact that 84 percent of Canadians feel that "people who are poor have a right to an adequate income to live on" (Bibby, 1995), they have also shown strong support for governments that have dramatically cut budgets in order to reduce financial deficits. Can you identify the value contradictions in the list of Canadian core values proposed by the Citizen's Forum?

IDEAL VERSUS REAL CULTURE What is the relationship between values and human behaviour? Sociologists stress that a gap always exists between ideal culture and real culture in a society.

***Ideal culture* refers to the values and standards of behaviour that people in a society profess to hold. *Real culture* refers to the values and standards of behaviour that people actually follow.** For example, we may claim to be law-abiding (ideal cultural value) but smoke marijuana (real cultural behaviour), or we may regularly drive over the speed limit but think of ourselves as "good citizens."

Most of us are not completely honest about how well we adhere to societal values. In a study known as the "Garbage Project," household waste was analyzed to determine the rate of alcohol consumption in a U.S. city. People were asked about their level of alcohol consumption, and in some areas of the city, very low levels of alcohol use were reported. However, when their garbage was analyzed, researchers found that in more than 80 percent of these households some beer had been consumed, and in more than half occupants threw out eight or more empty beer cans a week (Haviland, 1993:11–12). Obviously, this study shows a discrepancy between ideal cultural values and people's actual behaviour.

The degree of discrepancy between ideal and real culture is relevant to sociologists investigating social change. Large discrepancies provide a foothold for demonstrating hypocrisy (pretending to be what one is not or to feel what one does not feel). These discrepancies often are a source of social problems; if the discrepancy is perceived, leaders of social movements may utilize them to point out people's contradictory behaviour. For example, preserving our natural environment may be a core value, but our behaviour (such as littering highways and lakes) contributes to its degradation, as is further discussed in Chapter 17 ("Social Movements and Social Change").

NORMS

Values provide ideals or beliefs about behaviour but do not state explicitly how we should behave. Norms, on the other hand, do have specific behavioural expectations. ***Norms*** **are established rules of behaviour or standards of conduct.** *Prescriptive norms* state what behaviour is appropriate or acceptable. For example, persons making a certain amount of money are expected to file a tax return and pay any taxes they owe. Norms based on custom direct us to open a door for a person carrying a heavy load. By contrast, *proscriptive norms* state what behaviour is inappropriate or unacceptable. Laws that prohibit us from driving over the speed limit and "good manners" that preclude reading a newspaper during class are examples. Prescriptive and proscriptive norms operate at all levels of society, from our everyday actions to the formulation of laws.

FORMAL AND INFORMAL NORMS Not all norms are of equal importance; those that are most crucial are formalized. *Formal norms* are written down and involve specific punishments for violators. Laws are the most common type of formal norms; they have been codified and may be enforced by sanctions. ***Sanctions*** **are rewards for appropriate behaviour or penalties for inappropriate behaviour.** Examples of *positive sanctions* include praise, honours, or medals for conformity to specific norms. *Negative sanctions* range from mild disapproval to life imprisonment. In the case of law, formal sanctions are clearly defined and can be administered only by persons in certain official positions (such as police officers and judges) who are given the authority to impose the sanctions.

Norms considered to be less important are referred to as *informal norms*—unwritten standards of behaviour understood by people who share a common identity. When individuals violate informal norms, other people may apply informal sanctions. *Informal sanctions* are not clearly defined and can be applied by any member of a group (such as frowning at someone or making a negative comment or gesture).

FOLKWAYS Norms are also classified according to their relative social importance. ***Folkways*** **are informal norms or everyday customs that may be violated without serious consequences within a particular culture** (Sumner, 1959/1906). They provide rules for conduct but are not considered to be essential to society's survival. In Canada, folkways include using underarm deodorant, brushing one's teeth, and wearing appropriate clothing for a specific occasion. Folkways are not often enforced; when they are enforced, the resulting sanctions tend to be informal and relatively mild.

Folkways are very culture specific; they are learned patterns of behaviour that can vary markedly from one society to another. In Japan, for example, where the walls of restroom stalls reach to the floor, folkways dictate that a person should knock on the door before entering a stall (you cannot tell if anyone is inside without knocking). People in Canada find it disconcerting, however, when someone knocks on the door of the stall (Collins, 1991).

MORES Other norms are considered highly essential to the stability of society. ***Mores*** (pronounced MOR-ays) **are strongly held norms with moral and ethical connotations that may not be violated without serious consequences in a particular culture.** Since mores are based on cultural values and are considered crucial for the well-being of the group, violators are subject to more severe negative sanctions (such as ridicule, loss of employment, or imprisonment) than are those who fail to adhere to folkways. The strongest mores are referred to as taboos. ***Taboos* are mores so strong that their violation is considered to be extremely offensive and even unmentionable.** Violation of taboos is punishable by the group or even, according to certain belief systems, by a supernatural force. The incest taboo, which prohibits sexual or marital relations between certain categories of kin, is an example of a nearly universal taboo.

Folkways and mores provide structure and security in a society. They make everyday life more predictable and provide people with some guidelines for appearance and behaviour. As individuals travel in countries other than their own, they become aware of cross-cultural differences in folkways and mores. For example, women from Canada travelling in Muslim nations quickly become aware of mores, based on the Sharia (the edicts of the Koran), that prescribe the dominance of men over women. In Saudi Arabia, for instance, women are not allowed to mix with men in public. Banks have branches with only women tellers—and only women customers. In hospitals, female doctors are supposed to tend only to children and other women (Alireza, 1990; Ibrahim, 1990).

LAWS ***Laws* are formal, standardized norms that have been enacted by legislatures and are enforced by formal sanctions.** Laws may be either civil or criminal. *Civil law* deals with disputes among persons or groups. Persons who lose civil suits may encounter negative sanctions such as having to pay compensation to the other party or being ordered to stop certain conduct. *Criminal law*, on the other hand, deals with public safety and well-being. When criminal laws are violated, fines and prison sentences are the most likely negative sanctions.

Changes in law often reflect changes in culture. In the 1990s, increasing awareness of hate crimes based on racial/ethnic, religious, or sexual-orientation biases has led to increasing pressure on the federal government to establish uniform reporting requirements and to increase penalties for hate crimes (see Box 3.2).

In addition to material objects, all of the nonmaterial components of culture—symbols, language, values, and norms—are reflected in the popular culture of contemporary society.

POPULAR CULTURE

Before taking this course, what was the first thing you thought about when you heard the term *culture*? In everyday life, culture often is used to describe the fine arts, literature, or classical music. When people say that a person is "cultured," they may mean that the individual has a highly developed sense of style or aesthetic appreciation of the "finer" things.

POPULAR VERSUS HIGH CULTURE

Some sociologists use the concepts of high culture and popular culture to distinguish between different cultural forms. These ideal types are differentiated by their content, style, expressed values, and respective audiences (Gans, 1974; DiMaggio and Useem, 1978; Bourdieu, 1984; DiMaggio, 1987). *High culture* consists of classical music, opera, ballet, live theatre, and other activities usually patronized by elite audiences, composed primarily of members of the upper middle and upper classes, who have the time, money, and knowledge assumed to be necessary for its appreciation. ***Popular culture* consists of activities, products, and services that are assumed to appeal primarily to members of the middle and working classes.** These include rock concerts, spectator sports, movies, and television soap operas and situation comedies.

Some sociological examinations of high culture and popular culture focus primarily on the link between culture and social class. French sociologist Pierre Bourdieu's (1984) *cultural capital theory* views high culture as a device used by the

BOX 3.2 SOCIOLOGY AND LAW

Dealing with Hate Crimes

> Moles only come out in the dark when no one is watching. Jews only do their deeds when no one is watching. A mole, when mad, will strike back and have NO mercy when disturbed. Jews strike at any time and have NO mercy.

That excerpt from an examination answer penned by an Eckville, Alta., high-school student in 1982 is just one example of the lessons taught by former social studies teacher James Keegstra—lessons that launched a long and convoluted series of trials and appeals that finally ended [in February 1996]. In a unanimous decision, the Supreme Court of Canada upheld Keegstra's 1992 conviction in Alberta—his second—on charges of willfully inciting hatred against an identifiable group. "It ends a very ugly chapter in Alberta's history ... All groups in our multicultural society will rest easy tonight."

The Keegstra case began in the fall of 1982 when one Eckville parent, dismayed by what she had discovered in her son's social studies notebook, complained about the teacher to the local school board. In December of that year, Keegstra lost his teaching job; in January 1984, he was charged with hate-mongering. After a 70-day trial, he was convicted ... but three years later the Alberta Court of Appeal overturned the ruling after Keegstra's lawyer argued that Canada's so-called hate law was unconstitutional because it denies freedom of expression. Not according to the Supreme Court, which subsequently upheld the law's constitutionality and sent the case back to the provincial appeals court, which ordered a new trial. Keegstra was again found guilty, a decision that he successfully appealed two years later on grounds that the jury received inappropriate direction from the trial judge.

That decision set the stage for the Supreme Court ruling which also reaffirmed the high court's previous decision that Canada's anti-hate law is constitutional.

Keegstra, who now works as an automobile mechanic, remains unrepentant. Described in 1985 by the judge presiding over his original trial as "akin to a drug addict pushing drugs," he declared that he was "disappointed, because we were dealing with truths and now they've made me a criminal for telling the truth." While some Eckville residents expressed relief that the case was finally over, it is clear that certain aspects of Keegstra's ugly brand of "truth" continue to resonate. Before the initial complaint against him, he spread his anti-Semitic message among Eckville students for more than a decade. One of them told reporters that some of his teaching fell on fertile ground. "He was so strong about it that I believed what he believed. You basically accepted what you were being taught." While Keegstra's legal odyssey may have ended, he could face up to two years in jail.

The educational system is one of the primary institutions through which we are socialized or "acquire the culture." In this case, young students were in fact taught anti-semitism. Is it any surprise that there are subcultures of hate in our multicultural society?

Source: Kopvillem, 1996.

dominant class to exclude the subordinate classes. According to Bourdieu, people must be trained to appreciate and understand high culture. Individuals learn about high culture in upper middle- and upper-class families and in elite education systems, especially higher education. Once they acquire this trained capacity, they possess a form of cultural capital. Persons from poor and working-class backgrounds typically do not acquire this cultural capital. Since knowledge and appreciation of high culture is considered a prerequisite for access to the dominant class, its members can use their cultural capital to deny access to subordinate group members and thus preserve and reproduce the existing class structure (but see Halle, 1993).

Unlike high culture, popular culture is assumed to be far more widespread and accessible to everyone; for this reason, it is sometimes referred to as "mass culture." While the primary purpose of popular culture is entertainment, it also provides an avenue for people to express their hopes, fears, and anger. However, popular culture also may include racism, sexism, and nativism (hostility toward immigrants by native-born citizens) (Mukerji and Schudson, 1991). For example, "cruising the Internet" has become a new form of popular culture. Unfortunately, although this medium is for most Canadians a source of education and entertainment, it has also become a medium for hate groups to disseminate racist and homophobic ideology. For example, on the World Wide Web there are White Nationalist and One World Government resource pages (Chidley, 1995). Canadian law is just beginning to respond to hate crime in cyberspace. Police in Winnipeg laid the first Internet hate crime charges in 1996 after arresting a 17-year-old "Net surfer" known as "Inbred Jed" for threatening the life of a local gay activist over the Internet (Nairne, 1996:A1–A3). For sociologists, popular culture provides a window into the public consciousness. At times the view can be disturbing.

Forms of popular culture move across cultures. In fact, popular culture is the United States' second-largest export (Rockwell, 1994), and one of its largest importers is Canada. Sadly, we often assess the quality of popular culture on the basis of whether it is a Canadian or American product. Canadian artists, musicians, and entertainers know they have "made it" when they become part of American popular culture. Of the world's 100 most-attended films in 1993, for example, 88 were produced by U.S.-based film companies. Likewise, music, television shows, novels, and street fashions from the United States have become a part of Canadian culture.

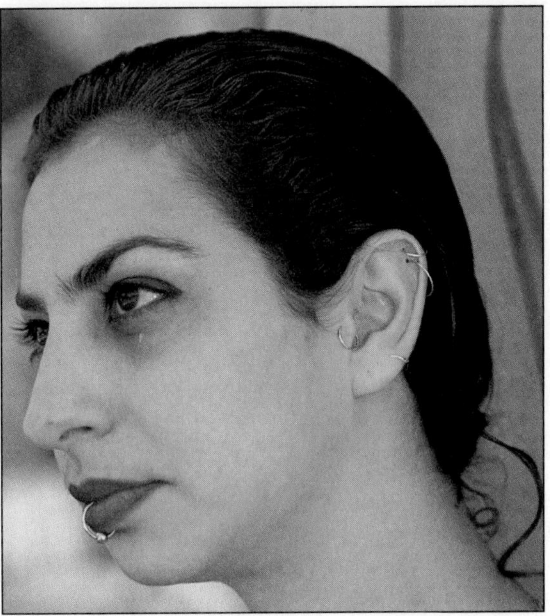

Is body piercing a fad, or might it become a more lasting feature of culture? How does it reinforce or challenge "mainstream" values and norms?

DIVERGENT PERSPECTIVES ON POPULAR CULTURE

According to many functionalist theorists, popular culture serves an important function in society: It may be the "glue" that holds society together. Regardless of their ethnicity, class, sex, or age, people are brought together (at least in spirit) to cheer teams competing in major sporting events such as the Stanley Cup or the Olympic Games. Television helps integrate immigrants into the mainstream culture, while longer-term residents become more homogenized as a result of seeing the same images and being exposed to the same beliefs and values (Gerbner et al., 1987).

Popular culture also may help us temporarily forget our everyday problems. In a recent study of Walt Disney World, anthropologist Stephen M. Fjellman (1992) found that such amusement parks allow people to forget that the outside world can be threatening. Even at night, they can walk without fear on the park's streets because virtually no crime exists and automobiles are not allowed. As Fjellman (1992:12) notes, "This freedom is enormously empowering." Various forms of popular culture provide people with opportunities to relax, be entertained, and exercise their abilities to think, feel, and remember (Fjellman, 1992).

Functionalist analysts point out, however, that popular culture also has dysfunctions. Popular culture may undermine core cultural values rather than reinforce them (see Christians, Rotzoll, and Fackler, 1987). For example, movies may glorify crime, rather than hard work, as the quickest way to get ahead. Excessive violence in music videos, movies, and television shows may be harmful to children and young people (Medved, 1992). From this perspective, popular culture may contribute to antisocial behaviour. Do some forms of popular culture promote hatred and violence in society? Recent controversies over rap music have focused on this issue, as discussed in Box 3.3.

Conflict theorists tend to view popular culture as part of the commercial system in which it is created (see Gans, 1974; Cantor, 1980, 1987). Corporations create popular culture in the same way that any other product or service is produced. Popular culture promotes consumption of *commodities*—objects outside ourselves that we purchase to satisfy our human needs or wants (Fjellman, 1992). For example, Fjellman found that park-goers at Walt Disney World spend as much money on merchandise as they do on admissions and rides. They purchase items ranging from Magic Kingdom pencils and Mickey Mouse hats to non-Disney kitchen accessories, flowers and plants, and clothing:

> Once inside the Magic Kingdom, it is the grown-ups who relax, who drop their guards and become childlike. They buy everything in sight, shoving off much of it on their kids, wearing some of it and stashing some of it as gifts for others ... The adults themselves lose control over not only the purse strings but their very sense of self. (Fjellman, 1992:162)

From this perspective, popular culture has been turned into a commodity; people come to believe that they *need* things they ordinarily would not purchase. Their desire is intensified by marketing techniques that promote public trust in products and services provided by a corporation such as the Walt Disney Company. Sociologist Pierre Bourdieu (1984:291) referred to this public trust as *symbolic capital:* "the acquisition of a reputation for competence and an image of respectability and honourability." Symbolic capital consists of culturally approved intangibles—such as honour, integrity, esteem, trust, and goodwill—that may be accumulated and used for tangible (economic) gain. Thus, people buy products at Walt Disney World (and Disney stores throughout the country) because they believe in the trustworthiness of the item ("These children's pyjamas are bound to be flame retardant; they came from the Disney Store") and the integrity of the company ("I can trust Disney; it has been around for a long time").

Other conflict theorists suggest that corporations do not create popular culture as much as they co-opt existing popular culture for their own economic gain. As communications scholar Herbert I. Schiller (1989:30) explained:

> Speech, dance, drama (ritual), music, and the visual and plastic arts have been vital ... features of human experience from earliest times. What distinguishes their situation in the industrial-capitalist era ... [is] the relentless and successful efforts to separate these elemental expressions of human creativity from their group and community origins for the purpose of selling them to those who can pay for them.

Schiller further argues that corporate control of arenas of culture, such as museums, theatres, performing arts centres, and public broadcasting stations, has resulted in the manipulation of people's consciousness and a form of censorship.

Although numerous scholars have examined the relationship between class and popular culture, few have investigated the intertwining relationship between ethnicity, gender, and popular culture. However, sociologist K. Sue Jewell (1993) linked images found in popular culture to negative stereotypes of black women. She suggested that cultural images depicting black women as mammies or domestics, whose primary purpose is to nurture others, affect their career prospects as early as middle school, when guidance counsellors and teachers give them little encouragement to succeed. Popular cultural icons such as Aunt Jemima, Uncle Ben (her male counterpart on rice boxes), and other "mammy trademarks" are

BOX 3.3 SOCIOLOGY AND MEDIA

Popular Culture, Rap, and Social Protest

Popular culture both reflects and affects the attitudes and concerns of people (Levin and McDevitt, 1993). While it is difficult to trace the beginnings of most forms of popular culture, rap is believed to have originated in the late 1970s in the South Bronx and Harlem areas of New York, where disc jockeys stirred dancers into a frenzy by shouting rhythmic rhymes, or raps, over the recorded music. During the 1980s, rap gained popularity and profitability as it began to describe the social, economic, and political conditions (such as drug addiction, material deprivation, teen pregnancy, and police brutality) that led to its emergence.

Today, rap is a multimillion-dollar business as major record labels—such as Atlantic, MCA, Columbia, and Warner Brothers—and MTV have cashed in on its popularity with young people in the suburbs as well as the central cities. Rap recording artists and performers make large sums of money; rapper Biz Markie, for example, stated that he makes $15,000 per performance on a "bad night" (Marriott, 1993).

"Gangsta rap" is a severe form of rap that advocates violence, exploitation of women, and hatred of the police. The first hardcore gangsta rap recording, "Straight Outta Compton," was recorded by the California-based group N.W.A. (Niggaz With Attitudes) in the late 1980s. Since that time, gangsta rap has been criticized for its harsh lyrics and violent themes. It received adverse publicity when a young man accused of killing a highway patrol officer used as his defence the fact that he had been listening to gangsta rap tapes, including those by the late rap artist Tupac Shakur, for hours before his encounter with the officer (Ward, 1993).

Although this man was convicted, the debate continues over the effects of gangsta rap. Some claim that it devalues women and reinforces negative stereotypes of blacks (see Carter, 1993; Marriott, 1993). However, bell hooks (1994) notes that the "sexist ... patriarchal ways of thinking and behaving that are glorified in gangsta rap are a reflection of the prevailing values in our society." Michael Eric Dyson (1993:15) is critical of the violence and sexist sentiments found in some rap music, but he also points out that rap has positive attributes:

> Rap is a form of profound musical, cultural, and social creativity. It expresses the desire of young black people to reclaim their history, reactivate forms of black radicalism, and contest the powers of despair and economic depression that presently besiege the black community. Besides being the most powerful form of black musical expression today, rap projects a style of self into the world that generates forms of cultural resistance and transforms the ugly terrain of ghetto existence into a searing portrait of life as it must be lived by millions of voiceless people. For that reason alone, rap deserves attention and should be taken seriously; and for its productive and healthy moments, it should be promoted as a worthy form of artistic expression and cultural projection and an enabling source of black juvenile and communal solidarity.

What other forms of music can you think of that express protest?

displayed on grocery store shelves, on antique cookie jars, and in advertising campaigns. Until 1968, Aunt Jemima retained the traditional mammy image; that year, "her complexion was lightened, her head rag was replaced with a head band, she was reduced in size, and her grin was replaced with a smile" (Jewell, 1993:183). In the late 1980s, the head band was removed, and she was given a contemporary hairstyle. Even with these changes in Aunt Jemima's appearance, Brent

Staples (1994:A14) argues that "racially charged imagery never fully loses its historical taint."

Antique mammy cookie jars exemplify the ambiguity between popular culture and high culture designations. Items of popular culture may come to be designated as high culture, and vice versa. Today, some mammy cookie jars are costly collector's items displayed in elite art galleries and museums. According to sociologists Chandra Mukerji and Michael Schudson (1991:35):

> ... a radical distinction between high culture and popular culture cannot be maintained. Aspects of popular culture become high culture over time (Charles Dickens, folk art, early manufactured furniture, jazz). Aspects of high culture become popular (Pachelbel's "Canon in D," Handel's *Messiah*). Common people have sophisticated and refined craft knowledge and artistic capabilities; elites have their own folk beliefs ...

While culture may contribute to permanence and stability, changes in material and nonmaterial culture also tend to bring about dramatic changes in society.

CULTURAL CHANGE AND DIVERSITY

We have examined the nature of culture within society, the defining components of culture, and the forcefulness of popular culture. Cultures do not generally remain static, however. There are many forces working toward change and diversity. Some societies and individuals adapt to this change, while others suffer culture shock and succumb to ethnocentrism.

CULTURAL CHANGE

Societies continually experience cultural change, at both material and nonmaterial levels. Moreover, a change in one area frequently triggers a change in other areas. For example, the personal computer has changed how we work and how we think about work; today, many people work at home—away from the immediate gaze of a supervisor. Ultimately, computer technology may change the nature of boss–worker relations. Such changes are often set in motion by discovery, invention, and diffusion.

Discovery **is the process of learning about something previously unknown or unrecognized.** Historically, discovery involved unearthing natural elements or existing realities, such as "discovering" fire or the true shape of the earth. Today, discovery most often results from scientific research. For example, discovery of a polio vaccine virtually eliminated one of the major childhood diseases. A future discovery of a cure for cancer or the common cold could result in longer and more productive lives for many people.

As more discoveries have occurred, people have been able to reconfigure existing material and nonmaterial cultural items through invention. ***Invention*** **is the process of reshaping existing cultural items into a new form.** Guns, video games, airplanes, and the Charter of Rights and Freedoms are examples of inventions that positively or negatively affect our lives today.

When diverse groups of people come into contact, they begin to adapt one another's discoveries, inventions, and ideas for their own use. ***Diffusion*** **is the transmission of cultural items or social practices from one group or society to another** through such means as exploration, military endeavours, the media, tourism, and immigration. To illustrate, piñatas, the decorated bowls or jars that are filled with candy and form part of the festivities at birthdays and other celebrations in Latin-American countries, can be traced back to the twelfth century when Marco Polo brought them back from China where they were used to celebrate the springtime harvest. In Italy, they were filled with costly gifts in a game played by the nobility. When the piñata travelled to Spain, it became part of Lenten traditions. In Mexico, it was used to celebrate the birth of the Aztec god Huitzilopochtli (Burciaga, 1993).

Today, children in many countries squeal with excitement at parties as they swing a stick at a piñata. In today's "shrinking globe," cultural diffusion moves at a very rapid pace as countries continually seek new markets for their products.

When a change occurs in the material culture of a society, nonmaterial culture must adapt to that change. Frequently, this rate of change is uneven, resulting in a gap between the two. Sociologist William F. Ogburn (1966/1922) referred to this disparity as ***cultural lag*****—a gap between the technical development of a society and its moral and legal institutions** (G. Marshall, 1994). The failure of nonmaterial culture to keep pace with material culture is linked to social conflict and problems in society. In Canada, medical treatment is a right of Canadian citizenship. In contrast, although the United States has some of the most advanced medical technology in the world, there is a lack of consensus regarding to whom it should be available. The debate centres on whether medical care is a privilege for which people must pay or a right of U.S. citizenship (or noncitizen residency). The number of Americans *not* covered by medical insurance (about 35 million) exceeds the entire population of Canada.

Christmas trees and other holiday symbols exemplify the way in which elements from diverse cultures take on new meanings through the process of diffusion. For instance, notice the European-looking Joseph and Mary, as well as the Greek columns, in this depiction of a manger in Bethlehem. Even the traditional date chosen to celebrate the birth of Jesus (to Christians, the "light of the world") is an adaptation of an ancient pagan celebration of the winter solstice (when the light of the returning sun conquers the darkness of winter).

CULTURAL DIVERSITY

Cultural diversity refers to the wide range of cultural differences found between and within nations. Cultural diversity between countries may be the result of natural circumstances (such as climate and geography) or social circumstances (such as level of technology and composition of the population). Some countries—such as Sweden—are referred to as *homogeneous societies*, meaning they include people who share a common culture and are typically from similar social, religious, political, and economic backgrounds. By contrast, other countries—including Canada—are referred to as *heterogeneous societies*, meaning they include people who are dissimilar in regard to social characteristics such as nationality, race, ethnicity, class, occupation, or education (see Figure 3.2).

Immigration contributes to cultural diversity in a society. Throughout its history, Canada has been a nation of immigrants. Over the past 150 years, more than 13 million "documented" (legal) immigrants have arrived here; innumerable people also have entered the country as undocumented immigrants. Immigration can cause feelings of frustration and hostility, especially in people who feel threatened by the changes that large numbers of immigrants may produce (Fleras and Elliott, 1996). Often, people are intolerant of those who are different from themselves. When societal tensions rise, people may look for others on whom

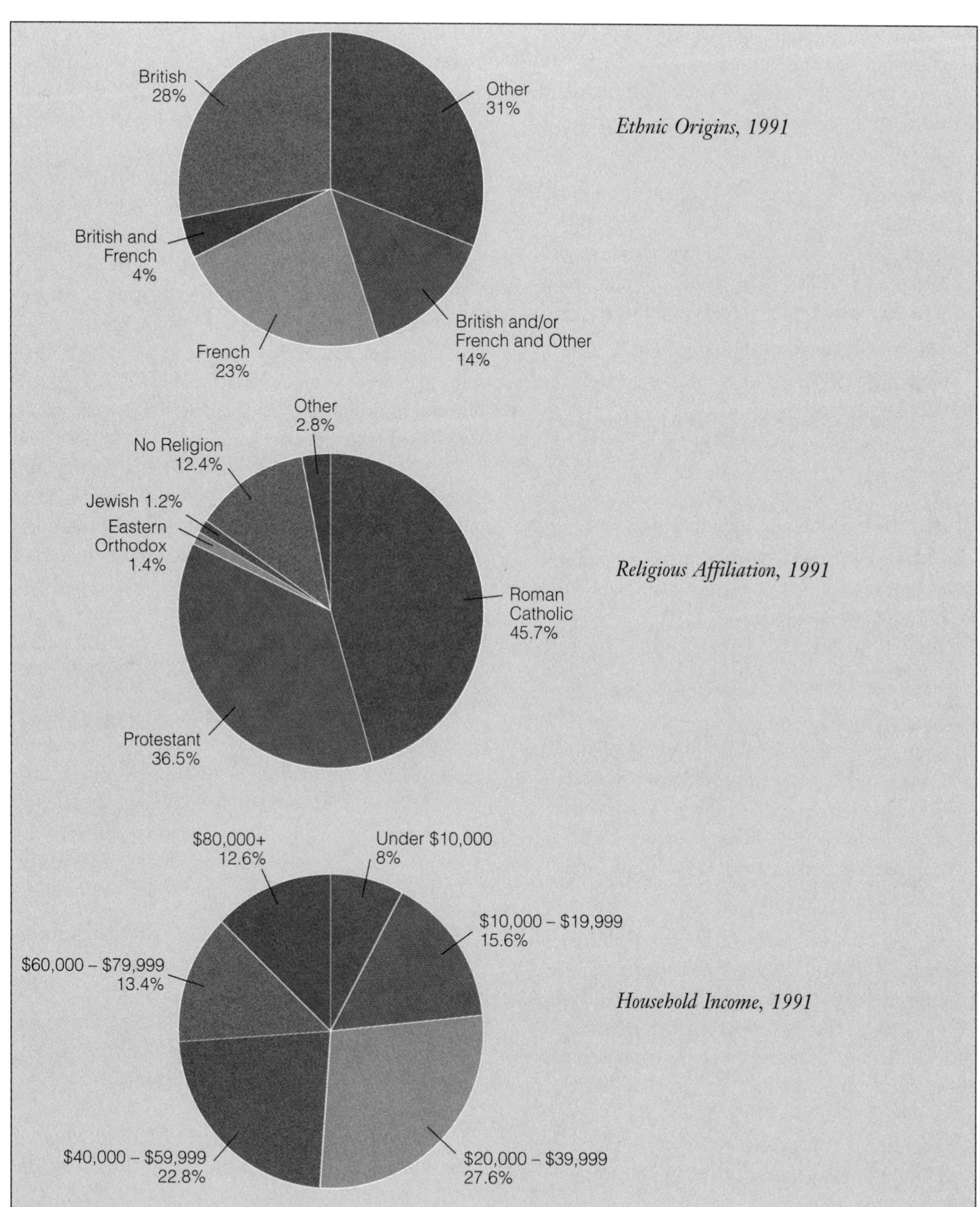

FIGURE 3.2

Heterogeneity of Canadian Society

Throughout history, Canada has been heterogeneous. Today, Canada is represented by a wide variety of social categories, including our religious affiliations, income levels, and ethnic origins.

Source: Statistics Canada, *Canada at a Glance*, 1995.

they can place blame—or single out persons because they are the "other," the "outsider," the one who does not "belong." Sociologist Adrienne Shadd described her experience of being singled out as an "other":

> Routinely I am asked, "Where are you from?" or "What nationality are you?" as if to be Black, you have to come from somewhere else. I respond that I'm "Canadian." ... I play along. The scenario usually unfolds as follows:
>
> "But where are you **originally** from?"
>
> "Canada."
>
> "Oh, *you* were born here. But where are your parents from?"
>
> "Canada"
>
> "But what about your grandparents?"
>
> As individuals delve further into my genealogy to find out where I'm "really" from, their frustration levels rise.
>
> "No, uh, I mean ... your *people*. Where do your *people* come from?"
>
> At this point, questioners are totally annoyed and/or frustrated. After all, Black people in Canada are supposed to come from "the islands," aren't they? For those of us living in large urban centres, there are constant reminders that we are not regarded as truly "Canadian." (1994:11)

Have you ever been made to feel like an "outsider"? Each of us receives cultural messages that may make us feel good or bad about ourselves or may give us the perception that we "belong" or "do not belong." However, in heterogeneous societies such as Canada, cultural diversity is inevitable. In Canada, this diversity has created some unique problems in terms of defining and maintaining our distinct Canadian culture.

CANADIAN CULTURE

Is there such a thing as a distinct Canadian culture? If so, what are the components of this culture? Harry Hiller (1991, 1995) suggests there are a number of structural features of Canadian society that preclude the development of a readily identifiable Canadian culture and that, instead, contribute to this country's "cultural ambiguity." First, **regionalism** is a significant divisive factor in Canada. The country's territory is so large and its population so dispersed that different regions (e.g., Western versus Eastern Canada) each have their own society with distinct historical origins and cultural attributes.

Second, Canada is described as a "nation of immigrants." Canada became one of the first officially multicultural nations with the passage in 1988 of the Multiculturalism Act (Elliot and Fleras, 1990). The policy, as set out in the Act, encourages Canadians to celebrate their differences and be proud that all members of this society contribute to Canada's cultural diversity. Although this policy was not legislated until 1988, the concept of our Canadian multicultural identity was first introduced on October 8, 1971, when then prime minister Pierre Trudeau said:

> There cannot be one cultural policy for Canadians of British or French origins, another for the originals, and yet a third for all others. For although there are two official languages, there is no official culture. Nor does any cultural group take precedence over another ... We are free to be ourselves. (quoted in Li, 1990:64)

This policy of multiculturalism advocates tolerance of and encouragement for all cultural groups as vital to Canadian society. However, it has been suggested that this policy detracts from the building of a strong national Canadian culture (Bibby, 1990). Are Canadianism and multiculturalism mutually exclusive?

The third factor identified by Hiller (1991) as working against a Canadian identity is what he refers to as the "duality of Canadian society." The history of conflict between French- and English-speaking Canadians, as reflected in Bill 101 (which made French Quebec's official language), the Quebec separatist movement and the results of the referendum on sovereignty, demonstrate that there are unresolved issues concerning whether Canada is composed of two cultures rather than one.

The final barrier to establishing a Canadian identity is Canada's proximity to the United States. Some have asked how Canada can maintain a unique culture despite its proximity to the world's most powerful economic and military nation (Fleras and Elliott, 1996). Most of Canada's population lives adjacent to the American border, making the influence of American culture on its northern neighbour inevitable.

It has been suggested that complex societies are more likely to produce subcultures. This is certainly the case in Canada where regional, ethnic, class, language, and religious subcultures combine to produce a highly diverse society.

SUBCULTURES A ***subculture*** **is a group of people who share a distinctive set of cultural beliefs and behaviours that differ in some significant way from that of the larger society.** Although members of subcultures participate in the mainstream society, they tend to associate with one another more frequently and more personally than with members of other groups. Occupational groups, such as lawyers; ethnic populations such as Italian Canadians; religious groups such as Orthodox Jews; people living in small rural communities: all of these are examples of subcultures. All of these groups will develop unique beliefs, norms, and values. We next look at one subculture—the Hutterites—to see how this group interacts with the dominant Canadian culture.

The Hutterites This subculture has fought for many years to maintain its distinct identity. They are the largest family-type communal grouping in the Western world, with over 20,000 members living in approximately 200 settlements (Curtis and Lambert, 1994). The Hutterites live on farms in western Canada and the United States where they practise their religious beliefs and maintain a relatively closed social network.

The Hutterites are considered a subculture because their values, norms, and appearance differ significantly from those of members of the dominant culture. They have a strong faith in God and reject worldly concerns. Their core values include the joy of work, the primacy of the home, faithfulness, thriftiness, tradition, and humility. Hutterites hold conservative views of the family, believing that women are subordinate to men, birth control is unacceptable, and wives should remain at home. Children are cherished and seen as an economic asset: they help with the farming and other work. Also central to their value system is the belief that communal living is necessary for people to be trained in proper obedience to God. Members of this group have communal rather than private property; nobody is permitted to individually own as much as a pair of shoes (Curtis and Lambert, 1994). The Hutterites also have a distinctive mode of dress which makes this subculture readily identifiable in Canadian society.

The Hutterites are aware that their values are distinct from those of most other Canadians and that they look different from other people; these differences, though, provide them with a collective identity and make them feel close to one another (Peter, 1987). However, the Hutterites do not attempt to achieve complete social isolation from the wider society. They are successful farmers who trade with people in the surrounding communities, and they buy modern farm machinery from outsiders. They also read newspapers, use telephones and utilize the services of non-Hutterite professionals (Curtis and Lambert, 1994).

COUNTERCULTURES Some subcultures actively oppose the larger society. A ***counterculture*** **is a group that strongly rejects dominant societal values and norms and seeks alternative lifestyles** (Yinger, 1960, 1982). Young people are most likely to join countercultural groups, perhaps because younger persons generally have less invested in the existing culture. Examples of countercultures include the beatniks of the 1950s, the flower children of the 1960s, the drug enthusiasts

At an early age, Hutterite children learn the distinctive values and norms of their subculture. Parents hope that their children will continue to honour Hutterite teachings as they reach their teenage years.

of the 1970s, and members of nonmainstream religious sects, or cults. Some countercultures (such as the Ku Klux Klan, skinheads, and the Nation of Islam) even engage in revolutionary political activities.

One of the countercultures closely associated with hate crimes is the skinheads, sometimes referred to as "neo-Nazi skinheads," who have been present in North America since the early 1980s. Skinheads primarily are young, white, working-class males who express group identity by wearing boots, jeans, suspenders, green flight jackets, and chains, and by shaving their heads or sporting "burr" haircuts. Core values of "hard-core" skinheads include racial group superiority, patriotism, a belief in the traditional roles of women and men, and justification of physical violence as a means of expressing anger toward immigrants, gay men and lesbians, people of colour, and Jews (Wooden, 1995). Some skinhead groups tend to engage in relatively spontaneous outbursts of violence; others are highly organized and motivated. These groups select leaders, hold regular meetings, distribute racist propaganda, and attend rallies sponsored by groups like the Ku Klux Klan and the White Aryan Resistance (Barrett, 1987).

The skinhead counterculture in Canada consists of three main groups: the Ku Klux Klan, the Western Guard, and a third group that includes a number of smaller organizations, such as the Canadian National Socialist Party (Barrett, 1987). All of these groups share the belief that the Aryan, or white, race is superior to others morally, intellectually, and culturally and that it is their destiny to dominate society.

Canadian neo-Nazi countercultural groups also believe that the survival of white society in this country is in jeopardy because of the practice of allowing "non-Aryans" into Canada. Skinheads, consequently, have been involved in a number of violent assaults and murders. For example, in 1993 three Tamil refugees were beaten in Toronto. One died as a result of the injuries inflicted and one was paralyzed (Henry et al., 1995).

Hard-core skinheads are a countercultural group because they focus on "white power" and other racist views that contradict the norms and

Members of white extremist countercultures such as these neo-Nazi skinheads in Germany speak an international language of intolerance of those who are different from themselves.

values of mainstream Canadian culture. However, not all skinheads share racist views; some identify themselves as SHARPS (Skinheads Against Racial Prejudice) or SARS (Skinheads Against Racism) (Wooden, 1995). Members of these groups have been attacked by hard-core skinheads because they refused to participate in violence against members of "out" groups.

CULTURE SHOCK

***Culture shock* is the disorientation that people feel when they encounter cultures radically different from their own** and believe they cannot depend on their own taken-for-granted assumptions about life. When people travel to another society, they may not know how to respond to that setting. For example, Napoleon Chagnon (1992) described his initial shock at seeing the Yanomamö (pronounced yah-noh-MAH-mah) tribe of South America for the first time in 1964.

The Yanomamö (also referred as the "Yanomami") are a tribe of about 20,000 South American Indians who live in the rain forest. Although Chagnon travelled in a small aluminum motorboat for three days to reach these people, he was not prepared for the sight that met his eyes when he arrived:

> I looked up and gasped to see a dozen burly, naked, sweaty, hideous men staring at us down the shafts of their drawn arrows. Immense wads of green tobacco were stuck between their lower teeth and lips, making them look even more hideous, and strands of dark-green slime dripped from their nostrils—strands so long that they reached down to their pectoral muscles or drizzled down their chins and stuck to their chests and bellies. We arrived as the men were blowing *ebene*, a hallucinogenic drug, up their noses. As I soon learned, one side effect of the drug is a runny nose. The mucus becomes saturated with the drug's green powder, and the Yanomamö usually just let it dangle freely from their nostrils to plop off when the strands become too heavy.
>
> Then the stench of decaying vegetation and filth hit me, and I was almost sick to my

The distinctiveness of the Yanomamö is evident in this picture of tribe members making bread for guests. Do you think you would experience culture shock upon encountering these people for the first time?

> stomach. I was horrified. What kind of welcome was this for someone who had come to live with these people and learn their way of life—to become friends with them? But when they recognized Barker [a guide], they put their weapons down and returned to their chanting, while keeping a nervous eye on the village entrances. (Chagnon, 1992:12–14)

The Yanomamö have no written language, system of numbers, or calendar. They lead a nomadic lifestyle, carrying everything they own on their backs. They wear no clothes and paint their bodies; the women insert slender sticks through holes in the lower lip and through the pierced nasal septum. Chagnon referred to the Yanomamo as a "fierce people" because they engaged in persistent aggression (such as club fighting, gang rape, and murder) within their own group and in continual warfare with outsiders (Chagnon, 1988).

When Chagnon returned to the Yanomamö in 1992, he found that they were threatened by diseases (such as malaria, venereal disease, and tuberculosis) and by environmental degradation. Seventy percent of the tribe's land in Brazil had been taken away from them, and their supplies of fish were poisoned by mercury contamination of rivers. Although the governments of Brazil and Venezuela enacted policies to save them from extinction by setting aside huge areas as a homeland for them (see Chagnon, 1992:248–255), in August 1993, about seventy of the Yanomamö were attacked and brutally killed by Brazilian gold miners in a massacre that produced a widespread outcry (Brooke, 1993a:Y3).

ETHNOCENTRISM

Many of us tend to make judgments about other cultures in terms of our own culture. ***Ethnocentrism* is the assumption that one's own culture and way of life are superior to all others** (Sumner, 1959/1906). From a functionalist viewpoint, ethnocentrism can serve a positive function in societies by promoting group solidarity and loyalty and by encouraging people to conform to societal norms and values. For example, nationalism and patriotism encourage people to think of their own nation as "the best." International sports competitions such as the Olympic Games, help to foster this idea.

On the other hand, ethnocentrism can be problematic for societies. Historically, people have regarded outsiders as "barbarians" or "primitive" because they were different. Until recently, for example, few people in the more developed nations have been interested in what indigenous peoples such as the Yanomamö might know; after all, what could nations with high levels of technology possibly learn from tribal cultures? Yet people in such cultures have devised ways to survive and flourish that constitute an important source of knowledge. Some have created methods of farming without irrigation; others hunt, fish, and gather food in the rain forest without destroying the delicate balance that maintains the ecosystem. Ethnocentrism is counterproductive when it blinds us to what other groups have to offer or when it leads to conflict, hostility, and war.

Ethnocentrism can be a problem within societies as well as between them when it leads to social isolation, prejudice, discrimination, and oppression of one group by another. People who have recently arrived in a country where their customs, dress, eating habits, or religious beliefs differ markedly from those of existing residents often find themselves the object of ridicule. Indigenous groups, such as Native Americans, also have been the target of ethnocentrism by other groups.

Recently, some sociologists have begun to study xenocentrism, or "reverse ethnocentrism." ***Xenocentrism* is the belief that the products, styles, or ideas of another society are better than those of one's own culture.** Examples include the desire for German-made cars by Canadian citizens, some of whom assert that North American manufacturers cannot make a decent car any more, and the embracing of American popular culture (television programs, movies, and books) as superior to Canadian popular culture.

CULTURAL RELATIVISM

An alternative to ethnocentrism and xenocentrism is ***cultural relativism*—the belief that the behaviours and customs of a society must be viewed and analyzed within the context of its own culture.** Cultural relativism is a part of the sociological imagination; researchers must be aware of the customs and norms of the society they are studying and then spell out their background assumptions so that others can spot possible biases in their studies.

Anthropologist Marvin Harris (1974, 1985) uses cultural relativism to explain why cattle, which are viewed as sacred, are not killed and eaten in India, where widespread hunger and malnutrition exist. From an ethnocentric viewpoint, we might conclude that cow worship is the cause of the hunger and poverty in India. However, Harris demonstrates that the Hindu taboo against killing cattle is very important to their economic system. Live cows are more valuable than dead ones because they have more important uses than as a direct source of food. As part of the ecological system, cows consume grasses of little value to humans. Then they produce two valuable resources—oxen (the neutered offspring of cows), to power the ploughs, and manure (for fuel and fertilizer)—as well as milk, floor covering, and leather. As Harris's study reveals, culture must be viewed from the standpoint of those who live in a particular society.

SOCIOLOGICAL ANALYSIS OF CULTURE

Sociologists regard culture as a central ingredient in human behaviour. Although all sociologists share a similar purpose, they typically see culture through somewhat different lenses as they are guided by different theoretical perspectives in their research. What do these perspectives tell us about culture?

A FUNCTIONALIST PERSPECTIVE

As previously discussed, functionalist perspectives are based on the assumption that society is a stable, orderly system with interrelated parts that serve specific functions. Anthropologist Bronislaw Malinowski (1922) suggested that culture helps people meet their *biological needs* (including food and procreation), *instrumental needs* (including law and education), and *integrative needs* (including religion and art). Societies in which people share a common language and core values are more likely to have consensus and harmony. However, all societies have dysfunctions that produce a variety of societal problems. Inequalities along class, racial, and gender lines often contribute to many of these problems. When a society contains numerous subcultures, discord results from a lack of consensus about core values and a failure to educate everyone about the positive value of cultural diversity. Resolution of such problems must come from families, schools, and other organizations charged with teaching the young and maintaining order and peace.

A strength of the functionalist perspective on culture is its focus on the needs of society and the fact that stability is essential for society's continued survival. A shortcoming is its overemphasis on harmony and cooperation and a lack of acknowledgment of societal factors that contribute to conflict and strife.

Many people in our society face the challenge of preserving a subcultural heritage while sharing in many of the values and norms of the dominant culture. The powwow is a means through which Native peoples can celebrate their unique culture and pass on cultural traditions to future generations.

A CONFLICT PERSPECTIVE

Conflict perspectives are based on the assumption that social life is a continuous struggle in which members of powerful groups seek to control scarce resources. Values and norms help create and sustain the privileged position of the powerful in society while excluding others. As early conflict theorist Karl Marx stressed, ideas are cultural creations of a society's most powerful members. According to conflict theorists, most people are not aware that they are being dominated because they have ***false consciousness*, which means that they hold beliefs they think**

promote their best interests when those beliefs actually are damaging to their interests. For example, when hate groups "blame" people located at the margins of society for society's problems, they shift attention away from persons in positions of political and economic power. Extremist groups may perpetuate the very "problem" they think exists. Thus, hate crimes may maintain the status quo by protecting the people who are responsible for making important decisions at the highest levels of society (Levin and McDevitt, 1993:234).

A strength of the conflict perspective is that it stresses how cultural values and norms may perpetuate social inequalities. It also highlights the inevitability of change and the constant tension between those who want to maintain the status quo and those who desire change. A limitation is its focus on societal discord and the divisiveness of culture.

AN INTERACTIONIST PERSPECTIVE

Unlike functionalists and conflict theorists, interactionists do not examine the functions of culture or the ways in which culture helps maintain the status of privileged groups while excluding others from society's benefits. Interactionists instead focus on a microlevel analysis that views society as the sum of all people's interactions. From this perspective, people create, maintain, and modify culture as they go about their everyday activities. Symbols make communication with others possible because they provide us with shared meanings.

According to interactionist theory, people continually negotiate their social realities. Values and norms are not independent realities that automatically determine our behaviour. Instead, we reinterpret them in each social situation we encounter. Hard-core skinheads defy dominant group norms and accept alternative norms of violence as an appropriate response to groups they consider "inferior." This interpretation of reality is reinforced by continual interaction with other hard-core skinhead groups (Farley, 1993a). Canada and the United States are not the only countries to experience these problems; as Box 3.4 points out, Western Europe is experiencing an upswing in hate crimes against "foreigners" by neo-Nazi skinheads and others.

An interactionist approach highlights how people maintain and change culture through their interactions with others. However, interactionism does not provide a systematic framework for analyzing how we shape culture and how it, in turn, shapes us. It also does not provide insight into how shared meanings are developed among people, and it does not take into account the many situations in which there is disagreement on meanings. Where the functional and conflict approaches tend to overemphasize the macrolevel workings of society, the interactionist viewpoint often fails to take into account these larger social structures.

In viewing culture from any of these perspectives, the impact of ethnicity, class, gender, religion, and age must be taken into account in examining people's experiences. In Canada, people have a wide array of experiences because they come from diverse backgrounds. However, simply by living in this country, most of us share some aspects of the dominant culture. This shared culture may be as basic as our use of Canadian currency or postage stamps. It may involve a core curriculum of subjects all children are required to take in elementary school. Shared culture for many individuals is framed at the subcultural level, where, for example, members of a particular church, private club, or other organization may have similar lifestyles and hold values in common with other members of the group.

CULTURAL PATTERNS FOR THE TWENTY-FIRST CENTURY

As we have discussed in this chapter, many changes are occurring in our Canadian culture.

BOX 3.4 SOCIOLOGY IN GLOBAL PERSPECTIVE

Hostility Toward Immigrants

Hate crimes have increased in the nations of Western Europe as well as in North America in recent years. Hundreds of thousands of people fleeing economic depression or political oppression in African and Southeast Asian countries have migrated to Western Europe, where attitudes toward immigrants have changed dramatically as their numbers have grown. In many countries, immigrants were previously seen as a source of cheap labour for jobs like ditch digging or street cleaning. Today, however, in many countries (including Canada) some people see immigrant workers as competing for scarce jobs in tough economic times and as draining the welfare, education, and health-care systems. Many immigrants do not have anywhere to go, as indicated by a Liberian man who stowed away on a freighter from Nigeria to get to Western Europe: "I don't know what to do. I can't go back [to Liberia, where civil wars have continued for a number of years]. I walk the street and I'm a dead man" (Darnton, 1993:A1).

In recent years, several political candidates in Western European nations have promised, if they are elected, to expel these "foreigners." A rising tide of racism and hate crimes waged by neo-Nazi skinheads against persons believed to be recent immigrants has bolstered their political claims that something must be done very soon. Hate speech often is based on nostalgia for a bygone era alleged to have been "comfortable, orderly, and virtually all white" (Darnton, 1993:A6). In actuality, changes in the ethnic makeup of Western Europe as nations occurred years ago; Turks, for instance have lived for generations in Germany, as have Pakistanis in Britain.

With dramatic increases in immigration, hate speech and crimes have skyrocketed. In Britain, the increase in tension has been particularly sharp in inner-city neighbourhoods, where most nonwhite immigrants have settled and where unemployment and recession have taken their greatest toll. The grandson of Winston Churchill publicly complained about the "relentless flow of immigrants" and noted that in the future, England would by characterized by "the muezzin ... calling Allah's faithful to the high street mosque for Friday prayers" (Schmidt, 1993:A2).

Other Western European countries, including Spain, Italy, and France, also have seen an increase in hate speech and crimes. For example, in Aravaca, a suburb of Madrid, *rapadas* (urban gang members) have shot undocumented Dominican immigrants living in abandoned buildings. Likewise, in Rome, "Nazi-skins" seek out Africans who sleep in the parks at night and beat them up, as well as burning down the residences of foreigners (Darnton, 1993:A6).

Western Europe faces a difficult, if not impossible, task if it tries to close the door to immigrants. A recent United Nations Population Fund report, for example, estimated that at least 100 million international migrants live outside the countries where they were born. The tide of people crossing borders to flee war, drought, and economic misery "could become the human crisis of our age," according to the report (quoted in Darnton, 1993:A6). Globally, then, it is very likely that immigration pressures will continue and that hate crimes will increase.

Increasing cultural diversity can either cause long-simmering racial and ethnic antagonisms to come closer to a boiling point or result in the creation of a truly multicultural society in which diversity is respected and encouraged. According to our ideal culture, Canada will "prosper in diversity." The Multicultural Act has legislated "cultural freedom." However, it has been suggested that this freedom is more "symbolic" than real (Roberts and Clifton, 1990). In the real culture, anti-immigration sentiment has risen in response to the estimated one-and-a-half million newcomers who have arrived in Canada over the past decade. Cultural diversity and global immigration are affecting economic and employment perceptions. Many people accuse newcomers of stealing jobs

Multiculturalism has been described as a policy that is more symbolic than real. In recent years, Canada has experienced increasing conflict and intergroup hostility as reflected in Native peoples' struggles to gain recognition as a unique society within Canadian culture and increasing anti-immigrant sentiments among Canadians.

and overutilizing the social service safety net at the Canadian taxpayers' expense. An opinion survey of 1800 Canadians, conducted by the federal immigration department, showed a "growing acceptance" of attitudes and practices that show a dislike of "foreigners." One-third of the respondents agreed that it was important to "keep out people who are different from most Canadians," while more than half were "really worried that they may become a minority if immigration is unchecked." Almost half said there were too many immigrants, even though they had underestimated the actual amount of immigration to Canada (Henry et al., 1995:88). These attitudes, quite clearly, are racist. Furthermore, they are not attitudes expressed by a fringe minority of right-wing hate mongers, but by a *representative* sample of Canadian citizens. Sociologist Adrienne Shadd comments:

> It always amazes me when people express surprise that there might be a "race problem" in Canada, or when they attribute the "problem" to a minority of prejudiced individuals. Racism is, and always has been, one of the bedrock institutions of Canadian society, embedded in the very fabric of our thinking, our personality. (Shadd, 1991:1)

If racism is part of our culture, one of our greatest challenges is to reduce the extent of intergroup hostility, tension, and conflict in order to create a *real,* rather than an *ideal,* multicultural society.

As we head into the twenty-first century, the issue of cultural diversity will increase in importance, especially in schools. Multicultural education that focuses on the contributions of a wide variety of people from different backgrounds will continue to be an issue from kindergarten through university. Public schools have incorporated a number of heritage languages into their curriculum. These schools will face the challenge of embracing widespread cultural diversity while conveying a sense of community and national identity to students.

CULTURE AND TECHNOLOGY

In the twenty-first century, technology will continue to profoundly affect culture. Television and radio, films and videos, and electronic communications (including the telephone, electronic mail, and fax) will continue to accelerate the flow of information and expand cultural diffu-

Is this Japanese amusement park a sign of a homogeneous global culture, or of cultural imperialism?

sion throughout the world. Global communication devices will move images of people's lives, behaviour, and fashions instantaneously among almost all nations (Petersen, 1994). Increasingly, television may become people's window on the world and, in the process, promote greater integration or fragmentation among nations. Integration occurs when there is a widespread acceptance of ideas and items—such as democracy, rock music, blue jeans, and McDonald's hamburgers—among cultures. By contrast, fragmentation occurs when people in one culture disdain the beliefs and actions of other cultures, such as the rejection by fundamentalist Muslims of Western cultural values, especially as shown in North American–based television shows, music, films, and videos. As a force for both cultural integration and fragmentation, technology will continue to revolutionize communications, but most of the world's population will not participate in this revolution (Petersen, 1994).

A GLOBAL CULTURE?

Some scholars have suggested that a single *global culture*—a worldwide interconnection of material and nonmaterial culture without regard for national identities or boundaries—may emerge in the twenty-first century (see Featherstone, 1990). Others note that global subcultures, such as those of science, business, and diplomacy, already exist and that people are "more at home in these placeless subcultures than in any traditional culture or nation or tribe" (Anderson, 1990:23). If this assumption is correct, these subcultures would create linkages around the world with "communities of shared interest, ideology, and information" (Anderson, 1990:23). However, some analysts do not believe that such widespread acceptance of a single culture will occur.

Critics argue that the world is not developing a homogeneous global culture, rather, other cultures are becoming Westernized. Political and religious leaders in some nations oppose this process, which they view as ***cultural imperialism*** **the extensive infusion of one nation's culture into other nations.** Some view the widespread infusion of the English language into countries that speak other languages as a form of cultural imperialism. A number of countries or states within them have sought to prevent English from overtaking their native language. For example, several of India's largest states have ordered that all official government work and correspondence must be conducted in Hindi (the dominant language of northern India) (McCarroll, 1993: 53). In Canada, conflict over the use of English in French-speaking Quebec is ongoing.

Perhaps the concept of cultural imperialism fails to take into account various cross-cultural influences. For example, Japanese management styles and cars are widely known in North America, and cultural diffusion of literature, music, clothing, and food has occurred on a global scale. A global culture, if it comes into existence, most likely will include components from many societies and cultures. It has been suggested that the "global culture is going to be one with a thin, fragile, and ever-shifting web of common ideas and values, and within that, incredible diversity—more diversity than there has ever been" (Anderson, 1990:25).

However, predictions of a global culture may be premature. Currently, a resurgence of *nationalism*, an ethnocentric belief that the political and economic rights of one's own nation morally supersede those of other nations, has occurred throughout the nations of Eastern Europe and the former Soviet Union. As these nations have experienced rapid change and economic decline, many people have identified more strongly with their original nationalities (as Russians, Armenians, Azerbaijanis, Georgians, or another of the hundreds of nationalities and ethnic groups in that part of the world) than as citizens of a single nation.

From a sociological perspective, the study of culture helps us not only understand our own "tool kit" of symbols, stories, rituals, and world views but expand our insights to include those of other people of the world who also seek strategies for enhancing their lives. If we understand how culture is used by people, how cultural elements constrain or facilitate certain patterns of action, what aspects of our cultural heritage have enduring effects on our action, and what specific historical changes undermine the validity of some cultural patterns and give rise to others, we can apply our sociological imagination not only to our own society but to the entire world (see Swidler, 1986).

CHAPTER REVIEW

Culture encompasses the knowledge, language, values, and customs passed from one generation to the next in a human group or society. Culture is essential for our individual survival because, unlike nonhuman animals, we are not born with instinctive information about how to behave and how to care for ourselves and others.

Culture can be a stabilizing force for society; it can provide a sense of continuity. However, culture also can be a force that generates discord, conflict, and violence.

- There are both material and nonmaterial expressions of culture. Material culture consists of the physical creations of society. Nonmaterial culture is more abstract and reflects the ideas, values, and beliefs of a society.

- Cultural universals are customs and practices that exist in all societies and include activities and institutions such as storytelling, families, and laws. Specific forms of these universals vary from one cultural group to another, however.
- Four key nonmaterial components are common to all cultures: symbols, language, values, and norms. Symbols express shared meanings; through them, groups communicate cultural ideas and abstract concepts. Language is a set of symbols through which groups communicate. Values are a culture's collective ideas about what is or is not acceptable. Norms are the specific behavioural expectations within a culture. Folkways are norms that express the everyday customs of a group, while mores are norms with strong moral and ethical connotations and are essential to the stability of a culture. Laws are formal, standardized norms that are enforced by formal sanctions.
- High culture consists of classical music, opera, ballet, and other activities usually patronized by the elite audiences. Popular culture consists of the activities, products, and services of a culture that appeal primarily to members of the middle and working classes.
- Culture change takes place in all societies. Change occurs through discovery and invention and through diffusion, which is the transmission of culture from one society or group to another.
- Cultural diversity exists within societies and across societies. Diversity is reflected through race, ethnicity, age, sexual orientation, religion, occupation, and so forth. A diverse culture also includes subcultures and countercultures. A subculture has distinctive ideas and behaviours that differ from the larger society to which it belongs. A counterculture rejects the dominant societal values and norms.
- Culture shock refers to the anxiety people experience when they encounter cultures radically different from their own. Ethnocentrism is the assumption that one's own culture is superior to others. Cultural relativism counters culture shock and ethnocentrism by viewing and analyzing another culture in terms of its own values and standards.
- Sociologists may examine culture through different theoretical lenses. A functional analysis of culture assumes that a common language and shared values help to produce consensus and harmony. According to some conflict theorists, culture may be used by certain groups to maintain their privilege and exclude others from society's benefits. Symbolic interactionists suggest that people create, maintain, and modify culture as they go about their everyday activities.
- While increasing cultural diversity in Canada has expanded the thinking of some individuals, it also has increased racial–ethnic antagonisms. As we look toward even more diverse and global cultural patterns in the twenty-first century, it is important to keep our sociological imaginations actively engaged.

KEY TERMS

counterculture **107**
cultural imperialism **117**
cultural lag **104**
cultural relativism **111**
cultural universals **88**
culture **82**
culture shock **109**
diffusion **103**
discovery **103**
ethnocentrism **111**
false consciousness **112**
folkways **97**
ideal culture **96**
invention **103**
language **90**
laws **98**
material culture **85**
mores **97**
nonmaterial culture **86**
norms **97**
popular culture **98**
real culture **96**
sanctions **97**
Sapir-Whorf hypothesis **90**
subculture **107**
taboos **98**
technology **85**
values **95**
value contradictions **96**
xenocentrism **111**

QUESTIONS FOR ANALYSIS AND UNDERSTANDING

1. Why is culture important to individuals? to groups?
2. What are some of the folkways and mores of your culture?
3. How do subcultures and countercultures differ from one another?
4. In the twenty-first century, will there be many separate cultures in Canada, or will there be one large and diverse culture?

QUESTIONS FOR CRITICAL THINKING

1. Would it be possible today to live in a totally separate culture in Canada? Could you avoid all influences from the mainstream popular culture or from the values and norms of other cultures? How would you be able to avoid any change in your culture?
2. Do fads and fashions in popular culture reflect and reinforce, or challenge and change the values and norms of a society? Consider a wide variety of fads and fashions: musical styles; computer and video games and other technologies; literature; and political, social, and religious ideas.
3. In Chapter 2, we examined sociological research and various studies on suicide. Suppose you wanted to find out why rates of suicide were higher in some cultures than others. What might you examine in each culture? Symbols, language, values, or norms? popular culture? fads? The amount of diversity in a culture? What would be the best way to conduct your research?

4. You are doing a survey analysis of neo-Nazi skinheads to determine the effects of popular culture on their views and behaviour. What are some of the questions you would use in your survey?

SUGGESTED READINGS

An interesting functionalist analysis of culture is provided by this anthropologist:

Marvin Harris. *Cannibals and Kings: The Origins of Cultures*. New York: Random House, 1977.

Marvin Harris. *Good to Eat: Riddles of Food and Culture*. New York: Simon & Schuster, 1986.

These authors analyze aspects of culture from diverse perspectives:

Reginald W. Bibby. *Mosaic Madness: The Poverty and Potential of Life in Canada*. Toronto: Stoddart Publishing, 1990.

Michael Eric Dyson. *Reflecting Black: African-American Cultural Criticism*. Minneapolis: University of Minnesota Press, 1993.

bell hooks. *Outlaw Culture: Resisting Representations*. New York: Routledge, 1994.

These books provide interesting insights on culture and demonstrate how fieldwork can be carried out in a wide variety of settings:

Napoleon A. Chagnon. *Yanamamö: The Last Days of Eden*. San Diego: Harcourt Brace Jovanovich, 1992.

Stephen M. Fjellman. *Vinyl Leaves: Walt Disney World and America*. Boulder, Colo.: Westview Press, 1992.

To find out more about subcultures, countercultures, and hate crimes see the following:

Stanley R. Barrett. *Is God a Racist? The Right Wing in Canada*. Toronto: University of Toronto Press, 1987.

William M. Kephart and William W. Zellner. *Extraordinary Groups: An Examination of Unconventional Life-Styles* (5th ed.). New York: St. Martin's Press, 1994.

Jack Levin and Jack McDevitt. *Hate Crimes: The Rising Tide of Bigotry and Bloodshed*. New York: Plenum Press, 1993.

Wayne S. Wooden. *Renegade Kids, Suburban Outlaws*. Belmont, Cal.: Wadsworth, 1995.

Chapter 4

SOCIALIZATION

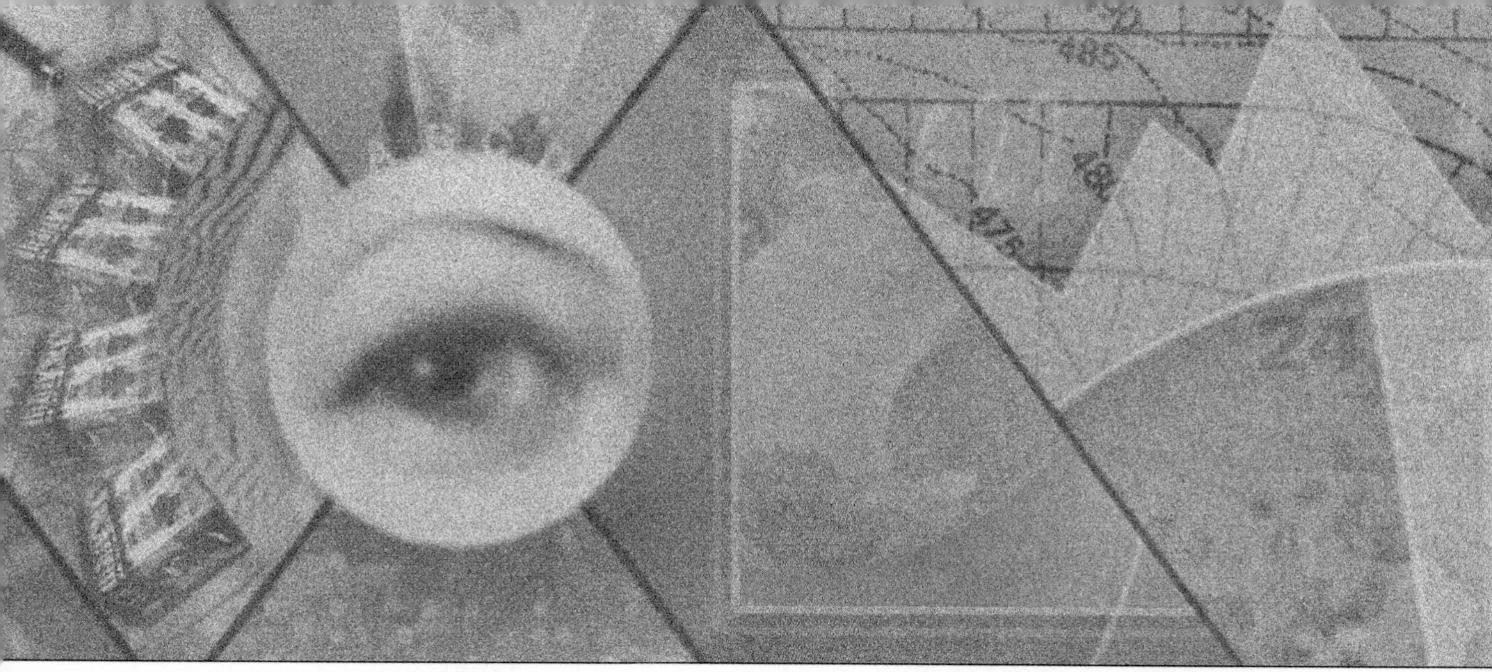

Sylvia Fraser, author of *My Father's House*, recalls her experiences of child abuse:

My daddy plays with my belly button, my daddy plays with my toes as he did when I was little: "This little piggy, that little piggy …" Now I lie on my daddy's bed, face buried in his feather pillow. I shiver, because the window is open, the lace curtains are blowing and I haven't any clothes on. My daddy lies beside me in his shorts and undershirt, smelling of talcum. He rubs against me, still hot and wet from his bath. My daddy breathes very loudly, the way he does when he snores, and his belly heaves like the sunfish I saw on the beach at Van Wagners. Something hard pushes up against me, then between my legs and under my belly. It bursts all over me in a sticky cream. I hold my breath, feeling sick like when you spin on a piano stool till the seat falls off. I hear God say: "You've been dirty, go naked!" When I pull up my daddy's pillow over my head I get feathers up my nose ...

Desperation makes me bold. At last I say the won't-love-me words: "I'm going to tell my mommy on you!"…

"Shut up! What will the neighbors think? If you don't shut up I'll … I'll … send you to the place where all bad children go. An orphanage where they lock up bad children whose parents don't want them any more."

"My mother won't let you!"

"Your mother will do what I say. Then you'll be spanked every night and get only bread and water."

That shuts me up for quite a while, but eventually I dare to see this, too, as a game for which there is an answer: "I don't care. I'll run away!"

My father needs a permanent seal for my lips, one that will murder all defiance. "If you say once more that you're going to tell, I'm sending that cat of yours to the pound for gassing!"

"I'll … I'll … I'll …"

The air swooshes out of me as if I have been punched. My heart is broken. My resistance is broken. Smoky's life is in my hands. This is no longer a game, however desperate. Our bargain is sealed in blood. (Fraser, 1987:8–11)

Child abuse is not just beatings—it includes physical abuse, sexual abuse, physical neglect, and emotional mistreatment (Wachtel, 1994). Such child abuse has a serious impact on a child's social growth, behaviour, and self-image—all of which develop within the process of socialization. Children who are abused rather than nurtured, trusted, and loved by their

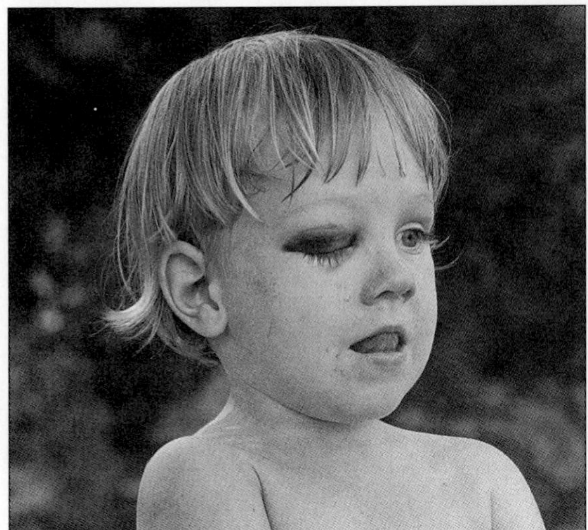

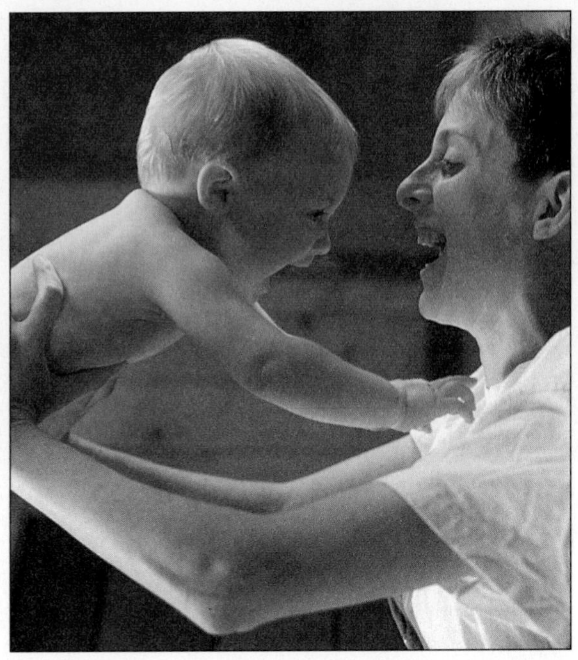

Human interaction is essential to the development of a positive self-concept; in abusive families, however, children may come to view abuse as "normal" everyday behaviour.

parents find it difficult to develop a positive self-image and learn healthy conduct because the appropriate models of behaviour, which parents normally provide, are absent. In some abusive families, children may be socialized to think that abuse is normal interactive behaviour.

In this chapter, we examine why socialization is so crucial, and we discuss both sociological and psychological theories of human development. We look at the dynamics of socialization—how it occurs and what shapes it. Throughout the chapter, we focus on child abuse and its impact on socialization. Before reading on, test your knowledge of child abuse by taking the quiz in Box 4.1.

QUESTIONS AND ISSUES

What purpose does socialization serve?

How do individuals develop a sense of self?

What happens when children do not have an environment that supports positive socialization?

How does socialization occur?

When are individuals completely socialized?

Who experiences resocialization?

WHY IS SOCIALIZATION IMPORTANT?

***Socialization* is the lifelong process of social interaction through which individuals acquire a self-identity and the physical, mental, and social skills needed for survival in society.** It is the essential link between the individual and society (Robertson, 1989). Socialization enables each of us to develop our human potential and learn the ways of thinking, talking, and acting that are essential for social living.

Socialization is essential for the individual's survival and for human development. The many people who met the early material and social needs of each of us were central to our establishing our own identity. During the first three years of our life, we begin to develop a unique identity and the ability to manipulate things and to walk. We acquire sophisticated cognitive tools for thinking and analyzing a wide variety of situations, and we

BOX 4.1 SOCIOLOGY AND EVERYDAY LIFE

How Much Do You Know About Child Abuse?

TRUE	FALSE	
T	F	1. The extent of child abuse has been exaggerated by the media.
T	F	2. Child abuse only occurs in lower-class families.
T	F	3. Men are always the perpetrators of sexual abuse and very seldom the victims.
T	F	4. Infants are Canada's most likely homicide victims.
T	F	5. Neglect is not a form of child abuse.
T	F	6. In a family in which child abuse occurs, all of the children are likely to be victims.
T	F	7. It is against the law to fail to report child abuse.
T	F	8. In most cases of sexual abuse, the perpetrator is known to the child.
T	F	9. People who are the victims of child abuse are more likely to become abusers themselves.
T	F	10. Some people are "born" abusers while others learn abusive behaviour from their family and friends.

Answers on page 126

learn effective communication skills. In the process, we begin a relatively long socialization process that culminates in our integration into a complex social and cultural system (Garcia Coll, 1990).

Socialization also is essential for the survival and stability of society. Members of a society must be socialized to support and maintain the existing social structure. From a functionalist perspective, individual conformity to existing norms is not taken for granted; rather, basic individual needs and desires must be balanced against the needs of the social structure. The socialization process is most effective when people conform to the norms of society because they believe this is the best course of action. In Chapter 3, we saw how people shape and are shaped by the knowledge, language, values, and customs within their cultures. Socialization enables a society to "reproduce" itself by passing on this cultural content from one generation to the next.

If we look at the diversity between societies (and even within our own society), we see an enormous variety of beliefs, values, and rules of behaviour. The content of socialization therefore differs greatly from one society to another. How people walk, talk, eat, make love, and wage war are all functions of the culture in which they are raised. At the same time, we also are influenced by our exposure to subcultures of class, ethnicity, religion, and gender. In addition, each of us has unique experiences in our families and friendship groupings. The kind of human being that we become depends greatly on the particular society and social groups that surround us at birth and

BOX 4.1 SOCIOLOGY AND EVERYDAY LIFE

Answers to the Sociology Quiz on Child Abuse

TRUE	FALSE	
T	**F**	1. *False.* Child abuse is a growing problem in Canada. No national estimates of the prevalence of child abuse are available. The research suggests that many incidents of child abuse are unreported and undetected.
T	**F**	2. *False.* Child abuse occurs in families from all social classes.
T	**F**	3. *False.* Men are not always the perpetrators of sexual abuse, and they may indeed be the victims. Many male victims of sexual abuse are abused by male abusers. However, in about 92 percent of reported sexual abuse cases, young girls and women are the victims; and in 98 percent of the cases, men are the perpetrators.
T	F	4. *True.* At a rate of 5.6 homicides per 100,000 infants, babies have a higher risk of being victims of homicide than older children, teens, or adults. The killers are most likely parents or step-parents.
T	**F**	5. *False.* Child abuse and child neglect are both types of child abuse. Neglect refers to the failure of a parent to provide minimally adequate care in terms of health, nutrition, shelter, education, supervision, affection, attention, or protection. Neglect may be as physically and mentally damaging as physical abuse.
T	**F**	6. *False.* In some families, one child repeatedly may be the victim of abuse while others are not. This is especially true with incest, whereby one daughter may be singled out for abuse by a father, stepfather, uncle, or other male relative.
T	F	7. *True.* In Canada, all of the provinces have mandatory reporting requirements. However, there has been inconsistent compliance with these legal mandates. All adults who believe or suspect that a child is in need of protection have a duty to report this to the authorities. Some provinces specify that professionals who are in contact with children must report suspected abuse cases or face a fine of up to $1000.
T	F	8. *True.* Data from police departments across Canada show that 81 percent of the child sexual assault victims knew their abuser. The largest group of offenders is fathers.
T	F	9. *True.* Although scholars disagree on this point, a number of studies have found that adults who were abused as children have a greater tendency to be violent and abusive when compared with those who were not abused.
T	**F**	10. *False.* No one is "born" to be an abuser. People learn abusive behaviour from their family and friends.

Sources: Based on Wolfe, 1987; Knudsen, 1992; Jackson, 1993; Begin 1994; Wachtel, 1994, Gunn and Linden, 1994; Rodgers and Kong, 1996; Durrant and Rose-Krasnor, 1995.

As this birthday celebration attended by four generations of family members illustrates, socialization enables society to "reproduce" itself.

during early childhood. What we believe about ourselves, our society, and the world is largely a product of our interactions with others.

HUMAN DEVELOPMENT: BIOLOGY AND SOCIETY

What does it mean to be "human"? To be human includes being conscious of ourselves as individuals with unique identities, personalities, and relationships with others. As humans, we have ideas, emotions, and values. We have the capacity to think and to make rational decisions. But what is the source of "humanness"? Are we born with these human characteristics, or do we develop them through our interactions with others?

When we are born, we are totally dependent on others for our survival. We cannot turn ourselves over, speak, reason, plan, or do many of the things that are associated with being human. Although we can nurse, wet, and cry, most small mammals also can do those things. As discussed in Chapter 3, we humans differ from nonhuman animals because we lack instincts and must rely on learning for our survival. Human infants have the potential for developing human characteristics if they are exposed to an adequate socialization process.

Every human being is a product of biology, society, and personal experiences—that is, of heredity and environment or, in even more basic terms, "nature" and "nurture." How much of our development can be explained by socialization? How much by our genetic heritage? Sociologists focus on how humans design their own culture and transmit it from generation to generation through socialization. By contrast, sociobiologists assert that nature, in the form of our genetic makeup, is a major factor in shaping human behaviour. ***Sociobiology* is the systematic study of how biology affects social behaviour** (Wilson, 1975). According to zoologist Edward O. Wilson, who pioneered sociobiology, genetic inheritance underlies many forms of social behaviour such as war and peace, envy and concern for others, and competition and cooperation. Most sociologists disagree with the notion that biological principles can be used to explain all human behaviour. Obviously, however, some aspects of our physical makeup—such as eye colour, hair colour, height, and weight—largely are determined by our heredity.

How important is social influence, or "nurture," in human development? There is hardly a behaviour that is not influenced socially.

Except for simple reflexes, such as dilation of the pupils and knee-jerk responses, most human actions are social, either in their causes or in their consequences. Even solitary actions such as crying or brushing our teeth are ultimately social. We cry because someone has hurt us. We brush our teeth because our parents (or dentist) told us it was important. Social environment probably has a greater effect than heredity on the way we develop and the way we act. However, heredity does provide the basic material from which other people help to mould an individual's human characteristics.

Our biological and emotional needs are related in a complex equation. Children whose needs are met in settings characterized by affection, warmth, and closeness see the world as a safe and comfortable place and other people as trustworthy and helpful. By contrast, infants and children who receive less-than-adequate care or who are emotionally rejected or abused often view the world as hostile and have feelings of suspicion and fear.

SOCIAL ISOLATION

Social environment, then, is a crucial part of an individual's socialization. Even nonhuman primates such as monkeys and chimpanzees need social contact with others of their species in order to develop properly. As we will see, appropriate social contact is even more important for humans.

ISOLATION AND NONHUMAN PRIMATES Researchers have attempted to demonstrate the effects of social isolation on nonhuman primates raised without contact with others of their own species. In a series of laboratory experiments, psychologists Harry and Margaret Harlow (1962, 1977) took infant rhesus monkeys from their mothers and isolated them in separate cages. Each cage contained two nonliving "mother substitutes" made of wire, one with a feeding bottle attached and the other covered with soft terry cloth but without a bottle. The infant monkeys instinctively clung to the cloth "mother" and would not abandon it until hunger drove them to the bottle attached to the wire "mother." As soon as they were full, they went back to the cloth "mother" seeking warmth, affection, and physical comfort.

The Harlows's experiments show the detrimental effects of isolation on nonhuman primates. When the young monkeys later were introduced to other members of their species, they cringed in the corner. Having been deprived of social contact with other monkeys during their first six months of life, they never learned how to relate to other monkeys or to become well-adjusted adult monkeys—they were fearful of or hostile toward other monkeys (Harlow and Harlow, 1962, 1977).

If nurture is needed for monkeys to develop normally, how much more important is it in the development of humans? We must be cautious about using nonhuman animal studies to draw inferences for human behaviour. Obviously, human beings are not monkeys. However, the Harlows's studies do show that, without socialization, monkeys do not learn normal social or emotional behaviour. And because humans rely more heavily on social learning than do monkeys, the process of socialization is even more important for us.

FERAL CHILDREN People have always been intrigued by accounts of *feral children*, who are assumed to have been raised by animals in the wilderness, isolated from human society. The Romans, for example, believed that the alleged founders of Rome (Romulus and Remus) had been raised by a wolf.

In 1798, hunters in Aveyron, a rural area of France, reported that a boy was running naked through a forest on all fours. The "Wild Boy of Aveyron" was believed to be about 11 years old and to have lived alone in the forest for five or six years. Jean-Marc Itard, a young doctor, took the boy into his home, named him Victor, and attempted to socialize him. Victor learned to speak a few words, to eat with a knife and fork, and to get along with the doctor and his housekeeper. However, from the time Victor was found until his death at the age of 40, he never was able to develop relationships with other people (Candland, 1993). In the late nineteenth and early twentieth century, other cases of feral children were reported in India, France, and elsewhere (see Singh and Zingg, 1942; Shattuck, 1980). The children were unable to talk, were afraid of other human beings, walked on all fours or slouched over, tore ravenously at their food, and drank by lapping water (Malson, 1972). Were these tales true? Have there really been feral children?

Social scientists generally agree that it is highly unlikely that feral children actually were raised by wild animals. They suggest that the children likely were abandoned by their parents shortly before they were found by others. The children already may have been abused or isolated from most human contact before they actually were abandoned (Bettelheim, 1959). However, documented cases of child abuse and neglect indicate that human infants without adequate social interaction with other human beings are unable to develop fully "human" characteristics.

Studies of feral and isolated children provide important insights into the effect of social isolation on human beings. One of the most widely known feral children was Victor, "The Wild Boy of Aveyron," shown here in an engraved portrait from Dr. Jean-Marc Itard's report of 1801.

ISOLATED CHILDREN Social scientists have documented cases of children who were deliberately raised in isolation. A look at the lives of two children who suffered such emotional abuse provides important insights into the effect of social isolation on human beings.

Anna Born in 1932 to an unmarried, mentally impaired woman, Anna was an unwanted child. She was kept in an attic-like room in her grandfather's house. Her mother, who worked on the farm all day and often went out at night, gave Anna just enough care to keep her alive; she received no other care. Sociologist Kingsley Davis (1940) described her condition when she was found in 1938:

> [Anna] had no glimmering of speech, absolutely no ability to walk, no sense of gesture, not the least capacity to feed herself even when the food was put in front of her, and no comprehension of cleanliness. She was so apathetic that it was hard to tell whether or not she could hear. And all of this at the age of nearly six years.

When she was placed in a special school and given the necessary care, Anna slowly learned to walk, talk, and care for herself. Just before her death at the age of 10, Anna reportedly could follow directions, talk in phrases, wash her hands, brush her teeth, and try to help other children (Davis, 1940).

Genie Almost four decades after Anna was discovered, Genie was found in 1970 at the age of 13. She had been locked in a bedroom alone, alternately strapped down to a child's potty chair or straitjacketed into a sleeping bag, since she was 20 months old. She had been fed baby food and beaten with a wooden paddle when she whimpered. She had not heard the sounds of human speech because no one talked to her and there was no television or radio in her home (Curtiss, 1977; Pines, 1981). Genie was placed in a pediatric hospital where one of the psychologists described her condition:

> At the time of her admission she was virtually unsocialized. She could not stand erect, salivated continuously, had never been toilet-trained and had no control over her urinary or bowel functions. She was unable to chew solid food and had the weight, height and appearance of a child half her age. (Rigler, 1993:35)

In addition to her physical condition, Genie showed psychological traits associated with neglect, as described by one of her psychiatrists:

> If you gave [Genie] a toy, she would reach out and touch it, hold it, caress it with her fingertips, as though she didn't trust her eyes. She would rub it against her cheek to feel it. So when I met her and she began to notice me standing beside her bed, I held my hand out and she reached out and took my hand and carefully felt my thumb and fingers individually, and then put my hand against her cheek. She was exactly like a blind child. (Rymer, 1993:45)

Extensive therapy was used in an attempt to socialize Genie and develop her language abilities (Curtiss, 1977; Pines, 1981). These efforts met with limited success: In the early 1990s, Genie was living in a board-and-care home for retarded adults (see Angier, 1993; Rigler, 1993; Rymer, 1993).

These cases are important to our understanding of the socialization process because they show that social isolation and neglect are extremely detrimental to young children. When infants are deprived of human contact, they do not develop the characteristics most of us think of as "human."

CHILD ABUSE

What do the words "child abuse" mean to you? Many people first think of cases that involve severe physical injuries or sexual abuse. However, "child abuse" is a general term used to describe a variety of injuries inflicted by a parent or caregiver. There are three types of abuse: physical abuse or battering; neglect; and sexual abuse. It is estimated that neglect is the most frequent form of child abuse (Wachtel, 1994). Child neglect occurs when a child's basic needs—including emotional warmth and security, adequate shelter, food, health care, education, clothing and protection—are not met, regardless of cause (Dubowitz et al., 1993:12). Neglect often involves acts of omission (where parents or caregivers fail to provide adequate physical or emotional care for children) rather than acts of commission (such as physical or sexual abuse). The cases of Anna and Genie demonstrate the devastating effect that parental neglect can have on a child's development.

What acts constitute child abuse or neglect? Throughout history and across cultures, perceptions of what constitutes abuse or neglect have differed. What might have been considered appropriate disciplinary action by parents in the past (such as following the adage "Spare the rod, spoil the child") today is viewed by many as child abuse. Still, many Canadian parents choose to use spanking as a form of discipline. Recent research on the use of corporal punishment has revealed that approximately 70 percent of Canadian parents have used physical punishment, although the majority indicate that it is ineffective to do so (Durrant, 1995).

Unfortunately, the federal government has yet to develop a standard definition of child abuse. Subsequently, there is a wide variety of interpretations interprovincially about what constitutes child abuse. In fact, as the debate surrounding Section 43 of the Criminal Code demonstrates (see Box 4.2), there is little agreement within Canadian society with regard to what constitutes child abuse.

SOCIALIZATION AND THE SELF

Without social contact, we cannot form a sense of self or personal identity. The *self* represents the sum total of perceptions and feelings that an

BOX 4.2 SOCIOLOGY AND LAW

Child Abuse Then and Now

Childhood in Canada does not always match our idealized cultural notion that children should be loved and protected by adults. Conduct ranging from extreme indifference and neglect to physical and sexual abuse of children has been commonplace throughout history.

Historically, society has viewed children as the property of their parents—to be treated as the parents wished. In the United States in the early 1600s, the "Stubborn Child Act" specified that the parents of a rebellious or stubborn child could petition the court for permission to put the child to death (Wolfe, 1987). Even without such a law, physical beatings often have been considered appropriate discipline for children. In fact, parents who did not beat their children were considered to be neglecting their parental duties (DeMause, 1975). Parents had absolute power and control over their children. Early Roman law referred to as *patria potestas* included the right of the father to give a child away or have the child put to death. Under an 18th century English common law, *parens patriae*, the father had an obligation to exercise guardianship over minors. Children were regarded as chattel.

It is only in the past 100 years that childhood has been recognized as a distinct period. The first legal challenge to the absolute rights of parents occurred in 1870 in New York when a social worker was forced to turn to the American Society for the Prevention of Cruelty to Animals as a means of obtaining legal sanctions against the parents of a neglected child. In response, the American Society for the Prevention of Cruelty to Children was founded. Shortly thereafter, in 1891, the Children's Aid Society was established in Toronto.

One of the most contentious current issues pertaining to child abuse revolves around Section 43 of the Criminal Code, which states:

> Every school teacher, parent or person standing in the place of a parent is justified in using force by way of correction toward a pupil or child, as the case may be, who is under his care, if the force does not exceed what is reasonable under the circumstances.

The original intention of Section 43 was the protection of the child from unreasonable force, not to sanction physical punishment by parents. However, those lobbying for the repeal of Section 43 argue that this provision gives parents the legal right to assault their children with impunity. Others argue that removing Section 43 would remove the protection that parents now have against criminal prosecution if they physically discipline their children.

"Reasonable force" is an ambiguous term. The research indicates that parents of abused children report that their actions were simply an extension of a parent's disciplinary role (Begin, 1994; Durrant, 1995).

In the Canadian courts, "reasonable force" is left for the judge to determine. Frequently the judges do so, in disregard of present-day attitudes. Section 43 has been used as a defense in court cases where children have been beaten black and blue. In one case presented to the Manitoba Court of Appeal in 1992, a judge decided that although the father had left severe bruises on his son, they were lighter than the beatings the judge had received as a child. The man was acquitted.

Source: Durrant, 1995; Mitchell, 1995

individual has of being a distinct, unique person—a sense of who and what one is. This sense of self (also referred to as *self-concept*) is not present at birth; it arises in the process of social experience. ***Self-concept* is the totality of our beliefs and feelings about ourselves** (Gecas, 1982). Four components comprise our self-concept: (1) the *physical* self ("I am tall"), (2) the *active* self ("I am good at soccer"), (3) the *social* self ("I am nice to others"), and (4) the *psychological* self ("I believe in

Our self-concept continues to be influenced by our interactions with others throughout our lives.

world peace"). Between early and late childhood, a child's focus tends to shift from the physical and active dimensions of self toward the social and psychological aspects (Lippa, 1994). Self-concept is the foundation for communication with others; it continues to develop and change throughout our lives (Zurcher, 1983).

Our *self-identity* is our perception about what kind of person we are. As we have seen, socially isolated children do not have typical self-identities because they have had no experience of "humanness." According to interactionists, we do not know who we are until we see ourselves as we believe others see us. We gain information about the self largely through language, symbols, and interaction with others. Our interpretation and evaluation of these messages is central to the social construction of our identity. However, we are not just passive reactors to situations, programmed by society to respond in fixed ways. Instead, we are active agents who develop plans out of the pieces supplied by culture and attempt to execute these plans in social encounters (McCall and Simmons, 1978). For example, once children learn about humour, they begin to tell jokes in order to entertain—or even shock—others.

SOCIOLOGICAL THEORIES OF HUMAN DEVELOPMENT

The perspectives of symbolic interactionists Charles Horton Cooley and George Herbert Mead help us understand how our self-identity is developed through our interactions with others.

THE LOOKING-GLASS SELF According to sociologist Charles Horton Cooley (1864–1929), the ***looking-glass self*** **refers to the way in which a person's sense of self is derived from the perceptions of others.** Our looking-glass self is not who we actually are or what people actually think about us; it is based on our *perception* of how other people think of us (Cooley, 1922/1902). Cooley asserted that we base our perception of who we are on how we think other people see us and on whether this seems good or bad to us.

As Figure 4.1 shows, the looking-glass self is a self-concept derived from a three-step process:

1. We imagine how our personality and appearance will look to other people. We may imagine that we are attractive or unattractive, heavy or slim, friendly or unfriendly, and so on.
2. We imagine how other people judge the appearance and personality that we think we present. This step involves our *perception* of how we think they are judging us. We may be correct or incorrect!
3. We develop a self-concept. If we think the evaluation of others is favourable, our self-concept is enhanced. If we think the evaluation is unfavourable, our self-concept is diminished (Cooley, 1922/1902).

According to Cooley, we use our interactions with others as a mirror for our own thoughts and actions; our sense of self depends on how we inter-

FIGURE 4.1

How the Looking-Glass Self Works

pret what they do and say. Consequently, our sense of self is not permanently fixed; it is always developing as we interact with others. A key component of Cooley's looking-glass self is the idea that the self results from a person's "imagination" of how others view her or him. As a result, we can develop self-identities based on incorrect, as well as correct, perceptions of how others see us.

ROLE-TAKING George Herbert Mead (1863–1931) extended Cooley's insights by linking the idea of self-concept to ***role-taking*****—the process by which a person mentally assumes the role of another person in order to understand the world from that person's point of view.** Role-taking often occurs through play and games, as children try out different roles (such as being mommy, daddy, doctor, or teacher) and gain an appreciation of them.

According to Mead (1934), in the early months of life, children do not realize that they are separate from others. They do, however, begin early on to see a mirrored image of themselves in others. Shortly after birth, infants start to notice things in the environment that have certain characteristics, such as contour, contrast, and movement.

Because the human face has all these characteristics, it is one of the first things many infants notice. We are most likely to observe the faces of those around us, especially the significant others whose faces start to have meaning, because they are associated with experiences like feeding and cuddling. ***Significant others*** **are those persons whose care, affection, and approval are especially desired and who are most important in the development of the self.** Gradually, we distinguish ourselves from our caregivers and begin to perceive ourselves in contrast to them. As we develop language skills and learn to understand symbols, we begin to develop a self-concept. When we can represent ourselves in our own minds as objects distinct from everything else, our self has been formed.

Mead divided the self into the "I" and the "me." The "I" is the subjective element of the self that represents the spontaneous and unique traits of each person. The "me" is the objective element of the self, which is composed of the internalized attitudes and demands of other members of society and the individual's awareness of those demands. Both the "I" and the "me" are needed to form the social self. The unity of the two constitutes the full development of the individual. According to Mead, the "I" develops first, and the "me" takes form during the three stages of self development:

1. During the *preparatory stage*, up to about age 3, interactions lack meaning, and children largely imitate the people around them. Children may mimic family members or others nearby, but they lack understanding of the meaning of their behaviour and are simply copying others. At this stage, children are *preparing* for role-taking.
2. In the *play stage*, from about age 3 to 5, children learn to use language and other symbols, thus enabling them to pretend to take the roles of specific people. At first, children tend to model themselves on significant others, typically members of their families, teachers, and other caregivers with whom they spend substantial amounts of time. Later, children may play at taking the roles of others, such as "doctor, "superhero," or "bad guy." At this stage, children begin to see themselves in relation to others, but they do not see role-taking as something they *have* to do.
3. During the *game stage*, which begins in the early school years, children understand not only their own social position but also the positions of others around them. In contrast to play, games are structured by rules, often are competitive, and involve a number of other "players." Children now learn a system of interdependent roles and ways of relating to many people and groups. At this time, they become concerned about the demands and expectations of others and of the larger society. Mead used the example of a baseball game to describe this stage because children, like baseball players, must take into account the roles of all the other players at the same time. They must plan their responses to the predicted actions of other players based on the "big picture" of the entire situation. Mead's concept of the ***generalized other*** **refers to the child's awareness of the demands and expectations of the society as a whole or of the child's subculture.** To return to Mead's baseball analogy, for instance, think of the 7-year-old's abstract ability to *simultaneously* consider the roles of other team members when the ball is hit to centre field.

Is socialization a one-way process? No, according to Mead. Socialization is a two-way process between society and the individual. Just as the society in which we live helps determine what kind of individuals we will become, we have the ability to shape certain aspects of our social environment and perhaps even the larger society.

SELF-CONCEPT AND CHILD ABUSE What happens when a child does not have a supportive environment in which to develop a positive self-concept? Inter-

According to sociologist George Herbert Mead, the self develops through three stages. In the preparatory stage, children imitate others; in the play stage, children pretend to take the roles of specific people; and in the game stage, children become aware of the "rules of the game" and the expectations of others.

actionists suggest that a child's self-concept is defined and evaluated through interaction with significant others, who are assumed to have the best interests of the child in mind. Positive parent–child relationships, for example, are characterized by a balance between positive and negative interactions and between discipline and emotional bonding. By contrast, child abuse occurs when there is an extreme imbalance in such interactions (Wolfe, 1987). According to interactionist analysis, although people may abuse or neglect children for many reasons, the primary "causes" are located within social interactions, especially between parent and child.

What is the relationship between childhood abuse and a person's self-concept as an adult? The dynamic interplay between individual, familial, and other social factors in relation to past events (such as exposure to abuse as a child) and present situations (such as a child who is "misbehaving") is important for understanding the long-term effects of child abuse (Wolfe, 1987). Consider this mother's story:

> I live in a middle-class neighborhood and have all the conveniences available to a modern-day housewife. I do not work outside the home, preferring to stay behind closed doors where it is safe. In all respects I should be a happily married woman and proud mother of two beautiful children. Unfortunately, this is not the case. …
>
> To my husband, I am an uncommunicative, frigid wife who has no desire to socialize or be sexually active with him. To my children, I am someone who barely tolerates their presence;

> who walks around with the belt in the hand, using it every time they step out of line, which is any time they are in my way or not being quiet; who constantly is verbally condemning them for something trivial they may have done; who violently attacks them, using my fists and wire kitchen whisks and kicking with my feet and then leaving them where they lay, crumpled in pain and misery, to wonder what they could have done to warrant such punishment. ... But how can I love them and hate to be around them at the same time? ...
>
> From the age of thirteen to the age of eighteen I was physically and sexually abused by both my mother and stepfather, and physically and sexually abused by both of my brothers, who were physically and emotionally abused also.
>
> ... How has my childhood affected my adulthood? It has deformed me. Not physically; the broken bones, cuts, and bruises have mended, the gunshot wounds have healed, leaving behind only small scars that I can cover up. It is the inner wounds that are still unhealed, visible by my inability to make friends, inability to form a close bond with my husband, and worst of all, unable to love my children in the way they were meant to be loved. For one can only teach what one has been taught, one can only give what one has been given. I was given only pain expressed in silent anger and depraved actions. Is that all I have to give to my children and my husband? I would gladly lay down my life in order to secure happiness for them. They are the innocent ones. (quoted in Fontana, 1991:23–24)

What happened in this woman's childhood socialization process that influences her adult behaviour? From an interactionist perspective, child abuse such as this can best be explained as the *result of an interaction* between the parent and child within a system that seldom provides alternate solutions (such as exposure to appropriate parental models, education, and social supports) or clear-cut restraints (such as laws, sanctions, and consequences) to the use of excessive force to resolve common child-rearing conflicts (Wolfe, 1987). In other words, if individuals do not learn appropriate models of parenting from their own families, then it can be difficult to learn them elsewhere.

EVALUATING INTERACTIONIST THEORIES How useful are interactionist perspectives such as Cooley's and Mead's in enhancing our understanding of the socialization process? Certainly, this approach contributes to our understanding of how the self develops. Cooley's idea of the looking-glass self makes us aware that our perception of how we *think* others see us is not always correct. Mead extended Cooley's ideas by emphasizing the cognitive skills acquired through role-taking. He stressed the importance of play and games, as children try out different roles and gain an appreciation of them. His concept of the generalized other helps us see that the self is a social creation. According to Mead (1934:196), "Selves can only exist in definite relations to other selves. No hard-and-fast line can be drawn between our own selves and the selves of others."

As with any theoretical approach, the viewpoints of interactionists such as Cooley and Mead have certain limitations. Some conflict theorists have argued that these theories are excessively conservative because they assume that what is good for dominant group members is good for everyone. For example, sociologist Anne Kaspar (1986) suggests that Mead's ideas about the social self may be more applicable for men than women. According to Mead's theory, both the "I" and the "me" are needed to form the social self, and there is no inherent conflict between the two. By contrast, Kaspar asserts that women experience inherent conflicts between the meanings they derive from their *personal experience* and those they take from the *culture*. She notes that "ideals of motherhood" that derive from culture may be in sharp contrast to the actual experiences of women as mothers. For many women, it is difficult to balance the idealized view of a mother as selfless, nurturing, and devoted to family with the realities of their own needs for autonomy, independence, and valued work in and outside the home (Kaspar, 1986).

How might ethnicity, class, religion, and other factors also contribute to inherent tensions between the meanings we derive from our personal experience and those we take from culture? People may be viewed as "deficient" or "poorly adjusted" if they do not accept uncritically the core values, norms, and behaviours of mainstream society. Many members of minority groups, for example, may be faced with an unhappy choice: maintain pride in one's ethnic roots and be shunned by members of the dominant group or "sell out" one's heritage in order to be accepted (Garcia Coll, 1990; Steinback, 1993; G. Williams, 1995).

PSYCHOLOGICAL THEORIES OF HUMAN DEVELOPMENT

Sociologist Cynthia Fuchs Epstein (1988:96) notes that "scholars in different disciplines often develop concepts and theories about the same subject matter without paying attention to each other's work." The social sciences may be able to contribute more to our understanding of human behaviour if we analyze the strengths and weaknesses of existing perspectives and integrate the most useful theories from other disciplines. Up to this point, we have discussed sociologically oriented theories; we now turn to psychological theories that have influenced contemporary views of human development.

PSYCHOANALYTIC PERSPECTIVE Sigmund Freud (1856–1939) is known as the founder of psychoanalytic theory. He lived in the Victorian era, during which biological explanations of human behaviour were prevalent. It also was an era of extreme sexual repression and male dominance when compared to contemporary North American standards. Freud's theory was greatly influenced by these cultural factors, as reflected in the importance he assigned to sexual motives in explaining behaviour.

Freud divided the mind into three interrelated parts: id, ego, and superego. The ***id*** **is the component of personality that includes all of the individual's basic biological drives and needs that demand immediate gratification.** The new-born child's personality is all id, and from birth, the child finds that urges for self-gratification—such as wanting to be held, fed, or changed—are not going to be satisfied immediately. The ***ego*** **is the rational, reality-oriented component of personality that imposes restrictions on the innate pleasure-seeking drives of the id.** The ego channels the desire of the id for immediate gratification into the most advantageous direction for the individual. The ***superego*****, or conscience, consists of the moral and ethical aspects of personality.** It is first expressed as the recognition of parental control and eventually matures as the child learns that parental control is a reflection of the values and moral demands of the larger society. When a person is well adjusted, the ego successfully manages the opposing forces of the id and the superego. Figure 4.2 illustrates Freud's theory of personality.

Freud acknowledged the importance of socialization when he pointed out that people's biological drives may be controlled by the values and moral demands of society that are learned primarily during childhood. However, his theory has been heavily criticized by many scholars. One criticism is that his work was based on unprovable assertions. For example, according to Freud's psychoanalytic theory, most incest reports represent the sexual fantasies of alleged victims (Roth, 1993). Freud assumed that his female patients' accounts of incest were figments of their imaginations, based on their own sexual desires. Sociologist Diana E.H. Russell (1986) has argued this assumption discounts the reality of incestuous abuse or, if discounting is impossible, blames the child.

PSYCHOSOCIAL DEVELOPMENT Erik H. Erikson (1902–1994) drew from Freud's theory and identified eight psychosocial stages of development. According to Erikson (1980/1959), each stage is accom-

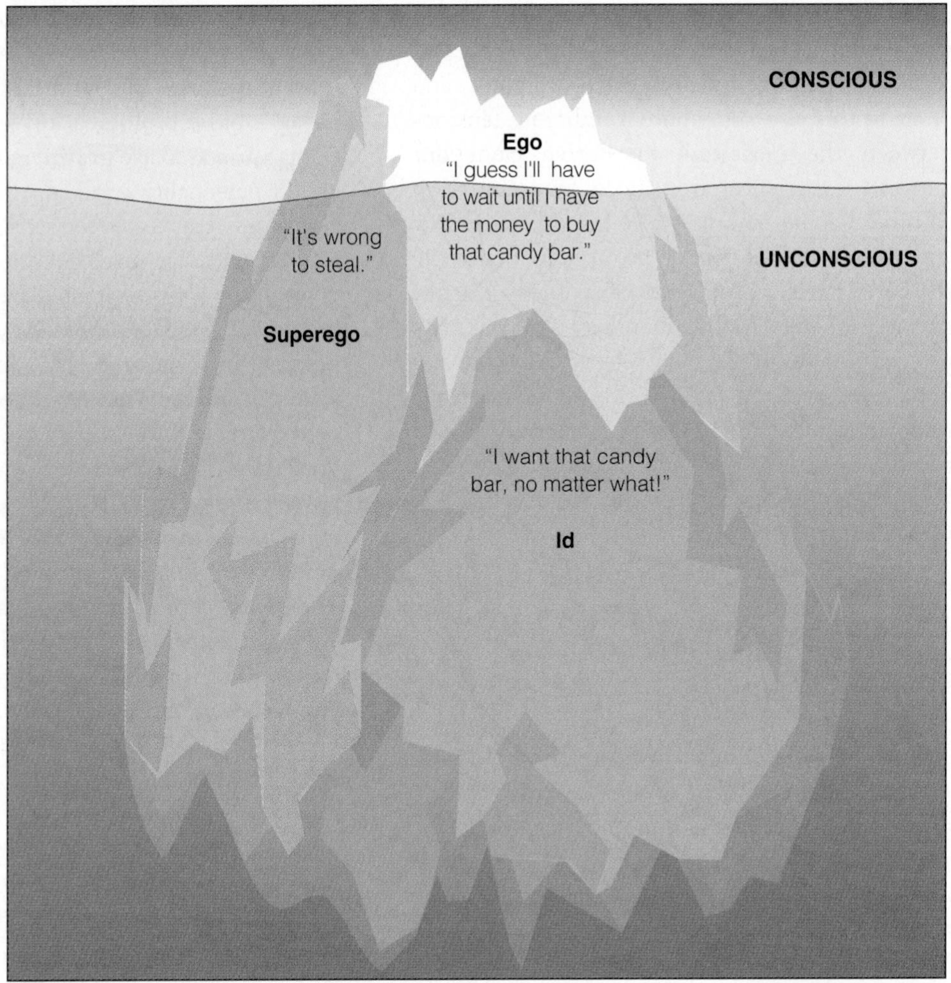

FIGURE 4.2

Freud's Theory of Personality

This illustration shows how Freud might picture a person's internal conflict over whether to commit an antisocial act such as stealing a candy bar. In addition to dividing personality into three components, Freud theorized that our personalities are largely unconscious—hidden away outside our normal awareness. To dramatize his point, Freud compared conscious awareness (portions of the ego and superego) to the visible tip of an iceberg. Most of personality—including all of the id, with its raw desires and impulses—lies submerged in our subconscious.

panied by a crisis or potential crisis that involves transitions in social relationships:

1. *Trust versus mistrust* (birth to age 1). If infants receive good care and nurturing (characterized by emotional warmth, security, and love) from their parents, they will develop a sense of trust. If they do not receive such care, they will become mistrustful and anxious about their surroundings.
2. *Autonomy versus shame and doubt* (age 1–3). As children gain a feeling of control over their behaviour and develop a variety of

physical and mental abilities, they begin to assert their independence. If they are allowed to explore their environment, children will grow more autonomous. If parents disapprove of or discourage them, children begin to doubt their abilities.

3. *Initiative versus guilt* (age 3–5). If parents encourage initiative during this stage, children develop a sense of initiative. If parents make children feel that their actions are bad or that they are a nuisance, children may develop a strong sense of guilt.
4. *Industry versus inferiority* (age 6–11). At this stage, children desire to manipulate objects and learn how things work. Adults who encourage children's efforts and praise the results—both at home and at school—produce a feeling of industry in children. Feelings of inferiority result when parents or teachers appear to view children's efforts as silly or a nuisance.
5. *Identity versus role confusion* (age 12–18). During this stage, adolescents attempt to develop a sense of identity. As young people take on new roles, the new roles must be combined with the old ones to create a strong self-identity. Role confusion results when individuals fail to acquire an accurate sense of personal identity.
6. *Intimacy versus isolation* (age 18–35). The challenge of this stage (which covers courtship and early family life) is to develop close and meaningful relationships. If individuals establish successful relationships, intimacy ensues. If they fail to do so, they may feel isolated.
7. *Generativity versus self-absorption* (age 35–55). Generativity means looking beyond oneself and being concerned about the next generation and the future of the world in general. Self-absorbed people may be preoccupied with their own well-being and material gains or be overwhelmed by "stagnation, boredom, and interpersonal impoverishment" (Erikson, 1968:138).
8. *Integrity versus despair* (maturity and old age). Integrity results when individuals have resolved previous psychosocial crises and are able to look back at their life as having been meaningful and personally fulfilling. Despair results when previous crises remain unresolved and individuals view their life as a series of disappointments, failures, and misfortunes.

Erikson's psychosocial stages broaden the framework of Freud's theory by focusing on social and cultural forces and by examining development throughout the life course. The psychosocial approach encompasses the conflicts that coincide with major changes in a person's social environment and describes how satisfactory resolution of these conflicts results in positive development. For example, if adolescents who experience an identity crisis are able to determine who they are and what they want from life, they may be able to achieve a positive self-identity and acquire greater psychological distance from their parents.

Critics have pointed out that Erikson's research was limited to white, middle-class respondents from industrial societies (Slugoski and Ginsburg, 1989). However, other scholars have used his theoretical framework to examine ethnic variations in the process of psychosocial development. Most of the studies have concluded that all children face the same developmental tasks at each stage but that ethnic minorities often have greater difficulty in obtaining a positive outcome because of experiences with racial prejudice and discrimination in society (Rotheram and Phinney, 1987). Although establishing an identity is difficult for most adolescents, one study found that it was especially problematic for children of recent South Asian immigrants who had experienced stress related to conflicting value systems and lifestyles (Kurian, 1991).

COGNITIVE DEVELOPMENT Jean Piaget (1896–1980), a Swiss psychologist, was a pioneer in the field of cognitive (intellectual) development. Cognitive theorists are interested in how people obtain, process, and use information—that is, in how we think. Cognitive development relates to changes over time in how we think.

Piaget (1954) believed that in each stage of development (from birth through adolescence), children's activities are governed by their perception of the world around them. His four stages of cognitive development are organized around specific tasks that, when mastered, lead to the acquisition of new mental capacities, which then serve as the basis for the next level of development. Piaget emphasized that all children must go through each stage in sequence before moving on to the next one, although some children move through them faster than others.

1. *Sensorimotor stage* (birth to age 2). During this period, children understand the world only through sensory contact and immediate action because they cannot engage in symbolic thought or use language. Toward the end of the second year, children comprehend *object permanence;* that is, they start to realize that objects continue to exist even when the items are out of sight.
2. *Preoperational stage* (age 2–7). In this stage, children begin to use words as mental symbols and to form mental images. However, they still are limited in their ability to use logic to solve problems or to realize that physical objects may change in shape or appearance while still retaining their physical properties. For example, Piaget showed children two identical beakers filled with the same amount of water. After the children agreed that both beakers held the same amount of water, Piaget poured the water from one beaker into a taller, narrower beaker and then asked them about the amounts of water in each beaker. Those still in the preoperational stage believed that the taller beaker held more water because the water line was higher than in the shorter, wider beaker. In this stage, children are *egocentric;* they see the world from their own perspective and do not realize that a situation may appear different to someone else.
3. *Concrete operational stage* (age 7–11). During this stage, children think in terms of tangible objects and actual events. They can draw conclusions about the likely physical consequences of an action without always having to try it out. Children grow less egocentric as they begin to take the role of others and start to empathize with the viewpoints of others.
4. *Formal operational stage* (age 12 through adolescence). By this stage, adolescents are able to engage in highly abstract thought and understand places, things, and events they have never seen. They can think about the future and evaluate different options or courses of action.

Piaget provided useful insights on the emergence of logical thinking as the result of biological maturation and socialization. However, critics have noted several weaknesses in Piaget's approach to cognitive development. For one thing, the theory says little about individual differences among children, nor does it account for cultural differences. For another, as psychologist Carol Gilligan (1982) has noted, Piaget did not take into account how gender affects the process of social development.

STAGES OF MORAL DEVELOPMENT Lawrence Kohlberg (b. 1927) elaborated on Piaget's theories of cognitive reasoning by conducting a series of studies in which respondents were presented with a moral dilemma. In one hypothetical case, a woman was near death from cancer. The local pharmacist had a drug that might save her life, but the woman's husband could not afford the cost. The pharmacist refused to sell the drug to him cheaper or to let him pay later. In desperation, the husband broke into the drug store and stole the drug. The respondents were asked to answer questions such as, "Should the husband have done that? Why?" Based on the responses, Kohlberg classified moral reasoning into three levels, each containing two specific stages. He argued that people must pass through each stage before going on to the next (Kohlberg, 1969, 1981).

1. *Preconventional level* (age 7–10). At this level, children give little consideration to the views of others. Kohlberg referred to the first stage of moral development as *punishment and obedience orientation* (punishment avoidance). Here, the child's judgment as to what is right or wrong is simply based on a fear of punishment. In this stage, when asked about stealing the drug from the pharmacist, a child might respond, "He shouldn't have stolen the drug; he may have to go to jail." Stage 2 of moral development is *naive instrumental hedonism* (need satisfaction). Here, the child believes that good conduct produces pleasure and bad conduct results in unwanted consequences. In this stage, a child might respond, "It's all right to steal the drug because she needs it and he wants her to live" (Kohlberg, 1969, 1981).
2. *Conventional level* (age 10 through adulthood). At this level, individuals are most concerned with how they are perceived by their peers. Stage 3 of moral development involves *"good-boy/nice-girl" morality* in which children believe that behaviour is good (or right) if it receives wide approval from significant others, including peers. At this stage, children confronted with the case of the dying wife express concern with how others would view the husband's behaviour if he did (or did not) steal the drug. Stage 4, *law-and-order orientation*, is based on how one conforms to rules and laws. Conforming to rules and laws is seen as being important in maintaining societal approval. At this stage, respondents tend to believe either that the husband should steal the drug because he personally would be responsible if the wife died or that he should not steal the drug because it is always wrong to steal.
3. *Postconventional level* (few adults reach this stage). At this level, people view morality in terms of individual rights. In stage 5, *social contract orientation*, ideals and principles are seen as having value that does not depend on the approval of others; rather, rights are seen as part of a social contract. On the one hand, people might respond to the hypothetical dilemma by saying that the husband is justified in taking the drug because the law really does not apply to circumstances such as these. On the other hand, they might reply that extreme circumstances do not justify taking the law into one's own hands. Stage 6, the final moral stage, is *universal ethical principles*, and "moral conduct" is judged by principles based on human rights that transcend government and laws. At this stage, the value of a human life (the wife's) would be compared with the right (of the pharmacist) to financial gain.

In expanding on Piaget's theories of cognitive development by analyzing stages of moral development, Kohlberg concluded that certain levels of cognitive development are essential before corresponding levels of moral reasoning can occur. However, higher stages of moral development do not necessarily accompany these advances in cognitive development.

Critics have challenged Kohlberg's concept of stages of moral development and his belief that these stages are linked to cognitive development. They also have questioned whether these stages are universal. Some researchers suggest that his "moral dilemmas" (such as the critically ill wife and the medical remedy) are too abstract for children. When questions are made simpler, or when children and adolescents are observed in natural (as opposed to laboratory) settings, they often demonstrate sophisticated levels of moral reasoning (Darley and Schultz, 1990; Lapsley, 1990).

GENDER AND MORAL DEVELOPMENT One of the major criticisms of Kohlberg's work came from psychologist Carol Gilligan (b. 1936), one of his former colleagues. According to Gilligan (1982), Kohlberg's research has key weaknesses. Because all of his subjects were male, his model was based solely on male responses. Gilligan stated that there is evidence of male–female differences with regard to morality. Girls might be concerned about the consequences that stealing or not stealing the drug might have on the man, his wife, and their children and thus frame an answer that would produce the least harm to them. For example, one female grade six student reasoned:

> If he stole the drug, he might save his wife then, but if he did, he might have to go to jail, and then his wife might get sicker again, and he couldn't get more of the drug ... So, they should really just talk it out and find some other way to make the money. (Gilligan, 1982)

To Kohlberg, this would be at about stage 3 of moral development. The older boys in the study approached the dilemma from the standpoint of abstract standards of right and wrong; to Kohlberg, this would be close to stage 6. The difference in responses does not indicate a "moral deficiency" on the part of either gender; rather, it results from different socialization and life experiences.

To correct what she perceived to be a male bias in Kohlberg's research, Gilligan (1982) examined morality in women by interviewing twenty-eight pregnant women who were contemplating having an abortion. Based on her research, Gilligan concluded that Kohlberg's stages do not reflect the ways many women think about moral problems. As a result, Gilligan identified three stages in female moral development. In stage 1, the woman is motivated primarily by selfish concerns ("This is what I want . . . this is what I need"). In stage 2, she increasingly recognizes her responsibility to others. In stage 3, she makes her decision based on her desire to do the greatest good for both herself and for others. Gilligan argued that men are socialized to make moral decisions based on abstract principles of justice ("What is the fairest to do?") while women are socialized to make such decisions on the basis of compassion and care ("Who will be hurt least?").

Subsequent research that directly compared women's and men's reasoning about moral dilemmas has supported some of Gilligan's assertions but not others. Most studies have found that both men and women use care-based reasoning *and* justice-based reasoning. Thus, Gilligan's argument that people make moral decisions according to both abstract principles of justice and principles of compassion and care is an important contribution to our knowledge about moral reasoning. Studies have not confirmed, however, that women are more compassionate than men (Tavris, 1993). One study concluded that a person's level of education is a better predictor of moral reasoning than gender (Walker, 1989).

In sum, Gilligan's research highlights the need to be aware of the possibility that some theories and conclusions about human development may not be equally applicable to males and females (Gilligan, Ward, and Taylor, 1988).

Although the sociological and psychological perspectives we have examined often have been based on different assumptions and have reached somewhat different conclusions, an important theme emerges from these models of cognitive and moral development—through the process of socialization, people learn how to take into account other people's perspectives.

AGENTS OF SOCIALIZATION

***Agents of socialization* are the persons, groups, or institutions that teach us what we need to know in order to participate in society.** We are exposed to many agents of socialization throughout our lifetime. Here, we look at the most pervasive ones in childhood—the family, the school, peer groups, and the mass media.

THE FAMILY

The family is the most important agent of socialization in all societies. As the discussions of child abuse have demonstrated, the initial love and nurturance we receive from our families are essential to normal cognitive, emotional, and physical development. Furthermore, our parents are our first teachers. From infancy, our families transmit cultural and social values to us. As discussed in Chapter 14 ("Families and Intimate Relationships"), families in Canada vary in size and structure. Some families consist of two parents and their biological children, while others consist of a single parent and one or more children. Still other families reflect changing patterns of divorce and remarriage, and an increasing number are comprised of same-sex partners and their children.

Functionalists emphasize that families are the primary locus for the procreation and socialization of children in industrialized nations. Most of us form an emerging sense of self and acquire most of our beliefs and values within the family context. We also learn about culture (including language, attitudes, beliefs, values, and norms) as it is interpreted by our parents and other relatives.

Families also are the primary source of emotional support. Ideally, people receive love, understanding, security, acceptance, intimacy, and companionship within families (Benokraitis, 1993:6). The role of the family is especially significant because young children have little social experience beyond its boundaries; they have no basis for comparison or for evaluating how they are treated by their own family.

To a large extent, the family is where we acquire our specific social position in society. From birth, we are a part of the specific ethnic, economic, religious, and regional subcultural grouping of our family. Studies show that families socialize their children somewhat differently based on ethnicity and class (Kohn, 1977, 1990; Kurian, 1991; Harrison et al., 1990). Sociologist Melvin Kohn (1977, 1990) has suggested that social class (as measured by parental occupation) is one of the strongest influences on what and how parents teach their children. On the one hand, working-class parents who are closely supervised and expected to follow orders at work typically emphasize to their children the importance of obedience and conformity. On the other hand, parents from the middle and professional classes, who have more freedom and flexibility at work, tend to give their children more freedom to make their own decisions and to be creative. Kohn concluded that differences in the parents' occupations were a better predictor of child-rearing practices than was social class itself.

Conflict theorists stress that socialization reproduces the class structure in the next generation. Children in poor and low-income families, for example, may be unintentionally socialized to believe that acquiring an education and aspiring to lofty ambitions are pointless because of existing economic conditions in the family (Ballantine, 1993). By contrast, middle- and upper-income families typically instill ideas of monetary and social success in children, as well as emphasizing the necessity of thinking and behaving in "socially acceptable" ways.

THE SCHOOL

It is evident that with the rapid expansion of specialized technical and scientific knowledge and the increased time children are in educational settings, schools continue to play an enormous role in the socialization of young people. For many people, the formal education process is an undertaking that lasts up to twenty years.

As the number of one-parent families and families in which both parents work outside the home has increased dramatically, the number of children in daycare and preschool programs also has grown rapidly. Currently, more than 50 percent of Canadian preschool children are in daycare, either in private homes or institutional settings, and this percentage continues to climb (Burke et al., 1994). Studies generally have found that daycare and preschool programs may have a positive effect on the overall socialization of children (Silverstein, 1991). These programs are especially beneficial for children from less-advantaged backgrounds in that they provide these children with valuable learning experiences not available at home. Many scholars also have found that children from all social classes and family backgrounds may benefit from learning experiences in early childhood education programs that they have not had in their homes.

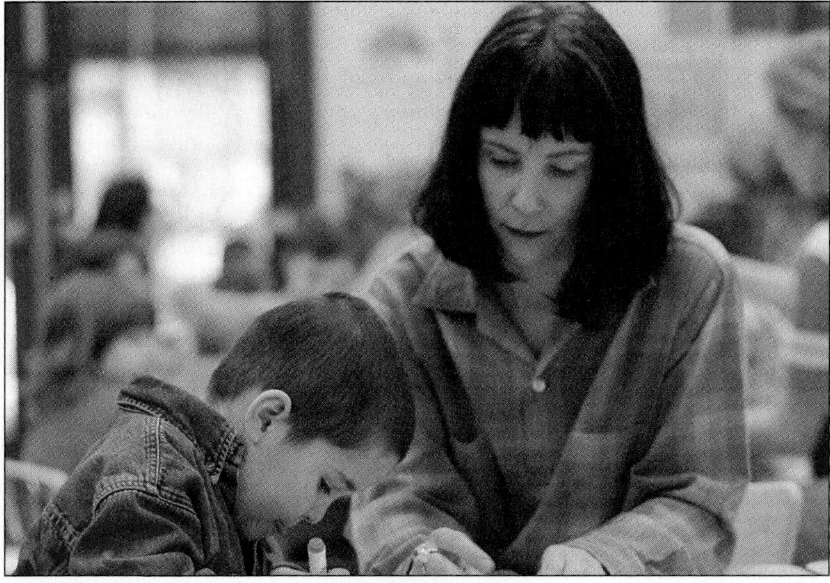

Daycare centres have become important agents of socialization for increasing numbers of children. Today, more than 50 percent of all Canadian preschool children are in daycare of one kind or another.

Schools teach specific knowledge and skills; they also have a profound effect on children's self-image, beliefs, and values. As children enter school for the first time, they are evaluated and systematically compared with one another by the teacher. A permanent, official record is kept of each child's personal behaviour and academic activities. From a functionalist perspective, schools are responsible for (1) socialization, or teaching students to be productive members of society, (2) transmission of culture, (3) social control and personal development, and (4) the selection, training, and placement of individuals on different rungs in the society (Ballantine, 1993).

In contrast, conflict theorists assert that students have different experiences in the school system, depending on their social class, ethnic background, the neighbourhood in which they live, their gender, and other factors. According to sociologist Stephen Richer (1988), much of what happens in school amounts to teaching a *hidden curriculum* in which children learn to value competition, materialism, work over play, obedience to authority, and attentiveness. Richer's study of Ottawa classrooms indicated that success in school may be based more on students' ability to conform to the hidden curriculum than their mastery of the formal curriculum. Therefore, students who are destined for leadership or elite positions acquire different skills and knowledge than those who will enter working-class and middle-class occupations (see Cookson and Persell, 1985).

Regardless of whether we see the educational process as positive or negative in its consequences, schools clearly do expand children's horizons beyond their family and immediate neighbourhood. In public school settings, children may become aware of the diverse cultures represented in Canada today. With this increased awareness, some people gain more tolerance for diversity; others begin to see those who are not just like them as people to be avoided at all costs. In elite, private school settings, students often only associate with others from similar backgrounds. As a participant in one study stated, "You don't go to private school just for your education. You go there to be separated from ordinary people" (Ostrander, 1984:85). In another study, students at elite boarding schools noted that networking with other people from similar backgrounds is a primary benefit of

The pleasure of hanging out with friends is not the only attraction of adolescent peer groups. Peer groups contribute to our sense of belonging and self-worth regardless of our age.

attending such schools (Cookson and Persell, 1985).

PEER GROUPS

As soon as we are old enough to have acquaintances outside the home, most of us begin to rely heavily on peer groups as a source of information and approval about social behaviour (Lips, 1989). A ***peer group* is a group of people who are linked by common interests, equal social position, and (usually) similar age.** In early childhood, peer groups often are composed of classmates in daycare, preschool, and elementary school. In adolescence, these groups typically are people with similar interests and social activities. As adults, we continue to participate in peer groups of people with whom we share common interests and comparable occupations, income, or social position.

Peer groups function as agents of socialization by contributing to our sense of "belonging" and our feelings of self-worth. Unlike families and schools, peer groups provide children and adolescents with some degree of freedom from parents and other authority figures (Corsaro, 1992). Peer groups also teach and reinforce cultural norms while providing important information about "acceptable" behaviour. The peer group is both a product of culture and one of its major transmitters (Elkin and Handel, 1989). In other words, peer groups simultaneously reflect the larger culture and serve as a conduit for passing on culture to young people.

Is there such a thing as "peer pressure"? Individuals must *earn* their acceptance with their peers by conforming to a given group's *own* norms, attitudes, speech patterns, and dress codes. When we conform to our peer group's expectations, we are rewarded; if we do not conform, we may be ridiculed or even expelled from the group. Conforming to the demands of peers frequently places children and adolescents at cross purposes with their parents. Sociologist William A. Corsaro (1992) notes that children experience strong peer pressure even during their preschool years. For example, children frequently are under pressure to obtain certain valued material possessions (such as toys, videotapes, clothing, or athletic shoes); they then pass this pressure on to their parents through emotional pleas to purchase the desired items. In this way, adult caregivers learn about the latest fads and fashions from children, and they may contribute to the peer culture by purchasing the items desired by the children (Corsaro, 1992). Socialization is not a one-way process from adults to children. Adults also learn from children.

MASS MEDIA

An agent of socialization that has a profound impact on both children and adults is the *mass media*, comprised of large-scale organizations that use print or electronic means (such as radio, television, or film) to communicate with large numbers of people. The media function as socializing agents in several ways: (1) they inform us about events, (2) they introduce us to a wide variety of people, (3) they provide an array of viewpoints on current issues, (4) they make us aware of products and services that, if we purchase them, supposedly will help us to be accepted by others, and (5) they entertain us by providing the opportunity to live vicariously (through other people's experiences). Although most of us take for granted that the media play an important part in contemporary socialization, we frequently underestimate the enormous influence this agent of socialization may have on children's attitudes and behaviour.

Recent estimates indicate that close to 100 percent of Canadian households have at least one television. Canadian viewers watch an average of 3.4 hours of television per day. Generally, women watch more television than men, and the elderly watch more than younger people. The amount of time people spend watching television, however, is high for all groups, including children and teenagers (Young, 1990). What effect does all of this "boob tube" viewing have on its viewers, especially the younger viewers?

Parents, educators, social scientists, and public officials have widely debated the consequences of watching television on young people. Television has been praised for offering numerous positive experiences to children. Some scholars suggest that television (when used wisely) can enhance children's development by improving their language abilities, concept formation skills, and reading skills and by encouraging prosocial development (Winn, 1985).

As Box 4.3 notes, however, television (and other media) not only can educate us about important social problems such as child abuse but also can sensationalize and trivialize such problems. Television also has been blamed for its potentially harmful effects, such as the declining rate of literacy, rampant consumerism, and increases in aggressive behaviour and in violent crime (Biagi, 1994).

Two theories have been most widely used to explain how televised consumerism and violence affect children's behaviour. The ***observational learning theory*** **states that we observe the behaviour of another person and repeat the behaviour ourselves.** Critics of television violence insist that viewing television violence contributes to aggressive and in some cases criminal behaviour of children and adolescents. For example:

> In October 1989, two Burlington, Ontario, teenagers murdered a 44-year-old department store executive in a gas-station kiosk as part of a bungled robbery. They killed the man by hitting him over the head more than 30 times with a fire extinguisher. During their trial, on charges of first-degree murder, one of the youths told the court that they thought they could knock the victim unconscious with a couple of blows. "We've seen it in the movies all the time. You hit him once and down he goes." (Jenish, 1992:40)

The ***catharsis theory*** presents an entirely different view of the effects of television viewing. Proponents of this view suggest that **violence in the media provides a catharsis. An individual's frustrations are relieved or purged through vicarious participation in media violence.** Alfred Hitchcock's defense of his own television program illustrates the catharsis position:

> One of the television's greatest contributions is that it brought murder back into the home

BOX 4.3 SOCIOLOGY AND MEDIA

Public Awareness of Child Abuse

The media have the potential for socializing large numbers of people regarding important social problems such as child abuse. In 1992, for example, *Scared Silent: Exposing and Ending Child Abuse*, hosted by Oprah Winfrey, was the first nonnews event ever to be shown simultaneously on prime-time television by three broadcast networks. The documentary, viewed by over 45 million people in North America, generated more than 112,000 telephone calls on the National Child Abuse Hotline in the five days following its airing. Local child abuse organizations also received thousands of calls.

The purpose of the film was to inform people about the nature of child abuse and to encourage them "to break the silence, to speak out, and stop further pain, injury, and death" (Rowe, 1992:11). Information about sexual, physical, and emotional abuse was provided through six true stories of intergenerational child abuse in which the victims and the perpetrators both were profiled.

Public response to this documentary shows the media's immense capacity for bringing important issues such as child abuse to our attention and providing us with information about how to prevent such violence and neglect. Arnold Shapiro, producer and co-writer of the program, noted that the "undeniable reality is that *all* of us are victims of child abuse because we all pay the price in dealing with victims who act out their rage and hurt on society. What begins as a family crisis becomes society's burden, expense and responsibility" (Rowe, 1992:11).

In addition to providing information about social problems, the media also have the potential for sensationalizing (and perhaps trivializing) cases of alleged child abuse. In 1993, for example, Michael Jackson, the superstar pop singer, was accused of sexual abuse by a 13-year-old boy. Instantly, the media sensationalized the case under the guise of providing the public with the latest information. The allegations regarding Jackson were discussed on network news programs and television talk shows. Among the new found (although temporary) celebrities to be interviewed were two of Michael Jackson's other young male friends, whose interviews received global coverage. They defended Jackson and stated that the accusations against him were false. They were instant celebrities because they each admitted that they had slept with Jackson without being molested (McGuigan, 1993).

When other stories such as this arise in the future, the media no doubt will continue to publicize (and perhaps sensationalize) allegations of child abuse because it is assumed that this is what people want to read about and see. As psychologist Melvin Guyer noted, "The public gets to be puritanical and voyeuristic at the same time. Their attitude is basically, 'This food is terrible, and there's not enough of it' " (Corliss, 1993:56).

Do highly publicized cases make us more aware of child abuse, or do they trivialize the genuine problem of child abuse in our society?

> where it belongs. Seeing a murder on TV can be good therapy. It can help work off one's frustrations. If you haven't any frustrations, the commercials will give you some. (quoted in Hagedorn, 1983:85)

Most children who watch television and movies have seen thousands of people injured or killed as a result of the aggressive behaviour of others. For example, Sylvester Stallone, Bruce Willis, and Arnold Schwarzenegger make violence look fun, sexy, and profitable. To illustrate, add up the body counts in the movies listed in Table 4.1.

A person who saw all of these movies would have witnessed at least 611 killings, plus hundreds of other nonfatal injuries. The increasing level of violence in movies has been mirrored in virtually all the mass media. For example, taboos about what can be said and what can be

Despite the apparent rise in televised violence, concern about the effects of violence on television are not new. This sardonic "Odd Bodkins" cartoon was published in 1964. (SOURCE: Dan O'Neill, *The Collective Unconscience of Odd Bodkins.* Glide Publications, 330 Ellis St., San Francisco, CA 94102. Copyright © 1973 by Chronicle Publishing Company.)

shown on television newscasts are collapsing. From automobile accidents, to homicide victims, to airplane crash survivors, no scene is too grisly or traumatic not to show viewers in the name of "the ratings."

Psychologist Albert Bandura (1973, 1986) found evidence that seeing violent behaviour desensitizes people to violence and may increase aggressive behaviour (at least temporarily) in some individuals. He concluded that desensitization is the result of *disinhibition*, a process that occurs when an individual's inhibitions or constraints are weakened by observing the behaviour of a model. For example, crosscultural studies have shown that children who watch numerous violent films display more aggressive behaviour than do those who were not exposed to the films (see Eron, 1987; Huesmann et al., 1987).

What we see on television and in films influences many different types of conduct. For example, the Walt Disney Company removed a scene from one of its films, *The Program* (in which several drunken college football players lie in the middle of a busy road to prove their toughness), after three American teenagers apparently attempted to imitate the scene. Unlike the movie hero, they did not walk away unharmed: one was killed, another paralyzed, and the third critically injured when hit by passing vehicles.

Undoubtedly, not only television and films but all mass media—including newspapers, magazines, radio, musical recordings, and books—socialize us in ways that we may or may not be consciously aware of. Figure 4.3 contrasts television "reality" with its real-life counterpart.

TABLE 4.1

Violence in Movies: Recent Body Counts

Film	Body Count
Last Action Hero	57 dead
Terminator 2	27 dead
Total Recall	76 dead
Robocop 2	81 dead
Rambo III	106 dead
Die Hard II	264 dead

Sources: Prothrow-Stith, 1991:30; and *Time*, 1993:22.

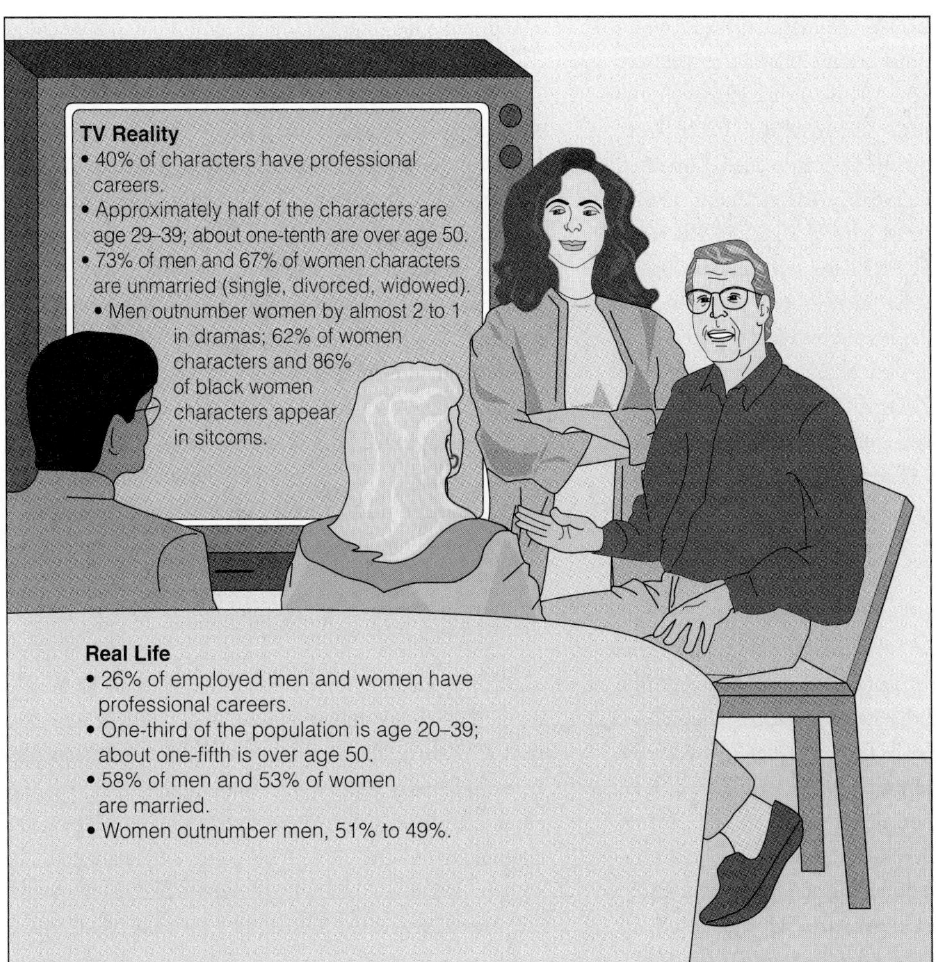

TV Reality
• 40% of characters have professional careers.
• Approximately half of the characters are age 29–39; about one-tenth are over age 50.
• 73% of men and 67% of women characters are unmarried (single, divorced, widowed).
• Men outnumber women by almost 2 to 1 in dramas; 62% of women characters and 86% of black women characters appear in sitcoms.
Real Life
• 26% of employed men and women have professional careers.
• One-third of the population is age 20–39; about one-fifth is over age 50.
• 58% of men and 53% of women are married.
• Women outnumber men, 51% to 49%.

FIGURE 4.3

Socialization through Television

GENDER SOCIALIZATION

If you had only one child, would you prefer for the child to be a boy or a girl? In most societies, parents prefer male children to female children based on cultural assumptions about sex differences (Steinbacher and Holmes, 1987). Is this because males inherently are superior to females? Not at all; parents acquire these gender preferences through ***gender socialization*, the aspect of socialization that contains specific messages and practices concerning the nature of being female or male in a specific group or society.** Gender socialization is important in determining what we *think* the "preferred" sex of a child should be and in influencing our beliefs about acceptable behaviours for males and females.

In some families, gender socialization starts before birth. Parents who learn the sex of the fetus through ultrasound or amniocentesis often purchase colour-coded and gender-typed clothes, toys, and nursery decorations in anticipation of their daughter's or son's arrival. After birth, parents may respond differently toward male and female infants; they often play more roughly with boys and talk more lovingly to girls (Eccles, Jacobs, and Harold, 1990). Throughout childhood and adolescence, boys and girls typically are assigned different household chores and given different privileges (such as how late they may stay out at night).

When we look at the relationship between gender socialization and social class, the picture becomes more complex. While some studies have found less rigid gender stereotyping in higher-income families (Seegmiller, Suter, and Duviant, 1980; Brooks-Gunn, 1986), others have found more (Bardwell, Cochran, and Walker, 1986). One study found that higher-income families are more likely than low-income families to give "male-oriented" toys (which develop visual–spatial and problem-solving skills) to children of *both* sexes (Serbin et al., 1990). Working-class families tend to adhere to more rigid gender expectations than middle-class families (Canter and Ageton, 1984; Brooks-Gunn, 1986).

Like the family, schools, peer groups, and the media contribute to our gender socialization. From kindergarten through college, teachers and peers reward gender-appropriate attitudes and behaviour. Sports reinforce traditional gender roles through a rigid division of events into male and female categories. The media also are a powerful source of gender socialization; from an early age, children's books, television programs, movies, and music provide subtle and not-so-subtle messages about "masculine" and "feminine" behaviour. Gender socialization is discussed in more depth in Chapter 10 ("Sex and Gender").

Scholars may be hesitant to point out differences in socialization practices among diverse ethnic and social class groupings because such differences typically have been interpreted by others to be a sign of inadequate (or inferior) socialization practices. Beliefs as to what is, and what is not, proper treatment of children vary from society to society around the world, as Box 4.4 explains.

SOCIALIZATION THROUGH THE LIFE COURSE

Why is socialization a lifelong process? Throughout our lives, we continue to learn. Each time we experience a change in status (such as becoming a university student or getting married), we learn a new set of rules, roles, and relationships. Even before we achieve a new status, we often participate in ***anticipatory socialization*—the process by which knowledge and skills are learned for future roles.** Many societies organize social experience according to age. Some have distinct *rites of passage,* based on age or other factors, that publicly dramatize and validate changes in a person's status. In Canada and other industrialized societies, the most common categories of age are infancy, childhood, adolescence, and adulthood (often subdivided into young adulthood, middle adulthood, and older adulthood).

INFANCY AND CHILDHOOD

Some social scientists believe that a child's sense of self is formed at a very early age and that it is difficult to change this view later in life. Interactionists emphasize that during infancy and early childhood, family support and guidance are crucial to a child's developing self-concept. In some families, children are provided with emotional warmth, feelings of mutual trust, and a sense of security. These families come closer to our ideal cultural belief that childhood should be a time of carefree play, safety, and freedom from economic, political, and sexual responsibilities. However, other families reflect the discrepancy between cultural ideals and reality—children grow up in a setting characterized by fear, danger, and risks that are created by parental neglect, emotional abuse, or premature economic and sexual demands (Knudsen, 1992). Violations of the incest taboo by a parent are an example of such abuse. Consider the experiences of Mariah, a victim of childhood incest, as she described them to a psychotherapist:

> When I was really little, I remember feeling a bit confused about my father. There were times when he'd hug and kiss me and tell me how special I was to him, and then there'd be other

BOX 4.4 SOCIOLOGY IN GLOBAL PERSPECTIVE

Child Abuse in Asia

How child abuse is viewed may depend on cultural values. Based on North American values, child treatment in many other nations would be defined as abuse. For example, child labour conditions in India are considered intolerable in Canada. In India, children as young as 4 may work at looms weaving carpets for up to fifteen hours a day (without a break) to earn 5 rupees or about 15 cents. In North America, this practice would be viewed as parents "selling" their children as "child labour." In Pakistan and Bangladesh, 4- to 8-year-old boys are sold as jockeys in camel races in Saudi Arabia. Bangladeshi girls ages 8 to 10 are auctioned into sexual slavery in the slums of Karachi. Many parents consider a pretty daughter or a strong son to be a financial asset. If a girl is considered to be pretty, she is sold into prostitution; if not, she is sold to a sweatshop. Overall, millions of children live in virtual slavery, toiling for little or no pay in brothels, fields, factories, mines, or stone quarries, or as domestic help.

In crosscultural terms, is this child abuse? In societies where poverty is endemic, the answer to this question is intertwined with the constant struggle with hunger. Cultural relativism, as discussed in Chapter 3, tells us that we should view this question from viewpoints other than our own. Some critics of child labour state that it perpetuates poverty, illiteracy, adult unemployment, and overpopulation. Others point out, however, that not working often means not eating. For example, Mohammad Sohrab, age 8, carries heavy loads of fish, rice, and vegetables from the market to shoppers' homes in Dhaka, the capital of Bangladesh, to earn the equivalent of $1 a day to support himself and his four younger brothers and sisters. Sohrab describes his life: "My mother is ill, my father is dead. The family will starve if I don't work. I hate to work. I want to play like other children."

Although all countries of South Asia have enacted laws against child labour, actual enforcement is lax. The ban on child labour does not cover agriculture, where about 75 percent of the child labourers are found. Officials in India estimate 20 million children, most of them below the age of 13, work in hazardous industries such as making matches, quarrying, tanning, firework-making, and carpet weaving. Child rights activists estimate the figure is closer to 55 million.

External pressures against child labour in Asia are rising. The United Nations International Labor Organization is attempting to force governments to acknowledge that child labour is a problem in their countries. Canadian child rights activist Craig Kielburger, founder of the group called Free The Children, toured Asia to speak out against child labour. This 13-year-old schoolboy from Ontario met with the prime minister in order to convince Mr. Chrétien that Canada should make a long-term commitment to protect child rights and ensure that goods imported by Canada were not the products of child labour and exploitation. Canada is exploring the possibility of "confronting the menace of child labour" by imposing restrictions on selected imports of products made by children.

Sources: Based on Moorhead, 1992; Schmetzer, 1992; Joshi, 1993; Hauser, 1996)

times when he'd call me "Dummy" or "Stupid Head" and yell at me to do household chores. …

When I was 6 years old my dad started touching me differently. … [He abused her sexually.] I was too afraid to turn my head to look at his face. He didn't speak to me while this happened. After he stopped moving he would gently say, "You're my special girl." So I figured that even though I was scared and uncomfortable, this was just something daddies do with their special daughters. Even so, I

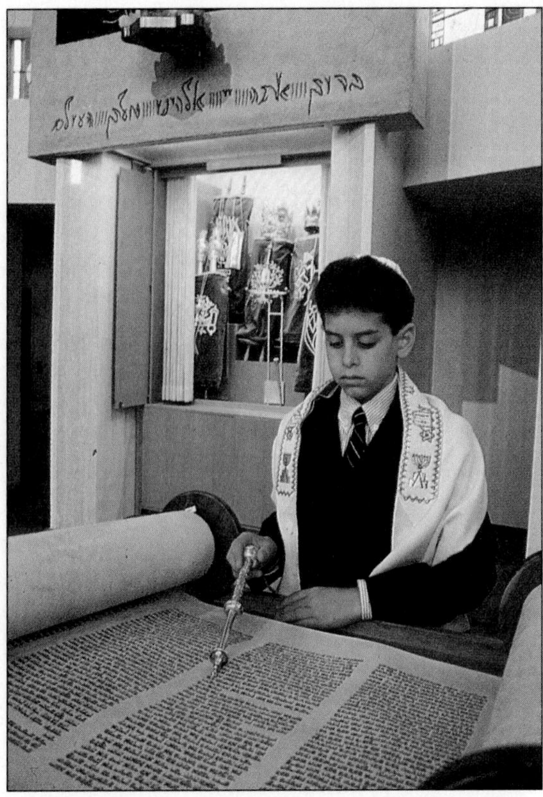

A Jewish boy's bar mitzvah is an outward manifestation of his attainment of the age of religious responsibility. Many societies have similar rites of passage that publicly dramatize changes in a person's status.

became very wary around my father. (quoted in Roth, 1993:2)

The father's incestuous conduct continued until Mariah left home at the age of 18 (Roth, 1993:6).

Abused children often experience low self-esteem, an inability to trust others, feelings of isolation and powerlessness, and denial of their feelings. However, the manner in which parental abuse affects children's ongoing development is subject to much debate and uncertainty. For example, some scholars and therapists assert that the intergenerational hypothesis—the idea that abused children will become abusive parents—is valid, but others have found little support for this hypothesis (Knudsen, 1992).

ADOLESCENCE

In industrialized societies, the adolescent (or teenage) years represent a buffer between childhood and adulthood. In Canada, no specific rites of passage exist to mark children's move into adulthood; therefore, young people have to pursue their own routes to self-identity and adulthood (Gilmore, 1990). Anticipatory socialization often is associated with adolescence, whereby many young people spend much of their time planning or being educated for future roles they hope to occupy. However, other adolescents (such as 15- and 16-year-old mothers) may have to plunge into adult responsibilities at this time. Adolescence often is characterized by emotional and social unrest. In the process of developing their own identities, some young people come into conflict with parents, teachers, and other authority figures who attempt to restrict their freedom. Adolescents also may find themselves caught between the demands of adulthood and their own lack of financial independence and experience in the job market. The experiences of individuals during adolescence vary according to their ethnicity, class, and gender. Based on their family's economic situation, some young people move directly into the adult world of work. However, those from upper-middle- and upper-class families may extend adolescence into their late twenties or early thirties by attending graduate or professional school and then receiving additional advice and financial support from their parents as they start their own families, careers, or businesses.

ADULTHOOD

One of the major differences between child and adult socialization is the degree of freedom of choice. If young adults are able to support themselves financially, they gain the ability to make more choices about their own lives. In early adulthood (usually until about age 40), people work toward their own goals of creating meaningful relationships with others, finding employment, and seeking personal fulfillment. Of course, young adults continue to be socialized by their parents, teachers, peers, and the media, but they also learn new attitudes and behaviours. For example, when we marry or have children, we learn new roles as partners or parents. Adults often learn about fads and fashions in clothing, music, and language from their children. Parents in one study indicated that they had learned new attitudes and behaviours about drug use, sexuality, sports, leisure, and ethnic issues from their university-aged children (Peters, 1985).

Workplace, or *occupational, socialization* is one of the most important types of adult socialization. Sociologist Wilbert Moore (1968) divided occupational socialization into four phases: (1) career choice, (2) anticipatory socialization (learning different aspects of the occupation before entering it), (3) conditioning and commitment (learning the "ups" and "downs" of the occupation and remaining committed to it), and (4) continuous commitment (remaining committed to the work even when problems or other alternatives may arise). This type of socialization tends to be most intense immediately after a person makes the transition from school to the workplace; however, this process continues throughout our years of employment. In the late 1990s, many people will experience continuous workplace socialization as a result of individuals having more than one career in their lifetime (Lefrançois, 1993).

Between the ages of 40 and 60, people enter middle adulthood, and many begin to compare their accomplishments with their earlier expectations. This is the point at which people either decide that they have reached their goals or recognize that they have attained as much as they are likely to achieve.

In older adulthood, some people are quite happy and content; others are not. Erik Erikson noted that difficult changes in adult attitudes and behaviour occur in the last years of life when people experience decreased physical ability, lower prestige, and the prospect of death. Older adults in industrialized societies have experienced ***social devaluation*—wherein a person or group is considered to have less social value than other groups.** Social devaluation is especially acute when people are leaving roles that have defined their sense of social identity and provided them with meaningful activity (Achenbaum, 1978).

It is important to note that not everyone goes through passages or stages of a life course at the same age. Sociologist Alice Rossi (1980) suggests that human experience is much more diverse than life course models suggest. She also points out that young people growing up today live in a different world, with a different set of opportunities and problems, than did the young people of previous generations (Epstein, 1988). Rossi further suggests that women's and men's experiences are not identical throughout the life course and that the life course of women today is remarkably different from that of their mothers and grandmothers because of changing societal roles and expectations. Life course patterns are strongly influenced by ethnicity and social class as well.

RESOCIALIZATION

***Resocialization* is the process of learning a new and different set of attitudes, values, and behaviours from those in one's previous background and experience.** It may be voluntary or involuntary. In either case, people undergo changes that are much more rapid and pervasive than the gradual adaptations that socialization usually involves.

VOLUNTARY RESOCIALIZATION

Resocialization is voluntary when we assume a new status (such as becoming a student, an employee, or a retiree) of our own free will. Sometimes, voluntary resocialization involves medical or psychological treatment or religious conversion, in which case the person's existing attitudes,

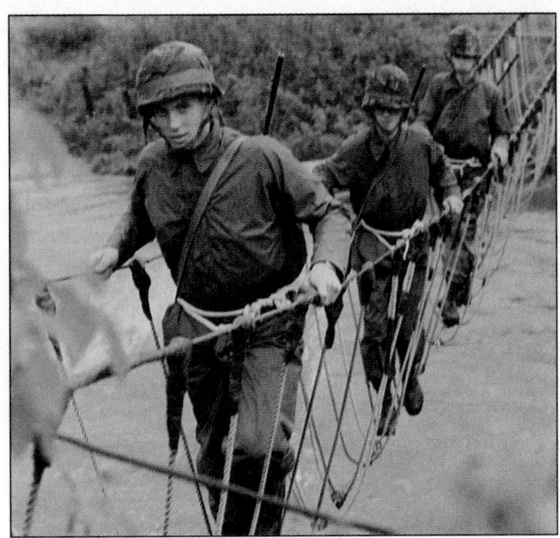

Recruits in this Canadian Armed Forces training exercise are resocialized through extensive, gruelling military drills and manoeuvres. What types of new values and behaviours do you think they are expected to learn?

beliefs, and behaviours must undergo strenuous modification to a new regime and a new way of life. For example, resocialization for adult survivors of emotional/physical child abuse includes extensive therapy in order to form new patterns of thinking and action, somewhat like Alcoholics Anonymous and its twelve-step program that has become the basis for many other programs dealing with addictive behaviour (Parrish, 1990).

INVOLUNTARY RESOCIALIZATION

Involuntary resocialization occurs against a person's wishes and generally takes place within a ***total institution*—a place where people are isolated from the rest of society for a set period of time and come under the control of the officials who run the institution** (Goffman, 1961a). Military boot camps, jails and prisons, concentration camps, and some mental hospitals are total institutions. In these settings, people are totally stripped of their former selves—or depersonalized—through a *degradation ceremony* (Goffman, 1961a). Inmates entering prison, for example, are required to strip, shower, and wear assigned institutional clothing. In the process, they are searched, weighed, fingerprinted, photographed, and given no privacy even in showers and restrooms. Their official identification becomes not a name but a number. In this abrupt break from their former existence, they must leave behind their personal possessions and their family and friends. The depersonalization process continues as they are required to obey rigid rules and to conform to their new environment.

After stripping people of their former identities, the institution attempts to build a more compliant person. A system of rewards and punishments (such as providing or withholding cigarettes and television or exercise privileges) encourages conformity to institutional norms. Some individuals may be rehabilitated; others become angry and hostile toward the system that has taken away their freedom. While the assumed purpose of involuntary resocialization is to reform persons so that they will conform to societal standards of conduct after their release, the ability of total institutions to modify offenders' behaviour in a meaningful manner has been widely questioned. In many prisons, for example, inmates may conform to the norms of the prison or of other inmates, but little relationship exists between those norms and the laws of society.

SOCIALIZATION IN THE TWENTY-FIRST CENTURY

In the twenty-first century, the family is likely to remain the institution that most fundamentally shapes and nurtures personal values and self-identity. However, parents increasingly may feel overburdened by this responsibility, especially without societal support—such as high-quality, affordable child care—and more education in parenting skills. Some analysts have suggested that there will be an increase in known cases of child abuse and in the number of children who experience delayed psychosocial development, learning difficulties, and emotional and behavioural problems. They attribute these increases to the dramatic changes occurring in the size, structure, and economic stability of families.

A central value-oriented issue facing parents and teachers as they attempt to socialize children is the growing dominance of the mass media and other forms of technology. For example, interactive television and computer networking systems will enable children to experience many things outside their own homes and schools and to communicate regularly with people around the world. If futurists are correct in predicting that ideas and information and access to them will be the basis for personal, business, and political advancement in the twenty-first century, people without access to computers and other information technology will become even more disadvantaged. This prediction raises important issues about the effects of social inequality on the socialization process. As we approach the twenty-first century, socialization—a lifelong learning process—can no longer be viewed as a "glance in the rearview mirror" or a reaction to some previous experience. With the rapid pace of technological change, we must not only learn about the past but learn how to anticipate—and consider the consequences of—the future (Westrum, 1991).

CHAPTER REVIEW

Socialization is the lifelong process through which individuals acquire their self-identity and learn the physical, mental, and social skills needed for survival in society. The kind of person we become depends greatly on what we learn during our formative years from our surrounding social groups and social environment.

- As individual human beings, we have unique identities, personalities, and relationships with others. Individuals are born with some of their unique physical characteristics; other characteristics and traits are gained during the socialization process.
- Each of us is a product of two forces: (1) heredity, referred to as "nature," and (2) the social environment, referred to as "nurture." While biology dictates our physical makeup, the social environment largely determines how we develop and behave. Social contact is essential in developing a self, or self-concept, which represents an individual's perceptions and feelings of being a distinct or separate person. Much of what we think about ourselves is gained from our interactions with others and from what we perceive others think of us.
- Charles Horton Cooley developed the image of the looking-glass self to explain how people see themselves through the perceptions of others. Our initial sense of self is typically based on how families perceive and treat us.
- George Herbert Mead linked the idea of self-concept to role playing and to learning the rules of social interaction. According to Mead, the self is divided into the "I" and the "me." The "I" represents the spontaneous and unique traits of each person. The "me" represents the internalized attitudes and demands of other members of society.
- While Cooley's and Mead's theories are sociologically based, other theories have a more psychological basis. Sigmund Freud divided the self into three interrelated forces (id,

ego, and superego); when a person is well adjusted, the three forces act in balance. Erik Erikson identified eight psychosocial stages of development, each of which is accompanied by a potential crisis or conflict in a person's social environment. Jean Piaget identified four cognitive stages of development; at each stage, children's activities are governed by how they understand the world around them.

- Lawrence Kohlberg classified moral development into six stages; certain levels of cognitive development are essential before corresponding levels of moral reasoning may occur. Carol Gilligan suggested that there are male–female differences regarding morality and identified three stages in female moral development.
- The people, groups, and institutions that teach us what we need to know in order to participate in society are called agents of socialization. The agents include the family, schools, peer groups, the media, the workplace, and so on.
- Our families, which transmit cultural and social values to us, are the most important agents of socialization in all societies: (1) procreating and socializing children, (2) providing emotional support, and (3) assigning social position.
- Schools are another key agent of socialization; they not only teach knowledge and skills but also deeply influence the self-image, beliefs, and values of children. Peer groups contribute to our sense of belonging and self-worth; they teach and reinforce cultural norms; and they are a key source of information about acceptable behaviour.
- The media function as socializing agents by (1) informing us about world events, (2) introducing us to a wide variety of people, and (3) providing an opportunity to live vicariously through other people's experiences.
- Social class, gender, and ethnicity are all determining factors in socialization practices. Social class is one of the strongest influences on what and how parents teach their children. Gender socialization strongly influences what we believe to be acceptable behaviour for females and males.
- Socialization is ongoing throughout the life course. We learn knowledge and skills for future roles through anticipatory socialization. Parents are socialized by their own children, and adults learn through workplace socialization. Resocialization is the process of learning new attitudes, values, and behaviours, either voluntarily or involuntarily.

KEY TERMS

agents of socialization **142**
anticipatory socialization **150**
catharsis theory **146**
ego **137**
gender socialization **149**
generalized other **134**
id **137**
looking-glass self **132**
observational learning theory **146**
peer group **142**
resocialization **153**
role-taking **133**
self-concept **131**
significant other **134**
social devaluation **153**
socialization **124**
sociobiology **127**
superego **137**
total institution **154**

QUESTIONS FOR ANALYSIS AND UNDERSTANDING

1. How much does biology, or genetics, influence a child's personality and behaviour?
2. What is the source of an individual's self-concept?
3. Why are there various theories of human development? Do any of the theories contradict other ones?
4. How can individuals who were abused as children be resocialized toward nurturing behaviour as adults?

QUESTIONS FOR CRITICAL THINKING

1. Consider the concept of the looking-glass self. How do you think others perceive you? Do you think most people perceive you correctly?
2. What are your "I" traits? What are your "me" traits? Which ones are stronger?
3. What are some different ways you might study the effect of toys on the socialization of children? How could you isolate the toy variable from other variables that influence children's socialization?
4. Is the attempted rehabilitation of criminal offenders—through boot camp programs, for example—a form of socialization or resocialization?

SUGGESTED READINGS

These books provide in-depth information on various aspects of socialization:

Carol Gilligan. *In a Different Voice: Psychological Theory and Women's Development.* Cambridge, Mass.: Harvard University Press, 1982.

Erving Goffman. *Asylums: Essays on the Social Situation of Mental Patients and Other Inmates.* Chicago: Aldine, 1961.

Bernice Lott. *Women's Lives: Themes and Variations in Gender Learning* (2nd ed.). Pacific Grove, Cal.: Brooks/Cole, 1994.

George Herbert Mead. *Mind, Self, and Society from the Standpoint of a Social Behaviouralist.* Charles W. Morris (ed.). Chicago: University of Chicago Press, 1962; orig. pub. 1934.

To find out more about the problem of child abuse:

Sylvia Fraser. *My Father's House: A Memoir of Incest and Healing.* Toronto: Doubleday, 1987.

Connie Guberman and Margie Wolfe (eds.). *No Safe Place: Violence Against Women and Children.* Toronto: Women's Press, 1985.

Dean D. Knudsen. *Child Maltreatment: Emerging Perspectives.* Dix Hills, N.Y.: General Hall, 1992.

David A. Wolfe. *Child Abuse: Implications for Child Development and Psychopathology.* Newbury Park, Cal.: Sage, 1987.

Chapter 5

SOCIAL STRUCTURE AND INTERACTION IN EVERYDAY LIFE

Social Structure: The Macrolevel Perspective

Components of Social Structure

Status

Roles

Groups

Social Institutions

Societies: Changes in Social Structure

Mechanical and Organic Solidarity

Gemeinschaft *and* Gesellschaft

Social Structure and Homelessness

Social Interaction: The Microlevel Perspective

Social Interaction and Meaning

The Social Construction of Reality

Ethnomethodology

Dramaturgical Analysis

The Sociology of Emotions

Nonverbal Communication

Changing Social Structure and Interaction in the Twenty-First Century

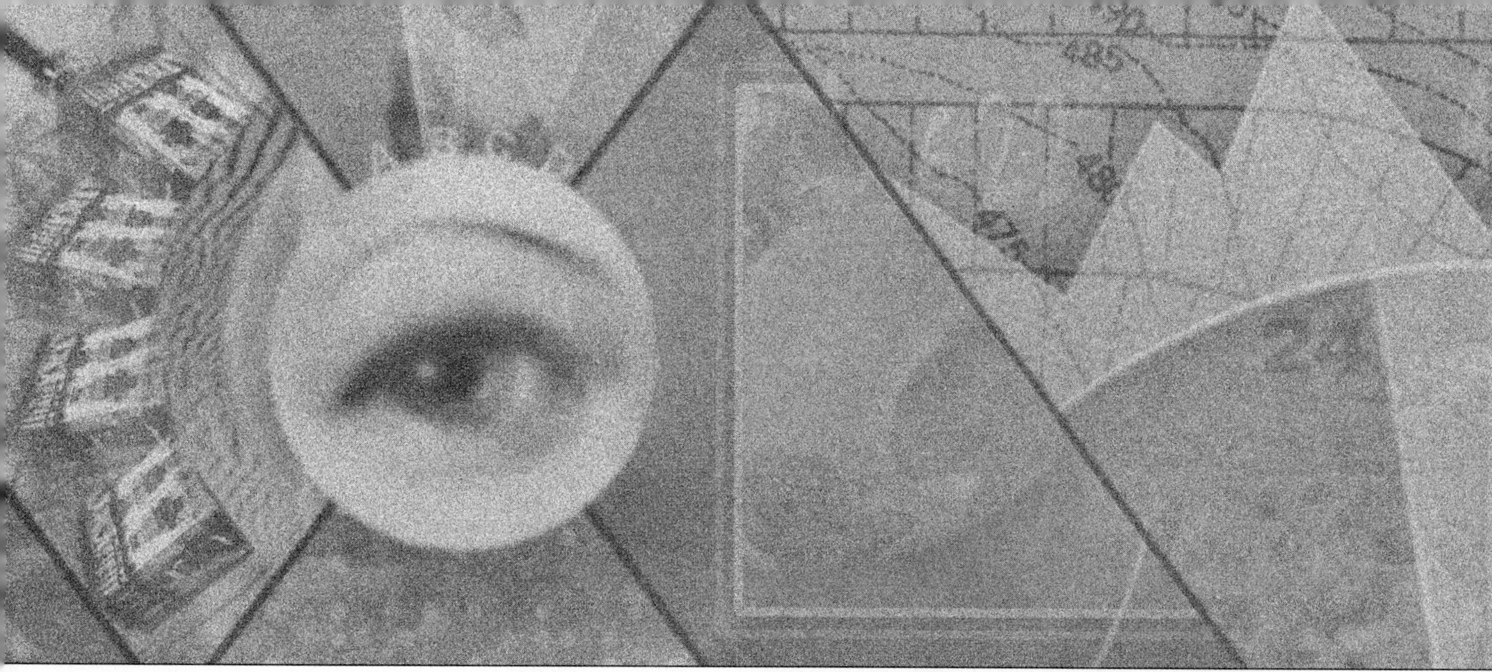

Twenty-year-old David moved to Vancouver looking for a job. He rented a bachelor apartment in the downtown core with most of his savings and set out to find a job. One evening he was robbed of all his belongings, including his life savings, which as meagre as they were, he had not bothered to deposit in the bank. David found himself without a place to stay, with his dreams in ruins. When he was interviewed, David had been homeless for three months. He was unable to go out to look for work. Demoralized, victimized, and too embarrassed to go to his family for assistance, he spent his days wandering the downtown areas of Vancouver. David describes his "drift" into homelessness:

> When I walked across the threshold of the shelter it was like someone had just hit me in the guts. I felt sick to my stomach. I'd read about homeless people but they were different, bums, and that wasn't me. Now, here I was just like them, one of them, a bum. It was a shock that has left me numb ever since. You know you're at rock bottom but you just can't shake it. You're homeless, a homeless person, that's your identity now, everything else just drops away. It's like the rest of your life never happened ... It'll probably take me months more to get out of this rut. I know I will, but it gets harder every day, you get used to it. (O'Reilly-Fleming, 1993:56)

David's activities reflect a specific pattern of social behaviour. All activities in life—including living in shelters, hostels, or "on the streets"—are social in nature. Homeless persons and domiciled persons (those with homes) live in social worlds that have predictable patterns of social interaction. ***Social interaction* is the process by which people act toward or respond to other people** and is the foundation for all relationships and groups in society. In this chapter, we look at the relationship between social structure and social interaction. In the process, homelessness is used as an example of how social problems occur and may be perpetuated within social structures and patterns of interaction.

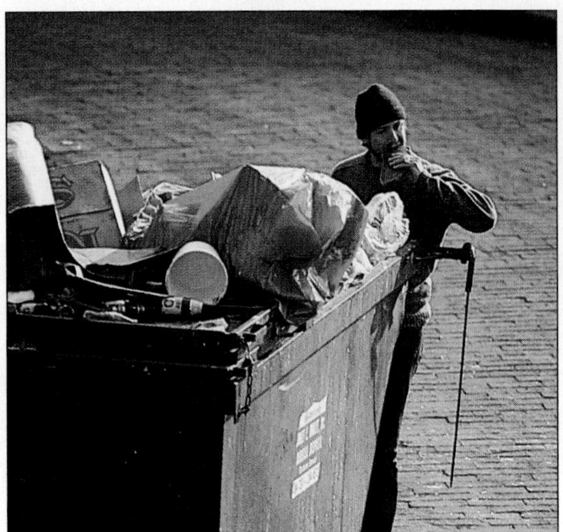

Although eating from a dumpster may appear to be an individual act, this behaviour—like all other activities in life—is affected by the larger patterns of social interaction and social structure found in society.

***Social structure* is the stable pattern of social relationships that exist within a particular group or society.** This structure is essential for the survival of society and for the well-being of individuals because it provides a social web of familial support and social relationships that connects each of us to the larger society. Many homeless people have lost this vital linkage. As a result, they often experience a loss of personal dignity and a sense of moral worth because of their "homeless" condition (Snow and Anderson, 1993).

Who are the homeless? Before reading on, take the quiz on homelessness in Box 5.1. The profile of Canada's homeless has changed dramatically in recent years. Our stereotypical image of "hobo," "bum," or "rubby" is far from an accurate reflection of our country's homeless population. Now included in the category of homeless are people who have never before had to depend on charity for food, clothing, and a roof over their heads. A major change is the sheer numbers of women that have been rendered homeless due to the severe housing crisis in major North American cities in the 1980s (Harman, 1989). Social workers have also tracked an increase in the number of single parents, again mostly women, with small children (Corelli, 1996).

Homeless people come from all walks of life. They live in cities, suburbs, and rural areas (Baum and Burnes, 1993). Contrary to popular myths, most of the homeless are not on the streets by choice or because they were deinstitutionalized by mental hospitals. A sizeable proportion of Canadian street people is made up of Native Canadian Indians, Inuit, and first-generation immigrants (Krotz, 1980). Not all of the homeless are unemployed. Many homeless people hold full- or part-time jobs but earn too little to afford housing (Shogren, 1993).

QUESTIONS AND ISSUES

What are the components of social structure?

How do societies maintain social solidarity and continue to function in times of rapid change?

Why do societies have shared patterns of social interaction?

How are daily interactions similar to being onstage?

Do positive changes in society occur through individual or institutional efforts?

SOCIAL STRUCTURE: THE MACROLEVEL PERSPECTIVE

Social structure provides the framework within which we interact with others. This framework is an orderly, fixed arrangement of parts that together comprise the whole group or society (see Figure 5.1). At the macrolevel, the social structure of a society has several essential elements: social institutions, groups, statuses, roles, and norms.

Functional theorists emphasize that social structure is essential because it creates order and predictability in a society (Parsons, 1951). Social

BOX 5.1 SOCIOLOGY AND EVERYDAY LIFE

How Much Do You Know About Homelessness?

TRUE	FALSE	
T	F	1. Many homeless people choose to be homeless.
T	F	2. There are an estimated 20,000 homeless people in Canada.
T	F	3. All homeless people are unemployed.
T	F	4. Most homeless people are mentally ill.
T	F	5. Older men over the age of 50 make up most of Canada's homeless population.
T	F	6. Most homeless people are alcoholics and substance abusers.
T	F	7. A large number of homeless people are dangerous.
T	F	8. Homelessness is a relatively new social problem in Canada.
T	F	9. One out of every four homeless people is a child.
T	F	10. Some homeless people have attended university.

Answers on page 162

structure also is important for our human development. As we saw in Chapter 4, we develop a self-concept as we learn the attitudes, values, and behaviours of the people around us. When these attitudes and values are part of a predictable structure, it is easier to develop that self-concept.

Social structure gives us the ability to interpret the social situations we encounter. For example, we expect our families to care for us, our schools to educate us, and our police to protect us. When our circumstances change dramatically, most of us feel an acute sense of anxiety because we do not know what to expect or what is expected of us. For example, newly homeless individuals may feel disoriented because they do not know how to function in their new setting. The person is likely to wonder, "How will I survive on the streets?" "Where do I go to get help?" "Should I stay at a shelter?" and "Where can I get a job?" Social structure helps people make sense out of their environment, even when they find themselves on the streets. As sociologists David Snow and Leon Anderson (1993) suggest in their study of unattached, homeless men, survival strategies are the product of the interplay between the resourcefulness and ingenuity of the homeless and local political and ecological constraints.

In addition to providing a map for our encounters with others, social structure may limit our options and place us in arbitrary categories not of our own choosing. Conflict theorists maintain that there is more to the social structure than is readily visible and that we must explore the deeper, underlying structures that determine social relations in a society. Karl Marx suggested that the way economic production is organized is the most important structural aspect of any society. In capitalistic societies where a few people control the labour of many, the social structure reflects a system of relationships of domination among cate-

BOX 5.1

Answers to the Sociology Quiz on Homelessness

TRUE	FALSE	
T	**F**	1. *False.* This myth is an example of "blaming the victim." Homelessness is a result of a number of social factors—namely, welfare cuts, an inadequate supply of low-rent housing, mass layoffs, and diminishing psychiatric services.
T	**F**	2. *False.* There are an estimated 20,000 homeless people in Montreal alone. It is very difficult to get an accurate estimate of the total number of homeless individuals in Canada given the transient status of these individuals.
T	**F**	3. *False.* Many homeless people are among the working poor. Minimum-wage jobs do not pay enough for an individual to support a family and pay for housing.
T	**F**	4. *False.* Approximately 20 percent of homeless people are mentally ill.
T	**F**	5. *False.* Single men over the age of 50 no longer represent the majority of the homeless. Homeless males now tend to be in their twenties and thirties. There has also been a dramatic increase in the number of single parents, mostly women, with small children.
T	**F**	6. *False.* Most homeless people are not heavy drug users. Estimates suggest that about one-fourth of the homeless are substance abusers. Many of these individuals are also mentally ill.
T	**F**	7. *False.* Most homeless people are among the least threatening members of society. They often are the victims, not the perpetrators, of crime.
T	**F**	8. *False.* Homelessness has always existed in Canada. However, the number of homeless people has increased or decreased with fluctuations in the economy. In the past, individuals without homes were referred to as "hobos," "tramps," and "vagrants"; today, they are lumped into the category of "homeless."
T	F	9. *True.* Children also comprise the fastest growing category of homeless people in North America.
T	F	10. *True.* Some homeless people have attended university. Some have even gone to graduate school. Many have completed high school.

Sources: Based on Harman, 1989; Liebow, 1993, O'Reilly-Fleming, 1993; and Corelli, 1996.

gories of people (for example, owner–worker and employer–employee).

Social structure creates boundaries that define which persons or groups will be the "insiders" and which will be the "outsiders." ***Social marginality* is the state of being part insider and part outsider in the social structure.** Sociologist Robert Park (1928) coined this term to refer to persons (such as immigrants) who simultaneously share the life and traditions of two distinct groups. Social marginality results in stigmatization. A ***stigma* is any physical or social attribute or sign that so devalues a person's social identity that it disqualifies that person from full social acceptance** (Goffman, 1963b). A convicted criminal, wearing a prison uniform, is an example of a person who has been stigmatized; the uniform says that the person has done something wrong and

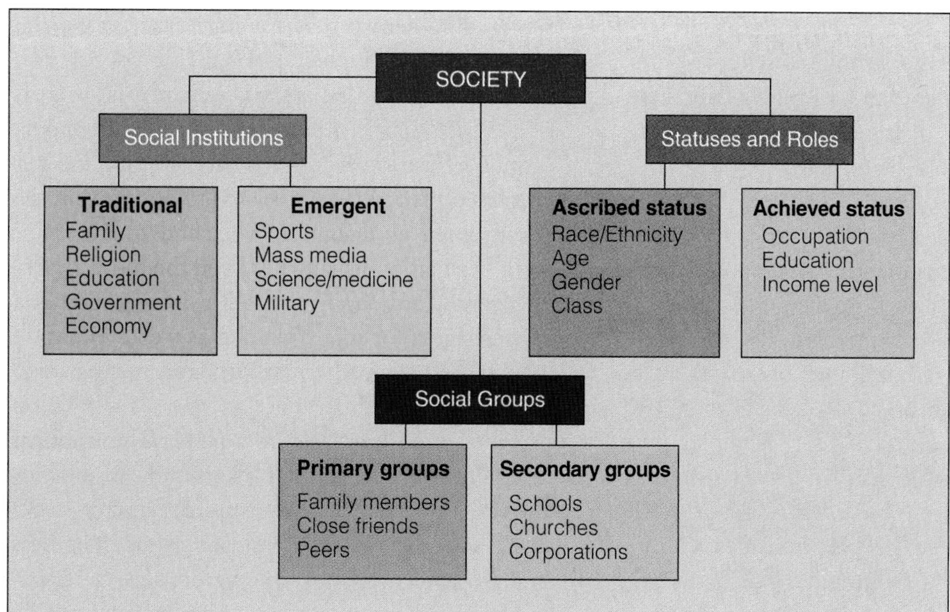

FIGURE 5.1

Social Structure Framework

should not be allowed unsupervised outside the prison walls.

COMPONENTS OF SOCIAL STRUCTURE

The social structure of a society includes its social positions, the relationships among those positions, and the kinds of resources attached to each of the positions. Social structure also includes all of the groups that make up society and the relationships among those groups (Smelser, 1988). We begin by examining the social positions that are closest to the individual.

STATUS

A ***status*** **is a socially defined position in a group or society characterized by certain expectations, rights, and duties.** Statuses exist independently of the specific people occupying them (Linton, 1936); the statuses of professional athlete, rock musician, professor, university student, and homeless person all exist exclusive of the specific individuals who occupy these social positions. For example, although thousands of new students arrive on university campuses each year to occupy the status of first-year student, the status of university student and the expectations attached to that position have remained relatively unchanged for most of the twentieth century.

Does the term *status* refer only to high-level positions in society? No, not in a sociological sense. Although many people equate the term *status* with high levels of prestige, sociologists use it to refer to *all* socially defined positions—high- and low-rank. For example, both the position of director of the Department of Health and Welfare in Ottawa, and that of a homeless person who is paid about five dollars a week (plus bed and board) to clean up the dining room at a homeless shelter are social statuses (see Snow and Anderson, 1993).

Take a moment to answer the question, "Who am I?" To determine who you are, you must think about your social identity, which is derived from the statuses you occupy and is based on your status set. A ***status set*** **is comprised of all the statuses that a person occupies at a given time.** For example, Marie may be a psychologist, a professor, a wife, a mother, a Catholic, a school volunteer, an Alberta resident, and a French Canadian. All of these socially defined positions constitute her status set.

ASCRIBED AND ACHIEVED STATUS Statuses are distinguished by the manner in which we acquire them. An ***ascribed status*** **is a social position conferred at birth or received involuntarily later in life,** based on attributes over which the individual has little or no control, such as ethnicity, age, and gender. Marie, for example, is a female born to French Canadian parents; she was assigned these statuses at birth. An ***achieved status*** **is a social position a person assumes voluntarily as a result of personal choice, merit, or direct effort.** Achieved statuses (such as occupation, education, and income) are thought to be gained as a result of personal ability or successful competition. Most occupational positions in modern societies are achieved statuses. For instance, Marie voluntarily assumed the statuses of psychologist, professor, wife, mother, and school volunteer. Not all achieved statuses, however, are positions most people would want to attain; being a criminal, a drug addict, or a homeless person, for example, is a negative achieved status.

Ascribed statuses have a significant influence on the achieved statuses we occupy. Ethnicity, gender, and age affect each person's opportunity to acquire certain achieved statuses. Those who are privileged by their positive ascribed statuses are more likely to achieve the more prestigious positions in a society. Those who are disadvantaged by their ascribed statuses may more easily acquire negative achieved statuses.

MASTER STATUS If we occupy many different statuses, how can we determine which is the most important? Sociologist Everett Hughes has stated that societies resolve this ambiguity by determining master statuses. A ***master status*** **is the most important status a person occupies;** it dominates all of the individual's other statuses and is the overriding ingredient in determining a person's general social position (Hughes, 1945). Being poor or rich is a master status that influences many other areas of life, including health, education, and life opportunities. Historically, the most common master statuses for women have related to positions in the family, such as daughter, wife, and mother. For men, occupation usually has been the most important status, although occupation increasingly is a master status for many women as well. "What do you do?" is one of the first questions many people ask when meeting one another. Occupation provides important clues to a person's educational level, income, and family background. An individual's ethnicity also may constitute a master status in a society in which dominant group members single out members of other groups as "inferior" on the basis of real or alleged physical, cultural, or nationality characteristics (see Feagin and Feagin, 1993).

Master statuses are vital to how we view ourselves, how we are seen by others, and how we interact with others. Beverley McLachlin is both a Supreme Court justice and a mother. Which is her master status? Can you imagine how she would react if attorneys arguing a case before the Supreme Court of Canada treated her as if she were a mother rather than a justice? Lawyers wisely use "Honourable Madam Justice" as her master status and act accordingly.

Master statuses confer high or low levels of personal worth and dignity on people. Those are not characteristics that we inherently possess; they are derived from the statuses we occupy. For those who have no residence, being a homeless person readily becomes a master status regardless of the person's other attributes. Homelessness is a stigmatized master status that confers disrepute on its occupant because domiciled people often believe a homeless person has a "character flaw." The circumstances under which someone becomes homeless determine the extent to which that person is stigmatized. For example, individuals who become homeless as a result of natural disasters (such as a hurricane or a brush fire) are not seen as causing their homelessness or as being a

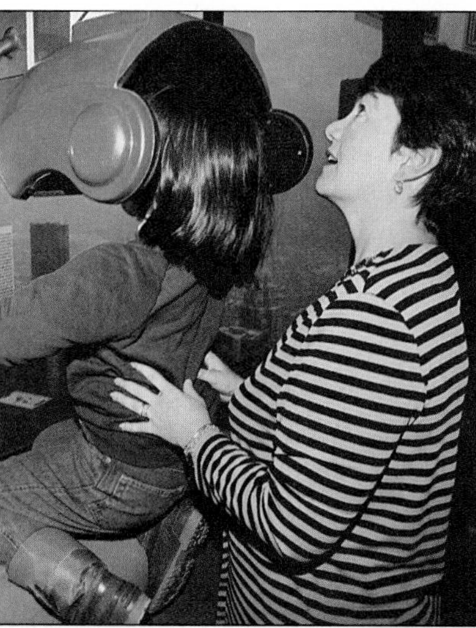

How does your perception of Sheila Copps's master status change when you compare these photographs?

threat to the community. Thus, they are less likely to be stigmatized. However, in cases in which homeless persons are viewed as the cause of their own problems, they are more likely to be stigmatized and marginalized by others. Snow and Anderson (1993:199) observed the effects of homelessness as a master status:

> It was late afternoon, and the homeless were congregated in front of [the Salvation Army shelter] for dinner. A school bus approached that was packed with Anglo junior high school students being bused from an eastside barrio school to their upper-middle and upper-class homes in the city's northwest neighborhoods. As the bus rolled by, a fusillade of coins came flying out the windows, as the students made obscene gestures and shouted, "Get a job." Some of the homeless gestured back, some scrambled for the scattered coins—mostly pennies—others angrily threw the coins at the bus, and a few seemed oblivious to the encounter. For the passing junior high schoolers, the exchange was harmless fun, a way to work off the restless energy built up in school; but for the homeless it was a stark reminder of their stigmatized status and of the extent to which they are the objects of negative attention.

STATUS SYMBOLS When people are proud of a particular social status they occupy, they often choose to use visible means to let others know about their position. ***Status symbols*** **are material signs that inform others of a person's specific status.** For example, just as wearing a wedding ring proclaims that a person is married, owning a Rolls-Royce announces that one has "made it." In North American society, people who have "made it" frequently want symbols to inform others of their accomplishments.

In our daily lives, status symbols both announce our statuses and facilitate our interactions with others. For example, medical students wear white lab jackets with plastic name tags identifying their status to all hospital personnel, patients, or visitors they encounter (Haas and Shaffir, 1995). The length and colour of a person's uniform in a hospital indicates the individual's status within the medical centre. Physicians wear longer white coats, medical students wear shorter white coats, laboratory technicians wear short blue coats, and so forth.

Status symbols for the domiciled and for the homeless may have different meanings. Among affluent persons, a full shopping cart in the grocery store and bags of merchandise from expensive department stores indicate a lofty financial position. By contrast, among the homeless, bulging shopping bags and overloaded grocery carts suggest a completely different status. Carts and bags are essential to street life; there is no other place to keep things, as shown by this description of Tamara, a homeless woman from a city in Ontario:

> I don't care much for the police. I get in fights with them a lot. They tell me to "move along" and I tell them I have a right to be there just like anyone else. One time in the subway station I was carrying two shopping bags full of clothes. I hadn't had a chance to wash them in a while, so they were a little dirty, but they were my clothes! A policeman, or it may have been a company cop, grabbed my bags and put them in the garbage. I put up a fight and told him to give them back to me. We ended up wrestling on the platform! Finally, he let his hands fall to his sides and I again demanded that he give me back my things. He went over to the garbage and took them out. (Harman, 1989:95)

For homeless women and men, possessions are not status symbols so much as they are a link with the past, a hope for the future, and a potential source of immediate cash. As Snow and Anderson (1993: 147) note, selling personal possessions is not uncommon among most social classes; members of the working and middle classes hold garage sales, and those in the upper classes have estate sales. However, when homeless persons sell their personal possessions, they do so to meet their immediate needs, not because they want to "clean house."

ROLES

Role is the dynamic aspect of a status. While we *occupy* a status, we *play* a role (Linton, 1936). **A *role* is a set of behavioural expectations associated with a given status.** For example, a carpenter (employee) hired to remodel a kitchen is not expected to sit down uninvited and join the family (employer) for dinner.

***Role expectation* is a group's or society's definition of the way a specific role *ought* to be played.** By contrast, ***role performance* is how a person *actually* plays the role.** Role performance does not always match role expectation. Some statuses have role expectations that are highly specific, such as that of surgeon or university professor. Other statuses, such as friend or significant other, have less structured expectations. The role expectations tied to the status of student are more specific than those for being a friend. Role expectations typically are based on a range of acceptable behaviour rather than on strictly defined standards.

Our roles are relational (or complementary); that is, they are defined in the context of roles performed by others. We can play the role of student because someone else fulfills the role of professor. Conversely, to perform the role of professor, the teacher must have one or more students.

Role ambiguity occurs when the expectations associated with a role are unclear. For example, it is not always clear when the provider–dependent aspect of the parent–child relationship ends. Should it end at age 18 or 21? When a person is no longer in school? Different people will answer these questions differently depending on their experiences and socialization, as well as on the parents' financial capability and psychological willingness to continue contributing to the welfare of their adult children.

Role ambiguity frequently occurs when a status is relatively new or is unacknowledged by a society. In Canada, such statuses include single parent, domestic partner (in the case of gay or lesbian couples), and homeless person. On one hand, for the homeless, the role of "street person" and the activities associated with it (such as day labour, panhandling, or scavenging) are devalued by society. On the other hand, some of the skills needed by the homeless for day-to-day survival (such as "street smarts") are valued in other contexts, such as a "wilderness survival course," where a person must be able to live in an unfamiliar and sometimes harsh environment with very limited resources. Such problems of role ambiguity often are closely linked with role conflict and role strain.

ROLE CONFLICT AND ROLE STRAIN Most people occupy a number of statuses, each of which has numerous role expectations attached. For example, Charles is a student who attends morning classes at the university, and he is an employee at a fast-food restaurant where he works from 3:00 to 10:00 P.M. He also is Stephanie's boyfriend, and she would like to see him more often. On December 7, Charles has a final exam at 7:00 P.M., when he is supposed to be working. Meanwhile, Stephanie is pressuring him to take her to a movie. To top it off, his mother calls, asking him to fly home because his father is going to have emergency surgery. How can Charles be in all of these places at once? Such experiences of role conflict can be overwhelming.

Role conflict **occurs when incompatible role demands are placed on a person by two or more statuses held at the same time.** When role conflict occurs, we may feel pulled in different directions. To deal with this problem, we may *prioritize* our roles and first complete the one we consider to be most important. Or we may *compartmentalize* our lives and "insulate" our various roles (Merton, 1968). That is, we may perform the activities linked to one role for part of the day, and then engage in the activities associated with another role in some other time period or elsewhere. For example, under routine circumstances, Charles would fulfill his student role for part of the day and his employee role for another part of the day. In his current situation, however, he is unable to compartmentalize his roles.

Role conflict may occur as a result of changing statuses and roles in society. Research has found that women who engage in behaviour that is gender-typed as "masculine" tend to have higher rates of role conflict than those who engage in traditional "feminine" behaviour (Basow, 1992). According to sociologist Tracey Watson (1987), role conflict sometimes can be attributed not to the roles themselves but to the pressures people feel when they do not fit into culturally prescribed roles. In her study of women athletes in college sports programs, Watson found role conflict in the traditionally incongruent identities of being a woman and being an athlete. Even though the women athletes in her study wore makeup and presented a conventional image when they were not on the basketball court, their peers in school still saw them as "female jocks," thus leading to role conflict.

Whereas role conflict occurs between two or more statuses (such as being homeless and being a temporary employee of a social services agency), role strain takes place within one status. ***Role strain*** **occurs when incompatible demands are built into a single status that a person occupies** (Goode, 1960). For example, many women experience role strain in the labour force because they hold jobs that are "less satisfying and more stressful than men's jobs since they involve less money, less prestige, fewer job openings, more career roadblocks, and so forth" (Basow, 1992:192). Similarly, married women may experience more role strain than married men, because of work overload, marital inequality with their spouse, exclusive parenting responsibilities, unclear expectations, and lack of emotional support.

Recent social changes may have increased role strain in men. In the family, men's traditional position of dominance has eroded as more women have entered the paid labour force and demanded more assistance in child-rearing and homemaking responsibilities. High rates of unemployment have produced problems for many men whose major role in the past was centred on their occupation.

Sexual orientation, age, and occupation frequently are associated with role strain. Lesbians and gay men often experience role strain because of the pressures associated with having an identity heavily stigmatized by the dominant cultural group (Basow, 1992). Women in their thirties may experience the highest levels of role strain; they face a large amount of stress in terms of role demands and conflicting work and family expectations (Basow, 1992). Dentists, psychiatrists, and police officers have been found to experience high levels of occupation-related role strain, which may result in suicide.

Caseworkers for the homeless also experience high levels of role strain. Stephanie Golden (1992: 61–62) found that caseworkers frequently became overwhelmed by the incompatible demands built into their role:

> I called an agency for someone and the man to whom I spoke was shockingly snide. He treated me like an idiot for asking a perfectly reasonable question. When I snapped back that he had no business talking to me like that, he was startled, for he had assumed that I was the [homeless] client and had responded in his habitual mode. He then apologized a little, enough at any rate to demonstrate that he was not always overbearing and offensive. Indeed, I dealt with many concerned caseworkers trying to help and even some who saw their clients as persons like themselves. But their job was brutalizing; those who lasted in it often had to become insensitive to some extent just to survive. The enormity of the suffering they saw and the awareness of how limited even their best efforts were in alleviating it, plus the frustration of repeatedly failing to counteract people's self-destructive behaviour, demoralized them too.

For caseworkers, as well as for many other people, performing the roles attached to even one status often produces a high degree of stress.

Individuals frequently distance themselves from a role they find extremely stressful or otherwise problematic. *Role distancing* occurs when people consciously foster the impression of a lack of commitment or attachment to a particular role and merely go through the motions of role performance (Goffman, 1961b). People use distancing techniques when they do not want others to take them as the "self" implied in a particular role, especially if they think the role is "beneath them." While Charles is working in the fast-food restaurant, for example, he does not want people to think of him as a "loser in a dead-end job." He wants them to view him as a college student who is working there just to "pick up a few bucks" until he graduates. When customers from the university come in, Charles talks to them about what courses they are taking, what they are majoring in, and what professors they have. He does not discuss whether the bacon cheeseburger is better than the chili burger. When Charles is really involved in role distancing, he tells his friends that he "works there but wouldn't eat there."

Role distancing is most likely to occur when people find themselves in roles in which the social identities implied are inconsistent with how they think of themselves or how they want to be viewed by others. Snow and Anderson found that role distancing was common among the homeless—especially the recently homeless. One 24-year-old man who had been homeless for only a few weeks commented:

> I'm not like the other guys who hang down at the Sally [Salvation Army]. If you want to know about the street people, I can tell you about them; but you can't really learn about street people from studying me, because I'm different. (1993:349)

These individuals often pursue employment opportunities in an effort to exit their role as a homeless person as quickly as possible.

ROLE EXIT ***Role exit*** **occurs when people disengage from social roles that have been central to their self-identity** (Ebaugh, 1988). Sociologist Helen Rose Fuchs Ebaugh studied this process by interviewing ex-convicts, ex-nuns, retirees, divorced men and women, and others who had exited voluntarily from significant social roles. According to Ebaugh, role exit occurs in four stages. The first stage is doubt, in which people experience frustration or burnout when they reflect on their existing roles. The second stage involves a search for alternatives; here, people may take a leave of absence from their work or temporarily separate from their marriage partner. The third stage is the turning point at which people realize that they must take some final action, such as quitting their job or getting a divorce. The fourth and final stage involves the creation of a new identity.

Exiting the "homeless" role often is very difficult. The longer a person remains on the streets, the more difficult it becomes to exit this role. Personal resources diminish over time. Personal possessions (such as tools, clothes, and identification papers) often are stolen, lost, sold, or pawned. Work experience and skills become outdated, and physical disabilities that prevent individuals from working are likely to develop on the streets. Consider Jacqueline Wisemen's comments on the sometimes unrealistic demands placed on homeless people to exit their role:

> The goal of all institutions on the loop is to get the charge "back into the system" or "back into the real world." But, what is the concept that the professional has of these men's real world? To them rehabilitation means: "Getting a job, a room, and maintaining sobriety." … How is he to get the job, the room, and avoid old drinking friends? How can he change from a today-oriented, no-social-stake person to a future-oriented, middle-class person? … How is he to feel a *part* of this middle-class society? (1979:229)

Of course, many of the homeless do not beat the odds and exit this role. Instead, they shift their focus from role exiting to survival on the streets.

GROUPS

Groups are another important component of social structure. To sociologists, a ***social group* consists of two or more people who interact frequently and share a common identity and a feeling of interdependence.** Throughout our lives, most of us participate in groups, from our families and childhood friends, to our university classes, to our work and community organizations, and even to society.

Primary and secondary groups are the two basic types of social groups. A ***primary group* is a small, less specialized group in which members engage in face-to-face, emotion-based interactions over an extended period of time.** Typically, primary groups include our family, close friends, and school or work-related peer groups. By contrast, a ***secondary group* is a larger, more specialized group in which members engage in more impersonal, goal-oriented relationships for a limited period of time.** Schools, churches, the military, and corporations are examples of secondary groups. In secondary groups, people have few, if any, emotional ties to one another. Instead, they come together for some specific, practical purpose, such as getting a degree or a pay cheque. Secondary groups are more specialized than primary ones; individuals relate to one another in terms of specific roles (such as professor and student) and more limited activities (such as course-related endeavours).

Social solidarity, or cohesion, relates to a group's ability to maintain itself in the face of obstacles. Social solidarity exists when social bonds, attractions, or other forces hold members of a group in interaction over a period of time (Jary and Jary, 1991). For example, if a local church is destroyed by fire and congregation members still worship together, in a makeshift setting, then they have a high degree of social solidarity.

Many of us build social networks from our personal friends in primary groups and our acquaintances in secondary groups. A ***social network* is a series of social relationships that link an individual to others.** Social networks work differently for men and women, for different ethnic groups, and for members of different social classes. Traditionally, visible minorities and women have been excluded from powerful "old-boy" social networks (Kanter, 1977; McPherson and Smith-Lovin, 1982, 1986). At the middle- and upper-class levels, individuals tap social networks to find employment, make business deals, and win political elections. However, social networks typically do not work effectively for poor and

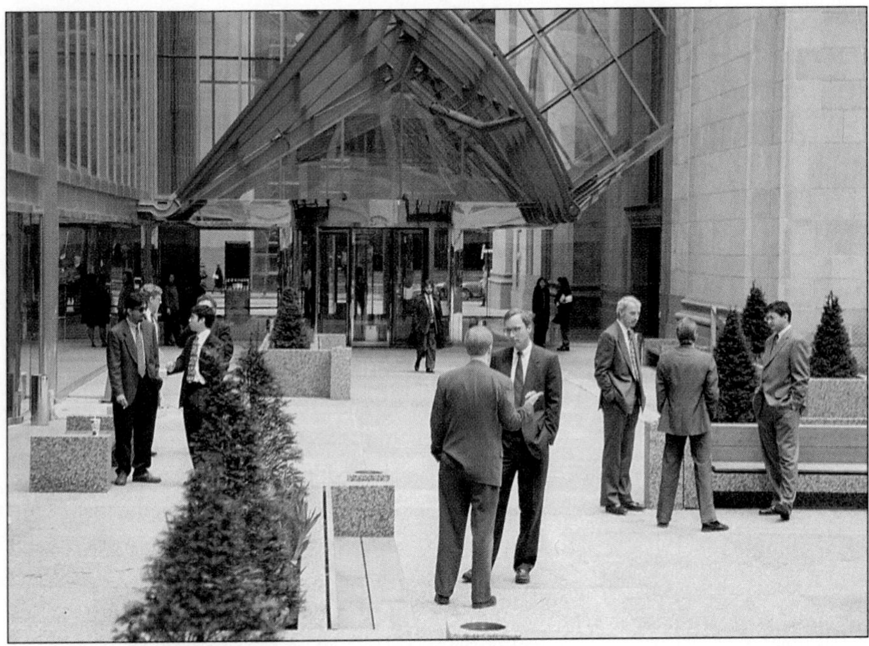

For many years, capitalism has been dominated by powerful "old-boy" social networks.

homeless individuals. Snow and Anderson (1993) found that homeless men have fragile social networks that are plagued with instability. They often do not even know each other's "real" names.

Sociological research on the homeless largely has emphasized the social isolation experienced by people on the streets. Sociologist Peter H. Rossi (1989) found that a high degree of social isolation exists because the homeless are separated from their extended family and former friends. Rossi noted that among the homeless who did have families, most either did not wish to return or believed that they would not be welcome. Most of the avenues for exiting the homeless role and acquiring housing are intertwined with the large-scale, secondary groups that sociologists refer to as formal organizations.

A ***formal organization*** **is a highly structured group formed for the purpose of completing certain tasks or achieving specific goals.** Many of us spend most of our time in formal organizations, such as universities, corporations, or the government. In Chapter 6 ("Groups and Organizations"), we analyze the characteristics of bureaucratic organizations; however, at this point, we should note that these organizations are a very important component of social structure in all industrialized societies. We expect such organizations to educate us, solve our social problems (such as crime and homelessness), and provide work opportunities.

Many formal organizations today have been referred to as "people-processing" organizations. For example, the Salvation Army and other caregiver groups provide services for the homeless and others in need. However, these organizations must work with limited monetary resources and at the same time maintain some control of their clientele. This control is necessary in order to provide their services in an orderly and timely fashion, according to a major at the Salvation Army:

> I'll sleep and feed almost anybody, but such help requires that they be deserving. Some

> people would say I'm cold-hearted, but I rule with an iron hand. I have to because these guys need to respect authority. ... The experience of working with these guys has taught us the necessity of rules in order to avoid problems. (Snow and Anderson, 1993:81)

Because of rules and policies, the "Sally" (as the Salvation Army sometimes is called) tends to close its doors to those who are currently inebriated, are chronic drunks, or are viewed as "troublemakers." Likewise, a number of the women's shelters have restrictions and regulations that some of the women feel deprive them of their personhood. One shelter used to require a compulsory gynecological examination of its residents (Golden, 1992). Another required that the women be out of the building by 7:00 A.M. and not return before 7:00 P.M. Fearful of violence among shelter residents or between residents and staff, many shelters use elaborate questionnaires and interviews to screen out potentially disruptive clients. Those who are supposed to benefit from the services of such shelters often find the experience demeaning and alienating. Nevertheless, organizations such as the Salvation Army and women's shelters do help people within the limited means they have available.

SOCIAL INSTITUTIONS

At the macrolevel of all societies, certain basic activities routinely occur—children are born and socialized, goods and services are produced and distributed, order is preserved, and a sense of purpose is maintained (Aberle et al., 1950; Mack and Bradford, 1979). Social institutions are the means by which these basic needs are met. A ***social institution*** **is a set of organized beliefs and rules that establish how a society will attempt to meet its basic social needs.** In the past, these needs have centred around five basic social institutions: the family, religion, education, the economy, and the government or politics. Today, mass media, sports, science and medicine, and the military also are considered to be social institutions.

What is the difference between a group and a social institution? A group is composed of specific, identifiable people; an institution is a standardized way of doing something. The concept of "family" helps to distinguish between the two. When we talk about your family or my family, we are referring to *a* family. When we refer to *the* family as a social institution, we are talking about ideologies and standardized patterns of behaviour that organize family life. For example, the family as a social institution contains certain statuses organized into well-defined relationships, such as husband–wife, parent–child, brother–sister, and so forth. Specific families do not always conform to these ideologies and behaviour patterns.

Functional theorists emphasize that social institutions exist because they perform five essential tasks:

1. *Replacing members.* Societies and groups must have socially approved ways of replacing members who move away or die. The family provides the structure for legitimated sexual activity—and thus procreation—between adults. The government also may participate in replacing members of society through immigration and other policies.

2. *Teaching new members.* People who are born into a society or move into it must learn the group's values and customs. The family is essential in teaching new members, but other social institutions educate new members as well. Schools pass on knowledge to the young so that they can act as members of society, while religious organizations transmit moral and spiritual values.

3. *Producing, distributing, and consuming goods and services.* All societies must provide and distribute goods and services for their members. The economy is the primary social institution fulfilling this need; the government often is involved in the regulation of economic activity.

4. *Preserving order.* Every group or society must preserve order within its boundaries and protect itself from attack by outsiders. The

Whose interests are served when residential and commercial properties in a city become more upscale? How might functionalists and conflict theorists differ in their interpretations of scenes like this one?

government legitimates the creation of law enforcement agencies to preserve internal order and some form of military for external defense.

5. *Providing and maintaining a sense of purpose.* In order to motivate people to cooperate with one another, a sense of purpose is needed. Some societies encourage the development of a sense of purpose through religious values, moral codes, or patriotism.

Although this list of functional prerequisites is shared by all societies, the institutions in each society perform these tasks in somewhat different ways depending on their specific cultural values and norms.

Conflict theorists agree with functionalists that social institutions originally are organized to meet basic social needs. They do not agree, however, that social institutions work for the common good of everyone in society. The homeless, for example, lack the power and resources to promote their own interests when they are opposed by dominant social groups. From the conflict perspective, social institutions such as the government maintain the privileges of the wealthy and powerful while contributing to the powerlessness of others (see Domhoff, 1983, 1990). For example, government policies in urban areas have benefited some people but exacerbated the problems of others. Urban renewal and transportation projects caused the destruction of low-cost housing and put large numbers of people "on the street" (Katz, 1989). Similarly, the shift in governmental policies toward the mentally ill and welfare recipients resulted in more people struggling—and often failing—to find affordable housing. Meanwhile, many wealthy and privileged bankers, investors, developers, and builders benefited at the expense of the low-income casualties of those policies.

Functionalist and conflict perspectives provide a macrosociological overview because they concentrate on large-scale events and broad social features. For example, sociologists using the macrosociological approach to study the homeless might analyze how social institutions have operated to produce current conditions. By contrast, the interactionist perspective takes a microsociological approach, asking how social institutions affect our daily lives. We will discuss the microlevel perspective in detail later in this chapter.

SOCIETIES: CHANGES IN SOCIAL STRUCTURE

Changes in social structure have a dramatic impact on individuals, groups, and societies. Social arrangements in contemporary societies have grown more complex with the introduction of new technology, changes in values and norms, and the rapidly shrinking "global village." How do societies maintain some degree of social solidarity in the face of such changes? Sociologists Emile Durkheim and Ferdinand Tonnies developed typologies to explain the processes of stability and change in the social structure of societies. A *typology* is a classification scheme containing two or more mutually exclusive categories that are used to compare different kinds of behaviour or types of societies. For example, Durkheim's classification of suicide into four types is a typology that helps to explain why people kill themselves intentionally (see Chapter 2).

MECHANICAL AND ORGANIC SOLIDARITY

As noted in Chapter 1, Emile Durkheim (1933/1893) was concerned with the question, "How do societies manage to hold together?" Durkheim asserted that preindustrial societies were held together by strong traditions and by the members' shared moral beliefs and values. As societies industrialized and developed more specialized economic activities, social solidarity came to be rooted in the members' shared dependence on one another. From Durkheim's perspective, social solidarity derives from a society's social structure, which, in turn, is based on the society's division of labour. *Division of labour* refers to how the various tasks of a society are divided up and performed. People in diverse societies (or in the same society at different points in time) divide their tasks somewhat differently, however, based on their own history, physical environment, and level of technological development.

To explain social change, Durkheim developed a typology that categorized societies as having either mechanical or organic solidarity. ***Mechanical solidarity* refers to the social cohesion in preindustrial societies, in which there is minimal division of labour and people feel united by shared values and common social bonds.** Durkheim used the term *mechanical solidarity* because he believed that people in such preindustrial societies feel a more or less automatic sense of belonging. Social interaction is characterized by face-to-face, intimate, primary-group relationships. Everyone is engaged in similar work, and little specialization is found in the division of labour.

***Organic solidarity* refers to the social cohesion found in industrial societies, in which people perform very specialized tasks and feel united by their mutual dependence.** Durkheim chose the term *organic solidarity* because he believed that individuals in industrial societies come to rely on one another in much the same way that the organs of the human body function interdependently. Social interaction is less personal, more status-oriented, and more focused on specific goals and objectives. People no longer rely on morality or shared values for social solidarity; instead, they are bound together by practical considerations.

GEMEINSCHAFT AND GESELLSCHAFT

Sociologist Ferdinand Tonnies (1855–1936) used the terms *Gemeinschaft* and *Gesellschaft* to characterize the degree of social solidarity and social control found in societies. Tonnies was especially concerned about what happens to social solidarity in a society when a "loss of community" occurs.

The *Gemeinschaft* (guh-MINE-shoft) is a traditional society in which social relationships are based on personal bonds of friendship and kinship and on intergenerational stability.

These relationships are based on ascribed rather than achieved status. In such societies, people have a commitment to the entire group and feel a sense of togetherness. Tonnies used the German term *Gemeinschaft* because it means "commune" or "community"; social solidarity and social control are maintained by the community. Members have a strong sense of belonging, but they also have very limited privacy.

By contrast, the ***Gesellschaft*** **(guh-ZELL-shoft) is a large, urban society in which social bonds are based on impersonal and specialized relationships, with little long-term commitment to the group or consensus on values.** In such societies, most people are "strangers" who perceive that they have very little in common with most other people. Consequently, self-interest dominates, and little consensus exists regarding values. Tonnies selected the German term *Gesellschaft* because it means "association"; relationships are based on achieved statuses, and interactions among people are both rational and calculated.

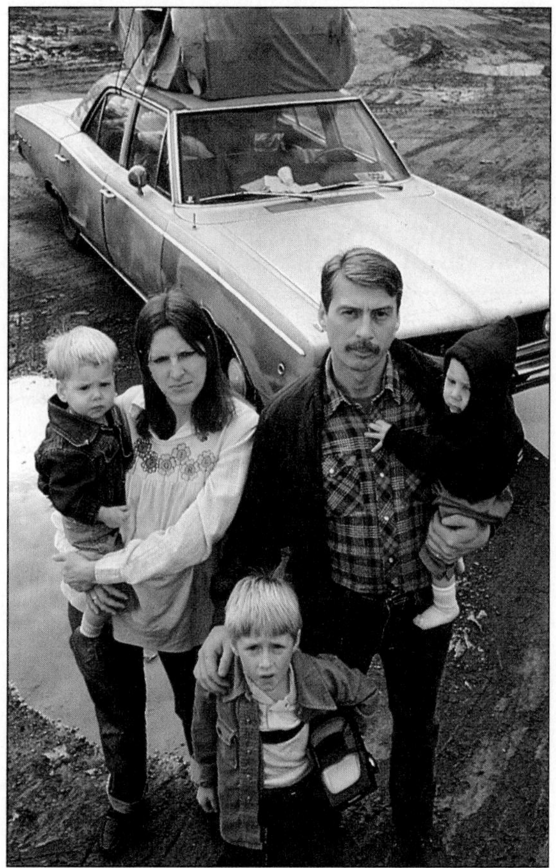

Contrary to a popular myth that most homeless people are single drifters, an increasing number of families now are homeless. This family lives in their car.

SOCIAL STRUCTURE AND HOMELESSNESS

In *Gesellschaft* societies such as Canada, a prevailing core value is that people should be able to take care of themselves. Thus, many people view the homeless as "throwaways"—as beyond help or as having already had enough done for them by society. Some argue that the homeless made their own bad decisions, which led them into alcoholism or drug addiction, and should be held responsible for the consequences of their own actions. In this sense, homeless people serve as a visible example to others to "follow the rules" lest they experience a similar fate (see White, 1992).

Alternative explanations for homelessness in *Gesellschaft* societies have been suggested. Elliot Liebow (1993) notes that homelessness is rooted in poverty; homeless people overwhelmingly are poor people who come from poor families. Homelessness is a "social class phenomenon, the direct result of a steady, across-the-board lowering of the standard of living of the working class and lower class" (Liebow, 1993:224). As the standard of living falls, those at the bottom rungs of society are plunged into homelessness. The problem is exacerbated by a lack of jobs. Of those who find work, a growing number work full-time, year-round, but remain poor because of substandard wages. Households living below the poverty line use most of their income for rent—if they are able to find accommodations that they can afford at all (Corelli, 1996). Clearly, there is no simple answer to the question about what should be done to help the homeless. Nor, as discussed in Box 5.2, is there any consensus as to what rights the homeless should have in our society, such as parks and sidewalks. The answers we derive as a society and as

BOX 5.2 SOCIOLOGY AND LAW

Vagrancy Laws versus Homeless Rights in Canada

Are homeless people in Canada allowed to sleep in parks and other public areas? Should homeless people be permitted to support themselves by panhandling on the street?

The tendency of societies to seek to control the homeless is reflected in the history of vagrancy laws. England's 1535 vagrancy statute offered a way to control poor and marginal members of society, as the following illustrates:

> and if any [ruffian] ... after having been once apprehended ... shall wander, loiter, or idle use [himself] and play the [vagabond] ... [he] shall be ... not only whipped again, but shall have the gristle of his right ear cut off. And if he shall again offend, he shall be committed to gaol till the next sessions; and being there convicted upon indictment, he shall have judgement to suffer pains and execution of death. (Chambliss, 1969:57)

This vagrancy statute was concerned with people who were suspected of being criminals, but couldn't be charged with any specific offense. Homeless individuals were those most suspect of being "potential criminals."

The concern of the vagrancy laws changed in the middle of the 18th century to those who were idle and unemployed. The laws were designed to control those who had no ties to society and who were considered likely to become involved in crime. Using vagrancy statutes, undesirables could be removed from the streets.

The laws were brought to North America in this form and for two centuries were used for purposes that might best be described as "social sanitation." In Canada, the following Criminal Code definition of vagrancy existed until the law was changed in 1972:

> 175(1) Every one commits vagrancy who
>
> a) not having any apparent means of support is found wandering abroad or trespassing and does not, when required, justify his presence in the place where he is found;
>
> b) begs from door to door or in a public place;
>
> c) being a common prostitute or night walker is found in a public place and does not, when required, give a good account of herself;
>
> d) supports himself in whole or in part by gaming or crime and has no lawful profession or calling by which to maintain himself;
>
> e) having at any time been convicted of an offense [describes sections dealing with child sexual offenses] ... is found loitering or wandering in or near a school ground, playground, public park, or bathing area.

In 1972 this Act was amended and Sections a–c were eliminated. As a result, the new vagrancy law is rarely used in Canada.

Why was the Act changed? Quite clearly, the revision was motivated by emerging concerns with civil liberties. The vagrancy statute was a bad law in that it was used primarily to punish people for what they were (idle, unemployed, homeless) rather than for any offenses that they had committed. The police, however, found these statutes useful in controlling panhandlers and prostitutes, who most people in society wished to see removed from the streets. In this case, law reformers felt that individual civil liberties were more important than the need to maintain order on the streets. Do you agree?

Source: Based on Chambliss, 1969.

individuals often are based on our social construction of this reality of life.

SOCIAL INTERACTION: THE MICROLEVEL PERSPECTIVE

So far in this chapter, we have focused on society and social structure from a macrolevel perspective. We have seen how the structure of society affects the statuses we occupy, the roles we play, and the groups and organizations to which we belong. We will now look at society from the microlevel perspective, which focuses on social interactions among individuals, especially in face-to-face encounters.

SOCIAL INTERACTION AND MEANING

When you are with other people, do you often wonder what they think of you? If so, you are not alone! Because most of us are concerned about the meanings others ascribe to our behaviour, we try to interpret their words and actions so that we can plan how we will react toward them (Blumer, 1969). We know that others have expectations of us. We also have certain expectations about them. For example, if we enter an elevator that has only one other person in it, we do not expect that individual to confront us and stare into our eyes. As a matter of fact, we would be quite upset if the person did so.

Social interaction within a given society has certain shared meanings across situations. For instance, our reaction would be the same regardless of *which* elevator we rode in *which* building. Sociologist Erving Goffman (1963b) described these shared meanings in his observation about two pedestrians approaching each other on a public sidewalk. He noted that each will tend to look at the other just long enough to acknowledge the other's presence. By the time they are about eight feet away from each other, both individuals will tend to look downward. Goffman referred to this behaviour as *civil inattention*—the ways in which an individual shows an awareness that others are present without making them the object of particular attention. The fact that people engage in civil inattention demonstrates that interaction does have a pattern, or *interaction order*, which regulates the form and processes (but not the content) of social interaction.

Does everyone interpret social interaction rituals in the same way? No. Ethnicity, gender, and social class play a part in the meanings we give to our interactions with others, including chance encounters on elevators or the street. Our perceptions about the meaning of a situation vary widely based on the statuses we occupy and our unique personal experiences. For example, sociologist Carol Brooks Gardner (1989) found that women frequently do not perceive street encounters to be "routine" rituals. They fear for their personal safety and try to avoid comments and propositions that are sexual in nature when they walk down the street. Members of visible minority groups also may feel uncomfortable in street encounters. A middle-class black university student described his experiences walking home at night from a campus job:

> So, even if you wanted to, it's difficult just to live a life where you don't come into conflict with others. ... Every day that you live as a black person you're reminded how you're perceived in society. You walk the streets at night; white people cross the streets. I've seen white couples and individuals dart in front of cars to not be on the same side of the street. Just the other day, I was walking down the street, and this white female with a child, I saw her pass a young white male about 20 yards ahead. When she saw me, she quickly dragged the child and herself across the busy street. ... [When I pass] white men tighten their grip on their women. I've seen people turn around and seem like they're going to take blows from me. ... So, every day you realize [you're black]. Even though you're not doing anything wrong; you're just existing. You're just a person. But you're a black person perceived in an unblack world. (Feagin, 1991:111–112)

Sharply contrasting perceptions of the same reality are evident in these scenes outside the Los Angeles Criminal Court building, site of the O.J. Simpson double homicide trial.

As this statement indicates, social encounters have different meanings for men and women, and individuals from different social classes and ethnic groups. Members of the dominant classes regard the poor, unemployed, and working class as less worthy of attention, frequently subjecting them to subtle yet systematic "attention deprivation" (Derber, 1983). The same can certainly be said about how members of the dominant classes "interact" with the homeless.

THE SOCIAL CONSTRUCTION OF REALITY

If we interpret other people's actions so subjectively, can we have a shared social reality? Some interaction theorists believe that there is very little shared reality beyond that which is socially created. Interactionists refer to this as the ***social construction of reality*—the process by which our perception of reality is shaped largely by the subjective meaning that we give to an experience** (Berger and Luckmann, 1967). This meaning strongly influences what we "see" and how we respond to situations.

Our perceptions and behaviour are influenced by how we initially define situations: We act on reality as we see it. Sociologists describe this process as the *definition of the situation*, meaning that we analyze a social context in which we find ourselves, determine what is in our best interest, and adjust our attitudes and actions accordingly. This can result in a ***self-fulfilling prophecy*—a false belief or prediction that produces behaviour that makes the originally false belief come true** (Thomas and Thomas, 1928:72). An example would be a person who has been told repeatedly that she or he is not a good student; eventually, this person might come to believe it to be true, stop studying, and receive failing grades.

People may define a given situation in very different ways, a tendency demonstrated by sociologist Jacqueline Wiseman (1970) in her study of "Pacific City's" skid row. She wanted to know how people who live or work on skid row (a run-down area found in all cities) felt about it. Wiseman found that homeless people living on skid row evaluated it very differently from the social workers who dealt with them there. On the one hand, many of the social workers "saw" skid row as a smelly, depressing area filled with men who were "down-and-out," alcoholic, and often physically and mentally ill. On the other hand, the men who lived on skid row did not see it in such a negative light. They experienced some degree of satisfaction with their "bottle clubs [and a] remarkably indomitable and creative spirit"—at least initially (Wiseman, 1970:18). Consider further Lesley Harman's initial reaction to her field research site, a facility for homeless women in an Ontario city:

> The initial shock of facing the world of the homeless told me much about what I took for granted ... The first day I lasted two very long hours. I went home and woke up severely depressed, weeping uncontrollably. (Harman, 1989:42)

In contrast, many of the women who lived there defined the situation of living in a hostel in very different terms. For example, one resident commented, "This is home to me because I feel so comfortable. I can do what I really want, the staff are very nice to me, everybody is good to me, it's home, you know?" (1989:91). As these studies show, we define situations from our own frame of reference, based on the statuses we occupy and the roles we play.

Dominant group members with prestigious statuses may have the ability to establish how other people define "reality" (Berger and Luckmann, 1967:109). For example, the media often set the tone for our current opinions about homelessness, either with negative stories about the problems the homeless "cause" or with "human interest" stories, as discussed in Box 5.3.

ETHNOMETHODOLOGY

How do we know how to interact in a given situation? What rules do we follow? Ethnomethodologists are interested in the answers to these questions. ***Ethnomethodology* is the study of the commonsense knowledge that people use to understand the situations in which they find themselves** (Heritage, 1984:4). Sociologist Harold Garfinkel (1967) initiated this approach and coined the term: *ethno* for "people" or "folk" and *methodology* for "a system of methods." Garfinkel was critical of mainstream sociology for not recognizing the ongoing ways in which people create reality and produce their own world. Consequently, ethnomethodologists examine existing patterns of conventional behaviour in order to uncover people's *background expectancies*, that is, their shared interpretation of objects and events, as well as their resulting actions (Zimmerman, 1992). According to ethnomethodologists, interaction is based on assumptions of shared expectancies. For example, when you are talking with someone, what expectations do you have that you will take turns? Based on your background expectancies, would you be surprised if the other person talked for an hour and never gave you a chance to speak?

To uncover people's background expectancies, ethnomethodologists frequently break "rules" or act as though they do not understand some basic rule of social life so that they can observe other people's responses. In a series of *breaching experiments*, Garfinkel assigned different activities to his students to see how breaking the unspoken rules of behaviour created confusion. In one experiment, when students participating in the study were asked, "How are you?" by persons not in the study, they were instructed to respond with very detailed accounts of their health and personal problems, as in this example:

> ACQUAINTANCE: How are you?
>
> STUDENT: How am I in regard to what? My health, my finances, my school work, my peace of mind, my ...
>
> ACQUAINTANCE (red in the face and suddenly out of control): Look! I was just trying to be polite. Frankly, I don't give a damn how you are. (Garfinkel, 1967:44)

In this encounter, the acquaintance expected the student to use conventional behaviour in answering the question. By acting unconventionally, the student violated background expectancies and effectively "sabotaged" the interaction.

The ethnomethodological approach contributes to our knowledge of social interaction by making us aware of subconscious social realities in our daily lives. However, a number of sociologists regard ethnomethodology as a frivolous approach to studying human behaviour because it is does not examine the impact of macrolevel social institutions—such as the economy and education—on people's expectancies. Women's studies scholars suggest that ethnomethodologists fail to do what they claim to: look at how social realities are created. Rather, they take ascribed statuses (such as ethnicity, class, gender, and age) as "givens," not as *socially created* realities. For example, in the experiments Garfinkel assigned to his students, he did not account for how gender affected their experiences. When Garfinkel asked students to reduce the distance between themselves and a nonrelative to the point that "their noses were almost touching," he ignored the fact that gender was as important to the encounter as was the proximity of the two persons. Scholars recently have emphasized that our expectations about reality are strongly influenced by our assumptions relating to gender, ethnicity, and social class (see Bologh, 1992).

DRAMATURGICAL ANALYSIS

Erving Goffman suggested that day-to-day interactions have much in common with being on stage or in a dramatic production. ***Dramaturgical analysis* is the study of social interaction that compares everyday life to a theatrical presentation.** Members of our "audience" judge our performance (Goffman, 1959, 1963a). Consequently, most of us attempt to play our role as well as possible and to control the impressions we give to others. *Impression management*, or ***presentation of self*, refers to people's efforts to present themselves to others in ways that are most favourable to their own interests or image.**

For example, suppose that a professor has returned graded exams to your class. Will you discuss the exam and your grade with others in the class? If you are like most people, you probably play your student role differently depending on whom you are talking to and what grade you received on the exam. In a study at the University of Manitoba, Daniel and Cheryl Albas (1988) analyzed how students "presented themselves" or "managed impressions" when exam grades are returned. Students who all received high grades ("Ace–Ace encounters") willingly talked with one another about their grades and sometimes engaged in a little bragging about how they had "aced" the test. However, encounters between students who had received high grades and those who had received low or failing grades ("Ace–Bomber encounters") were uncomfortable. The Aces felt as if they had to minimize their own grade. Consequently, they tended to attribute their success to "luck" and were quick to offer the Bombers words of encouragement. On the other hand, the Bombers believed that they had to praise the Aces and hide their own feelings of frustration and disappointment. Students who received low or failing grades ("Bomber–Bomber encounters") were more comfortable when they talked with one another because they could share their negative emotions. They often indulged in self-pity and relied on face-saving excuses (such as an illness or an unfair exam) for their poor performances (Albas and Albas, 1988).

In Goffman's terminology, *face-saving behaviour* refers to the strategies we use to rescue our performance when we experience a potential or actual loss of face. When the Bombers made excuses for their low scores, they were engaged in face-saving; the Aces attempted to help them save face by asserting that the test was unfair or that it was only a small part of the final grade. Why would the Aces and Bombers both participate in face-saving behaviour? In most social interactions, all role players have an interest in keeping the "play" going so that they can maintain their overall definition of the situation in which they perform their roles.

Goffman noted that people consciously participate in *studied nonobservance*, a face-saving technique in which one role player ignores the flaws in another's performance to avoid embarrassment *for everyone* involved. Most of us remember times when we have failed in our role and know that it is likely to happen again; thus, we may be more forgiving of the role failures of others.

Social interaction, like a theatre, has a front stage and a back stage. The *front stage* is the area where a player performs a specific role before an audience. The *back stage* is the area where a player is not required to perform a specific role because it is out of view of a given audience. For example, when the Aces and Bombers were talking with each other at school, they were on the "front

BOX 5.3 SOCIOLOGY AND MEDIA

The Homeless and the Holidays

Why do newspaper and television stories on the homeless proliferate in November, December, and January, as shown in Figure 1? Journalists may find the plight of the homeless more newsworthy during the cold winter months and the holiday season because of the stark contrast between their situation and that of the domiciled. Homeless people constitute "human interest" stories for the holiday season. Members of the press barrage service providers at "soup kitchens" and homeless shelters for interviews and stories about "Jimmy G." or "Sherry P.," and volunteers are shown as they serve turkey dinners to the homeless on Thanksgiving.

From one viewpoint, the media serve an important function by keeping the public aware of the plight of homeless people. A recent television public service announcement featured homeless people in New York. The commercial begins with a voice singing, "New York, New York," the first line of a song from a popular Broadway musical that emphasized the importance of success. Next, the camera shows that the voice singing, "Start spreading the news, I'm leaving today," belongs to a homeless man sitting on a bench. Then, line by line, the rest of the song is sung by a series of homeless men and women in tattered clothing. Gradually, the disparity between being *home* and being *homeless* for the holidays (and every other day) is made vivid. Then, after one homeless person sings, "If I can make it there, I'll make it anywhere," the screen abruptly fades to black. The words to the next line of the song appear, addressing the viewer: "It's up to you, New York, New York. The Coalition for the Homeless." Similar media campaigns for the homeless have utilized billboards, newspapers, and magazines. One newspaper ad and billboard poster had a drawing of Jesus above the headline, "How can you worship a homeless man on Sunday and ignore one on Monday?"

From another viewpoint, the media perpetuate negative images and myths about the homeless. In some articles and news stories, the homeless are depicted as drug addicts, alcoholics, or con artists who choose to be homeless. Photographs of homeless women and men in alcohol- or drug-induced stupors lying on park benches, heat grates, and the street reinforce these stereotypes. After decrying the societal problems caused by the homeless, one journalist suggested quarantining homeless men on military bases. By using the money currently spent on shelters for this purpose, this writer continued, the men would receive required medical treatment and an education in ethics, philosophy, art, and music.

What do you think about the media's coverage of the homeless? Does extensive coverage during the holiday season perhaps appeal to the "guilty conscience" of individuals who have a place to live while the homeless do not?

Sources: Based on Leonard and Randell, 1992; Elliott, 1993; Hamill, 1993; and Snow and Anderson, 1993.

stage." When they were in the privacy of their own residences, they were in "back stage" settings—they no longer had to perform the Ace and Bomber roles and could be themselves.

The need for impression management is most intense when role players have widely divergent or devalued statuses. As we have seen with the Aces and Bombers, the participants often play different roles under different circumstances and keep their various audiences separated from one another. If one audience becomes aware of other roles that a person plays, the impression being given at that time may be ruined. For example, homeless people may lose jobs or the opportunity to get them when their homelessness becomes known. One woman, Kim, had worked as a receptionist in a doctor's office for several weeks but was fired when the doctor learned that she was living in a shelter. According to Kim, the doctor told her, "If I had known you lived in a shelter, I

BOX 5.3 SOCIOLOGY AND MEDIA

Continued

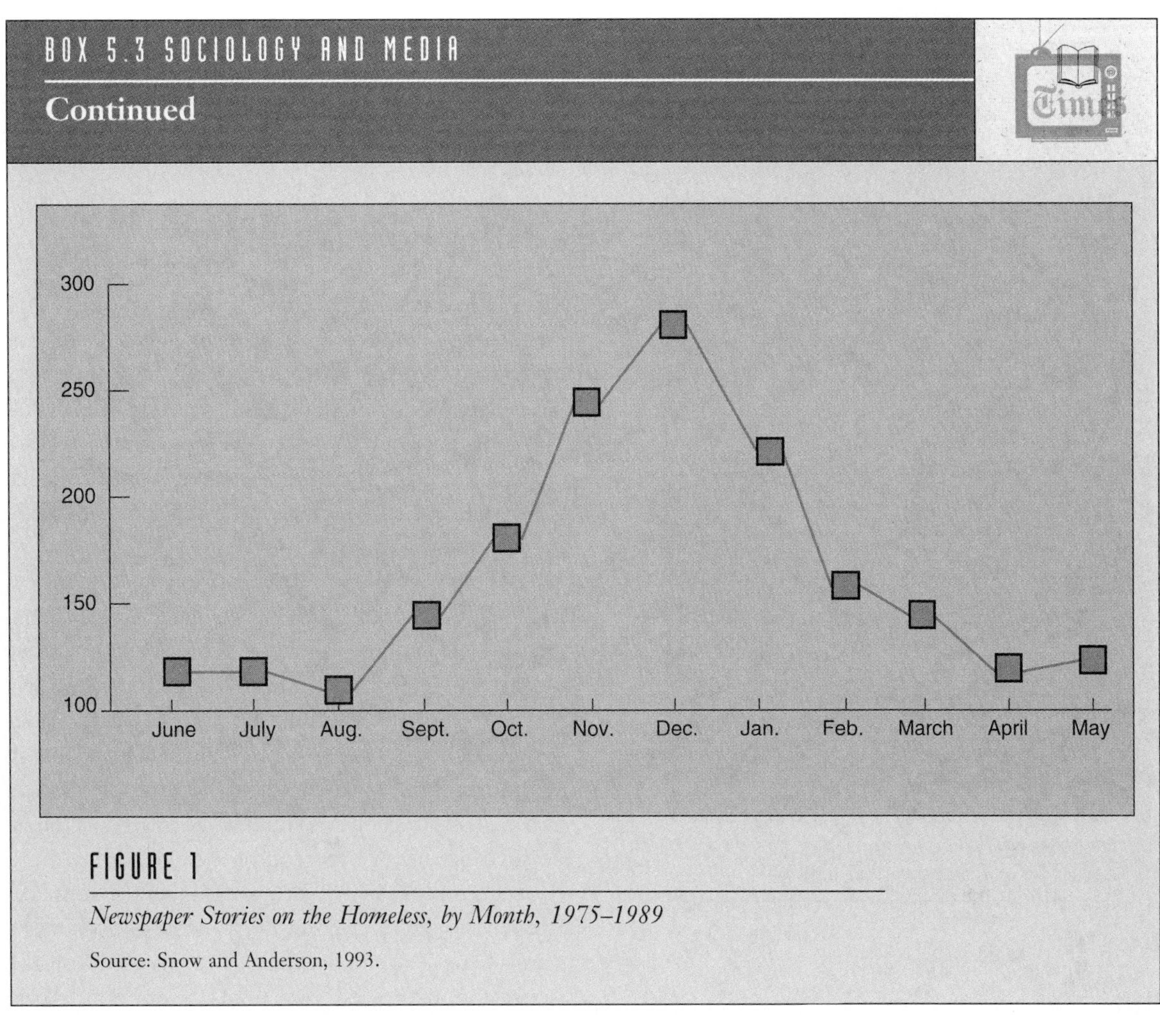

FIGURE 1

Newspaper Stories on the Homeless, by Month, 1975–1989

Source: Snow and Anderson, 1993.

would never have hired you. Shelters are places of disease" (Liebow, 1993:53–54).

For face-saving purposes, many homeless individuals create justifications to give meaning to their actions or the settings in which they find themselves. To "salvage the self," the homeless often use one of three adages; "I'm down on my luck"; "What goes around, comes around"; and "I've paid my dues" (Snow and Anderson, 1993: 204). "I'm down on my luck" means that the role does not really fit the person, as one homeless man stated: "It ain't my fault I'm on the streets. I didn't choose to become homeless. I just had a lot of bad luck. And that ain't my fault. ... It can happen to anyone, you know!" (Snow and Anderson, 1993:205). Others may salvage the self by embellishing stories about past or current occupational and financial accomplishments or sexual and drinking exploits. They may fantasize about the future regarding employment, money, material possessions, and women. One of the most prominent role fantasies is of becoming rich (Snow and Anderson, 1993). However, the homeless do not passively accept the roles into which they are cast. For the most part, they attempt—as we all do—to engage in impression management in their everyday life.

The dramaturgical approach helps us think about the roles we play and the audiences who judge our presentation of self. Like all other

Biker gangs like the Hell's Angels are very good at impression management. How do you think their front and back stage roles differ?

approaches, it has its critics. Sociologist Alvin Gouldner (1970) criticized this approach for focusing on appearances and not the underlying substance. Others have argued that Goffman's work reduces the self to "a peg on which the clothes of the role are hung" (see Burns, 1992) or have suggested that this approach does not place enough emphasis on the ways in which our everyday interactions with other people are influenced by occurrences within the larger society. For example, if a political official belittles the homeless as being lazy and unwilling to work, it may become easier for people walking down a street to do likewise. Goffman's defenders counter that he captured the essence of society because social interaction "turns out to be not only where most of the world's work gets done, but where the solid buildings of the social world are in fact constructed" (Burns, 1992:380). Goffman's work was influential in the development of the sociology of emotions, a relatively new area of theory and research.

THE SOCIOLOGY OF EMOTIONS

Why do we laugh, cry, or become angry? Are these emotional expressions biological or social in nature? To some extent, emotions are a biologically given sense (like hearing, smell, and touch), but they also are social in origin. We are socialized to feel certain emotions, and we learn how and when to express (or not express) those emotions (Hochschild, 1983:219).

How do we know which emotions are appropriate for a given role? Sociologist Arlie Hochschild (1983) suggests that we acquire a set of *feeling rules,* which shape the appropriate emotions for a given role or specific situation. These rules include how, where, when, and with whom an emotion should be expressed. For example, for the role of a mourner at a funeral, feeling rules tell us which emotions are required (sadness and grief, for example), which are acceptable (a sense of relief that the deceased no longer has to suffer), and which are unacceptable (enjoyment of the occasion expressed by laughing out loud) (see Hochschild, 1983:63–68).

Feeling rules also apply to the role of student. Albas and Albas (1988) examined the rules that exist regarding the emotions or feelings students experience during exam time. They concluded that when students believe that their level of anxiety is not at the "optimal level," they will engage in *emotional labour*. This term refers to the work that students will do to suppress or enhance the intensity, duration, or direction of their emotions (in this case, anxiety). The emotional labour done by students appears overwhelmingly to be in reducing the emotion rather than enhancing it. Individuals learn the student feeling rules regarding "exam anxiety" informally through their interactions with other students (Albas and Albas, 1988).

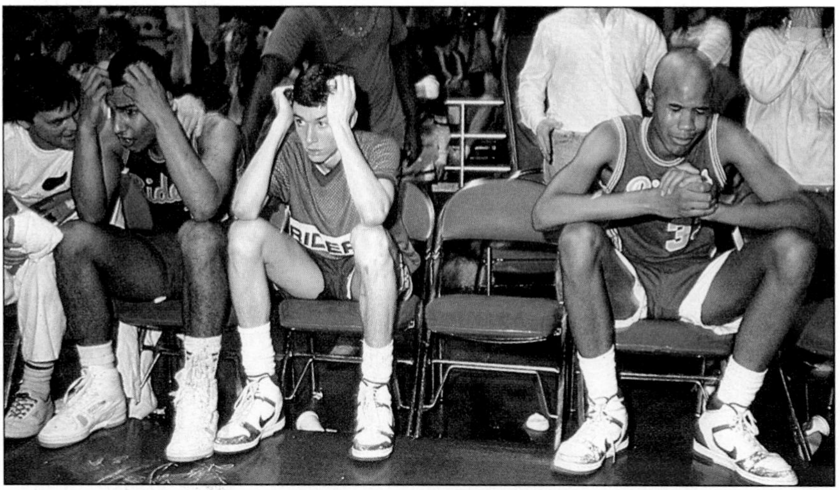

Is it acceptable for men to cry? In our society, males generally learn to suppress strong displays of emotion in everyday life. But in certain settings, such as high-stakes athletic competition, the same behaviour may be seen as perfectly natural.

Emotional labour may produce feelings of estrangement from one's "true" self. C. Wright Mills (1956) suggested that when we "sell our personality" in the course of selling goods or services, we engage in a seriously self-alienating process. Hochschild uses the following case to demonstrate the potential negative effects of emotional labour:

> A businessman asked a flight attendant, "Why aren't you smiling?" She looked at him in the eye. "I'll tell you what. You smile first, and then I'll smile." The businessman smiled at her. "Good," she replied. "Now freeze and hold that for fifteen hours." Then she walked away. (Hochschild, 1983:192)

In other words, the "commercialization" of our feelings may dehumanize our work role performance and create alienation and contempt that spill over into other aspects of our life (Smith and Kleinman, 1989).

Those who are unemployed and homeless also are required to engage in emotional labour. Governmental agencies and nonprofit organizations that function as caregivers to the homeless sometimes require emotional labour (such as feelings of gratitude or penitence) from their recipients. Homeless people have been denied social services even when they were eligible and have been asked to leave shelters when they did not show the appropriate deference and gratitude toward staff members (Liebow, 1993).

Do all people experience and express emotions the same way? It is widely believed that women express emotions more readily than men; as a result, very little research has been conducted to determine its accuracy. In fact, women and men may differ more in the way they *express* their emotions than in their actual feelings (Fabes and Martin, 1991). Differences in emotional expression also may be attributed to socialization; the extent to which men and women have been taught that a given emotion is appropriate (or inappropriate) for their gender no doubt plays an important part in their perceptions (Lombardo et al., 1983).

Social class also is a determinant in managed expression and emotion management. Emotional labour is emphasized in middle- and upper-class families. Since middle- and upper-class parents often work with people, they are more likely to teach their children the importance of emotional labour in their own careers than are working-class parents, who tend to work with things, not people (Hochschild, 1983). Ethnicity is also an important factor in emotional labour. Members of minority groups spend much of their life engaged in emotional labour, because racist attitudes and discrimination make it continually necessary to manage one's feelings.

Clearly, Hochschild's contribution to the sociology of emotions helps us understand the social context of our feelings and the relationship between the roles we play and the emotions we experience. However, her thesis has been criticized for overemphasizing the *cost* of emotional labour and the emotional controls that exist *outside* the individual (Wouters, 1989). The context in which emotions are studied and the specific emotions examined are important factors in determining the costs and benefits of emotional labour.

NONVERBAL COMMUNICATION

In a typical stage drama, the players not only speak their lines but also convey information by nonverbal communication. In Chapter 3, we discussed the importance of language; now we will look at the messages we communicate without speaking. ***Nonverbal communication* is the transfer of information between persons without the use of speech.** It includes not only visual cues (gestures, appearances) but also vocal features (inflection, volume, pitch) and environmental factors (use of space, position) that affect meanings (Wood, 1994). Facial expressions, head movements, body positions, and other gestures carry as much of the total *meaning* of our communication with others as our spoken words do (Wood, 1994:151).

Nonverbal communication may be intentional or unintentional. Actors, politicians, and salespersons may make deliberate use of nonverbal communication to convey an idea or "make a sale." We also may send nonverbal messages through gestures or facial expressions or even our appearance without intending to let other people know what we are thinking.

FUNCTIONS OF NONVERBAL COMMUNICATION Nonverbal communication often supplements verbal communication (Wood, 1994). Head and facial movements may provide us with information about other people's emotional states, and others receive similar information from us (Samovar and Porter, 1991a). We obtain first impressions of others from various kinds of nonverbal communication, such as the clothing they wear and their body positions.

Our social interaction is regulated by nonverbal communication. Through our body posture and eye contact, we signal that we do or do not wish to speak to someone. For example, we may look down at the sidewalk or off into the distance when we pass homeless persons who look as if they are going to ask for money.

Nonverbal communication establishes the relationship between people in terms of their responsiveness to and power over one another (Wood, 1994). For example, we show that we are responsive toward or like another person by maintaining eye contact and attentive body posture and perhaps by touching and standing close. By contrast, we signal to others that we do not wish to be near them or that we dislike them by refusing to look them in the eye or stand near them. We can even express power or control over others through nonverbal communication. Goffman (1956) suggested that *demeanour* (how we behave or conduct ourselves) is relative to social power. People in positions of dominance are allowed a wider range of permissible actions than are their subordinates, who are expected to show deference. *Deference* is the symbolic means by which subordinates give a required permissive response to those in power; it confirms the existence of inequality and reaffirms each person's relationship to the other (Rollins, 1985).

FACIAL EXPRESSION, EYE CONTACT, AND TOUCHING Deference behaviour is important in regard to facial expression, eye contact, and touching. This type of nonverbal communication is symbolic of our relationships with others. Who smiles? Who stares? Who makes and sustains eye contact? Who touches whom? All of these questions relate to demeanour and deference; the key issue is the status of the person who is *doing* the smiling, star-

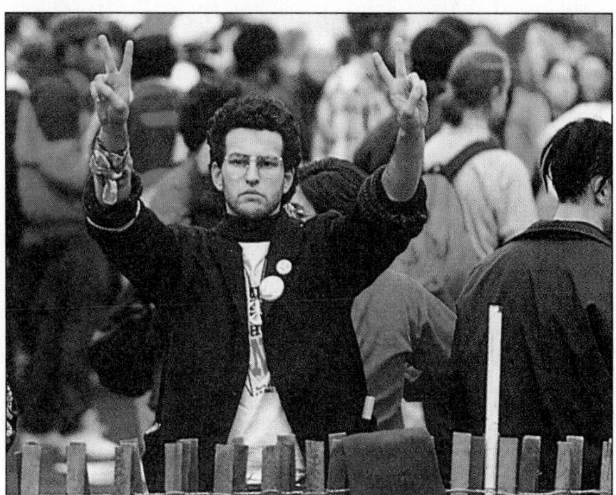

Nonverbal communication may be thought of as an international language. What message do you receive from the facial expression, body position, and gestures of each of these people? Is it possible to misinterpret their messages?

ing, or touching relative to the status of the recipient (Goffman, 1967).

Facial expressions, especially smiles, also reflect gender-based patterns of dominance and subordination in society. Women typically have been socialized to smile and frequently do so even when they are not actually happy (Halberstadt and Saitta, 1987). Jobs held predominantly by women (including flight attendant, secretary, elementary school teacher, and nurse) are more closely associated with being pleasant and smiling than are "men's jobs." In addition to smiling more frequently, many women tend to tilt their heads in deferential positions when they are talking or listening to others. By contrast, men tend to display less emotion through smiles or other facial expressions and instead seek to show that they are "reserved and in control" (Wood, 1994:164).

Women are more likely to sustain eye contact during conversations (but not otherwise) as a means of showing their interest in and involvement with others. By contrast, men are less likely to maintain prolonged eye contact during conversations but are more likely to stare at other people (especially men) in order to challenge them and assert their own status (Pearson, 1985).

Eye contact can be a sign of domination or deference. For example, in a participant observation study of domestic (household) workers and their employers, sociologist Judith Rollins (1985) found that the domestics were supposed to show deference by averting their eyes when they talked to their employers. Deference also required that they present an "exaggeratedly subservient demeanour" by standing less erect and walking tentatively.

Touching is another form of nonverbal behaviour that has many different shades of meaning. Gender and power differences are evident in tactile communication from birth. Studies have shown that touching has variable meanings to parents: Boys are touched more roughly and playfully, while girls are handled more gently and protectively (Condry, Condry, and Pogatshnik, 1983). This pattern continues into adulthood, with women touched more frequently than men. Sociologist Nancy Henley (1977) attributed this pattern to power differentials between men and women and to the nature of women's roles as mothers, nurses, teachers, and secretaries. Clearly, touching has a different meaning to women than to men (Stier and Hall, 1984). Women may hug and touch others to indicate affection and emotional support, while men are more likely to touch others to give directions, assert power, and express sexual interest (Wood, 1994:162). The "meaning" we give to touching is related to its "duration, intensity, frequency, and the body parts touching and being touched" (Wood, 1994:162).

PERSONAL SPACE Physical space is an important component of nonverbal communication. Anthropologist Edward Hall (1966) analyzed the physical distance between people speaking to one another and found that the amount of personal space people prefer varies from one culture to another. ***Personal space*** **is the immediate area surrounding a person that the person claims as private.** Our personal space is contained within an invisible boundary surrounding our body, much like a snail's shell. When others invade our space, we may retreat, stand our ground, or even lash out, depending on our cultural background (Samovar and Porter, 1991a). Hall (1966) observed that North Americans have different "distance zones":

1. *Intimate distance* (contact to about 18 inches): reserved for spouses, lovers, and close friends, for purposes of lovemaking, comforting, and protecting.
2. *Personal distance* (18 inches to 4 feet): reserved for friends and acquaintances, for purposes of ordinary conversation, card playing, and similar activities.
3. *Social distance* (4 to 12 feet): marks impersonal or formal relationships, such as in job interviews and business transactions.
4. *Public distance* (beyond 12 feet): marks an even more formal relationship and makes interpersonal communication nearly impossible. This distance often denotes a status difference between dignitaries or speakers and their audience or the general public.

Hall makes the distinction between "contact" and "noncontact" cultures and emphasizes that people from different cultures have different distance zones. Contact cultures are characterized by closer physical distance in interaction, more frequent eye contact and touch, and greater voice volume. Representatives of contact cultures include Arabs, Southern Europeans, and the French. Canadians, Asians, and the British are examples of noncontact cultures who typically interact at greater distances with less eye contact and touch, and lower voice volume (Hall, 1966).

What happens to personal distance when individuals from contact and noncontact cultures interact? This question is particularly important in our multicultural society where members of different ethnic subcultures interact on a regular basis. One study examined this question by observing members of a contact culture (Franco-Manitobans) with a noncontact culture (Anglo-Manitobans) interacting in their natural setting. Albas and Albas (1989) reported that the subjects, in an attempt to comply with the expectations of others, would adjust their "distance zone" when interacting with someone from a different cultural group.

Power differentials are also reflected in personal space and privacy issues. With regard to age, adults generally do not hesitate to enter the personal space of a child (Thorne, Kramarae, and Henley, 1983). Similarly, young children who invade the personal space of an adult tend to elicit a more favourable response than do older uninvited visitors (Dean, Willis, and la Rocco, 1976). The need for personal space appears to increase with age (Baxter, 1970; Aiello and Jones, 1971), although it may begin to decrease at about age 40 (Heshka and Nelson, 1972).

In sum, all forms of nonverbal communication are influenced by gender, ethnicity, social class, and the personal contexts in which they occur. While it is difficult to generalize about people's nonverbal behaviour, we still need to think about our own nonverbal communication patterns. Recognizing that differences in social interaction exist is important. We should be wary of making value judgments—the differences are simply *differences*. Learning to understand and respect alternative styles of social interaction enhances our personal effectiveness by increasing the range of options we have for communicating with different people in diverse contexts and for varied reasons (Wood, 1994).

CHANGING SOCIAL STRUCTURE AND INTERACTION IN THE TWENTY-FIRST CENTURY

The social structure in North America has been changing rapidly in recent decades. Currently, there are more possible statuses for persons to occupy and roles to play than at any other time in history. Although achieved statuses are important as we enter the twenty-first century, ascribed statuses still have a significant impact on the options and opportunities people have.

Ironically, at a time when we have more technological capability, more leisure activities and types of entertainment, and more quantities of material goods available for consumption than ever before, many people experience high levels of stress, fear for their lives because of crime, and face problems such as homelessness. In a society that can send astronauts into space to perform complex scientific experiments, is it impossible to solve some of the problems that plague us here on earth? Homelessness is not just a problem in Canada and the United States, however. As shown in Box 5.4, other industrialized nations share the problem.

Individuals and groups often show initiative in trying to solve some of our pressing problems. For example, Ellen Baxter has single-handedly tried to create housing for hundreds of New York City's homeless by reinventing well-maintained, single-room-occupancy residential hotels to provide cheap lodging and social services (Anderson, 1993). However, individual initiative alone will not solve all our social problems in the twenty-first century. Large-scale, formal organizations must become more responsive to society's needs.

At the microlevel, we need to regard social problems as everyone's problem; if we do not, they have a way of becoming everyone's problem anyway. When we think about "the homeless," for example, we are thinking in a somewhat misleading manner. "The homeless" suggests a uniform set of problems and a single category of poor people. Jonathan Kozol (1988:92) emphasizes that "their miseries are somewhat uniform; the squalor is uniform; the density of living space is uniform. [However, the] uniformity is in their mode of suffering, not in themselves."

What can be done about homelessness in the twenty-first century? Martha R. Burt, director of the Urban Institute's 1987 national study of urban homeless shelter and soup kitchen users, notes that we must first become dissatisfied with explanations that see personal problems as the cause of homelessness. Many people in the past have suffered from poverty, mental illness, alcoholism, physical handicaps, and drug addiction, but they have not become homeless.

BOX 5.4 SOCIOLOGY IN GLOBAL PERSPECTIVE

Homelessness in Japan and France

Homelessness is a problem not only in Canada and the United States but also in virtually all industrialized nations. Homeless people sleep on the sidewalks and warm air vents in Tokyo and Paris, as well as in Vancouver, Toronto, and Chicago. While many people in Canada feel fear, resentment, or compassion fatigue regarding the homeless, the Japanese and French are just becoming aware of the problem.

In Japan, volunteers feed many of the homeless to make up for the absence of any type of governmental assistance. Recently, the number of homeless people has increased significantly, even with Japan's high per capita income of over $28,000 annually. However, the Japanese economy has dipped into its deepest slump since World War II, and this recession has forced many Japanese companies to do away with their previous guarantee of lifetime employment for their workers. Layoffs and so-called voluntary retirement have produced many unemployed workers who are over the age of 50. Although the Japanese government does not keep records of the homeless, some experts estimate that persons over the age of 50 account for more than half of the homeless population. In order to have a roof over their heads, many near-homeless men rent cheap hotel rooms for as long as they can afford them. In the short term, the extremely high cost of housing in Japan makes the homeless problem even worse. If homelessness becomes a long-term problem, government initiatives will be inevitable.

Like Japan, France has experienced a high rate of homelessness caused at least in part by a downturn in the economy and massive immigration by refugees from war-torn countries. Paris has set up camps for the homeless in two underground subway stations and offers free showers in public baths. Charity groups have mobilized soup vans and expanded their shelters. A group of social workers known as the Companions of the Night has set up a meeting place where homeless people can meet and talk all night if they so desire. The homeless in Paris are highly visible as they sleep in doorways, subways, garages, and shelters. Some ride the train all night long in order to remain warm and to get some sleep. Many of the homeless in France blame their problems on a welfare state that went astray and on an overregulated society that stifled individual initiative.

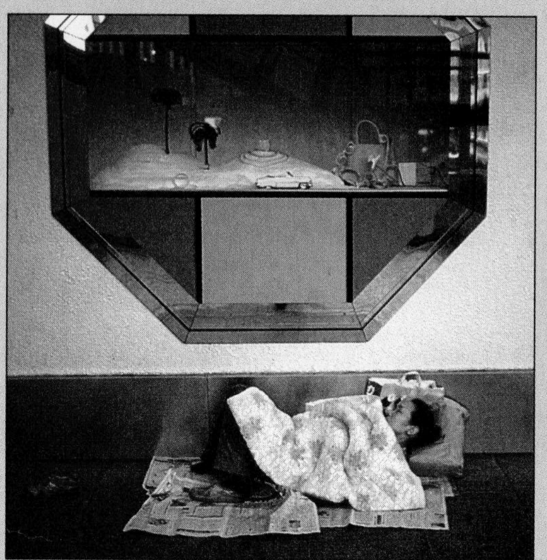

Although this familiar scene could have taken place in any major city, this homeless person sleeps in front of a Tokyo shop patronized by wealthy Japanese.

Thus far, compassion fatigue does not appear to have set in either in Tokyo or in Paris. While the French government has taken a role in ameliorating the problems faced by homeless people, the Japanese government has done little as yet. Volunteers in both countries are actively involved in working with the homeless. Do you think compassion fatigue is inevitable in all countries? Can volunteers and charities alone solve major problems such as homelessness?

Sources: Based on Greenwald, 1993; and Simons, 1993a.

In order to understand homelessness, it is necessary to examine the changes in large-scale structural factors that contribute to personal problems at the microlevel. There is a constant interplay between individual effects and institutional responses. Changes in our economic system—including welfare cuts, a shrinking supply of low-rent housing, high unemployment rates, and diminishing mental health services—have created the largest homeless population in our history.

At a Montreal conference of social activists, delegates vowed to fight government cuts in social services. "Our governments are making the underprivileged pay for the debt," they say (Corelli, 1996:48). They argue that effects of welfare cuts will be realized not only at the individual level, but also at the structural level as responsibility is shifted onto the correctional and health care systems. If the social service/welfare system is ill-prepared or ill-equipped to deal with the needs of the homeless, these effects will be felt in other systems. Individuals may develop mental health problems in response to the financial stresses of homelessness, or, alternatively, homeless people may become involved in criminal activities to supplement the income lost from welfare cuts. In order to create any type of positive change, it necessary for Canadians to recognize that "private troubles" and "public issues" are intimately connected. Unfortunately, as the director of a Calgary food bank commented, "The whole mentality of our society has changed. It's much easier now to step over people in the street" (Corelli, 1996:48).

The future of this country rests on our collective ability to deal with major social problems at both the macrolevel and the microlevel of society.

CHAPTER REVIEW

The stable patterns of social relationships within a particular society make up its social structure. Social structure is a macrolevel influence because it shapes and determines the overall patterns in which social interaction occurs. Social interaction refers to how people within a society act and respond to one another. This interaction is a microlevel dynamic—between individuals and groups—and is the foundation of meaningful relationships in society.

- Social structure provides an ordered framework for society and for our interactions with others. It has several essential components: roles, statuses, groups, and social institutions. While social structure gives us the ability to interpret the social situations we encounter, it also may limit our options and place us in arbitrary categories. Social marginality occurs when people are partly in and partly out of the social structure.
- A status is a specific position in a group or society and is characterized by certain expectations, rights, and duties. An ascribed status is acquired at birth or involuntarily later in life. An achieved status is assumed voluntarily as a result of personal choice, merit, or direct effort. Ascribed statuses—gender, class, and ethnicity, for example—influence the achieved statuses we occupy. A role is the set of behavioural expectations associated with a given status. While we occupy a status, we play a role. Role expectation is society's definition of how a role ought to be played. Role performance is how the role is actually played.
- A social group consists of two or more people who interact frequently and share a common identity and sense of interdependence. A formal organization is a highly structured group formed to complete certain tasks or achieve specific goals.

- A social institution is a set of organized beliefs and rules that establish how a society attempts to meet its basic needs. The family, religion, education, the economy, and the government are considered established social institutions. Mass media, sports, science and medicine, and the military increasingly are included as social institutions.
- According to functionalist theorists, social institutions perform several prerequisites of all societies: replace members; teach new members; produce, distribute, and consume goods and services; preserve order; and provide and maintain a sense of purpose. Conflict theorists, however, note that social institutions do not work for the common good of all individuals. Institutions may enhance and uphold the power of some groups but exclude others, such as the homeless.
- Although changes in social structure may dramatically affect individuals and groups, societies manage to maintain some degree of stability. According to Durkheim, mechanical solidarity refers to social cohesion in preindustrial societies, in which people are united by shared values and common social bonds. Organic solidarity refers to the cohesion in industrial societies, in which people perform specialized tasks and are united by mutual dependence.
- According to Ferdinand Tonnies, the *Gemeinschaft* is a traditional society in which relationships are based on personal bonds of friendship and kinship and on intergenerational stability. The *Gesellschaft* is an urban society in which social bonds are based on impersonal and specialized relationships, with little group commitment or consensus on values.
- Social interaction within a society, particularly face-to-face encounters, is guided by certain shared meanings of how we should behave. Social interaction also is marked by nonverbal communication, which is the transfer of information between people without using speech. Ethnicity, gender, and social class often influence perceptions of meaning, however.
- According to Erving Goffman's dramaturgical analysis, our daily interactions are similar to dramatic productions. Presentation of self refers to efforts to present our own self to others in ways that are most favourable to our own interests or self-image.
- Feeling rules shape the appropriate emotions for a given role or specific situation. Our emotions are not always private, and specific emotions may be demanded of us on certain occasions.

KEY TERMS

achieved status **164**
ascribed status **164**
dramaturgical analysis **179**
ethnomethodology **178**
formal organization **170**
Gemeinschaft **173**
Gesellschaft **174**
master status **164**
mechanical solidarity **173**
nonverbal communication **184**
organic solidarity **173**
personal space **186**
presentation of self **179**
primary group **169**
role **166**
role conflict **167**
role exit **168**
role expectation **166**
role performance **166**
role strain **167**
secondary group **169**
self-fulfilling prophecy **177**
social construction of reality **177**
social group **169**
social institution **171**
social interaction **159**
social marginality **162**
social network **169**
social structure **160**
status **163**
status set **163**
status symbol **165**
stigma **162**

QUESTIONS FOR ANALYSIS AND UNDERSTANDING

1. Does social structure create order and predictability in society, or does it create boundaries that define which groups are insiders and which are outsiders?
2. How do role and status differ? What are your ascribed, achieved, and master statuses? What are your roles?
3. What formal organizations affect the lives of homeless people? How so?

QUESTIONS FOR CRITICAL THINKING

1. Think of a person you know well who often irritates you or whose behaviour grates on your nerves (it could be a parent, friend, relative, teacher). First, list that person's statuses and roles. Then, analyze his or her possible role expectations, role performance, role conflicts, and role strains. Does anything you find in your analysis help to explain his or her irritating behaviour? (If not, change your method of analysis!) How helpful are the concepts of social structure in analyzing individual behaviour?
2. Are structural problems responsible for homelessness, or are homeless individuals responsible for their own situation?
3. You are conducting field research on gender differences in nonverbal communication styles. How are you going to account for variations among age, ethnicity, and social class?
4. When communicating with other genders, ethnic groups, and ages, is it better to express and acknowledge different styles or to develop a common, uniform style?

SUGGESTED READINGS

These books provide interesting insights on social interaction and the social construction of reality:

Peter L. Berger and Thomas Luckmann. *The Social Construction of Reality: A Treatise in the Sociology of Knowledge.* Garden City, N.Y.: Doubleday/Anchor Books, 1967.

Erving Goffman. *The Presentation of Self in Everyday Life.* New York: Doubleday, 1959.

David A. Karp and William C. Yoels. *Sociology and Everyday Life.* Itasca, Ill.: Peacock, 1986.

The process of leaving a significant role and establishing a new identity is examined in this book:

Helen Rose Fuchs Ebaugh. *Becoming an EX: The Process of Role Exit.* Chicago: University of Chicago Press, 1988.

To find out more about the problem of homelessness:

Lars Eighner. *Travels with Lizbeth.* New York: St. Martin's Press, 1993.

David A. Snow and Leon Anderson. *Down on Their Luck: A Case Study of Homeless Street People.* Berkeley: University of California Press, 1993.

Lesley D. Harman. *When a Hostel Becomes a Home: Experiences of Women.* Toronto: Garamond Press, 1989.

Thomas O'Reilly-Fleming. *Down and Out in Canada: Homeless Canadians.* Toronto: Canadian Scholars Press, 1993.

Chapter 6

GROUPS AND ORGANIZATIONS

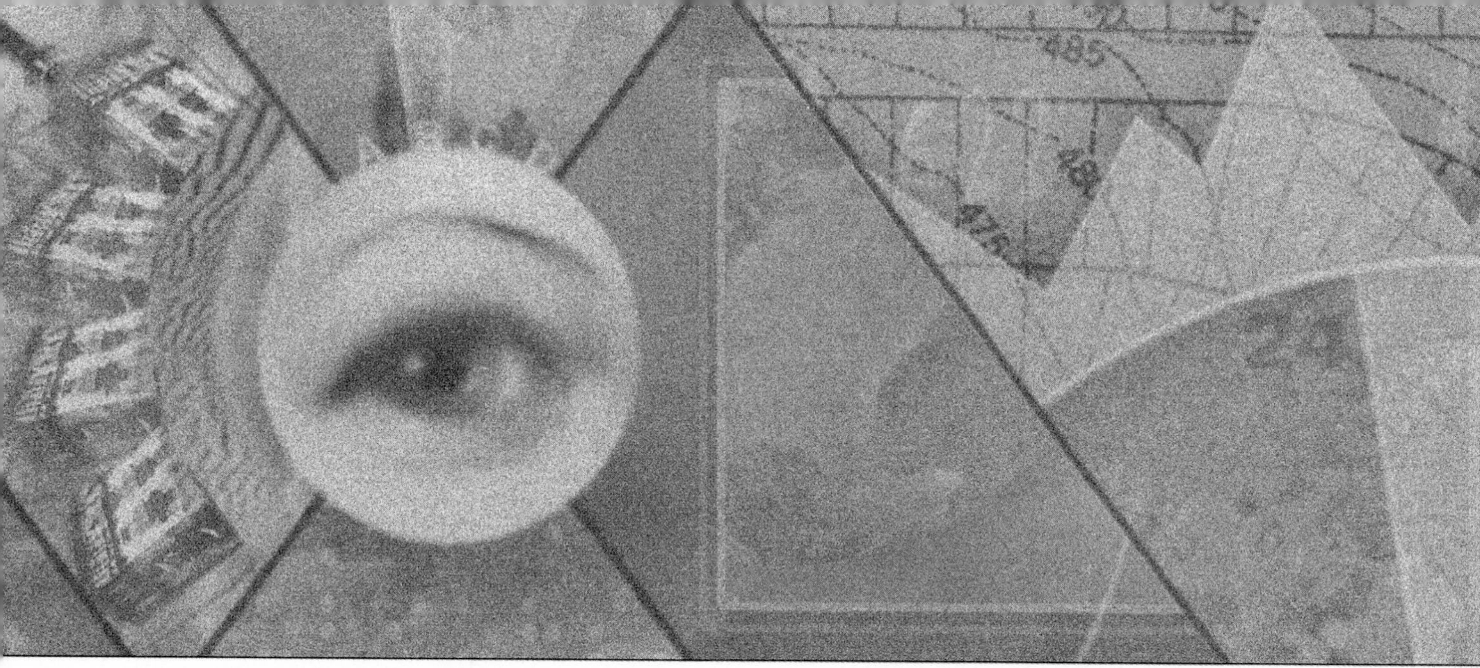

Kimberly had just entered graduate school when she had a lengthy ordeal with the professor who supervised her academic work:

My ordeal began … when … I made the decision to pursue graduate study … What I did not imagine is that I would be battling with a monster. That monster is sexual harassment—a vicious beast that lives in a dark cave called society, where it is often hidden, making its capture all the more difficult. Many find it easier to deny its existence than to battle it.

My harasser, a forty-two-year-old professor, carried the beast within himself … Throughout the seven months I was enrolled in his classes, I was subjected to seduction, violent threats, and emotional abuse. Nearly every day, he commented on my looks and my sexuality. In computer class, he put his arms around me and rubbed his body back and forth against me … He gave me a lower final grade than I'd earned "so that [I'd] have to come and complain." … He made repeated references to "whipping" and "handcuffing" me, and to the pleasure he would receive from "punishing" me … All of this was "fun" to him, and he repeatedly told me how "special" I was that he had chosen me.

Ironically, it was his most frightening threat that gave me the strength to stand up to him. When I finally told him that his behaviour was becoming obvious to other students, he became enraged. He threatened my life if I told anybody what he had done. He was being considered for tenure and knew that his misconduct, if reported, would put that decision in great jeopardy … (Langelan, 1993:267–271)

Although sexual harassment is not a new phenomenon, it has only recently been recognized as a problem in our society. The internationally televised controversy between U.S. Supreme Court nominee Clarence Thomas and his accuser, Anita Hill, in October 1991 increased public awareness of sexual harassment.

Sexual harassment can occur in any organizational sphere. Sexual harassment may include, but is not limited to, sexually oriented gestures; sexist remarks, jokes, or innuendo; inappropriate touching; taunting someone's body, appearance, dress, or characteristics; or display of pornographic material. In short, sexual harassment is unwanted sexual attention. There was no name to label these acts until 1976 when feminists coined the term "sexual harassment" (MacKinnon, 1979).

It is difficult to define sexual harassment because individual experiences of sexual harassment are interpreted subjectively, not objectively. A specific behaviour may or may not be interpreted or perceived as sexual harassment. For

BOX 6.1 SOCIOLOGY AND LAW

Sexual Harassment and the Law

Sexual harassment is not a criminal offence in Canada. Sexual harassment is considered an infringement of human (civil) rights, and constitutes sex discrimination. Sexual harassment is sexual discrimination because it is precisely because of the victim's sex that the harassment takes place (Wishart, 1993:187). The Canadian Human Rights Act was amended on July 1, 1983, to provide protection against sexual harassment. Across the country, Human Rights Boards prohibit sexual harassment. However, the board's rulings are not binding so the courts decide whether sexual harassment has taken place. Some have argued for the improvement of sexual harassment legislation (Wishart, 1993).

Sexual harassment is sometimes direct and blatant (*quid pro quo* harassment), but can also occur in more subtle forms. In Canada, sexual harassment in the workplace is distinguished as either sexual coercion or sexual annoyance. Sexual coercion involves some direct consequence for the worker's employment status—some gain, loss, or benefit (Wishart, 1993:186). Sexual annoyance is sexually related conduct viewed as intimidating, offensive, or hostile to an employee (Wishart, 1993:186). Subtle behaviour may create an environment that is intimidating, hostile, or offensive, and unreasonably interferes with an individual's performance. This form of sexual harassment is inherently ambiguous (Macionis et al., 1994). An example would be a workplace filled with sexual slurs, insults, and innuendo or pornographic pictures visibly displayed. Researchers have found that sexual harassment is often structured by power differentials (McDaniel and Roosmalen, 1985). However, sexual harassment may also occur among peers, i.e., colleagues or fellow students.

Sexual harassment undermines the mutual respect, cooperation, and understanding that ideally should characterize the workplace and educational institutions. Many employers across the country are establishing anti-harassment policies that specify intolerable behaviours. The Canadian Auto Workers, Ford, General Motors, and Chrysler began a woman's advocate program to assist women experiencing sexual harassment and other problems (*Toronto Star*, December 6, 1994:A2).

Universities across Canada do not condone sexual harassment and have implemented procedures for reporting cases. Usually, an investigations officer will hear the complaint and, after investigating the incident, take disciplinary measures if appropriate. For instance, at the University of Toronto, a Sexual Harassment Coalition has been formed that has developed recommendations for a sexual harassment grievance procedure.

In Ontario, sexual harassment is now considered a commensurable injury at the workplace as a result of the Supreme Court of Canada's ruling in favour of Bonnie Robichaud (Dekeseredy and Hinch, 1991:127). The court ruled that employers are responsible for providing a healthy working environment. Now businesses governed by federal and provincial human rights legislation must create systems that deal with all kinds of discrimination. Unions have recently been integral in the fight against sexual harassment. Many unions are committed to women's programs, such as equal pay for work of equal value and harassment policies.

Sexual harassment is part of a society-wide pattern of behaviour that should give way to more equal treatment of all people. Sexual harassment exists within a society where attitudes condone violence toward women. In our culture, men are encouraged to be sexually assertive, while women tend to be socialized into more passive sexual roles. Is having a law against sexual harassment sufficient to stop such incidents?

instance, in one context a glance or comment may be perceived as appropriate, where in another the same behaviour would be deemed sexual harassment. If a woman defines a situation as sexual harassment, she has perceived it to be unwanted sexual attention. Both men and women can be sexually harassed but, overwhelmingly, women are victims, and men perpetrators.

The issue of sexual harassment raises questions about the degree of responsibility groups and organizations have for the behaviour of their members. Al McLean, former speaker of the Ontario legislature, resigned his position after being accused of sexual harassment by a member of his staff.

What does the complex problem of sexual harassment have to do with a chapter on groups and organizations? When we apply our sociological imagination to this problem, we see that harassment is not always isolated behaviour on the part of a "misguided" individual. While it may exist in a one-on-one setting, harassment also is found in many groups, both small and large. In Kimberly's situation, the harasser used his position in an organization (the university) to sexually harass someone within that organization (a student).

QUESTIONS AND ISSUES

What constitutes a social group?

How are groups and their members shaped by group size, leadership style, and pressures to conform?

What group dynamics contribute to sexual harassment?

What purposes does bureaucracy serve?

How might an alternative form of organization differ from existing ones?

SOCIAL GROUPS

Three strangers are standing at a street corner waiting for a traffic light to change. Do they constitute a group? Five hundred women and men are first-year graduate students at a university. Do they constitute a group? In everyday usage, we use the word *group* to mean any collection of people. According to sociologists, however, the answer to these questions is no; individuals who happen to share a common feature or to be in the same place at the same time do not constitute social groups.

GROUPS, AGGREGATES, AND CATEGORIES

As we saw in Chapter 5, a *social group* is a collection of two or more people who interact frequently with one another, share a sense of belonging, and have a feeling of interdependence. Several people waiting for a traffic light to change constitute an ***aggregate*—a collection of people who happen to be in the same place at the same time but share little else in common.** Shoppers in a department store and passengers on an airplane flight also are examples of aggregates. People in aggregates share a common purpose (such as purchasing items or arriving at their destination) but generally do not interact with one another, except perhaps briefly. The first-year graduate students, at least initially, constitute a ***category*—a number of people who may never have met one another but share a similar characteristic** (such as education level, age, ethnicity, and gender). Men and women make up categories, as do First Nations peoples, and victims of sexual or racial harassment. Categories are not social groups because the people in them usually do not create a social structure or have anything in common other than a particular trait.

Occasionally, people in aggregates and categories form social groups. People within the category known as "graduate students," for instance, may become an aggregate when they get together for an orientation to graduate school. Some of them may form social groups as they interact with one another in classes and seminars, find that they have mutual interests and concerns, and develop a sense of belonging to the group.

The number and diversity of social groups within society is enormous, especially when you consider that a social group may contain as few as two members and that the purposes for which they are formed are so wide-ranging. Women who have been the victims of sexual harassment (a category), for example, have created social groups for the purpose of confronting harassment. In one situation, women who lived in the same apartment complex (an aggregate) learned that they all had been sexually harassed by the same apartment manager. To fight back, they formed a nonprofit group known as WRATH (Women Refusing to Accept Tenant Harassment) to help people who had experienced sexual harassment in housing. As this example shows, an aggregate or category over time may become a formal organization with a specific structure and clear-cut goals. A *formal organization*, you will recall, is a highly structured group formed for the purpose of achieving specific goals in the most efficient manner. Colleges, factories, corporations, the military, and government agencies are examples of formal organizations. Before we examine formal organizations, however, we need to know more about groups in general and the ways in which they function.

TYPES OF GROUPS

As you will recall from Chapter 5, groups have varying degrees of social solidarity and structure. This structure is flexible in some groups and more rigid in others. Some groups are small and personal; others are large and impersonal. We more closely identify with the members of some groups than we do others.

PRIMARY AND SECONDARY GROUPS Sociologist Charles H. Cooley (1962/1909) used the term *primary group* to describe a small, less specialized group in which members engage in face-to-face, emotion-based interactions over an extended period of time. We have primary relationships with other individuals in our primary groups—that is, with our *significant others*, who frequently serve as role models.

In contrast, you will recall, a *secondary group* is a larger, more specialized group in which the members engage in more impersonal, goal-oriented relationships for a limited period of time. The size of a secondary group may vary. Twelve students in a graduate seminar may start out as a secondary group but eventually become a primary group as they get to know one another and communicate on a more personal basis. Formal organizations are secondary groups, but they also contain many primary groups within them. For example, how many primary groups do you think there are within the secondary group setting of your university?

INGROUPS AND OUTGROUPS All groups set boundaries by distinguishing between insiders who are members and outsiders who are not. Sociologist William Graham Sumner (1959/1906) coined the terms *ingroup* and *outgroup* to describe people's feelings toward members of their own and other groups. An ***ingroup* is a group to which a person belongs and with which the person feels a sense of identity.** An ***outgroup* is a group to**

These Olympic teams graphically illustrate the concept of ingroups and outgroups. Each Olympic team can be seen as an ingroup that helps to give its members a sense of belonging and identity—feelings that are strengthened by the presence of clearly defined outgroups (competing teams).

which a person does not belong and toward which the person may feel a sense of competitiveness or hostility. Distinguishing between our ingroups and our outgroups helps us establish our individual identity and self-worth. Likewise, groups are solidified by ingroup and outgroup distinctions; the presence of an enemy or hostile group binds members more closely together (Coser, 1956).

Group boundaries may be formal, with clearly defined criteria for membership. For example, a country club that requires applicants for membership to be recommended by four current members, to pay a $25,000 initiation fee, and to pay $1,000 per month membership dues has clearly set requirements for its members. The club may even post a sign at its entrance that states "Members Only," and use security personnel to ensure that nonmembers do not encroach on its grounds. Boundary distinctions often are reflected in symbols such as emblems or clothing. Members of the country club are given membership cards to gain access to the club's facilities or to charge food to their account. They may wear sun visors and shirts with the country club's logo on them. All of these symbols denote that the bearer/wearer is a member of the ingroup; they are status symbols.

Group boundaries are not always as formal as they are in a private club. Friendship groups, for example, usually do not have clear guidelines for membership; rather, the boundaries tend to be very informal and vaguely defined.

Ingroup and outgroup distinctions may encourage social cohesion among members, but they also may promote classism, racism, sexism, and ageism. Ingroup members typically view themselves positively and members of outgroups negatively. These feelings of group superiority, or *ethnocentrism*, are somewhat inevitable. However, members of some groups feel more free than others to act on their beliefs. If groups are embedded in larger groups and organizations, the large organization may discourage such beliefs and their consequences (Merton, 1968). Conversely, organizations covertly may foster these ingroup/outgroup distinctions by denying their existence or by failing to take action when misconduct occurs. For example, take the case of sexual harassment in a Winnipeg plant:

> In Winnipeg, Manitoba, recently two male employees were fired from a Canada Safeway bread plant for accusations of sexual harassment against female employees. One of the men allegedly exposed himself, stalked, and gave photographs of his anatomy to a female employee. Accusations against the other man include repeatedly making lewd and suggestive

> comments to female employees and inappropriately touching them. The female employee said that 10 or 12 women on the work floor have taken stress leave from work over the last five years because of the abuse. Men outnumber women on the shop floor by about eight to one. The United Food and Commercial Workers union spokesperson explained that, "the system of dealing with sexual-harassment complaints failed in this case because of the influential position one of the accused men held with the union." These incidents were not brought to the attention of the union management. Female employees say that the atmosphere at the plant discouraged women from coming forward to report incidents of harassment. One stated "we were terrified ... they told us not to do it and we didn't know any better ... they kept saying they'll deal with it, but they never did. And we didn't know anything about our rights." (Owen, 1996b)

Female employees stated that the company has failed to take claims of sexual harassment seriously. One anonymous employee indicated that the abuse (both verbal and physical) occurred over a number of years before the union or company took action. In this case, male co-workers seem to have developed an ingroup from which the female employees were not only categorically excluded but also made the object of the group's ridicule. In a work environment, ingroups can provide support for group members. Those who are denied membership in the group, however, may find it impossible to perform their job effectively.

REFERENCE GROUPS Ingroups provide us not only with a source of identity but also with a point of reference. A ***reference group*** **is a group that strongly influences a person's behaviour and social attitudes, regardless of whether that individual is an actual member.** When we attempt to evaluate our appearance, ideas, or goals, we automatically refer to the standards of some group. Sometimes, we will refer to our membership groups, such as family or friends. Other times, we will rely on groups to which we do not currently belong but that we might wish to join in the future, such as a social club or a profession. We also may have negative reference groups. For many people, the Ku Klux Klan and neo-Nazi skinheads are examples of negative reference groups because most people's racial attitudes compare favourably with such groups' blatantly racist behaviour.

Reference groups help explain why our behaviour and attitudes sometimes differ from those of our membership groups. We may accept the values and norms of a group with which we identify rather than one to which we belong. We also may act more like members of a group we want to join than members of groups to which we already belong. In this case, reference groups are a source of anticipatory socialization. Many people have more than one reference group and often receive conflicting messages from them about how they should view themselves. For most of us, our reference group attachments change many times during our life course, especially when we acquire a new status in a formal organization.

GROUP CHARACTERISTICS AND DYNAMICS

What purpose do groups serve? Why are individuals willing to relinquish some of their freedom to participate in groups? According to functionalists, people form groups to meet instrumental and expressive needs. *Instrumental*, or task-oriented, needs cannot always be met by one person, so the group works cooperatively to fulfill a specific goal. Think, for example, of how hard it would be to function as a one-person football team or to single-handedly build a skyscraper. Groups help members do jobs that are impossible to do alone or that would be very difficult and time-consuming at best. In addition to instrumental needs, groups also help people meet their *expressive*, or emotional, needs, especially for self-expression and support from family, friends, and peers.

While not disputing that groups ideally perform such functions, conflict theorists suggest that groups also involve a series of power relationships whereby the needs of individual members may not be equally served. Symbolic interactionists focus on how the size of a group influences the kind of interaction that takes place among members.

We now will look at certain characteristics of groups, such as how size affects group dynamics.

Throughout life, our most intense relationships occur in dyads. The ties we share with another person are either strengthened or weakened by the attitudes and behaviour of other acquaintances.

GROUP SIZE

The size of a group is one of its most important features. Interactions are more personal and intense in a ***small group*, a collectivity small enough for all members to be acquainted with one another and to interact simultaneously.**

Sociologist Georg Simmel (1950/1917) suggested that small groups have distinctive interaction patterns that do not exist in larger groups. According to Simmel, in a ***dyad*—a group composed of two members**—the active participation of both members is crucial for the group's survival. If one member withdraws from interaction or "quits," the group ceases to exist. Examples of dyads include two people who are best friends, married couples, and domestic partnerships. Dyads provide members with a more intense bond and a sense of unity not found in most larger groups.

When a third person is added to a dyad, a ***triad*, a group composed of three members,** is formed. The nature of the relationship and interaction patterns change with the addition of the third person. In a triad even if one member ignores another or declines to participate, the group can still function. In addition, two members may unite to create a coalition that can subject the third member to group pressure to conform. A *coalition* is an alliance created in an attempt to reach a shared objective or goal. If two members form a coalition, the other member may be seen as an outsider or intruder. In extreme cases, certain types of harassment may be fostered in triadic relationships in which two harassers reinforce each other's behaviour and make the third member of the group the "outsider." Like dyads, triads can exist as separate entities or be contained within formal organizations.

As the size of a group increases beyond three people, members tend to specialize in different tasks, and everyday communication patterns change. For instance, in groups of more than six or seven people, it becomes increasingly difficult for everyone to take part in the same conversation; therefore, several conversations likely will take place simultaneously. Members also are likely to take sides on issues and form a number of coalitions. In groups of more than ten or twelve people, it becomes virtually impossible for all members to participate in a single conversation unless one person serves as moderator and facilitates the discussion. As shown in Figure 6.1, when the size of the group increases, the number of possible social interactions also increases.

Although large groups typically have less social solidarity than small ones, they may have more power. However, the relationship between size and power is more complicated than it might

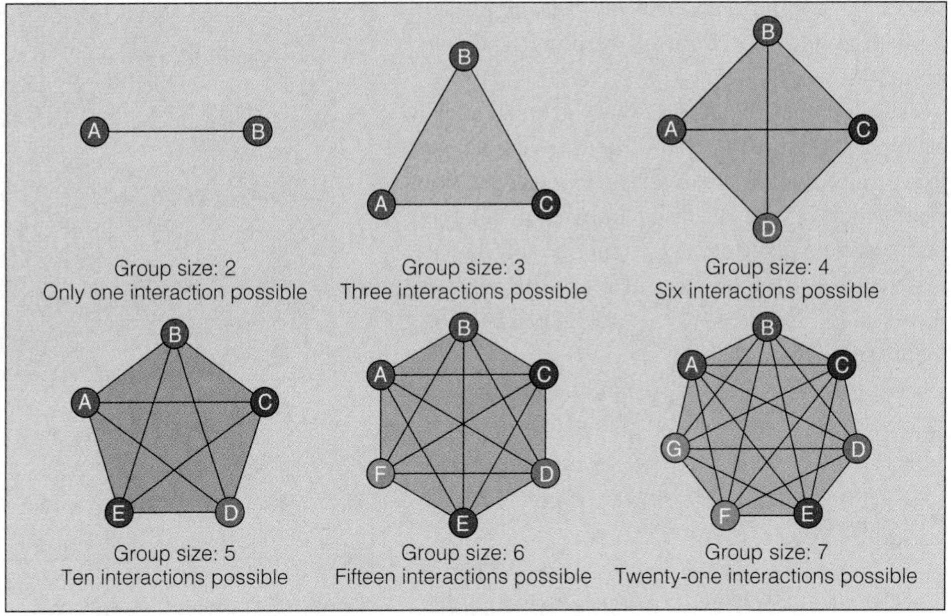

FIGURE 6.1

Growth of Possible Social Interaction Based on Group Size

initially seem. The power relationship depends on both a group's *absolute* size and its *relative* size (Simmel, 1950/1902; Merton, 1968). The absolute size is the number of members the group actually has; the relative size is the number of potential members. Suppose, for example, that three hundred people (out of many thousands) who have been the victims of sexual harassment band together to protest government and demand more stringent enforcement of harassment laws. Although three hundred people is a large number in some contexts, opponents of this group would argue that the low turnout demonstrated that harassment is not as big a problem as some might think. At the same time, the power of a small group to demand change may be based on a "strength in numbers" factor if the group is seen as speaking on behalf of a large number of other people (who also are voters).

Larger groups typically have more formalized leadership structures. Their leaders are expected to perform a variety of roles, some related to the internal workings of the group and others related to external relationships with other groups.

GROUP LEADERSHIP

What role do leaders play in groups? Leaders are responsible for directing plans and activities so that the group completes its task or fulfills its goals. Primary groups generally have informal leadership. For example, most of us do not elect or appoint leaders in our own families. Various family members may assume a leadership role at various times or act as leaders for specific tasks. In traditional families, the father or eldest male is usually the leader. However, in today's more diverse families, leadership and power are more diverse, and power relationships may be quite different, as discussed in Chapter 14 ("Families and Intimate Relationships"). By comparison, leadership in secondary groups (such as colleges, governmental agencies, and corporations) involves a clearly defined chain of command with written responsibilities assigned to each position in the organizational structure.

LEADERSHIP FUNCTIONS Both primary and secondary groups have some type of leadership or positions that enable certain people to be leaders, or at least to wield power over others. From a functionalist perspective, if groups exist to meet the instrumental and expressive needs of their members, then leaders are responsible for helping the group meet those needs. ***Instrumental leadership* is goal- or task-oriented;** this type of leadership is most appropriate when the group's purpose is to complete a task or reach a particular goal. ***Expressive leadership* provides emotional support for members;** this type of leadership is most appropriate when the group is dealing with emotional issues, and harmony, solidarity, and high morale are needed. Both kinds of leadership are needed for groups to work effectively. Traditionally, instrumental and expressive leadership roles have been limited by gender socialization. Instrumental leadership has been linked with men while expressive leadership has been linked with women. Social change in recent years has somewhat blurred the distinction between gender-specific leadership characteristics, but these outdated stereotypes have not completely disappeared (Basow, 1992).

LEADERSHIP STYLES Three major styles of leadership exist in groups: authoritarian, democratic, and laissez-faire. ***Authoritarian leaders* make all major group decisions and assign tasks to members.** These leaders focus on the instrumental tasks of the group and demand compliance from others. In times of crisis, such as a war or natural disaster, authoritarian leaders may be commended for their decisive actions. In other situations, however, they may be criticized for being dictatorial and for fostering intergroup hostility. By contrast, ***democratic leaders* encourage group discussion and decision making through consensus building.** These leaders may be praised for their expressive, supportive behaviour toward group members, but they also may be blamed for being indecisive in times of crisis.

Laissez-faire literally means "to leave alone." ***Laissez-faire leaders* are only minimally involved in decision making and encourage group members to make their own decisions.** On the one hand, laissez-faire leaders may be viewed positively by group members because they do not flaunt their power or position. On the other hand, a group that needs active leadership is not likely to find it with this style of leadership, which does not work vigorously to promote group goals (White and Lippitt, 1953, 1960).

Studies of kinds of leadership and decision-making styles have certain inherent limitations. They tend to focus on leadership that is imposed externally on a group (such as bosses or political leaders) rather than leadership that arises within a group. Different decision-making styles may be more effective in one setting than another. Imagine, for example, attending a university class in which the professor asked the students to determine what should be covered in the course, what the course requirements should be, and how students should be graded. It would be a difficult and cumbersome way to start the semester; students might spend the entire semester negotiating these matters and never actually learn anything.

GROUP CONFORMITY

To what extent do groups exert a powerful influence in our lives? As discussed in Chapters 3 and 4, groups have a significant amount of influence over our values, attitudes, and behaviour. In order to gain and then retain our membership in groups, most of us are willing to exhibit a high level of conformity to the wishes of other group members. ***Conformity* is the process of maintaining or changing behaviour to comply with the norms established by a society, subculture, or other group.** We often experience powerful pressure from other group members to conform. In some situations, this pressure may be almost overwhelming.

In several studies (which would be impossible to conduct today for ethical reasons), researchers found that the pressure to conform may cause group members to say they see something that is contradictory to what they actually are seeing or to do something they otherwise would be unwilling to do. As we look at two of these studies, ask yourself what you might have done if you had been involved in this research.

ASCH'S RESEARCH Pressure to conform is especially strong in small groups in which members want to fit in with the group. In a series of experiments conducted by Solomon Asch (1955, 1956), the pressure toward group conformity was so great that participants were willing to contradict their own best judgment if the rest of the group disagreed with them.

One of Asch's experiments involved groups of undergraduate men (seven in each group) who allegedly were recruited for a study of visual perception. All of the men were seated in chairs. However, the person in the sixth chair did not know that he was the only actual subject; all of the others were assisting the researcher. The participants first were shown a large card with a vertical line on it and then a second card with three vertical lines (see Figure 6.2). Each of the seven participants was asked to indicate which of the three lines on the second card was identical in length to the "standard line" on the first card.

In the first test with each group, all seven men selected the correct matching line. In the second trial, all seven still answered correctly. In the third trial, however, the subject became very uncomfortable when all of the others selected the incorrect line. The actual subject could not understand what was happening and became even more confused as the others continued to give incorrect responses on eleven out of the next fifteen trials.

If you had been in the position of the subject, how would you have responded? Would you have continued to give the correct answer, or would you have been swayed by the others? When Asch (1955) averaged the responses of the fifty actual subjects who participated in the study, he found that about 33 percent routinely chose to conform to the group by giving the same (incorrect) responses as Asch's assistants. Another 40 percent gave incorrect responses in about half of the trials. Although 25 percent always gave correct responses, even they felt very uneasy and "knew that something was wrong." In discussing the experiment afterwards, most of the subjects who gave incorrect responses indicated that they had known the answers were wrong but decided to go along with the group in order to avoid ridicule or ostracism.

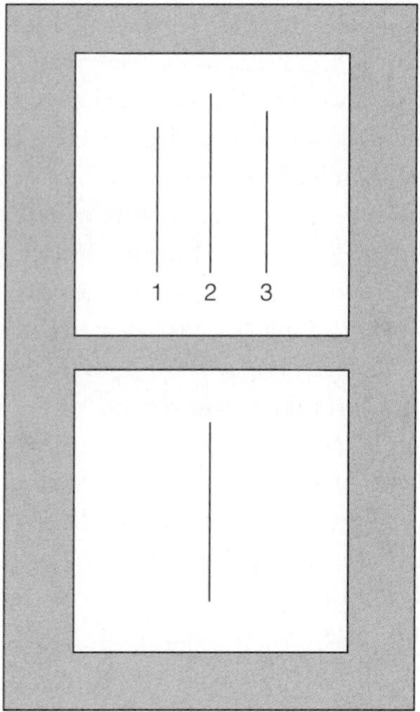

FIGURE 6.2

Asch's Cards

Source: Asch, 1955.

After conducting additional research, Asch concluded that the size of the group and the degree of social cohesion felt by participants were important influences on the extent to which individuals respond to group pressure. In dyads, for example, the subject was much less likely to conform to an incorrect response from one assistant than in four-member groups. This effect peaked in groups of approximately seven members and then leveled off (see Figure 6.3). Not surprisingly, when groups were not cohesive (when more than one member dissented), group size had less

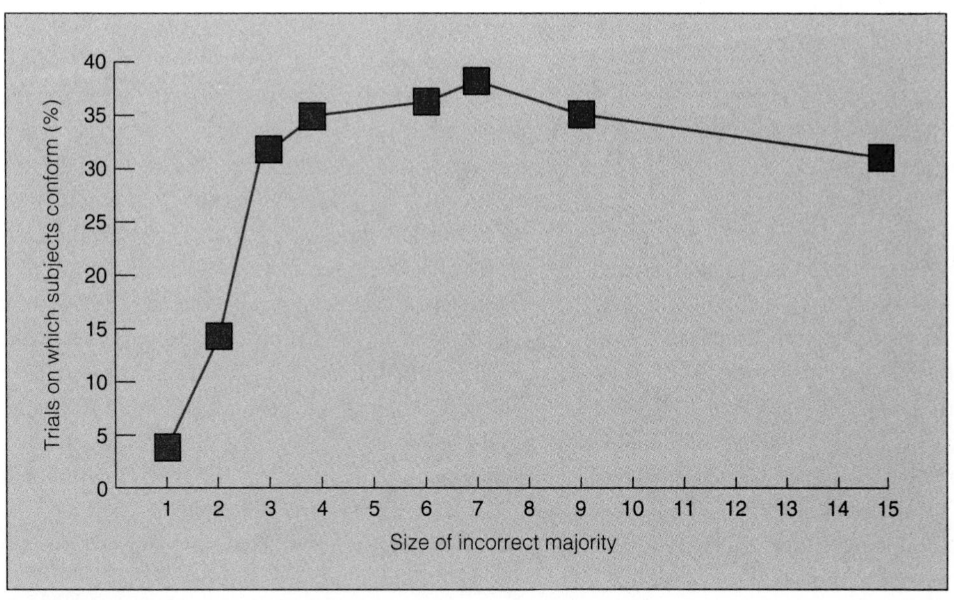

FIGURE 6.3

Effect of Group Size in the Asch Conformity Studies

As more people are added to the "incorrect" majority, subjects' tendency to conform by giving wrong answers increases—but only up to a point. Adding more than seven people to the incorrect majority does *not* further increase subjects' tendency to conform—perhaps because subjects are suspicious about why so many people agree with one another.

Source: Asch, 1955.

effect. If even a single assistant did not agree with the others, the subject was reassured by hearing someone else question the accuracy of incorrect responses and was much less likely to give a wrong answer himself.

One contribution of Asch's research is the dramatic way in which it calls our attention to the power that groups have to produce a certain type of conformity referred to as compliance. *Compliance* is the extent to which people say (or do) things so that they may gain the approval of other people. Certainly, Asch demonstrated that people will bow to social pressure in small-group settings. From a sociological perspective, however, the study was flawed because it involved deception about the purpose of the study and about the role of individual group members. Moreover, the study included only male college students, thus making it impossible for us to generalize its findings to other populations, including women and people who were not undergraduates. Would Asch's conclusions have been the same if women had participated in the study? Would the same conclusions be reached if the study were conducted today? We cannot answer these questions with certainty, but the work of Solomon Asch and his student, Stanley Milgram, have had a lasting impact on social science perceptions about group conformity and obedience to authority.

MILGRAM'S RESEARCH How willing are we to do something because someone in a position of authority has told us to do it? How far are we willing to go in following the demands of that individual? Stanley Milgram (1963, 1974) conducted a series of controversial experiments to find answers to these questions about people's obedience to authority. *Obedience* is a form of compliance in which people follow direct orders from someone in a position of authority.

Milgram's subjects were men who had responded to an advertisement for participants in an experiment. When the first (actual) subject arrived, he was told that the study concerned the effects of punishment on learning. After the second subject (an assistant of Milgram's) arrived, the two men were instructed to draw slips of paper from a hat to get their assignments as either the "teacher" or the "learner." Because the drawing was rigged, the actual subject always became the teacher, and the assistant the learner. Next, the learner was strapped into a chair with protruding electrodes that looked something like an electric chair. The teacher was placed in an adjoining room and given a realistic-looking but nonoperative shock generator. The "generator's" control panel showed levels that went from "Slight Shock" (15 volts) on the left, to "Intense Shock" (255 volts) in the middle, to "DANGER: SEVERE SHOCK" (375 volts), and finally "XXX" (450 volts) on the right.

The teacher was instructed to read aloud a pair of words and then repeat the first of the two words. At that time, the learner was supposed to respond with the second of the two words. If the learner could not provide the second word, the teacher was instructed to press the lever on the shock generator so that the learner would be punished for forgetting the word. Each time the learner gave an incorrect response, the teacher was supposed to increase the shock level by 15 volts. The alleged purpose of the shock was to determine if punishment improves a person's memory.

What was the maximum level of shock that a "teacher" was willing to inflict on a "learner"? The learner had been instructed (in advance) to beat on the wall between himself and the teacher as the experiment continued, pretending that he was in intense pain. The teacher was told that the shocks might be "extremely painful" but that they would cause no permanent damage. At about 300 volts, when the learner quit responding at all to questions, the teacher often turned to the experimenter to see what he should do next. When the experimenter indicated that the teacher should give increasingly painful shocks, 65 percent of them administered shocks all the way up to the "XXX" (450-volt) level (see Figure 6.4). By this point in the process, the teachers frequently were sweating, stuttering, or biting on their lip. According to Milgram, the teachers (who were free to leave whenever they wanted to) continued in the experiment because they were being given directions by a person in a position of authority (a university scientist wearing a white coat).

What can we learn from Milgram's study? The study provides evidence that obedience to authority may be more common than most of us would like to believe. None of the "teachers" challenged the process before they had applied 300 volts. Almost two-thirds went all the way to what could have been a deadly jolt of electricity if the shock generator had been real. For many years, Milgram's findings were found to be consistent in a number of different settings and with variations in the research design (Miller, 1986).

This research once again raises some questions originally posed in Chapter 2 concerning research ethics. As was true of Asch's research, Milgram's subjects were deceived about the nature of the study in which they were being asked to participate. Many of them found the experiment extremely stressful. Such conditions cannot be ignored by social scientists because subjects may receive lasting emotional scars from such research. It would be virtually impossible today to obtain permission to replicate this experiment in a university setting.

GROUP CONFORMITY AND SEXUAL HARASSMENT Social scientists recently have begun to conduct experiments and engage in other types of research to help them understand the behaviour behind and the circumstances of sexual harassment. We have looked at some aspects of sexual harassment already in this chapter, but what are your percep-

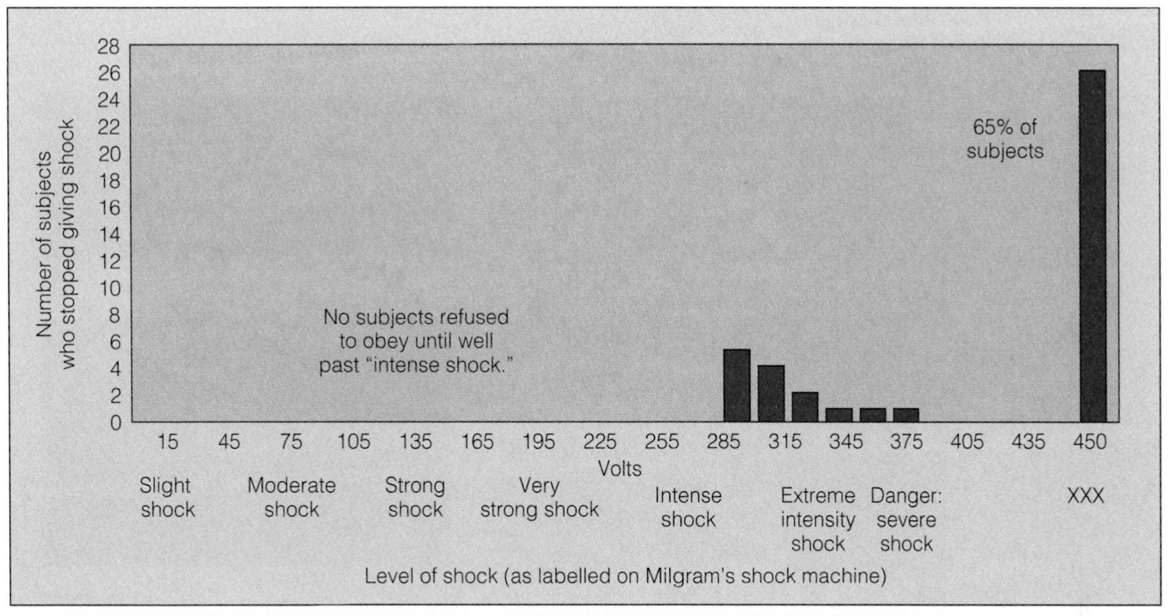

FIGURE 6.4

Results of Milgram's Obedience Experiment

Even Milgram was surprised by subjects' willingness to administer what they thought were severely painful and even dangerous shocks to a helpless "learner."

Source: Milgram, 1963.

tions about this complex social problem? Before reading further, take the quiz on sexual harassment in Box 6.2.

Psychologist John Pryor (*PBS*, 1992b) has conducted behavioural experiments on university campuses to examine the social dynamics of harassment. In one of his studies, a graduate student (who actually was a member of the research team) led research subjects to believe that they would be training undergraduate women to use a computer. The actual purpose of the experiment was to observe whether the trainers (subjects) would harass the women if given the opportunity and encouraged to do so. By design, the graduate student purposely harassed the women (who also were part of the research team), setting an example for the subjects to follow.

Pryor found that when the "trainers" were led to believe that sexual harassment was condoned and then were left alone with the women, they took full advantage of the situation in 90 percent of the experiments. Shannon Hoffman, one of the women who participated in the research, felt vulnerable because of the permissive environment created by the men in charge:

> It was very uncomfortable for me. I realized that had it been out of the experimental setting that, as a woman, I would have been very nervous with someone that close to me and reaching around me. So it kind of made me feel a little bit powerless as far as that goes because there was nothing I could do about it. But I also realized that in a business setting, if this person really was my boss, that it would be harder for me to send out the negative signals or whatever to try to fend off that type of thing. (*PBS*, 1992b)

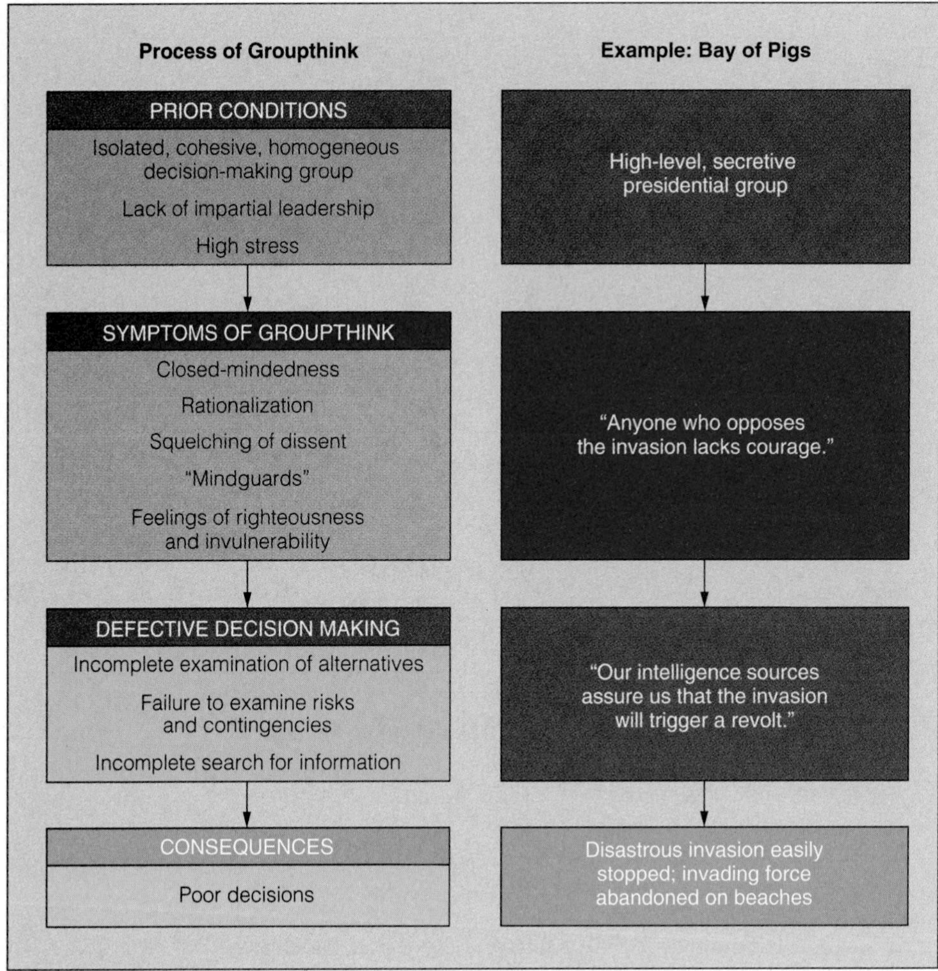

FIGURE 6.5

Janis's Description of Groupthink

In Janis's model, prior conditions such as a highly homogeneous group with a committed leadership can lead to potentially disastrous "groupthink," which short-circuits careful and impartial deliberation. Janis believed that the dynamics of groupthink played a major role in the decision of the Kennedy administration to back an ill-advised invasion of Cuba in 1961.

This research suggests a relationship between group conformity and harassment. Sexual harassment is more likely to occur when it is encouraged (or at least not actively discouraged) by others. When people think they can get away with it, they are more likely to engage in such behaviour.

GROUPTHINK As we have seen, individuals often respond differently in a group context than they might if they were alone. Social psychologist Irving Janis (1972, 1989) examined group decision making among political experts and found that major blunders in U.S. history may be attributed to pressure toward group conformity. To describe

BOX 6.2 SOCIOLOGY AND EVERYDAY LIFE

How Much Do You Know About Sexual Harassment?

TRUE	FALSE	
T	F	1. Few women are sexually harassed in today's society.
T	F	2. Sexual harassment is relatively easy to define and study.
T	F	3. Sexual harassment in the workplace is a problem experienced only by women.
T	F	4. A female student is repeatedly asked out by a male in her dormitory. She has made it clear that she is not interested, yet he persists in his requests. She may be a victim of sexual harassment.
T	F	5. In the media, women are always depicted as the victims of sexual harassment and men as the perpetrators.
T	F	6. A professor who invites a student to go out on a date even though the student has previously refused to go out in the past may have committed sexual harassment.
T	F	7. It is safe to assume that the statistics for the incidence of sexual harassment present an accurate representation of the actual occurrence of sexual harassment.
T	F	8. The only way that an organization can be sure that sexual harassment does not occur is to limit relationships among participants, whether they are students and faculty or employees and supervisors.
T	F	9. Women who are sexually harassed often experience it as an isolated occurrence and suffer no lasting effects after the incident.
T	F	10. Sexual harassment that occurs in an organization reflects the dynamics of interaction in that institution and influences in the larger society.

Answers on page 210

this phenomenon, he coined the term ***groupthink*—the process by which members of a cohesive group arrive at a decision that many individual members privately believe is unwise.** Why not speak up at the time? Members usually want to be "team players." They may not want to be the ones who undermine the group's consensus or who challenge the group's leaders. Consequently, members often limit or withhold their opinions and focus on consensus rather than on exploring all of the options and determining the best course of action. Figure 6.5 summarizes the dynamics and results of groupthink.

Groupthink frequently occurs in situations in which the leader is powerful and the decision-making group is relatively small and highly cohesive. According to Janis (1972), loyalty to a group can prevent members from voicing controversial questions. Before the 1961 ill-fated Bay of Pigs invasion, to maintain consensus and group harmony, several U.S. policy advisors withheld their objections from president John F. Kennedy.

BOX 6.2 SOCIOLOGY AND EVERYDAY LIFE

Answers to the Sociology Quiz on Sexual Harassment

TRUE	FALSE	
T	**F**	1. *False.* The Violence Against Women Survey conducted by Statistics Canada in 1994 found that 89 percent of the women surveyed were sexually harassed, abused, or assaulted. Kelly (1988) found the prevalence rate to be 87 percent in her study of British women. She also found sexual harassment to be more common than physical or sexual assaults.
T	**F**	2. *False.* There are a myriad of behaviours that may constitute sexual harassment. Given the ambiguity of defining sexual harassment in objective terms, it is difficult to research the prevalence of this phenomenon.
T	**F**	3. *False.* Sexual harassment in the workplace is a problem for both men and women; however, women are more likely to be the victims. Women are nine times more likely to quit their jobs because of sexual harassment, five times more likely to transfer, and three times more likely to lose their jobs.
T	F	4. *True.* It is sexual harassment when certain behaviour is perceived as unwelcome sexual attention. She has indicated that his requests are unwelcome, but he continues to ask.
T	**F**	5. *False.* Recently, the media (especially novels, television talk shows, and movies) have depicted a few women as the perpetrators of sexual harassment. However, women are still more likely to be shown as victims rather than as harassers.
T	F	6. *True.* If the student believes that rejection may result in adverse academic action, such as a bad grade or recommendation, this situation could constitute sexual harassment. Also, if the student feels violated and feels the invitations are unwanted sexual attention, this occurrence could be sexual harassment.
T	**F**	7. *False.* Many victims of sexual harassment are either unsure whether they have been sexually harassed, or are afraid to report the incident. These cases remain undetected. The actual rates of sexual harassment are therefore higher than the estimates reported. It is estimated that 90 percent of sexual harassment victims are unwilling to come forward in fear of retaliation (such as losing a job or receiving a failing grade) or a loss of privacy.
T	**F**	8. *False.* Not only would it be virtually impossible to restrict interpersonal relationships in this way, but placing such limitations on relationships would not free an organization of sexual harassment. Instead, it might create an oppressive environment in which harassers simply used more covert methods.
T	**F**	9. *False.* The effects of sexual harassment can linger long past the actual incident to remind women of their vulnerability to assault (Kelly, 1988). The human costs of sexual harassment extend beyond the immediate situation to include physical, emotional, and psychological effects, and other consequences.
T	F	10. *True.* Sociologists look further than the walls of institutions where sexual harassment takes place and recognize it as a larger social problem. Looking at the larger social context, we can see a society where acts of violence against women are widespread and still, for the most part, being accepted.

Sources: Based on Lightle and Doucet, 1992; Women's Action Coalition, 1993; Statistics Canada, 1994c; Kelly, 1988.

The group "unanimously" voted to invade Cuba. They reached a consensus on the surface, but had divergent opinions concerning the proposed attack. Janis quotes one of the participants as stating later: "Our meeting was taking place in an atmosphere of assumed consensus. Had one senior advisor opposed the venture, I believe Kennedy would have cancelled it. Not one spoke up." Individuals did not voice their opposition, hence questioning the group's original assumptions, to avoid disrupting group harmony (Robertson, 1977:145).

FORMAL ORGANIZATIONS

Over the past century, the number of formal organizations has increased dramatically in Canada and other industrialized nations. Everyday life previously was centred in small, informal, primary groups, such as the family and the village. With the advent of industrialization and urbanization (as discussed in Chapter 1), people's lives became increasingly dominated by large, formal, secondary organizations. A *formal organization*, you will recall, is a highly structured secondary group formed for the purpose of achieving specific goals in the most efficient manner. Formal organizations (such as corporations, schools, and government agencies) usually keep their basic structure for many years in order to meet their specific goals.

TYPES OF FORMAL ORGANIZATIONS

We join some organizations voluntarily and others out of necessity. Sociologist Amitai Etzioni (1975) classified formal organizations into three categories—normative, coercive, and utilitarian—based on the nature of membership in each.

NORMATIVE ORGANIZATIONS We voluntarily join normative organizations when we want to pursue some common interest or gain personal satisfaction or prestige from being a member. Voluntary membership is one of the central features of normative associations. Members function as unpaid workers. Women, being historically excluded from the labour force, have played a central role in normative organizations. In 1987, there were 5.3 million Canadians in volunteer positions. The majority (56 percent) of these volunteers were women (Vanier Institute of the Family, 1994). A widely diverse range of normative organizations exist in Canada. These include political parties, activist groups, religious organizations, and educational associations.

People join normative organizations for a number of reasons, some of which may be: to advance a particular cause the group represents; to gain a sense of purpose and identity; or to promote social change. Many women have joined together to form women's interest groups across the country and were influential in establishing what was formerly called the National Action Committee on the Status of Women. Anti-racist coalitions are another example of an organization that fights for a particular cause, in this case to eradicate racism. Members of the environmental movement have formed various organizations such as Greenpeace and the Sierra Club to support their cause. Normative organizations have also formed to address nuclear disarmament, animal testing, endangered species, and ozone depletion. One animal rights organization in Canada is the People Acting for Animal Liberation. Gay rights organizations have formed across the country to advocate human rights for gay men and women, and an end to homophobia and hate crimes directed against gays and lesbians. First Nations groups have organized and are advocating for better social, economic, and health conditions for their people.

There are several well-known humanitarian voluntary organizations in Canada, including the Red Cross, Easter Seals, Shriners, Big Brothers and Big Sisters, and the Canadian Cancer Society. Members volunteer their time for the good of helping others. For example, the Shriners fund twenty-two nonprofit hospitals across North America, including three for young burn victims.

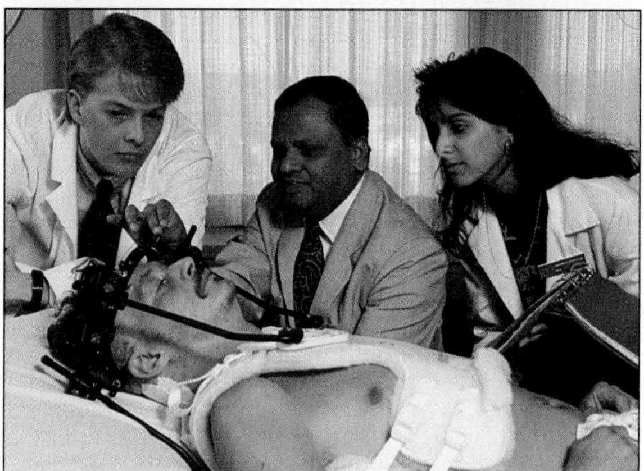

Normative organizations rely on volunteers to fulfill their goals; these volunteers (left) make Red Cross work possible in Honduras, Central America. Coercive organizations rely on involuntary recruitment; these young men (upper right) were remanded to this juvenile correctional centre (a total institution). Utilitarian organizations provide material rewards to participants; in teaching hospitals such as this (lower right), physicians, medical students, and patients all hope they may benefit from involvement with the organization.

The Rotary Club and Kiwanis are examples of other normative organizations. Membership in these groups is more exclusive than the others mentioned.

Since participation in the organization is voluntary, few formal control mechanisms exist for enforcing norms on members. As a result, people tend to change affiliations rather frequently. They may change groups when personal objectives have been fulfilled or when other groups might better meet their individual needs.

COERCIVE ORGANIZATIONS Unlike normative organizations, people do not voluntarily become members of *coercive organizations*—associations people are forced to join. Total institutions, such as boot camps, prisons, and some mental hospitals, are examples of coercive organizations. As discussed in Chapter 4, the assumed goal of total institutions is to resocialize people through incarceration. These environments are characterized by restrictive barriers (such as locks, bars, and security guards) that make it impossible for people

Although telephone- and computer-based procedures have streamlined the registration process at many schools, for many students registration exemplifies the worst aspects of academic bureaucracy. Yet students and other members of the academic community depend upon the "bureaucracy" to establish and administer procedures that enable the complex system of the university to operate smoothly.

to leave freely. When people leave without being officially dismissed, their exit is referred to as an "escape."

In coercive organizations, both men and women frequently are sexually harassed and violently assaulted. Inmates and patients who have been involuntarily committed to mental hospitals often find themselves powerless not only in comparison with organizational employees (such as guards and attendants) but also in relationship to other, more experienced, residents. Even in institutions where such behaviour is relatively rare, there is widespread fear of sexual victimization (Bowker, 1980).

UTILITARIAN ORGANIZATIONS We voluntarily join *utilitarian organizations* when they can provide us with a material reward we seek. To make a living or earn a university degree, we must participate in organizations that can provide us these opportunities. Although we have some choice regarding where we work or attend school, utilitarian organizations are not always completely voluntary. For example, most people must continue to work even if the conditions of their employment are less than ideal.

BUREAUCRACIES

As we approach the twenty-first century, the bureaucratic model of organization remains the most universal organizational form in government, business, education, and religion. A ***bureaucracy*** **is an organizational model characterized by a hierarchy of authority, a clear division of labour, explicit rules and procedures, and impersonality in personnel matters.**

When we think of a bureaucracy, we may think of "buck-passing," such as occurs when we are directed from one office to the next without receiving an answer to our question or a solution to our problem. We also may view a bureaucracy in terms of "red tape" because of the situations in which there is so much paperwork and so many incomprehensible rules that no one really understands what to do. However, the bureaucracy originally was not intended to be this way; it was seen as a way to make organizations *more* productive and efficient.

As noted in Chapter 1, German sociologist Max Weber (1968/1922) was interested in the historical trend toward bureaucratization that accelerated during the Industrial Revolution. To

Weber, the bureaucracy was the most "rational" and efficient means of attaining organizational goals because it contributed to coordination and control. According to Weber, ***rationality* is the process by which traditional methods of social organization, characterized by informality and spontaneity, gradually are replaced by efficiently administered formal rules and procedures.** It can be seen in all aspects of our lives, from small colleges with perhaps a thousand students to multinational corporations employing many thousands of workers worldwide.

In his study of bureaucracies, Weber relied on an ideal-type analysis, which he adapted from the field of economics. **An *ideal type* is an abstract model that describes the recurring characteristics of some phenomenon** (such as bureaucracy). To develop this ideal type, Weber abstracted the most characteristic bureaucratic aspects of religious, educational, political, and business organizations. For example, to develop an ideal type for bureaucracy in higher education, you would need to include the relationships among governing bodies (such as boards of regents or trustees), administrators, faculty, staff, and students. You also would have to include the rules and policies that govern the school's activities (such as admissions criteria, grading policies, and graduation requirements). Although no two schools would have exactly the same criteria, the ideal-type constructs would be quite similar. Weber acknowledged that no existing organization would exactly fit his ideal type of bureaucracy (Blau and Meyer, 1987).

IDEAL CHARACTERISTICS OF BUREAUCRACY Weber set forth several ideal-type characteristics of bureaucratic organizations. Although bureaucratic realities often differ from these ideal characteristics, Weber's model highlights the organizational efficiency and productivity that bureaucracies strive for. The model has been criticized for not taking into account informal networks (Roethlisberger and Dickson, 1939; Blau and Meyer, 1987). However, it is not surprising that these patterns largely are ignored in Weber's theory of bureaucracy; he constructed an idealized model that deliberately overlooked imperfections and unintended outcomes (Blau and Meyer, 1987).

Division of Labour Bureaucratic organizations are characterized by specialization, and each member has a specific status with certain assigned tasks to fulfill. This division of labour requires the employment of specialized experts who are responsible for the effective performance of their duties.

In a university, for example, a distinct division of labour exists between the faculty and administration. Faculty members primarily are responsible for teaching students and conducting research. Upper-level administrators are responsible for external relations with business and community leaders, fund-raising activities, and internal governance (such as control of the budget, allocation of space, and appointments of deans, department heads, and faculty), while lower-level administrators are responsible for the day-to-day operations of the school.

Hierarchy of Authority In the sense that Weber described hierarchy of authority, or chain of command, it includes each lower office being under the control and supervision of a higher one. Sociologist Charles Perrow (1986) has noted that all groups with a division of labour are hierarchically structured. Although the chain of command is not always followed, "in a crunch, the chain is there for those higher up to use it." Authority that is distributed hierarchically takes the form of a pyramid; those few individuals at the top have more power and exercise more control than do the many at the lower levels. Hierarchy inevitably influences social interaction. Those who are lower in the hierarchy report to (and often take orders from) those above them in the organizational pyramid. Persons at the upper levels are responsible not only for their own actions but also for those of the individuals they supervise. Hierarchy has been described as a graded system of interpersonal relationships, a society of unequals in which scarce rewards become even more scarce further down the hierarchy (Presthus, 1978).

In a university, student–faculty relationships are based on both hierarchical and professional authority patterns. Professors have power based on their academic credentials and knowledge. For example, they are required to provide syllabi and other written course information that inform students about grading policies, attendance requirements, reading and testing schedules, and other expectations they must meet. Faculty members also have some degree of academic freedom and self-governance. At the same time, they are hierarchically arranged within the faculty in ranks of instructor, assistant professor, associate professor, and full professor. In the university's vertical chain of command, they also have a position. Suppose that a student has a complaint about an instructor. The chain of command in most universities would require that the student first speak with the department head or division chair, then to the dean of the university, and, occasionally, even to the vice president of academic affairs, provost, or president.

Rules and Regulations Weber asserted that rules and regulations establish authority within an organization. These rules typically are standardized and provided to members in a written format. In theory, written rules and regulations offer clear-cut standards for determining satisfactory performance. They also provide continuity so that each new member does not have to reinvent the necessary rules and regulations.

In higher education, student handbooks, catalogs, and course syllabi provide students with information about the school's rules, regulations, and academic expectations. Faculty and administrators also are provided with policy and procedures manuals that spell out their rights and obligations.

Qualification-Based Employment Bureaucracies hire staff members and professional employees based on specific qualifications. Favoritism, family connections, and other subjective factors not relevant to organizational efficiency are not acceptable criteria for employment. Individual performance is evaluated against specific standards, and promotions are based on merit as spelled out in personnel policies.

In universities, faculty members and administrators are hired based on their academic background and technical qualifications. Many faculty members in universities have tenure or other legal guarantees against arbitrary dismissal.

Impersonality A detached approach should prevail toward clients so that personal feelings do not interfere with organizational decisions. Officials must interact with subordinates based on their official status, not on their personal feelings about them.

Impersonality can be seen in standardization of test scores for admission to graduate schools across North America, and undergraduate programs in the United States. Standardized examinations for graduate and professional schools include the Graduate Records Exam (GRE), Law School Admission Test (LSAT), and the Medical College Admission Test (MCAT). These criteria supposedly are impartially applied, and individuals are admitted based on their ability to perform in a given academic setting. However, questions may have a class, ethnic, or gender bias, and thus make it harder for some to achieve a high score.

INFORMAL STRUCTURE IN BUREAUCRACIES When we look at an organizational chart, the official, formal structure of a bureaucracy is readily apparent. In practice, however, a bureaucracy has patterns of activities and interactions that cannot be accounted for by its organizational chart. These have been referred to as *bureaucracy's other face* (Page, 1946).

An organization's ***informal structure*** **is composed of those aspects of participants' day-to-day activities and interactions that ignore, bypass, or do not correspond with the official rules and procedures of the bureaucracy.** An example is an informal "grapevine" that spreads information (with varying degrees of accuracy) much faster than do official channels of communication, which tend to be slow and unresponsive. The informal structure also has been referred to as *work culture* and includes the ideology and practices of workers on the job. It is the "informal, customary values and rules [that] mediate the formal authority structure of the workplace and distance workers from its impact" (Benson, 1983:185). Workers create this work culture in order to confront, resist, or adapt to the constraints of their jobs, as well as to guide and interpret social relations on the job (Zavella, 1987).

In some situations, informal networks may be a means of dealing with an issue such as sexual harassment. For example, Jim, a computer programmer, was talking with a woman in his office about sexual harassment when she surprised him by stating that the "most obnoxious person" in the office was his boss, who had stared almost exclusively at her breasts when he talked to her for half an hour one day. Jim describes how he used the informal structure to help his colleague with this problem:

> I decided to act on her comment. … [However,] this was kind of tricky, because the guy is essentially my boss. I met with him privately. I told him that I was not asked to talk to him and that I was not going to pursue it further, but that I would certainly want to know if negative feedback was getting around about me, so I wanted him to know what a friend had told me. I quietly described the incident and mentioned that she was offended. I suggested that his eye-contact was on the undisciplined side and that he might want to be aware of how he looked at people.
>
> His response was defensive. He had some demeaning comments to make about the woman, too. I listened patiently, then pointed out that, just like his wife, women did notice how they were being treated, and he might want to consider being more aware.
>
> Today the woman came and thanked me for talking to him. He had gone up to her and apologized. (Langelan, 1993:212–213)

HAWTHORNE STUDIES AND INFORMAL NETWORKS The existence of informal networks was first established by researchers in the Hawthorne studies. As you will recall from Chapter 2, the Hawthorne effect takes place when research subjects modify their behaviour because they know that they are being observed. The Hawthorne studies also made social scientists aware of the effect of informal networks on workers' productivity.

In this particular study, researchers observed fourteen men in the "bank wiring room" who were responsible for making parts of switches for telephone equipment. Although management had offered financial incentives to encourage the men to work harder, the men persisted in working according to their own informal rules and sanctions. For example, they tended to work rapidly in the morning and ease off in the afternoon. They frequently stopped their own work to help another person who had fallen behind. When they got bored, they swapped tasks so that their work was more varied. They played games and made bets on the horse races and on baseball. Two competing cliques formed in the room, each with its own separate games and activities.

Why did these men insist on lagging behind even when they had been offered financial incentives to work harder? Perhaps they feared that the required productivity levels would increase if they showed that they could do more. Some of them also may have feared that they would lose their jobs if the work was finished more rapidly. One fact stood out in the study: The men's productivity level was clearly related to the pressure they received from other members of their informal networks. Those who worked too hard were called "speed kings" and "rate busters"; individuals who worked too slowly were referred to as "chiselers." Those who broke the informal norm against telling a supervisor about someone else's shortcomings were called "squealers." Negative sanctions in the form of "binging" (striking a person on the shoulder) made the workers want to adhere to the informal norms of their clique. Ultimately, the level of productivity was determined by the workers' informal networks, not by the levels set by management (Roethlisberger and Dickson, 1939; Blau and Meyer, 1987).

POSITIVE AND NEGATIVE ASPECTS OF INFORMAL STRUCTURE Is informal structure good or bad? Should it be controlled or encouraged? Two schools of thought have emerged with regard to these questions. One approach emphasizes control (or eradication) of informal groups; the other suggests that they should be nurtured. Traditional management theories are based on the assumption that people basically are lazy and motivated by greed. Consequently, informal groups must be controlled (or eliminated) in order to ensure greater worker productivity. Proponents of this view cite the bank wiring room study as an example of the importance of controlling informal networks.

By contrast, the other school of thought asserts that people are capable of cooperation. Thus, organizations should foster informal groups that permit people to work more efficiently toward organizational goals. Chester Barnard (1938), an early organizational theorist, focused on the functional aspects of informal groups. He suggested that organizations are cooperative systems in which informal groups "oil the wheels" by providing understanding and motivation for participants. In other words, informal networks serve as a means of communication and cohesion among individuals, as well as protecting the integrity of the individual (Barnard, 1938; Perrow, 1986).

The *human relations approach*, which is strongly influenced by Barnard's model, views informal networks as a type of adaptive behaviour workers engage in because they experience a lack of congruence between their own needs and the demands of the organization (Argyris, 1960). Organizations typically demand dependent, childlike behaviour from their members and strive to thwart the members' ability to grow and achieve "maturity" (Argyris, 1962). At the same time, members have their own needs to grow and mature. Informal networks help workers to fill this void. Large organizations would be unable to function without strong informal norms and relations among participants (Blau and Meyer, 1987).

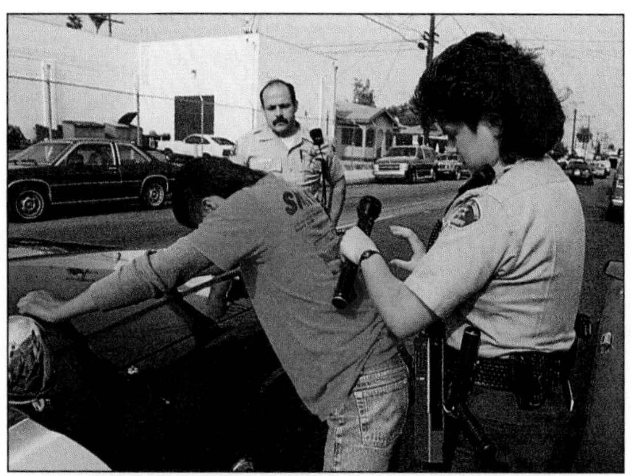

Sociologists have found that women in law enforcement are less likely than men to be included in informal networks and more likely to be harassed on the job. Are these two factors related? What steps could be taken to reduce the problems of harassment and lack of networks?

More recent studies have confirmed the importance of informal networks in bureaucracies. While some scholars have argued that women and visible minorities receive fairer treatment in larger bureaucracies than they do in smaller organizations, others have stressed that they may be categorically excluded from networks that are important for survival and advancement in the organization (Kanter, 1977; South et al., 1982; Benokraitis and Feagin, 1986; Feagin, 1991). A female firefighter describes how detrimental, and even hazardous, it is for workers to be excluded from such informal networks because of ethnicity, gender, or other attributes:

> I had sort of a "Pollyanna" view of how long it would take before women were really accepted in these nontraditional, very male-dominated jobs [such as being a firefighter]. One always thinks that once I and the other women prove that we can do the job well, people will just accept us and we'll all fit in ... [However,] I went to a firehouse where the men refused to eat with me. They would not talk to me. On one occasion my protective gear had been tampered with. It was always a big question as

> to whether in fact you have anyone there to back you up when you needed them. (*PBS*, 1992b)

White women and visible minorities who are employed in positions traditionally held by white men (such as firefighters, police officers, and factory workers) often experience categoric exclusion from the informal structure. Not only do they lack an informal network to "grease the wheels," they also may be harassed and endangered by their co-workers. In sum, the informal structure is critical for employees—whether they are allowed to participate in it or not.

SHORTCOMINGS OF BUREAUCRACIES

As noted previously, Weber's description of bureaucracy was intentionally an abstract, idealized model of a rationally organized institution. However, the very characteristics that make up this "rational" model have a dark side that frequently has given this type of organization a bad name (see Figure 6.6). Three of the major problems of bureaucracies are (1) inefficiency and rigidity, (2) resistance to change, and (3) perpetuation of ethnic, class, and gender inequalities (see Blau and Meyer, 1987).

INEFFICIENCY AND RIGIDITY Bureaucracies experience inefficiency and rigidity at both the upper and lower levels of the organization. The self-protective behaviour of officials at the top may render the organization inefficient. One type of self-protective behaviour is the monopolization of information in order to maintain control over subordinates and outsiders. Information is a valuable commodity in organizations. Budgets and long-range plans theoretically are based on relevant information, and decisions are made based on the best available data. However, those in positions of authority guard information because it is a source of power for them—others cannot "second-guess" their decisions without access to relevant (and often "confidential") information (Blau and Meyer, 1987).

This information blockage is intensified by the hierarchical arrangement of officials and workers. While those at the top tend to use their power and authority to monopolize information, they also fail to communicate with workers at the lower levels. As a result, they often are unaware of potential problems facing the organization and of high levels of worker frustration. Meanwhile, those at the bottom of the structure hide their mistakes from supervisors, a practice that ultimately may result in disaster for the organization.

Policies and procedures also contribute to inefficiency and rigidity. Sociologists Peter M. Blau and Marshall W. Meyer (1987) have suggested that bureaucratic regulations are similar to bridges and buildings in that they are designed to withstand far greater stresses than they will ever experience. Accordingly, bureaucratic regulations are written in far greater detail than is necessary, in order to ensure that almost all conceivable situations are covered. ***Goal displacement*** **occurs when the rules become an end in themselves rather than a means-to-an-end, and organizational survival becomes more important than achievement of goals** (Merton, 1968). Administrators tend to overconform to the rules because their expertise is knowledge of the regulations, and they are paid to enforce them. Officials are most likely to emphasize rules and procedures when they fear that they may lose their jobs or a "spoils system" that benefits them. They also fear that if they bend the rules for one person, they may be accused of violating the norm of impersonality and engaging in favoritism (Blau and Meyer, 1987).

Inefficiency and rigidity occur at the lower levels of the organization as well. Workers often engage in *ritualism;* that is, they become most concerned with "going through the motions" and "following the rules." According to Robert Merton (1968), the term ***bureaucratic personality*** **describes those workers who are more concerned with following correct procedures than they are with getting the job done correctly.** Such workers usually are able to handle routine situations effectively but frequently are

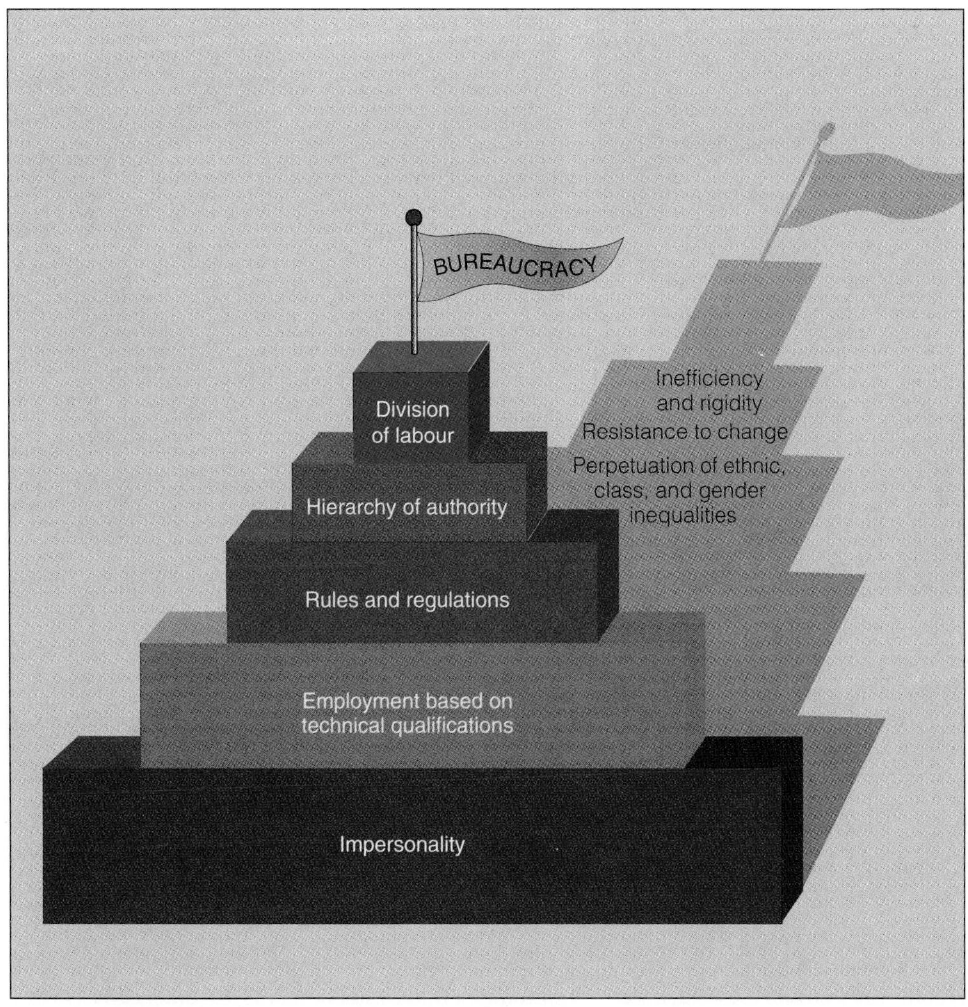

FIGURE 6.6

Characteristics and Effects of Bureaucracy

The very characteristics that define Weber's idealized bureaucracy can create or exacerbate the problems that many people associate with this type of organization.

incapable of handling a unique problem or an emergency. Thorstein Veblen (1967/1899) used the term *trained incapacity* to characterize situations in which workers have become so highly specialized, or have been given such fragmented jobs to do, that they are unable to come up with creative solutions to problems. Workers who have reached this point also tend to experience bureaucratic alienation—they really do not care what is happening around them.

Sociologists have extensively analyzed the effects of bureaucracy on workers. While some may become alienated, others may lose any identity apart from the organization. Sociologist William H. Whyte, Jr. (1957) coined the term *organization man* to identify an individual whose

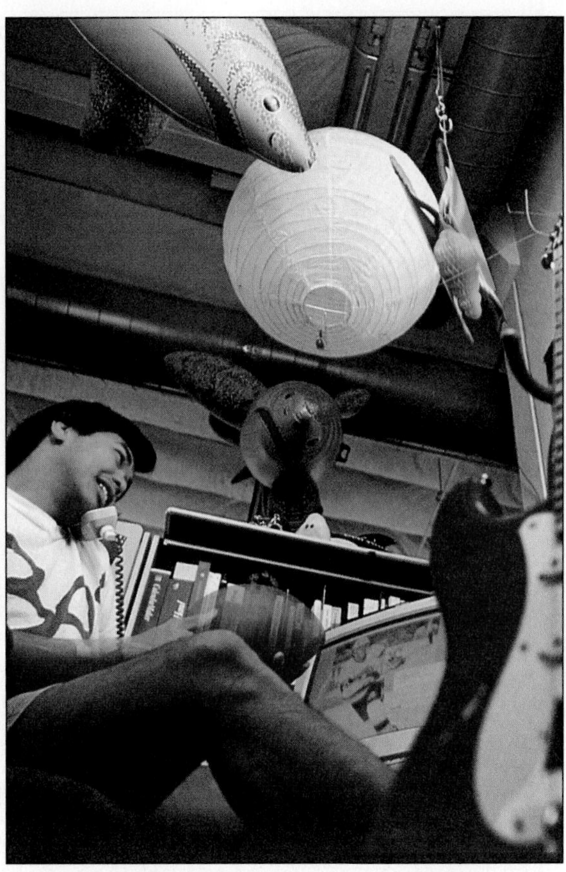

The "organization man" of the 1990s varies widely in manner and appearance, as shown in the contrast between the blue-suited chief executive officer of IBM, Louis V. Gerstner, Jr., and this casually clad employee at Apple Computer.

life is controlled by the corporation. C. Wright Mills (1959) suggested that employees become "cheerful robots" when they are controlled by an organization. Other scholars have argued that most workers do not reach these extremes.

RESISTANCE TO CHANGE Once bureaucratic organizations are created, they tend to resist change. Although the formal structure may help an organization survive during periods of crisis, it also may undermine creativity and profitability. In a study of 152 architectural firms, sociologist Judith R. Blau (1984) found that the same characteristics that made these firms most likely to survive an economic recession also made them the least likely to become highly profitable. Although the large, well-established firms had the corporate clients and the resources to withstand difficult economic times, their greater overhead made them less inclined than smaller firms to take risks. While some of the risky ventures taken by the smaller firms led to greater profits, others led to bankruptcy.

Resistance to change occurs in all bureaucratic organizations, including schools, trade unions, businesses, and government agencies. This resistance not only makes bureaucracies virtually impossible to eliminate but also contributes to bureaucratic enlargement. Because of the assumed relationship between size and importance, officials tend to press for larger budgets and more staff and office space. To justify growth, administrators and managers must come up with more tasks for workers to perform. Ultimately, the outcome predicted by "Parkinson's Law" is fulfilled: "Work expands to fill the time available for its completion" (Parkinson, 1957).

Resistance to change also may lead to incompetence. Based on organizational policy, bureaucracies tend to promote people from within the organization. As a consequence, a person who performs satisfactorily in one position is promoted to a higher level in the organization. Eventually, people reach a level that is beyond their own knowledge, experience, and capabilities. This process has been referred to as the "Peter Principle": People "rise to the level of their incompetence" (Peter and Hull, 1969:25). However, neither the Peter Principle nor Parkinson's Law has been systematically tested by sociologists. Although each may contain some truth, if they were completely accurate, all bureaucracies would be run by incompetents.

PERPETUATION OF ETHNIC, CLASS, AND GENDER INEQUALITIES Some bureaucracies perpetuate inequalities of ethnicity, class, and gender because this form of organizational structure creates a specific type of work or learning environment. This structure typically was created for middle- and upper-middle-class white men, who for many years were the predominant organizational participants.

Ethnic Inequalities In a recent study of 209 middle-class African-Americans in the United States, sociologist Joe R. Feagin (1991) found that *entry* into dominant white bureaucratic organizations should not be equated with thorough *integration.* Instead, many have experienced an internal conflict between the bureaucratic ideals of equal opportunity and fairness and the prevailing norms of discrimination and hostility that exist in many organizations. Harish Jain has done extensive research on employment discrimination in Canada. His findings indicate that racial minorities encounter both entry-level discrimination (hiring) and post-employment (on the job) discrimination in the workplace, including lack of promotions, transfers, salary increases, and job ghettoization (Jain, 1985). Other research has found that visible minorities are more adversely impacted than dominant-group members by hierarchical bureaucratic structures. These studies have been conducted in a number of organizational settings, ranging from medical schools to canning factories to corporations (see Kendall and Feagin, 1983; Zavella, 1987; and S. Collins, 1989). We will continue our discussion of the impact of organizations on visible minorities in Chapter 9 ("Ethnicity").

Social Class Inequalities Like racial inequalities, social class divisions may be perpetuated in bureaucracies (Blau and Meyer, 1987). Sociologists have explored the impact of labour market conditions on the kinds of jobs and wages available to workers. The theory of a "dual labour market" has been developed to explain how social class distinctions are perpetuated through different types of employment. Middle- and upper-middle-class employees are more likely to work in industries characterized by higher wages, more job security, and opportunities for advancement. By contrast, poor and working-class employees work in industries characterized by low wages, lack of job security, and few opportunities for promotion. Even though the "dual economy" is not a perfect model for explaining class-based organizational inequalities, it does illuminate how individuals' employment not only reflects their position in the social class but also perpetuates it. Peter Blau and Marshall Meyer (1987:160–161) conclude that "over time, then, organizational conditions reinforce social stratification… . Bureaucracies create profound differences in the life chances of the people working in them."

Gender Inequalities Gender inequalities also are perpetuated in bureaucracies. Sociologist Rosabeth Moss Kanter (1977) analyzed how the power structure of bureaucratic hierarchies can negatively impact white women and visible minorities when they are underrepresented within an organization. In such cases, they tend to be more visible ("on display") and to feel greater pressure not to make mistakes or stand out too much. They also may find it harder to gain credibility, particularly in management positions. As a result, they are more likely to feel isolated, to be excluded from informal networks, and to have less access to mentors and to power through alliances. By contrast, affluent white men generally are seen as being "one of the group." They find it easier to gain credibility, to join informal networks, and to find sponsorships (Kanter, 1977:248–249).

Gender inequality in organizations has additional consequences. People who lack opportunities for integration and advancement tend to be pessimistic and to have lower self-esteem. They seek satisfaction away from work and are less likely to promote change at work. Believing they have few opportunities, they resign themselves to staying put and surviving at that level. By contrast, those who enjoy full access to organizational opportunities tend to have high aspirations and high self-esteem. They feel loyalty to the organization and typically see their job as a means for mobility and growth.

In addition, women working in occupations and professions traditionally dominated by men have a greater likelihood of becoming the victims of sexual harassment. Although many instances of such harassment of women are reported in the media, the media may disproportionately cover situations in which a man is the subject of the harassment, as discussed in Box 6.3. Reports of overt harassment of women have come from virtually all occupational areas, including the armed forces, coal mines, corporate offices, universities, and factories (Lott, 1994). While a specific act of sexual harassment may seem minor to those who consider it to be an "isolated situation," one blatantly discriminatory act often is combined with a number of subtle and covert behaviours as well.

Covert and subtle harassment is even more difficult to document. To study conductors and train operators for a major rapid transit system, Marian Swerdlow (1989) spent four years working as a conductor. She found that the men (who comprised 96 percent of these employees) did not engage in overt harassment. However, they routinely engaged in subtle harassment, such as sexualizing work relationships, exaggerating women's errors, depicting women's routine competence as exceptional, and perpetuating a myth that women received special "preference" in hiring.

Frequently, complaints of harassment are disregarded or downplayed by employers and supervisors. When officials fail to pursue grievances, they give the impression of endorsing or condoning the harassment through their inaction (Janofsky, 1993: F1, F6). Although sexual harassment violates equal opportunity employment laws, enforcement is difficult given an employer's economic power to reward or punish a woman employee.

Many women do not report incidents of harassment because they fear that they may lose their job or suffer retaliation from their boss or co-workers. When harassment occurs in the workplace, women may simply quit their jobs. Those who experience harassment in university may drop a class, change majors, or transfer to another institution in order to escape the harasser. Women who are visible minorities face double jeopardy in that they may experience both racial discrimination and sexual harassment (Benokraitis and Feagin, 1986:126).

The bottom line is that sexual or racial harassment undermines the goal of gender equality in the workplace and in education. Consequently, organizations must be proactive in establishing guidelines for what is considered acceptable and unacceptable behaviour. The elimination of sexual harassment must be viewed as desirable not only for moral, legal, and financial reasons but also essential for creating and maintaining a positive organizational atmosphere for all participants (see Riggs, Murrell, and Cutting, 1993). Ultimately, gender and racial equality in the workplace reflects the "ideal" characteristics of bureaucracy, as well as being guaranteed by law in Canada.

BUREAUCRACY AND OLIGARCHY

Max Weber believed that bureaucracy was a necessary evil because it achieved coordination and control and thus efficiency in administration (Blau and Meyer, 1987). Sociologist Charles Perrow (1986) has suggested that bureaucracy produces a high standard of living for persons living in industrialized countries because of its superiority as a "social tool over other forms of

BOX 6.3 SOCIOLOGY AND MEDIA

The 5 Percent Factor: Sexual Harassment, Media Style

> "I didn't harass her. She harassed me."
>
> "I'm sure," Blackburn said, "it may have *seemed* like that to you at the time but—"
>
> "Phil, I'm telling you. She did everything but rape me." He paced angrily. "Phil: *she* harassed *me*." (Crichton, 1994:129)

In this scene from the best-selling novel *Disclosure*, by Michael Crichton, later a major motion picture, Tom Sanders explains that he has been the victim of sexual harassment by his female boss. The heart of the story is that Sanders, a successful married male executive in his forties at a computer company in Seattle, rejects the sexual advances of his new female boss who, in turn, falsely claims that she is the victim of sexual harassment by Tom. The fact that they had been lovers ten years earlier complicates the situation.

A likely story in real life? Seldom, if ever. Although the author claims that his novel is based on an actual incident, he has acknowledged that sexual harassment of men by women is a rarity. In a newspaper interview, Crichton noted:

> Statistically, 25 percent of harassment cases are brought by men, and the majority of those are against other men. *Five percent* of all harassment cases are brought by men against women. I think we live in a society in which it is perceived that if a man is coming on to a woman she's being stressed, but if a woman comes on to a man he's lucky. The reality is not necessarily that way.
>
> On all sides here there are unexamined issues and unstated feelings, feelings that people don't even know they have. You bring this out by reversing the ordinary roles. Let everybody see what the other side feels like. The goal, really, is to do something about harassment. (quoted in Weinraub, 1994:B1)

If we assume that these figures are correct and that approximately 5 percent of all harassment cases are brought by men against women, why would this novel and movie be so popular? Perhaps role reversals do give us more insight into an issue. Conversely, they may reinforce what some people already want to believe.

For the majority of sexual harassment victims in the workplace—women—this fictionalized role reversal may trivialize their genuine problems. Victims often retreat into a passive or sullen acceptance in which their self-confidence is undermined and their long-term career opportunities are damaged. If, at the same time, harassment victims are bombarded by media images of women making false accusations against men even as they themselves are harassing others, the claims of genuine victims may sound more shallow and unsubstantiated—even to the victims themselves. Certainly, men can be the victims of sexual harassment. However, since far fewer women are in managerial and supervisory positions where they conceivably could use their power and authority over men, the likelihood is far greater that they will be the victims rather than the perpetrators of such harassment.

Critics have suggested that novels and movies such as *Disclosure*, instead of "doing something" about sexual harassment, merely sell books, movie tickets, and videotapes. Recently, some television news programs have attempted to widen media coverage of sexual harassment issues. Some of these programs came as a response to *Disclosure*, to show how seldom women are accused of sexual harassment compared with men. What do you think the role of the media should be regarding such issues?

Sources: Based on Crawford, 1993; and Weinraub, 1994.

organization." Bureaucratic characteristics (such as a hierarchy of authority, a clear division of labour, explicit rules and procedures, and impersonality in personnel matters) may contribute to organizational efficiency or they may produce gridlock.

Weber, however, was not completely favourable toward bureaucracies. He believed such organizations stifle human initiative and creativity, thus producing an "iron cage." Bureaucracy also places an enormous amount of unregulated and often unperceived social power in the hands of a very few leaders. Such a situation is referred to as an oligarchy—the rule of the many by the few.

Why do a small number of leaders at the top make all of the important organizational decisions? According to German political sociologist Robert Michels (1949/1911), all organizations encounter the ***iron law of oligarchy*—the tendency to become a bureaucracy ruled by the few.** His central idea was that those who control bureaucracies not only wield power but also have an interest in retaining their power. In his research, Michels studied socialist parties and labour unions in Europe before World War I and concluded that even some of the most radical leaders of these organizations had a vested interest in clinging to their power. In this case, if the leaders lost their power positions, they once again would become manual labourers.

According to Michels, the hierarchical structure of bureaucracies and oligarchies go hand in hand. On the one hand, power may be concentrated in the hands of a few people because rank-and-file members inevitably must delegate a certain amount of decision-making authority to their leaders. Leaders then have access to information that other members do not have. They also have "clout," which they may use to protect their own interests, sometimes at the expense of the interests of others. On the other hand, oligarchy may result when individuals have certain outstanding qualities that make it possible for them to manage, if not control, others. The members choose to look to their leaders for direction; the leaders are strongly motivated to maintain the power and privileges that go with their leadership positions.

Is the iron law of oligarchy correct? Many scholars believe that Michels overstated his case. The leaders in most organizations do not have unlimited power. Divergent groups within a large-scale organization often compete for power, and informal networks can be used to "go behind the backs" of leaders. In addition, members routinely challenge, and sometimes remove, their leaders when they are not pleased with their actions.

AN ALTERNATIVE FORM OF ORGANIZATION

Many organizations have sought new and innovative ways to organize work more efficiently than the traditional hierarchical model. In the early 1980s, there was a movement in North America to *humanize bureaucracy*—to establish an organizational environment that develops rather than impedes human resources. More humane bureaucracies are characterized by (1) less rigid hierarchical structures and greater sharing of power and responsibility by all participants, (2) encouragement of participants to share their ideas and try new approaches to problem solving, and (3) efforts to reduce the number of people in dead-end jobs, train people in needed skills and competencies, and help people meet outside family responsibilities while still receiving equal treatment inside the organization (Kanter, 1977, 1983, 1985). However, this movement may have been overshadowed by the perceived strengths of another organizational model.

For several decades, the Japanese model of organization has been widely praised for its innovative structure. A number of social scientists and management specialists concluded that guaranteed lifetime employment and a teamwork approach to management were the major reasons Japanese workers had been so productive since the end of World War II, when Japan's economy was in shambles. When the North American manufacturing sector weakened in the 1980s, the Japanese system was widely discussed as an alternative to the prevalent North American hierarchical organizational structure. Let's briefly compare the characteristics of large Japanese corporations with their North American–based counterparts.

LIFETIME EMPLOYMENT Until recently, many large Japanese corporations guaranteed their workers permanent employment after an initial proba-

The contrasting styles of baseball players in North America and Japan reflect profound differences in organizational culture. People in North America tend to value individualism over the group, while people in Japan focus primarily on the group and deemphasize individual accomplishment in favour of teamwork and collective success.

tionary period. Thus, Japanese employees often remained with the same company for their entire career, whereas their North American counterparts often changed employers every few years. Japanese workers felt obligated to remain with their company and not to leave for more pay or a better position elsewhere, as frequently occurred in Canada and the United States. Likewise, Japanese employers in the past had an obligation not to "downsize" by laying off workers or to cut their wages. Unlike top managers in North America who gave themselves pay raises, bonuses, and so on even when their companies were financially strapped and laying off workers, Japanese managers took pay cuts. When financial problems occurred, Japanese workers frequently were reassigned or retrained by their company. Since many people retire in Japan at about age 55, the typical length of employment at one corporation for most workers is about thirty to thirty-five years.

According to advocates, the Japanese system encourages worker loyalty and a high level of productivity. Managers move through various parts of the organization and acquire technical knowledge about the workings of many aspects of the corporation, unlike their North American counterparts who tend to become highly specialized (Sengoku, 1985). Clearly, permanent employment has its advantages for workers. They do not have to worry about losing their jobs or having their wages cut. Employers benefit by not having to compete with one another to keep workers. Further, corporate trade secrets are more secure because employees do not leave one company and join another that produces a similar product. By contrast, in North America, many trade secrets have been carried not only from company to company within Canada and the United States but across nations as global economic competition has increased dramatically.

QUALITY CIRCLES Small workgroups made up of about five to fifteen workers who meet regularly with one or two managers to discuss the group's performance and working conditions are known as *quality circles.* The purpose of this team approach to management is both to improve product quality and to lower product costs. Workers are motivated to save the corporation money because they, in turn, receive bonuses or higher wages for their efforts. Quality circles have been praised for creating worker satisfaction, helping employees develop their potential, and improving productivity (Krahn and Lowe, 1996). Because quality circles focus on both productivity and worker satisfaction, they (at least ideally) meet the needs of both the corporation and the workers. While many Japanese corporations have utilized quality circles to achieve better productivity, many North American-based corporations have implemented automation in hopes of controlling the quality of their products.

LIMITATIONS Will the Japanese organizational structure continue to work over a period of time? Recently, the notion of lifetime employment has become problematic as an economic recession forced some Japanese factories to close and other companies ran out of subsidiaries willing to take on workers for "reassignment" (Sanger, 1994:E5). Also, sociologist Robert Coles (1979) has suggested that the Japanese model does not actually provide workers with more control over the corporation. While it may give them more control over their own work, production goals set by managers still must be met.

Although the possibility of implementing the Japanese model in North American-based corporations has been widely discussed, its large-scale acceptance is doubtful. Cultural traditions in Japan have focused on the importance of the group rather than the individual. Workers in North America are not likely to embrace this idea because it directly conflicts with the value of individualism so strongly held by many in this country (Krahn and Lowe, 1996). North American workers also are unwilling to commit themselves to one corporation for their entire work life. Moreover, men typically fare much better than women in Japanese corporations in which, due to patrimony, many women have found themselves excluded from career-track positions (Brinton, 1989).

Canada and the United States have a history of labour–management disputes that have not existed in Japan. Consequently, managers tend to be opposed to proposals that enhance worker participation in the decision-making process. Also, successful managers often do not make good team leaders. If managers previously have been pitted against workers in manufacturing plants, for instance, they are less likely to think that they should build consensus and encourage group decision making (Stern, 1993). Furthermore, workers sometimes equate employee participation with more work for them. For example, in the cellular phone industry, the workers see themselves as being responsible not only for producing telephones but also for maintaining quality control and plantwide production levels.

In spite of these limitations, more organizations in North America are turning to a more participatory style of management. The incentives for such changes exist because many of the corporations experience greater worker satisfaction and higher productivity and profits (see Florida and Kenney, 1991).

NEW ORGANIZATIONS FOR THE TWENTY-FIRST CENTURY

What kind of "Help Wanted" ad might a company run in the twenty-first century? As discussed in Box 6.4, an employment advertisement may give us clues about the business that placed the ad. One journalist has suggested that a want ad in the next century might read something like this: "WANTED: Bureaucracy basher, willing to challenge convention, assume big risks, and rewrite the accepted rules of industrial order" (Byrne, 1993:76). Organizational theorists have suggested a *horizontal* model for corporations in which both hierarchy and functional or depart-

BOX 6.4 SOCIOLOGY IN GLOBAL PERSPECTIVE

Sexual Harassment Crosses Global Boundaries

Item: A help wanted advertisement in a Moscow newspaper lists the following job qualifications: computer skills, typing, English and German. Applicants should be 18 to 25, 5 foot 7 and have long hair. "There will be a contest." (Stanley, 1994)

Item: A report released in 1992 by the International Labor Office states that sexual harassment pervades the international workplace, but only 7 of the 23 industrialized nations included in the survey have laws that deal specifically with the problem. (Mollison, 1992)

Analysts note that sexual harassment is an everyday occurrence in organizations worldwide. According to the International Labor Office report, women by far are the most likely targets of sexual harassment; an estimated 6 to 8 percent of women workers in industrialized nations have been forced out of their jobs by this problem. The report states that "generations of women have suffered from unwanted sexual attention at work and from offensive behaviour based on their gender. But it is only in the last 20 years that this conduct has been given a name" (Mollison, 1992:A2). This international study also found that some men—especially young men, black men, and gay men—face sexual harassment in the workplace.

In Moscow, the advertisement described above is not an isolated occurrence. Analysts report that a workplace climate of "sexual swaggering and bullying" prevails in many organizations; groping a secretary or requiring a clerk to discuss a pay raise after work in a hotel room is not unusual in many Russian businesses (Stanley, 1994). Igor M. Bunin, author of a recent study on Russian businessmen, states that some women do not view sexual harassment as a problem: "Women view their bodies as a way of furthering their careers—that's just the way it is" (Stanley, 1994:1). However, many Russian women do not agree. As Irina, a graphic designer who quit her job at a Moscow publishing house because her boss kept grabbing her and pressuring her to sleep with him, stated, "I can understand that men want to look ... But they shouldn't be allowed to do something to me that I don't want" (Stanley, 1994:1). Although sexual harassment—defined as a boss demanding sexual favours from subordinates—is a criminal offense in Russia, it is rarely enforced.

Sexual harassment has been given different names in different countries: In Italy, for example, it is called "sexual molestation"; in France, it is called "sexual blackmail"; and in the former Czechoslovakia, it is referred to as "bad interpersonal relationships" (Mollison, 1992). Whatever the name, however, it increasingly is being recognized around the world as a problem, for both victims and their employers. When the employee is harassed, she or he may decide that the only way out of the situation is to change jobs; that not only hurts that person's career but also may create a morale problem for the remaining employees.

Sources: Based on Mollison, 1992; Langelan, 1993; and Stanley, 1994.

mental boundaries largely would be eliminated. Seven key elements of the horizontal corporation have been suggested: (1) work would be organized around "core" processes, not tasks; (2) the hierarchy would be flattened; (3) teams would manage everything and be held accountable for measurable performance goals; (4) performance would be measured by customer satisfaction, not profits; (5) team performance would be rewarded; (6) employees would have regular contact with suppliers and customers; and (7) all employees would be trained in how to use available information effectively to make their own decisions (Byrne, 1993:76–79).

In the horizontal structure, a limited number of senior executives would still fill support roles (such as finance and human resources) while everyone else would work in multidisciplinary teams and perform core processes (such as product development or sales generation). Organizations would have fewer layers between company heads and the staffers responsible for any given process. Performance objectives would be related to the needs of customers; people would be rewarded not just for individual performance but for skills development and team performance. If such organizations become a reality, organizational charts of the twenty-first century will more closely resemble a pepperoni pizza, a shamrock, or an inverted pyramid than the traditional pyramid-shaped stack of boxes connected by lines.

Currently, most corporations are hybrids of vertical and horizontal organizational structures; however, a number of companies appear to be moving toward the horizontal model. If the horizontal model is widely implemented, this will constitute one of the most significant changes in organizational structure since the Industrial Revolution.

What is the best organizational structure for the future? Of course, this question is difficult to answer because it requires the ability to predict economic, political, and social conditions. Nevertheless, we can make several observations. Ultimately, everyone has a stake in seeing that organizations operate in as humane a fashion as possible and that channels for opportunity are widely available to all people regardless of ethnicity, gender, or class. Workers and students alike can benefit from organizational environments that make it possible for people to explore their joint interests without fear of being harassed or being pitted against one another in a competitive struggle for advantage.

CHAPTER REVIEW

Groups are a key element of our social structure, and much of our social interaction takes place within them. Sociologists define a social group as a collection of two or more people who interact frequently, share a sense of belonging, and depend on one another.

- People who happen to be in the same place at the same time are considered an aggregate. Those who share a similar characteristic are considered a category. While aggregates and categories are groupings of people, they are not considered social groups.
- Primary groups are small and personal, and members engage in emotion-based interactions over an extended period. Secondary groups are larger and more specialized, and members have less personal and more formal, goal-oriented relationships. Ingroups are groups to which we belong and with which we identify. Outgroups are groups we do not belong to or perhaps feel hostile toward.
- In small groups, all members know one another and interact simultaneously. In groups with more than three members, communication dynamics change and members tend to assume specialized tasks. Large groups often have less social solidarity than small groups, but they tend to have

more power and more formalized leadership roles.

- Instrumental leadership is goal- or task-oriented and is an appropriate style for action-oriented groups. Expressive leadership is concerned with providing emotional support for members and works well when harmony and high morale are important for a group.
- Authoritarian leaders make major decisions and assign tasks to individual members. Democratic leaders encourage discussion and collaborative decision making. Laissez-faire leaders are minimally involved and encourage members to make their own decisions.
- Groups may have significant influence on members' values, attitudes, and behaviours. In order to maintain ties with a group, many members are willing to conform to norms established and reinforced by group members. The tendency for group members to conform may create a work atmosphere that allows for sexual harassment. It also may lead to a groupthink style whereby members of a cohesive group arrive at a collective decision that individual members personally believe is wrong or unwise.
- A bureaucracy is a formal organization characterized by hierarchical authority, division of labour, explicit procedures, and impersonality. According to Max Weber, bureaucracy supplies a rational means of attaining organizational goals because it contributes to coordination and control.
- A bureaucracy also has an informal structure, which includes the daily activities and interactions that bypass the official rules and procedures. Informal networks may enhance productivity or may be counterproductive to the organization. Informal networks also may be detrimental to those who are excluded from them, typically any minority within the organization.
- There are three major shortcomings of bureaucracies. They may be inefficient and rigid, particularly when an organization's survival becomes more important than the achievement of its goals. They may resist change, which can lead to bureaucratic enlargement or incompetence. And they may perpetuate class, ethnic, and gender inequalities.
- An oligarchy is the rule of the many by the few. In bureaucracies with an oligarchical structure, those in control have not only power but also a great interest in maintaining that power.
- Recent trends have generated interest in more innovative bureaucratic structures. The movement to humanize bureaucracy has focused on developing, rather than impeding, human resources. The Japanese model of organization emphasizes company loyalty and a teamwork approach to management.
- As we approach the twenty-first century, some organizational theorists are advocating a horizontal model for bureaucracy that emphasizes teamwork, informed employee decision making, and customer satisfaction. Ultimately, all of us benefit from organizations that operate humanely and that include opportunities for all, regardless of ethnicity, gender, or class.

KEY TERMS

aggregate **197**
authoritarian leaders **203**
bureaucracy **213**
bureaucratic personality **218**
category **198**
conformity **203**
democratic leaders **203**
dyad **201**
expressive leadership **203**
goal displacement **218**
groupthink **209**
ideal type **214**
informal structure **215**
ingroup **198**
instrumental leadership **203**
iron law of oligarchy **224**
laissez-faire leaders **203**
outgroup **198**
rationality **214**
reference group **200**
small group **201**
triad **201**

QUESTIONS FOR ANALYSIS AND UNDERSTANDING

1. What are your ingroups, outgroups, and reference groups? Which two groups have the most influence on your behaviour, values, and attitudes?
2. What are the differences between group solidarity and group conformity? What are some specific examples of group solidarity? Of group conformity?
3. How does Max Weber's ideal-type bureaucracy compare with actual bureaucracies?
4. Should informal structure be encouraged or discouraged? Why?

QUESTIONS FOR CRITICAL THINKING

1. Who might be more likely to conform in a bureaucracy, those with power or those wanting more power?
2. Although there has been much discussion recently concerning what is and what is not sexual harassment, it has been difficult to reach a clear consensus on what behaviours and actions are acceptable. What are some specific ways both women and men can avoid contributing to an atmosphere of sexual harassment in organizations? Consider team relationships, management and mentor relationships, promotion policies, attitudes, behaviour, dress and presentation, and after-work socializing.
3. Do the insights gained from Milgram's research on obedience outweigh the elements of deception and stress that were forced on its subjects?
4. If you were forming a company based on humane organizational principles, would you base the promotional policies on merit and performance or on affirmative action goals?

SUGGESTED READINGS

Organizations are examined from a variety of perspectives in these interesting books:

Wallace Clement. *The Canadian Corporate Elite*. Toronto: McClelland and Stewart, 1975.

Kathy E. Ferguson. *The Feminist Case Against Bureaucracy*. Philadelphia: Temple University Press, 1984.

Richard H. Hall. *Organizations: Structures, Processes, and Outcomes*. Englewood Cliffs, N.J.: Prentice-Hall, 1991.

Rosabeth Moss Kanter. *Men and Women of the Corporation*. New York: Basic Books, 1993; orig. pub. 1977.

Rosabeth Moss Kanter. *When Giants Learn to Dance: Mastering the Challenges of Strategy, Management, and Careers in the 1990s*. New York: Simon & Schuster, 1989.

Gifford Pinchot and Elizabeth Pinchot. *The End of Bureaucracy and the Rise of the Intelligent Organization*. San Francisco: Berrett-Koehler, 1993.

To find out more about sexual harassment:

Clare Brant and Yun Lee Too (eds.). *Rethinking Sexual Harassment*. Boulder, Colo.: Pluto Press, 1994.

Celia Morris. *Bearing Witness: Sexual Harassment and Beyond—Everywoman's Story*. Boston: Little, Brown, 1994.

Kerry Segrave. *The Sexual Harassment of Women in the Workplace, 1600 to 1993*. Jefferson, N.C.: McFarland, 1994.

Susan L. Webb. *Shockwaves: The Global Impact of Sexual Harassment*. New York: MasterMedia, 1994.

Chapter 7

DEVIANCE AND CRIME

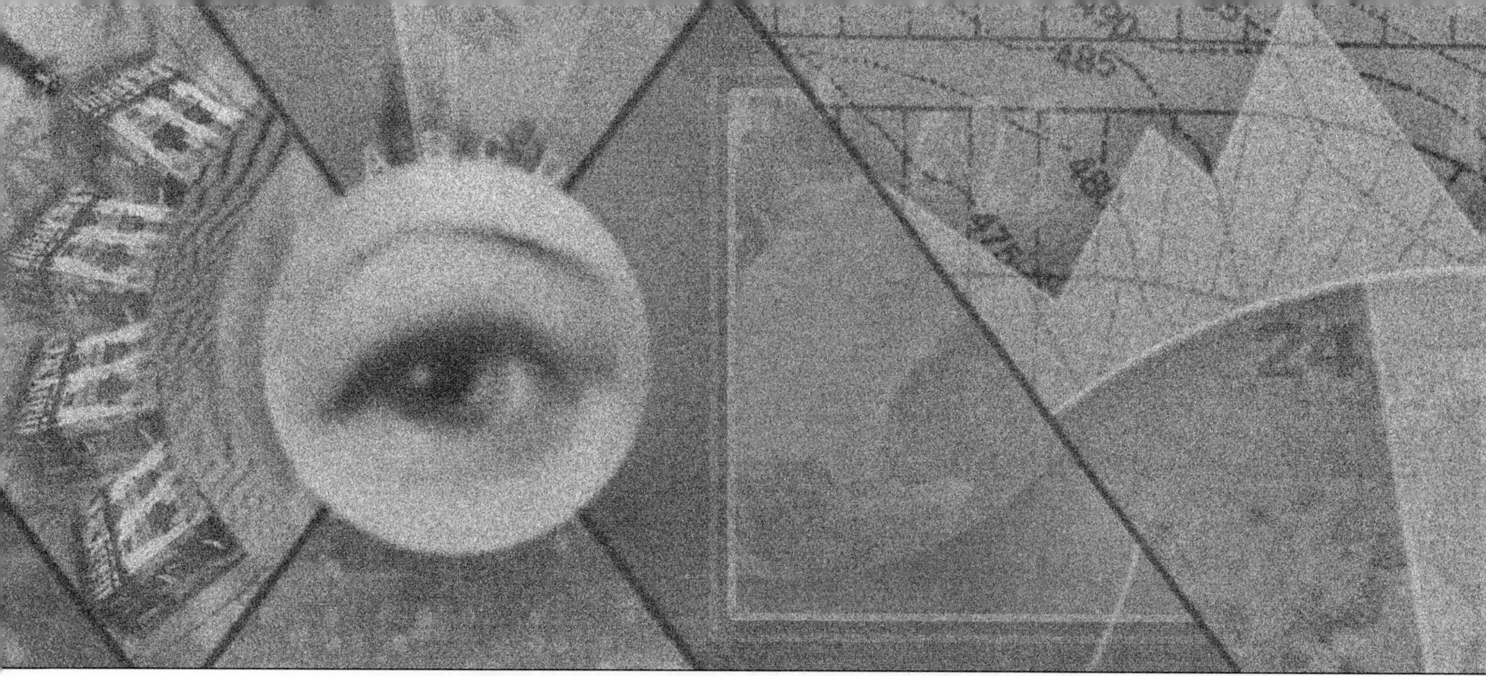

When most of us think of organized crime, we think of biker gangs or perhaps the Italian Mafia. In reality, however, organized crime has many other faces. In Canada, active organized crime groups come from many different racial and ethnic backgrounds including Russian, Colombian, Chinese, Vietnamese, Italian, French-Canadian, Turkish, and many others. These groups have many things in common, including a willingness to use violence—a willingness that is evident from the following account:

Constable Peter Yuen, a member of the Metropolitan Toronto Police Service, was working undercover in a gaming house, monitoring off-track betting while police backup units waited outside. During this operation, four hooded Vietnamese gang members burst into the room and ordered the gamblers to hand over their valuables. The robbers found Yuen's police badge and ordered him to kneel with his hands behind his head. Yuen recalled the events that followed:

"I was kicked in the face until my shirt was soaked in blood." Then, one of the robbers forced the barrel of a .45 calibre automatic into Yuen's mouth, while another held a .357 magnum to his temple. Said Yuen: "They were shouting that I was a traitor for serving the white authorities and that I deserved to die." Yuen then heard a gun click and heard an assailant remark, "Goodbye copper." But the assault abruptly ceased when another of the robbers noticed that the building was surrounded by police. Two of the suspects were arrested at the scene, but the police ultimately chased one of Yuen's attackers into a bush area where he hid by burying himself in mud and breathing through a piece of straw. Police found him after 30 minutes using tracking dogs.

Forensic tests on the pistol showed that the gangster had indeed pulled the trigger, but that the bullet in the chamber had not fired ... Concluded Yuen, who was named Toronto's Policeman of the Year ... for his bravery during the attack: "I have no doubt that they would have done me in if they had not been interrupted." (Kaihla, 1991:21)

The problem of organized crime is certainly not unique to Canada. This problem has existed for centuries and

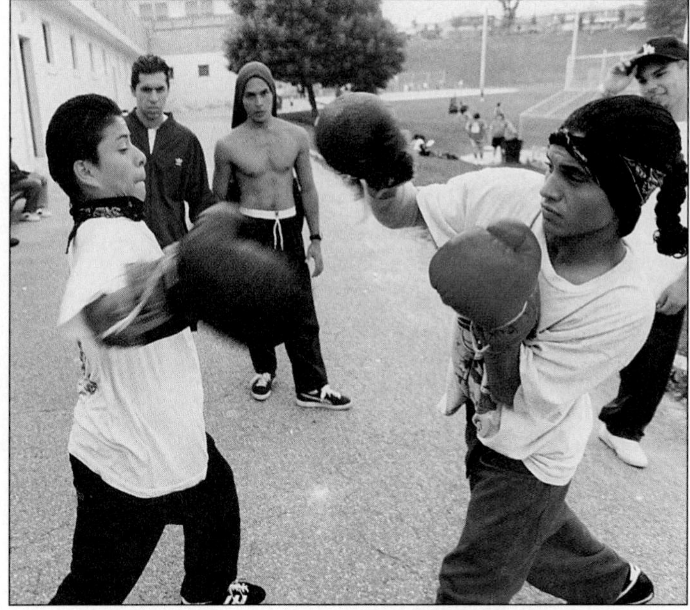

According to sociologists, deviance is relative—in other words, it varies according to time, place, group, and circumstance. In this controlled aggression program for youth gang members in Toronto, Ontario, aggression has been defined as normative rather than deviant.

today such gangs operate around the world. *Organized crime* is not a distinct type of crime, but a process or method for committing crimes. Margaret Beare defines organized crime as "ongoing activity, involving a continuing criminal conspiracy, with a structure greater than any single member, with the potential for corruption and/or violence to facilitate the criminal process" (1996a:15). For many years, organized crime and other types of crime and deviance have been of special interest to sociologists. Many of the issues they have examined remain important today: What is deviant behaviour, and how does it differ from criminal behaviour? Why are some people considered to be "deviants" or "criminals" while others are not? In this chapter, we look at the relationship between conformity, deviance, and crime. Before reading on, take the quiz on organized crime, deviance, and crime in Box 7.1.

QUESTIONS AND ISSUES

What is deviant behaviour?

How do sociologists explain deviant and criminal behaviour?

When is deviance considered a crime?

How do sociologists classify crime?

How does the criminal justice system deal with crime?

How can we begin to solve the crime problem in the twenty-first century?

WHAT IS DEVIANCE?

How do societies determine what behaviour is acceptable and unacceptable? As discussed in previous chapters, all societies have norms that govern acceptable behaviour. If we are to live and to work with others these rules are necessary. We must also have a reasonable expectation that other people will obey the rules. Think of the chaos that would result if each driver decided which side of the road she would drive on each day, or which stop sign he would decide to obey. Most of us usually conform to the norms our group prescribes. Of course, not all members of the group obey all the time. All of you have broken many rules, sometimes even important ones.

BOX 7.1 SOCIOLOGY AND EVERYDAY LIFE

How Much Do You Know About Crime and Organized Crime?

TRUE	FALSE	
T	F	1. Official statistics accurately reflect the amount of crime in Canada.
T	F	2. Most organized criminals are affiliated with the Italian Mafia.
T	F	3. Organized crime exists largely to provide goods and services demanded by "respectable" members of the community.
T	F	4. Rates of murder and other violent crime have been steadily rising for the past twenty years.
T	F	5. Because of their concern with a variety of charitable causes, biker gangs such as the Hell's Angels have become less of a social threat.
T	F	6. During Canada's great cigarette smuggling epidemic of 1992 and 1993, our major cigarette companies exported cigarettes to the United States that they knew would be smuggled back into Canada.
T	F	7. Canada's most prolific serial killer was a Hell's Angel who killed forty-three people, but served only seven years of a sentence for manslaughter.
T	F	8. Many organized crime groups are made up of people from the same ethnic group.
T	F	9. In Russia, organized crime is so pervasive that it is a threat to the future economic and political life of that country.
T	F	10. Most of the money made by organized criminals comes from gambling and loansharking.

Answers on page 236

These violations are dealt with through various mechanisms of ***social control*****—systematic practices developed by social groups to encourage conformity and to discourage deviance.** One form of social control takes place through the process of socialization whereby individuals *internalize* societal norms and values. A second form of social control occurs through the use of negative sanctions to punish rule-breakers and nonconforming acts. Although the purpose of social control is to ensure some level of conformity, all societies still have some degree of ***deviance*****—any behaviour, belief, or condition that violates cultural norms** (Adler and Adler, 1995).

We are most familiar with *behavioural* deviance based on a person's intentional or inadvertent actions. For example, a person may engage in intentional deviance by drinking too much or

BOX 7.1 SOCIOLOGY AND EVERYDAY LIFE

Answers to the Sociology Quiz on Crime and Organized Crime

TRUE	FALSE	
T	**F**	1. *False*. Although official statistics provide a variety of information about crime in Canada, they reflect only crimes that are *reported* to police, not all the offences that are *committed*. Studies have shown that less than half of all crimes are reported to the police.
T	**F**	2. *False*. The Italian Mafia has a global influence on organized crime. However, it is one of many different organized crime groups.
T	F	3. *True*. If not for public demand for illegal drugs, gambling, tax-free liquor and cigarettes, and the other goods and services supplied by organized crime, illegal profits would largely disappear.
T	**F**	4. *False*. While crime rates generally rose through the 1980s, they have declined steadily throughout the 1990s.
T	**F**	5. *False*. The Hell's Angels have used high-profile activities like toy runs for children to improve their public image. However, they are one of the most ruthless and profitable criminal organizations in North America.
T	F	6. *True*. The vast majority of cigarettes smuggled into Canada were legally manufactured here and exported into the United States. Executives of one of Canada's largest manufacturers, Imperial Tobacco, said explicitly that they wanted to ensure that their cigarettes were the ones smuggled back into Canada.
T	F	7. *True*. Yves (Apache) Trudeau was a contract killer who received a lenient sentence in exchange for information about other Montreal underworld figures. (For more on this case, see Box 7.4 on page 268.)
T	F	8. *True*. Many different nationalities are involved in Canadian organized crime, including Russian, Iranian, Chinese, Vietnamese, Colombian, Jamaican, and Italian. Restricting membership to one's own group provides a number of advantages. For one thing, interpersonal ties based in ethnic communities and language differences make it difficult for law enforcement to infiltrate with the groups. The ethnic ties also facilitate the development of international crime networks.
T	F	9. *True*. After the fall of Communism, the lack of meaningful economic institutions and the failure of the criminal justice system created conditions favourable to organized crime. Organized criminals control many of the new businesses in Russia and have powerful links to the government.
T	**F**	10. *False*. The importation and distribution of illegal drugs is the main source of funds for organized crime.

Sources: Based on Evans and Himelfarb, 1996; Lavigne, 1987; and Stamler, 1996.

shoplifting or in inadvertent deviance by losing the rent money at a video lottery terminal or laughing during a solemn occasion.

Although we usually think of deviance as a type of behaviour, people may be regarded as deviant if they express *radical* or *unusual beliefs*. For example, members of cults (such as Moonies and satanists) and of far-right- or far-left-wing political groups may be considered deviant when their religions or political beliefs become known to people with more conventional cultural views. For instance, school teachers James Keegstra and Malcolm Ross were removed from their classrooms for expressing anti-Semitic beliefs including denying that the Holocaust actually occurred.

People may be regarded as deviant because of specific *characteristics* or *conditions* that they have had since birth (such as a physical disability or minority status in a racist society) or have acquired (such as contracting AIDS) (Adler and Adler, 1994). Sociologist Rose Weitz (1993) has suggested that persons with AIDS live with a stigma that affects their relationships with family members, friends, lovers, colleagues, and health-care workers. To avoid or reduce stigma, many people with AIDS attempt to conceal their illness, learn when and to whom they should reveal their illness, change their social networks, or work to convince others that they are still functioning social beings (Weitz, 1993). As Weitz's observation suggests, individuals considered to be "deviant" by one group may be conformists in another group. Organized crime gangs are no exception; members who shun mainstream cultural beliefs and values may conform routinely to codes of dress, attitude (such as defiant individualism), and behaviour (Jankowski, 1991). The Hell's Angels provide a graphic example of such conformity within a group.

According to sociologists, deviance is *relative*—that is, an act becomes deviant when it is socially defined as such. Definitions of deviance vary widely from place to place, from time to time, and from group to group. For example, you may have played the Pick 3 lottery. To win, you must pick a three-digit number matching the one drawn by the government lottery agency. Television commercials encourage us to risk our money on this game from which the government profits. Several years ago, the same game was called the numbers racket and was the most popular form of gambling in many low-income neighbourhoods. The two main differences between now and then are: the game used to be run by organized criminals, and these criminals paid the winners a higher share of the take than the government now does.

Deviance can be difficult to define. Good and evil are not two distinct categories. The two overlap, and the line between deviant and nondeviant can be very *ambiguous*. For example, how do we decide someone is mentally ill? What if your brother begins to behave in a strange fashion? You notice that he occasionally yells at people for no apparent reason, and keeps changing topics when you talk to him. He begins to wear clothes that don't match and phones you in the middle of the night to talk about people on the street who are threatening him. How would you respond to this change in behaviour? Would it make any difference if you knew that your brother was drinking heavily at the time or that he was under a lot of stress at work? Would it make a difference if he behaved this way once a year or twice a week? When would you decide that he had a problem and should seek help? What is the difference between someone who is eccentric and someone who is mentally ill? These questions reflect the difficulty we have in defining deviance.

Deviant behaviour also varies in its degree of seriousness, ranging from mild transgressions of folkways, to more serious infringements of mores, to quite serious violations of the law. Have you kept a library book past its due date or cut classes? If so, you have violated folkways. Others probably view your infraction as relatively minor; at most, you might have to pay a fine or receive a lower grade. Violations of mores—such as falsifying a university application or cheating on an examination—are viewed as more serious infractions and are punishable by stronger sanctions, such as academic probation or expulsion. Some forms of deviant behaviour are officially defined as crimes. A ***crime* is a behaviour that violates criminal law and is punishable with fines, jail terms, and other sanctions**. Crimes range from minor (such as running an illegal bingo game or telling fortunes) to major offences (such as sexual assault and murder). A subcategory, ***juvenile delinquency*, refers to a violation of law by young people under the age of 18**.

When sociologists study deviance, they do not judge certain kinds of behaviour or people as "good" or "bad." Instead, they attempt to learn what types of behaviour are defined as deviant, who does the defining, how and why people become deviants, and how society deals with deviants (Schur, 1983). People have always been fascinated and troubled by crime and deviance, and theorists from a wide variety of different perspectives have tried to understand and explain deviant behaviour. In this chapter, we present several sociological explanations of deviance. While each focuses on the role of social groups in creating deviance, these theories are quite different from one another. However, each contributes in its own way to our understanding of deviance. No one perspective is a comprehensive explanation of all deviance, and in many respects the theories presented in this chapter can be considered as complementary.

FUNCTIONALIST PERSPECTIVES ON DEVIANCE

STRAIN THEORY: GOALS AND THE MEANS TO ACHIEVE THEM

As discussed in Chapter 1, Durkheim (1964a/1895) introduced the concept of *anomie* to describe a social condition in which people experience a sense of futility because social norms are weak, absent, or conflicting. Sociologist Robert Merton's (1938, 1968) strain theory is based on Durkheim's assertion that the macrolevel structure of a society can produce social pressures that result in a higher rate of deviant behaviour. According to ***strain theory*, people feel strain when they are exposed to cultural goals that they are unable to obtain because they do not have access to culturally approved means of achieving those goals**. The goals may be material possessions and money; the approved means may include an education and jobs. When denied legitimate access to these goals, some people seek access through deviant means.

Sociologist Margaret Beare (1996a) has used Merton's strain theory to explain the increased involvement of Canadian Mohawks in the organized crime of smuggling during the early 1990s. In order to raise revenue and to discourage smoking, Canadian governments had for decades imposed high taxes on cigarettes. As a result, the cost of cigarettes had become very high, particularly in comparison with prices in the United States. To save money, many of those addicted to cigarettes turned to the contraband market. By 1993 more than one-quarter of the cigarettes consumed in Canada were purchased illegally. In Ontario and Quebec, residents of some First Nations communities were among the major sources of these contraband cigarettes.

Because of the high unemployment and lack of legitimate opportunities in most First Nations communities, deviance had become an attractive option to some community members who saw smuggling as a means of achieving the goal of financial success. Akwesasne Chief Mike Mitchell described the financial opportunity in a CBC interview:

> The money—it's unbelievable the money you can make and it's so easy ... You can buy a pack of cigarettes on the American side of the reservation for $1.58 and you go across here in Cornwall and you have to buy it for close to $7.00 a pack, same pack, within a short distance of each other, so no one is surprised that all this is happening. (cited in Beare, 1996b:272)

The business of getting the cigarettes into Canada was facilitated by a number of factors. First, Cana-

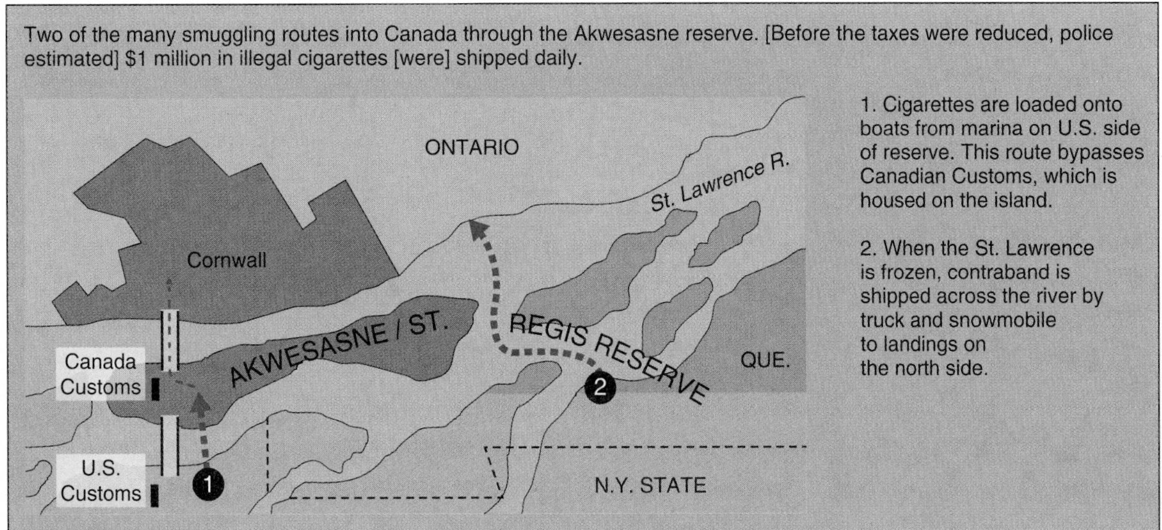
Two of the many smuggling routes into Canada through the Akwesasne reserve. [Before the taxes were reduced, police estimated] $1 million in illegal cigarettes [were] shipped daily.
ONTARIO
St. Lawrence R.
Cornwall
AKWESASNE / ST. REGIS RESERVE
Canada Customs
U.S. Customs
QUE.
N.Y. STATE
1. Cigarettes are loaded onto boats from marina on U.S. side of reserve. This route bypasses Canadian Customs, which is housed on the island.
2. When the St. Lawrence is frozen, contraband is shipped across the river by truck and snowmobile to landings on the north side.

FIGURE 7.1

Smuggling Routes

Reprinted with permission—The Toronto Star Syndicate.

dian cigarette manufacturers were eager to ship Canadian brands into the United States knowing that the cigarettes would be smuggled back into Canada. Second, the location of some reserves was ideal. The Mohawk reserve at Akwesasne, for example, straddles the Ontario–Quebec and Canada–U.S. borders (Figure 7.1), and the geography of the St. Lawrence River at Akwesasne makes detection difficult. Third, First Nations peoples can purchase for personal use unlimited amounts of tax-free tobacco in the United States. While this tobacco was and is supposed to remain on the reserve, at the height of the smuggling epidemic, much of it became part of the contraband trade. Finally, the jurisdictional disputes over law enforcement, which were so apparent during the 1990 Oka crisis in Quebec, reduced the ability of the police to work effectively. Beare feels that the smuggling was also facilitated by feelings of injustice against federal and provincial governments on the part of the Mohawks, which allowed them to justify their deviant behaviour.

While substantial tax cuts have dramatically reduced the incidence of cigarette smuggling, the networks and expertise developed by the smugglers have remained, and many, having made linkages with other organized criminals, have turned to smuggling other commodities including drugs, alcohol, and firearms. This has helped create illegitimate opportunity structures (see Figure 7.1) on some reserves that may attract others into the world of organized smuggling.

OPPORTUNITY THEORY: ACCESS TO ILLEGITIMATE OPPORTUNITIES

Expanding on Merton's strain theory, sociologists Richard Cloward and Lloyd Ohlin (1960) have suggested that for deviance to occur people must have access to ***illegitimate opportunity structures*—circumstances that provide an opportunity for people to acquire through illegitimate activities what they cannot get**

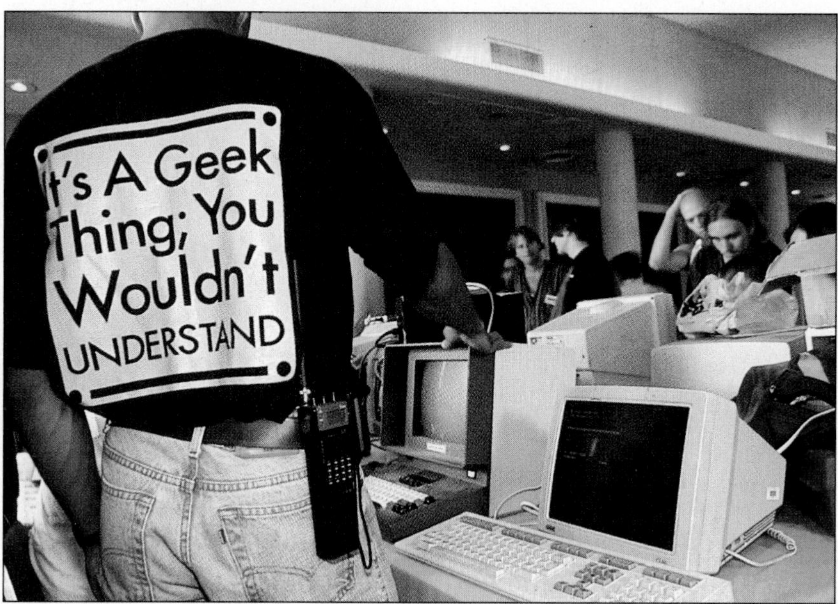

For some people the "information superhighway" is a new avenue of illegitimate opportunity. While only a fraction of "hackers" engage in deviant behaviour, computer mischief and crime demonstrate how new opportunity structures can elicit new forms of deviance.

through legitimate channels. For example, members of some communities may have insufficient legitimate means to achieve conventional goals of status and wealth but have much greater access to illegitimate opportunity structures—such as theft, drug dealing, or robbery—through which they can achieve these goals. The situation at Akwesasne provided a very lucrative opportunity structure for the minority of community members who chose to use it. However, more typically, illegitimate opportunities are often situational and small-scale, as the following description an East Coast youth gave of his delinquent behaviour demonstrates:

> We used to break into places. I was drunk on every one of them jobs. We never really planned it, we just broke in. The one I remember most clearly is when we broke into the Lougheed Drive-In. I was drunk then so I can't remember everything. We just wanted to do a break, so we did a break to get more booze for the next day. It was after dark and hardly anybody was there—this was 3:00 in the morning. We busted open the door, because there's no alarm system in it—we checked all that out—we just busted the door with a crowbar. We got in there and we searched everywhere and we didn't find nothing, there wasn't no money there. Then we saw the cigarette machine so we said, "Let's take this." So the six of us picked it up and threw it in the back of the trunk—we had an old shitbox of a car—and took off. We got $35.00 out of it and around 200 packs of cigarettes. We dumped it in a field in there by Kmart on Ryerson Road. We bought a bottle of Seagram's—I know it was Seagram's because I drank half—I just drank it all down. You just get drunk, you get blackouts. You're nervous doing breaks. I never really wanted to be involved with them: mostly I just told them I'd be lookout. One time we all

> broke in this place: I was out watching and the boys went in, and then a cop car and two paddy wagons came down the road. I said, "Boys, the cops are coming," and I beat it. The boys all got caught. (Leyton, 1979:124)

According to Cloward and Ohlin (1960), three different forms of delinquent subcultures—criminal, conflict, and retreatist—emerge based on the type of illegitimate opportunities available in a specific area. The criminal subculture focuses on economic gain and includes acts such as theft, extortion, and drug dealing. Sociologist Elijah Anderson (1990) suggested that the "drug economy [is an] employment agency superimposed on the existing gang network" for many young men who lack other opportunities. For young men who grow up in a gang subculture, running drug houses and selling drugs on street corners becomes a source of illegitimate opportunity. Using the money from these "jobs," they can support themselves and their families as well as purchase material possessions to impress others. When illegitimate economic opportunities are not available, gangs may become conflict subcultures that fight over turf (territory) and adopt a value system of toughness, courage, and similar status-enhancing qualities. Those who lack the opportunity or ability to join one of these gangs may turn to retreatist activities such as drinking and drug use.

Opportunity theory expands strain theory by pointing out the relationship between deviance and the availability of illegitimate opportunity structures. Some recent studies of gangs have supported this premise by pointing out that gang membership provides some women and men in low-income central-city areas with an illegitimate means to acquire money, entertainment, refuge, physical protection, and escape from living like their parents (Jankowski, 1991; Esbensen and Huizinga, 1993). In a study of women's gangs in Detroit, criminologist Carl Taylor (1993) found that gangs provide a support system otherwise unavailable for unemployed and sometimes homeless women. According to criminologist Anne Campbell (1984:267), gangs are a "microcosm of American society, a mirror image in which power, possession, rank, and role ... are found within a subcultural life of poverty and crime."

CONTROL THEORY: SOCIAL BONDING

Why do people *not* engage in deviant behaviour? In an effort to answer this question, sociologist Walter Reckless (1967) developed a theory of social control, which states that certain factors draw people toward deviance while others "insulate" them from such behaviour. According to Reckless, people are drawn to deviance by poverty, unemployment, and lack of educational opportunity. They also may be influenced by members of deviant subcultures, media depictions of deviant behaviour, and their own feelings of frustration, hostility, or inferiority. However, many people do not turn to deviance because they are insulated by *outer containments* such as supportive family and friends, reasonable social expectations, and supervision by others and by *inner containments* such as self-control, a sense of responsibility, and resistance to unlawful diversions.

Extending Reckless's containment theory, sociologist Travis Hirschi (1969) developed a theory suggesting that deviant behaviour is minimized when people have strong bonds that bind them to families, school, peers, churches, and other social institutions. ***Social bond theory*** **holds that the probability of deviant behaviour increases when a person's ties to society are weakened or broken.** According to Hirschi, social bonding consists of (1) *attachment* to other people, (2) *commitment* to conventional lines of behaviour such as schooling and job success, (3) *involvement* in conventional activities, and (4) *belief* in the legitimacy of conventional values and norms. Although Hirschi did not include females in his study, others who have replicated his study with both females and males have found that the theory appears to explain the delinquency of both (see Linden and Fillmore, 1981).

While Hirschi's theory did not differentiate between bonds to conventional and to deviant others, several researchers have modified the theory and have suggested that the probability of crime or delinquency increases when a person's social bonds are weak and when peers promote antisocial values and deviant behaviour (Linden and Fillmore, 1981). Gang members may bond with one another rather than with persons who subscribe to dominant cultural values. As one gang member explains:

> Before I joined the gang, I could see that you could count on your boys to help in times of need and that meant a lot to me. And when I needed money, sure enough they gave it to me. Nobody else would have given it to me; my parents didn't have it, and there was no other place to go. The gang was just like they said they would be, and they'll continue to be there when I need them. (Jankowski, 1991:42)

INTERACTIONIST PERSPECTIVES ON DEVIANCE

As we discussed in Chapter 4, interactionists focus on how people develop a self-concept and learn conforming behaviour through the process of socialization. According to interactionists, deviance is learned in the same way as conformity—through interaction with others.

DIFFERENTIAL ASSOCIATION THEORY

More than fifty years ago, sociologist Edwin Sutherland (1939) developed a theory to explain how people learn deviance through social interaction. ***Differential association theory*** **states that individuals have a greater tendency to deviate from societal norms when they frequently associate with persons who favour deviance over conformity**. According to Sutherland, people learn the necessary techniques and the motives, drives, rationalizations, and attitudes of deviant behaviour from people with whom they associate. Letkemann (1973), for example, described how a former Canadian penitentiary resident learned the now-obsolete art of safecracking:

> Prior to doing his first "can" [safe] [he] bugged an older safecracker in prison "until he finally divulged how to do it." This instruction, he added was "not like a teacher–student, it was just a matter of discussion during work."
>
> When he left the prison he went back to his regular partner and described to him what he had learned about safes. His partner said this was ridiculous but [he] persuaded him to come along: "I followed the instructions to the letter. It opened—we were both overcome with it all—the ease of it all!"
>
> This first job had been a punch job [breaking into a safe without explosives]—technically the simplest. Following this [he] and his partner "opened many doors by trial and error." ... This went on for four years; they had not yet used explosives, nor had they ever been caught punching safes. They became increasingly eager to try explosives since they found so many safes that couldn't be opened any other way.
>
> During this time, [he] was associating with other safecrackers ... He eventually asked another safecracker whether he could borrow some grease [nitroglycerine]. "I wouldn't admit that I knew nothing about it." He obtained the grease and chose a small safe, but was unsuccessful. The next day, he discussed his problem with some more experienced safecrackers. He found he had used too long a fuse and was advised to use electric knockers [detonators]. This he did with success." (Letkemann, 1973:136)

Another example of this learning of deviance—the acquisition of certain attitudes and the mastery of techniques—is provided in Box 7.2, which discusses how in Japan, younger organized crime gang members serve apprenticeships to older members of their organizations.

Differential association is most likely to result in criminal activity when a person has frequent, intense, and long-lasting interaction with others who violate the law. When there are more factors favouring violation of the law than there are opposing it, the person is more likely to become a criminal. Ties to other deviants can be particularly important in the world of organized crime, where the willingness of peers to stand up for one another can be critical in maintaining power in the face of violent opposition from competitors. Daniel Wolf, an anthropologist who rode with The Rebels, an Edmonton biker gang, describes this solidarity:

> For an outlaw biker, the greatest fear is not of the police; rather, it is of a slight variation of his own mirror image: the patch holder [full-fledged member] of another club. Under slightly different circumstances those men would call each other "brother." But when turf is at stake, inter-club rivalry and warfare completely override any considerations of the common bonds of being a biker—and brother kills brother. None of the outlaws that I rode with enjoyed the prospect of having to break the bones of another biker. Nor did they look forward to having to live with the hate–fear syndrome that dominates a conflict in which there are no rules. I came to realize that the willingness of an outlaw to lay down his life in these conflicts goes beyond a belligerent masculinity that brooks no challenge. When a patch holder defends his colours, he defends his personal identity, his community, his lifestyle. When a war is on, loyalty to the club and one another arises out of the midst of danger, out of apprehension of possible injury, mutilation, or worse. Whether one considers this process as desperate, heroic, or just outlandishly foolish and banal does not really matter. What matters is that, for patch holders, the brotherhood emerges as a necessary feature of their continued existence as individuals and as a group. (1996:11)

Differential association theory contributes to our knowledge of how deviant behaviour reflects the individual's learned techniques, values, attitudes, motives, and rationalizations. However, critics question why many individuals who have had extensive contact with people who violate the law still conform most of the time. They also assert that the theory does not adequately assess possible linkages between social inequality and criminal behaviour.

LABELLING THEORY

Two complementary processes are involved in the definition of deviance. First, some people act (or are believed to act) in a manner contrary to the expectations of others. Second, others disapprove of and try to control this contrary behaviour. Part of this social control process involves labelling people as deviants. A very important contribution to the study of deviance was made by sociologists who asked the question, "Why are some people labelled as deviants while others are not?" ***Labelling theory*** **suggests that deviants are those people who have been successfully labelled as such by others**. The process of labelling is directly related to the power and status of those persons who *do* the labelling and those who are *being labelled*. Behaviour, then, is not deviant in and of itself; it is defined as such by a social audience (Erikson, 1962). According to sociologist Howard Becker (1963), *moral entrepreneurs* are persons who use their own views of right and wrong to establish rules and label others as deviant. These rules are enforced on persons with less power.

William Chambliss (1973) witnessed the labelling process when he observed members of two groups of high school boys: the "Saints" and the "Roughnecks." Both groups were "constantly occupied with truancy, drinking, wild parties, petty theft, and vandalism." Overall, the Saints committed more offences than the Roughnecks, but the Roughnecks were labelled as troublemakers by school and law enforcement officials while the Saints were seen as being likely to succeed. Unlike the Roughnecks, none of the Saints was ever arrested.

Chambliss attributed this contradictory response by authorities to the fact the Saints came from "good families," did well in school, and thus were forgiven for their "boys will be boys"–type behaviour. By contrast, the Roughnecks came from lower-income families, did poorly in school, and generally were viewed negatively. Although both groups engaged in similar behaviour, only the Roughnecks were stigmatized by a deviant label.

Another study of juvenile offenders also found that those from lower-income families were more likely to be arrested and indicted than were middle-class juveniles who participated in the same kinds of activities (Sampson, 1986). The criminal justice system frequently takes into account such factors as the offender's family life, educational achievement (or lack thereof), and social class in deciding how to deal with youthful offenders. The individuals most likely to be apprehended, labelled as delinquent, and prosecuted are people of colour who are young, male, unemployed, and undereducated and who reside in urban high-crime areas (Vito and Holmes, 1994).

The concept of secondary deviance is important to labelling theory because it suggests that when people accept a negative label or stigma that has been applied to them, the label may contribute to the type of behaviour it initially was meant to control. According to sociologist Edwin Lemert (1951), ***primary deviance* is the initial act of rule-breaking. *Secondary deviance* occurs when a person who has been labelled a deviant accepts that new identity and continues the deviant behaviour**. For example, a person may smoke marijuana, not be labelled as deviant, and subsequently decide to forgo such an act in the future. Secondary deviance occurs if the person smokes marijuana, is labelled a "pothead," accepts that label, and then continues to smoke marijuana.

One contribution of labelling theory is that it calls attention to the way in which social control and personal identity are intertwined: labelling may contribute to the acceptance of deviant roles and self-images. Critics argue that this theory does not explain what causes the original acts that make up primary deviance. Nor does it provide insight into why some people accept deviant labels and others do not (Cavender, 1995).

While interactionist perspectives are concerned with how people learn deviant behaviour, identities, and social roles through interaction with others, conflict theorists are interested in how certain kinds of people and behaviour, and not others, come to be defined as deviant.

CONFLICT PERSPECTIVES ON DEVIANCE

Who determines what kinds of behaviour are deviant or criminal? According to conflict perspectives, people in positions of power maintain their advantage by using the law to protect their own interests. Conflict theorists suggest that lifestyles considered deviant by political and economic elites often are defined as illegal. From this perspective, law defines and controls two distinct categories of people: (1) *social dynamite*—persons who have been marginalized (including rioters, labour organizers, gang members, and criminals)—and (2) *social junk*—members of stigmatized groups (such as welfare recipients, the homeless, and persons with disabilities) who are costly to society but relatively harmless (Spitzer, 1975). Conflict theorists note that the activities of poor and lower-income individuals are more likely to be defined as criminal than those of persons from middle- and upper-income backgrounds. For example, in low-income central-city areas in the United States, alcohol abuse is more prevalent among white youths than among African American youths, who prefer drugs (Pope, 1995). Currently, drug possession and use is a crime while alcohol use is not a criminal offence. Since drug offences account for the largest number of young

BOX 7.2 SOCIOLOGY IN GLOBAL PERSPECTIVE

Street Youths, *Bosozoku*, and *Yakuza* in Japan

Criminologists have identified three categories of gangs of Japan: youth gangs, *bosozoku* (hot-rod gangs), and *yakuza* (networks of adult male criminal organizations). In Japanese society, where high levels of conformity are expected, youth groups and gangs deliberately draw public attention to their deviant status, according to criminologist Joachim Kersten (1993:281):

> Minimal elements of deviance like smoking in public or in school, change of hairstyle, change of school uniform, body language, and gestures become statements of rebellious style. Youth gangs or cliques in Western cities may use specific accessories to signify the general philosophy of the group (e.g., cowboy boots, studded belts or jackets emphasizing machismo, emblems indicating ethnicity, the repulsive SS runes or Nazi swastikas worn by bikers or skinheads demonstrating racially superior status). In the United States and some Western nations, for gang members, fashion is generally secondary to focal concerns like machismo, toughness, ethnic issues, and turf. In contrast, for street corner youth gangs in Japan like yankee or *shibukaji*, and to an even higher degree for *bosozoku*, style and fashion of dress and vehicles have central relevance to their groups.

Youth gang members, who are between the ages of 14 and 20, want to separate themselves from mainstream society. Although these gangs may include females, the focus is on masculinity and male prowess. *Bosozoku* are males (and a very few females) aged 17 to 20, whose activities centre on nightly high-speed, high-noise, and high-risk rides on motorcycles and in customized cars as they are chased by the police. Members who reach the age of 20 are considered too old for the group and must find something else to do or join the *yakuza*, which is made up of adults with younger persons in apprentice roles. One Japanese man, Hayashi, describes his move from the youth gang to the *yakuza*:

> My life as a *yakuza* [organized crime gang member] began with difficulty, when as a young delinquent I joined a gang. The *oyabun* [parent figure or godfather] didn't like me ... I wanted to be a gambler, but for a long time after joining the family I wasn't allowed to gamble. First I helped with the cooking and cleaning ...
>
> After some months of cleaning duty, I got a position doing *tachiban* [standing guard], but on cold winter days it was difficult. Finally, when new members joined our gang, I was able to do *zoriban* [arranging shoes in order]. These moves were important. For the first time I was not in the house, cleaning. Unless you take these steps, you could not become a card dealer ...
>
> ... So this is the work of outlaws. The *oyabun* can't teach you anything unless you learn yourself. But one must pledge total obedience. To do that you must receive sake from the boss, with a third person as a witness. It is a very important ceremony ... *Yakuza* tradition will never cease because we're different from ordinary people. That's why we joined this world. And we share the same idea that if we make one big mistake we die together. (quoted in Kaplan and Dubro, 1987:142–144)

Nearly one-third of the *yakuza's* recruits come from the *bosozoku*. In 1992, an anti-*yakuza* law was passed that sought to prevent forcible recruitment practices used by organized crime members to fill their lower ranks with members from youth gangs (Kersten, 1993).

people held in confinement facilities, this distinction disproportionately affects African American youth.

THE CRITICAL APPROACH

Although Karl Marx wrote very little about deviance and crime, many of his ideas are found in a critical approach that has emerged from earlier Marxist and radical perspectives on criminology. The critical approach is based on the assumption that the criminal justice system protects the power and privilege of the capitalist class.

As we saw in Chapter 1, Marx based his critique of capitalism on the inherent conflict that he believed existed between the capitalists and the working class. According to Marx, social institutions (such as law, politics, and education) make up a superstructure in society that legitimizes the class structure and maintains the capitalists' superior position in it. Crime is an expression of the individual's struggle against the unjust social conditions and inequality produced by capitalism.

According to sociologist Richard Quinney (1974, 1979, 1980), people with economic and political power define as criminal any behaviour that threatens their own interests. The powerful use law to control those who are without power. For example, drug laws enacted early in the twentieth century were passed and enforced in an effort to control immigrant workers, particularly the Chinese, who were more inclined than most other residents of Canada to smoke opium. The laws were motivated by racism more than by a real concern with drug use (Cook, 1969). By contrast, while the Canadian government passed anticombines legislation in 1889, in response to concerns expressed by labour and small business people about the growing power of monopoly capitalists, the law had no impact on major companies who engaged in price-fixing and other means of limiting competition. Having symbolic anticombines laws on the books merely shored up the government's legitimacy by making it appear responsive to public concerns about big business (Smandych, 1985).

Why do people commit crimes? Some critical theorists believe that the affluent commit crimes because they are greedy and want more than they have. Corporate or white-collar crimes such as stock market manipulation, land speculation, and fraudulent bankruptcies and crimes committed on behalf of organizations often involve huge sums of money and harm many people. By contrast, street crimes such as robbery and aggravated assault generally involve small sums of money and cause harm to limited numbers of victims (Bonger, 1969). According to these theorists, the poor commit street crimes in order to survive; they find that they cannot afford the necessary essentials such as food, clothing, shelter, and health care. Thus, some crime represents a rational response by the poor to the unequal distribution of resources in society (Gordon, 1973). Further, living in poverty may lead to violent crime and victimization *of the poor by the poor*. For example, violent gang activity may be a collective response of young people to seemingly hopeless poverty (Quinney, 1979).

Recently, critical conflict theorists have examined the relationship between class, race, and crime. Many street crimes are committed by persons of colour who are more affected by poverty, unemployment, and racism than other groups. Some scholars argue that bias against the poor (especially people of colour living in poverty) contributes to the greater likelihood of their arrest and conviction than that of more affluent whites.

In sum, the critical approach argues that criminal law protects the interests of the affluent and powerful. The way laws are written and enforced benefits the capitalist class by ensuring that individuals at the bottom of the social class structure do not infringe on the property or threaten the safety of those at the top (Reiman, 1984). However, critics assert that critical theorists have not shown that powerful economic and political elites actually manipulate law making and enforcement for their own benefit. Rather, people of all classes share a consensus about the criminality of certain acts. For example, laws that prohibit murder, rape, and armed robbery protect not only middle- and upper-income people but also low-income people, who frequently are the victims of such violent crimes (Klockars, 1979).

FEMINIST APPROACHES

Can theories developed to explain male behaviour help us understand female deviance and crime? According to some feminist scholars, the answer is no. The few early studies that were conducted on "women's crimes" focused almost exclusively on prostitution and attributed the cause of this crime to women's biological or psychological "inferiority." As late as the 1980s, researchers were still looking for unique predisposing factors that led women to commit crime, which was often seen as individual psychopathology rather than as a response to their social environment. These theories, which reinforce existing female stereotypes, have had a negative impact on both our understanding and our treatment of female offenders.

A new interest in women and deviance developed in 1975 when two books—Freda Adler's *Sisters in Crime* and Rita James Simons's *Women and Crime*—declared that women's crime rates were going to increase significantly as a result of the women's liberation movement. Although, this so-called *emancipation theory* of female crime has been strongly criticized by subsequent analysts (Comack, 1996a), Adler's and Simons's works encouraged feminist scholars (both women and men) to examine the relationship between gender, deviance, and crime more closely. While there is no single feminist perspective on deviance and crime, three schools of thought have emerged.

Liberal feminism explains women's deviance and crime as a rational response to gender discrimination experienced in work, marriage, and interpersonal relationships. Some female crimes may be attributed to women's lack of educational and job opportunities and stereotypical expectations about what roles women should have in society. For example, a woman is no more likely to be a big-time drug dealer or an organized crime boss than she is to be a corporate director (see Daly and Chesney-Lind, 1988; Simpson, 1989).

Radical feminism suggests that patriarchy (male domination over females) keeps women more tied to family and home, even if women also work full-time. Based on this approach, prostitution might be explained as a reflection of society's sexual double standard, whereby it is acceptable for a man to pay for sex but unacceptable for a woman to accept money for such services. Although prostitution laws in Canada define both the prostitute and the customer as violating the law, women are far more likely than men to be arrested, brought to trial, convicted, and sentenced for prostitution-related offences.

The third school of feminist thought, *socialist feminism*, notes that women are exploited by capitalism and patriarchy. Because most females have relatively low-wage jobs and few economic resources, crimes such as prostitution and shoplifting become a means to earn money or acquire consumer products. Instead of freeing women from their problems, however, prostitution institutionalizes women's dependence on men and results in a form of female sexual slavery (Vito and Holmes, 1994).

Recently, some feminist scholars have observed that these schools of feminist thought have not placed sufficient emphasis on race and ethnicity in their analyses. As a result, some recent studies have focused on the simultaneous effects of race, class, and gender on deviant behaviour. Regina Arnold attributes many of the women's offences to living in families in which sexual abuse, incest, and other violence left them few choices except to engage in deviance. Economic marginality and racism also contributed to their victimization. "To be young, Black, poor, and female is to be in a high-risk category for victimization and stigmatization on many levels" (Arnold, 1990:156). These findings are reinforced by a recent study in which Elizabeth Comack examined the relationship between women's earlier victimization in their family and their subsequent involvement in the criminal justice system. The incidence of prior victimization was pervasive among women incarcerated in a provincial jail. To examine the problem in detail, Comack interviewed twenty-four women. The abuse suffered by the women was connected to their criminal behaviour in several ways. Some women turned to crime as a means of coping with their histories of abuse. "Meredith" had been sexually abused by her father since the age of four or five. She was in jail for fraud and had been involved in drug use and prostitution:

> Some people are violent, some people take it out in other ways, but that was my only way to release it. It was like, it's almost orgasmic, you know, you'd write the cheques, and you'd get home and you'd go through all these things and it's like, "There's so much there. I have all these new things to keep my mind off. I don't have to deal with the old issues." And so you do it. And it becomes an escape. (Comack, 1996b:86)

Others break the law in the course of resisting abuse. "Janice" had been raped as a teenager and turned to alcohol as a means of coping. Serving time for manslaughter, she recounts the circumstances of the offence:

> ... well I was at a party, and this guy, older, older guy, came, came on to me. He tried telling me, "Why don't you go to bed with me. I'm getting some money, you know." And I said, "No." And then he started hitting me and then he raped me and then (pause) I lost it. Like I just, I went, I got very angy and I snapped. And I started hitting him. I threw a coffee table on top of his head and then I stabbed him, and then I left. (Comack, 1996b:96)

While abuse was strongly related to the womens' law violations, Comack also found that race and class were factors contributing to the criminal behaviour of many of the women; most were aboriginal and poor.

We have examined functionalist, interactionist, and conflict perspectives on deviance and crime (see Concept Table 7.A). These explanations help us to understand the causes and consequences of certain kinds of behaviour; however, they also make us aware of the limitations of our knowledge about deviance and crime. It has been said that there is "no crime without law." In other words, if a law does not exist that prohibits a specific act, it is not a crime to engage in that behaviour. Crime, like other types of deviance, can be analyzed only within a specific social context. Behaviour may be deviant but not criminal (such as claiming to have been abducted by space aliens), criminal but not necessarily deviant (such as smoking marijuana), or both criminal and deviant (such as committing murder).

CRIME CLASSIFICATION AND STATISTICS

The law divides crime into different categories. We will look first at the legal classifications of crime and then at categories typically used by sociologists and criminologists.

HOW THE LAW CLASSIFIES CRIME

The law divides crime into summary conviction and indictable offences. The distinction between the two is based on the seriousness of the crime. *Indictable offences* include serious crimes such as homicide, sexual assault, robbery, and break and enter. *Summary conviction offences* are relatively minor offences, including fraudulently obtaining food from a restaurant, causing a disturbance, and wilfully committing an indecent act. Summary conviction offences are punishable by a fine of up to $2000 and/or six months in jail.

HOW SOCIOLOGISTS CLASSIFY CRIME

Sociologists categorize crimes based on how they are committed and how society views the offences. We will examine four types: (1) conven-

CONCEPT TABLE 7.A

Theoretical Perspectives on Deviance

	Theory	Key Elements
Functionalist Perspectives		
Robert Merton	Strain theory	Deviance occurs when access to the approved means of reaching culturally approved goals is blocked. Innovation, ritualism, retreatism, or rebellion may result.
Richard Cloward/ Lloyd Ohlin	Opportunity theory	For deviance to occur, people must have the opportunity. Access to illegitimate opportunity structures varies, and this helps determine the nature of the deviance in which a person will enagage.
Travis Hirschi	Social control/social bonding	Social bonds keep people from becoming criminals. When ties to family, friends, and others become weak, an individual is most likely to engage in criminal behaviour.
Interactionist Perspectives		
Edwin Sutherland	Differential association	Deviant behaviour is learned in interaction with others. A person becomes delinquent when exposure to lawbreaking attitudes is more extensive than exposure to law-abiding attitudes.
Howard Becker	Labelling theory	Acts are deviant or criminal because they have been labelled as such. Powerful groups often label less powerful individuals.
Edwin Lemert	Primary/secondary deviance	Primary deviance is the initial act. Secondary deviance occurs when a person accepts the label of "deviant" and continues to engage in the behaviour that initially produced the label.
Conflict Perspectives		
Karl Marx Richard Quinney	Critical approach	The powerful use law and the criminal justice system to protect their own class interests.
Kathleen Daly Meda Chesney-Lind	Feminist approach	Historically, women have been ignored in research on crime. Liberal feminism views women's deviance as arising from gender discrimination; radical feminism focuses on patriarchy; and socialist feminism emphasizes the effects of capitalism and patriarchy on

tional, or street, crime, (2) occupational, or white-collar, and corporate crime, (3) organized crime, and (4) political crime. As you read about these types of crime, ask yourself how you feel about them. Should each be a crime? How stiff should the sanctions be against each type?

CONVENTIONAL CRIME When people think of crime, the images that most commonly come to mind are of ***conventional* or *street crime*, which includes offences such as robbery, assault, and break and enter**. These are the crimes that occupy most of the time and attention of the criminal justice system. Obviously, all street crime does not occur on the street; it frequently occurs in the home, workplace, and other locations.

Violent crime consists of actions involving force or the threat of force against others, including murder, sexual assault, robbery, and aggravated assault. Violent crimes are probably the most anxiety-provoking of all criminal behaviour. Victims often are physically injured or even lose their lives; the psychological trauma may last for years after the event (Parker, 1995). Violent crime receives the most sustained attention from law enforcement officials and the media (see Warr, 1995). And, while much attention may be given to, and fears aroused by, the violent stranger, the vast majority of violent crime victims actually are injured by someone whom they know: family members, friends, neighbours, or co-workers (Silverman and Kennedy, 1993).

Property crimes include break and enter, theft, motor vehicle theft, and arson. While violent crime receives the most publicity, property crimes are much more common. In most property crimes, the primary motive is to obtain money or some other desired valuable.

"Morals" crimes involve an illegal action voluntarily engaged in by the participants, such as prostitution, illegal gambling, the private use of illegal drugs, and illegal pornography. Many people assert that such conduct should not be labelled as a crime; these offences often are referred to as "victimless crimes" because they involve exchanges of illegal goods or services among willing adults (Schur, 1965).

However, morals crimes can include children and adolescents as well as adults. Young children and adolescents may unwillingly become child pornography "stars" or prostitutes. Members of juvenile gangs often find selling drugs to be a lucrative business in which getting addicted and/or arrested is merely an occupational hazard.

OCCUPATIONAL AND CORPORATE CRIME Although sociologist Edwin Sutherland (1949) developed the theory of white-collar crime almost fifty years ago, it was not until the 1980s that the public really became aware of its nature. ***Occupational* or *white-collar crime* consists of illegal activities committed by people in the course of their employment or financial dealings.**

At the heart of much white-collar crime is a violation of positions of trust in business or government (Shapiro, 1990). These activities include pilfering (employee theft of company property or profits), soliciting bribes or kickbacks, and embezzling. In the past decade, computers have created even greater access to such illegal practices. Some white-collar criminals set up businesses for the sole purpose of victimizing the general public, engaging in activities such as land swindles, securities thefts, and consumer fraud.

In addition to acting for their own financial benefit, some white-collar offenders become involved in criminal conspiracies designed to improve the market share or profitability of their companies. This is known as ***corporate crime*—illegal acts committed by corporate employees on *behalf* of the corporation and with its support**. Examples include antitrust violations; false advertising; infringements on patents, copyrights, and trademarks; price fixing; and financial fraud. These crimes are a result of deliberate decisions made by corporate personnel to enhance resources or profits at the expense of competitors, consumers, and the general public.

The cost of white-collar and corporate crimes far exceeds that of street crime. Gabor (1994) reports that tax evasion costs Canadians about $30 billion a year, which is greater than the federal deficit. The failure of a number of savings and loan institutions in the United States, many of which were caused by the criminal misconduct of their owners, will cost American taxpayers hundreds of billions of dollars. At the individual level, while few bank robbers get away with more than a few thousand dollars, Julius Melnitzer, a London, Ontario, lawyer, defrauded Canadian banks of $90 million in order to support his lavish lifestyle.

Corporate crimes can also be very costly in terms of lives lost and injury. Laureen Snider (1988) found that occupational deaths are the third leading cause of death in Canada. She attributes at least half of these deaths to unsafe and illegal working conditions. Working conditions in the mining industry, for example, have been especially dangerous. Decades ago, large numbers of Canadian miners died because their employers failed to protect them from mine hazards. Coal miners died of black lung, a condition caused by inhaling coal dust, and fluorspar miners died from the effects of inhaling silica dust in unventilated mineshafts. Not only did the mine owners fail to provide safe working conditions, but company doctors were also told not to advise the miners of the seriousness of their illnesses. The loss of 26 miners in a preventable explosion at Nova Scotia's Westray mine in 1992 suggests some mine owners have yet to put their employees' lives above profits.

One reason many employers have been reluctant to implement required safety measures is because the penalties for violating workplace health and safety laws are so light. Consider the case of Silco, an Edmonton-based construction company. In 1994, a Silco employee fell to his death from a homemade man-basket attached to an unstable crane boom. The company had received three different orders to improve their safety practices earlier that year, but had ignored all of them, including a stop-work order the month of the accident. Despite Silco's obvious negligence, the company received only a fine of $6,000 for its part in the employee's death (Ward, 1996).

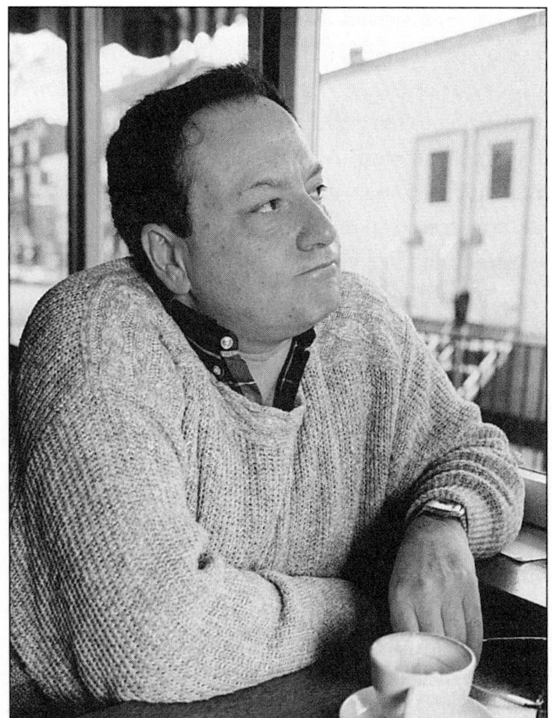

While few bank robbers get away with more than a few thousand dollars, white-collar criminal Julius Melnitzer was able to defraud Canadian banks of $90 million.

Although people who commit occupational and corporate crimes can be arrested, fined, and sent to prison, many people do not regard such behaviour as "criminal." People who tend to condemn street crime are less sure of how their own (or their friends') financial and corporate behaviour should be judged. At most, punishment for such offences is usually a fine or a relatively brief prison sentence at a minimum-security facility. The case of Michael Milken shows the typical sanctions for white-collar crimes. After his 1990s conviction for illegal insider trading, Milken, a former high-paid executive with a large U.S. investment banking firm, was ordered to pay $600 million in fines and restitution and sentenced to ten years in prison. He was released from a minimum-security prison after less than two years to do community service and still retained enough money from his crimes to remain one of the country's richest men. Milken also taught a graduate business seminar in which one of his students demonstrated many people's ambivalence toward white-collar and corporate offenders: "[Milken] is a great man—a martyr, not a crook. It's not fair, punishing him simply because society cannot understand how one man could make $500 million in a single year" (Clines, 1993a:9).

In many corporate crimes it is more difficult to attach individual blame than in conventional (street) crimes. It is far easier to determine who was responsible for a sexual assault or a robbery than to determine the specific individuals who are responsible for complex price-fixing arrangements between companies. For example, a scheme by Canada's largest flour-milling companies to fix prices on flour sold to the government for food aid to Third World countries continued for more than a decade and involved very complex business arrangements. In some respects, individual blame is irrelevant in most corporate crimes because usually it is the corporation that is prosecuted, not the individual manager.

One final point that can be made about white-collar crime is that the concept also fits people who wear blue collars. Because of this, some have suggested that *occupational crime* may be a more accurate term. Many tradespeople defraud the government by doing work "off the books" in order to avoid provincial sales tax and the Goods and Services Tax. Some blue-collar businesses have bad records of consumer fraud. Robert Sikorsky (1990), who travelled across Canada and visited 152 automobile repair shops, documented an appalling degree of misconduct in this business. Before each visit, he disconnected the idle air control in his car, which triggered a warning light on the instrument panel. The repair needed was obvious and simple—reinsert the connector. But, more than half the shops Sikorsky visited performed unnecessary work, overcharged him for work, or lied about the work that had been done. In one case he was presented with an estimate of $570.

ORGANIZED CRIME ***Organized crime*** **is a business operation that supplies illegal goods and services for profit**. Organized crime includes drug trafficking, prostitution, liquor and cigarette smuggling, loan-sharking, money laundering, and large-scale theft, such as truck hijacking (Simon and Eitzen, 1993). No single organization controls all organized crime; rather, many groups operate at all levels of society. Organized crime thrives because there is great demand for illegal goods and services. This public demand has produced illicit supply systems with global connections. These activities are highly profitable, since groups that have a monopoly over goods and services the public strongly desires can set their own price. Legitimate competitors are excluded because of the illegality; illegitimate competitors are controlled by force.

The deadly nature of organized crime has been shown in Montreal, which has been the scene of a major turf war between two rival biker gangs: the Rock Machine and the Hell's Angels. The two gangs have been engaged in a battle for control of a large segment of the city's illegal drug market. During January and February of 1995, the battle took a particularly bloody turn as rival gang members died at a rate of almost one a week as a result of car bombings, shootings, and stabbings. Along with their illegal enterprises, organized crime groups have infiltrated the world of legitimate business. Known linkages between legitimate businesses and organized crime exist in banking, hotels and motels, real estate, garbage collection, vending machines, construction, delivery and long-distance hauling, garment manufacturing, insurance, stocks and bonds, vacation resorts, and funeral parlours (National Council on Crime and Delinquency, 1969). In addition, law enforcement and government officials may be corrupted through bribery, campaign contributions, and favours intended to buy them off, although this has been much less of a problem in Canada than in many other countries.

POLITICAL CRIMES The term ***political crime*** **refers to illegal or unethical acts involving the misuse of power by government officials, or illegal/unethical acts perpetrated against the government by outsiders seeking to make a political statement, undermine the government, or overthrow it.** Government officials may use their authority unethically or illegally for material gain or political power. They may engage in graft (taking advantage of political position to gain money or property) through bribery, kickbacks, or "insider" deals that financially benefit them. For example, several members of the Mulroney government were charged with bribery, influence peddling, and abuse of public trust, and many allegations have been made that the former prime minister and other senior officials were involved in these activities and in subsequent coverups (Corrado, 1996).

Other types of corruption have been costly for taxpayers, including dubious use of public funds and public property, corruption in the regulation of commercial activities (such as food inspection), graft in zoning and land use decisions, and campaign contributions and other favours to legislators that corrupt the legislative process. While some political crimes are for personal material gain, others (such as illegal wiretapping and political "dirty tricks") are aimed at gaining or maintaining political office or influence.

Some acts committed by agents of the government against persons and groups believed to be threats to national security also are political crimes. Four types of political deviance have been attributed to some officials: (1) secrecy and deception designed to manipulate public opinion, (2) abuse of power, (3) prosecution of individuals due to their political activities, and (4) official violence, such as police brutality against people of colour or the use of citizens as unwilling guinea pigs (Simon and Eitzen, 1993).

Political crimes also include illegal or unethical acts perpetrated against the government by outsiders seeking to make a political statement or to undermine or overthrow the government. Examples include treason, acts of political sabotage, and certain types of environmental protests. During the 1960s, the Front de Libération du Québec (FLQ) tried to bring about an independent Quebec through terrorism (Corrado, 1996). Several people were killed in bombings, and in 1970 the FLQ precipitated the October Crisis by kidnapping James Cross, a British trade official, and Pierre Laporte, a provincial cabinet minister. Laporte was killed, and the federal government invoked the War Measures Act, which suspended certain civil liberties in order to deal with the crisis. While the FLQ's acts were clearly criminal, debate continues about whether the government was justified in using the War Measures Act, or whether invoking it also constituted a political crime aimed at defeating the Quebec nationalist movement.

CRIME STATISTICS

While citizens, police, and policy makers all wish to know how much crime there is and what forms this crime takes, those who commit crimes normally try to conceal their actions. It is always difficult to gather statistics about crime and to get access to the social worlds of criminals. Thus our information about crime will always be incomplete and we can never be certain that it is completely accurate. Our main sources of information about crime are police statistics, victimization surveys, and self-reports.

OFFICIAL STATISTICS Our most important source of crime data is the *Canadian Uniform Crime Reports* (CUCR) system, which summarizes crimes reported to all Canadian police departments. The CUCR is compiled by the Canadian Centre for Justice Statistics, which is part of Statistics Canada. This system collects information on almost all criminal code offences as well as on violations of federal and provincial statutes. Most of our public information about crime comes from the CUCR. When we read that the homicide rate in British Columbia is higher than the national average, or that in 1993, over three million offences were reported to the police, this information is usually based on CUCR data. Figure 7.2 shows trends in violent and property crimes, and Figure 7.3 shows Canada's homicide rates. While most Canadians think that crime is increasing, these charts show that it has begun to decline in the past few years. The decline is particularly significant in the case of homicide where 1995 rates were the lowest they have been in twenty-five years.

Crime figures should be interpreted very cautiously. While one can have confidence in homicide statistics, the accuracy of other crime statistics is less certain. Since many policy decisions by governments, as well as decisions by individuals about their personal safety, are based on CUCR statistics, it is important to recognize their limitations.

The major weakness of the CUCR is that police statistics always underreport the actual amount of crime. The vast majority of offences reported in the CUCR come to the attention of the police from the reports of victims of crime, and victims do not report all crimes. Furthermore, reporting of crime is inconsistent from place to place and from time to time. Official crime rates are the result of a criminal act, a complaint by a victim or witness, and a response by the criminal justice system. A change in any of these will lead to an increase or decrease in crime rates. This makes it very difficult to make sense of crime patterns and trends.

For example, Figure 7.2 shows that rates of reported violent crimes increased significantly in Canada during the late 1980s and early 1990s. In fact, they almost doubled between 1980 and 1990. While we don't know the real number of these crimes, we do know that at least part of the increase in reported crime is due to the fact that violence against women is now reported more often than it used to be (Linden, 1994). In the mid-1980s, many provincial governments directed police in their provinces to lay charges in all suspected cases of domestic violence. The procedures police were directed to use in laying these charges have been made progressively more effective since they were first implemented. This visible support by the justice system may have encouraged more victims to report spousal assaults. The impact of these changes can be seen in Winnipeg, where the police have instituted a mandatory charging policy and where the province has set up a special family violence court to facilitate the processing of spouse abuse cases. The number of domestic violence cases dealt with by this court rose from 1444 in 1990, the first year of the court's operation, to 3387 three years later (Ursel, 1996). It is likely that this increase was entirely due to changes in the reporting and recording of domestic assaults and not to any actual increase in family violence.

Another weakness of official statistics is that many crimes committed by persons of higher socioeconomic status are routinely handled by administrative or quasi-judicial bodies or by civil courts. To avoid negative publicity, many companies prefer to deal privately with offences like embezzlement committed by their employees, and these cases are never reported to the police. As a result, many elite crimes are never classified as "crimes," nor are the business people who commit them labelled as "criminals."

VICTIMIZATION SURVEYS The weaknesses of the CUCR have led to other methods of measuring crime, the most important of which is the victimization survey. Because a major problem with the CUCR is the fact that many people do not report their victimization, some governments began to carry out large surveys in which members of the public were directly asked whether they had been victims of crime. In the largest Canadian survey, less than 42 percent of the victimizations reported by respondents had been reported to the police (Evans and Himelfarb, 1996). Thus reported crimes are only the "tip of the iceberg." People told interviewers they did not report crimes because they considered the incident too minor, because they felt it was a personal matter, because they preferred to deal with the problem in another way, or because they did not feel the police could do anything about the crime. Victimization

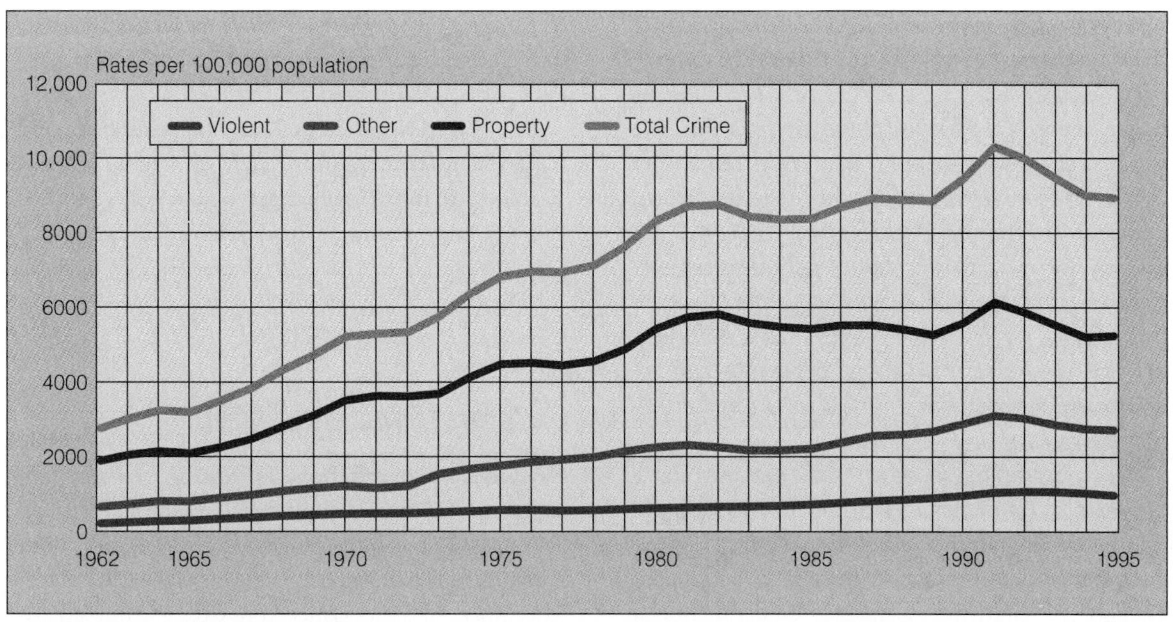

FIGURE 7.2

Canadian Crime Rates, 1962–1995

Reproduced by authority of the Minister of Industry, 1996, Statistics Canada, from Uniform Crime Reporting Survey, Canadian Centre for Justice Statistics, *Juristat*, Cat. no. 85-002, 1994.

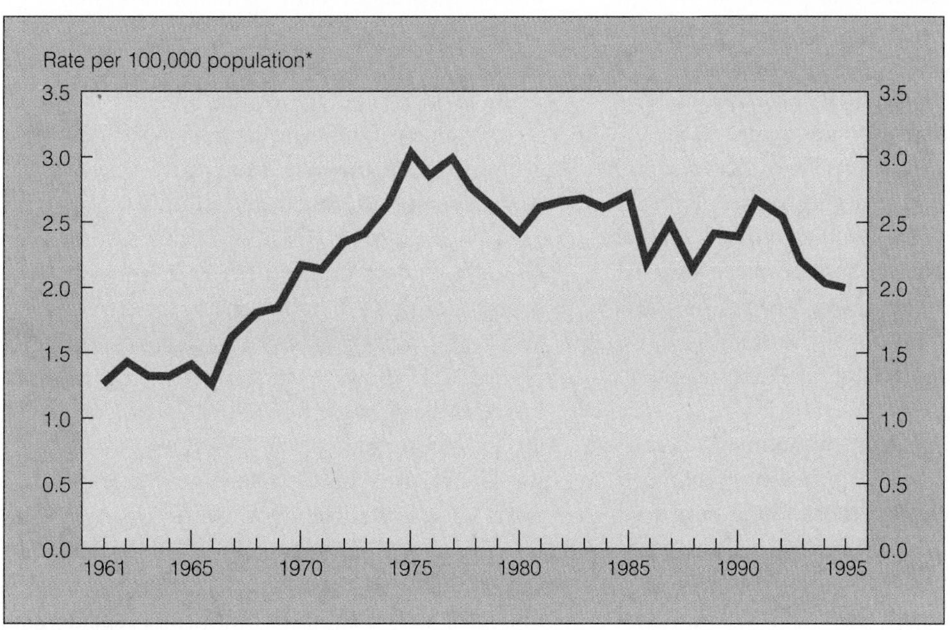

FIGURE 7.3

Canadian Homicide Rates, 1961–1995

As of 1971, population estimates were adjusted to reflect new methods of calculation.

Reproduced by authority of the Minister of Industry, 1996, Statistics Canada, from Homicide Survey, Policing Services Program, Canadian Centre for Justice Statistics, *Juristat*, Cat. no. 85-002, August 1995.

surveys provide us with information about crimes that have not been officially reported, so they provide more accurate statistics of crime than do police records. However, these surveys do have some weaknesses: people may not remember minor types of victimization; they may not report honestly to the interviewer; and they do not provide any information about "victimless crimes" such as drug use and illegal gambling. Despite these flaws, victimization surveys have shed new light on the extent of criminal behaviour and are a valuable complement to other ways of counting crimes.

For example, victimization surveys have provided additional information that has helped us to understand the increase in violent crimes discussed above. Victimization surveys conducted as part of Statistics Canada's General Social Survey showed that despite an increase of about 25 percent in the CUCR reported assault rate between 1988 and 1993, the rate of assault victimizations reported in the survey actually declined slightly during this period (Kingsley, 1996). While both police statistics and victimization surveys have their weaknesses, you can see how analyses of data from the CUCR and from the General Social Survey allow us to tentatively conclude that assaults are not increasing in Canada. Rather, a combination of government policies that encourage the reporting and charging of assailants in domestic violence cases and increased public attention to the problem of spousal abuse have led to increased reporting and recording of these assaults. Assaults have probably not increased, we are simply doing a better job of counting them.

SELF-REPORTS Studies based on anonymous self-reports of criminal behaviour also reveal much higher rates of crime than those found in official statistics. For example, self-reports tend to indicate that adolescents of all social classes violate criminal laws. However, official statistics show that those who are arrested and placed in juvenile facilities typically have limited financial resources, have repeatedly committed serious offences, or both (Hindelang, Hirschi, and Weis, 1981; Steffensmeier and Streifel, 1991). Youth court statistics may also reflect class and racial biases in criminal justice enforcement. Not all young people who commit offences are apprehended and referred to court. Children from white, affluent families are more likely to have their cases handled outside the juvenile justice system (for example, a youth may be sent to a private school or hospital rather than to a juvenile correctional facility).

STREET CRIMES AND CRIMINALS

Given the limitations of official statistics, is it possible to determine who commits crimes? We have much more information available about conventional or street crime than elite crime; therefore, statistics concerning street crime do not show who commits all types of crime. Age, gender, class, and race are important factors in official statistics pertaining to street crime. These are known as *correlates of crime*, that is, they are factors associated with criminal activity. One method of testing theories of crime is to see how well they explain these correlates.

AGE AND CRIME The age of the offender is one of the most significant factors associated with crime. Arrests increase from early adolescence, peak in young adulthood, and steadily decline with age. There is some variation in this pattern—for example, violent crimes peak at a later age than property crimes—but the general pattern is almost always the same. Crime is a young person's game. Figure 7.4 shows that property crimes peak between the ages of 18 to 24, while violent crimes are most common among 25- to 34-year-olds.

The relationship between age and criminality exists in every society for which we have data (Hirschi and Gottfredson, 1983). Adolescence and early adulthood are the peak times for both offending and victimization. Possible explanations for this are the physical effects of aging, which make some criminal activity more difficult, and the realization by older chronic offenders that further arrests will result in very long jail

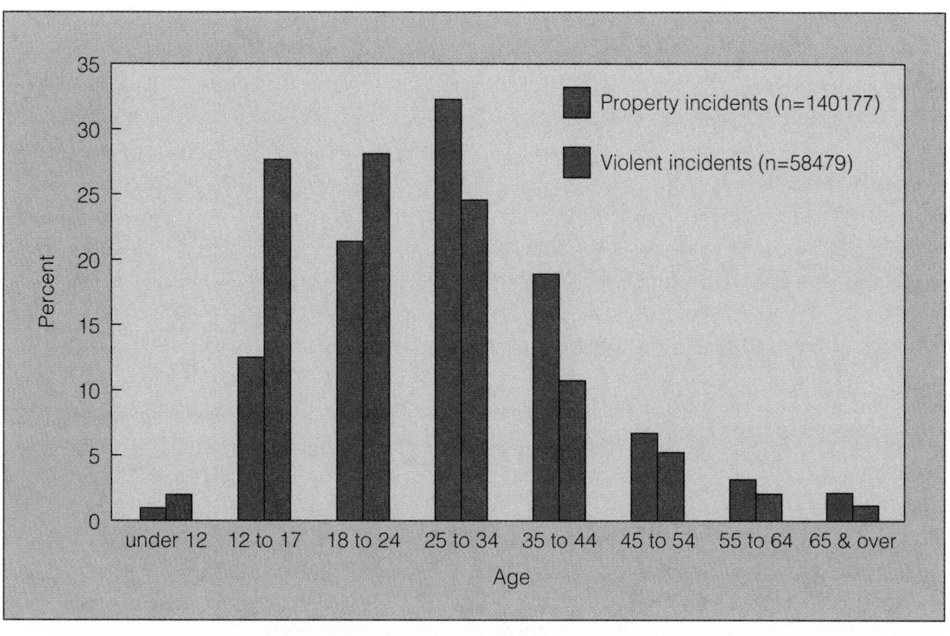

FIGURE 7.4

Age of Accused, Property and Violent Incidents, 1992

Reproduced with permission of the Minister of Industry, 1996, Statistics Canada, from *Canadian Crime Statistics*, Cat. no. 85-205.

sentences. Perhaps the best explanation for maturational reform, though, is related to the different social positions of youth and adults. Adolescents are between childhood and adult life. They have few responsibilities and no clear social role. Adolescence is also a time when young people are breaking away from the controls of their parents and others and preparing to live on their own. As we age, we begin to acquire commitments and obligations that limit our freedom to choose a lifestyle that includes crime.

GENDER AND CRIME Another consistent correlate of crime is gender. Most crimes are committed by males. Females are more likely to be victims than offenders. As with age and crime, this relationship has existed in almost all times and cultures. However, while the age distribution is remarkably stable, considerably more variation in male/female crime ratios exists in different places, at different times, and for different types of crime.

In 1993, men made up 81 percent of those charged with crimes in Canada (Chard, 1995). As Figure 7.5 shows, the degree of involvement of males and females varies substantially for different crimes. The most important gender differences in arrest rates are reflected in the proportionately greater involvement of men in violent crimes and major property offences.

The difference between male and female crime rates has narrowed over the past three decades. Hartnagel (1996) compared the rate of male and female adults charged with a variety of offences in 1968 and in 1992, and found that crime rates for females increased much more rapidly than for males during this period. The percentage of Criminal Code offences committed by females increased from 9 percent to 18 percent. While there was virtually no change in the proportion of

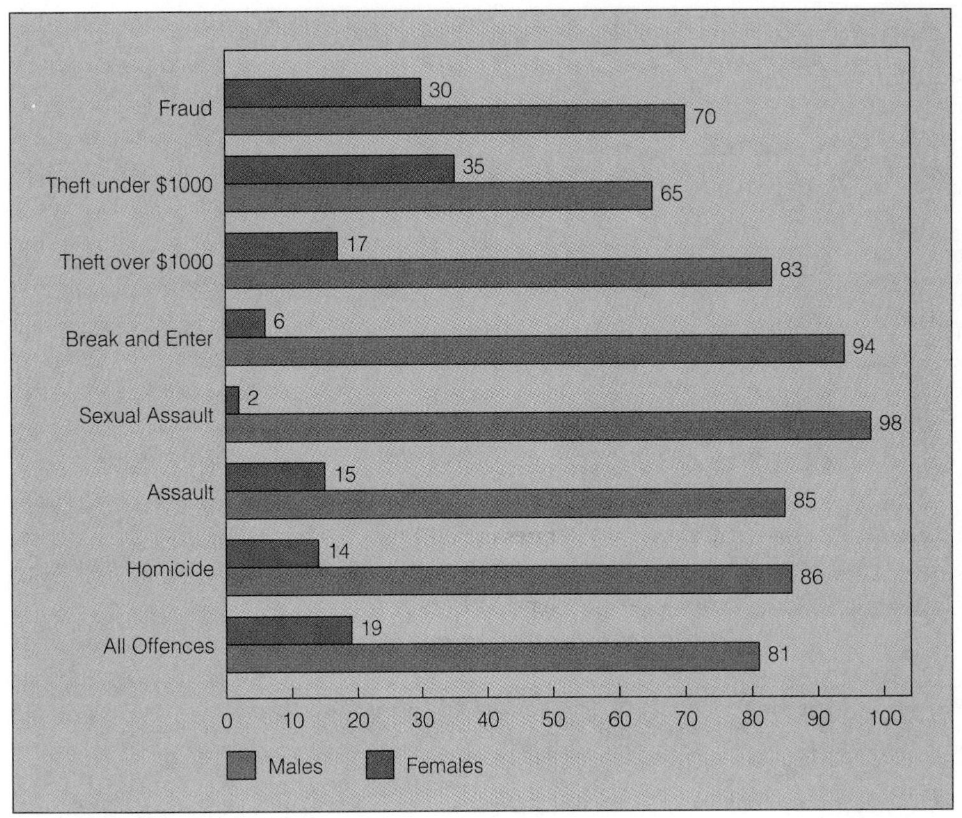

FIGURE 7.5

Arrests by Sex, 1993 (Selected Criminal Offences)

Reproduced by authority of the Minister of Industry, 1996, Statistics Canada, from *Juristat*, Cat. no. 85-002, volume 15, no. 10, 1995.

females charged with homicide (11 percent versus 12 percent), the proportion of women charged with serious theft (9 percent to 18 percent), fraud (11 percent to 29 percent,) and minor theft (22 percent to 34 percent) changed substantially.

What has caused this change in the sex distribution of crime? One clue comes from cross-cultural data showing very large differences in sex ratios of criminal involvement in different parts of the world. While the ratio of male to female crime in North America and Western Europe is between 5:1 and 10:1, ratios as high as 20,000:1 have been reported elsewhere. The ratios are highest (meaning that male rates of crime are much higher than those of females) in countries having the greatest differences between the roles of men and women. Where women follow traditional roles in which their lives are centred exclusively on the home, their crime rates are very low. On the other hand, where women's lives are more similar to men's, their crime rates will be higher. This is consistent with the change in women's crime rates over the past several decades in Canada, where the role of women has come to resemble that of men.

While role convergence may explain some of the reduction in the gap between male and female crime rates, the rate of convergence has slowed and it does not seem likely that women will ever become as involved in crime as men, or that they will adopt male patterns of crime, particularly for violent crime. The increase in female crime has been the greatest for property crimes such as theft and fraud. These two categories include offences commonly committed by females such as shoplifting, credit card fraud, and passing bad cheques, which are among the least serious property offences. Comack (1996a) has concluded that this reflects the feminization of poverty rather than any convergence of men's and women's roles. As you will see in Chapter 8, the number of poor, female single parents is growing, and some of these women may commit crime in order to support themselves and their children. Thus, much of the increase in female crime may simply reflect the economic marginalization of women. That women are not all relinquishing their traditional feminine roles in a patriarchal society is evident, moreover, from the fact that when women are arrested for serious violent and property crimes, they are often accomplices to males who organized the crime and instigated its commission (Steffensmeier and Allan, 1995).

While female crime rates have increased more rapidly than male crime rates, it is important to remember that the numbers seem more dramatic than they are because the percentage changes are based on very low numbers of female crimes in earlier decades. Women have a long way to go to reach parity in crime with men.

SOCIAL CLASS AND CRIME Criminologists have long debated the relationship between social class and crime. Many theories of crime are based on the assumption that crime is economically motivated and that poverty will lead to criminal behaviour. Unfortunately, the evidence concerning the impact of economic factors on crime is not entirely clear. We do know that persons from lower socioeconomic backgrounds are more likely to be arrested for violent and property crimes. However, we also know that these types of crimes are more likely to come to the attention of the police than are the white-collar and corporate crimes that are more likely to be committed by members of the upper class. Because the vast majority of white-collar and corporate crimes are never reported, we do not have the data to adequately assess the relationship between class and crime.

Before looking at some of the data on social class and crime we do have, let us briefly consider several other economic variables. Does crime increase during times of high unemployment? Do poor cities, provinces, and countries have higher crime rates than richer communities? The answer to both these questions is no. Historically, crime rates are at least as likely to rise during periods of prosperity as during recessionary times (Nettler, 1984). We are also as likely to find high crime rates in rich countries as in poor ones. The world's wealthiest countries, the United States and Japan, have very different crime rates. Compared with other countries, crime in the United States is very high and crime in Japan is very low. Within Canada, the poor provinces of Newfoundland and New Brunswick have crime rates far lower than the rich provinces of British Columbia and Alberta (see Figure 7.6). Hartnagel (1996) has concluded that the *degree of inequality*—poverty amid affluence—is a better predictor of crime than is the amount of poverty.

We know that lower-class people are overrepresented in arrest and prison admission statistics. However, we do not know if this is because lower-class people commit more crimes, or because the justice system treats them more harshly. To get closer to actual behaviour, researchers developed the self-report measures discussed earlier. There is some disagreement about the conclusions that should be drawn from this research, most of which has used adolescent subjects. Some feel that self-report research shows almost no correlation between class and delinquency and crime, and attributes class differences in official measures to bias in the criminal justice system (Tittle et al., 1978). However, other research (Elliott and Ageton, 1980; Thornberry and Farnworth, 1982) has supported the view that crime is more frequent in the lower class. Based on the results of these and many other studies, the most likely conclu-

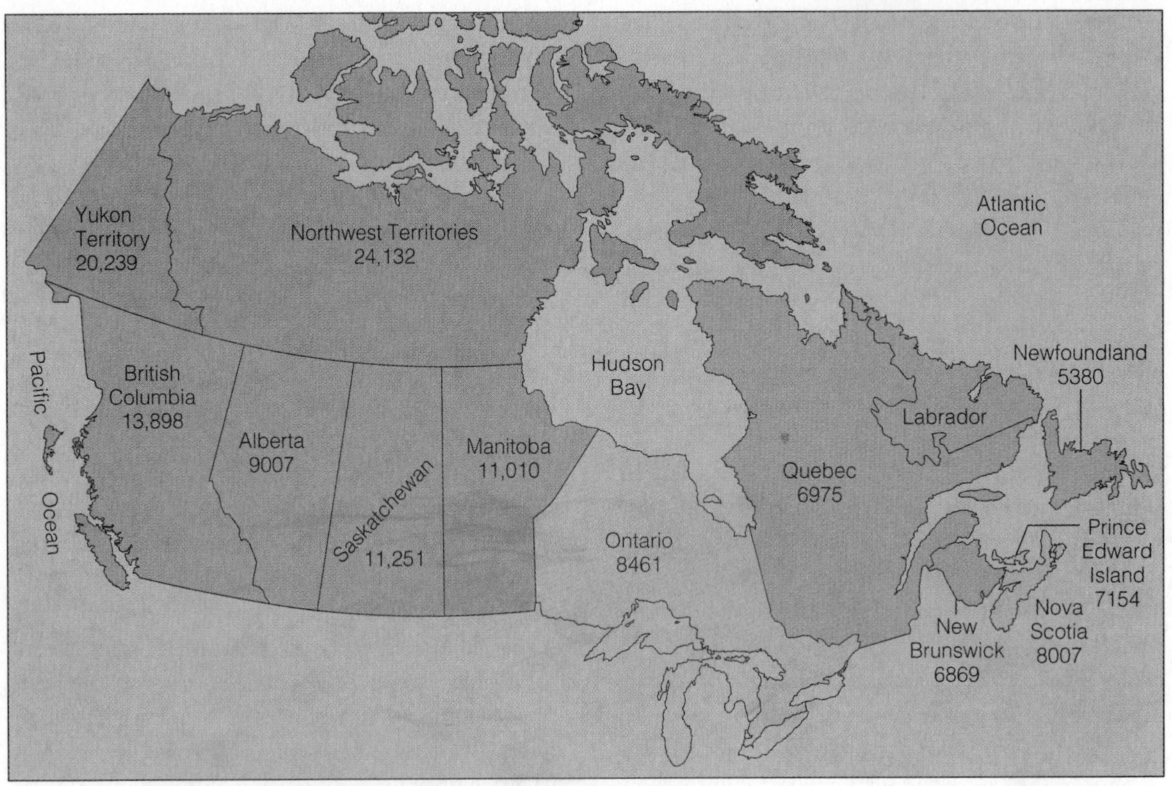

FIGURE 7.6

Crime Rates Per 100,000 Population (Criminal Code excluding traffic)

Reproduced by authority of the Minister of Industry, 1996, Statistics Canada, from *Canadian Crime Statistics*, Cat. no. 85-205, 1995.

sion is that for the vast majority of people, class and crime or delinquency are not related. People from all classes break the law, at least occasionally. However, those who engage in frequent and serious offending are most likely to come from the very bottom of the class ladder—from an underclass that is severely disadvantaged economically, educationally, and socially.

This conclusion is supported by the work of several researchers who have conducted field studies among street youth in several countries including Canada, the United States, and Britain. U.S. research has focused on the role of chronic unemployment and discrimination in the development of street gangs in Hispanic (Vigil, 1990) and African American (E. Anderson, 1994) communities. Subcultures that encourage and facilitate crime have developed in response to the long-term poverty so common in many American communities. Compared to the bleak legitimate opportunities available to them, criminal opportunities, particularly from the drug trade, can be very attractive. The Canadian research involved studies of street youth in Toronto (Hagan and McCarthy, 1992) and Edmonton (Baron, 1994). These studies found that many street youth were from lower-class families and were on the streets because of poor relationships at home and at school. Their life on the streets often leads to delinquency because of the need to survive and

BOX 7.3 SOCIOLOGY AND MEDIA

"If It Bleeds, It Leads": Fear of Crime and the Media

Most Canadians learn about crime through the media rather than from first-hand experience. Stories on television and radio, and in newspapers, magazines, and books shape our views about crime and criminals. However, the media do not simply "report" the news. Editors and reporters select the crime news we hear about and construct the way in which this news is presented to us.

Unfortunately, the picture of crime we receive from the media is very inaccurate. For example, while most crime is property crime, most stories in the media deal with violent crime. Typical of research in this area was a review of all the crime-related stories reported over two months in an Ottawa newspaper (Gabor, 1994). Over half the stories focused on violent crimes, particularly murders. However, violent crimes actually made up only 7 percent of reported crimes in Ottawa and the city averaged just six murders per year. While violent crimes were overreported, property crimes rarely received much attention, and white-collar and political crimes were almost never written about.

Why do the media misrepresent crime? The primary goal of the media is to make profits by selling advertising. Stories that attract viewers or readers will boost ratings and circulation even if these stories do not represent the reality of crime. The informal media rule, "If it bleeds, it leads," reflects the fact that the public are fascinated by sensationalized, bloody stories such as mass murders or attacks against helpless senior citizens. Commenting on his experience with the media, the executive director of a provincial legal society said, "If there's no blood and gore, or there's no sex, it's not newsworthy. And if it falls into the category of being newsworthy, then they have to show the dead body. They've got to show the corpse" (McCormick, 1995:182).

The media's misrepresentation of crime has several consequences. First, Canadians greatly overestimate the amount of violent crime that is committed and have a fear of crime that is more intense than the risk of victimization justifies. One survey found that the vast majority of Canadians (75 percent) felt that most crimes are accompanied by violence, though the true figure is less than 10 percent (Doob and Roberts, 1983). Crime stories lead us to see Canada as a violent and dangerous place. Our fears are reinforced by the global coverage of violence. Television can instantly bring us events from anywhere and violent crimes such as the bus bombings by Hamas terrorists in Israel and the murder of 16 children in Dunblane, Scotland, are reported as immediately and as thoroughly as if they had happened in our own communities.

Paul Rosen, who was Paul Bernardo's lawyer, faces the media during Bernardo's trial.

The media also provide us with a distorted stereotype of offenders. Violent crimes are most often committed by relatives, friends, and acquaintances, not by the anonymous stranger so many of us fear. Consider even our image of the mass murderer. Everybody in Canada knows about Clifford Olson and Paul Bernardo. However, few recognize the names of Clifford Frame, Gerald Phillips, and Roger Parry, who may have been responsible for the deaths of 26 miners in the 1992 Westray mine disaster in Nova Scotia. In their coverage of the Westray affair, journalists focused on the tragedy and on the dangers of mining rather than on the safety concerns many miners had before the explosion, the pressure managers exerted on miners to work underground despite these concerns, and the role of government in funding the mine and its failure to investigate safety concerns.

Our fear of crime and our image of the criminal have an impact on government policy toward crime. Actual crime trends are irrelevant—if the public feels crime is out of control, it demands that government do something about it. While crime rates are declining, a combination of increasing media coverage of crime and pressure from a variety of interest groups has led the federal government to consider tightening several laws including those concerning immigration, young offenders, and firearms.

Sources: Based on Kappeler, Blumberg, and Potter (1996); and McCormick (1995).

also because engaging in crime provides them with a sense of control they do not get in other facets of their lives.

A unique victimization survey further reinforces this conclusion. In 1993, Statistics Canada conducted the national Violence Against Women Survey, for which more than 12,000 women were interviewed (Johnson, 1996). Several findings supported the view that violence is greatest in the lower class. First, men with high-school educations assaulted their wives at twice the rate of men with university degrees. Second, men who were out of work committed assaults at twice the rate of men who were employed. Third, men in the lowest income category (less than $15,000 a year) assaulted their wives at twice the rate of men with higher incomes. However, above this $15,000 level, there was no relationship between income and crime. This again suggests that the highest crime rates can be found at the very bottom of the economic ladder.

RACE AND ETHNICITY AND CRIME In societies with culturally heterogeneous populations, some ethnic and racial groups will have higher crime rates than others (Nettler, 1984). For example, in the United States, African Americans and Hispanics are overrepresented in arrest data. In 1993, African Americans made up about 12 percent of the U.S. population but accounted for about 28 percent of all arrests and 45 percent of arrests for violent crimes (FBI, 1994). Hispanics comprised about 7 percent of the U.S. population and accounted for about 13 percent of all arrests. Over two-thirds of their arrests were for crimes such as alcohol- and drug-related offences, larceny, and disorderly conduct. In 1993, less than 2 percent of all arrests were of Asian Americans or Pacific Islanders, while 1 percent were of Native Americans.

Statistics Canada does not routinely collect data about racial and ethnic correlates of crime, so we know relatively little about the situation in Canada. In addition to data about Native Canadians, which will be discussed later, there have been two recent studies dealing with minorities and crime. The first of these studies, which examined race and ethnicity in the federal prison system, found that offenders from nonaboriginal, visible ethnic minorities were *underrepresented* in the federal correctional system's population (Thomas, 1992). Specifically, the study found that in 1989, 5.2 percent of the federal corrections population were members of ethnic minority groups, while these groups made up over 6.3 percent of the general population. Two groups that were overrepresented, however, were those whose ethnic origins were West Indian and Central and South American. The second study, which examined provincial youth and adult correctional centres in British Columbia, arrived at similar findings. Only 8.2 percent of the prison population were members of nonaboriginal, visible ethnic minorities, yet these groups made up 13.5 percent of the province's population. Eleven percent of B.C. inmates were not born in Canada, a characteristic they shared with over 22 percent of the general population of the province.

While statistics on other minorities are limited, there are extensive data on aboriginal peoples. This is in part due to the documentation that resulted from special inquiries held to find out whether actions toward aboriginal people by the justice system in several provinces have been discriminatory. Many studies have demonstrated the *overinvolvement* of aboriginal people (Hartnagel, 1996); a typical finding is that while natives make up about 2 percent of the population in 1991, they make up about 24 percent of persons held in custody after being convicted of a crime (Brantingham, Mu, and Verma, 1995). In their study of Canadian homicides, Silverman and Kennedy found that aboriginal people are involved in homicides in proportions that are at least five times greater than their representation in the population (1993). Hyde and LaPrairie (1987) showed that aboriginal and nonaboriginal people had different patterns, as well as different rates, of crime. Aboriginal people had more social disorder offences (many of which were alcohol-related), fewer property offences, and more violent offences. Other researchers found a great deal of variation in aboriginal crime rates between different communities and parts of the country (Wood and Griffiths, 1996).

What is the reason for these racial and ethnic differences in crime rates? One answer is that there has often been discrimination against minority groups. The treatment of blacks in South Africa and in the southern United States throughout much of this century and the previous one are obvious examples. Discrimination against aboriginal people in Canada, Australia, and New Zealand has also been well-documented by commissions of inquiry. Members of minority groups, who tend to be poor, may go to prison for minor offences if they are unable to pay fines. A report by the Law Reform Commission of Canada (1974) found that in 1970 and 1971 over half of all natives admitted to Saskatchewan jails were incarcerated for nonpayment of fines. While this type of discrimination may be unintentional, it is nonetheless real. The justice system also tends to focus its efforts on the types of crimes that are committed by low-income people rather than on white-collar and corporate crimes, so members of poor minority groups may be overrepresented in crime statistics. Discrimination likely accounts for some, but not all, of the high rates of criminality of some minority groups.

To provide a further explanation, consider again the case of Canada's aboriginal people. Their situation is, of course, unique but the same kinds of factors may apply in other contexts. While a number of theories have been advanced to explain aboriginal overinvolvement (Hartnagel, 1996; Wood and Griffiths, 1995), consider the following explanation, which has been drawn from social control theory. Canada's aboriginal people have far less power and fewer resources than other Canadians. They must cope with systems of education and religion that are imposed on them from outside their cultural communities and are not compatible with native customs and traditions. In the past, forced attendance at residential schools and forced adoption outside the community have weakened family ties. Crippling rates of unemployment in many areas mean no job ties, and school curricula that are irrelevant to the lives of native students mean that children do not become attached to their schools. Under these conditions, strong social bonds are difficult to develop and high rates of crime can be predicted. As Manitoba's Aboriginal Justice Inquiry concluded: "From our review of the information available to us ... we believe that the relatively high rates of crime among Aboriginal people are a result of the despair, dependency, anger, frustration and sense of injustice prevalent in Aboriginal communities, stemming from the cultural and community breakdown that has occurred over the past century" (Hamilton and Sinclair, 1991:91).

REGION AND CRIME Crime is not evenly distributed around the globe. Some countries have much higher crime rates than others, and within countries there are often significant differences among regions. Unfortunately, because different countries have such varying methods of reporting and recording crime, international comparisons are difficult. The most reliable measure for comparison is homicide rates, which are reported in a reasonably similar fashion in most countries. Canada's homicide rate of about 2 per 100,000 people is relatively low by world standards. It is about a quarter of the U.S. rate, but about one-and-a-half times that of the United Kingdom. The highest rates of homicide are typically found in the less economically developed countries, although the high rate in the United States is a notable exception.

Major regional differences in crime rates exist within Canada. As shown in Figure 7.6 (see page 260), crime rates are highest in the West and the North, and lowest in Atlantic Canada. These interprovincial differences have existed for many years.

THE CRIMINAL JUSTICE SYSTEM

The criminal justice system includes the police, the courts, and prisons. However, the term *criminal justice system* is misleading because it implies that law enforcement agencies and courts constitute one large, integrated system, when it is actually a collection of "somewhat interrelated, semi-autonomous bureaucracies," each of which possesses considerable discretion to do as it wishes (Sheley, 1991:334). *Discretion* refers to the use of personal judgment by police officers, prosecutors, judges, and other criminal justice system officials regarding whether and how to proceed in a given situation.

THE POLICE

Most people think the main function of the police is to enforce the law. That is indeed one of their functions, but there are several others including order maintenance and the provision of social services. Order maintenance refers to keeping the peace. For example, stopping arguments, controlling the areas where skid-row alcoholics drink, and making a group of boisterous teenagers move away from the parking lot of a convenience store are all order maintenance activities. While the main concern in law enforcement is arresting a suspect, the main concern in order maintenance is to restore peace in the community. In difficult situations, arrest may be one means of doing this, but arresting someone is only a means to an end rather than an end in itself. The service role is also an important one and consists of many different activities including finding lost children, counselling crime victims, and notifying next of kin in fatal accidents.

Two questions you might ask are: Why do the police have such a broad range of responsibilities? and What, if anything, do these activities have in common? To answer the first question, the following list offers several reasons why the police have the broad responsibilities they do:

1. The police are one of the few public agencies open twenty-four hours a day.
2. In many cases, the police are serving clients that other agencies may not be interested in. The poor, the homeless, and the mentally ill may become police clients almost by default. If no other agency will gather drunks who pass out on downtown streets, the police must do it.
3. The police may not be well-informed about, or have access to, other agencies that could handle some of their cases.
4. Historically, the role of the police has been to keep the peace. Sir Robert Peel, the founder of the first municipal police force, in London, England, stressed a service-oriented philosophy, and this tradition has persisted.

The second question, What ties these diverse activities together?, is best answered by looking at two dimensions of the police role. First, the police have the *authority* (and often the duty) to intervene in situations where something must be done immediately. This authority is the same whether the incident is an armed robbery in progress, a naked man standing on a busy street screaming at people, or a complaint that someone's pet boa constrictor has just appeared in someone else's bedroom. Second, the authority is backed up by *non-negotiable force*. If someone refuses to go along with what a police officer suggests, the officer can use force (usually arrest) to back up his or her demands. Even professional caregivers may resort to calling the police when clients refuse to cooperate with them. Once the situation gets into the hands of the police, there may be nobody else to call so they have to resolve the situation themselves. Egon Bittner has nicely summed up the role of the patrol officer: "What policemen do appears to consist of rushing to the scene of any crisis whatever, judging its needs in accordance with canons of common sense reasoning, and imposing solutions upon it without regard to resistance or opposition" (1980:137).

Given the enormous range of activities with which the police are involved, you can see that the police have a high degree of discretion. Police managers, for one thing, have *administrative discretion* over how they organize their department and use their resources. If few resources are dedicated to commercial crime, few white-collar offenders

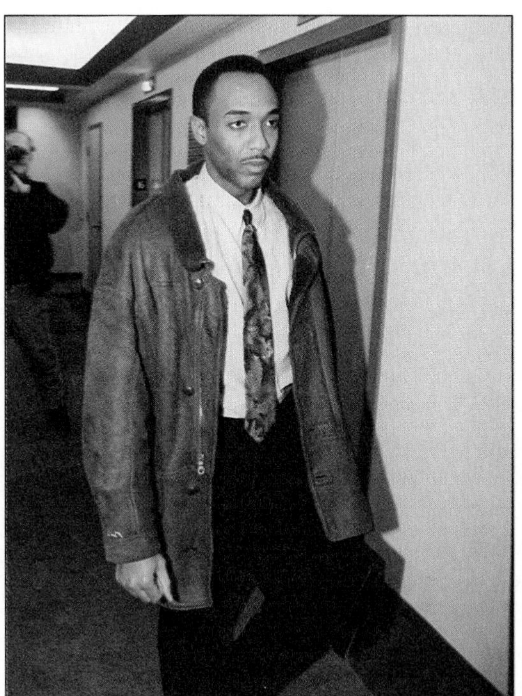

Does the justice system discriminate against members of racial minority groups? City-TV assignment editor Dwight Drummond attends a public inquiry into his wrongful arrest during a drug bust in October 1993.

will be apprehended. If a department only rewards its members for law-enforcement tasks, they will not do as good a job on order maintenance and service activities. Second, police officers exercise a great deal of *individual discretion* in that they often have to decide which rules to apply and how to apply them. Many of the situations in which the police use their discretion have very low visibility. Their supervisors are unlikely to observe them or to find out many details about how individual officers use their discretion. For example, if a police officer stops a driver for speeding and the driver has alcohol on his or her breath, several outcomes are possible. The police officer may warn the person and tell them to go straight home; write a speeding ticket; or administer a breathalyzer and lay charges of impaired driving. If the officer elects not to administer the breathalyzer, the supervisor will never know how that officer has used discretion.

The use of discretion by the police is unavoidable. This is not a problem if discretion is dispensed equitably and in a manner consistent with both community standards and the rule of law. However, if it is based on extra-legal factors such as race or class, or if it is used to favour certain individuals over others, it can be considered *discriminatory* and is an abuse of police powers. Issues of racial discrimination have generated the most discussion in Canada in recent years as inquiries have been held in many cities following police shootings of minority group members. But discrimination may not be deliberate. For example, Tim Quigley has described what he calls the overpolicing of aboriginals:

> Police use race as an indicator for patrols, for arrests, detentions ... For instance, police in cities tend to patrol bars and streets where Aboriginal people congregate, rather than the private clubs frequented by white business people ... This does not necessarily indicate that the police are invariably racist (although some are) since there is some empirical basis for the police view that proportionately more Aboriginal people are involved in criminality. But to operate patrols or to allocate police on ... [this] basis ... can become a self-fulfilling prophecy: patrols in areas frequented by the groups that they believe are involved in crimes will undoubtedly discover some criminality; when more police are assigned to detachments where there is a high Aboriginal population, their added presence will most assuredly detect more criminal activity." (1994:273–274)

THE COURTS

Criminal courts decide the guilt or innocence of those accused of committing a crime. In theory, justice is determined in an adversarial process in which the prosecutor (a lawyer who represents the state) argues that the accused is guilty and the defence lawyer asserts that the accused is innocent. Each side presents its position, the position is debated, and evidence is introduced to support each position. Proponents of the adversarial system feel this system best provides a just decision about guilt or innocence.

The essence of the adversarial system can be seen in the defence lawyer's role, which is to do all he or she can do to help the accused. This role was described by Lord Brougham, who was the defence lawyer in an 1821 case that could have had disastrous consequences for the British government had his defence been successful:

> An advocate, in the discharge of his duty, knows but one person in all the world, and that person is his client. To save that client by all means and expedients, and at all hazards and costs to their persons, and amongst them, to himself, is his first and only duty; and in performing this duty he must not regard the alarm, the torments, the destruction which he may bring upon others. Separating the duty of a patriot from that of an advocate, he must go on reckless of the consequences, though it should be his unhappy fate to involve his country in confusion." (cited in Greenspan, 1982:201)

We can add to Lord Brougham's comment that in an adversarial system the defence lawyer is obliged to fulfil this duty to the client without concern for the client's actual guilt or innocence.

Most of those working in the courts strongly defend the adversarial system and see it as one of the cornerstones of a free and democratic society. Many of the procedures that seem to restrict the ability of the court to get at the "truth," such as the rule that accused persons cannot be forced to testify against themselves, were adopted to prevent the arbitrary use of state power against the accused. However, some critics feel that our system does not deal adequately with crime because it places more emphasis on winning than on doing what is best for the accused, for the victim, and for society. Very few people who watched the O.J. Simpson trial could disagree with at least some aspects of this criticism.

Not all Western countries use the adversarial court system. Several European countries use systems in which the judge takes a much more active role in ensuring that justice is done. Jim Hackler (1994), one of the most articulate critics of Canada's courts, has described the court process in Switzerland, for example. In Switzerland, the police investigation is directed by a magistrate and the police gather information relevant to both sides of the case. While the accused lacks some of the protection of our system, the defence has access to all information about the case and can request through the magistrate that the police gather additional information. At the trial, the judge leads the questioning and there is much more concern with getting at the truth, and less on the legal constraints of the kind that exist in our system. The holistic approach to justice advocated by many aboriginal people is another alternative to the very technical and legalistic system that now prevails in our courts. This approach takes into account what is best for the victim, the accused, and the community rather than simply applying formal legal rules and procedures.

PUNISHMENT

Punishment **is any action designed to deprive a person of things of value (including liberty) because of some offence the person is thought to have committed** (Barlow, 1987:421). Punishment is seen as serving four functions:

1. *Retribution* imposes a penalty on the offender. Retribution is based on the premise that the punishment should fit the crime: the greater the degree of social harm, the more the offender should be punished. An individual who murders, for example, should be punished more severely than one who shoplifts.

2. *Social protection* results from restricting offenders so they cannot commit further crimes. If someone is in prison, they are no longer a threat to those of us on the outside. However, a high rate of offending *within* the prison exists, so imprisonment does not necessarily put an end to criminal behaviour.

3. *Rehabilitation* seeks to return offenders to the community as law-abiding citizens; however, rehabilitation programs are not a priority for governments or prison officials and the few rehabilitation programs that exist are typically underfunded. While many Canadian prisons offer some training to inmates, the job skills (such as agricultural work) that may be learned in prison typically do not transfer to the outside world, nor are offenders given much assistance in finding work that fits their skills once they are released.

4. *Deterrence* seeks to reduce criminal activity by instilling a fear of punishment. *Specific deterrence* is intended to deter the individual offender from reoffending. For example, a judge may sentence a wife abuser to six months in jail to teach him not to repeat his abuse. *General deterrence* is intended to deter all of us who see the example set by the justice system. For example, a judge may decide that convenience store robberies are getting out of hand and give one offender a severe sentence to set an example for others.

There is no question that the law deters. You do not deliberately park where you know your car will be towed away, and you do not speed if you see a police car behind you. However, the law does not deter as well as we might hope because the *certainty* of being arrested and convicted for most crimes is low. Most crimes do not result in arrests and, perhaps surprisingly, most arrests do not result in convictions. It is difficult to increase the certainty of punishment, so we try to tinker with the severity of punishment instead. Most "law and order" politicians talk about getting tough on crime by increasing penalties rather than by making punishment more certain. However, increasing the average penalty for robbery by a year will not likely reduce robbery rates if most robberies do not result in a conviction and a jail sentence.

We know less about the impact of law as a specific deterrent. That is, does serving a prison sentence make it less likely that a person will commit a crime in the future? While we do know that a large proportion of criminals are *recidivists* (repeat offenders), we do not know how many would repeat if they had not been in prison.

Most convicted criminals today are out on either *probation* (supervision of their everyday lives instead of serving a prison term) or *parole* (early release from prison). If offenders violate the conditions of their probation or parole, they may be required to serve their full sentence in prison.

The disparate treatment of the poor and some racial minorities is evident in the prison system. We have seen that incarceration rates for aboriginal people are disproportionately higher than those for whites. Disparate treatment of women also is evident. Women make up only a small minority of Canada's prison population—in 1994 there were 13,550 male inmates in federal penitentiaries compared with 323 females (Correctional Services of Canada, 1995). These small numbers mean that in some respects men are treated better than women in prison. Women's prisons, for example, offer far fewer educational and training programs than do men's prisons. The small number of women inmates makes it difficult to offer a wide range of programs. Until recently, there was only one federal prison for women in Canada, so all female offenders receiving a sentence of two years or more were sent to Kingston rather than staying in their own provinces, closer to family and friends. Since the majority of female inmates are single parents (which is not true of male inmates), long periods of incarceration far away from home and family place a special burden on female inmates (Comack, 1996a).

BOX 7.4 SOCIOLOGY AND LAW

Let's Make a Deal: Bargaining for Justice

The image most of us have of the court process is that those who are arrested and charged will go to trial. This trial will be held in a courtroom packed with spectators and will be contested by highly trained and articulate lawyers arguing the fine points of law before a judge and jury. However, this image is far from the truth. Trials are relatively rare and most cases are decided by guilty pleas. A high proportion, probably the majority, of these guilty pleas result from plea bargaining.

Plea bargaining is the process of negotiating a guilty plea. Informal, private discussions are held between the defence and the prosecution in an attempt to reach a mutually agreeable outcome in which both parties receive concessions. For the accused, plea bargaining may mean that the severity of the penalty will be reduced. A negotiated guilty plea also relieves the anxiety of waiting for sentencing, as the outcome of the case is agreed on ahead of time. The accused may also wish to save the expense and publicity of a trial, especially if the likely result is conviction. For the prosecution, plea bargaining saves time, which is crucial in our overloaded courts. If all cases went to trial, the backlog would be endless. It is likely that busier courts will give more lenient deals as the accused will have more bargaining power. The crown, or prosecuting, attorney may also bargain if the prosecution's case is weak. For example, if a key witness is very reluctant to testify or would not make a good impression on a judge or jury, the prosecution may bargain to ensure the defendant does not get off.

Plea bargaining has been widely criticized on the grounds that it subverts the aims of the criminal justice system by rewarding the guilty and penalizing those who elect to maintain their innocence and go to trial. The Law Reform Commission of Canada, among other groups, has recommended its abolition. However, despite this criticism the practice continues and some argue that the system could not work without it.

Plea bargaining has been particularly criticized in cases where guilty people are given light sentences in exchange for testimony against their partners in crime. The twelve-year sentence given to Karla Homolka in exchange for her testimony against Paul Bernardo is an example of this type of bargaining. While the Homolka case was controversial because of her direct involvement with Bernardo's killings, some cases are even more questionable because someone heavily involved in criminal activity receives a lenient disposition in exchange for information about others who are less involved.

Consider the case of Yves (Apache) Trudeau, for example. A former Hell's Angel, of the notorious Laval, Quebec, chapter, Trudeau is probably the most prolific killer in Canada's history. Trudeau admitted to forty-three gang-related killings and was able to negotiate a plea bargain in which the Crown accepted guilty pleas to forty-three counts of manslaughter and gave a commitment that he would be released with a new identity after serving seven years in jail. Trudeau agreed to cooperate with the police after learning he was the target of other Hell's Angels who had already killed six members of his chapter. In exchange for police protection, a comfortable cell, and a light sentence, Trudeau agreed to tell what he knew about the operation of the Hell's Angels and other Montreal organized crime groups. Two other members of the Laval chapter, Michel Blass and Gilles Lachance, also received plea bargains in exchange for their testimony against other gang members. While the police and prosecutors would argue that plea bargaining was the only way to convict other Hell's Angels and to reduce the influence of the gang, the practice of making deals with killers raises some difficult moral and ethical questions.

Sources: Based on Griffiths and Verdun-Jones, 1994; Lavigne, 1987; and Stamler, 1996.

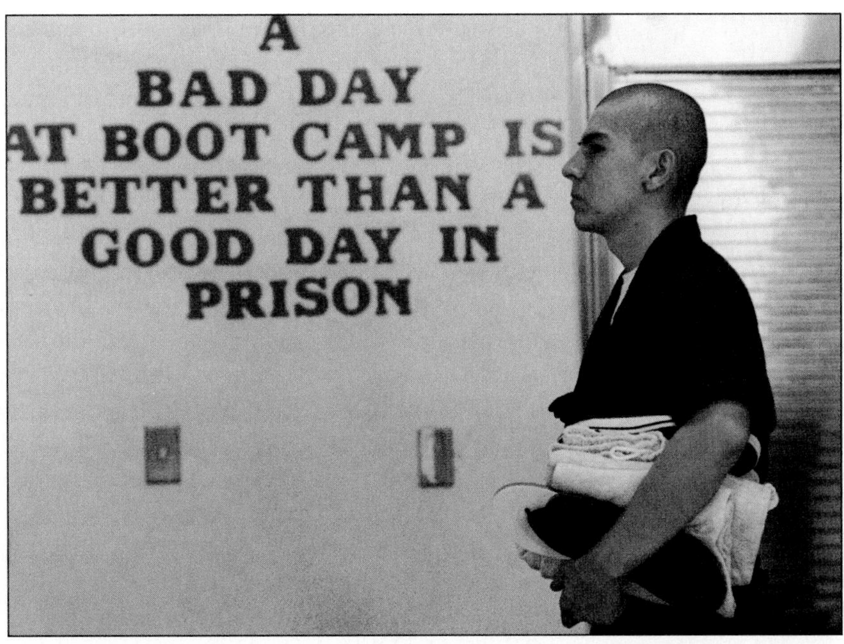

In recent years, military-style boot camps have been used as an alternative to prison and long jail terms for nonviolent offenders under age 30. Critics argue that structural solutions—not stop-gap measures—are needed to reduce crime in the twenty-first century.

COMMUNITY CORRECTIONS

Canada has a much higher rate of incarceration than most other industrialized countries. A recent study of nine countries ranked Canada third highest, following the United States and Switzerland, and ahead of (in descending order of incarceration rates) Northern Ireland, Australia, Scotland, England, Denmark, and Sweden (Mihorean and Lipinski, 1992). While our rate is double that of Sweden, it is only one-third as high as that of the United States.

Because our rates are higher than those of many other countries, some have suggested that Canada should move toward a greater use of community corrections. These dispositions include programs such as victim–offender reconciliation, mediation, and restitution programs as alternatives to incarceration. The movement toward community-based sanctions has been driven by three major concerns. First, these programs are much cheaper than incarceration. It costs about $50,000 to keep a person in a federal penitentiary for a year. In its 1996 budget, the Quebec government announced that it was going to close several provincial prisons and increase the use of community-based programs as part of its program of controlling the provincial deficit. The second concern is humanitarian. Prison life is very unpleasant and it can be unfair to send people to jail for relatively minor offences. Finally, an offender may benefit from being able to maintain ties with family and community, and these ties may make subsequent involvement in crime less likely.

DEVIANCE AND CRIME IN THE TWENTY-FIRST CENTURY

Among the questions pertaining to deviance and crime facing us as we approach the twenty-first century are: Is the solution to our "crime problem" more law and order? and, What impact will the global economy have on crime?

Although many Canadians agree that crime is one of our most important problems, they are divided over what to do about it. Some of the frustration about crime might be based on unfounded fears that the crime rate has been rising in the past few years, whereas it has actually declined. However, it is still far too high.

One thing is clear: the existing criminal justice system cannot solve the "crime problem." If most crimes do not result in arrest, most arrests do not result in convictions, and most convictions do not result in a jail term, the "lock 'em up and throw away the key" approach has little chance of succeeding. Nor does the high rate of recidivism among those who have been incarcerated speak well for the rehabilitative efforts of our existing correctional facilities. We can look to the United States to see a very expensive social experiment. Massive numbers of people are being locked up for very long periods of time and prison populations are increasing much more rapidly than in other countries. Between 1980 and 1990, the American prison population grew by 121 percent, while in Canada the increase was 14 percent (Mihorean and Lipinski, 1992). Since 1990, American prison populations have continued to increase. Many states have passed "three strikes and you're out" laws that impose a mandatory life sentence for anyone convicted of a third felony. Each inmate convicted under these laws will cost about $1.5 million to keep in prison for the rest of his or her life.

An alternative to this approach begins with the realization that the best way to deal with crime is to ensure that it doesn't happen. Instead of longer sentences, military-style boot camps or other stop-gap measures, *structural solutions*—such as more and better education and jobs, affordable housing, more equality and less discrimination, and socially productive activities—are needed to reduce street crime in the next century. The best approach for reducing delinquency and crime ultimately would be prevention: to work with young people *before* they become juvenile offenders, to help them establish family relationships, build self-esteem, choose a career, and get an education that will help them pursue that career.

Perhaps the major trend that will affect the type of crime we will see in the future is the globalization of the economy and of communications. Organized crime has spread from one country to another; the drug trade is a vast international business. With the aid of satellites and computers, financial crimes can be committed from anywhere in the world, and may be almost impossible to punish because of competing jurisdictions and different laws. The reduction of border controls in trading alliances such as the European Community makes it easier for criminals to move from one country to another.

Globalization may affect crime in many other ways. The transition to a global economy has devastated the job market in many countries. Traditional, secure manufacturing jobs have either been moved to countries in which lower wages are paid or they have disappeared altogether, and poorly paid and insecure jobs in the service sector are the jobs that remain. This loss of good jobs has, in turn, affected families and communities and may result in increased criminality. In many countries changes in taxation and social welfare policies, intended to increase global competitiveness, have increased social inequality. This inequality may also lead to crime.

CHAPTER REVIEW

All societies have norms to reinforce and help teach acceptable behaviour. Deviant behaviour is any act that violates established norms. Deviance varies from culture to culture and in degree of seriousness. Crime is seriously deviant behaviour that violates written laws and that is punishable by fines, incarceration, or other sanctions.

- Sociologists are interested in what types of behaviour are defined by societies as "deviant," who does that defining, how individuals become deviant, and how those individuals are dealt with by society.
- Strain theory focuses on the idea that the structure of a society can produce pressures that result in deviant behaviour. When denied legitimate access to cultural goals, such as a good job or nice home, people may engage in illegal behaviour to obtain them. Opportunity theory suggests that access to illegitimate opportunity structures varies, and this access helps determine the nature of deviance in which a person will engage.
- According to social control theories, everyone is capable of committing crimes, but social bonding keeps many from doing so. People bond to society through their attachments to family and to other social institutions such as the church and school. When a person's bonds to society are weakened or broken, the probability of deviant behaviour increases.
- Differential association theory states that individuals have a greater tendency to deviate from societal norms when they frequently associate with persons who tend toward deviance instead of conformity.
- According to labelling theory, deviant behaviour is that which is labelled deviant. The process of labelling is related to the relative power and status of those persons who do the labelling and those who are labelled. Those in power may use their power to label the behaviour of others as deviant.
- Conflict perspectives on deviance examine inequalities in society. According to the critical approach, the legal order protects those with political and economic power and exploits persons from lower classes.
- Feminist approaches to deviance examine the relationship between gender and deviance. Liberal feminism explains female deviance as a rational response to gender discrimination experienced in work, marriage, and interpersonal relationships. Radical feminism suggests that patriarchy (male domination of females) contributes to female deviance, especially prostitution. Socialist feminism states that exploitation of women by patriarchy and capitalism is related to their involvement in criminal acts such as prostitution and shoplifting.
- Law divides crimes into summary conviction and indictable offences. Indictable offences are serious crimes, and punishment may involve a lengthy prison term. Summary conviction offences are less serious crimes and receive less serious punishment.
- Conventional, or street, crime includes violent crimes, property crimes, and morals crimes. Occupational, or white-collar, crimes are illegal activities committed by people in the course of their employment or financial dealings. Corporate crimes are illegal acts committed by company employees on behalf of the corporation and with its support. Organized crime is a business operation that supplies illegal goods and services for profit. Political crime refers to illegal or unethical acts involving the misuse of power by government officials, or illegal or unethical acts perpetrated against the government by

outsiders seeking to make a political statement, undermine the government, or overthrow it.

- Official crime statistics are taken from the Canadian Uniform Crime Reporting survey that lists crimes reported to the police. We also collect information about crime through victimization surveys that interview households to determine the incidence of crimes, including those not reported to police. Studies show that many more crimes are committed than are officially reported.
- Age is a key factor in crime. Persons under 25 have the highest rates of crime. Persons arrested for assault and homicide generally are older, and white-collar criminals usually are older because it takes time to acquire the professional position and skill needed to commit occupational crime.
- Women have much lower rates of crime than men.
- Persons from lower socioeconomic backgrounds are more likely to be arrested for violent and property crimes; corporate crime is more likely to occur among upper socioeconomic classes.
- The criminal justice system includes the police, the courts, and prisons. These agencies often have considerable discretion in dealing with offenders. The police often use discretion in deciding whether to act on a situation. Prosecutors and judges use discretion in deciding which cases to pursue and how to handle them.

KEY TERMS

conventional or street crime **250**
corporate crime **250**
crime **238**
deviance **235**
differential association theory **242**
illegitimate opportunity structures **239**
juvenile delinquency **238**
labelling theory **243**
occupational or white-collar crime **250**
organized crime **252**
political crime **253**
primary deviance **244**
punishment **266**
secondary deviance **244**
social bond theory **241**
social control **235**
strain theory **238**

QUESTIONS FOR ANALYSIS AND UNDERSTANDING

1. What role do the media play in our perception of crime?
2. How does the expectation that some people, such as gang members, are deviant contribute to any crimes they commit?
3. How are organized crime and corporate crime conspiracies similar? (Consider the concept of "groupthink" from Chapter 6.) How are they different?
4. How does police use of discretion help police officers handle deviant and criminal behaviour?

QUESTIONS FOR CRITICAL THINKING

1. What factors account for the increase in organized crime throughout the world? How can society best deal with this type of crime?
2. Should so-called victimless crimes, such as prostitution and recreational drug use, be decriminalized? Do these crimes harm society?
3. Several commissions have recommended that aboriginal people have a separate justice system? Do you agree? How do you think such a system would operate?
4. As a sociologist armed with a sociological imagination, how do you propose to deal with the problem of crime in Canada? What programs would you suggest enhancing? What programs would you reduce?

SUGGESTED READINGS

These books provide additional insights on many of the crime and justice issues discussed in this chapter:

Beare, Margaret. 1996. *Criminal Conspiracies: Organized Crime in Canada.* Toronto: Nelson Canada.

Dubro, James. 1985. *Mob Rule: Inside the Canadian Mafia.*

Fleming, Thomas. 1985. *The New Criminologies in Canada: State, Crime and Control.* Toronto: Oxford University Press.

Gabor, Thomas. 1994. *Everybody Does It! Crime by the Public.* Toronto: University of Toronto Press.

Griffiths, Curt T., and Simon N. Verdun-Jones. 1994. *Canadian Criminal Justice* (2nd ed.). Toronto: Harcourt Brace and Company.

Hackler, James C. 1994. *Crime and Canadian Public Policy.* Scarborough: Prentice Hall.

Hamilton, Allen C., and C. Murray Sinclair. 1991. *Report of the Aboriginal Justice Inquiry of Manitoba*, Vol. 1. Winnipeg: Queen's Printer.

Jackson, Margaret A., and Curt T. Griffiths (eds.). *Canadian Criminology.* Toronto: Harcourt Brace.

Johnson, Holly. 1996. *Dangerous Domains: Violence Against Women in Canada.* Toronto: Nelson Canada.

Kennedy, Leslie W., and Vincent F. Sacco. *Crime Counts: A Criminal Event Analysis.* Toronto: Nelson Canada.

Lavigne, Yves. 1987. *Hell's Angels: Taking Care of Business.* Toronto: Ballantine Books.

Linden, Rick. 1996. *Criminology: A Canadian Perspective* (3rd ed.). Toronto: Harcourt Brace and Company.

McCormick, Chris. 1995. *Constructing Danger: The Mis/Representation of Crime in the News.* Halifax: Fernwood Publishing.

Silverman, Robert, and Leslie Kennedy. 1993. *Deadly Deeds: Murder in Canada.* Scarborough: Nelson Canada.

Silverman, Robert, James J. Teevan, and Vincent F. Sacco. 1996. *Crime in Canadian Society* (5th ed.). Toronto: Harcourt Brace and Company.

Snider, Laureen. 1993. *Bad Business: Corporate Crime in Canada.*

Wolf, Daniel. 1991 *The Rebels: A Brotherhood of Outlaw Bikers*

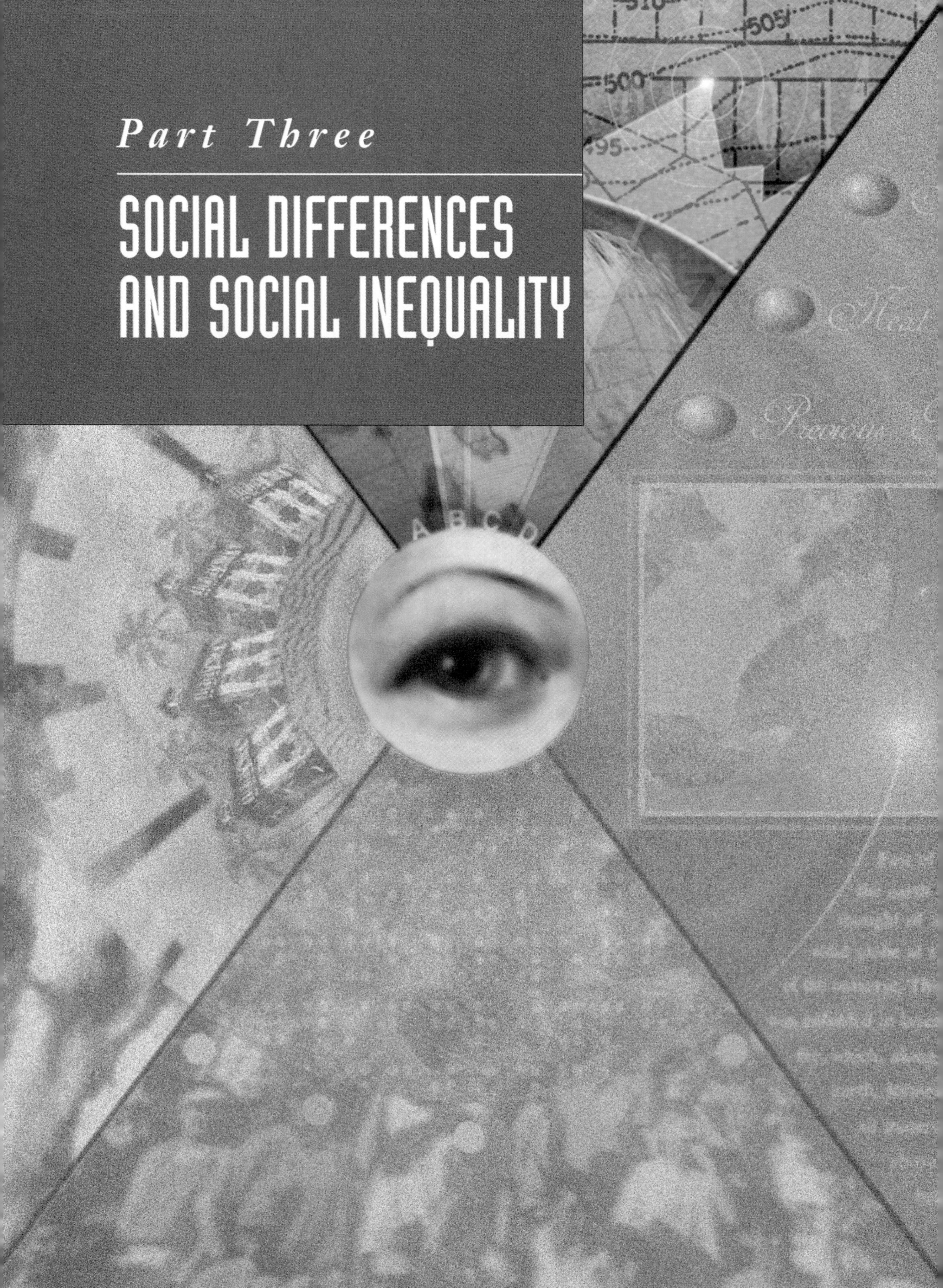
Part Three
SOCIAL DIFFERENCES
AND SOCIAL INEQUALITY

Chapter 8

SOCIAL STRATIFICATION AND CLASS

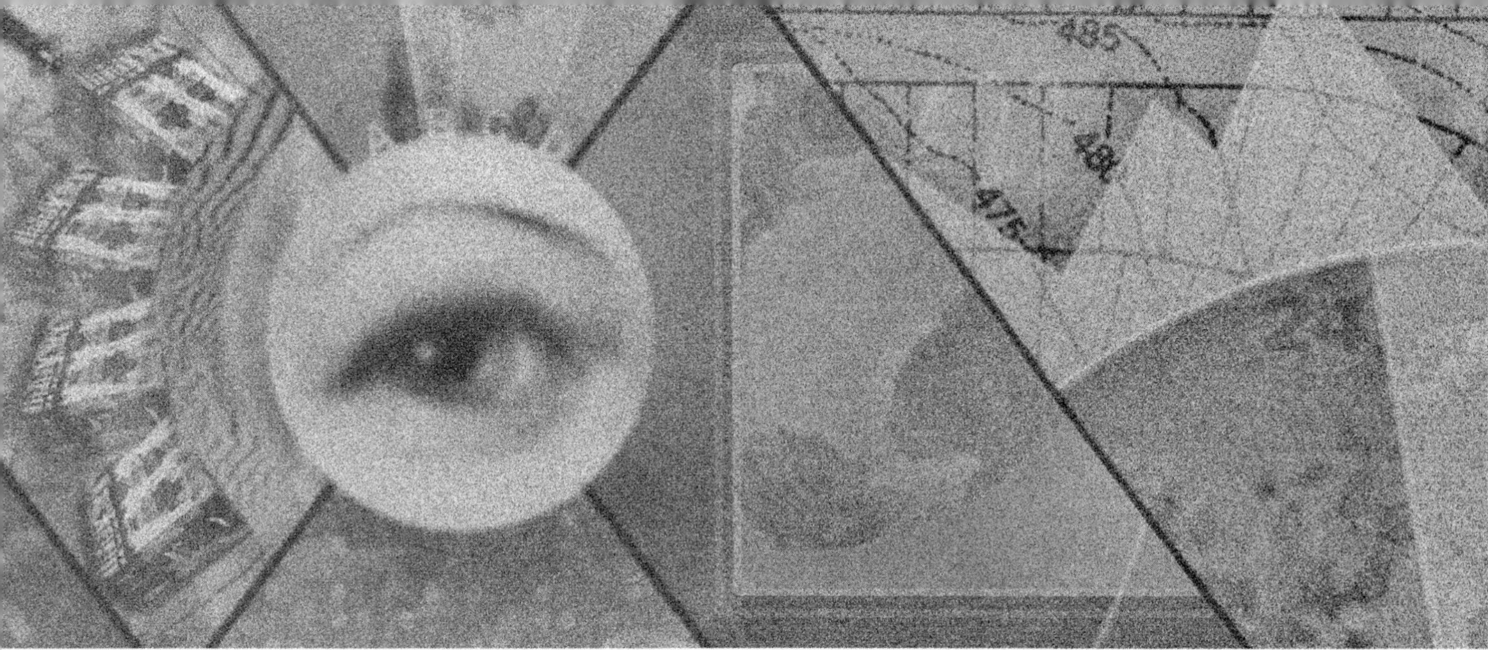

Sally is a 29-year-old single mother who lives with her 8-year-old son Sean in Toronto. She is one of many Canadians who has experienced downward mobility—moving from a comfortable middle-class lifestyle to a life of poverty. Sally talks about her life in a motel, her struggle to survive, and the impact of poverty on her young son:

He just hates it. He's not used to living like this. My son always had the best of everything; now from the best of everything he's got nothing … Everytime I look at Sean I think no, I can't let myself down or this kid's even gonna suffer more. This kid's seen more in his eight years. At his age I'd never seen half of this … This is no place for a child at all. There's prostitutes. I hear a lot of fights … I look at myself and Sean and I think at eight years old I'd had no worries … If Sean needs a pair of shoes or boots, well, I got him a pair of boots for $4 over there [the Goodwill Store] and a jacket. I had to say "Well Sean, you need your winter coat, your winter boots so like no, I can't buy this kind of meat and no, I can't buy jam 'cause we need that for your winter boots.

A constant theme in Sally's discussion of her impoverished life is the tremendous sense of guilt and failure she feels over what she sees as her inability to provide adequately for her child. These feelings, which are not uncommon, are most apparent in her comments on using a food bank:

It was my fault, but I had to bring Sean down there. I couldn't leave him in the motel alone. I brought him down there and Sean just looked at me like he was disgusted with me, for the first time I really saw disgust in that kid's face. I didn't say anything to him 'cause I knew exactly how he was feeling. (O'Reilly-Fleming, 1993:147–149)

When we examine social stratification and social inequality in Canada, it becomes apparent that Sally and Sean's situation is not unique. Poverty affects people's lives, their sense of self, and their most important relationships with others. The emotional, physical, and social toll that poverty takes is most apparent among children. The evidence suggests that the years spent in childhood poverty will have long-term consequences for the life chances of children like Sean. The most recent estimates indicate that in 1994, 1.3 million of Canada's children were growing up poor (National Council of Welfare, 1996). Children represent more than one-quarter of our poor and the child poverty rate in Canada is the second highest in the industrialized world, topped only by that of the United States (Duffy and Mandell, 1996). In 1989, the House of Commons unanimously resolved "to seek to achieve the goal of eliminating poverty among Canadian children by the year 2000" (Hughes, 1995:779). Do you think that this is a realistic goal? In this chapter we will attempt to answer this question by examining more closely the relationship between social stratification, social inequality, and child poverty.

Before reading on, test your knowledge of poverty in Canada by taking the quiz in Box 8.1.

QUESTIONS AND ISSUES

Do all societies have some type of stratification system?

How do prestige, power, and wealth determine social class?

What role does ownership of resources play in a conflict perspective on class structure?

How are social stratification and poverty linked?

What is the extent of social inequality in Canada?

WHAT IS SOCIAL STRATIFICATION?

***Social stratification* refers to the persistent patterns of social inequality within a society, perpetuated by the manner in which wealth, power, and prestige are distributed and passed on from one generation to the next** (Krahn, 1995b). Sociologists examine the social groups that make up the hierarchy in a society and seek to determine how inequalities are structured and persist over time (Jary and Jary, 1991).

Max Weber's term ***life chances* describes the extent to which persons within a particular layer of stratification have access to important scarce resources.** *Resources* are anything valued in a society, ranging from money and property to medical care and education; they are considered to be scarce because of their unequal distribution among social categories. If we think about the valued resources available in Canada, Sally's life chances are readily apparent. As one analyst suggested, "Poverty narrows and closes life chances. The victims of poverty experience a kind of arteriosclerosis of opportunity. Being poor not only means economic insecurity, it also wreaks havoc on one's mental and physical health" (Ropers, 1991:25). Our life chances are intertwined with our class, race, gender, and age.

Social stratification in one form or another exists in all societies. Individuals are ranked or assigned status within a society on the basis of a number of different characteristics. For example, all societies distinguish among people by age. Young children typically have less authority and responsibility than older persons. Older persons, especially those without wealth or power, may find themselves at the bottom of the social hierarchy. Similarly, all societies differentiate between females and males: women often are treated as subordinate to men. Age and gender are examples of *ascribed status*—that is, a status that is assigned to an individual, typically at birth. Ascribed status is not chosen or earned and cannot be changed. Can you think of other ascribed statuses you may have?

Individuals are also ranked on the basis of *achieved status*—a changeable status that is achieved on the basis of how well an individual performs in a particular role. Examples of achieved statuses are occupational statuses such as accountant, lawyer, professor, as well as other earned roles such as mother, husband, Olympic athlete, or armed robber. There is an element of

BOX 8.1 SOCIOLOGY AND EVERYDAY LIFE

How Much Do You Know About Poverty in Canada?

TRUE	FALSE	
T	F	1. Winning the war on poverty is an unrealistic goal.
T	F	2. Individuals over the age of 65 have the highest rate of poverty.
T	F	3. Men account of two out of three impoverished adults in Canada.
T	F	4. Most poor children live in female-headed, single-parent households.
T	F	5. The Canadian cities with the highest rates of child poverty are Winnipeg, Montreal, and Saskatoon.
T	F	6. Poverty is predominantly a rural phenomenon.
T	F	7. A large proportion of people receiving social assistance are able to work.
T	F	8. Children living in poverty are more likely to be abused and/or neglected.
T	F	9. Poverty is a new phenomenon in Canada.
T	F	10. Welfare benefits provide enough income for recipients to live comfortably.

Answers on page 280

choice in each of these roles. Can you identify your achieved statuses? The degree of significance of achieved and ascribed statuses will vary in different systems of stratification.

SYSTEMS OF STRATIFICATION

One of the most important characteristics of systems of stratification is their degree of flexibility. Sociologists distinguish among such systems based on the extent to which they are open or closed. In an *open system*, the boundaries between levels in the hierarchies are more flexible and may be influenced (positively or negatively) by people's achieved statuses. Open systems are assumed to have some degree of social mobility. ***Social mobility* is the movement of individuals or groups from one level in a stratification system to another** (Rothman, 1993). This movement can be either upward or downward. ***Intergenerational mobility* is the social movement experienced by family members from one generation to the next.** By contrast, ***intragenerational* mobility is the social movement of individuals within their own lifetime.** In a *closed system*, the boundaries between levels in the

BOX 8.1 SOCIOLOGY AND EVERYDAY LIFE

Answers to the Sociology Quiz on Poverty

TRUE	FALSE	
T	**F**	1. *False.* Statistics Canada estimated that the cost of bringing all poor people out of poverty in 1994 would have been $15.2 billion. According to the National Council of Welfare that is a huge but not outrageous amount of money relative to government spending in Canada.
T	**F**	2. *False.* As a group, children have a higher rate of poverty than the elderly. Government programs such as old age security are indexed to inflation, while many of the programs for the young have been scaled back or eliminated. However, many elderly individuals do live in poverty.
T	**F**	3. *False.* Women, not men, account for two out of three impoverished adults in Canada. The reasons include the lack of job opportunities for women, lower pay for women than men for comparable jobs, lack of affordable day care for children, and sexism in the workplace.
T	**F**	4. *False.* In 1994, 703,000 poor children were living in two-parent families, compared with 539,000 in female-headed single-parent households. However, the *rate* of poverty is highest for female-headed single-parent families.
T	F	5. *True.* In these three cities, one-quarter of preschool-aged children are poor.
T	F	6. *True.* Images of poverty as a rural phenomenon are out of date. In 1994, approximately 7 out of every 10 poor families lived in a city with a population of 100,000 or more.
T	**F**	7. *False.* The poor are stereotyped by many as being lazy and not wanting to work. In reality only a fraction of welfare recipients are able-bodied adults who are capable of working. Rather than looking at the structural characteristics of society, people cite the alleged personal attributes of the poor as the reason for their plight.
T	F	8. *True.* A literature review on poverty and child abuse concluded that poverty debilitates families and can be a "catalyst and intensifier of child maltreatment" (Volpe, 1989:12).
T	**F**	9. *False.* Poverty has been a constant feature throughout the history of Canada.
T	**F**	10. *False.* Welfare payments across Canada fall far below the low-income cut-offs.

Sources: Based on Harman, 1995a; Lochhead and Shillington, 1996; National Council of Welfare, 1996; and Volpe, 1989.

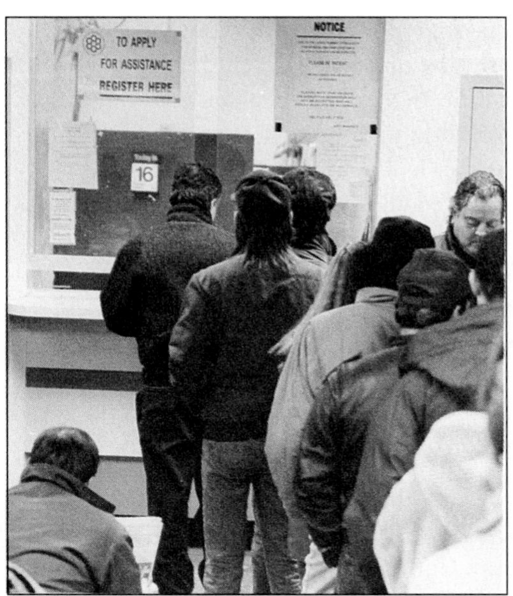

"Social stratification" may seem to be an abstract concept, but it is an everyday reality for these individuals standing in line at a welfare office.

hierarchies of social stratification are rigid, and people's positions are set by ascribed status.

Open and closed systems are ideal-type constructs; no actual stratification system is completely open or closed. The systems of stratification we will examine—caste and class—are characterized by different hierarchical structures and varying degrees of mobility. Let's examine these systems of stratification to determine how people acquire their positions in each and what potential for social movement they have.

THE CASTE SYSTEM

Caste is a closed system of social stratification. A ***caste system*** **is a system of social inequality in which people's status is permanently determined at birth based on their parents' ascribed characteristics.** Vestiges of caste systems exist in contemporary India and South Africa.

In India, caste is based in part on occupation; thus, families typically perform the same type of work from generation to generation. By contrast, the caste system of South Africa was based on racial classifications and the belief of white South Africans (Afrikaners) that they were morally superior to the black majority. Until the 1990s, the Afrikaners controlled the government, the police, and the military by enforcing ***apartheid*****—the separation of the races**. Blacks were denied full citizenship and restricted to segregated hospitals, schools, residential neighbourhoods, and other facilities. Whites held almost all of the desirable jobs; blacks worked as manual labourers and servants.

In a caste system, marriage is *endogamous*, meaning that people are allowed to marry only within their own group. In India, parents traditionally have selected marriage partners for their children. In South Africa, interracial marriage was illegal until 1985.

Cultural beliefs and values sustain caste systems. In India, the Hindu religion reinforced the caste system by teaching that people should accept their fate in life and work hard as a moral duty. Caste systems grow weaker as societies industrialize; the values reinforcing the system break down, and people start to focus on the types of skills needed for industrialization.

As we have seen, in closed systems of stratification, group membership is hereditary, and it is almost impossible to move up within the structure. Custom and law frequently perpetuate privilege and ensure that higher-level positions are reserved for the children of the advantaged (Rothman, 1993:171).

THE CLASS SYSTEM

The ***class system*** **is a type of stratification based on the ownership and control of resources and on the type of work people do** (Rothman, 1993). At least theoretically, a class system is more open than a caste system because the boundaries between classes are less distinct than the boundaries between castes. In a class system, status comes at least partly through achievement rather than entirely by ascription.

In class systems, people may become members of a class other than that of their parents through both intergenerational and intragenerational mobility, either upward or downward. *Horizontal mobility* occurs when people experience a gain or loss in position and/or income that does not produce a change in their place in the class structure. For example, a person may get a pay increase and a more prestigious title but still not move from one class to another. In contrast, movement up or down the class structure is *vertical mobility*. Martin, a commercial artist who owns his own firm, is an example of vertical, intergenerational mobility:

> My family came out of a lot of poverty and were eager to escape it ... My [mother's parents] worked in a sweatshop. My grandfather to the day he died never earned more than $14 a week. My grandmother worked in knitting mills while she had five children ... My father quit school when he was in eighth grade and supported his mother and his two sisters when he was twelve years old. My grandfather died when my father was four and he basically raised his sisters. He got a man's job when he was twelve and took care of the three of them. (quoted in Newman, 1993:65)

Martin's mobility reflects the ideal of upward mobility, according to which we can move beyond our origins and become more "successful" than our parents.

People also may experience downward mobility for any number of reasons, including a lack of jobs, lower wages and employment instability, marriage to someone with fewer resources and less power than oneself, and changing social conditions (Ehrenreich, 1989; Newman, 1988, 1993). Laura, who was born in the 1950s and who grew up believing in the dream of success, finds instead that she has experienced downward mobility:

> I'll never have what my parents had. I can't even dream of that. I'm living a lifestyle that's way lower than it was when I was growing up and it's depressing. You know it's a rude awakening when you're out in the world on your own ... Even if you are a hard worker and you never skipped a beat, you followed all the rules, did everything they told you you were supposed to do, it's still horrendous. They lied to me. You don't get where you were supposed to wind up. At the end of the road it isn't there. I worked all these years and then I didn't get to candy land. The prize wasn't there, damn it. (quoted in Newman, 1993:3)

In Canadian society we are socialized to believe that hard work is the key to personal success. Conversely, we are also taught that individuals who fail, who do not achieve success, do so as a result of their own personal inadequacies. Poverty is attributable to personal defect and it is up to the individual to find a way to break the "cycle of poverty." Do you agree? Or do you think structural factors in Canadian society affect the degree of success individuals achieve? Anthropologist Katherine Newman (1993:11) has identified several factors that affect the level of material success an individual achieves. She attributes the downward mobility experienced by Laura and others of her generation to "escalating housing prices, occupational insecurity, blocked mobility on the job, and the cost-of-living squeeze that has penalized the boomer generation, even when they have more education and better jobs than their parents." Ascribed statuses such as race/ethnicity, gender, and religion also affect people's social mobility. We will look at the ideals versus the realities of social mobility as we continue to examine the class structure in Canada.

CRITERIA FOR CLASS MEMBERSHIP

What is your social class? Early sociologists grappled with the definition of class and the criteria for determining people's location within the social stratification system. Many people in this country do not like to talk about social class. Some even deny that class distinctions exist, leading some analysts to refer to class as the "last dirty secret" (see Forcese, 1986; Parenti, 1994). Most people like to think of themselves as middle class; it puts them in a comfortable middle position—neither rich nor poor. Both Karl Marx and Max Weber viewed class as an important determinant of social inequality and social change, and their works have had a profound influence on contemporary class theory.

KARL MARX: RELATION TO MEANS OF PRODUCTION

For Karl Marx, class position is determined by people's work situation, or relationship to the means of production. As previously discussed, Marx suggested that capitalistic societies are comprised of two classes—the capitalists and the workers. The capitalist class, or *bourgeoisie*, consists of those who own the means of production—the land and capital necessary for factories and mines, for example. The working class, or *proletariat*, consists of those who must sell their labour to the owners in order to earn enough money to survive (see Figure 8.1).

According to Marx, class relationships involve inequality and exploitation. The workers are exploited as capitalists maximize their profits by paying workers less than the resale value of what they produce but do not own. Furthermore, later in the Industrial Revolution, mechanization reduced the cost of producing products, and so machines replaced many workers (Tucker, 1979). When people's labour no longer is needed, the newly created surplus of workers becomes a "reserve army." These unemployed workers, who are a readily available source of cheap labour, can be used by capitalists as a "weapon" against employees who demand pay raises or better working conditions. The presence of the reserve army keeps wages low and creates even greater profits for members of the capitalist class.

Marx predicted that the exploitation of workers by the capitalist class ultimately would lead to the destruction of capitalism. He argued that when the workers realized that capitalists were the source of their oppression, they would overthrow the capitalists and their agents of social control, including the government. The workers then would take over the state and create a more egalitarian society.

Why has no workers' revolution occurred? One critic has suggested that workers traditionally have sought to become a part of the system rather than to overthrow it (Beeghley, 1989). According to sociologist Ralf Dahrendorf (1959), capitalism may have persisted because it has changed significantly since Marx's time. Individual capitalists no longer own and control factories and other means of production; today, ownership and control largely have been separated. For example, contemporary multinational corporations are owned by a multitude of stockholders but run by paid officers and managers.

According to Marx, the capitalist class maintained its position at the top of the class structure by control of the society's *superstructure*, which is comprised of the government, schools, churches, and other social institutions that produce and disseminate ideas perpetuating the existing system of exploitation. For Marx, "The ideas of the ruling class are in every epoch the ruling ideas" (quoted in Tucker, 1979:172).

Marx had a number of important insights into capitalist societies. First, he recognized the economic basis of class systems (Gilbert and Kahl, 1993). Second, he noted the relationship between people's location in the class structure and their values, beliefs, and behaviour. Finally, he acknowledged that classes may have opposing (rather than complementary) interests. For example, capitalists' best interests are served by a decrease in labour costs and other expenses and a corresponding increase in profit; workers' best interests are served by well-paid jobs, safe working conditions, and job security.

Marx's views make us aware of macrolevel economic conditions that may influence large

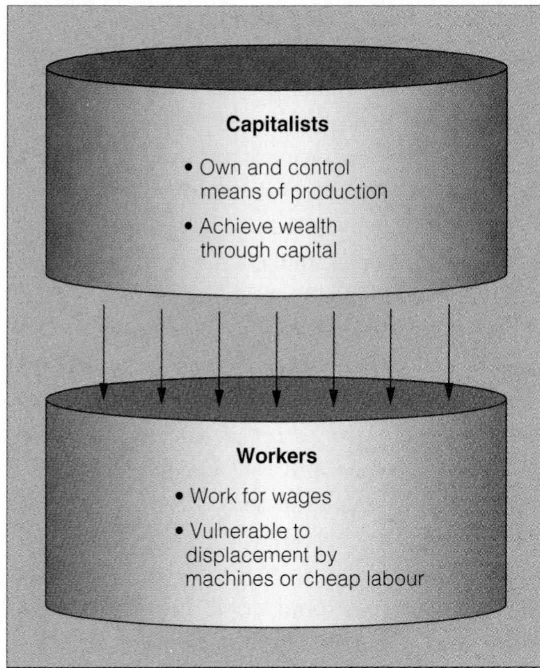

FIGURE 8.1

Marx's View of Stratification

Although the exploitation of workers by the capitalist class has not led to the destruction of capitalism, it has led to numerous labour strikes. Here, Ontario public sector workers fight with police in an attempt to move their protests to the provincial legislature.

numbers of oppressed people to recognize their common condition and to act politically to change it. According to political scientist Michael Parenti (1994:66), the absence (thus far) of a class revolution ... does not mean that workers are not exploited by capitalists or that people's class position does not mould the conditions of their lives. People who work for a living do fight back; struggles between the classes are continual even if they do not result in revolution as Marx predicted (Parenti, 1994).

MAX WEBER: WEALTH, PRESTIGE, AND POWER

Max Weber agreed with Marx's assertion that economic factors are important in understanding individual and group behaviour. However, Weber emphasized that no one factor (such as economic divisions between capitalists and workers) was sufficient for defining people's location within the class structure. As a result, he developed a multidimensional approach to social stratification that focused on the interplay among wealth, prestige, and power in determining a person's class position.

Wealth **is the value of all of a person's or family's economic assets, including income, personal property, and income-producing property.** Weber placed people who have a similar level of wealth and income in the same class. For example, he identified a privileged commercial class of *entrepreneurs*—wealthy bankers, ship owners, professionals, and merchants who possess similar financial resources. He also described a class of *rentiers*—wealthy individuals who live off their investments and do not have to work. According to Weber, entrepreneurs and rentiers have much in common. Both are able to purchase expensive consumer items, control other people's opportunities to acquire wealth and property, and monopolize costly status privileges (such as education) that provide contacts and skills for their children.

Weber divided those who work for wages into two classes: the middle class and the working class. The middle class consists of white-collar workers, public officials, managers, and professionals. The working class consists of skilled, semiskilled, and unskilled workers.

***Prestige* is the respect with which a person or status position is regarded by others.** Fame, respect, honour, and esteem are the most common forms of prestige. A person who has a high level of prestige is assumed to receive deferential and respectful treatment from others. Weber suggested that individuals who share a common level of social prestige belong to the same status group regardless of their level of wealth. They tend to socialize with one another, marry within their own group of social equals, spend their leisure time together, and safeguard their status by restricting outsiders' opportunities to join their ranks (Beeghley, 1989).

***Power* is the ability of people or groups to achieve their goals despite opposition from others.** The powerful shape society in accordance with their own interests and direct the actions of others (Tumin, 1953). Social power in modern societies is held by bureaucracies; individual power depends on a person's position within the bureaucracy. Weber suggested that the power of modern bureaucracies was so strong that even a workers' revolution (as predicted by Marx) would not lessen social inequality (Hurst, 1992).

Wealth, prestige, and power are separate continuums on which people can be ranked from high to low, as shown in Figure 8.2. Individuals may be high on one dimension while being low on another. For example, people may be very wealthy but have little political power (for example, a recluse who has inherited a large sum of money). They also may have prestige but not wealth (for instance, a university professor who receives teaching excellence awards but lives on a relatively low income). In Weber's multidimensional approach, people are ranked on all three dimensions.

Although power, wealth, and prestige are independent of one another, one may be used to acquire the others. Wealth, for example, can be used to gain power or prestige; the "charitable rich" in Canada acquire prestige by their financial contributions to and voluntary activities on behalf of nonprofit groups, such as symphony orchestras, museums, hospitals, and charities (Odendahl, 1990). Similarly, people may use their prestige to gain wealth. For example, celebrity athletes and entertainers often make their fortunes by endorsing products.

Weber's analysis of social stratification contributes to our understanding by emphasizing that people behave according to both their economic interests and their values. He added to Marx's insights by developing a multidimensional explanation of the class structure and identifying additional classes. Both Marx and Weber emphasized that capitalists and workers are the primary players in a class society, and both noted the importance of class to people's life chances. However, they saw different futures for capitalism and the social system. Marx saw these structures being overthrown; Weber saw the increasing bureaucratization of life even without capitalism.

THEORIES OF STRATIFICATION

Why are all societies stratified? The functionalist perspective sees stratification as an inevitable and even necessary feature of society. The conflict perspective, influenced by Karl Marx, sees stratification as avoidable, unnecessary, and the source of most human conflict. Gerhard Lenski (1966) has offered a third approach that combines elements of both functionalism and conflict theory.

THE FUNCTIONALIST APPROACH TO SOCIAL STRATIFICATION

Fifty years ago, Kingsley Davis and Wilbert Moore developed a theory of social stratification that has been debated ever since. Davis and

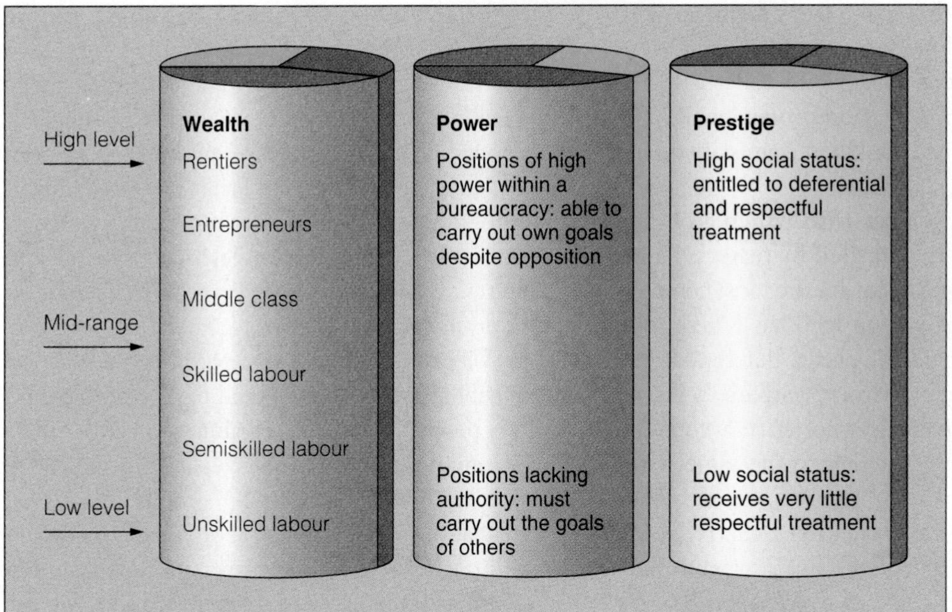

FIGURE 8.2

Weber's Multidimensional Approach to Social Stratification

According to Max Weber, wealth, power, and prestige are separate continuums. Individuals may rank high in one dimension and low in another, or they may rank high or low in more than one dimension. Also, individuals may use their high rank in one dimension to achieve a comparable rank in another.

Moore (1945) suggested that social stratification is not only universal but also functionally necessary for all societies. How can social inequality be beneficial to a society? The *Davis–Moore thesis*, which has become the definitive functionalist explanation for social inequality, can be summarized as follows:

1. All societies have important tasks that must be accomplished and certain positions that must be filled.
2. Some positions are more important for the survival of society than others.
3. The most important positions must be filled by the most qualified people.
4. The positions that are the most important for society and that require scarce talent, extensive training, or both, must be the most highly rewarded.
5. The most highly rewarded positions should be those that are functionally unique (no other position can perform the same function) and on which other positions rely for expertise, direction, or financing.

Davis and Moore use the physician as an example of a functionally unique position. Doctors are very important to society and require extensive training, but individuals would not be motivated to go through years of costly and stressful medical training without incentives to do so. The Davis–Moore thesis assumes that social stratification results in ***meritocracy*—a hierarchy in which all positions are rewarded based on people's ability and credentials.**

An important contribution of the Davis–Moore thesis is that it directs attention to the distribution of social prestige based on occupation. Yet occupational prestige rankings may not actually be based on the importance of a position to society. The highest ratings may be given to professionals—such as physicians and lawyers—because they have many years of training in their fields and some control of their own work, not because these positions contribute the most to society. According to some scholars, members of the medical profession have created a professional monopoly that has contributed significantly to their income and prestige throughout most of the twentieth century (see Freidson, 1970, 1986; Starr, 1982).

Critics have suggested that the Davis–Moore thesis ignores inequalities based on inherited wealth and intergenerational family status (Rossides, 1986). The thesis assumes that economic rewards and prestige are the only effective motivators for people and fails to take into account other intrinsic aspects of work, such as self-fulfilment (Tumin, 1953). It also does not adequately explain how such a reward system guarantees that the most qualified people will gain access to the most highly rewarded positions.

What about people who have not been able to maximize their talents and skills because they were born in impoverished circumstances and received a substandard education (see Kozol, 1991)? The functionalist approach generally ignores such questions because it does not consider structural factors (such as racial discrimination, lack of job opportunities, and inadequate funding of many schools) that may contribute to the persistence of inequality in society. Some conflict approaches attempt to fill this gap.

THE CONFLICT EXPLANATION OF SOCIAL STRATIFICATION

Conflict approaches, especially those based on Marxist theories, identify ownership or nonownership of the means of production as the distinguishing feature of classes. From this perspective, classes are social groups organized around property ownership and control of the workplace. Conflict theory is based on the assumption that social stratification is created and maintained by one group in order to protect and enhance its own economic interests. Societies are organized around classes in conflict over scarce resources. Stratification exists only because the rich and powerful are determined to hang on to more than their share of scarce resources. Inequality results from the more powerful exploiting the less powerful.

From a conflict perspective, people with economic and political power are able to shape and distribute the rewards, resources, privileges, and opportunities in society for their own benefit. Conflict theorists do not believe that inequality serves as a motivating force for people; they argue that powerful individuals and groups use ideology to maintain their favoured positions at the expenses of others. A stratified social system is accepted because of the dominant ideology of the society, the set of beliefs that explain and justify the existing social order (Marchak, 1975). Core values in Canada emphasize the importance of material possessions, hard work, and individual initiative to get ahead, and behaviour that supports the existing social structure. These same values support the prevailing resource distribution system and contribute to social inequality.

Conflict theorists note that laws and informal social norms also support inequality in Canada. For the first half of the twentieth century, for example, both legalized and institutionalized segregation and discrimination reinforced employment discrimination and produced higher levels of economic inequality. Although laws have been passed to make these overt acts of discrimination illegal, many forms of discrimination still exist in educational and employment opportunities.

THE EVOLUTIONARY APPROACH

Gerhard Lenski (1966) developed a theory of power and privilege to explain social stratification and inequality. Lenski's theory, referred to as the *evolutionary approach*, combined elements from both conflict theory and functionalism.

Lenski recognized power and conflict much more explicitly than did Davis and Moore. Although he used the term *class*, he focused more on the concept of ruling elites in society and how they managed to maintain control over society's wealth and power (Krahn, 1995b).

Lenski begins with the idea that people generally are more rewarded by fulfilling their own wants and ambitions rather than by addressing the needs of others. He acknowledged that it may be possible to socialize human beings so that they do not behave in this way, but he also pointed out that it remains an almost universal feature of social life. Most of the things that people want (wealth, power, prestige) are scarce. In other words, the demand exceeds the supply. Therefore, some conflict over how these limited resources are distributed is inevitable. The result is social inequality. Sometimes this inequality is functional for a society. However, Lenski points out, forms of stratification persist long after their functional benefit has ended. Most societies are much more stratified than they need to be.

Lenski traced the evolution of social stratification and argued that the type and form it takes is related to the society's means of economic production or technological base. Lenski shows how the nature of stratification varies from one type of society to another.

HUNTING AND GATHERING SOCIETIES People in these societies depend on materials taken directly from nature for their food, clothing, and shelter. Their technology consists of primitive tools such as digging sticks, bows and arrows, traps, and fishing equipment. Members of these societies are nomadic—as soon as local resources are used up, they move on in pursuit of more. In simple hunting and gathering societies, the few resources of the society were distributed primarily on the basis of need. There is no surplus wealth, and therefore no opportunity for some people to become wealthier than others. Consequently, hunting and gathering societies are the least stratified, especially in the dimensions of property and power. The main criteria for inequality in these societies are age and sex. But the overall stratification system is simple and fairly egalitarian.

SIMPLE HORTICULTURAL SOCIETIES As societies became more technologically complex, more resources were produced than were needed to fulfil the basic needs of the society. Further, it is possible to accumulate property in horticultural societies because people are not having to move when resources are depleted. In these societies "specialists," such as producers of harpoons, canoes, drums, or art appear for the first time. With increasing "division of labour" comes increased inequality as some roles are assigned more prestige or power than others. In horticultural and pastoral societies a surplus product is available and chieftainships emerge as powerful families obtain control over surplus—an advantage also known as resources *privilege*. As a result, differences in property, power, and prestige among members are marked.

AGRICULTURAL SOCIETIES These societies are much larger, much more specialized, much richer, and much more stratified than are simple horticultural societies. The primary reason for these differences is related to technological advancement—specifically the production of metal tools. The metal plough dramatically increased yields from farming. Because a small number of farmers can produce enough food to support a large number of people, a relatively small portion of the population needs to be involved in food production. The most important consequence of increased productivity is the creation of permanent armies and elaborate governmental structures. Classes of professional soldiers and government officials appear. A number of governmental levels are created—from the king down to the local village headman. In simple horticultural societies a great deal of wealth is based on the accumulation of wives. With advances in production, it becomes profitable to own people in order the gain the surplus wealth from their labour. It is in these societies that slavery first appears. In agricultural societies the status of heredity rises dramatically. Cattle, land, slaves, and even primitive forms of money can be passed from one generation to another. Therefore, each generation can accumulate more wealth through inheritance. These societies are the first to exhibit hereditary classes and very marked inequalities of power, property, and prestige. The more complex agricultural societies developed highly structured governing and tax collecting systems through which the ruling elites accumulated wealth at the expense of the less privileged. The result is that the society becomes divided into strata.

INDUSTRIAL SOCIETIES In their earliest form, industrial societies had similar stratification systems to that of agricultural societies. Kings continued to rule and impoverished factory workers replaced impoverished peasantry as the source of surplus wealth. However, as the result of industrialization and increasingly complex technology, the trend toward increasing inequality was reversed (Lenski, 1966). Industrial societies became less stratified than agricultural societies and this trend has continued.

The specific cause of this reversal was that the owners of the means of production, the ruling elite, could no longer control the production process directly and were forced to rely on educated managers and specialized technical workers to maintain production. This change curtailed the power of the ruling classes. Individuals and groups were introduced to ideas of democracy, which led them to demand a larger share of the profits they were helping to produce (Krahn, 1995b). The ruling elite gave in to these demands because they could not produce without the educated, skilled workers. Second, industrialized societies are much more productive—therefore there is more wealth to divide or, as Lenski points out, the elite could "make economic concessions in relative terms without necessarily suffering any loss" (Lenski, 1966:314). In industrial societies the importance of ascribed status is diminished while achieved status is emphasized. Universal education systems have been created to facilitate upward mobility based on individual merit rather than on ascribed characteristics.

THE CANADIAN CLASS STRUCTURE

How many social classes exist in Canada? No broad consensus exists about how to characterize the class structure in this country. Sociologists differ in the methods used to determine people's relative positions in the class structure.

Three methods may be used to determine people's placement in the class structure: the subjective, the reputational, and the objective. In the *subjective method*, people are asked to locate themselves in the class structure. However, when Canadians are questioned about their social class, most will say, in effect, that "There is no such thing as social class in Canada. We're all equal" (Spencer, 1993:166). In the *reputational method*, people are asked to place other individuals in their community (based on their reputation) into social classes. Using the *objective method*, researchers assign individuals to social classes based on predetermined criteria (occupation, source and amount of income, amount of education, and type and area of residence, for example). Analysts often use ***socioeconomic status*** **(SES), a combined measure that attempts to classify individuals, families, or households in terms of indicators such as income, occupation, and education,** to determine class location. As you might expect, different occupations have significantly different levels of status or prestige (see Table 8.1). For the past forty years, these ratings have been remarkably consistent across societies and among subgroups in Canada (Spencer, 1993). These prestige rankings have become the foundation for status attainment research, which uses sophisticated statistical measurements to assess the influence of family background and education on people's occupational mobility and success (see Curtis et al., 1993). *Status attainment research* focuses on the process by which people ultimately reach their position in the class structure. Based largely on studies of men, this research uses the father's occupation and the son's education and first job as primary determinants of the eventual class position of the son. Obviously, family back-

TABLE 8.1

Prestige Rankings of Selected Occupations in Canada

Occupation	Score
Provincial premier	90
Physician	87
University professor	85
Judge	83
Lawyer	82
Architect	78
Catholic priest	73
Civil engineer	73
Physiotherapist	72
Bank manager	71
Owner of a manufacturing plant	69
Registered nurse	65
Economist	62
Public school teacher	60
Social worker	55
Computer programmer	54
Policeman	52
Electrician	50
Bookkeeper	49
Ballet dancer	49
Someone who lives on inherited wealth	46
Farm owner and operator	44
Machinist	44
Plumber	43
Bank teller	42
Typist	42
Barber	39
Carpenter	39
Automobile repairman	38
Bus driver	36
Trailer truck driver	33
Used car salesman	31
Restaurant cook	30
Private in the army	28
Assembly-line worker	28
Clerk in a store	27
Logger	25
Cod fisherman	23
Waitress	20
Bartender	20
Janitor	17
Someone who lives on social assistance	7

Source: Adapted from Pineo and Porter, 1979.

ground is the central factor in this process because the son's education and first job are linked to the family's economic status. In addition, the family's location in the class system is related to the availability of social ties that may open occupational doors for the son.

Although they have been widely employed in sociological research, status attainment models have several serious limitations. One is the focus of this research on the occupational prestige of traditionally male jobs and the exclusion of women's work, which often has been unpaid. A woman's social class position typically has been linked to that of her father or husband, irrespective of her own work.

Status attainment research also has been criticized for its overly optimistic image of society, whereby high rates of social mobility exist and opportunities are available for all people (Knottnerus, 1993:255). The social structure is pictured as a fluid system in which people are free to seek their goals, especially their occupational goals, in a growing middle class. People are social actors motivated by the desire to attain occupational status and material consumer items that are valued status symbols (Knottnerus, 1993). Status attainment research takes a benign view of contemporary industrial society and assumes that success is within the grasp of virtually all people if they work hard enough. However, examination of the different social classes in Canada suggests otherwise. Figure 8.3 outlines the four broad social classes in Canada: the upper class, the middle class, the working class, and the lower class, which includes the working poor and the underclass.

THE UPPER (OR CAPITALIST) CLASS

The upper class is the wealthiest and most powerful class in Canada. Approximately 3 to 5 percent of the population is included in this class, whose members own substantial income-producing assets and operate at both the national and international level. People in this class have

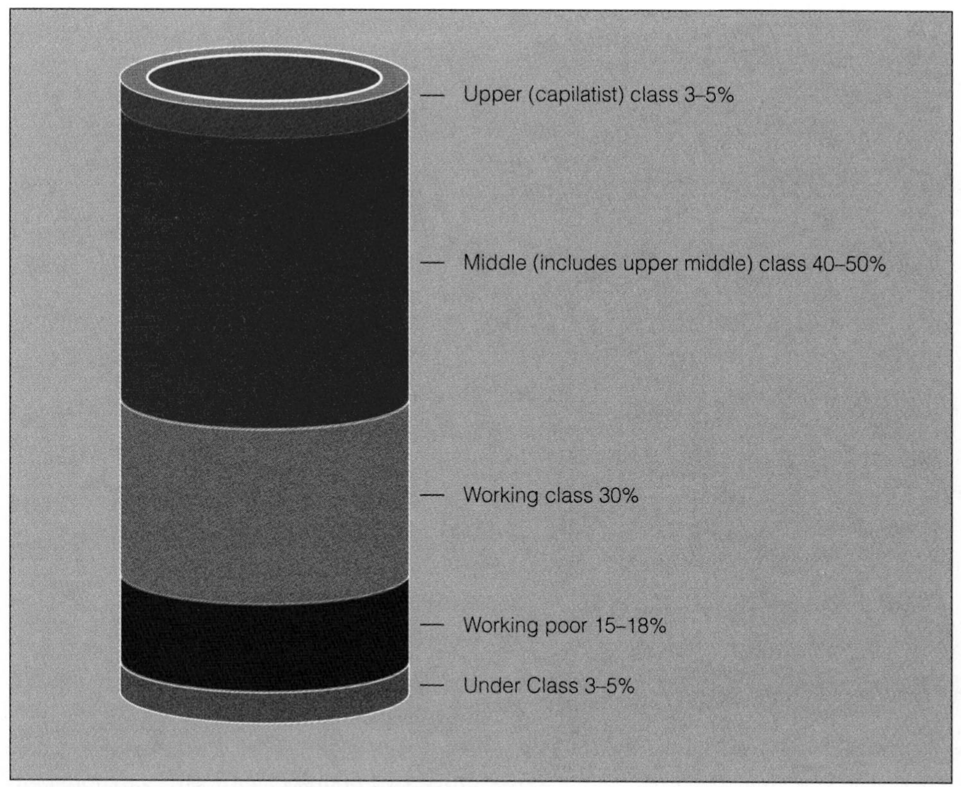

FIGURE 8.3

Stratification Based on Education, Occupation, and Income

an influence on the economy and society far beyond their numbers (Gilbert and Kahl, 1993).

Some models further divide the upper class into upper-upper ("old money") and lower-upper ("new money") categories (Warner and Lunt, 1941; Coleman and Rainwater, 1978). Only 1 percent of the population are members of the upper-upper class. They come from prominent families, which possess great wealth that they have held for several generations. Canada has some of the wealthiest families in the world. For example, in 1989, the *Financial Post* estimated the worth of the Irving and Ken Thomson families at 8 billion and 6.4 billion, respectively (Dyck, 1996). Family names—such as Bronfman, Eaton, and Weston—are well known and often held in high esteem. Persons in the upper-upper class tend to have strong feelings of ingroup solidarity. They belong to the same exclusive clubs and support high culture (such as the opera, symphony orchestras, ballet, and art museums). Their children are educated at private schools such as Upper Canada College in Toronto and at prestigious universities; many acquire strong feelings of privilege from birth, as author Lewis H. Lapham (1988:14), who is upper-class, states:

> Together with my classmates and peers, I was given to understand that it was sufficient accomplishment merely to have been born. Not that anybody ever said precisely that in so many words, but the assumption was plain enough, and I could confirm it by observing the mechanics of the local society. A man might become a drunkard, a concert pianist or an owner of companies, but none of these

Wealthy businessman and investor Ross Perot of Dallas, Texas, is an example of how members of the upper class can exert a disproportionate influence on politics and the economy. In 1992, he spent millions of dollars of his own money to finance an independent bid for the U.S. presidency. Many commentators believe that his mere presence continues to affect policy decisions in both of the major political parties.

occupations would have an important bearing on his social rank.

Children of the upper class are socialized to view themselves as different from others; they also learn that they are expected to marry within their own class (Warner and Lunt, 1941; Baltzell, 1958; Mills, 1959; Domhoff, 1970, 1983).

Members of the lower-upper class may be extremely wealthy but have not attained as much prestige as members of the upper-upper class. The "new rich" have earned most of their money in their own lifetimes as entrepreneurs, presidents of major corporations, sports or entertainment celebrities, or top-level professionals. Some members of the lower-upper class aspire to gain the respect of the upper-upper class members. In the early 1990s, for example, American-billionaire real estate developer Donald Trump purchased a 118-room Florida estate and entertained members of the upper-upper class in hopes of being invited to join the elite Palm Beach Bath and Tennis Club. After Trump was shunned by club members, he disdainfully remarked to a journalist that the old-line rich are "frivolous and boring" (Kunen, 1990:31).

THE MIDDLE CLASS

This is the largest group: an estimated 40 to 50 percent of Canada's population is in this class. Once again, this group is sometimes divided into the upper-middle class and the lower-middle class. Persons in the upper-middle class often are highly educated professionals who have built careers as physicians, attorneys, stockbrokers, or corporate managers. Others derive their income from family-owned businesses. A combination of three factors qualifies people for the upper-middle class: university degrees, authority and independence on the job, and high income. Of all the class categories, the upper-middle class is the one that is most shaped by formal education.

In past decades, a high-school diploma was necessary to qualify for most middle-class jobs. Today, the community college degree has supplemented the high school diploma as an entry-level job requirement in a number of middle-class occupations such as medical technicians, nurses, legal and medical secretaries, lower-level managers, semiprofessionals, and nonretail salesworkers. Traditionally, most middle-class occupations have been relatively secure and provided more opportunities for advancement (especially with increasing levels of education and experience) than working-class positions. Recently, however, four factors have diminished the chances for material success for this class: (1) escalating housing prices, (2) occupational insecurity, (3) blocked mobility on the job, and (4) the cost-of-living squeeze that has penalized younger workers, even when they have more education and better jobs than their parents (Newman, 1993). Consider, for example,

Socioeconomic status in Canada is often determined on the basis of income, education, and occupation. Can you assess the socio-economic status of the individuals in these photographs?

Brenda and Amancio Irizarry, who are struggling to get by on a combined pretax income of $38,000 a year. Although they make more money than their parents did, the Irizarrys cannot afford to buy a house, have no savings, and have never taken a vacation together. They are working hard to send their daughter, Michelle, to a community college. As Mrs. Irizarry explains:

> We didn't have a college fund for Michelle. You see commercials on television saying to start [saving] when the baby is born. But because of the unforeseen things that happen in life, it's impossible to save money. (quoted in Jones, 1995:9)

Michelle appreciates her parents' efforts but eventually wants much more for herself:

> I don't want to live like this the rest of my life ... I mean, they have morals and are trying to make it. But unless they hit the Lotto, this is how it's going to be the rest of their lives. And that's sad, to think that's it. This is as good as it's going to get. (quoted in Jones, 1995:9)

Michelle has not given up; she is determined to become a social worker and have a nice place to live (Jones, 1995). As this example suggests, class distinctions between the middle and working classes are less clear than those between other classes due to overlapping characteristics (Gilbert and Kahl, 1993).

THE WORKING CLASS

The core of this class is composed of people who hold relatively unskilled blue-collar and white-collar jobs. Members of the working class include clerks and salespeople who, in Gilbert and Kahl's words (1993), "have routine, mechanized tasks which require little skill beyond literacy and a short period of on-the-job training" and some workers in the service sector. Also included in the working class are ***pink-collar occupations*****—relatively low-paying, nonmanual, semiskilled positions primarily held by women,** such as day-care workers, checkout clerks, cashiers, and waitpersons. An estimated 30 percent of the Canadian population is in the working class.

Working-class families earn less than middle-class families and have less financial security, especially because of layoffs and plant closings. Few members have training beyond a high-school diploma, and many have less, thus making other job opportunities scarce (Gilbert and Kahl, 1993).

THE LOWER CLASS

The lower class account for about 20 percent of the Canadian population. Included in this group are the working poor and the underclass.

Members of the working poor live from just above to just below the poverty line; they hold unskilled jobs, seasonal migrant employment in agriculture, lower-paid factory jobs, and service jobs (such as counter help at restaurants). Employed single mothers often belong to this class; consequently, children are overrepresented in this category. Visible minorities, native peoples, and recent immigrants are also overrepresented among the working poor (Ross, Shillington, and Lochhead, 1994). The working poor tend to live from paycheque to paycheque and have so little left that they are unable to save money for emergencies; periodic unemployment is a constant problem.

Gilbert and Kahl (1993:316) describe people in the underclass as poor, seldom employed, and caught in long-term deprivation "from low education, low employability, low income, and eventually, low self-esteem." Some are unable to work because of age or disability; others experience discrimination based on race/ethnicity. Single mothers are overrepresented in this class because of the lack of jobs, affordable child care, and many other impediments to the mother's future and that of her children. People without a "living wage" often must rely on the welfare system for survival. About 3 to 5 percent of the population is in this category; the chances of the children moving out of poverty are estimated at fifty-fifty (Gilbert and Kahl, 1993).

While some young people are hopeful that they can acquire well-paid, meaningful jobs that

BOX 8.2 SOCIOLOGY AND MEDIA

Campaign 2000 and Child Poverty

What effect do you think advertising can have on public awareness of social issues such as child poverty? Can advertising accomplish anything other than increasing our desires for products we often do not need?

Campaign 2000 is a unique Canadian campaign to achieve implementation of the 1989 House of Commons resolution to end child poverty by the year 2000. This campaign has been important in giving child poverty a high profile. Public support for action has been reaching unprecedented levels. A recent national opinion poll found that 89 percent of Canadians believe that alleviating child poverty should be a priority for the federal government.

The media have played an important role in bringing this issue to the forefront of the political arena. High-profile Canadians such as children's entertainers Sharon, Lois and Bram were recruited as Campaign 2000 ambassadors. The Body Shop of Canada co-sponsored two national awareness and political action campaigns, as well as organizing and paying for Campaign 2000's postcard protest that used the slogans "Light a Fire Under the Powers that Be" and "Kids Can't Vote—You Can." The campaign also consisted of stores displaying giant posters, disseminating fact sheets and media releases, and selling T-shirts. During the 1993 federal election campaign, Body Shop customers were encouraged to tell the candidates in their riding that "specific public policies must be formulated to end child and family poverty in Canada." Those who wanted to could also write their name and address on a preprinted postcard. Sixty thousand postcards delivered to parliament demanded that government "raise and protect the basic living standards of families in all regions" and "improve the life chances of all children in Canada." Since the election, Campaign 2000 has continued to lobby the federal government to make the elimination of child poverty a priority. According to one of the Body Shop's directors, "We're trying to act as a catalyst or even an irritant to prompt some real political action." Have they been successful? Can an advertising campaign have an affect on government decision making? To date, the success of this campaign has been marginal. Although Prime Minister Chrétien did identify child poverty and Campaign 2000 in a discussion paper on improving social security, to date, Ottawa has yet to take the first step in putting an end to child poverty in Canada.

Source: Koch, 1993.

will help them escape poverty, others view their futures with pessimism and uncertainty. They may have levelled aspirations, as author Jay MacLeod (1988) learned when he asked members of two male teenage peer groups from underclass families what their lives would be like in twenty years. Three of them replied (in separate interviews):

> STONEY: Hard to say, I could be dead tomorrow. Around here, you gotta take life day by day.
>
> BOO-BOO: I dunno. I don't want to think about it. I'll think about it when it comes.
>
> SHORTY: Twenty years? I'm gonna be in jail. (MacLeod, 1988:61)

Those who discussed work saw it solely as a means to an end—money (MacLeod, 1988).

INEQUALITY IN CANADA

Throughout human history, people have argued about the distribution of scarce resources in society. Disagreements often centre on whether the share we get is a fair reward for our efforts and hard work (Braun, 1991). As we have seen, functionalists argue that people who receive the greatest rewards generally deserve them because of their extensive years of education or possession of specialized knowledge, skills, or talent. In contrast, conflict theorists view the current means of distribution as unfair. Especially unfair to them are mechanisms such as inheritance, whereby wealthy families are able to pass down large amounts of money to children who may have done nothing more than be born into the "right" family. Recently, however, both schools of thought have agreed on one point—the rich get richer. To understand how this happens, we first must take a closer look at income and wealth in Canada.

UNEQUAL DISTRIBUTION OF INCOME AND WEALTH

Money is essential for acquiring goods and services. People without money cannot purchase food, shelter, clothing, medical care, legal services, education, and the other things they need or desire. Money—in the form of both income and wealth—is very unevenly distributed in Canada. Among prosperous nations, Canada ranks fourth highest in terms of inequality of income distribution. The United States has the greatest inequality of income distribution (Ross, Shillington, and Lochhead, 1994).

INCOME *Income* is the economic gain derived from wages, salaries, income transfers (governmental aid such as social assistance, Canada Pension Plan payments), and ownership of property (Beeghley, 1989). Economist Paul Samuelson has noted that, "If we made an income pyramid out of a child's blocks, with each layer portraying $500 of income, the peak would be far higher than Mount Everest, but most people would be within a few feet of the ground" (quoted in Samuelson and Nordhaus, 1989:644).

Dennis Gilbert and Joseph Kahl (1993:93) compare the distribution of income to a "national pie that has been sliced into portions, ranging in size from stingy to generous, for distribution among segments of the population." One way of measuring income inequality is to divide the population into five equal groups or quintiles, and to indicate the share of total income received by each group. As shown in Figure 8.4, in 1992 the wealthiest 20 percent of households received over 40 percent of the total income "pie," while the poorest 20 percent of households received less than 5 percent of all income. The top 10 percent received 22 percent of all income—an amount greater than was received by the bottom 40 percent of all households (Statistics Canada, 1991b). Figure 8.4 also reveals the remarkable stability of income distribution over time.

There is considerable regional variation in income in Canada. As shown in Map 8.1, the average family income is highest in Ontario, British Columbia, and Alberta and lowest in the Atlantic provinces.

Income distribution also varies by race/ethnicity. Table 8.2, which shows the average incomes of the largest nineteen ethnic groups in Canada, makes it apparent that race and ethnicity are important determinants of social position. Jews rank first with average incomes of $37,146, more than double the income of both aboriginal peoples and Latin Americans, who rank lowest (Driedger, 1996). The categories that have the lowest average incomes are almost exclusively visible minorities. It is also clear from the data that native peoples are particularly disadvantaged (Frideres, 1993). The average income of a native person in Canada is less than two-thirds the average income of a non-Native.

WEALTH Income is only one aspect of wealth. Wealth includes property such as buildings, land, farms, houses, factories, and cars, as well as other assets such as money in bank accounts, corporate stocks, bonds, and insurance policies. Wealth is computed by subtracting all debt obligations and converting the remaining assets into cash. For most people in Canada, wealth is invested primarily in property that generates no income, such as a house or a car. In contrast, the

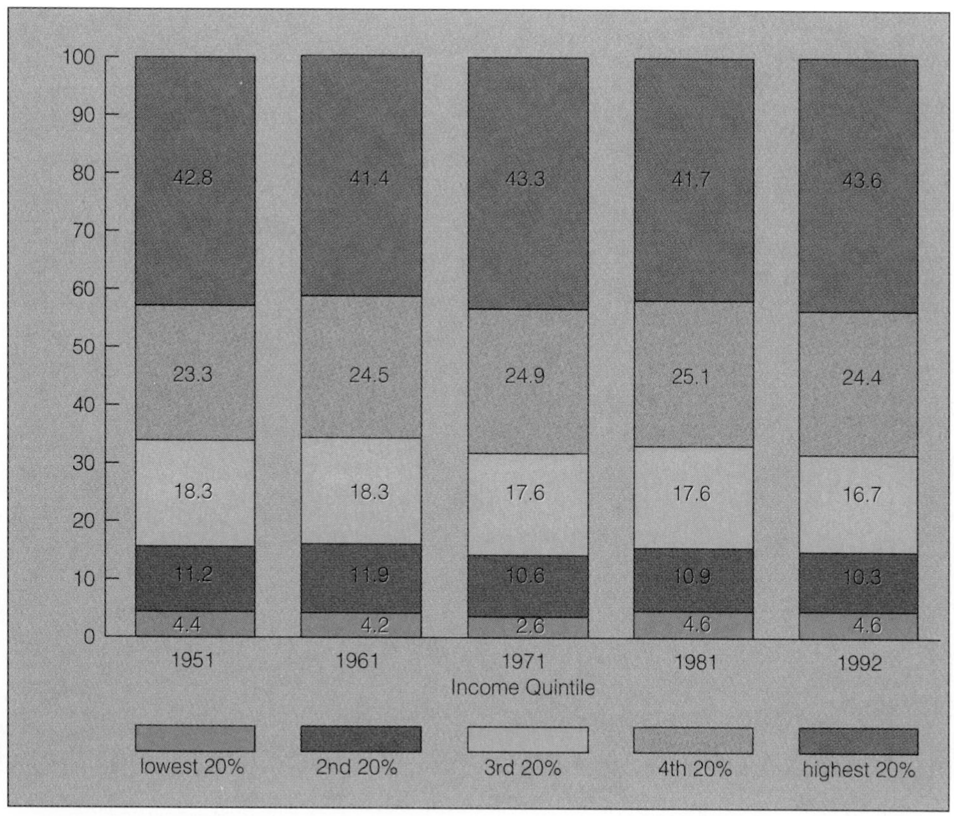

FIGURE 8.4

Income Distribution by Quintile, Families and Unattached Individuals, Canada, 1951–1992

Reproduced by authority of the Minister of Industry, 1996, Statistics Canada, from *Income Distribution by Size in Canada*, Cat. no. 13-207.

wealth of an elite minority often is in the form of income-producing property.

Research on the distribution of wealth in Canada reveals that wealth is more unevenly distributed among the Canadian population than is income. The combined wealth of a small number of Canada's richest individuals and families, shown in Table 8.3, is over $23 billion. In other words, a limited number of people own or control a very large portion of the wealth in Canada. Antonious and Crowley (1986), for example, demonstrated that more than two-thirds of the largest Canadian corporations were controlled by a single owner. At least half of these owners were families. Richardson's (1990) analysis of corporate ownership in Canada reported similar findings. He noted that in 1985 over three-quarters of the assets of Canada's largest nonfinancial corporations were controlled by only 17 large business enterprises. Eleven of the 17 enterprises were controlled by a single owner.

Table 8.4 outlines the unequal distribution of wealth in Canada. The poorest 10 percent had no assets and owed money. The wealthiest 10 percent on the other hand, had more than 50 percent of the wealth in Canada.

For the upper class, wealth often comes from inheritance. The majority of the wealthiest people in Canada are inheritors, with some at least three or four generations removed from the original

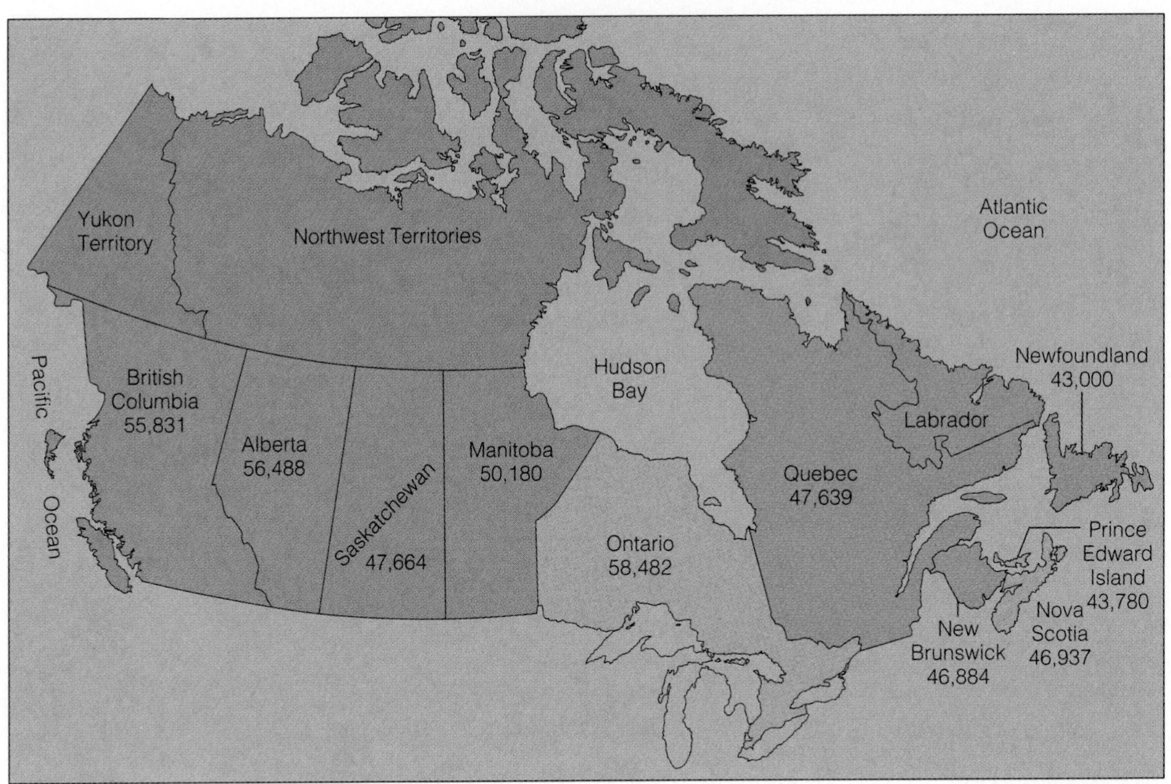

MAP 8.1

Regional Variation in Average Family Income

Reproduced by authority of the Minister of Industry, 1996, Statistics Canada, from *Select Income Statistics*, Cat. no. 93-331, 1991.

fortune (Dyck, 1996). After inheriting a fortune, John D. Rockefeller, Jr., stated, "I was born into [wealth] and there was nothing I could do about it. It was there, like air or food or any other element. The only question with wealth is what to do with it" (quoted in Glastris, 1990:26).

Whether we consider distribution of income or wealth, though, it is relatively clear that social inequality is a real, consistent, and enduring feature of life in Canadian society (Harman, 1995a).

CONSEQUENCES OF INEQUALITY

Income and wealth are not simply statistics; they are intricately related to our individual life chances. Persons with a high income or substantial wealth have more control over their lives. They have greater access to goods and services; they can afford better housing, more education, and a wider range of medical services. Similarly, as discussed in Box 8.3, those with greater access to economic resources fare better when dealing with the criminal justice system (Reiman, 1979; Gabor 1994; Linden, 1995). Persons with less income, especially those living in poverty, must spend their limited resources to acquire the basic necessities of life.

HEALTH AND NUTRITION People who are wealthy and well educated and who have high-paying jobs are much more likely to be healthy than are poor people. As people's economic status increases, so does their health status. The poor have shorter life

TABLE 8.2

Mean Wage Incomes of Canadian Employed Male Population Aged 20–60 by Ethnic Group, 1981–1991

Ethnic Group	Annual Income 1981	Annual Income 1991
Jewish	$19,054	$37,146
Ukrainian	17,109	34,110
German	16,887	31,506
Dutch	16,461	30,888
Multiple British/French*	16,556	30,649
British	17,360	30,420
Multiple non British/French**	16,190	29,928
Polish	17,095	29,656
Italian	15,588	29,550
Other European	15,776	28,458
French	15,389	27,222
Portuguese	14,776	26,926
Chinese	14,120	26,392
South Asian	—	25,718
Other E/SE Asia	—	24,080
Black/Caribbean	14,442	23,346
Arab/West Asian	—	21,284
Aboriginal	—	18,779
Latin American	—	16,460

* Multiple British/French refers to individuals who have both British and French ethnic origins.

** Multiple non British/French refers to individuals having mixed ethnic origins that *do not* include French or English.

Reproduced by authority of the Minister of Industry, 1996, Statistics Canada, from 1981 and 1991 Census of Canada.

expectancies and are at greater risk for chronic illnesses such as diabetes, heart disease, and cancer, as well as for infectious diseases such as tuberculosis.

Children born into poor families are at much greater risk of dying during their first year of life. Some die from disease, accidents, or violence. Others are unable to survive because they are born with low birth weight, a condition linked to birth defects and increased probability of infant mortality (Rogers, 1986). Low birth weight in infants is attributed, at least in part, to the inadequate nutrition received by many low-income pregnant women. Most of the poor do not receive preventive medical and dental checkups; many do not receive adequate medical care after they experience illness or injury. Furthermore, many high-poverty areas lack an adequate supply of doctors and

BOX 8.4 SOCIOLOGY AND LAW

The Rich Get Richer and the Poor Get Prison

In Canada, the capacity of all federal and provincial prisons is slightly over 25,000, while the country's population is approximately 29 million. This means that less than one in every thousand Canadians can be incarcerated at any given time. The result is that prisons must be used selectively.

How does social class effect the likelihood of being sent to prison? Are there different sets of rules operating in the criminal justice system—one for the rich and one for the poor? According to Jeffery Reiman author of *The Rich Get Richer and the Poor Get Prison: Ideology, Class and Criminal Justice* (1979), economic power is the central factor in determining whether a person will go to prison for a criminal offence. Reiman supports this premise with data that reveals that in the United States the prison populations are comprised overwhelmingly from the franks of society's disadvantaged. He states:

For the same criminal behavior, the poor are more likely to be arrested; if arrested, they are more likely to be charged; if charged, more likely to be convicted; if convicted, more likely to be sentenced to prison; and if sentenced, more likely to be given longer prison terms than members of the middle and upper classes. In other words, the image of the criminal population one sees in our nation's jails and prisons is an image distorted by the shape of the criminal justice system itself. It is the face of evil reflected in a carnival mirror, but it is no laughing matter. (1979:97)

What effect does social class play in the processing of accused persons in the Canadian criminal justice system? According to criminologist Thomas Gabor, the justice system in Canada also favours the middle and upper class—those who have the financial resources to protect their best interests. For example, in the case of young offenders, police are more likely to refer lower-class youths to juvenile court. Youth from wealthier homes are more likely to be dealt with informally. Poor defendants are less likely to be able to afford bail and are therefore more likely to remain in jail until their case goes to trial (this may be several months). The poor must rely on legal-aid lawyers who have large case-loads and little time to prepare cases for trial. The sentencing state also favours individuals of higher social standing. Crimes committed by middle-and upper-class persons e.g., embezzlement, fraud, income tax evasion) usually earn lighter sentences than those more likely to be committed by the poor (e.g., robbery, burglary).

In short, white-collar criminals have been very successful in ensuring that their interests are reflected in the law and its enforcement. As criminologist Rick Linden discusses, the crimes committed by higher status criminals are much less likely to be labelled criminal:

A storekeeper who sells a turkey labelled 12 kg which actually weights 11 kg may not be prosecuted; if he or she actually is, the charge will be breach of a regulatory offence with relatively minor penalties. However, someone caught stealing a kilogram of turkey meat will be charged with the criminal offence of theft. Doctors who fraudulently bill provincial health insurance plans are usually disciplined by their professional body, while someone who fraudulently receives welfare is subject to criminal prosecution. (1995:219)

It is evident that social class plays a significant role in terms of the type of punishment, if any, offenders receive for their crime. However, as Gabor notes, other factors such as the type and severity of the offence are also important considerations:

Even poor people are selectively punished. The poor people we find in prisons have been incarcerated for murder, robbery, theft, burglary, drug offences and the like; they are rarely punished for assaulting their wives, abusing their children, or stealing from their employers. Thus, the type of infraction one commits, too, is important in the selection of people for legal proceedings. (1994:290)

Arrest, detention, and sentencing decisions are extremely complex and involve a number of legal (prior record, severity of offence, type of offence) and non-legal (social class, age, demeanour, gender) factors. Therefore, although we can say that social class effects an individual's chances of going to prison, it is difficult to determine the degree of influence this non-legal factor has.

Source: Gabor, 1994; Reiman, 1979; Linden, 1995.

TABLE 8.3

Major Canadian Entrepreneurs: Their Principal Businesses and Estimated Wealth

Name	Principal Business	Wealth ($billion)
Kenneth Roy Thomson	Newspapers, Hudson's Bay Co.	7.5
Three Irving brothers	Gas stations, oil refineries	6.0
Garry Weston	Baking, grain trade, packaged foods	2.7
Charles Bronfman	Seagram, Cineplex Odeon	2.7
Four Eaton brothers	T. Eaton Co.	1.4
Edward S. (Ted) Rogers	Rogers Communications	1.3
Galen Weston	Grocery stores, packaged foods	1.3

Source: Hagedorn 1994.

TABLE 8.4

Wealth Distribution in Canada, 1970, 1977, 1989

Decile Shares	Wealth (Net Worth) of Family Units and Others		
	1970	1977	1989
1. Poorest 10%	–1.0	–0.6	–0.4
2.	0.0	0.1	0.1
3.	0.30	0.6	0.6
4.	2.3	1.7	1.8
5.	3.0	3.6	3.6
6.	5.4	6.0	5.7
7.	8.3	8.6	8.2
8.	11.8	12.0	11.6
9.	17.6	17.5	17.6
10. Wealthiest 10%	53.3	50.6	51.2

The data for three years may not be strictly comparable for family units and unattached individuals. Net worth = total assets minus debts, where total assets includes financial assets (deposits, bonds, stocks, mortgages, cash), business equity, and real and personal estate.

Sources: *Reflections on Canadian Incomes*. 1980. Ottawa: Industry Canada, p. 352. Adapted with the permission of the Minister of Public Works and Government Services Canada, 1996.

medical facilities. The higher death rates among native peoples in Canada are partly attributable to unequal access to medical care and nutrition.

Although the precise relationship between class and health is not known, analysts suggest that people with higher income and wealth tend to smoke less, exercise more, maintain a healthy body weight, and eat nutritious meals. As a category, more affluent persons tend to be less depressed and face less psychological stress, conditions that tend to be directly proportional to income, education, and job status (*Mental Medicine*, 1994).

Good health is basic to good life chances, and adequate amounts of nutritious food are essential for good health. Hunger is related to class position and income inequality. After spending 60 percent of their income on housing, low-income families are often unable to provide enough food for their children. Consider the following comments by a mother on her attempts to manage her food budget:

> Juice wars we have at our place. "You can't have that extra glass of juice." They bring somebody in the house and the three of them are having a glass of juice and that's all there is for the rest of the week. And there they are just drinking it down, and you're going, "Oh my God, don't they understand anything?" (Duffy and Mandell, 1996:100)

The number of food banks in Canada has grown from 1 in 1981 to more than 300 in 1996. This increase clearly indicates that many Canadians are unable to meet their nutritional needs (Kitchen et al., 1991; Oderkirk,1992).

EDUCATION Educational opportunities and life chances are directly linked. Some functionalist theorists view education as the "elevator" to social mobility. Improvements in the educational achievement levels (measured in number of years of schooling completed) of the poor, visible minorities, and women have been cited as evidence that students' abilities now are more important than their class, race, or gender. From this perspective, inequality in education is declining, and students have an opportunity to achieve upward mobility through achievements at school (see Hauser and Featherman, 1976).

Functionalists generally see the education system as flexible, allowing most students the opportunity to attend university if they apply themselves (Ballantine, 1993).

In contrast, most conflict theorists stress that schools are agencies for reproducing the capitalist class system and perpetuating inequality in society (Bowles and Gintis, 1976; Bowles, 1977). From this perspective, education perpetuates poverty. Parents with limited income are not able to provide the same educational opportunities for their children as are families with greater financial resources. Author Jonathan Kozol (1991, quoted in Feagin and Feagin, 1994:191) documented the effect of educational inequality on students:

> Kindergartners are so full of hope, cheerfulness, high expectations. By the time they get into fourth grade, many begin to lose heart. They see the score, understanding they're not getting what others are getting ... They see suburban schools on television ... They begin to get the point that they are not valued much in our society. By the time they are in junior high, they understand it. "We have eyes and we can see; we have hearts and we can feel ... We know the difference."

Poverty exacts such a toll that many young people will not have the opportunity to finish high school, much less enter college.

POVERTY

When many people think about poverty, they think of people who are unemployed or on welfare. However, many hardworking people with full-time jobs live in poverty. In 1994, 216,000 unattached persons and 71,000 attached (i.e., who were in families) Canadians were poor even though they were working (National Council of Welfare, 1994). Statistics Canada uses the term "low-income cut-off" to measure poverty. According to this measure, any individual or family that spends more than 56.2 percent of their income on food, clothing, and shelter is considered to be living in poverty. Statistics Canada also calculates different low-income cut-off lines based on community size and size of family—both factors affect the cost of living. In 1994, the income cut-offs for a family of four ranged from $20,905 in rural areas to $30,708 in cities of more than 500,000. Based on these low-income cut-offs, nearly 4.8 million children, women, and men—one in every six Canadians—were living in poverty in 1994. "In a country as rich as Canada," says the National Council of Welfare, "these figures bear witness to the failure of successive federal, provincial and territorial governments to provide for the well-being of a significant portion of the people they were elected to represent" (1995:1).

When sociologists define poverty, they distinguish between absolute and relative poverty. ***Absolute poverty*** **exists when people do not have the means to secure the most basic necessities of life.** This definition comes closest to that used by the federal government. Absolute poverty often has life-threatening consequences, such as when a homeless person freezes to death on a park bench. By comparison, ***relative poverty*** **exists when people may be able to afford basic necessities but still are unable to maintain an average standard of living** (Harman, 1995a).

As Duffy and Mandell point out (1996:99), being poor means much more than getting by at some arbitrary level of income and understanding poverty demands more than a statistical overview. Poverty is primarily about deprivation, as this woman's comments reveal:

> There are times when I am so scared that I'm not going to find a job, I think, "What the hell is wrong with me? … I can get scared to death … I have periods of insomnia. I'll get very short tempered with my husband and with the children.
>
> If I say "no" to the children, they feel very depressed when they see other children taking things to school. The children feel very disappointed. They kind of lose love for you. They think that you don't love them. (Duffy and Mandell,1996:102)

WHO ARE THE POOR?

Poverty in Canada is not randomly distributed, but rather is highly concentrated among certain groups of people—specifically, women, children, persons with disabilities, and native Canadians. When people belong to more than one of these categories, for example, native children, their risk of poverty is even greater.

AGE Today, children are at much greater risk of living in poverty than are adults aged 16 to 64 (National Council of Welfare, 1996). A generation ago, persons over age 65 were at greatest risk of being poor; however, increased government transfer payments and an increase in the number of elderly retiring with personal private pension plans has led to a decline in poverty among the elderly. Even so, older women are twice as likely as older men to be poor.

The age category most vulnerable to poverty today is that of the young. While the overall poverty rate in 1994 was about 17 percent, the rate for children under the age 18 was 19.1 percent. This means more than 1.3 million Canadian children are living in poverty (National Council of Welfare, 1996). A large number of children hover just above the official poverty line. The precarious position of native children is even more striking. Shillington (1991) estimated that approximately 51 percent of Native children (both on and off reserves) are living in poverty.

Children as a group are poorer now than they were at the beginning of the 1980s (see Table 8.5), and this is true whether they live in one- or two-parent families. The majority of poor children live in two-parent families in which one or both parents are employed. However, children in

TABLE 8.5

Poverty Trends—Children Under 18

Year	Number Living in Poverty	Poverty Rate
1980	984,000	14.9%
1981	998,000	15.2
1982	1,155,000	17.8
1983	1,221,000	19.0
1984	1,253,000	19.6
1985	1,165,000	18.3
1986	1,086,000	17.0
1987	1,057,000	16.6
1988	987,000	15.4
1989	934,000	14.5
1990	1,105,000	16.9
1991	1,210,000	18.3
1992	1,218,000	18.2
1993	1,415,000	20.8
1994	1,334,000	19.1

Source: *Poverty Profile 1994.* Ottawa: National Council of Welfare, Spring 1996. Reprinted by permission.

single-parent households headed by women are much likelier to be living in poverty. Despite efforts such as Campaign 2000 (see Box 8.2) and the promise to alleviate child poverty by the year 2000 made by the House of Commons in 1989—which sparked the campaign—the future for poor children does not look bright. These children are poor because their parents are poor, and one of the main reasons for poverty among adults is a lack of good jobs. Government cuts to unemployment insurance benefits and employment programs will affect not only those who need these services but also the children of these individuals.

GENDER About two-thirds of all adults living in poverty in Canada are women. As Figure 8.5 shows, in 1994, single-parent families headed by women had a 57.3 percent poverty rate compared with an 11.3 percent rate for two-parent families. Furthermore, women are among the poorest of the poor. Poor single mothers with children under 18 are the worst off, living $8,535 below the poverty line in 1994. Sociologist Diana Pearce (1978) coined a term to describe this problem: the ***feminization of poverty*** **refers to the trend in which women are disproportionately represented among individuals living in poverty.** According to Pearce (1978), women have a higher risk of being poor because they bear the major economic burden of raising children as single heads of households but earn only 70 cents for every dollar a male worker earns—a figure that has changed little over four decades. More women than men are unable to obtain regular, full-time, year-round employment, and the lack of adequate, affordable day care exacerbates this problem.

While some women are victims of chronic poverty, others are among the "new poor" who

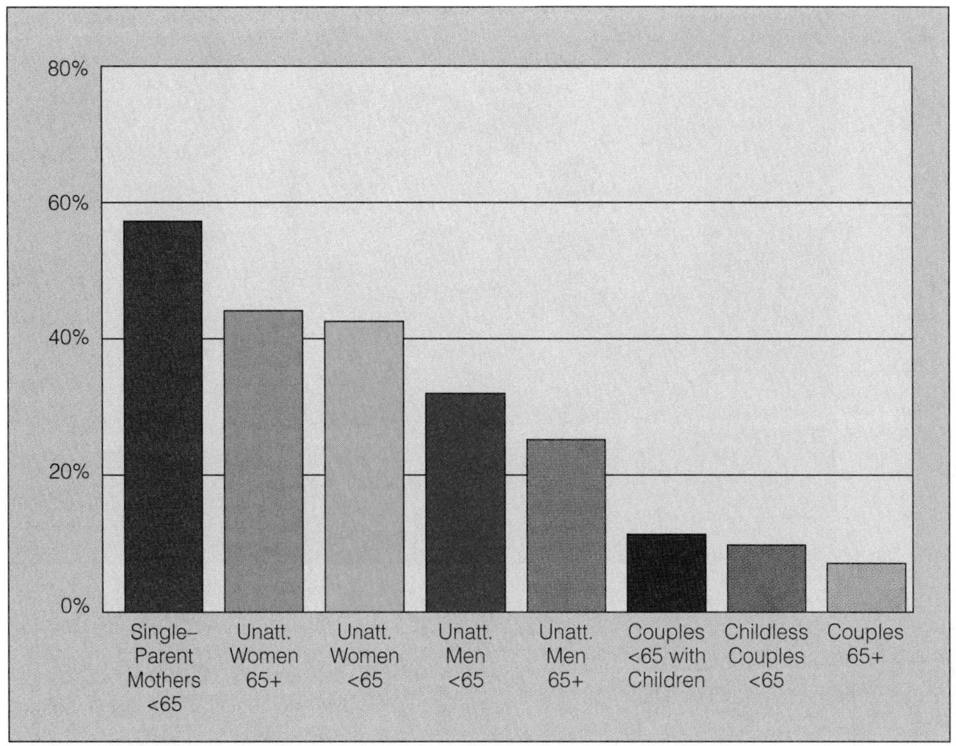

FIGURE 8.5

Poverty Rates by Family Types, 1994

Source: *Poverty Profile 1994.* Ottawa: National Council of Welfare, Spring 1996. Reprinted by permission.

have experienced "event-driven poverty" as a result of marital separation, divorce, or widowhood (Bane, 1986). Sociologist Lenore Weitzman (1985) has suggested that no-fault divorce laws have placed many women in financial jeopardy because supposedly "equal" settlements did not take into account women's lesser earning capabilities, especially if they had been out of the workforce taking care of young children at home. The Economic Council of Canada's five-year survey of Canadian incomes found that women's incomes (adjusted for family size) dropped by about 39 percent when they separated or divorced. Three years after the marriage breakup, women's incomes were still 27 percent below their earlier level. In contrast, men's incomes, increased by an average of 7 percent three years after the breakup (Duffy and Mandell, 1996:98).

Certain groups of women experience "multiple jeopardy," a term used to refer to the even greater risk of poverty faced by women who are immigrants, disabled, visible minorities, or native Canadians (Gerber, 1990).

RACE/ETHNICITY According to some stereotypes, most of the poor and virtually all welfare recipients are visible minorities. Such stereotypes are perpetuated, however, because a disproportionate percentage of the impoverished in Canada are native Canadians and recent immigrants. Native people in Canada are among the most severely disadvantaged persons. About one-half live below the poverty line, and some live in conditions of extreme poverty. In 1990, 47.2 percent of native peoples living on reserves had incomes of below

The "feminization of poverty" refers to the fact that two out of three impoverished adults in North America are women. Should we assume that poverty is primarily a women's issue? Why or why not?

$10,000 per year, compared with about one-quarter (27.7 percent) of all Canadian individuals. Also, the unemployment rate for native persons in Canada ranges from 40 to 60 percent, while the national average is about 10 percent. In sum, "to be Native in Canada is to face a strong likelihood of poverty" (Harman, 1995a:259).

PERSONS WITH DISABILITIES Awareness that persons with disabilities are discriminated against in the job market has increased in recent years. As a result, they now constitute one of the recognized "target groups" in efforts to eliminate discrimination in the workplace. However, the effects of this systemic discrimination continue to be felt by disabled persons as they are still, as a group, vulnerable to poverty (Harman, 1995a). As discussed in Chapter 11 ("Aging and Persons with Disabilities"), adults with disabilities have significantly lower incomes than nondisabled Canadians. In 1991, 42.7 percent of all disabled persons aged 15 to 64 had incomes below $10,000 compared with only 34.9 percent of all Canadians in this age group (Ross, Shillington, and Lochhead, 1994). Once again, when gender and disability are combined, we find that women with disabilities are doubly disadvantaged (Harman, 1995a).

ECONOMIC AND STRUCTURAL SOURCES OF POVERTY

Poverty has both economic and structural sources. The low wages paid for many jobs is the major cause: one-third of all families living in poverty are headed by someone who is employed (National Council of Welfare, 1996). In 1972, minimum-wage legislation meant that a worker who worked 40 hours a week, 52 weeks a year could earn a yearly income 20 percent over the poverty line. By 1991, the same worker would have to work 50 hours a week for 52 weeks simply to reach the poverty line (Kitcher et al., 1991:36). In other words, a person with full-time employment in a minimum-wage job cannot keep a family of four above the official poverty line.

Structural problems contribute to both unemployment and underemployment. Automation in the industrial heartland of Quebec and Ontario has made the skills and training of thousands of workers obsolete. Many of these workers have become unemployable and poor. Corporations have been deinvesting in Canada, and millions of people have lost their jobs as a result. Economists refer to this displacement as the *deindustrialization of North America* (Bluestone and Harrison, 1982).

Even as they have closed their Canadian factories and plants, many corporations have opened new facilities in other countries where "cheap labour" exists because people of necessity will work for lower wages. ***Job deskilling*****—a reduction in the proficiency needed to perform a specific job that leads to a corresponding reduction in the wages for that job**—has resulted from the introduction of computers and other technology (Hodson and Parker, 1988). The shift from manufacturing to service occupations has resulted in the loss of higher-paying positions and their replacement with lower-paying and less secure positions that do not offer the wages, job stability, or advancement potential of the disappearing manufacturing jobs. Many of the new jobs are located in the suburbs, thus making them inaccessible to central-city residents. In addition, the lack of affordable high-quality day care for women who need to earn an income means that many jobs are inaccessible, especially to women who are single parents. The problems of unemployment, underemployment, and poverty-level wages are even greater for visible minorities and young people (Collins, 1990).

SOLVING THE POVERTY PROBLEM

In 1996, the International Year for the Eradication of Poverty, the National Council of Welfare made four recommendations to address the issue of poverty in Canada. The Council indicated that in order to achieve any dramatic reductions in poverty it is necessary for all levels of government to change their priorities and their attitudes toward poor people. The recommendations directed at "mounting and winning the war on poverty" were outlined as follows:

1. *Government should make a special effort to promote realistic portraits of poor people.* A faltering economy and family breakups have added greatly to the ranks of the poor in recent years. In this context, it is wrong to condone false and degrading stereotypes of poor people.
2. *Governments should look to tax expenditures rather than cuts in social programs as the prime means for reducing their deficits.* Governments should stop cutting social programs that provide help to the least fortunate members of our society. It is unfair to ask poor people to "pay their share" of the cost of deficit reduction.
3. *Governments should agree to work collectively to fight poverty.* It makes sense for governments to work together rather than passing on their own financial problems to other governments. In the early 1980s the federal government started putting pressure on provincial governments with a series of cuts to cost-shared programs. Many provinces offset the effects of these costs by cutting funds to local governments, school districts, and hospitals.
4. *Governments should add fighting poverty to their list of immediate economic priorities.* Given the resources available to governments, there is no reason that fighting poverty should have to wait while governments grapple with reducing the deficit, lowering interest rates, or creating jobs. The reality is that poor people cannot wait five, ten, or twenty years for their concerns to be addressed. (National Council of Welfare, 1996:86)

How to reform welfare has been debated for the past two decades. A lack of consensus exists regarding both the definition of the problem and the possible solutions for it. While the political debates rage on, welfare recipients attempt to survive as best they can while clinging to their own version of success. Such dreams keep people alive, as one women living in poverty, Sara, indicated when she shared her dream for herself and her son:

> I got my vision, I got my dreams, and there are days when I feel down like I really can't make it. I'm nothing—you know, I'm tired,

BOX 8.4 SOCIOLOGY IN GLOBAL PERSPECTIVE

Poverty in Brazil: The Effects on Women and Children

According to the United Nations, most of the roughly 100 million homeless people in the world are women and children, and another 600 million live in impoverished conditions in inadequate and unhealthy shelters. The United Nations Center for Human Settlement published a report indicating that of the 1.3 billion people living in poverty, 70 percent are women and girls. They referred to this as the global feminization of poverty, further indicating that women and girls are also the most rapidly growing group of impoverished. Some 50,000 people—mostly women and children—die daily because of poor shelter, polluted water, and bad sanitation. The report estimated that if housing could be brought up to a minimum standard, there would be 5 million fewer deaths and 2 million fewer disabilities per year. Women are relegated to homelessness or squatter-status in many parts of the world where they cannot legally own or inherit land, cannot obtain bank loans, receive much lower wages than men, and often are abandoned to raise children on their own. Women are often also the prime targets of political upheavals, making up 70 to 80 percent of the world's 23 million refugees.

What is life like for these women? Persons in all nations have hopes and dreams for their children and grandchildren. Doralice Moreira de Souza is a 47-year-old woman whose hands are gnarled from years of cutting a daily quota of five tons of sugar cane in Conceicao de Macabu, Brazil. She has a dream for Alan, her 10-year-old grandson: "I would like him to study, so that when he grows up, he won't end up like a slave like me." However, Alan's life chances already are seriously limited because of economic conditions and labour exploitation in his country. Today, slavery flourishes in rural and other isolated areas of Brazil—on sugarcane plantations and ranches, in gold mines, and in the charcoal industries of the Amazon. The sugarcane fields in which Doralice works are harvested by farm workers who toil from sunup to sundown and sleep in hammocks strung in cow stalls. Their employer, an alcohol distillery owner, does not pay wages for their work. Workers instead receive scrip, which they can redeem for food. Because landowners need to ensure that they will have a readily available supply of cheap labour, they bind labourers by encouraging them to run up unpayable debts at company-owned stores or canteens. As a Rio de Janeiro prosecutor looking into labour law violations stated, "In the 19th century, the chains were metal. Today, the chains are debt—the worker has to repay his transportation, his tools, his food" (Brooke, 1993b:3).

What is life like for the children living in poverty in Brazil? Sociologist Martha Huggins (quoted in Henslin, 1996) describing the brutal conditions in which these children live, said that in the Brazilian slum areas both adults and children rummage through garbage dumps to find enough decaying food to keep themselves alive, and hordes of homeless children roam the streets, begging, stealing, shining shoes—anything to survive. These children, according to Huggins, are considered by middle and upper class Brazilians as part of the "dangerous classes" because they threaten the status quo. These children, who loiter in front of businesses, shoplift, or sell items on the street in competition with storeowners, are considered to be nothing but trouble. Since there are no social institutions in this country to provide for these children, one monstrous "solution" has been to kill them. Each year the Brazilian police and death squads murder about 2,000 children. These murders are often preceded by ritual torture.

As these tragic examples demonstrate, poverty is the world's deadliest disease. How should First world nations respond to global world poverty?

Source: Based on Brooke, 1993b; Henslin and Nelson, 1996; and Osterman, 1995.

I'm tired and it's too hard. But it's like I have goals—I want to be something different from what I have right now ... I guess to be somebody in poverty, to see that generation that's coming behind us—it's sad, it's real sad, what do they have to strive for? I just got to believe I only can make the difference ... even though obviously the system doesn't really want you to succeed ... I can become what statistics has designed me to be, a nothing, or I can make statistics a lie ... Today, I am making statistics a lie. (quoted in Polakow, 1993:73)

SOCIAL STRATIFICATION IN THE TWENTY-FIRST CENTURY

Will social inequality in Canada increase in the twenty-first century? Many social scientists predict that existing trends point to an increase. First, the purchasing power of the dollar has stagnated or declined since the early 1970s. As families started to lose ground financially, more family members (especially women) entered the labour force in an attempt to support themselves and their families (Gilbert and Kahl, 1993). Economist Robert Reich (1993:145) has noted that the employed have been travelling on two escalators—one going up and the other going down—in recent years. The gap between the earnings of workers and the income of managers and top executives has widened (Feagin and Feagin, 1994:56).

Second, wealth continues to become more concentrated at the top of the Canadian class structure. As the rich have grown richer, more people have found themselves among the ranks of the poor. Structural sources of upward mobility are shrinking while the rate of downward mobility has increased. The main problem in redistributing wealth and income in Canada is that the middle and upper classes may have to accept less so that others can have more (Krahn, 1995). This is a tough, if not impossible, sell in a society like that of Canada, in which the ability to acquire material goods is as highly valued as it is.

Are we sabotaging our future if we do not work constructively to eliminate poverty? It has been said that a chain is no stronger than its weakest link. If we apply this idea to the problem of poverty, it is to our advantage to see that those who cannot find work or do not have a job that provides a living wage receive adequate training and employment. Children of today, the adults of tomorrow, need education, health care, and safety as they grow up.

Reich (1993) emphasizes that the growth in single-parent lower-income families cannot continue to be used as an explanation for the widening gap between the rich and the poor. He argues instead that the persistence of economic inequality is related to profound global economic changes. Box 8.4 discusses the impact of poverty on women and children in Third World countries. In this chapter, we have focused primarily on social stratification in Canada; however, in Chapter 12 ("Economy and Work"), we examine the connections between wealth and poverty in the developed nations (such as Canada and the United States) and in the less developed nations of the world.

As mentioned at the beginning of this chapter, the House of Commons passed a motion stating a goal of eliminating poverty among children by the year 2000 (Kitcher et al., 1991). As we approach the twenty-first century, are we close to reaching the goals outline in Campaign 2000? Canada's response to poverty has been contradictory. One would expect that in working toward eliminating poverty action would be taken to address the structural causes of poverty—high unemployment and an inadequate set of child and family social policies. Instead, the federal government has cut federal social supports (such as subsidized day care, unemployment benefits, and family allowance) (Kitcher et al., 1991), leaving families to bear the burden of poverty. Almost one-fifth of the children in this country continue to grow up poor, in circumstances that seriously jeopardize their chances of becoming happy and productive citizens. As Marsden and Robertson state in their report *Children in Poverty: Toward a Better Future*,

> Children are the future of any society. There is no sounder investment in Canada's future than an investment in our children. It is disturbing … that the necessity of solving child poverty must be justified in monetary or "bottom line" terms. Nevertheless, if that is required, the figures speak for themselves—but poor children cannot." (Marsden and Robertson, 1991:6)

CHAPTER REVIEW

Stratification is the hierarchical arrangement of large social groups based on their control over basic resources. Most of us are linked to the social hierarchies of class, race, gender, and age, and people are treated differently based on where they are positioned within these hierarchies.

- A key characteristic of systems of stratification is the extent to which the structure is flexible. In an open system, boundaries between levels in hierarchies are more flexible and may be influenced by people's achieved statuses. In a closed system, boundaries between levels are rigid, and people's positions are set by ascribed status. Social mobility is the movement of individuals or groups from one level to another in a stratification system.
- The caste system is a closed system in which people's status is determined at birth based on their parents' position in society. The class system, which exists in Canada, is a type of stratification based on ownership of resources and on the type of work people do. Class systems are characterized by unequal distribution of resources and by movement up and down the class structure through social mobility.
- Karl Marx and Max Weber acknowledged social class as a key determinant of social inequality and social change. For Marx, people's relationship to the means of production determines their class position. Weber developed a multidimensional concept of stratification that focuses on the interplay of wealth, prestige, and power.
- Functionalist perspectives on the Canadian class structure view class as broad groupings of people who share similar levels of privilege on the basis of their roles in the occupational structure. According to the Davis–Moore thesis, stratification exists in all societies, and some inequality is not only inevitable but also necessary for the ongoing functioning of society. The positions that are most important within society and that require the most talent and training must be highly rewarded.
- Conflict perspectives on the Canadian class structure are based on the assumption that social stratification is created and maintained by one group in order to enhance and protect its own economic interests. Conflict theorists measure class according to people's relationships with others in the production process.
- The stratification of society into different social groups results in wide discrepancies in income and wealth and in variable access to available goods and services. People with

high incomes or wealth have greater opportunity to control their own lives. People with lower incomes have fewer life chances and must spend their limited resources to acquire basic necessities.

- Many people with full-time jobs live in poverty. Sociologists distinguish between absolute poverty and relative poverty. Absolute poverty exists when people do not have the means to secure the basic necessities of life. Relative poverty exists when people may be able to afford basic necessities but still are unable to maintain an average standard of living.
- Age, gender, race/ethnicity, and disability tend to be factors in poverty. Children have a greater risk of being poor than do the elderly, while women have a higher rate of poverty than do men. Although whites account for approximately two-thirds of those below the poverty line, native peoples and visible minorities account for a share of the impoverished in Canada that is disproportionate to their numbers.
- As the gap between rich and poor and between employed and unemployed widens, social inequality clearly will increase in the twenty-first century.

KEY TERMS

absolute poverty **303**
apartheid **281**
caste system **281**
class system **281**
feminization of poverty **304**
intergenerational mobility **279**
intragenerational mobility **279**
job deskilling **307**
life chances **278**
meritocracy **286**
pink-collar occupations **294**
power **285**
prestige **285**
relative poverty **303**
social mobility **279**
social stratification **278**
socioeconomic status (SES) **289**
wealth **284**

QUESTIONS FOR ANALYSIS AND UNDERSTANDING

1. Why do all societies have some form of stratification?
2. Marx predicted that exploited workers eventually would overthrow the capitalists. Why has no such revolution occurred in Canada? What challenges to stratification have occurred in Canada in the twentieth century?
3. How can you determine your class location according to the class structure models of Marx and Weber? Which model seems most accurate?
4. What is the meaning of the phrase *the feminization of poverty*?

QUESTIONS FOR CRITICAL THINKING

1. Based on the functionalist model of class structure, what is the class location of each of your ten closest friends or acquaintances? What is their location in relation to yours? to one another? What does their location tell you about friendship and social class?
2. Should employment be based on merit, need, or affirmative action policies?
3. What might happen in Canada in the twenty-first century if the gap between rich and poor continues to widen?

SUGGESTED READINGS

These texts provide more in-depth information about social stratification:

Wallace Clement. *The Canadian Corporate Elite: An Analysis of Economic Power.* Toronto: McClelland & Stewart, 1975.

Dennis Forcese. *The Canadian Class Structure.* Toronto: McGraw-Hill Ryerson, 1986.

Charles E. Hurst. *Social Inequality: Forms, Causes, and Consequences.* Boston: Allyn & Bacon, 1992.

John Porter. *The Vertical Mosaic: An Analysis of Social Class and Power in Canada.* Toronto: University of Toronto Press, 1965.

A wide diversity of viewpoints on the intertwining of race, class, and gender in social stratification are found in these readers:

Margaret L. Andersen and Patricia Hill Collins (eds.). *Race, Class, and Gender: An Anthology* (2nd ed.). Belmont, Cal.: Wadsworth, 1995.

James E. Curtis, Edward Grabb, and Neil Guppy (eds). *Social Inequality in Canada: Patterns, Problems, Policies* (2nd ed.). Scarborough, Ont.: Prentice-Hall, 1993.

For more information on poverty in Canada, see:

David P. Ross and Richard Shillington. *The Canadian Fact Book on Poverty.* Ottawa: Canadian Council on Social Development, 1994.

Chapter 9

RACE AND ETHNICITY

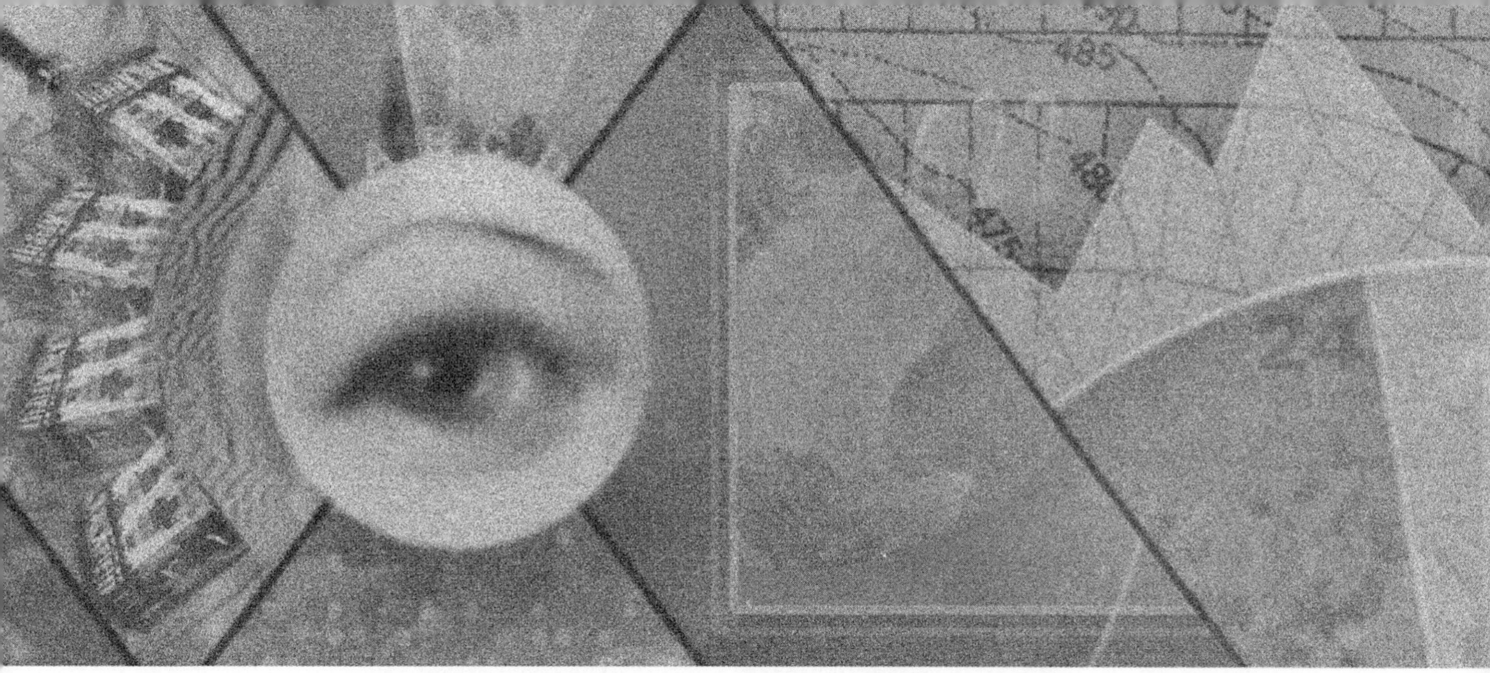

In the following personal narrative, Valerie Bedassigae Pheasant discusses her experiences with racism and the impact of these experiences on both her mother and herself:

> I sat on the banister railing for what felt like an eternity, watching my mother. As silently as I crept to watch, I left. I wondered why she did not dance for us. That was the first and only time I saw my mother dance with abandon. What I did see was a gradual freezing of her emotions and a treacherous walk with silence. Her metamorphosis had happened before our eyes and we were unable to stop it. Why didn't she yell at them? Why didn't she tell them—no? Where did the fire go? When was it that the dancing stopped?
>
> The cocoon that encased my mother was woven by inside thoughts that constricted her more strongly than anything tangible in the human world. Inside thoughts reacting to outside action generated towards our family's Nativeness. Blatant racist remarks and statements by women who did not care to know us. Each word, each comment diminished her capacity to speak—she moved slower and slower ... My mother liked to play bingo at the church hall occasionally. I went with her ... It was hard to find seats. We found some. We looked around at the other women at the table. Nobody said hello. They looked and I looked back ... The other women talked amongst themselves in what resembled a huddle. They glanced furtively in our direction. We sat and waited—I watched. Whispers. Whispers coming from the huddle. Whispers that called out, too loud, clanging in my ears, "Smells like Indians!" Instinctively, I breathed in deeply. Did they mean us? I could see them staring at us. My mother's head was down. Tears? I knew it was us. We moved to another table. We do not speak about what was said about us. We do not recognize them. We cannot give them more power. My anger grows. My mother's spirit staggers. (1994:35–36)

Canada is a diverse and complex society composed of racially and ethnically different groups. Our country has a reputation

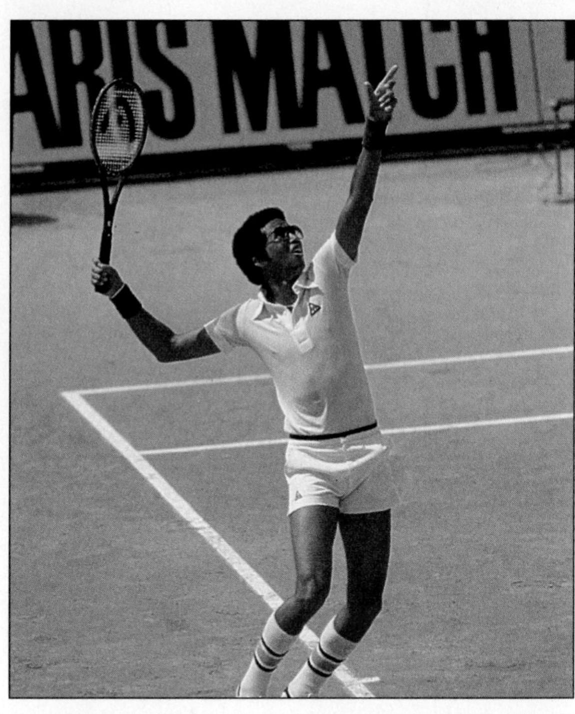

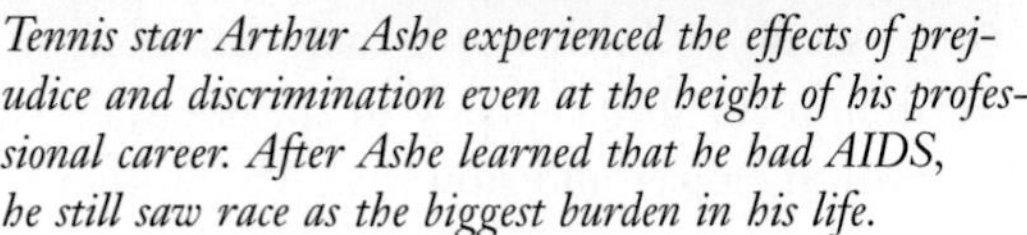
Tennis star Arthur Ashe experienced the effects of prejudice and discrimination even at the height of his professional career. After Ashe learned that he had AIDS, he still saw race as the biggest burden in his life.

as a tolerant and compassionate country whose success in race and ethnic relations has received worldwide admiration. Canadians profess to be colour-blind: the refrain "race doesn't matter here" is widely endorsed (James and Shadd, 1994:47). Is it surprising, therefore, to read the above personal narrative, in which it is suggested that native people in Canada experience racism as part of their everyday life? As Fleras and Elliott comment, "From afar, Canada looks idyllic; up close, the picture changes. Dig deeper and one can unearth a country that has little to boast about in the treatment of minorities" (1996:17). In this chapter racism will be central to the discussion of race and ethnicity. One of the most important and reliable sources of data on racism is the victims who have experienced it directly (Henry et al., 1996). Therefore, we will explore the subjective impact of race and ethnicity on people's lives—and examine whether those effects are changing. Before reading on, test your knowledge about racism in Canada by taking the quiz in Box 9.1.

QUESTIONS AND ISSUES

How significant is race in Canadian society?

How do race and ethnicity differ?

What accounts for prejudice?

How does discrimination differ from prejudice?

How are racial and ethnic relations analyzed from a sociological perspective?

What are the unique experiences of racial and ethnic groups in Canada?

RACE AND ETHNICITY

What is "race"? Some people think it refers to skin colour (the Caucasian "race"); others use it to refer to a religion (the Jewish "race"), nationality (the British "race"), or the entire human

BOX 9.1 SOCIOLOGY AND EVERYDAY LIFE

How Much Do You Know About Racism in Canada?

TRUE	FALSE	
T	F	1. There is only one kind of racism in Canada.
T	F	2. The majority of Canadians view racism as a significant social problem.
T	F	3. Racism in Canada is a result of immigration.
T	F	4. Racism occurs only in times of economic decline and recession.
T	F	5. Policies of multiculturalism are insufficient to address the problems of racism.
T	F	6. No civil rights movement existed in Canada.
T	F	7. Affirmative action programs directed at hiring visible minorities are a form of reverse discrimination.
T	F	8. Visible minorities are the likeliest victims of racism.
T	F	9. Incidents of anti-Semitism (racism directed at Jews) have increased in the past decade.
T	F	10. Slavery has never existed in Canada.

Answers on page 318

species (the human "race") (Marger, 1994). A ***race* is a category of people who have been singled out as inferior or superior, often on the basis of physical characteristics such as skin colour, hair texture, and eye shape** (Newman, 1995).

A number of difficulties arise when thinking in terms of race. First, race is defined by perceived skin colour: white or nonwhite (S. Lee, 1993). While one category exists for "whites" (who vary considerably in actual skin colour and physical appearance), all of the remaining categories are considered "nonwhite." This classification system, which took hold in such predominantly "white" countries as Canada, the United States, and the countries of Europe, is now outdated because of the growing presence in those countries of ethnic groups who fit neither category (Starr, 1987, 1992).

Second, use of the term *race* implies that racial purity exists. Although we may assume that we can distinguish between people on the basis on racially defined physical characteristics, biology confirms that most Canadians, like people all over the world, are genetically mixed. The combined effects of migration, immigration, and intermarriage have made it impossible to draw a line around human populations, with certain characteristics on one side, but not on the other (Martin and Franklin, 1983). Consider the confusion the concept of race created for Lawrence Hill:

BOX 9.1 SOCIOLOGY AND EVERYDAY LIFE

Answers to the Sociology Quiz on Racism in Canada

TRUE	FALSE	
T	**F**	1. *False.* Racism takes many forms. More subtle forms of racism such as institutional or systemic racism remain prevalent in Canadian society.
T	F	2. *True.* A recent poll indicated that 75 percent of Canadians considered racism a serious social problem.
T	**F**	3. *False.* The argument here is that if immigration is curbed, racism will decrease. However, even before Canada began allowing large-scale immigration, racism existed in the relationship between white colonial settlers and aboriginal peoples.
T	**F**	4. *False.* Racism has been practised systematically in Canada since this country was formed—even in times of economic prosperity. For example, in the early 1950s, despite an economic boom, Chinese and Japanese citizens were regarded as "enemy aliens."
T	F	5. *True.* To expect that programs supporting cultural retention can also achieve racial equality and harmony is unrealistic.
T	**F**	6. *False.* In the 1940s and 1950s organizations such as the Windsor Council on Group Relations, the National Unity Association of Chatham-Dresden-North Buxton, and the Negro Citizens' Association of Toronto fought segregation in housing and employment, as well as fighting racist immigration laws.
T	**F**	7. *False.* For affirmative action policies to be a form of reverse discrimination, they would have to require employers to discriminate against better-qualified whites and give an unfair advantage to visible minorities. Affirmative action is directed not at discrimination, but at elimination of a long history of employment practices that result in preferential treatment to white candidates.
T	**F**	8. *False.* In Canada both aboriginal people and visible minorities are subjected to racism. Which group is victimized more is difficult to measure.
T	F	9. *True.* In the past decade, the League for Human Rights of B'nai B'rith has monitored the number and types of anti-Semitic incidents that have occurred in all regions of Canada. They report a significant increase in anti-Semitic incidents of all kinds.
T	**F**	10. *False.* Slavery was introduced in Canada by the French in 1608. Sixteen legislators in the first Parliament of Upper Canada owned slaves. Slavery existed in Quebec, New Brunswick, Nova Scotia, and Ontario until the early nineteenth century.

Sources: Henry et al., 1995; Fleras and Elliott, 1996.

Even as a boy, I sensed that terms such a "mulatto," "half-Black" and "part-Black" denied my fullness as a person. I recognized the absurdity of calling somebody "one-half" or "one-quarter" or "one-eighth" Black ... One couldn't assign this colour to the heart and that colour to the liver. And at the same time, a person like me couldn't be all white

> and not Black, or all Black and not White, unless society imposed one colour on me. (1994:47)

The true diversity of the population is not revealed when multiracial individuals in Canada are placed in vague categories such as "other" (S. Lee, 1993). The concept of race is a social creation rather than a biological reality. Nevertheless, individuals like Lawrence Hill struggle to define themselves according to arbitrary racial classifications in an attempt clarify their identity.

The third problem with thinking in terms of race is that official racial classifications may over time create a sense of group membership or "consciousness of kind" for people within a somewhat arbitrary classification. When people of European descent were classified as "white," some began to see themselves as different from those classified as "nonwhite." Consequently, Jewish, Italian, and Irish immigrants may have felt more a part of the northern European white mainstream in the late nineteenth and early twentieth centuries. Whether Chinese Canadians, Japanese Canadians, and Filipino Canadians come to think of themselves collectively as "Asian Canadians" because of official classifications remains to be seen (S. Lee, 1993).

How do you classify yourself with regard to race? For an increasing number of people, this is a difficult question to answer. What if you were asked about your ethnic origin or your ethnicity? The Canadian census, unlike that of the United States, collects information on ethnic origin rather than race. Race refers only to physical characteristics, but the concept of ethnicity refers to cultural features. These features may include language, religion, national origin, distinctive foods, a common heritage, music, dress, or any other distinctive cultural trait. An ***ethnic group*, then, is a collection of people who, as a result of their shared cultural traits and a high level of interaction, regard themselves and are regarded as a cultural unit** (Robertson, 1977). As Table 9.1 demonstrates, almost 8 million Canadians reported multiple ethnic origins. As a result, collecting data on ethnic origin is not a simple task. In the table, data from the 1991 census reveal that almost 30 percent of Canadians reported multiethnic origins. As a result, future generations will be more likely to have a mixed racial and ethnic heritage. One student stated the dilemma this may pose as follows:

> I am part French, part Cherokee Indian, part Filipino, and part black. Our family taught us to be aware of all these groups, and just to be ourselves. But I have never known what I am. People have asked if I am a Gypsy, or a Portuguese, or a Mexican, or lots of other things. It seems to make people curious, uneasy, and sometimes belligerent. Students I don't even know stop me on campus and ask, "What are you, anyway?" (quoted in Davis, 1991:133)

Ethnic groups share five main characteristics: (1) unique cultural traits (such as language, clothing, holidays, or religious practice, (2) a sense of community, (3) a feeling of ethnocentrism, (4) ascribed membership from birth, and (5) territoriality, or a tendency to occupy a distinct geographic area by choice or for protection.

Although the distinction between ethnicity and race appears obvious—one is cultural, the other biological—they are often used interchangeably. Many people, for example, believe that Jews constitute a race although their distinctiveness pertains to cultural characteristics, primarily religious beliefs as well as a history of persecution.

SOCIAL SIGNIFICANCE OF RACE AND ETHNICITY

How important are race and ethnicity in Canada? According to sociologists Augie Fleras and Jean Leonard Elliott:

> Most Canadians appear ambivalent about the race concept. The concept carries a negative connotation that conflicts with the virtues of an achievement-oriented, upwardly mobile society. Many dislike the underlying message

TABLE 9.1

Selected Ethnic Origins of Canadians, 1991

Canada		
Total population	26,994,045	Percentage
Single origin*	19,199,790	71.1
French	6,129,680	22.7
English	3,958,405	14.7
German	911,560	3.4
Scottish	893,125	3.3
Canadian	765,095	2.8
Italian	750,055	2.8
Irish	725,660	2.7
Chinese	586,645	2.2
Ukrainian	406,645	1.5
North American Indian	365,375	1.4
Dutch	358,180	1.3
East Indian	324,840	1.2
Polish	272,810	1.2
Portuguese	246,890	0.9
Jewish	245,840	0.9
Black**	214,265	0.8
Filipino	157,250	0.6
Greek	151,150	0.6
Hungarian	100,725	0.4
Vietnamese	84,005	0.3
Métis	75,150	0.2
Inuit	30,085	0.1
Other single origins	1,446,355	
Multiple origins	7,794,250	28.9

* *Single origin* means the same ethnic origin is claimed on both maternal and paternal sides.

** The Census gives respondents the option of choosing Black as one of the ethnic categories.

Reproduced by authority of the Minister of Industry, 1996, Statistics Canada, from *Ethnic Origins*, Cat. no. 93-315, 1991.

> of race: That is, the most important thing about a person is an accident of birth, something beyond control, and that alone should determine job status, and privilege. (1996:37)

It is easy to suggest that race is insignificant if one is not a member of a racial minority. But, whether we like to acknowledge it or not, race does matter. It matters because it provides privilege and power for some. Fleras and Elliott discuss the significance of being white and enjoying what has sometimes been referred to as *white privilege*:

> Think for a moment about the privileges associated with whiteness, many of which are taken for granted and unearned by accident of birth. Being white means you can purchase a home in any part of town and expect cordial treatment rather than community grumblings about the neighborhood "going to pot." Being white saves you the embarrassment of going into a shopping mall with fears of being followed, frisked, monitored, or finger printed. Being white means you can comment on a variety of topics without someone impugning your objectivity or motives. You can speak your mind with little to lose if things go wrong. Being white enables you to display righteous anger in dealing with colleagues, yet not incur snide remarks about "aggression" or "emotional stability" ... Being white gives you the peace of mind that your actions are not judged as a betrayal or a credit to your race. Finally, being white provides the satisfaction of cruising around late at night without attracting unnecessary police attention (1996:35).

Ethnicity, like race, is a basis of hierarchical ranking in society and an "extremely critical determinant of who gets 'what there is to get' and in what amounts" (Marger, 1994:18). John Porter (1965) described Canada as a "vertical mosaic," made up of different ethnic groups wielding varying degrees of social and economic power, status, and prestige. Porter's extensive analysis of ethnic groups in Canada revealed a significant degree of ethnic stratification with some ethnic groups heavily represented in the upper strata, or elite, and other groups heavily represented in the lower strata. The dominant group holds power over other (subordinate) ethnic groups. Ethnic stratification is one dimension of a larger system of structured social inequality, as examined in Chapter 8.

MAJORITY AND MINORITY GROUPS

The terms *majority group* and *minority group* are widely used, but what do they actually mean? To sociologists, a ***majority* (or *dominant*) *group* is one that is advantaged and has superior resources and rights in a society** (Feagin and Feagin, 1993). In Canada, whites with northern European ancestry (often referred to as Euro-Canadians, white Anglo-Saxon Protestants, or WASPs) are considered a majority group. A ***minority* (or *subordinate*) *group* is one whose members, because of physical or cultural characteristics, are disadvantaged and subjected to unequal treatment by the dominant group and who regard themselves as objects of collective discrimination** (Wirth, 1945). All visible minorities and white women are considered minority group members in Canada. The term *visible minority* refers to an official government category of nonwhite non-Caucasian individuals. Included in this category are blacks, Chinese, Japanese, Koreans, Filipinos, Indo-Pakistanis, West Asians and Arabs, Southeast Asians, Latin Americans, and Pacific Islanders (Fleras and Elliott, 1996:279). Aboriginal people form a separate category.

Although the terms *majority group* and *minority group* are widely used, their actual meanings are not clear. In the sociological sense, *group* is misleading because people who merely share ascribed racial or ethnic characteristics do not constitute a group. Further, *majority* and *minority* have meanings associated with both numbers and domination. Numerically speaking, *minority* means that a group is smaller in number than a dominant group. However, in countries such as South Africa and India, this has not historically been true. Those running the country were of a race (in South Africa) or caste (in India) with far fewer members than the masses that they ruled. Consequently, the use of these terms from a standpoint of dominance is more accurate. In this context, majority and minority refer to relationships of advantage/disadvantage and power/exploitation.

Wagley and Harris (1958) have summarized five important characteristics of minorities:

1. Minorities are subordinate segments of complex societies.
2. They have special physical or cultural traits that are usually held in low esteem by the dominant majority.
3. They are self-conscious units bound together by special traits.
4. Membership is transmitted by descent, capable of affiliating succeeding generations.
5. By choice or necessity, members usually marry within the group. (quoted in Driedger, 1994:300)

According to these characteristics, Hutterites, aboriginals, blacks, and Jews are minorities in Canada. While we all belong to an ethnic group or groups, not everyone belongs to a minority group. Minority status is a reflection of the lack of power of a group. Many sociologists prefer to use the terms *dominant group* and *subordinate group* because they more precisely reflect the importance of power in the relationships (Feagin and Feagin, 1993).

COMPONENTS OF RACIAL AND ETHNIC CONFLICT

PREJUDICE

***Prejudice* is a negative attitude based on preconceived notions about members of selected groups.** Prejudice partially stems from our attempts to create some order in our lives by classifying others. However, prejudices **(pre +**

judgments) are judgments that are irrational and rigid insofar as they are supported by little or no direct evidence. Prejudice can be directed against a range of social or personal characteristics including social class, gender, sexual orientation, occupation, religion, political affiliation, age, race, or ethnicity. These attitudes may be either felt or expressed. ***Racial prejudices* involve beliefs that certain racial groups are innately inferior to others or have a disproportionate number of negative traits.** Prejudice is often reinforced by *stereotypes*—overgeneralizations about the appearance, behaviour, or other characteristics of all members of a group.

Although all stereotypes are hurtful, negative stereotypes are particularly harmful to minorities. As Fleras and Elliott comment, "Power and privilege provide a protective layer. For minorities, however, stereotyping is a problem. Each negative image or unflattering representation reinforces their peripheral position within an unequal society" (1996:69). Consider the following conversation:

> Sabra: So, you think I'm not like the rest of them ...
>
> Alex: Well, when I see you, I don't see your colour. I don't see you as a South Asian. You're not like the rest of them ...
>
> Sabra: Oh, so, I'm more like you and less like, should I say it, "a real South Asian." You see, although you are not saying it, your statement reveals that you have some preconceived ideas of South Asians, the people I'm supposed to be so unlike. This means that whatever your preconceived ideas are of South Asians, they make South Asians less acceptable, less attractive, and less appealing to you than I. Well, this is not just stereotyping, this is racist stereotyping. (Desai, 1994:191)

How do people learn of stereotypes? As Box 9.3 illustrates, the media are a major source of racial and ethnic stereotypes. Another source is ethnic jokes, which portray minorities in a derogatory manner, not necessarily intentionally, but because such humour by definition is simplistic and prone to exaggeration. Take a moment and think of an ethnic joke you have heard. Do you think this joke is harmful? Would you tell the joke to a member of the minority group that the joke is about? If not, chances are that you have some level of awareness that these jokes are damaging. Consider the comments of Paul, a student in a race and ethnic relations course at a Canadian university:

> If I laugh at a joke that uses a Black … because I associate a stereotype with what has been said, I am a bigot. For example, what do you call a Black guy in a new car? A thief. Funny, eh? No, the joke itself is not funny, but it makes reference to a stereotype about Blacks that they're all thieves, which I do find funny ... That kind of joke is not funny. It does not point out a funny stereotype of a certain race ... it is pure malice and cruelty against a specific group. The fact that it was Blacks mattered little. Am I a bigot? I don't know what I am anymore. (James, 1995:107)

Prejudice is often present in ***ethnocentrism*—the belief in the superiority of one's own culture compared with that of others.** Ethnocentrism involves the evaluation of all groups and cultures in terms of one's own cultural standards and values. What is wrong with believing that your cultural values are preferable to those of others? Such a belief is, after all, a source of pride. The problem with ethnocentrism is that your standards are used as a frame of reference for negatively evaluating the behaviour of other groups. Not surprisingly, these groups will be evaluated negatively as backward, immoral, primitive, or irrational. In short, although ethnocentrism promotes group cohesion and morale, it is also a major source of intergroup hostility and conflict.

DISCRIMINATION

While prejudice refers to attitudes and beliefs, discrimination refers to the process by which these negative attitudes are put into practice.

BOX 9.2 SOCIOLOGY AND MEDIA

Racism in the Media

The media are one of the most powerful sources of information in society, tremendously influencing the way we look at the world, how we understand it, and the manner in which we experience and relate to it. In other words, the media provide a "window on the world." For many Canadians, the media are the primary source of information about racial and ethnic groups. For example, the media relay information about who racial minorities are, what they want, why, how they propose to achieve their goals, and with what consequences for Canadian society. Racial minorities have accused Canada's mass media of slanted coverage; descriptions of the coverage have ranged from unfair and inadequate to racist. The following are examples of how journalist Doug Collins has discussed visible minorities and aboriginal peoples in his columns in the *North Shore News*:

> The result is that Vancouver is becoming a suburb of Asia; Toronto, once the Queen City of English Canada, has become the tower of Babel, with every race except ours bawling for special rights and receiving them. Montreal is a target for the enlightened folk of Haiti. And the politicians wouldn't care if voodooism became the leading religion.

> The Third World is occupying the classrooms of much of the Lower Mainland. This is clear from the statistics and the pictures on TV. Hardly a White face in sight. Which should tell you something about why we have to have free lunches. But no one wants to say it.

> What saving the country boils down to is handing out more dough to the French and the ever-squawking Indians who know they are dealing with dummies and never had it so good until we turned up and showed them the wheel.

> The issue is whether the Holocaust took place. In other words, whether the Hitler regime deliberately set out to kill all the Jews it could get its hands on, and that 6,000,000 died as a result. More and more, I am coming to the conclusion that it [the Holocaust] didn't. (Darling thoughts that could land a guy in jail in this free country of ours!)

Though a complaint against Collins was filed with the British Columbia Press Council, the council dismissed it. In 1993, the British Columbia Organization to Fight Racism (BCOFR) was appalled when it learned that the governor general of Canada had presented Collins with an award that honours Canadians who have made a significant contribution to their fellow citizens, their community, or Canada. Collins was described as a "controversial columnist for the *North Shore News* who forces people to think for themselves and re-evaluate commonly held opinions."

Apparently, freedom of the press is considered so sacred a trust that the media believe they have the right to communicate racist content. Is there an effective way to reconcile the apparently contradictory goals of freedom of expression and freedom from discrimination? If not, perhaps we need to reexamine which of these goals should take priority.

Source: Henry et al., 1996.

***Discrimination* involves actions or practices of dominant group members (or their representatives) that have a harmful impact on members of a subordinate group** (Feagin and Feagin, 1994). For example, people who are prejudiced toward East Indians, Jews, or native people may refuse to hire them, rent an apartment to them, or allow their children to play with them. In these instances, discrimination involves the differential treatment of minority group members not because of their ability or merit, but because of irrelevant characteristics such as skin colour or language preference.

Discriminatory actions vary in severity from the use of derogatory labels to violence against individuals and groups. Discrimination takes two basic forms: *de jure*, or legal discrimination, which is encoded in laws; and *de facto*, or informal discrimination, which is entrenched in social customs and institutions. De jure discrimination has been backed by explicitly discriminatory laws such as the Chinese Exclusionary Act, which restricted immigration to Canada on the basis of race, or the Nuremberg laws passed in Nazi Germany, which imposed restrictions on Jews. The Indian Act provides another example of *de jure* discrimination. According to the Act, status Indian women lost their "status rights" if they married someone who was not a status Indian, while status Indian men did not. An amendment to the Indian Act in 1985 ended this legalized sex discrimination. Section 15 of the Charter of Rights and Freedom prohibits discrimination on the basis of race, ethnicity, or origin. As a result, many cases of de jure discrimination have been eliminated. De facto discrimination is more subtle and less visible to public scrutiny and, therefore, much more difficult to eradicate.

Prejudice and discrimination do not always go hand in hand. Discrimination can exist without prejudice, and prejudice may flourish without expressing itself in discriminatory actions (Fleras and Elliott, 1996). This was demonstrated in a classic study conducted in the early 1930s. Richard LaPiere travelled around the United States with a Chinese couple, stopping at over 250 restaurants and hotels along the way. The pervasive anti-Oriental prejudice of the time led LaPiere to assume that the travellers would be refused service in most of the hotels and restaurants at which they intended to stop. However, LaPiere was wrong—only one establishment refused service to LaPiere and his friends. Several months later LaPiere sent letters to all the establishments they had visited, asking if they would serve "members of the Chinese race" as guests in their establishments. Ninety-two percent of the establishments that had earlier accepted LaPiere and his guests replied that Chinese people would not be welcome. This study is one of many examples of sociological research that reveals the discrepancy between what people say and what they do (Robertson, 1977).

As shown in Figure 9.1, sociologist Robert Merton (1949) identified four combinations of attitudes and responses. *Unprejudiced nondiscriminators* are not personally prejudiced and do not discriminate against others. These are individuals who believe in equality for all. *Unprejudiced discriminators* may have no personal prejudices but still engage in discriminatory behaviour because of peer group pressure or economic, political, or social interests. For example, an employee who has no personal hostility toward members of certain groups but is encouraged not to hire them by senior management. *Prejudiced nondiscriminators* hold personal prejudices but do not discriminate due to peer pressure, legal demands, or a desire for profits. Such individuals are often referred to as "timid bigots" because they are reluctant to translate their attitudes into action (especially when prejudice is considered to be "politically incorrect"). Finally, *prejudiced discriminators* hold personal prejudices and actively discriminate against others. For example, the landlord who refuses to rent an apartment to a native couple and then readily justifies his actions on the basis of racist stereotypes of native people.

RACISM

Racism is a complex phenomenon that displays itself in a number of different forms. In his book *Is God a Racist?: The Right Wing in Canada*, Stanley Barrett discusses one of the less recognizable forms:

> If racists as a category all wore horns, the battle against them would be a great deal easier ... The type that chilled me the most, in fact, was not the hard-nosed bully who wanted to kick somebody's teeth in, but rather the highly educated man, wealthy and sophisticated, who sat sipping his cognac while elaborating on the nobility of the

	Prejudiced attitude?	Discriminatory behaviour?
Unprejudiced nondiscriminator	No	No
Unprejudiced discriminator	No	Yes
Prejudiced nondiscriminator	Yes	No
Prejudiced discriminator	Yes	Yes

FIGURE 9.1

Merton's Typology of Prejudice and Discrimination

white race and the necessity of excising the "mud people" from our midst. (1987:16)

Racism involves elements of prejudice, ethnocentrism, stereotyping, and discrimination. For example, racism is present in the belief that some racial or ethnic groups are superior while others are inferior; this belief is a prejudice. Racism may be the basis for unfair treatment toward members of a racial or ethnic group. In this case the racism involves discrimination. The interplay of these four elements creates a structural situation whereby groups are assigned role and status positions on the basis of their ascribed characteristics of race/ethnicity. Fleras and Elliott (1996) developed the most inclusive definition of racism, which incorporates both racial prejudice and discrimination. They define ***racism*** **as "an organized set of beliefs about the innate inferiority of some racial groups, combined with the power to transform these ideas into practices that deny or exclude equality of treatment on the basis of race"** (1996:98). Fleras and Elliott (1996) identify five different types of racism: rednecked, polite, subliminal, institutionalized, and systemic.

REDNECKED RACISM Rednecked racism is the kind of racism that most people associate with the term racist, that is, the kind of old-fashioned racism that prevailed in the American "deep South." ***Rednecked racism*** **is overt racism and may take the form of public statements about the "inferiority" of members of a racial or ethnic group.** For example, Al Campanis (former Los Angeles Dodgers general manager) repeatedly stated on national television that African Americans "lacked the necessities" to handle coaching and management positions. Jimmy "the Greek" Snyder (a former television sports analyst) declared that African Americans make good football running backs because they were bred during slavery to have big, strong thighs. Roger Staubach (former Dallas Cowboys quarterback) wrote that white football players have higher IQs than African American players 100 percent of the time (Lapchick, 1991). Although each of these incidents created a public outcry, such racist beliefs remain a part of the fabric of U.S. society (Feagin and Sikes, 1994).

What about Canada? Though racism is a bad word in Canadian society and acknowledging its existence here may be an affront to our Canadian identity, instances of rednecked racism are readily available. Racist, white supremacist groups including the White Aryan Nation, the Western Guard, and the Ku Klux Klan are active in Canada. These groups have relied on violence to create an environment of fear and hatred against minorities throughout the Canada and the United States. According to Warren Kinsella (1994), white hate groups disseminate their hate propaganda primarily through telephone hotlines, the Internet, and disinformation campaigns by hatemongers. White supremacist groups perceive themselves as the "saviours of the White race and Western Christian civilization" (Barrett, 1987:90). They believe that the survival of white society is in jeopardy because of the practice of allowing "non-Aryans" into Canada (see Chapter 3 for more on hate groups).

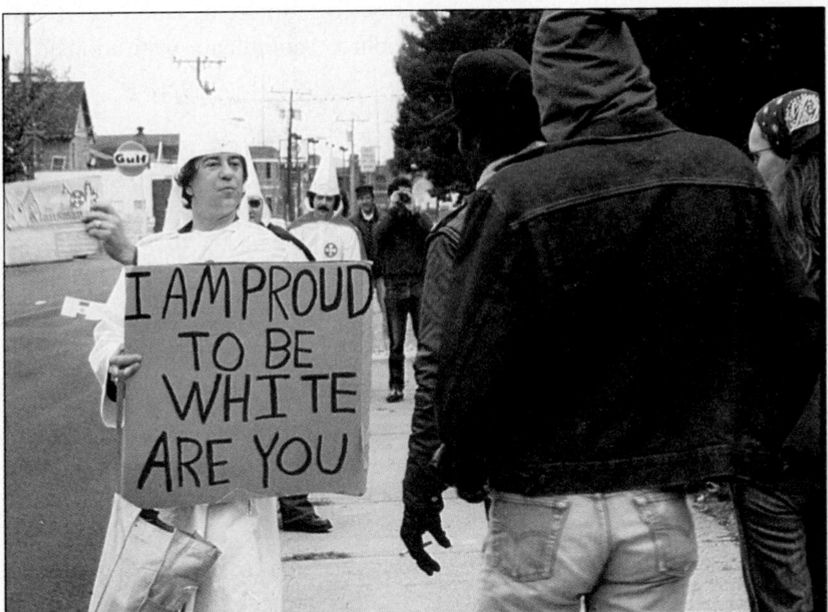

Members of white supremacy groups such as the Ku Klux Klan are rednecked racists; they often use members of subordinate racial and ethnic groups as scapegoats for societal problems over which they have no control.

White supremacist groups are not the only rednecked racists in Canada. Barrett (1987) suggests that the ideology of these right-wing groups may reflect the opinions of other Canadians. A 1988 survey of racist attitudes in Canada found that 19 percent of Canadians agree with "research findings" that assert Orientals superiority to whites, who were, in turn, "found" superior to blacks. In addition, 13 percent of those surveyed indicated they would exclude nonwhite groups from immigrating to Canada; 7 percent would not vote for a black political candidate; and 9 percent would not vote for a Chinese candidate (Henry et al., 1996).

Why does rednecked racism survive? Because this type of racist is not bothered by accusations of racism—in fact they may even boast about such a label. Research suggests, however, that this type of racism is becoming increasingly unacceptable in Canadian society. For this reason, it is being displaced by more subtle but equally destructive forms of racism.

POLITE RACISM Although blatant racial slurs may have been acceptable in the past, few people today will tolerate the open expression of racism. Both the Charter of Rights and Freedoms, as previously mentioned, and human rights legislation (see Box 9.3) have served as legal inhibitors to the expression of racist ideology or active racial discrimination. In Canada, overt acts of discrimination are now illegal. While blatant forms of racism have dissipated to some extent, less obvious expressions of bigotry and stereotyping remain prevalent in our society. Although the Charter and human rights legislation were designed to eliminate racism, they may have had the unintentional effect of "moving racism into the closet." As Fleras and Elliott explain, "Racist slurs ('those kind of people ... ') are now couched in a way that allows us to talk around or disguise our criticism of others by using somewhat more muted (polite) tones" (1996:74). ***Polite racism* is an attempt to disguise a dislike of others through behaviour that appears to be nonprejudicial.** This type of racism may be operating when people of colour are ignored or turned down for jobs or promotions on a regular basis. A number of studies over the past two decades have examined the extent of racial prejudice and discrimination in the workplace. In the well-known study *Who Gets Work?* by Henry and Ginzberg (1984), black and white job seekers with similar job qualifications were sent to apply for entry positions advertised in a major newspaper. An analysis of the results of several hundred applications and interviews revealed that whites received job offers three times more often than did black job applicants. In addition, telephone callers with accents, particularly those from South Asia and the Caribbean, were often screened out when they phoned to inquire about a job vacancy. This study was replicated in 1989 and the findings were much more favourable with blacks slightly favoured in job offers: 20 compared with 18 offers to whites. However, individuals with accents were still more likely to be screened out prior to being selected for an interview (Economic Council of Canada, 1991).

SUBLIMINAL RACISM ***Subliminal racism* involves an unconscious criticism of minorities.** Like passive racism, it is communicated indirectly. However, whereas polite racism involves a conscious attempt to put down minorities, subliminal racism is unintended. For this reason, subliminal racism is sometimes referred to as "democratic racism" (Henry et al., 1995) or "nonracist racism." Subliminal racism is not directly expressed, but is demonstrated in opposition to progressive minority policies (such as Canada's immigration policy) or programs (such as employment equity or affirmative action). For example, refugees are not condemned in blunt racist terminology, but their entry into Canada is viewed as taking unfair advantage of Canada's generosity. The decision by the Royal Canadian Mounted Police (RCMP) to allow Sikh officers to wear turbans while on duty resulted in petitions tabled in the House of Commons, which were signed by 250,000 Canadians and which protested "that a handful of Sikhs wearing turbans would crack up the RCMP" (Henry et al., 1996:136). How so, you ask? The petitioners said they had nothing against Sikhs, but that turbans were "unCanadian," "an affront to majority values," "excessively demanding," and "too costly," among other things. Racist pins and calendars with depictions of turban-clad Mounties began appearing across Canada (Henry et al., 1996).

Subliminal racism, more than any other type of racism, demonstrates an ambiguity concerning racism. For example, a national survey conducted in 1993 for the Canadian Council of Christians and Jews found that while Canadians generally saw themselves as tolerant of other cultures and races, three-quarters believed that racism was a serious problem in Canada. At the same time three-quarters of the 1200 respondents rejected the concept of multiculturalism, and half agreed with the statement: "I am sick and tired of some groups complaining about racism being directed at them." In addition, 41 percent agreed with the description of themselves as "tired of ethnic minorities being given special treatment" (Henry et al., 1996:138). Values that support racial equality are publicly affirmed, while at the same time there is resentment at the prospect of moving over and making space for newcomers is also present. Subliminal racism enables individuals to maintain two apparently conflicting values—one rooted in the egalitarian virtues of justice and fairness, the other in beliefs that result in resentment and selfishness (Fleras and Elliott, 1996).

INSTITUTIONALIZED RACISM ***Institutionalized racism* is made up of the rules, procedures, and practices that directly and deliberately prevent minorities from having full and equal involvement in society.** These actions are routinely carried out by a number of dominant group members based on the norms of the immediate organization or community (Feagin and Feagin, 1993). In a recent class-action lawsuit against an international restaurant chain, Robert Norton, a former manager, made this statement:

> I am a white male formerly employed as a manager with Denny's restaurants ... While employed with Denny's I was instructed by my district manager to implement policies designed to limit or discourage black patronage.

> Instructions on policies applied to black customers were given at district meetings and, to a greater degree, individually at the restaurants by district managers ... During these meetings the term "blackout" was used on many occasions in the presence of district and regional managers ... In time, I heard the term with enough frequency to learn that "blackout" was used by Denny's management to refer to a situation where too many black customers were in the restaurant.
>
> At district meetings ... we were taught to avoid blackouts by requiring black customers to pay for their meals in advance or simply close the restaurant for a few hours when we started getting too many black customers. (quoted in Labaton, 1994:E4)

These practices of direct institutional racism were built into the organization's procedures and conveyed to employees for implementation. Although in that lawsuit a large out-of-court settlement was reached (*New York Times*, 1993b), discrimination such as this continues (see also Feagin and Vera, 1995).

In 1991, the Canadian Civil Liberties Association (CCLA) examined institutionalized discrimination in employment agencies. The CCLA randomly selected agencies in four cities in Ontario and asked whether the agencies would agree to refer only white people for the jobs that needed to be filled. Eleven of the fifteen agencies surveyed agreed to accept discriminatory job orders. The following are examples of the agencies' responses:

> It is discrimination, but it can be done discreetly without anyone knowing. No problem with that.
>
> That's no problem. It's between you and me. I don't tell anyone; you don't tell anyone.
>
> You are paying to see the people you want to see.
>
> Absolutely—definitely ... that request is pretty standard here.
>
> That's not a problem. Appearance means a lot, whether it's colour or overweight people. (quoted in Henry et al., 1996:142)

What happens in actual cases of agencies using such discriminatory employment practices? Recently a complaint laid with the Ontario Human Rights Commission against two employment agencies in Toronto drew public attention to this issue. A settlement was reached in which the agencies agreed to develop policies against accepting discriminatory job requests, and employees received training in race relations and employment equity.

Research now suggests that minorities are much less likely to be directly victimized by blatant institutional racism. Institutions can no longer openly discriminate against minorities without attracting legal sanctions, negative publicity, or consumer resistance (Fleras and Elliott, 1996). However, as the previous examples demonstrate, institutional racism continues to exist.

SYSTEMIC RACISM ***Systemic racism* refers to practices that have a harmful impact on subordinate group members even though the organizationally prescribed norms or regulations guiding these actions initially were established with no intent to harm.** Systemic racism is entrenched in the structure (rules, organization), function (norms, goals), and process (procedures) of many social institutions. These institutions may have standards that have the unintended effect of excluding members of minority groups (Fleras and Elliott, 1996). For example, occupations such as police officer and firefighter had minimum weight, height, and educational requirements for job applicants. These criteria resulted in discrimination because they favoured white applicants over members of many minority groups, as well as males over females. Though valid reasons may have existed for imposing these restrictions, these criteria remain unfair and exclusionary. Other examples of systemic racism include the requirement of a college or university degree for nonspecialized jobs, employment regulations that require people to work on their Sabbath, and the policy of only recognizing university degrees and trade diplomas obtained in North America.

Systemic racism (as well as other forms of systemic discrimination) is normally reflected in statistical underrepresentation of certain groups within an institution or organization. For example, a given group may represent 15 percent of the general population but only 2 percent of those promoted to upper management positions in a large company. Efforts to eliminate this kind of disproportionate representation are the focus of employment equity legislation. The target groups for employment equity in Canada are visible minorities, women, persons with disabilities, and aboriginal peoples. Strategies may include modified admissions tests and requirements, enhanced recruitment of certain target groups, establishment of hiring quotas for particular minority groups, or specialized training or employment programs for specific target groups. The most recent analysis of employment equity programs indicates that these programs have had the most significant effect on women and aboriginal peoples, while people with disabilities have made the fewest gains. As for members of visible minorities, although they have higher levels of education on average than do other Canadians and very high labour force participation rates, they continue to be concentrated in low-status, low-paying occupations (Henry et al., 1996). It is important to note that effects of systemic discrimination on specific visible minority groups in Canada vary substantially, with blacks experiencing the greatest disadvantage in income and Asian groups, the least (Boyd, 1992). Table 9.2 outlines the different forms of racism.

THEORETICAL EXPLANATIONS OF PREJUDICE, DISCRIMINATION, AND RACISM

How do people's prejudices develop? Is prejudice a personality characteristic of a select number of individuals or can entire groups or societies collectively display prejudice? Psychologists and sociologists have addressed these questions in their attempts to explain conflicts between groups.

SCAPEGOAT THEORY Are some people more prejudiced than others? To answer this question, some theories focus on how individuals may transfer their internal psychological problems onto an external object or person (Feagin and Feagin, 1993).

The *frustration-aggression hypothesis* states that people who are frustrated in their efforts to achieve a highly desired goal will respond with a pattern of aggression toward others (Dollard et al., 1939). The object of their aggression becomes the ***scapegoat*—a person or group that is incapable of offering resistance to the hostility or aggression of others** (Marger, 1994). Scapegoats often are used as substitutes for the actual source of the frustration. For example, members of subordinate racial and ethnic groups often are blamed for societal problems (such as unemployment or an economic recession) over which they have no control.

SOCIAL LEARNING According to some interactionists, prejudice results from *social learning*; in other words, it is learned from observing and imitating significant others, such as parents and peers. Initially, children do not have a frame of reference from which to question the prejudices of their relatives and friends. When they are rewarded with smiles or laughs for telling derogatory jokes or making negative comments about outgroup members, children's prejudiced attitudes may be reinforced. In the following commentary, a university student discusses how his prejudices were developed:

> I don't fancy myself as a redneck who goes around killing Blacks à la KKK, nor do I participate in Gay-bashing or any other type of physical outbursts aimed at any particular race or ethnic group. Where I am prejudiced is through all the stereotypes. Women and

TABLE 9.2

The Faces of Racism

	What: Core Slogan	Why: Degree of Intent	How: Style of Expression	Where: Magnitude and Scope	When: Locus of Expression
Rednecked Racism	"X get out!"	conscious	personal and explicit	personal	interpersonal
Polite Racism	"Sorry, the job is taken."	moderate	discreet and subtle	personal	interpersonal
Subliminal Racism	"I'm not racist, but ..."	ambivalent	oblique	cultural	value conflicts
Institutional Racism	"X need not apply."	deliberate	blatant	institutional	rewards and entitlements
Systemic Racism	"We treat everyone the same here."	unintentional	impersonal	societal	rules and procedures

Source: Fleras and Elliott, 1996, 84.

> Chinese people can't drive. Pakistanis smell bad. Blacks are thieves and smell bad. Italians either build houses or kill people for a living.
>
> Most of these stereotypes were fed to me over time by my parents and my older brother. I didn't know what the word stereotype meant then. I took these "phrases of wisdom" as truths and they altered my view of people. Prejudice is learned, not instinctive. (James, 1995:60)

AUTHORITARIAN PERSONALITY Do some people have personality patterns that predispose them to prejudice? In the late 1940s, psychologist Theodore W. Adorno and his colleagues (1950) tried to answer this question.

Adorno tested his subjects on three dimensions: fascism, ethnocentrism, and anti-semitism. The findings indicated that people whose scores on any one of the dimensions were high also tended to have high scores on the others. In other words, if someone was prejudiced against Jews, they were also likely to be prejudiced against other minority groups, to favour strong authoritarian leadership (fascism), and to view their cultural traditions and norms as superior to all others.

Adorno concluded that highly prejudiced individuals tend to have an ***authoritarian personality*****, which is characterized by excessive conformity, submissiveness to authority, intolerance, insecurity, a high level of superstition, a propensity for stereotyping, and rigid thinking** (Adorno et al., 1950). This personality, more-

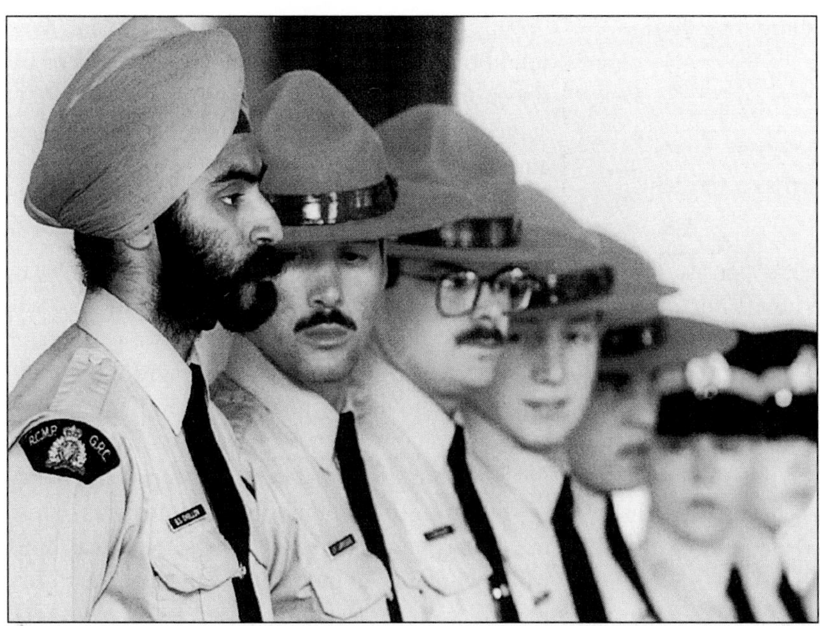

The decision by the RCMP to allow Sikh officers to wear turbans in uniform resulted in subliminal racism. Racist pins and calendars with turban-clad mounties appeared across Canada, and 250,000 Canadians signed a petition protesting that the turbans were "unCanadian."

over, is most likely to develop in a family environment in which dominating parents who are anxious about status use physical discipline but show very little love in raising their children (Adorno et al., 1950). Other scholars have linked prejudiced attitudes to traits such as being submissive to authority, extreme anger toward outgroups, and conservative religious and political beliefs (Altemeyer, 1981, 1988; Weigel and Howes, 1985).

CULTURAL THEORY OF PREJUDICE Can prejudice be a cultural trait? Do Canadians have ethnic or racial prejudices? Berry, Kalin, and Taylor found that most Canadians, whatever their ethnic origin, tend to have a positive perception and a positive attitude toward the two charter groups—French and English Canadians (1977). These groups seem to serve as a model to other ethnic groups as to what it means to be a Canadian. In other words, Canadians are prejudiced in favour of the charter groups (Rosenburg, 1995). How do Canadians feel about other ethnic groups?

Emory Bogardus (1968) studied the effects of culturally rooted prejudices on interpersonal relationships and developed the concept of social distance to measure levels of prejudice. ***Social distance*** **refers to the extent to which people are willing to interact and establish relationships with members of racial and ethnic groups other than their own** (Park and Burgess, 1921). Bogardus (1925, 1968) developed a scale to measure social distance in specific situations. Using the scale, he asked respondents to answer yes or no to the following seven questions with regard to members of various racial and ethnic groups:

1. I would marry or accept as a close relative.
2. I would accept as a close friend.
3. I would accept as a next-door neighbour.
4. I would accept in my school or church.

5. I would accept in my community but would not have contact with.
6. I would accept as a resident of my country but not in my community.
7. I would not accept at all even as a resident of my country.

He found that some groups were consistently ranked as more desirable than others for close interpersonal contact. More recently, analysts have found that whites who accept racial stereotypes desire greater social distance from people of colour than do whites who reject negative stereotypes (Krysan and Farley, 1993). While the Bogardus social distance scale has been used in numerous studies around the world, use of the scale for social distance research in Canada has been limited. Driedger and Mezoff's 1981 study of students in nine Winnipeg high school found that students were much more willing to marry persons of European than of non-European origin (see Table 9.3). In other words, these students made racial distinctions between whites and nonwhites in their marriage preferences. The students also made social distance distinctions within the European category. The high school students were three times more willing to marry Americans than Jews. A small number of the students demonstrated extreme prejudice in their wishes to prohibit certain groups from entering Canada. About 2 percent of students were in favour of excluding the Dutch and blacks, while 11 percent wished to restrict Jews. The restriction of Jews appeared to be based on religious or ethnic prejudice (Driedger, 1996). In a second study Driedger (1982) used the social distance scale to measure prejudice among University of Manitoba students. Seventy-five percent of the students surveyed indicated that they were willing to either marry or be a close friend of persons in each of the twenty groups. Very few students desired only minimal contact with other groups. Almost none wanted to ban others from Canada. However, once again, more than half of the students were willing to marry into groups of European origin, while only one-quarter were willing to marry into groups of non-European origin. Scholars have found that increased contact may have little or no effect on existing prejudices and, in some circumstances, can even lead to an increase in prejudice and conflict.

CONFLICT PERPECTIVES Conflict theorists focus on economic stratification and access to power in their analyses of race and ethnic relations. According to conflict theories, prejudice is a product of social conflict among competing groups. Prejudice is used to justify the oppression of minorities.

The Split-Labour-Market Theory Who benefits from the exploitation of minorities? Dual or split-labour-market theory states that both white workers and members of the capitalist class benefit from the exploitation of minorities. ***Split labour market*** **refers to the division of the economy into two areas of employment, a primary sector or upper tier, composed of higher-paid (usually dominant group) workers in more secure jobs, and a secondary sector or lower tier, made up of lower-paid (often subordinate group) workers in jobs with little security and hazardous working conditions** (Bonacich, 1972, 1976). According to this perspective, white workers in the upper tier may use racial discrimination against nonwhites to protect their positions. These actions most often occur when upper-tier workers feel threatened by lower-tier workers hired by capitalists to reduce labour costs and maximize corporate profits. In the past, immigrants were a source of cheap labour that employers could use to break strikes and keep wages down. Agnes Calliste (1987) applied the split-labour-market theory in her study, "Sleeping Car Porters In Canada." Calliste found a doubly submerged split labour market, with three levels of stratification in this area of employment. While "white" trade unions were unable to restrict access to porter positions on the basis of race, they were able to impose differential pay scales. Consequently, black porters received less pay than white porters, even though they were doing the same work. Furthermore, the labour market was doubly

TABLE 9.3

Degrees-of-Distance-from-others Preferences of Winnipeg High-School Students

Ethnic Groups[a]		Marry	Have as Close Friend	Have as Neighbour	Work with on Job	Have as Acquaintance	Have as Visitor Only	Debar From Nation
		Social Distance Scale (Bogardus) Willingness to: Percentages						
European origin	American	75	14	5	2	2	2	2
	British	65	20	6	4	2	3	1
	Scandinavian	56	24	8	6	3	2	1
	Dutch	53	25	11	5	4	1[b]	1
	Polish	51	26	9	6	4	2	2
	Ukrainian	50	28	9	6	4	2	2
	French	50	24	9	6	6	2	5
	German	48	25	11	7	4	3	2
	Italian	44	28	10	7	6	3	3
	Russian	41	27	11	7	6	3	5
	Jewish	28	34	12	7	9	4	7
Non-European Origin	Negro (Black)	29	49	11	6	3	1	1
	Mexican (Hispanic)	29	37	14	8	6	4	1
	Japanese	26	44	14	7	6	2	2
	Filipino	26	40	13	9	6	4	2
	Chinese	25	45	13	7	5	2	2
	West Indian	23	43	13	9	8	3	3
	Indo-Pakistani	23	42	13	10	8	3	2
	Aboriginal	22	41	10	10	10	3	4
	Eskimo (Inuit)	19	45	13	10	8	3	2

[a] Ingroup evaluations were deleted (e.g., the British in the sample did not evaluate their own group).
[b] The Ns in any one cell never dropped below 20.

Source: Leo Driedger, *Multi-Ethnic Canada*. Toronto: Oxford University Press, 1996, p. 266. Reprinted with permission.

submerged because black immigrant workers from the United States received even less pay than both black and white Canadian porters. Throughout history, higher-paid workers have responded with racial hostility and joined movements to curtail immigration and thus do away with the source of cheap labour (Marger, 1994).

Proponents of the split-labour-market theory suggest that white workers benefit from racial and ethnic antagonisms. However, these analysts typi-

BOX 9.3 SOCIOLOGY AND LAW

Human Rights Legislation in Action

Human rights legislation is grounded on the premise that all human beings are full and equal persons. As such, all persons have a fundamental right to life and freedom, equality, and dignity in all life pursuits. What legal recourse do individuals have who experience a violation of these basic human rights? How effective is present human rights legislation in curtailing these violations? These questions can be addressed by examining of legal cases that have been brought forward by minority claimants under the provisions of human rights legislation in Canada.

In the first example, a claim of racial discrimination was made against a Victoria restaurant and the Victoria police by a black citizen of Canada. The complainant, born in St. Vincent, holds master's degrees from two Canadian universities and works as a health coordinator in British Columbia. While visiting Victoria, the complainant, a registered guest at a motor inn, went into the restaurant at the inn and sat down at the only available table. All other tables were occupied by nonblack patrons. He placed his order with a waiter, but within five minutes was informed by a waitress that he would have to move so that she could seat two other persons at his table. He refused to move because he could see no other table available and because he had not, as yet, received his order. The police were called. Victoria police questioned him about his citizenship, threatened him with deportation, searched and handcuffed him, and then took him to jail and locked him up for eight hours. The complainant brought his case to the B.C. Human Rights Council, which found that the only reasonable inference that could be drawn was that the complainant was the subject of racial discrimination. The complainant was awarded $2000 for humiliation, embarrassment, and damage to his self-respect in the settlement of his claim against both the restaurant and the police. Do you think the amount awarded is sufficient compensation for the harm done in this case? Do you think this amount will deter future racist actions on the part of the organizations sanctioned? If not, what do you think an appropriate settlement would be?

This case demonstrates that under human rights legislation the employer (the restaurant) is held responsible for the discriminatory acts of employees. In other words, what appeared to be a case of individual discrimination or racism was treated as an act of institutional racism. Thus, the onus is on those who control organizations to ensure that their employees respect the human rights of all persons. Do you agree?

A second and somewhat parallel case involves a claim filed with the Canadian Human Rights Commission that alleged institutional discrimination on the part of the RCMP. A Chinese Canadian, who was born in Halifax, filed a complaint of racial discrimination under the (federal) Canadian Human Rights Act, because an RCMP officer, who had stopped him for a driving offence, asked him whether he was a Canadian citizen and whether he was born in Canada. An internal RCMP investigation following the lodging of the complaint revealed that the RCMP officer in question customarily interrogated members of visible ethnic minorities in the same way when he stopped them for speeding. The commission found that the officer's action was not an isolated case, but represented accepted RCMP practice. The commission concluded that the RCMP discriminated against suspects on the basis of racial origin and that such discrimination was unjustifiable. The commission ordered the RCMP to cease the practice in question and to issue a directive to this effect to all members of the force. The commission also recommended that the RCMP provide educational instruction to members of the force on the right to equal treatment of citizens from visible minorities. The RCMP was ordered to pay the complainant $250 for hurt and affront to dignity. What do you think of the penalty in this case?

Source: Adapted with permission from Kallen, 1991.

cally do not examine the interactive effects of race, class, and gender in the workplace.

RECENT PERSPECTIVES FOCUSING ON RACE AND GENDER The term *gendered racism* refers to the interactive effect of racism and sexism in the exploitation of women of colour. According to social psychologist Philomena Essed (1991), women's particular position must be explored within each racial or ethnic group, because their experiences will not have been the same as the men's in each grouping.

All workers are not equally exploited by capitalists. Gender and race or ethnicity are important in this exploitation. For example, jobs are race-typed and gender-typed. Consider a registered nurse and a custodian in a hospital. What race and gender are they likely to be? Did a white woman and a man of colour come to mind? Most jobs have similar race and gender designations. Often, the jobs people hold are linked to their class, race, and gender. Consequently, the effect of class on our life changes is inseparable from the effects of our gender and race or ethnicity. The split labour market, then, involves not only class but also race, ethnicity, and gender (Amott and Matthaei, 1991). Historically, the high-paying primary labour market has been monopolized by white men. People of colour and most white women more often hold lower-tier jobs. Below that tier is the underground sector of the economy, characterized by illegal or quasi-legal activities such as drug trafficking, prostitution, and working in sweatshops that do not meet minimum wage and safety standards. Many undocumented workers and some white women and people of colour attempt to earn a living in this sector (Amott and Matthaei, 1991).

PATTERNS OF INTERACTION BETWEEN RACIAL AND ETHNIC GROUPS

When racially or ethnically different groups come into sustained contact with one another, patterns of interaction evolve. Race and ethnic relations may follow many different patterns ranging from harmonious co-existence to outright conflict or cultural annihilation. Box 9.4 discusses global conflicts between different racial/ethnic groups.

ASSIMILATION ***Assimilation* is a process by which members of subordinate racial and ethnic groups become absorbed into the dominant culture.** To some analysts, assimilation is functional because it contributes to the stability of society by minimizing group differences that otherwise might result in hostility and violence (Gordon, 1964).

Assimilation occurs at several distinct levels, including the cultural, structural, biological, and psychological levels. *Cultural assimilation*, or *acculturation*, occurs when members of an ethnic group adopt dominant group traits, such as language, dress, values, religion, and food preferences. Cultural assimilation in this country initially followed an "Anglo-conformity" model; members of subordinate ethnic groups were expected to conform to the culture of the dominant white Anglo-Saxon population (Gordon, 1964). However, some groups such as native peoples and the Québécois have refused to be assimilated and are struggling to maintain their unique cultural identity.

Structural assimilation, or *integration*, occurs when members of subordinate racial or ethnic groups gain acceptance in everyday social interaction with members of the dominant group. This type of assimilation typically starts in large, impersonal settings such as schools and workplaces and only later (if at all) results in close friendships and intermarriage. *Biological assimilation*, or *amalgamation*, occurs when members of one group marry those of other social or ethnic groups. Biological assimilation has been more complete in some other countries, such as Mexico and Brazil, than in Canada.

Psychological assimilation involves a change in racial or ethnic self-identification on the part of an individual. Rejection by the dominant group may prevent psychological assimilation by members of some subordinate racial and ethnic groups, especially those with visible characteris-

BOX 9.4 SOCIOLOGY IN GLOBAL PERSPECTIVE

Worldwide Racial and Ethnic Conflicts in the 21st Century

Throughout the world, many racial and ethnic groups are seeking self-determination—the right to choose their own way of life. As many nations currently are structured, however, self-determination is impossible.

The cost of the struggle for self-determination is the loss of life and property in ethnic warfare. In recent years, the Cold War has given way to dozens of small wars over ethnic dominance. In Europe, for example, ethnic violence has persisted in Bosnia-Herzegovina, Croatia, Spain, Britain (between the Protestant majority and the Catholic minority in Northern Ireland), Romania, Russia, Moldova, and Georgia. Hundreds of thousands of people have died from warfare, disease (such as the cholera epidemic in war-torn Rwanda), and refugee migration.

Ethnic wars exact a high price even for survivors, whose life chances can become bleaker even after the violence subsides. In the ethnic conflict between Abkhazians and Georgians in the former Soviet Union, for example, as many as two thousand people have been killed and over eighty thousand displaced. Ironically, the Abkhazians previously had been known for their longevity and good mental health—many live into their nineties or more, possibly because of their healthy lifestyle and positive attitudes toward aging (Benet, 1971). More recently, ethnic war has devastated Chechnya, an area that attempted to secede from Russia despite Russia's claim of sovereignty. Such ethnic wars likely will continue into the twenty-first century (Bonner, 1994).

Not all analysts view the future this bleakly. Some predict that nations including Canada, the United States, Great Britain, Japan, and Germany will suppress ethnic violence with the assistance of the United Nations, which will serve a peacekeeping function by monitoring and enforcing agreements between rival factions (Binder, 1993).

Conflict between Protestants and Catholics in Northern Ireland has continued for hundreds of years. Here, Londonderry Protestants approach the Catholic Bogside neighbourhood as tensions rose in August 1996.

Caribana parade marchers exemplify the concept of ethnic pluralism—maintaining their distinct identity even as they share in many elements of mainstream culture.

tics such as skin colour or facial features that differ from those of the dominant group.

ETHNIC PLURALISM Instead of complete assimilation, many groups share elements of the mainstream culture while remaining culturally distinct from both the dominant group and other social and ethnic groups. ***Ethnic pluralism* is the co-existence of a variety of distinct racial and ethnic groups within one society.**

Equalitarian pluralism, or *accommodation*, is a situation in which ethnic groups co-exist in equality with one another. Switzerland has been described as a model of equalitarian pluralism; over 6 million people with French, German, and Italian cultural heritages peacefully co-exist there (Simpson and Yinger, 1972).

Has Canada achieved equalitarian pluralism? The Canadian Multiculturalism Act of 1988 stated that "[A]ll Canadians are full and equal partners in Canadian society." The Department of Multiculturalism and Citizenship was established in 1991 with the goal of encouraging ethnic minorities to participate fully in all aspects of Canadian life and at the same time maintain their distinct ethnic identities and cultural practices. The objective of multiculturalism is to "promote unity through diversity." Multiculturalism programs provide funding for education, consultative support, and a range of activities including heritage language training, race relations training, ethnic policing and justice, and ethnic celebrations. In recent years multiculturalism policies have been under increasing attack. Neil Bissoondath, author of *Selling Illusions: The Cult of Multiculturalism in Canada* (1994), suggests that multiculturalism does not promote equalitarian pluralism. Rather, he argues, multiculturalism is divisive, and says that it ghettoizes visible minorities, fosters racial animosity, and detracts from national unity. Bissoondath further maintains that a policy of multiculturalism emphasizes our differences rather than our similarities as Canadians. In a 1995 survey 66 percent of respondents disagreed with the following statement: "The government should provide funding to ethnic groups so that they can protect their traditions and language." On the other hand, 20 percent agreed with it; and 14 percent were undecided (Dyck, 1996:199).

INTERNAL COLONIALISM Conflict theorists use the term ***internal colonization*** **to refer to a situation in which members of a racial or ethnic group are conquered or colonized and forcibly placed under the economic and political control of the dominant group.** Groups that have been subjected to internal colonialism remain in subordinate positions longer than groups that voluntarily migrated to Canada.

Native peoples in Canada were colonized by Europeans and others who invaded their lands and conquered them. In the process, natives lost property, political rights, aspects of their culture, and often their lives (Blauner, 1972). The capitalist class acquired cheap labour and land through this government-sanctioned racial exploitation (Blauner, 1972). The effects of past internal colonialism are reflected today in the number of native people who live on government reservations.

The experiences of internally colonized groups are unique in three ways: (1) they have been forced to exist in a society other than their own; (2) they have been kept out of the economic and political mainstream, so that it is difficult for them to compete with dominant group members; and (3) they have been subjected to severe attacks on their own culture, which may lead to its extinction (Blauner, 1972).

SEGREGATION Segregation, exists when specific ethnic groups are set apart from the dominant group and have unequal access to power and privilege (Marger, 1994). ***Segregation*** **is the spatial and social separation of categories of people by race, ethnicity, class, gender, and/or religion.** Segregation may be enforced by law (*de jure*) or by custom (*de facto*). An example of de jure segregation was the *Jim Crow laws*, which legalized the separation of the races in all public accommodations (including hotels, restaurants, transportation, hospitals, jails, schools, churches, and cemeteries) in the southern United States after the Civil War (Feagin and Feagin, 1993). Segregation denied African Americans access to opportunities in many areas, including education, jobs, health care, and politics.

De jure segregation of blacks is also part of the history of Canada. Blacks in Canada lived in largely segregated communities in Nova Scotia, New Brunswick, and Ontario where racial segregation was evident in the schools, government, the workplace, residential housing, and elsewhere. Segregated schools continued in Nova Scotia until the 1960s. Residential segregation was legally enforced through the use of racially restrictive convenants attached to deeds and leases. Separation and refusal of service were common in restaurants, theatres, and recreational facilities (Henry et al., 1995). Sociologist Adrienne Shadd describes her experience of growing up in North Buxton, Ontario, in the 1950s and 1960s:

> When we would go into the local ice cream parlour, the man behind the counter would serve us last, after all the Whites had been served, even if they came into the shop after us. Southwestern Ontario may as well have been below the Mason-Dixon line in those days. Dresden, home of the historic Uncle Tom's cabin, made national headlines in 1954 when Blacks tested the local restaurants after the passage of the Fair Accommodation Practices Act and found that two openly refused to serve them. This came as no surprise, given that for years certain eateries, hotels, and recreational clubs were restricted to us, and at one time Blacks could only sit in designated sections of movie theatres (usually the balcony) if admitted at all. (Shadd, 1991:1)

One of the most blatant examples of segregation in Canada is the federal government reserve system for status Indians, by which native peoples were segregated on reserves in remote areas.

Although legally sanctioned forms of racial segregation have been all but eliminated, de facto segregation, which is enforced by custom, still exists.

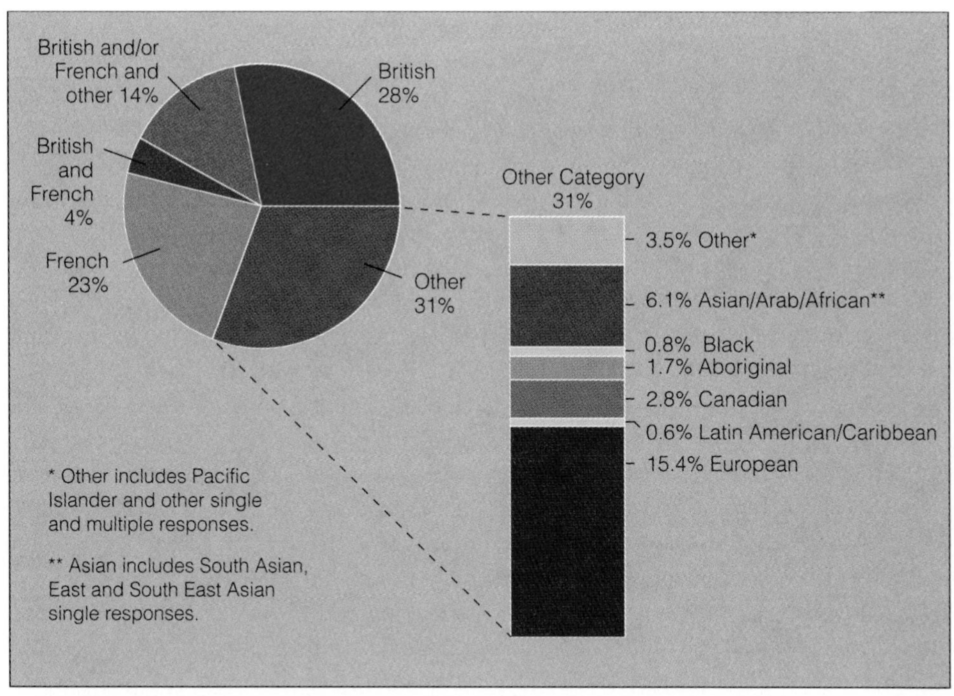

FIGURE 9.2

Percentage Distribution of Population by Ethnic Origin, Canada, 1991

Source: Reproduced by authority of the Minister of Industry, 1996, Statistics Canada, from *Canada's Changing Immigrant Population*, Cat. no. 96-311E, 1991.

GENOCIDE ***Genocide* is the deliberate, systematic killing of an entire people or nation** (Schaefer, 1993:23). It occurs when people are considered to be unworthy to live because of their race or ethnicity. Examples of genocide include the killing of thousands of native Americans by white settlers in North America and the extermination of six million European Jews, known as the Holocaust, in Nazi Germany. In other instances, approximately two million people were slaughtered in the "killing fields" of Cambodia between 1975 and 1980 and in 1994 more than 500,000 children, women, and men were brutally killed in Rwanda in what has been described as *mass genocide*. More recently, the term *ethnic cleansing* has been used to define a policy of "cleansing" geographic areas (as in Bosnia-Herzegovina) by forcing persons of other races or religions to flee—or die (Schaefer, 1995).

ETHNIC GROUPS IN CANADA

At the turn of the century, the Canadian population was predominantly made up of French Canadians (30.7 percent) and British Canadians (57 percent). As Figure 9.2 indicates, in 1991 approximately one-third of Canada's population claimed ethnic origins other than French or British. Given the diversity of our population, imposing any kind of conceptual order on a discussion of ethnic groups in Canada is difficult. A detailed historical account of the unique experiences of each group is beyond the scope of this chapter (see Driedger, 1996). Instead, we will look briefly at some of the unique ethnic groups in Canada. In the process, we will examine a brief history of racism with respect to each group.

FIRST NATIONS

Canada's native peoples are believed to have migrated to North America from Asia an estimated 40,000 years ago (Dyck, 1996). Native peoples are an extremely diverse group. Today, the term *native*, *First Nations*, or *aboriginal* refers to approximately fifty-five sovereign peoples including the Inuit, Cree, Micmac, Blackfoot, Iroquois, and Haida. Other categories of native peoples are status Indians (those Indians with legal rights under the Indian Act), nonstatus Indians (those without legal rights), Métis, and Inuit. Those who settled in the southern part of Canada, the Yukon, and the Mackenzie Valley, can be termed *North American Indians*. Those located in the eastern Arctic and northern islands, who were formerly referred to as Eskimos, are now referred to as *Inuit*. A third category, *Métis*, who mostly live on the Prairies, are descendants of Indian and non-Indian unions (primarily French settlers and Indian women).

When European settlers (or invaders) arrived on this continent, the native inhabitants' way of life was changed forever. Experts estimate that between one and twelve million natives lived in North America at this time; however, their numbers had been reduced to less than 240,000 by 1900 (Churchill, 1994). What factors led to this drastic depopulation?

GENOCIDE, FORCED MIGRATION, AND FORCED ASSIMILATION Native people have been the victims of genocide and forced migration. Many native Americans either were massacred or died from European diseases (such as typhoid, smallpox, and measles) and starvation (Wagner and Stearn, 1945; Cook, 1973). In battle, native people often were no match for the Europeans, who had the latest weaponry (Amott and Matthaei, 1991). Europeans justified their aggression by stereotyping the natives as "savages" and "heathens" (Takaki, 1993).

Entire nations were forced to move in order to accommodate the white settlers. The "Trail of Tears" was one of the most disastrous of the forced migrations to occur in the United States. In the coldest part of the winter of 1832, over half of the Cherokee Nation died during or as a result of their forced relocation from the southeastern United States to the Indian Territory in Oklahoma (Thornton, 1984). The colonization of the native population was far less brutal in Canada than in the United States. However, as Weinfeld comments, "It is not clear whether this more benign conquest left aboriginals in Canada any better off than their counterparts in the United States in the long run" (1995:4.8).

The relations between native people and the newcomers in Canada were governed by treaties. Indian rights were clearly defined in the Royal Proclamation of 1763, which divided up the territory acquired by Britain. In a large area called Indian Territory, the purchase or settlement of land was forbidden without a treaty. This is sometimes called the principle of "voluntary cession" (Dyck, 1996:154). Scholars note that the government broke treaty after treaty as it engaged in a policy of wholesale removal of indigenous nations in order to clear the land for settlement by Anglo-Saxon "pioneers" (Green, 1977; Churchill, 1994). The 1867 Constitution Act gave jurisdiction over Indians and lands reserved for the Indians to the federal government. The Canadian government then passed the Indian Act of 1876, which provided for federal government control of almost every aspect of Indian life. According to Frances Henry and her colleagues, this Act "introduced institutionalized racism in the relationship between Canada and its aboriginal peoples that continues to flourish today" (1996:60). The regulations under the Act included prohibitions against owning land, voting, and purchasing and consuming alcohol. Later provisions prevented native people from leaving reserves without permission and a ticket from the agent (Bolaria and Li, 1988).

The Indian Act was designed to promote assimilation; native peoples were to adopt the cultural attitudes and norms of the dominant culture and give up their own cultural traditions (including their values, customs, and language). For example, the Indian Act outlawed the Potlatch ceremony, which provided a central organizing framework in which new leaders were installed, wealth was distributed, names were given and recorded, political councils were held and decisions made, history instruction was provided and spiritual guidance was given. (Henry et al., 1996)

Native American children were placed in residential boarding schools to facilitate their assimilation into the dominant culture. The Jesuits and other missionaries who ran these schools believed that aboriginal peoples should not be left in their "inferior" natural state and considered it their mission to replace aboriginal culture with Christian beliefs, values, rituals, and practices (Bolaria and Li, 1988). Many native children who attended these schools were sexually, physically, and emotionally abused. They were not allowed to speak their language or engage in any of their traditional cultural practices. The coercive and oppressive nature of this educational experience is one of the most blatant examples of institutionalized racism (Henry et al., 1996:62). The Indian Act institutionalized the reserve system and divided native people into two categories by law: status Indians and nonstatus Indians. *Status Indians*—people legally defined as Indians—include treaty Indians and registered Indians outside treaty areas, are registered on band lists held by the Department of Indian Affairs. *Nonstatus Indians* have Indian ancestry but not legal status, as a result of either intermarriage with whites or of abandoning their legal status. Many native peoples today reject these legal distinctions as artificially imposed by European colonizers and their laws (Weinfeld, 1995).

NATIVE PEOPLES TODAY Currently more than one million native people live in Canada. Table 9.4 indicates specifically how this population breaks down.

There are several native Indian tribal groups, living in nearly 600 bands. Although the majority of registered Indians live on reserves, the majority of the total aboriginal population live off reserves. The native population is unevenly distributed across Canada, with the heaviest concentrations of aboriginal Canadians in western and northern Canada, as Table 9.5 indicates.

TABLE 9.4

Native Peoples in Canada, 1993

Status Indians on reserve	**326,444**
Status Indians off reserve	226,872
Nonstatus Indians	405,000
Métis	192,100
Inuit	50,800
	1,201,216

Source: Dyck, 1996.

As discussed in Chapter 8, native peoples are the most disadvantaged racial or ethnic group in Canada in terms of income, employment, housing, nutrition, and health. The life chances of native peoples who live on reservations are especially limited. They have the highest rates of infant mortality and death by exposure and malnutrition. They also have high rates of tuberculosis, alcoholism, and suicide. The overall life expectancy of aboriginal Canadians is ten years shorter than that of non-natives; this is largely due to poor health services and inadequate housing on reserves (Dyck, 1996). Native peoples also have had very limited educational opportunities (the functional illiteracy of aboriginal peoples is 45 percent compared with the overall Canadian rate of 17 percent) and they have a very high rate of unemployment (their jobless rate averages nearly 70 percent) (Henry et al., 1996).

In spite of the odds against them, many native peoples resist oppression. National organizations like the Assembly of First Nations, Inuit Tapirisat, the Native Council of Canada, and the Métis National Council have been instrumental in bringing the demands of those they represent into the

TABLE 9.5

Distribution by Province and Territory of Those Reporting Aboriginal Origins, 1991

	North American Indian	Métis	Inuit	Total	Percent of Provincial Population	Percent of Aboriginal Canadians
Newfoundland	5 840	1 605	6 455	13 100	2.3%	1.3%
P.E.I.	1 670	190	80	1 885	1.5%	0.2%
Nova Scotia	19 950	1 590	770	21 885	2.4%	2.2%
New Brunswick	11 830	980	445	12 820	1.8%	1.3%
Quebec	112 590	19 475	8 485	137 615	2.0%	13.7%
Ontario	220 140	26 905	5 245	243 555	2.4%	24.3%
Manitoba	76 370	45 575	900	116 195	10.6%	11.6%
Saskatchewan	69 385	32 840	540	96 580	9.8%	9.6%
Alberta	99 655	56 310	2 820	148 220	5.8%	14.8%
British Columbia	149 565	22 295	1 990	169 035	5.2%	16.9%
Yukon	5 870	565	170	6 358	23.0%	0.6%
N.W.T.	11 100	4 315	21 355	35 390	61.4%	3.5%
Total	783 980	212 650	49 260	1 002 675	3.7%	100%

*Note: Data obtained from the Department of Indian and Northern Affairs reported a higher number of aboriginal people in 1993.

Reproduced by authority of the Minister of Industry, 1996, Statistics Canada, from *Profile of Canadian Aboriginal Population,* Cat. no. 94-325, 1995.

political and constitutional arenas. Of these demands, the major ones have been and still are self-government, aboriginal rights, and the resolution of land claims (see Frideres, 1993). Meanwhile, native women's groups such as the Native Women's Association of Canada have publicized the harmful conditions (including child sexual abuse, incest, and wife battering) that exist on reserves.

One of the first major successes in the quest for self-determination is the creation of Nunavut (which means "our land"). The vision of Nunavut came to be in 1993 when the Nunavut Land Claims Agreement was signed. Under the terms of this agreement, the Inuit will receive title to 350,000 square kilometres of land in the Northwest Territories, including mineral rights to 36,000 square kilometres. The agreement also provides financial compensation of $1.14 billion. The territorial government will be controlled by the Inuit with the assistance of a system of cooperatives and the Inuit Broadcasting Corporation. Nunavut is a positive step for the Inuit in establishing their rights of self-determination over their unique culture.

Life chances are extremely limited for native peoples who live in native communities. These boys are participating in the pole twist—a traditional Inuit game. Despite their athletic prowess, it is unlikely that they will become members of professional sports teams—a ticket to success for many.

CHARTER EUROPEANS

WHITE ANGLO-SAXON PROTESTANTS (BRITISH CANADIANS) Whereas native peoples have been among the most disadvantaged peoples, white Anglo-Saxon Protestants (WASPs) have been the most privileged group in this country. Although many English settlers initially came to North America as indentured servants or as prisoners, they quickly emerged as the dominant group, creating a core culture (including language, laws, and holidays) to which all other groups were expected to adapt. Most WASPs do not think of themselves as having race or ethnicity. As one young woman commented, "I don't think of myself as white, I don't feel superior. I just felt normal" (quoted in Fleras and Elliott, 1996:35). The experience of being a WASP in Canadian society is an experience of privilege. But few Canadians are likely to acknowledge this privileged status—nor that it is derived from skin colour. Even fewer are prepared to concede that whiteness is directly related to the underprivileged status of others (Fleras and Elliott, 1996). The following student's comments, however, reflect a definite awareness of what it means to be a white Anglo-Saxon male:

> I am a member of a majority group that has a great deal of power ... It is White culture that I experience day to day and the very fact that discrimination is rarely an issue for me personally results in my own racial identity becoming an invisible thing. The powerful people within my experience, directly or indirectly—the politician, the employer, the teacher, the social worker—are invariably White. I know that my race will not be an issue with most of the people I must deal with, as I know we will have a commonality from the start. Being in the majority in all three origins [White, English, Canadian], there is also a good chance that either culturally, ethnically or both, our backgrounds will be similar. Neither will I expect my values or behavior to be an issue because I fit into the "norm." (James, 1995:47)

Class, Gender, and WASPs Like members of other racial and ethnic groups, not all WASPs are alike. Social class and gender affect their life chances and opportunities. For example, members of the working class and the poor do not have political and economic power; men in the capitalist class do. Likewise, WASP women have not always had the same rights as the men of their group. Women historically were viewed as the property of men and were denied equal protection under the law and the right to vote. In short, while WASP women have the privilege of a dominant racial position, they do not have the gender-related privileges of men (Amott and Matthaei, 1991).

FRENCH CANADIANS The European colonization of Canada began with the exploration and settlement of New France. In 1608, the first permanent settlement in New France was established at Quebec City, by Samuel de Champlain. France's North American empire extended from Hudson Bay to Louisiana. However, borders were constantly being moved, as a result of ongoing territorial disputes between New France and the English colonies.

Following the British conquest of the French in Canada in the Seven Years' War (1756–1763), Canada became a British dominion and the French found themselves in an inferior position (Weinfeld, 1995). The French were able to maintain French civil law, language, and religion; however, the overall economic, social and political power passed to English Canada. Although officially under British control, the competition between French and English Canadians continued until Confederation in 1867.

The British North America Act formally acknowledged the rights and privileges of the French and British as the founding or *charter groups* of Canadian society. With Confederation, it was assumed that in the future French- and English-speaking groups would co-exist and complement one another. However, during the period between Confederation and World War II, the French struggled for cultural survival because English-speaking Canadians controlled the major economic institutions in both English Canada and Quebec.

During the period known as the Quiet Revolution (1960–1966), Quebec nationalism grew sharply. Under the leadership of newly elected Premier Jean Lesage in 1960, Quebec began undergoing a rapid process of modernization. During this time the authority of the Catholic Church over the educational system was reduced as the Quebec government established a department of education. More French Canadians began pursuing higher education, particularly in business and science. The church also lost some of its influence over moral issues which was reflected in a declining birth rate and an increase in common-law marriages. Finally, nonfrancophone immigrants were challenging French culture by choosing to learn English, and having their children learn English, rather than French. The result? Francophones came to view their language and the culture as endangered. They recognized that the French language and culture in Quebec had to be protected. As a result, they rejected their Canadian identity and adopted a distinctly Québécois identity.

In 1976, Quebec elected the separatist Parti Québécois. First on party leader René Lévesque's agenda was the introduction and passage of Bill 101, a controversial law that established French as the sole official language in Quebec. In addition, children of new immigrants to Quebec had to be taught in French. In 1980, the Lévesque government held a referendum on whether to negotiate a relationship of "sovereignty association" with Canada. The proposal was rejected, but the matter was not resolved (see Chapter 13). A second referendum, held on October 30, 1995, also ended in a loss for the sovereignists, but this time by a narrow margin of only 1 percent.

French Canadians Today Today approximately 25 percent of the Canadian population is francophone, 85 percent of which is located in Quebec. Many Quebec nationalists now see independence or separation as the ultimate protection against cultural and linguistic assimilation, as well as the route to economic power. As political scientist Rand Dyck comments,

> [G]iven its geographic concentration in Quebec and majority control of a large province, and given their modern-day self-consciousness and self-confidence, the French fact in Canada cannot be ignored. If English Canada wants Quebec to remain a part of the country, it cannot go back to the easy days of pre-1960 unilingualism." (1996:185)

French Canadians have at least forced Canada to take its second language and culture seriously, which is an important step towards attaining cultural pluralism. "In the case of the French in Canada, assimilation was tried but failed" (Driedger, 1996:105).

CANADA'S IMMIGRANTS

Home to approximately 4.33 million foreign-born immigrants, Canada is well described as a land of immigrants. Canada's policies towards some of these immigrant groups have been far from exemplary. In fact, initial Canadian immigration policies have been described as essentially racist in orientation, assimilationist in intent, and segregationist in content (Fleras and Elliott, 1996). A "racial pecking order" sorted out potential immigrants on the basis of racial characteristics and capacity for assimilation (Lupul, 1988). As much energy was expended in keeping out certain "types" as was put into encouraging others to settle (Whitaker, 1991). A preferred category as the that of *white ethnics*—a term coined to identify immigrants who came from European countries other than England, such as Scotland, Ireland, Poland, Italy, Greece, Germany, Yugoslavia, and Russia and other former Soviet republics. Immigration from "white" countries was encouraged to ensure the British character of Canada. With the exception of visa formalities, this category of "preferred" immigrants was virtually exempt from entry restrictions. On the other hand, Jews and Mediterranean populations required special permits for entry, and Asian populations were admitted grudgingly, mostly to serve as cheap labour for Canadian capitalist expansion. The restrictions regarding the Chinese, Japanese, and Jews highlighted the racist dimension of Canada's early immigration policies.

ASIAN CANADIANS The Canadian census uses the term *Asian* to designate the many diverse groups with roots in Asia and the Pacific Islands. Chinese and Japanese immigrants were among the earliest Asian Canadians. Filipinos, Asian Indians, Koreans, Vietnamese, Cambodians, Pakistanis, and Indonesians have arrived more recently.

Chinese Canadians The initial wave of Chinese immigration began in the 1850s, when Chinese men were "pushed" from China by harsh economic conditions and "pulled" to Canada by the promise of gold in British Columbia and employment opportunities. Nearly 16,000 Chinese were brought to Canada at this time to lay track for the Canadian Pacific Railway. The work was brutally hard and dangerous, living conditions were appalling, food and shelter were insufficient, and due to scurvy and smallpox there was a high fatality rate. These immigrants were "welcomed" only as long as there was a shortage of white workers. However, they were not permitted to bring their wives and children with them or to have sexual relations with white women, because of the fear they would spread the "yellow menace" (Henry et al., 1995). After the railroad was built, the welcome mat was quickly rolled up.

The Chinese were subjected to extreme prejudice and were referred to by derogatory terms such as "coolies," "heathens," and "Chinks." Some were attacked by working-class whites who feared they would lose their jobs to Chinese immigrants. In 1885 the federal government passed its first anti-Chinese bill, the purpose of which was to limit Chinese immigration. Other hostile legislation included a range of racist exclusionary policies including prohibiting the Chinese from voting, serving in public office, serving on juries, participating in white labour unions, and working in the professions of law and pharmacy. In 1888, a head tax was imposed on all Chinese males arriving in Canada. In 1903, the tax was raised to $500 from $100 in a further attempt to restrict entry to Canada. Not until after World War II were such "objectionable discrimination" policies removed from the Immigration Act. After immigration laws were further relaxed in the 1960s, the second and largest wave of Chinese immigration occurred, with immigrants coming primarily from Hong Kong and Taiwan.

Japanese Canadians Japanese immigrants began arriving in Canada in large numbers after Chinese immigration tapered off. Like Chinese immigrants two decades earlier, the Japanese were viewed as a threat by white workers and became victims of stereotyping and discrimination.

In 1907 an organization known as the Asiatic Exclusion League was formed with the mandate of restricting admission of Asians to Canada. Following the arrival of a ship carrying over a thousand Japanese and a few hundred Sikhs, the league carried out a demonstration that precipitated a race riot. A "gentlemen's agreement," negotiated in 1908, permitted entry only of certain categories of Japanese on a fixed quota basis.

Japanese Canadians experienced one of the most vicious forms of discrimination ever sanctioned by Canadian law. During World War II, when Canada was at war with Japan, nearly 23,000 people of Japanese ancestry (13,300 of whom were Canadian-born) were placed in internment camps because they were seen as a security threat (Takaki, 1993). They remained in the camps for more than two years despite the total lack of evidence that they posed a danger to this country. Many of the camps were situated in remote locales in British Columbia, Alberta, and Manitoba; they had guard towers, and were surrounded by barbed-wire fences. This action was a direct violation of the citizenship rights of these Japanese who were born in Canada. Ironically, only the Japanese were singled out for such harsh treatment; German immigrants avoided this fate even though Canada was at war with both. After the war, restrictions were placed on where Japanese Canadians could settle and some were forcibly sent back to Japan. Four decades after these events, the Canadian government issued an apology for its actions and agreed to pay $20,000 to each person who had been placed in an internment camp (Henry et al., 1995).

East Indians East Indians also had to deal with discriminatory immigration laws. One of these laws was the "continuous passage" rule of 1908, which specified that East Indians could immigrate only if they came directly from India and did not stop at any ports on the way. This law made it almost impossible for them to enter the country, since no ships made direct journeys from India. East Indians who did manage to immigrate to Canada faced hostile employers and distrustful

As more Chinese Canadians have made gains in education and employment, many have also made a conscious effort to increase awareness of Chinese culture and to develop a sense of unity and cooperation. This Chinese Dragon parade exemplifies this desire to maintain traditional celebrations.

citizens. Their property and businesses were frequently attacked, and they were denied citizenship and the right to vote in British Columbia until 1947 (Henry et al., 1995).

Jewish Canadians In 1942, Canada closed its doors to Jews fleeing Hitler and the Holocaust. A ship carrying Jewish refugees from Europe attempted to land in Halifax and was denied entrance. During the 1930s Canada admitted fewer Jewish refugees as a percentage of its population than any other Western country. Jews who did immigrate experienced widespread discrimination in employment, business, and education. Other indicators of anti-Semitism included restrictions on where Jews could live, buy property, and attend university. According to Abella and Troper (1982), signs posted along Toronto's beaches warned "No dogs or Jews allowed." Many hotels and resorts had policies prohibiting Jews as guests (Abella and Troper, 1982, quoted in Henry et al., 1995:74). Despite the discrimination and racism to which Jews were

TABLE 9.6

Principal Sources of Immigrants to Canada, Selected Years (Percentage)

	Britain	Europe	Asia	Caribbean
1957	38.6	52.6	1.3	0.4
1967	28.0	43.8	9.3	3.9
1977	15.7	19.8	21.0	10.4
1987	5.6	19.1	44.3	7.4
1992	2.8	14.9	55.1	5.9

Source: Dyck, 1996:193.

subjected, Jewish Canadians today have attained a level of education and income considerably above the Canadian average.

IMMIGRATION TRENDS FROM 1929 TO THE PRESENT The Great Depression, which began in 1929, prompted the implementation of restrictive measures to further limit new immigrants to those from the preferred groups. According to Henry et al. (1995):

> Canadian immigration policy continued to be racist in the 1930s. The dominant and pervasive mindset underlying the policy and the administrative and political framework was "Whites Only." White immigrants from Britain were bestowed with preferential treatment, followed by White immigrants from the United States and France. Only if these traditional sources of immigration proved insufficient would the government consider admitting White Europeans from countries other than France and Britain. (1995:74)

Changes to the Immigration Act in 1962 opened the door to immigration on a nonracial basis. Education, occupation, and language skills replaced race or national origin as the criteria for admission. In 1967, a *points system* was introduced whereby immigrants were rated according to the totals of points given for the following: job training, experience, skills, level of education, knowledge of English or French, degree of demand for the applicant's occupation, and job offers. This new act opened the doors to those from previously excluded countries. As Table 9.6 and Figure 9.3 show, Canadian immigration patterns changed dramatically because of this new immigration policy. Whereas in 1957, over 90 percent of the immigrants were from Britain or continental Europe, by 1992, the percentage of immigrants from these source countries had fallen to 17 percent. In contrast, in 1957, Asian and Caribbean immigrants accounted for less than 2 percent of immigrants to Canada, but by 1992, this figure had risen to over 60 percent (see Figure 9.2). However, while changes in Canada's immigration laws altered Canada's ethnic composition, the domination of the Euro-Canadian majority in the stratification system has not been altered significantly. While Euro-Canadian and French-Canadian groups have been able to achieve upward mobility into middle- and upper-class social posi-

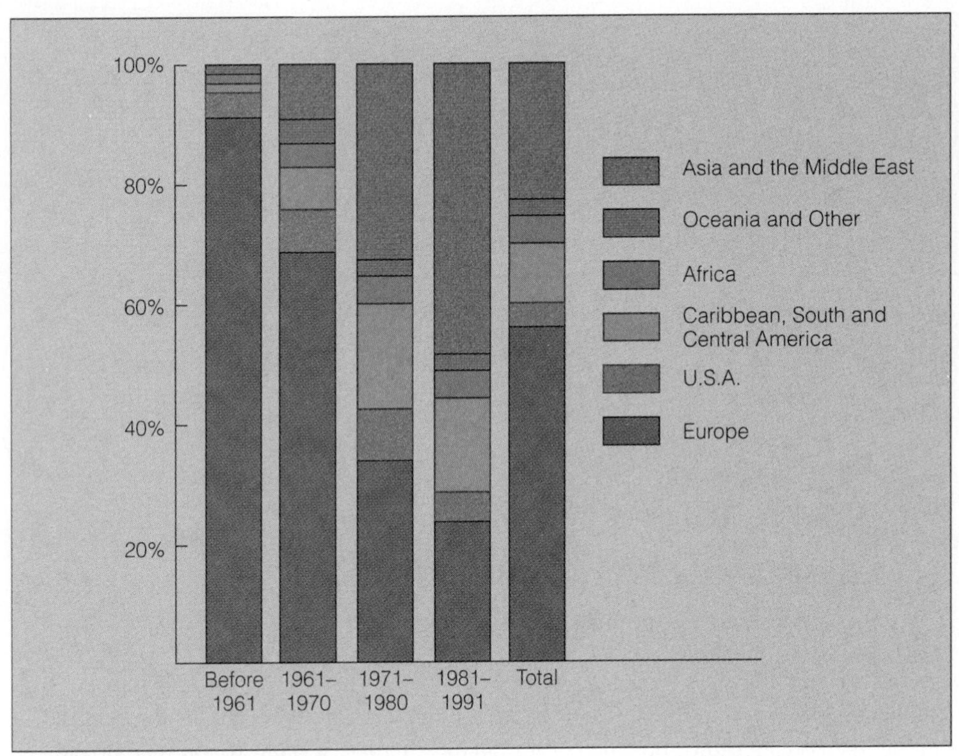

FIGURE 9.3

Immigrant Population by Place of Birth and Period of Immigration, 1991

Reproduced by authority of the Minister of Industry, 1996, Statistics Canada, from *Canadian Social Trends*, Cat. no. 11-008E, Summer 1993.

tions, the lower status of many visible minority groups has been virtually unchanged (for further discussion of ethnic stratification see Chapter 8).

RACIAL AND ETHNIC DIVERSITY IN CANADA IN THE TWENTY-FIRST CENTURY

Racial and ethnic diversity is increasing in Canada. This changing demographic pattern is largely the result of the elimination of overtly racist immigration policies and the opening up of immigration to Third World countries. Canada has evolved from a country largely inhabited by whites and aboriginal peoples to a country made up of people from more than seventy countries. Today, more than two-thirds of racial-minority immigrants come from Asia. The Chinese comprise the largest group, with 1.3 million people, followed by South Asians (East Indians, Pakistanis, Sri Lankans, and Bangladeshis) and blacks, with 1.1 million each. The next largest groups are West Asians and Arabs, Filipinos, Southeast Asians, and Latin Americans. The number of Latin American immigrants is expected to grow fourfold by the turn of the century (Henry et al., 1996). Almost all immigrants to Canada live in cities. In fact, 66 percent of immigrants who came here between 1981 and 1991 live in Toronto (39 percent), Montreal (14 percent), and Vancouver (13 percent). As Figure 9.4 shows, projections for the year 2001 are that nearly half of the popu-

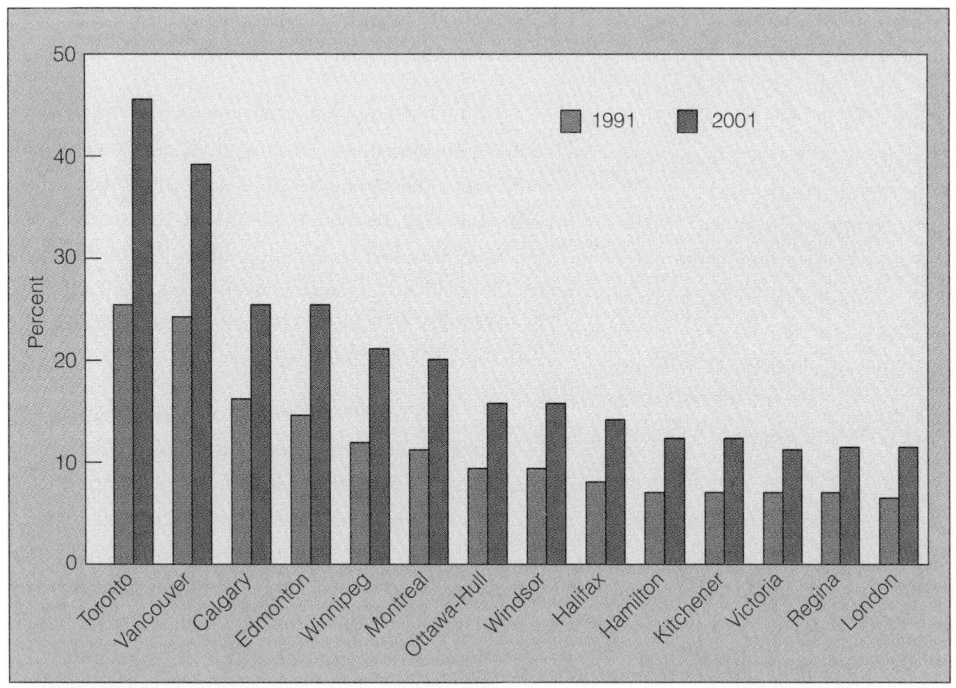

FIGURE 9.4

Racial Minorities in Selected Census Metropolitan Areas, 1991 and 2001 (Projected)

Source: T.J. Samuals, *Visible Minorities in Canada: A Projection.* Toronto: Race Relations Advisory Council on Advertising, Canadian Advertising Foundation, 1992. Reprinted by permission.

lation of Toronto and nearly two-fifths of the population of Vancouver will be composed of visible minorities. By the year 2000, visible minorities will make up over 10 percent of the total population of Canada, in contrast to 6.3 percent in 1986.

What effect will these changes have on racial and ethnic relations? Several possibilities exist. On the one hand, conflict between whites and people of colour may become more overt and confrontational. Certainly, the concentration of visible minorities will mean that these groups will become more visible than ever in some Canadian cities. Increasing contact may lead to increased intergroup cohesion and understanding or it may bring on racism or prejudice. The rapid political changes and the global economic recession of the 1990s have made people fearful about their future and may cause some to blame "foreigners" for their problems. Interethnic tensions among members of subordinate groups in urban areas may increase as subordinate groups continue to face economic deprivation and discrimination. People may continue to use *sincere fictions*—personal beliefs that reflect larger societal mythologies, such as "I am not racist" or "I have never discriminated against anyone"—even when these are inaccurate perceptions (Feagin and Vera, 1995). Concerns about violence, crime, welfare, education, housing, and taxes may be encompassed in the larger issue of race (Edsall and Edsall, 1992).

On the other hand, there is reason for cautious optimism. Throughout Canadian history, subordinate racial and ethnic groups have struggled to gain the freedom and rights that previously were withheld from them. Today, employment equity programs are alleviating some of the effects of past discrimination against minority groups as well as addressing systemic and institutional forms of racism that exist in employment. Movements made up of both whites and people of colour continue to oppose racism in everyday life, to seek to heal divisions among racial groups, and to teach children about racial tolerance (Rutstein, 1993). Many groups hope not only to affect their own countries but also to contribute to worldwide efforts to end racism (Ford, 1994).

To eliminate racial discrimination, it will be necessary to equalize opportunities in schools and workplaces. As Michael Omi and Howard Winant have emphasized:

> Today more than ever, opposing racism requires that we notice race, not ignore it, that we afford it the recognition it deserves and the subtlety it embodies. By noticing race we can begin to challenge racism, with its ever-more-absurd reduction of human experience to an essence attributed to all without regard for historical or social context. (1994:158)

The challenge of trying to keep together a nation composed of people divided by ethnicity, language, and even region, is a monumental task—one that will not be resolved in the near future (Rosenburg, 1995). Nevertheless, the elimination of racial/ethnic conflict should be an important government and public priority. Why? Because, as Norman Buchignani explains:

> There is an argument for the elimination of racism which transcends the question of harm to its victims. Racism is a moral issue, which reflects on Canadian society at large. Like sexism, racism ties us morally and intellectually to centuries-old legitimations and patterns of subordination which simply have no morally justifiable place in today's world. The persistence of racism diminishes us all (1991:200).

CHAPTER REVIEW

Issues of race and ethnicity permeate all levels of interaction in Canada. A race is a category of people who have been singled out as inferior or superior, often on the basis of physical characteristics such as skin colour, hair texture, or eye shape. An ethnic group is a collection of people who, as a result of their shared cultural traits and high level of mutual interaction, regard themselves as a cultural unity.

- Race and ethnicity are ingrained in our consciousness. They often form the basis of hierarchical ranking in society and determine who gets what resources: employment, housing, education, and social services.
- A majority or dominant group is an advantaged group that has superior resources and rights in society. A minority or subordinate group is a disadvantaged group whose members are subjected to unequal treatment by the majority group. The terms *dominant* and *subordinate* reflect the importance of power in relationships.
- Prejudice is a negative attitude based on preconceived notions about members of selected groups. Prejudice is often reinforced by stereotypes and is present in ethnocentric attitudes.

- Discrimination involves actions or practices of dominant group members that have a harmful impact on members of a subordinate group. Whereas prejudice involves attitudes, discrimination involves actions. Discriminatory actions range from name-calling to violent actions. Discrimination can be either de jure (encoded in law) or de facto (informal).
- Racism refers to an organized set of beliefs about the innate inferiority of some racial groups combined with the power to discriminate on the basis of race. There are many different ways in which racism may manifest itself including: rednecked racism, polite racism, subliminal racism, institutional racism, and systemic racism.
- According to the frustration-aggression hypothesis of prejudice, people frustrated in their efforts to achieve a highly desired goal may respond with aggression toward others, who then become scapegoats. Another theory of prejudice focuses on the authoritarian personality, which is marked by excessive conformity, submissiveness to authority, intolerance, insecurity, superstition, and rigid thinking. According to social learning theory, prejudice is learned from significant others, such as parents and close friends. Emory Bogardus developed the social distance scale to measure prejudiced attitudes toward different ethnic groups. From a conflict perspective, prejudice arises as a result of competition among different social groups for scarce and valued resources. Some conflict theorists have suggested that class, which is connected to the economy and jobs, is more crucial than race in explaining the unequal life chances of visible minorities. According to split-labour-market theory, white workers and members of the capitalist class benefit from the exploitation of people of colour (the lower tier).
- When ethnically diverse groups come into contact with one another, several different patterns of interaction may evolve, including assimilation, ethnic pluralism, internal colonialism, segregation, and genocide. All of these patterns of interaction have existed at some point in Canadian history. However, the pattern that best describes this interaction in Canada today is ethnic pluralism. There is some debate, though, over whether a policy of multiculturalism has moved us closer to equalitarian pluralism.
- Native people suffered greatly from the actions of European settlers, who seized their lands and made them victims of forced migration and genocide. Native people today lead lives characterized by poverty and lack of opportunity. White Anglo-Saxon Protestants are the most privileged group in Canada, although social class and gender affect their life chances. White ethnics, whose ancestors migrated from southern and eastern European countries, gradually have made their way into the mainstream of Canadian society. At present, Francophones represent 25 percent of the Canadian population, the majority of whom live in Quebec. The struggle to receive recognition of their unique language and culture has been ongoing and is reflected in the increasing identification of Québécois with the separatist movement.
- Canada's early immigration policies were described as racist and included exclusionary policies directed at Asian populations including Chinese, Japanese, and East Indians as well as Jews. "White ethnics" who came from European countries comprised the preferred category of immigrants. Changes to the Immigration Act in 1962 involving the implementation of a points system opened the door to immigration on a nonracial basis.
- Canada is becoming more ethnically and racially diverse. It remains to be seen whether the conflict between dominant and subordinate groups becomes more overt or whether the nation is able to heal divisions and work effectively to end racial discrimination.

KEY TERMS

assimilation **335**
authoritarian personality **330**
discrimination **323**
ethnic group **319**
ethnic pluralism **337**
ethnocentrism **322**
genocide **339**
institutionalized racism **327**
internal colonialization **338**
majority (dominant) group **321**
minority (subordinate) group **321**
polite racism **326**
prejudice **321**
race **317**
racial prejudice **322**
racism **325**
rednecked racism **325**
scapegoat **329**
segregation **338**
social distance **331**
split labour market **332**
subliminal racism **327**
systemic racism **328**

QUESTIONS FOR ANALYSIS AND UNDERSTANDING

1. How are ethnicity and race crucial components of stratification?
2. Why do some racial and ethnic groups continue to experience subjugation while others do not? Consider the concepts of forced subjugation and voluntary migration.

QUESTIONS FOR CRITICAL THINKING

1. Do you consider yourself defined more strongly by your race or by your ethnicity? How so?
2. Given that minority groups have some common experiences, why is there such deep conflict between certain minority groups?
3. What would need to happen in Canada, both individually and institutionally, for a positive form of ethnic pluralism to flourish in the twenty-first century?

SUGGESTED READINGS

For an in-depth analysis of race and ethnic relations, these texts are excellent:

Leo Driedger, *Multi-Ethnic Canada: Identities and Inequalities*. Don Mills, Ont.: Oxford University Press, 1996.

Carl E. James and Adrienne Shadd (eds.). *Talking About Difference: Encounters in Culture, Language and Identity*. Toronto: Between the Lines, 1994.

Peter S. Li (ed.). *Race and Ethnic Relations in Canada*. Toronto: Oxford University Press, 1990.

Martin N. Marger. *Race and Ethnic Relations: American and Global Perspectives*. Belmont, Cal.: Wadsworth, 1994.

These recent books provide excellent discussions on racism in Canada:

Stanley R. Barrett. *Is God a Racist? The Right Wing in Canada*. Toronto: University of Toronto Press, 1987.

Augie Fleras and Jean Leonard Elliott. *Unequal Relations: An Introduction to Race, Ethnic and Aboriginal Dynamics in Canada* (2nd ed.). Scarborough, Ont.: Prentice-Hall, 1996.

Frances Henry, Carol Tator, Winston Mattis, and Tim Rees. *The Colour of Democracy: Racism in Canadian Society*. Toronto: Harcourt Brace, 1995.

Carl James. *Seeing Ourselves: Exploring Race, Ethnicity and Culture*. Toronto: Thompson Publishing, 1995.

Ormond McKague (ed.). *Racism in Canada*. Saskatoon: Fifth House, 1991.

For additional information on the experiences of specific racial and ethnic groups:

Menno Boldt. *Surviving as Indians: The Challenge of Self-Government*. Toronto: University of Toronto Press, 1993.

James S. Frideres (ed.). *Native Peoples in Canada: Contemporary Conflicts* (4th ed.). Scarborough, Ont.: Prentice-Hall, 1993.

Chapter 10

SEX AND GENDER

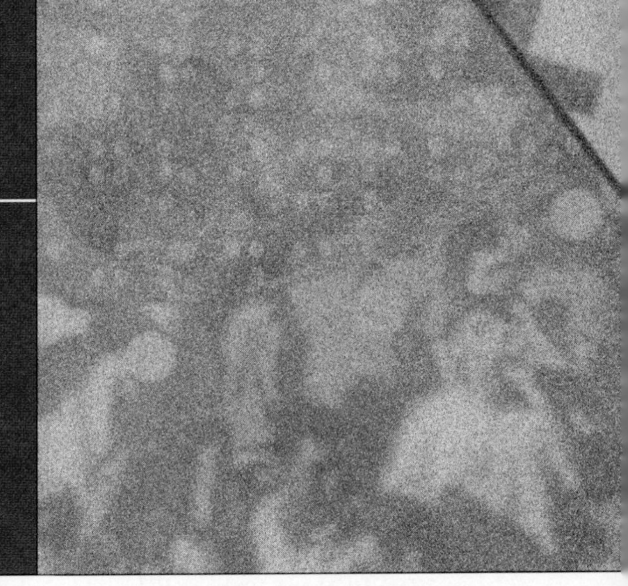

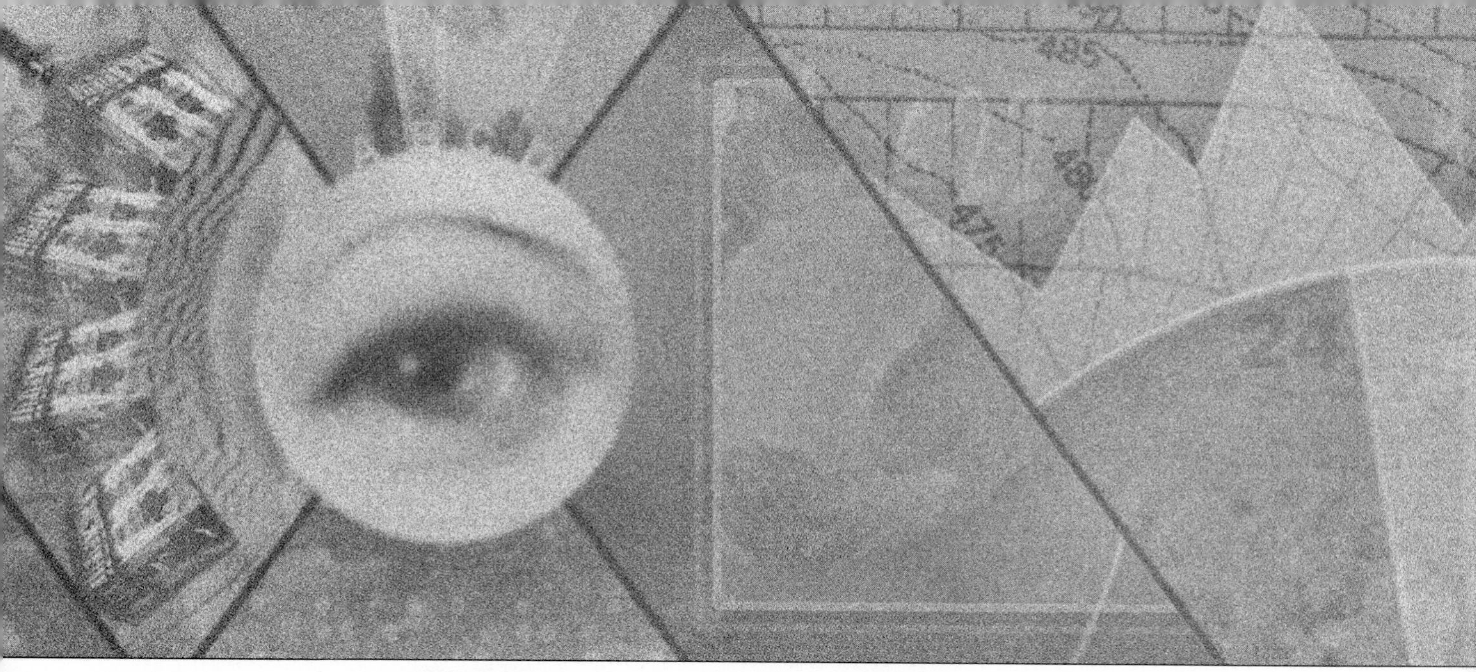

Naomi Wolf, author of *The Beauty Myth*, discusses the pressure she experienced as a young girl to conform or measure up to a culturally defined standard of femininity:

It was dead easy to become an anorexic ... At thirteen I was taking in the calorie equivalent of the food energy available to the famine victims of the siege of Paris. I did my schoolwork diligently and kept quiet in the classroom. I was a wind-up obedience toy. Not a teacher or principal or guidance counselor confronted me with an objection to my evident deportation in stages from the land of the living ... Anorexia was the only way I could see to keep the dignity in my body that I had had as a kid, and that I would lose as a woman. It was the only choice that really looked like one: By refusing to put on a woman's body and receive a rating, I chose not to have all my future choices confined to little things, and not to have choices made for me, on the basis of something meaningless to me. But as time went on, my choices grew smaller and smaller. Beef bouillion or hot water with lemon? The bouillion had twenty calories—I'd take the water. The lemon had four; I could live without it. Just. (Wolf, 1990:202–205)

Why would a young girl be so intensely fearful of becoming a woman that she would starve herself to avoid it? In Canada, an estimated 5 percent of women have an eating disorder. Another 10 to 20 percent have symptoms of eating disorders (Marble, 1995). Approximately 95 percent of those who develop eating disorders are women. Men are not immune to these pressures though they respond in a very different manner than women. An estimated 83,000 Canadian youths—mostly young men—take muscle-building steroids (Nemeth et al., 1994).

Eating disorders are strongly linked to social and cultural pressures. In our society, thinness is associated with beauty, happiness, and success. We live in a culture in which the body is a means of assessing an individual's value or worth. As Wolf says, a person's weight may be "fair game" for jokes even in an era when remarks about race, sex, or religion are considered unacceptable. Discrimination against people on the basis of appearance has been referred to as one of the last acceptable forms of prejudice (Stolker, 1992). People who deviate significantly from existing weight and appearance norms often are devalued and objectified by others. *Objectification* is the process of treating people as if they were objects or things, not human beings. We objectify people when we judge them on the basis of their status in a stigma-

TABLE 10.1

The Objectification of Women

General Aspects of Objectification

Women are responded to primarily as "females," while their personal qualities and accomplishments are of secondary importance.

Women are seen as being "all alike."

Women are seen as being subordinate and passive, so things can easily be "done to a woman"—for example, discrimination, harassment, and violence.

Women are seen as easily ignored, dismissed, or trivialized.

Objectification Based on Cultural Preoccupation with "Looks"

Women often are seen as the objects of sexual attraction, not full human beings—for example, when they are stared at.

Women are seen by some as depersonalized body parts—for example, "a piece of ass."

Depersonalized female sexuality is used for cultural and economic purposes—such as in the media, advertising, fashion and cosmetics industries, and pornography.

Women are seen as being "decorative" and status-conferring objects, to be sought (sometimes collected) and displayed by men and sometimes by other women.

Women are evaluated according to prevailing, narrow "beauty" standards and often feel pressure to conform to appearance norms.

Source: Schur, 1983.

laden category (such as a "fat slob" or a "hundred–pound weakling"), rather than on the basis of their individual qualities or actions (Schur, 1983). In our society, objectification of women is especially common (see Table 10.1).

Studies suggest that men and women may have negative perceptions about their body size, weight, and appearance (Marble, 1995; Nemeth et al., 1994) Many men compare themselves unfavourably to muscular bodybuilders and believe that they need to gain weight or muscularity, which for some is associated with masculinity and power (Basow, 1992; Klein, 1993). For women, however, body image is an even greater concern. Women may compare themselves unfavourably to slender stars of film and television and believe that they need to lose weight. Men are less likely to let concerns about appearance affect how they feel about their own competence, worth, and abilities; among women, dislike of their bodies may affect self-esteem and feelings of self-worth (Mintz and Betz, 1986).

Why do women and men feel differently about their bodies? Cultural differences in appearance norms may explain women's greater concern; they tend to be judged more harshly, and they know it

BOX 10.1 SOCIOLOGY AND EVERYDAY LIFE

How Much Do You Know About Body Image and Gender?

TRUE	FALSE	
T	F	1. Most people have an accurate perception of their own physical appearance.
T	F	2. Recent studies show that up to 95 percent of men express dissatisfaction with some aspect of their bodies.
T	F	3. Many young girls and women believe that being even slightly overweight makes them less feminine.
T	F	4. Physical attractiveness is a more central part of self-concept for women than for men.
T	F	5. Virtually no men have eating problems such as anorexia and bulimia.
T	F	6. Thinness has always been the "ideal" body image for women.
T	F	7. Women bodybuilders have gained full acceptance in society.
T	F	8. In school, boys are more likely than girls to ridicule people about their appearance.
T	F	9. Canada has laws prohibiting employment discrimination on the basis of weight.
T	F	10. Young girls and women very rarely die as a result of anorexia or bulimia.

Answers on page 358

(Wolf, 1990). Throughout their lives, men and women receive different cultural messages about body image, food, and eating. Men are encouraged to eat while women are made to feel guilty about eating (Basow, 1992). In North America, the image of female beauty as childlike and thin is continually flaunted by the advertising industry; the job market reinforces it through overt and covert discrimination against women who do not fit the image (Thompson, 1994). Women of all ethnic groups, classes, and sexual orientations regard their weight as a crucial index of their acceptability to others (Thompson, 1994; Wood, 1994).

Body image is only one example of the many socially constructed differences between men and women—differences that relate to gender (a social concept) rather than to a person's biological makeup, or sex. In this chapter, we examine the issue of gender: what it is and how it affects us. Before reading on, test your knowledge about gender and body image by taking the quiz in Box 10.1.

Answers to the Sociology Quiz on Body Image and Gender

TRUE	FALSE	
T	**F**	1. *False.* Many people do not have a very accurate perception of their own bodies. For example, many young girls and women think of themselves as fat when they are not. Some young boys and men tend to believe that they need well-developed chest and arm muscles, broad shoulders, and a narrow waist.
T	F	2. *True.* In recent studies, up to 95 percent of men believed they needed to improve some aspect of their bodies.
T	F	3. *True.* More than half of all adult women in North America are currently dieting, and over three-fourths of normal-weight women think they are too fat. Recently, very young girls have developed similar concerns. For example, 80 percent of Grade 4 girls in one study were watching their weight.
T	F	4. *True.* Women have been socialized to believe that being physically attractive is very important. Studies have found that weight and body shape are the central determinants of women's perception of their physical attractiveness.
T	**F**	5. *False.* Some men do have eating problems such as anorexia and bulimia. These problems have been found especially among gay men and male fashion models and dancers.
T	**F**	6. *False.* The "ideal" body image for women has changed a number of times. A positive view of body fat has prevailed for most of human history; however, in the twentieth century in North America, this view has given way to "fat aversion."
T	**F**	7. *False.* Although bodybuilding among women has gained some degree of acceptance, women bodybuilders still are expected to be very "feminine" and not to overdevelop themselves.
T	F	8. *True.* Boys are especially likely to ridicule girls whom they perceive to be "unattractive" or overweight.
T	**F**	9. *False.* To date Canada has no laws that specifically prohibit employment discrimination on the basis of weight.
T	**F**	10. *False.* Although the exact number is not known, many young girls and women do die as a result of starvation, malnutrition, and other problems associated with anorexia and bulimia. These are considered life-threatening behaviours by many in the medical profession.

Sources: Based on Lips, 1993; Fallon, Katzman, and Wooley, 1994; Kilbourne, 1994; and Seid, 1994.

QUESTIONS AND ISSUES

What is the difference between sex and gender?

How do expectations about female and male appearance reflect gender inequality?

How do a society's resources and economic structure influence gender stratification?

What are the primary agents of gender socialization?

How does the contemporary workplace reflect gender stratification?

How do functionalist, conflict, and feminist perspectives on gender stratification differ?

SEX AND GENDER

The word *sex* often is used to refer to the biological attributes of men and women (Epstein, 1988). Gender often is used to refer to the distinctive qualities of men and women (masculinity and femininity) that are culturally created (Epstein, 1988; Marshall, 1994).

SEX

***Sex* refers to the biological and anatomical differences between females and males.** At the core of these differences is the chromosomal information transmitted at the moment a child is conceived. The mother contributes an X chromosome and the father either an X (which produces a female embryo) or a Y chromosome (which produces a male embryo). At birth, male and female infants are distinguished by ***primary sex characteristics:* the genitalia used in the reproductive process.** At puberty, an increased production of hormones results in the development of ***secondary sex characteristics:* the physical traits (other than reproductive organs) that identify an individual's sex.** For women, these include larger breasts, wider hips, and narrower shoulders; a layer of fatty tissue throughout the body; and menstruation. For men, they include development of enlarged genitals, a deeper voice, greater height, a more muscular build, and more body and facial hair (see Lott, 1994:17–32).

These changes produce an acute awareness of sexuality. During this time, many young people become aware of their ***sexual orientation*—a preference for emotional–sexual relationships with members of the opposite sex (heterosexuality), the same sex (homosexuality), or both (bisexuality)** (Lips, 1993). Some researchers believe that sexual orientation is rooted in biological factors that are present at birth (Pillard and Weinrich, 1986); others believe that sexuality has both biological and social components and is not preordained at birth (Golden, 1987). Sexual orientation is examined in Chapter 14 ("Families and Intimate Relationships").

Sex is not always clear–cut. Occasionally, a hormone imbalance before birth produces a ***hermaphrodite*—a person in whom sexual differentiation is ambiguous or incomplete** (Renzetti and Curran, 1995). Hermaphrodites tend to have some combination of male and female genitalia. In one case, for example, a chromosomally normal (XY) male was born with a penis just one centimetre long and a urinary opening similar to that of a female (Money and Ehrhardt, 1972). Some people may be genetically of one sex but have a gender identity of the other. That is true for a ***transsexual*, a person who believes that he or she was born with the body of the wrong sex.** Some transsexuals take hormone treatments or have a sex change operation to alter their genitalia in order to achieve a body congruent with their own sense of sexual identity (Basow, 1992).

Western societies acknowledge the existence of only two sexes; some other societies recognize three—men, women, and *berdaches* (or *hijras* or *xaniths*), biological males who behave, dress, and work and are treated in most respects as women. The closest approximation of a third sex in Western societies is a ***transvestite*, a male who lives as a women or a female who lives as a man but does not alter the genitalia.** Although transves-

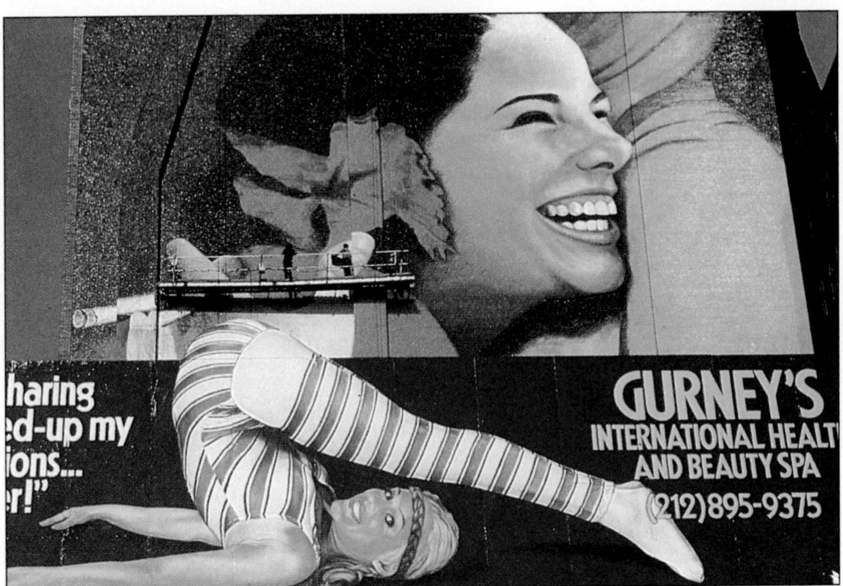

No wonder many women are extremely concerned about body image; even billboards communicate cultural messages about their appearance.

tites are not treated as a third sex, they often "pass" for members of that sex because their appearance and mannerisms fall within the range of what is expected from members of the other sex (Lorber, 1994).

GENDER

Gender **refers to the culturally and socially constructed differences between females and males found in the meanings, beliefs, and practices associated with "femininity" and "masculinity."** Although biological differences between women and men are very important, most "sex differences" actually are socially constructed "gender differences" (Gailey, 1987). According to sociologists, social and cultural processes, not biological "givens," are most important in defining what females and males are, what they should do, and what sorts of relations do or should exist between them (Ortner and Whitehead, 1981; Lott, 1994). Sociologist Judith Lorber (1994:6) summarizes the importance of gender:

> Gender is a human invention, like language, kinship, religion, and technology; like them, gender organizes human social life in culturally patterned ways. Gender organizes social relations in everyday life as well as in the major social structures, such as social class and the hierarchies of bureaucratic organizations.

Virtually everything social in our lives is *gendered:* people continually distinguish between males and females and evaluate them differentially (Eitzen and Zinn, 1995). Gender is an integral part of the daily experiences of both women and men (Kimmel and Messner, 1992).

A microlevel analysis of gender focuses on how individuals learn gender roles and acquire a gender identity. ***Gender role*** **refers to the attitudes, behaviour, and activities that are socially defined as appropriate for each sex and are learned through the socialization process** (Lips, 1993). For example, in Canadian society, males traditionally are expected to demonstrate aggressiveness and toughness while females are expected to be passive and nurturing. ***Gender identity*** **is a person's perception of the self as**

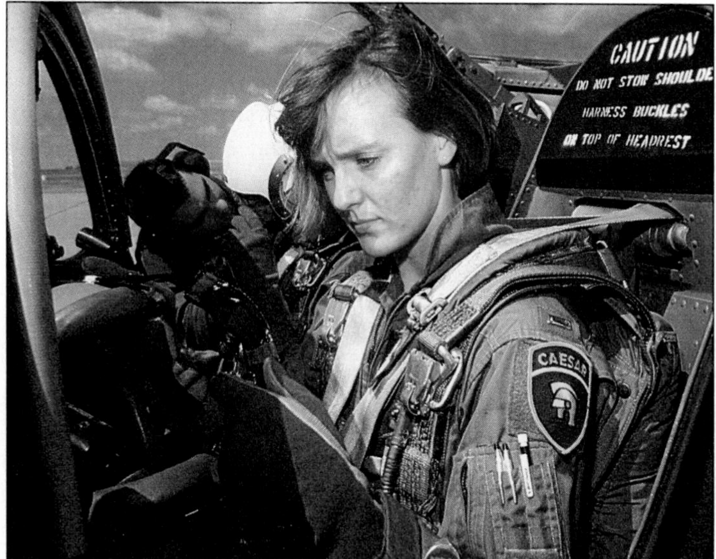

The way society views women's role in war illustrates how gender belief systems change over time as gender roles change.

female or male. Typically established between 18 months and 3 years of age, gender identity is a powerful aspect of our self–concept (Cahill, 1986; Lips, 1993). Although this identity is an individual perception, it is developed through interaction with others. As a result, most people form a gender identity that matches their biological sex: most biological females think of themselves as female, and most biological males think of themselves as male. Body consciousness is a part of gender identity (Basow, 1992). ***Body consciousness* is how a person perceives and feels about his or her body;** it also includes an awareness of social conditions in society that contribute to this self-knowledge (Thompson, 1994). Consider, for example, these comments by Steve Michalik, a former Mr. Universe:

> I was small and weak, and my brother Anthony was big and graceful, and my old man made no bones about loving him and hating me ... The minute I walked in from school, it was, "You worthless little s--t, what are you doing home so early?" His favorite way to torture me was to tell me he was going to put me in a home. We'd be driving along ... and we'd pass a building with iron bars on the windows, and he'd stop the car and say to me, "Get out. This is the home we're putting you in." I'd be standing there sobbing on the curb—I was maybe eight or nine at the time. (quoted in Klein, 1993:273)

As we grow up, we become aware, as Michalik did, that the physical shape of our bodies subjects us to the approval or disapproval of others. While being small and weak may be considered positive attributes for women, they are considered negative characteristics for "real men."

A macrolevel analysis of gender examines structural features, external to the individual, that perpetuate gender inequality. These structures have been referred to as *gendered institutions*, meaning that gender is one of the major ways by which social life is organized in all sectors of society. Gender is embedded in the images, ideas, and language of a society and is used as a means to divide up work, allocate resources, and distribute power. For example, every society uses gender to assign certain tasks—ranging from child rearing to warfare—to females and to males.

These institutions are reinforced by a *gender belief system* that includes all of the ideas regarding masculine and feminine attributes that are held to be valid in a society. This belief system is legitimated by religion, science, law, and other societal values (Lorber, 1994). For example, gendered belief systems may change over time as gender roles change. Fathers are taking a larger role in the care of young children today, and there is a much greater acceptance of this change in roles. However, popular stereotypes about men and women, as well as cultural norms about gender-appropriate appearance and behaviour, serve to reinforce gendered institutions in society (Deaux and Kite, 1987).

THE SOCIAL SIGNIFICANCE OF GENDER

Like ethnicity, gender is a social construction with important consequences in everyday life. Just as stereotypes regarding race/ethnicity have built-in notions of superiority and inferiority, gender stereotypes hold that men and women are inherently different in attributes, behaviour, and aspirations. Stereotypes define men as strong, rational, dominant, independent, and less concerned with their appearance. Women are stereotyped as weak, emotional, nurturing, dependent, and anxious about their appearance.

The social significance of gender stereotypes is illustrated by eating problems. The three most common eating problems are anorexia, bulimia, and obesity. With *anorexia*, a person has lost at least 25 percent of body weight due to a compulsive fear of becoming fat (Lott, 1994). With *bulimia*, a person binges by consuming large quantities of food and then purges the food by induced vomiting, excessive exercise, laxatives, or fasting (Renzetti and Curran, 1992). With *obesity*, individuals are 20 percent or more above their desirable weight, as established by the medical profession. For a 5-foot-4-inch woman, that is about twenty-five pounds; for a 5-foot-10-inch man, about thirty pounds (Burros, 1994:1).

Sociologist Becky W. Thompson argues that, based on stereotypes, the primary victims of eating problems are presumed to be white, middle-class, heterosexual women. However, such problems also exist among visible-minority women, working-class women, lesbians, and some men. According to Thompson, explanations regarding the relationship between gender and eating problems must take into account a complex array of social factors, including gender socialization and women's responses to problems such as racism and emotional, physical, and sexual abuse (Thompson, 1994; see also, Wooley, 1994).

Bodybuilding is another gendered experience. *Bodybuilding* is the process of deliberately cultivating an increase in mass and strength of the skeletal muscles by means of lifting and pushing weights (Mansfield and McGinn, 1993). In the past, bodybuilding was predominantly a male activity; musculature connoted power, domination, and virility (Klein, 1993). Today, an increasing number of women engage in this activity. As gendered experiences, eating problems, and bodybuilding have more in common than we might think. Historian Susan Bordo (1993) has noted that the anorexic body and the muscled body are not opposites; instead, they exist on a continuum because they are united against a "common platoon of enemies: the soft, the loose; unsolid, excess flesh." The *body* is objectified in both compulsive dieting and bodybuilding (Mansfield and McGinn, 1993:53).

SEXISM

***Sexism* is the subordination of one sex, usually female, based on the assumed superiority of the other sex.** Sexism directed at women has three components: (1) negative attitudes toward women, (2) stereotypical beliefs that reinforce, complement, or justify the prejudice, and (3) discrimination—acts that exclude, distance, or keep women separate (Lott, 1994).

Can men be victims of sexism? Although women are more often the target of sexist remarks and practices, men can be victims of sexist assumptions. As social psychologist Hilary M. Lips (1993:11) notes, "Sexism cuts both ways; for example, the other side of the prejudiced attitude that [usually bars] women from combat positions in the military is the attitude that it is somehow less upsetting to have male soldiers killed than to have female soldiers killed."

Like racism, sexism is used to justify discriminatory treatment. When women participate in what is considered gender-inappropriate endeavours in the workplace, at home, or in leisure activities, they often find that they are the targets of prejudice and discrimination. Obvious manifestations of sexism are found in the undervaluing of women's work, in hiring and promotion practices that effectively exclude women from an organization or confine them to the bottom of the organizational hierarchy, and in the denial of equal access for women to educational opportunities (Armstrong and Armstrong, 1994). Some people feel that pornography serves to perpetuate sexism by portraying women as objects. Box 10.4 addresses how the law in Canada deals with this rather complex issue. Women who attempt to enter nontraditional occupations (such as firefighting, welding, and steelworking) or professions (such as dentistry and architecture) often encounter hurdles that men do not face. Women may experience discrimination because they are perceived to be "out of place." Consider the following comments from a male steelworker in Hamilton regarding the hiring of female steelworkers:

> It's dirty, heavy, it's no climate for a woman. The men's world is a little rougher than the women's. Physically a man is in better shape. Men are more mechanically minded ... There is nothing wrong with women, it's just that sometimes with heavy work ... if you take the overall picture, masculinity has always been the man's. It doesn't mean that he has more brains because that is not true, but muscularity. I think that women should be outside. It is no place for women. I hate it. (Livingston and Luxton, 1995:190)

Sexism is interwoven with ***patriarchy*—a hierarchical system of social organization in which cultural, political, and economic structures are controlled by men.** By contrast, ***matriarchy* is a hierarchical system of social organization in which cultural, political, and economic structures are controlled by women;** however, few (if any) societies have been organized in this manner (Lengermann and Wallace, 1985). Patriarchy is reflected in the way men may think of their position as men as a given while women may deliberate on what their position in society should be. As sociologist Virginia Cyrus (1993:6) explains, "Under patriarchy, men are seen as 'natural' heads of households, political candidates, corporate executives, university presidents, etc. Women, on the other hand, are men's subordinates, playing such supportive roles as housewife, mother, nurse, and secretary." Gender inequality and a division of labour based on male dominance are nearly universal, as we will see in the following discussion on the origins of gender-based stratification.

GENDER STRATIFICATION IN HISTORICAL PERSPECTIVE

How do tasks in a society come to be defined as "men's work" or "women's work"? Three factors are important in determining the gendered division of labour in a society: (1) the type of subsistence base, (2) the supply of and demand for labour, and (3) the extent to which women's child-rearing activities are compatible with certain types of work. *Subsistence* refers to the means by which a society gains the basic necessities of life, including food, shelter, and clothing (Nielsen, 1990). The three factors vary according to a society's *technoeconomic base*—the level of technology and the organization of the economy in a given society.

TABLE 10.2

Technoeconomic Bases of Society

	Hunting and Gathering	Horticultural and Pastoral	Agrarian	Industrialized
Change from Prior Society	—	Use of hand tools, such as digging stick and hoe	Use of animal-drawn plows and equipment	Invention of steam engine
Economic Characteristics	Hunting game, gathering roots and berries	Planting crops, domestication of animals for food	Labour-intensive farming	Mechanized production of goods
Control of Surplus	None	Men begin to control societies	Men who own land or herds	Men who own means of production
Inheritance	None	Shared—patrilineal and matrilineal	Patrilineal	Patrilineal
Control over Procreation	None	Increasingly by men	Men—to ensure legitimacy of heirs	Men—but less so in later stages
Women's Status	Relative equality	Decreasing in move to pastoralism	Low	Low

Source: Adapted from Lorber, 1994:140.

Four such bases have been identified: hunting and gathering societies, horticultural and pastoral societies, agrarian societies, and industrial societies, as shown in Table 10.2.

HUNTING AND GATHERING SOCIETIES

The earliest known division of labour between women and men is in hunting and gathering societies. While the men hunt for wild game, women gather roots and berries (Nielsen, 1990). A relatively equitable relationship exists because neither sex has the ability to provide all of the food necessary for survival. When wild game is nearby, both men and women may hunt (Basow, 1992). When it is far away, hunting becomes incompatible with child rearing (which women tend to do because they breast-feed their young), and women are placed at a disadvantage in terms of contributing to the food supply (Lorber, 1994). In most hunting and gathering societies, women are full economic partners with men; relations between them tend to be cooperative and relatively egalitarian (Chafetz, 1984). Little social stratification of any kind is found because people do not acquire a food surplus.

A few hunting and gathering societies remain, including the Bushmen of Africa, the aborigines of Australia, the Yanomami of South America, and the Kaska Indians of Canada. However, some analysts predict that these groups will cease to exist by the twenty-first century (Lenski, Lenski, and Nolan, 1991). Native peoples in Canada had very successful hunting and gathering societies prior to European inhabitation. Sadly, few native cultures have been able to maintain this egalitarian system.

HORTICULTURAL AND PASTORAL SOCIETIES

In horticultural societies, which first developed ten to twelve thousand years ago, a steady source of food becomes available. People are able to grow their own food because of hand tools, such as the digging stick and the hoe. Women make an important contribution to food production because hoe cultivation is compatible with child care. A fairly high degree of gender equality exists because neither sex controls the food supply (Basow, 1992).

When inadequate moisture in an area makes planting crops impossible *pastoralism*—the domestication of large animals to provide food—develops. Herding primarily is done by men, and women contribute relatively little to subsistence production in such societies. In some herding societies, women have relatively low status; their primary value is their ability to produce male offspring so that the family lineage can be preserved and enough males will exist to protect the group against attack (Nielsen, 1990).

Social practices contribute to gender inequality in horticultural and pastoral societies. Male dominance is promoted by practices such as menstrual taboos, bridewealth, and polygyny (Nielsen, 1990). *Polygyny*—the marriage of one man to multiple wives—contributes to power differences between women and men. A man with multiple wives can produce many children who will enhance his resources, take care of him in his "old age," and become heirs to his property (Nielsen, 1990). *Menstrual taboos* place women in a subordinate position by segregating them into menstrual huts for the duration of their monthly cycle. Even when women are not officially segregated, they are defined as "unclean." *Bridewealth*—the payment of a price by a man for a wife—turns women into property that can be bought and sold. The man gives the bride's family material goods or services in exchange for their daughter's exclusive sexual services and his sole claim to their offspring.

In contemporary horticultural societies, women do most of the farming while men hunt game, clear land, work with arts and crafts, make tools, participate in religious and ceremonial activities, and engage in war (Nielsen, 1990). A combination of horticultural and pastoral activities is found in some contemporary societies in Asia, Africa, the Middle East, and South America. These societies are characterized by more gender inequality than in hunting and gathering societies but less than in agrarian societies (Nielsen, 1990: 36–39).

AGRARIAN SOCIETIES

In agrarian societies, which first developed about eight to ten thousand years ago, gender inequality and male dominance become institutionalized. The most extreme form of gender inequality developed about five thousand years ago in societies in the fertile crescent around the Mediterranean Sea (Lorber, 1994). Agrarian societies rely on agriculture—farming done by animal-drawn or energy-powered plows and equipment. Because agrarian tasks require more labour and greater physical strength than horticultural ones, men become more involved in food production. It has been suggested that women are excluded from these tasks because they are viewed as too weak for the work and because child-care

Gender inequality is intertwined with the tasks that come to be defined as "men's work" or "women's work." In hunting and gathering societies such as the Yanomami of South America, there is a relatively equitable division of labour between women and men. Gender inequality becomes more distinct in pastoral and horticultural societies and increases in agrarian societies, as exemplified by the practice of purdah *found primarily among Hindus and Muslims. Gender inequality reaches a peak in industrialized societies, represented here by the "cult of true womanhood" of the late nineteenth century.*

responsibilities are considered incompatible with the full-time labour that the tasks require (Nielsen, 1990).

Why does gender inequality increase in agrarian societies? Scholars cannot agree on an answer; some suggest that it results from private ownership of property. When people no longer have to move continually in search of food, they can acquire a surplus. Men gain control over the disposition of the surplus and the kinship system, which serves men's interests (Lorber, 1994). The importance of producing "legitimate" heirs to inherit the surplus increases significantly, and women's lives become more secluded and restricted as men attempt to ensure the legitimacy of their children. Premarital virginity and marital fidelity are required; indiscretions are punished (Nielsen, 1990). Other scholars argue that male dominance existed before the private ownership of property (Firestone, 1970; Lerner, 1986).

The division of labour between women and men is very distinct in contemporary agrarian societies in places such as Burma and parts of the Middle East. There, women's work takes place in the private sphere (inside the home) and men's work occurs in the public sphere, providing them with more recognition and greater formal status.

Four practices in agrarian societies contribute to subordination of women. *Purdah*, found primarily among Hindus and Muslims, requires the seclusion of women, extreme modesty in apparel, and the visible subordination of women to men. Women must show deference to men by walking behind them, speaking only when spoken to, and eating only after the men have finished a meal (Nielsen, 1990).

Footbinding is the custom of thwarting the growth of a female's feet that was practised in China beginning around A.D. 1000 and continuing into the early twentieth century. The toes of young girls are bent under and continually bound tighter to the soles of their feet. As a result, women may experience extreme pain as their toenails grow into their feet or develop serious infections due to lack of blood circulation (Dworkin, 1974).

Suttee (most common in parts of India) is the sacrificial killing of a widow upon the death of her husband. Although some women allegedly choose to make this sacrifice, others are tied to their husband's funeral pyre. The practice is justified on the basis that the widow's sins in a former life are responsible for her husband's death. However, the actual purpose is to ensure that the husband's male relatives, rather than the widow, inherit his property (Nielsen, 1990:43–44).

Genital mutilation is a surgical procedure performed on young girls as a method of sexual control (Nielsen, 1990). The mutilation involves cutting off all or part of a girl's clitoris and labia, and in some cases stitching her vagina closed until marriage (Simons, 1993b). Often justified on the erroneous belief that the Koran commands it, these procedures are supposed to ensure that women are chaste before marriage and have no extramarital affairs after marriage. Genital mutilation has resulted in the maiming of many females, some of whom died as a result of hemorrhage, infection, or other complications. It is still practised in more that twenty-five countries. Box 10.2 discusses genital mutilation of women around the world.

In sum, male dominance is very strong in agrarian societies. Women are secluded, subordinated, and mutilated as a means of regulating their sexuality and protecting paternity. Most of the world's population currently lives in agrarian societies in various stages of industrialization.

INDUSTRIAL SOCIETIES

An *industrial society* is one in which factory or mechanized production has replaced agriculture as the major form of economic activity (Nielsen, 1990:49). As societies industrialize, the status of women tends to decline further. Industrialization in Canada created a gap between the nonpaid work performed by women at home and the paid work that increasingly was performed by men and unmarried girls (Krahn and Lowe, 1993; Armstrong and Armstrong, 1994). When families needed extra money, their daughters worked in the textile mills until they married. Once married, women were expected to leave the paid work force. In 1931, for example, only 3.5 percent of married Canadian women were in the paid labour force (Baker and Lero, 1996). As it became more difficult to make a living by farming, many men found work in the factories, where their primary responsibility often was supervising the work of women and children. Men began to press for a clear division between "men's work" and "women's work," as well as corresponding pay differentials (higher for men, lower for women).

In Canada, the division of labour between men and women in the middle and upper classes became much more distinct with industrialization (Vanier Institute of the Family, 1994). The men were responsible for being "breadwinners," the women were seen as "homemakers." In this new "cult of domesticity" (also referred to as the "cult of true womanhood"), the home became a private, personal sphere in which women created a haven for the family (Amott and Matthaei, 1991). Those who supported the cult of domesticity argued that women were the natural keepers of the domestic sphere and that children were the mother's responsibility. Meanwhile, the "breadwinner" role placed enormous pressure on men to support their

BOX 10.2 SOCIOLOGY IN GLOBAL PERSPECTIVE

Women and Human Rights: Female Genital Mutilation

> The little girl, entirely nude, is immobilized in the sitting position on a low stool by at least three women. One of them has her arms tightly around the little girl's chest, two others hold the child's thighs apart by force, in order to open the vulva. The child's arms are tied behind her back, or immobilized by two other women guests. Then the old woman takes her razor and excises the clitoris. The infibulation follows: the operator cuts with her razor from top to bottom of the small lip and then scrapes the flesh from the inside of the large lip. The nymphotomy and scraping are repeated on the other side of the vulva. The little girl howls and writhes in pain, although strongly held down. The operator wipes the blood from the wound and the mother, as well as the guests, "verify" her work, sometimes putting their fingers in. The opening left for urine and menstrual blood is minuscule. Then the practitioner applies a paste and ensures the adhesion of the large lips by means of acacia thorn, which pierces one lip and passes through into the other. She sticks in three or four in this manner down the vulva. These thorns are then held in place either by means of a sewing thread or horsehair. Paste is again put on the wound. Exhausted, the little girl is then dressed and put on a bed. The operation lasts from 15 to 20 minutes according to the ability of the old woman and the resistance put up by the child. (Tomasevski, 1993:85)

Now in her early thirties, Selma recalls enduring this procedure in Sudan at age 8, screaming and resisting to no avail: "They held me down. It was painful. I had some anesthetic, but I felt it all" (Rowley, 1994:A9).

As we approach the twenty-first century, the traditional ritual of female genital mutilation is performed on more than 2 million girls and women a year. The World Health Organization estimates that 85–115 million women have had their genitals mutilated. Although the practice occurs primarily in twenty-eight African nations and in some areas of Asia, cases of genital mutilation among families of recent immigrants from Africa and Asia have been reported in the United States, Canada, Europe, and Australia.

In 1993, attorney Linda Weil-Curiel made the following statement at the Paris trial of a mother accused of allowing the mutilation of her daughter (a practice brought to France by African immigrants): "This is butchery invented to control women ... It's a form of violence we would never allow here against white girls. If immigrants cut off a girl's ear in the name of tradition, there would be an outcry. But here the sex of a future woman is cut off and people are willing to defend it or turn away" (quoted in Simons, 1993b:A4).

Some view genital mutilation as a deeply embedded ritual that must be understood in terms of the culture involved. These practices may be perpetrated on young girls because of centuries-old customs dictating that girls must be kept chaste and that, without the ritual, they will not get a husband and their family will not get a dowry. A spokesperson for the World Health Organization noted that respect for other cultures is needed but that such practices must be challenged when they threaten people's health. What do you think? Should the United Nations protest the genital mutilation practised by countries belonging to the organization? When this practice occurs in Canada, should the parents be charged with child abuse, or should they be excused because of their cultural background?

Sources: Based on Simons, 1993b; Tomasevski, 1993; Greenhouse, 1994; and Rowley, 1994.

families—being a good provider was considered to be a sign of manhood. However, this gendered division of labour increased the economic and political subordination of women (Bernard, 1995). As a result, many women focused their efforts on acquiring a husband who was capable of bringing home a good wage. Single women and widows and their children tended to live a bleak existence, crowded into rundown areas of cities, where they were unable to support themselves on their meagre wages.

While industrialization was a source of upward mobility for many whites, most racial and ethnic minorities were left behind. The cult of domesticity, for example, was distinctly white and middle or upper class. White families with the financial means to do so hired domestic servants to do much of the household work. In the early 1900s, many black women (as well as white non-English-speaking European women) were employed as household servants (Das Gupta, 1995). Consequently, the cult of true womanhood not only increased women's dependence on men but also became the source of discrimination against women from minority groups.

The shift from an agricultural to an urban society also had an effect on gender body consciousness. People who worked in offices often became sedentary and exhibited physical deterioration from their lack of activity. As gymnasiums were built to fight this lack of physical fitness, a new image of masculinity developed. Whereas the "burly farmer" or "robust workman" previously had been the idealized image of masculinity, now the middle-class man who exercised and lifted weights came to embody the ideal of masculinity (Klein, 1993).

In the late nineteenth century, middle-class women began to become preoccupied with body fitness (Bordo, 1993:184; Seid, 1994). As industrialization progressed and food became more plentiful, the social symbolism of body weight and size changed. Previously, it had been considered a sign of high status to be somewhat overweight, but now a slender body reflected an enhanced social status. To the status-seeking middle-class man, a slender wife became a symbol of the husband's success. Historian Susan Bordo (1993:193) has suggested that "social power had come to be less dependent on the sheer accumulation of material wealth and more connected to the ability to control and manage the labor and resources of others. At the same time, excess body weight came to be seen as reflecting moral or personal inadequacy, or lack of will" (see also Banner, 1983). Today, women's bodies (even in bodybuilding programs) are supposed to be "inviting, available, and welcoming" while men's bodies should be "self-contained, active and invasive" (MacSween, 1993:256).

In sum, from hunting and gathering societies to contemporary industrial societies, women's status relative to men has declined. Today, patriarchy and male dominance remain pervasive. These existing patterns of inequality are perpetuated through the process of gender socialization.

GENDER AND SOCIALIZATION

We learn gender-appropriate behaviour through the socialization process. Our parents, teachers, friends, and the media all serve as gendered institutions that communicate to us our earliest, and often most lasting, beliefs about the social meanings of being male or female and thinking and behaving in masculine or feminine ways. Some gender roles have changed dramatically in recent years; others remain largely unchanged over time.

Many parents prefer boys to girls because of stereotypical ideas about the relative importance of males and females to the future of the family and society (Achilles, 1996). Although some parents prefer boys to girls because they believe old myths about the biological inferiority of females, research suggests that social expectations also play a major role in this preference. We are socialized to believe that it is important to have a son, especially as a first or only child. For many years, it was assumed that a male child could support his parents in their later years and carry on the family name.

Across cultures, boys are preferred to girls, especially when the number of children that parents can have is limited by law or economic conditions. For example, in China, which strictly regulates the allowable number of children to one per family, a disproportionate number of female fetuses are aborted (Basow, 1992). In India, the practice of aborting female fetuses is widespread, and female infanticide occurs frequently (Achilles, 1996). As a result, both India and China have a growing surplus of young men who will face a shortage of women their own age (Shenon, 1994).

In North America, some sex selection no doubt takes place through abortion. However, most women seek abortions because of socioeconomic factors, problematic relationships with partners, health-related concerns, and lack of readiness or ability to care for a child (or another child) (Lott, 1994).

GENDER SOCIALIZATION BY PARENTS

From birth, parents act toward children on the basis of the child's sex. Baby boys are perceived to be less fragile than girls and tend to be treated more roughly by their parents. Girl babies are thought to be "cute, sweet, and cuddly" and receive more gentle treatment (MacDonald and Parke, 1986). When girl babies cry, parents respond to them more quickly, and parents are more prone to talk and sing to girl babies (Basow, 1992). However, one study ("The Favored Infants," 1976) found ethnic–racial variations within cultures of these socialization patterns.

Children's clothing and toys reflect their parents' gender expectations. Boys' clothing, for example, is more "masculine" and functional and features male activities and characters (baseball players and superheros) while girls' clothing is more "feminine" and dainty (floral fabrics, lace, and bows) and has female characters. Gender–appropriate toys for boys include blocks and building sets, trucks and other vehicles, sports equipment, and war toys such as guns and soldiers (Richardson and Simpson, 1982). Girls' toys include "Barbie" dolls, play makeup, and homemaking items. Parents' choices of toys for their children are not likely to change in the near future. A group of university students in a recent study was shown slides of toys and asked to decide which ones they would buy for girls and boys. Most said they would buy guns, soldiers, jeeps, carpenter tools, and red bicycles for boys; girls would get baby dolls, dishes, sewing kits, jewellery boxes, and pink bicycles (Fisher-Thompson, 1990).

Boys are encouraged to engage in gender–appropriate behaviour; they are not to show an interest in "girls'" activities. For example, one father was dismayed when he bought his 4–year–old son a Ninja Turtle shaving kit, only to see the little boy head straight for the bathroom, sit on the edge of the tub, and start to shave his legs (*Austin American–Statesman*, 1994).

Differential treatment leads to differential development. A doll or a stuffed animal in a girl's hand calls for "hugging, stroking, and tender loving care"; a ball in a boy's hand "demands bouncing, throwing, and kicking" (Lott, 1994:40). When children are old enough to help with household chores, they often are assigned different tasks. Maintenance chores (such as mowing the lawn) are assigned to boys while domestic chores (such as shopping, cooking, and cleaning the table) are assigned to girls. Chores also may become linked with future occupational choices and personal characteristics. Girls who are responsible for domestic chores such as caring for younger brothers and sisters may learn nurturing behaviours that later translate into employment as a nurse or schoolteacher. Boys may learn about mechanics and other types of technology that lead to different career options.

Just as appropriate "masculine" or "feminine" behaviour is learned through interaction with parents and other caregivers, inappropriate behaviour such as eating problems can be learned from parents. Nicole Annesi tells how she learned about binging and purging from her mother:

> I was seven years old the first time I was exposed to my mother's bulimia. It was after dinner one evening. After Mom and I cleared the table ... she quickly disappeared into the bathroom ... What was unusual about these visits was that they became consistent. After each meal Mom would visit the bathroom and come out a few minutes later looking pale, yet refreshed ...
>
> So after the dishes were cleared away that evening, I disappeared into the bathroom. I hid in the tub, behind the navy blue, opaque curtain ... like clockwork, in she came. I peered between the curtains to find my mother bent over the toilet, like she was going to get sick or something. And then I watched her ... She placed a popsicle stick down her throat and made herself sick. How weird, I thought to myself. Mom comes into the bathroom every night to stick one of these doctor sticks down her throat! ...
>
> I began to do some thinking myself ... I knew when I got sick, afterwards my stomach would flatten out. I felt lighter. So one day after school I ate a bag of Pecan Sandies. I stuffed myself until I couldn't swallow. Afterwards I made my way to the upstairs bathroom and locked the door behind me. I turned on the faucet so that nothing could be heard ... That day I became a seven-year-old bulimic. (Annesi, 1993:91–93)

Many parents are aware of the effect that gender socialization has on their children and make a conscientious effort to provide nonsexist experiences for them. For example, one study found that mothers with nontraditional views encourage their daughters to be independent (Brooks-Gunn, 1986). Many fathers also take an active role in socializing their sons to be thoughtful and caring individuals who do not live by traditional gender stereotypes. However, peers often make nontraditional gender socialization much more difficult for parents and children (see Rabinowitz and Cochran, 1994).

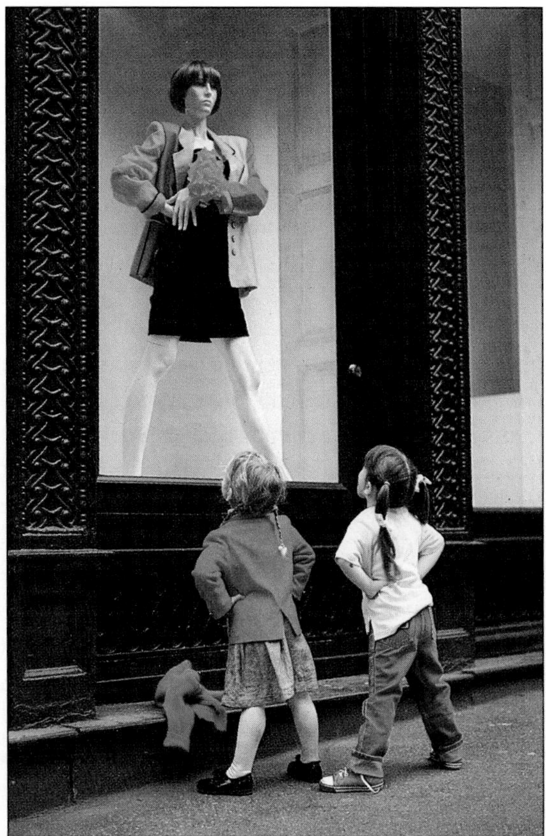

From an early age, a number of societal influences encourage us to learn gender-appropriate behaviour.

PEERS AND GENDER SOCIALIZATION

Peers help children learn prevailing gender role stereotypes, as well as gender-appropriate and –inappropriate behaviour. During the school years, same-sex peers have a powerful effect on how children see their gender roles (Maccoby and Jacklin, 1987); children are more socially acceptable to their peers when they conform to gender stereotypes (Martin, 1989). It is within the "peer culture" that children learn appropriate gender norms and gender roles (Adler et al., 1995).

Male peer groups place more pressure on boys to do "masculine" things than female peer groups place on girls to do "feminine" things (Fagot, 1984). For example, girls wear jeans and other "boy" clothes, play soccer and softball, and engage in other activities traditionally associated with males. But, if a boy wears a dress, plays hopscotch with girls, and engages in other activities associated with being female, he will be ridiculed by his peers. This distinction between the relative value of boys' and girls' behaviours strengthens the cultural message that masculine activities and behaviour are more important and more acceptable (Wood, 1994).

During adolescence, peers often are more influential agents of gender socialization than adults. Peers are thought to be especially important in boys' development of gender identity (Maccoby and Jacklin, 1987). Male bonding that occurs during adolescence is believed to reinforce masculine identity (Gaylin, 1992) and to encourage gender-stereotypical attitudes and behaviour (Huston, 1985; Martin, 1989). For example, male peers have a tendency to ridicule and bully others about their appearance, size, and weight. One woman painfully recalled walking down the halls at school when boys would flatten themselves against the lockers and cry, "Wide load!" At lunchtime, the boys made a production of watching her eat lunch and frequently made sounds like pig grunts or moos (Kolata, 1993). Because peer acceptance is so important for both males and females during their first two decades, such actions can have very harmful consequences for the victims.

As young adults, men and women still receive many gender-related messages from peers. Among university students, for example, peers play an important role in career choices and the establishment of long-term, intimate relationships. Male peers may pressure other men to participate in "male bonding" rituals that are derogatory toward women (DeKeseredy and Kelly, 1995). For example, fraternity initiations may require pledges to participate in behaviour ranging from "showing their manhood" to gang rapes (O'Sullivan, 1993). Some of the research suggests that male peers are often unable to show a man how to effectively interact intimately with other people (Tannen, 1990; DeKeseredy and Kelly, 1995).

Peer groups for both women and men on university campuses are organized largely around gender relations (Holland and Eisenhart, 1990). In a study that followed a number of women students at two universities, anthropologists Dorothy C. Holland and Margaret A. Eisenhart (1990) found that the peer system propelled women into a world of romance in which their attractiveness to men counted most; the women were subjected to a "sexual auction block." While peers initially did not influence the women's choices of majors and careers, they did influence whether the women continued to pursue their initial goals, changed their course of action, or were "derailed" (Holland and Eisenhart, 1981, 1990).

If Holland and Eisenhart's research can be generalized to other colleges and universities, peer pressure often is at its strongest in relation to appearance norms. As other researchers have shown, peer pressure can strongly influence a person's body consciousness. Women in university often feel pressure to be very thin, as Karen explains:

> "Do you diet?" asked a friend [in my first year of university], as I was stuffing a third homemade chocolate chip cookie in my mouth. "Do you know how many calories there are in that one cookie?"
>
> Stopping to think for a moment as she and two other friends stared at me, probably wanting to ask me the same question, I realized that I really didn't even know what a calorie was …
>
> From that moment, I'd taken on a new enemy, one more powerful and destructive than any human can be. One that nearly fought me to the death—my death …
>
> I just couldn't eat food anymore. I was so obsessed with it that I thought about it every second … In two months, I'd lost thirty pounds … Everyone kept telling me I looked great …
>
> I really didn't realize that anything was wrong with me … There were physical things occurring in my body other than not having

> my period anymore. My hair was falling out and was getting thinner … I would constantly get head rushes every time I stood up … When my friends would all go out to dinner or to a party I stayed home quite often, afraid that I might have to eat something, and afraid that my friends would find out that I didn't eat. (Twenhofel, 1993:198)

Feminist scholars have concluded that eating problems are not always psychological "disorders" (as they are referred to by members of the medical profession). Instead, eating (or not eating) may be a strategy for coping with problems such as unrealistic social pressures about slenderness (see Orbach, 1978; Chernin, 1981; Hesse-Biber, 1989) and/or social injustices caused by racism, sexism, and classism in society (Thompson, 1994).

TEACHERS AND SCHOOLS AND GENDER SOCIALIZATION

From kindergarten through university, schools operate as gendered institutions. Teachers provide important messages about gender through both the formal content of classroom assignments and informal interaction with students. Sometimes, gender-related messages from teachers and other students reinforce gender roles that have been taught at home; however, teachers also may contradict parental socialization. During the early years of a child's schooling, the teachers' influence is very powerful; many children spend more hours per day with their teachers than they do with their own parents.

One of the messages teachers may communicate to students is that boys are more important than girls. Research spanning the past twenty years shows that unintentional gender bias occurs in virtually all educational settings. ***Gender bias*** **consists of showing favouritism toward one gender over the other.** Researchers consistently find that teachers devote more time, effort, and attention to boys than to girls (Sadker and Sadker, 1994). Males receive more praise for their contributions and are called on more frequently in class, even when they do not volunteer. Very often, boys receive attention because they call out in class, demand help, and sometimes engage in disruptive behaviour (Sadker and Sadker, 1994). Teachers who do not negatively sanction such behaviour may unintentionally encourage it. Boys learn that when they yell out an answer without being called on, their answer will be accepted by the teacher; girls learn that they will be praised when they are compliant and wait for the teacher to call on them. If they call out an answer, they may be corrected with comments such as, "Please raise your hand if you want to speak" (Sadker and Sadker, 1994).

The content of teacher–student interaction is very important. In a multiple-year study of more than one hundred Grade 4, Grade 6, and Grade 8 students, education professors Myra and David Sadker (1984) identified four types of teacher comments: praise, acceptance, remediation, and criticism. They found that boys typically received more of all four types of teacher comments than did girls. Teachers also gave more precise and penetrating replies to boys; by contrast, teachers used vague and superficial terms such as "OK" when responding to girls. Because boys receive more specific and intense interaction from teachers, they may gain more insights than girls into the strengths and weaknesses of their answers and thus learn how to improve their responses.

Teacher–student interactions influence not only students' learning but also their self-esteem (Sadker and Sadker, 1985, 1986, 1994). A comprehensive study of gender bias in schools suggested that girls' self-esteem is undermined in school through such experiences as (1) a relative lack of attention from teachers, (2) sexual harassment by male peers, (3) the stereotyping and invisibility of females in textbooks, especially in science and math texts, and (4) test bias based on assumptions about the relative importance of quantitative and visual-spatial ability, as compared with verbal ability, that lessen girls' chances of being admitted to the university of their choice and awarded scholarships. White males may have better self-esteem because they receive more teacher attention than all other student groups (Sadker and Sadker, 1994).

Teachers also influence how students treat one another during school hours. Many teachers use sex segregation as a way to organize students, resulting in unnecessary competition between females and males (Eyre, 1992). In addition, teachers also may take a "boys will be boys" attitude when females complain of sexual harassment. Even though sexual harassment is prohibited by law, and teachers and administrators are obligated to investigate such incidents, the complaints may be dealt with superficially. If that happens, the school setting can become a hostile environment rather than a site for learning (Sadker and Sadker, 1994).

Most problems that exist in prekindergarten through high school also are found in colleges and universities. University professors often pay more attention to men than women in their classes (Wylie, 1995). Women are also subjected to a number of "exclusionary tactics," such as being called on less frequently and receiving less encouragement than men, or being interrupted, ignored, or devalued (Wylie, 1995). Researchers have found that women university professors (approximately 22 percent of university teachers) encourage a more participatory classroom environment and do a better job of including both women and men in their interactions (Statham, Richardson, and Cook, 1994). However, a study, which has come to be known as the "Chilly Climate Report" conducted at the University of Western Ontario, found that the university classroom is a "chilly" climate for women students, who often experience a drop in self-esteem as a result of their academic experiences. One graduate student reported that she felt "totally demoralized ... a failure ... I forget, even now, that I used to be seen as a powerful person. I lost my sense of personal power and self worth in the four years I was there" (Backhouse et al., 1995:127).

Despite these obstacles, women are more likely than men to earn a university degree. As Table 10.3 shows, in 1991, 58 percent of all bachelor's degrees awarded in Canada went to women.

TABLE 10.3

University Degrees Granted

	1994	
Bachelor's and first professional degrees		
Males	53,483	(42%)
Females	73,055	(58%)
Total	126,538	
Master's degrees		
Males	10,901	(51%)
Females	10,391	(49%)
Total	21,292	
Earned doctorates		
Males	2,453	(70%)
Females	1,099	(30%)
Total	3,552	

Source: Statistics Canada, 1995.

This pattern is relatively recent. It was not until 1988 that women's enrolment in university surpassed men's (Wylie, 1995). Women also received nearly half of the Master's degrees granted in 1994, which is up from 43 percent in 1982. Women remain substantially underrepresented at the doctoral level—earning less than one-third of the PhD's in 1994 (Wannell and Caron, 1996).

Most fields of study retain a male or female orientation, even though there has been a blending of fields of study in recent years. The proportion of women has been increasing in many traditionally male fields (including physics, meteorology, engineering, architecture, and dentistry), yet remains comparatively small. Women are more concentrated in nursing, home economics, most social sciences, public health, education, journalism, and fine arts. The mix of men and women is relatively equal in some of the fields that lead to high-paying jobs such as law, medicine, and optometry (Wannell and Caron, 1996). These recent trends should be reflected in future reductions in earnings gaps between men and women.

SPORTS AND GENDER SOCIALIZATION

Children spend more than half of their nonschool time in play and games, but the type of games played differs with the child's sex. Studies indicate that boys are socialized to participate in highly competitive, rule-oriented games with a larger number of participants than games played by girls. Girls have been socialized to play exclusively with others of their own age, in groups of two or three, in activities such as hopscotch and jump rope that involve a minimum of competitiveness (Adler, 1995).

From elementary school through high school, boys are encouraged to play competitive sports such as hockey and football. For males, competitive sports becomes a means of "constructing a masculine identity, a legitimated outlet for violence and aggression, and an avenue for upward mobility" (Lorber, 1994:43). Patricia Adler and her colleagues' participant observation study (1995) of two elementary school classrooms indicated that the most important factor affecting the boys' popularity or social status was athletic ability. Recently, more girls have started to play soccer, hockey, and baseball, and in the future, even more girls and women will participate in sports formerly regarded as exclusively "male" activities. However, even with these changes, women athletes have to manage a contradictory status of being both "women" and "athletes." One study found that women university basketball players dealt with this contradiction by dividing their lives into segments. On the basketball court, the women "did athlete": they pushed, shoved, fouled, ran hard, sweated, and cursed. Off the court, they "did woman": after the game, they showered, dressed, applied makeup, and styled their hair, even if they were only getting in a van for a long ride home (Watson, 1987).

Women athletes juggle contradictory statuses. According to one study, women university basketball players "did athlete" on the court and "did woman" after the game.

According to sociologist Judith Lorber (1994:41), "Sports illustrate the ways bodies are gendered by social practices and how the female body is socially constructed to be inferior." Most sports are rigidly divided into female and male events. Assumptions about male and female physiology and athletic capabilities influence the types of sports in which members of each sex are encouraged to participate. For example, women who engage in activities that are assumed to be "masculine" (such as bodybuilding) may either ignore their critics or attempt to redefine the activity or its result as "feminine" or womanly (Duff and Hong, 1984; Klein, 1993). Some women bodybuilders do not want their bodies to get "overbuilt." They have learned that they are more likely to win women's bodybuilding competitions if they look and pose "more or less along the lines of fashion models" (Klein, 1993:179). How strongly some female gymnasts internalize this idealized body image was reflected by the death of 22-year-old Christy Henrich, a former nationally ranked gymnast. At the time of her death, she weighed less than sixty pounds, the victim of anorexia and bulimia; her mother said, "[Christy] was going to do whatever it took, no matter what the price. She could endure any pain" (quoted in Amdur, 1994:B9).

MASS MEDIA AND GENDER SOCIALIZATION

The media are a powerful source of gender stereotyping. While some critics argue that the media simply reflect existing gender roles in society, others point out that the media have a uniquely persuasive ability to shape ideas. Think of the impact that television has on children who are estimated to spend one-third of their waking time watching it. Children from working-class families spend significantly more time in front of the television than those from the middle class (Basow, 1992).

From children's cartoons to adult shows, television programs are sex-typed and white-male oriented. More male than female roles are shown, and male characters act strikingly different from female ones. Males are typically more aggressive, constructive, and direct and are rewarded for their actions. In contrast, females are depicted as acting deferentially toward other people or as manipulating them through helplessness or seductiveness to get their way (Basow, 1992). Because advertisers hope to appeal to boys, who constitute more than half of the viewing audience for some shows, many programs feature lively adventure and lots of loud noise and violence. Even educational programs such as "Sesame Street" and "Barney," in which most of the characters have male names and masculine voices and participate in "boy's activities," may perpetuate gender stereotypes.

While attempts have been made by media "watchdogs" and some members of the media itself to eliminate sexism in children's programming, adult daytime and prime-time programs (which children frequently watch) have received less scrutiny. Soap operas are a classic example of programs that stereotype gender. In them, women are depicted as emotional, nurturing, and unable to make a decision; men are forceful and more oriented toward problem solving. Daytime talk shows such as "Donahue" and "Oprah" may trivialize important issues of sex and gender under the guise of letting people air their grievances and opinions and of having experts who set the record straight (Basow, 1992).

In prime-time television, a number of significant changes in the past three decades have reduced gender stereotyping; however, men still outnumber women as leading characters. Men, for the most part, have been police officers, detectives, attorneys, doctors, and businessmen. In recent years, women in professional careers have been overrepresented, which may give the erroneous impression that most women in the workforce are in executive, managerial, and professional positions; in the "real world," most employed women work in low-paying, low-status jobs (Basow, 1992). In most programs, women's appearance is considered very important and frequently is a topic of discussion in the program itself. Advertising reinforces the notion that women can never be too young or too thin, as discussed in Box 10.3.

Advertising—whether on television and billboards or in magazines and newspapers—can be very persuasive. The intended message is clear to many people: if they embrace traditional notions of masculinity and femininity, their personal and social success is assured; and if they purchase the right products and services, they can enhance their appearance and gain power over other people. For example, the \$20-billion-per-year cosmetics industry uses ads depicting the "truly feminine woman" as needing a "plethora of beauty aids to help her look younger and more attractive to men" (Wolf, 1990). Such ads may play an important role in adult gender socialization.

BOX 10.3 SOCIOLOGY AND MEDIA

"You've Come a Long Way, Baby!"

> In a television commercial, two little French girls are shown dressing up in the feathery finery of their mothers' clothes. They are exquisite little girls, flawless and innocent, and the scene emphasizes both their youth and the natural sense of style often associated with French women. (The ad is done in French, with subtitles.) One of the girls, spying a picture of the other girl's mother, exclaims breathlessly, "Your mother, she is so slim, so beautiful? Does she eat?" The daughter, giggling, replies, "Silly, just not as much," and displays her mother's helper, a bottle of diet pills. "Aren't you jealous?" the friend asks. Dimpling, shy, yet self-possessed, deeply knowing, the daughter answers, "Not if I know her secrets." (Bordo, 1993:99)

Women are bombarded with such advertisements and commercials for weight-loss products and programs. This ad is especially problematic, however, because it suggests that very young girls should begin learning to control their weight by the use of some "secret" (Bordo, 1993:99). Viewers must use their imagination about how the mother looks, but the message is clear: Her "slim ... beautiful" appearance can belong to any woman who purchases this product. According to media scholar Jean Kilbourne (1994:395):

> The current emphasis on excessive thinness for women is one of the clearest examples of advertising's power to influence cultural standards and consequent individual behavior. Body types, like clothing styles, go in and out of fashion, and are promoted by advertising ... The images in the mass media constantly reinforce the latest ideal—what is acceptable and what is out of date ... Advertising and the media indoctrinate us in these ideals, to the detriment of most women.

Today's ideal body type is unattainable except for the thinnest 5 percent of all women. Clearly, the dramatic increase in eating problems in recent years cannot be attributed solely to advertising and the mass media; however, their potential impact on young girls and women in establishing role models with whom to identify is extremely important (Kilbourne, 1994:398).

Recurring themes in advertising campaigns directed at women include the need for diet products and the fear of fat, reinforced by the theme of guilt (Kilbourne, 1994:404). The messages in these ads may even be contradictory. Virginia Slims cigarette advertisements say, "You've come a long way, baby!" even though they are marketing an addictive and unhealthy product (Kilbourne, 1994:413). In one ad, a slim, elegant African American woman holds up a lighted cigarette. The caption states, "Decisions are easy. When I get to a fork in the road, I eat." The ad suggests that this woman can make decisions easily; she can eat and not experience negative consequences simply because she smokes a particular brand of cigarettes. Nor are such ads new; for most of this century, cigarettes have been marketed to women and young girls as a way to control their weight. In 1928, for example, Lucky Strike cigarette ads stated, "To keep a slender figure, no one can deny ... reach for a Lucky instead of a sweet" (Kilbourne, 1994:413).

As women have attempted to gain power and freedom, advertising has worked to reduce the political to the personal. If people buy the right products and get their individual acts together, everything will be fine. As Kilbourne (1994) notes, "The advertisers will never voluntarily change, because it is profitable for women to feel terrible about themselves. Thus, we need to educate everyone to be critical viewers of advertising and the mass media."

Sources: Based on Barthel, 1988; Moog, 1990; Bordo, 1993; and Kilbourne, 1994.

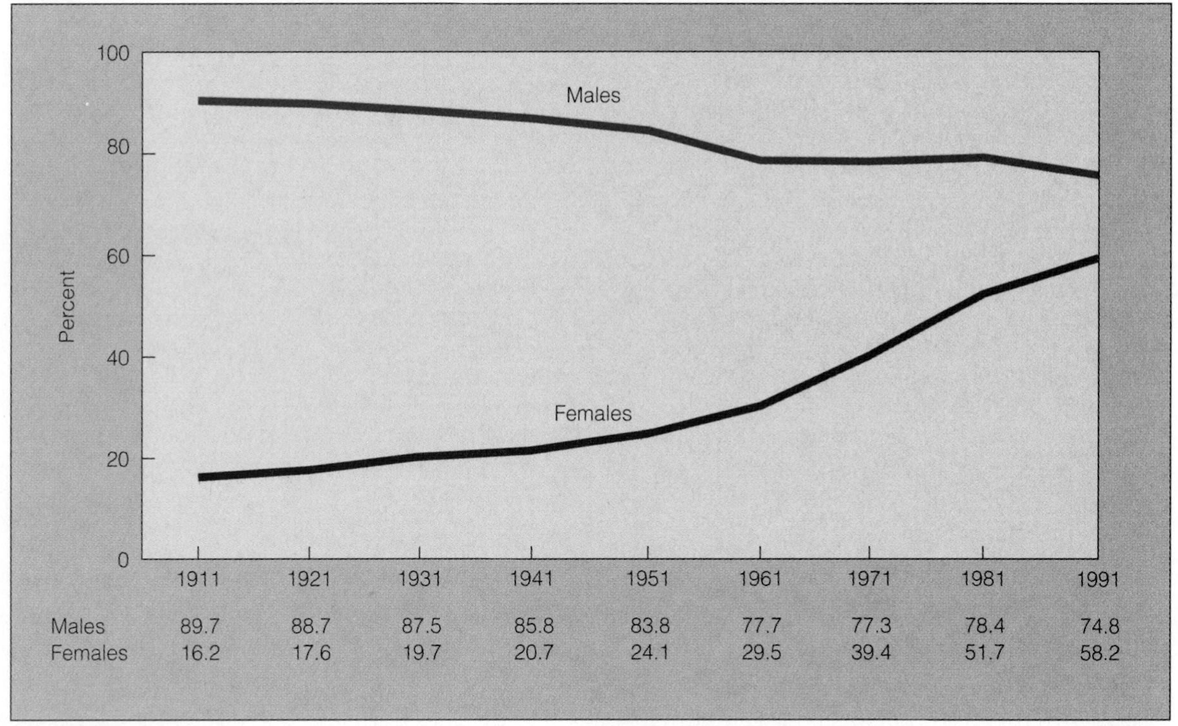

	1911	1921	1931	1941	1951	1961	1971	1981	1991
Males	89.7	88.7	87.5	85.8	83.8	77.7	77.3	78.4	74.8
Females	16.2	17.6	19.7	20.7	24.1	29.5	39.4	51.7	58.2

FIGURE 10.1

Labour Force Participation Rates, Males and Females Aged 15 and Over, 1911–1991

Prepared by the Centre for International Statistics. © The Vanier Institute of the Family. Reprinted by permission.

A knowledge of how we develop a gender-related self-concept and learn to feel, think, and act in feminine or masculine ways is important for an understanding of ourselves. Examining gender socialization makes us aware of the impact of our parents, sibling, teachers, friends, and the media have on our own perspectives about gender. However, the gender socialization perspective has been criticized on several accounts. Childhood gender-role socialization may not affect people as much as some analysts have suggested. For example, the types of jobs people take as adults may have less to do with how they were socialized in childhood than it does with how they are treated in the workplace. From this perspective, women and men will act in ways that bring them the most rewards and produce the fewest punishments (Reskin and Padavic, 1994). Also, gender socialization theories can be used to blame women for their own subordination (Eitzen and Baca Zinn, 1995). For example, if we assume that women's problems can all be blamed on women themselves, existing social structures that perpetuate gender inequality will be overlooked. We will now examine a few of those structural forces.

CONTEMPORARY GENDER INEQUALITY

According to feminist scholars, women experience gender inequality as a result of economic,

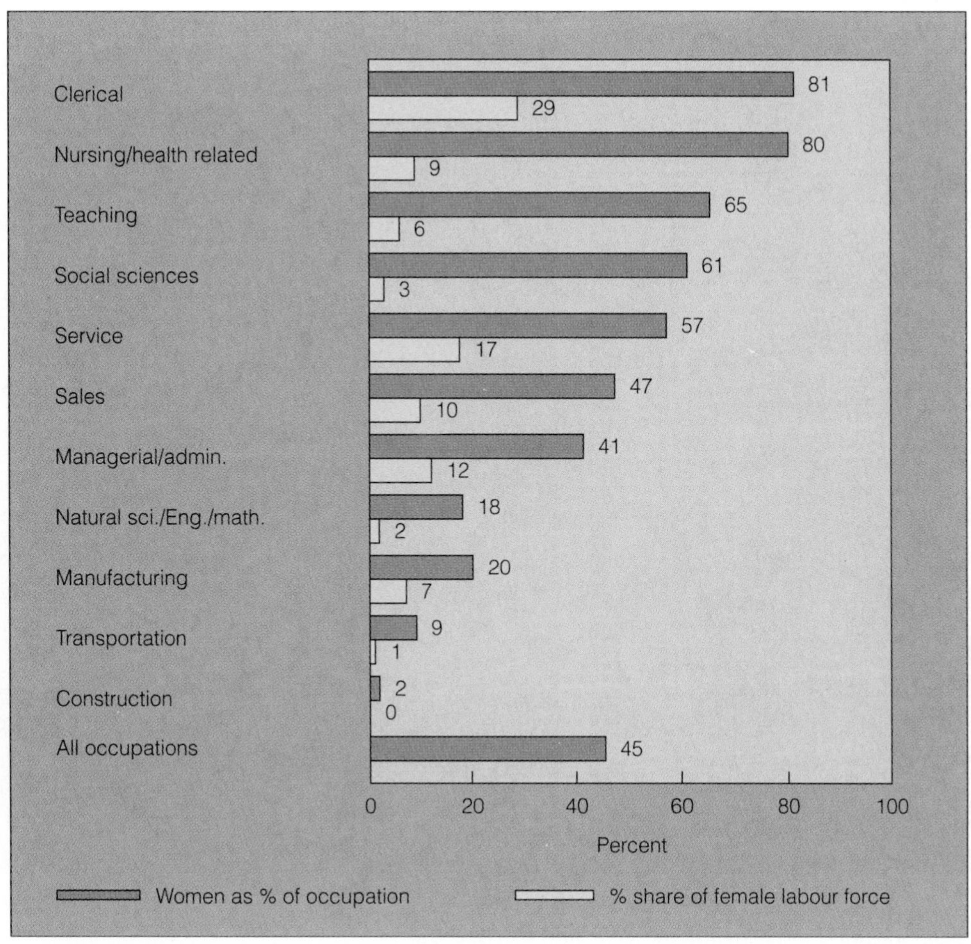

FIGURE 10.2

Employment Concentration and Occupational Distribution of Women, Canada, 1991

Note: Manufacturing = processing, machining, fabricating, materials handling, and other crafts. Unclassified occupations omitted.

Reproduced by authority of the Minister of Industry, 1996, Statistics Canada, from *The Labour Force Annual Averages* 1991, Cat. no. 71-220.

political, and educational discrimination (Luxton, 1980; Smith, 1987; Richer & Weir, 1995). Women's position in the Canadian work force reflects their overall subordination in society.

GENDERED DIVISION OF PAID WORK

The workplace is another example of a gendered institution. As Figure 10.1 demonstrates, the number of Canadian women entering the paid workforce in the past thirty years has risen substantially. Most Canadian women continue to be employed in traditional female occupations and, contrary to popular myth, "few women have moved into more prestigious and better-paying jobs" (Armstrong, 1993:129). Although more women are in professional occupations than ever before, they remain concentrated in lower-paying,

What stereotypes are associated with men in female-oriented occupations? With women in male-oriented occupations? Do you think such stereotypes will change in the near future?

traditionally female jobs. In 1993, 71 percent of all working women were employed in teaching, nursing, and health-related occupations, clerical work, or sales and service occupations (Statistics Canada, 1994a). Since 1950, there has been an increase of only 1.4 percent in the proportion of women employed in professional and technical jobs, most of which are lower-paying technical positions (Armstrong, 1993:129).

Gender–segregated work refers to the concentration of women and men in different occupations, jobs, and places of work (Krahn and Lowe, 1993). In 1991, for example, 81 percent of all clerical jobs in Canada were held by women (see Figure 10.2). In the same year, men were overrepresented in jobs in the natural sciences, engineering, and mathematics and made up 82 percent of the professionals in these fields (Zukewich Ghalam, 1994). However, women have made gains in several professional occupations in which few women have worked in the past. In 1993, for example, women accounted for 26 percent of all doctors, dentists, and other health-diagnosing and treating professionals, up from 18 percent in 1982 (Statistics Canada, 1994a).

Although the degree of gender segregation in parts of the professional labour market has declined since the 1970s (Sokoloff, 1992), racial-

TABLE 10.4

Women's Earnings as a Percentage of Men for Full-Time, Full-Year Workers, 1971–1992

Year	%
1971	59.7
1976	59.1
1981	63.7
1986	65.8
1989	65.8
1991	69.6
1992	71.8

Reproduced by authority of the Minister of Industry, 1996, Statistics Canada, from *Earnings of Men and Women*, Cat. no. 13-217.

ethnic segregation has remained deeply embedded in the social structure. However, the relationship between visible minority status and occupational status is complex and varies by gender. Although visible minority males are overrepresented in both lower- and higher-status occupations, nonwhite women are heavily overrepresented in lower-paying, low-skilled jobs (Krahn and Lowe, 1993).

Workplace gender segregation is not unique to Canada. For example, in Sweden, the country with the highest rate of women's paid labour force participation in the world, gender segregation is even greater (Borchorst and Siim, 1987). To eliminate gender-segregated jobs in the United States, more than half of all men and women workers would have to change occupations (Reskin and Hartmann, 1986). Across cultures, men are less active than women in crossing the gender barrier in employment (Kauppinen-Toropainen and Lammi, 1993).

Occupational segregation—the division of jobs into categories with distinct working conditions—results in women having separate and unequal jobs (Armstrong and Armstrong, 1994). The pay gap between men and women is the best-documented consequence of gender-segregated work (Krahn and Lowe, 1993). Most women work in the secondary sector of the labour market, which consists of low-paying jobs with few benefits and very little job security or job advancement. As described in Chapter 9, the primary sector or upper tier of the labour market consists of well-paid jobs with good benefits, job security, and the possibility of future advancement. Because many employers assume that men are the breadwinners, men are expected to make more money than women in order to support their families. For many years, women have been viewed as supplemental wage earners in a male-headed household, regardless of the woman's marital status. Consequently, women have not been seen as legitimate workers but mainly as wives and mothers (Lorber, 1994).

Gender-segregated work affects both men and women. Men often are kept out of certain types of jobs. Those who enter female-dominated occupations often have to justify themselves and prove that they are "real men." They have to fight stereotypes ("Is he gay? Lazy?") about why they are interested in such work (Williams, 1993:3). Even if these assumptions do not push men out of female-dominated occupations, they affect how the men manage their gender identity at work. For example, men in occupations such as nursing emphasize their masculinity, attempt to distance themselves from female colleagues, and try to move quickly into management and supervisory positions (Williams, 1989, 1993).

Occupational gender segregation contributes to stratification in society. Job segregation is structural; it does not occur simply because individual workers have different abilities, motivations, and material needs. As a result of gender and racial segregation, employers are able to pay many visible minority males and females less money, promote them less often, and provide fewer bene-

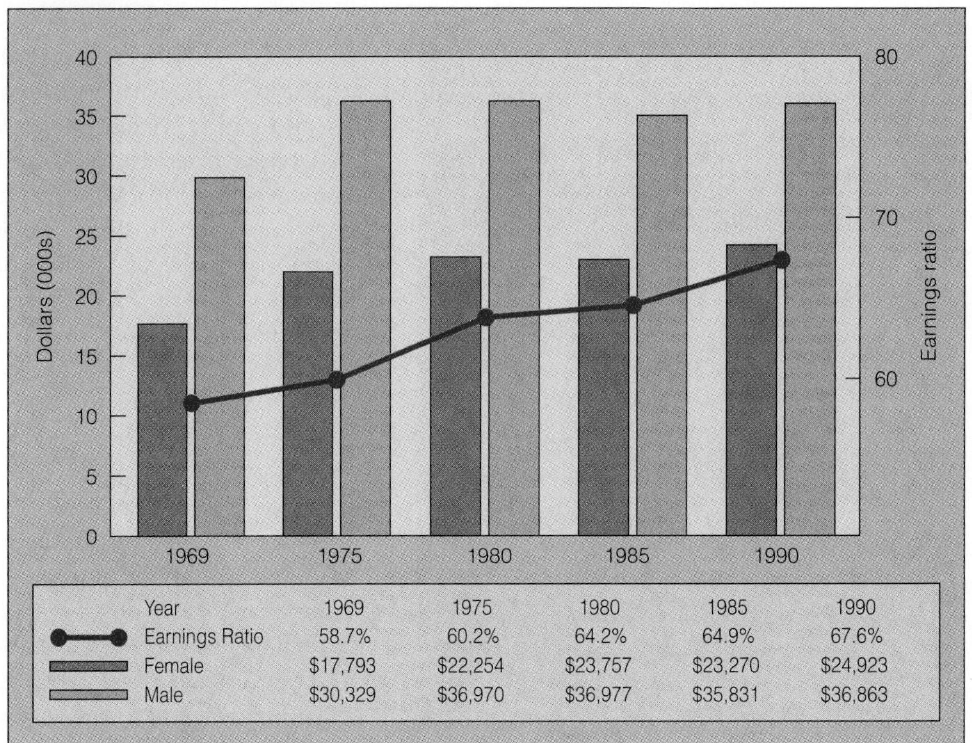

Year	1969	1975	1980	1985	1990
Earnings Ratio	58.7%	60.2%	64.2%	64.9%	67.6%
Female	$17,793	$22,254	$23,757	$23,270	$24,923
Male	$30,329	$36,970	$36,977	$35,831	$36,863

FIGURE 10.3A

Average Earnings in Constant (1990) Dollars for Full-time, Full Year Canadian Workers, by Gender, 1969–1990*

* Full-time = 30 or more hours weekly; full-year = 49–52 weeks annually (50–52 weeks prior to 1981). Earning ratio: female earnings as a percentage of male earnings.

Reproduced by authority of the Minister of Industry, 1996, Statistics Canada, from *Earnings of Men and Women 1990*, Cat. no. 13-217.

fits. If they demand better working conditions or wages, workers often are reminded of the number of individuals (members of Marx's "reserve army") who would like to have their jobs.

PAY EQUITY AND EMPLOYMENT EQUITY

Occupational segregation contributes to a second form of discrimination—the ***wage gap, a*** **a term referring to the disparity between women's and men's earnings.** It is calculated by dividing women's earnings by men's to yield a percentage, also known as the *earnings ratio* (Reskin and Padavic, 1994). Table 10.4 and Figure 10.3A show that there has been some improvement in this earnings ratio over the past two decades, but the progress has been slow. In 1992, women who worked full time for the whole year still earned only 71.8 percent of what similarly employed men earned (Parkinson and Drislane, 1996). To make matters worse, the earnings ratio actually underestimates the actual differences in pay between men and women because it does not take into account fringe benefits. If fringe benefits are included, the wage gap between men and women is actually increasing as more women enter the labour force (Armstrong, 1993). Among older workers, the wage gap between men and women

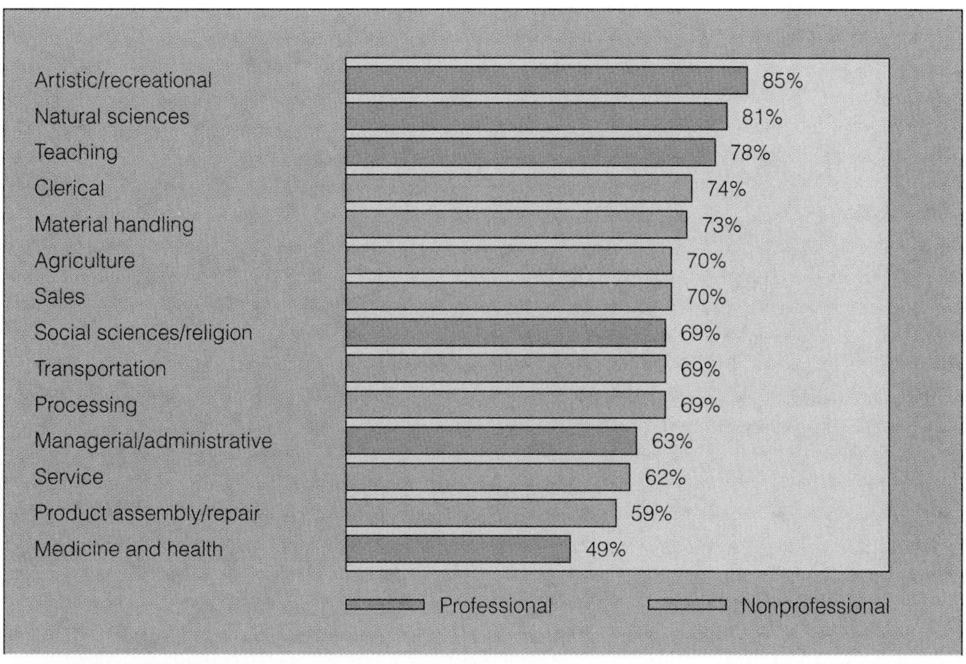

FIGURE 10.3B

Earnings of Women as a Percentage of Those of Men,[1]

[1]Includes earnings of full-time, full-year workers.

Reproduced by authority of the Minister of Industry, 1996, Statistics Canada, from *Earnings of Men and Women*, Cat. no. 13-217.

is larger. Women's earnings tend to rise more slowly than men's when they are younger and then drop off when women reach their late thirties and early forties, while the wages of men tend to increase as they age (Vanier Institute of the Family, 1994). Because women's overall pay relative to men's has increased by about a penny a year for the past ten years, it might seem that women's earnings have taken a noticeable move upwards. However, this decrease in wage disparity can be attributed to the fact that men's earnings have declined since the 1970s while women's have climbed slowly (Roos and Reskin, 1992). Some hope for the future is offered by the fact that recent figures indicate that there was no earnings difference between single men and women with university educations (Statistics Canada, 1994).

Pay equity or, as it is sometimes called ***comparable worth*** **is the belief that wages ought to reflect the worth of a job, not the gender or race of the worker** (Kemp, 1994). Pay equity is a proactive policy that requires employers to assess the extent of pay discrimination and then adjust wages so that women are fairly compensated (Krahn and Lowe, 1993:183). How do you determine the amount of pay discrimination? One way is to compare the actual work of women's and men's jobs and see if there is a disparity in the salaries paid for each. To do this, analysts break a job into components—such as the education, training, and skills required, the extent of responsibility for others' work, and the working conditions—and then allocate points for each (Lorber, 1994). For pay equity to exist, men and women in occupations that receive the same number of points should be paid the same. As the Ontario New Democrat government's Green Paper on Pay Equity put it, pay equity legislation was to be designed "as a positive remedy to address a historical imbalance—the correlation between being a

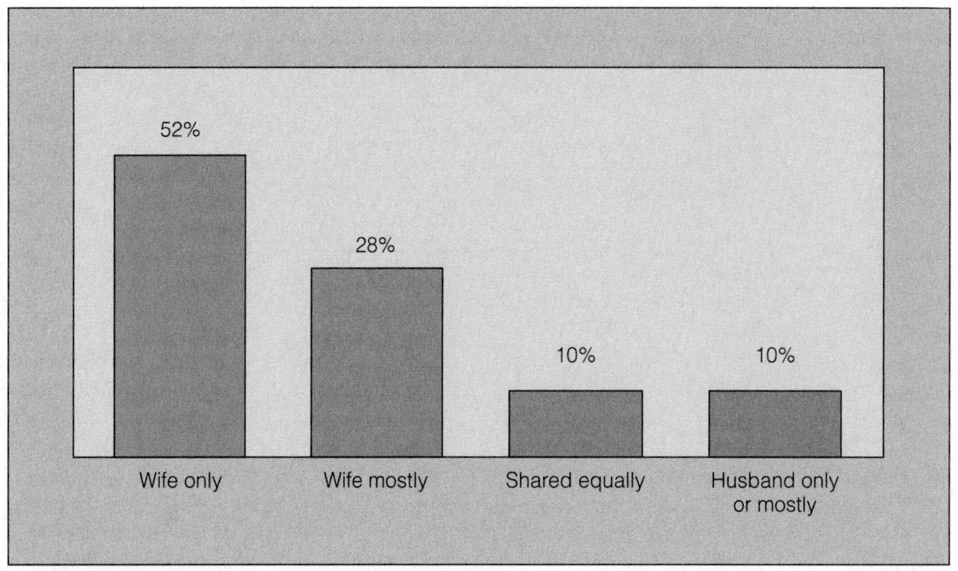

FIGURE 10.4

Responsibility for Housework in Dual-Earner Families with Both Spouses Employed Full Time, 1990

Reproduced by authority of the Minister of Industry, 1996, Statistics Canada, from *1990 General Social Survey,* Cat. no. 11-612.

female employee and receiving lower wages" (Krahn and Lowe, 1993:183).

Pay equity legislation has now been implemented in most provinces. However, as Figure 10.3B demonstrates, pay equity exists for very few occupations. For example, in 1991, for every dollar earned by men, women earned 78 cents as teachers, 62 cents as lawyers, 72 cents as accountants, and 91 cents as university professors.

A second strategy for addressing inequality in the workplace is ***employment equity,*** which, according to the 1984 Royal Commission on Equality of Employment is **a strategy to eliminate the effects of discrimination and to fully open the competition for job opportunities to those who have been excluded historically** (Krahn and Lowe, 1995:180). The target groups for employment equity are: visible minorities, persons with disabilities, aboriginal peoples, and women. In comparison with pay equity, which addresses wage issues only, employment equity covers a range of employment issues such as recruitment, selection, training, development, and promotion. Employment equity also addresses issues pertaining to conditions of employment such as compensation, layoffs, and disciplinary action (Boyd, 1995). However, the 1986 Employment Equity Act covers only employers within the federal government, including federal Crown corporations, banks, and companies that have federal government contracts. This represents only about 11 percent of the Canadian labour force (Boyd, 1995:24). Although these policies represent a start in the right direction, male resistance and poor regulation and enforcement have resulted in minimal progress toward gendered employment equity. A more detailed discussion of the gendered nature of the workplace is in Chapter 12 ("The Economy and Work").

PAID WORK AND FAMILY WORK

As previously discussed, the first big change in the relationship between family and work occurred with the Industrial Revolution and the

BOX 10.4 SOCIOLOGY AND LAW

Obscenity and Women's Equality

Is pornography harmful? If so, who does it harm? Is all pornographic material obscene or just some of it? Does it result in exploitation and further objectification of women in our society? In the Canadian courts, the jury on these issues is still out.

The Criminal Code originally defined obscene material as that which involves, "the undue exploitation of sex." What exactly constitutes "undue exploitation of sex"? This is yet to be resolved in the courts, despite millions of dollars of litigation dating back forty years when the legislation was originally enacted. Until recently, judges had the responsibility of assessing what was decent and what was indecent in obscenity cases. In other words, obscenity was in the eye of the beholder and varied with the times.

This changed in 1992 with the landmark Supreme Court of Canada case R vs. Butler. David Butler, the owner of a Winnipeg pornography shop was charged with 250 counts of possessing and trafficking in obscene hard-core videos and magazines. Owning and distributing obscene material carries a maximum penalty of two years in jail. Butler was acquitted on 242 counts and convicted on eight. Unsatisfied with this result, Butler appealed his convictions up to the Supreme Court of Canada, arguing that pornographic material is protected from prosecution because of the guarantee of freedom of expression in the Charter of Rights and Freedoms.

The outcome of the Butler case was influenced by the Women's Legal Education and Action Fund (LEAF). In an official brief, LEAF asked the Supreme Court to uphold the obscenity law on the basis that some forms of pornography promoted violence against women. However, as LEAF acknowledged, the research evidence is ambiguous—it neither proves nor disproves this claim.

The Supreme Court agreed with LEAF and in a unanimous decision, upheld the obscenity law and the court's rights to censor pornographic material that is defined as obscene. However, according to Justice Sopinka, who authored the Supreme Court ruling, only the worst types of pornography should be outlawed "not because it offends against morals but because it is perceived by public opinion to be harmful to society, particularly women (Verberg, 1994:26). If an obscene work threatened the equality of women, censorship was justified.

A more explicit definition of obscenity resulted from Butler's Supreme Court challenge. First, any material that mixes explicit sex and violence, or includes children, should be ruled obscene. Second, materials that involve explicit sex and degradation are obscene if they are deemed to encourage violence or other harm against women. Finally, other sexually explicit material is permissible.

The ruling in the Butler decision has resulted in increasingly liberal interpretations of obscenity laws. Why? Now in order to obtain a conviction on an obscenity charge, the prosecution has to prove that a certain work causes harm. This is a defense counsel's dream, as one Toronto criminal lawyer comments, "Dirty pictures don't cause anything" (Kaihla, 1994:30).

What do you think? In a downtown Toronto shop called "Books," an entire wall is devoted to bondage videos. One of the selections is entitled *Women Ruled By Men*. On the cover are two nude women strapped back to back by a series of chains. One of them has what looks like a horse's bit in her mouth, held there by a strap around her head. Another selection features "Sir Michael" in a dungeon with whips and chains hanging from the wall, pulling open the negligee of a young women gagged with heavy, knotted rope. The cover reads "Join Sir Michael as he teases, torments, humiliates and disciplines some of the most beautiful and submissive women who have fallen under his powerful will" (Kaihla, 1994:30).

Are these videos harmful? How would you go about proving in a courtroom that these images are harmful?

Sources: Kaihla, 1994; Verburg, 1994.

rise of capitalism. The cult of domesticity kept many middle- and upper-class women out of the work force during this period. Working-class and poor women primarily were the ones who had to deal with the work/family conflict. Today, however, the issue spans the entire economic spectrum (Reskin and Padavic, 1994). The typical married woman in Canada combines paid work in the labour force and family work as a homemaker. Although this change has occurred at the societal level, individual women bear the brunt of the problem.

Even with dramatic changes in women's workforce participation, the sexual division of labour in the family remains essentially unchanged. While most married women now share responsibility for the breadwinner role, many men do not accept their share of domestic responsibilities (Armstrong, 1993; Marshall, 1995; Luxton, 1995). Consequently (and as Figure 10.4 demonstrates), many women have a "double day" or "second shift" because of their dual responsibilities for paid and unpaid work (Hochschild, 1989). Working women have less time to spend on housework; if husbands do not participate in routine domestic chores, some chores simply do not get done or get done less often. While the income many women earn is essential for the economic survival of their families, they still must spend part of their earnings on family maintenance, such as day-care centres, fast-food restaurants, and laundries, in an attempt to keep up with their obligations (Bergmann, 1986).

Especially in families with young children, domestic responsibilities consume a great deal of time and energy. Although some kinds of housework can be put off, the needs of children often cannot be ignored or delayed. When children are ill or school events cannot be scheduled around work, parents (especially mothers) may experience stressful role conflicts ("Shall I be a good employee or a good mother?"). Many working women care not only for themselves, their husbands, and their children but also for elderly parents or in-laws. Some analysts refer to these women as "the sandwich generation"—caught between the needs of their young children and elderly relatives.

Although both men and women profess that working couples should share household responsibilities, researchers find that family demands remain mostly women's responsibility, even among women who hold full-time paid employment. Many women try to solve their time crunch by forgoing leisure time and sleep. When Arlie Hochschild interviewed working mothers, she found that they talked about sleep "the way a hungry person talks about food" (1989:9).

PERSPECTIVES ON GENDER STRATIFICATION

Sociological perspectives on gender stratification vary in their approach to examining gender roles and power relationships in society. Some focus on the roles of women and men in the domestic sphere; others note the inequalities arising from a gendered division of labour in the workplace. Still others attempt to integrate both the public and private spheres into their analyses.

FUNCTIONALIST AND NEOCLASSICAL ECONOMIC PERSPECTIVES

As seen earlier, functionalist theory views men and women as having distinct roles that are important for the survival of the family and society. The most basic division of labour is biological: men are physically stronger while women are the only ones able to bear and nurse children. Gendered belief systems foster assumptions about appropriate behaviour for men and women and may have an impact on the types of work women and men perform.

THE IMPORTANCE OF TRADITIONAL GENDER ROLES According to functional analysts such as Talcott Parsons (1955), women's roles as nurturers and caregivers are even more pronounced in contemporary industrialized societies. While the husband performs the *instrumental* tasks of providing economic support and making decisions, the wife assumes the *expressive* tasks of providing affection and emotional support for the family. This division of family labour ensures that important societal tasks will be fulfilled; it also provides stability for family members.

This view has been adopted by a number of conservative analysts. George F. Gilder (1986) argues that traditional gender roles are important not only for individuals but also for the economic and social order of society. He asserts that relationships between men and women are damaged when changes in gender roles occur, and family life suffers as a consequence. According to Gilder, women provide for the socialization of the next generation; if they do not, society's moral fabric will decay, resulting in higher rates of crime, violence, and drug abuse. From this perspective, the traditional division of labour between men and women is the natural order of the universe (Kemp, 1994).

THE HUMAN CAPITAL MODEL Functionalist explanations of occupational gender segregation are similar to neoclassical economic perspectives, such as the human capital model (Horan, 1978; Kemp, 1994). According to this model, individuals vary widely in the amount of human capital they bring to the labour market. *Human capital* is acquired by education and job training; it is the source of a person's productivity and can be measured in terms of the return on the investment (wages) and the cost (schooling or training) (Stevenson, 1988; Kemp, 1994).

From this perspective, what individuals earn is the result of their own choices (the kinds of training, education, and experience they accumulate, for example) and of the labour market need (demand) for and availability (supply) of certain kinds of workers at specific points in time. For example, human capital analysts argue that women diminish their human capital when they leave the labour force to engage in childbearing and childcare activities. While women are out of the labour force, their human capital deteriorates from nonuse. When they return to work, women earn lower wages than men because they have fewer years of work experience and have "atrophied human capital" because their education and training may have become obsolete (Kemp, 1994:70).

Other neoclassical economic models attribute the wage gap to such factors as (1) the different amounts of energy men and women expend on their work (women who spend much energy on their family and household have less to put into their work), (2) the occupational choices women make (choosing female-dominated occupations so that they can spend more time with their families), and (3) the crowding of too many women into some occupations (suppressing wages because the supply of workers exceeds demand) (Kemp, 1994).

EVALUATION OF FUNCTIONALIST AND NEOCLASSICAL ECONOMIC PERSPECTIVES Although Parsons and other functionalists did not specifically endorse the gendered division of labour, their analysis views it as natural and perhaps inevitable. Critics argue, however, that problems inherent in traditional gender roles, including the personal role strains of men and women and the social costs to society, are minimized by this approach. For example, men are assumed to be "money machines" for their families when they might prefer to spend more time in child-rearing activities. Also, the woman's place is assumed to be in the home, an assumption that ignores the fact that many women hold jobs due to economic necessity.

In addition, the functionalist approach does not take a critical look at the structure of society (especially the economic inequalities) that make educational and occupational opportunities more available to some than to others. Furthermore, it fails to examine the underlying power relations between men and women or to consider the fact that the tasks assigned to women and to men are unequally valued by society (Kemp, 1994). Similarly, the human capital model is rooted in the premise that individuals are evaluated based on their human capital in an open, competitive

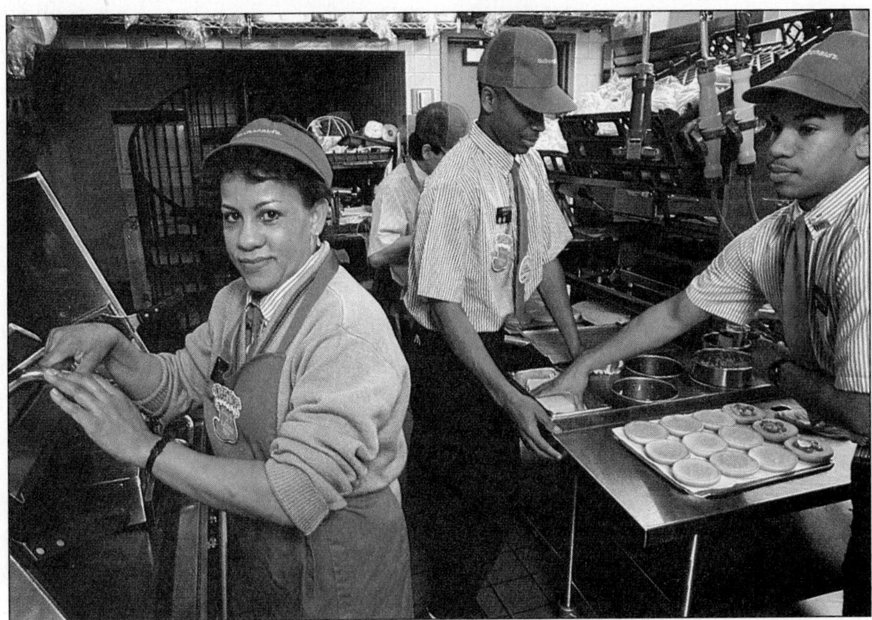

The disparity between women's and men's earnings is even greater for women of colour. Feminists who analyze ethnicity, class, and gender suggest that equality will occur only when all women are treated more equitably.

market where education, training, and other job-enhancing characteristics are taken into account. From this perspective, those who make less money (often men of ethnic minority groups and all women) have no one to blame but themselves. According to sociologist Alice Kemp (1994:76).

> If women have children to care for, it is a situation they freely chose and will have to work out for themselves. That jobs and professions have been structured to reflect men's lives and circumstances is seldom recognized; instead women are conceptualized as somehow different from men in their motivations and preference for income.

Critics note that, instead of blaming people for their choices, we must acknowledge other realities. Wage discrimination occurs in two ways: (1) The wages are higher in male-dominated jobs, occupations, and segments of the labour market, regardless of whether women take time for family duties, and (2) in any job, women and members of some minority groups will be paid less (Lorber, 1994).

CONFLICT PERSPECTIVES

According to many conflict analysts, the gendered division of labour within families and in the workplace results from male control of and dominance over women and resources. Differentials between men and women may exist in terms of economic, political, physical, and/or interpersonal power. The importance of a male monopoly in any of these arenas depends on the significance of that type of power in a society (Richardson, 1993). In hunting and gathering and horticultural societies, male dominance over women is limited because all members of the society must work in order to survive (Collins, 1971; Nielsen, 1990). In agrarian societies, however, male sexual dominance is at its peak. Male heads of household gain a monopoly not only on physical power but also on economic power, and women become sexual property.

Although men's ability to use physical power to control women diminishes in industrial societies, men still remain the heads of household and control the property. In addition, men gain more power through their predominance in the most highly paid and prestigious occupations and the highest elected offices. In contrast, women have the ability to trade their sexual resources, companionship, and emotional support in the marriage market for men's financial support and social status; as a result, however, women as a group, remain subordinate to men (Collins, 1971; Nielsen, 1990).

All men are not equally privileged; some analysts argue that women and men in the upper classes are more privileged, because of their economic power, than men in lower-class positions and members of some minority groups (Lorber, 1994). In industrialized societies, persons who occupy elite positions in corporations, universities, the mass media, and government or who have great wealth have the most power (Richardson, 1993). Most of these are men, however.

Conflict theorists in the Marxist tradition assert that gender stratification results from private ownership of the means of production; some men not only gain control over property and the distribution of goods but also gain power over women. According to Friedrich Engels and Karl Marx, marriage serves to enforce male dominance. Men of the capitalist class instituted monogamous marriage (a gendered institution) so that they could be certain of the paternity of their offspring, especially sons, whom they wanted to inherit their wealth. Feminist analysts have examined this theory, among others, as they have sought to explain male domination and gender stratification.

FEMINIST PERSPECTIVES

***Feminism*—the belief that women and men are equal and that they should be valued equally and have equal rights**—is embraced by many men as well as women. Gender is viewed as a socially constructed concept that has important consequences in the lives of all people (Craig, 1992). According to sociologist Ben Agger (1993), men can be feminists and propose feminist theories; both women and men have much in common as they seek to gain a better understanding of the causes and consequences of gender inequality.

As discussed in Chapter 7 ("Deviance and Crime"), feminist perspectives vary in their analyses of the ways in which norms, roles, institutions, and internalized expectations limit women's behaviour. Taken together, they all seek to demonstrate how women's personal control operates even within the constraints of relative lack of power (Stewart, 1994). Although subordination and oppression have significant consequences in women's lives, feminist theorists note that these are not the *only* features of women's lives (Fine, 1987, 1989). We will now look at the main types of feminist theory and examine the focus of each.

LIBERAL FEMINISM In liberal feminism, gender equality is equated with equality of opportunity. Liberal feminism strives for sex equality through the elimination of laws that differentiate people by gender. The roots of women's oppression lie in women's lack of equal civil rights and educational opportunities. Only when these constraints on women's participation are removed will women have the same chance of success as men. This approach notes the importance of gender-role socialization and suggests that changes need to be made in what children learn from their families, teachers, and the media about appropriate masculine and feminine attitudes and behaviour. Liberal feminists fight for better child-care options, a woman's right to choose an abortion, and elimination of sex discrimination in the workplace. This approach has been criticized for ignoring class and race distinctions among women (Basow, 1992), as well as power differentials between men and women (Kemp, 1994).

RADICAL FEMINISM According to radical feminists, male domination causes all forms of human oppression, including racism and classism (Tong,

1989). Radical feminists often trace the roots of patriarchy to women's childbearing and child-rearing responsibilities, which make them dependent on men (Firestone, 1970; Chafetz, 1984). In the radical feminist view, men's oppression of women is deliberate, and ideological justification for this subordination is provided by other institutions such as the media and religion. For women's condition to improve, radical feminists claim, patriarchy must be abolished. If institutions currently are gendered, alternative institutions—such as women's organizations seeking better health and day care and shelters for victims of domestic violence and sexual assault—should be developed to meet women's needs. Major strengths of this perspective include its emphasis on the importance of the work women do in the home and its identification of the primary site of women's oppression as in the home and in women's intimate relations with men (Kemp, 1994). However, a weakness of this approach is its lack of attention to occupational gender segregation and other gender-related issues in the workplace. Critics also have noted that it ignores the significant differences in power and privilege among various groups of women, such as those between white women and women of colour.

SOCIALIST FEMINISM Socialist feminists suggest that women's oppression results from their dual roles as paid *and* unpaid workers in a capitalist economy. In the workplace, women are exploited by capitalism; at home, they are exploited by patriarchy (Kemp, 1994). Women are easily exploited in both sectors; they are paid low wages and have few economic resources. Gendered job segregation is "the primary mechanism in capitalist society that maintains the superiority of men over women, because it enforces lower wages for women in the labour market" (Hartmann, 1976:139). As a result, women must do domestic labour either to gain a better-paid man's economic support or to stretch their own wages (Lorber, 1994). According to socialist feminists, the only way to achieve gender equality is to eliminate capitalism and develop a socialist economy that would bring equal pay and rights to women. However, as discussed in Chapter 12 ("Economy and Work"), this is not the case in existing socialist nations.

This perspective is valuable for its suggestion that women may be oppressed simultaneously in their homes and in the labour market. It also provides insights on the gendered division of labour in the workplace and the "second shift" in the home. However, it has been criticized for its "catchall" use of the term *patriarchy* to explain women's subordination (Ramazanoglu, 1989), as well as for neglecting race and ethnicity in its examination of gender and class relations (Kemp, 1994).

FEMINIST PERSPECTIVES ON EATING PROBLEMS As noted earlier, feminist analysts suggest that eating problems are not just individual "disorders" but relate to the issue of subordination (see Orbach, 1978; Fallon, Katzman, and Wooley, 1994). This analysis focuses on the relationship between eating problems and patriarchy (male dominance) in the labour force and family. Eating problems cannot be viewed solely as psychological "disorders" but rather are symbolic of women's personal and cultural oppression. Anorexia and bulimia reflect women's (and sometimes men's) denial of other problems, disconnection from other people, and disempowerment in society (Peters and Fallon, 1994:353).

Feminist scholars have begun to look at ways in which race/ethnicity may be linked to eating problems (Root, 1990). In contrast, most early research focused on the problems of white, middle- to upper-class females; women from minority groups were, at most, mentioned in a footnote (for example, see Brumberg, 1988). In a recent study of women with eating problems, sociologist Becky Thompson (1992, 1994) found that more than half the women from minority groups had been victims of sexual abuse, racism, anti-Semitism, and/or homophobia. However, she suggests that it is impossible to determine a single explanation about socialization and eating problems among ethnic minority women.

Eating problems also may be associated with social class and sexual orientation. For example, some lower-class women may view binge eating as a momentary reprieve from poverty and other worries. Some lesbians may develop eating problems in rebellion against cultural expectations that attempt to force heterosexuality or at least heterosexual values on them, in sharp contradiction to their own sexual identities (Thompson, 1994). Two feminist studies comparing lesbian and heterosexual women found that both groups are influenced by cultural pressures to be thin but that lesbians tend to be more satisfied with their bodies and to desire a somewhat higher ideal weight (Brand, Rothblum, and Solomon, 1992; Herzog et al., 1992). Gay men, on the other hand, may be more prone to eating problems because of the importance some place on low body weight and/or physical attractiveness (see Shisslak and Crago, 1992).

Feminist perspectives focus on the prevention of eating problems and a re-evaluation of existing therapies. However, feminist authors Naomi Wolf (1990) and Susan Faludi (1991) have suggested that the current social order may have a vested interest in promoting, rather than preventing, eating problems among women. Wolf (1994) argues that emphasis on thinness is a response to the threat posed by women's efforts to gain courage, self-esteem, and a sense of effectiveness. By contrast, dieting leads to passivity, anxiety, and low self-esteem—traits valued in women by the dominant culture.

Feminists argue that, to prevent eating problems—as well as other mental and physical problems of women—societal changes are needed. These changes relate to work (such as equal pay, and the elimination of sexual harassment and discrimination) and the family (child-care programs and deterrence of sexual violence, for example) (Wolf, 1990; Shisslak and Crago, 1994). As Thompson (1994:5) notes:

> Most women are relegated to sex-segregated jobs that pay them less well than men are paid for comparable work. What is typically referred to as the "glass ceiling" in employment is actually a euphemism for real men's bodies blocking most women's advancement. These barriers, coupled with educational systems that still steer girls away from mathematics, science, and competitive sports, help explain why adolescent girls' self-esteem declines as boys' self-esteem increases. In this context, eating problems signal women's many hungers—for recognition, achievement, and encouragement. It is no surprise that appetites and food take on a metaphorical significance in a society in which women typically are responsible for food preparation and yet are taught to deny themselves ample appetites.

EVALUATION OF CONFLICT AND FEMINIST PERSPECTIVES Conflict and feminist perspectives provide insights into the structural aspects of gender inequality in society. While functionalist approaches focus on the characteristics of individuals, the conflict and feminist approaches emphasize factors external to individuals that contribute to the oppression of women. These approaches also examine the ways in which the workplace and the home are gendered.

Conflict theory has been criticized for emphasizing the differences between men and women without taking into account their commonalities. Feminist approaches have been criticized for their emphasis on male dominance without a corresponding analysis of the ways in which some men also may be oppressed by patriarchy and capitalism. Some theorists in men's studies have attempted to overcome this deficit by exploring how gender domination includes "men's subordination and denigration of other men as well as men's exploitation of women" (Brod, 1987; Kimmel and Messner, 1992; Lorber, 1994:4).

GENDER ISSUES IN THE TWENTY-FIRST CENTURY

In the past thirty years, women have made significant progress in the labour force (Gee,

1996). Laws have been passed to prohibit sexual discrimination in the workplace and school. Affirmative action programs have made women more visible in education, government, and the professional world. More women are entering the political arena as candidates instead of as volunteers who "answer the telephone and lick stamps" in the campaign offices of male candidates (Lott, 1994:341).

Many men have joined movements to raise their consciousness not only about men's concerns but also about the need to eliminate sexism and gender bias. Many men realize that what is harmful to women also may be harmful to men. For example, women's lower wages in the labour force suppress men's wages as well; in a two-paycheque family, women who are paid less contribute less to the family's finances, thus placing a greater burden on men to earn more money.

In the midst of these changes, many gender issues remain unresolved. In the labour force, gender segregation may increase if the number of female-dominated jobs—such as information clerk, nurses' aide, and fast-food restaurant worker—continues to grow. If men lose jobs in the blue-collar sector as factories relocate to other countries or close entirely, they may seek jobs that primarily have been held by women. Although this situation might lead to less gender segregation, the loss of desirable jobs ultimately is not in anyone's interest (Reskin and Padavic, 1994:172). As men see the number and quality of "men's jobs" shrink, they also may become more resistant to women's entry into what have customarily been male jobs (Reskin and Padavic, 1994:172).

The pay gap between men and women should continue to shrink, but this may be due in part to decreasing wages paid to men (Armstrong and Armstrong, 1994). Employers and governments will continue to implement family-leave policies, but these will not relieve women's domestic burden in the family. The burden of the "double day" or second shift" has led many women to work part time in an attempt to reconcile family–work contradictions. This choice increases or maintains occupational segregation, low pay with minimal or no benefits, and marginalized treatment (Gee, 1995).

Reflecting on the changes in gender relations that have occurred over the past century, some may agree with the saying 'We've come a long way, baby." However, as the next century approaches and we consider the challenges that lie ahead. Many will also agree "We still have a long way to go" in constructing a society in which gender equality prevails (Gee, 1995).

CHAPTER REVIEW

Sex refers to the biological categories and manifestations of femaleness and maleness; gender refers to the socially constructed differences between females and males. In short, sex is what we (generally) are born with; gender is what we acquire through socialization. Issues of sex and gender affect our beliefs about weight and appearance.

- Although biological distinctions between males and females are important, most of what we think of as sex differences are socially constructed gender differences associated with ideas of masculinity and femininity. Gender role encompasses the attitudes, behaviours, and activities that are socially assigned to each sex and that are learned through socialization. Gender identity is an individual's perception of self as either female or male. Body consciousness, a part of gender identity, is how an individual perceives and feels about her or his body. This consciousness is influenced by the expectations and approval of others.

- Gendered institutions are those structural features that perpetuate gender inequality. Gender is socially significant because it leads to differential treatment of men and women. Like racism, sexism often is used to justify discriminatory treatment. Sexism is linked to patriarchy, a hierarchical system in which cultural, political, and economic structures are male-dominated.
- In most hunting and gathering societies, fairly equitable relationships exist because neither sex has the ability to provide all of the food necessary for survival. In horticultural societies, hoe cultivation is compatible with child care, and a fair degree of gender equality exists because neither sex controls the food supply. In agrarian societies, male dominance is very apparent; agrarian tasks require more labour and physical strength, and women often are excluded from these tasks because they are viewed as too weak or too tied to child-rearing activities. In industrialized societies, a gap exists between nonpaid work performed by women at home and paid work performed by men and women.
- The key agents of gender socialization are parents, peers, teachers and schools, sports, and the media, all of which tend to reinforce stereotypes of appropriate gender behaviour. Differential treatment leads to differential development. Parents often treat girls more gently than boys, dress them differently, buy them gendered toys, and assign them gendered chores. During adolescence, peers tend to be stronger agents of socialization than adults. Gender bias occurs unintentionally in virtually all educational settings.
- Some argue that the media merely reinforce existing gender roles while others claim the media shape these roles. Television shows tend to be sex–typed and male-oriented. Advertising sends a message to viewers that if they embrace traditional notions of masculinity and femininity, their personal and social success is ensured.
- Gender inequality results from economic, political, and educational discrimination against women. In most workplaces, jobs are either gender segregated or the majority of employees are of the same gender. While the degree of gender segregation in the professional workplace has declined since the 1970s, racial and ethnic segregation remains deeply embedded.
- Many women work in lower-paying, less prestigious jobs than men. This occupational segregation leads to a disparity, or pay gap, between women's and men's earnings. Even when women are employed in the same job as men, on average they do not receive the same, or comparable, pay. The typical married working woman in Canada does both paid work in the labour force and unpaid work as a homemaker. Many women have a "second shift" because of their dual responsibilities for paid and unpaid work.
- According to functional analysts, women's roles as caregivers in contemporary industrialized societies are crucial in ensuring that key societal tasks are fulfilled. While the husband performs the instrumental tasks of economic support and decision making, the wife assumes the expressive tasks of providing affection and emotional support of the family. According to conflict analysis, the gendered division of labour within families and the workplace—particularly in agrarian and industrial societies—results from male control and dominance over women and resources.
- Although feminist perspectives vary in their analyses of women's subordination, they all advocate social change to eradicate gender inequality. In liberal feminism, gender equality is connected to equality of opportunity.

In radical feminism, male dominance is seen as the cause of oppression. According to socialist feminists, women's oppression results from their dual roles as paid and unpaid workers.

KEY TERMS

body consciousness **361**
comparable worth **382**
employment equity **383**
feminism **389**
gender **360**
gender bias **373**
gender identity **360**
gender role **360**
hermaphrodite **359**
matriarchy **363**
patriarchy **363**
primary sex characteristics **359**
secondary sex characteristics **359**
sex **359**
sexism **362**
sexual orientation **359**
transsexual **359**
transvestite **359**
wage gap **381**

QUESTIONS FOR ANALYSIS AND UNDERSTANDING

1. Why is gender equality found in hunting and gathering societies while gender inequality is found in industrial societies?
2. Why are peers often much stronger agents of gender socialization than parents?
3. Why are many jobs gender stratified?
4. What are the major differences among the feminist perspectives on gender stratification? Which perspectives reflect your experiences?

QUESTIONS FOR CRITICAL THINKING

1. Do the media reflect societal attitudes on gender, or do the media determine and teach gender behaviour? (As a related activity, watch television for several hours and list the roles women and men play in the shows watched and in the advertisements.)
2. Review the concept of cultural relativism in Chapter 3. Should the Canadian government and human rights groups such as Amnesty International protest genital mutilation in those countries in which it is practised and should the government withhold any funding or aid destined for those nations until they cease the practice?
3. Examine the various academic departments at your university. What is the gender breakdown of the faculty in selected departments? What is the gender breakdown of undergraduates and graduates in those departments? Are there major differences among the social sciences, science, and humanities departments? What can you come up with to explain your observations?

SUGGESTED READINGS

These well-written books provide in-depth information on various issues raised in this chapter:

Sandra L. Bem. *The Lenses of Gender: Transforming the Debate on Sexual Inequality.* New Haven, Conn.: Yale University Press, 1993.

Michael S. Kimmel and Michael A. Messner (eds.). *Men's Lives.* New York: Macmillan, 1992.

Claire M. Renzetti and Daniel J. Curran. *Women, Men, and Society.* Boston: Allyn & Bacon, 1995.

A comprehensive look at media depictions of men and masculinity is found in this book:

Steve Craig (ed.). *Men, Masculinity, and the Media.* Newbury Park, Cal.: Sage, 1992.

Women's and men's work is examined in these interesting books:

Pat Armstrong and Hugh Armstrong. *The Double Ghetto: Canadian Women and Their Segregated Work.* Toronto: McClelland & Stewart, 1994.

Christine L. Williams. *Still a Man's World: Men Who Do Women's Work.* Berkeley: University of California Press, 1995.

The unequal treatment of females in schools and universities is explored in these books:

Jane Gaskell and Arlene McLaren. *Women and Education.* Calgary: Detselig, 1992.

Stephen Richer and Lorna Weir. *Beyond Political Correctness: Toward the Inclusive University.* Toronto: University of Toronto Press, 1995.

Best-sellers dealing with feminism, appearance norms, and communication between women and men include these books:

Susan Faludi. *Backlash: The Undeclared War Against American Women.* New York: Crown, 1991.

Deborah Tannen. *You Just Don't Understand: Women and Men in Conversation.* New York: Morrow, 1990.

Deborah Tannen. *Talking From 9 to 5.* New York: Morrow, 1994.

Naomi Wolf. *The Beauty Myth: How Images of Beauty Are Used Against Women.* New York: Morrow, 1990.

These books provide a more personal approach to the experiences of men and women:

Bernice Lott. *Women's Lives: Themes and Variations in Gender Learning* (2nd ed.). Pacific Grove, Cal.: Brooks/Cole, 1994.

Fredric E. Rabinowitz and Sam V. Cochran. *Man Alive: A Primer of Men's Issues.* Pacific Grove, Cal., Brooks/Cole, 1994.

For additional information on eating problems:

Kim Chernin. *The Obsession: Refections on the Tyranny of Slenderness.* New York: Harper & Row, 1981.

Leslea Newman (ed.). *Eating Our Hearts Out: Personal Accounts of Women's Relationship to Food.* Freedom, Cal.: The Crossing Press, 1993.

Susie Orbach. *The Hungry Self: Women, Eating, and Identity.* New York: Times Books/Random House, 1985.

For additional information on the bodybuilding subculture:

Alan M. Klein. *Little Big Men: Bodybuilding Subculture and Gender Construction.* Albany: State University of New York Press, 1993.

Chapter 11

AGING AND PERSONS WITH DISABILITIES

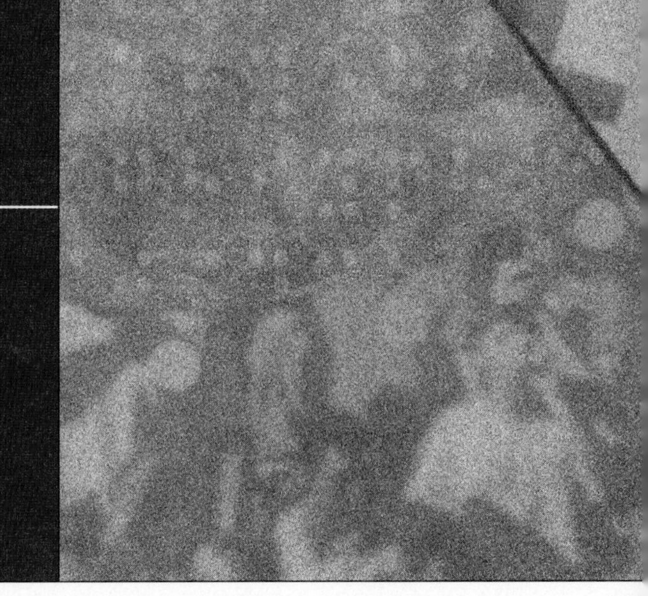

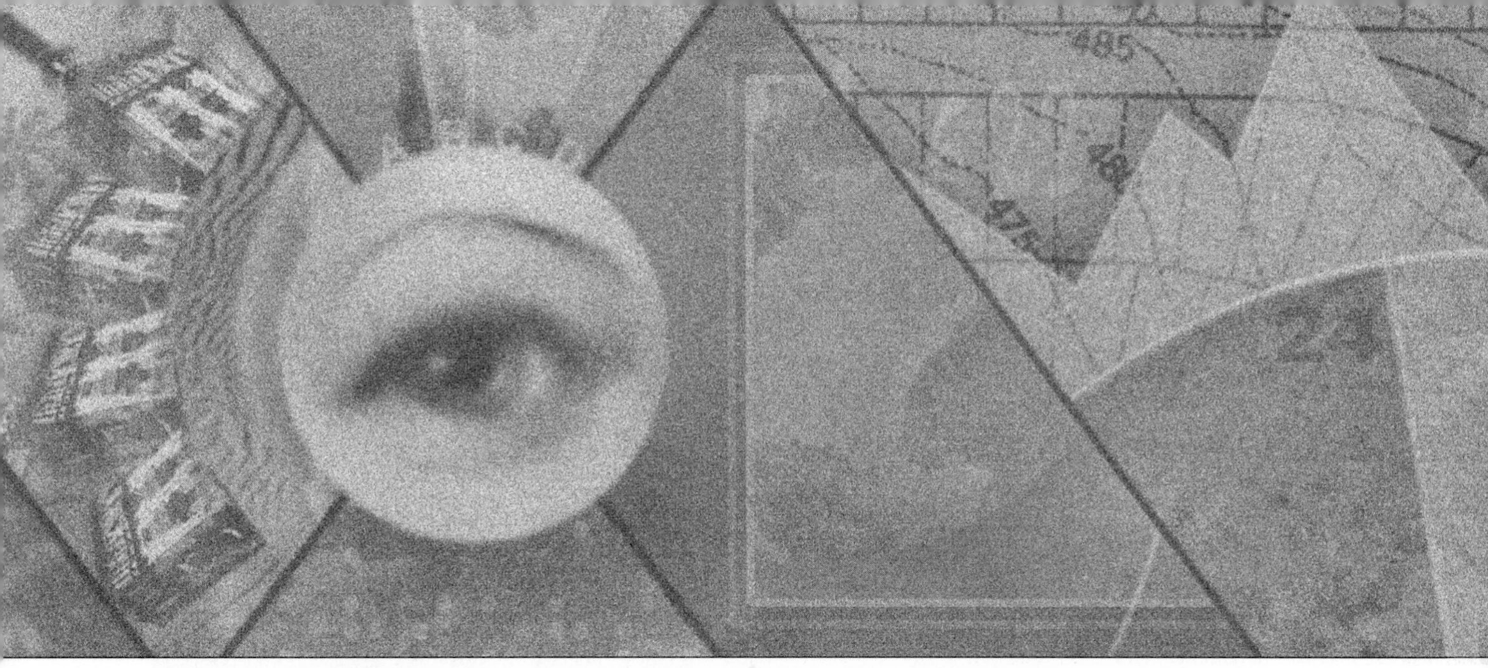

Basha, an 89-year-old woman, explains how her days get started:

> Every morning, I wake up in pain. I wiggle my toes. Good. They still obey. I open my eyes. Good. I can see. Everything hurts but I get dressed. I walk down to the ocean. Good. It's still there. Now my day can start. About tomorrow I never know. After all, I'm eighty-nine. I can't live forever. (quoted in Myerhoff, 1994:1)

Most people do not live to Basha's age and thus may never experience the feelings that she describes regarding aging. Likewise, many people will never have to cope with a disability. Susan Wendell describes her personal experience with disability:

> In 1985, I fell ill overnight with what turned out to be a disabling chronic disease. In the long struggle to come to terms with it, I had to learn to live with a body that felt entirely different to me—weak, tired, painful, nauseated, dizzy, unpredictable. I learned at first by listening to other people with chronic illnesses or disabilities; suddenly able-bodied people seemed to be profoundly ignorant of everything I most needed to know. Although doctors told me there was a good chance I would eventually recover completely, I realized after a year of waiting to get well, hoping to recover my healthy body was a dangerous strategy. I began slowly to identify with my new disabled body and learn to work with it. As I moved back into the world, I also began to experience the world as structured for people who have no weaknesses. The process of encountering the able-bodied world lead me gradually to identify myself as a disabled person, and to reflect upon the nature of the disability … (Wendell, 1995:455)

Basha and Susan are confronting the problems associated with aging and disability. If we apply our sociological imagination to their experiences, we see that problems associated with growing older or experiencing disability are not just personal problems but also public issues. Older individuals and persons with a disability often are discriminated against and denied access to rights and resources that are taken for granted by younger persons and individuals without disabilities. In this chapter, we examine two types of social stratification: age-based and disability-based inequalities. In some instances, the two intertwine in a form of dual marginalization. We also will examine how people seek dignity, autonomy, and empowerment in a society that often devalues those who do not fit the ideal norms of youth, beauty, physical fitness, and self-sufficiency. Before reading on, test your knowledge about aging, disability, and empowerment by taking the quiz in Box 11.1.

Many older persons seek dignity, autonomy, and empowerment in a society that values youth, beauty, physical fitness, and self-sufficiency.

QUESTIONS AND ISSUES

How does functional age differ from chronological age?

How does age determine a person's roles and statuses in society?

What is the source of most disabilities?

How is disability viewed by society?

What actions can be taken to bring about a more equitable society for older people and persons with a disability?

AN OVERVIEW OF AGING AND PERSONS WITH DISABILITIES

Aging and disability are not synonymous. ***Aging* is the physical, psychological, and social processes associated with growing older** (Atchley, 1994). As people age, they do not *inevitably* become disabled. A ***disability* is a physical or health condition that stigmatizes or causes discrimination** (Shapiro, 1993). Not all disabilities limit people physically, and many disabilities are not visible to others. Likewise, most Canadians over the age of 55 generally report high levels of well-being as measured by their health, happiness, and satisfaction with life (Keight and Landy, 1994).

Nevertheless, older people and persons with a disability share some important concerns. First, both may be targets of prejudice and discrimination based on commonly held myths about aging and physical capabilities. Older persons may be viewed as "handicapped" solely on the basis of their age; persons with certain types of disabilities are perceived as much older than their actual age because of physical or psychological frailties associated with their disability. Second, both groups may need assistance from others and support from society. Finally, many older people and persons with a disability have used similar methods to gain individual dignity and autonomy. At one time or another, all of us will be affected by aging or disability. According to sociologist Rose Weitz (1995), the ongoing aging of the population and the increasing ability of medical technology to

BOX 11.1 SOCIOLOGY AND EVERYDAY LIFE

How Much Do You Know About Aging, Disability, and Empowerment?

TRUE	FALSE	
T	F	1. Most older persons have serious physical or mental disabilities.
T	F	2. Women in Canada have a longer life expectancy than men.
T	F	3. Scientific studies have documented the fact that women age faster than men.
T	F	4. The majority of older people have income below the poverty line.
T	F	5. Studies show that advertising no longer stereotypes older persons.
T	F	6. Positive stereotypes regarding persons with disabilities may produce negative results.
T	F	7. After women reach menopause, they may enjoy sexual activity more than when they were younger.
T	F	8. Individuals with disabilities are less likely to be physically or sexual abused.
T	F	9. Older people stand a higher risk of criminal victimization than people in other age groups.
T	F	10. Having a disability inevitably shortens a person's life expectancy.

Answers on page 400

keep people of all ages alive means that many of us can expect to live for a number of years with illness and disability, whether our own or that of our parents, children, or friends. We will look first at aging and then at disability.

THE SOCIAL SIGNIFICANCE OF AGE

"How old are you?" This is one of the most frequently asked questions in our society. Beyond indicating how old or young a person is, age is socially significant because it defines what is appropriate for or expected of people at various stages. Moreover, while it is an ascribed status, age is one of the few ascribed statuses that changes over time.

When we hear the word *age*, most of us think of ***chronological age*—a person's age based on date of birth** (Atchley, 1994). In everyday life, however, we gain a general idea of a person's age based on ***functional age*—observable individual attributes such as physical appearance, mobility, strength, coordination, and mental capacity that are used to assign people to age categories** (Atchley, 1994). Because we typically do not have access to other people's birth certifi-

BOX 11.1 SOCIOLOGY AND EVERYDAY LIFE

Answers to the Sociology Quiz on Aging and Disability

TRUE	FALSE	
T	**F**	1. *False.* In Canada, approximately 46 percent of people 65 or over have a disability—the majority of which are classified as mild or moderate disabilities.
T	F	2. *True.* In 1994, female life expectancy (at birth) was 81 years, as compared with 74 years for males.
T	**F**	3. *False.* No studies have documented that women actually age faster than men. However, some scholars have noted a "double standard" of aging that places older women at a disadvantage with respect to older men because women's worth in the North American culture is defined in terms of physical appearance.
T	**F**	4. *False.* The 1991 poverty rate for seniors was 15 percent, which is down from 33 percent reported in 1980. However, females are at a greater risk of living in poverty than males.
T	**F**	5. *False.* Studies have shown that advertisements frequently depict older people negatively—for example, as sickly or silly.
T	F	6. *True.* Disability rights advocates have pointed out that the image of people with disabilities as being "wheelchair racers" and "supercrips" does not reflect the struggles faced by people with disabilities in everyday life.
T	F	7. *True.* Women may enjoy sexual activity more after menopause because their sexual enjoyment now is separated from the possibility of pregnancy.
T	**F**	8. *False.* Research indicates that people with disabilities are at greater risk of physical and sexual abuse. In one survey, 39 percent of married women with a disability reported being physically or sexually abused, compared with 27 percent of nondisabled women.
T	**F**	9. *False.* Older people had only one-sixth the rate of violent and personal victimizations compared to all adults, and one-twelfth the rate of the 16–24 age group.
T	**F**	10. *False.* Many people with one or more disabilities live out the full life expectancy of their birth cohort. Some conditions do not change, such as the loss of a limb, hearing loss, or visual impairments; others may be progressive in nature and may eventually result in death, such as potentially disabling chronic conditions (e.g., cardiovascular disease, rheumatoid arthritis, and cancer among older people).

Sources: N.A.S.A., 1989; Novak, 1993; Rodgers and Kong, 1996; Statistics Canada, Cat. No. 82-554.

cates to learn their chronological age, we often use visible characteristics—such as youthful appearance or gray hair and wrinkled skin—as our criteria for determining whether someone is "young" or "old." As historian Lois W. Banner (1993:15) suggests, "Appearance, more than any other factor, has occasioned the objectification of aging. We define someone as old because he or she looks old." Feminist scholars have noted that functional age works differently for women and men—as they age, men may be viewed as distinguished or powerful while women may be viewed as old or grandmotherly.

TRENDS IN AGING

Not only do people get older, but societies age, too. Between the turn of the century and 1991, Canada's older population multiplied over ten times. Today, older Canadians make up more than one-tenth of the population (Novak, 1993). This makes Canada's population one of the oldest in the world, and population projections suggest that the Canadian society will age even more in the next fifty years (Novak, 1993) (see Figure 11.1a).

Over the past decades, the median age (the age at which half the people are younger and half are older) increased by over three years, from 29.6 in 1981 to 33.5 in 1991. This change was partly a result of the baby boomers (people born between 1946 and 1964) moving into middle age, and partly a result of more people living longer. As shown in Figure 11.1b, the number of older people (age 65 and above) increased dramatically between 1901 and 1991 (McKie, 1993). Especially fast growing has been the population over age 85.

Referred by some analysts as the *greying of Canada*, the aging of the Canadian population resulted from an increase in life expectancy combined with a decrease in birth rates (McKie, 1994). ***Life expectancy* is the average length of time a group of individuals of the same age will live.** Based on the death rates in the year of birth, life expectancy shows the average length of life of a ***cohort*—a group of people born within a specified period of time.** Cohorts may be established on the basis of one-, five-, or ten-year intervals; they may also be defined by events taking place at the time of their birth, such as the "Depression era" babies or baby boomers (Moody, 1994). For the cohort born in 1987, for example, life expectancy at birth was 79.7 for females and 73.0 for males. Figure 11.1c outlines the sex differences in life expectancy. There are also ethnic differences in the elderly in Canada. The two "oldest" ethnic groups in the country are people claiming Jewish or Polish ancestry. Native peoples have very "young" populations with less than 4 percent aged 65 and over (Driedger and Chappell, 1987). Although the life expectancy of Native peoples in Canada has improved over the past 50 years, higher rates of illness, disability, and suicide—attributed to poverty, inadequate health care, and greater exposure to environmental risk factors—still persist (Bobet, 1994).

At the turn of the century, about 5 percent of the Canadian population was over age 65; in 1981, that number had risen to approximately 10 percent. As Figure 11.1b shows, in 1991, approximately 12 percent of the population was age 65 or over. By the year 2031, according to projections, about 22 percent of the population will be at least 65 (Norland, 1994).

Since the beginning of the twentieth century, life expectancy has steadily increased as industrialized nations developed better water and sewage systems, improved nutrition, and made tremendous advances in medical science. Economic development that contributed to the lower death rate also was a force in lowering the birth rate. In industrialized nations, children are viewed as an economic liability; they cannot contribute to the family's financial well-being and must be supported.

The current distribution of the Canadian population is depicted in the "age pyramid" in Figure 11.1d. If, every year, the same number of people are born as in the previous year and a certain number die in each age group, the plot of the population distribution should be pyramid-shaped. As you will note, however, Figure 11.1d

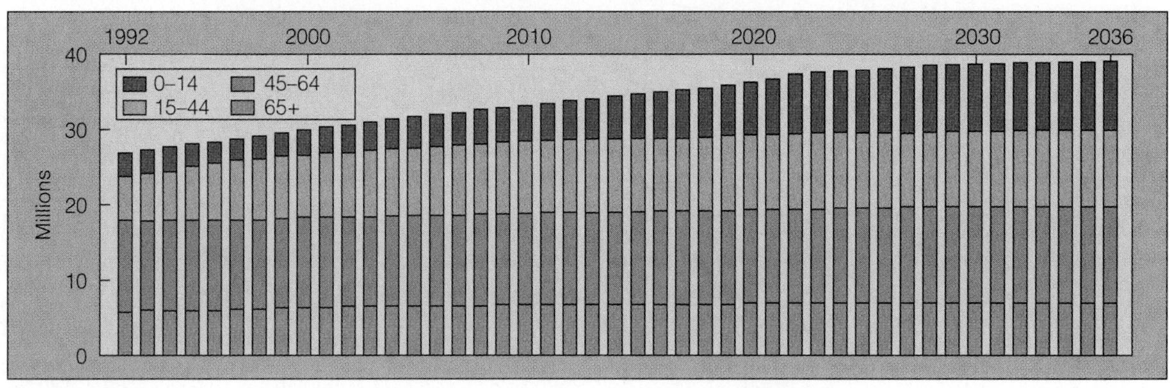

FIGURE 11.1A

Projected Population by Age Group, 1992–2036

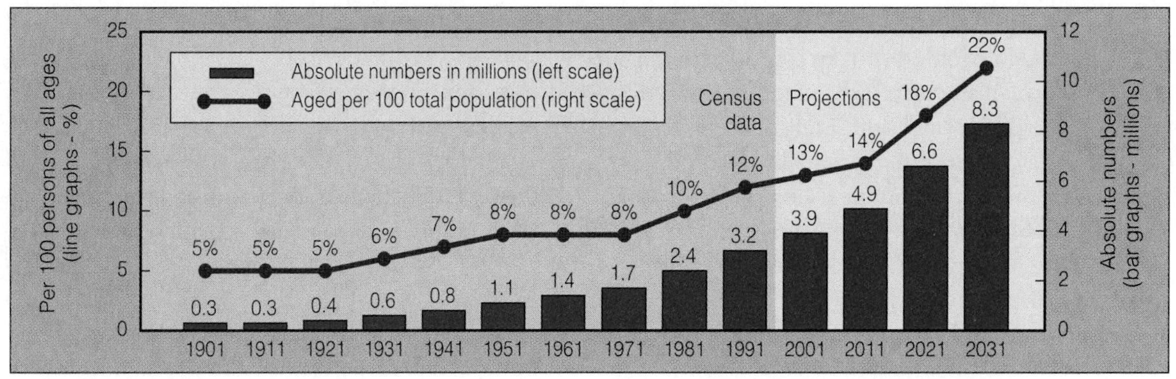

FIGURE 11.1B

Population 65 and Over, Canada, 1900–2031

is not a perfect pyramid, but rather reflects declining birth rates among post–baby boomers.

As a result of changing population trends, research on aging has grown dramatically in the past fifty years. *Gerontology* is the study of aging and older people. A subfield of gerontology, ***social gerontology* is the study of the social (nonphysical) aspects of aging,** including such topics as the societal consequences of an aging population and the personal experience of aging (Novak, 1993). According to gerontologists, age is viewed differently from society to society and changes over time.

AGE IN HISTORICAL PERSPECTIVE

People are assigned to different roles and positions based on the age structure and role structure in a particular society. *Age structure* is the number of persons of each age level within the society; *role structure* is the number and type of positions available to them (Riley and Riley, 1994). Over the years, the age continuum has been chopped up into finer and finer points. Two hundred years ago, people divided the age spectrum into "babyhood," a *very* short childhood, and then adulthood. What we would consider "child-

FIGURE 11.1C

Evolution of Life Expectancy by Age and Sex, Canada, 1921–1991

Year	Males – At Birth –	Females
1921	58.8	60.6
1926	60.5	62.3
1931	60.0	62.1
1941	63.0	66.3
1951	66.4	70.9
1961	68.4	74.3
1971	69.4	76.5
1981	71.9	79.0
1985–1987	73.0	79.7
1989–1991	73.9	80.5

FIGURE 11.1D

Age Groups as Percentages of Population, 1991

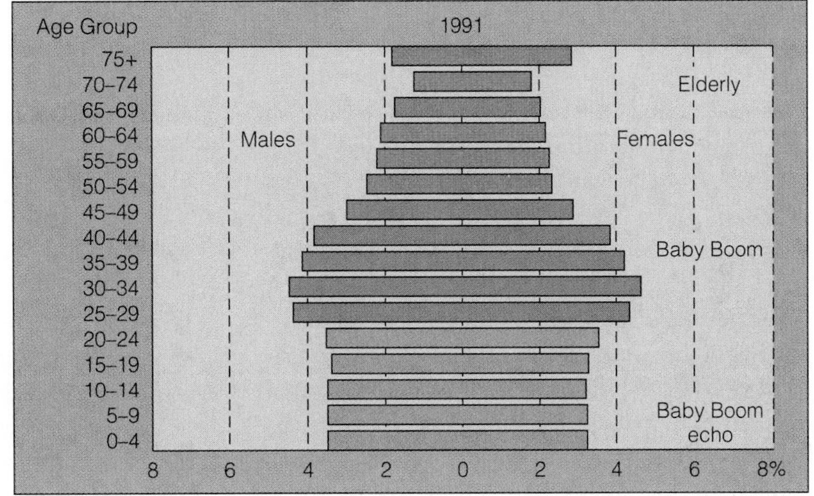

Sources: Fig. 11.1A: Statistics Canada, *Canadian Social Trends*, 1993; Fig. 11.1B: Norland, 1994 and Statistics Canada; Fig. 11.1C: Norland, 1994; and Fig. 11.1D: McVey and Kalbach, 1995.

hood" today was very different two hundred years ago when agricultural societies needed a large number of strong arms and backs to work on the land to ensure survival. When 95 percent of the population had to be involved in food production, categories such as toddlers, preschoolers, preteens, teenagers, young adults, the middle-aged, or older persons did not exist.

If the physical labour of young persons is necessary for society's survival, then young persons are considered "little adults" and are expected to act like adults and do adult work. Older persons also are expected to continue to be productive for the benefit of the society for as long as they are physically able. In pre-industrial societies, persons of all ages help with the work, and little training is necessary for the roles that they fill. During the seventeenth and eighteenth centuries in North America, for example, older individuals helped with the work and were respected because they were needed—and because few people lived that long (Gratton, 1986).

AGE IN CONTEMPORARY SOCIETY

In industrialized societies, the skills necessary for many roles are more complex and the number of unskilled positions is more limited. Consequently, children are expected to attend school and learn the necessary skills for future employment rather than perform unskilled labour. Further, older persons are expected to retire so that younger persons can take their places. However, when older persons have fewer productive roles to fill, inequality may increase. For example, the trend in recent years to "downsize" the work force has contributed to pressure on some older workers to retire early, thereby saving employers money and preserving jobs for young workers. Such "early retirement" is not always voluntary and may pose significant economic risks for individuals who find that they cannot live on their pensions and that employment is not available because employers won't hire older workers.

In North America, age differentiation is based on narrowly defined categories, such as infancy, childhood, adolescence, young adulthood, middle adulthood, and later adulthood. These narrowly defined age categories have had a profound effect on our perceptions of people's capabilities, responsibilities, and entitlements. What is considered appropriate for or expected of people at various ages is somewhat arbitrarily determined and produces ***age stratification*****—the inequalities, differences, segregation, or conflict between age groups** (Atchley, 1994). We will now examine some of those strata.

ADOLESCENCE In contemporary industrialized countries, adolescence roughly spans the teenage years, although some analysts place the lower and upper ages at 15 and 24 (Corr, Nabe, and Corr, 1994). As compared with pre-industrial societies in which 7-year-old children were expected to do adult work, adolescence today is a period in which the individual is neither treated as a child nor afforded full status as an adult (Chudacoff, 1989). Adolescents are expected to continue their education and perhaps hold a part-time job while they do so.

YOUNG ADULTHOOD Young adulthood, which follows adolescence and lasts to about age 39, is socially significant because, during this time, people are expected to get married, have children, and get a job. For some young adults, this may be easier than for others. As previously discussed, ethnicity and gender strongly influence people's opportunities to engage in these activities. Today, age may be less of a determinant of when people enter or leave basic social structures of work, education, and family.

MIDDLE ADULTHOOD Prior to the twentieth century, life expectancy in Canada was only about 47 years, so the concept of middle adulthood—people between the ages of 40 and 65—did not exist until fairly recently. Normal changes in appearance occur during these years; although these changes have little relationship to a person's health or physical functioning, they are socially significant to many people (Lefrançois, 1993).

People may experience a change of life in this stage. Women undergo *menopause*—the cessation of the menstrual cycle caused by a gradual decline in the body's production of the "female" hormones estrogen and progesterone. Menopause typically occurs between the mid-forties and the early fifties and signals the end of a woman's childbearing capabilities. Some women may experience irregular menstrual cycles for several years, followed by hot flashes, retention of body fluids, swollen breasts, and other aches and pains. Other women may have few or no noticeable physical symptoms. The psychological aspects of menopause often are as important as any physical effects. In one study, Anne Fausto-Sterling (1985) concluded that many women respond negatively to menopause because of negative stereotypes associated with menopausal and postmenopausal women. These stereotypes make the natural process of aging in women appear abnormal when compared with men's aging process. Actually, many women experience a new interest in sexual activity because they no longer have to worry about the possibility of becoming pregnant.

Men undergo a *climacteric* in which the production of the "male" hormone testosterone decreases. Some have argued that this change in hormone levels produces nervousness and depression in men; however, it is not clear whether these emotional changes are due to biological changes or to a more general "midlife crisis" in which men assess what they have accomplished (Benokraitis, 1993). Ironically, even as these biological changes may have a liberating effect on some people, they also may reinforce societal stereotypes of older people, especially women, as "sexless."

Middle adulthood for most people represents the time during which (1) they have the highest levels of income and prestige, (2) they leave the problems of child rearing behind them and are content with their spouse of many years, and (3) they may have grandchildren who give them another tie to the future. Even so, persons during middle adulthood know that, given society's current structure, their status may begin to change significantly when they reach the end of that period of their lives.

LATE ADULTHOOD Late adulthood is generally considered to begin at age 65—the "normal" retirement age. *Retirement* is the institutionalized separation of an individual from an occupational position, with continuation of income through a retirement pension based on prior years of service (Atchley, 1994). Retirement means the end of a status that long has been a source of income and a means of personal identity. Perhaps the loss of a valued status explains why many retired persons introduce themselves by saying, "I'm retired now, but I was a (banker, lawyer, plumber, supervisor, and so on) for forty years."

Some gerontologists subdivide late adulthood into three categories: (1) the "young-old" (ages 65–74), (2) the "old-old" (ages 75–85), and (3) the "oldest-old" (over age 85) (see Moody, 1994). Although these are somewhat arbitrary divisions, the "young-old" are less likely to suffer from disabling illnesses, while some of the "old-old" are more likely to suffer such illnesses (Belsky, 1990). A recent study found, however, that the prevalence of disability among those 85 and over decreased during the 1980s due to better health care.

The rate of biological and psychological changes in older persons may be as important as their chronological age in determining how they are perceived by themselves and others. As adults grow older, they actually become shorter, partly because bones that have become more porous with age develop curvature. A loss of three inches in height is not uncommon. As bones become more porous, they also become more brittle; simply falling may result in broken bones that take longer to heal. With age, arthritis increases, and connective tissue stiffens joints. Wrinkled skin, "age spots," gray (or white) hair, and midriff bulge appear; however, people may use Oil of Olay, Clairol, or Buster's Magic Tummy Tightener in the hope of avoiding looking older (Atchley, 1994).

Older persons also have increased chances of heart attacks, strokes, and cancer, and some diseases affect virtually only persons in late adulthood. Alzheimer's disease (a progressive and irreversible deterioration of brain tissue) is an example; about 55 percent of all organic mental disorders in the older population are caused by Alzheimer's (Atchley, 1994). Persons with this disease have an impaired ability to function in everyday social roles; eventually, they cease to be able to recognize people they have always known and lose all sense of their own identity. Finally, they may revert to a speechless, infantile state such that others must feed them, dress them, sit them on the toilet, and lead them around. The disease has no known cause and, currently, there is no cure. Over a quarter million Canadians suffer from Alzheimer's disease and related dementias. By the year 2030, it is estimated that this number will grow to three-quarters of a million.

The time and attention needed to care for someone who has Alzheimer's disease or who simply no longer can leave home without help can be staggering. Daniel Heinrichs, a full-time caregiver for his wife, explains what caring for Norah was like:

> My wife Norah was afflicted with Alzheimer's disease. She could no longer function as a person in our marriage. Slowly I had to take over the various duties she had performed. After that I took over her financial affairs. Then I had to care for her personally: choosing, buying, and looking after clothing, dressing and undressing her, combing her hair, and feeding her. Slowly our conversation ceased. She could not think rationally any more. She could not understand the words that were being used, and she did not know the names of objects she saw. She no longer knew who I was either. "Norah is gone, there is nothing left of your marriage. You need to look after yourself again," is advice that I have heard and felt. Fortunately, I did not yield to this advice. Despite all of Norah's disabilities, we continued to have a rich and enjoyable experience together. I learned to communicate with Norah in other ways. How I spoke the words said more than their actual meaning. She watched for the smile on my face and the fun in my voice. My disposition had more effect on her than my words. She let me put my arm around her and hold her hands whenever I desired, or needed to do so ... Now Norah is gone, but I'm glad that I stayed with her "... till death do us part." (Heinrichs, 1996:48)

Fortunately, most older people do not suffer from Alzheimer's and are not incapacitated by their physical condition. Only about 5 percent of older people live in nursing homes, about 10 percent have visual impairment, and about 50 percent have some hearing loss (Naeyaert, 1990; Lou, 1990; Novak, 1993). Although most older people experience some decline in strength, flexibility, stamina, and other physical capabilities, much of that decline does not result simply from the aging process and is avoidable; with proper exercise, some of it is even reversible (Lefrançois, 1993).

With the physical changes come changes in the roles that older adults are expected (or even allowed) to perform. For example, people may lose some of the abilities necessary for driving a car safely, such as vision or reflexes. Although it is not true of all older persons, the average individual over age 65 does not react as rapidly as the average person who is younger than 65 (Lefrançois, 1993).

The physical and psychological changes that come with increasing age can cause stress. According to Erik Erikson (1963), older people must resolve a tension of "integrity versus despair." They must accept that the life cycle is inevitable, that their lives are nearing an end, and that achieving inner harmony requires accepting both one's past accomplishments and past disappointments. Mark Novak interviewed several older people about what he termed "successful aging." One respondent, Joanne, commented:

> For me getting older was very painful at first because I resisted change. Now I'm changed, and it's okay. I would say I have a new freedom ... I thought I had no limits, but for me a great learning [experience] was recognizing my limits. It was a complete turnover, almost like a rebirth. I guess I've learned we're all weak really. At least we should accept that—being weak—and realize, "Hey, I'm only a fragile human being." (Novak, 1995:125)

Like many older people, Joanne has worked to maintain her dignity and autonomy. Otherwise, according to Erikson, late adulthood may turn into a time of despair—of being bitter and disappointed because it is too late to change what happened, and therefore a time of being afraid of dying.

INEQUALITIES RELATED TO AGING

In previous chapters, we have seen how prejudice and discrimination may be directed toward individuals based on ascribed characteristics—such as ethnicity or gender—over which they have no control. The same holds true for age.

AGEISM

Stereotypes regarding older persons reinforce ***ageism*—prejudice and discrimination against people on the basis of age, particularly when they are older persons** (Butler, 1975). Ageism against older persons is rooted in the assumption that people become unattractive, unintelligent, asexual, unemployable, and mentally incompetent as they grow older (Comfort, 1976).

Ageism is reinforced by stereotypes, whereby people have narrow, fixed images of certain groups. One-sided and exaggerated images of older people are used repeatedly in everyday life. Older persons often are stereotyped as thinking and moving slowly; as bound to themselves and their past, unable to change and grow; as being unable to move forward and often moving backward (Belsky, 1990). They are viewed as cranky, sickly, and lacking in social value (Atchley, 1994); as egocentric and demanding; as shallow and enfeebled, aimless and absent-minded (Belsky, 1990).

The media contribute to negative images of older persons, many of whom are portrayed as doddering, feebleminded, wrinkled, and laughable men and women, literally standing on their last legs (Lefrançois, 1993). This is especially true with regard to advertising. In one survey, 40 percent of respondents over age 65 agreed that advertising portrays older people as unattractive and incompetent (Pomice, 1990). According to the advertising director of one magazine, "Advertising shows young people at their best and most beautiful, but it shows older people at their worst" (quoted in Pomice, 1990:42). Of older persons who do appear on television, most are male; only about one in ten characters appearing to be age 65 or older is a woman, conveying a subtle message that older women especially are unimportant (Pomice, 1990).

Stereotypes also contribute to the view that women are "old" ten or fifteen years sooner than men (Bell, 1989). The multibillion-dollar cosmetics industry helps perpetuate the myth that age reduces the "sexual value" of women but increases it for men. Men's sexual value is defined more in terms of personality, intelligence, and earning

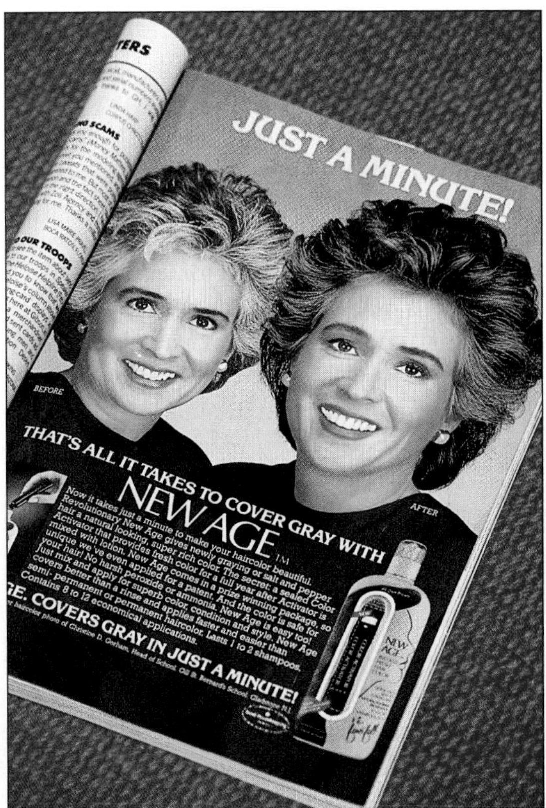

For many years, advertisers have bombarded women with messages about the importance of a youthful appearance. Increasingly, men, too, are being targeted by advertising campaigns that play on fears about the "ravages" of aging.

power than physical appearance. For women, however, sexual attractiveness is based on youthful appearance. By idealizing this "youthful" image of women and playing up the fear of growing older, sponsors sell thousands of products that claim to prevent the "ravages" of aging.

Negative stereotypes of older persons often are held by many young people. In one study, William C. Levin (1988) showed photographs of the same man (disguised to appear as ages 25, 52, and 73 in various photos) to a group of college students and asked them to evaluate these (apparently different) men for employment purposes. Based purely on the photographs, the "73-year-old" was viewed by many of the students as being less competent, less intelligent, and less reliable than the "25-year-old" and the "52-year-old."

Although not all people act on appearances alone, Patricia Moore, an industrial designer, found that many do. At age 27, Moore disguised herself as an 85-year-old woman by donning age-appropriate clothing and placing baby oil in her eyes to create the appearance of cataracts. With the help of a makeup artist, Moore supplemented the "aging process" with latex wrinkles, stained teeth, and a gray wig. For three years, "Old Pat Moore" went to various locations, including a grocery store, to see how people responded to her:

> When I did my grocery shopping while in character, I learned quickly that the Old Pat Moore behaved—and was treated—differently from the Young Pat Moore. When I was 85, people were more likely to jockey ahead of me in the checkout line. And even more interesting, I found that when it happened, I didn't say anything to the offender, as I certainly would at age 27. It seemed somehow, even to me, that it was okay for them to do this to the Old Pat Moore, since they were undoubtedly busier than I was anyway. And further, they apparently thought it was okay, too! After all, little old ladies have plenty of time, don't they? And then when I did get to the checkout counter, the clerk might start yelling, assuming I was deaf, or becoming immediately testy, assuming I would take a long time to get my money out, or would ask to have the price repeated, or somehow become confused about the transaction. What it all added up to was that people feared I would be trouble, so they tried to have as little to do with me as possible. And the amazing thing is that I began almost to believe it myself. . . . I think perhaps the worst thing about aging may be the overwhelming sense that everything around you is letting you know that you are not terribly important any more. (Moore with Conn, 1985:75–76)

If we apply our sociological imagination to Moore's study, we find that "Old Pat Moore's" experiences reflect what many older persons already know—it is other people's *reactions* to their age, not their age itself, that places them at a disadvantage.

Many older people buffer themselves against ageism by continuing to view themselves as being in middle adulthood long after their actual chronological age would suggest otherwise. In one study of people aged 60 and over, 75 percent of the respondents stated that they thought of themselves as middle-aged and only 10 percent viewed themselves as being old. When the same people were interviewed again ten years later, one-third still considered themselves to be middle-aged. Even at age 80, one out of four men and one out of five women said that the word *old* did not apply to them; this lack of willingness to acknowledge having reached older age is a consequence of ageism in society (Belsky, 1990).

WEALTH, POVERTY, AND AGING

How have older people as a group fared economically in recent decades? There is no easy answer to this question. The elderly comprise an extremely heterogeneous group. Some of Canada's wealthiest individuals are old. There are also a significant number of this country's older citizens who are poor or near poor. The image of our elderly population living the "high life" on the backs of our younger population is a misnomer that only serves to perpetuate ageism.

In order to accurately access the economic situation of older people, it is necessary to address two questions. First, has the economic situation of older Canadians improved? Yes—rather dramatically. The income of people over the age of 65 has improved in the past two decades. In fact, the income for Canadians aged 65 and over has risen faster than that of the rest of the population since the early 1970s.

The second question is whether older Canadians are able to maintain a satisfactory standard of living. The answer to this question is more complex. If we compare wealth (all economic resources of value, whether they produce cash or not) with income (available money or its equivalent in purchasing power), we find that older people tend to have more wealth but less income than younger people. For example, older people are more likely to own a home that has increased substantially in market value; however, some may not have the available cash to pay property taxes, to buy insurance, and to maintain the property (Moody, 1994). According to recent Statistics Canada reports (1990c), elderly couples have an average income of $34,000, as compared with $50,000 for all nonelderly couples. In short, although some older Canadians are able to maintain a reasonable standard of living, they do not have higher incomes than the rest of the population.

It is important to remember that although the economic situation of seniors has improved, 15 percent of all people over the age of 65 have low incomes. Changes to government income transfer programs, expansion of tax-sheltered RRSPs, and increased investment returns have reduced the incidence of low income among older people in Canada since the early 1970s (Ng, 1994). Furthermore, while income has risen in the past few years for older people in general, certain groups still have incomes below the poverty line in old age. Older people from lower-income backgrounds, people who cannot speak English or French, people with limited education, and people in small towns tend to have low incomes. Very old people, women, and unattached individuals (Figure 11.2a) often live below the poverty line (Novak, 1993).

THE FEMINIZATION OF POVERTY

> One conclusion stands out from all the facts and figures [about aging and poverty]: Poverty in old age is largely a woman's problem, and is becoming more so every year. (National Council of Welfare, c.f. Novak, 1993:239)

The poverty rate for elderly women is double the poverty rate of elderly men. *Unattached* elderly women are at the greatest risk of poverty with a rate that is double that of married elderly women (see Figure 11.2b). Why do women have such low incomes in old age? According to the National Council of Welfare, "after a lifetime spent taking care of their spouses and children, these women who had no opportunity to become financially self-sufficient are now abandoned by the generation that benefited most from their work" (quoted in Novak, 1993:239).

Although middle-aged and older women make up an increasing portion of the workforce, they are paid substantially less than men their age, receive raises at a slower pace, and still work largely in gender-segregated jobs (see Chapter 10). As a result, women do not garner economic security for their retirement years at the same rate that men do. These factors have contributed to the economic marginality of the current cohort of older women (Novak, 1993).

In a recent study, gerontologists Melissa A. Hardy and Lawrence E. Hazelrigg (1993) found that gender was more directly related to poverty in older persons than was ethnicity, educational background, or occupational status. Hardy and Hazelrigg (1993) suggested that many women who are now age 65 or over spent their early adult lives as financial dependents of husbands or as working nonmarried women trying to support themselves in a culture that did not see women as the heads of households or sole providers of family income. Because they were not viewed as being responsible for the family's financial security, women were paid less; therefore, older women may rely on inadequate income replacement programs originally designed to treat them as dependents. Furthermore, women tend to marry men who are older than themselves, and women live longer than men. Consequently, nearly half of all women over age 65 are widowed and living alone on fixed incomes. The result? According to the National Council of Welfare, "after fifty years or so of unpaid, faithful service a women's only reward is likely to be poverty" (quoted in Novak, 1993:241). In 1988, 50 percent of women aged 75 and over, most of them widows, lived in poverty. As Novak stresses, "this figure does not include people who live in institutions; if it did, the poverty rate would be higher" (1993:241).

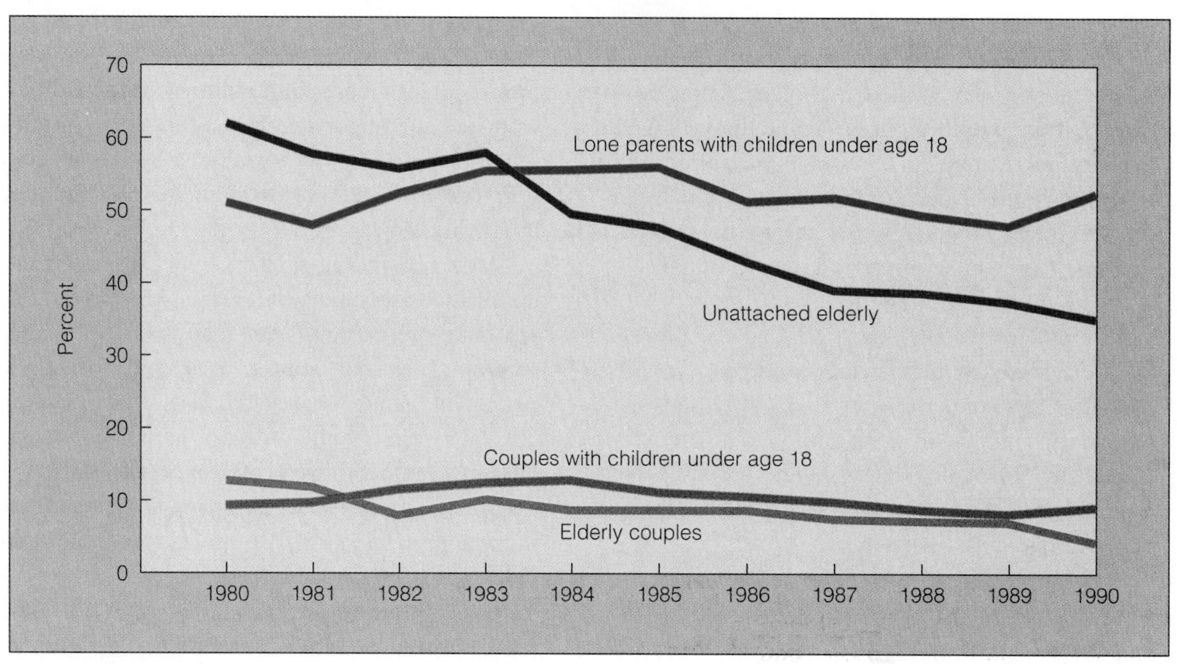

FIGURE 11.2A

Incidence of Low Income (1978 base), by Family Type, 1980–1990

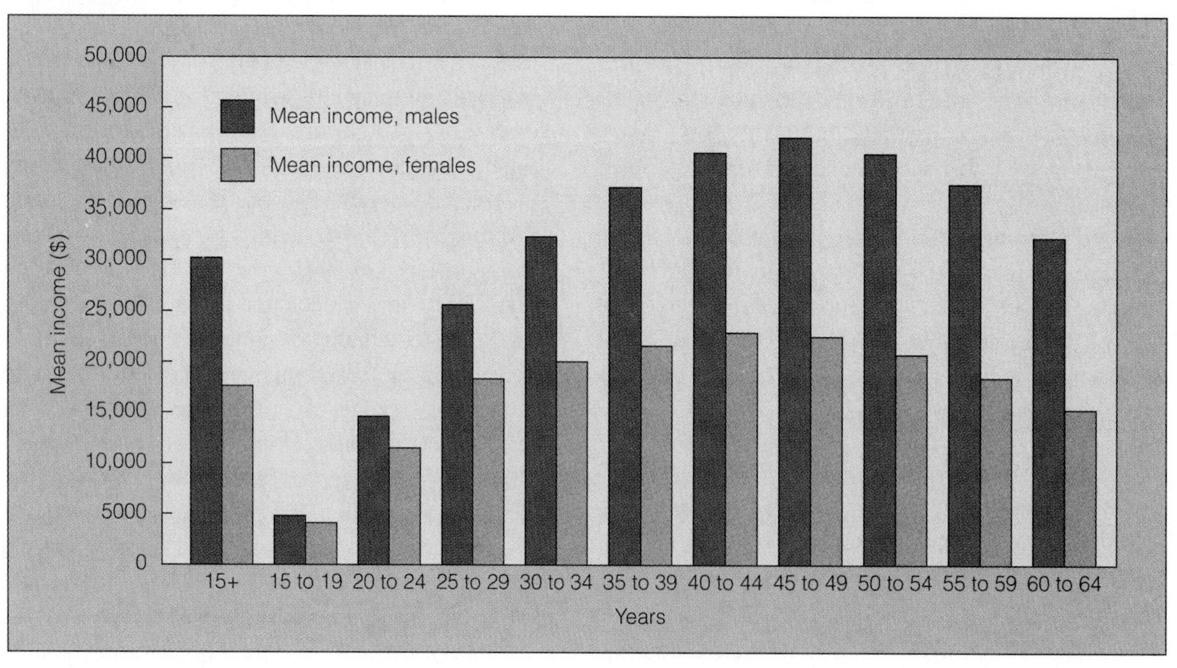

FIGURE 11.2B

Population and Mean 1990 Income by Age and Sex, Canada, 1991 Census Data

Sources: Fig. 11.2a: Statistics Canada, Cat. No. 13-207 and unpublished data.

Fig. 11.2b: 1991 Census of Canada special tabulations. J.A. Norland, *Profile of Canada's Seniors.* Statistics Canada, Cat. no. 96-312E.

Young women today will be much better equipped to deal with the financial pressures of old age as a result of a number of structural changes in Canadian society. The majority of women are working in the paid labour force, they have begun to enter male-dominated professions, and more of them belong to private pension plans (Connelly and MacDonald, 1990).

ELDER ABUSE

Abuse and neglect of older persons has received increasing public attention in recent years, due both to the increasing number of older people and to the establishment of more vocal groups to represent their concerns. ***Elder abuse* refers to physical abuse, psychological abuse, financial exploitation, and medical abuse or neglect of people age 65 or older** (Patterson and Podnieks, 1995).

The elderly are often referred to as "hidden victims" of intimate violence (DeKeseredy, 1996). It is difficult to determine the extent of abuse of older persons. Many victims are understandably reluctant to talk about it. One study used a cross-Canada telephone survey of elderly persons living in private houses (Podnieks, 1989). Four percent of a randomly selected sample reported some form of abuse. Although this may appear to be a small percentage, 4 percent of all seniors living in private dwellings translates into 98,000 Canadians. Many cases of abuse are chronic or repetitive. Podnieks reported that only 25 percent of the victims of elder abuse had reported the incident to the police. In only one case was a criminal charge laid. The most common reasons for not reporting the incident were that it was not serious enough to report to the police or it was a private family matter. The research indicates that elder abuse tends to be concentrated among those over age 75 (Steinmetz, 1987). In most cases the abuse is inflicted by a relative and is approximately equally distributed between children or grandchildren and spouses (Patterson and Podnieks, 1995). Almost two-thirds of the victims were men even though there are far more women in the elderly population. Abusers usually live with the victim and have often cared for the victim for a long time.

Elder abuse traditionally has been associated with high levels of impairment on the part of the older person (Harris, 1990), but studies have found little evidence to support that conclusion (Pedrick-Cornell and Gelles, 1982). Sociologist Karl Pillmer found that there was no support for another common misconception: that dependency on the part of the older person leads to abuse. In fact, victims of abuse were more likely than nonvictims to report that they lived with a person with serious health, emotional, or alcohol abuse problems. Furthermore, the abusers are very likely to be dependant on the older person for housing and financial assistance (Pillemer, 1985).

Although the risk of criminal victimization is much lower for individuals over the age of 65 than their younger counterparts, older people report more fear of crime. For example, the Canadian Urban Victimization Survey found that almost 60 percent of the people over 65 indicated that they felt unsafe walking alone at night (Johnson, 1990). Older unattached women with low incomes and fair-to-poor health reported the most fear of criminal victimization (Podnieks,1989). There are a number of factors that may lead to this fear. According to Novak, "loss of social networks due to retirement, widowhood, and staying home may lead to increased fear of crime" (1993:8). Furthermore, cases of abuse and neglect of older people are highly dramatized in the media because of their extremely disturbing nature. However, the media coverage may also serve to create a fear of victimization that does not fit the facts regarding elder abuse. Finally, the consequences of victimization may be more serious. A young person who is knocked down by a stranger may get up unharmed, while an older person may be seriously hurt in a similar incident.

What happens as we grow older? Activity theory assumes we will find substitutes for our previous roles and activities. Disengagement theory assumes we will detach ourselves from social roles and prepare for death. Which scenario do you prefer for your future?

SOCIOLOGICAL PERSPECTIVES ON AGING

Sociologists and social gerontologists have developed a number of explanations regarding the effects of aging. Some of the early theories were based on a microlevel analysis of how individuals adapt to changing social roles. More recent theories have used a macrolevel approach to examine the inequalities produced by age stratification at the societal level.

FUNCTIONALIST PERSPECTIVES ON AGING

Functionalist explanations of aging focus on how older persons adjust to their changing roles in society. According to sociologist Talcott Parsons (1960), the roles of older persons need to be redefined by society. He suggested that devaluing the contributions of older persons is dysfunctional for society; older persons often have knowledge and wisdom to share with younger people.

How does society cope with the disruptions resulting from its members growing older and dying? According to ***disengagement theory*, older persons make a normal and healthy adjustment to aging when they detach themselves from their social roles and prepare for their eventual death** (Cumming and Henry, 1961). Gerontologists Elaine C. Cumming and William E. Henry (1961) noted that disengagement can be functional for both the individual and society. The withdrawal of older persons from the work force, for example, provides employment opportunities for younger people. Disengagement also facilitates a gradual and orderly transfer of statuses and roles from one generation to the next; an abrupt change would result in chaos. Retirement, then, can be thought of as recognition for years of service and acknowledgment that the person no longer fits into the world of paid work (Williamson, Duffy

Rinehart, and Blank, 1992). The younger workers who move into the vacated positions have received more up-to-date training—for example, the computer skills that are taught to most younger people today.

Critics of this perspective object to the assumption that all older persons want to disengage while they still are productive and gain satisfaction from their work. Disengagement may be functional for organizations but not for individuals. A corporation that has compulsory retirement may be able to replace higher-paid, older workers with lower-paid, younger workers but retirement may not be beneficial for some older workers. Contrary to disengagement theory, a number of studies have found that activity in society is *more* important with increasing age.

INTERACTIONIST PERSPECTIVES ON AGING

Interactionist perspectives examine the connection between personal satisfaction in a person's later years and a high level of activity. ***Activity theory* states that people tend to shift gears in late middle age and find substitutes for previous statuses, roles, and activities** (Havighurst, Neugarten, and Tobin, 1968). From this perspective, older people have the same social and psychological needs as middle-aged people and thus do not want to withdraw unless restricted by poor health or disability.

Whether they invest their energies in grandchildren, travelling, hobbies, or new work roles, social activity among retired persons is directly related to longevity, happiness, and health (Palmore, 1981). Psychologist and newspaper columnist Eda LeShan observed a difference in the perceptions of people who do and do not remain active:

> The Richardsons came for lunch: friends we hadn't seen for twenty years. ... Helen and Martin had owned and worked together in a very fine women's clothing shop. ... Having some mistaken notion they were getting too old and should retire and "enjoy themselves," they sold the business ten years ago.
>
> During lunch, Larry and I realized we were dealing with two seriously depressed people, in excellent health but with no place to go. When Larry asked Helen what she'd been doing, she replied bitterly, "Who has anything to do?" Martin said sadly he was sorry he gave up tennis ten years ago; if he'd kept it up he could still play. ...
>
> We were embarrassed to indicate we were still so busy that we couldn't see straight. They seemed genuinely shocked that we had no plans to retire at seventy-one and seventy-four. (LeShan, 1994:221–222)

Studies have confirmed LeShan's suggestion that healthy people who remain active have a higher level of life satisfaction than do those who are inactive or in ill health (Havighurst, Neugarten, and Tobin, 1968). Among those whose mental capacities decline later in life, deterioration is most rapid in people who withdraw from social relationships and activities.

A variation on activity theory is the concept of *continuity*—that people are constantly attempting to maintain their self-esteem and lifelong principles and practices and that they simply adjust to the feedback from and needs of others as they grow older (Williamson, Duffy Rinehart, and Blank, 1992). From this perspective, aging is a continuation of earlier life stages rather than a separate and unique period. Thus, values and behaviours that have been important to an individual previously will continue to be so as the person ages. People also may turn to their ethnic culture to help them deal with physical changes, role changes, and bereavement issues in their later years. For example, studies have found that the church serves an important function in reducing loneliness, providing support systems, and enhancing self-image in older black persons (Gelfand, 1994).

Other interactionist perspectives focus on role and exchange theories. Role theory poses the question, What roles are available for older people? Some theorists have noted that industrialized, urbanized societies typically do not have roles for older people (Cowgill, 1986). Analysts examining the relationship between ethnicity and aging have found that many older persons are able to find active roles within their own ethnic group. While their experiences may not be valued in the larger society, they are esteemed within their ethnic subculture because they provide a rich source of knowledge of ethnic lore and history. For example, Mildred Cleghorn, an 80-year-old Native woman, passes on information to younger people by use of dolls:

> I decided ... to show that we were all not the same, by making dolls that said we were just as different as our clothes are different. I made four dolls ... representing the four tribes there—then seven more ... for the tribes living here. Now, over the years, I have a collection of forty-one fabric dolls, all different tribes. The trouble is there are thirty-two more to go! (quoted in Mucciolo, 1992:23)

Cleghorn's unique knowledge about the various First Nations has been a valuable source of information for young aboriginal people who otherwise might be unaware of the great diversity found among First Nations peoples. According to sociologist Donald E. Gelfand (1994), older people can "exchange" their knowledge for deference and respect from younger people.

CONFLICT PERSPECTIVES ON AGING

Conflict theorists view aging as especially problematic in contemporary capitalistic societies. As people grow older, their power tends to diminish unless they are able to maintain wealth. Consequently, those who have been disadvantaged in their younger years become even more so in late adulthood. Women age 75 and over are among the most disadvantaged because they often must rely solely on government support payments, having outlived their spouses and sometimes their children (Harrington Meyer, 1990).

Underlying the capitalist system is an ideology that assumes that all people have equal access to the means of gaining wealth and that poverty results from individual weakness. When older people are in need, they may be viewed as not having worked hard enough or planned adequately for their retirement. The family and the private sector are seen as the "proper" agents to respond to their needs. To minimize the demand for governmental assistance, these services are made punitive and stigmatizing to those who need them (Atchley, 1994). Class-based theories of inequality assert that government programs for older persons stratify society on the basis of class. Feminist approaches claim that these programs perpetuate inequalities on the basis of gender and ethnicity in addition to class (Harrington Meyer, 1994).

Conflict analysis draws attention to the diversity in the older population. Differences in social class, gender, and ethnicity divide older people just as they do everyone else. Wealth cannot forestall aging indefinitely, but it can soften the economic hardships faced in later years. The conflict perspective adds to our understanding of aging by focusing on how capitalism devalues older people, especially women. Critics assert, however, that this approach ignores the fact that industrialization and capitalism have greatly enhanced the longevity and quality of life for many older persons.

If we apply our sociological imagination to problems associated with aging, we find that these are not isolated situations shared by only a few people. Individuals cannot solve all of the problems associated with growing older or, in some cases, becoming a person with a disability. Some older persons initially may not see commonalities between their experiences and those of persons with a disability; however, if they have a problem that overlaps both categories, their perceptions may change. Eda LeShan (1994) explains:

> People like me sometimes need a hard lesson. Having just recently moved ... I looked forward eagerly to swimming at the local

BOX 11.2 SOCIOLOGY AND LAW

Murder or Mercy Killing?

In November 1994, Robert Latimer, a Saskatchewan farmer, was sentenced to a minimum of 10 years in jail after being convicted of second-degree murder for killing his severely disabled 12-year-old daughter, Tracy. Latimer never denied killing his daughter, who suffered both mentally and physically from cerebral palsy.

On October 24, 1993, while his wife and his other three children attended a Sunday morning church service, Latimer put Tracy in the cab of a pickup truck and left the motor running. Using a hose, he filled the cab with carbon monoxide fumes. By doing so, Latimer told police at the time of his arrest, he had finally ended his daughter's suffering. He also unwittingly triggered an emotional debate between Canadians who believe that no one has the right to take another person's life and those who believe he acted out of compassion. Latimer's lawyer argued that the girl was in such pain that the action constituted mercy killing. Latimer's supporters donated more than $60,000 to cover his legal bills—others circulated a clemency petition. Supporters appealed to the Federal cabinet to pardon Latimer under what is known as a "Royal Prerogative" contained in the Criminal Code. Under the provisions, a person convicted of murder may ask the cabinet for a full pardon or a reduced sentence. One supporter commented, "The severity of the sentence struck me. The justice system has gone off the rails."

Groups that represent disabled Canadians have a very different interpretation of this case—they say Latimer deserves no mercy. The president of the Association for Community Living argued that if Latimer's conviction were overturned or his sentenced reduced, it could encourage others to take similar action against the disabled. Theresa Ducharme, president of the Winnipeg-based People in Equal Participation Inc., argues, "The Criminal Code is there to protect the lives of all people. When it comes to the disabled, people seem to believe they should not uphold the law. According to the lawyer for the Saskatchewan Voice of the Disabled and the Council of Canadians with Disabilities, "The issue is whether the parents or guardians of disabled children have the discretion to terminate their dependents lives. We can't carve out the kind of exceptions in law that Mr. Latimer's supporters want without declaring open season on the handicapped." All three of these advocacy groups were successful in obtaining intervenor status at Latimer's appeal. At the Saskatchewan Court of Appeal, Latimer's lawyer contended the trial judge erred in telling the jury to follow the law strictly, and in denying that Latimer "had the legal right to commit suicide for his daughter, by virtue of her complete absence of physical and mental abilities." The Appeal Court did not agree. Latimer's conviction was upheld.

Perhaps Liberal MP Gordon Kirkby expressed it best: "We'll get into trouble trying to decide whose life is worth living. People may try to fairly judge a life's quality, but human beings don't have the wisdom to make those kinds of judgements."

Sources: Fennell, 1995; Woodward, 1995; Blinch, 1995.

YMCA. ... I was sure many of the members would be old ladies like me. ... Much to my surprise I discovered I had two choices: Either I would have to climb down a ladder, which I couldn't do because of arthritic feet, or I could paddle about in the "old people's pool," which was small and kept at 87 degrees. I am, at seventy, one helluva good swimmer. I just can't deal with ladders, and the hot pool was too debilitating and had no room for swimming laps. I got my membership fee back. ...

What do you know—I am one of the disabled! Unfortunately we imperfect humans often have to experience something ourselves before we get the full significance of a problem. (LeShan, 1994:132–133)

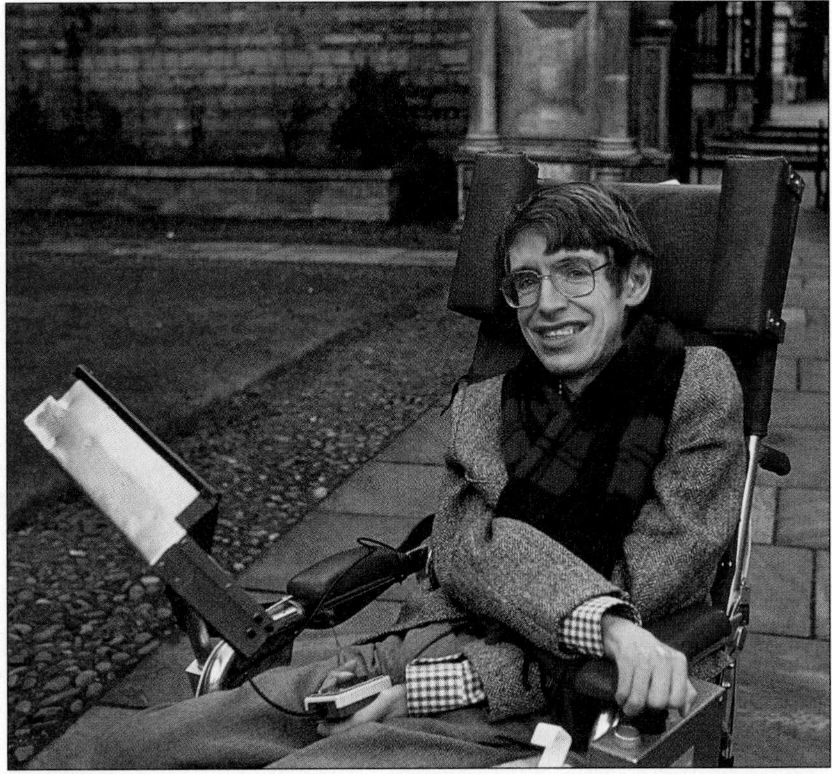

Does life expectancy take on a different meaning for persons with chronic disabilities? While he was still in college, British theoretical physicist Stephen Hawking learned he had Lou Gehrig's disease (amyotrophic lateral sclerosis). Hawking went on to develop a quantum theory of gravity that forever changed our view of the universe and caused Hawking to be considered one of the leading figures in modern cosmology.

THE SOCIAL SIGNIFICANCE OF DISABILITY

What is a disability? There are many different definitions. In business and government, it often is defined in terms of work—for instance, "an inability to engage in gainful employment." Medical professionals tend to define it in terms of organically based impairments—the problem being entirely within the body (Albrecht, 1992). However, not all disabilities are visible to others or necessarily limit people physically. The definition set forth at the start of this chapter (a physical or health condition that stigmatizes or causes discrimination) helps us view disability as residing primarily (although not exclusively) in social attitudes and in social and physical environments (Weitz, 1995). In other words, disability is socially created through everyday experiences that create barriers for individuals with disabilities. According to Blackford (1996), the social system and its planners have failed to provide the universal access that is needed so that people with disabilities can participate fully in all aspects of life. For example, in an elevator, the buttons may be beyond the reach of persons using a wheelchair. In this context, disability derives from the fact that certain things have been made inaccessible to some people (Weitz, 1995). Michael Oliver (1990) used the term *disability oppression* to describe the barriers that exist for disabled persons in Canadian society. These include economic hardship (from such things as the additional costs of accessibility devices, transportation, and attendant care; or employment discrimination), inadequate government assistance programs, and negative social attitudes toward disabled persons. According to disability rights advocates, disability must be thought of in terms of how society causes or contributes to the problem—not in terms of what is "wrong" with the person with a disability (see Box 11.2).

TABLE 11.1

Disabled Persons in Canada, Ages 15–65, 1990–91

Characteristics	Percentage
Age	
15–34 years	29.4
35–54 years	43.2
55–64 years	27.4
Type of Disability	
Severe	14
Moderate	32
Mild	54
Nature of Disability	
Mobility	52
Agility	50
Cognitive disability (includes intellectual, mental health, or learning disability	32
Hearing	25
Vision	9
Speaking	8
*Note: totals do not add up to 100 as disabled persons may have more than one disability.	
Marital status	
Never Married	24
Married/Common Law	61
Divorced	7
Separated	4
Widowed	4
Employment Status	
Unemployed	52
Employed	48
Level of Schooling	
University degree	6
High-school diploma	19
Some post-secondary	35

Reproduced by authority of the Minister of Industry, 1996, Statistics Canada, from *Report on Canadian Health and Disability Survey*, Cat. no. 82-555.

DISABILITY IN HISTORICAL PERSPECTIVE

Historically, different societies dealt with disabilities on the basis of their culture, values, and technology. For example, in the Neolithic period, some persons with disabling illnesses had a hole drilled in their skull to provide an escape route for the evil spirits that were assumed to cause the problem (McElroy and Townsend, 1989; Albrecht, 1992). During the Middle Ages, disabilities were seen as an expression of God's displeasure, so the clergy dealt with medical problems.

The mode of subsistence in a society is a major determinant of the types of disabilities and the social responses to them. In some hunting and gathering societies, impairments are viewed as punishment for past transgressions, and people with disabilities may be banished or killed; in others, they are fully integrated into the group (Albrecht, 1992). In pastoral societies, the migratory life inherent in continually moving herds of cattle, sheep, or goats to new locations for grazing may have serious consequences for those with an immobilizing disability. By contrast, in horticultural and agrarian societies, in which people settle down to cultivate crops and raise domestic animals, fewer stigmas are associated with disabilities (Albrecht, 1992). At the same time, however, as stable communities are developed, epidemics related to poor sanitation and overcrowding are more likely to occur. For example, during the early stages of industrialization, urban density, lack of adequate sanitation, and poverty all contribute to a rise in the rate of chronic illness and physical disability (Albrecht, 1992).

DISABILITY IN CONTEMPORARY SOCIETY

An estimated 4.2 million or 15.5 percent of the population in Canada have one or more physical or mental disabilities. This number continues to increase for several reasons. First, with advances in medical technology, many people who formerly would have died from an accident or illness now survive, although with an impairment. Second, as more people live longer, they are more likely to experience diseases (such as arthritis) that may have disabling consequences (Albrecht, 1992). Third, persons born with serious disabilities are more likely to survive infancy because of medical technology. However, less than 15 percent of persons with a disability today were born with it; accidents and disease account for most disabilities in this country.

Although anyone can become disabled, some people are more likely to be or to become disabled than others. Native people have higher rates of disability than whites, especially more serious disabilities; persons with lower incomes also have higher rates of disability (Bolaria and Bolaria, 1994). However, "disability knows no socioeconomic boundaries. You can become disabled from your mother's poor nutrition or from falling off your polo pony," says Patrisha Wright, a spokesperson for the Disability Rights Education and Defense Fund (quoted in Shapiro, 1993:10).

For persons with chronic illness and disability, life expectancy may take on a different meaning. Knowing that they likely will not live out the full life expectancy for persons in their age cohort, they may come to "treasure each moment," as does James Keller, a baseball coach:

> In December 1992, I found out I have Lou Gehrig's disease—amyotrophic lateral sclerosis, or ALS. I learned that this disease destroys every muscle in the body, that there's no known cure or treatment and that the average life expectancy for people with ALS is two to five years after diagnosis.
>
> Those are hard facts to accept. Even today, nearly two years after my diagnosis, I see myself as 42-year-old career athlete who has always been blessed with excellent health. Though not an hour goes by in which I don't see or hear in my mind that phrase "two to five years," I still can't quite believe it. Maybe my resistance to those words is exactly what gives me the strength to live with them and the will to make the best of every day in every way. (Keller, 1994)

As Keller's comments illustrate, disease and disability are intricately linked.

Environment, lifestyle, and working conditions all may contribute to either temporary or chronic disability. For example, air pollution in automobile-clogged cities leads to a higher incidence of chronic respiratory disease and lung damage, which may result in severe disability in some people. Eating certain types of food and smoking cigarettes increase the risk for coronary and cardiovascular diseases (Albrecht, 1992). In contemporary industrial societies, workers in the second tier of the labour market (primarily recent immigrants, white women, and visible minorities) are at the greatest risk for certain health hazards and disabilities. Employees in data processing and service-oriented jobs also may be affected by work-related disabilities. The extensive use of computers has been shown to harm some workers' vision; to produce joint problems such as arthritis, low-back pain, and carpal tunnel syndrome; and to place employees under high levels of stress that may result in neuroses and other mental health problems (Albrecht, 1992).

Nearly one out of six people in Canada have a "chronic health condition which, given the physical, attitudinal, and financial barriers built into the social system, makes it difficult to perform one or more activities generally considered appropriate for persons of their age" (Nessler, 1994). Can a person in a wheelchair have equal access to education, employment, and housing? If public transportation is not accessible to those in wheelchairs, the answer certainly is no. As disability rights activist Mark Johnson put it, "Black people fought for the right to ride in the front of the bus. We're fighting for the right to get on the bus" (quoted in Shapiro, 1993:128).

Living with disabilities is a long-term process. For infants born with certain types of congenital (present at birth) problems, their disability first acquires social significance for their parents and caregivers. In a study of children with disabilities in Israel, sociologist Meira Weiss (1994) challenged the assumption that parents automatically bond with infants, especially those born with visible disabilities. She found that an infant's appearance may determine how parents will view the child. Parents are more likely to be bothered by external, openly visible disabilities than by internal or disguised ones; some of the parents are more willing to consent to or even demand the death of an "appearance-impaired" child (Weiss, 1994). According to Weiss, children born with internal (concealed) disabilities at least initially are more acceptable to parents because they do not violate the parents' perceived body images of their children. Weiss's study provides insight into the social significance people attach to congenital disabilities.

Many disability rights advocates argue that persons with a disability have been kept out of the mainstream of society. They have been denied equal opportunities in education by being consigned to special education classes or special schools. For example, people who grow up deaf often are viewed as disabled; however, many members of the deaf community instead view themselves as a "linguistic minority" that is part of a unique culture (Lane, 1992; Cohen, 1994). They believe they have been restricted from entry into schools and the work force, not due to their own limitations, but by societal barriers. Why are disabled persons excluded? Susan Wendell offers an explanation:

> In a society which idealizes the body, the physically disabled are often marginalized. People learn to identify with their own strengths (by cultural standards) and to hate, fear, and neglect their own weaknesses. The disabled are not only de-valued for their de-valued bodies; they are constant reminders to the able-bodied of the negative body—of what the able-bodied are trying to avoid, forget, and ignore . . . In a culture which loves the idea that the body can be controlled, those who cannot control their bodies are seen (and may see themselves) as failures. (1995:458)

Among persons who acquire disabilities through disease or accidents later in life, the social significance of their disability can be seen in how they initially respond to their symptoms and diagnosis, how they view the immediate situation and their future, and how the illness and disability affect their lives. According to Wendell:

> Disabled people can participate in marginalizing ourselves. We can wish for bodies we do not have, with frustration, shame, self-hatred. We can feel trapped in the negative body; it is our internalized oppression to feel this. Every (visibly or invisibly) disabled person I have talked to has felt this; some never stop feeling it. (1995:458)

When confronted with a disability, most people adopt one of two strategies—avoidance or vigilance. Those who use the avoidance strategy deny their condition so as to maintain hopeful images of the future and elude depression; for example, some individuals refuse to participate in rehabilitation following a traumatic injury because they want to pretend that it does not exist (Weitz, 1995). By contrast, those using the vigilant strategy actively seek knowledge and treatment so that they can respond appropriately to the changes in their bodies (Weitz, 1995).

SOCIOLOGICAL PERSPECTIVES ON DISABILITY

What causes some people to react negatively toward a person with a disability? To answer that question, we will examine the issue from three different perspectives.

FUNCTIONALIST PERSPECTIVES ON DISABILITY

The early analytical work on persons with a disability was based on Talcott Parsons's concept of the *sick role* (Albrecht, 1992). According to Parsons, to have a functioning social system, all persons must fulfill their appropriate social roles. When individuals are ill (or disabled), they are consigned to the sick role. Persons who assume the sick role (1) are not responsible for their condition, (2) are temporarily exempt from their normal roles and obligations, (3) must try to get well, and (4) must seek competent help from a medical professional to hasten the process of getting well (Parsons, 1951). This is referred to as the *medical model* of disability because persons with disabilities in effect become chronic patients under the supervision of doctors and other medical personnel, subject to a doctor's orders or a program's rules, and not to their own judgment (Shapiro, 1993). From this perspective, disability is deviance.

INTERACTIONIST PERSPECTIVES ON DISABILITY

The deviance framework also is apparent in some interactionist perspectives. According to interactionists, persons with a disability experience role ambiguity because many people equate disability with deviance (Murphy et al., 1988). By labelling persons with a disability as "deviant," other people can avoid them or treat them as outsiders. Society marginalizes persons with a disability because they have lost old roles and statuses and are labelled as "disabled" persons.

According to sociologist Eliot Freidson (1965), how they are labelled results from three factors: (1) their degree of responsibility for their impairment, (2) the apparent seriousness of their condition, and (3) the perceived legitimacy of the condition. Freidson concluded that the definitions of and expectations for persons with a disability are socially constructed factors.

CONFLICT PERSPECTIVES ON DISABILITY

From a conflict perspective, persons with a disability are members of a subordinate group in conflict with persons in positions of power in the government, the health care industry, and the rehabilitation business, all of whom are trying to control their destinies (Albrecht, 1992). Those in positions of power have created policies and artificial barriers that keep people with disabilities in a subservient position (Asch, 1986; Hahn, 1987). Moreover, in a capitalist economy, disabilities are big business. When people with disabilities are defined as a social problem and public funds are spent to purchase goods and services for them, rehabilitation becomes a commodity that can be bought and sold (Albrecht, 1992). The private sector, including pharmaceutical companies, medical supply companies, and others, can reap huge profits from persons with disabilities. To cease to be subservient, people with disabilities must band together to force changes through laws and public policies to alter public attitudes toward disabilities (Albrecht, 1992).

From this perspective, persons with a disability are objectified. They have an economic value as consumers of goods and services that allegedly will make them "better" people. Many persons with a disability endure the same struggle for resources faced by visible minorities, women, and older persons. Individuals who hold more than one of these ascribed statuses, combined with experiencing disability, are doubly or triply oppressed by capitalism.

INEQUALITIES RELATED TO DISABILITY

As we have seen, prejudice about disability interferes with the everyday life of many people. For example, Marylou Breslin, executive director of the American Disability Rights Education and Defense Fund, was wearing a businesswoman's suit, sitting at the airport in her battery-powered wheelchair, and drinking a cup of coffee while waiting for a plane. A woman walked by and plunked a coin in the coffee cup that Breslin held in her hand, splashing coffee on Breslin's blouse (Shapiro, 1993). Why did the woman drop the coin in Breslin's cup? The answer to this question is found in stereotypes built on lack of knowledge about or exaggeration of the characteristics of persons with a disability.

BOX 11.3 SOCIOLOGY AND MEDIA

Stereotypes, Disability, and Fund-Raising

"Jerry's got to go. Jerry's got to go."

Many of the protesters were in wheelchairs; some wore Jerry Lewis masks with a "no" symbol across his face while others carried signs that stated "Not Jerry's kids" as they demonstrated outside a store owned by one of the corporate sponsors of the 1994 "Stars Across America" telethon for the Muscular Dystrophy Association.

The telethon raised $47.1 million for muscular dystrophy research, so why were members of ADAPT, a national group that promotes the rights of people with disabilities, protesting? As with all disputes, there are at least two sides to the story, and the Jerry Lewis telethon is no exception.

How did Jerry Lewis, a comedian, get involved with a telethon anyway? It all started in 1959 when the parents of Evan Kemp, Jr., and other children with muscular dystrophy and similar conditions put together a telethon on a television station in Cleveland to raise money for medical research. The telethon initially featured entertainers and celebrities who asked viewers to send in contributions. Jerry Lewis took over the telethon in 1966 and turned it into an extravaganza. In addition to including celebrities, Lewis began to introduce children with muscular dystrophy to nationwide television audiences. In the process, he repeatedly pointed out the tragic number of children who died from this disease. Each year, Lewis raised large sums of money by introducing cute, huggable "kids" on crutches and in wheelchairs and appealing to viewers to "give from the heart!"

Controversy over the telethon arose when Evan Kemp, Jr., became an outspoken critic of the telethon and Lewis's fund-raising methods. In 1981, Kemp wrote, "By arousing the public's fear of the handicap itself, the telethon makes viewers more afraid of handicapped people. Playing to pity may raise money, but it also raises walls of fear between the public and us" (quoted in Shapiro, 1993:21). Over the next decade, disability rights advocates decried the "pity approach" to raising money. Some adults especially felt demeaned when Lewis began to refer to both adults and children as "Jerry's kids." Eventually, Lewis modified his approach. Now he told stories of hope and courage about children who did well at school and adults who succeeded at work. "Poster children" were renamed "national goodwill ambassadors"; however, stories of impending doom for persons with muscular dystrophy still were told.

If Lewis's annual telethons were criticized by many people, why weren't they discontinued? The answer is simple—money! Without these televised appeals, the Muscular Dystrophy Association would have raised far less money over the past three decades. As one journalist noted, "Let's ask this question of the [protesters] who would like to see Lewis drummed out of the telethon: Just who is going to keep this cash machine going?" (quoted in Shapiro, 1993:23). Other groups, including the National Easter Seal Society and United Cerebral Palsy Association, developed telethons based on Lewis's model, although they have used a softer focus on persons with a disability.

Regardless of how it is done, some disability rights advocates do not approve of dividing the world into the "abled" and "disabled." As Marilynn Phillips, a former polio "poster child," stated, "There are no good plantations and there are no good telethons" (quoted in Shapiro, 1993:24).

Do you think telethons perpetuate stereotypes about persons with a disability? Why or why not?

Sources: Based on Shapiro, 1993.

STEREOTYPES BASED ON DISABILITY

Stereotypes of persons with a disability fall into two categories. The first category consists of deformed individuals who also may be horrible deviants. Horror movies are an example. In the *Nightmare on Elm Street* movies, the villain was turned into a hateful, sadistic killer because of disfigurement resulting from a fire. Even lighter fare such as the *Batman* movies depict villains as

BOX 11.4 SOCIOLOGY IN GLOBAL PERSPECTIVE

The Politics of Disability in China

Fang Zheng, China's discus champion among athletes with disabilities, speaks about being barred from entering an international athletic competition in 1994 after Communist Party officials discovered that his disability occurred during the June 4, 1989, Tiananmen Square uprising in which prodemocracy students and workers were demonstrating for greater freedom:

> I am the champion. ... Even though I was injured on June 4, I should be treated the same as any other disabled man, but, in reality, the situation has proved to be different. There should be no connection between the injury and the cause of my injury. ...
>
> I have never suffered from feelings of pessimism. Even though losing my legs means there are many obstacles in my life, I still feel that I can make a useful contribution. I can still do a lot of things to help other people. ...
>
> I am very fond of sports, it has been my hobby since I was a child and so I was excited about my chance to participate in the [Far East and South Pacific Games]. But I had no idea that there would be such a strong political coloration surrounding the competition. (quoted in Tyler, 1994:A3)

His legs were crushed (and later amputated) when a Chinese Army tank ran him down and dragged him thirty feet as it plunged into the crowd to suppress the dissenters. When questioned by journalists, Chinese sports ministry officials denied that Fang had qualified in the discus event. However, it was learned that Fang's previous record-breaking throw was 27 meters, as compared with the winning 12.1 meters of the only entrant in the competition.

Fang's exclusion from the competition captured international media attention; it also made people more aware of how limited the rights of persons with a disability may be in countries such as China. For example, wheelchair ramps and special facilities are virtually nonexistent. Fang had to build his own ramp to bridge the two-step walk-up to the entrance of his apartment. While the international games for athletes with disabilities was a part of China's campaign to improve its international image, some journalists declared that the effort had failed in light of Fang's predicament.

Source: Based on Tyler, 1994.

individuals with disabilities: the Joker, disfigured by a fall into a vat of acid, and the Penguin, born with flippers instead of arms (Shapiro, 1993).

According to the second category of stereotypes, persons with a disability are to be pitied. As discussed in Box 11.3, fund-raising activities by many charitable organizations whose goal is to *help* those with disabilities have contributed to this latter perception. The "poster child" campaigns are an example. They show a photograph of a friendly looking child with a visible disability and appeal for donations to help cure and care for such children. However, persons with disabilities often disapprove of this approach. "The poster child says it's not okay to be disabled," argues Cyndi Jones. "It says this could happen to you, your child, or your grandchild. But it says, if you just donate some money, the disabled children will go away" (quoted in Shapiro, 1993:14). Jones had been the March of Dimes poster child when she was age 5. She appeared on a national telethon during which she touched the nation's hearts and tapped its pocketbooks and wallets by dropping her crutches and taking a few wobbly steps before falling with a thud to the stage (Shapiro, 1993). The clear message was, Help children such as this valiant little girl by contributing money.

Even apparently positive stereotypes become harmful to persons with a disability. An example is what some disabled persons refer to as "super-

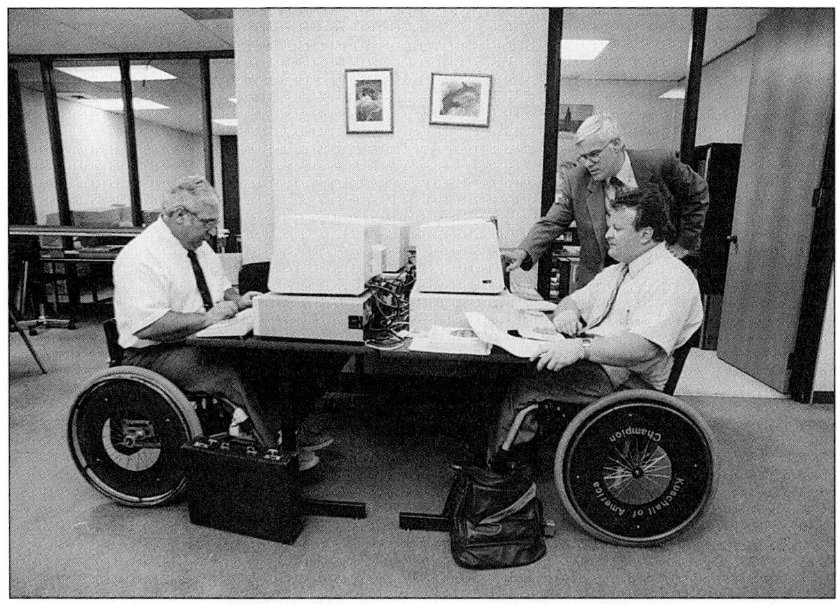

The problem of unemployment is particularly severe for persons with disabilities. Affirmative action programs such as this computer training course have had some success in alleviating employment discrimination and creating employment opportunities for disabled persons.

crips"—people with severe disabilities who seem to excel despite the impairment and who receive widespread press coverage in the process. Disability rights advocates note that such stereotypes do not reflect the day-to-day reality of most persons with disabilities, who must struggle constantly with smaller challenges (Shapiro, 1993). Box 11.4 examines a conflict between a Chinese athlete with a disability and Communist Party officials and provides a unique insight into the politics of disability.

PREJUDICE AND DISCRIMINATION BASED ON DISABILITY

Prejudice against persons with disabilities may result in either subtle or overt discrimination. Examples of the latter include the owner of a zoo who refused to admit children with mental disabilities to the monkey house, claiming that they scared the monkeys; a restaurant owner who asked a woman with cerebral palsy to leave because her appearance was disturbing to other diners; and an airline employee who threw an elderly amputee onto a baggage dolly ("like a sack of potatoes," his daughter noted) rather than helping him into a wheelchair so that he could board a plane (Shapiro, 1993).

Treating persons with disabilities as asexual is a more subtle type of discrimination (Matthews, 1983). Margaret Nosek, a medical school professor, conducted research on sexuality issues faced by women with physical disabilities such as spina bifida, cerebral palsy, postpolio, amputation, spinal cord injuries, and multiple sclerosis. This was of special interest to Nosek, who was born with a neuromuscular disease that required her to use a wheelchair from the fifth grade on. According to Nosek, her father used to tell her that no one would ever marry her, so she had better excel academically (Karkabi, 1993).

Nosek found that other women with disabilities had similar experiences, not only in their families but also with some medical professionals (especially in obstetrics and gynecology) who treat women with disabilities as if they were asexual beings. For example, she found that women had been advised either to have hysterectomies or not to have children because they were perceived as being unfit mothers:

> One woman had her baby when her doctor was not in town. As she was wheeled into the oper-

> ating room, the doctor who was to deliver her baby suggested she have her tubes tied.
>
> Another new mom was in the hospital with her baby. A nurse came in and said, "Let me hold the baby till the mother comes back." (Karkabi, 1993)

Despite her research findings and her own experiences with discrimination, Nosek remains optimistic:

> I used to feel a brotherhood with all people with disabilities, but now I feel a sisterhood because I realize my disability is no worse than other disadvantages, like poverty, battering or lack of education. I'm firmly convinced that a lack of education is much worse than a disability. I'm living proof of that. (Karkabi, 1993:E8)

Acquiring an education can help some persons with disabilities gain employment. However, many persons with disabilities encounter employment bias in hiring, salaries, and promotions.

INCOME, EMPLOYMENT, AND DISABILITY

> Being disabled remains a substantial impediment to finding and keeping a job in Canada. While a significant proportion of those with disabilities are employed, disabled people are much less likely to be working than their nondisabled peers. As well, gaps between the employment levels of disabled and nondisabled populations exist regardless of sex, age, or educational attainment. (Gower, 1990:218)

In recent years, the role of disabled persons in the Canadian labour force has expanded. Technology has made it possible for disabled persons to perform a wider variety of jobs, and special training has become more readily available. However, compared with nondisabled adults, a much smaller proportion of the disabled population is employed. Today, about 50 percent of working-age persons with a disability in Canada are unemployed (H.A.L.S., 1991). Most unemployed disabled persons believe that they could and would work if offered the opportunity. However, even when persons with a disability are able to find jobs, they typically earn less than persons without a disability (Yelin, 1992).

Level of education has a major impact on the employment levels of disabled persons. There are particularly large differences in employment rates for disabled and nondisabled persons with low levels of education. This difference is relatively easy to understand. We know that in our society people with little education are more likely to have jobs requiring manual labour. A physical disability would represent a serious obstacle to employment in these occupations.

It is difficult to assess exactly how education is related to employment for disabled persons. In some cases, the disability will have occurred after the individual had obtained his or her education. In other instances, the type and degree of disability may affect the level of education an individual can attain. This is especially true in the case of the mentally handicapped (Gower, 1990). Finally, as a result of negative stereotyping of disabled persons, many individuals may be perceived to be incapable of succeeding in educational pursuits. Sociologist Susan Wendell sums it up best:

> Disabled people are placed in a double-bind: they have access to inadequate resources because they are unemployed or underemployed, and they are unemployed or underemployed because they lack the resources that would enable them to make their full contribution to society. (1995:456)

Affirmative action programs in the public and private service sectors have made some limited progress in alleviating the discrimination that disabled persons encounter with respect to employment. However, some of these attempts have only served to reinforce negative images of disabled persons. For example, the well-known restaurant chain McDonald's has trademarked the term "McJobs" to refer only to the employment of individuals with disabilities. In response, a leader in the disability community in Canada commented:

> They are in a state of denial if they think that "McJobs" is not patronizing and humiliating to people with a disability. We want to integrate in an equal fashion, and not through some fancy public relations label. Do they have McXecutives, too? (Anderson, 1996:17)

Given the inequities in employment and education, it is no surprise that disabled adults generally have lower incomes than other Canadians. In 1990, disabled men aged 15 and over had a total average income of $20,000, compared with $26,210 for adults without disabilities. The difference was not as great among women (H.A.L.S, 1991). This does not mean that women who are disabled are in a better economic situation. Rather, according to sociologist Lesley Harman:

> Physical disability is an almost guaranteed route to poverty for women. Disabled women are less likely to be married than are disabled men or able-bodied women; if they are alone, they are less likely to be employed and therefore will depend on the state for their material existence. Disabled single mothers often find it difficult to find affordable, accessible housing. (1995b:409)

The income gap between people with and without disabilities narrows after retirement age. However, this is more a reflection of decreases in income for the nondisabled populations in retirement than an improvement in economic circumstances for disabled persons. In Canada, only a small minority of the disabled population receive any form of disability-related pension (Nessler, 1994).

LIVING ARRANGEMENTS AND LONG-TERM CARE FACILITIES

Living arrangements are a central issue for many persons with severe disabilities. Sometimes, having an accessible bathroom and kitchen or space for specialized equipment means the difference between living independently and requiring a round-the-clock attendant or living in an institutionalized setting.

INDEPENDENT LIVING CENTRES

Originating in the 1970s, the independent living movement has encouraged innovative living arrangements for persons with a disability. Independent living is based on the concept that persons with a disability should have the chance to live like other people and work independently. Independent living centres help people with disabilities to find attendants, housing, and employment so that they can be independent of relatives and institutions.

Technological advances also have made it possible for more persons with a disability to live independently. Computerized voice recognition devices allow persons who are paralyzed to control their environment. Optical character recognition computers help persons who have visual impairments. Motorized wheelchairs can be controlled by sip-and-puff air tubes; and persons with paralysis can exercise by means of computerized electrical stimulation devices attached to nerves and joints (Shapiro, 1993).

HOME CARE, SUPPORT SERVICES, AND DAY CARE

Many persons with a severe disability, as well as frail, older people, live alone or in a family setting where care is provided informally by family or friends. Relatives (especially women) provide most of the care (Glazer, 1990). Many women caregivers are employed outside the home; some are still raising a family. Recently, the responsibilities of informal caregivers have become more complex. For frail, older persons, for example, family members often are involved in nursing regimes—such as chemotherapy and tube-feeding—that previously were performed in hospitals (Glazer, 1990). Only about 7 percent of frail,

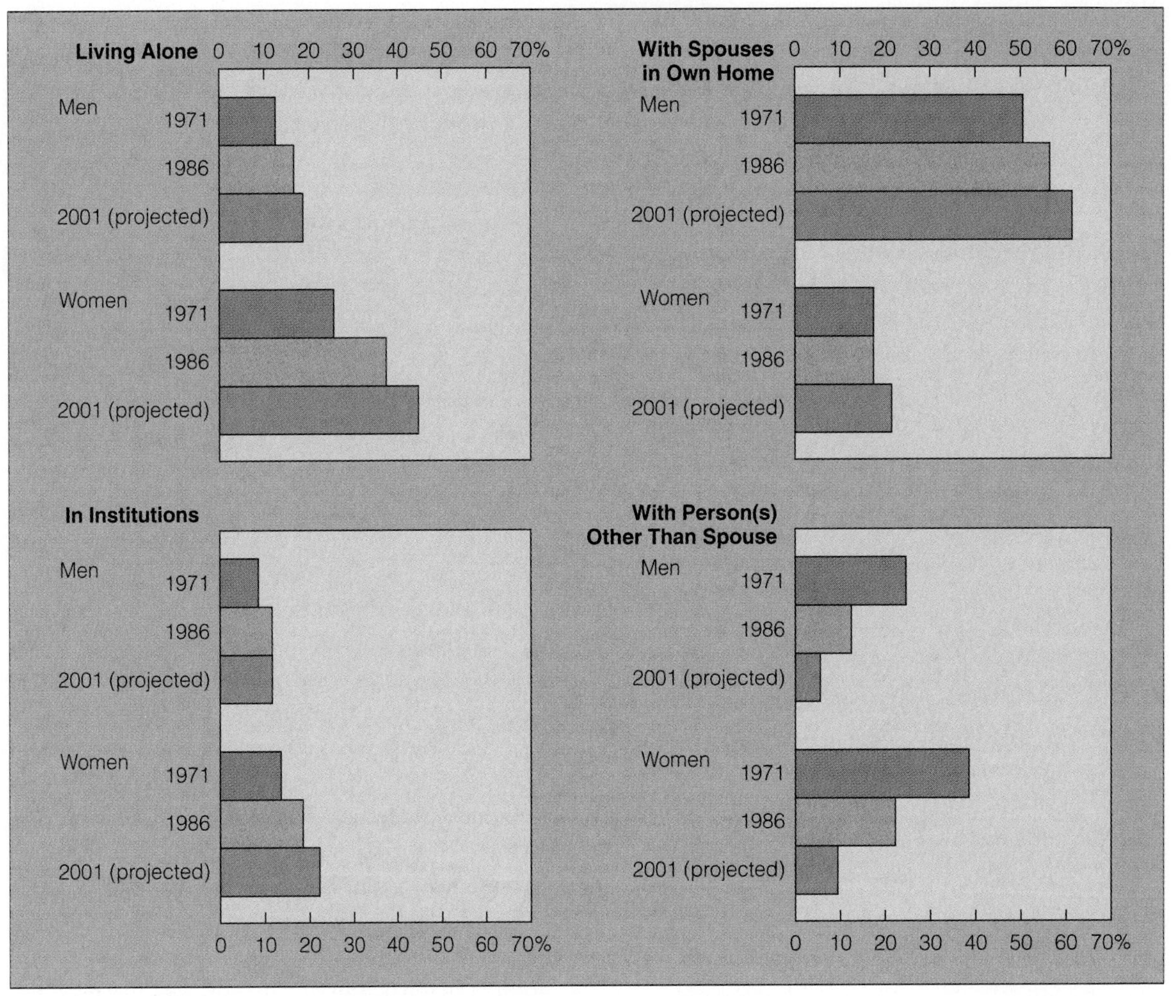

FIGURE 11.3

Living Arrangements of Population Aged 75 and Over, by Sex, 1971, 1986 and 2001.

Reproduced by authority of the Minister of Industry, 1996, Statistics Canada, from *Canadian Social Trends*, Cat. no. 11-008, 1993.

older persons are currently in nursing homes (Priest, 1993).

Support services help older individuals and persons with a disability cope with the problems in their day-to-day care. These services are very expensive even when they are provided through government-funded programs, hospitals, or community organizations.

For older persons, homemaker services perform basic chores (such as light housecleaning and laundry); other services (such as Meals on Wheels) deliver meals to homes. Some programs provide balanced meals at set locations, such as churches, synagogues, or senior centres. Some of these programs have been criticized, however, for their failure to provide meals that take into account the diverse ethnic backgrounds of the people they serve (Gelfand, 1994).

Day-care centres also have been developed to help older persons maintain as much dignity and

What does the concept of nursing homes imply about the ability of residents to live out their lives with dignity and respect?

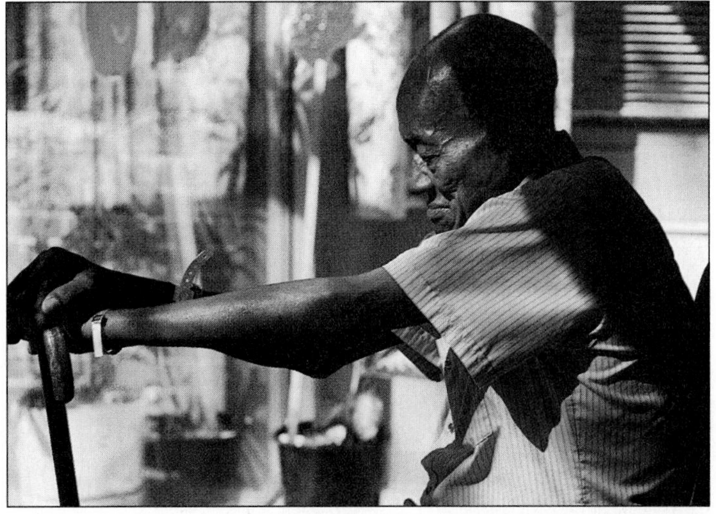

autonomy as possible. These centres typically provide transportation, activities, some medical personnel (such as a licensed practical nurse) on staff, and nutritious meals.

NURSING HOMES

Nursing homes are the most restrictive environment for older persons and persons of all ages with disabilities. Most nursing homes have been set up to care for frail, older persons, not younger individuals with disabilities such as head and spinal cord injuries and cerebral palsy. Nursing homes have been referred to as "the new black holes of isolation and despair for young people with disabilities" (Shapiro, 1993:240). Even for young people whose families struggle to keep them at home, living in a nursing home may be a part of their future if their parents become physically or financially unable to care for them or they outlive their parents (Shapiro, 1993).

Many nursing home residents have major physical and/or cognitive problems that prevent them from living in any other setting or do not have available caregivers in their family. Women are more likely to enter nursing homes because of their greater life expectancy, higher rates of chronic illness, and higher rates of widowhood.

Nursing homes have been criticized for a lack of consideration for residents' ethnic backgrounds by staff members performing their daily tasks (Gelfand, 1994). For example, members of different ethnic groups have specific ways in which they prefer to be addressed. When someone violates these rules of etiquette, the older person may view the behaviour as a deliberate insult. Likewise, if members of the nursing home staff do not respect the older person's desire for privacy, particularly in regard to dressing, toileting, and bathing, the perception of disrespect grows even stronger (Gelfand, 1994). Language barriers often exist between nursing home assistants and the older nursing home residents; many of the assistants are recent immigrants and do not speak the same language as the residents (MacLean and Bonar, 1995).

Nursing homes may not be the solution to anyone's problem. Cases of neglect, excessive use of physical restraints, overmedication of patients, and other complaints have been rampant in many of the homes. Author Betty Friedan (1993:516) stresses that even the best-run nursing homes "deny the personhood of age [because they] reify the image of age as inevitable decline and deterioration."

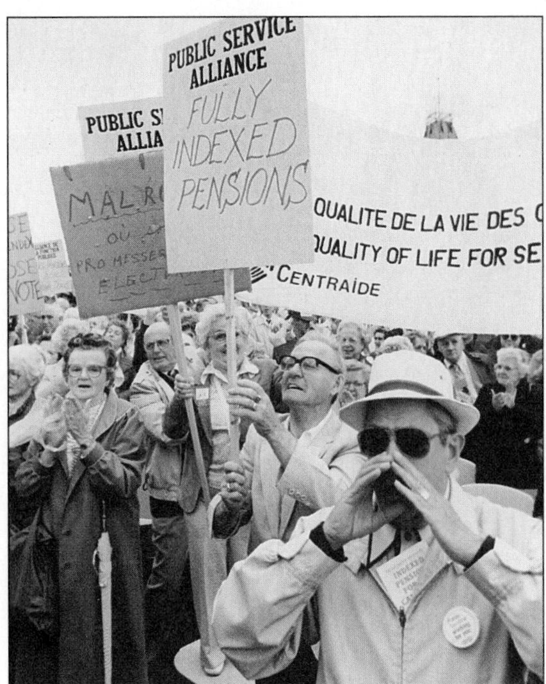

Older persons and persons with disabilities both seek to be fully accepted as participants in everyday life, as this seniors protest demonstrates.

DEATH AND DYING

Historically, death has been a common occurrence at all stages of the life course. Until the twentieth century, the chances that a newborn child would live to adulthood were very small. Poor nutrition, infectious diseases, accidents, and natural disasters took their toll on men and women of all ages. In contemporary, industrial societies, however, death is looked on as unnatural because it largely has been removed from everyday life. Most deaths now occur among older persons and in institutional settings. The association of death with the aging process has contributed to ageism in our society; if people can deny aging, they feel they can deny death (Atchley, 1994).

In the past, explanations for death and dying were rooted in custom or religious beliefs; today, they have been replaced by medical and legal explanations and definitions, and ongoing medical and legal battles.

The Canadian courts have not yet successfully resolved a number of controversial issues that relate to the right to die with dignity. Should parents of incompetent persons in permanent vegetative states have the legal right to refuse medical treatment? Should individuals suffering from an incurable, terminal illness have the right to decide when their life should end? The Supreme Court of Canada recently considered this question in the case of Sue Rodriquez, a British Columbia woman suffering from Lou Gehrig's disease. The court decided that the right to life, liberty, and security of the person (as outlined in the Charter of Rights and Freedoms) does not include the right to take action that will end one's life. Furthermore, the court decided that prohibition of physician-assisted suicide did not constitute cruel and unusual treatment. However, the lack of consensus over this complex issue was reflected in a strong dissenting vote expressed by four of the nine justices. Justice Beverley McLachlin wrote:

> The denial to Sue Rodriquez of a choice available to others cannot be justified. Such a denial deprived Sue Rodriquez of her security of the person (the right to make decisions concerning her own body which affect only her own body) in a way that offended the principles of fundamental justice. (Bolton, 1995:391)

After the Supreme Court declined her challenge for a legal physician-assisted suicide, Rodriquez took her own life with the help of an anonymous doctor and NDP MP and right-to-die advocate Svend Robinson. Currently, the Criminal Code specifies that anyone who counsels or "aids and abets" a suicide is guilty of an indictable offense and subject to 14 years in prison (McGovern, 1995). The patient's consent can not be used as a defense.

There is no national standard for determining when life support measures should be ended. Thousands of people are in some kind of permanent vegetative state today, and many thousands more are faced with terminal illnesses. As a result, many people have chosen to have a say in how their own lives might end by signing a *living will*—a document stating their wishes about the medical circumstances under which their life should be terminated. Most provinces recognize living wills. Many issues pertaining to the quality of life and to death with dignity may remain unresolved as we approach the twenty-first century.

How do people cope with dying? To answer this question, psychiatrist Elisabeth Kübler-Ross (1969) proposed five stages: (1) denial ("Not me!"), (2) anger ("Why me?"), (3) bargaining ("Yes me, but ... "—negotiating for divine intervention), (4) depression and sense of loss, and (5) acceptance. She pointed out that these stages are not the same for all people; some of them may exist at the same time. Kübler-Ross (1969:138) also stated that "the one thing that usually persists through all these stages is hope."

Kübler-Ross's stages were attractive to the general public and the media because they provided common responses to a difficult situation. On the other hand, her stage-based model also generated a great deal of criticism. Some have pointed out that these stages have never been conclusively demonstrated or comprehensively explained. Others have noted that there are many ways in which people cope with dying, not just five.

Criticisms notwithstanding, Kübler-Ross's perspective made the process of dying an acceptable topic for public discussion and helped facilitate the hospice movement in the 1970s (Weitz, 1995). A ***hospice*** **is a homelike facility that provides supportive care for patients with terminal illnesses.** The hospice philosophy asserts that people should participate in their own care and have control over as many decisions pertaining to their life as possible. Pain and suffering should be minimized, but artificial measures should not be used to sustain life. This approach is family based and provides support for family members and friends, as well as for the person who is dying (see Corr, Nabe, and Corr, 1994). Although the hospice movement has been very successful, critics claim that the movement has exchanged much of its initial philosophy and goals for social acceptance and financial support (Finn Paradis and Cummings, 1986; Weitz, 1995).

AGING AND DISABILITY IN THE TWENTY-FIRST CENTURY

The size of the older population in Canada will increase dramatically in the early decades of the twenty-first century. By the year 2031, there will be an estimated 8 million persons age 65 and older, as compared with 3.2 million in 1991. Thus, combined with decreasing birth rates, during the next sixty years, most of the population growth will occur in the older age cohorts. More people will survive to age 85, and more will even reach the 95-and-over cohort (Norland, 1994).

In the twenty-first century, approximately one in every four people will be 65 or over. How will this affect life in Canada? First, there will be a much greater demand on social resources and programs that provide support to the elderly. Some have suggested that unless steps are taken to meet the health care needs of millions of additional older people, our society will face a monumental health care crisis in the next century. However, others have stressed that changes in the health care system, like changes in the population, occur gradually. Therefore, the health care system will have a long time to adjust to the increasing demands of the next century (Barer et al., 1995).

One of the most positive consequences of the "greying of Canada" is that there will be considerably less age segregation. The younger population today has limited contact with older people. When the elderly comprise one-quarter of the population, there will be much more interaction between individuals of all age groups. This increased information regarding older people and the effects of aging should lead to dramatic decreases in both ageism and negative stereotypes of old age.

Who will assist persons with needs they cannot meet themselves? Family members in the future may be less willing or able to serve as caregivers. Women, the primary caregivers in the past, are faced with not just double but *triple* workdays if they attempt to combine working full-time with caring for their children and assisting older relatives or persons with disabilities. Even "superwomen" have a breaking point—no one has unlimited time, energy, and will to engage in such demanding activities for extended periods of time.

As biomedical research on aging and disabilities continues, new discoveries in genetics may eliminate life-threatening diseases and make early identification of others possible. Technological advances in the diagnosis, prevention, and treatment of Alzheimer's disease may revolutionize people's feelings about growing older (Butler, 1987; Atchley, 1993). Advances in medical technology may lead to a more positive outlook on aging and disability.

If these advances occur, will they help everyone or just some segments of the population? This is a very important question for the future. As we have seen, many of the benefits and opportunities of living in a highly technological, affluent society are not available to all people. Classism, racism, sexism, and ageism all serve to restrict individuals' access to education, medical care, housing, employment, and other valued goods and services in society.

For older persons and individuals with disabilities, the issues discussed in this chapter are not merely sociological abstractions; they are an integral part of their everyday lives. Older people have resisted ageism through organizations such as the New Horizons Program, the Senior's Independence Program, and the Gray Panthers. In the disability rights movement, alliances have been forged among individuals and groups representing hundreds of different disabilities. Organizations such as Disabled Persons International, National Educational Association of Disabled Students (NEADS), and Council of Canadians with Disabilities Act have brought many persons with disabilities together, at least briefly, for a common cause—to end discrimination and gain opportunities for all people with disabilities. As Joseph Shapiro (1993) has suggested in the title of his book, *No Pity*, persons with a disability (like older persons) do not want pity; what they insist on is "common respect and the opportunity to build bonds to their communities as fully accepted participants in everyday life."

CHAPTER REVIEW

Aging and disability are not synonymous terms.

Aging refers to the physical, psychological, and social processes associated with growing older; a disability is a physical or health condition that stigmatizes or causes discrimination. Older people and persons with a disability may share certain commonalities: (1) both may be the targets of prejudice and discrimination; (2) both may be viewed as "handicapped"; (3) both may need assistance from others and support from society; and (4) both have used similar methods to gain individual dignity and autonomy. At one time or another, all of us will be affected by aging or disability.

- Gerontology is the study of aging and older people. Social gerontology is the study of the social (nonphysical) aspects of aging, including the consequences of an aging population and the personal experience of aging.
- In pre-industrial societies, people of all ages are expected to share the work, and the contributions of older people are valued. In industrialized societies, however, older people often are expected to retire so that younger people may take their place.
- Age differentiation in Canada is based on narrowly defined categories, such as adolescence, young adulthood, middle adulthood,

and late adulthood. Ageism is prejudice and discrimination against people on the basis of age, particularly when they are older persons. Ageism is reinforced by stereotypes of older people. Elder abuse includes physical abuse, psychological abuse, financial exploitation, and medical abuse or neglect of people age 65 or older. Passive neglect is the most common form of abuse.

- Functionalist explanations of aging focus on how older persons adjust to their changing roles in society; gradual transfer of statuses and roles from one generation to the next is necessary for the functioning of society. Activity theory, a part of the interactionist perspective, states that people change in late middle age and find substitutes for previous statuses, roles, and activities. This theory claims that people do not want to withdraw unless restricted by poor health or disability. Conflict theorists link the loss of status and power experienced by many older persons to their lack of ability to produce and maintain wealth in a capitalist economy.
- There are about 4.2 million persons with a disability in Canada, and this number continues to increase due to advances in medical technology. Many people with disabilities have been kept out of the mainstream of society, often by being assigned to special schools and barred from traditional jobs.
- According to functionalists, to have a functioning social system, all people must perform their appropriate social roles. Those who are sick or disabled cannot perform their designated roles and are thus confined to a sick role. According to interactionists, some people want to distance themselves from individuals with disabilities, so they avoid them and treat them as if they were deviant in some way. According to the conflict perspective, those with disabilities are viewed as members of a subordinate group. Persons in power create policies and barriers that keep people with disabilities in subservient positions.
- People with disabilities often face discrimination and employment bias. About one half of working-age persons with a disability in Canada are unemployed; those who are employed typically earn less than persons without a disability. Independence, self-sufficiency, and mainstreaming have been the principles guiding the disability rights movement. These beliefs are embedded in the independent living movement, which assumes that persons with a disability should be able to live and work independently.
- Many persons with a disability and many older persons live alone or in an informal family setting. Support services and day care help older individuals who are frail or disabled cope with their day-to-day care, although many older persons do not have the financial means to pay for these services. Nursing homes are the most restrictive environment for older persons and persons with disabilities. Many nursing home residents have major physical and/or cognitive problems that prevent them from living in any other setting or do not have available caregivers in their family.
- In industrial societies, death has been removed from everyday life and is often regarded as unnatural. Elisabeth Kübler-Ross proposed five stages of coping with dying: denial, anger, bargaining, depression, and acceptance. Hospices help people who are dying participate in their own care.

KEY TERMS

activity theory **413**
ageism **407**
age stratification **404**
aging **398**
chronological age **399**
cohort **401**
disability **398**
disengagement theory **412**
elder abuse **411**
functional age **399**
hospice **429**
life expectancy **401**
social gerontology **402**

QUESTIONS FOR ANALYSIS AND UNDERSTANDING

1. Why does activity theory contain more positive assumptions about older persons than does disengagement theory?
2. How are employment, poverty, and disability related?
3. How will the size of the older population in Canada affect society in the twenty-first century?

QUESTIONS FOR CRITICAL THINKING

1. Is it necessary to have a mandatory retirement age?
2. In your own thinking, what constitutes a disability?
3. Analyze your own grandparents (or other older persons you know well or even yourself if you are older) in terms of disengagement theory and activity theory. Which theory seems to provide the most insights? Why?

SUGGESTED READINGS

Texts and readers that give insightful coverage of aging and diversity include:

Robert C. Atchley. *Social Forces and Aging: An Introduction to Social Gerontology* (7th ed.). Belmont, Cal.: Wadsworth, 1994.

Mark Novak. *Aging and Society: A Canadian Perspective*. Scarborough, Ont.: Nelson Canada, 1993.

Susan McDaniel. *Canada's Aging Population*. Toronto: Butterworths, 1986.

Harry R. Moody. *Aging: Concepts and Controversies.* Thousand Oaks, Cal.: Pine Forge Press, 1994.

Eleanor Palo Stoller and Rose Campbell Gibson. *Worlds of Difference: Inequality in the Aging Experience.* Thousand Oaks, Cal.: Pine Forge Press, 1994.

To learn more about aging in global perspective:

Steven M. Albert and Maria G. Cattell. *Old Age in Global Perspective: Cross-Cultural and Cross-National Views.* New York: G.K. Hall, 1994.

These popular books on age and aging are written in an easy-to-read format:

Betty Friedan. *The Fountain of Age.* New York: Simon & Schuster, 1993.

Jayne E. Maugans. *Aging Parents, Ambivalent Baby Boomers: A Critical Approach to Gerontology.* Dix Hills, N.J.: General Hall, 1994.

To find out more about the disability rights movement, these books are suggested:

Michael Oliver. *The Politics of Disablement.* London: MacMillan, 1990.

Joseph P. Shapiro. *No Pity: People with Disabilities Forging a New Civil Rights Movement.* New York: Times Books, 1993.

Part Four

SOCIAL INSTITUTIONS

Chapter 12

THE ECONOMY AND WORK

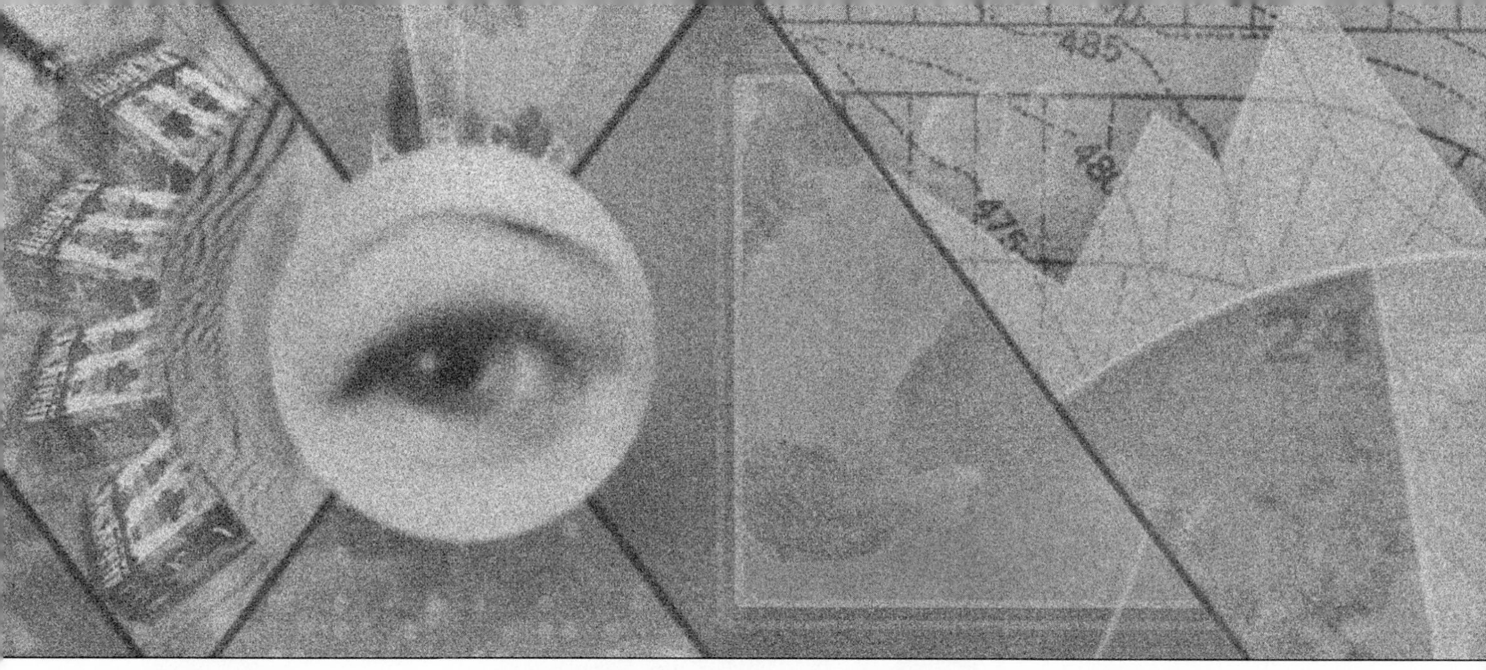

Wilfred Popoff was the associate editor of Saskatoon's *Star Phoenix* until Conrad Black's Hollinger Corporation purchased the newspaper in early 1996 and immediately reduced the size of its staff. Popoff (1996:A22) describes how he, a senior employee with more than 30 years of service, was dismissed:

> I can only attribute my sudden firing, within several months of possible retirement, a dignified retirement I had seen so many others receive, to total abandonment of common civility, a phenomenon more and more prevalent today. You see, I was fired not because of anything I did or didn't do, but because of the need to cut costs in the quest for fantastic profits. And how the affair was stage-managed tells more than one wishes to know about the uncivil environment surrounding contemporary capitalism.
>
> On a Friday afternoon all employees, about 300 in all, received a terse letter from the boss commanding attendance at a meeting in a hotel the following morning. The arrangement was reminiscent of military occupations portrayed in countless movies. The vanquished are summoned to the market square where officers of the occupying army register all people and direct them to various camps. In our case the officers were employees of a consulting firm, also strangers, who directed employees to various rooms, separating survivors from those marked for elimination. Of course, I was in the second group, although none of us knew what fate awaited us. Eventually the boss entered, gripped the lectern and read a brief statement: We were all finished, the decision was final.
>
> Not only were we finished, our place of work a few blocks away had been locked up, incapacitating our entry cards, and was under guard. We could never go back except to retrieve our personal belongings, and this under the watchful eye of a senior supervisor and one of the newly retained guards. I felt like a criminal. In my time I had managed large portions of this company, had represented it the world over and, until the previous day, had authority to spend its money. Now I couldn't be trusted not to snitch a pencil or note pad. … The current phenomenon known as downsizing is threatening to hurt capitalism by depriving it of the very thing it needs most: a market. This, however, speaks to the stupidity of capitalism today, not its abandonment of civility. But perhaps there is a connection.

In the wake of the Industrial Revolution, many thoughtful observers were dismayed by the mechanization of work and its effects on the dignity of workers. Filmmaker Charlie Chaplin bitingly satirized the new relationship between workers and machines in the classic Modern Times.

Many Canadians have faced unemployment over the past decade because of slow economic growth and deficit cutting by governments. However, Popoff and his colleagues at the *Star Phoenix* lost their jobs for another reason that has become very common: corporate cost-cutting. Although the paper had been quite profitable under its previous owners, new owner Conrad Black wished to cut costs and increase profits so he and other shareholders would receive a greater return on their investment. Firing staff is often the quickest route to short-term profits, so the termination consultants were called.

Unemployment shows the linkage between the economy and work. Changes in the economy affect the lives of most people. Those who lose their jobs will feel an acute sense of financial and personal loss. For many people, work helps define who they are; the first question usually asked of someone with whom one is speaking for the first time is, Where do you work? or What do you do for a living? Job loss may cause people to experience financial crises that could include the loss of their cars and homes to bankruptcy and foreclosure, as well as bringing on personal problems such as depression and divorce.

In this chapter, we will discuss the economy and the world of work—how people feel about their work, how the work world is changing, and what impact these changes may have on university students and other current and future workers. In the process, we will explore the impact that workers' resistance to management practices through labour union activism has had on work in contemporary society. Before reading on, test your knowledge about the economy, work, and worker resistance and activism by taking the quiz in Box 12.1.

QUESTIONS AND ISSUES

How do economics and sociology overlap?

What are the key assumptions of capitalism and socialism?

What contributes to job satisfaction and to work alienation?

What is the individual's role in the workforce?

Why does unemployment occur?

How do workers attempt to gain control over their work situation?

BOX 12.1 SOCIOLOGY AND EVERYDAY LIFE

How Much Do You Know About the Economy and the World of Work?

TRUE	FALSE	
T	F	1. Most factory workers are aware of the part their work plays in the overall production process.
T	F	2. Professions are largely indistinguishable from other occupations.
T	F	3. Workers' skills usually are upgraded when new technology is introduced in the workplace.
T	F	4. Many of the new jobs being created in the service sector pay poorly and offer little job security.
T	F	5. New computer-based technologies will create more jobs than they eliminate.
T	F	6. Labour unions probably will not exist in the twenty-first century.
T	F	7. Few workers resist work conditions that they consider to be oppressive.
T	F	8. New office technology has made it possible for clerical workers to function with little or no supervision.
T	F	9. Unions were established in Canada with the full cooperation of industry and government who recognized the need to protect the interests of workers.
T	F	10. Assembly lines are rapidly disappearing from all sectors of the Canadian economy.

Answers on page 438

THE ECONOMY

The ***economy* is the social institution that ensures the maintenance of society through the production, distribution, and consumption of goods and services.** *Goods* are tangible objects that are necessary (such as food, clothing, and shelter) or desired (such as VCRs and electric toothbrushes). *Services* are intangible activities for which people are willing to pay (such as dry cleaning, a movie, or medical care). While some services are produced by human labour (the plumber who unstops your sink, for example), others primarily are produced by capital (such as communication services provided by a telephone company). *Labour* consists of the physical and intellectual services, including training, education, and individual abilities, that people contribute to the production process (Boyes and Melvin, 1994). *Capital* is wealth (money or property) owned or used in business by a person or corporation. Obviously, money, or financial capital, is needed to invest in the physical capital (such as machinery,

BOX 12.1 SOCIOLOGY AND EVERYDAY LIFE

Answers to the Sociology Quiz on the Economy and the World of Work

TRUE	FALSE	
T.	**F.**	1. *False.* Most factory workers view their work as fragmented and specialized, and they do not understand what part their work plays in the overall production process.
T	**F**	2. *False.* Professions have five characteristics that distinguish them from other occupations: (1) abstract, specialized knowledge, (2) autonomy, (3) self-regulating, (4) authority over clients and subordinate occupational groups, and (5) a degree of altruism.
T	**F**	3. *False.* Jobs often are deskilled when new technology (such as bar code scanners or computerized cash registers) is installed in the workplace. Some of the workers' skills are no longer needed because a "smart machine" now provides the answers (such as how much something costs or how much change a customer should receive). Even when new skills are needed, the training is usually minimal.
T	F	4. *True.* Many of the new jobs being created in the service sector, such as nurses' aide, child-care worker, hotel maid, and fast-food server, offer little job security and low pay.
T	**F**	5. *False.* Many experts believe that the number of jobs will be dramatically reduced because of the impact of technology.
T	**F**	6. *False.* Sociologists who have examined organized labour generally predict that unions will continue to exist; however, their strength may wane in the global economy.
T	**F**	7. *False.* Many workers resist work conditions that they believe are unjust or oppressive. Many have joined unions or participated in other types of pro-worker organizations; others have engaged in sabotage.
T	**F**	8. *False.* Clerical workers still work under supervision; however, they may not even know when they are being observed because of new technology. For example, a supervisor may examine a clerk's work on a computer network without the employee knowing about it, and an airline reservationist's supervisor may listen in on selected conversations with customers.
T	**F**	9. *False.* The struggle to unionize in Canada was always difficult and often bloody. Governments often worked with employers to make union organizing difficult.
T	**F**	10. *False.* According to some scholars, assembly lines will remain a fact of life for businesses ranging from fast-food restaurants to high-tech semiconductor plants.

Sources: Based on Garson, 1989; Zuboff, 1988; Hodson and Sullivan, 1990; Feagin and Feagin, 1994; and Rifkin, 1995.

equipment, buildings, warehouses, and factories) used in production. For example, a person who owns a thousand shares of Bell Canada stock owns financial capital, but these shares also represent an ownership interest in Bell's physical capital.

THE SOCIOLOGY OF ECONOMIC LIFE

Perhaps you are wondering how a sociological perspective on the economy differs from the study of economics. Although aspects of the two disciplines overlap, each provides a unique perspective on economic institutions. Economists attempt to explain how the limited resources and efforts of a society are allocated among competing ends (G. Marshall, 1994). To economists, an imbalance exists between people's wants and society's ability to meet those wants. To illustrate, think about university registration. How many of you would like to have the "perfect" schedule—with the classes you want at the times you want, and with "preferred" professors? How many of you actually manage to arrange such a schedule? What organizational constraints make it impossible for everyone to have what they need or want? Some economists suggest this answer: "The most important fact of economics is the law of scarcity: there will never be enough resources to meet everyone's wants" (Ruffin and Gregory, 1988:31). Universities do not have the financial or human resources to provide everything that students (or faculty) want.

While economists focus on the complex workings of economic systems (such as monetary policy, inflation, and the national debt), sociologists focus on interconnections among the economy, other social institutions, and the social organization of work. At the macrolevel, sociologists may study the impact of multinational corporations on industrialized and developing nations. At the microlevel, sociologists might study people's satisfaction with their jobs. To better understand the Canadian economy, we will examine how economic systems came into existence and how they have changed over time.

HISTORICAL CHANGES IN ECONOMIC SYSTEMS

In all societies, the specific method of producing goods is related to the technoeconomic base of the society, as discussed in Chapter 10. In each society, people develop an economic system, ranging from simple to very complex, for the sake of survival.

PREINDUSTRIAL ECONOMIES Hunting and gathering, horticultural and pastoral, and agrarian societies are all preindustrial economic structures (previously discussed in Chapter 8, "Social Stratification"). Most workers engage in ***primary sector production*—the extraction of raw materials and natural resources from the environment**. These materials and resources typically are consumed or used without much processing.

The *production* units in hunting and gathering societies are small; most goods are produced by family members. The division of labour is by age and gender (Hodson and Sullivan, 1990). The potential for producing surplus goods increases as people learn to domesticate animals and grow their own food. In horticultural and pastoral societies, the economy becomes distinct from family life. The distribution process becomes more complex with the accumulation of a *surplus* such that some people can engage in activities other than food production. In agrarian societies, production is related primarily to producing food. However, workers have a greater variety of specialized tasks, such as warlord or priest; for example, warriors are necessary to protect the surplus goods from plunder by outsiders (Hodson and Sullivan, 1990). Surplus goods are distributed through a system of *barter*—the direct exchange of goods or services considered of equal value by the traders. However, bartering is limited as a method of distribution; equivalencies are difficult to determine (how many fish equal one rabbit?) because there is no way to assign a set value to the items being traded. As a result, *money*, a medium of exchange with a relatively fixed value, came into use in order to facilitate the distribution of goods and services in society.

INDUSTRIAL ECONOMIES Industrialization brings sweeping changes to the system of production and distribution of goods and services. Prior to the 19th century, people did not *have* jobs, they *did* jobs (Bridges, 1994). Thus industrial production caused a dramatic change in the nature of work. Drawing on new forms of energy (such as steam, gasoline, and electricity) and technology, factories proliferate as the primary means of producing goods. Wage labour is the dominant form of employment relationship; workers sell their labour to others rather than working for themselves or with other members of their family. In a capitalist system, this means that the product belongs to the factory owner and not to those whose labour creates that product.

Most workers engage in ***secondary sector production*****—the processing of raw materials (from the primary sector) into finished goods**. For example, steel workers process metal ore; auto workers then convert the ore into automobiles, trucks, and buses. In industrial economies, work becomes specialized and repetitive, activities become bureaucratically organized, and workers primarily work with machines instead of with one another.

This method of production is very different from craftwork, where individual artisans perform all steps in the production process. Think of the difference between a skilled artisan, who creates a wide variety of intricate metal castings from handmade sand mouldings, and a relatively unskilled foundry worker who operates a moulding machine. The transition from craft to assembly line in the metalwork trade is described by Craig Heron:

> By the 1920s ... the role of the artisan in the foundry had been reduced to only those few tasks which could not be turned over to machines and handymen ... As early as 1909, Josiah Beare, a young union moulder in Hamilton, told a workmate: "Jim, I have worked too hard in my time; the pace is set too fast for the average man to keep up, and I am a nervous wreck"; he died six weeks later of [what was referred to as] "heart trouble." Half a century later Joe Davidson, future leader of [the union for] Canada's postal workers, arrived in Hamilton as an experienced Scottish moulder and discovered "the more intense style of working" at Canada Iron Foundries; in nearby Dundas, he found, "The motto was 'produce or else' and every day was a mad race, the men working like beasts." (Heron, 1993:10)

Although more goods are produced in a shorter period of time on an assembly line, individual workers begin to see themselves as part of the machinery, not as human beings. We will explore this issue later in the chapter.

Mass production results in larger surpluses that benefit some people and organizations but not others. Goods and services become more unequally distributed because some people can afford anything they want and others can afford very little. Nations engaging primarily in secondary sector production also have some primary sector production, but they may rely on less industrialized nations for the raw materials from which to make many products.

In many countries, industrialization had a major impact on women's lives. In preindustrial times much of the production took place within the household and men and women often worked together. Factories separated production from the household, causing a gendered division of labour; men became responsible for the family's income and women for domestic tasks. In Canada, however, home-based production had never been widespread outside the agricultural sector. The resource-based economy was already male-oriented, so industrialization brought little change (Cohen, 1993).

During the first half of this century, Canada shifted from a primary sector economy to one focused on manufacturing and service industries. By 1951, 47 percent of Canadian workers were employed in the service sector, an additional 31 percent were employed in manufacturing, and the remaining 22 percent worked in primary indus-

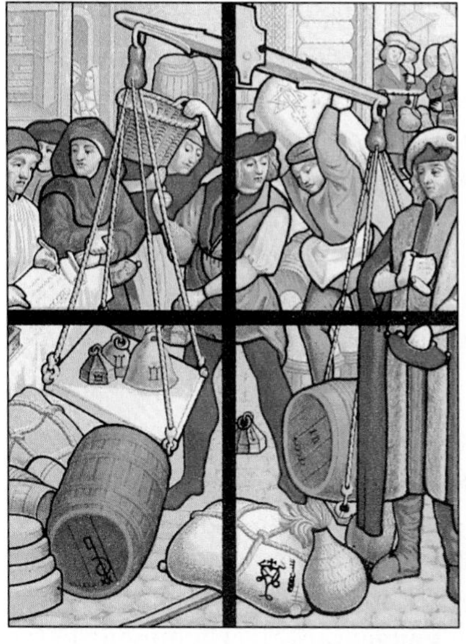

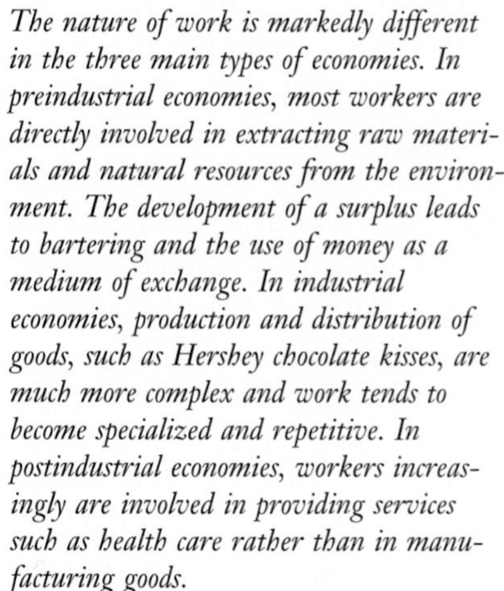

The nature of work is markedly different in the three main types of economies. In preindustrial economies, most workers are directly involved in extracting raw materials and natural resources from the environment. The development of a surplus leads to bartering and the use of money as a medium of exchange. In industrial economies, production and distribution of goods, such as Hershey chocolate kisses, are much more complex and work tends to become specialized and repetitive. In postindustrial economies, workers increasingly are involved in providing services such as health care rather than in manufacturing goods.

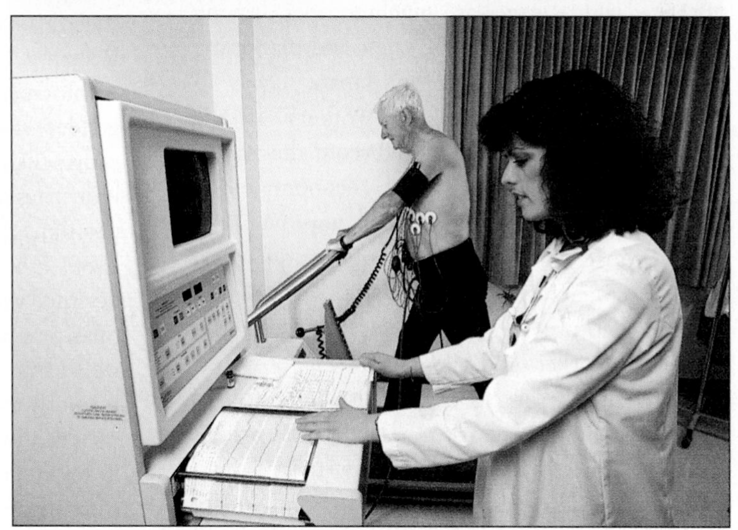

tries. By 1991, only 6 percent of workers remained in primary industries, while 23 percent were employed in manufacturing, and fully 71 percent worked in service industries (Krahn and Lowe, 1993). We now have what has been called a *postindustrial economy*.

POSTINDUSTRIAL ECONOMIES A postindustrial economy is based on ***tertiary sector production*—the provision of services rather than goods**—as a primary source of livelihood for workers and profit for owners and corporate shareholders. Tertiary sector production includes a wide range of activities, such as fast-food service, transportation, communication, education, real estate, advertising, sports, and entertainment.

Over two decades ago, sociologist Daniel Bell (1973) predicted that the manufacturing sector of the U.S. economy would be replaced by a service and information processing sector, based on technical skills and higher education (the "postindustrial society"). Bell suggested that professionals, scientists, and technicians would proliferate and that many blue-collar and lower-paying, second-tier service sector positions gradually would disappear. These changes would bring about greater economic stability and fewer class conflicts. Workers' feelings of alienation would be alleviated by greater participation in the decision-making process.

A number of factors created the service economy. Mechanization and technological innovation have allowed fewer workers to produce more in both the manufacturing and primary sectors. Robots have replaced assembly line workers and tractors and factory ships have enabled farmers and fishers to produce more than their predecessors. The expansion of our economy and the increased leisure time available have increased the demand for a wide variety of services. Finally, much of the low-skill production is now done offshore, where wages are much cheaper, leaving components such as design, sales, and marketing in North America, Europe, and Japan.

Highly skilled "knowledge workers" in the service economy have benefited from the stable, less alienating postindustrial economy Bell predicted. However, these benefits have not been felt by those who do routine production work, such as manufacturing and data entry, and workers who provide personal services, including restaurant workers and sales clerks. The positions filled by these workers of the service sector, as mentioned previously, form a second tier where labour is typically unskilled and poorly paid. And these are positions Bell predicted would gradually disappear. In his study of the "McDonaldization" of society, however, sociologist George Ritzer (1993) suggests that the number of lower-paid, second-tier service sector positions actually has increased. Many jobs in the service sector emphasize productivity, often at the expense of workers. Fast-food restaurants are a case in point, as the manager of a McDonald's explains:

> As a manager I am judged by the statistical reports which come off the computer. Which basically means my crew labour productivity. What else can I really distinguish myself by? ... O.K., it's true, you can over spend your [maintenance and repair] budget; you can have a low fry yield; you can run a dirty store, every Coke spigot is monitored. Every ketchup squirt is measured. My costs for every item are set. So my crew labour productivity is my main flexibility ... Look, you can't squeeze a McDonald's hamburger any flatter. If you want to improve your productivity there is nothing for a manager to squeeze but the crew. (quoted in Garson, 1989:33–35)

"McDonaldization" is built on many of the ideas and systems of industrial society, including bureaucracy and the assembly line (Ritzer, 1993).

Also contrary to Bell's prediction, class conflict and poverty may well increase in postindustrial societies (see Touraine, 1971; Thompson, 1983). Recently, researchers also have found that employment in the service sector remains largely gender segregated and that skills degradation, rather than skills upgrading, has occurred in many industries where women hold a large number of positions (Steiger and Wardell, 1995). In the 1980s the relative wages paid to younger workers declined very sharply (Myles, 1991). Machines and off-shore production have eliminated many of the well-paying manufacturing jobs that were formerly available to young people with low levels of education and training. These people now work in lower-paying service sector jobs. It is too early to tell whether these young workers will become more prosperous as they move on in their careers or whether this wage restructuring is permanent. To gain a better understanding of how our economy works today, we now turn to an examination of contemporary economic systems and their interrelationship in an emerging global economy.

CONTEMPORARY ECONOMIC SYSTEMS

During the twentieth century, capitalism and socialism have been the principal economic models in industrialized countries. Sociologists often use two criteria—property ownership and market control—to distinguish between types of economies. Keep in mind, however, that no society has a purely capitalist or socialist economy.

CAPITALISM

***Capitalism* is an economic system characterized by private ownership of the means of production, from which personal profits can be derived through market competition and without government intervention.** Most of us think of ourselves as "owners" of private property because we own a car, a stereo, or other possessions. However, most of us are not capitalists; we *spend money* on the things we own, rather than *making money* from them. Capitalism is not simply the accumulation of wealth, but is the "use of wealth ... as a means for gathering more wealth" (Heilbroner, 1985:35). Relatively few people own income-producing property from which a profit can be realized by producing and distributing goods and services. Everyone else is a consumer. "Ideal" capitalism has four distinctive features: (1) private ownership of the means of production, (2) pursuit of personal profit, (3) competition, and (4) lack of government intervention.

PRIVATE OWNERSHIP OF THE MEANS OF PRODUCTION Capitalist economies are based on the right of individuals to own income-producing property, such as land, water, mines, and factories and to "buy" people's labour. The early Canadian economy was based on the sale of *staples*—goods associated with primary industries including lumber, wheat, and minerals. Economist Harold Innis (1930) showed how the early Canadian economy was driven by the demands for raw materials by the colonial powers of France and Britain. This began early in Canada's history; in 1670 a British royal charter gave the privately held Hudson's Bay Company exclusive control over much of what is now western Canada, which was the source of the very lucrative fur trade.

In the early stages of industrial capitalism (1850–1890), virtually all of the capital for investment was individually owned, and a few individuals and families controlled all the major trade and financial organizations in Canada. Under early monopoly capitalism (1890–1940), most ownership rapidly shifted from individuals to huge ***corporations*—large-scale organizations that have legal powers, such as the ability to enter into contracts and buy and sell property, separate from their individual owners**. During this period, major industries came under the control of a few corporations owned by shareholders. For example, the automobile industry in North America came to be dominated by the "Big Three"—General Motors, Ford, and Chrysler. Industrial development in Canada lagged behind that of many other countries as business focused on exporting raw materials and importing finished products. Many of the industries that did establish themselves in Canada were branch plants of large American and British corporations whose profits flowed back to their home countries. Economist Kari Levitt (1970) was among the first to show how this foreign private investment posed a threat to Canadian sovereignty as fundamental economic decisions were made outside the country.

In advanced monopoly capitalism (1940–present), ownership and control of major industrial and business sectors has become increasingly concentrated. *Economic concentration* is the degree to which a relatively small number of corporations controls a disproportionately large share of a nation's economic resources. There are about 400,000 corporations in Canada; the top 100 control 67 percent of Canadian business assets, while the other 399,900 account for the remaining 33 percent of these assets. The level of corporate concentration in Canada is far higher than that of our major trading partners, the United States, Germany, and Japan (Richardson, 1992).

Today, ***multinational corporations*—large companies that are headquartered in one country and have subsidiaries or branches in other countries**—play a major role in the economies and governments of many nations.

BOX 12.2 SOCIOLOGY AND MEDIA

Labour Unions in the Cartoon World

How fairly are unions portrayed by the media? While many people think of the media as being "liberal" in its treatment of political issues, scholars recently have found that organized labour has marginal and mostly negative images in movies, on television, and in the press, including cartoons. In his examination of how cartoonists over the past century have depicted unions and their leaders, William J. Puette (1992) concluded that labour union leadership has traditionally been viewed with the same contempt as corrupt politicians.

Some of the earliest cartoon images of labour can be traced to the work of Thomas Nast, a political cartoonist for *Harper's Weekly* from 1862 to 1885. Nast's original male labourer wore a "white, flat-topped, four cornered, paper machinists' cap and carried a cylindrical dinner pail," an image later replaced by a hard hat and lunch box. A recurring theme in Nast's cartoons was that union organizers were communists trying to destroy capitalism. In the 1878 cartoon "Always Killing the Goose that Lays the Golden Egg," the labourer, with the golden egg of his wages in his pocket, is depicted as being tricked by the communist into killing the goose of capitalism. Notice the slogans on the wall—"Labor Is Capital" and "Up with the Red Flag."

Cartoonists became even less sympathetic toward the labour movement as it grew stronger.

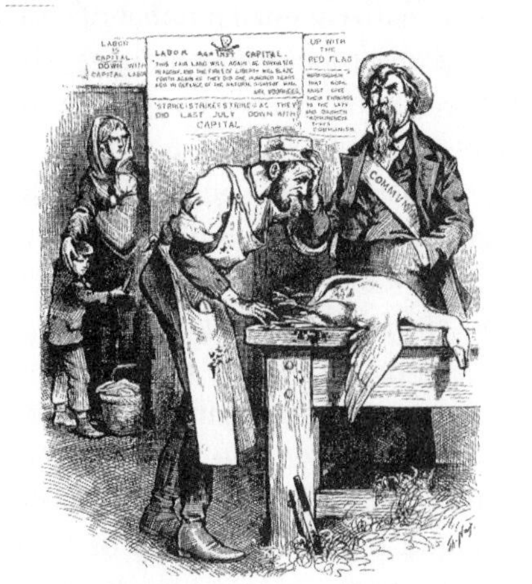

ALWAYS KILLING THE GOOSE THAT LAYS THE GOLDEN EGG
Communistic Statesman (*without responsibility*). "Nothing in it after all; it's too bad; I thought he was just full of them."

SOURCE: Thomas Nast, *Harper's Weekly*, March 16, 1878, Vol. 22, p. 205.

In the twentieth century, labour leaders typically have been depicted as greedy and power hungry or as corrupt and violent, and union members and leaders as fat and slovenly—images that convey a strong class bias against working-class people.

When the Teamsters Union (predominantly made up of truck drivers and related personnel) was discredited based on charges of engaging in corrupt management practices and other criminal activity, cartoonists' image of labour unions shifted to one of corruption and linkages to organized crime. Paul Conrad's 1986 cartoon had no caption but showed a "Welcome Teamsters Convention" sign on the wall of a prison.

As compared with political cartoons, how do labour unions fare in comic strips? According to Puette, comic strip artists typically take fairly liberal positions on just about everything except labour unions. For example, in 1990, the "Cathy" strip, which usually is liberal on political and social issues, showed Cathy's friends suffering from a contractor's disruption of their home because "the drywall suppliers are on strike and it'd be 10 weeks before we could repair any holes!" (quoted in Puette, 1992:91).

Some comic strips have used snakes to represent organized labour. In a 1985 "B.C." strip by Johnny Hart, a caveman (who is leaning over a rock labelled "Union Headquarters") is approached by a snake who wants to join because "Striking is my 'Biz'."

Other comic strips have taken up the stereotypes of crime-committing labour leaders, strike-happy workers, or sloppy or lazy union members. For example, in a 1990 "Geech" strip by Jerry Bittle, two slovenly deliverymen are bringing a box marked "Fragile" and "This end up" upside down into a man's house. When he tells them to be careful, they tell him "Not to worry. We're union." After they drop the box with a big "Crash," the man says, "I thought you said not to worry." Their reply is, "We're not. We're union."

Puette (1992:99) concludes that "a class bias lies behind the generally negative treatment accorded to labour unions in the comic strips ... Because the media are staffed and regulated by predominantly white male professionals, it is little wonder that the dominant portrayal of the labour movement is essentially managerial in its sympathies." His findings are in keeping with Michael Parenti's (1986)

BOX 12.2 SOCIOLOGY AND MEDIA

Continued

conclusion that unions are always portrayed in the media as the greedy ones; capitalists are never characterized as relentlessly accumulating as much of the wealth created by labour as possible. Parenti states (1986:81), "The impression of who is giving and who is grabbing is inverted in a business-owned press that portrays management as making 'offers' and labour as making 'demands.' The struggles between workers and bosses are called 'labour problems' and 'labour disputes,' never 'management disputes'—even when it is management that refuses to negotiate a contract—as is often the case."

Sources: Based on Parenti, 1986; and Puette, 1992.

SOURCE: Geech © Universal Press Syndicate. Reprinted with permission. All rights reserved.

Multinational corporations also are referred to as *transnational corporations* because they sell and produce goods abroad. These corporations are not dependent on the labour, capital, or technology of any one country and may move their operations to countries where wages and taxes are lower and potential profits are higher. Corporate considerations of this kind help to explain why many jobs formerly located in Canada have been moved to developing nations where, because few employment opportunities exist, workers will accept jobs at significantly less pay than would Canadians.

PURSUIT OF PERSONAL PROFIT A tenet of capitalism is the belief that people are free to maximize their individual gain through personal profit; in the process, the entire society will benefit from their activities (Smith, 1976/1776). Economic development is assumed to benefit both capitalists and workers, and the general public also benefits from public expenditures (such as for roads, schools, and parks) made possible through an increase in business tax revenues.

During the period of industrial capitalism, however, specific individuals and families (not the general public) were the primary recipients of profits. For many generations, descendants of some of the early industrial capitalists have benefited from the economic deeds (and misdeeds) of their ancestors. For example, the Seagram distillery's fortune was based on the profits made from bootlegging during Prohibition. In early monopoly capitalism, some stockholders derived massive profits from companies that held near-monopolies on specific goods and services. In advanced (late) monopoly capitalism, profits have become even more concentrated as a few large corporations control more of the market through expansion and the acquisition of competitors.

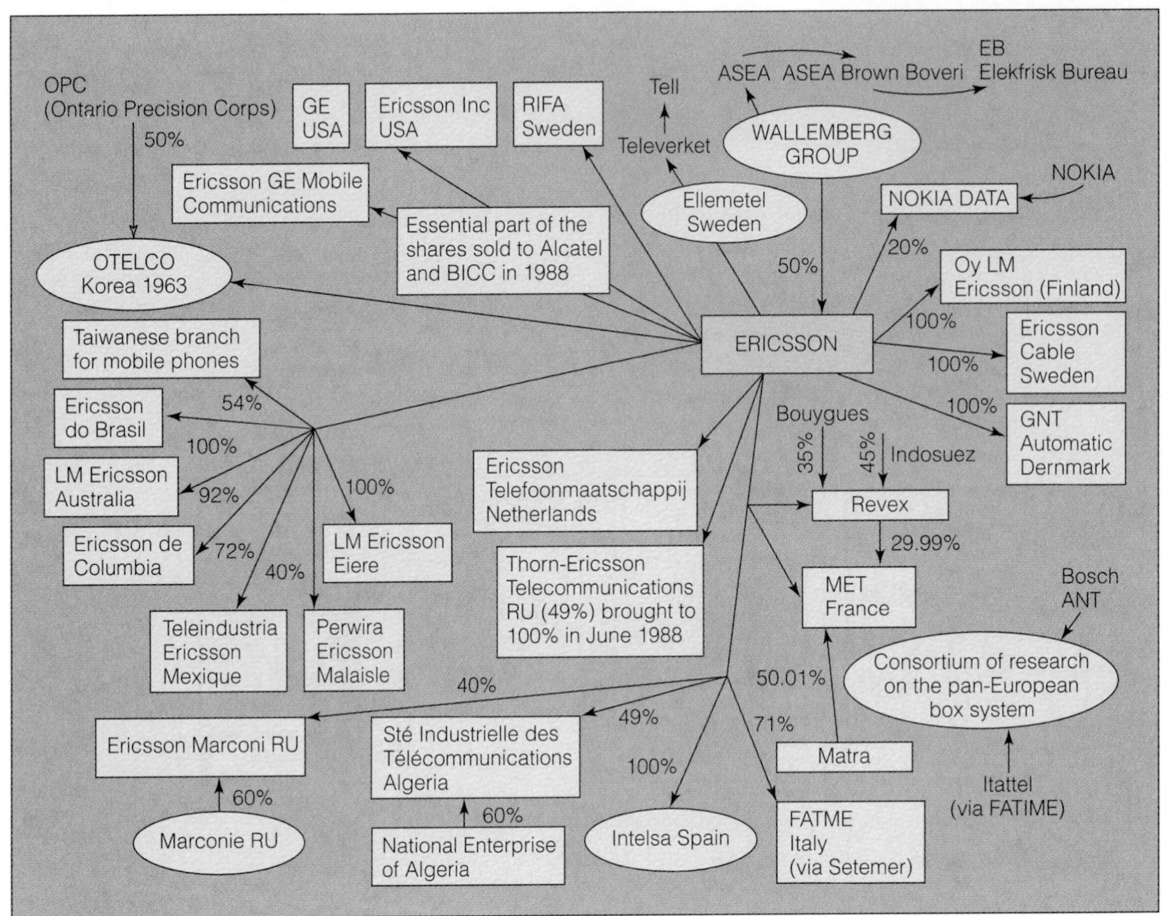

FIGURE 12.1

The Telecommunications Giant, Ericsson, is Typical of Today's Multinational Corporations that have Interests Throughout the World.

Global telecommunications are controlled by a small number of companies such as Ericsson. Other economic sectors are similarly dominated by a few global giants.

Source: The Group of Lisbon, 1995. *Limits to Competition.* Cambridge, Mass.: The MIT Press.

COMPETITION In theory, competition acts as a balance to excessive profits. When producers vie with one another for customers, they must be able to offer innovative goods and services at competitive prices. However, from the time of early industrial capitalism, the trend has been toward less, rather than more, competition among companies; profits are higher when there is less competition. In early monopoly capitalism competition was diminished by increasing concentration *within* a particular industry. Today, Microsoft Corp. so dominates certain areas of the computer software industry so that it has virtually no competitors in those areas.

How do large companies restrict competition? One way is by temporarily setting prices so low that weaker competitors are forced out of business. Ultramar, which owns 1400 gasoline stations in Quebec and Atlantic Canada, started a gasoline price war that saw gas prices in Quebec fall from 63 to 19.9 cents per litre in 1996. One Nova Scotia independent station owner complained that Ultra-

TABLE 12.1

The Music Industry's Big Six

Company	Country	Leading Artists	1992 Worldwide Music Sales[a]
Sony	Japan	Mariah Carey Michael Jackson Bruce Springsteen	$3.5 billion
Philips (Polygram)	Netherlands	Def Leppard Billy Ray Cyrus Amy Grant	$3.3 billion
Time Warner	United States	R.E.M. Led Zeppelin Natalie Cole	$3.2 billion
Bertelsmann (RCA)	Germany	Whitney Houston Kenny G Taylor Dayne	$2.5 billion
Thorn/EMI	United Kingdom	M.C. Hammer Vanilla Ice Pink Floyd	$2.2 billion
Matsushita (MCA)	Japan	Guns N' Roses Wynonna Judd Nirvana	$300 million

[a]Some totals include music publishing and contributions from other areas, such as videos.

Source: Biagi, 1994:248.

mar was charging him 50 cents a litre for wholesale gasoline, while it was retailing its own gasoline at a nearby station for 42.9 cents per litre. While this provides a temporary benefit to consumers, it reduces competition by forcing small retailers out of the market. The large companies recoup their losses when the competition has disappeared.

What appears to be competition among producers *within* an industry actually may be "competition" among products, all of which are produced and distributed by relatively few corporations. Much of the beer in Canada is produced by Molsons and Labatts, who use a wide variety of different brand names for their products. An ***oligopoly*** **exists when several companies overwhelmingly control an entire industry**. An example is the music industry, in which a few giant companies are behind many of the labels and artists known to consumers (see Table 12.1). More specifically, a ***shared monopoly*** **exists when four or fewer companies supply 50 percent or more of a particular market** (Eitzen and Baca Zinn, 1995).

In advanced monopoly capitalism, mergers also occur *across* industries: corporations gain near-monopoly control over all aspects of the production and distribution of a product by acquiring both the companies that supply the raw materials and the companies that are the outlets for its products. For example, an oil company may hold leases on the land where the oil is pumped out of the ground, the plants that convert the oil into gasoline, and the individual gasoline stations that sell the product to the public. By acting as producers, wholesalers, and retailers, companies such as Ultramar are able to maintain control over their markets and their competition.

Corporations with control both within and across industries often are formed by a series of mergers and acquisitions across industries. These corporations are referred to as ***conglomerates*—combinations of businesses in different commercial areas, all of which are owned by one holding company**. Media ownership is a case in point: companies such as Time Warner and Paramount Communications have extensive holdings in radio and television stations, cable television companies, book publishing firms, and film production and distribution companies, to name only a few. Similarly, a small number of companies control most of Canada's newspapers. The government, the business community, and the public do not seem disturbed by the fact that these major media outlets are run by a small number of Canada's wealthiest businessmen.

While the government and the business community seem content with this control of the media by a few rich white males, do you think they would accept the same degree of control of the media by feminists, trade unions, or religious fundamentalists?

Competition is reduced over the long run by ***interlocking corporate directorates*—members of the board of directors of one corporation who also sit on the board(s) of other corporations**. Interlocking directorates diminish competition by producing interdependence. Individuals who serve on multiple boards often are able to forge cooperative arrangements that benefit their corporations but not necessarily the general public. When several corporations are controlled by the same financial interests, they are more likely to cooperate with one another than to compete. Canadian business has a very high degree of integration at the board level, with the five big banks serving as the principal centres linking the different corporate sectors (Richardson, 1992).

LACK OF GOVERNMENT INTERVENTION Proponents of capitalism say that ideally capitalism works best without government intervention in the market place. This policy of laissez-faire was advocated by economist Adam Smith in his 1776 treatise *An Inquiry into the Nature and Causes of the Wealth of Nations*. Smith argued that when people pursue their own selfish interests, they are guided "as if by an invisible hand" to promote the best interests of society (see Smith, 1976/1776). Today, terms such as *market economy* and *free enterprise* often are used, but the underlying assumption is the same: that free market competition, not the government, should regulate prices and wages.

However the "ideal" of unregulated markets benefiting all citizens has been seldom realized. Individuals and companies in pursuit of higher profits have run roughshod over weaker competitors, and small businesses have grown into large monopolistic corporations. Accordingly, government regulations were implemented in an effort to curb the excesses of the marketplace brought about by laissez-faire policies. While its effectiveness can be debated, Canada has a Competitions Bureau with the mandate of ensuring that corporations compete fairly.

Ironically, much of what is referred to as government intervention has been in the form of aid to business. Canadian governments have always been intimately involved with business. To encourage settlement of the West, the government gave subsidies and huge tracts of land to the Canadian Pacific Railway to encourage the construction of a national railway. Many corporations receive government assistance in the form of public subsidies and protection from competition by tariffs, patents, and trademarks. Government intervention in the 1990s has included billions of dollars in tax credits for corporations, large subsidies or loan guarantees to manufacturers, and subsidies and tariff protection for farmers. Overall, most corporations have gained much more than they have lost as a result of government involvement in the economy.

SOCIALISM

***Socialism* is an economic system characterized by public ownership of the means of production, the pursuit of collective goals, and centralized decision making.** Like "pure" capitalism, "pure" socialism does not exist. Karl Marx described socialism as a temporary stage en route to an ideal communist society. Although the terms *socialism* and *communism* are associated with Marx and often are used interchangeably, they are not identical. Marx defined communism as an economic system characterized by common ownership of all economic resources (G. Marshall, 1994). In *The Communist Manifesto* and *Das Kapital*, he predicted that the working class would become increasingly impoverished and alienated under capitalism. As a result, the workers would become aware of their own class interests, revolt against the capitalists, and overthrow the entire system (see Turner, Beeghley, and Powers, 1995). After the revolution, private property would be abolished and capital would be controlled by collectives of workers who would own the means of production. The government (previously used to further the interests of the capitalists) no longer would be necessary. People would contribute according to their abilities and receive according to their needs (Marx and Engels, 1967/1848; Marx, 1967/1867). Over the years, state control was added as an organizing principle for communist societies. This structure is referred to as a system of "state socialism." The reasons state socialism in the former Soviet Union did not evolve into a communist economic system are discussed in the following sections.

PUBLIC OWNERSHIP OF THE MEANS OF PRODUCTION In a truly socialist economy, the means of production are owned and controlled by a collectivity or the state, not by private individuals or corporations. Prior to the early 1990s, the state owned all the natural resources and almost all the capital in the Soviet Union. In the 1980s, for example, state-owned enterprises produced more than 88 percent of agricultural output and 98 percent of retail trade, and owned 75 percent of the urban housing space (Boyes and Melvin, 1994). At least in theory, goods were produced to meet the needs of people. Access to housing and medical care were considered a right.

Leaders of the former Soviet Union and some Eastern European nations decided to abandon government ownership and control of the means of production because the system was unresponsive to the needs of the marketplace and offered no incentive for increased efficiency (Boyes and Melvin, 1994). Shortages and widespread unrest led to the reform movement headed by Soviet President Mikhail Gorbachev in the late 1980s.

In the 1990s, Russia and other states in the former Soviet Union have attempted to privatize ownership of production. In *privatization*, resources are converted from state ownership to private ownership; the government takes an active role in developing, recognizing, and protecting private property rights (Boyes and Melvin, 1994).

PURSUIT OF COLLECTIVE GOALS Ideal socialism is based on the pursuit of collective goals, rather than on personal profits. Equality in decision making replaces hierarchical relationships (such as between owners and workers or political leaders and citizens). Everyone shares in the goods and services of society, especially necessities such as food, clothing, shelter, and medical care based on need, not on ability to pay. In reality, however, few societies can or do pursue purely collective goals.

CENTRALIZED DECISION MAKING Another tenet of socialism is centralized decision making. In theory, economic decisions are based on the needs of society; the government is responsible for facilitating the production and distribution of goods and services. Central planners set wages and prices to ensure that the production process works. When problems such as shortages and unemployment arise, they can be dealt with quickly and effectively by the central government (Boyes and Melvin, 1994).

Centralized decision making is hierarchical. In the former Soviet Union, for example, broad economic policy decisions were made by the highest authorities of the Communist Party, who also held political power. The production units (the enterprises and farms) at the bottom of the structure had little voice in the decision-making process. Wages and prices were based on political priorities and eventually came to be completely unrelated to actual supply and demand.

The collapse of state socialism in the former Soviet Union was due partly to the declining ability of the Communist Party to act as an effective agent of society and partly to the growing incompatibility of central planning with the requirements of a modern economy (see Misztal, 1993). While the socialist system as practised in the Soviet Union was not sustainable, privatization has proven difficult. Only a few years after centralized decision making was abolished in Russia, people are faced with soaring unemployment and crime rates, and the prices of goods and services have risen greatly. The armed motorcades of Communist Party leaders from the past have been replaced by the limousines of business people with their armed escorts. Organized criminal groups have muscled their way into business and trade; many workers feel their future is very dim. According to a 30-year-old machinist in Moscow: "I was raised in a country that cared about its workers ... Life used to be simple, but we had a deal. We worked hard, and the company took care of the rest" (Specter, 1994b:A6).

MIXED ECONOMIES

As we have seen, no economy is truly capitalist or socialist; most economies are mixtures of both. A ***mixed economy*** **combines elements of a market economy (capitalism) with elements of a command economy (socialism)**. Sweden and France have mixed economies, sometimes referred to as ***democratic socialism*****—an economic and political system that combines private ownership of some of the means of production, governmental distribution of some essential goods and services, and free elections**. Government ownership in Sweden, for example, is limited primarily to railroads, mineral resources, a public bank, and liquor and tobacco operations (Feagin and Feagin, 1994). Compared with capitalist economies, however, the government in a mixed economy plays a larger role in setting rules, policies, and objectives.

The government also is heavily involved in providing services such as medical care, child care, and transportation. In Sweden, for example, all residents have health insurance, housing subsidies, child allowances, paid parental leave, and day-care subsidies. National insurance pays medical bills associated with work-related injuries, and workplaces are specially adapted for persons with disabilities. College tuition is free, and public funds help subsidize cultural institutions such as theatres and orchestras ("General Facts on Sweden," 1988; Kelman, 1991). While Sweden has a very high degree of government involvement, all industrial countries have assumed many of the obligations to provide support and services to its citizens. However, there are very significant differences in the degree to which these services are provided among these countries; for example, Canada provides medical care to all its citizens, but over 30 million Americans have no health insurance at all. While Canada is much closer to a welfare state than the United States, the benefits provided by our government are less than those provided in most Western European countries.

PERSPECTIVES ON ECONOMY AND WORK

Functionalists, conflict theorists, and interactionists view the economy and the nature of work from a variety of perspectives. In this section, we examine functionalist and conflict views; in the next section, we focus on the interactionist perspective on the social organization of work.

THE FUNCTIONALIST PERSPECTIVE

Functionalists view the economy as a vital social institution because it is the means by which needed goods and services are produced and distributed. When the economy runs smoothly, other parts of society function more effectively. However, if the system becomes unbalanced, such as when demand does not keep up with production, a maladjustment occurs (in this case, a surplus). Some problems may be easily remedied in the marketplace (through "free enterprise") or through government intervention (such as buying and storing excess production of butter and cheese). However, other problems, such as periodic *peaks* (high points) and *troughs* (low points) in the business cycle, are more difficult to resolve. The *business cycle* is the rise and fall of economic activity relative to long-term growth in the economy (McEachern, 1994).

From this perspective, peaks occur when "business" has confidence in the country's economic future. During a peak, or *expansion* period, the economy thrives: plants are built, raw materials are ordered, workers are hired, and production increases. In addition, upward social mobility for workers and their families becomes possible. For example, some workers hope their children will not have to follow their footsteps into the factory. Ben Hamper (1992:13) describes how GM workers felt:

> Being a factory worker in Flint, Michigan, wasn't something purposely passed on from generation to generation. To grow up believing that you were brought into this world to follow in your daddy's footsteps, just another chip-off-the-old-shoprat, was to engage in the lowest possible form of negativism. Working the line for GM was something fathers did so that their offspring wouldn't have to.

The dream of upward mobility is linked to peaks in the business cycle. Once the peak is reached, however, the economy turns down because too large a surplus of goods has been produced. In part, this is due to *inflation*—a sustained and continuous increase in prices (McEachern, 1994). Inflation erodes the value of people's money, and they no longer are able to purchase as high a percentage of the goods that have been produced. Because of this lack of demand, fewer goods are produced, workers are laid off, credit becomes difficult to obtain, and people cut back on their purchases even more, fearing unemployment. Eventually, this produces a distrust of the economy, resulting in a *recession*—a decline in an economy's total production that lasts six months or longer. To combat a recession, the government lowers interest rates (to make borrowing easier and to get more money back into circulation) in an attempt to spur the beginning of the next expansion period.

THE CONFLICT PERSPECTIVE

Conflict theorists view business cycles and the economic system differently. From a conflict perspective, business cycles are the result of capitalist greed. In order to maximize profits, capitalists suppress the wages of workers. As the prices of the products increase, the workers are not able to purchase them in the quantities that have been produced. The resulting surpluses cause capitalists to reduce production, close factories, and lay off workers, thus contributing to the growth of the reserve army of the unemployed, whose presence helps to reduce the wages of the remaining workers. In 1994, for example, some trucking companies claimed that they could not afford to pay union truck drivers $17 an hour, so they hired nonunion freight carriers who made about $9 an hour. Drivers such as Tim Hart claimed that pay was the only difference between his work and that of a union driver: "I bust my tail, doing the exact same thing the union drivers do. And they make double what I do. It bothers me. I mean, if those companies can afford to pay that much, why can't mine?" (quoted in Johnson, 1994:10). This practice of contracting out—governments and corporations hiring outside workers to do some jobs rather than using existing staff—has become a favourite cost-cutting technique. In today's economy, it is easy to find someone who will do the work more cheaply than existing employees whose seniority and wages have increased over time, often because of the efforts of unions.

Much of the pressure to reduce costs has come from shareholders, and many observers have seen the firing or deskilling of workers as symptoms of class warfare; the rich are benefiting at the expense of the poor. The rich have indeed thrived; those with large amounts of capital have seen their fortunes increase dramatically. However, the largest shareholders in many companies are pension plans whose assets belong to workers from the private and public sectors; so, in essence some workers have lost their jobs to enhance the retirement benefits of other workers. Bob Bertram, vice president of the Ontario Teachers Pension Plan, puts the matter very succinctly:

> We believe the board of directors is representing us as owners and they have a duty to maximize share wealth for us. If it's not going to be looking after our interests first and foremost, then we will invest elsewhere ... Companies aren't put together to create jobs. The No.1 priority is creating shareholder wealth. (Ip, 1996:B1)

THE SOCIAL ORGANIZATION OF WORK

Sociologists who focus on microlevel analyses are interested in how the economic system and the social organization of work affect peoples' attitudes and behaviour. Interactionists, in particular, have examined the factors that contribute to a person's job satisfaction or feeling of alienation.

JOB SATISFACTION AND ALIENATION

According to interactionists, work is an important source of self-identity for many people; it can help people feel positive about themselves or it can cause them to feel alienated. *Job satisfaction* refers to people's attitudes toward their work, based on (1) their job responsibilities, (2) the organizational structure in which they work, and (3) their individual needs and values (Hodson and Sullivan, 1990). Studies have found that worker satisfaction is highest when employees have some degree of control over their work, when they are part of the decision-making process, when they are not too closely supervised, and when they feel that they play an important part in the outcome (Kohn et al., 1990). The reasons contract administrator Beth McEwen gives for liking her job, for example, bear this out:

> I've worked for employers who couldn't care if you were gone tomorrow—who let you think your job could be done by anyone because 100,000 people out there are looking for work. But here, there's always someone to help you if you need assistance, and they're open to letting you set out your own job plan that suits what they're after and what you're trying to accomplish. They know every person goes about a job in a different way. (quoted in Maynard, 1987:121)

Job satisfaction often is related to both intrinsic and extrinsic factors. Intrinsic factors pertain to the nature of the work itself, while extrinsic factors include such things as vacation and holiday policies, parking privileges, on-site day-care centres, and other amenities that contribute to workers' overall perception that their employer cares about them.

Alienation occurs when workers' needs for self-identity and meaning are not met and when work is done strictly for material gain, with no accompanying sense of personal satisfaction. According to Marx, workers dislike having very little power and no opportunities to make workplace decisions. This lack of control contributes to an ongoing struggle between workers and employers. Job segmentation, isolation of workers, and the discouragement of any type of pro-worker organizations (such as unions) further contribute to feelings of helplessness and frustration. Some occupations may be more closely associated with high levels of alienation than others.

OCCUPATIONS

***Occupations* are categories of jobs that involve similar activities at different work sites** (Reskin and Padavic, 1994). There are hundreds of different types of occupations. Historically, occupations have been classified as blue collar and white collar. Blue-collar workers primarily were factory and craftworkers who did manual labour; white-collar workers were office workers and professionals. However, contemporary workers in the service sector do not easily fit into either of these categories; neither do the so-called pink-collar workers, primarily women, who are employed in occupations such as preschool teacher, dental assistant, secretary, and clerk (Hodson and Sullivan, 1990).

PROFESSIONS

What occupations are professions? Athletes who are paid for playing sports are referred to as "professional athletes." Dog groomers, pest exterminators, automobile mechanics, and nail technicians (manicurists) also refer to themselves as professionals. Although sociologists do not always agree on exactly which occupations are professions, they do agree that the number of people categorized as "professionals" has grown dramatically since World War II. According to sociologist Steven Brint (1994), the contemporary professional middle class includes most doctors, natural scientists, engineers, computer scientists, certified public accountants, economists, social scientists, psychotherapists, lawyers, policy experts of various sorts, professors, at least some journalists and editors, some clergy, and some artists and writers.

CHARACTERISTICS OF PROFESSIONS ***Professions* are high-status, knowledge-based occupations** that have five major characteristics (Freidson, 1970, 1986; Larson, 1977):

1. *Abstract, specialized knowledge.* Professionals have abstract, specialized knowledge of their field, based on formal education and interaction with colleagues. Education provides the credentials, skills, and training that allow professionals to have job opportunities and to assume positions of authority within organizations (Brint, 1994).
2. *Autonomy.* Professionals are autonomous in that they can rely on their own judgment in selecting the relevant knowledge or the appropriate technique for dealing with a problem. Consequently, they expect patients, clients, or students to respect that autonomy.
3. *Self-regulation.* In exchange for autonomy, professionals theoretically are self-regulating. All professions have licensing, accreditation, and regulatory associations that set professional standards and that require members to adhere to a code of ethics as a form of public accountability. Realistically, however, professionals often are constrained by organizational power structures. Many work within large-scale bureaucracies that have rules, policies, and procedures to which professionals, like everyone else, must adhere. However, they are still accountable to their professional associations for standards of practice and conduct.
4. *Authority.* Because of their authority, professionals expect compliance with their directions and advice. Their authority is based on mastery of the body of specialized knowledge and on their profession's autonomy: professionals do not expect the client to argue about the professional advice rendered. Professionals also have authority over persons in subordinate occupations; for example, doctors control much of the work of nurses and others in the health-care field.
5. *Altruism.* Ideally, professionals have concern for others. The term *altruism* implies some degree of self-sacrifice whereby profession-

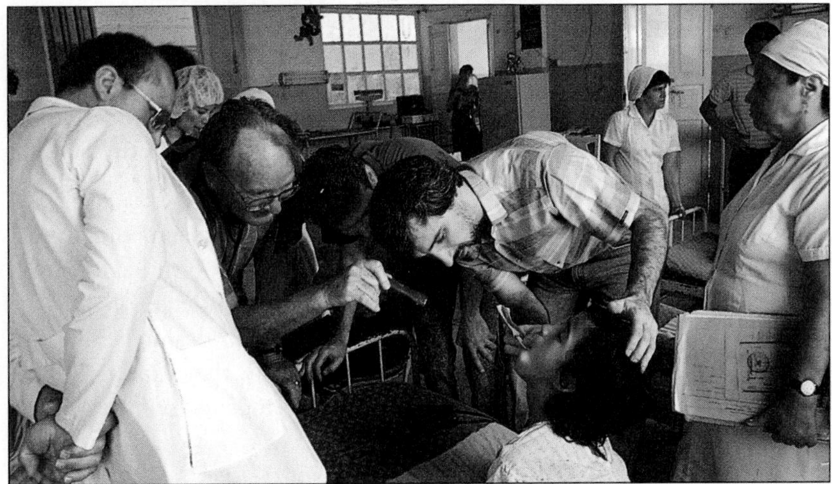

Professionals are expected to share their knowledge and display concern for others. These surgeons have volunteered their services to people in Ecuador.

als go beyond self-interest or personal comfort so that they can help a patient or client (Hodson and Sullivan, 1990). Professionals also have a responsibility to protect and enhance their knowledge and to use it for the public interest.

In the past, job satisfaction among professionals generally has been very high because of relatively high levels of income, autonomy, and authority. In the future, professionals may either become the backbone of a postindustrial society or suffer from "intellectual obsolescence" if they cannot keep up with the knowledge explosion (Leventman, 1981).

Women have made significant gains in the professions. Katherine Marshall found that the number of women employed in traditionally male-dominated professions in Canada rose by 42 percent between 1981 and 1986, compared with a 9 percent increase for men. Women's share of employment rose from 17 percent to 21 percent among doctors, from 8 percent to 14 percent among dentists, and from 16 percent to 22 percent among lawyers (Marshall, 1990). These percentages have increased since 1986 and will continue to grow, as women now make up over half of the students now studying in many professional schools (see Chapter 15, "Education and Religion").

MANAGERS AND THE MANAGED

A wide variety of occupations are classified as "management" positions. The generic term *manager* often is used to refer to executives, managers, and administrators (Hodson and Sullivan, 1990). At the upper level of a workplace bureaucracy are *executives*, who control the operation of their organizations. *Administrators* often work for governmental bureaucracies or organizations dealing with health, education, or welfare (such as hospitals, colleges and universities, and nursing homes) and usually are appointed. *Managers* typically have responsibility for workers, physical plants, equipment, and the financial aspects of a bureaucratic organization. Women have increasingly gained access to management positions at this level, especially in middle management positions. In 1993, 42 percent of those working in management and administrative positions in Canada were women, up from 29 percent in 1982 (Statistics Canada, 1994).

MANAGEMENT IN BUREAUCRACIES Managers are essential in contemporary bureaucracies in which work is highly specialized and authority structures are hierarchical (see Chapter 6). Managers often control workers by applying organizational rules. Workers at each level of the hierarchy take orders from their immediate superiors and perhaps give orders to a few subordinates. Upper-level managers typically are responsible for coordination of activities and control of workers. The *span of control*, or the number of workers a manager supervises, is affected by the organizational structure and by technology. Some analysts believe hierarchical organization is necessary to coordinate the activities of a large number of people; others suggest that it produces apathy and alienation among workers (Blauner, 1964). Lack of worker control over the labour process was built into the earliest factory systems through techniques known as scientific management (Taylorism) and mass production (Fordism).

SCIENTIFIC MANAGEMENT (TAYLORISM) At the beginning of the twentieth century, industrial engineer Frederick Winslow Taylor revolutionized management with a system he called *scientific management*. In an effort to increase productivity in factories, Taylor did numerous *time-and-motion* studies of workers he considered to be reasonably efficient. From these studies, he broke down each task into its most minute components to determine the "one best way" of doing each of them. Workers then were taught to perform the tasks in a concise series of steps. Skilled workers became less essential since unskilled workers could be trained by management to follow routinized procedures. The process of breaking up work into specialized tasks and minute operations contributed to the *deskilling* of work and shifted much of the control of knowledge from workers to management (Braverman, 1974). As this occurred, workers increasingly felt powerless (Westrum, 1991).

The *differential* piece-rate system, a central component of scientific management in which workers were paid for the number of units they produced, further contributed to the estrangement between workers and managers. Taylor believed that this system would reduce the antagonism workers felt about direct supervision and control by managers. However, just the opposite often tended to occur: workers felt distrustful and overworked because managers often increased the number of pieces required when workers met their quotas. Overall, scientific management amplified the divergent interests of management and workers rather than lessening them (Zuboff, 1988). Management became even more removed from workers with the advent of mass production.

MASS PRODUCTION THROUGH AUTOMATION (FORDISM) *Fordism*, named for Henry Ford, the founder of the Ford Motor Company, incorporated hierarchical authority structures and scientific management techniques into the manufacturing process (Collier and Horowitz, 1987). Assembly lines, machines, and robots became a means of *technical control* over the work process (Edwards, 1979). The *assembly line*, a system in which workers perform a specialized operation on an unfinished product as it is moved by conveyor past their workstation, increased efficiency and productivity. On Ford's assembly line, for example, a Model T automobile could be assembled in one-eighth the time formerly required. Ford broke the production process of the Model T into 7882 specific tasks (Toffler, 1980). This fragmentation of the labour process meant that individual workers had little to do with the final product. The assembly line also allowed managers to control the pace of work by speeding up the line when they wanted to increase productivity. As productivity increased, however, workers began to grow increasingly alienated as they saw themselves becoming robot-like labourers (Collier and Horowitz, 1987). However, dramatically increased productivity allowed Ford to give pay raises, which kept workers relatively content, while his own profits steadily rose. Without mass consumers there could be no mass production; Ford recognized that better wages would allow the workers to buy his products.

The role of contemporary managers was strongly influenced by the development of the assembly line and mass production techniques, which made it possible to use interchangeable parts in a variety of products. According to sociologist George Ritzer (1993), the assembly line and machine technology have even come to dominate work settings such as fast-food restaurants. Burger King, for example, uses a conveyor belt to cook hamburgers, and food is produced in assembly line fashion. McDonald's has a soft-drink dispenser with a sensor that shuts off when the glass is full so that the employee does not have to make this decision (Ritzer, 1993). What do managers do in such a highly rationalized, technically controlled setting? Their task is limited because the restaurant's system is designed to be error-free. George Cohon, the president of McDonald's of Canada, describes how the system works:

> A McDonald's outlet is a machine that produces, with the help of unskilled machine attendants, a highly polished product. Through painstaking attention to total design and facilities planning, everything is built integrally into the technology of the system. The only choice open to the attendant is to operate it exactly as the designers intended." (Globe and Mail, 1990:B80)

Of course, managers also hire workers, settle disputes, and take care of other tasks, but in many work settings, automation has dramatically deskilled their jobs (Garson, 1989; Zuboff, 1988; Ritzer, 1993).

Automation also has contributed to increased surveillance of employees. With computer networks, managers can measure productivity without employees even realizing it. Whereas early forms of management involved direct supervision of workers, technology now makes it possible for a limited number of managers to control many more workers (see Zuboff, 1988).

THE LOWER TIER OF THE SERVICE SECTOR AND MARGINAL JOBS

Positions in the lower tier of the service sector are characterized by low wages, little job security, few chances for advancement, and higher unemployment rates. Typical lower-tier positions include janitor, waitress, messenger, sales clerk, typist, file clerk, farm labourer, and textile worker.

According to the employment norms of this country, a job should (1) be legal, (2) be covered by government work regulations, such as minimum standards of pay, working conditions, and safety standards, (3) be relatively permanent, and (4) provide adequate pay with sufficient hours of work each week to make a living (Hodson and Sullivan, 1990). However, many lower-tier service sector jobs do not meet these norms and therefore are marginal. ***Marginal jobs*** **differ from the employment norms of the society in which they are located**; an example in the Canadian labour market is that of personal service workers.

PERSONAL SERVICE WORKERS Service workers often are viewed by customers as subordinates or personal servants. Frequently, they are required to wear a uniform that reflects their status as a clerk, food server, maid, or porter. In 1991, more than 3 million workers in Canada were employed in the retail trade and other consumer services. Occupational segregation by gender (see Chapter 10) and by age is clearly visible in personal service industries. Thirty-two percent of working women were employed in this sector, compared with 21 percent of men (Statistics Canada, 1992). Younger workers are more likely than older people to work in this sector, as they pay for their studies with part-time work or use these low-level positions as a means of entering the labour force.

INTERNATIONALIZATION OF MARGINAL JOBS Some manufacturing jobs also may be marginalized. Marginal jobs are more likely to be found in peripheral industries than in core, or essential, industries. Peripheral industries tend to be in highly competitive industries (such as garment or microelectronics manufacturing) that operate in markets where prices are subject to sudden, intense fluctuations and where labour is a significant part of the cost of the goods sold (Hodson and Sullivan, 1990).

Although "high-tech" occupations (such as engineering and computer technology) are viewed by some as the wave of the future, many jobs in this field are marginal. Assembly line jobs in high-

Robots at this Honda factory exemplify the deskilling of jobs through automation. What are managers' responsibilities in workplaces such as this?

tech industries often are boring, low-paying, and hazardous. These industries also are more likely to export jobs to other regions of the country or to developing nations, where labour costs are lower. The term *global assembly line* is used to describe situations in which corporations hire workers, usually girls and young women, in developing nations at very low wages to work under hazardous conditions. Despite the grim work environment such jobs represent a temporary respite from grinding poverty for many workers (Ehrenreich and Fuentes, 1981; Women Working Worldwide, 1991).

To gain the same benefits of "cheap labour," some Canadian companies hire women who have recently migrated to this country. While many work for low wages in factories, their lack of language and job skills, and the shortage of affordable child care makes these women vulnerable to companies that will hire them as *homeworkers*, that is, they perform the work these companies require at home. As such, they are not protected by employment standards legislation. Many expensive fashion labels sell clothing that is made by homeworkers who are paid less than the minimum wage. A 1991 study of Chinese-Canadian garment workers in Toronto found that their hourly wages averaged $4.50, they did not get vacation pay or overtime, and their employers did not make contributions on their behalf to unemployment insurance or to the Canada Pension Plan (Dagg and Fudge, 1992).

CONTINGENT WORK

***Contingent work* is part-time work or temporary work** that offers advantages to employers but that can be detrimental to the welfare of workers. Contingent work is found in every segment of the workforce, including colleges and universities, where tenure-track positions are fewer in number than in the past and a series of one-year, non-tenure-track appointments at the lecturer or instructor level has become a means of livelihood for many professionals. The federal government is part of this trend, as is private enterprise. For example, the health-care field continues to undergo significant change, as governments try to cut health costs. Nurses, personal care homeworkers, and others in this field increasingly are employed through temporary agencies as their jobs are contracted out.

Employers benefit by hiring workers on a part-time or temporary basis; they are able to cut costs, maximize profits, and have workers available only when they need them. As some companies have cut their workforce, or downsized, they have replaced regular employees who had higher salaries and full benefit packages with part-time and hourly employees who receive lower wages and no benefits. Although some people voluntar-

Occupational segregation by race and gender is clearly visible in personal service industries, such as restaurants and fast-food chains. Women and people from ethnic minorities are disproportionately represented in marginal jobs such as waitperson or fast-food server—jobs that do not meet societal norms for minimum pay, benefits, or security.

ily work part-time (such as through job sharing and work sharing), many people are forced to do so because they lack opportunities for full-time employment. Sociologist Harvey Krahn (1995) found that between 1976 and 1994, the number of part-time jobs increased at an average rate of 6.9 percent annually, whereas the rate was 1.5 percent for full-time jobs. By 1994 nearly 17 percent of the labour force worked part-time.

A Statistics Canada survey reveals that most part-time workers are young people and that women are much more likely than men to hold part-time jobs. Women account for nearly 70 percent of all part-time workers. More than one-third, or 500,000 of these women, wanted full-time employment (Statistics Canada, 1994).

Temporary workers make up the fastest-growing segment of the contingent work force, and the number of agencies that "place" them have increased dramatically in the last decade. The agencies provide workers on a contract basis to employers for an hourly fee; workers are paid a portion of this fee.

In 1994, almost one million Canadians (9 percent of all employees) were temporary workers (Krahn, 1995). Men and women were equally likely to hold temporary employment. Temporary workers usually have lower wages and fewer benefits than permanent, full-time employees in the same field. Many employers enjoy the flexibility provided by temporary employees. In examining this perspective, Zeidenberg (1990) interviewed Kathy Sayers, the co-owner of a Vancouver technical writing company that relies heavily on temporary employees, and found, in the case of this enterprise, that

> When the [economic] downturn hits, International Wordsmith will be ready and able to retrench quickly and wait out the storm. It won't have a big payroll to cut, nor high overhead costs. "It takes a load off your mind and lets you sleep easier," says Sayers, "when your company has a plan to deal with a change in the economic weather." When the economy perks up ... the partners will quickly hire more temporary employees for stints lasting weeks or months. (Zeidenberg, 1990:31)

While employers find it easier to cope with changes in the economy using such methods, their temporary employees have no economic security and can find themselves quickly unemployed during economic hard times.

UNEMPLOYMENT

There are three major types of unemployment—cyclical, seasonal, and structural. *Cyclical unemployment* occurs as a result of lower rates of production during recessions in the business cycle; although massive layoffs initially occur, some of the workers eventually will be rehired, largely depending on the length and severity of the recession. *Seasonal unemployment* results from shifts in the demand for workers based on conditions such as the weather (in agriculture, the construction industry, and tourism) or the season

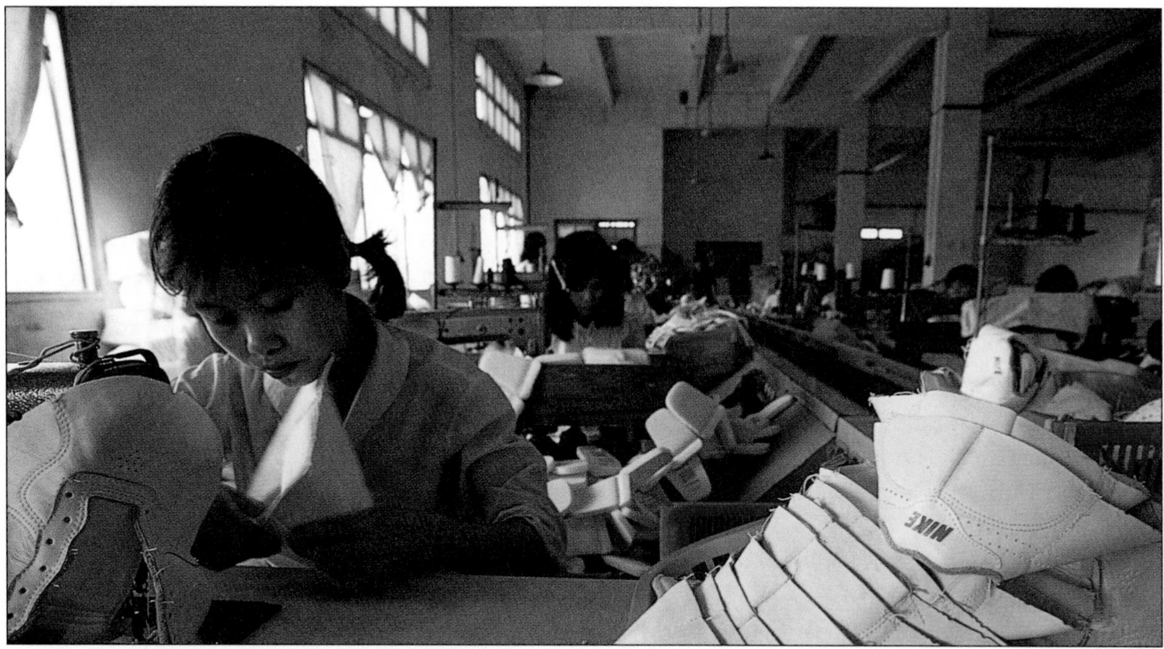

Workers in developing nations—often women or young girls—make or assemble a number of products sold in North America and other developed nations. Workers in China make many Nike products; in the United States, Nike employees are primarily involved in nonmanufacturing work, including research, design, and retailing.

(holidays and summer vacations). Both of these types of unemployment tend to be relatively temporary in nature.

By contrast, structural unemployment may be relatively permanent. *Structural unemployment* arises because the skills demanded by employers do not match the skills of the unemployed or because the unemployed to not live where the jobs are located (McEachern, 1994). This type of unemployment often occurs when a number of plants in the same industry are closed or new technology makes certain jobs obsolete. For example, workers previously employed in the Nova Scotia coal industry or in the Ontario steel industry found that their job skills did not transfer to other types of industries when their mines and plants closed. Workers who lose their jobs when a factory closes down or moves or when their positions or shifts are abolished experience *worker displacement.* Between 1981 and 1984, nearly 500,000 Canadian workers were displaced. The most frequent reasons for displacement were the closure or relocation of a plant and reductions in workload. By 1986, almost two-thirds of these workers had new jobs, often at lower rates of pay, while the remaining third had either left the workforce or were still unemployed (Picot and Wannell, 1990). Structural unemployment often results from *capital flight*—the investment of capital in foreign facilities, as previously discussed. Today, many workers fear losing their jobs, exhausting their unemployment benefits, and still not being able to find another job.

The ***unemployment rate*** **is the percentage of unemployed persons in the labour force actively seeking jobs.** The unemployment rate is not a complete measure of unemployment because it does not include those who have become discouraged and have stopped looking for work, nor does it count students, even if they are looking for employment. Unemployment rates vary by year, region, gender, race, age, and with the presence of a disability.

- *Yearly variations*. The Canadian unemployment rate reached a post–World War II high in the early 1980s, when it climbed above 11 percent. The rate declined to below 8 percent in 1988 and for most of the 1990s has been above 10 percent. In July 1996, 10 percent of the workforce was unemployed.
- *Regional differences*. Canada's regions have widely different rates of unemployment. Newfoundland has traditionally been the highest, with rates that are frequently above 20 percent. Rates in the other Atlantic provinces and in Quebec are also usually higher than the Canadian average. British Columbia, Alberta, and Ontario often have the lowest rates as their economies have been the most successful at creating jobs.
- *Gender*. Male and female unemployment rates have been very similar for the past two decades. While women formerly had higher rates than men, their rates have recently been slightly lower than those of male workers (Statistics Canada, 1994).
- *Race*. Data from the 1986 census showed that visible minorities (a category that does not include aboriginals) had an unemployment rate that was only slightly higher than the national average. However, despite higher levels of education, their average employment income was lower than for Canadians overall. Aboriginal Canadians had rates of unemployment that were more than double the national average (Moreau, 1994).
- *Age*. Youth have higher rates of unemployment than older persons. Unemployment rates for people aged 15 to 24 are as much as 50 percent higher than the overall unemployment rate.
- *Presence of a disability*. People with disabilities were much less likely to be employed than other Canadians. According to a 1990 study by David Gower (1990), while 640,000 disabled persons aged 15 to 64 were employed, their employment rate was only about two-thirds that of the nondisabled population. Even those with jobs were often underemployed in jobs below their qualifications.

Canada's unemployment rates have historically been higher than those of most other industrial countries. In the mid-1990s these rates remain much higher than those of the United States and Japan. However, unemployment has risen to unusually high levels in many European countries in recent years, and, by comparison, Canada's rates are low.

WORKER RESISTANCE AND ACTIVISM

In their individual and collective struggles to improve their work environment and gain some measure of control over their own work-related activities, workers have used a number of methods. Many have joined labour unions to gain strength through collective actions.

LABOUR UNIONS

As workers grew tired of toiling for the benefit of capitalists instead of for themselves, some of them banded together to form labour unions in the middle of the nineteenth century. Craftspeople such as printers, tailors, and blacksmiths were the first to organize, and their efforts led to the passage of the Trade Unions Act in 1872, which legalized union activity in Canada. A ***labour union*** **is a group of employees who join together to bargain with an employer or a group of employers over wages, benefits, and working conditions**. Although the unions made significant gains for workers, media images of labour unions often have not been favourable (see Box 12.2).

During the period of monopoly capitalism, as industries such as automobile and steel manufac-

BOX 12.3 SOCIOLOGY AND LAW

Labour Unions and the Law

Labour unions have existed in Canada since the 1800s, when groups of craft workers began to organize in an effort to earn higher wages and achieve better working conditions. The law discouraged collective bargaining (under common law, collective action by workers was treated as criminal conspiracy) and unions had almost no influence until the 1872 Unions Act removed many of the restrictions on their activity. Following passage of this Act, labour unions grew in size and strength as factory workers banded together to bargain with management on a more meaningful basis. However, as the repression of the Winnipeg General Strike illustrated, union influence remained limited.

Collective bargaining implies that union and management face each other as equals; only in this way can an equitable agreement be reached. When management does not meet the union's demands, the members of the union may strike—walk off the job in order to cripple the employer's production (or, in the case of services such as airlines, curtail the service). The extent to which a strike is successful depends on many factors, including the percentage of workers who stop working, the number of replacements who can be hired, the surplus (if any) of goods the employer has on hand to "weather" the strike, and the ability of the striking workers to survive economically over what may be a protracted period of time. Thus, a strike is, in effect, a duel between the union and management; who prevails, and to what extent, depends on who "blinks" or wears out first.

The legislative framework within which collective bargaining takes place is critical in ensuring its fairness. Canada's labour laws did not support a system of full-scale collective bargaining until the end of the Second World War. Since labour law is a provincial matter, it is difficult to impose national policies. However, during the war, Prime Minister Mackenzie King recognized the importance of labour stability and in 1944 used the federal government's extraordinary wartime powers to pass the National War Labour Order, which dramatically liberalized labour relations. While the legislation was no longer valid after the war, it was used as a model by the federal and most provincial governments when post-war labour laws were drafted.

The post-war legislation established the rights of workers to join and form unions and to bargain collectively with their employer under fair conditions. Governments also restricted the rights of workers and employers in order to avoid work stoppages. Strikes and lockouts were prohibited during the period of a collective agreement, and a provision was made for compulsory mediation and/or conciliation during disputes. This legislation had a significant impact on the union movement; union membership increased dramatically and collective bargaining began to play a vital role in the labour market.

Union membership in the United States has declined dramatically compared with Canada. At least some of this difference can be attributed to labour law. First, it is more difficult for U.S. workers to unionize. American law requires a certification campaign before workers vote on unionization. During this campaign, employers are able to use a variety of methods to discourage unionization. In Canada, certification as a union can be accomplished if the union simply signs up a majority of workers as members. Second, American workers have less power than Canadian workers to force employers to bargain in good faith. Third, in the United States many companies have moved their businesses and factories to states whose laws discourage unionization. In Canada, provincial laws are still relatively consistent, though this may change under more ideologically right-wing governments.

While unions are stronger in Canada than in the United States, the power of labour is still quite limited. This is illustrated by the Anti-Inflation Act of 1975–1978. To control inflation and to ensure labour stability, the federal government introduced legislation that suspended collective bargaining and imposed wage controls on all Canadian workers even though this meant the denial of previously won bargaining rights. Once this precedent had been set, governments were not reluctant to restrict bargaining of public sector workers during times of economic difficulty. Federal government salaries have been virtually frozen during most of the 1990s and many provincial governments demanded wage rollbacks from employees in order to balance their budgets, including (in 1993) the labour-backed NDP government in Ontario. Many private sector employers eagerly followed the example set by federal and provincial governments. As a result, the incomes of Canadian families declined significantly between 1990 and 1996.

Sources: Panitch and Swartz (1993); Wieler (1986).

turing shifted to mass production, workers realized that they needed more power to improve poor working conditions. The suppression of the Winnipeg General Strike in 1919 and the employment crisis during the Depression of the 1930s had devastated unions. Those that remained were typically based in the United States and usually organized to benefit specific trades such as bricklayers and carpenters. One of the most important events in Canadian labour history was the United Automobile Workers (UAW) strike against General Motors in 1937 in Oshawa, Ontario (Abella, 1974). At the beginning of 1937, there was no union at the Oshawa plant, and workers had suffered their fifth consecutive wage cut while General Motors had announced record profits. When the company announced that the assembly line would be speeded up to produce 32 units per hour instead of the 27 it had been producing, the men stopped work and organizers started a Canadian chapter of the UAW.

An unusual feature of the strike was the involvement on behalf of GM of the premier of Ontario, Mitchell Hepburn. He hoped to crush the strike and stop the spread of industrial unions in Ontario. His fear of unions is clear from following statement at a press conference (Abella, 1974:106):

> We now know what these [union] agitators are up to. We are advised only a few hours ago that they are working their way into the lumber camps and pulp mills and our mines. Well, that has got to stop and we are going to stop it! If necessary we'll raise an army to do it.

Hepburn did raise an army. He recruited hundreds of men into the provincial police; the newcomers were irreverently called "Hepburn Hussars" and "Sons of Mitches." Despite the premier's efforts, the union won the strike and received a contract that became a model for unions throughout Canada. This also marked the beginning of *industrial unionism,* in which all workers in a particular industry, covering a wide variety of different trades, belonged to a single union. This gave the workers a great deal of bargaining power because a strike could shut down an entire industry.

Industrial unions faced a long struggle to organize. Relations between workers and managers were difficult and violence against workers was often used to fight unionization. Ultimately, organizers were successful, and unions have been credited with gaining an eight-hour workday and a five-day work week, health and retirement benefits, sick leave and unemployment insurance, and workplace health and safety standards for many employees. Most of these gains have occurred through *collective bargaining*—negotiations between employers and labour union leaders on behalf of workers. In some cases, union leaders have called strikes to force employers to accept the union's position on wages and benefits. While on strike, workers may picket in front of the workplace to gain media attention, to fend off "scabs" (nonunion workers) who might take over their jobs, and in some cases to discourage customers from purchasing products made or sold by their employer. Studies documenting strikes and lockouts reveal that incidences have fluctuated widely between 1919 and 1990. During the 1970s and 1980s, Canada's record of labour problems was much higher than in most other industrial countries. However, in recent years, strike activity has diminished significantly as the recession and corporate restructuring made it unlikely that a successful strike would mean major gains for workers, many of whom were happy to even have a job. Many recent strikes have been a result of workers trying to protect their jobs during a time of cutbacks. Labour relations in the health care field have been particularly difficult in a number of provinces, as governments have been trying to reduce health costs by cutting people or by contracting out services to lower-paying private companies.

Union membership has grown dramatically throughout this century. In 1990, over 36 percent of the nonagricultural paid workforce belonged to unions. Union membership grew dramatically during the two world wars, when labour shortages and economic growth made union expansion easy, and in the 1970s when governments allowed public servants to unionize (Krahn and Lowe, 1993). However, union membership has declined during the 1980s and 1990s as economic recessions and massive layoffs in government and industry have reduced the numbers of unionized workers and severely weakened the bargaining power of unions. You have seen that jobs have shifted from manufacturing and manual work to the service sector where employees have been less able to unionize. While white-collar workers in the public sector such as teachers and civil servants have successfully organized, white-collar workers in the private sector remain largely unorganized. For example, only 4 percent of workers in banks and other financial services belong to unions. While women are less likely than men to be members of a union, they have accounted for most of the growth in union membership over the past decade. In 1991, 31 percent of all female paid workers were unionized, compared with 39 percent of male paid workers (Statistics Canada, 1994).

Difficult times may lie ahead for unions; the growing diversity of the workforce; the increase in temporary and part-time work, the threat of global competition, the ease with which jobs can be moved from one country to another, and the replacement of jobs with technology are just a few of the challenges that lie ahead. The next decade will be a critical time in the future of the labour movement. How do you think union leaders can change their organizations to meet the new realities of the world of work?

The rate of union membership among workers in Canada is higher than in Japan and the United States, but far lower than in most Western European countries. About 90 percent of all workers in Sweden belong to unions, as do 50 percent in Great Britain, almost 40 percent in Germany, and about 33 percent in Switzerland and Japan. Thirty years ago, the union membership rate in the United States was the same as in Canada, but it is now less than half. American industry has been very antiunion, and state and federal laws have not protected the rights of workers to unionize (see Box 12.3).

In most industrialized countries, collective bargaining by unions has been dominated by men. However, in many countries, including Sweden, Germany, Austria, and Great Britain, women workers have made important gains as a result of labour union participation, as discussed in Box 12.4.

THE GLOBAL ECONOMY IN THE TWENTY-FIRST CENTURY

Will the nature of work change in the twenty-first century? What are Canada's future economic prospects? What about the global economy? Although sociologists do not have a crystal ball with which to predict the future, some general trends can be suggested.

THE END OF WORK?

Corporations around the world have eliminated millions of jobs in the 1990s for a variety of different reasons. Only the most efficient companies can flourish in an era when the globalization of trade has meant that competition can now come from anywhere in the world. Downsizing has also become fashionable, and even profitable companies feel pressure to reduce costs. Perhaps most importantly, technology has enabled workers to be replaced with machines. Because of these trends, economist and futurist Jeremy Rifkin (1995) thinks that work as we know it is coming to an end. Rifkin feels that we are moving into a postindustrial, information-based economy in which factory work, clerical work, middle management, and many other traditional jobs will soon fall victim to technology. Bank machines will replace tellers, robots will replace factory workers, and electronic scanners will replace cashiers. When agriculture became mechanized, displaced workers found jobs in industry; when industry turned to computers, service jobs were available. However, the information age does not hold the

BOX 12.4 SOCIOLOGY IN GLOBAL PERSPECTIVE

Women and Labour Activism

We are learning to use the system, and well we should for it has certainly used us.—Tish Sommers

Even among the most industrialized nations in the world—such as Sweden, Great Britain, the United States, Germany, and Canada—almost all union negotiators are men. The issues most often brought forward by these negotiators are those affecting "all" workers, often to the exclusion of issues that primarily affect women. Take, for example, the issue of the shorter workweek. Most women who do not have child-rearing responsibilities, as well as most men, want a shorter *workweek,* while most women who have child-rearing responsibilities prefer a shorter *workday* so that they can share child-care duties with other persons.

In recent years, however, some women union members in industrialized countries have become much more savvy at "using the system." Initially, most improvements in women's work opportunities came through legislation. Subsequently, collective bargaining provided a new vehicle through which women could press for needed changes. For example, through labour–management negotiations, workers have bargained for higher safety standards in the workplace than those required by law. However, struggles over what are perceived to be "women's issues" often produce conflict among union leaders. Many male union leaders typically saw certain issues as just that—"women's issues." Ironically, some of their perceptions began to change as they became more aware that some of the health and safety problems in many factories, mines, and other work settings also affected men.

Once a health or safety issue is viewed as affecting men, it often is redefined as a "labour market issue" rather than a "women's issue." Clearly, employed women share many workplace hazards with men because they work in the same factories or offices or services. Other problems are unique to women because of gender segregation in employment or because of the potential risks associated with pregnancy and certain jobs.

European unions have made many advances in dealing with some of these problem areas. For example, German and Austrian unions have been instrumental in instituting inspection systems to identify work hazards. In Germany and Sweden, unions have bargained for relief from "repetitive motion" injuries such as carpal tunnel syndrome (a hand and wrist disorder associated with excessive use of computer keyboards and typewriters) for thousands of women computer operators. Men in the manufacturing sector also benefited from the negotiations because their work is repetitive and may lead to back, leg, hand, and eye injuries. The important role that unions can play in improving workplace health has been demonstrated in Saskatchewan where it was shown that safety could be improved by giving workers greater control over their jobs.

In European countries and in Canada, the number of women in unions is increasing at a faster rate than for men; but women are still less likely than men to belong to unions. Thirty-nine percent of Canadian men belong to unions compared with 31 percent of women (Statistics Canada, 1994). Canadian women have had some success in attaining leadership roles and serving on the national boards of unions. As a result, women's issues, including pay equity and maternity leave, have recently been addressed in collective bargaining.

Women workers in industrialized nations currently fare much better than their counterparts in other parts of the global economy. In many situations, workers have been denied the right to organize and unionize in free trade zones and home-based production industries. Some nations have no labour laws dealing with minimum wages, maternity benefits, equal pay, and leave; others have not enforced existing laws. In some Asian countries, for example, women migrant workers who are exempt from many regulations do most of the back-breaking, repetitive work on plantations. Because they are brought in from another cultural context, they often experience triple discrimination based on race, class, and gender. In the global economy, many working women (along with men) lack not only union representation but also basic human rights.

Sources: Based on Cook, Lorwin, and Daniels, 1992; National Safety Council, 1992; Sass, 1986; and Tomasevski, 1993.

same potential for jobs. Some *knowledge workers*—the engineers, technicians, and scientists who are leading us into the information age—will gain, but there may be little work for the rest of us. We will have an elite workforce, not a mass workforce. The elites will be well paid; Microsoft's Bill Gates, for example, made an astounding $25-billion in a little over a decade. However, the majority have not received the benefits of the postindustrial society. Many people do not have jobs, and those with jobs have seen declines in their purchasing power. Nathan Gardels fears that the unemployed face economic irrelevance: "We don't need what they have and they can't buy what we sell" (quoted in Rifkin, 1995:215).

Two questions arise from Rifkin's analysis. First, what does society do with the millions of people who may not be needed by employers? Second, how do we persuade the top 20 percent, who are receiving the benefits of productivity gains, to share them with the bottom 80 percent who are bearing the burden of change? One possible answer to the first question is to gradually shorten the workweek to 30 hours for the same pay using productivity gains to pay the bill. Earlier technological revolutions resulted in reduced hours of work—from eighty hours per week in the nineteenth century to the current level of forty hours per week. Leisure, rather than formal work, would become the focus of peoples' lives. The second possibility is to redefine what we now consider as work. Rifkin suggests that countries should turn to the nonprofit *civil sector*—community service activities now largely carried out by volunteers—as a source of jobs. The civil sector includes activities such as social services, health care, education, the arts, and assisting the disadvantaged. Not only would this create jobs, but it would strengthen our communities. Recognizing these benefits, the government of Quebec has implemented programs to encourage welfare and unemployment insurance recipients to take jobs in *l'économie sociale* (Rifkin's civil sector). This may become a model for other provinces.

What incentives exist to encourage those benefitting from increased productivity to change? The after-tax purchasing power of Canadians has declined during the past decade and the lack of jobs means that the number of potential customers may decline. Recall that Henry Ford recognized that only well-paid workers could buy his cars. Without customers nobody will be able to buy the products created by the new technology. Many economists blame the depression of the 1930s on the failure of business leaders to recognize that they had to share the benefits of increased productivity with their workers (Rifkin, 1995) and the same threat may now exist.

Increased inequality may also destabilize society. As British journalist Victor Keegan has observed, "A world in which the majority of people are disenfranchised will not be a pleasant or safe place for the rich minority" (1996:D4). The United States, which has the greatest disparity between rich and poor in the industrialized world, now incarcerates about 2 percent of its adult male population (Epstein, 1996), yet still has a much higher crime rate than most other industrialized countries. Recent riots in Jakarta, Indonesia, were begun by young people who were angry at the growing gap between rich and poor and at their own lack of opportunity (Stackhouse, 1996). Rifkin argues that the rich can either use some of their gains to create a fortress economy or they can use the same money to prevent it. Edward Luttwak has contrasted these two different approaches to the distribution of wealth:

> When I go to a gas station in Japan, five young men wearing uniforms jump on my car. They not only check the oil but also wash the tires and wash the lights. Why is that? Because government doesn't allow oil companies to compete by price, and therefore they have to compete by service ... I pay a lot of money for the gas.
>
> Then I come to Washington, and in Washington gas is much cheaper. Nobody washes the tires, nobody does anything for me, but here, too, there are five young men ... standing around, unemployed, waiting to rob my car. I still have to pay for them,

through my taxes, through imprisonment, through a failed welfare system ... But in Japan at least they clean my car." (1996:24)

Also, the public, unions, and some politicians have begun to protest the growing trend toward paying executives enormous salaries while their workers are being laid off or having their wages cut. Public pressure may eventually force a redistribution of the costs and benefits of the shift to a new economy. Blaming the Second World War on economic crises, a policymakers built a postwar economy designed to promote both growth and equity (Epstein, 1996) . The resulting decades of stability and prosperity may help serve as a model for the future.

Rifkin's view of the future may be wrong; others are more optimistic that the period of downsizing is only a temporary one and that the economy will soon begin to create new, well-paying jobs. However, the scenario he foresees is a plausible one and his work points out the way in which fundamental changes in our economy can affect all of us.

THE CANADIAN ECONOMY

Many of the trends we have examined in this chapter will produce dramatic changes in the organization of the economy and work in the next century. Canadian industry will continue to compete with companies around the globe for a share of international trade, and the jobs that go with this trade. As globalization and the technological revolution continue, workers increasingly may be fragmented into two major labour market divisions: (1) those who work in the innovative, primary sector and (2) those whose jobs are located in the growing secondary, marginal sector. Knowledge will increasingly become the factor that differentiates the rich from the poor. In the innovative sector, increased productivity will be the watchword as corporations respond to heightened international competition. In the marginal sector, alienation will grow as temporary workers, sometimes professionals, look for avenues of upward mobility or at least a chance to make their work life more tolerable.

Labour unions will be increasingly less able to help workers unless the unions embark on innovative programs to recruit new members, improve their image, and recover their former political clout (Hodson and Sullivan, 1990). The participation of women in the labour force will continue to increase, and women will continue to make inroads into the professions and senior levels of management. Part-time work, job sharing, and work from the home—the "electronic cottage" will likely continue to grow.

GLOBAL ECONOMIC INTERDEPENDENCE AND COMPETITION

Borderless markets and industries defy political boundaries. For example, Japanese cars may be produced in Canada and the United States using components that can be made virtually anywhere in the world. Capital and jobs can move very rapidly, so governments have much less power to intervene in markets.

Most futurists predict that multinational corporations will become even more significant in the global economy of the twenty-first century. As they continue to compete for world market share, these corporations will become even less aligned with the values of any one nation. Those who advocate increased globalization typically focus on its potential impact on developed countries, not the effect it may have on the 80 percent of the world's population that resides in less developed and developing countries. Persons in developing countries may become increasingly resentful when they are bombarded with media images of Western affluence and consumption; billions of "have nots" may feel angry at the "haves"—including the employees and managers of multinational companies living and working in their midst (Kennedy, 1993).

The chasm between rich and poor nations probably will widen in the twenty-first century as developed countries purchase fewer raw materials from developing countries and more products and services from one another. This change will take place because raw materials of all sorts are no longer as important to manufacturers in developed nations. Oil, for example, may become less important as a power source with the development of solar power and other types of energy. Initial losers in the global marketplace may be the Arab states of the Middle East, where economies will become less stable and elites and workers much poorer when the petroleum age comes to an end (Kennedy, 1993).

In recent years, the average worker in Canada and other developed countries has benefited more than have workers in less developed and developing countries from global economic growth. The average citizen of Switzerland, for example, has an income several hundred times that of a resident of Ethiopia. More than a billion of the world's people live in abject poverty; for many, this means attempting to survive on less than $370 a year (Kennedy, 1993). According to a recent United Nations Report, the total wealth of the world's 358 billionaires equals the combined incomes of the poorest 45 percent of the world's population—2.3 billion people (United Nations Development Program, 1996). While some countries, including many in Southeast Asia and Latin America, will begin to enter the developed world, others, particularly in Africa, will continue to fall farther behind the rest of the world.

The impact of globalization on Canada has been the subject of an interesting debate, part of which concerns whether our economy has benefited from agreements such as the North American Free Trade Agreement (NAFTA), which involves Canada, the United States, and Mexico. We know that the economies of Canada and the United States are becoming more closely linked: the amount of trade is steadily increasing and the border has become almost irrelevant to business. Those looking for opportunities to expand business are increasingly looking south rather than east or west. For example, the Manitoba government placed a high priority on building a four-lane highway south to the United States, while parts of the Trans-Canada Highway in Manitoba remain with only two lanes. This is symbolic of the fact that most of our provincial economies are more dependent on exports to other countries than on exports to other provinces.

The economic consequences of NAFTA will not be known for decades. Critics complained that NAFTA would bring an end to medicare and to our social safety net and would dramatically reduce environmental standards. During the first few years following the 1989 implementation of the agreement with the United States that preceded NAFTA, a great number of manufacturing jobs were lost, just as opponents of the deal had predicted. However, these were also years when Canada's economy was in a recession, and when high interest rates and the high value of the Canadian dollar made our exports uncompetitive. More recently, as a result of low interest rates, a low dollar, and more competitive industry, Canada is exporting far more to the United States than we import and export-related jobs are creating economic growth. We do not know if the future will bring increased prosperity to all three countries, or whether factors like the low wages paid to workers in Mexico and the southern United States will result in jobs permanently moving out of Canada.

Regardless of the impact of globalization on individual countries, the process will almost inevitably continue. A global workplace is emerging in which telecommunications networks will link workers in distant locations. In the developed world, the skills of some professionals will transcend the borders of their own countries. For example, there is a demand for the services of international law specialists, engineers, and software designers across countries. Even as nations become more dependent on one another, they also will become more competitive in the economic sphere. While the prospects for greater economic equality do not appear hopeful, perhaps we should not be unduly pessimistic. According to sociologist G. William Domhoff (1990:285), "If history teaches us anything, it is that no one can predict the future."

CHAPTER REVIEW

The economy is the social institution that ensures the maintenance of society through the production, distribution, and consumption of goods and services. Historically, there have been four basic economic systems: hunting and gathering, horticultural and pastoral, agrarian, and industrial. In primary sector production, workers extract raw materials and natural resources from the environment and use them without much processing. Industrial societies engage in secondary sector production, which is based on the processing of raw materials (from the primary sector) into finished goods. Postindustrial societies engage in tertiary sector production by providing services rather than goods. Much of the Canadian economy is moving from a manufacturing orientation to a service orientation.

- Sociologists often use the criteria of property ownership and market control to distinguish between types of economies. In the twentieth century, capitalism and socialism have been the main economic systems in industrialized countries. Capitalism is characterized by ownership of the means of production, pursuit of personal profit, competition, and limited government intervention. Socialism is characterized by public ownership of the means of production, the pursuit of collective goals, and centralized decision making. In mixed economies, elements of a capitalist, market economy are combined with elements of a command, socialist economy. These mixed economies often are referred to as democratic socialism.
- According to functionalists, the economy is a vital social institution because it is the means by which needed goods and services are produced and distributed. Business cycles represent the necessary rise and fall of economic activity relative to long-term economic growth. Conflict theorists view business cycles as the result of capitalist greed. In order to maximize profits, capitalists suppress the wages of workers who, in turn, cannot purchase products, making it necessary for capitalists to reduce production, close factories, lay off workers, and adopt other remedies that are detrimental to workers and society. Interactionists focus on the microlevel of the economic system, particularly on the social organization of work and its effects on workers' attitudes and behaviour.
- For many people, jobs and professions are key influences on self-identity. Many workers experience job satisfaction when they like their job responsibilities and the organizational structure in which they work and when their individual needs and values are met. Alienation occurs when workers do not gain a sense of self-identity from their jobs and when their work is done completely for material gain and not for personal satisfaction.
- Occupations are categories of jobs that involve similar activities at different work sites. The primary labour market consists of well-paying jobs with good benefits that have some degree of security and the possibility of advancement. The secondary labour market consists of low-paying jobs with few benefits and very little job security or possibility of advancement. Professions are high-status, knowledge-based occupations characterized by abstract, specialized knowledge, autonomy, authority over clients and subordinate occupational groups, and a degree of altruism.
- According to the employment norms of a society, jobs should be legal, be covered by government regulations, be relatively permanent, and provide adequate hours and pay in order to make a living. Marginal jobs are those that differ significantly from these

norms. Contingent work is part-time work and temporary work that offers advantages to employers but may be detrimental to workers.

- The history of capitalism and labour unions are closely intertwined. A labour union is a group of employees who join together to bargain with an employer or a group of employers over wages, benefits, and working conditions. Women workers have turned to various forms of resistance and activism in order to overcome workplace alienation, to improve the workplace environment, and to gain some control over their work activities.

KEY TERMS

capitalism **443**
conglomerates **448**
contingent work **457**
corporations **443**
democratic socialism **450**
economy **437**
interlocking corporate directorates **448**
labour union **460**
marginal jobs **456**
mixed economy **450**
multinational corporations **443**
occupations **453**
oligopoly **447**
primary sector production **439**
professions **453**
secondary sector production **440**
shared monopoly **447**
socialism **448**
tertiary sector production **441**
unemployment rate **459**

QUESTIONS FOR ANALYSIS AND UNDERSTANDING

1. What are the crucial differences between capitalism and socialism in regard to property ownership and market control?
2. What is the difference between an occupation and a profession? What are some newly emerging occupations? Professions?
3. How do labour unions enhance the quality of the workplace for employees? How might they be a detriment to the workplace?

QUESTIONS FOR CRITICAL THINKING

1. If you were the manager of a computer software division, how might you encourage innovation among your technical employees? How might you encourage efficiency? If you were the manager of a fast-food restaurant, how might you increase job satisfaction and decrease job alienation among your employees?
2. Using Chapter 2 as a guide, design a study to determine the degree of altruism in certain professions. What might be your hypothesis? What

variables would you study? What research methods would provide the best data for analysis?

3. What types of occupations will have the highest prestige and income in 2020? The lowest prestige and income? What, if anything, does your answer reflect about the future of the Canadian economy?
4. Many occupations will change or disappear in the future. Think of a specific occupation or profession and consider its future. For example, what will be the role of the librarian when books, journals, and abstracts are all instantly accessible on the Internet?

SUGGESTED READINGS

A very good general book on the sociology of work is:

Harvey J. Krahn and Graham S. Lowe. *Work, Industry, and Canadian Society*. Scarborough, Ont.: Nelson Canada, 1993.

These books provide more information about capitalism:

Peter L. Berger. *The Capitalist Revolution: Fifty Propositions About Prosperity, Equality, and Liberty*. New York: Basic Books, 1986.

Harry Braverman. *Labour and Monopoly Capital: The Degradation of Work in the Twentieth Century*. New York: Monthly Review Press, 1974.

Karl Marx. *Selected Writings in Sociology and Social Philosophy*. Thomas B. Bottomore and Maximilian Rubel (eds.). New York: McGraw-Hill, 1964.

Books that provide interesting insights on the sociology of work include:

Patrick Burman. *Killing Time, Losing Ground: Experiences of Unemployment*. Toronto: Wall and Thompson, 1988.

Barbara Garson. *The Electronic Sweatshop: How Computers Are Transforming the Office of the Future into the Factory of the Past*. New York: Penguin Books, 1989.

Ben Hamper. *Rivethead: Tales from the Assembly Line*. New York: Time Warner, 1992.

Jeremy Rifkin. *The End of Work*. New York: G.P. Putnam's Sons, 1995.

Studs Terkel. *Working: People Talk About What They Do All Day and How They Feel About What They Do*. New York: Ballantine Books, 1985.

Scholarly works on labour unions include:

Irving Abella. *On Strike: Six Key Labour Struggles in Canada 1919-1949*. Toronto: James Lewis and Samuel, 1974.

Berch Berberoglu (ed.). *The Labor Process and the Control of Labor: The Changing Nature of Work Relations in the Late Twentieth Century*. Westport, Conn.: Praeger, 1993.

Chapter 13

POLITICS AND GOVERNMENT

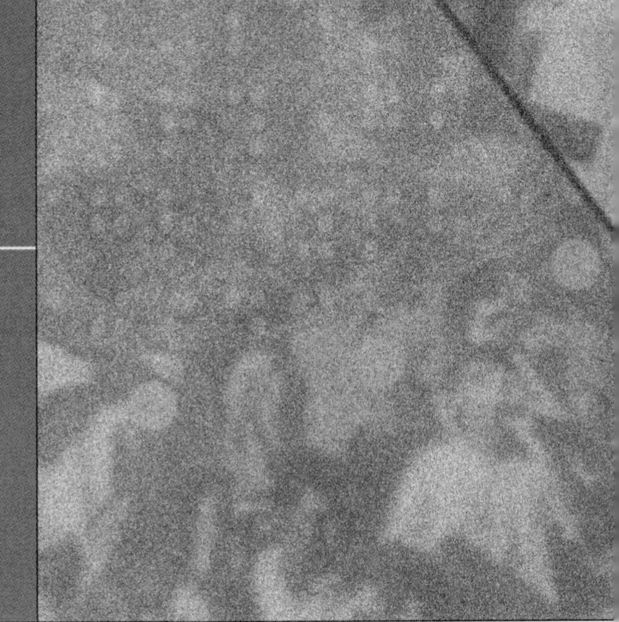

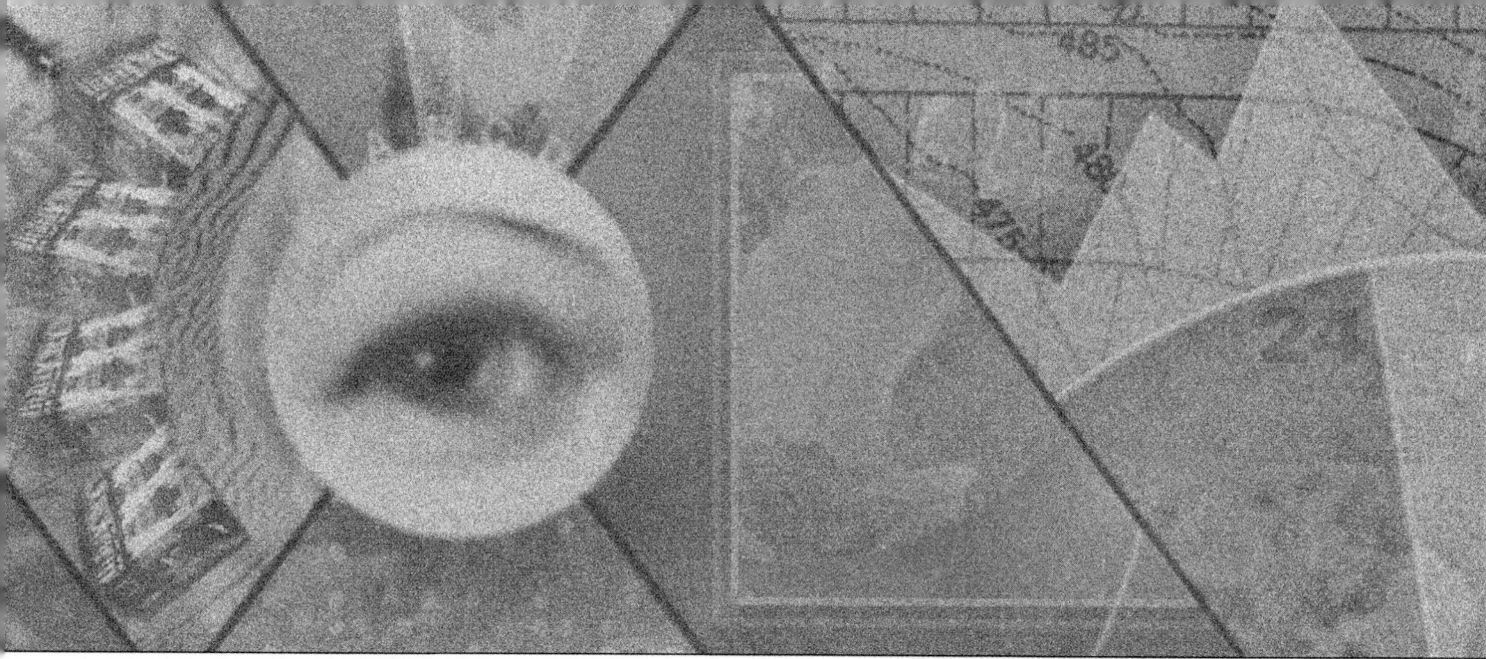

Compared with most other nations, Canada has had a very peaceful political history. However, there have been instances of political violence. During the 1960s and early 1970s, a group called the Front de Libération du Quebec (FLQ) committed a number of terrorist acts, which culminated in the kidnapping of a British diplomat and the murder of a Quebec cabinet minister. One of the intellectual leaders of the FLQ was Pierre Vallières. In *White Niggers of America,* a book he wrote in prison following his arrest for the murder of a woman who died in one of the terrorists bomb attacks carried out by the FLQ, Vallières outlined some of the grievances of the Quebec separatists:

In writing this book I claim to do no more than bear witness to the determination of the workers of Quebec to put an end to three centuries of exploitation, of injustices borne in silence, of sacrifices accepted in vain, of insecurity endured with resignation; to bear witness to their new and increasingly energetic determination to take control of their economic, political, and social affairs and to transform into a more just and fraternal society this country, Quebec, which is theirs, this country where they have always been the overwhelming majority of citizens and producers of the "national" wealth, yet where they never have enjoyed the economic power and social freedom to which their numbers and labor entitle them. (1971:17)

While this sounds much like the rhetoric of present-day separatists, the FLQ was different because its members also adhered to a revolutionary Marxist ideology, which they used to justify their violence. Vallières, who saw himself as a political prisoner, rather than as a "common criminal," described the two goals of his movement in this way:

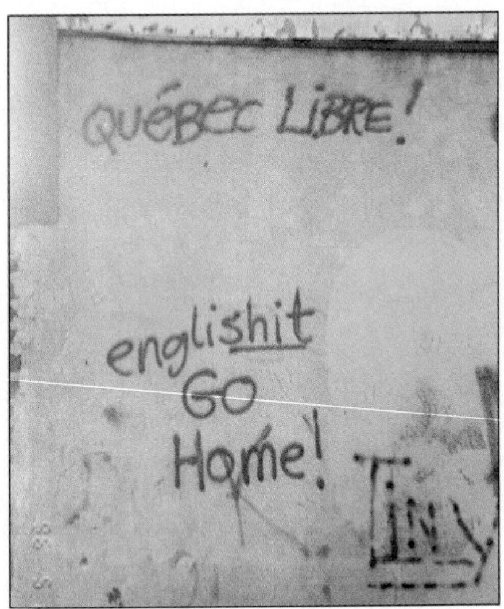

Tension between Anglophone and Francophone Montrealers has increased since the 1995 referendum. Many separatists are angry at the English and ethnic voters who refused to support independence.

> The FLQ is … the armed avant-garde of the exploited classes of Quebec: the workers, the farmers, the petty white-collar workers, the students, the unemployed, and those on welfare—that is, at least 90 percent of the population. The FLQ is struggling not only for the political independence of Quebec, but also and inseparably for the revolution, a total revolution which will give all power to the workers and students in a free, self-administering, and fraternal society. Only a total revolution will make it possible for the Québécois, in collaboration with the other peoples of the earth, to build a Quebec that is truly free, truly sovereign. (1971:258–259)

While few now share Vallières's views about the need for a violent revolution, many Quebeckers still dream of independence. Feeling their culture threatened by the influence of English-speaking North America, separatists believe they can only fulfil their destiny as a distinct "people" through political independence. While the separatists lost the October 1995 referendum by the narrowest of margins and were supported by a large majority of French-speaking voters, the feelings of Quebeckers remain ambivalent. For example, a poll conducted in June 1996 found that two-thirds of Quebeckers wanted their province to remain part of the country. However, the same poll showed that 55 percent would vote for separation. These data reflect Quebec comedian Yvon Deschamps's perception that what Québécois really want is an independent Quebec within a strong and united Canada. They also suggest that some flexibility from the other provinces concerning Quebec's place in Canada would ensure that our country stays together, as many Quebeckers would clearly prefer constitutional reform to separation.

This chapter is about political and state institutions. Political institutions are concerned with the exercise of power, and state institutions are the means through which that power is exercised. Modern nations face tremendous political challenges. Resolving the place of Quebec in (or out) of Confederation is but one of the political issues facing Canadians. In this chapter, we will discuss some of these issues and describe the political system through which Canadians will deal with them. We will also examine other systems of government. Before reading on, test your knowledge about political issues and state institutions by taking the quiz in Box 13.1.

QUESTIONS AND ISSUES

What is the relationship between power and authority? Why do people accept authority?

What are the major political systems?

Whose interests are reflected in political decisions?

How is government shaped by political parties and political attitudes?

BOX 13.1 SOCIOLOGY AND EVERYDAY LIFE

How Much Do You Know About Political Issues and State Institutions?

TRUE	FALSE	
T	F	1. Organizations in which authority is based on the charismatic qualities of particular leaders can be unstable, and these kinds of organizations often fail.
T	F	2. In Canada, our constitutional right to freedom of speech means that any kind of pornography or hate literature can be legally distributed.
T	F	3. While authoritarian governments still exist in many countries, democratic government has become more widespread throughout the world during the past decade.
T	F	4. In Canada, members of the governing party are free to vote against the government in Parliament whenever they wish.
T	F	5. Canada's aboriginal peoples have been able to vote in federal elections since 1867, the year of Confederation.
T	F	6. Governments tend to make their decisions based on a broadly representative sampling of the opinions of all citizens.
T	F	7. Canada has had a female prime minister.
T	F	8. Canada is one of the few nations in the world that has had as its official Opposition in Parliament a political party dedicated to the breakup of the country.
T	F	9. A higher proportion of Canadians vote in federal elections than do most of the citizens of other industrialized countries.
T	F	10. Under most proposals for aboriginal self-government, aboriginal groups in Canada would have total control over their territory and would be considered sovereign nations.

Answers on page 476

Why is nationalism such an important force in the world today?

What is the place of democracy in the twenty-first century?

POLITICS, POWER, AND AUTHORITY

***Politics*—is the social institution through which power is acquired and exercised by some people and groups.** In contemporary soci-

BOX 13.1 SOCIOLOGY AND EVERYDAY LIFE

Answers to the Sociology Quiz on Political Issues and State Institutions

TRUE	FALSE	
T	F	1. *True.* Many political and religious movements that are held together by the personal qualities of their leader fail when the leader dies, retires, or is found to be "ordinary."
T	**F**	2. *False.* While the Canadian Charter of Rights and Freedoms does guarantee the freedom of speech, all freedoms are subject to "reasonable limits." Our courts have interpreted this to allow governments some powers of censorship.
T	F	3. *True.* The movement toward democratic government speeded up dramatically with the fall of the Berlin Wall in 1989 and the subsequent breakup of the Soviet Union. A number of countries in Africa and in Central and South America have also become democracies since that time.
T	**F**	4. *False.* In the United States members of Congress who belong to the same party as the president often vote against the president. However, in Canada party discipline is imposed on those who vote against their leader.
T	**F**	5. *False.* Aboriginal people did not have voting rights in federal elections until 1960.
T	**F**	6. *False.* Special interest groups and various elites in society have far more influence on government policy than do average citizens.
T	F	7. *True.* Kim Campbell was prime minister of Canada in 1993. When Brian Mulroney retired from politics, Campbell took over the leadership of the Progressive Conservative Party and automatically became prime minister. However, she was defeated in an election held a few months later, so we have still never had a woman *elected* prime minister.
T	F	8. *True.* In 1993 the Bloc Québécois won the second highest number of seats in the federal election and become the official opposition. The main purpose of the Bloc is to promote the separation of Quebec from Canada.
T	**F**	9. *False.* Canada's voter turnout rate is substantially higher than that of the United States, but lower than most other industrialized countries.
T	**F**	10. *False.* Some aboriginal groups, including some Quebec Mohawks, do argue that they have the status of sovereign nations, but most aboriginal people have a more limited view of self-government.

Sources: Boldt, 1993; and Dyck, 1996.

eties, the government is the primary political system. ***Government* is the formal organization that has the legal and political authority to regulate the relationships among members of a society and between the society and those outside its borders.** Some social scientists refer to government as the ***state*—the political entity that possesses a legitimate monopoly over the use of force within its territory to achieve its goals.**

How does a sociological perspective on politics and government differ from that of political

Two solitudes: Quebec Premier Lucien Bouchard and Prime Minister Jean Chrétien are the two people responsible for Canada's future as a nation. Does the body language in this photo suggest that cooperation is likely?

science? Although some areas of political science overlap with political sociology, the focus of the two is somewhat different.

POLITICAL SCIENCE AND POLITICAL SOCIOLOGY

For most of the twentieth century, *political science* primarily has focused on power and its distribution in different types of political systems. Some political scientists focus on the operation of the federal government and the operative political processes (including political parties, public opinion, elections, and political participation). Other political scientists compare and contrast political systems in different countries. Still others analyze the interrelationships between national governments, multinational corporations, and international organizations such as the United Nations.

By contrast, ***political sociology*** **is the area of sociology that examines the nature and consequences of power within or between societies**, as well as the social and political conflicts that lead to changes in the allocation of power (Orum, 1988). In other words, sociologists focus on the social circumstances of politics and explore the *interrelationships* between politics and social structures: How is politics shaped by events in society? In turn, how does politics shape events? From the perspective of political sociology, the political arena and its actors are intertwined with all other social institutions, including the economy, family, education, and religion.

Even as we distinguish between political sociology and political science, we should note that some political scientists have broadened their focus to include sociological concerns, such as the importance of socialization, the mass media, and collective behaviour in shaping people's political participation (see Greenberg and Page, 1993). Political sociologists and political scientists agree that the "essence of politics is power" (Orum, 1988). Thus, to understand politics, we first must examine the nature and distribution of power in society.

POWER AND AUTHORITY

Power **is the ability of persons or groups to carry out their will even when opposed by**

others (Weber, 1968/1922). Through the use of power, people's actions are channelled in one direction rather than another on the assumption that meeting some collective goal is more important than satisfying individual needs and wishes. Consequently, power is a *social relationship* that involves both leaders and followers. Power also is a dimension in the structure of social stratification. Persons in positions of power control valuable resources of society—including wealth, status, comfort, and safety—and are able to influence the actions of others by awarding or withholding those resources (Dye and Zeigler, 1993).

The most basic form of power is force or military might. Initially, force may be used to seize and hold power. Max Weber suggested, however, that force is not the most effective long-term means of gaining compliance, because those who are being ruled do not accept as legitimate those who are doing the ruling. Consequently, most leaders do not want to base their power on force alone; they seek to legitimize their power by turning it into authority.

Authority **is power that people accept as legitimate rather than coercive**. People have a greater tendency to accept authority as legitimate if they are economically or politically dependent on those who hold power. They also may accept authority more readily if it reflects their own beliefs and values (Turner, Beeghley, and Powers, 1995). *Legitimation* refers to the process by which power is institutionalized and given a moral foundation to justify its existence. Weber outlined three *ideal types* of authority—charismatic, traditional, and rational-legal—each of which has a different basis of legitimacy and a different means of administration.

CHARISMATIC AUTHORITY According to Weber, ***charismatic authority*** **is power legitimized on the basis of a leader's exceptional personal qualities** or the demonstration of extraordinary insight and accomplishment, which inspire loyalty and obedience from followers. To Weber, charismatic individuals are able to "identify themselves with the central facts or problems of people's lives [and through the force of their personalities] communicate their inspirations to others and lead them in new directions" (Turner, Beeghley, and Powers, 1995:214–215). Charismatic leaders may be politicians, soldiers, and entertainers, among others (Shils, 1965; Bendix, 1971).

From Weber's perspective, a charismatic leader may be either a tyrant or a hero. Thus, charismatic authority has been attributed to such diverse historical figures as Jesus Christ, Napoleon, Julius Caesar, Adolf Hitler, Winston Churchill, and Martin Luther King, Jr. Among the most charismatic leaders in Canadian politics have been Pierre Trudeau and Lucien Bouchard. Bouchard's personal appeal almost led to a separatist victory in the 1995 referendum, which, under the distinctly uncharismatic Jacques Parizeau, looked to be heading for defeat.

Since women seldom are permitted to assume positions of leadership in patriarchal political and social structures, they are much less likely to become charismatic leaders. Famous women who had charismatic appeal include Joan of Arc, Mother Teresa, Indira Gandhi of India, Evita Peron of Argentina, and Margaret Thatcher of the United Kingdom. Kim Campbell's strong performance as Minister of Justice and her personality gave her a charismatic appeal, which, in turn, helped her to win the leadership of the Progressive Conservative Party and become Canada's first woman prime minister. However, the fleeting nature of such appeal was illustrated in the 1993 election when the campaign performance of Campbell and her party was too weak to overcome the negative feelings Canadians held about the government of her predecessor, Brian Mulroney. The Conservatives were reduced to only two seats in Parliament and their future as a party remains in doubt.

Charismatic authority generally tends to be temporary and unstable; it derives primarily from individual leaders (who may change their minds, leave, or die) and from an administrative structure usually limited to a small number of faithful followers. For this reason, charismatic authority often becomes routinized. The ***routinization of***

***charisma* occurs when charismatic authority is succeeded by a bureaucracy controlled by a rationally established authority or by a combination of traditional and bureaucratic authority** (Turner, Beeghley, and Powers, 1995). According to Weber (1968/1922:1148), "It is the fate of charisma to recede ... after it has entered the permanent structures of social action." However, charisma cannot always be successfully transferred to organizations; many organizations, particularly religious ones, fail when the leader departs.

TRADITIONAL AUTHORITY In contrast to charismatic authority, ***traditional authority* is power that is legitimized by respect for long-standing custom**. In preindustrial societies, the authority of traditional leaders, such as kings, queens, pharaohs, emperors, and religious dignitaries, usually is grounded in religious beliefs and established practices. For example, British kings and queens historically have traced their authority from God. Members of subordinate classes obey a traditional leader's edicts out of economic and political dependency and sometimes personal loyalty. However, custom and religious beliefs are sufficient to maintain traditional authority for extended periods of time only as long as people share similar backgrounds and accept this type of authority as legitimate.

Weber noted that traditional authority may be either patriarchal or patrimonial. In systems of *patriarchy*, men are assumed to have authority in the household and in other small groups. In systems of *patrimony*, traditional authority rests in larger social structures that require administrators (such as personal aides who are loyal to the ruler) to carry out edicts. Although patrimonial systems largely have become extinct (or ceremonial, as in the case of the English monarchy), patriarchal systems still remain as a source of authority. One of the ironies of modern life occurred, for example, in the Persian Gulf War when military women from several countries including Canada risked their lives for countries (Kuwait and Saudi Arabia) where women are not allowed to drive vehicles or to vote (Eisenstein, 1994).

As societies industrialize, traditional authority is challenged by a more complex division of labour and by the wider diversity of people who now inhabit the area as a result of migration. In industrialized societies, people do not share the same viewpoint on many issues and tend to openly question traditional authority. As the division of labour becomes more complex, political and economic institutions become increasingly interdependent (Durkheim, 1933/1893).

Weber predicted that traditional authority would inhibit the development of capitalism. He stressed that capitalism cannot fully develop when rules are not logically established, when officials follow rules arbitrarily, and when leaders are not technically trained (Weber, 1968/1922; Turner, Beeghley, and Powers, 1995). Weber believed that capitalism worked best in systems of rational-legal authority.

RATIONAL-LEGAL AUTHORITY According to Weber, ***rational-legal authority* is power legitimized by law or written rules and regulations**. Rational-legal authority is also called *bureaucratic authority*. As you will recall from Chapter 6, bureaucracies are characterized by a clear-cut division of labour, hierarchy of authority, formal rules, impersonal enforcement of rules, and job security based on a person's technical qualifications. In rational-legal authority, power is legitimized by procedures; if leaders obtain their positions in a procedurally correct manner (such as by election or appointment), they have the right to act.

In Canada, our political system gives rational-legal authority to the office of the prime minister, for example, by specifying the procedures by which persons hold the office as well as its duties and limitations. Rational-legal authority also is held by other elected or appointed government officials and by officers in a formal organization. However, authority is invested in the *office*, not in the *person* who holds the office. For example, when the Conservatives lost the 1993 federal election, Kim Campbell passed on the power of the office

Max Weber's three types of authority are shown here in global perspective. Charismatic authority is exemplified by a gospel preacher in the United States whose leadership depends on personal qualities. Sultan Ali Mirah of Ethiopia is an example of traditional authority sanctioned by custom. Australian Supreme Court justices (shown here at the opening of Parliament in Perth, Australia) represent rational-legal authority, which depends on established rules and procedures.

of prime minister to Jean Chrétien and no longer had any involvement in government.

In a rational-legal system, bureaucracy is the apparatus responsible for creating and enforcing rules in the public interest. Weber believed that rational-legal authority was the only means to attain "efficient, flexible, and competent regulation under a rule of law" (Turner, Beeghley, and Powers, 1995:218). Weber's three types of authority are summarized in Concept Table 13.A.

The "rule of law" differs in various situations and organizations. For example, the unique needs of the military as a specialized society separate from civilian society are used as a justification for policies that, in civilian life, would be a violation of rights. For example, in most military forces a soldier can be tried and imprisoned for not showing up for work. This penalty far exceeds that which most of you would expect to receive if you missed a day of school or work, but reflects the need for discipline during times of combat.

Are all citizens guaranteed certain liberties and rights? The Charter of Rights and Freedoms, which is entrenched in the Canadian Constitution, guarantees Canadians *fundamental freedoms*, including the freedoms of the press, speech, assembly, and religion; *democratic rights*, including the right to vote; *mobility rights*, which guarantee Canadians the right to live in any province; *legal rights*, including the presumption of innocence and the right to a fair trial; and *equality rights* prohibiting discrimination on the basis of race,

CONCEPT TABLE 13.A

Weber's Three Types of Authority

	Description	Examples
Charismatic	Based on leaders' personal qualities Temporary and unstable	Napoleon Adolf Hitler Martin Luther King, Jr.
Traditional	Legitimized by long-standing custom Subject to erosion as traditions weaken	Patrimony (authority resides in traditional leader supported by larger social structures, as in old British monarchy) Patriarchy (rule by men occupying traditional positions of authority, as in the family)
Rational-legal	Legitimized by rationally established rules and procedures Authority resides in the office, not the person	Modern British Parliament Canadian prime minister, parliament, federal bureaucracy

age, gender, sexual orientation, or religion (Dyck, 1996). These rights normally cannot be violated by government or the state, and the courts have the power to invalidate legislation that violates a citizen's rights and freedoms. However, Canadian courts have considerable discretion, as rights are not absolute but subject to "reasonable limits." That is, governments can pass laws that may violate citizens' rights if the courts find it reasonable for the government to do so. For example, the court has found it reasonable for governments to limit the freedoms of Holocaust deniers and pornographers. On the other hand, governments have the power to overrule the Charter and the courts through the "notwithstanding clause," which governments can use to pass legislation that conflicts with some parts of the Charter. The notwithstanding clause was used, for example, by the Quebec government to maintain its laws limiting English-language signs after the Supreme Court of Canada ruled these laws unconstitutional.

POLITICAL SYSTEMS IN GLOBAL PERSPECTIVE

Political systems as we know them today have evolved slowly. In the earliest societies, politics was not an entity separate from other aspects of life. As we will see, however, all groups have some means of legitimizing power.

Hunting and gathering societies do not have political institutions as such because they have very little division of labour or social inequality. Leadership and authority are centred in the family and clan. Individuals acquire leadership roles due to personal attributes such as great physical strength, exceptional skills, or charisma (Lenski, Lenski, and Nolan, 1991).

Political institutions first emerged in agrarian societies as they acquired surpluses and developed greater social inequality. Elites took control of politics and used custom or traditional authority to justify their position. When cities developed circa 3500–3000 B.C.E., the *city-state*—a city whose power extended to adjacent areas—became the centre of political power. Both the Roman and Persian empires comprised a number of city-states, each of which had its own monarchy. Thus, in these societies, political authority was decentralized. After each of these empires fell, the individual city-states lived on.

Nation-states, as we know them, began to develop in Spain, France, and England between the twelfth and fifteenth centuries (see Tilly, 1975). A *nation-state* is a unit of political organization that has recognizable national boundaries and whose citizens posses specific legal rights and obligations. Nation-states emerge as countries develop specific geographic territories and acquire greater ability to defend their borders. Improvements in communication and transportation make it possible for people in a larger geographic area to share a common language and culture. As charismatic and traditional authority are superseded by rational-legal authority, legal standards come to prevail in all areas of life, and the nation-state claims a monopoly over the legitimate use of force (Kennedy, 1993).

Approximately 190 nation-states currently exist throughout the world; today, everyone is born, lives, and dies under the auspices of a nation-state (see Skocpol and Amenta, 1986). Four main types of political systems are found in nation-states: monarchy, authoritarianism, totalitarianism, and democracy.

MONARCHY

***Monarchy* is a political system in which power resides in one person or family and is passed from generation to generation through lines of inheritance.** Monarchies are most common in agrarian societies and are associated with traditional authority patterns. However, the relative power of monarchs has varied across nations, depending on religious, political, and economic conditions. *Absolute monarchs* claim a hereditary right to rule (based on membership in a noble family) or a divine right to rule (in other words, a God-given right to rule that legitimizes the exercise of power). In *limited monarchies*, rulers depend on powerful members of the nobility to retain their thrones. Unlike absolute monarchs, limited monarchs are not considered to be above the law. In *constitutional monarchies*, the royalty serve as symbolic rulers or heads of state while actual authority is held by elected officials in the national parliaments. In such present-day monarchies as the United Kingdom, Sweden, Japan, and the Netherlands, members of royal families primarily perform ceremonial functions.

AUTHORITARIANISM

***Authoritarianism* is a political system controlled by rulers who deny popular participation in government.** A few authoritarian regimes have been absolute monarchies in which rulers claimed a hereditary right to their position. Today, Saudi Arabia and Kuwait are examples of authoritarian absolute monarchies. *Dictatorships*, in which power is gained and held by a single individual, also are authoritarian in nature. Pure dictatorships are rare: all rulers need the support of the military and the backing of business elites to maintain their position. *Military juntas* result when military officers seize power from the government, as has happened in recent years in Nigeria, Chile, and Haiti. Authoritarian regimes may be relatively short-lived; some nations may move toward democracy while others may become more totalitarian.

TOTALITARIANISM

***Totalitarianism* is a political system in which the state seeks to regulate all aspects of people's public and private lives.** Totalitarianism relies on modern technology to monitor and control people; mass propaganda and electronic surveillance are widely used to influence peoples' thinking and control their actions. One example of a totalitarian regime was the National Socialist (Nazi) party in Germany during World War II, where military leaders sought to control all aspects of national life, not just government operations. Other examples include the former Soviet Union and contemporary Iraq under Saddam Hussein's regime.

To keep people from rebelling, totalitarian governments enforce conformity: people are denied the right to assemble for political purposes; access to information is strictly controlled; and secret police enforce compliance, creating an environment of constant fear and suspicion. Economic class is another factor in totalitarian control. For example, the Nazi party gained support from members of the middle class who wanted to maintain the status quo while enhancing their own position. By contrast, in the former Soviet Union, the working class sought to eliminate class distinctions, a belief that fit well with Soviet ideology of collective ownership. Sometimes, the relationship between political and economic systems is complex. For example, the People's Republic of China today appears to be readying itself for global competition by embracing some aspects of capitalism (and consumerism) while maintaining strict control over its citizens and blocking their efforts to embrace democracy as it did so ruthlessly in 1989 at Tiananmen Square (see Arendt, 1973; Soper, 1985; McLeod, 1994; Piturro, 1994).

DEMOCRACY

***Democracy* is a political system in which the people hold the ruling power either directly or through elected representatives.** The literal meaning of democracy is "rule by the people" (from the Greek words *demos*, meaning "the people," and *kratein*, meaning "to rule"). In an ideal-type democracy, people would actively and directly rule themselves. *Direct participatory democracy* requires that citizens be able to meet regularly to debate and decide the issues of the day. Historical examples of direct democracy might include ancient Athens or a town meeting in colonial New England; however, the extent to which such meetings actually reflected the wishes of most people has been the subject of scholarly debate. Moreover, the impracticality of involving an entire citizenry in direct decision making becomes evident in nations containing millions of adults. If all thirty million people in Canada came together in one place for a meeting, for example, they would occupy an area of 30 square kilometres, and a single round of five-minute speeches would require hundreds of years. At this rate, people would be born, grow old, and die while waiting for a single decision to be made. Even an electronic town hall meeting in which people were linked through the telephone, television, or the Internet would be enormously complicated to organize.

In most democratic countries, including Canada, people have a voice in the government through *representative democracy*, whereby citizens elect representatives to serve as bridges between themselves and the government. In a representative democracy, elected representatives are supposed to convey the concerns and interests of those they represent, and the government is expected to be responsive to the wishes of the people. Elected officials are held accountable to the people through elections.

However, representative democracy is not always equally accessible to all people in a nation. Throughout Canada's history, for example, members of subordinate groups have been denied full participation in the democratic process. Aboriginals, women, Asians, and East Indians have in the past been prohibited from voting. Today, the Charter of Rights and Freedoms guarantees that all Canadians have the right to democratic participation.

Even representative democracies are not all alike. As compared to the winner-takes-all elections in Canada, which are decided by who wins the most votes in each constituency, many European elections are based on a system of *proportional representation*, meaning that each party is represented in the national legislature according to the *proportion* of votes received by each political party. For example, a party that won 40 percent of the vote would receive 40 percent of the seats in a legislative body, and a party receiving 20 percent of the votes would receive 20 percent of the seats. (By contrast, in the 1993 Canadian federal election, the Progressive Conservatives won two seats with 16 percent of the total vote, while the Bloc Québécois won 54 seats with only 14 percent of the vote.) Systems based on proportional representation increase the power of minority parties because they still have a chance of gaining representation in the legislature even though they would not have sufficient strength to win any particular constituency. Israel has a system that encourages a wide range of minority parties, and an election is usually followed by a long period of negotiation before a coalition is formed representing a majority of seats in the country's parliament, the Knesset. This bargaining can give a great deal of power to small parties representing only a fraction of the population, as their participation in a coalition may determine which of the two major parties forms the government.

The specific form of representative democracies also varies. Canada is a *constitutional monarchy* whose head of state is the Queen, a hereditary ruler who is represented in Canada by the governor general. The governor general is appointed by the Queen but recommended by the prime minister, and has a role that is largely ceremonial, as our elected parliament actually governs the country. By contrast, the United States and France are *republics*, whose heads of state are elected and share governing power with the legislature.

Another major difference between Canada and the United States is that our system is a *parliamentary* one in which the prime minister is the leader of the party that wins the most seats in the House of Commons. This system is based on parliamentary discipline, which ensures that the policies favoured by the prime minister will become law. If government members oppose these policies, they have the opportunity to debate them in private caucus meetings, but are normally bound to vote with the government in the House. Party discipline can be harsh; in 1996, John Nunziata was expelled from the Liberal Party by Prime Minister Jean Chrétien for voting against the government's budget. By contrast, U.S. legislators often vote against their party's program.

When Canada adopted the British parliamentary system, the Fathers of Confederation also implemented an important feature of the American system—both Canada and the United States are *federations*, with a division of power between the central government and provincial or state governments. Other countries, including Britain and Italy, are *unitary states*, which means they have a single central political authority. While John A. Macdonald, our first prime minister, would have preferred a centralized unitary state, this was opposed by Quebec and the Maritimes, which wished to protect their distinctive identities. The British North America Act of 1867 established the distribution of powers between federal and provincial governments.

Some countries have one-party democracies that appear to be democratic because they hold periodic elections. However, the outcome of these elections is a foregone conclusion; voters get to select from candidates belonging to only one party. For example, in the former Soviet Union, all candidates belonged to the Communist party; in Iraq, all candidates are aligned with Saddam Hussein's Baathist party.

During the past decade, democracy has spread very rapidly, particularly in formerly Communist states. Communism was a one-party system that often maintained its power through repressive means. Since the fall of the Berlin Wall in 1989, the countries of the former Soviet bloc in Eastern Europe, as well as others such as Nicaragua and Zambia have established democratic governments. While Communist governments remain in a number of countries including China and Cuba, pressures for democratization are strong around the globe.

If nothing else, the economic and social success of the democratic states serves as a model for those wishing to reform their own governments. Historically and today, capitalism is best served by a democratic system and most countries initiating reforms are moving to capitalism. Full control over property and free markets are necessary and these are not compatible with an absolutist state. The global revolution in communications has also facilitated democratization. Nondemocratic governments may wish to keep their citizens cut off from developments elsewhere in the world. However, satellite television, fax machines, and the Internet make it impossible to control or close off communications, and global culture, including democratic ideals, continues to spread.

PERSPECTIVES ON POWER AND POLITICAL SYSTEMS

Is political power in Canada concentrated in the hands of the few or distributed among the many? Sociologists and political scientists have suggested many different answers to this question; however, two prevalent models of power have emerged: pluralist and elite.

FUNCTIONALIST PERSPECTIVES: THE PLURALIST MODEL

The pluralist model is rooted in a functionalist perspective, which assumes that people share a consensus on central concerns, such as freedom and protection from harm, and that the government serves important functions in society that no other institution can fulfil. According to Emile Durkheim (1933/1893), the purpose of government is to socialize people to become good citizens, to regulate the economy so that it operates effectively, and to provide the necessary services for citizens. Contemporary functionalists state the four main functions of government as follows: (1) maintaining law and order, (2) planning and directing society, (3) meeting social needs, and (4) handling international relations, including warfare.

If government at national, provincial, and local levels is responsible for these functions, what role do people play in the political system? What keeps the government from becoming all-powerful? What happens when people do not agree on specific issues or concerns? Functionalists suggest that divergent viewpoints lead to a system of political pluralism in which the government functions as an arbiter between competing interests and viewpoints. According to the ***pluralist model*****, power in political systems is widely dispersed throughout many competing interest groups** (Dahl, 1961). Many of these are ***special interest groups*****—political coalitions made up of individuals or groups that share a specific interest they wish to protect or advance with the help of the political system** (Greenberg and Page, 1993). Examples of special interest groups include the Business Council on National Issues, the Canadian Labour Congress, the National Action Committee on the Status of Women, and the Assembly of First Nations.

Some feel that pressure group activity is increasingly replacing individual and party activity in Canada's political system. Our country is so large and so diverse that we have always had a highly pluralistic society, and political scientist Rand Dyck (1996) predicts that pluralism will become even more important in the future. Our ethnic diversity is growing (see Chapter 16), and groups representing women, the French, aboriginals, ethnics, and many others are challenging the elitism of the past. Interest groups are now part of our political culture and their influence has been enhanced through legislation such as the Charter of Rights and Freedoms, which guarantees them a voice in political affairs.

While a pluralistic system ensures the voice of many groups will be heard, it does not always work as fairly as political theorists might wish. For example, there are many more groups representing business interests than there are groups representing the interests of the lower class (Dyck, 1996). While this does not mean that government actions always reflect the interests of the powerful, it does mean that the weak must work much harder to be heard. Another potential problem with a highly pluralistic system is that if people turn away from broad social values to those of particular economic, cultural, racial, and gender groups—a process known as *identity politics*—society may become too fragmented. Signs of a backlash to this fragmentation can be seen in the success of the Reform Party in Alberta during the 1993 Federal election, which was largely a response to the concern of right-wing voters with the power of special interest groups (Harrison, Johnston, and Krahn, 1996). The challenge ahead is to build a society that embraces all minorities while retaining a sense of national community.

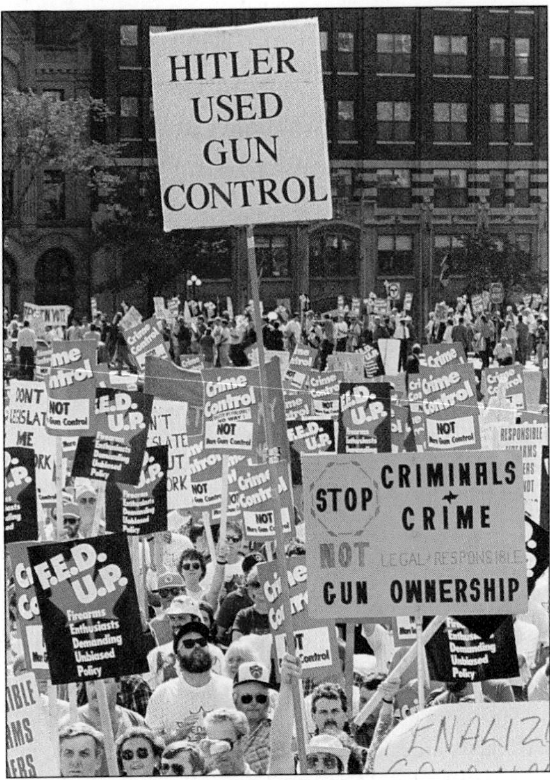

In addition to direct contact with legislators (the "inside game"), special interests like the "gun lobby" try to influence policymaking by mobilizing constituents and stirring up public opinion (the "outside game"). Recent years have seen a proliferation of single-issue groups like those on both sides of the gun control issue. The strong feelings of gun owners are shown in this Ottawa rally.

KEY ELEMENTS Political scientists Thomas R. Dye and Harmon Zeigler (1993) have summarized the key elements of pluralism as follows:

- Decisions are made on behalf of the people by leaders who engage in a process of bargaining, accommodation, and compromise.
- Competition among leadership groups (such as in business, labour, education, law, medicine, consumer organizations, and government) protects people by making the abuse of power by any one group more difficult. These groups often operate as *veto groups* that attempt to protect their own interests by keeping others from taking actions that would threaten those interests.
- People can influence public policy by voting in elections, participating in existing special interest groups, or forming new ones to gain access to the political system.
- Power is widely dispersed in society. Leadership groups that wield influence on some decisions are not the same groups that may be influential in other decisions.
- Public policy is not always based on majority preference; rather, it reflects a balance among competing interest groups.

From a pluralist perspective, representative democracy (coupled with the checks and balances provided by our legal system, and the division of governmental powers between a central government and smaller units such as provinces and municipalities) ensures that no one group can overpower the others and that individual rights are protected.

SPECIAL INTEREST GROUPS Special interest groups help people advocate their own interests and further their causes. Of the thousands of special interest groups in Canada, some (such as environmental groups) seek a collective good while others (such as the cigarette manufacturers lobby) have a relatively narrow focus. Broad categories of social interest groups include banking, business, education, energy, the environment, health, labour, persons with a disability, religious groups, retired persons, women, and those espousing a specific ideological viewpoint; obviously, many groups overlap in interests and membership. Within each of these categories are numerous subgroups. In education, for example, different special interest groups represent teachers, parents, school administrators, universities, professors, vocational and technical schools, and students. Despite their claims to objectivity, members of the media also represent interest groups. Box 13.2 shows how the media portray different sides in the separatism debate.

Special interest groups also are referred to as *pressure groups* (because they put pressure on political leaders) and *lobbies*. The term *lobby* derives from the tradition of interest groups' representatives (*lobbyists*) cornering legislators in the lobbies and hallways of legislative buildings (Greenberg and Page, 1993). Lobbies often are referred to in terms of the organization they represent or the single issue on which they focus—for example, the "gun lobby" and the "dairy lobby."

Lobbying can be conducted as either an inside or an outside game. The *inside game*, refers to situations in which interest group representatives are in direct contact with officials in the government and try to build influence on the basis of personal relationships. This method is typically used by corporations who often hire former government officials to lobby their former colleagues. In the *outside game*, interest groups attempt to pressure officials by mobilizing their constituents to telephone or write letters demanding a specific course of action, by stirring up public opinion, and by getting their membership involved in activities to make their wishes known (Greenberg and Page, 1993). This method is often used by more broadly based groups such as environmentalists or anti-abortion groups.

Advocates of the pluralist model point out that special interest groups provide a "voice" for people who otherwise might not be heard by elected officials at the national, provincial, and local level. However, many special interest groups have specific economic stakes in public policy. Professional groups (such as the Canadian Bankers' Association) wield power with policymakers on issues that they feel may affect their economic well-being (such as increased competition in the banking industry). As discussed in Chapter 12, labour unions have asserted their claims in the hope of protecting the jobs of their members and gaining maximum wages and benefits.

Over the past two decades, special interest groups have become more involved in "single-issue politics," in which political candidates often are supported or rejected solely on the basis of their views on a specific issue—such as abortion, gun control, gay and lesbian rights, or the environment. Single-issue groups derive their strength from the intensity of their beliefs; leaders have little room to compromise on issues. Some of these groups have been very effective; about a decade ago, a quickly organized group of seniors were able to make the government back down on its plans to change the law that provided automatic cost-of-living increases to old age pensioners.

CONFLICT PERSPECTIVES: ELITE MODELS

Although conflict theorists acknowledge that the government serves a number of important purposes in society, they assume that government

BOX 13.2 SOCIOLOGY AND MEDIA

The Media and Separatism

The mass media have a major influence on politics. Most of us are aware that the media can distort events; this is particularly true of television, which is Canadians' main source of political information. Television news is very brief—items rarely last more than a minute or two—and producers try to show pictures that are interesting, exciting, and visually appealing. This means that any political messages must be short and simple. Since most political issues are very complex, they are inevitably oversimplified and distorted by television.

Media bias is a particular problem when reporters favour one side of a political debate. This has been the case in the battle over Quebec separatism. Many of those who work in Quebec's French-language media are ardent nationalists and their stories reflect their political views. Another problem is owners can impose their views on reporters. For example, Pierre Péladeau is one of Quebec's wealthiest and most influential publishers. When he was accused of rebuking the staff of one of his papers for their stories praising Jews, Péladeau's defence was that he was not anti-Semitic, but that he wanted his papers to focus on stories about francophones. Since Quebec Jews are typically English-speaking, stories about them should not take up too much space in his papers.

On the other side, the English-language media are very much opposed to the sovereignty of Quebec and their work reflects a pro-unity position. That the French and English media in Quebec can differ dramatically in their reporting of the same event was shown in their coverage of a June 1996 rally of federalists on Parliament Hill in Ottawa. *The Gazette*, Montreal's leading English-language newspaper, reported that 12,000 people had attended a federalist "love-in." Their front-page photo showed a girl in front of the flag-waving crowd. In the girl's hand was a sign saying "Separation: It's Over." Contrast this with *Le Devoir*, a French-language paper, which reported that 6,000 people had attended the rally. On the front page was a photo of a protester wearing a Lucien Bouchard mask and carrying a cane. Another man appeared to be kicking him in the leg. The spin the media put on events, as in this case, makes it difficult to separate reality from media bias.

The importance of the media in the battle for the hearts, minds, and votes of Quebeckers is indicated by the ongoing controversy over the role of the Canadian Broadcasting Corporation (CBC) in the unity debate. In 1967, the Liberal government gave the CBC the explicit mandate of promoting national unity and the Canadian identity. This led at times to political interference by the federal government in coverage by Radio-Canada, the French-language network of the CBC. While national unity has since been removed from the CBC's mission, the media remain an important part of our national debate.

Sources: Picard, 1996; Raboy, 1992; and Richler, 1991.

exists for the benefit of wealthy or politically powerful elites who use the government to impose their will on the masses. According to the ***elite model*****, power in political systems is concentrated in the hands of a small group of elites and the masses are relatively powerless**. Early Italian sociologists Vilfredo Pareto (1848–1923) and Gaetano Mosca (1858–1941) were among the first to show that concentration of power may be inevitable within societies. Pareto first used the term *elite* to refer to "the few who rule the many" (G. Marshall, 1994). Similarly, Karl Marx claimed that under capitalism, the government serves the interests of the ruling (or capitalist) class that controls the means of production.

KEY ELEMENTS Elite models are based on the following assumptions (Dye and Zeigler, 1993):

- Decisions are made by the elite, which possesses greater wealth, education, status, and other resources than do the "masses" it governs.
- Consensus exists among the elite on the basic values and goals of society; disagreements arise only over the means to achieve those values and goals. However, most people in a society do not necessarily share the elite consensus on these important social concerns.
- The masses have little influence over the elite and public policy. The masses are seen as uninterested in and uninformed about the issues facing society; the elite is in the best position to make important decisions.
- Power is highly concentrated at the top of a pyramid-shaped social hierarchy; those at the top of the power structure come together to set policy for everyone.
- Public policy reflects the values and preferences of the elite, not the preferences of the people. The elite uses the media to shape the political attitudes of the masses.

From this perspective, a few of the "best and brightest" among the masses may rise to elite positions by acquiring the requisite education, experience leadership skills, and other attributes of the elite (Dye and Zeigler, 1993). However, those who do not share the attitudes, political philosophy, gender, or race of the elites will not succeed in this way.

C. WRIGHT MILLS AND THE POWER ELITE Sociologist C. Wright Mills (1959) was among the first to formulate and test ideas concerning power elites. Mills examined the power structure of the United States and concluded that a power elite occupied the upper echelon of the power pyramid. The ***power elite*** **is composed of leaders at the top of business, the executive branch of the federal government, and the military**. Of these three, Mills speculated that the "corporate rich" (the highest-paid officers of the biggest corporations) were the most powerful because of their unique ability to parlay the vast economic resources at their disposal into political power. At the middle level of the pyramid, Mills placed the legislative branch of government, special interest groups, and local opinion leaders. The bottom (and widest layer) of the pyramid is occupied by the unorganized masses who are relatively powerless and vulnerable to economic and political exploitation.

Mills emphasized that individuals who make up the power elite have similar class backgrounds and interests; many of them also interact on a regular basis. Members of the power elite are able to influence many important decisions, including federal spending. Other researchers (Hunter, 1953) have identified elites who control decision making at local community levels; so, the view of elite domination can be extended to all levels of government.

G. WILLIAM DOMHOFF AND THE RULING CLASS According to sociologist G. William Domhoff (1978), the *ruling class* is made up of the corporate rich, who make up less than 1 percent of the population. Domhoff uses the term *ruling class* to signify a relatively fixed group of privileged people who wield sufficient power to constrain political processes and serve underlying capitalist interests. By contrast, *governing power* refers to the everyday operation of the political system; who *governs* is much less important than who *rules*.

Like Mills, Domhoff asserted that individuals in the upper echelon are members of a business class that owns and controls large corporations. The intertwining of the upper class and the corporate community produces economic and social cohesion. Economic interdependence among members of the ruling class is rooted in common stock ownership and is visible in interlocking corporate directorates that serve as a communication network (Domhoff, 1983; Clement, 1975). Members of the ruling class also are socially linked with one another. They attend the same schools, belong to the same clubs, and frequently socialize together. Consider the example of Power Corporation, which is controlled by Paul Desmarais,

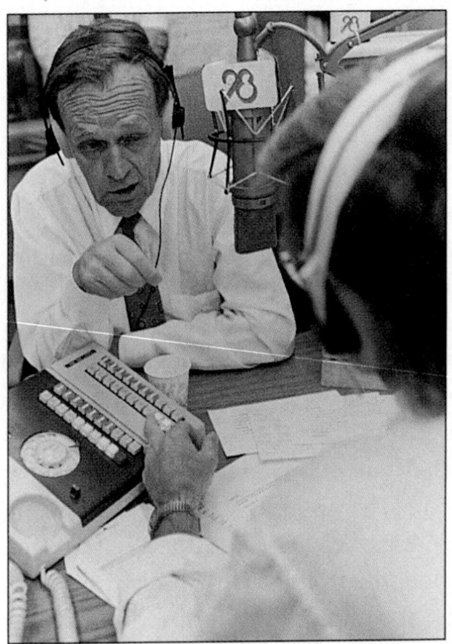

Political leaders often avoid contact with "average voters." When was the last time you saw a prime minister at a public forum or press conference where his policies could be challenged? This is one of Prime Minister Chrétien's rare visits to an open-line radio show.

who is a close friend of former prime ministers Pierre Trudeau and Brian Mulroney, and of Prime Minister Jean Chrétien—in fact, Desmarais's son is married to Chrétien's daughter. A wide variety of senior politicians and government bureaucrats move back and forth between senior Power Corporation positions and government service. With these contacts, Desmarais certainly has no difficulty in having his views heard by those responsible for Canada's governmental policy. Fox and Ornstein (1986) have documented an extensive network of links between large corporations and the federal Cabinet, the Senate, and the federal bureaucracy. These links grew over the three decades they studied. They found far fewer links between provincial governments and the corporate world.

According to Domhoff (1983), the corporate rich influence the political process in three ways. First, they affect the candidate selection process by helping to finance campaigns and providing favours to political candidates. Second, through participation in the special interest process, the corporate rich are able to obtain favours, tax breaks, and favourable regulatory rulings. Finally, the corporate rich in Canada may gain access to the policy-making process through their appointments to governmental bodies such as the Senate. While the economic elites are not in agreement on all issues, they do agree on the need to ensure an economic climate that favours their continuing accumulation of wealth. Fox and Ornstein conclude that the state is not simply an instrument or tool of the capitalists, but that there are important structural connections between the state and corporations that often help capitalists shape legislation to their benefit.

Today, some members of the ruling class influence international politics through their involvement in banking, business services, and law firms that have a strong interest in overseas sales, investments, or raw materials extraction (Domhoff, 1990). The power of transnational corporations has become an important factor in class analyses of the modern state.

CLASS CONFLICT PERSPECTIVES Most contemporary elite models are based on the work of Karl Marx; however, there are divergent viewpoints about the role of the state within the Marxist (or class conflict) perspective. On the one hand, *instrumental Marxists* argue that the state invariably acts to perpetuate the capitalist class. From this perspective, capitalists control the government through special interest groups, lobbying, campaign financing, and other types of "influence peddling" to get legislatures and the courts to make decisions favourable to their class (Miliband, 1969; Domhoff, 1970). In other words, the state exists only to support the interests of the dominant class (Marger, 1987).

On the other hand, *structural Marxists* contend that the state is not simply a passive instrument of the capitalist class. Because the state must simultaneously preserve order and maintain a positive climate for the accumulation of capital, not all decisions can favour the immediate wishes of the dominant class (Quadagno, 1984; Marger, 1987). For example, at various points in the history of this country, the state has had to institute social welfare programs, regulate business, and enact policies that favour unions in order to placate people and maintain "law and order." Ultimately, however, such actions serve the long-range interests of the capitalists by keeping members of subordinate groups from rebelling against the dominant group (O'Connor, 1973).

CRITIQUE OF PLURALIST AND ELITE MODELS

Pluralist and elite models share some basic assumptions about the nature of power and its distribution. Both models assume that decisions are made through interactions among key actors from the upper echelons of larger-scale organizations and institutions in society. Both models agree that these leaders are not everyday citizens and that public policy usually reflects the interests of these organizations (Dye and Zeigler, 1993).

Pluralist and elite models each make a unique contribution to our understanding of power. The pluralist model emphasizes that many different groups, not just elected officials, compete for power and advantage in society. This model also shows how coalitions may shift over time and how elected officials may be highly responsive to public opinion on some occasions (Eitzen and Zinn, 1995). However, critics counter that the pluralist model is naive in its assumption that diverse interest groups balance one another out. They note that our system only has the appearance of pluralism and that it is, in fact, remarkably elitist for a society that claims to value ordinary people's input (Domhoff, 1983). A wide disparity exists between the resources and political clout of "Big Business" when compared with those of interest groups that represent infants and children or persons with a disability, for example. According to critics, consensus is difficult, if not impossible, in populations consisting of people from different classes, religions, and racial-ethnic and age groups.

Mills's power elite model highlights the interrelationships of the economic, political, and military sectors of society and makes us aware that the elite may be a relatively cohesive group. Similarly, Domhoff's ruling class model emphasizes the role of elites in setting and implementing policies that benefit the capitalist class. Power elite models call our attention to a central concern in contemporary Canadian society: the ability of democracy and its ideals to survive in the context of the increasingly concentrated power held by capitalist oligarchies (see Chapter 12).

One important critique of elite models is that social change does not always favour the dominant groups in our society. For example, women have won many battles over the past two decades despite the degree of control which males have had over the corporate and political spheres. The success of the women's movement supports the pluralist claim that nonelites can organize to force change.

FEMINIST PERSPECTIVES

Political theorists have focused much of their attention on class issues. British sociologist Mary McIntosh (1978) was among the first to argue that gender issues were also important. McIntosh felt that the state supported a system in which women were controlled in the household, where they performed unpaid labour that helped supply a cheap workforce for the capitalist system. Until they achieved some political power, women would inevitably be subordinated by the patriarchal state.

Women have long been excluded from the political process. The Elections Act of 1903 said that "No woman, criminal, or lunatic can vote," and Canadian women were not permitted to vote in federal elections until 1918. Most provinces began allowing women to vote at around this time, though in Quebec women were not enfranchised until 1940. With the vote, women also received the right to run for election. However, few ran, and even fewer were successful. Only 27 women were elected to the federal Parliament between 1921 and 1968. Since that time, significant progress has been made; almost 20 percent of the Members of Parliament (MPs) elected in 1993 were women. But women have not yet reached the highest political positions. While Canada has had one woman prime minister (Kim Campbell) and two provincial premiers, only one of these three, Catherine Callbeck of Prince Edward Island, was actually elected to the position. Women have been much more successful at the municipal level; many of Canada's mayors are women. The poor representation of women in Canadian political office is typical of most western countries. The major exception is the Scandinavian countries where women make up about 30 percent of the membership of the national parliaments. The issue is not simply one of representation. The absence of women in our legislatures has meant that many gender-related issues have not received sufficient attention. Issues like day-care policy, pay equity, the feminization of poverty, and violence against women and children have only recently begun to receive the attention they deserve. In theory, male legislators, whose constituents are over 50 percent women, could have pursued these issues. However, as you will read in Chapter 14, male MPs found the subject of wife battering a joking matter. The attitudes reflected in that incident make the prospects of progressive change without more women legislators look dim.

POLITICS AND GOVERNMENT IN CANADA

The Canadian political process consists of formal elements, such as the duties of the prime minister and the legislative process, and informal elements, such as the role of political parties in the election process. We now turn to an examination of these informal elements, including political parties, political socialization, and voter participation.

POLITICAL PARTIES

A ***political party* is an organization whose purpose is to gain and hold legitimate control of government;** it usually is composed of people with similar attitudes, interests, and socio-economic status. A political party (1) develops and articulates policy positions, (2) educates voters about issues and simplifies the choices for them, and (3) recruits candidates who agree with those policies, helps those candidates win office, and holds the candidates responsible for implementing the party's policy positions. In carrying out these functions, a party may try to modify the demands of special interests groups, build a consensus that could win majority support, and provide simple and identifiable choices for the voters on election day. Political parties create a *platform*, a formal statement of the party's political positions on various social and economic issues.

The party that wins the most seats in an election forms the government; the party with the next largest number of seats becomes the official Opposition. Since Confederation, two political parties, the Liberals and the Progressive Conservatives, have dominated the Canadian political system. Although one party may control the government for several terms, at some point the voters elect the other party and control shifts. From time to time, other parties have gained some strength. At various times the New Democratic Party (NDP) and the Social Credit Party had some political strength, but neither had enough seats to form the official Opposition. However, in the 1993 election, the Progressive Conservatives were reduced to only two seats. The Bloc Québécois, a party that favours Quebec separation, became the official Opposition and the Reform Party, which mainly represents politically disaffected Western Canadians, also won significant representation.

IDEAL TYPE VERSUS REALITY Ideally, political parties will offer clear alternatives to the electorate—alternatives that reflect the aspirations, concerns, and viewpoints of the population. For several reasons, this is usually not the case. First, the two major parties rarely offer voters clear policy alternatives. Most voters view themselves as being close to the centre of the political spectrum (extremely liberal being the far left of that spectrum and extremely conservative being the far right). Although the definitions of liberal and conservative vary over time, *liberals* tend to focus on equality of opportunity and the need for government regulation and social safety nets. By contrast, *conservatives* are more likely to emphasize economic liberty and freedom from government interference (Greenberg and Page, 1993). However, because most voters consider themselves moderates, neither party has much incentive to move very far from the middle. Parties like the NDP and Reform, which choose to maintain some ideological purity, run the risk of being marginalized and are very unlikely to win a national election. While these parties have not won electoral power, they have been successful in having their ideas implemented. During the 1960s and 1970s, many of the social policies advocated by the NDP were implemented by Liberal and Progressive Conservative governments. More recently, the Reform Party has been much more successful in having its deficit-cutting agenda implemented by federal and provincial governments than it has been in convincing Canadians it should be given the power to run the country.

This staying near the centre of the political spectrum and the co-optation of opposing parties' policy ideas mean that Canadian elections tend to be fought over issues of leadership rather than of fundamental political principles. The most notable recent exception to this is instructive. A major issue of the 1988 election was the Canada–U.S. free trade agreement; a pact removing the barriers to the sale of goods and services between Canada and the United States. The Progressive Conservatives, who ultimately won the election, strongly supported the Canada-U.S. Free Trade Agreement, while their main opponents, the Liberals, opposed it. However, when the Liberals did eventually take power in 1993 they quickly "studied" the North American Free Trade Agreement (NAFTA), the successor to the earlier pact, which was also negotiated by the Conservatives and opposed by the Liberals, expressed their support for it, and since then have been ardent free traders, seeking to expand NAFTA to Chile.

The second reason the two major political parties do not offer clear alternatives that reflect the viewpoints of the population is that most political parties are dominated by active elites who are not representative of the general population. Many represent special interests and tend to come from the upper echelons of society. Thus the poor, women, and racial minorities have not been included in drafting party policy or in selecting party leaders. One study (Lele et al., 1979) looked at attendance at Liberal, Progressive Conservative, and NDP conventions and found that participation at none of them was representative of the Canadian population. Similarly, Members of Parliament are disproportionately male and from the upper and middle classes (Guppy et al., 1987). Many people involved in politics today tend to work outside the traditional party structure, often in single-issue interest groups. Organizations like the National Action Committee for the Status of Women, Greenpeace, and various aboriginal groups have been very effective in advancing their agendas and in getting grassroots involvement without attaching themselves to a particular political party.

Finally, our electoral system effectively limits the degree to which a diversity of views will be reflected in our legislatures. In those political systems with proportional representation (discussed earlier in this chapter), minority parties have a much greater chance of electing candidates to the legislature. It is interesting to speculate on what impact proportional representation would have on our political system.

Despite the fact that the Liberals and Progressive Conservatives may not have all of the ideal characteristics of political parties, they have both flourished—at least until the Conservatives were decimated in the 1993 election. Whether the Bloc Québécois and the Reform Party retain their

When people move from one country to another, they learn new political attitudes, values, and behaviour. This citizenship ceremony was held in Quebec City during National Citizenship Week. What role do you think these new Canadians will play in Quebec politics?

current representation, or whether the Progressive Conservatives regain their role as a major political force, remains to be seen.

POLITICS AND THE PEOPLE

Why do some people vote and others do not? How do people come to think of themselves as being conservative, moderate, or liberal? Key factors include individuals' political socialization, attitudes, and participation.

POLITICAL SOCIALIZATION ***Political socialization*** **is the process by which people learn political attitudes, values, and behaviour**. For young children, the family is the primary agent of political socialization, and children tend to learn and hold many of the same opinions as their parents. By the time children reach school age, they typically identify with the political party (if any) of their parents (Burnham, 1983). As they grow older, other agents of socialization including peers, teachers, and the media, begin to affect children's political beliefs. Over time, these other agents may cause people's political attitudes and values to change, and they may cease to identify with the political party of their parents. Even for adults, political socialization continues through the media, friends, neighbours, and colleagues in the workplace.

POLITICAL ATTITUDES In addition to the socialization process, people's socioeconomic status affects their political attitudes, values, beliefs, and behaviour. For example, individuals who are very poor or who are unable to find employment tend to believe that society has failed them and therefore to be indifferent toward the political system (Zipp, 1985; Pinderhughes, 1986). Believing that casting a ballot would make no difference to their own circumstances, they do not vote.

In general, voters tend to select candidates and political parties based on social and economic issues they consider important to their lives. *Social issues* are those relating to moral judgments or civil rights, ranging from abortion rights to equal rights for homosexuals. Other social issues include the rights of people of colour and persons with a disability, capital punishment, and gun control. Persons with a liberal perspective on social issues, for example, tend to believe that women have the right to an abortion (at least under certain circumstances), that criminals should be rehabilitated and not just punished, and that the government has an obligation to protect the rights of subordinate groups. Conservatives tend to believe in limiting individual rights on social issues and to oppose social programs that they see as promoting individuals on the basis of minority status rather than merit. Based on these distinctions, Liberals and New Democrats are more likely to seek passage of social programs that make the government a more active participant in society, promoting social welfare and equality. By contrast, Progressive Conservative and Reform Party members are more likely to act according to the belief that government should limit its involvement in social issues.

Economic issues fall into two broad categories: (1) the amount that should be spent on government programs and (2) the extent to which these programs should encourage a redistribution of income and assets. Those holding liberal political views believe that without government intervention, income and assets would become concentrated in the hands of even fewer people and that the government must act to redistribute wealth, thus ensuring that everyone gets a "fair slice" of the economic "pie." In order to accomplish this, they envision that larger sums of money must be raised and spent by the government on such programs. Conservatives contend that such programs are not only unnecessary but also counterproductive. That is, programs financed by tax increases decrease people's incentive to work and to be innovative, and make people dependent upon the government.

You will remember that the main parties tend toward the centre and that their policies are often not ideologically distinct on either social or economic issues. The Progressive Conservatives, who ideologically favour spending restraint, ran up the largest budget *deficits* in Canadian history before they were voted out of office in 1993. The Liberals, on the other hand, after winning the election, implemented the largest budget *cuts* in Canadian history in order to reduce the deficit, despite the impact of these cuts on the social programs that have traditionally received their support. The immediate demands of political reality are often more important in determining government policy than is political philosophy.

Social class is correlated with political attitudes. People in the upper classes tend to be more conservative on economic issues and more liberal on social issues. Upper-class conservatives generally favour equality of opportunity but do not want their own income and assets taxed heavily to abolish poverty or societal problems that they believe some people bring upon themselves. Most of Canada's social programs faced opposition from corporate and upper-class interests, and some of these groups have led the call for cuts to these programs in the 1990s. By contrast, people in the lower classes tend to be conservative on social issues, such as capital punishment or abortion rights, but liberal on economic issues, such as increasing the minimum wage and expanding social programs.

Despite these tendencies, there is probably less of a connection between voting behaviour and social class in Canada than in many other industrialized countries. The Liberal Party has typically attracted voters from all classes, while the NDP gets a high proportion of its support from skilled and unskilled labour. Even so, more voters from the skilled and unskilled labour classes usually vote for other parties than they do for the New Democrats. In fact, Canadian voters tend to be somewhat fickle at the polls and frequently switch parties. For example, comparing the 1988 and 1993 federal elections, more voters switched parties than voted for the same party they had chosen in the earlier election (Pammett, 1993). This is the reason the Progressive Conservatives, who had won the 1988 election, were reduced to only two seats in Parliament in the 1993 election.

Why is the association between class and voting so low in Canada? Canadian voters appear to be influenced more by individual leaders or particular issues and events than by loyalties to a particular party's philosophy. This conclusion is supported by the results of one study (Clarke et al., 1991) in which it was found that class, gender, ethnicity, religion, community size, and age all had some effect on Canadians' voting preferences, but much less than such political variables as prior voting record, concern about immediate issues, and the image of the party leader.

Another reason for the weak connection between class and voting is that the mainstream parties, particularly the Liberals, have been able to incorporate many of the reforms suggested by more class-based parties into their own platforms. For example, government medical care, which was introduced in Saskatchewan by the CCF (Co-operative Commonwealth Federation) party—now the New Democratic Party—was subsequently adopted by the Liberals, who implemented it at the national level.

Finally, sociologist Rick Ogmundson (1975) explained the weak link between class and voting as resulting from what he called the *subjective class vote*. Using survey data, he found that people often believed they were voting for a party that reflected their interests, even though more objective measures of the party's position indicated that this was not the case. According to Ogmundson and Ng (1982), the subjective class vote in Canada was about as high as it was in the United Kingdom, which is usually thought to have a high degree of class politics. Ogmundson's work is supported by research showing that support for the NDP was more strongly related to belief in class ideology, including support for unions and an egalitarian philosophy than it was to the actual class position of the voters (Nakhaie and Arnold, 1996).

POLITICAL PARTICIPATION Democracy has been defined as a government "of the people, by the people, and for the people." Accordingly, it would stand to reason that "the people" would actively participate in their government at any or all of four levels: (1) voting, (2) attending and taking part in political meetings, (3) actively participating in political campaigns, and (4) running for or holding political office. Participation is important as elections are the means through which citizens can make their views known to politicians. Participation also helps to legitimate the political process; those who vote share a responsibility for, and an interest in, the outcome of the election. In Canada, about 75 percent of those eligible to vote exercise that right in federal elections. The participation rate is slightly higher for provincial elections and much lower for municipal elections. While our 75 percent participation rate means that most Canadians do get involved in the electoral process, many western industrial countries have even greater participation rates. For example, in Western European countries participation rates are normally 80 to 90 percent. The United States has one of the lowest voter participation rates of all Western nations. About 60 percent of eligible voters participated in the 1992 U.S. elections.

Why do many eligible voters in North America stay away from the polls? During any election, some voting-age persons do not go to the polls due to illness, disability, lack of transportation, or absenteeism. However, these explanations do not account for why many other people do not vote. According to some analysts, people may not vote because they are satisfied with the status quo or because they are apathetic and uninformed—they lack a basic understanding of both public issues and the basic process of government. Surveys of voters typically show that the majority of Canadians have little knowledge of the candidates or the issues. This lack of knowledge makes it difficult for many people to cast a meaningful ballot, so they simply stay away from the polls.

By contrast, others argue that people stay away from the polls because they feel alienated from politics at all levels of government—federal, provincial, and local. They believe that government does not care about issues that concern them and that only the elites or special interest groups have any influence.

Participation in politics is influenced by gender, age, race/ethnicity, and socioeconomic status (SES). The rate of participation increases as a person's SES increases. One explanation for the higher rates of political participation at higher SES levels is that higher levels of education may give people a better understanding of government processes, a belief that they have more at stake in the political process, and greater economic resources to contribute to the process.

GOVERNMENTAL BUREAUCRACY

When most people think about political power, they overlook one of its major sources—the governmental bureaucracy. As previously discussed, Weber's rational-legal authority finds its contemporary embodiment in bureaucratic organizations. Negative feelings about bureaucracy are perhaps strongest when people are describing the "red tape" and "faceless bureaucrats" in government with whom they must deal. But who are these "faceless bureaucrats," and what do they do?

CHARACTERISTICS OF THE FEDERAL GOVERNMENT BUREAUCRACY

Bureaucratic power tends to take on a life of its own. During the nineteenth century, the government had a relatively limited role. The scope of government was extended greatly during the Great Depression in the 1930s to deal with labour–management relations, public welfare, and regulation of financial markets. With dramatic increases in technology and increasing demands from the public that the government "do something" about problems facing society, the government has grown still more in recent decades. Today, even with reductions in size, the federal bureaucracy employs more than two hundred thousand people.

Our federal government is divided into departments such as Finance, National Defence, Foreign Affairs, Human Resources Development, and Health. While the number of departments varies as governments change, there are usually between twenty and twenty-five, and each is headed by a minister who is a member of the prime minister's cabinet. The prime minister and the cabinet make up the political executive; most decisions come from cabinet and the power of MPs who are not ministers is quite limited. Ministers do not usually have any expertise in their area of responsibility, so they rely very heavily on members of their departmental bureaucracy for advice. Even strong ministers may have difficulty imposing their ideas on a bureaucracy consisting of thousands of people with a great deal of expertise, who have permanent jobs in their departments, and who have seen many ministers come and go.

The governmental bureaucracy has been able to perpetuate itself and expand because many of its employees have highly specialized knowledge and skills and cannot be replaced easily by outsiders. Also, Canada decided almost a century ago to rely on a professional civil service rather than follow a *political patronage* system in which civil servants are replaced when a new party assumes power. Following a change of president and, as a result, a change also in the party affiliation of the president, in the United States, thousands of changes will be made at the senior levels of the U.S. bureaucracy; in Canada it is rare to see more than one or two senior officials lose their jobs during such transitions.

While patronage is not an issue within the civil service, the government bases many of its appointments on party loyalty rather than on the principle of merit. Appointments to the Senate are perhaps the most obvious example, but appointments to the judiciary and to a wide variety of regulatory boards and commissions are also based on political ties. While opposition parties loudly complain about patronage, when they get into power they usually follow the same practices as their predecessors.

The swearing-in of the new cabinet in January 1996. In our system of parliamentary democracy, power rests in the hands of the prime minister and the cabinet. Individual members of parliament have little influence on government policy.

A major issue concerning our government bureaucracy is the extent to which it represents Canadian society. Traditionally, the civil service, like other sectors of our society, has been controlled by white, English-speaking males. The first major change to this was the involvement of francophones. The Official Languages Act of 1969 mandated a bilingual government and most senior officials are, as a result, required to be fluent in both official languages. Francophones were given preference in hiring and promotion until the imbalance was redressed, and language training was required for many unilingual government employees. The federal civil service now has a higher proportion of francophones than does the Canadian population.

Women now make up almost half the civil service. While they are still underrepresented in senior management positions, women have made substantial gains in recent years. For example, Jocelyne Bourgon, a woman, is the clerk of the Privy Council, the top position in the civil service, and pay equity programs have ensured that women are fairly paid. The federal government has also passed employment equity legislation, the aim in which is to increase the representation in the federal public service of women, aboriginals, people with disabilities, and visible minorities.

In addition to civil servants, who are directly employed by the government, the public bureaucracy also includes many bureaucrats who are employed by Crown corporations and by regulatory agencies. Crown corporations include organizations such as the Canadian Broadcasting Corporation, the Canada Mortgage and Housing Corporation, the Canadian Wheat Board, and Canada Post. Regulatory agencies include agencies such as the Atomic Energy Control Board, the National Parole Board, and the Immigration and Refugee Board. Many policy decisions affecting all Canadians are made by these corporations and agencies, which do not directly respond to day-to-day political direction.

MAJOR POLITICAL ISSUES IN CANADA: QUEBEC SEPARATISM AND ABORIGINAL SELF-GOVERNMENT

THE QUIET REVOLUTION AND QUEBEC NATIONALISM

Because of our former colonial status and the dissatisfaction of many Quebec nationalists with the current political structure, constitutional matters have been much more prominent in Canada than in most other countries. The following review of events from the early 1960s onwards will set the stage for the very close results of the 1995 referendum on separation. They are events that even after the referendum continue to play a major role in the political, economic, and social life in Canada.

The constitutional crisis of recent years were set in motion by the Quiet Revolution, which began in Quebec in the 1960s. The term of Premier Jean Lesage (1960-1966) saw a dramatic change. Prior to 1960, Quebec had been a very traditional society. The Catholic Church and the family were at the core of French-Canadian society; economic power was in the hands of English Canadians. In a very short time Quebec underwent a dramatic transformation into a secular, urban society with a modern educational system, public health and welfare programs, and a provincially controlled electric power system. A new sense of nationalism was used as a core ideology to justify the expanded role of the state. This nationalism was clearly expressed in the 1962 Liberal campaign slogan *maîtres chez nous* ("masters in our own house"). Economic and social reform would strengthen French culture. The state would replace the church at the heart of Quebec society. To pursue its agenda of renewal, the Quebec government began demanding, and receiving, more control over matters traditionally managed by the federal government.

As Quebec became more like the rest of North America in most other respects, language came to be its major distinguishing factor, assuming both a real and a symbolic role in the province's political future. English was the language of business in the province, and French-Canadian owners and managers were rare. In a series of legislative steps beginning in the 1960s, the provincial government moved to ensure that French became the language of business. The goal was stated clearly in the White Paper (that is, a government policy document) that preceded a major piece of language legislation, Bill 101, which was adopted in 1977:

> The Quebec that we wish to build will be essentially French. The fact that the majority of the population is French will be distinctly visible: at work, in communications, in the country. It is also a country where the traditional division of powers, especially in matters concerning the economy, will be modified: the use of French will not be generalized simply to hide the predominance of foreign powers over Francophones; this usage will accompany, will symbolize a reconquest by the Francophone majority of Quebec of the hold which returns to it on the levers of the economy. (cited in Cook, 1995:133)

By any measure, the Quiet Revolution has been a success. A large body of legislation now protects the French language in Quebec. Regulations requiring immigrant children to attend French-language schools and restrictions on the use of English on commercial signs have reinforced the dominant role of the French language in Quebec. Quebeckers have gained control over the economy and other major social institutions including culture, politics, and government.

While the transformation of Quebec was remarkably rapid, it was not rapid enough for some. Nationalist groups, which began to emerge in the 1960s, saw independence as the only means by which Quebec could fulfil its destiny. At the same time, another vision was offered by Quebeck-

Aboriginal leaders have played a prominent role in Canadian politics during the past decade. As questions of self-government, aboriginal rights, and land claims have been considered, two of the most important leaders have been Grand Chief Ovide Mercredi of the Assembly of First Nations and Elijah Harper, now a member of the federal parliament.

ers like Pierre Trudeau who felt that Quebec's aspirations could best be fulfilled within Canada. For Trudeau, cultural survival did not depend on political sovereignty; a strong federal government, which actively promoted bilingualism, was the best guarantee that French would survive in a predominantly English North America. As prime minister, Trudeau in 1969 brought in the Official Languages Act, which made the federal public service bilingual. This provided opportunities for francophones and helped to ensure that Canadians in all parts of the country could receive services in either language. The government also began to encourage French immersion programs in schools in English Canada.

These changes met with vociferous resistance among some English Canadians. Consider matters from the perspective of those opposed to bilingualism: as Quebec was becoming more autonomous and less bilingual, the need for bilingualism was being promoted throughout the rest of the country (Dyck, 1996). Unilingual anglophone civil servants had to learn French if they wished to be promoted and bilingualism was clearly a major part of the federal political agenda. Many felt that Quebec was blackmailing the federal government at the expense of the other provinces. With extreme Quebec nationalists on one side and those in the rest of Canada who were tired of "having French forced down their throats" on the other, the stage was set for several decades of constitutional debate (see Box 13.3).

ABORIGINAL SELF-GOVERNMENT

Canada's constitutional debate has focused on the role of our "two founding peoples"—the English and the French. Aboriginal peoples have strongly objected to this view of Canadian history. Anthropologist Olive Dickason, a Métis, has pointed out that when the Europeans first came to North America, fifty-five aboriginal First Nations were on the continent. Each of these nations had its own government, territory, culture, and language. But aboriginal objections to the notion of two founding peoples do not focus only

BOX 13.3 SOCIOLOGY AND LAW

Quebec and Constitutional Reform

Pierre Trudeau attempted several times to achieve a constitutional arrangement that was acceptable to Quebec and the other provinces. Among the critical issues were (1) the division of powers between the federal and provincial governments—most provinces, particularly Quebec, wanted more power decentralized to the provinces; (2) language rights, with Quebec wanting the power to limit individual rights on language matters; and (3) a formula for amending the constitution—Quebec wanted a veto over constitutional changes that might affect the French language and culture. The election of René Lévesque's separatist government in 1976 further complicated the already difficult negotiations over these matters. Following the failure of the Yes side in Quebec's first referendum on sovereignty-association in 1980, Trudeau repatriated Canada's constitution from Britain in 1982. While the 1982 Constitution Act, including the Charter of Rights, applied to Quebec, the government of Quebec had not consented to it.

In 1984 Brian Mulroney, another prime minister from Quebec, sought to modify the constitution to make it acceptable to Quebec. For his part, Quebec's Premier Robert Bourassa set out the following five demands for his province's inclusion:

- recognition of Quebec as a distinct society,
- increased control over immigration,
- participation in Supreme Court appointments,
- a veto on constitutional changes, and
- the ability to opt out of national programs operating in areas that fall within provincial jurisdiction.

Despite some reservations, in 1987 the provincial premiers all agreed to support these demands in the Meech Lake Accord. Prior to implementation, the Accord had to be passed by all provincial legislatures within a three-year period. A great deal of public debate took place during this period; many opponents were concerned the Accord gave Quebec and other provinces too much power, while others complained of insufficient consultation with the public, and that the interests of groups such as aboriginals and women had not been advanced by the Accord. Ultimately, the Accord failed when Elijah Harper, an aboriginal member of the Manitoba legislature, did not allow its passage. Harper opposed the Accord because it gave Quebec recognition as a distinct society and with it the special status that aboriginal people had sought for themselves. Aboriginal people were not opposed to Quebec's demands, but were frustrated because their own demands had been ignored.

The Mulroney government made a second attempt at bringing Quebec into the constitutional fold. Following a broad process of consultation, the provincial premiers once again met with their federal counterparts to discuss constitutional reform. The resulting Charlottetown Accord included four major components:

- a Canada clause that recognized Quebec as a distinct society,
- a reformed and elected Senate,
- recognition of the inherent right of aboriginals to self-government, and
- increased decentralization of federal powers.

The Accord was defeated in a national referendum in 1992. Dyck (1996) attributes the defeat as much to public hostility against politics and politicians as to the substance of the Accord. Many people felt that politicians should be more concerned with economic and social issues than with esoteric matters such as the federal–provincial division of powers and constitutional amending formulae. Ironically, the failure of the Charlottetown Accord meant that constitutional issues would remain on the national agenda for years to come.

Sources: Cook, 1995; and Dyck, 1996.

on the historical issue of which groups were here first. The more important concern is which groups will have political power in the future. Quebec claims a special status that entitles it to certain powers to govern its own people, and also certain rights within the federation such as having three Quebec members of the Supreme Court. Aboriginal peoples also claim a unique status based on their position as Canada's First Nations and have, because of that position, pursued their right to self-government.

While the issue of self-government is extremely complex, some background will help in understanding the broad issues involved. In 1763, the British government issued a royal proclamation that formed the basis for the negotiation of treaties with aboriginal groups. Without a background in European law, native peoples did not realize that title to the land had passed to the Crown. They were, however, still entitled to the use and benefit of that land through their "aboriginal title" (Boldt, 1993). Following Confederation, aboriginal peoples came under the control of the government. The mechanism for this control, the Indian Act, was passed in 1876 and gave government bureaucrats almost total control over native peoples. The Act even went so far as to define a "person" as "an individual other than an Indian" (Hamilton and Sinclair, 1991).

The consequences of the Indian Act were profound. For example, aboriginal children were forced to attend residential schools (which meant that generations of children were not raised with their families); traditional religious practices were restricted; native people did not fully control their own land and could not sell agricultural products off the reserve; and the government imposed a "pass system," which restricted the right of Native peoples to travel off their reserves. Native peoples did not have full voting rights in federal elections until 1960. As sociologist Menno Boldt has observed, contemporary "Indian powerlessness has its roots in Canada's Indian policies" (1993:xvii).

In the 1960s, the federal government began to review its policies concerning native peoples. A White Paper, tabled in 1969, proposed assimilation of native peoples. Treaties were to be dropped, reserves were to become like neighbouring nonaboriginal communities, and aboriginal rights and aboriginal land titles were to be discarded. The "aboriginal problem" would disappear, it was thought, if aboriginal people became, in Pierre Trudeau's words, "Canadians as all other Canadians" (Boldt, 1993). Reaction to this paper marked a watershed in aboriginal politics. A national campaign, which ultimately forced the government to drop its proposals, became a countrywide movement and the formation of several pan-Indian organizations, including the Assembly of First Nations, were formed (Hamilton and Sinclair, 1991). Rather than accepting the federal government's assimilationist model, aboriginal leaders embraced nationalism. Self-government, aboriginal rights, and land claims became the rallying points of the movement.

Some Indian leaders, particularly among the Mohawks, view their bands as separate nations that have sovereign control over their lands. However, most proponents of aboriginal self-government take the more limited view that their First Nations status gives them the "inherent" right to self-government within the Canadian federation (Boldt, 1993). They feel their status as Canada's first people, who were never conquered and who signed voluntary treaties with the Crown, entitles them to the right of self-determination and to protection of their culture and customs. These rights are not *granted* by the Canadian government, but are inherently theirs. On the other hand, the positions of the federal and the provincial governments have been that the right to self-determination could only be extended as powers delegated to aboriginal people by government through legislation or constitutional change. Further, the powers that would be granted by government would extend only to powers now held by municipal governments rather than the much broader powers sought by aboriginal peoples. It is difficult to predict where the current process of ending the colonial rule of aboriginals will lead. One major change will occur in 1999, when Inuit in the Northwest Territories take over government of the newly created Nunavut Territory, encompassing over 350,000 square kilometres of land in the Eastern Arctic. While the federal government accepted the inherent nature of aboriginals' right to self-government in 1995 and are committed to dismantling the Department of Indian Affairs and Northern Development, the future form of that government is not at all clear—not even among Aboriginal people themselves. Also, many problems must be solved along the way, including decisions about how the growing number of urban aboriginals will be included, the applicability of the Canadian Charter of Rights and Freedoms to aboriginal communities, and sources of funding for this new order of government. The possible separation of Quebec also creates some interesting issues. While the separatists argue strongly for their right to self-determination and their recognition as a "people," they do not accept that aboriginals in the resource-rich northern part of Quebec have the same right.

POLITICAL ISSUES FOR THE TWENTY-FIRST CENTURY

Will the governments of modern nation-states simply become obsolete in the twenty-first century? Although there has been some erosion of the powers of developed nations and an increase in the transnational nature of politics and the economy, scholars such as Paul Kennedy (1993:134) argue that

> the nation-state remains the primary locus of identity for most people; regardless of who their employer is and what they do for a living, individuals pay taxes to the state, are subject to its laws, serve (if need be) in its armed forces, and can travel only by having its passport. Moreover, as new challenges emerge ... people turn instinctively (at least in the democracies) to their own governments to find "solutions."

However, the nature of the new challenges facing many governments makes it increasingly difficult for them to control events. For example, how do nations deal with terrorism within their borders, such as the 1995 bombing in Oklahoma City that resulted in the deaths of more than 150 people, including many infants and children at an on-site day-care centre, and the terrorist attacks carried out in England by the Irish Republican Army? In the aftermath of tragedies such as these, governments' responsibility for protecting citizens but not violating their basic freedoms was widely examined in national debates that inevitably will continue into the twenty-first century.

Likewise, how are nations to deal with the proliferation of arms and nuclear weapons in other countries? Will some of the missiles and warheads fall into the hands of terrorists? What should be done with the masses of nuclear waste being produced? No easy answers are forthcoming. International agencies, such as the United Nations, the World Bank, and the International Monetary Fund, face many of the same problems that individual governments do—including severe economic constraints and extreme differences of opinion among participants. Without some form of effective international control, it will be impossible to ensure that future generations are protected from environmental threats such as global warming, and water and air pollution.

Another issue that will continue to trouble many countries is nationalism. Can Canada make an accommodation with Quebec? How will European countries adapt to the loss of national powers within the European Community? Will groups continue to make war to support their nationalistic aspirations? (Some of the more troubling aspects of nationalism are discussed in Box 13.4.) The issues surrounding nationalism must be resolved if we are to continue to move toward the dream of a peaceful world.

The twenty-first century will be a challenging one for politicians and for the citizens they represent. Can countries like Russia and Mexico, with their very weak democracies, cope with the conflicts inherent in the transition to a market

BOX 13.4 SOCIOLOGY IN GLOBAL PERSPECTIVE

Nationalism Around the World

Historian Ramsay Cook has observed that "Everyone belongs somewhere. Yet much of the conflict in the history ... of mankind has been about who belongs where" (Cook, 1995:9). Cook goes on to discuss the role of nationalism in justifying one's place in the world. Nationalism, he says, is a "doctrine asserting that humanity is naturally divided into groups with common characteristics and that by virtue of those collective traits they have a right to exercise control—sovereignty—over the particular place" (1995:9). Most Canadians have heard Lucien Bouchard and other Quebec separatists state that the Québécois constitute a "people" who must have sovereignty over their territory if their destiny is to be fulfilled. The desire for separation from Canada in Quebec is a manifestation of nationalism.

Quebec nationalists are not the only people trying to take control of what they see as their territory. Punjabis in India, Tamils in Sri Lanka, and Palestinians in the Middle East are just a few of the hundreds of nationalist groups active in the world today. Authority or justification for their claims is usually given to or provided by God, language, culture, or history. However, what ultimately decides things is power. This power may be political—the Czech Republic and Slovakia separated after a democratic vote—but more typically, it is military, as with the Iraqis and the Turks who in this way prevented the Kurds from establishing a separate homeland.

Nationalism can be a unifying force—many countries, including Germany and Italy, were formed in the late nineteenth century though the unification of smaller states with similar language and cultural backgrounds. Diverse groups were brought together under a common flag. However, nationalism can also be divisive—and often deadly. Societies based on national identity can easily become intolerant to those who do not share the same ethnicity, religion, or culture. Millions have died at the hands of oppressive nationalists. Historically, most wars have been between countries; today they are almost all *within* countries.

Successful nationalist movements often carry with them the seeds of their own destruction. Yugoslavia is a case in point. Prior to 1989, the diverse elements of the country had been held together by the Communist regime. However, when the communist domination of Eastern Europe ended, the Croats and Muslims in Yugoslavia decided to break away from the Serb-dominated Communist government and created the independent states of Croatia and Bosnia-Herzegovina. However, after years of living within the common boundaries of Yugoslavia, each of the new countries had significant ethnic minorities within its borders. These minorities in turn claimed their independence and the ensuing carnage has cost hundreds of thousands of lives and has added the words "ethnic cleansing" to our vocabulary. Ethnic cleansing is a chilling final solution to the minority problem—you simply kill or expel every man, woman, and child of a different religious or cultural background who has the misfortune of remaining within your territory.

War has become a means of expressing national identities, and grievances dating back hundreds or even thousands of years have become the justification for brutal mass murder. As large nation-states become less relevant in an era of globalization and homogenization, they lose their ability to unify. People search for a collective identity at the local level. Unfortunately, this identity is often grounded on exclusion—those who are not like us are not tolerated.

Where this will lead is uncertain. It is difficult to imagine the nationalist process continuing indefinitely. Fewer than 200 countries now exist; if every linguistic group became a nation, there would be about 8,000 countries.

Source: Cook, 1995.

economy? Will politicians around the globe be able to manage the changes that lie ahead when actions occurring elsewhere may profoundly affect their cultures, economies, and political systems? Even countries that wish to close themselves off to outside influences must still be involved in global trade and will be unable to control what is seen, read, and heard by their citizens because of the communications revolution. Can they restore people's faith in the ability of the political system to deal with issues such as jobs, crime, and social services before voters become too cynical and critical to care which party manages their country?

CHAPTER REVIEW

Power is the ability of persons or groups to carry out their will even when opposed by others. Politics is the social institution through which power is acquired and exercised by some people or groups. Government is the formal organization that has the legal and political authority to regulate the relationships among members in a society. A strong relationship between politics and power exists in all countries.

- Most leaders seek to legitimize their power through authority, so that those who are governed accept the legitimacy of those doing the governing. Max Weber identified three types of authority. Charismatic authority is power legitimized on the basis of the leader's exceptional personal qualities, which inspire loyalty and obedience from followers. Traditional authority is power legitimized by respect for custom and is often found in patriarchal or patrimonial systems. Rational-legal authority is power legitimized by rationally established rules and procedures and is the basis of the political system in Canada.
- There are four main types of contemporary political systems. In a monarchy, one person is the ruler of the nation, although in constitutional monarchies, the royalty serve as symbolic rulers. In authoritarian systems, rulers tolerate little or no public opposition and generally cannot be removed from office by legal means. In totalitarian systems, the state seeks to regulate all aspects of society and to monopolize all societal resources in order to control completely both public and private life. In a democratic system, the powers of government are derived from the consent of all the people.
- There are two key perspectives on how power is distributed in Canada: pluralist, which is aligned with the functionalist perspective, and elitist, which is aligned with the conflict perspective. According to the pluralist model, power is widely dispersed throughout many competing interest groups. People influence policy by voting, joining special interest groups and political campaigns, and forming new groups. According to the elite model, power is concentrated in a small group of elites, while the masses are relatively powerless. The elites possess greater resources than the masses, and public policy reflects their preferences. The power elite is made up of influential business leaders, key government leaders, and the military.
- The vast governmental bureaucracy is a major source of power. The bureaucracy cannot always be tightly controlled by elected politicians because bureaucrats have a high degree of technical knowledge and permanent employment in government.

KEY TERMS

authoritarianism **482**
authority **478**
charismatic authority **478**
democracy **483**
elite model **488**
government **476**
monarchy **482**
pluralist model **485**
political party **492**
political socialization **494**
political sociology **477**
politics **475**
power **477**
power elite **489**
rational-legal authority **479**
routinization of charisma **478**
special interest groups **485**
state **476**
totalitarianism **483**
traditional authority **479**

QUESTIONS FOR ANALYSIS AND UNDERSTANDING

1. What are the key assumptions of charismatic authority, traditional authority, and rational-legal authority?
2. What elements of the Canadian political system reinforce the notion of a pluralist model power? What elements reinforce the elite model?
3. What influences an individual's political attitudes and party affiliation?
4. How does the Canadian government bureaucracy both enhance and impede the goals of democracy?

QUESTIONS FOR CRITICAL THINKING

1. Who is ultimately responsible for decisions and policies that are made in a democracy such as Canada: the people or their elected representatives?
2. How would you design a research project that studies the relationship between campaign contributions to elected representatives and their subsequent voting records? What would be your hypothesis? What kinds of data would you need to gather? How would you gather accurate data?
3. How does your school (or workplace) reflect a pluralist or elite model of power and decision making?
4. How is it possible to be a liberal on some issues and a conservative on others? Do you tend to be both liberal and conservative?

SUGGESTED READINGS

These books examine politics from a sociological perspective:

G. William Domhoff. *The Power Elite and the State: How Policy Is Made in America.* New York: Aldine de Gruyter, 1990.

Anthony M. Orum. *Introduction to Political Sociology: The Social Anatomy of the Body Politic* (3rd ed.). Englewood Cliffs, N.J.: Prentice-Hall, 1988.

In-depth information about politics and government is provided in this political science text:

Rand Dyck. *Canadian Politics: Critical Approaches* (2nd ed.). Toronto: Nelson Canada, 1996.

Two books that are helpful in understanding aboriginal political issues are:

Boldt, Menno. *Surviving as Indians: The Challenge of Self-Government.* Toronto: University of Toronto Press, 1993.

Olive Dickason. *Canada's First Nations.* Toronto: McClelland and Stewart, 1992.

For a good overview of Quebec separatism and related issues, you can read:

Ramsay Cook. *Canada, Quebec and the Uses of Nationalism* (2nd ed.). Toronto: McClelland and Stewart, 1995.

Marcel Rioux. *Quebec in Question.* Toronto: James Lorimer and Company, 1971.

Chapter 14

FAMILIES AND INTIMATE RELATIONSHIPS

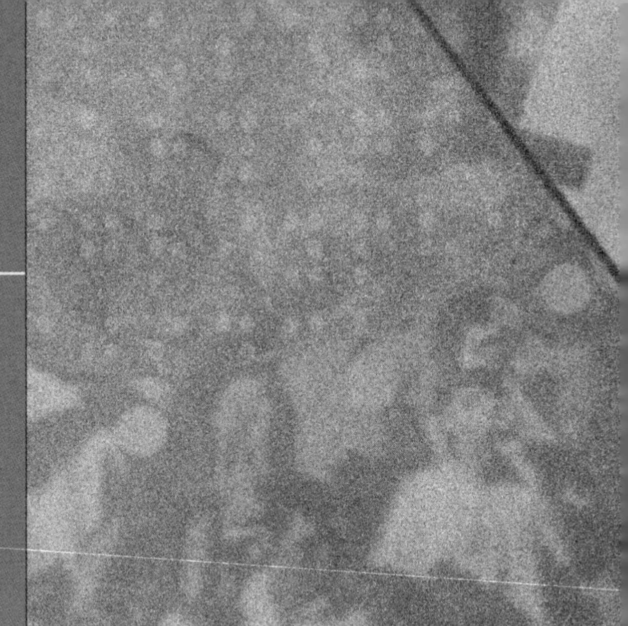

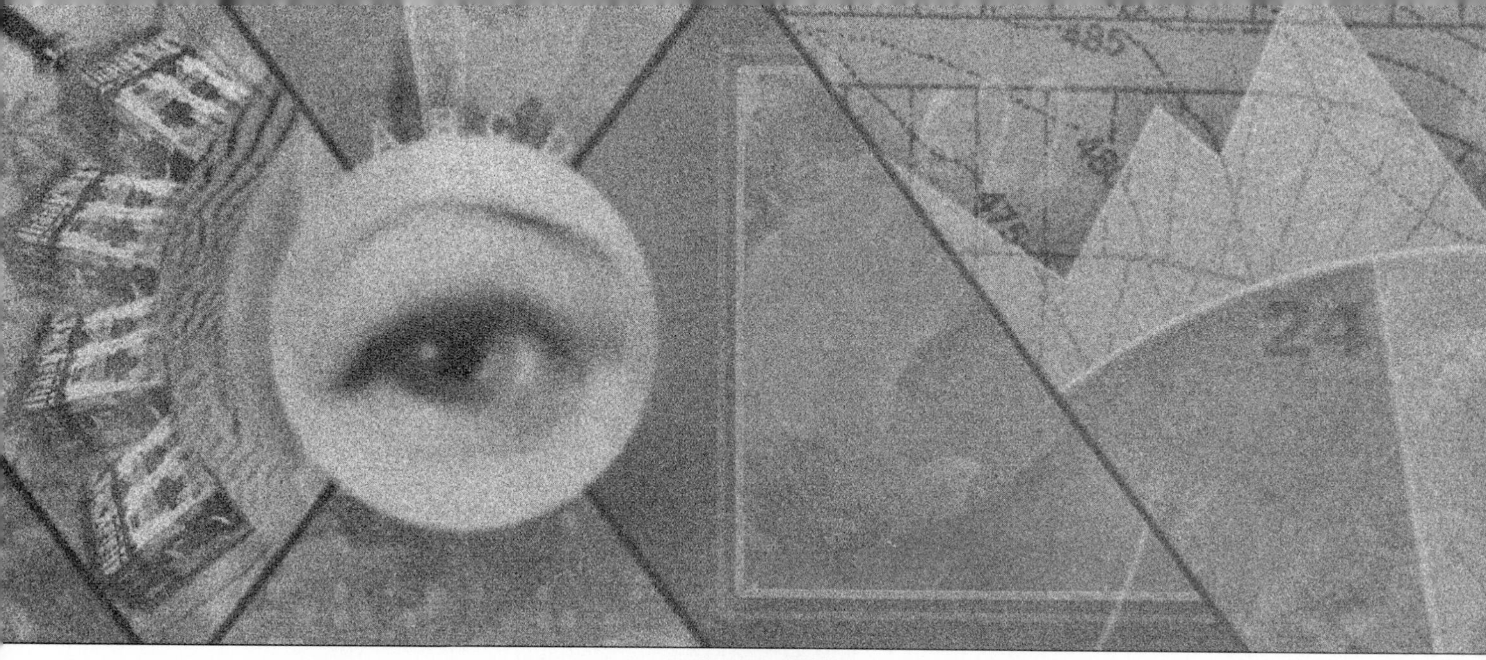

There was a time not long ago when wife battering was a laughing matter for some of Canada's political leaders. On May 12, 1982, when the issue of wife battering was raised in the House of Commons and described as a serious crime suffered by one out of ten Canadian women, laughter erupted throughout the House (MacLeod, 1987:3). It is hard to understand this reaction when we consider the following account from a survivor of wife abuse:

I couldn't believe my husband had hit me. I just kept asking, is this the same man who loves me so much that he can't stand it if another man talks to me? It was really easy for me to accept his explanation that he'd had a hard day at work and a little too much to drink. I couldn't see anything else without having to ask if he really did love me, and that was just too painful. It wasn't until much later, years of violence later, that I could see that the way he loved me—his jealousy, his possessiveness—were also part of the violence. (MacLeod, 1994:224)

Consider, too, another woman's comments on the power of wife abuse to degrade women:

The thing that's most hurting for me is the way he makes me feel so dirty, so filthy. He treats me like a dog, worse even. He tells me I'm ugly and worthless. He spits on me. It's not enough to hit me and kick me. He spits on me. Sometimes I think the hitting is better than being made to feel so low. (MacLeod, 1987:12)

The experiences of these women are not isolated incidents. In 1981 the Canadian Advisory Council on the Status of Women released its first report on wife abuse, entitled *Wife Battering in Canada: The Vicious Circle*. Its author, Linda MacLeod, estimated that each year a million Canadian women are beaten by their husbands. These beatings involve women being "kicked, punched, beaten, burned, threatened, knifed and shot, not by strangers who break into their houses or accost them on dark streets, but by husbands and lovers they've spent many years with—years with good times as well as bad" (MacLeod, 1980:6). The results of the Violence Against Women Survey showed that, in 1993, 29 percent of all women who had ever been

Despite the idealized image of "the family," North American families have undergone many changes in the twentieth century, as exemplified by the "divorce" of 12-year-old Gregory Kingsley from his mother. Here Gregory leaves the courthouse after an Orlando, Florida, judge approved his request.

married or had lived with a man in a common-law relationship had experienced at least one episode of violence by a husband or a live-in partner. This figure represents over 2.6 million Canadian women (Johnson, 1996a:136).

As the narratives at the beginning of the chapter demonstrate, wife abuse involves vicious attacks, not only against one's body, but against one's mind and image of self. Yet these attacks occur within the most intimate and important of all social institutions—the family. Many families experience a wide variety of additional problems, including high rates of divorce, teen pregnancy, substance abuse, and child abuse and neglect. Family life, which is central to our existence, is, therefore, far more complicated than the idealized image of families found in the media and used as examples in many political discussions. While some families provide their members with love, warmth, and satisfying emotional experiences, others may be hazardous to the individual's physical and mental well-being. Because of this dichotomy in family life, sociologists have described families as both a "haven in a heartless world" (Lasch, 1977) and a "cradle of violence" (Gelles and Straus, 1988).

In this chapter, we examine the diversity and complexity of families as we approach the twenty-first century. In the process, we will focus on wife abuse and other problems facing families today. Before reading on, test your knowledge about wife abuse by taking the quiz in Box 14.1.

QUESTIONS AND ISSUES

Why is it difficult to define family?

How do marriage patterns vary across cultures?

What are the key assumptions of functionalist, conflict/feminist, and interactionist perspectives on families?

What significant trends affect many Canadian families today?

BOX 14.1 SOCIOLOGY AND EVERYDAY LIFE

How Much Do You Know About Wife Abuse in Canada?

TRUE	FALSE	
T	F	1. The extent of wife abuse in Canada has been exaggerated by the media.
T	F	2. Men batter their wives because of poor impulse control.
T	F	3. A woman who has witnessed violence against her mother is more likely to be involved in an abusive relationship.
T	F	4. Women are more likely to be killed by a stranger than by a family member.
T	F	5. It is illegal in Canada for a husband to rape his wife.
T	F	6. It is rare for women to be assaulted by their intimate partners when they are pregnant.
T	F	7. Wife abuse occurs primarily in the lower classes.
T	F	8. Women "ask for it": they drive men to commit violence against them.
T	F	9. One of the strongest risk factors of wife abuse is the age of the couple.
T	F	10. In cases of domestic assault the victim is responsible for deciding if the abuser will be charged.

Answers on page 512

Why do some analysts argue that the family as we know it will become extinct in the twenty-first century?

FAMILIES IN GLOBAL PERSPECTIVE

For many years, a standard sociological definition of *family* has been a group of people who are related to one another by bonds of blood, marriage, or adoption and who live together, form an economic unit, and bear and raise children (Benokraitis, 1993). Many people believe that this definition should not be expanded—that social approval should not be extended to other relationships simply because the persons in those relationships wish to consider themselves a family. However, others challenge this definition because it simply does not match the reality of family life in contemporary society (Lynn, 1996; Vanier Institute of the Family, 1994). Today's families include many types of living arrangements and relationships, including single-parent households, unmarried couples, lesbian and gay couples, and multiple-generation families that include grandparents, parents, and children, for example. A number of legal challenges have been launched in Canada regarding the definitions of marriage and spouse by same-sex couples who, because they are

BOX 14.1 SOCIOLOGY AND EVERYDAY LIFE

Answers to the Sociology Quiz on Wife Abuse in Canada

TRUE	FALSE	
T	**F**	1. *False.* Wife abuse is widespread in Canada. According to the 1993 Violence Against Women Survey, 29 percent of married women have been physically or sexually assaulted by their partners.
T	**F**	2. *False.* Most wife abusers even when drunk avoid hitting their wives in the company of others, avoid leaving visible bruises on them, and assault their wives when their children are asleep. This suggests excellent impulse control.
T	F	3. *True.* Research indicates that women who witness violence against their mothers are more likely to become involved in abusive relationships.
T	**F**	4. *False.* The risk of being killed by a spouse is nine times greater than that of being killed by a stranger. This finding led one researcher to conclude that "intimacy can be dangerous to one's health."
T	F	5. *True.* As a result of revisions to the law in 1986, it is now illegal for a husband to force his wife to have sex.
T	**F**	6. *False.* According to the 1993 Violence Against Women Survey, women frequently report being punched or kicked in the stomach by their husbands when they are pregnant.
T	**F**	7. *False.* Wife abuse crosses all socioeconomic lines, although it is more common among people at the very bottom of the income scale.
T	**F**	8. *False.* Stress and conflict are part of any relationship. Violence is never an appropriate way to solve a problem, and no one deserves to be beaten.
T	F	9. *True.* Young women aged 18 to 24 are four times more likely to be victims of wife assault. The same pattern holds for violent partners—men aged 18 to 24 show the highest rates of violence.
T	**F**	10. *False.* Once the police learn of the offence, they decide if charges will be laid. Many Canadian jurisdictions have implemented a "zero tolerance" policy, which directs that charges be laid in all domestic violence cases.

Sources: Based on Rodgers and Kong, 1996; Johnson, 1996; DeKeseredy and Hinch, 1991.

not legally married, have been denied the rights and benefits accorded to other families. To accurately reflect the reality of family life, we need a more encompassing definition of what constitutes a family. Accordingly, we will define ***families* as relationships in which people live together with commitment, form an economic unit and care for any young, and consider their identity to be significantly attached to the group.** Sexual expression and parent–children relationships are a part of most, but not all, family relationships (based on Benokraitis, 1993; Lamanna and Riedmann, 1994).

In our study of families, we will use our sociological imagination to see how our personal experiences are related to the larger happenings in our society. At the microlevel, each of us has our own "biography," based on our experience

While the relationship between a husband and wife is based on legal ties, relationships between parents and children may be established either by blood ties or by legal ties.

within a family; at the macrolevel, our families are embedded in a specific social context that has a major impact on them (Aulette, 1994). We will examine the institution of the family at both of these levels, starting with family structure and characteristics.

FAMILY STRUCTURE AND CHARACTERISTICS

In preindustrial societies, the primary form of social organization is through kinship ties. ***Kinship*** **refers to a social network of people based on common ancestry, marriage, or adoption.** Through kinship networks, people cooperate so that they can acquire the basic necessities of life, including food and shelter. Kinship systems also can serve as a means by which property is transferred, goods are produced and distributed, and power is allocated.

In industrialized societies, other social institutions fulfil some of the functions previously taken care of by the kinship network. For example, political systems provide a structure of social control

THE FAR SIDE By GARY LARSON
"Bob and Ruth! Come on in .... Have you met Russell and Bill, our 1.5 children?"

The Far Side © 1988; Distributed by Universal Press Syndicate. Reprinted with permission.

and authority, and economic systems are responsible for the production and distribution of goods and services. Consequently, families in industrialized societies serve fewer and more specialized purposes than do families in preindustrial societies. Contemporary families are responsible primarily for regulating sexual activity, socializing children, and providing affection and companionship for family members.

FAMILIES OF ORIENTATION AND PROCREATION During our lifetime, many of us will be members of two different types of families—a family of orientation and a family of procreation. The ***family of orientation*** **is the family into which a person is born and in which early socialization usually takes place**. While most people are related to members of their family of orientation by blood ties, those who are adopted have a legal tie that is patterned after a blood relationship (Aulette, 1994). The ***family of procreation*** **is the family a person forms by having or adopting children** (Benokraitis, 1993). Both legal and blood ties are found in most families of procreation. The relationship between a husband and wife is based on legal ties; however, the relationship between a parent and child may be based on either blood ties or legal ties, depending on whether the child has been adopted (Aulette, 1994).

Some sociologists have emphasized that "family of orientation" and "family of procreation" do not encompass all types of contemporary families. Instead, as Kath Weston (1991) notes, many gay men and lesbians have *families we choose*—social arrangements that include intimate relationships between couples and close familial relationships among other couples and other adults and children. According to sociologist Judy Root Aulette (1994), "families we choose" include both blood ties and legal ties, but they also include fictive kin-persons who are not actually related by blood but are accepted as family members. For example, fictive kin are included in this woman's plans for procreation:

> When I go to have a kid, I'm not gonna have my sisters as godparents. I'm gonna have people that are around me, that are gay. No, I call on my inner family—my community, or whatever—to help me with my life. So there's definitely a family. And you're building it, it keeps getting bigger and bigger. (quoted in Weston, 1991:108)

In her study of lesbian and gay families, Weston found fictive kin to be part of an extended family network.

EXTENDED AND NUCLEAR FAMILIES Sociologists distinguish between extended and nuclear families based on the number of generations that live within a household. An ***extended family*** **is a family unit composed of relatives in addition to parents and children who live in the same household.** These families often include grandparents, uncles, aunts, or other relatives who live in close proximity to the parents and children, making it possible for family members to share resources. In horticultural and agricultural societies, extended fami-

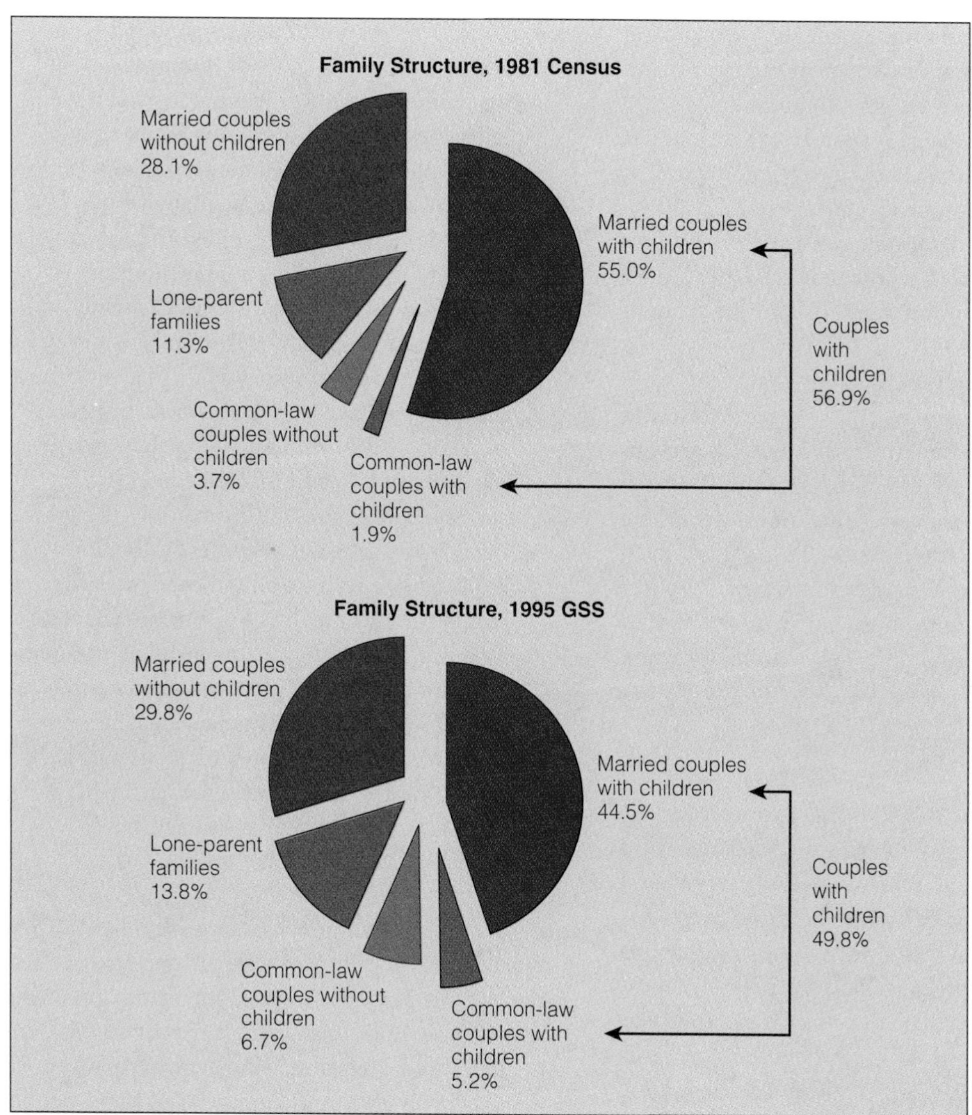

FIGURE 14.1

Family Structure

Source: Based on 1981 Census and 1995 General Social Survey. Reproduced by authority of the Minister of Industry, 1996, Statistics Canada, from *General Social Survey*, Cat. no. 11-612, 1995.

lies are extremely important; having a large number of family members participate in food production may be essential for survival. Today, extended family patterns are found in Latin America, Africa, Asia, and some parts of Eastern and Southern Europe (Busch, 1990).

A ***nuclear family* is a family composed of one or two parents and their dependent children, all of whom live apart from other relatives.** A traditional definition specifies that a nuclear family is made up of a "couple" and their dependent children; however, this definition became outdated as a significant shift occurred in the family structure. As shown in Figure 14.1, in 1995, about 50 percent of all households were composed of married couples with children under the age of 18. The second-largest family type, at 29 percent, were married couples without children living at home. This group consisted of childless couples and couples whose children no longer lived at home (empty-nesters) (Vanier Institute of the Family, 1994).

Nuclear families are smaller than they were twenty years ago; whereas the average family size in 1971 was 3.7 persons, in 1991 it was 3.1 persons (Statistics Canada, 1995). This decrease has been attributed to declining fertility rates, economic factors (i.e., the cost of having children, an indicator of which is the increased number of households in which both husband and wife work outside of the home), and delayed childbearing.

MARRIAGE PATTERNS

Across cultures, families are characterized by different forms of marriage. ***Marriage* is a legally recognized and/or socially approved arrangement between two or more individuals that carries certain rights and obligations and usually involves sexual activity.** In most societies, marriage involves a mutual commitment by each partner, and linkages between two individuals and families are publicly demonstrated.

In Canada, the only legally sanctioned form of marriage is ***monogamy*—a marriage between two partners of the opposite sex.** For some people, marriage is a lifelong commitment that ends only with the death of a partner. In long-term monogamous relationships, losing a marital partner may be the most difficult experience of a person's life. For example, author Robert Kotlowitz (1994:85–86) described the day that he and his wife of forty-three years learned that she had inoperable cancer:

> That evening, we sit in the living room together, comfortably sipping vodka while we talk. Dinner will wait. Perhaps we will eat later, perhaps not. There is suddenly a lot to say to each other, a lot of questions about her benefits, medical insurance, sick leave, and workload; and questions about family burial plots. She raises the last issue without perceptible strain—like so many of our friends, we have long avoided the subject.
>
> We talk on, raising the questions as we have done for the past two weeks while waiting for the diagnosis. But tonight is different; tonight we are finally at grips with the indisputable fact—not guesswork or projections or wishful thinking—that has arrived in our lives today with biblical force, like a sudden rain of fire and brimstone. It has been working on us relentlessly for hours, although we try to pretend otherwise. In fact, sitting in our living room now, face to face, we are unashamedly tearful as the questions and answers continue; but my wife's voice remains as even, as level, as an empty sheet of white paper on which she might be inscribing the exact nature of her awful plight. I marvel at her calm, as I have marveled for 43 years.

Members of some religious groups believe that marriage is literally "forever"; if one spouse dies, the surviving spouse is precluded from marrying anyone else. For others, marriage is a commitment of indefinite duration. Through a pattern of marriage, divorce, and remarriage, some people practice *serial monogamy*—a succession of marriages in which a person has several spouses over a lifetime but is legally married to only one person at a time.

***Polygamy* is the concurrent marriage of a person of one sex with two or more members of the opposite sex** (G. Marshall, 1994). The most prevalent form of polygamy is ***polygyny*—the concurrent marriage of one man with two or more women.** Polygyny has been practised in a number of societies, including by some in parts of Europe until the Middle Ages. More recently, some marriages in Islamic societies in Africa and Asia have been polygynous; however, the cost of providing for multiple wives and numerous children makes the practice impossible for all but the wealthiest men. In addition, because roughly equal numbers of women and men live in these areas, this nearly balanced sex ratio tends to limit polygyny.

Polygyny brings prestige to the men through their wives' work and the children they produce. Some researchers assert that women also benefit from polygyny because agricultural and domestic work can be shared among wives, and educated women can have children but remain independent from their husbands (Mackintosh, 1979). Others argue that polygyny is an oppressive practice, existing only for the purpose of men's sexual advantage and the ongoing oppression of women (see Thiam, 1986).

The second type of polygamy is ***polyandry*—marriage of one woman with two or more men.** Polyandry is very rare; when it does occur it usually takes place in societies in which men greatly outnumber women because of high rates of female infanticide. Polyandry often involves the marriage of a woman to two or more brothers. For example, among the Nayar and Toda in South India in the late nineteenth century, a woman who married a man also became the wife of his brothers (even those born after the marriage). Everyone lived in the same household and rotated sexual privileges. The oldest brother was considered to be the legal father of the first two or three children; other brothers became the legal fathers of subsequent children. Even after marriage, women were considered members of their mother's household, and the children's lineage was traced through the mother's side of the family (Cassidy and Lee, 1989).

DESCENT AND INHERITANCE

Even though a variety of marital patterns exist across cultures, virtually all forms of marriage establish a system of descent so that kinship can be determined and inheritance rights established. In preindustrial societies, kinship is usually traced through one parent (unilineally). The most common pattern of unilineal descent is ***patrilineal descent*—a system of tracing descent through the father's side of the family.** Patrilineal systems are set up in such a manner that a legitimate son inherits his father's property and sometimes his position upon the father's death. In nations such as India, where boys are seen as permanent patrilineal family members while girls are seen only as temporary family members, girls tend to be considered more expendable than boys (O'Connell, 1994). Even with the less common pattern of ***matrilineal descent*—a system of tracing descent through the mother's side of the family**—women may not control property. However, inheritance of property and position usually is traced from the maternal uncle (mother's brother) to his nephew (mother's son). In some cases, mothers may pass on their property to daughters.

By contrast, in industrial societies, kinship usually is traced through both parents (bilineally). The most common form is ***bilateral descent*—a system of tracing descent through both the mother's and father's sides of the family.** This pattern is used in Canada for the purpose of determining kinship and inheritance rights; however, children typically take the father's last name.

POWER AND AUTHORITY IN FAMILIES

Descent and inheritance rights are intricately linked with patterns of power and authority in families. The most prevalent forms of familial power and authority are patriarchy, matriarchy, and egalitarianism. A ***patriarchal family* is a family structure in which authority is held by the eldest male (usually the father).** The male authority figure acts as head of the household and holds power and authority over the women and children as well as over other males. A ***matriarchal family* is a family structure in which authority is held by the eldest female (usually the mother).** In this case, the female authority figure acts as head of the household. Although there has been a great deal of discussion about matriarchal families, scholars have found no historical evidence to indicate that true matriarchies ever existed.

The most prevalent pattern of power and authority in families is patriarchy. Across cultures, men are the primary (and often sole) decision makers regarding domestic, economic, and social concerns facing the family. The existence of patriarchy may give men a sense of power over their own lives, but it also can create an atmosphere in which some men feel greater freedom to abuse women and children (Daly and Chesney-Lind, 1988). An excerpt from a letter comedian Louie Anderson wrote to his deceased father in hopes of overcoming the anger and sadness he felt about the abuse in his family describes this kind of behaviour:

> You know, my earliest memory in life is when I was five years old. I was hiding under the kitchen table with [a brother] while you were hitting Mom. You slapped her across the face and called her a whore. Your voice thundered through our tiny duplex like a violent storm. I remember [another brother] bolted in the front door and pinned you against the refrigerator. "Don't ever, ever, do that again!" he yelled right into your droopy face.
>
> The rest of us watched in horror from the other room. I don't know what frightened us more. That you hit Mom. Or that, once you sobered up and realized what had happened, you'd get drunk and angry all over again. (quoted in David, 1994:98–99)

Anderson and his mother and ten brothers and sisters constantly lived in fear of one man—the father.

While many people live in families where love and mutual concern are expressed every day, other people experience frightening, and sometimes violent, encounters with their "loved ones" on a routine basis. According to some feminist scholars and journalists, hostility and violence perpetrated by men against women and children is the result of patriarchal attitudes, economic hardship, rigid gender roles, and societal acceptance of aggression (Johnson, 1996; Lynn and O'Neill, 1995; MacLeod, 1987; Smith, 1996). Women also can perpetrate violence against family members; however, the majority of domestic violence cases involve male perpetrators and female victims (Johnson, 1996; DeKeseredy, 1996).

An ***egalitarian family*** **is a family structure in which both partners share power and authority equally**. Recently, a trend toward more egalitarian relationships has been evident in a number of countries as women have sought changes in their legal status and increased educational and employment opportunities. Some degree of economic independence makes it possible for women to delay marriage or to terminate a problematic marriage (Richardson, 1996). Among gay and lesbian couples, power and authority issues also are important. While some analysts suggest that legalizing marriage among gay couples would reproduce more egalitarian relationships, others argue that such marriages would reproduce inequalities in power and authority found in conventional heterosexual relationships (see Aulette, 1994).

RESIDENTIAL PATTERNS

Residential patterns are interrelated with the authority structure and method of tracing descent in families. ***Patrilocal residence*** **refers to the custom of a married couple living in the same household (or community) as the husband's family**. Across cultures, patrilocal residency is most common. Few societies have residential patterns known as ***matrilocal residence*—the custom of a married couple living in the same household (or community) as the wife's parents**. In industrialized nations such as Canada, most couples hope to live in a ***neolocal residence*—the custom of a married couple living in their own residence apart from both the husband's and the wife's parents**. For many couples, however, economic conditions, availability of housing, and other considerations may make neolocal residency impossible, at least initially.

To this point, we have examined a variety of marriage and family patterns found around the world. Even with the diversity of these patterns, most people's behaviour is shaped by cultural rules pertaining to endogamy and exogamy. ***Endogamy* refers to cultural norms prescribing that people marry within their own social group or category.** In Canada most people practice endogamy: they marry people who come from the same social class, racial-ethnic group, religious affiliation, and other categories considered important within their own social group. ***Exogamy* refers to cultural norms prescribing that people marry outside their own social group or category**. However, certain types of exogamy may result in social ridicule or ostracism from the group, such as marriage outside one's own racial-ethnic group or religion. For example, although the number of interracial marriages in Canada is growing as the country becomes more diverse, they are still viewed negatively by members of some groups (Ramu, 1993). Regardless of the exact patterns followed by families around the world, virtually all share certain common purposes and may have somewhat similar consequences for individual members.

PERSPECTIVES ON FAMILIES

The ***sociology of family* is the subdiscipline of sociology that attempts to describe and explain patterns of family life and variations in family structure.** Functionalist perspectives emphasize the functions that families perform at the macrolevel of society, while conflict and feminist perspectives focus on families as a primary source of social inequality. By contrast, interactionists examine microlevel interactions that are integral to the roles of different family members.

FUNCTIONALIST PERSPECTIVES

Functionalists emphasize the importance of the family in maintaining the stability of society and the well-being of individuals. According to Emile Durkheim, marriage is a microcosmic replica of the larger society; both marriage and society involve a mental and moral fusion of physically distinct individuals (Lehmann, 1994). Durkheim also believed that a division of labour contributed to greater efficiency in all areas of life—including marriages and families—even though he acknowledged that this division imposed significant limitations on some people.

Talcott Parsons was a key figure in developing a functionalist model of the family. According to Parsons (1955), the husband/father fulfils the *instrumental role* (meeting the family's economic needs, making important decisions, and providing leadership) while the wife/mother fulfils the *expressive role* (running the household, caring for children, and meeting the emotional needs of family members).

Contemporary functionalist perspectives on families derive their foundation from Durkheim and Parsons. Division of labour makes it possible for families to fulfil a number of functions that no other institution can perform as effectively. In advanced industrial societies, families serve four key functions:

1. *Sexual regulation*. Families are expected to regulate the sexual activity of their members and thus control reproduction so that it occurs within specific boundaries. At the macrolevel, incest taboos prohibit sexual contact or marriage between certain relatives. For example, virtually all societies prohibit sexual relations between parents and their children and between brothers and sisters. However, some societies exclude remotely related individuals such as second and third cousins from such prohibitions. Sexual regulation of family members by the family is supposed to protect the *principle of legitimacy*—the belief that all children should have a socially and legally recognized father (Malinowski, 1964/1929).
2. *Socialization*. Parents and other relatives are responsible for teaching children the neces-

BOX 14.2 SOCIOLOGY AND MEDIA

The Simpsons: An All-American Family

In one episode of "The Simpsons," the popular animated television series, Marge Simpson (the wife and mother) reads a "checklist for family problems" to Homer (the husband and father):

MARGE: Do you need a beer to fall asleep?
HOMER: Thank you, that'd be nice.
MARGE: Do you ever hide beer around the house?

[Homer removes a beer from the top of the commode in the bathroom.]

MARGE: Do you ever fantasize that you are someone else?

[Homer looks in the mirror, humming the tune "Can-Can."]

MARGE: Homie, I'd like you to do something for me. I want you to give up beer for a month.
HOMER: You got it! No deer for a month.
MARGE: Did you say "beer" or "deer"?
HOMER: Deer.

In this exchange, Marge represents the dutiful working-class wife who hopes to get her husband to drink less. Homer blissfully ignores her hints and suggestions because he finds that beer relaxes him after a stressful day at work. On other occasions, Homer talks with Bart (the son) and Lisa (the oldest daughter) about his drinking:

HOMER: ... Daddy has to go to a beer-drinking contest today.
BART: Think you'll win?
HOMER: Son, when you participate in sporting events, it's not whether you win or lose, it's how drunk you get.
BART: Gotcha. ...

The fictional Simpson family is one of the most popular working-class families of all time; however, several decades ago, "The Simpsons" could never have been shown on television. The earliest family comedies (such as "Father Knows Best," "The Adventures of Ozzie and Harriet," and "Leave It to Beaver") idealized the white middle-class nuclear family and depicted the father as a *superdad.* The children were respectful as compared with Bart, who says exactly what is on his mind. These early shows offered endless images of "adoring and endearing couples who were blessed with squeaky-clean kids" (Medved, 1992:129); they created a powerful and lasting vision of how the nuclear family is *supposed to be.* Unlike Homer Simpson, the male characters in 1950s and 1960s family shows were never shown consuming alcoholic beverages.

Beginning in the late 1960s and early 1970s, some situation comedies based on working-class families depicted fathers quite differently from the superdads of the middle-class. Working-class fathers were more likely to have a few beers or to talk about being "hung over" from their "night out with the boys." Working-class fathers routinely were depicted as inept or made the butt of jokes. As for Homer Simpson, his bumbling but well-intentioned behaviour has endeared him to many viewers, who feel that his character captures the essence of many men's existence. Similarly, many women identify with the overworked and underappreciated Marge Simpson who, even as a cartoon character, realistically shows that raising a family can be a tough but rewarding experience. "The Simpsons" reflects a working-class, "we-stick-together-and-survive-on-our-own" ethic.

Sources: Based on Cantor and Cantor, 1992; Coontz, 1992; Duffy, 1992; and Medved, 1992.

sary knowledge and skills to survive. The smallness and intimacy of families makes them best suited for providing children with the initial learning experiences they need.

3. *Economic and psychological support.* Families are responsible for providing economic and psychological support for members. In preindustrial societies, families are economic

production units; in industrial societies, the economic security of families is tied to the workplace and to macrolevel economic systems. In recent years, psychological support and emotional security have been increasingly important functions of the family (Chafetz, 1989).

4. *Provision of social status*. Families confer social status and reputation on their members. These statuses include the ascribed statuses with which individuals are born, such as race/ethnicity, nationality, social class, and sometimes religious affiliation. One of the most significant and compelling forms of social placement is the family's class position and the opportunities (or lack thereof) resulting from that position. Examples of class-related opportunities include access to quality health care, higher education, and a safe place to live.

Functionalist explanations of family problems examine the relationship between family troubles and a decline in other social institutions. Changes in the economy, in religion, in the educational system, in the law, or in government programs all can contribute to family problems. For example, the wife of a man who was laid off from his job and was unable to find work for about a year describes the consequences for her family:

> So he took this job as a dishwasher in this restaurant. It's one of those new kind of places with an open kitchen, so there he was, standing there washing dishes in front of everybody. I mean, we used to go there to eat sometimes, and now he's washing the dishes and the whole town sees him doing it. He felt so ashamed, like it was such a come-down that he'd come home even worse than when he wasn't working. (Rubin, 1994:219)

Media depictions of how members of working-class families may attempt to deal with the frustration of everyday life are discussed in Box 14.2.

Functionalists assert that erosion of family values may occur when the institution of religion becomes less important in everyday life. Likewise, changes in law (such as recognition of "no fault" divorce) contribute to high rates of divorce and dramatic increases in single-parent households. According to some functionalists, children are the most affected by these trends because they receive less nurturance and guidance from their parents (see Popenoe, 1993).

CONFLICT AND FEMINIST PERSPECTIVES

Conflict and feminist analysts view functionalist perspectives on the role of the family in society as idealized and inadequate. Rather than operating harmoniously and for the benefit of all members, families are sources of social inequality and conflict over values, goals, and access to resources and power (Benokraitis, 1993).

According to some conflict theorists, families in capitalist economies are similar to workers in a factory. Women are dominated by men in the home in the same manner that workers are dominated by capitalists and managers in factories (Engels, 1972). While childbearing and care for family members in the home contributes to capitalism, these activities also reinforce the subordination of women through unpaid (and often devalued) labour. Other conflict analysts are concerned with the effect that class conflict has on the family. The exploitation of the lower classes by the upper classes contributes to family problems such as high rates of divorce and overall family instability.

Feminist perspectives on inequality in families focus on patriarchy rather than class. From this viewpoint, men's domination over women existed long before private ownership of property and capitalism (Mann, 1994). Women's subordination, which consists of control over women's labour power (or production) and reproduction, is rooted in patriarchy (Ursel, 1992). The dependency created in a patriarchal family system is demonstrated by one husband's comments in Meg Luxton's study of families in Flin Flon, Manitoba: "You'd never work like I do. That's hard work, real work that earns money. And that money keeps you alive. Don't you forget it" (Luxton, 1980:164). As these comments demonstrate, men may feel that they have earned special priviledges as a result of their breadwinner status (Smith, 1985; Luxton, 1995).

Many women resist male domination. Women can control their reproductive capabilities through contraception and other means, and they can take control of their labour power from their husbands by working for wages outside the home (Mann, 1994). However, men are often reluctant to relinquish their status as family breadwinner. Why? Although only 15 percent of families in Canada are supported solely by a male breadwinner (Bradbury, 1996), many men continue to construct their ideal of masculinity around this cultural value (Livingston and Luxton, 1995). Meg Luxton and D.W. Livingston examined the attitudes of male and female steelworkers to the introduction of women in the labour force of Stelco, a steelworking company in Hamilton, Ontario. The male steelworkers did not object to women's economic role as long as it was defined simply as earning money. However, when female steelworkers also seemed to be challenging the "ideal" roles of male breadwinner/female homemaker, the men were much less positive. Some men expressed direct antagonism to women steelworkers, arguing that they posed a direct threat to men's breadwinner power. In the words of one of the men surveyed:

> There were a lot of men who could do those jobs. We've had quite a few cases of women who have gone to Stelco to work whose husbands work there. There were a lot of men who have families who got laid off. That's what most guys object to—I was laid off, she's taking over my job. They were making \$500 to \$600 a week. You lose your house, you lose your car, you lose your wife ... (Livingston and Luxton, 1995:190)

Conflict and feminist perspectives on families primarily focus on the problems inherent in relationships of dominance and subordination. Specifically, feminist theorists have developed explanations that take into account the unequal political relationship between women and men in families and outside of families (Comack, 1996). Some feminist analysts explain family violence as a conscious strategy used by men to control women and perpetuate gender inequality (Harris, 1991; Smith, 1996). According to Lisa Freedman, the reason men batter women, simply put, is:

> ... because they can ... Their perceived role as the "head of the household" tells them that they can batter in order to "control" their spouses. And though society does not encourage battering, social institutions do tacitly condone it. (Freedman, 1985)

Box 14.3 examines how the Criminal Justice System has responded to the issue of wife abuse.

To remedy problems such as wife battering, the subordination of women in all areas of society would have to be eliminated. A starting point might be the elimination of factors fostering violence, such as media images that "convey strong messages that men are sexual predators and sexually dominant in their relationships with women" (Johnson, 1996:7). These messages serve to "glorify and romanticize assaults and other violent behavior" (Aulette, 1994:329).

INTERACTIONIST PERSPECTIVES

Early interactionists viewed the communication process in families as integral to the roles that different family members play. Interactionists examine the roles of husbands, wives, and children as they act out their own part and react to the actions of others. From this perspective, what people think, as well as what they say and do, is very important in understanding family dynamics.

According to sociologists Peter Berger and Hansfried Kellner (1964), interaction between marital partners contributes to a shared reality. Although newlyweds bring separate identities to a marriage, over time they construct a shared reality as a couple. In the process, the partners rede-

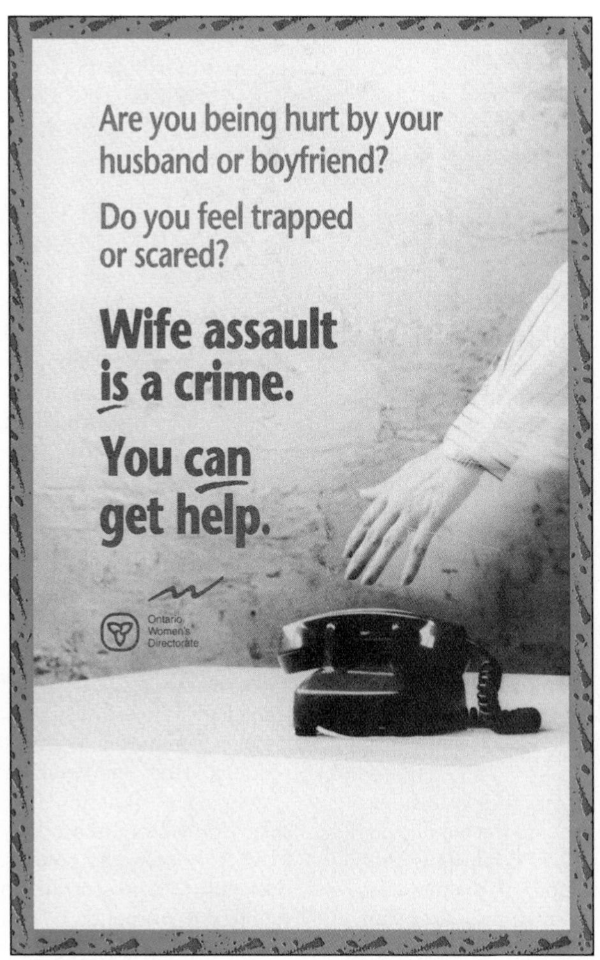

Although public awareness of domestic violence has increased in recent years, society is far from finding an effective solution for this pressing social problem.

fine their past identities to be consistent with new realities. Development of a shared reality is a continuous process, taking place not only in the family but in any group in which the couple participates together. Divorce is the reverse of this process; couples may start with a shared reality and, in the process of uncoupling, gradually develop separate realities (Vaughan, 1985).

Interactionists explain family relationships in terms of the subjective meanings and everyday interpretations people give to their lives. As sociologist Jessie Bernard (1982/1973) pointed out, women and men experience marriage differently. While a husband may see his marriage very positively, his wife may feel less positive about her marriage, and vice versa. Researchers have found that husbands and wives may give very different accounts of the same event, and their "two realities" frequently do not coincide (Safilios-Rothschild, 1969).

How do interactionists view problems within the family? Some focus on the terminology used to describe these problems, examining the extent to which words convey assumptions or "realities"

BOX 14.3 SOCIOLOGY AND LAW

The Criminal Justice System's Response to Domestic Abuse

Historically, wife abuse was seen as a private family matter. For centuries the law permitted the male head of the house to use force against his wife and children, who by law were considered to be the man's property. The expression "rule of thumb" comes from English common law, which specified that a man was authorized to beat his wife with a stick, as long as the stick was no thicker than his thumb. Wife abuse was not seen as a serious threat to the social order and therefore did not require legal intervention. Police reacted to calls for assistance with frustration or apathy, viewing responses to "domestic" calls as a waste of valuable time and resources. Their primary role in these cases was to calm the people involved and restore order. The general perception was that battered women could simply leave an abusive relationship if they wanted to. But if they chose to remain in the situation, one could conclude that the abuse was not that serious.

The women's movement was responsible for bringing the issue of wife abuse into the public and political arenas during the 1970s. Campaigns and protests led to the organization of shelters for victims and also forced governments to alter the criminal justice system's response to wife abuse. The movement identified the double standard that existed in the justice system—if a man hit another man he was charged with assault, but if he hit his wife, it was a private family matter. The first step in providing protection to women in their own homes occurred in the early 1980s, when the first mandatory charging policies were implemented. At the same time, sexual assault laws were changed so that men could be charged with sexually assaulting their wives, and the Canada Evidence Act was revised to permit wives to testify against their husbands. *Mandatory charging policies* give police the authority to lay charges against a suspect where there is reasonable and probable grounds to believe that an assault has occurred regardless of whether there are witnesses to the crime. Before these policies were implemented, the onus was on the abused spouse to lay charges. Many women decided against having their husbands charged because they feared provoking them to further violence. As a result, charges were not laid unless the injuries were serious or there were witnesses to the assault.

Mandatory charging policies were intended to improve the way the criminal justice system responded to cases of domestic violence. They were also intended to encourage women to report these offences by demonstrating that their abuse would be taken seriously. In addition, the arrest of violent men was expected to deter them from further assaults on their wives. Arrest makes the man's violence public—something that most men don't want.

How effective have these policies been in reducing the incidence of wife abuse? The Violence Against Women survey provides some answers. This survey, conducted by Statistics Canada in 1993, involved 12,300 telephone interviews with Canadian women. Respondents were asked about violence committed by husbands and common-law partners, dates, and boyfriends, other known men, and strangers (Johnson, 1996). The results of this survey provide an indication of the effectiveness of mandatory changing policies. First of all, it found that only 26 percent of domestic assaults were reported to the police. Of those incidents reported, only 28 percent resulted in criminal charges. However, once charges were laid, the majority proceeded to court. Female victims surveyed indicated that the response of the police was effective in decreasing or stopping the violence in 45 percent of cases. There was no change in the men's behaviour in 40 percent of cases, and the violence actually increased in 10 percent of the cases. As the results indicate, despite the implementation of mandatory changing policies, wife abuse is still highly underreported and a significant number of abusers are not deterred by arrest.

Tragically, typical of the 10 percent of cases in which violence increased is that of Rhonda Lavoie, who was murdered by her estranged husband, Ron Lavoie. After he murdered his wife, Lavoie took his own life. Incidents such as these are all too common in Canada and elsewhere. Such tragedies demonstrate that there are still inadequacies in the justice system's response to wife abuse. Rhonda Lavoie was a victim of wife abuse; she had been beaten before

BOX 14.3 SOCIOLOGY AND LAW

Continued

and had sought help from the police. Ron Lavoie had been charged, but was out on bail at the time of the murder-suicide. The system was unable to protect Rhonda Lavoie from her husband. By granting him bail, the courts decided that he was not a threat to her.

There are no easy solutions to a crime as complex as wife abuse. As Holly Johnson explains:

> Wife battering is not a crime like any other. Unlike crimes that occur outside the milieu of the family, victims are living with their assailants; they often have strong emotional, financial, and physical bonds; many share children; and very often they want the relationship to continue. All of these factors create complications for both victims and police officers called to the scene of the crime. The difficulties are exacerbated in situations where community-level supports for the victim and her children are lacking. Mandatory charging policies and the best intentions on the part of the police officer may have little effect on alleviating the violence over the long term if the woman lives in an area with no shelters or counselling services for either herself or her husband, and if she has no family support, no financial resources, and no foreseeable way of supporting herself and her children ... Without other community supports working cooperatively with the efforts of the criminal justice system to address the problem, many feel these efforts are only temporary. (Johnson, 1996a:215)

Sources: Johnson, 1996; and Ursel, 1993.

about the nature of the problem. For example, violence between men and women in the home often is referred to as *spouse abuse* or *domestic violence*. However, these terms imply that women and men play equal roles in the perpetration of violence in families, overlooking the more active part men usually play in such aggression. In addition, the term *domestic violence* suggests that this is the "kind of violence that women volunteer for, or inspire, or provoke" (Jacobs, 1994:56). Some scholars and activists use terms such as *wife battering* or *wife abuse* to highlight the gendered nature of such behaviour (see Macleod, 1987). However, others argue that *battered woman* suggests a "woman who is more or less permanently black and blue and helpless" (Jacobs, 1994:56).

Analysts using a social constructionist approach note that definitions concerning family violence are not only socially constructed but also have an effect on how people are treated. In one study of a shelter for battered women, analysts found that workers made decisions about whom to assist and how to assist them based on their own understanding of what constitutes a "real" battered woman (Loseke, 1992). In fact, the term "stitch rule" is used by some shelter workers in reference to the belief that if a person does not require stitches, she is not hurt (DeKeseredy and Hinch, 1991).

Other interactionists have examined ways in which individuals communicate with one another and interpret these interactions. According to Lenore Walker (1979), females are socialized to be passive and males are socialized to be aggressive long before they take on the adult roles of battered and batterer. Even women who have not been socialized by their parents to be helpless and passive, however, may be socialized into this behaviour by abusive husbands. Three factors contribute to the acceptance of the roles of batterer and battered: (1) low self-esteem on the part of both people involved, (2) a limited range of behaviours (he only knows how to be jealous and possessive; she only knows how to be dependent and anxious to make everyone happy), and (3) a belief by both in stereotypic gender roles (she should be feminine and pampered; he should be aggressive and dominant). Other analysts suggest that this pattern is changing as women are gaining paid employment and becoming less dependent on their husbands or male companions for economic support.

Concept Table 14.A summarizes these sociological perspectives on the family. Taken together, these perspectives on the social institution of families help us understand both the good and bad sides of familial relationships. Now we shift our focus to love, marriage, intimate relationships, and family issues in Canada.

CANADIAN FAMILIES AND INTIMATE RELATIONSHIPS

Consider the following facts about families in Canada:

- Eighty-four percent of Canadians live in a family as a spouse, a parent, or a never-married child. This has declined from 89 percent in 1971 (Vanier Institute of the Family, 1994).
- Many Canadians are now marrying more than once. One out of every four men and women who married in 1990 had been previously married (LaNovara, 1995).
- An increasing number of Canadians are choosing to delay marriage. In 1994, the average marrying age for women was 30.1, whereas it was 22 in 1971. For men the average age at marriage in 1994 was 32.6, while it was 25 in 1971 (LaNovara, 1995; Statistics Canada, 1996a).
- The proportion of lone-parent families is on the rise. Between 1981 and 1995, the number of lone-parent families in Canada went from 712,000 to 1.1 million (General Social Survey, 1995).
- Between 1981 and 1995, the number of common-law families almost tripled to 997,000 from 355,000 (General Social Survey, 1995).

As these facts illustrate, families are changing dramatically in Canada. When we examine the traditional stages through which many families move, these patterns clearly will not apply to all families. Let's look first at how people develop intimate relationships.

DEVELOPING INTIMATE RELATIONSHIPS

It has been said that we are "in love with love" or that couples in our culture suffer from a "romantic love complex" (Goode, 1959). This term refers to the fact that in Western society, it is expected that love will form the basis of a lifelong relationship and that the bonds between the couple will be deep and intense (Albas and Albas, 1992). Perhaps this is so because our culture emphasizes *romantic love*—"a deep and vital emotion resulting from significant need satisfaction, coupled with a caring for and acceptance of the beloved, and resulting in an intimate relationship" (Lamanna and Riedmann, 1994:648).

During the Industrial Revolution in the late nineteenth century, people came to view work and home as separate spheres in which different feelings and emotions were appropriate (Coontz, 1992). The public sphere of work—men's sphere—emphasized self-reliance and independence. In contrast, the private sphere of the home—women's sphere—emphasized the giving of services, the exchange of gifts, and love. Accordingly, love and emotions became the domain of women, and work and rationality the domain of men (Lamanna and Riedmann, 1994).

Although the roles of women and men have changed dramatically in the twentieth century,

CONCEPT TABLE 14.A

Theoretical Perspectives on Families

	Focus	Key Points	Perspective on Family Problems
Functionalist	Role of families in maintaining stability of society and individuals' well-being	In modern societies, families serve the functions of sexual regulation, socialization, economic and psychological support, and provision of social status.	Family problems are related to changes in social institutions such as the economy, religion, education, and law/government.
Conflict/Feminist	Families as sources of conflict and social inequality	Families both mirrror and help to perpetuate social inequalities based on class and gender.	Family problems reflect social patterns of dominance and subordination.
Interactionist	Family dynamics, including communication patterns and subjective meanings people assign to events	Interactions within families create a shared reality.	How family problems are perceived and defined depends on patterns of communication, the meanings people give to roles and events, and individuals' interpretations of family interactions.

they still may not share the same perceptions about romantic love today. Hatkoff and Lasswell (1979), for example (see also Hatfield, 1995), conducted 554 interviews of men and women age 18 to 60 and concluded that there are gender differences in the way love is conceptualized. Specifically, they found that men were more romantic and self-centred lovers. In contrast, women were found to be more practical and dependent lovers. Neither gender was particularly altruistic. (See Concept Table 14.B for definitions of six types of love.) More recent research indicates that men and women have similar expectations in their intimate relationships. As Hatfield concludes:

> Everyone, male *and* female, wants love *and* sex, intimacy *and* control. Yet, if one is determined, one can detect slight differences between the genders. Women may be slightly more concerned with love; men with sex. Women may be somewhat more eager for a deeply, intimate relationship than are men. (Hatfield, 1995:273)

Overall, though current research identifies far more similarities than differences in the feelings of men and women about love and intimacy (Hatfield, 1995).

Love, intimacy, and sexuality are closely intertwined. Intimacy may be psychic ("the sharing of minds") or sexual, or both. Although sexuality is an integral part of many intimate relationships, perceptions about sexual activities vary from one culture to the next and from one era to another. For example, kissing is found primarily in Western cultures; many African and Asian cultures view kissing negatively (Reinisch, 1990).

What is love? In Western society, an idealized picture of romantic love can be found as early as the Middle Ages. Do you think that people today have a different perspective on love?

Scholars have suggested that there are six dominant sexual standards in North America (Altman, 1982; Kelly, 1992; Aulette, 1994):

1. *Heterosexual*: Sexual attraction should be limited to members of the opposite sex.
2. *Romantic*: Sex and love should go together.
3. *Marital*: Marriage should include sex; sex outside of marriage is designated as *pre*marital or *extra*marital sex.
4. *Two-person*: Sex must involve two (but no more than two) people.
5. *Coital*: Sexual intercourse should occur between a man and a woman, with coitus being the ultimate sexual act.
6. *Orgasmic*: People should experience orgasm as the climax of sexual interactions; if not, something is wrong.

These dominant sexual ideologies continue to have a strong impact on how people think and feel about sexual conduct. In recent years, the sociological aspects of human sexuality have been examined in a subdiscipline known as *sociology of sexuality*—the "study of sexual attitudes and behavior, the contexts in which these occur, and the social organization of sexual relations at the individual, community, and societal level" (Schneider and Gould, 1987:23).

For over forty years, the work of biologist Alfred C. Kinsey was considered the definitive research on human sexuality, even though some of his methodology had serious limitations. More recently, the National Opinion Research Center at the University of Chicago conducted the National Health and Social Life Survey (see Laumann et al., 1994; Michael et al., 1994). Based on interviews with more than 3,400 men and women aged 18 to 59, this random survey tended

CONCEPT TABLE 14.B

Six Types of Love

Romantic Love	Romantic lovers believe in love at first sight. They're in love with love. They can remember when they met, how they met, and what their partners were wearing when they first touched. They expect their partners to remember, too. Romantic lovers want to know everything about their beloved; to share their joys and sorrows and their experiences. They identify totally with one another. They are thoroughly committed to their lovers. Theirs is a sexual kind of love. Romatic lovers try hard to please their loved ones. They give generous presents.
Self-Centred Love	Self-Centred lovers play at love affairs as they play at games. They try to demonstrate their skills or superiority; they try to win. Such lovers may keep two or three lovers on the string at one time. For them, sex is self-centred and exploitative. As a rule, such lovers have only one sexual routine. If that doesn't work, they move up to new sexual partners. Self-centred lovers care about having fun. They get frightened off if someone becomes dependent on them or wants commitment. If a partner ends the relationship, they take loss gracefully: "You win a few, you lose a few—there'll be another one along in a minute."
Dependent Love	Dependent lovers are obsessed. They are unable to sleep, eat, or even think. The dependent lover has peaks of excitement, but also depths of depression. They are irrationally jealous, and become extremely anxious when their loved ones threaten to leave, even for a short time.
Companionate Love	Companionate lovers are basically good friends. They take it for granted that their relationships will be permanent. The companionate relationship is *not* an intensely sexual one. Sex is satisfying, but not compelling. Temporary separations are not a great problem. If their relationship breaks up, such lovers remain close and caring friends for the rest of their lives.
Practical Love	Practical lovers are intensely pragmatic. They look realistically at their own assets, assess their market value, and set off to get the best possible deal in their partners. They are faithful in love so long as the loved one is a good bargain. Practical lovers think carefully about education, make sensible decisions about family size, and so on. They carefully check out their future in-laws and relatives.
Altruistic Love	Altruistic lovers are forgiving. They assume the best. If their lovers cause them pain, they assume the lovers didn't mean to do so. Altruistic lovers are always supportive, self-sacrificing. They care enough about their lovers' happiness to give them up, if their lovers have a chance for greater happiness elsewhere.

Source: E. Hatfield 1995.

to reaffirm the significance of the dominant sexual ideologies. Most respondents reported that they engaged in heterosexual relationships, although 9 percent of the men said they had had at least one homosexual encounter resulting in orgasm. While 6.2 percent of men and 4.4 percent of women said that they were at least somewhat attracted to others of the same gender, only 2.8 percent of men and 1.4 percent of women identified themselves as gay or lesbian. According to the study, persons who engaged in extramarital sex found their activities to be more thrilling than those with their marital partner, but they also felt guilty. Persons in sustained relationships such as marriage or cohabitation found sexual activity to be the most satisfying emotionally and physically.

COHABITATION AND DOMESTIC PARTNERSHIPS

Attitudes about cohabitation have changed in the past two decades. Although cohabitation is still defined by the Canadian census as the sharing of a household by one man and one woman who are not related to each other by kinship or marriage, many sociologists now use a more inclusive definition. For our purposes, we will define ***cohabitation*** **as referring to a couple who live together without being legally married**. Between 1981 and 1995, the number of common-law families almost tripled to 997,000 from 355,000. In 1995, common-law families represented almost 12 percent of all Canadian families, up from 5.9 percent in 1981 (General Social Survey, 1995). The proportion of people in common-law unions varies considerably by province (see Figure 14.2). In 1995, Quebec had the highest percentage; there, 21 percent of families were living common-law. At 7.9 percent, common-law unions were least common in Ontario (General Social Survey, 1995).

Those most likely to cohabit are young adults between the ages of 15 and 24. In 1990, nearly 82 percent of all 15–19 year olds in a couple union were living common-law (Stout, 1994). Cohabitation is also common among Canadian university and college students, an estimated 25 percent of whom report having cohabited at some time. While "living together" or living common-law is often a prelude to marriage for young adults, common-law unions are also becoming a popular alternative both to marriage and to remarriage following divorce or separation (Stout, 1994).

For couples who plan to get married eventually, cohabitation usually follows the *two-stage marriage* pattern set out by anthropologist Margaret Mead, who argued that dating patterns in North America are not adequate preparation for marriage and parenting responsibilities. Instead, Mead suggested that marriage should occur in two stages, each with its own ceremony and responsibilities. In the first stage, the *individual marriage*, two people would make a serious commitment to each other but agree not to have children during this stage. In the second stage, the *parental marriage*, the couple would decide to have children and to share responsibility for their upbringing (Lamanna and Riedmann, 1994).

Today, some people view cohabitation as a form of "trial marriage." For others, however, cohabitation is not a first step toward marriage. For example, one study found that slightly more than 50 percent of such relationships culminate in marriage; about 37 percent of couples break up; and 10 percent were still ongoing at the time of the survey (London, 1991). In another study, 39 percent of the relationships among never-married individuals and 30 percent of the relationships among formerly married individuals broke up in less than a year (Bumpass, Sweet, and Cherlin, 1991).

Does cohabitation contribute to marital success? Some studies have found that cohabitation has little or no effect on marital adjustment, emotional closeness, satisfaction, and intimacy (White, 1987). However, other evidence suggests that couples who cohabit have less chance of marital success than those who do not (Burch and Madan, 1986). In a study that examined the relationship between cohabiting before marriage and the likelihood of divorce, researchers concluded that those who had cohabited were both less satisfied with their marriage and less committed to the institution of marriage than those who married without having first cohabited (Baker, 1996). The researchers theorized that cohabitation may contribute to people's individualistic attitudes and

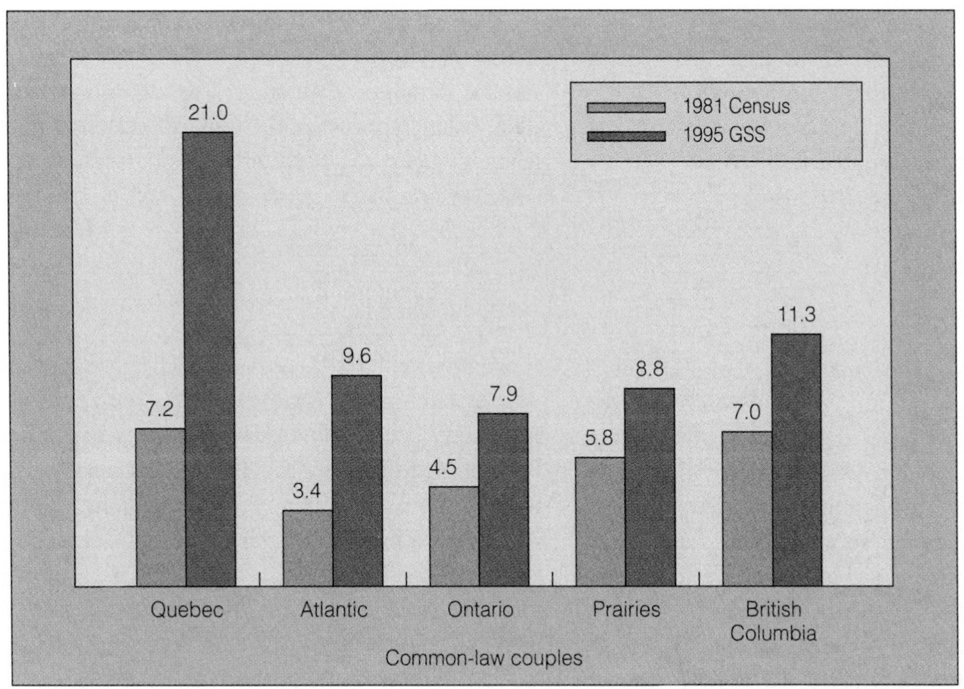

FIGURE 14.2

Common-law Couples as a Proportion of Total Families, by Region

Reproduced by authority of the Minister of Industry, 1996, Statistics Canada, from *1981 Census* and *1995 General Social Survey*, Cat. no. 11-612.

values while making them more aware that alternatives to marriage exist (Axinn and Thornton, 1992; Thomson and Colella, 1992).

In Canada and the United States, many lesbian and gay couples cohabit because they cannot enter into legally recognized marital relationships. Recently, some gay and lesbian activists have sought recognition of ***domestic partnerships*—household partnerships in which an unmarried couple lives together in a committed, sexually intimate relationship and is granted the same rights and benefits as those accorded married heterosexual couples** (Gerstel and Gross, 1995; O'Brien and Weir, 1995). Benefits such as health and life insurance coverage are extremely important to *all* couples, as Gayle, a lesbian, points out:

> It makes me angry that [heterosexuals] get insurance benefits and all the privileges, and Frances [her partner] and I take a beating financially. We both pay our insurance policies, but we don't get discounts that other people get and that's not fair. (quoted in Sherman, 1992:197)

Despite the failure of the law to recognize gay marriages, many lesbian and gay couples consider themselves married and living in lifelong commitments. To make their commitment public, some couples exchange rings and vows under the auspices of churches. The Metropolitan Community Church in Toronto is one such church. Other couples, like Gayle and Frances, do not feel the need to be married. As Gayle says,

> Within my home I feel married to Frances, but I don't consider us "married." The marriage part is still very heterosexual to me. One of the reasons I don't like to associate

> with marriage is because heterosexual marriage seems to be in trouble. It's like booking passage on the Titanic. Frances is my life partner; that's how I'm accustomed to thinking of her. (quoted in Sherman, 1992:189–190)

MARRIAGE

Why do people get married? Couples get married for a variety of reasons. Some do so because they are "in love," desire companionship and sex, want to have children, feel social pressure, are attempting to escape from a bad situation in their parents' home, or believe that they will have more money or other resources if they get married. These factors not withstanding, the selection of a marital partner actually is fairly predictable. As previously discussed, most people in Canada tend to choose marriage partners who are similar to themselves. ***Homogamy*** **refers to the pattern of individuals marrying those who have similar characteristics, such as race/ethnicity, religious background, age, education, or social class.** However, homogamy provides only the general framework within which people select their partners; people are also influenced by other factors. For example, some researchers claim that people want partners whose personalities match their own in significant ways. Thus, people who are outgoing and friendly may be attracted to people with those same traits. However, other researchers claim that people look for partners whose personality traits differ from but complement their own.

Regardless of the individual traits of marriage partners, research indicates that communication and emotional support are crucial to the success of marriages. Common marital problems include lack of emotional intimacy, poor communication, and lack of companionship. One study concluded that for many middle- and upper-income couples, women's paid work was critical to the success of their marriages. People who have a strong commitment to their work have two distinct sources of pleasure—work and family. For members of the working class, however, work may not be a source of pleasure. For all women and men, balancing work and family life is a challenge (Baker and Lero, 1996).

HOUSEWORK

Approximately 62 percent of all marriages in Canada are ***dual-earner marriages*****—marriages in which both spouses are in the labour force** (see Figure 14.3). Most employed women hold full-time, year-round jobs. Even when their children are very young, most working mothers are employed full time. For example, in 1991, over 60 percent of employed mothers with children under the age of 3 were working full time (Vanier Institute of the Family, 1994).

As discussed in Chapter 10, many married women leave their paid employment at the end of the day and go home to perform hours of housework and child care. Sociologist Arlie Hochschild (1989) refers to this as the ***second shift*****—the domestic work that employed women perform at home after they complete their workday on the job.** Thus, many married women today contribute to the economic well-being of their families and also meet many, if not all, of the domestic needs of family members by cooking, cleaning, shopping, taking care of children, and managing household routines. According to Hochschild, the unpaid housework women do on the second shift amounts to an extra month of work each year. The results from the General Social Survey (1990) indicated that Canadian women assume more responsibility for housework as the number of children in the family increases. This pattern is consistent regardless of whether the woman is employed full time or part time (Marshall, 1995). However, women with higher levels of education were less likely to assume full responsibility for domestic chores in dual-earner families. Similarly, husbands with higher education were more likely to share responsibility for

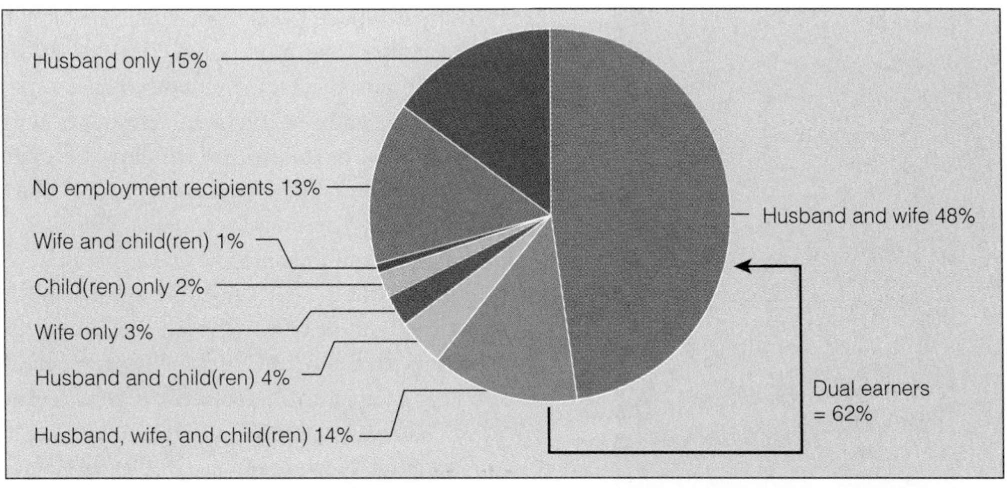

FIGURE 14.3

Earners in Canadian Husband–Wife Families, 1990

Source: Prepared by the Centre for International Statistics, Canadian Council on Social Development. Reproduced by permission.

household chores. Marshall suggests that this equality in terms of housework may be a reflection of more equality in terms of income earned (1995:305).

In recent years, more husbands have attempted to share some of the household and child-care responsibilities, especially in families in which the wife's earnings are essential to family finances (Perry-Jenkins and Crouter, 1990). In contrast, husbands who see themselves as the primary breadwinners are less likely to share housework with their wives. Even when husbands share some of the household responsibilities, however, they typically spend much less time in these activities than do their wives (Marshall, 1995). (See Figure 14.4 and Figure 14.5.) Women and men perform different household tasks, and the deadlines for their work vary widely. Recurring tasks that have specific times for completion (such as bathing a child or cooking a meal) tend to be the women's responsibility, whereas men are more likely to do the periodic tasks that have no highly structured schedule (such as mowing the lawn or changing the oil in the car) (Hochschild, 1989; Marshall, 1994). Men also are more reluctant to perform undesirable tasks such as scrubbing the toilet or diapering a baby, or to give up leisure pursuits.

Couples with more egalitarian ideas about women's and men's roles tend to share more equally in food preparation, housework, and child care (Wright et al., 1992). For some men, the shift to a more egalitarian household occurs gradually, as Wesley, whose wife works full time, explains:

> It was me taking the initiative, and also Connie pushing, saying "Gee, there's so much that has to be done." At first I said, "But I'm supposed to be the breadwinner," not realizing she's also the breadwinner. I was being a little blind to what was going on, but I got tired of waiting for my wife to come home to start cooking, so one day I surprised the hell out [of] her and myself and the kids, and I had supper waiting on the table for her. (quoted in Gerson, 1993:170)

Women employed fulltime who are single parents probably have the greatest burden of all; they have complete responsibility for the children and the household, often with little or no help from ex-husbands or relatives.

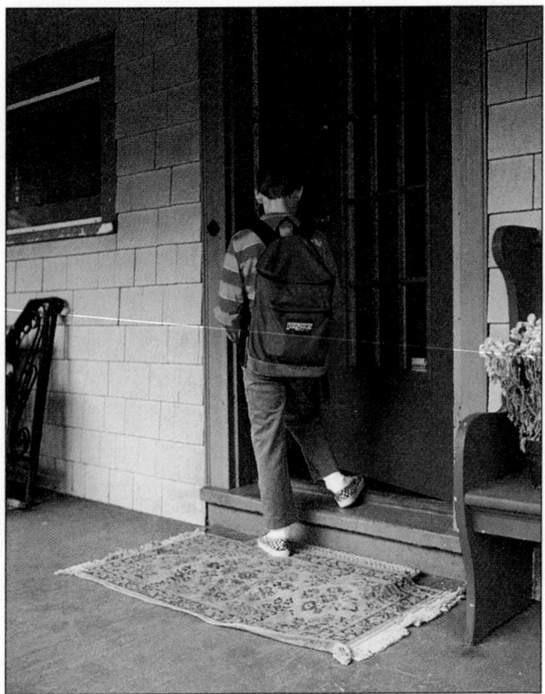

Dual-earner marriages are a challenge for many children as well as their parents. While parents are at work, latchkey children often are at home alone.

PARENTING

Not all couples become parents. Those who decide not to have children often consider themselves to be "child-free," while those who want to have children but cannot do so may consider themselves "childless." Research on voluntary childlessness in Canada reveals that one-third of childless couples decide before marriage that they do not want children (Veevers, 1980). Couples remain childless for a number of reasons including the view that pregnancy is a form of illness, or a condition that reduces one's sexual appeal; the association of motherhood with dependency or incompetence; and the interference of children with career advancement, travelling, and marital stability. Do couples need to have children to be happy? According to the research, the answer is no. Studies have found that child-free couples report greater marital satisfaction than do couples with children (Ramu, 1984) However, despite this fact, childless couples experience higher rates of divorce. Although only about 20 percent of couples are childless, between 50 to 70 percent of divorces in Canada are obtained by childless couples (Adams, 1990).

Involuntary childlessness has become increasingly common in recent years. Couples may be involuntarily childless as a result of infertility. ***Infertility* is defined by medical professionals as one year of attempting to achieve pregnancy without success** (Achilles, 1996). The Royal Commission on New Reproductive Technologies found that 7 percent of Canadian couples were infertile (Vanier Institute of the Family, 1994). Reasons for this increase include infertility related to delayed childbirth, side effects of contraceptives, and decreased sperm counts, possibly related to environmental pollutants (Gee, 1994).

According to sociologist Charlene Miall (1986), women who are involuntarily childless engage in "information management" to combat the social stigma associated with childlessness. Their tactics range from avoiding people who make them uncomfortable to revealing their infertility so that others will not think of them as "selfish" for being childless. People who are involuntarily childless may choose to become parents by adopting a child.

ADOPTION Adoption is a legal process through which the rights and duties of parenting are transferred from a child's biological and/or legal parents to new legal parents. This procedure gives the adopted child all of the rights of a biological child. In most adoptions, a new birth certificate is issued, and the child has no future contact with the biological parents. In Canada, adoption is regulated provincially. Therefore, adopted persons' access to information regarding their "biological parents" varies, as does their desire to access this information (Jackson, 1993).

Matching children who are available for adoption with prospective adoptive parents can be difficult. The available children have specific needs,

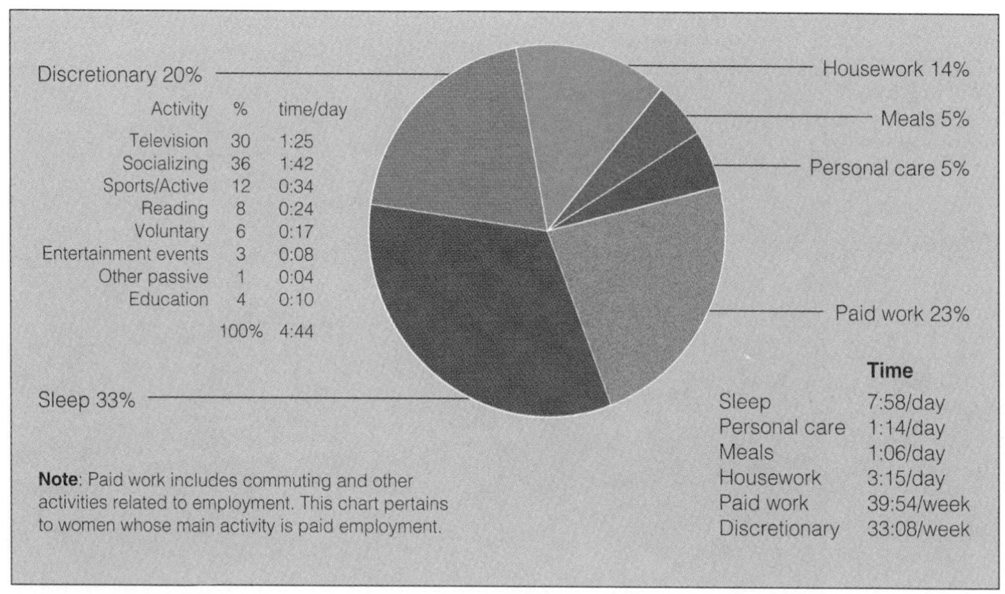

FIGURE 14.4

Average Weekly Time Use: Employed Canadian Women, 1992

Source: Prepared by the Centre for International Statistics, Canadian Council on Social Development. Reproduced by permission.

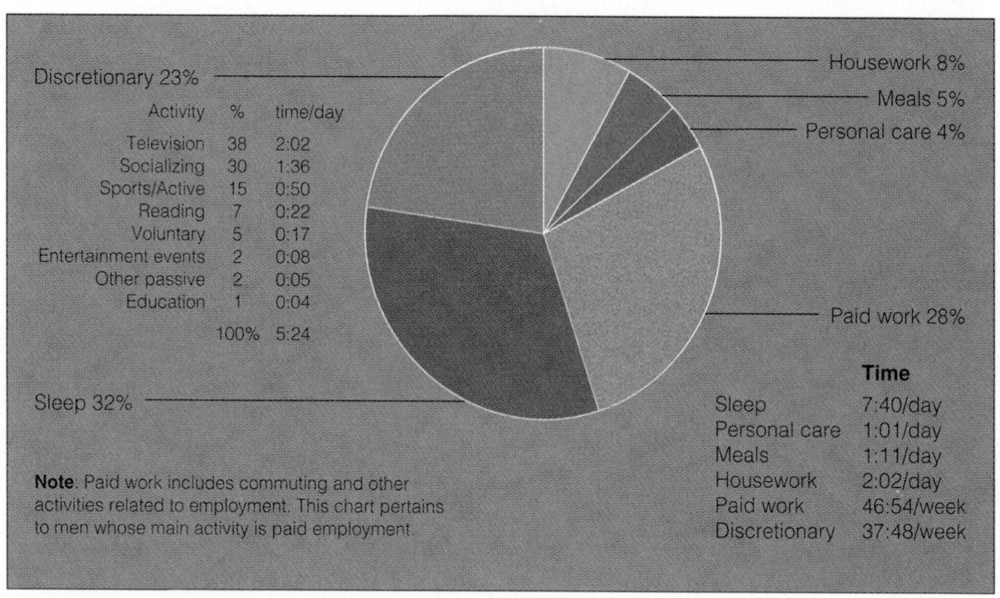

FIGURE 14.5

Average Weekly Time Use: Employed Canadian Men, 1992

Source: Prepared by the Centre for International Statistics, Canadian Council on Social Development. Reproduced by permission.

Adoption is a complex legal process for most parents; it can be even more complicated for gay and lesbian couples.

and the prospective parents often set specifications on the type of child they want to adopt. Ironically, while thousands of children are available for adoption each year in North America, prospective parents seek out children in developing nations such as Romania, South Korea, and India. The primary reason is that the available children in Canada are thought to be "unsuitable." They may have disabilities or illnesses, or their undesirability may be due to their being nonwhite (most prospective parents are white) or too old (Zelizer, 1985). In addition, fewer infants are available for adoption today than in the past because better means of contraception exist, abortion is more readily available, and more single parents decide to keep their babies. Consequently, the demand for adoptive children is growing, while the supply of children available for adoption is shrinking. In Canada, there are three applicants for each public adoption and almost as many for private adoptions. In addition, in 1990, an estimated 2000 to 5000 Canadians were actively pursuing international adoptions. This trend toward private adoptions (which are more costly) means that adoption is increasingly becoming a parenting option available only to the wealthy (Vanier Institute of the Family, 1994).

NEW REPRODUCTIVE TECHNOLOGIES The availability of a variety of reproductive technologies is having a dramatic impact on traditional concepts of the family and parenthood. The three basic categories of reproductive technology are: (1) those that inhibit or prevent the development of new life (birth control, sterilization, and abortion), (2) those that monitor new life (ultrasound, amniocentesis, fetal monitoring, and fetal surgery), and (3) those that involve the creation of a new life (artificial insemination, in vitro fertilization). The procedures used in the creation of new life are referred to as methods of **assisted reproduction** (Achilles, 1996). These procedures have raised some controversial ethical issues in terms of what role medical science should play in the creation of human life (Eichler, 1996).

Artificial insemination is the oldest, simplest, and most common type of assisted reproduction. Artificial insemination simply replaces sexual intercourse. Semen is obtained from either the male partner or a semen donor and is inserted into a woman's vagina at the time of her ovulation. The woman is often given fertility drugs prior to insemination to increase the chances of conception. It has been suggested that the word "artificial" is misleading and that a more accurate term for this procedure would be "alternative insemination" (Achilles, 1996:349). Donor insemination is not a new procedure, as the first recorded case was in 1884.

There are several complex issues concerning the moral, legal, and social implications of artificial insemination. For one thing, the Roman Catholic Church considers donor insemination adulterous. Another problem is that in most cases the woman is given no information about the donor and the donor is not told if a pregnancy has occurred. The result of this anonymity is that neither mother nor the individuals conceived through donor insemination will have access to information regarding the biological father. Finally, the laws in most provinces do not provide protection for the participants in this procedure, with the exception of Quebec, where the child is legally considered to be the child of the "social" father, and in the Yukon, where donors are protected from possible legal action by offspring or donor sperm recipients (Achilles, 1996).

The term *test-tube baby* is often used incorrectly to describe babies conceived through *in vitro* fertilization. An actual test-tube baby would require conception, gestation, and birth to occur outside of a woman's body. To date, this technology has not been developed (Achilles, 1996). In vitro (Latin for "in glass") fertilization involves removing an egg from a woman, fertilizing the egg with the sperm in a petri dish, and then implanting the fertilized eggs (embryos) into the woman. This process has been described as "stressful, invasive, and financially and emotionally draining" (Achilles, 1996:354). Furthermore, the success rate for this procedure is very low: one Canadian study reports a live birth rate of approximately 15 percent (Bryant, 1990). Critics of this procedure have suggested that this rate is no better than the probability of an infertile couple's having a child without medical intervention.

Another alternative available to couples with fertility problems is the use of a surrogate, or substitute, mother to carry a child for them. Surrogate parenting is correctly referred to as a *preconception contract*, which involves a legal agreement between the woman who will bear the child and a woman or couple who have been unable to become pregnant (Achilles, 1996). There are two types of surrogacy. In *traditional surrogacy* the surrogate is artificially inseminated with the father's sperm. In this case, the egg is the surrogate's. The child is biologically related to the surrogate and the father. This type of surrogacy is typically used in cases were the woman is infertile or when there is a risk of passing on a serious genetic disorder from mother to child. In the second type of surrogacy, *gestational surrogacy*, the sperm and the eggs from the infertile couple are transferred to the surrogate using an assisted reproductive technology (such as in vitro fertilization). With gestational surrogacy the surrogate carries the child but is not biologically or genetically related to it. The genetic parents are the man and woman whose eggs and sperm were donated to the surrogate. Sound confusing? Part of the reason we have so much difficulty with these new reproductive technologies is because they are just that—new. They are new to our society and also new to our concept of the family. In fact, our language has yet to develop accurate terminology to incorporate all of these new alternatives. For example, is "mother" an accurate term for the gestational surrogate mother? What does the term "parent" mean? For many, surrogacy involves serious ethical, legal, religious, and emotional considerations. It is also time-consuming, invasive, and expensive, with costs usually starting at around $15,000.

Legislation outlawing surrogate motherhood was introduced in June 1996. Included in this legislation is also a recommendation to ban commercial trade in eggs, sperm, and embryos. The bill is the government's long-awaited response to the 1993 report of the Royal Commission on New Reproductive Technologies. This legislation was not yet passed at the time of writ-

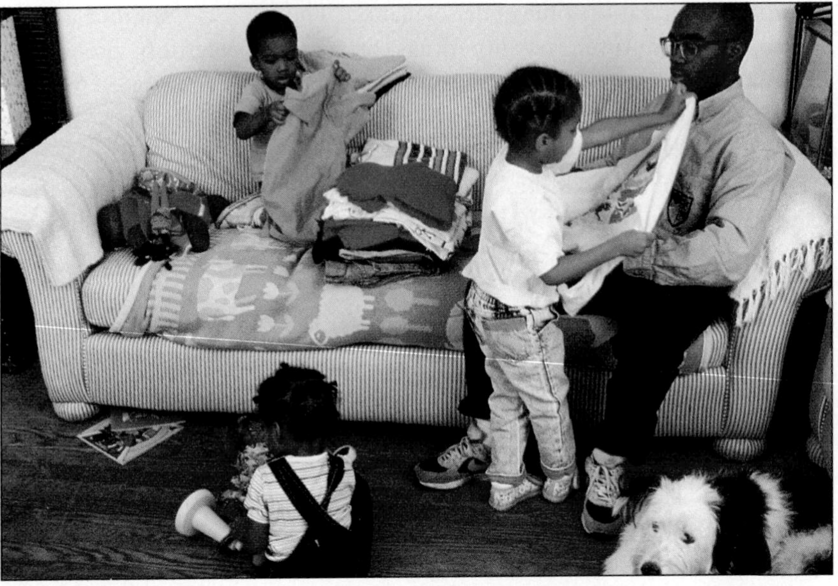

In recent years, many more fathers and mothers alike have been confronting the unique challenges of single parenting.

ing. The laws pertaining to surrogacy are still evolving and so far are inadequate in terms of addressing the complexities of these new family relationships. Nevertheless, these new reproductive technologies have enabled some infertile couples to become parents. For them, the benefits far outweigh the costs.

SINGLE-PARENT HOUSEHOLDS According to Marcil-Gratton, "Families built around the enduring relationship of a man and a woman have been disintegrating from the beginnings of time, leaving one parent to take responsibility" (1993:73). However, in recent years, single- or one-parent households have increased significantly due to divorce and to births outside of marriage. Single-parenting is not a new phenomenon in Canada. Recent estimates suggest that up to one-third of all Canadian mothers will be single parents at some stage in their lives (Marcil-Gratton, 1993).

Even for a person with a stable income and a network of friends and family to help with child care, raising a child alone can be an emotional and financial burden. Single-parent households headed by women have been stereotyped by some journalists, politicians, and analysts as being problematic for children. In 1995, 13.8 percent of Canadian households are headed by a single parent who is divorced, separated, widowed, or who has never been married (General Social Survey, 1996). Eighty-two percent of lone-parent families are headed by a mother (Oderkirk and Lochhead, 1995). According to sociologists Sara McLanahan and Karen Booth (1991), children in mother-only families are more likely than children in two-parent families to have poor academic achievement, higher school absentee and dropout rates, higher early marriage and parenthood, and higher divorce rates, and more drug and alcohol abuse. But living in a one-parent family is *not* the cause of all this. Lone-parent families comprise almost half of all low-income families (Oderkirk, 1994). The difficulties experienced by children of single mothers are more likely the result of living in poverty than of the absence of a parent. Many other factors—including discrimination, unsafe neighbourhoods, and high crime rates—contribute to these problems.

Lesbian mothers and gay fathers are counted in some studies as single parents; however, they often share parenting responsibilities with same-sex partners. Due to homophobia (hatred and fear of homosexuals and lesbians), lesbian mothers and gay fathers are more likely to lose custody to a heterosexual parent in divorce cases (Arnup, 1995; Epstein, 1996). In any case, many gay men in the United States and Canada are fathers. Some gay men are married natural fathers, others are single gay men who have adopted children on their own, and still others are gay couples who have adopted children. Very little research exists on gay fathers; what does exist tends to show that noncustodial gay fathers try to maintain good relationships with their children (Bozett, 1988).

Single fathers who do not have custody of their children may play a relatively limited role in the lives of those children. While some remain actively involved in their children's lives, others may become "Disneyland daddies" who spend time with their children in recreational activities and buy them presents for special occasions but have a very small part in the children's day-to-day lives. Sometimes, this limited role is by choice, but more often, it is caused by workplace demands on time and energy, the location of the ex-wife's residence, and the limitations placed on the visitation arrangements.

Currently, men head about 18 percent of lone-parent families; among many of the men, a pattern of "involved fatherhood" has emerged (Gerson, 1993). For example, in a study of men who became single fathers because of their wifes' deaths, desertion, or relinquishment of custody, sociologist Barbara Risman (1987) found that the men had very strong relationships with their children.

TWO-PARENT HOUSEHOLDS Parenthood in Canada is idealized, especially for women. According to sociologist Alice Rossi (1992), maternity is the mark of adulthood for women, whether or not they are employed. By contrast, men secure their status as adults by their employment and other activities outside the family (Hoffnung, 1995).

For families in which a couple truly shares parenting, children have two primary caregivers. Some parents share parenting responsibilities by choice; others share out of necessity because both hold full-time jobs. Some studies have found that the taking of an active part in raising the children by fathers is beneficial not only for the mothers (who then have a little more time for other activities) but also for the fathers and the children. The men benefit through increased access to children and the greater opportunity to be nurturing parents (Coltrane, 1989).

Children in two-parent families are not guaranteed a happy childhood simply because both parents reside in the same household. Children whose parents argue constantly, are alcoholics, or abuse them may be worse off than children in single-parent families in which the environment is more conducive to their well-being. For example, Gary Crosby, son of the late singer and movie actor Bing Crosby, grew up in a wealthy two-parent family that, for all outward appearances, would have been the envy of others. However, Crosby's mother fought an ongoing battle with alcoholism while his father was on the road entertaining. In Crosby's words,

> I always breathed more easily when [my father] packed up his bags and golf clubs and left for a while. It meant there was one less person to mete out punishment, another pair of eyes that wouldn't be scrutinizing me to find something wrong. And when he was away, Mom might start hitting the bottle early and be in bed for the night by the time I got back from school. Then I wouldn't have to face either of them. (Crosby and Firestone, 1994:238)

As this example shows, even in a two-parent family, children can have strong feelings of isolation and stress. While members of some families continue to live with these unresolved problems, others see divorce as a solution.

TRANSITIONS IN FAMILIES

As we have seen, marriage may be an arrangement of love and intimacy or a generally unhappy situation. Differences in power and privilege can produce marital conflicts. Some analysts attribute problems in the family to the empty-nest syndrome, which supposedly occurs after children leave home. According to some scholars, mothers experience a lowered sense of well-being and higher levels of depression and alcohol abuse because of this family transition. Researchers in Japan have noted similar experiences among Japanese women, as discussed in Box 14.4. Other scholars have suggested, however, that the empty-nest theory is incorrect: couples may have greater marital satisfaction after children leave home (see Glenn, 1991). In any case, a common consequence of marital strife and unhappiness is divorce.

DIVORCE

Divorce is the legal process of dissolving a marriage that allows former spouses to remarry if they so choose. Prior to 1968 it was difficult to obtain a divorce in Canada. A divorce was granted only on the grounds of adultery. In 1968 the grounds for divorce were expanded to include marital breakdown (i.e., desertion, imprisonment, or separation of three or more years) and marital offences (physical or mental cruelty). In 1985 the Divorce Act introduced "no fault" provisions that made marital breakdown the sole ground for divorce. Under no-fault divorce laws, proof of "blameworthiness" is no longer necessary. However, when children are involved, the issue of "blame" may assume greater importance in the determination of parental custody.

Have you heard statements such as "One out of every two marriages ends in divorce"? Statistics might initially appear to bear out this statement. In 1994, for example, 159,316 Canadian couples married and 78,880 divorces were granted (Statistics Canada, 1996a; 1996b) However, comparing the number of marriages with the number of divorces from year to year can be misleading. The couples who are divorced in any given year are very unlikely to come from the group that married that year. In addition, in years when the economy is in a recession people may delay getting married but not divorced (McVey and Kalbach, 1995). Some people also may go through several marriages and divorces, thus skewing the divorce rate. The likelihood of divorce goes up with each subsequent marriage in the serial monogamy pattern.

In order to accurately assess the probability of a marriage ending in divorce it is necessary to use what is referred to as a *cohort approach*. This approach establishes probabilities based on assumptions about how the various age groups (cohorts) in society might behave, given their marriage rate, their age at first marriage, and their responses to various social, cultural, and economic changes. Canadian estimates based on a cohort approach are that 30 to 40 percent of marriages will end in divorce (Richardson, 1996:230).

CAUSES OF DIVORCE Why do divorces occur? As you will recall from Chapter 2, sociologists look for correlations (relationships between two variables) in attempting to answer questions such as this. Existing research has identified a number of factors at both the macro- and microlevel that make some couples more or less likely to divorce. At the macrolevel, societal factors contributing to higher rates of divorce include changes in social institutions, such as religion, the family, and the legal system. Some religions have taken a more lenient attitude toward divorce, and the social stigma associated with divorce has lessened. Further, as we have seen in this chapter, the family institution has undergone a major change that has resulted in less economic and emotional dependency among family members—and thus reduced a barrier to divorce. And, as Figure 14.6 demonstrates, the liberalization of divorce laws in Canada has had a dramatic impact on the divorce rate.

At the microlevel, a number of factors contribute to a couple's "statistical" likelihood of becoming divorced. Some of the primary social characteristics of those most likely to get divorced include:

- Marriage at an early age (15–19) (Balakrishnan et al., 1987)

BOX 14.4 SOCIOLOGY IN GLOBAL PERSPECTIVE

Family Life in Japan

Traditionally, Japanese women have been socialized to fulfil the "good wife/wise mother" role and find satisfaction primarily in marriage and motherhood. Although Japan is experiencing many social changes, traditional values still dictate that a Japanese girl is not a woman until she marries. Popular culture supports this ideal as well. For example, smiling newlyweds and wistful brides routinely are featured in magazine ads for wedding halls.

Japanese women who currently are in the age 40–50 cohort were taught *amae*—the belief that a very strong bond should exist between a mother and her children because the dependence a child learns for the mother can be transferred to the group as the child grows older. As a result, many of these mothers gave almost twenty-four-hour-a-day care and attention to their children, including picking them up immediately when they cried and always being there for them.

However, after the children leave home, many Japanese mothers feel that they have lost their sense of purpose (*ikigai*) and begin to search for something else to occupy their time. After years of diapering babies, overseeing homework, and meeting all of the needs of their children, many women lack self-confidence and marketable skills. Consequently, middle age becomes a time of crisis. While some take classes to widen their horizons, others may turn to drinking, out of fear of rejection or feelings of depression and boredom. At this time, some husbands are at the height of their careers and are working long hours or entertaining clients.

Today, many younger women in Japan are employed. Like women in Canada, however, they often have a second shift of housework averaging three hours a day as compared with husbands' eight minutes a day. However, traditional roles increasingly are being challenged by women (and some men) in Japan. Many more children now are entrusted to child-care centres whereas in the past it was unthinkable to have strangers take care of one's children. As is true with many changes in Japanese society today, the long-term effects of this change are as yet unknown.

Sources: Based on Kitano and Chi, 1986-87; Shorto, 1991; Kitano et al., 1992; Benokraitis, 1993; and Jung, 1994.

Although Japanese women have been socialized to fulfil the "good wife/wise mother" role in the past, many Japanese women currently are employed and face the same "double shift" as many Canadian women.

- A short acquaintanceship before marriage (Grover, 1985)
- Disapproval of the marriage by relatives and friends (Goode, 1976)
- Limited economic resources and low wages (Nett, 1993)
- A high-school education or less (although deferring marriage to attend college may be more of a factor than education per se) (Burch and Madan, 1987)
- Previous marriages (Richardson, 1996)
- The presence of children (depending on their gender and age at the beginning of the marriage) (Rankin and Maneker, 1985; Morgan, Lye, and Condran, 1988; Martin and Bumpass, 1989)

The interrelationship of these and other factors is complicated. For example, the effect of age is intertwined with economic resources; persons from families at the low end of the income scale tend to marry earlier than those at more affluent income levels. Thus, the question becomes whether age itself is a factor or whether economic resources are more closely associated with divorce.

CONSEQUENCES OF DIVORCE As discussed in previous chapters, divorce may have a dramatic economic and emotional impact on family members. The exact number of children affected by divorce in Canada is difficult to determine because no official information is available on out-of-court custody decisions. In 1990, approximately 34,000 Canadian children were involved in divorce cases in which the courts made custody decisions. In eight out of ten of these cases, the mother was awarded custody (Vanier Institute of the Family, 1994:45). Parental joint custody is also an option for some divorcing couples. When joint custody is a voluntary arrangement and when there is motivation to make it work, it has benefits for both children and parents (Richardson, 1996). Joint custody allows the children to maintain regular contact with both parents, which can ease the adjustment to the marriage breakup, and give parents more time to adjust to their new lives. However, this arrangement may also create unique problems for children, as author David Sheff (1995:64) explains:

> My son began commuting between his two homes at age 4. He travelled with a Hello Kitty suitcase with a pretend lock and key until it embarrassed him. He graduated to a canvas backpack filled with a revolving arsenal of essential stuff: books and journals, plastic vampire teeth, "Star Trek" Micro Machines, a Walkman, CD's, a teddy bear.
>
> The commuter flights . . . were the only times a parent wasn't lording over him, so he was able to order Coca-Cola, verboten at home. But such benefits were insignificant when contrasted with his preflight nightmares about plane crashes.
>
> Like so many divorcing couples, we divided the china and art and our young son. First he was ferried back and forth between our homes across town, and then, when his mother moved to Los Angeles, across the state. For the eight years since, he has been one of the thousands of children with two homes, two beds, two sets of clothes and toys and two toothbrushes.

Clearly, children from lower-income families would not have the benefit of these plane trips and two sets of amenities. Nevertheless, for most children, divorce is a difficult experience. Furthermore, some children experience more than one divorce during their childhood because one or both of their parents may remarry and subsequently divorce again.

Divorce not only changes relationships for the couple involved but also for other relatives. In some divorces, grandparents feel that they are the big losers. To see their grandchildren, the grandparents have to keep in touch with the parent who has custody. In-laws are less likely to be welcome and may be seen as being on the "other side" simply because they are the parents of the ex-spouse. Recently, some grandparents have sued for custody of minor grandchildren. They generally

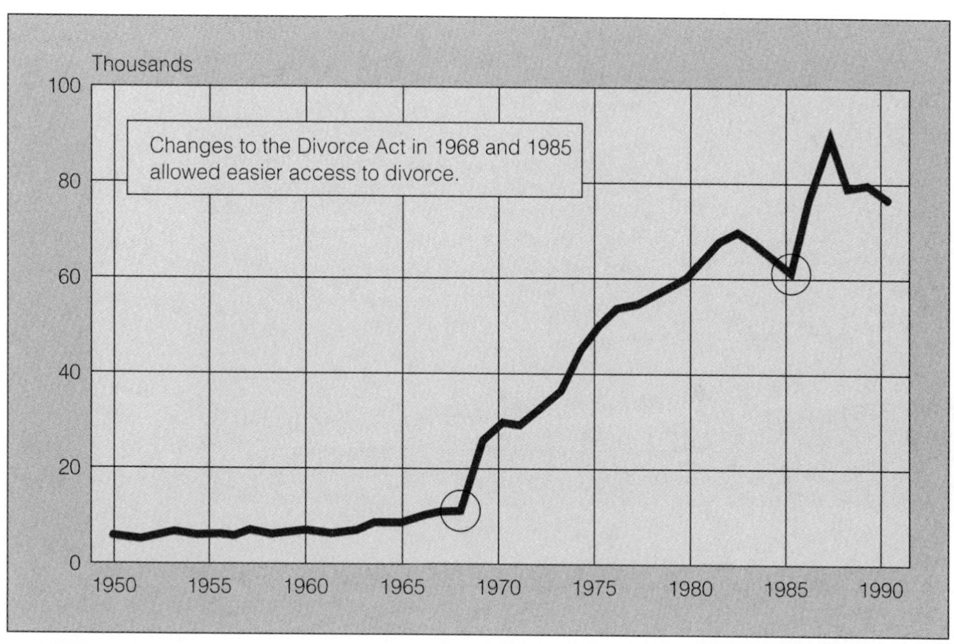

FIGURE 14.6

Divorces in Canada, 1950–1990

Source: Prepared by the Centre for International Statistics, Canadian Council on Social Development. Reproduced by permission.

have not been successful except in cases where questions existed about the emotional stability of the biological parents or the suitability of a foster care arrangement.

The consequences of divorce are not entirely negative. For some people, divorce may be an opportunity to terminate destructive relationships. For others, it may represent a means to achieve personal growth by enabling them to manage their lives and social relationships and establish their own identity. Consider the comments of this separated, single mother of two:

> It was amazing once I got my affairs in order and got my apartment. It was like the clouds parted and the sun came out. It was so amazing. I think it was the best thing that I ever did for myself. Through that whole marriage I don't think I had this much self-esteem. Everybody says, Oh, it's a tragedy. It's not a tragedy. It's a growing thing. It probably could have happened sooner. I'm glad it didn't happen later. I probably would have been a wreck. (quoted in Lynn, 1996:56)

Elizabeth Church (1996) suggests that, given the divorce rate in Canada, divorce should no longer be viewed as a deviant act, but should, rather, be considered a normal part of many people's lives. Church suggests that divorce, for some individuals, is part of their normal life cycle. She stresses that viewing divorce in this way does not deny that divorce and remarriage cause significant upheaval in people's lives. Both divorce and remarriage are generally very painful and difficult events for some members of the family (Church, 1996:86).

REMARRIAGE

Remarriage has been described as "the triumph of hope over experience" (Spencer, 1993:223). Most people who divorce remarry

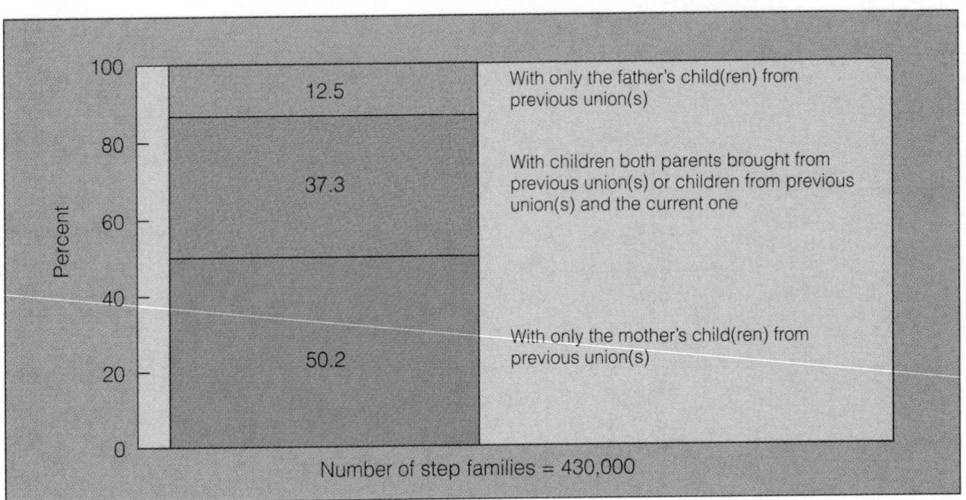

FIGURE 14.7

Step Families, by Type, 1995

Reproduced by authority of the Minister of Industry, 1996, Statistics Canada, from *1996 General Social Survey*, Cat. no. 11-612.

(McVey and Kalbach, 1995), and most divorced people remarry others who have been divorced (London and Wilson, 1988). For example, in the early 1990s, more than 40 percent of all marriages in Canada involved a previously married bride and/or groom. An estimated 76 percent of men and 64 percent of women will remarry and 75 percent of them will do so within three years of their divorce (Gorlick, 1995). Remarriage rates vary by gender. At all ages, a greater proportion of men than women remarry, but both often do so relatively soon after their divorce. Remarriage is also effected by age level and level of education. Among women, the older a woman is at the time of divorce, the lower the likelihood of her remarrying. Women who have not graduated from high school and have young children tend to remarry relatively quickly; by contrast, women with a university degree and without children are less likely to remarry (Nett, 1993).

As a result of divorce and remarriage, complex family relationships often are created. Some become stepfamilies or *blended families*, which consist of a husband and wife, children from previous marriages, and children (if any) from the new marriage. In Canada, an estimated 10 percent of families have at least one stepchild living with the family (General Social Survey, 1996). This figure does not include "occasional" stepchildren—those who visit on weekends and holidays (Church, 1996). Despite the increasing number of stepfamilies, they have been largely ignored in discussions of the family. The 1995 General Social Survey was one of the first to include the category "stepfamily" when collecting data to profile Canadian families. Figure 14.7 outlines the different types of stepfamilies. The 1991 Canadian census ignored stepfamilies (Church, 1996), classifying as families only those in which there are legally married, common-law, or single-parent heads of households.

At least initially, levels of family stress in stepfamilies may be fairly high because of rivalry among the children and hostility directed toward stepparents or ex-spouses (Church, 1996). As Hazel, a new stepparent explains:

> Laura [ex-wife] would come over after school to visit with the children [Hazel's stepchildren] during the times the children were living with us. I felt really uncomfortable about having her in the house when I wasn't home ... I would sit at work imagining that she was going through my kitchen cupboards, and it bothered me so much that George told Laura he didn't want her in the house unless we were there. So then she got mad and refused to come into the house at all and would stay in the car and honk the horn for Kathleen and Noel to come out. They got angry with me and told their father that I was unreasonable and I ended up feeling like the wicked stepmother. (quoted in Church, 1996:91)

In spite of these problems, however, many blended families succeed. The family that results from divorce and remarriage typically is a *complex binuclear family* in which children may have a biological parent and a stepparent, biological siblings and stepsiblings, and an array of other relatives including aunts, uncles, and cousins (Church, 1996).

According to sociologist Andrew Cherlin (1992), the norms governing divorce and remarriage are ambiguous. Because there are no clear-cut guidelines, people must make decisions about family life (such as whom to invite to birthday celebrations or weddings) based on their own beliefs and feelings about the people involved.

SINGLEHOOD

While marriage at increasingly younger ages was the trend in Canada during the first half of the twentieth century, by the 1960s the trend had reversed, and many more adults were remaining single. Figure 14.8 shows the increase in single households between 1951 and 1991. Currently, approximately 25 percent of households in Canada are one- or single-person households. However, this estimate includes people who are divorced, widowed, and those who have never married. Given the fact that nine out of ten Canadians marry at some time in their lives, single status is often temporary. An estimated 10 percent of the population will remain single throughout their lives (Nett, 1993).

Some never-married singles remain single by choice. Reasons include more opportunity for a career (especially for women), the availability of sexual partners without marriage, the belief that the single lifestyle is full of excitement, and the desire for self-sufficiency and freedom to change and experiment (Stein, 1976, 1981). Some scholars have concluded that individuals who prefer to remain single hold more individualistic values and are less family-oriented than those who choose to marry. Friends and personal growth tend to be valued more highly than marriage and children (Alwin, Converse, and Martin, 1985; Nett, 1993). Other never-married singles remain single out of necessity. Being single is an economic necessity for those who cannot afford to marry and set up their own household. Structural changes in the economy have limited the options of many working-class young people. Even some university and college graduates have found that they cannot earn enough money to set up a household separate from that of their parents.

NATIVE CANADIAN FAMILIES

The family has been described as a uniquely human invention (Nett, 1993). Sadly, in the case of native families in Canada, the destruction of the family has also been a human creation. Consider the following comments from a young native person:

> What happened to this "one big family" that the village once was? Our ancestors used to help each other and share with each other. My dad speaks of gatherings when he was young. Everyone shared the moose or the thousands of fish caught. (Fiske and Johnny, 1996:226)

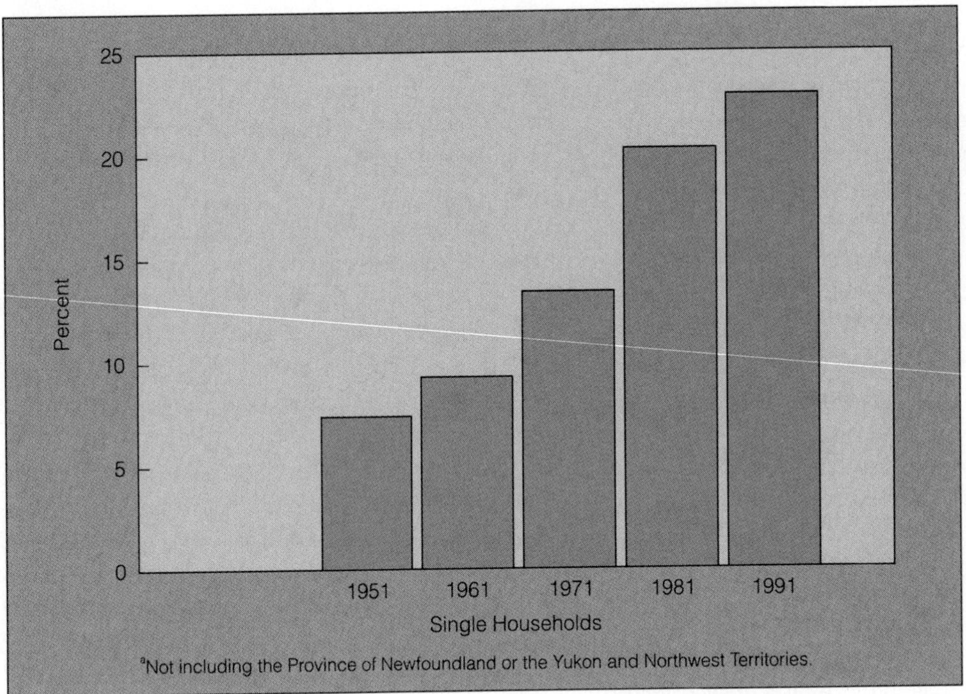

FIGURE 14.8

Selected Households Statistics for Canada, Single Households in Canada, 1951–1991

Reproduced by authority of the Minister of Industry, 1996, Statistics Canada, from *Census of Canada, 1941, 1951, 1961, 1971, 1981, and 1991.*

It is difficult to discuss native families given the fact that native peoples in Canada are by no means a homogeneous group. Native peoples are composed of many distinct nations with different histories, cultures, economic bases, and languages (DasGupta, 1995). However, one characteristic that was universal to these diverse groups was the importance of family ties. Prior to the arrival of the Europeans in Canada, native families were highly organized and stable. In native communities, the extended family was seen as central to both the individual and the community. The concept of family was defined very broadly. For example, to the Ojibwa, *family* referred to individuals who worked together and were bound together by responsibility and friendship as well as kinship ties. Family size averaged between 20 and 25 persons (Shkilnyk, 1985). A bandmember describes the economic cooperation and sharing that once existed within the Ojibwa family:

> Trapping kept the family together because everyone in the family had something to do; the man had to lay traps and check them; the woman skinned the animals, cooked, and looked after the kids. The grandparents helped with the kids; they taught them manners, how to behave, and told them stories about our people. The kids, if they were old enough, had work to do. (Shkilnyk, 1985:81)

Fishing and farming were other modes of production that promoted interdependence and cooperation within extended family units. Under this extended and cooperative family system native families were extremely successful in ensuring the survival and well-being of their members. Four hundred years after contact with the European settlers, the current state of family disruption is evident when you consider the following data. The proportion of native children who are removed from their homes as a result of parental abuse or neglect is ten times that of non-native children; the proportion of native children who commit suicide is seven times the rate of non-native children; wife abuse among native peoples is said to be at least seven times the national average; and mass disclosures of previously hidden sexual and physical abuse of native children are being made (Timpson, 1995:9). How did this happen? Joyce Timpson, who has studied these problems, believes they are not separate, individual problems with individual causes and requiring individual solutions, but that they reflect generations of cultural and spiritual destruction (1995:9).

The Canadian government, with the help of Christian churches, used invasive measures to "remake Aboriginal cultures and societies in the image of European cultures and societies" (Royal Commission on Aboriginal Peoples, 1995:26). Das Gupta (1995) explains that the destruction of traditional native family formations was at the centre of this approach. Families were displaced from their traditional lands and denied access to the resources that were central to the economic survival of the extended family unit. When they refused to give up their cultural identity— that is, when they refused to assimilate—they paid a price: marginalization within Canada. Native families were uprooted from land that was sacred to them and moved to reserves (Royal Commission on Aboriginal Peoples, 1995). The two institutions which have played key roles in the destruction of native family formations are the schools and the child welfare agencies (Das Gupta, 1995). Native children were removed from their families and placed in residential schools (where they were often sexually and physically abused) or adopted by non-native families. Generations of native children were separated from their families and their communities, and this separation also served to sever links with native culture and languages.

After generations of cultural and spiritual destruction, native peoples are now reclaiming their culture. They have also united behind the goal of self-government, especially in the areas of social services and child welfare (Das Gupta, 1995). In contrast with the ideologies inherent in the practices of non-native government agencies, native peoples believe in maintaining the ties between children and their natural parents, as well as caring for children within their native communities. This they see as essential to the rebuilding of native families in Canada. As we near the twenty-first century, many native communities are striving to return to the practices and values that traditionally nourished native family life: respect for women and children, mutual responsibility, and, above all, the general creed of sharing and caring (Royal Commission of Aboriginal Peoples, 1995:81).

FAMILY ISSUES IN THE TWENTY-FIRST CENTURY

As we have seen, families and intimate relationships have changed dramatically during the twentieth century. Some people believe that family as we know it is doomed. Others believe that a return to traditional values will save this important social institution and create greater stability in society. Family diversity is perceived as an indication that Canadian families are in "decline" or "crisis." However, as sociologist Ellen Gee reminds us, "Family diversity is the norm in Canadian society, past and present. Only for a short period in history ... did Canadian families approach uniformity, centered around near-universal marriage and parenthood, family "intactness" and highly differentiated gender roles" (1995:80). The diversity in Canadian families has simply taken on new forms, with increases in common-law unions, divorce, and lone-parent and blended families.

One of the most notable changes in the past fifty years has been the increase in dual-wage earner families. The labour force participation rate of women, particularly married women, has increased dramatically. However, regardless of women's labour force participation, women are still primarily responsible for child care and domestic chores (Marshall, 1990). The absence of adequate affordable child care, inflexible work hours, and parental leave policies means that work is structured in ways that are not "user friendly" for family life (Gee, 1995:102). A challenge for families in the next century is to find ways to reconcile family and work contradictions. As gender roles continue to change, we can expect to see a greater degree of egalitarianism within the family.

One of the most disturbing issues that will continue to affect the quality and stability of family relationships in the future is family violence. The latter part of this century has been marked by the "discovery" of the dark side of the family—child abuse (including physical, sexual, and emotional abuse), wife abuse, and elder abuse. As Elizabeth Comack notes:

> The ideal of the family as a "private domain" and a "resting place" or "sanctuary" has been shattered by the finding that violence in the home is a frequent occurence in contemporary society, and that violence between adults is systematically and disproportionately directed against women. (Comack, 1996a:155)

We live in a society that tolerates, condones, and perpetuates violence. We now have the knowledge that the family is not immune to this violence. "When violence is recognized by both men and women as pervasive, systemic, and unnecessary, change can begin" (Lynn and O'Neill, 1995:300). The challenge of the next century is to reduce the incidence of family violence.

The final issue to consider as we approach the twenty-first century is the impact of new reproductive technologies on families. As Margrit Eichler comments, "there is probably no other recent social development which has a potentially more far-reaching impact on the very nature of the family, on our understandings as to what it means to be a parent, and on the rights and obligations attached to this status" (1988a:280). New reproductive technologies have the capacity to revolutionize family life. Whether or not people will choose to take advantage of the possibilities, and whether or not governments will allow certain services to be delivered, remains to be seen (Baker, 1996).

Regardless of problems facing families in the twenty-first century, the family remains the central institution in the lives of most Canadians. A recent national opinion poll found that over three-quarters of Canadians regard the family as the most important thing in their lives, more important than their career or religion. Ninety-two percent of the respondents with young children at home indicated that the family is becoming more important to them. Finally, an overwhelming majority demonstrated their faith in the family by indicating that they want to marry and have children (although fewer children). Individuals in families are now freer to establish the kinds of family arrangements that best suit them. As Robert Brym concludes, "This does not spell the end of the family but the possibility that improved family forms can take shape" (1996:158).

CHAPTER REVIEW

Today's families include many types of living arrangements and relationships. Families may be defined as relationships in which people live together with commitment, form an economic unit and care for any young, and consider their identity to be significantly attached to the group. In preindustrial societies, the primary form of social organization is through kinship ties. In industrialized societies, other social institutions fulfil some of the functions previously taken care of by the kinship network.

- The family of orientation is the family into which a person is born; the family of procreation is the family a person forms by having or adopting children. An extended family is a family unit composed of relatives in addition to parents and children who live in the same household. A nuclear family is a family composed of one or two parents and their dependent children, all of whom live apart from other relatives.
- Monogamy is a marriage between two partners, usually a woman and a man. In Canada, monogamy is the only form of marriage sanctioned by law. Even though a variety of marital patterns exist across cultures, virtually all forms of marriage establish a system of descent so that kinship can be determined and inheritance rights established.
- Functionalists emphasize the importance of the family in maintaining the stability of society and the well-being of the individuals. Functions of the family include sexual regulation, socialization, economic and psychological support, and provision of social status. Conflict and feminist perspectives view the family as a source of social inequality and an arena for conflict over values, goals, and access to resources and power. Interactionists explain family relationships in terms of the subjective meanings and everyday interpretations people give to their lives.
- Families are changing dramatically in Canada. Cohabitation has increased significantly in the past two decades. With the increase in dual-earner marriages, women increasingly have been burdened by the second shift—the domestic work that employed women perform at home after they complete their workday on the job.
- Divorce is the legal process of dissolving a marriage. At the macrolevel, changes in social institutions may contribute to an increase in divorce rates; at the microlevel, factors contributing to divorce include age at marriage, length of acquaintanceship, economic resources, education level, and parental marital happiness. Most people who divorce get remarried, especially if they are under the age of 35. Divorce has contributed to greater diversity in family relationships, including stepfamilies or blended families and the complex binuclear family.
- Extended family networks are often important in native Canadian families, although factors such as age and class may reduce such family ties. Although all families share certain characteristics, each family is unique.

KEY TERMS

bilateral descent **517**
cohabitation **530**
domestic partnerships **531**
dual-earner marriages **532**
egalitarian family **518**
endogamy **519**
exogamy **519**
extended family **514**
families **512**
family of orientation **514**
family of procreation **514**
homogamy **532**
infertility **534**
kinship **513**
marriage **516**
matriarchal family **517**
matrilineal descent **517**
matrilocal residence **518**
monogamy **516**
neolocal residence **518**
nuclear family **515**
patriarchal family **517**
patrilineal descent **517**
patrilocal residence **518**
polyandry **517**
polygamy **516**
polygyny **516**
second shift **532**
sociology of family **519**

QUESTIONS FOR ANALYSIS AND UNDERSTANDING

1. How do functionalists, conflict, feminist, and interactionist perspectives explain family problems?
2. How are families changing in Canada?
3. What role do extended family networks play in contemporary families?

QUESTIONS FOR CRITICAL THINKING

1. In your own thinking, what constitutes an ideal family?
2. Suppose you wanted to find out about women's and men's perceptions about love and marriage. What specific issues might you examine? What would be the best way to conduct your research?
3. Is the family as we know it about to become extinct?

SUGGESTED READINGS

These comprehensive textbooks offer in-depth information on families and intimate relationships:

Nijole V. Benokraitis. *Marriage and Families: Changes, Choices, and Constraints.* Englewood Cliffs, N.J.: Prentice-Hall, 1993.

Emily Nett. *Canadian Families: Past and Present.* Toronto: Butterworths, 1993.

G.N. Ramu. *Marriage and the Family in Canada Today*. Scarborough, Ont.: Prentice Hall, 1993.

These books provide new insights on the diversity of family life:

Judy Root Aulette. *Changing Families*. Belmont, Cal.: Wadsworth, 1994.

K. Ishwaran. *Family and Marriage: Cross-Cultural Perspectives.* Toronto: Thompson Educational Publishing, 1992.

Marion Lynn. *Voices: Essays on Canadian Families*. Scarborough Ont.: Nelson, 1996.

A historical perspective on Canadian families may be found in:

Jane Ursel. *Private Lives, Public Policy: 100 Years of State Intervention in the Family.* Toronto: Women's Press, 1992.

For additional information about family problems, see:

Arlie Russell Hochschild. *The Second Shift: Working Parents and the Revolution at Home*. New York: Viking/Penguin, 1989.

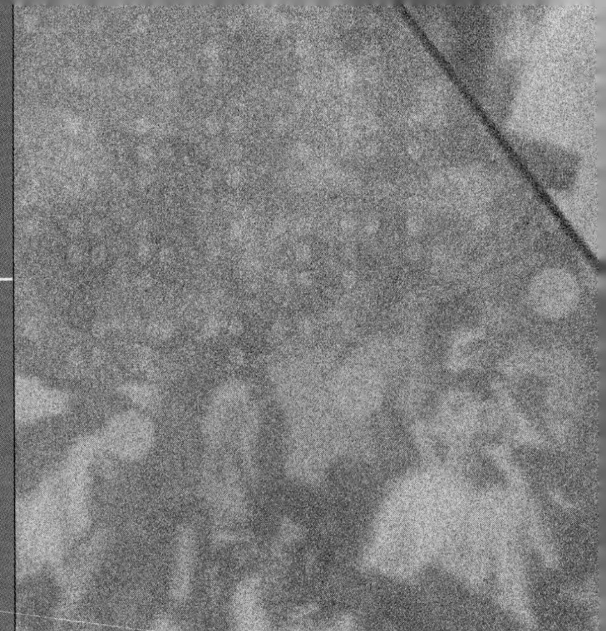

Chapter 15

EDUCATION AND RELIGION

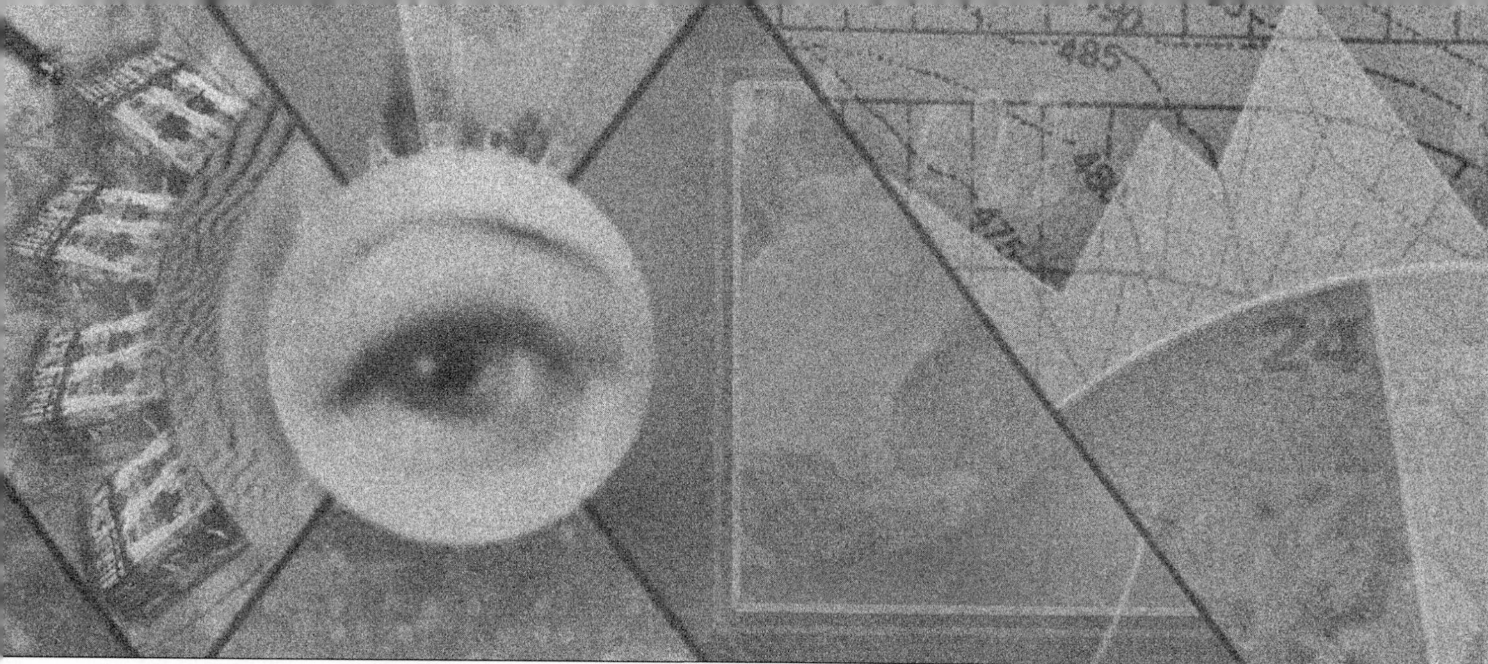

Historically, the institutions of religion and education have been closely interconnected. In fact, religion was largely responsible for the development and maintenance of educational institutions in Canada. Religious instruction was considered an essential component of "becoming educated." Which religion was to be taught was relatively simple—it was Christianity in either its Catholic or Protestant form. Today, things are not that simple—while the majority of Canadians still are Christians, with Catholics making up 45.7 percent and Protestants 36.2 percent, other religions such as Hinduism, Islam, Buddhism, Confucianism, Sikhism, and others too numerous to mention are now part of our Canadian mosaic (Statistics Canada, 1996). Currently, there is no consensus among Canadians regarding what role religion should play in education.

Efforts to create a more pluralistic religious environment within the school system have been "riddled with tension, stress, and frustration" (Fleras and Elliott, 1992). Should students receive religious instruction in the classroom? If so, which religions should be included? Should prayer be offered in schools? Should participation in prayer be voluntary or compulsory? In our multiethnic society, these questions are becoming increasingly difficult to answer. Some parents feel that religious instruction is necessary, suggesting that secularization in the public school system is contributing to a declining morality. These parents advocate compulsory religious instruction, but only in a mainstream Christian faith, as described by the following woman:

> It bothers me what they are teaching kids in school. They are changing history around.

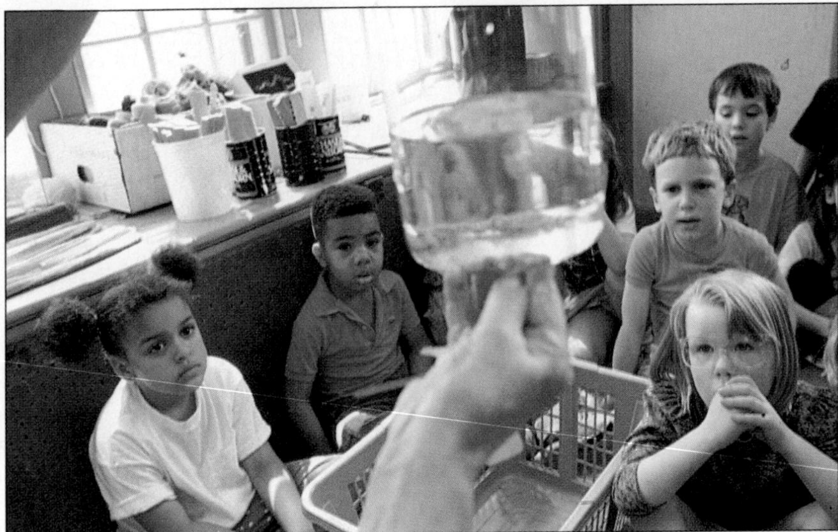

Debates about what children should be taught in schools have taken place throughout the history of North American public education. The issue of teaching creationism versus evolution in science classrooms is only one example of the intersection of religion and education.

> This country was founded on God. The people that came and founded this country were Godly people, and they have totally taken that out of history. They are trying to get rid of everything that ever says anything about God to please someone who is offended by it. That bothers me. (quoted in Roof, 1993:98)

Others strongly disagree with this mother's view on public schools and argue instead that religion and religious instruction in any form have no place in a secular school system. Proponents of this point of view suggest that in our multicultural society no religion should be espoused or endorsed. How might students and teachers who come from diverse religious and cultural backgrounds feel about instruction or organized prayer in public schools? Rick Nelson, a teacher in the public school system, explains his concern about the potential impact of group prayer on students in his classroom:

> I think it really trivializes religion when you try to take such a serious topic with so many different viewpoints and cover it in the public schools. At my school we have teachers and students who are Hindu. They are really devout, but they are not monotheistic. I am not opposed to individual prayer by students. I expect students to pray when I give them a test. They need to do that for my tests. But when there is group prayer who's going to lead the group? And if I had my Hindu students lead the prayer, I will tell you it will disrupt many of my students and their parents. It will disrupt the mission of my school, unfortunately, if my students are [forced] to participate in a group Hindu prayer. (CNN, 1994)

This argument is only one in a lengthy history of debates about the appropriate relationship between public education and religion in Canada. For many years, controversies have arisen periodically over topics such as moral education, anti-Semitism, sex education, school prayer, and the subject matter of textbooks and library books.

Who is to decide what should be taught in public schools? What is the purpose of education? Of religion? In this chapter, we examine education and religion, two social institutions that have certain commonalities both as institutions and as objects of sociological inquiry. Before reading on, test your knowledge about the impact religion has had on education in Canada by taking the quiz in Box 15.1

QUESTIONS AND ISSUES

What common concerns are shared by the social institutions of religion and education in Canada?

What are the key assumptions of functionalist and conflict perspectives on education?

How might educational tracking become a self-fulfilling prophecy for some people?

What unique functions might religion serve that no other institution can fulfil?

How do religious groups differ in organizational structure?

What actions could be taken to resolve debates over religious values and public education?

AN OVERVIEW OF EDUCATION AND RELIGION

Education and religion are powerful and influential forces in contemporary societies. Both institutions impart values, beliefs, and knowledge considered essential to the social reproduction of individual personalities and entire cultures (Bourdieu and Passeron, 1990). Education and religion both grapple with issues of societal stability and social change, reflecting society even as they attempt to shape it. Education and religion also share certain commonalities as objects of sociological study; for example, both are socializing institutions. While early socialization primarily is informal and takes place within our families and friendship networks, as we grow older, socialization passes to the more formalized organizations created for the specific purposes of education and religion.

Areas of sociological inquiry that specifically focus on these institutions are (1) the *sociology of education*, which primarily examines formal education or schooling in industrial societies, and (2) the *sociology of religion*, which focuses on religious groups and organizations, on the behaviour of individuals within these groups, and on ways in which religion is intertwined with other social institutions (Roberts, 1995). Let's start our examination by looking at formal education in historical perspective.

EDUCATION IN HISTORICAL PERSPECTIVE

***Education* is the social institution responsible for the systematic transmission of knowledge, skills, and cultural values within a formally organized structure.** In all societies, people must acquire certain knowledge and skills in order to survive. In less developed societies, these skills might include hunting, gathering, fishing, farming, and self-preservation. In contemporary, developed societies, knowledge and skills often are related to the requirements of a highly competitive job market. Although informal education has taken place throughout human history, education within formal academic settings such as schools is a relatively recent occurrence.

BOX 15.1 SOCIOLOGY AND EVERYDAY LIFE

How Much Do You Know About the Impact of Religion on Education in Canada?

TRUE	FALSE	
T	F	1. Provincial governments in Canada do not fund separate religious schools.
T	F	2. Virtually all contemporary sociologists have advocated the separation of moral teaching from academic subject matter.
T	F	3. The federal government has limited control over how funds are spent by school districts because most of the money comes from the provinces.
T	F	4. Enrolment in parochial schools has decreased in Canada as interest in religion has waned.
T	F	5. In Canada, the public school system recognizes only Christian religious holidays.
T	F	6. The number of children from religious backgrounds other than Christianity and Judaism has grown steadily in public schools over the past three decades.
T	F	7. Debates over textbook content focus only on elementary education because of the vulnerability of young children.
T	F	8. Increasing numbers of parents are instructing their own children through home schooling because of their concerns about what public schools are (or are not) teaching their children.
T	F	9. Most members of the baby boom generation have no religious affiliation today because they received no religious instruction in school.
T	F	10. Prayer in public schools in Canada is offered on a voluntary basis.

Answers on page 557

EARLY FORMAL EDUCATION

Perhaps the earliest formal education occurred in ancient Greece and Rome, where philosophers such as Socrates, Plato, and Aristotle taught elite males the necessary skills to become thinkers and orators who could engage in the art of persuasion (Ballantine, 1993). Between the fall of the Roman Empire and the beginning of the Middle Ages, formal education existed only in the castles of wealthy lords, where young knights were trained in the skills of military conflict and chivalrous behaviour; other children were trained through apprenticeships in merchant and craft

BOX 15.1 SOCIOLOGY AND EVERYDAY LIFE

Answers to the Sociology Quiz on Religion and Education

TRUE	FALSE	
T	**F**	1. *False.* Schools operated by the Catholic church are provincially funded in Alberta, Ontario, Saskatchewan, Yukon, and the Northwest Territories.
T	**F**	2. *False.* Obviously, contemporary sociologists hold strong beliefs and opinions on many subjects; however, most of them do not think it is their role to advocate specific stances on a topic. Early sociologists were less inclined to believe that they had to be "value-free." For example, Durkheim strongly advocated that education should have a moral component and that schools had a responsibility to perpetuate society by teaching a commitment to the common morality.
T	F	3. *True.* Under the terms of the British North America Act, education is a provincial responsibility. Public school revenue comes from local funding through property taxes and provincial funding from a variety of sources. The federal government is responsible for maintaining schools for native people, running a military college, funding adult education programs, and overseeing educational programs in federal penitentiaries.
T	**F**	4. *False.* In recent years, just the opposite has happened. As parents have begun feeling that their children were not receiving the type of education the parents desired for them in public schools, parochial schools have flourished. Both Christian schools and Jewish parochial schools, usually known as Hebrew day schools or yeshivas, have grown rapidly over the past decade.
T	**F**	5. *False.* Some schools have also recognized Jewish holidays. However, this has resulted in conflict, as other religious groups also want to see their religious holidays formally recognized.
T	F	6. *True.* Although about 83 percent of Canadians aged 18 and over describe their religion as one of the forms, or denominations, of Christianity, the number of those who either adhere to no religion (12.5 percent) or who are Jewish, Muslim/Islamic, Sikh, Buddhist, or Hindu has increased significantly.
T	**F**	7. *False.* Attempts to remove textbooks occur at all levels of schooling. A recent case involved the removal of Chaucer's "The Miller's Tale" and Aristophanes' *Lysistrata* from a high school curriculum.
T	F	8. *True.* Some parents choose home schooling for religious reasons; others embrace it for secular reasons, including fear for their children's safety and concerns about the quality of public schools.
T	**F**	9. *False.* Most baby boomers did receive religious instruction, either in private schools or in public schools where prayer and Bible reading took place. Many have returned to religion today because of a feeling that "something was missing" from their lives.
T	F	10. *True.* Parents must sign consent forms for their children to participate in prayers in public schools.

Sources: Based on Johnson, 1994; Ballantine, 1993; Greenberg and Page, 1993; Kosmin and Lachman, 1993; Roof, 1993; Sullivan, 1993; and Gibbs, 1994.

guilds (Ballantine, 1993). During the Middle Ages, the first colleges and universities were developed under the auspices of the church. This crucial linkage between education and religion introduced the concept of human depravity into the curriculum; to curtail people's "sinful nature," teachers used authoritarian methods of instruction and discipline (Ballantine, 1993). The history of education in Canada begins with attempts by Jesuit priests and missionaries to "civilize" native children and the children of colonists. During this time, the church was central to the institution of education. Many of Canada's oldest universities and colleges were founded by churches. The oldest is King's College, an Anglican college in Nova Scotia founded in 1789. Laval University was founded in 1852 by the Jesuits (Gaskell, 1994).

The Renaissance and the Industrial Revolution had a profound impact on education. During the Renaissance, the focus of education shifted from human depravity to the importance of developing well-rounded and liberally educated people. With the rapid growth of industrial capitalism and factories during the Industrial Revolution, it became necessary for workers to have basic skills in reading, writing, and arithmetic. In Canada, the school reformers of the late 1800s were concerned that the "classical curriculum did not reflect the realities of the new economic order ... Education, thus, began to be viewed as essential for national economic growth" (Gilbert, 1989:105). Ontario school reformer Egerton Ryerson promoted free schooling for all children, arguing that sending rich and poor children to the same schools would bring people closer together and create more harmony (Tepperman, 1994). By 1920, education was compulsory for all Canadian children up to the age of sixteen.

Also, by the 1920s, a "core" curriculum—including mathematics, social sciences, natural sciences, and English—had been introduced. This curriculum is reflected in today's "back to basics" movement that calls for teaching the three R's ("reading, 'riting, and 'rithmetic") and enforcing stricter discipline in schools. Some educational analysts praise this curriculum, but others argue that it emphasizes Western culture and Euro-Canadian history to the exclusion of the culture and history of all other groups and cultures.

CONTEMPORARY EDUCATION IN CANADA

In addition to teaching the basics, Canadian schools today teach a myriad of topics, ranging from computer skills to AIDS prevention. Many educators believe that their job description now encompasses numerous tasks that previously were performed by families and other social institutions. As Ruth Prale, an elementary reading specialist, notes:

> A teacher today is a social worker, surrogate parent, a bit of disciplinarian, a counselor, and someone who has to see to it that they eat. Many teachers are mandated to teach sex education, drug awareness, gang awareness. And we're supposed to be benevolent. And we haven't come to teaching yet! (quoted in Collins and Frantz, 1993:83)

Like Prale, many parents are critical of changes that have taken place in schools since their youth. Some argue that public schools used to teach moral education and hold organized classroom prayers. To these parents, the shift from moral education to value-neutral education is equivalent to abandoning the country's religious heritage and moral foundation. However, the tricky question remains, which religion should be taught? The 1960 Bill of Rights guarantees the right to religious freedom, and the Charter of Rights and Freedoms and human rights legislation prohibit discrimination on the basis of religion. Various minority groups have argued that these constitutional provisions give parents of all religious backgrounds the right to determine the education of their children. This right, they feel, includes the establishment of separate schools, which would be provincially funded in the same way that Catholic schools are financed by some provincial governments. The response of the provincial governments generally has been to permit some degree of religious instruction—

however, determining the nature and scope of the instruction is proving difficult. Numerous recent incidents have forced the issue of what is acceptable and what is not. For example, to promote a multicultural environment, several schools in Toronto decided to exclude all references to Christian symbols or doctrine from their annual Christmas celebrations. One Toronto high school renamed its Christmas assembly a "holiday assembly" and eliminated all references to Christianity. Another school banned the singing of religious Christmas carols on the grounds that references to Christianity would upset the non-Christian children (over 30 percent of the school population). As discussed in Box 15.2, the issue of which religious holidays are recognized in public schools is being played out in the courts. The overall effect of such incidents has been the increased secularization of the public school system. For example, in 1990 the Ontario Court of Appeal ruled against religious instruction in public elementary schools because it violates an individual's rights to freedom of religion (Fleras and Elliott, 1992). In 1995, Newfoundlanders voted to eliminate church-run schools in favour of a public, nondenominational education system. Newfoundland was at that time the only province in Canada that still had a church-run educational system.

SOCIOLOGICAL PERSPECTIVES ON EDUCATION

Sociologists have divergent perspectives on the purpose of education in contemporary society. Functionalists suggest that education contributes to the maintenance of society and provides people with an opportunity for self-enhancement and upward social mobility. Conflict theorists argue that education perpetuates social inequality and benefits the dominant class at the expense of all others. Interactionists focus on classroom dynamics and the effect of self-concept on grades and aspirations.

THE FUNCTIONALIST PERSPECTIVE ON EDUCATION

Functionalists view education as one of the most important components of society. According to Durkheim, education is the "influence exercised by adult generations on those that are not yet ready for social life" (Durkheim, 1956:28). As noted previously, Durkheim also asserted that moral values are the foundation of a cohesive social order and that schools have the responsibility of teaching a commitment to the common morality. Although his work entitled *Moral Education* was not completed before his death, contemporary sociologists Jonathan H. Turner, Leonard Beeghley, and Charles H. Powers (1995:46) have summarized his views on this topic as follows:

> The commitment to the common morality must be learned in schools, where the teacher operates as the functional equivalent of the priest. The teacher gives young students an understanding of and a reverence for the nature of the society and the need to have a morality that regulates passions and provides attachments to groupings organized to pursue societal goals. Such educational socialization must assure that the common morality is a part of the students' motivational needs ... their cognitive orientations ... and their self-control processes.

From this perspective, teachers are the functional equivalent of priests in teaching students about morality. Students must be taught to put the group's needs ahead of their individual desires and aspirations. Like Durkheim, contemporary functionalists suggest that education has specific functions in society, both manifest and latent.

MANIFEST FUNCTIONS OF EDUCATION Some purposes of education are ***manifest functions*—open, stated, and intended goals or consequences of activities within an organization or institution.** An example of a manifest function in education is

BOX 15.2 SOCIOLOGY AND LAW

A Legal Challenge to Religious Holidays in Schools

Like millions of other young Canadians, 14-year-old Aysha Bassuny returns to school this [September]. But the Ottawa Board of Education has delayed the start of her school year for two days so that Jewish students can observe the Jewish New Year—Rosh Hashanah. Bassuny is one of many in Ottawa's Islamic community who are angry that the board has refused to consider extending them a similar courtesy by closing schools for two Muslim holy days. "It's not fair," says Bassuny, a Grade 10 student at suburban Brookfield High School, who wears the traditional Islamic head scarf, the hijab. "I have to miss school for my holy days and the Jewish kids don't. You cannot have it for one group and not the other."

The Islamic Schools Federation of Ontario, which represents independent Muslim schools, agrees with the irate teenager. In July, the federation launched a lawsuit against the Ottawa Board of Education alleging that the rights of Muslims to freedom of conscience and religion under the Charger of Rights have been undermined by the board's actions. The lawsuit, which is scheduled to be heard on Oct. 25 by the Ontario Court General Division, argues that schools with significant numbers of Muslim students—according to the federation, there are 2,250 students of Muslim faith in Ottawa's public schools, compared with about 410 Jews—should be required to observe two important Islamic holidays. Whatever the lower court decides, its ruling is expected to be appealed, possibly all the way to the Supreme Court of Canada. In that event, the Ottawa case could eventually determine whether the Charter forces public school boards across Canada to treat all religions identically.

The dispute began in April 1994, when the Ottawa board agreed to what seemed at the time to be a modest request from Ottawa's Jewish community—to delay the start of the school year so that Jewish students could observe Rosh Hashanah without missing the crucial first two days of school (until now, only the Christian holidays of Christmas and Good Friday have been observed by public schools, meaning that students of other religions have been forced to miss a day of school in order to observe their own holy days). According to Jewish community leader Ron Singer, the request was entirely reasonable, because it did not mean a permanent change in the school year: the Jewish calendar is based on the cycles of the moon, and Rosh Hashanah coincides with the opening of school only once every 40 years. Observes Singer: "This is an extremely rare occurrence that happens twice in a century."

It may have seemed reasonable to Singer, but not to Ottawa's 18,000-strong Muslim community, which threatened legal action unless the decision was reversed or Muslims accommodated by the closing of schools on two of their holy days: March 3, the end of Ramadan, and May 11, which coincides with the annual pilgrimage to Mecca. Seven other public boards in Ontario agreed to delay the school year, although the neighbouring Carleton board did not. The Islamic federation chose Ottawa as a test case, believing that a victory there would set a precedent all across the country.

The lawyer for the Federation of Islamic Schools of Ontario said last week that the issue is simply one of equity. He rejected arguments by Jewish groups that their request for a one-time delay to the school year was far less than the Muslim demand for two new permanent school holidays each year. "The issue," Binavince said, "is the recognition of two religions, Christian and Jewish, and the rejection of another, Muslim."

But Singer says the goals of Ottawa Muslims are not so clear-cut: "If they just wanted holidays for themselves, it's legitimate. But to threaten legal action unless the holiday is taken away from the Jews ... " He leaves the sentence deliberately hanging. Those involved in the dispute recognize that, if taken to its logical extreme, the rapid growth of Canada's Muslim, Buddhist, Hindu, and Sikh communities could lead to a school year with as many as 15 religious holidays. One school board member concedes that "it's a tough problem." And one that an increasingly multicultural society will be unable to avoid. [To date this case remains unresolved.]

Source: Adapted from Fisher, 1994.

the teaching of specific subjects, such as science, mathematics, reading, history, and English. Education serves five major manifest functions in society:

1. *Socialization.* From kindergarten through university, schools teach students the student role, specific academic subjects, and political socialization. By kindergarten, children learn the appropriate attitudes and behaviour for the student role (Ballantine, 1993). In primary and secondary schools, students are taught specific subject matter appropriate to their age, skill level, and previous educational experience. At the university/college level, students focus on more detailed knowledge of subjects they have previously studied while also being exposed to new areas of study and research. Throughout their schooling, students receive political socialization in the form of history and civics lessons in good citizenship and patriotism, as discussed in Chapter 13.

2. *Transmission of culture.* Schools transmit cultural norms and values to each new generation and play an active part in the process of assimilation, whereby recent immigrants learn the dominant cultural values, attitudes, and behaviour so that they can be productive members of society. However, questions remain as to whose culture is being transmitted. Because of the great diversity in the Canada today, it is virtually impossible to define a single culture, as was discussed in Chapter 3.

3. *Social control.* Schools are responsible for teaching values such as discipline, respect, obedience, punctuality, and perseverance. Schools teach conformity by encouraging young people to be good students, conscientious future workers, and law-abiding citizens. Teaching conformity rests primarily with classroom teachers, as Adele Jones (1994:23), a high school math teacher, explains:

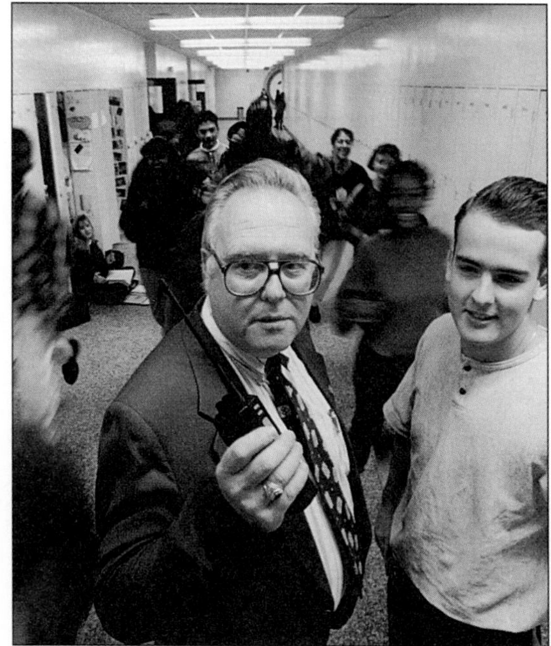

Although schools may contribute to social control in society, today's school officials find control increasingly difficult to maintain. This Toronto school has implemented a cooperative program operated by staff and students.

> I tell kids from the start that I'm not out to fail them, but they've got to understand certain concepts in order to go on to college. If they do four things, they'll do fine: pay attention in class, do their homework, study, and ask questions. They need to understand that quizzes count, that coming to class shows a commitment to learn, that doing homework, studying for tests, and participating in class tell me they want to learn ... I set my standards high so my kids can do likewise; is it therefore my fault if they choose not to do the work?

4. *Social placement.* Schools are responsible for identifying the most qualified people to fill available positions in society. As a result,

students are channelled into programs based on individual ability and academic achievement. Graduates receive the appropriate credentials for entry into the paid labour force.

5. *Change and innovation.* Schools are a source of change and innovation. As student populations change over time, new programs are introduced to meet societal needs; for example, sex education, drug education, and multicultural studies have been implemented in some schools to help students learn about pressing social issues. Innovation in the form of new knowledge is required of colleges and universities. Faculty members are encouraged, and sometimes required, to engage in research and share the results with students, colleagues, and others. In medical schools, for example, innovative technologies (such as new drugs) and new techniques (such as gene splicing) are developed and tested. Similarly, sociological research contributes to our knowledge of crime, family life, social movements, and discrimination, to name only a few areas.

LATENT FUNCTIONS OF EDUCATION In addition to manifest functions, all social institutions, including schools, have some ***latent functions*—hidden, unstated and sometimes unintended consequences of activities within an organization or institution**. Education serves at least three latent functions:

1. *Restricting some activities.* Early in the twentieth century, all provinces passed *mandatory education laws* that require children to attend school until they reach a specified age (usually 16) or until they complete a minimum level of formal education (generally completion of Grade 8). The assumption was that an educated citizenry and workforce are necessary for the smooth functioning of democracy and capitalism. Out of these laws grew one latent function of education, which is to keep students off the street and out of the full-time job market for a number of years, thus helping keep unemployment within reasonable bounds (Braverman, 1974).

2. *Matchmaking and production of social networks.* Because schools bring together people of similar ages, social class, and race/ethnicity, young people often meet future marriage partners and develop social networks there that may last for many years.

3. *Creation of a generation gap.* Students may learn information in school that contradicts beliefs held by their parents or their religion. Debates over the content of textbooks and library books, as well as arguments over creationism and evolution, typically centre on information that parents deem unacceptable for their children. When education conflicts with parental attitudes and beliefs, a generation gap is created if students embrace the newly acquired perspective.

Functionalists acknowledge that education has certain dysfunctions. Some analysts argue that Canadian schools are not teaching reading, writing, and mathematics skills at the high levels that are needed in the workplace and the global economy. For example, in a study of mathematical and science competence among 13-year-olds, Canadian students ranked ninth among the fifteen countries tested (see Table 15.3), even though Canada spends more on education than some of the countries that ranked ahead of it (Fennell, 1993; Stevenson and Stigler, 1992). A reason for this may lie in the fact that students from other countries such as Korea, Japan, and Taiwan, who usually outperform Canadian students, have schools that are more structured and instruction that focuses more on drill and practice. Ironically, however, Japanese educational officials recently noted that rigidity in schools often contributes to a lack of student creativity, an area where Canadian and American students continue to excel (Celis, 1994).

THE CONFLICT PERSPECTIVE ON EDUCATION

In contrast to the functionalist perspective, conflict theorists argue that schools perpetuate class, racial-ethnic, and gender inequalities in society, as some groups seek to maintain their privileged position at the expense of others (Guppy, 1984; Ballantine, 1993).

REPRODUCTION OF CLASS Conflict theorists argue that education is a vehicle for reproducing existing class relationships. According to French sociologist Pierre Bourdieu, students have differing amounts of ***cultural capital*—social assets that include values, beliefs, attitudes, and competencies in language and culture** (Bourdieu and Passeron, 1990). Cultural capital involves "proper" attitudes toward education, socially approved dress and manners, and knowledge about books, art, music, and other forms of high and popular culture. Middle- and upper-income parents endow their children with more cultural capital than do working-class and poverty-level parents. Because cultural capital is essential for acquiring an education, children with less cultural capital have fewer opportunities to succeed in school. For example, standardized tests, which are used for grouping students by ability and for assigning students to classes, often measure students' cultural capital rather than their "natural" intelligence or aptitude. Many Canadian schools practise "streaming" or ***tracking*—the categorical assignment of students based on test scores, previous grades, or both, to different types of educational programs**. The educational justification for streaming is that it is easier to teach students with similar abilities. In elementary schools children are sorted into ability groups—often disguised with names such as the Robins and the Bluejays. Children, of course, quickly learn the values attached to these labels—the Robins are the smart ones and the Bluejays ... well ... In junior high and in high school, students continue to be tracked into specific courses and educational programs. At the secondary level, the streaming consists of separating students into three streams: technical and vocational programs, general-level programs, and university entrance programs.

According to conflict analysis, streaming actually works to perpetuate inequality rather than to encourage individual achievement according to ability. Much research challenges the efficacy of streaming and instead points out its discriminatory biases. For one thing, as education scholar Jeannie Oakes has noted, streaming defines half of all students as below average (1985:86–89). What factors determine which "track" a student is placed in? Student records, test scores, dress, appearance, parental background, sex, and ethnicity combine in very complex ways to affect teacher expectations and evaluations of student potential (Gomme, 1995). In addition, a considerable amount of research suggests that socioeconomic background has as much to do with streaming as does individual merit (Bowles and Gintis, 1976; Oakes, 1985; Porter, 1987). Students in lower tracks tend to come from lower-class and minority backgrounds. In contrast, students from affluent families typically are placed in university-bound streams. Oakes (1985:86–89) also found that tracking affects students' perceptions of classroom goals and achievements, as the following statements from high- and low-track students suggest:

> I want to be a lawyer and debate has taught me to dig for answers and get involved. I can express myself. (High Track English).
>
> To understand concepts and ideas and experiment with them. Also to work independently. (High Track Science).
>
> To behave in class. (Low Track English).
>
> To be a better listener in class. (Low Track English).
>
> I have learned that I should do my questions for the book when he asks me to. (Low Track Science).

The research also indicates that streaming is particularly detrimental to the educational experiences of some ethnic minorities (Baril and Mori,

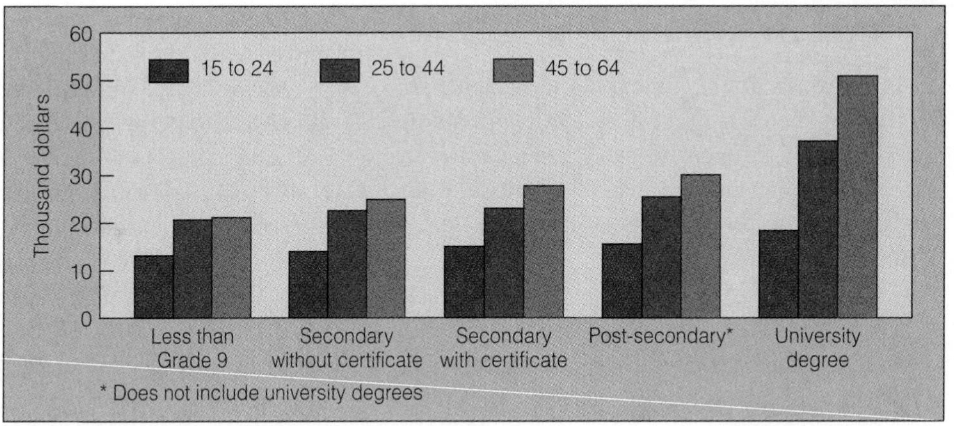

FIGURE 15.1

Average Annual Income for Full-time Workers, by Level of Schooling and Age Group, 1985

*1986 is last date for which data is available

Source: Secretary of State, Canada, 1992.

1991). Shamai (1992) examined the educational attainment of different ethnic groups in Canada and found that native people, Ukrainians, French, and Italians have lower-than-average years of schooling. Native peoples are the most disadvantaged group, with nearly 80 percent having less than a secondary education and only 5 percent ever going to college or university (Tepperman, 1994). People from Jewish, Chinese, and Japanese backgrounds have higher-than-average educational attainment and are much more likely to attend university.

Awareness of these effects has resulted in numerous destreaming initiatives across the country. For example, in 1993 the Ontario Ministry of Education and Training began a destreaming program of one grade per year starting with Grade 9. These initiatives are being met with some opposition by parents, teachers, and school boards, who are concerned that children will receive lower-quality education in destreamed classrooms. However, the benefits of destreaming may outweigh the costs, when we consider the perceptions and lowered expectations of students on the "low tracks," brought on by years of tracking.

THE HIDDEN CURRICULUM According to conflict theorists, the ***hidden curriculum*** **is the transmission of cultural values and attitudes, such as conformity and obedience to authority, through implied demands found in rules, routines, and regulations of schools** (Snyder, 1971).

Social Class and the Hidden Curriculum

Although students from all social classes are subjected to the hidden curriculum, working-class and poverty-level students may be most adversely affected (Cookson and Hodges Persell, 1985; Ballantine, 1993; Polakow, 1993). Stephen Richer (1988) studied the hidden curriculum in classrooms in Ottawa. He determined that the hidden curriculum in the early grades encourages students to be competitive, materialistic, to value work over play, and to show deference to authority. Richer suggests that the hidden curriculum favours students from middle- and upper-class backgounds over those from lower-class backgrounds. Why? The research indicates that students from lower-class backgrounds are less motivated, especially when the rewards for effort are symbolic rather than material. The lower-class culture also places more emphasis on the present as opposed to the future and emphasizes cooperation rather than competition. In contrast, middle-class children are socialized to act competitively, defer gratification, and pursue symbolic rewards. Therefore, these children are much more likely both to conform to the value system of the hidden curriculum and to receive the rewards of conforming: more praise, support, and positive attention in the classroom. Lower-class children, on the other hand, are more often subjected to discipline and authority. As a result, these students are less successful in school and may be disqualified from higher education and barred from obtaining the credentials necessary for well-paid occupations and professions (Bowles and Gintis, 1976).

Credentialism Canada has been described as a *credentials society*, that is, a society in which the acquisition of academic credentials is essential to upward mobility and success. The term ***credentialism* refers to the requirement that a person hold some particular diploma or degree as a condition of employment.** In a credentials society such as ours, skills and ability do not exist without a degree attached. Conflict theorists point out that the credentials required often bear little resemblance to the actual skills and responsibilities of the job. Why then are degrees so important? They are important because without them access to prestigious, high-paying jobs is limited (see Figure 15.1). According to Randall Collins (1979), credentials serve a gatekeeping function. That is, professional groups such as those consisting of doctors, lawyers, and accountants exclude anyone without the proper education in order to regulate the labour market and keep wages high. The result is a process of social selection in which class advantage and social status are linked to the possession of academic credentials (Collins, 1979; G. Marshall, 1994). According to conflict theorists, credentialism is not driven by the actual need for increased knowledge but rather by the promotion of vested interests—in income, prestige, autonomy and power—of professional groups.

TABLE 15.1

University Degrees Granted, by Field of Study and Sex, 1994

Canada	**178,074**	
Male	76,470	43%
Female	101,604	57%
Social Sciences	**69,586**	
Male	30,701	44%
Female	38,885	56%
Education	**30,383**	
Male	9,140	30%
Female	21,279	70%
Humanities	**23,057**	
Male	8,416	37%
Female	14,641	63%
Health professions and occupations	**12,183**	
Male	3,475	29%
Female	8,708	71%
Engineering and applied sciences	**12,597**	
Male	10,285	82%
Female	2,312	18%
Agriculture and biological sciences	**10,087**	
Male	4,309	43%
Female	5,778	57%
Mathematics and physical sciences	**9,551**	
Male	6,697	70%
Female	2,854	30%
Fine and applied arts	**5,308**	
Male	1,773	33%
Female	3,535	67%
Arts and sciences	**5,322**	
Male	1,710	32%
Female	3,612	68%

Reproduced by authority of the Minister of Industry, 1996, Statistics Canada, from CANSIM cross-classified table 00580602, 1996.

"Rich" schools and "poor" schools are readily identifiable by their buildings, equipment, and size of classes. What are the social consequences of unequal funding for schools?

Credentialism is closely related to ***meritocracy*—a social system in which status is assumed to be acquired through individual ability and effort** (Young, 1994/1958). Persons who acquire the appropriate credentials for a job are assumed to have gained the position through *what they know*, not *who they are* or *who they know*.

Gender Bias and the Hidden Curriculum In Chapter 10, we examined the ways in which gender bias in schools has a negative impact on female students. According to conflict theorists, gender bias is embedded in both the formal and the hidden curriculum of schools. Although most females in Canada have a greater opportunity for education than those living in developing nations, their educational opportunities are not equal to those of males in their social class (see Gaskell and McLaren, 1987). Through reading materials, classroom activities, and treatment by teachers and peers, female students learn that they are less important than male students. For example, such expressions as "scientists and their wives" or the "businessman's lunch" identify science and business as masculine activities. This kind of stereotyping is often unintentional or hidden in the sense that the discussion is not about gender relations (Guppy, 1995:472). The result, however, is the same, the reinforcement of gender-segregated stereotypes. As a result of pressure from women's groups, a number of advisory groups have been appointed to screen educational texts. The research evidence suggests that material used in the classrooms in the 1990s has become more diverse and less stereotyped (Gaskell et al., 1995).

The hidden curriculum has also been used to explain why so few women study mathematics and science at the postsecondary level. At the elementary and secondary levels of schools males and females are enrolled in roughly equal numbers. Over time, differential treatment undermines females' self-esteem and discourages them from taking certain courses, such as math and science courses, which usually are dominated by male teachers and students (Raffalli, 1994). For example, teachers tend to give girls less attention while encouraging boys to be problem solvers and asking them complicated questions. As a result, females tend to take fewer courses in these areas or drop them because they are uninterested (Fennema and Leder, 1990). Further evidence suggests that teachers and guidance counsellors encourage women to make educational and occupational choices that are consistent with traditional gender roles. Table 15.1 shows that in 1994 women received only 18 percent of the degrees awarded in engineering and applied sciences and 30 percent of degrees awarded in mathematics and physical sciences.

Canada is not unique in its lack of equality in educational opportunities for women. Literacy rates for women in developing nations reflect the belief that women do not need to read or possess knowledge that might contribute to their nation's social and economic development. These perceptions tend to be reinforced by strong religious beliefs, as discussed in Box 15.3.

SOCIAL CLASS IN HIGHER EDUCATION Even for students who complete high school, access to colleges and universities is determined not only by prior academic record but also by the ability to pay. Although public institutions such as community colleges and universities are funded primarily by tax dollars, the cost of attending such institutions has increased dramatically over the past decade. Even with the lower cost of attending community colleges, the enrolment of low-income students at these institutions has dropped since the 1980s as a result of declining scholarship funds and the necessity for many students to work full- or part-time to finance their education. In contrast, not only do students from affluent families have no trouble funding their education at Canadian institutions, but they are also more likely to attend prestigious private colleges or universities outside of Canada where tuition fees alone may be more than $20,000 per year (Fennell, 1993).

Thus, the ability to pay for a university education reproduces the class system. Some students lack access to higher education because of a lack of money; those who do attend university are stratified according to their ability to pay. In addition, a study of Ontario high-school students by Porter, Porter, and Blishen (1982) showed a strong relationship between family occupational status and the likelihood of university attendance. Seventy-eight percent of the higher-class students were in university-track programs, compared with only 40 percent of the lower-class students. Parents' occupational attainment is also strongly correlated to the university attendance of their children. Richer (1988) found in his sample of 19-to-21-year-olds that 67.5 percent of those whose fathers had university degrees were attending college or university, while only 18.2 percent of those whose fathers did not complete high school were attending a postsecondary institution. These patterns of inequality, of course, repeat themselves as seen in Figure 15.1, which shows average earnings of workers (by level of education). In sum, to conflict theorists, education reproduces social inequalities that create a stratified class structure in Canadian society.

THE INTERACTIONIST PERSPECTIVE ON EDUCATION

Sociologists examining education from an interactionist perspective may focus on classroom dynamics, examining the interpretations that students and teachers give to their interactions with one another. Interactionists also are interested in the effect of students' self-concept on their grades and aspirations.

EDUCATION AND THE SELF-FULFILLING PROPHECY For some students, schooling may become a self-fulfilling prophecy. According to sociologist Robert Merton (1968), a ***self-fulfilling prophecy*** **is an unsubstantiated belief or prediction resulting in behaviour that makes the originally false belief come true.** For example, if a teacher (as a result of stereotypes based on the relationship between IQ and race) believes that some students of colour are less capable of learning, that teacher (sometimes without even realizing it) may treat them as if they were incapable of learning.

What is the effect of teacher expectations on students? Does the practice of tracking or streaming students lead to self-fulfilling prophecies for individual students? Social psychologist Robert Rosenthal (1969) designed an experiment to answer these questions. Rosenthal told teachers at an elementary school that he had developed a new test that would identify those children who were likely to "spurt ahead" during the next year. The children were then tested and the teachers were provided with a list of the names of the "spurters" and were instructed to watch their progress without revealing their expectations to the students or the students' parents in any way. In fact, the test had no predictive value, and the names that Rosenthal provided had been selected at random. The only characteristic that distinguished these children from their classmates was the teachers' expectation of success. A year later, Rosenthal found marked academic gains among the "spurters." He concluded that the teachers had changed their attitudes toward these children in subtle ways and had influenced their progress as a result. In other words, the teachers' expectations had created a self-fulfilling prophecy. Rosenthal's findings, however, became controversial because attempts to replicate his experiment produced mixed results. But a good deal of research confirms that positive teacher expectations generally create more successful students (Snyder, 1991).

EDUCATION AND LABELLING In the past, IQ testing has resulted in labelling of students. For example, studies in the United States found that many African American and Mexican American children were placed in special education classes on the basis of IQ scores even when they simply could not understand the tests. Similar research in Canada indicates that in elementary schools, special education classes are filled with children from visible minority groups, and in high schools visible minority students are overrepresented in the technical and vocational streams (Curtis, Livingston, and Smaller, 1992). According to labelling theory, terms such as *learning disabled* are social constructions that lead to stigmatization and may be incorporated into the everyday interactions of teachers, students, and parents (Carrier, 1986; Coles, 1987). Labels placed on students by educators may indeed become a self-fulfilling prophecy if students become convinced that they are less intelligent and thus less capable than others. However, some programs have been shown to have a positive effect on students who scored lower on IQ tests. For example, a study in Ypsilanti, Michigan, found that preschool programs such as Head Start had a lasting impact on children: they were less likely to be absent from school or be classified as retarded and were more likely to graduate from high school and become employed (Passell, 1994).

A self-fulfilling prophecy also can result from labelling students as "gifted." Gifted students are considered to be those with above-average intellectual ability, academic aptitude, creative or productive thinking, or leadership skills (Ballantine, 1993). When some students are labelled as better than others, they may achieve at a higher level because of the label. Ironically, such labelling also may result in discrimination against these students. For example, according to law professor Margaret Chon (1995:238), the "myth of the super human Asian" creates a self-fulfilling prophecy for some Asian American students in the United States:

> When I was in college, I applied to the Air Force ROTC program. I was given the most complete physical of my life [and] I took an intelligence test. When I reported back to the ROTC staff, they looked glum. What is it? I thought. Did the physical turn up some life-threatening defect? It turned out I had gotten the highest test score ever at my school. Rather than feeling pleased and flattered, I felt like a sideshow freak. The recruiters were not happy either. I think our reactions had a lot to do with the fact that I did not resemble a typical recruit. I am a women of East Asian, specifically Korean, descent. They did not want me in ROTC no matter how "intelligent" I was.

According to Chon, painting Asian Americans as superintelligent makes it possible for others to pretend they do not exist: "Governments ignore us because we've already made it. Schools won't recruit us because we do so well on the SATs [standardized achievement tests]. Asian Americans seem almost invisible, except when there is a

BOX 15.3 SOCIOLOGY IN GLOBAL PERSPECTIVE

Religion and Women's Literacy in Developing Nations

Education is a powerful agent of progress. Literacy is the most basic and necessary of learning skills.—Maria Luisa Jauregui de Gainza, Literacy Specialist, UNESCO

Women's literacy has been referred to as the "challenge of the decade." *Functional illiteracy* refers to a lack of basic literacy and numeracy skills that are essential for proper functioning—such as the ability to read or write or to make sense of written material (Ballara, 1992: 1). Organizations such as the United Nations believe that the education of women in developing nations is a high priority not only for national development but also for the well-being of children and families.

An estimated 95 percent of all illiterate people are concentrated in the developing nations of Southeast Asia and sub-Saharan Africa. Here, one-third of all women are illiterate, as compared with one-fifth of the men. In the least developed nations, 79 percent of adult women are illiterate. Even with organizations such as the United Nations Educational, Scientific and Cultural Organization (UNESCO) attempting to eradicate illiteracy, the problem remains.

Many factors stand in the way of women's literacy, including religious beliefs that subordinate women and emphasize a traditional gendered division of labor, such as "care of children, maintenance of the household, care of older family members and the ill, servicing their husband and his relevant kin, maintenance of the network of familial ties, and servicing of the community" (Ballara, 1992:x). Religions that confine women's activities to domestic tasks and stress their role as wives and mothers often limit their access to education and produce feelings of low self-esteem and isolation.

Ultimately, the main reason most women (and men) are illiterate is poverty; daily survival becomes far more important than learning how to read or compute math problems. Some analysts have found that schools in the poorest developing nations are becoming even more impoverished. Some countries have a two-tier system: (1) in rural areas, a grossly inadequate school system that may be state-run or attached to a local temple or mosque, where religious education often is the primary goal, and (2) in urban areas, a better school system that may be patterned after Western schools such as those found in England or France and that serves the children of the nation's elite population.

Women throughout the world experience a lack of educational opportunities. In hopes of increasing women's literacy in Nepal, Save the Children Foundation provides adult education classes.

Is there hope for the future? Media campaigns and numerous projects are actively seeking to promote literacy. Perhaps a greater awareness of the problem is the first step toward eradication of it. Are the problems of women in developing nations in any way related to your life? Using your sociological imagination, can you think of ways in which their "fate" might be intertwined with yours?

Sources: Based on Ballara, 1992; and Ballantine, 1993.

grocery store boycott—or when we're touted as the model minority" (Chon, 1995:239–240).

Studies of girls labelled as "gifted" have found that many routinely deny their intelligence because they feel that academic achievement might keep them from being popular with others (see Eder, 1985; Eder and Parker, 1987). Ashley Reiter, a first-place winner in a national mathematics competition, described her middle school years as a "smart girl's torture chamber":

> No one would speak to me. I wouldn't even go into the cafeteria for lunch. Long tables stretched the length of the whole room, but wherever I sat, people acted as if I wasn't in the right place. So I would go to the library. It was definitely not cool to be smart in seventh and eighth grade, especially for a girl. Some kids thought they would lose their reputation just by speaking to someone smart. (quoted in Sadker and Sadker, 1994:93)

Some analysts suggest that girls receive subtle cues from adults that lead them to attribute success to *effort* while boys learn to attribute success to their *intelligence* and *ability*. Conversely, girls attribute their own failure to lack of ability while boys attribute failure to lack of effort (Sadker and Sadker, 1994).

Others argue that boys and girls who are high in achievement may be the victims of *anti-intellectualism*—hostility or opposition toward persons assumed to have great mental ability or toward subject matter thought to necessitate significant intellectual ability or knowledge for its comprehension. Advocates of the teaching of creationism, textbook censorship, and organized prayer in public schools have been charged with anti-intellectualism. Removing evolution from the curriculum in order to teach creationism has been described as tantamount to "educational deprivation" for children (Scott, 1992). School prayer and censorship of textbooks have been topics of protracted debate in education and religion in recent years because they are issues with many macro- and microlevel implications.

CURRENT ISSUES IN CANADIAN EDUCATION

Across Canada, thousands of alarmed parents are voicing their concerns regarding the provincial public education systems which, they maintain, are doing a poor job of teaching their children (Fennell, 1993). Although parents may have always been difficult to please, Table 15.2 shows that more and more parents have, over the past twenty years, become dissatisfied with the quality of their children's education. Most of the criticism is directed at inadequate educational standards and dropout rates.

Inadequate Standards A Decima poll conducted in 1993 surveyed 500 university students and found that only 52 percent felt that high school had prepared them properly for university. What is missing? According to a University of Toronto engineering student, not enough emphasis is placed on reading and writing. "Grammar might be worth only five marks on a paper ... If you want help you really have to motivate yourself" (Fennell, 1993:24). Much of the blame for inadequate standards is directed at *child-centred education*—a system that encourages students to progress at their own rate. Critics of child-centred education argue that because this system does not impose clear standards, it has become unaccountable and is producing children who cannot read and write. However, according to education specialists such as Patricia Holborn, a teaching consultant at Simon Fraser University:

> The child-centered system prepares children to be more than just good readers and writers. Unlike more traditional approaches where children learn by memorization, child-centered programs teach children to think and learn independently or co-operatively. (quoted in Fennell, 1993:24)

Critics of child-centred teaching methods also point to the declining skills of students. For example, the publishing firm Nelson Canada, which tested Grade 8 students periodically on a variety of basic skills from reading comprehension to

TABLE 15.2

Parents' Dissatisfaction with Children's Education, 1973, 1978, 1992

Are you satisfied or dissatisfied with the education children are getting today?

Canada	Satisfied	Dissatisfied	Don't know
1992	35%	56%	9%
1978	34	53	13
1973	51	41	8
Regional breakdown (1992)			
Atlantic	41	54	6
Quebec	37	55	8
Ontario	30	61	10
Prairies	49	45	6
B.C.	25	63	12

Note: percentages may not add to 100, due to rounding.
Reprinted with permission—The Toronto Star Syndicate.

TABLE 15.3

Educational Standards Survey of 13-Year-Olds: Ranking of 15 Nations, including Canada, 1994*

SCIENCE Ranking	Average Score	MATH	Average Score
1. South Korea	78%	South Korea	73%
2. Taiwan	76	Taiwan	73
3. Switzerland	74	Switzerland	71
4. Hungary	73	Soviet Union	70
5. Soviet Union	71	Hungary	68
6. Slovenia	70	France	64
7. Italy	70	Italy	64
8. Israel	70	Israel	63
9. Canada	69	Canada	62**
10. France	69	Scotland	61
11. Scotland	68	Ireland	61
12. Spain	68	Slovenia	57
13. United States	67	Spain	55
14. Ireland	63	United States	55
15. Jordan	57	Jordan	40

*Based on results of a random sample of 3000 students from each country who answered more than 100 questions.

**Prince Edward Island did not participate in the mathematics competition.

Source: U.S. Department of Education and National Science Foundation.

TABLE 15.4

Grade 8 Test-Score Percentage Declines, 1966–1991*

Vocabulary	–2%
Mathematics	–6%
Reading Comprehension	–9%
Writing Skills	–11%

*Based on periodic tests of Grade 8 students from all provinces except Quebec, conducted by Nelson Canada.
Source: *Nelson Canada.*

mathematics, found that skills declined in all areas between 1966 and 1991 (see Table 15.4). In addition, the rate of ***functional illiteracy*****—which means that reading and writing skills are inadequate to carry out everyday activities** (such as reading a newspaper, filling out a form, or following written instructions)—is alarmingly high. A 1989 survey that looked at literacy skills used in daily activities reported that 29 per cent of Canadians between the ages of 16 and 24 lacked the basic skills to read a newspaper. And, a report by the Economic Council of Canada estimated that more than one million functionally illiterate young people will come out of Canada's schools over the next ten years (Fennel, 1993).

Dropout Rates Critics of the public school system also point to the fact that too many students drop out before finishing high school. A 1991 survey, in which 9460 individuals between the ages of 18 and 20 were interviewed about their school attendance and educational attainment, reported Canada's dropout rate at 18 percent (Gilbert and Orok, 1993). The report also indicated that almost half of the school leavers were unhappy with their decision to leave school, mainly because they recognized the value of an education after they dropped out. In fact, many of the individuals reported that they intended to "drop back in" to school and complete the educational requirements necessary to get a better job. Apparently, the school leavers experienced the realities of dropping out in a credentials-based society. Although critics of the public education system point to high dropout rates as proof of the public education system's failure, dropout rates in Canada have actually declined since the 1950s when approximately 70 percent of students were not completing high school (Fennell, 1993).

EDUCATIONAL REFORM Efforts to address the problems in the public school system have met with varying results. At the same time, more and more parents who have the financial resources to do so are choosing to put their children in private schools. Other dissatisfied parents have joined lobby groups in order to promote a return to a more traditional education system with an emphasis on the three R's. Provincial strategies to improve the quality of education and reduce the number of dropouts do, in some cases, support this back-to-basics philosophy. For example, in Alberta, Manitoba, Nova Scotia, and New Brunswick, education officials are moving toward programs that place more emphasis on standardized testing and instruction in the core subjects—such as reading and writing. On the other hand, other provinces such as Ontario and British Columbia are moving toward more liberal, child-centred policies. Under the Year 2000 program in British Columbia, standard grades are being abolished from kindergarten to Grade 3 and report cards for younger students will not include grades (Fennell, 1993). In short, the debate continues. But, as Richard Dodds, past president of the Canadian Education Association, commented, "I think the school system is doing a great job, but one of these days we're going to have to sit down and decide what it is we want from our schools" (Fennell, 1993:26).

RELIGION IN HISTORICAL PERSPECTIVE

***Religion* is a system of beliefs, symbols, and rituals, based on some sacred or supernatural realm, that guides human behaviour, gives meaning to life, and unites believers into a community** (Durkheim, 1947/1912). For many people, religious beliefs provide the answers for seemingly unanswerable questions about the meaning of life and death.

RELIGION AND THE MEANING OF LIFE

Religion seeks to answer important questions such as why we exist, why people suffer and die, and what happens when we die. Whereas science and medicine typically rely on existing scientific evidence to respond to these questions, religion seeks to explain suffering, death, and injustice in the realm of the sacred. According to Emile Durkheim, the term ***sacred* refers to those aspects of life that are extraordinary or super-**

natural—in other words, those things that are set apart as "holy." People feel a sense of awe, reverence, deep respect, or fear for that which is considered sacred. Across cultures and in different eras, many things have been considered sacred, including invisible gods, spirits, specific animals or trees, altars, crosses, holy books, and special words or songs that only the initiated could speak or sing (Collins, 1982). Those things that people do not set apart as sacred are referred to as ***profane*****—the everyday, secular or "worldly" aspects of life** (Collins, 1982). Thus, whereas sacred beliefs are rooted in the holy or supernatural, secular beliefs have their foundation in scientific knowledge or everyday explanations. In the debate between creationists and evolutionists, for example, advocates of creationism view it as a belief founded in sacred (Biblical) teachings while advocates of evolutionism assert that their beliefs are based on provable scientific facts.

In addition to beliefs, religion is also composed of symbols and rituals. According to anthropologist Clifford Geertz (1966), religion is a set of cultural symbols that establish powerful and pervasive moods and motivations to help people interpret the meaning of life and establish a direction for their behaviour. People often act out their religious beliefs in the form of ***rituals*****—symbolic actions that represent religious meanings** (McGuire, 1992). Rituals range from songs and prayers to offerings and sacrifices that worship or praise a supernatural being, an ideal, or a set of supernatural principles (Roberts, 1995). Rituals differ from everyday actions in that they have very strictly determined behaviour. According to sociologist Randall Collins (1982:34), "In rituals, it is the forms that count. Saying prayers, singing a hymn, performing a primitive sacrifice or a dance, marching in a procession, kneeling before an idol or making the sign of the cross—in these, the action must be done the right way."

CATEGORIES OF RELIGION While it is difficult to establish exactly when religious rituals first began, anthropologists have concluded that all known groups over the past 100,000 years have had some form of religion (Haviland, 1993). Religions have been classified into four main categories based on their dominant belief: simple supernaturalism, animism, theism, and transcendent idealism (McGee, 1975). In very simple preindustrial societies, religion often takes the form of ***simple supernaturalism*****—the belief that supernatural forces affect people's lives either positively or negatively**. This type of religion does not acknowledge specific gods or supernatural spirits but focuses instead on impersonal forces that may exist in people or natural objects. For example, simple supernaturalism has been used to explain mystifying events of nature, such as sunrises and thunderstorms, and the ways in which some objects may bring a person good or bad luck. By contrast, ***animism*** **is the belief that plants, animals, or other elements of the natural world are endowed with spirits or life forces having an impact on events in society**. Animism is identified with early hunting and gathering societies and with many Native American societies, in which everyday life was not separated from the elements of the natural world (Albanese, 1992).

The third category of religion is ***theism*****—a belief in a god or gods**. Horticultural societies were among the first to practise ***monotheism*****—a belief in a single, supreme being or god who is responsible for significant events such as the creation of the world**. Three of the major world religions—Christianity, Judaism, and Islam—are monotheistic. By contrast, Hinduism, Shinto, and a number of indigenous religions of Africa are forms of ***polytheism*****—a belief in more than one god** (see Table 15.5). The fourth category of religion, transcendent idealism, is nontheistic because it does not focus on worship of a god or gods. ***Transcendent idealism*** **is a belief in sacred principles of thought and conduct**. Principles such as truth, justice, affirmation of life, and tolerance for others are central tenets of transcendent idealists, who seek an elevated state of consciousness in which they can fulfil their true potential.

Throughout the world, people seek the meaning of life through traditional and nontraditional forms of religion. These Italian spiritual seekers are meeting together at a Mayan ruin in quest of harmonic convergence.

SOCIOLOGICAL PERSPECTIVES ON RELIGION

Whereas school attendance is compulsory up to a certain grade level, people can choose whether they want to participate in organized religion in Canada. Nevertheless, according to sociologist Meredith B. McGuire (1992:3), religion as a social institution is a powerful, deeply felt, and influential force in human society. Sociologists study the social institution of religion because of the importance religion holds for many people; they also want to know more about the influence of religion on society, and vice versa (McGuire, 1992). For example, some people assume that the introduction of prayer or religious instruction in public schools would have a positive effect on the teaching of values such as honesty, compassion, courage, and tolerance because these values could be given a moral foundation. Historically, however, society has strongly influenced the practice of religion in Canada through court rulings and laws that have limited religious activities in public settings, including schools.

The major sociological perspectives have different outlooks on the relationship between religion and society. Functionalists typically emphasize the ways in which religious beliefs and rituals can bind people together. Conflict explanations suggest that religion can be a source of false consciousness in society. Interactionists focus on the meanings that people give to religion in their everyday life.

TABLE 15.5

Major World Religions

Religion	Current Followers	Founder/ Date	Beliefs
Christianity	1.7 billion	Jesus Christ; 1st century C.E.	Monotheistic. Jesus is the Son of God. Through good moral and religious behavior (and/or God's grace), people achieve eternal life with God.
Islam	950 million	Muhammad; ca. 610 C.E.	Monotheistic. Muhammad received the Koran (scriptures) from God. On Judgment Day, believers who have submitted to God's will, as revealed in the Koran, will go to an eternal Garden of Eden.
Hinduism	719 million	No specific founder; ca. 1500 B.C.E.	Polytheistic. Brahma (creator), Vishnu (preserver), and Shiva (destroyer) are divine. Union with ultimate reality and escape from eternal reincarnation are achieved through yoga, adherence to scripture, and devotion.
Buddhism	309 million	Siddhartha Gautama; 6th to 5th centuries B.C.E.	Nontheistic. Through meditation and adherence to the Eightfold Path (correct thought and behavior), people can free themselves from desire and suffering, escape the cycle of eternal rebirth, and achieve nirvana (enlightenment).
Judaism	18 million	Abraham, Isaac, and Jacob; ca. 2000 B.C.E.	Monotheistic. God's nature and will are revealed in the Torah (Hebrew scripture) and in his intervention in history. God has established a covenant with the people of Israel, who are called to a life of holiness, justice, mercy, and fidelity to God's Law.
Confucianism	5.9 million	K'ung Fu-Tzu (Confucius); 6th to 5th centuries B.C.E.	Neither polytheistic nor monotheistic. The sayings of Confucius (collected in the *Analects*) stress the role of virtue and order in the relationships between individuals, their families, and society.

THE FUNCTIONALIST PERSPECTIVE ON RELIGION

Emile Durkheim was one of the first sociologists to emphasize that religion is essential to the maintenance of society. He suggested that religion was a cultural universal found in all societies because it met basic human needs and served important societal functions.

DURKHEIM ON RELIGION In *The Elementary Forms of the Religious Life* (1947/1912:47), Durkheim defined religion as "a unified system of beliefs and practices relative to sacred things, that is to say, things set apart and forbidden—beliefs and practices which unite into one single moral community all those who adhere to them." According to Durkheim, all religions share three elements: (1) beliefs held by adherents, (2) practices (rituals) engaged in collectively by believers, and (3) a moral community based on the group's shared beliefs and practices pertaining to the sacred.

For Durkheim, the central feature of all religions is the presence of sacred beliefs and rituals that bind people together in a collectivity. In his studies of the religion of the Australian aborigines, for example, Durkheim found that each clan had established its own sacred totem, which included kangaroos, trees, rivers, rock formations, and other animals or natural creations. To clan members, their totem was sacred; it symbolized some unique quality of their clan. People developed a feeling of unity by performing ritual dances around their totem, which caused them to abandon individual self-interest. Durkheim suggested that the correct performance of the ritual gives rise to religious conviction. Religious beliefs and rituals are *collective representations*—group-held meanings that express something important about the group itself (McGuire, 1992:177). Because of the intertwining of group consciousness and society, functionalists suggest that religion is functional because it meets basic human needs.

FUNCTIONS OF RELIGION From a functionalist perspective, religion has three important functions in any society: (1) providing meaning and purpose to life, (2) promoting social cohesion and a sense of belonging, and (3) providing social control and support for the government.

Meaning and Purpose Religion offers meaning for the human experience. Some events create a profound sense of loss on both an individual basis (such as injustice, suffering, and the death of a loved one) and a group basis (such as famine, earthquake, economic depression, or subjugation by an enemy). Inequality may cause people to wonder why their own personal situation is no better than it is. Most religions offer explanations for these concerns. Explanations may differ from one religion to another, yet each tells the individual or group that life is part of a larger system of order in the universe (McGuire, 1992). Some (but not all) religions even offer hope of an afterlife for persons who follow the religion's tenets of morality in this life. Such beliefs help make injustices in this life easier to endure.

In a study of religious beliefs among baby boomers (born between 1946 and 1964), religion and society scholar Wade Clark Roof (1993) found that a number of people had returned to organized religion as part of a personal quest for meaning. Roof notes that they were looking "for something to believe in, for answers to questions about life," as reflected in this woman's comments:

> Something was missing. You turn around and you go, is this it? I have a nice husband, I have a nice house; I was just about to finish graduate school. I knew I was going to have a very marketable degree. I wanted to do it. And you turn and you go, here I am. This is it. And there were just things that were missing. I just didn't have stimulation. I didn't have the motivation. And I guess when you mentioned faith, I guess that's what was gone. (quoted in Roof, 1993:158)

Social Cohesion and a Sense of Belonging Religious teachings and practices, by emphasizing shared symbolism, help promote social cohesion. An example is the Christian ritual of

The shared experiences and beliefs associated with religion have helped many groups maintain a sense of social cohesion and a feeling of belonging in the face of prejudice and discrimination.

communion, which not only commemorates a historical event but also allows followers to participate in the unity ("communion") of themselves with other believers (McGuire, 1992). All religions have some forms of shared experience that rekindle the group's consciousness of its own unity.

Religion has played an important part in helping members of subordinate groups develop a sense of social cohesion and belonging. For example, in the late 1980s and early 1990s, Russian Jewish immigrants to Canada have found a sense of belonging in some congregations. Even though they did not speak the language of their new country, they had religious rituals and a sense of history in common with others in the congregation. Korean immigrants are forming their own congregations in Canada. In Calgary, the Baptist minister at a church with a congregation made up of 1500 Korean Calgarians, comments, "The church is more than a Christian institution, it is also a means of cultural fellowship. It is a place to feel comfortable. They are in a strange country and here there is friendship" (Nemeth et al., 1993:33). Shared experiences such as these strengthen not only the group but also the individual's commitment to the group's expectations and goals (McGuire, 1992).

Social Control and Support for the Government How does religion help bind society together and maintain social control? All societies attempt to maintain social control through systems of rewards and punishments. Sacred symbols and beliefs establish powerful, pervasive, long-lasting motivations based on the concept of a general order of existence (Geertz, 1966). In other words, if individuals consider themselves to be part of a larger order that holds the ultimate meaning in life, they will feel bound to one another (and past and future generations) in a way that otherwise might not be possible (McGuire, 1992).

Religion also helps maintain social control in society by conferring supernatural legitimacy on the norms and laws in society. In some societies, social control occurs as a result of direct collusion between the dominant classes and the dominant religious organizations. Niccolo Machiavelli, an influential sixteenth-century statesman and writer, wrote that it was "the duty of princes and heads of republics to uphold the foundations of religion in their countries, for then it is easy to keep their people religious, and consequently well conducted and united" (quoted in McGuire, 1992:218). As discussed in Chapter 13, absolute monarchs often have claimed a divine right to rule.

According to Marx and Weber, religion serves to reinforce social stratification in a society. For example, according to Hindu belief, a person's social position in their current life is a result of behaviour in a former life.

THE CONFLICT PERSPECTIVE ON RELIGION

While many functionalists view religion as serving positive functions in society, some conflict theorists view religion negatively.

KARL MARX ON RELIGION For Marx, *ideologies*—"systematic views of the way the world ought be"—are embodied in religious doctrines and political values (Turner, Beeghley, and Powers, 1995:135). These ideologies also serve to justify the status quo and retard social change. The capitalist class uses religious ideology as a tool of domination to mislead the workers about their true interests. For this reason, Marx wrote his now famous statement that religion is the "opiate of the masses." People become complacent because they have been taught to believe in an afterlife in which they will be rewarded for their suffering and misery in this life. Although these religious teachings soothe the masses' distress, any relief is illusory. Religion unites people under a "false consciousness," according to which they believe they have common interests with members of the dominant class (Roberts, 1995).

MAX WEBER ON RELIGION Whereas Marx believed that religion retarded social change, Weber argued just the opposite. For Weber, religion could be a catalyst to produce social change. In *The Protestant Ethic and the Spirit of Capitalism* (1976/1904–1905), Weber asserted that the religious teachings of John Calvin were directly related to the rise of capitalism. Calvin emphasized the doctrine of *predestination*—the belief that, even before they are born, all people are divided into two groups, the saved and the damned, and only God knows who will go to heaven (the elect) and who will go to hell. Because people cannot know whether they will be saved, they tend to look for earthly signs that they are among the elect. According to the Protestant ethic, those who have faith, perform good works, and achieve economic success are more likely to be among the chosen of God. As a result, people work hard, save their money, and do not spend it on worldly frivolity; instead they reinvest it in their land, equipment, and labour (Chalfant, Beckley, and Palmer, 1994).

The spirit of capitalism grew in the fertile soil of the Protestant ethic. Even as people worked ever harder to prove their religious piety, structural conditions in Europe led to the Industrial Revolution, free markets, and the commercialization of the economy—developments that worked hand in hand with Calvinist religious teachings. From this viewpoint, wealth was an unintended consequence of religious piety and hard work.

With the contemporary secularizing influence of wealth, people often think of wealth and material possessions as the major (or only) reason to work. Although no longer referred to as the "Protestant" ethic, many people still refer to the "work ethic" in somewhat the same manner that Weber did. For example, political and business leaders in Canada often claim that the work ethic is dead.

Like Marx, Weber was acutely aware that religion could reinforce existing social arrangements, especially the stratification system. The wealthy can use religion to justify their power and privilege: it is a sign of God's approval of their hard work and morality (McGuire, 1992). As for the poor, if they work hard and live a moral life, they will be richly rewarded in another life. The Hindu belief in reincarnation is an example of religion reinforcing the stratification system. Because a person's social position in the current life is the result of behaviour in a former life, the privileges of the upper class must be protected so that each person may enjoy those privileges in another incarnation (McGuire, 1992).

From a conflict perspective, religion tends to promote conflict between groups and societies. The new religious right in Canada, for example, has incorporated both the priestly and prophetic functions into its agenda. While calling for moral reform, the various organizations also are calling the nation back to a covenant with God (Roberts, 1995). According to McGuire (1992), Weber's distinction between people's "class situation" (stratification based on economic factors) and "status situation" (stratification based on lifestyle, honour, and prestige) is useful in understanding how the new religious right can press for change while at the same time demanding a "return" to traditional family values and prayer in public schools. McGuire (1992:217) suggests that members of "new right" religious organizations may feel that their status (relative prestige or honour) is "threatened by changing cultural norms and seek to re-establish the ideological basis of their status."

According to conflict theorists, conflict may be *between* religious groups (for example, anti-Semitism), *within* a religious group (for example, when a splinter group leaves an existing denomination), or between a religious group and *the larger society* (for example, the conflict over religion in the classroom). Conflict theorists assert that, in attempting to provide meaning and purpose in life while at the same time promoting the status quo, religion is used by the dominant classes to impose their own control over society and its resources (McGuire, 1992). Many feminists object to the patriarchal nature of most religions; some advocate a break from traditional religions, while others seek to reform religious language, symbols, and rituals to eliminate the elements of patriarchy (Renzetti and Curran, 1992).

THE INTERACTIONIST PERSPECTIVE ON RELIGION

Thus far, we have been looking at religion primarily from a macrolevel perspective. Interactionists focus their attention on a microlevel analysis that examines the meanings that people give to religion in their everyday life.

RELIGION AS A REFERENCE GROUP For many people, religion serves as a reference group to help them define themselves. Religious symbols, for example, have meaning for large bodies of people. The Star of David holds special significance for Jews, just as the crescent moon and star do for Muslims and the cross does for Christians. For individuals as well, a symbol may have certain meaning beyond that shared by the group. For instance, a symbol given to a child may have special meaning when he or she grows up and faces war or other crises. It may not only remind the adult of a religious belief but also create a feeling of closeness with a relative who is now deceased. It has been said that the symbolism of religion is so very powerful because it "expresses the essential facts of our human existence" (Collins, 1982:37).

HIS RELIGION AND HER RELIGION Not all people interpret religion in the same way. In virtually all religions, women have much less influence in establishing social definitions of appropriate gender roles both within the religious community and in the larger community (McGuire, 1992). Therefore, women and men may belong to the same religious group, but their individual religion will not necessarily be a carbon copy of the group's entire system of beliefs. In fact, according to McGuire (1992:112), women's versions of a certain religion probably differ markedly from men's versions. For example, whereas an Orthodox Jewish man may focus on his public ritual roles and his discussion of sacred texts, Orthodox Jewish women have few ritual duties and are more likely to focus on their responsibilities in the home. Consequently, the meaning of being Jewish may be different for women than for men.

Religious symbolism and language typically create a social definition of the roles of men and women. For example, religious symbolism may depict the higher deities as male and the lower deities as female. Sometimes, females are depicted as negative, or evil, spiritual forces. For example, the Hindu goddess Kali represents men's eternal battle against the evils of materialism (Daly, 1973). Historically, language has defined women as being nonexistent in the world's major religions. Phrases such as "for all men" in Catholic and Episcopal services gradually have been changed to "for all"; however, some churches retain the traditional liturgy. Although there has been resistance, especially by women, to some of the terms, overall inclusive language is less common than older male terms for God (Briggs, 1987).

Many women resist the subordination they have experienced in organized religion. They have worked to change the existing rules that have excluded them or placed them in a clearly subordinate position.

TYPES OF RELIGIOUS ORGANIZATIONS

Religious groups vary widely in their organizational structure. While some groups are large and somewhat bureaucratically organized, others are small and have a relatively informal authority structure. Some require total commitment of their members; others expect members to have only a partial commitment. Sociologists have developed typologies or ideal types of religious organization to enable them to study a wide variety of religious groups. The most common categorization sets forth four types: ecclesia, church, sect, and cult.

ECCLESIA

Some countries have an official or state religion known as the ***ecclesia*—a religious organization that is so integrated into the dominant culture that it claims as its membership all members of a society**. Membership in the ecclesia occurs as a result of being born into the society, rather than by any conscious decision on the part of individual members. The linkages between the social institutions of religion and government often are very strong in such societies. Although no true ecclesia exists in the contemporary world, the Anglican church (the official church of England), the Lutheran church in Sweden and Denmark, the Catholic church in Spain, and Islam in Iran and Pakistan come fairly close.

THE CHURCH–SECT TYPOLOGY

To help explain the different types of religious organizations found in societies, Ernst Troeltsch (1960/1931) and his teacher, Max Weber (1963/1922), developed a typology that distinguishes between the characteristics of churches and sects (see Table 15.6). Unlike an ecclesia, a church is not considered to be a state religion; however, it may still have a powerful influence on political and economic arrangements in society. **A *church* is a large, bureaucratically organized religious body that tends to seek accommodation with the larger society in order to maintain some degree of control over it.** Church membership largely is based on birth;

TABLE 15.6

Characteristics of Churches and Sects

Characteristic	Church	Sect
Organization	Large, bureaucratic organization, led by a professional clergy	Small, faithful group, with high degree of lay participation
Membership	Open to all; members usually from upper and middle classes	Closely guarded membership, usually from lower classes
Type of Worship	Formal, orderly	Informal, spontaneous
Salvation	Granted by God, as administered by the church	Achieved by moral purity
Attitude Toward Other Institutions and Religions	Tolerant	Intolerant

children of church members typically are baptized as infants and become lifelong members of the church. Older children and adults may choose to join the church, but they are required go through an extensive training program that culminates in a ceremony similar to the one that infants go through. Leadership is hierarchically arranged, and clergy generally have many years of formal education. Churches have very restrained services that appeal to the intellect rather than the emotions (Stark, 1992). Religious services are highly ritualized; they are led by clergy who wear robes, enter and exit in a formal processional, administer sacraments, and read services from a prayer book or other standardized liturgical format.

Midway between the church and the sect is a ***denomination*—a large, organized religious body characterized by accommodation to society but frequently lacking the ability or intention to dominate society** (Niebuhr, 1929). Denominations have a trained ministry, and while involvement by lay members is encouraged more than in the church, their participation usually is limited to particular activities, such as readings or prayers. Denominations tend to be more tolerant and less likely than churches to expel or excommunicate members. This form of organization is most likely to thrive in societies characterized by religious pluralism—a situation in which many religious groups exist because they have a special appeal to specific segments of the population. Perhaps because of its diversity, Canada has more denominations than most other countries.

A ***sect* is a relatively small religious group that has broken away from another religious organization to renew what it views as the original version of the faith**. Unlike churches, sects offer members a more personal religion and an intimate relationship with a supreme being, depicted as taking an active interest in the individual's everyday life. Whereas churches use formalized prayers, often from a prayer book, sects have informal prayers composed at the time they are given. Also, whereas churches typically appeal to members of the upper classes, and denominations to members of the middle and upper classes, sects seek to meet the needs of people who are low in the stratification system—that is, the masses (Stark, 1992).

According to the church–sect typology, as members of a sect become more successful economically and socially, their religious organization also is likely to focus more on this world and less on the next. If some members of the sect do not achieve financial success, they may feel left behind as other members and the ministers shift their priorities. Eventually, this process will weaken some organizations, and people will split off to create new, less worldly versions of the group, which will be more committed to "keeping the faith." Those who defect to form a new religious organization may start another sect or form a cult (Stark and Bainbridge, 1981).

CULTS

A ***cult*** **is a religious group with practices and teachings outside the dominant cultural and religious traditions of a society**. Although many people view cults negatively, some major religions (including Judaism, Islam, and Christianity) and some denominations (such as the Mormons) started as cults. Cult leadership is based on charismatic characteristics of the individual, including an unusual ability to form attachments with others (Stark, 1992:417). An example is the religious movement started by Reverend Sun Myung Moon, a Korean electrical engineer who believed that God had revealed to him that Judgment Day was rapidly approaching. Out of this movement, the Unification church, or "Moonies," grew and flourished, recruiting new members through their personal attachments to present members (Stark, 1992). Some recent cult leaders have not fared well, including Jim Jones, whose ill-fated cult ended up committing mass suicide in Guyana, and David Koresh of the also ill-fated Branch Davidians in Waco, Texas (see Chapter 2).

Over time, some cults undergo transformation into sects or denominations. For example, cult leader Mary Baker Eddy's Christian Science church has become an established denomination with mainstream methods of outreach, such as a "Christian Science Reading Room" strategically placed in an office building or shopping mall, where persons who otherwise might know nothing of the organization learn of its beliefs during their routine activities.

TRENDS IN RELIGION IN CANADA

CANADA'S RELIGIOUS MOSAIC

Canada has been described as a "monopolized mosaic." Until the end of the nineteenth century, Canada was a country with a religious population made up almost entirely of Protestants and Catholics. The Roman Catholic Church was the dominant religious force during the early settlement of Canada, a situation that continued well into the nineteenth century. With the arrival of the United Empire Loyalists from the American colonies in the 1780s, the Protestant population in Canada became larger than the French-Catholic population. The turning point, with respect to the dominance of the Protestant churches occurred after World War II. Their combined share declined from 51 percent in 1951 to 36 percent in 1991, and the most rapid decline occurred during the most recent decade (McVey and Kalbach, 1995). Changes in the population of the major religious groups in Canada are illustrated in Figure 15.2. Today, Catholics, at 46 percent of the population, are the largest religious group in Canada.

Other religions than Christianity, however, were practised in Canada prior to European colonization. Aboriginal peoples were excluded from the earliest census collections. Even so, in 1891, almost 2 percent of Canadians reported practising religions other than Christianity. In 1991, almost

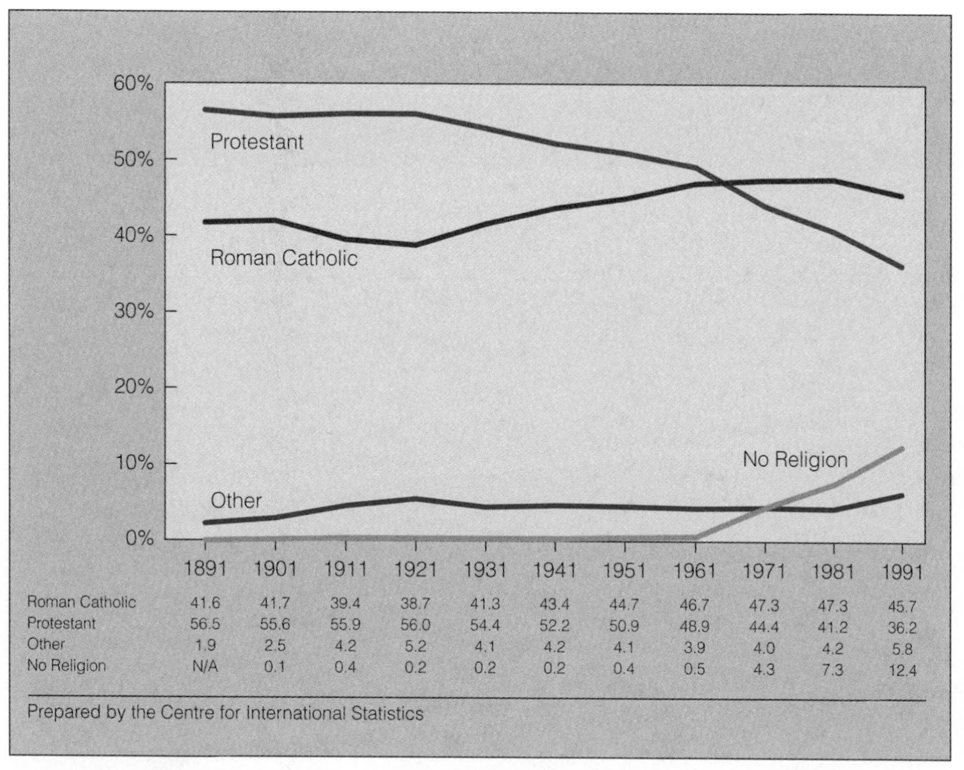

	1891	1901	1911	1921	1931	1941	1951	1961	1971	1981	1991
Roman Catholic	41.6	41.7	39.4	38.7	41.3	43.4	44.7	46.7	47.3	47.3	45.7
Protestant	56.5	55.6	55.9	56.0	54.4	52.2	50.9	48.9	44.4	41.2	36.2
Other	1.9	2.5	4.2	5.2	4.1	4.2	4.1	3.9	4.0	4.2	5.8
No Religion	N/A	0.1	0.4	0.2	0.2	0.2	0.4	0.5	4.3	7.3	12.4

FIGURE 15.2

Religious Affiliation in Canada

Source: Vanier Institute of the Family, 1994. Reprinted by permission.

6 percent of Canadians were affiliated with "other" religions, including Eastern Orthodox, Judaism, and Eastern non-Christian religions such as Islam, Buddhism, Hinduism, Sikhism, and parareligious groups (see Table 15.6). Among non-Christian religions, Judaism has shown a significant increase in followers, rising from 16,493 in 1901 to 318,065 in 1991. Eastern non-Christian religious populations have grown significantly since the 1960s as a result of the liberalization of immigration law in Canada, as have the numbers of those who fall under the category "no religion," going from 56,679 in 1951 to almost 3.4 million in 1991 (McVey and Kalbach, 1995). Does this mean that Canadians are rejecting religion? An answer to this question can be found in examining other recent trends in religion in Canada.

RELIGION AND SCIENTIFIC EXPLANATIONS

During the Industrial Revolution, scientific explanations began to compete with religious views of life. Rapid growth in scientific and technological knowledge gave rise to the idea that science ultimately would answer questions that previously had been in the realm of religion. Many scholars believed that increases in scientific knowledge would result in ***secularization*—the process by which religious beliefs, practices, and institutions lose their significance in sectors of society and culture** (Berger, 1967). Secularization involves a decline of religion in everyday life and a corresponding increase in organizations that are highly bureaucratized, fragmented, and impersonal (Chalfant, Beckley, and Palmer, 1992).

TABLE 15.6

Population by Religion

	1981		1991	
Total Population	24,083,495	100.0%	26,994,045	100.0%
Catholic	**11,402,605**	**47.3**	**12,335,255**	**45.7**
Roman Catholic	11,210,385	46.5	12,203,620	45.2
Ukrainian Catholic	190,585	0.8	128,390	0.5
Other Catholic	1,630	0.0	3,235	0.0
Protestant	**9,914,575**	**41.2**	**9,780,715**	**36.2**
United Church	3,758,015	15.6	3,093,120	11.5
Anglican	2,436,375	10.1	2,188,110	8.1
Presbyterian	812,105	3.4	636,295	2.4
Lutheran	702,900	2.9	636,205	2.4
Baptist	696,845	2.9	663,360	2.5
Pentecostal	338,790	1.4	436,435	1.6
Other Protestant	1,169,545	4.9	2,127,190	7.9
Eastern non-Christian	**305,890**	**1.3**	**747,455**	**2.8**
Islam	98,165	0.4	253,260	0.9
Buddhist	51,955	0.2	163,415	0.6
Hinduism	69,505	0.3	157,010	0.6
Sikhism	67,715	0.3	147,440	0.5
Other eastern non-Christian	18,550	0.1	26,330	0.1
Eastern Orthodox	**361,565**	**1.5**	**387,395**	**1.4**
Judaism	296,425	1.2	318,065	1.2
Parareligious groups	**13,450**	**0.1**	**28,155**	**0.1**
No religious affiliation	1,783,530	7.4	3,386,365	12.5
Other religions	**5,465**	**0.0**	**10,640**	**0.0**

*Based on sample data, which exclude institutional residents.

Reproduced by authority of the Minister of Industry, 1996, Statistics Canada, from *Religions in Canada*, Cat. no. 93-319.

In Canada, some people argue that science and technology have overshadowed religion, but others point to the resurgence of religious beliefs and an unprecedented development of alternative religions in recent years (Kosmin and Lachman, 1993; Roof, 1993; Singer and Lalich, 1995).

RELIGIOSITY

As we have seen, religion in Canada is very diverse. Pluralism and religious freedom are among the cultural values most widely espoused. However, is Canada a religious society? The answer depends on how you look at things, such as research that shows that church attendance, public confidence in church leadership, and church influence have all gradually declined since the late 1940s (Bibby, 1987 and 1990). On the other hand, one poll, conducted in 1993 by historian George Rawlyk, found Canada to be an overwhelmingly Christian nation, not only in name, but in belief (Nemeth et al., 1993:32). This poll also revealed that Canadians are not rejecting religion per se, but rather they are rejecting the way in which religion is practised. According to Rawlyk, "What we've caught here is Canadian religion changing fundamentally before our eyes" (Nemeth et al., 1993:32). The poll findings also indicated that, while fewer than a quarter of Canadians attend weekly religious services, eighty percent affirm their belief in God and seventy-five percent indicated their belief in the death and the resurrection of Jesus, the basic tenet of Christianity. Furthermore, almost a third of the adult population claims to pray daily and more than half read the Bible or other religious literature at least occasionally. It seems then that Christianity persists, but in a radically transformed way. According to sociologist Reginald Bibby, 60 percent of Canadians practise what he calls *specialized consumption*. For example, Canadians continue to look to churches for what have been referred to as "rites of passage" ceremonies such as baptisms, confirmations, marriages, and funerals. Canadians are into what Bibby describes as "religion à la carte," by which he means that people are increasingly drawing on religion as a consumer item, adopting a belief here and a practice there.

According to Bibby (1987), since the late 1940s the percentage of Canadians with ties to organized religion has dropped to 25 percent from 60 percent. But, Bibby adds, "All surveys indicate that there's a high, high level of receptivity to spirituality. So we can only assume those needs are being met elsewhere" (cited in McDonald, 1994:42). Many Canadians, predominantly the baby boomers, are becoming involved in what has been referred to as the "new spirituality." Indicators of this trend are revealed in Bibby's research (1996). According to theologian Tom Harper:

> There is a huge spiritual quest going on. There's a lot of attempts at quick fixes and spiritual junk food as well. But even the silly fringe is part of it ... People seem intuitively aware that something is missing in their lives, and there's a reaction against traditional religion. (quoted in McDonald, 1994:42)

FUNDAMENTALISM

The rise of a new fundamentalism has occurred at the same time that a number of mainline denominations have been losing membership. The term *religious fundamentalism* refers to a conservative religious doctrine that opposes intellectualism and worldly accommodation in favour of restoring a traditional otherworldly focus. In Canada, fundamentalism has been gaining popularity, primarily among Protestants, but also among Roman Catholics and Jews. Whereas "old" fundamentalism usually appealed to people from lower-income, rural backgrounds, the "new" fundamentalism appears to have a much wider following among persons from all socioeconomic levels, geographical areas, and occupations. "New-right" fundamentalists have been especially critical of *secular humanism*—a belief in the perfectibility of human beings through their own efforts rather than through a belief in God and a religious conversion. According to fundamentalists, "creeping" secular humanism has been most visible in the public schools, which, instead of offering children a fair and balanced picture, are teaching things that seem to the child to prove their parents' lifestyle and religion are inferior and perhaps irrational (Carter, 1994:52). The new-right fundamentalists claim that banning the teaching of Christian beliefs in the classroom while teaching things that are contrary to their faith is an infringement on their freedom of religion (Jenkinson, 1979). As we have seen in this chapter, the debate continues over what should be taught and what practices (such as Bible reading and prayer) should be permitted in public schools. The selection of textbooks and library materials is an especially controversial issue. Starting in the 1960s, books considered to have racist and sexist biases were attacked by civil rights activists and feminists. Soon thereafter, challenges were brought by extremely conservative groups such as the Educational Research Analysts and Eagle Forum to protest the use of books that they alleged had "factual inaccuracies" (such as a criticism of the free enterprise system) or morally objectionable subject matter or language (see Hefley, 1976; Shor, 1986; Wong, 1991; Bates, 1994). This debate, along with the message of fundamentalism, has been transformed into an international issue because of the growth of the electronic church and the Internet, as discussed in Box 15.4.

WOMEN IN THE MINISTRY

> I believe in God, the Father Almighty, Creator of Heaven and Earth, and in Jesus Christ, His only Son. (MacDonald, 1996:47)
>
> A woman can't represent Christ. Men and women are totally different—that's not my fault—and Jesus chose men for his disciples. (MacDonald, 1996:47)

The above quotations relate to two issues that are becoming increasingly important to women in today's society: the gender inclusiveness of Christianity and Judaism and the absence of women in significant roles within religious institutions. These contentious issues are leading many women to reject mainstream religion in search of a spirituality that reflects the experiences of both women and men. In churches, synagogues, and even Buddhist Zendos, women are demanding an end to the traditions that do not reflect their historic role and their ongoing stake in the divine. Some women are choosing alternative spiritual belief systems, while others are working from within the church to create change. The battles have been intense and polarizing. In 1992, the Church of England allowed the ordination of women priests. In response, a British vicar made a point of telling the media that he would "burn the bloody bitches" (MacDonald, 1996:47).

Despite opposition, some advances have been made. In the United States, there are at least 300 priestless Roman Catholic parishes. The majority are headed by women, specifically nuns (Wallace, 1991). It is predicted that by the year 2000, close to 25 percent of Christian pastors in the United States may be women. In 1994, the Vatican flatly rejected female ordination and more gender-neutral language in the Catholic Church. Given the dominance of the Roman Catholic Church in Canada, the growth in the proportion of female clergy here is likely to be more gradual (Currie and Stackhouse, 1996). Nonetheless, 25 percent of ordained United Church ministers and approximately 10 percent of Anglican priests in Canada are women (Nason-Clark, 1993). The Baptist, Lutheran, and Presbyterian churches in Canada have begun to ordain women as well. However, once ordained, these women still face an uphill battle: they continue to be offered junior positions, are paid lower wages, and are not promoted to more prestigious posts (Nason-Clark, 1993). Not all religions are as resistant to woman in the clergy. For example, Reform Judaism has ordained women as rabbis since the early 1970s. Native Canadian religions have traditionally given status to women in spiritual leadership.

According to sociologists Raymond Currie and John Stackhouse (1996), there is little doubt that the future role of religion will depend significantly on the ability of religious institutions to respond to the changing role of women in society.

EDUCATION AND RELIGION IN THE TWENTY-FIRST CENTURY

This chapter ends as it began by noting that education and religion will remain important social institutions as we enter the twenty-first century. Also remaining, however, will be the controversies that we have discussed—controversies that your generation must attempt to resolve.

With regard to education, questions will remain about what should be taught, not only in terms of preparing your children for their adult lives and the world of work but also in regard to

BOX 15.4 SOCIOLOGY AND MEDIA

In the Media Age: The Electronic Church and the Internet

In a single telecast, I preach to millions more than Christ did in His entire lifetime.—Billy Graham (quoted in Roberts, 1995:360)

Television and the Internet are transforming both religion and education in the United States and Canada. Although television has been used as a medium of communication by ministers since the 1950s, the *electronic church* has far surpassed most people's wildest estimates by becoming a multi-million-dollar industry with audiences ranging in size from 10 million to 130 million.

When religious services first were televised, many were church services conducted by a local congregation and carried by a regional television station primarily for the benefit of shut-ins and those who had no "church home" in the community. In the 1950s and early 1960s, the few nationally televised religious programs featured people like the Rev. Bishop Fulton J. Sheen, an established spokesperson for the Roman Catholic Church, or evangelists such as Billy Graham who "happened" to be televised while conducting a revival or "crusade" in some remote part of the world.

By comparison, most contemporary televangelists are entrepreneurs whose success hinges on presenting a message that "sells well" and generates the extremely large sums of money needed to keep the "television ministry" profitable. Rather than attempting to change viewers' beliefs, many televangelists attempt simply to confirm them. In the 1970s and 1980s, televangelists like Jerry Falwell, Oral Roberts, Jim and Tammy Faye Bakker, James Robison, Jimmy Swaggart, and Pat Robertson offered audiences a sense of belonging; for a certain sum of money, people could become "members" of the "700 Club" or "partners" in the "P.T.L. (Praise the Lord) Club" with Jim and Tammy Faye Bakker.

Even while some televangelists were discredited or, as in the case of Jim Bakker, convicted of felonies, others took their place not only to proclaim the "gospel" but also to become spokespersons for a political agenda. For example, Pat Robertson argued on the "700 Club" that the U.S. First Amendment "says nothing . . . about separation of church and state! Merely that Congress can't set up a national religion." Robertson also has referred to public schools as "agencies for the promotion of . . . the humanist religion" (quoted in Kosmin and Lachman, 1993: 194). Robertson formed the Christian Coalition, which has become actively involved in the election of school board members and other political officials at the state and national levels. In 1993, Robertson's Christian Coalition was reported to have a membership of 350,000 in over seven hundred affiliated chapters in all fifty of the United States; in 1992 alone, this organization raised more than $13 million. However, some televangelists, including Robertson, have lost viewers and supporters because of the way in which they intertwine religion and politics. Although they tend to take very conservative political positions, some of their viewers come from lower-income backgrounds and disagree with their politics.

By comparison, the Internet, the computer information network designed by the U.S. Defense Department and run by the federal government, is just having an impact on religion and education. As more schools gain access to the Internet, they are able to provide their students with a wide variety of opportunities and information that otherwise would not be available. The Internet has tremendous potential, but it also raises new questions and concerns. "Cyberspace battles" may occur because many books not available on the shelves of school libraries are available through the Internet. Some religious groups have begun pressing for limits to the types of information available on this network, or at least to limit access to the types of information available to young people—and even to college students. Do you think that there should be restrictions on what you, as a college student, can receive over the Internet?

Sources: Based on Hadden and Swann, 1981; Frankl, 1987; Hadden and Shupe, 1988; McGuire, 1992; Kosmin and Lachman, 1993; Tidwell, 1993; Bates, 1994; and Roberts, 1995.

the values to which you want your child exposed. Unlike many other countries, no central authority in Canada decides the curriculum to be taught to all students nationwide. Rather, each province enacts its own laws and regulations, with local school boards frequently making the final determination. Accordingly, no general standards exist as to what is to be *taught* to students or how, although many provinces now have adopted levels as to what (as a minimum) must be *learned* in order to graduate from high school.

The debate over what should be taught obviously is not limited to just religious and moral issues; rather, it includes the entire curriculum. If, as critics assert, academic achievement in Canada compares unfavourably with the level of achievement by students in many other countries, what can be done to change it? Some policy initiatives have been introduced in the public school system that should result in an improvement in the quality of education. For example, *compensatory education programs*, including preschool, remedial, or extra education programs, which provide additional learning assistance to assist disadvantaged children, have been designed to offset the effects of poverty, deprivation, and disadvantage on school performance (Guppy, 1995). Although these programs were tried in the 1970s and dismissed as complete failures, more recent compensatory programs have had more positive results. As we approach the twenty-first century, we also have witnessed some changes in both the formal and hidden school curricula such as eliminating textbooks that portray minority groups in a discriminatory or sexist manner.

School enrolments will continue to grow and diversify as baby boomers continue to have children and immigration to Canada creates an increasingly ethnically diverse population of students. The challenge for the next century lies in finding ways to facilitate learning in a pluralistic school system—meeting the needs of students in terms of their distinct cultural, linguistic, and religious traditions. However, as Neil Guppy says,

> Education will always be contentious. Disputes over the social function of schooling will persist. As the social and economic problems of Canadian society multiply, schools will come to be viewed as a source of salvation capable of solving problems such as increasing crime, economic decline, and the spread of AIDS. However, no school program can adequately satisfy the range of ideals people may wish education to achieve. (1995:475)

Analysts of religion have reached similar conclusions about the future of religion:

> Whatever the future holds, this generation's struggle over values and commitment is not over—if for no other reason than that the memories of the past live on as reminders of who they are and where they came from ... [People] know that religion, for all its institutional limitations, holds a vision of life's unity and meaningfulness, and for that reason will continue to have a place in their narrative. In a very basic sense, religion itself was never the problem, only social forms of religion that stifle the human spirit. The sacred lives on and is real to those who can access it. (Roof, 1993:261)

In the twenty-first century, religious organizations will continue to be important in the lives of many people. However, the influence of religious beliefs and values will be felt even by those who claim no religious beliefs of their own. In many nations the rise of religious nationalism has led to the blending of strongly held religious and political beliefs. Although the rise of religious nationalism is occurring throughout the world, it is especially strong in the Middle East, where Islamic nationalism has spread rapidly (Juergensmeyer, 1993).

In Canada, the influence of religion will be evident in ongoing battles over school prayer, abortion, gay rights, and women's issues, among others. On some fronts, religion may unify people;

on others, it may contribute to confrontations among individuals and groups. Legal scholar Stephen L. Carter (1994) suggests that tensions between religion and other social institutions are not necessarily negative. According to him, pervasive, totalitarian states find all conflict threatening and often remove religious liberty quickly when a statist dictator takes control. For Canada, however, one of our most cherished freedoms is religious liberty. Maintaining an appropriate balance between the social institutions of education and religion will be an important challenge in this country in the twenty-first century.

CHAPTER REVIEW

Education and religion are powerful and influential forces in society. Both institutions impart values, beliefs, and knowledge considered essential to the social reproduction of individual personalities and entire cultures.

- Education is the social institution responsible for the systematic transmission of knowledge, skills, and cultural values within a formally organized structure. By the 1920s, free public education in Canada was built around a "core" curriculum that included mathematics, social sciences, natural sciences, and English. More recently, many other subjects (ranging from computer skills to AIDS prevention) have been added.
- According to functionalists, education has both manifest functions (socialization, transmission of culture, social control, social placement, and change and innovation) and latent functions (keeping young people off the streets and out of the job market, matchmaking and producing social networks, and creating a generation gap). From a conflict perspective, education is used to perpetuate class, racial-ethnic, and gender inequalities through tracking ability grouping and a hidden curriculum that teaches subordinate groups conformity and obedience. According to interactionists, education may be a self-fulfilling prophecy for some students, such that these students come to perform up—or down—to the expectations held for them by teachers.
- Religion is a system of beliefs, symbols, and rituals, based on some sacred or supernatural realm, that guides human behaviour, gives meaning to life, and unites believers into a community. Religions have been classified into four main categories based on their dominant belief: simple naturalism, animism, theism, and transcendent idealism. During the Industrial Revolution, scientific explanations began to compete with religious views of life, resulting in secularization—religious beliefs, practices, and institutions losing their significance in some sectors of society.
- According to functionalists, religion has three important functions in any society: (1) providing meaning and purpose to life, (2) promoting social cohesion and a sense of belonging, and (3) providing social control and support for the government. From a conflict perspective, religion can have negative consequences in that the capitalist class uses religion as a tool of domination to mislead workers about their true interests. However, Max Weber believed that religion could be a catalyst for social change. Interac-

tionists examine the meanings that people give to religion and the meanings they attach to religious symbols in their everyday life.

- Religious organizations can be categorized as ecclesia, churches, denominations, sects, and cults. Some of the world's major religions started off as cults built around a charismatic leader.

KEY TERMS

animism **573**

church **581**

credentialism **565**

cult **582**

cultural capital **563**

denomination **581**

ecclesia **580**

education **555**

functional illiteracy **571**

hidden curriculum **564**

latent functions **562**

manifest functions **560**

meritocracy **566**

monotheism **573**

polytheism **573**

profane **573**

religion **572**

rituals **573**

sacred **572**

sect **581**

secularization **583**

self-fulfilling prophecy **568**

simple supernaturalism **573**

theism **573**

tracking **563**

transcendent idealism **573**

QUESTIONS FOR ANALYSIS AND UNDERSTANDING

1. What are the major functions of education and religion for individuals and for societies? Why do these functions tend to overlap in Canada?
2. Why do some theorists believe that education is a vehicle for decreasing social inequality while others believe that education reproduces existing class relationships?
3. How is religion changing in Canadian society?
4. How do people become members of different types of religious organizations? What is the relationship between religious affiliations and social class?

QUESTIONS FOR CRITICAL THINKING

1. Why does so much controversy exist over what should be taught in Canadian public schools?
2. How are the values and attitudes you learned from your family reflected in your beliefs about education and religion?
3. How would you design a research project to study the effects of fundamentalist religion on everyday life? What kind of data would be most accessible?
4. If Durkheim, Marx, and Weber were engaged in a discussion about education and religion, on what topics might they agree? On what topics would they disagree?

SUGGESTED READINGS

These books provide more information about the sociology of education and the sociology of religion:

Jeanne H. Ballantine. *The Sociology of Education: A Systematic Analysis* (3rd ed.). Englewood Cliffs, N.J.: Prentice-Hall, 1993.

Reginald Bibby. *Fragmented Gods: The Poverty and Potential of Religion in Canada*. Toronto: Irwin, 1996.

Daniel U. Levine and Robert J. Havighurst. *Society and Education* (8th ed.). Boston: Allyn & Bacon, 1992.

W.E. Hewitt (ed.). *The Sociology of Religion: A Canadian Focus*. Toronto: Butterworths, 1993.

Keith A. Roberts. *Religion in Sociological Perspective*. Belmont, Cal.: Wadsworth, 1995.

A recent book on social inequality in education is:

Jane S. Gaskell and Arlene Tigar McLaren. (eds.). *Women and Education: A Canadian Perspective*. Calgary: Detselig, 1987.

Recent books on various aspects of religion include:

Barry A. Kosmin and Seymour P. Lackman. *One Nation Under God: Religion in Contemporary American Society*. New York: Crown, 1993.

Wade Clark Roof. *A Generation of Seekers: The Spiritual Journeys of the Baby Boom Generation*. San Francisco: HarperSanFrancisco, 1993.

Margaret Thaler Singer with Janja Lalich. *Cults in Our Midst*. San Francisco: Jossey-Bass, 1995.

Part Five

SOCIAL DYNAMICS AND SOCIAL CHANGE

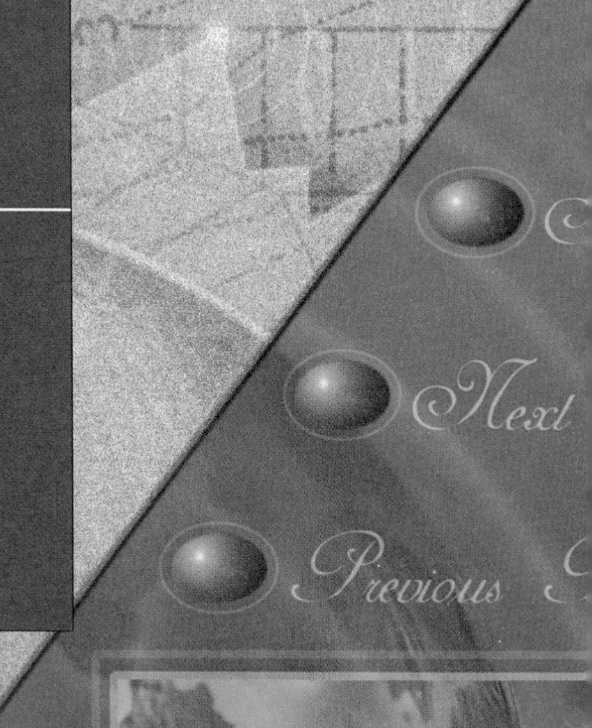

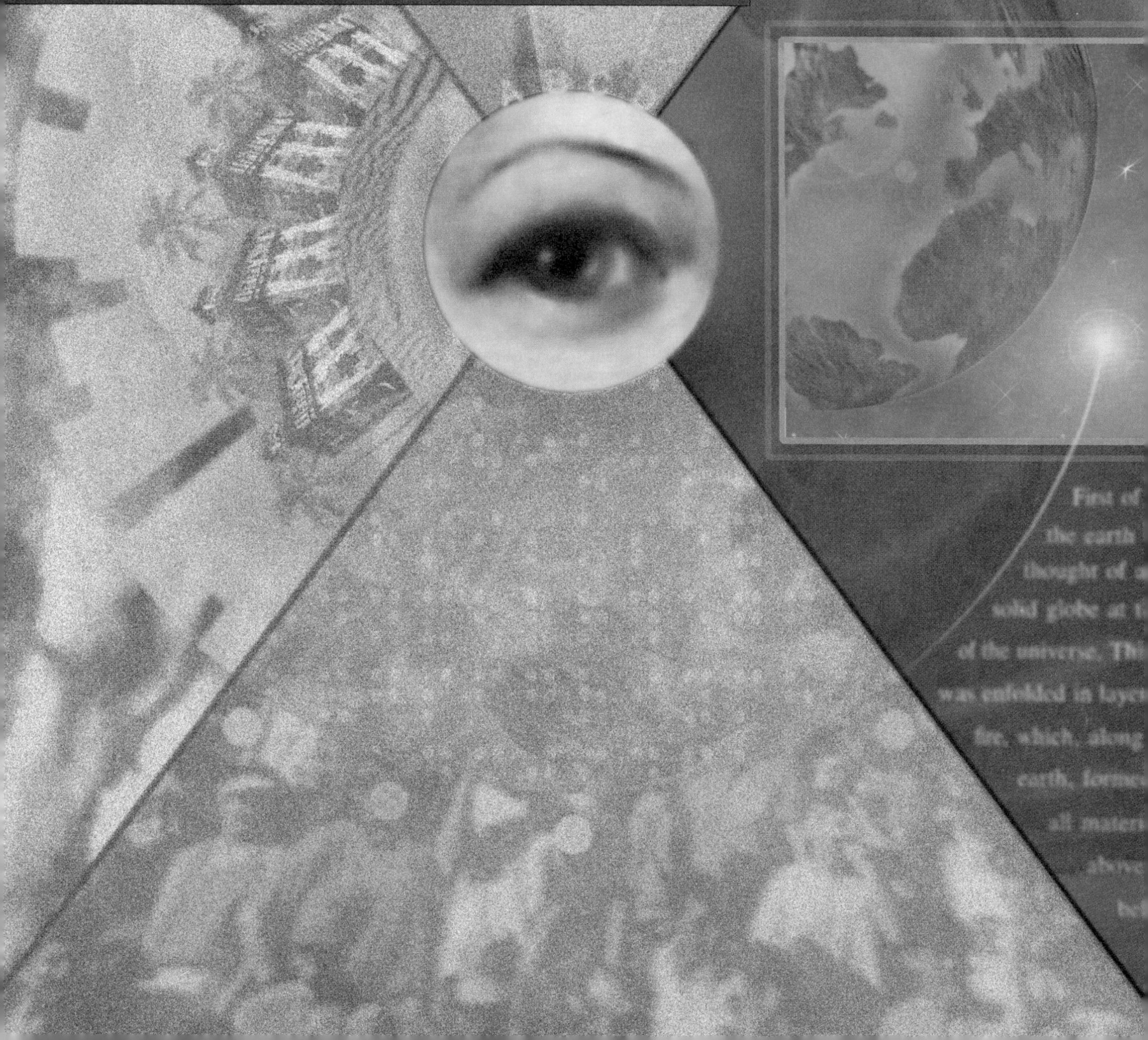

Chapter 16

POPULATION AND URBANIZATION

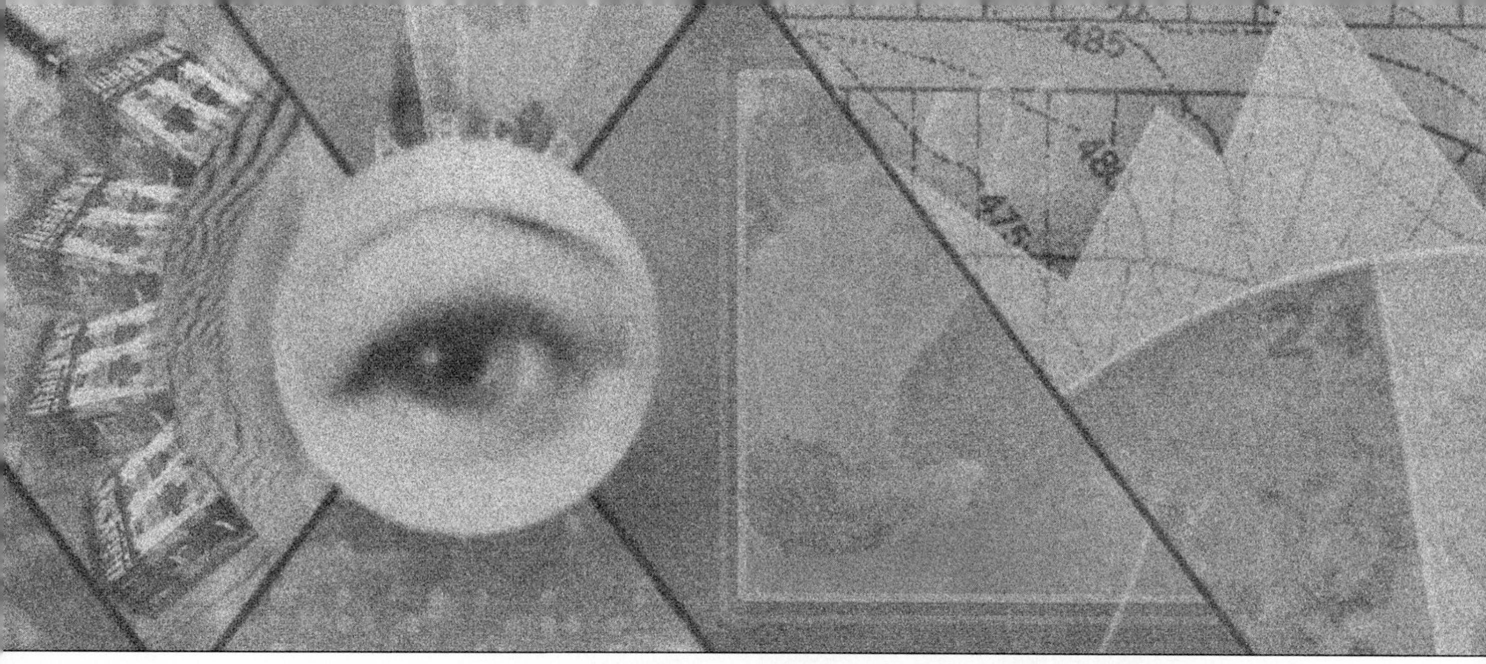

Moving to a new country and a new culture can be difficult, but the transition is easier for those who have support from others who share the same experience. Consider the contrast between the lives of the two women quoted below. The following excerpt is from an interview with the child of a Sikh woman:

> My mother had it hard when I was growing up. We had a small rented farm in the Okanagan Valley, where there were then very few Sikhs. I made friends with Canadians at school. Since I knew English fluently I often talked with the neighbours, as did my father. Mother wasn't so lucky. She never learned English well enough to communicate easily, so never really had any good Canadian friends. There were so few other Sikh families around that she had little contact with them either. For her, the family was everything. (Buchignani, Indra, and Srivastiva, 1985:76)

In the next excerpt a woman who moved from Hong Kong to a Canadian city with a large middle-class Chinese community talks about her Chinese friends in Canada:

> I feel we have more in common with each other. We often get together and reminisce about our lives in Hong Kong. We also laugh about our ignorance of Canadian culture and the little faux pas that we get ourselves into. Other times, we exchange information about schools, dentists, and other practical knowledge. Or we marvel at the high price we now pay for little things such as cooking wares and stockings. I have a feeling of solidarity when I talk to these people. They understand where I'm coming from. (Man, 1996:290)

The presence of others from one's former home plays a large role in determining where new immigrants settle in Canada. This has meant that cities such as Toronto and Vancouver have very high proportions of recent immigrants, while other communities have almost none. This is just one example of the impact that immigration has on our society. However, immigration is just one of the *demographic factors* that are changing Canada and the rest of the world. The phenomena of births, deaths, and the move-

This AIDS memorial in Toronto is a striking reminder that AIDS has taken a toll on individuals, families, cities, and nations. In some countries, AIDS is a significant cause of population mortality.

ment of people interact to affect us all in very complex ways.

In this chapter, we will explore the dynamics of population growth and urban change. In this process we will periodically focus on immigration and its importance to Canadian society. Before reading on, test your knowledge about the causes and consequences of immigration by taking the quiz in Box 16.1.

QUESTIONS AND ISSUES

What causes global population growth?

How are people affected by population changes?

Why is HIV/AIDS referred to as a global-human problem?

How do ecological/functionalist models and political economy/conflict models differ in their explanation of urban growth?

What is meant by the experience of urban life, *and how do sociologists seek to explain this experience?*

What are the best-case and worst-case scenarios regarding population and urban growth in the twenty-first century, and how might some of the worst-case scenarios be averted?

What has been the impact of the baby boom on Canada's population?

DEMOGRAPHY: THE STUDY OF POPULATION

Although population growth has slowed in Canada, the world's population of almost 5.7 billion in 1994 is increasing by 94 million people per year. By 2015 an estimated 1.7 billion additional people will live in the less-developed nations of the world, while the population in developed nations will increase by only 120 million people. This means that as we approach the twenty-first century, people in different parts of the world face dramatically different futures. While many people in developing countries face starvation because of rapidly increasing popula-

BOX 16.1 SOCIOLOGY AND EVERYDAY LIFE

How Much Do You Know About Immigration to Canada?

TRUE	FALSE	
T	F	1. Immigrants usually become a drain on the taxpayer because they have high rates of welfare use.
T	F	2. Immigrants are not evenly distributed across the country, because many prefer to settle in large cities.
T	F	3. Most immigrants to Canada are refugees.
T	F	4. Canada has had rates of immigration in the past that were higher than current rates.
T	F	5. There is no limit to the number of family-sponsored immigrants who are allowed into Canada.
T	F	6. Immigrants have lower rates of crime than other Canadians.
T	F	7. If we do not maintain rates of immigration that are high by world standards, our population will eventually decline.
T	F	8. About 3 percent of Canada's population was not born in Canada.
T	F	9. Canada welcomed hundreds of thousands of Jewish refugees fleeing Nazi persecution during World War II.
T	F	10. Most countries of the world have open immigration and citizenship policies like those of Canada.

Answers on page 598

tions, Canadians have a much different problem. Because of very low birth rates, our population is aging and there are concerns about how a relatively small number of young workers will support large numbers of elderly people.

Why does the population grow rapidly in some nations? What are the consequences of low birth rates in industrialized countries? What impact does immigration have on the immigrants and on the country of destination? What effect might a widespread AIDS crisis have on world population? How large will our cities be in twenty years? These questions are of interest to scholars who specialize in the study of ***demography*—the subfield of sociology that examines population size, composition, and distribution**. Many sociological studies use demographic analysis as a component in the research design.

Increases or decreases in population can have a powerful impact on the social, economic, and political structures of societies. Demographers define *population* as a group of people who live in a specified geographic area. Only three variables can change a population: *fertility* (births), *mortal-*

BOX 16.1 SOCIOLOGY AND EVERYDAY LIFE

Answers to the Sociology Quiz on Immigration

TRUE	FALSE	
T	**F**	1. *False.* Immigrants are less likely to be on welfare than people born in Canada. A study by the Economic Council of Canada using the 1986 census found that the proportion of welfare recipients among recent immigrants (12.5 percent) is smaller than among people born in Canada (13.8 percent). Immigrants are more highly educated and more likely to be working than native-born Canadians.
T	F	2. *True.* Immigrants are more likely to settle in large cities. A high proportion of immigrants live in Toronto, Vancouver, and Montreal.
T	**F**	3. *False.* In 1994, only 8 percent of immigrants to Canada were refugees.
T	F	4. *True.* Immigration rates fluctuate widely and at times in the past they have been much higher than they are today.
T	**F**	5. *False.* Each year the government determines the number of family-sponsored immigrants who will be admitted.
T	F	6. *True.* Immigrants were significantly underrepresented in the population of those incarcerated in the federal correctional system in 1989 and 1991.
T	F	7. *True.* Birth rates in Canada are currently below replacement level. When the baby boom generation begins to die (after 2025), Canada will lose population unless we give entry to about 250,000 immigrants each year.
T	**F**	8. *False.* About 16 percent of Canadian residents were born in other countries.
T	**F**	9. *False.* While most Canadians are proud of this country's record in accepting refugees, our policies were not always as liberal as they are today. Very few Jewish refugees were admitted to Canada during the Holocaust.
T	**F**	10. *False.* Canada has one of the highest rates of legal immigration in the world. Most countries discourage immigration and many will not give citizenship to anyone not born to parents who themselves are citizens of that country.

Sources: Based on Abella and Troper, 1982; Beaujot, 1991; Economic Council of Canada, 1991; Gordon and Nelson, 1993; Matas, 1995; and McVey and Kalbach, 1995.

ity (deaths), and *migration* (movement from one place to another).

FERTILITY

***Fertility* is the actual level of childbearing for an individual or a population.** The level of fertility in a society is based on biological and social factors, the primary biological factor being the number of women of childbearing age (usually between ages 15 and 45). Although men obviously are important in the reproductive process, women's behaviour is used as the measure of fertility because pregnancy and childbirth are more easily counted than is biological fatherhood. Other biological factors affecting fertility include

Women tend to have more children in agricultural regions of the world, such as Kenya, where children's labour is essential to the family's economic survival and child mortality rates are very high.

the general health and level of nutrition of women of childbearing age. Social factors influencing the level of fertility include the roles available to women in a society and prevalent viewpoints regarding what constitutes the "ideal" family size.

Based on biological capability alone, most women could produce twenty or more children during their childbearing years. *Fecundity* is the potential number of children that could be born if every woman reproduced at her maximum biological capacity. Fertility rates are not as high as fecundity rates because people's biological capabilities are limited by social factors such as practising voluntary abstinence and refraining from sexual intercourse until an older age, as well as by contraception, voluntary sterilization, abortion, and infanticide (Davis and Blake, 1956). Additional social factors affecting fertility include significant changes in the number of available partners for sex and/or marriage (as a result of war, for example), increases in the numbers of women of childbearing age in the workforce, and high rates of unemployment.

In some countries, governmental policies also affect the fertility rate. For example, China's one-child policy requires IUDs (intrauterine devices) for women of childbearing age with one child, sterilization (most often performed on women) for couples with two children, and abortions for women pregnant without authorization. According to estimates, more than 30 million abortions, sterilizations, and IUD insertions occur each year in China. In some cases, Chinese birth control officials have been coercive in their efforts to control population in that nation (see Mosher, 1994). A preference for male children, especially when parents are permitted only one child, has led to practices, such as female infanticide, which are creating an imbalance in sex ratios. In the future, many Chinese men will experience difficulty in finding a marital partner.

The most basic measure of fertility is the ***crude birth rate*****—the number of live births per 1000 people in a population in a given year**. In 1991, the crude birth rate in Canada was 15 per 1000, compared with a post-World-War-II high rate of 28 per 1000 in 1956 and around 40 per 1000 at the time of Confederation. This measure is referred to as a "crude" birth rate because it is based on the entire population and is not "refined" to incorporate significant variables affecting fertility, such as age, marital status, religion, or race/ethnicity. To refine this measure, demographers use the *age-specific birth rate*—the number of live births per 1000 women in a specific age group. For example, in 1991, the birth rate for women aged 20 to 24 was 83 per 1000 women, as compared with 234 per 1000 women in the same age range in 1961. This rate enables demographers to note changes in patterns of fertility between age cohorts. For example, in 1961 most births occurred among women aged 20 to 24; in 1991, most births occurred among women aged 25 to 29, and an increase in the proportion of births occurring among women aged 30 to 44 was reported (McVey and Kalbach, 1995). This pattern of births occurring at later ages has some very important consequences. For example, family size will be smaller because women effectively have fewer years in which to have children.

In most of the industrialized world, women are having fewer children. Crude birth rates in Japan and Spain are 11 per 1000; in the United Kingdom and France they are 13 per 1000 (about the same as Canada), and in the United States they are 15 per 1000. However, families are much larger in underdeveloped, agricultural regions of the world where children's labour is essential to a family's economic survival and child mortality rates are still very high. Countries with high crude birth rates (more than 40 per 1000) include Nigeria, Pakistan, and Ethiopia (Colombo, 1996).

MORTALITY

The primary cause of world population growth in recent years has been a decline in ***mortality*—the incidence of death in a population.** The simplest measure of mortality is the ***crude death rate*—the number of deaths per 1000 people in a population in a given year.** Mortality rates have declined dramatically in the last two hundred years. In 1867, the crude death rate in Canada was 21 deaths per 1000—half what it had been one hundred years earlier. By 1991 the death rate had dropped to 7 per 1000 (McVey and Kalbach, 1995). This decline has been due the fact that infectious diseases such as malaria, polio, cholera, tetanus, typhoid, and measles have been virtually eliminated by improved nutrition, sanitation, and personal hygiene and by vaccination. As the burden of communicable diseases has steadily declined, the major causes of death in the developed world are now chronic and degenerative diseases such as heart disease and cancer, Table 16.1 illustrates how this trend has affected Canada.

While mortality rates have dropped significantly in the less developed and developing nations, they are still 2 or 3 times higher than those of developed countries. In many countries, infectious diseases remain the leading cause of death; in some areas, mortality rates are increasing rapidly as a result of HIV/AIDS and a resurgence of tuberculosis. At least 14 million people, primarily in Africa and Asia, have been identified as being HIV-positive since the virus was first identified in 1981; this number may rise to 40 million people by 2000 (Altman, 1994).

In addition to the crude death rate, demographers often measure the ***infant mortality rate*—the number of deaths of infants under 1 year of age per 1000 live births in a given year.** The infant mortality rate is an important reflection of a society's level of preventive (prenatal) medical care, maternal nutrition, childbirth procedures, and neonatal care for infants, and it is often used by sociologists as a measure of the level of a country's social development. The impact of modernization on infant mortality rates has been dramatic. In 1921 the infant mortality rate in Canada was 102 deaths per 1000 live births; by 1991 it had declined to 6 per 1000 live births. This can be compared with rates of 8 per 1000 in the United States; 7 in France, Spain, and the United Kingdom; and 4 in Japan.

Underdeveloped countries with high birth rates also have high infant mortality rates. For example, the infant mortality rates for Nigeria, Haiti, and Ethiopia are (respectively) 111, 109, and 106 per 1000 live births (Colombo, 1996).

TABLE 16.1

Leading Causes of Death, Canada, 1881 and 1991

Rank	1880–81*	Rank	1991
1	Consumption (Tuberculosis)	1	Heart attack
		2	All other forms of Coronary heart disease
2	Diphtheria		
3	Lung Disease	3	Lung and throat cancer
4	Old Age	4	Stroke
5	Brain Disease	5	Pneumonia
6	Heart & Blood Disease	6	Breast Cancer
7	Scarlet Fever	7	Colon Cancer
8	Croup	8	Diabetes
9	Bowel Disease	9	Heart Failure
10	Debility	10	Motor Vehicle Accidents

*Includes P.E.I., N.B., N.S., Que., Ont., Man., B.C., and the Territories

Reproduced by authority of the Minister of Industry, 1996, Statistics Canada, adapted from Morality—*Summary List of Cases, 1991,* Cat. no. 84-209.

Infant mortality rates and crude death rates are high among Canada's aboriginal population, who suffer severe social disadvantages compared with the rest of the population, and who often lack access to health-care services. In 1981, the infant mortality rate for registered Indians (that is, aboriginal Canadians recognized as such by the federal government) was 17 per 1000 live births, which was nearly double the rate of the Canadian population as a whole (Beaujot, 1991).

Our declining mortality rates have led to substantial increases in *life expectancy*, which is an estimate of the average lifetime in years of people born in a specific year. For persons born in Canada in 1986, for example, life expectancy at birth was about 77 years, as compared with 79 years in Japan and 45 years or less in many poor African nations. Within Canada, life expectancy is lower for aboriginal people. On average, aboriginals live about 10 years less than the nonaboriginal population. Life expectancy also varies by sex; for example, females born in Canada in 1994 could expect to live about 81 years as compared with 75 years for males (Statistics Canada, 1996).

MIGRATION

***Migration* is the movement of people from one geographic area to another for the purpose of changing residency.** Migration affects the size and distribution of population in a given area. *Distribution* refers to the physical location of people throughout a geographic area. In Canada, people are not evenly distributed throughout the country; most Canadians live in densely populated areas while much of the country is sparsely populated. *Density* is the number of people living in a specific geographic area. Density may be measured by the number of people who live per room, per block, or per square mile.

Migration may be either international (movement between two nations) or internal (movement within national boundaries). When people migrate internationally, demographers refer to the country they leave as their *country of origin*; the country they enter is known as their *country of destination*. International migration often is very difficult; people must either meet stringent entrance requirements, run the risk of being arrested for entering a country illegally, or acquire refugee status based on persecution or a well-founded fear of persecution for political or religious beliefs in their country of origin (Weeks, 1992).

Migration involves two types of movement: immigration and emigration. ***Immigration* is the movement of people into a geographic area to take up residency**, while ***emigration* is the movement of people out of a geographic area to take up residency elsewhere.**

INTERNAL MIGRATION Internal migration has occurred throughout Canada's history and has significantly changed the distribution of our population over time. In the late nineteenth and early twentieth centuries, a major population shift occurred as Canada was transformed from a rural to an urban nation. At the time of Confederation, about 80 percent of the population resided in rural areas; by 1991, almost 80 percent were urban. While Canada is now an urban country, the degree of urbanization among the provinces varies, ranging from 82 percent of the population of Ontario to only 40 percent of Prince Edward Island residents (McVey and Kalbach, 1995).

Along with movement from rural to urban areas, we have also seen extensive migration from one province to another. Between 1981 and 1991 British Columbia and Ontario attracted the most internal migrants. All other provinces except Alberta lost more internal migrants than they gained. The provinces with the highest rates of loss were Newfoundland, Saskatchewan, and New Brunswick.

Many factors cause people to move from one part of the country to another. Better job opportunities in other parts of the country is a major cause of movement from rural to urban areas, and the booming economies of British Columbia, Alberta, and Ontario have drawn migrants from provinces with fewer opportunities. For decades, people from the Atlantic provinces have moved to Ontario in search of work. Between 1990 and 1996, 87 percent of the new jobs in Canada were created in British Columbia and Alberta, which have between them only 22 percent of the population (*Globe and Mail*, 1996). Based on these statistics, the 1996 census is expected to show continuing high rates of internal migration to these two western provinces. While jobs explain many of our internal migration patterns, other reasons for internal migration are climate and lower living costs, which tend to be particularly important for retired persons.

INTERNATIONAL MIGRATION People migrate either voluntarily or involuntarily. *Pull* factors at the international level, such as a democratic government, religious freedom, employment opportunities, or a more temperate climate, may draw voluntary immigrants into a nation. *Push* factors at the international level, such as political unrest, violence, war, famine, plagues, and natural disasters, may encourage people to leave one area and relocate elsewhere. Involuntary, or forced, migration usually occurs as a result of political oppression, such as when Jews fled Nazi Germany in the 1930s or when Haitians left their country to escape the Cedras regime in the 1990s. Slavery is the most striking example of involuntary migration; the ten to twenty million Africans transported forcibly to the Western Hemisphere prior to 1800 did not come by choice.

Most of Canada's thirty million people are immigrants or the descendants of immigrants. Thus, immigration has been a critical factor in the country's growth and development. Our immigration policy is one of the most open in the

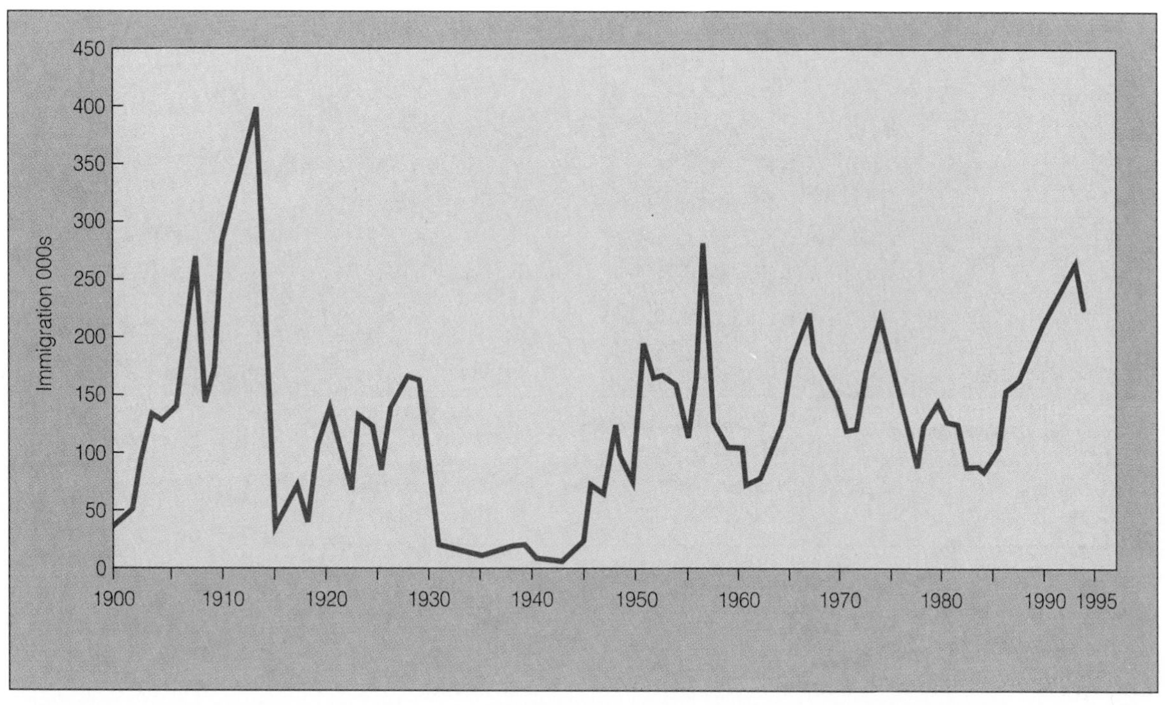

FIGURE 16.1

Annual Levels of Canadian Immigration, 1900–1994

Source: Jean Dumas, *Rapport sur l'état de la population du Canada, 1990,* Statistics Canada, Cat. no. 91-209 (Ottawa: Minister of Supply and Services, 1990), p. 2; Roderic Beaujot, K.G. Basavarajappa, and Ravi B.P. Verma, *Current Demographic Analysis: Income of Immigrants in Canada,* Statistics Canada, Cat. no. 91-527 (Ottawa: Minister of Supply and Services, 1988), p. 7. Adapted from *Population Change in Canada* by R. Beaujot.

world, and we have much higher rates of legal immigration than almost any other country. Immigrants comprise 16 percent of Canada's population (McVey and Kalbach, 1995).

Figure 16.1 shows that immigration levels throughout this century have fluctuated a great deal. Economic conditions, wars, pressures from refugees, and changes in government policies have all contributed to these shifts. Following the end of the economic depression in 1896, the government began to promote immigration to encourage settlement of the West. In the years before World War I as many as 400,000 people immigrated to Canada, a number which has never been exceeded. Most of these immigrants were European and many of them settled the farms, towns, and cities of the Prairie provinces. The beginning of World War I caused a precipitous decline in immigration. While numbers increased again after the war, the Great Depression and World War II meant very low levels of immigration for almost twenty years. During this period more people left Canada than arrived here. Immediately after World War II, immigration rates again climbed. Canada built a large industrial capacity during the war, and the postwar economy was very strong. Skilled foreign workers were needed to help with the expansion. Political instability and economic difficulty in Europe meant that many people were willing to leave to find a better life elsewhere. The postwar immigration peak in 1956–57 was a result both of Canada's acceptance of great numbers of refugees who were escaping the unsuccessful Hungarian Revolution and of its providing a home

Political unrest, violence, and war are "push" factors that encourage people to leave their country of origin. Shown here, a shipload of Liberian refugees await political asylum in Ghana, and Bosnian refugees flee Serb-held parts of Sarajevo. Civil wars are causing massive population movement.

for British subjects leaving Egypt following the Suez crisis.

Until 1962 Canada's immigration regulations permitted discrimination on the basis of racial and ethnic origin (see Box 16.2). At various times, Chinese, Japanese, and East Indians were prohibited from immigrating to Canada, and the 1953 Immigration Act allowed the government to bar entry on the grounds of race, ethnicity, or even "peculiar customs, habits, modes of life or methods of holding property" (Beaujot, 1991:109). Preference was given to whites, particularly those of British origin. These discriminatory restrictions were lifted in 1962, and from then on the face of immigration changed dramatically. Compare the source countries of immigrants arriving in 1957 with those of immigrants who came in 1991, as shown in Table 16.2. Whereas, in 1957, the vast majority of immigrants were whites from northern Europe, in 1991 immigrants to Canada came from all over the world and represented many different ethnic groups and cultures. While this diversity would not have been possible under the old rules, the factors "pushing" immigrants have also changed. For the past thirty years, most western European countries have had very strong economies, low unemployment rates, and stable governments. Living under these conditions, people have had little reason to emigrate. At the same time, conditions in many other parts of the world are less favourable, so emigration to Canada is seen positively. Most of the countries from which we drew immigrants in 1991 had some combination of political turmoil, war, or poverty.

During most of the 1990s the number of immigrants coming to Canada has remained relatively stable at between 200,000 and 250,000 persons. This is the result of government policy aimed at achieving a stable population in the future in the face of declining birth rates and an aging population.

POPULATION COMPOSITION

Changes in fertility, mortality, and migration affect the ***population composition*—the biological and social characteristics of a population**, including age, sex, ethnic origin, marital status, education, occupation, income, and size of household.

One measure of population composition is the ***sex ratio*—the number of males for every hundred females in a given population**. A sex ratio of 100 indicates an equal number of males and females. If the number is greater than 100, there are more males than females; if it is less than

BOX 16.2 SOCIOLOGY AND LAW

Immigration and the Law in Canada

Canadians can be proud of having welcomed immigrants from around the globe. However, the record has not been consistently good; at times in the past our immigration policy has been exclusionary and racist.

Shortly after the turn of the century, some Canadians began to express concerns about immigration from the Far East (China) and South Asia (India). The first Chinese immigrated to Canada in the 1850s; many were recruited to work as labourers during the construction of the Canadian Pacific Railway. South Asians began to immigrate to Canada in 1903. While the numbers of both groups were small, these immigrants were treated very poorly and subjected to discrimination. British Columbia, where the two groups were largely concentrated, passed a number of laws restricting the rights of Chinese and Japanese. For example, the Chinese and Japanese were denied the right to vote in 1872 and 1895 respectively, and many restrictions were imposed on their right to work. The federal government levied a head tax on the Chinese in 1885 to restrict their immigration and in 1923 passed the Chinese Immigration Act which virtually disallowed new immigration from the Far East.

In response to a resolution passed at a public meeting in Vancouver that "the influx of Asiatics is detrimental and hurtful to the best interest of the Dominion, from the standpoint of citizenship, public morals, and labour conditions" (Ghosh and Kanungo, 1992:6), in 1910 the federal government made several amendments to the Immigration Act that were intended to reduce immigration from India. The most explicitly racist section of the Act allowed the government to:

> (c) prohibit for a stated period, or permanently, the landing in Canada ... of immigrants belonging to any race deemed unsuited to the climate or requirements of Canada, or of immigrants of any specified class, occupation or character."

While these regulations now seem appalling, Canadians were no worse than most other Western countries, which also had very restrictive immigration policies. Backed by many leading scientists of the day was the view that Anglo-Saxons were biologically superior, and the admission of other races was seen as a danger to these white democracies.

Many Canadians are also unaware that for many years our immigration policy restricted the admission of Jews. This was because of anti-Jewish sentiment and because Jews settled in urban areas and rejected the rural settlement preferred by the government. Regulations approved between 1919 and 1923 blocked the admission of Jews from Europe. These rules made family sponsorship more difficult and restricted all independent immigrants from Europe except for farmers. Under the section of the law that allowed the regulation of "races which cannot be assimilated without social or economic loss to Canada," Jews were placed in a Special Permit Class that essentially prohibited immigration. Even during the World War II, when millions of Jews were being exterminated in Europe, Canada would not open its doors to Jewish refugees. No country made the immigration of Jews a priority during the Holocaust, but Canada's record was particularly poor. Between 1933 and 1945 Canada admitted fewer than 5,000 Jews, whereas during the same period 200,000 were allowed into the United States and 70,000 into the United Kingdom. Despite significant and vocal support among Canadians for taking action to save Jewish refugees, then Prime Minister Mackenzie King and his cabinet refused. The attitude of the government is summed up in the words of a senior Canadian official who was speaking with journalists in early 1945. When asked how many Jews would be admitted to Canada following the war, his response was "None is too many" (Abella and Troper, 1982:xxi).

Sources: Based on Abella and Troper, 1982; Ghosh and Kanungo, 1992; Statutes of Canada, 1910 c. 27.

TABLE 16.2

Canadian Immigrants' Countries of Origin, 1957 and 1991

1957				1991*			
Rank	Country	Number of people	% of total immigration	Rank	Country	Number of people	% of total immigration
1	U.K.	108,989	38.6	1	Hong Kong	22,147	9.7
2	Hungary	31,643	11.2	2	Poland	15,479	6.8
3	Germany	28,430	10.0	3	China	13,727	6.0
4	Italy	27,740	9.8	4	India	12,790	5.6
5	Netherlands	11,934	4.2	5	Philippines	12,127	5.3
6	U.S.	11,008	3.9	6	Lebanon	11,940	5.2
7	Denmark	7,683	2.7	7	Vietnam	8,934	3.9
8	France	5,869	2.0	8	U.K.	7,460	3.3
9	Austria	5,714	2.0	9	El Salvador	6,926	3.0
10	Greece	5,460	1.9	10	Sri Lanka	6,774	3.0
	TOTAL	**282,164**			**TOTAL**	**228,557**	

*1991 preliminary figures.

Reprinted with permission from Rose Zgodzinski, "Where Immigrants Came From." *The Globe and Mail* (June 20, 1996): A2; and reproduced by authority of the Minister of Industry, 1996, Statistics Canada, from *Canada Yearbook*, Cat. no. 11-402.

100, there are more females than males. In Canada, the sex ratio in 1991 was 97, which means there were about 97 males per 100 females. Although approximately 106 males are born for every 100 females, higher male mortality rates mean there are more females than males in the population.

For demographers, sex and age are significant population characteristics; they are key predictors of fertility and mortality rates. The age distribution of a population has a direct bearing on the demand for schooling, health, employment, housing, and pensions. The distribution of a population can be depicted in a ***population pyramid*—a graphic representation of the distribution of a population by sex and age**. Population pyramids are a series of bar graphs divided into five-year age cohorts; the left side of the pyramid shows the number or percentage of males in each age bracket; the right side provides the same information for females. The age/sex distribution in Canada and other developed nations such as France does not have the appearance of a classic pyramid, but rather is more rectangular or barrel-shaped. By contrast, less developed or developing nations, such as Mexico and Iran, which have high fertility and mortality rates, do fit the classic population pyramid. Figure 16.2 illustrates the demographic compositions of France, Mexico, and Iran. (Population pyramids for Canada are shown later in this chapter in Figure 16.4.)

As societies modernize, there is a time lag between the decrease in the death rate and a corresponding decrease in the birth rate. During this time lag, populations often grow very rapidly. The rate of population growth in a society is determined by a combination of fertility, mortality, and migration. The age and sex composition of the population affects each of these processes. If a large number of young people are in their prime reproductive years, the crude birth rate will rise because a large number of children will be

FIGURE 16.2

Population Pyramids for Mexico, Iran, and France

Source: Weeks, 1992.

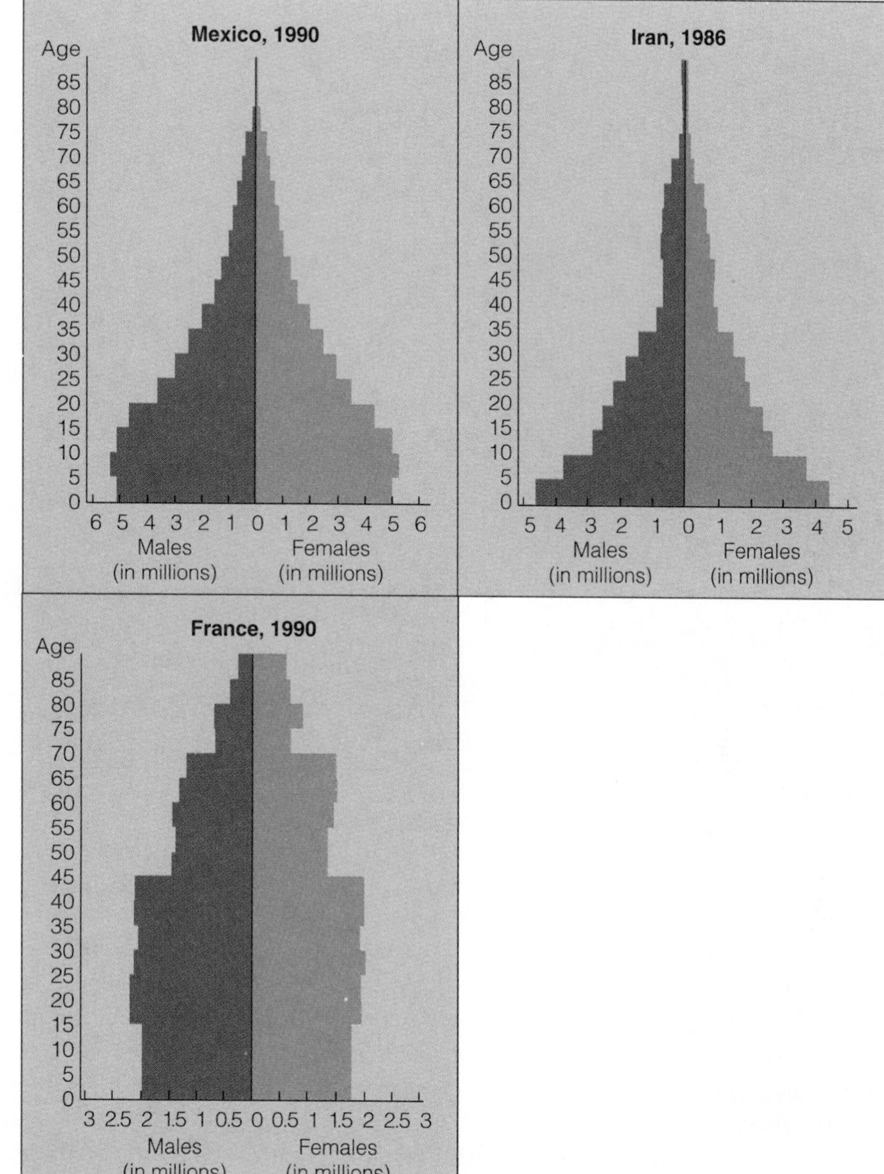

produced relative to the total population. In a population with a relatively small proportion of young people and a high proportion of older people, a substantial number of deaths will occur each year because of the large number of individuals moving into the higher-risk years. Thus, even if the society has a high life expectancy, the crude death rate will be higher because of the proportion of older people. Young adults are more likely to migrate than older persons, a factor that also affects the size of a specific population.

THE BABY BOOM AND THE BABY BUST

One very simple fact will help you to understand many things about Canadian society: every year you get one year older, and, more

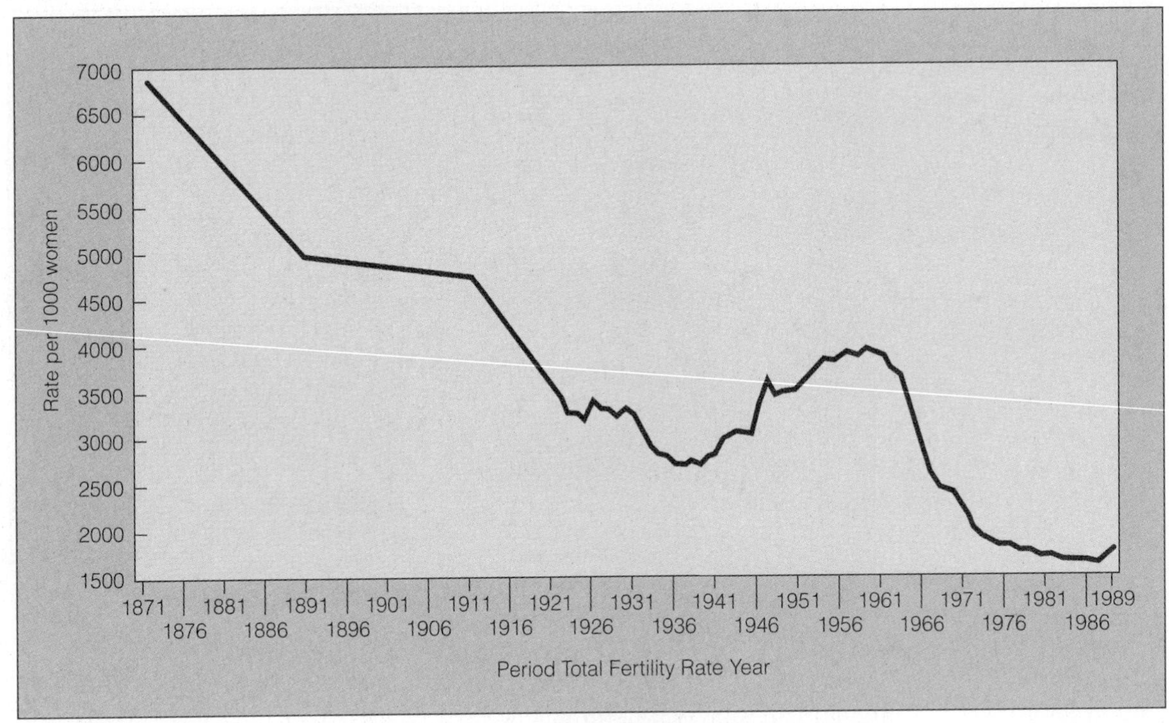

FIGURE 16.3

Period Total Fertility Rate for 1871–1989

Source: Romaniuc, 1994:121–22; Beaujot and McQuillan, 1982:54; Dumas, 1990b:18.

importantly, so does everyone else. Until recently, the age structure of the population was something of a hidden factor. While age differences among individuals were obvious, researchers and planners often failed to recognize the impact of changes in the *age structure* of the population.

One of the most significant demographic changes in Canadian history was the *baby boom*—the dramatic increase in births that occurred between 1946 and 1966. The boom was caused by young couples who married and began having families in the years immediately following the war. The high birth rates of the baby boom were followed by the *baby bust*, which saw birth rates fall to the very low levels where they remain today. While many demographic changes are subtle and take place over a long period of time, the baby boom was a rapid reversal of a long-term downward trend in birth rates. This increase is shown in Figure 16.3. By the end of the boom in 1966, one-third of all the people in Canada had been born in the preceding fifteen years.

The baby boom and baby bust have had a dramatic impact on the age structure, which can be seen in the series of population pyramids in Figure 16.4. The top pyramid shows the population of Canada toward the end of the baby boom in 1961. There are large numbers of young people because of the boom. The relatively small number of people aged 15 to 24 is the result of low birth rates during the Depression and World War II. In the 1981 pyramid, we can see the consequences of the baby boom and the drop in fertility rates that followed. The pyramid for 2006 shows an increased number of older people as the oldest baby boomers approach 60. Finally, in the 2031 pyramid, mortality has begun to affect the baby boomers, and the survivors are now 70 to 90 years of age.

BOX 16.3 SOCIOLOGY IN GLOBAL PERSPECTIVE

Immigration Policies of Canada and Other Countries

Canadian immigration laws and policies are among the most open in the world. Each year Canada accepts just under 1 percent of our population as immigrants and all have the right to obtain citizenship. Israel takes in about 2 percent of its population annually, while the other two leading destination countries for immigrants, Australia and the United States, each accept less than one-half of a percent of their populations. Most of the world's countries accept few or no immigrants, though many do accept refugees, at least on a temporary basis. Receiving countries react to immigration in three different ways.

The first is *differential exclusion*, according to which immigrants are allowed in certain areas of society, chiefly the labour market, but denied access to other areas such as health care, education, and social benefits. Immigrants in these countries are primarily refugees and guest workers who are admitted for specified periods to do work that members of the resident population cannot or will not perform. Germany, for example, imports workers from many countries, especially Turkey. Citizenship is based on ethnicity. German ancestry entitles an immigrant to automatic citizenship. However, even the German-born children of guest workers were not entitled to automatic citizenship until 1993 and naturalization of non-Germans is extremely rare. The result of this is the permanent marginalization of hundreds of thousands of people who are essentially permanent residents but who cannot become citizens. Japan, which has strongly emphasized the need for ethnic purity, has similar policies, but has treated its immigrant workers much more harshly than has Germany. Koreans, many of whom are third- and fourth- generation Japanese, have suffered severe discrimination.

The second immigration model is *assimilationist*, whereby immigrants are incorporated into the host society through a one-sided process of change. Immigrants are expected to become the same as the majority. Canada used to follow this policy, but today France probably follows this model the most closely. Immigrants to France can obtain citizenship after five years of residence, and children born in France automatically become citizens at 18 years of age unless they give up this right. All citizens are expected to accept the French language and culture. This model became strained as large numbers of immigrants, particularly those from North Africa, became economically marginalized and victimized by racism. When assimilation did not bring the benefits received by other citizens, some of these immigrants turned to organizations based on cultural identity as a way of ensuring a political voice.

The third model is *pluralism*, according to which immigrants are encouraged to form ethnic communities that can have equal rights while retaining their diversity in language, culture and other matters. Citizenship is readily given to legal immigrants, and even to children of illegal immigrants. Countries following this model differ in the degree to which cultural differences are supported by the state. In the United States, such differences are tolerated but are not supported directly by the government. On the other hand, both Australia and Canada have multicultural policies whereby the rights of ethnic communities are actively supported.

Source: Castles, 1995.

The baby boom has had a profound impact on virtually every aspect of our society. To help understand the impact of the baby boom, think of it as a twenty-year bulge in the population pyramid. Each year, this bulge moves one year up the pyramid as the baby boom cohort ages. You can easily track this bulge in the population pyramids in Figure 16.4. Some demographers have used the analogy of a pig that has been swallowed by a python to describe the way in which the baby boom generation has moved up the population pyramid. It is interesting to compare Canada's

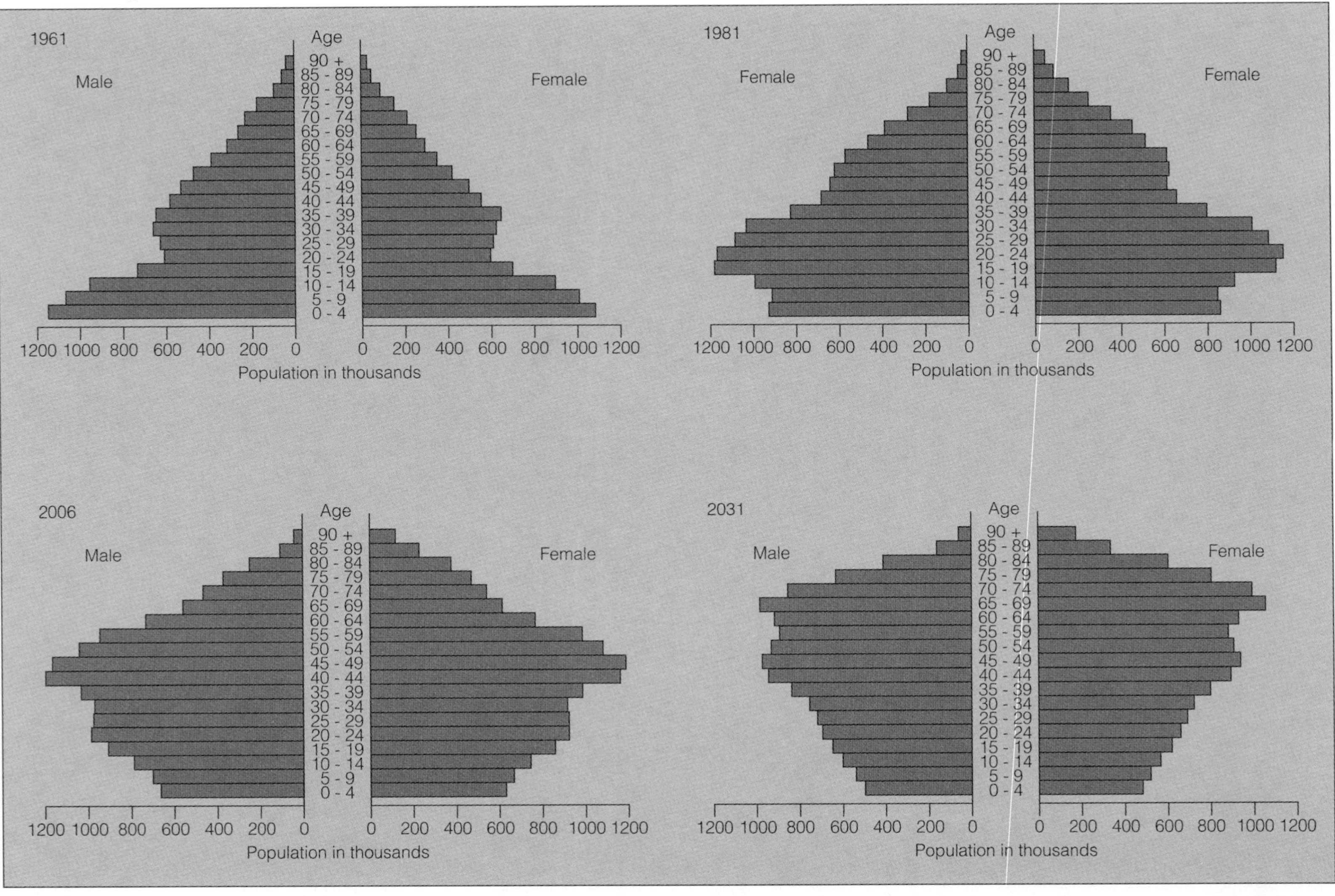

FIGURE 16.4

Population by Age and Sex, Canada, 1961 and 1981 (Census), 2006 and 2031

Reproduced by authority of the Minister of Industry, 1996, Statistics Canada, from *Population Projections for Canada, Provinces and Territories 1984–2006*, Cat no. 91-520; and from *1961 Census Bulletin* 1.2-2.

demographic structure with those of other countries. For example, you can see from Figure 16.3 that Mexico and Iran, which are developing societies, have a constant baby boom—they are continually adding young people to the population as their population rapidly expands. On the other hand, France did not have a baby boom after the war, so its age structure is quite different from Canada's. The age structure of many European countries is much like that of France; besides Canada, the only other countries that had a baby boom were Australia and the United States.

The baby boom has transformed society in many different ways. Because it has always been the largest age group, the baby boom generation has had a tremendous impact. Beginning in the late 1940s, many businesses saw their markets expand. Manufacturers of baby food, diapers, and children's toys flourished and obstetricians were in great demand. As the cohort aged, school construction increased dramatically and teaching jobs were plentiful. By the mid-1960s university enrolments began to climb and many new universities opened to meet the demand. You will recall from Chapter 7 ("Deviance and Crime") that crime rates also began to increase at this time. The explanation is that the baby boomers had entered the 15 to 24 age group during which criminal behaviour is most common. In the mid-1970s house prices rose quickly in most Canadian cities, as the baby boomers began to settle down and raise families.

Because of the baby bust, many of these changes reversed in the 1980s. Schools that had been built to house the soaring numbers of children in the 1960s were forced to close twenty years later and school boards are still trying to deal with an oversupply of teachers. By the 1990s both university enrolments and crime rates had begun to decline. Virtually throughout Canada, house prices have dropped or remained stable for much of the past decade. Radio stations that had catered to the baby boomers when they were young began to play "golden oldies" to keep this large audience. Corporations that had targeted youthful consumers have begun to reorient their products and their advertising to appeal to an older market. Clothing manufacturers are now offering their products in "relaxed fit" sizes as middle-aged spread begins to hit the baby boomers, and fast food chains are developing products to appeal to older people. The sight of television commercials showing Ronald McDonald on a golf course is a sure sign of the consumer power of the baby boom generation. In fact golf, and other modestly active forms of recreation such as travel, gardening, and birdwatching are replacing more active sports like tennis and downhill skiing in popularity as the baby boomers begin to slow down in middle age.

What of the future? The baby boom cohort is now entering middle age and the first of its members will reach 65 in the year 2012. As you have read in Chapter 11 ("Aging and Disability"), our society will soon begin to have a much higher proportion of older persons than it does today. In 1971, about 8 percent of Canadians were 65 and over; by 2011 the percentage will be 16 percent; and by 2036 it will likely stabilize at almost 25 percent. Over this period, the average age of the population will have increased quite dramatically. The *median age* of the population is the age that divides the population in two—half are above and half are below. The median age of the population in 1971 was 25 years and by 2036 will be 45 years (Beaujot, 1991).

The aging of our population is causing concern in a number of areas. Since the elderly are the biggest users of health care, governments are trying to get health costs under control before the baby boomers begin to reach the age where they begin to have serious health concerns. Those responsible for the Canada Pension Plan are now planning ways to increase contribution rates or to decrease benefits so the Plan can stay in operation. The baby boomers will remain politically powerful until mortality lessens their impact on the ballot box, and some observers have predicted that there may be tensions between the generations as governments elected by the aging baby boomers transfer resources from the young to the elderly. The chances of this happening will be reduced if governments and individuals begin planning now for the society we will have in the future. For example, expensive hospital costs may be reduced if we increase the availability to the elderly of less costly home care. Increased participation in private pension plans and Registered Retirement Savings Plans will lessen the dependence of future retirees on the government.

One final trend worth noting is the *baby boom echo*—the children of the baby boomers. You can see this echo in Figure 16.4, which shows a relatively large cohort following about twenty years behind the baby boom. Even though the baby boomers had far fewer children than their parents (about 1.66 children per family compared with more than 3 children for their parents), there were so many of them that their children are having a significant impact. The leading edge of the echo generation were about 15 years old in 1996, so they will have an impact on such things as high school and university enrolments and crime rates over the next two decades.

THE BABY BOOM AND IMMIGRATION POLICY One consequence of our current low birth rate is possible depopulation. Fertility of 2.1 children per woman is needed to ensure the replacement of a population. Two children will replace the parents, and the additional 0.1 compensates for deaths that occur before potential parents reach reproductive age. This level of fertility will eventually lead to a stable population with zero population growth except for that caused by migration. In Canada, our fertility is now 1.7 children per woman, which will not provide replacement of our population. If this level of fertility remains constant for the next several decades, Canada will begin losing population when the baby boomers begin to die. You can see this in the 2031 population pyramid in Figure 16.4. At present, besides losing population through death, we also lose about 60,000 each year to emigration.

As Figure 16.1 shows, during the 1990s Canada admitted from 200,000 to 250,000 immigrants annually. This number was chosen because demographers have calculated that to stabilize the population we need about 250,000 immigrants a year. Thus, the baby bust has had an important impact on our immigration policies.

POPULATION GROWTH IN A GLOBAL CONTEXT

What are the consequences of global population growth? Scholars do not agree on the answer to this question. Some biologists have warned that earth is a finite ecosystem that cannot support the 10 billion people predicted by 2050; however, some economists have emphasized that free-market capitalism is capable of developing innovative ways to solve such problems. This debate is not a new one; for several centuries, strong opinions have been voiced about the effects of population growth on human welfare.

THE MALTHUSIAN PERSPECTIVE

English clergyman and economist Thomas Robert Malthus (1766–1834) was one of the first scholars to systematically study the effects of population. Displeased with the societal changes brought about by the Industrial Revolution in England, Malthus (1965/1798:7) anonymously published *An Essay on the Principle of Population, As It Affects the Future Improvement of Society*, in which he argued that "the power of population is infinitely greater than the power of the earth to produce subsistence [food] for man."

According to Malthus, the population, if left unchecked, would exceed the available food supply. He argued that the population would increase in a geometric (exponential) progression (2, 4, 8, 16 ...), while the food supply would increase only by an arithmetic progression (1, 2, 3, 4 ...). In other words, a *doubling effect* occurs: two parents can have four children, sixteen grandchildren, and so on, but food production increases by only one acre at a time. Thus, population growth inevitably surpasses the food supply, and the lack of food ultimately ends population growth and perhaps eliminates the existing population (Weeks, 1992). Even in a best-case scenario, overpopulation results in poverty.

However, Malthus suggested that this disaster might be averted by either positive or preventive checks on population. *Positive checks* are mortality risks such as famine, disease, and war; *preventive checks* are limits to fertility. For Malthus, the only acceptable preventive check was *moral restraint*; people should practise sexual abstinence before marriage and postpone marriage as long as possible in order to have only a few children. Although Malthus later found data disproving his model and wrote essays modifying his earlier statements, his original text is more widely cited (Keyfitz, 1994).

Malthus has had a lasting impact on the field of population studies. Most demographers refer to his dire predictions when they examine the relationship between fertility and subsistence needs (Davis, 1955). Overpopulation is still a daunting problem that capitalism and technological advances thus far have not solved, especially in underdeveloped and developing nations with rapidly growing populations and very limited resources.

THE MARXIST PERSPECTIVE

According to Karl Marx and Friedrich Engels, the food supply is not threatened by overpopulation; technologically, it is possible to produce the food and other goods needed to meet the demands of a growing population. Marx and Engels viewed poverty as a consequence of the exploitation of workers by the owners of the means of production. They argued, for example, that England had poverty because the capitalists skimmed off some of the workers' wages as profits. The labour of the working classes was used by capitalists to earn profits, which, in turn, were used to purchase machinery that could replace the workers, rather than supply food for all.

From this perspective, overpopulation occurs because capitalists desire to have a surplus of workers (an industrial reserve army) so as to suppress wages and force workers concerned about losing their livelihoods to be more productive. Marx believed that overpopulation would contribute to the eventual destruction of capitalism: unemployment would make the workers dissatisfied, resulting in a class consciousness based on their shared oppression and in the eventual overthrow of the system. In a socialist regime, enough food and other resources would be created to accommodate population growth.

According to some contemporary economists, the greatest crisis today facing underdeveloped and developing nations is capital shortage, not food shortage. Through technological advances, agricultural production has reached the level at which it can meet the food needs of the world if food is distributed efficiently. Capital shortage refers to the lack of adequate money or property to maintain a business; it is a problem because the physical capital of the past no longer meets the needs of modern economic development. Formerly, self-contained rural economies survived on local labour, using local materials to produce the capital needed for other labourers. For example, in a typical village, a carpenter made the loom needed by the weaver to make cloth. Today, in the global economy, the one-to-one exchange between the carpenter and the weaver is lost. With an antiquated, locally made loom, the weaver cannot compete against electronically controlled, mass-produced looms. Therefore, the village must purchase capital from the outside using its own meagre financial resources. In the process, the complementary relationship between labour and capital is lost; modern technology brings with it steep costs and results in village noncompetitiveness and underemployment (see Keyfitz, 1994).

Marx and Engels made a significant contribution to the study of demography by suggesting that poverty, not overpopulation, is the most important issue with regard to food supply in a capitalist economy. Although Marx and Engels offer an interesting counterpoint to Malthus, some scholars argue that the Marxist perspective is self-limiting because it attributes the population problem solely to capitalism. In actuality, nations

BOX 16.4 SOCIOLOGY AND MEDIA

Immigration and the Media

Just after the turn of the century, a great deal of hostility was directed at nonwhite immigrants. The media actively promoted this racism by publishing inflammatory articles about racial minorities. These articles not only affected public opinion, but were also used by legislators to justify laws that targeted minority immigrants. The work of Judge Emily Murphy of Edmonton, the first woman judge in the British Empire, was particularly influential. A series of five articles which she wrote and were published in *Maclean's* magazine shaped Canada's drug laws throughout the 1920s; their effects live on in our present narcotics legislation. These articles also shaped the attitudes of Canadians toward nonwhite immigrants by attributing the drug problem to Chinese and black "villains" who, according to Judge Murphy, were trying to spread the drug habit in order to seduce white women and to destroy the Anglo-Saxon way of life.

Judge Murphy felt that nonwhite immigrants were a threat to the Canadian way of life. In *Maclean's*, she wrote of a detective who had a special talent for smelling cooked opium. Two of the detective's cases involved a "Chinaman" and a beautiful young girl he found smoking opium under a piano case and a "negro" smoking opium in a wardrobe with a "white woman on either side of him." Her articles were illustrated with photographs of opium smokers (almost all of whom were women and/or nonwhite men) and cartoons (which were also racially demeaning). Each article featured a caricature of a Chinese opium smoker with smoke coming out of each ear. She saw the Chinese drug pedlar as one who was perhaps unknowingly carrying out the wishes of his superiors who were trying to bring about the "downfall of the white race." The "Negroes coming into Canada," she wrote "have similar ideas."

The same conspiratorial view was advanced by other media. For example, in 1911, the *Montreal Herald* responded to the immigration of 58 black women domestics from Guadeloupe by reporting that the "dark-skinned domestics were the advanced guard for others to follow."

That these views were so freely expressed in the media certainly made it easy for politicians and members of the public to follow the same racist line. The views, moreover, help to explain why Canada had racially based immigration policies for much of this century.

Sources: Based on Calliste, 1993/94; Murphy, 1922; and Cook, 1969.

An opium addict

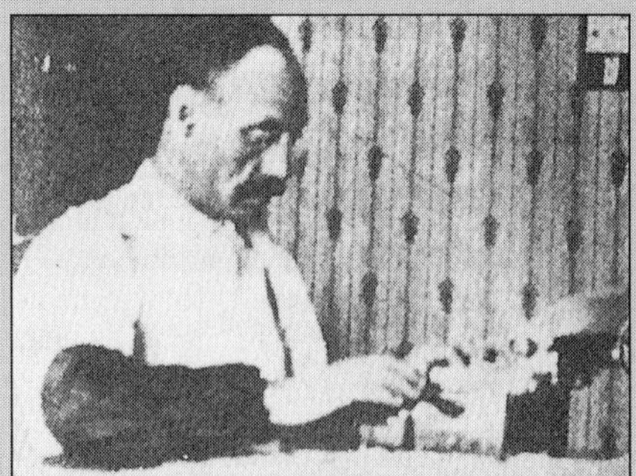

The keeper of an opium den

These photographs appeared in Judge Murphy's book The Black Candle *(Murphy, 1992), which, like her articles published in Maclean's in the 1920s, were used by legislators to justify laws that targeted minority immigrants.*

FIGURE 16.5

The Demographic Transition

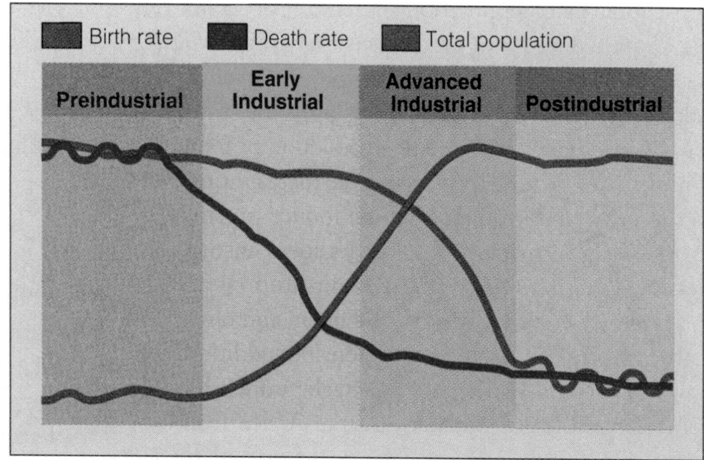

with socialist economies also have demographic trends similar to those in capitalist societies.

THE NEO-MALTHUSIAN PERSPECTIVE

More recently, *neo-Malthusians* (or "new Malthusians") have re-emphasized the dangers of overpopulation. Among the best known are biologists Paul Ehrlich and Anne H. Ehrlich (1991), who have suggested that the world population is following an *exponential growth pattern* because (much like Malthus's idea of geometric progression) "children ... remain in the population and themselves have children." To neo-Malthusians, the earth is "a dying planet" with too many people and too little food, and environmental degradation (Ehrlich, 1971). From the time of Christ to 1840, the doubling time of the population was 1,250 years, while at current growth rates the earth's population will double every 42 years (Grindstaff and Trovato, 1994). Overpopulation and rapid population growth result in global environmental problems, ranging from global warming and rain forest destruction to famine and vulnerability to epidemics such as AIDS (Ehrlich and Ehrlich, 1991). Environmental problems will worsen as countries such as India and China, with their large populations, modernize and begin to use resources at a rate closer to that of industrialized countries.

Throughout history, population growth and epidemic diseases have interacted to shape human destiny. People are extremely vulnerable to disease if they already are debilitated from inadequate nutrition, unclean water supplies, poor medical care, and lack of sanitation. However, even the richest inhabitants of a developed nation are not immune to such diseases. As the AIDS epidemic has demonstrated, HIV does not discriminate among class, race, gender, or age.

Are the neo-Malthusians correct? Will population increases leave many populations vulnerable to mass death through starvation and disease? Some possible outcomes are found in the work of Thomas Homer-Dixon, a University of Toronto political scientist who is often placed in the neo-Malthusian camp. Homer-Dixon feels that increases in population and resource consumption will lead to significant environmental changes including scarcities of soil, water, and climatic instability (1993). The strains caused by these scarcities may lead to unrest, including war, revolution, ethnic violence, and riots. The gloominess of this scenario is tempered by the fact that Homer-Dixon does not feel that population disaster is inevitable. Human social and technical ingenuity can overcome or at least delay the consequences of population increase. For example, despite decades of predictions that China will be unable to support its population, the average caloric intake in China has been rising as the country has massively increased its production of food. Unfortunately, there is no guarantee that solutions to the predicted problems will be found. Ingenuity itself is a function of a country's social institutions and in many countries, these institutions are too fragmented or too lacking in human and physical resources to solve their problems. In addition, political turmoil has been an obstacle; unrest has kept many countries in sub-Saharan Africa from progressing and, without major reform, their future is gloomy. For the same reasons, Homer-Dixon is more pessimistic about the future of India than of China because, he feels, India's social institutions are endangered by religious and caste cleavages. Ultimately, the future of humanity will depend on both national and international action to solve the problems created by population growth and environmental damage.

DEMOGRAPHIC TRANSITION THEORY

Some scholars who disagree with the neo-Malthusian viewpoint suggest that the theory of demographic transition offers a more accurate picture of future population growth. ***Demographic transition* is the process by which some societies have moved from high birth and death rates to relatively low birth and death rates as a result of technological development**. Although demographic transition theory initially was applied to population changes brought about by the Industrial Revolution in Western Europe and North America, it recently has emerged as a dominant perspective in contemporary demography (Weeks, 1992). Demographic transition is linked to four stages of economic development (see Figure 16.5):

- *Stage 1: Preindustrial societies.* Little population growth occurs because high birth rates are offset by high death rates. Children are viewed as an economic asset because of their ability to work, but infant and child mortality rates are high due to lack of sanitation and poor nutrition. Life expectancy is around 30 years.
- *Stage 2: Early industrialization.* Significant population growth occurs because birth rates remain relatively high while death rates decline. Improvements in health, sanitation, and nutrition produce a substantial decline in infant mortality rates. Overpopulation is likely to occur because more people are alive than the society has the ability to support. However, social institutions continue to promote high fertility. Although this stage occurred over a century ago in Europe, many developing nations—especially in Africa, Asia, and Latin America—currently are in this stage.
- *Stage 3: Advanced industrialization and urbanization.* Very little population growth occurs because both birth rates and death rates are low. The birth rate declines as couples control their fertility through contraception and become less likely to adhere to religious directives against their use. Children are not viewed as an economic asset; they consume income rather than producing it. Societies in this stage attain zero population growth—the point at which no population increase occurs from year to year.
- *Stage 4: Postindustrialization.* Birth rates continue to decline as more women gain full-time employment and the cost of raising children continues to increase. The population grows very slowly, if at all, because the decrease in birth rates is coupled with a stable death rate.

Debate continues as to whether this evolutionary model accurately explains the stages of population growth in all societies. Advocates note that demographic transition theory highlights the relationship between technological development and population growth, which make Malthus's predictions obsolete. Scholars also point out that demographic transitions occur at a faster rate in now-developing nations than they previously did in the nations that already are developed. Critics suggest that demographic transition theory best explains development in Western societies. Many regions of the Third World may never achieve a steady growth in social and economic wealth unless fertility levels first decline, so other routes to population control must be found.

Timothy Weiskel (1994) has pointed out that we should not expect that developing countries will follow the same path as Western nations, as they have very different demographic histories and their population dynamics operate within very different historical, cultural, and economic circumstances. Weiskel notes that women's status and education, along with active family planning programs, have been more important than overall economic growth as causes of declining fertility.

DEMOGRAPHY AND PUBLIC POLICY

China has dramatically reduced its rate of population growth because of its one-child-per-family policy, not because of technological advances and urbanization—80 percent of the Chinese population still resides in rural areas. China's one-child policy is an example of public policy that is based on demographic knowledge. The Chinese government recognized that with more than one billion people, the country could not continue to sustain high birth rates. To avoid the consequences of overpopulation suggested by Malthus, they developed a number of policies to convince couples to have only one child. This is a very harsh measure (if successful, it would mean that Chinese society would no longer have brothers, sisters, aunts, uncles, or cousins), which conflicts with both the strong value placed on the family in Chinese society and with the practical need for several children to help support the parents in old age. However, the government decided that the need for the survival of the nation was more important than the rights of Chinese citizens to have the number of children they wished.

We have discussed some of the ways in which Canada must change its policies to cope with the health and retirement demands of the aging baby boomers. While many government policies are related to population trends, one kind of policy you might not think of as relating to these trends is that which concerns the relationship between Quebec and the rest of Canada. Demographic analysis has, however, played a very large part in French/English politics over the past three decades.

Traditionally, Quebec has constituted about one-third of Canada's population. For many years, it had a higher birth rate than the other provinces. This meant increasing numbers of French-speaking Quebeckers—what some have called "the revenge of the cradle"—and it ensured a strong political voice for Quebec and helped maintain the dominance of the French language in Quebec. However, following the Quiet Revolution in the 1960s in Quebec (see Chapter 13, "Politics and Government"), the influence of the Catholic Church diminished and the province became increasingly secular. Birth rates declined dramatically, to a level far lower than that of most other provinces, reaching a low of 1.4 children per family in 1985 (Romaniuc, 1994). Like the rest of Canada, Quebec sought to make up for this shortage of births by increasing immigration. However, to the dismay of the Quebec government, many immigrants to Quebec chose to learn English rather than French. The French-speaking population continued to drop and now makes up less than one-quarter of Canada's total population. In response, the government passed Bill 101, which restricted the use of English and which required immigrants to send their children to French-language schools. Much of the nationalism in Quebec can be explained by Quebeckers' fears that the French language and culture will disappear in the vast North American sea of English.

While the French/English question will remain with us in some form for some time, demographic trends may create other sources of policy debate and political division. For example, most of the political and economic power in Canada has been centred in Ontario and Quebec. With the shift in jobs and population to Western Canada (British Columbia and Alberta now have more jobs than Quebec), we can anticipate that the West will begin to demand that its interests be reflected more broadly in national policies.

URBANIZATION AND THE GROWTH OF CITIES

Urban sociology **is a subfield of sociology that examines social relationships and political and economic structures in the city.** According to urban sociologists, a city is a relatively dense and permanent settlement of people who secure their livelihood primarily through nonagricultural activities. The Canadian census definition of urban is "communities with a population of 1,000 or more and a population density of 400 per square kilometre or greater" (Kalbach, and McVey, 1995). Definitions such as this one vary from country to country, making comparisons difficult. At any rate, this definition does not really correspond with the common notion of urban, which is "city living." The census term that defines our cities is *census metropolitan area*, or CMA. A *CMA* is "a very large urban area, together with adjacent urban and rural areas that have a high degree of economic and social integration with that urban area" (Statistics Canada, 1991:117). Canada has 25 CMAs, which in 1991 ranged in size from 3.9 million people in Toronto to 124,000 in Thunder Bay.

Although cities have existed for thousands of years, only about 3 percent of the world's population lived in cities two hundred years ago, as compared with almost 50 percent today. In Canada, the population is even more concentrated: almost 80 percent of us live in areas defined as urban; about 60 percent in CMAs; and about 30 percent in the three major metropolitan areas of Toronto, Montreal, and Vancouver. Since Confederation, at which time our population was roughly 16 percent urban (Stone, 1967), Canada has become steadily more urbanized. (As defined in Chapter 1, *urbanization* is the process by which an increasing proportion of a population lives in cities rather than rural areas.) To understand the process by which increasing numbers of people have become urban residents, we first need to examine how cities began.

EMERGENCE AND EVOLUTION OF THE CITY

Cities are a relatively recent innovation as compared with the length of human existence. The earliest humans are believed to have emerged anywhere from 40,000 to one million years ago, and permanent human settlements are believed to have first begun about 8000 B.C.E. However, some scholars date the development of the first city between 3500 and 3100 B.C.E., depending largely on whether a formal writing system is considered a requisite for city life (Sjoberg, 1965; Weeks, 1992; Flanagan, 1995).

According to sociologist Gideon Sjoberg (1965), three preconditions must be present in order for a city to develop:

1. *A favourable physical environment*, including climate and soil favourable to the development of plant and animal life and an adequate water supply to sustain both
2. *An advanced technology* (for that era) that could produce a social surplus in both agricultural and nonagricultural goods
3. *A well-developed social organization*, including a power structure, in order to provide social stability to the economic system

Based on these prerequisites, Sjoberg places the first cities in the Middle Eastern region of Mesopotamia or in areas immediately adjacent to it at about 3500 B.C.E. However, not all scholars concur; some place the earliest city, in Jericho (located in present-day Jordan), at about 8000 B.C.E. with a population of about six hundred

Toronto's Highway 401 at rush hour illustrates the development of postindustrial cities in which people commonly commute long distances to work.

people (see Kenyon, 1957). As Sjoberg points out, however, Jericho had no known formal writing system; therefore, a political structure and an economy (both essential to the establishment of a city) would not have been able to function effectively (see also Childe, 1957).

The earliest cities were not large by today's standards. The population of the larger Mesopotamian centres was between five and ten thousand (Sjoberg, 1965). The population of ancient Babylon (probably founded around 2200 B.C.E.) may have grown as large as 50,000 people; Athens may have held 80,000 people (Weeks, 1992). Four to five thousand years ago, cities with at least 50,000 people existed in the Middle East (in what today is Iraq and Egypt) and Asia (in what today is Pakistan and China), as well as in Europe. About 3,500 years ago, cities began to reach this size in Central and South America.

PREINDUSTRIAL CITIES

The largest preindustrial city was Rome; by 100 C.E., it may have had a population of 650,000 (Chandler and Fox, 1974). With the fall of the Roman Empire in 476 C.E., the nature of European cities changed. Seeking protection and survival, those persons who lived in urban settings typically did so in walled cities containing no more than 25,000 people. For the next six hundred years the urban population continued to live in walled enclaves, as competing warlords battled for power and territory during the "dark ages." Slowly, as trade increased, cities began to tear down their walls. Some walled cities still exist; Quebec City is the only walled city on this continent.

Preindustrial cities were limited in size by a number of factors. For one thing, crowded conditions and a lack of adequate sewage facilities increased the hazards from plagues and fires, and death rates were high. For another, food supplies were limited. In order to generate food for each city resident, at least fifty farmers had to work in the fields (Davis, 1949), and animal power was the only means of bringing food to the city. Once foodstuffs arrived in the city, there was no effective way to preserve them. Finally, migration to the city was difficult. Many people were in serf, slave, and caste systems that bound them to the land. Those able to escape such restrictions still faced several weeks of travel to reach the city, thus making it physically and financially impossible for many people to become city dwellers.

In spite of these problems, many preindustrial cities had a sense of *community*—a set of social relationships operating within given spatial boundaries or locations that provide people with a sense of identity and a feeling of belonging. The cities were full of people from all walks of life, both rich and poor, and they felt a high degree of social integration. You will recall that Ferdinand Tonnies (1940/1887) described such a community as *Gemeinschaft*—a society in which social relationships are based on personal bonds of friendship and kinship and on intergenerational stability, such that people have a commitment to the entire group and feel a sense of togetherness. In this type of society the person who sells you groceries may also be your neighbour, an elder in your church, and a relative by marriage. When you visit the store, your grocery purchase will be handled in a very personal fashion. By contrast, industrial cities were characterized by Tonnies as *Gesellschaft*—a society characterized by impersonal and specialized relationships, with little long-term commitment to the group or consensus on values (see Chapter 5). In *Gesellschaft* societies, even neighbours are "strangers" who feel they have little in common with one another. Your transaction at the grocery store will be handled much more formally in this type of society.

Canadian communities arose as settlement extended to new parts of this large country. Until the building of the Canadian Pacific Railway, much of Canada was accessible only by water, so most of our settlements, including those that have grown into large cities, were in areas with access to waterways. Transportation routes were particularly important for a colony whose main function was sending large quantities of raw materials such as timber, wheat, and beaver pelts overseas to European markets. Virtually all of our large cities are located on oceans, lakes, or large rivers.

INDUSTRIAL CITIES

The Industrial Revolution changed the nature of the city. Factories sprang up rapidly as production shifted from the primary, agricultural sector to the secondary, manufacturing sector. With the advent of factories came many new employment opportunities not available to people in rural areas. In fact, factories required a concentration of population to act as a labour force. Emergent technology, including new forms of transportation and agricultural production, made it easier for people to leave the countryside and move to the city. Between 1700 and 1900, the population of many European cities mushroomed. Although the Industrial Revolution did not start in North America until the mid-nineteenth century, the effect was similar. Between 1871 and 1911 the population of Toronto grew by 700 percent and that of Montreal by 450 percent (Nader, 1976). By 1911 both cities had roughly 500,000 people and were on their way to becoming major metropolises. A ***metropolis* is one or more central cities and their surrounding suburbs that dominate the economic and cultural life of a region.** A ***central city* is the densely populated centre of a metropolis.**

The growth of cities during the industrial period was something of a mixed blessing. As cities grew in size and density, overcrowding, poor sanitation, and lack of a clean water supply often led to the spread of epidemic diseases and contributed to a high death rate. In Europe, mortality rates were higher in cities than in rural areas until the nineteenth century, and this remains the case in many cities in the developing world today.

POSTINDUSTRIAL CITIES

Since the 1950s, postindustrial cities have emerged in technologically advanced countries, the economies of which have gradually shifted from secondary (manufacturing) production to tertiary (service and information-processing) production. As more traditional industries such as textile manufacturing, steel producing, and many different types of light manufacturing have become obsolete or moved to other countries with lower wages, cities have had to either change or face decline. For example, cities in New Brunswick have been economically devastated by the loss of many jobs in traditional industries such as shipbuilding and railroad maintenance, as well as in resource industries associated with the fishing industry. The province has tried to counteract these losses by moving into the technologically based field of telephone call centres, which perform tasks such as telephone marketing and airline-reservation handling.

Postindustrial cities are dominated by "light" industry, such as computer software manufacturing; information-processing services, such as airline and hotel reservation services; educational complexes; medical centres; convention and entertainment centres; and retail trade centres and shopping malls. Most families do not live in close proximity to a central business district. Technological advances in communication and transportation make it possible for middle- and upper-income individuals and families to have more work options and to live greater distances from the workplace. Some futurists feel that communications technology, along with the retirement plans of the baby boomers, may soon lead to a degree of deurbanization. People who do not have to be physically present in the city centre each day may find a rural or semirural lifestyle an attractive alternative to the commuting and high housing prices that are a part of life in a large city.

PERSPECTIVES ON URBANIZATION AND THE GROWTH OF CITIES

Urban sociology follows in the tradition of early European sociological perspectives that compared social life with biological organisms or ecological processes. Auguste Comte, for example, pointed out that cities are the "real organs" that make a society function. Emile Durkheim applied natural ecology to his analyses of *mechanical solidarity*, which is characterized by a simple division of labour and shared religious beliefs such as is found in small agrarian societies, and *organic solidarity*, which is characterized by interdependence based on the elaborate division of labour found in large, urban societies (see Chapter 5). These early analyses became the foundation for ecological models/functionalist perspectives in urban sociology.

FUNCTIONALIST PERSPECTIVES: ECOLOGICAL MODELS

Functionalists examine the interrelations among the parts that make up the whole; therefore, in studying the growth of cities, they emphasize the life cycle of urban growth. Like the social philosophers and sociologists before him, University of Chicago sociologist Robert Park (1915) based his analysis of the city on *human ecology*—the study of the relationship between people and their physical environment. According to Park (1936), economic competition produces certain regularities in land use patterns and population distributions. Applying Park's idea to the study of urban land use patterns, sociologist Ernest W. Burgess (1925) developed the concentric zone model, an ideal construct that attempted to explain why some cities expand radially from a central business core.

CONCENTRIC ZONE MODEL Burgess's *concentric zone model* is a description of the process of urban growth that views the city as a series of circular areas or zones, each characterized by a different type of land use, that developed from a central core (see Figure 16.6a). *Zone 1* is the central business district and cultural centre (retail stores, financial institutions, hotels, and theatres, for example), in which high land prices cause vertical growth in the form of skyscrapers. *Zone 2* is the zone of transition. As the city expanded, houses formerly occupied by wealthy families were divided into rooms that now are rented to recent immigrants and poor persons; this zone also contains wholesale light manufacturing and marginal business (such as secondhand stores, pawnshops, and taverns). *Zone 3* contains

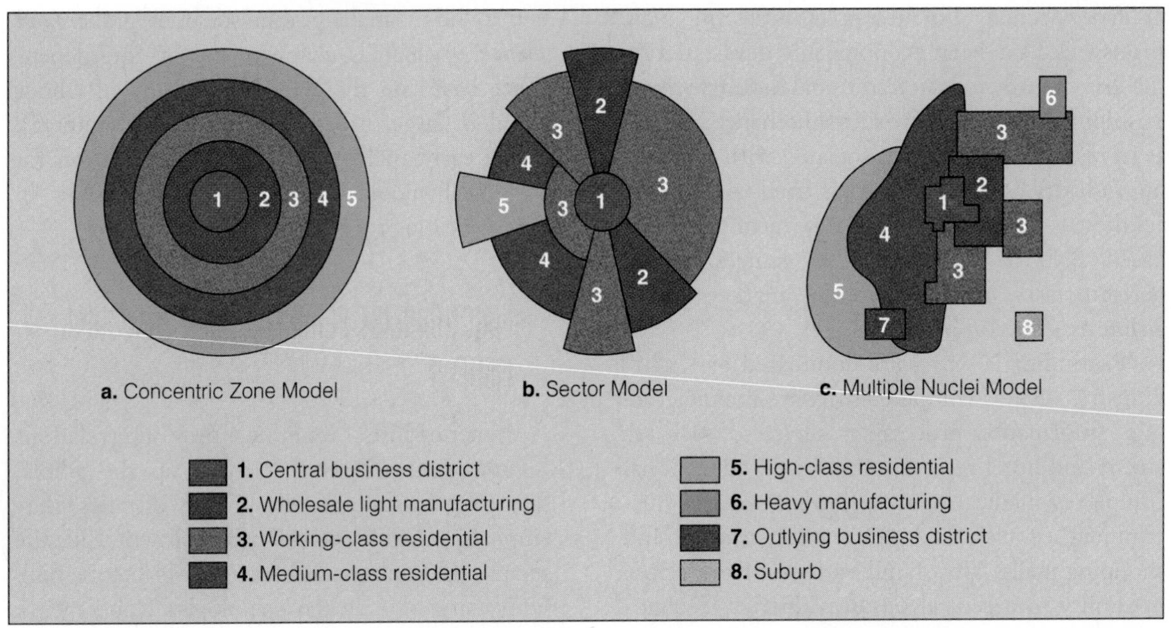

FIGURE 16.6

Three Models of the City

Adapted from Harris and Ullman, 1945.

working-class residences and shops and ethnic enclaves, such as Little Italy. *Zone 4* is composed of homes for affluent families, single-family residences of white-collar workers, and shopping centres. *Zone 5* is a ring of small cities and towns populated by persons who commute to the city to work and by people living on estates.

Two important ecological processes are involved in the concentric zone theory: invasion and succession. ***Invasion* is the process by which a new category of people or type of land use arrives in an area previously occupied by another group or land use** (McKenzie, 1925). For example, Burgess noted that recent immigrants and low-income individuals "invaded" zone 2 which were formerly occupied by wealthy families. ***Succession* is the process by which a new category of people or type of land use gradually predominates in an area formerly dominated by another group or activity** (McKenzie, 1925). In zone 2, for example, when some of the single-family residences were sold and subsequently divided into multiple housing units, the remaining single-family owners moved out because the "old" neighbourhood had changed. As a result of their move, the process of invasion was complete and succession had occurred.

Invasion and succession theoretically operate in an outward movement: those who are unable to "move out" of the inner rings are those without upward social mobility, so that the central zone ends up being primarily occupied by the poorest residents—except when gentrification occurs. ***Gentrification* is the process by which members of the middle and upper-middle classes move into the central city area and renovate existing properties**. Centrally located, naturally attractive areas are the most likely candidates for gentrification. To urban ecologists, gentrification is the solution to revitalizing the central city. To conflict theorists, gentrification creates additional hardships for the poor by depleting the amount of affordable housing available and "pushing" them out of the area (Flanagan, 1995).

The concentric zone model demonstrates how economic and political forces play an important part in the location of groups and activities, and it shows how a large urban area can have internal differentiation (Gottdiener, 1985). However, the model is most applicable to older cities that experienced high levels of immigration early in the twentieth century (Queen and Carpenter, 1953). No city, including Chicago (on which the model is based), entirely conforms to this model.

THE SECTOR MODEL In an attempt to examine a wider range of settings, urban ecologist Homer Hoyt (1939) studied the configuration of 142 cities. Hoyt's *sector model* emphasizes the significance of terrain and the importance of transportation routes in the layout of cities. According to Hoyt, residences of a particular type and value tend to grow outward from the centre of the city in wedge-shaped sectors, with the more expensive residential neighbourhoods located along the higher ground near lakes and rivers or along certain streets that stretch in one direction or another from the downtown area (see Figure 16.6b). By contrast, industrial areas tend to be located along river valleys and railroad lines. Middle-class residential zones exist on either side of the wealthier neighbourhoods. Finally, lower-class residential areas occupy the remaining space, bordering the central business area and the industrial areas.

THE MULTIPLE NUCLEI MODEL According to the *multiple nuclei model* developed by urban ecologists Chauncey Harris and Edward Ullman (1945), cities do not have one centre from which all growth radiates, but rather they have numerous centres of development based on specific urban needs or activities (see Figure 16.6c). As cities began to grow rapidly, they annexed formerly outlying and independent townships that had been communities in their own right. In addition to the central business district, other nuclei developed around activities such as an educational institution, a medical complex, or a government centre. Residential neighbourhoods may exist close to or far away from these nuclei. A wealthy residential area may be located near a high-priced shopping centre, for instance, while less-expensive housing must locate closer to industrial and transitional areas of town. This model fits some urban areas such as Metropolitan Toronto, which has large nuclei such as the business district of North York. It also applies to a number of communities such as Edmonton, which have nuclei around universities. However, critics suggest that it does not provide insights about uniformity of land use patterns among cities and relies on an after-the-fact explanation of why certain activities are located where they are (Flanagan, 1995).

DIFFERENCES BETWEEN CANADIAN AND U.S. CITIES The models of urban growth discussed above were developed to explain the growth of U.S. cities. They do not fit preindustrial cities (most of which have their slums on the outskirts of the city rather than in the central core) nor do they fit cities such as those in Europe that were relatively large before they industrialized. Because they developed on the same continent and at about the same time, there are many similarities between Canadian and American cities, but the models probably do not apply as well to Canadian cities, which differ from U.S. cities in the following important ways (Gillis, 1995; Wolfe, 1992):

1. Canadian cities are higher in density, which means they have less urban sprawl. It is cheaper to provide services in compact cities, and commuting to work is far easier.
2. The core areas of Canadian cities are much healthier than those in the United States. In many U.S. cities, residents have moved to the suburbs to avoid crime, high taxes, and other inner-city problems. This has created what some observers refer to as "doughnut cities," with poor central core areas that have no industry, no job opportunities, poor schools, deteriorated housing, and no tax

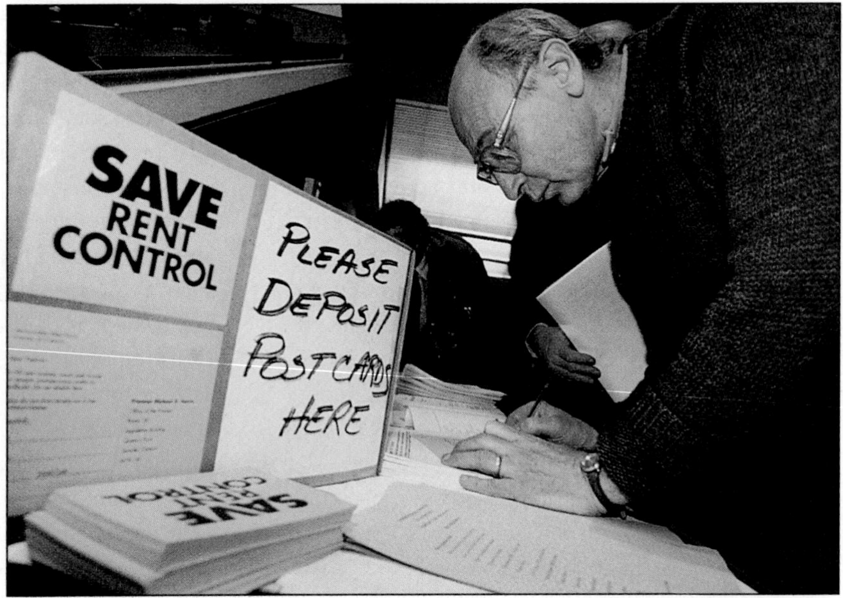

According to conflict theorists, members of the capitalist class make decisions that limit the choices of ordinary citizens, such as how affordable or unaffordable their housing will be. However, scenes like this show that tenants may become active participants in class conflict over the usage of urban space.

base to help improve things. The strength of our urban core is a major reason Canadian cities have much lower crime rates than American cities.

3. Urban Canadians rely on public transit more than do Americans, though both countries are far behind European cities in public transit use. Because of this, our cities are less divided by freeways than American urban areas.
4. Racial tension has been far less pronounced in Canada than in the United States, where it has led to many problems including urban riots and "white flight" to the suburbs.
5. Canadian and U.S. public housing policies have been very different. With a few exceptions, such as Toronto's Regent Park and Montreal's Jeanne Mance, governments in Canada have not built large-scale, high-rise developments. Public housing in Canada has taken the form of small, infill projects in established neighbourhoods. These are small housing developments typically consisting of small apartment buildings or row housing, which are built in established neighbourhoods. Thus we have not faced the problem of large numbers of economically disadvantaged people crowded into areas that can easily be neglected by the rest of society.

CONTEMPORARY URBAN ECOLOGY Urban ecologist Amos Hawley (1950) revitalized the ecological tradition by linking it more closely with functionalism. According to Hawley, urban areas are complex and expanding social systems in which growth patterns are based on advances in transportation and communication. For example, commuter railways and automobiles led to the decentralization of city life and the movement of industry from the central city to the suburbs (Hawley, 1981).

Other urban ecologists have continued to refine the methodology used to study the urban environment. *Social area analysis* examines urban populations in terms of economic status, family status, and ethnic classification (Shevky and Bell, 1966). For example, middle- and upper-middle-class parents with school-aged children tend to cluster together in "social areas" with a "good" school district; young single professionals may prefer to cluster in the central city for entertainment and nightlife.

The influence of human ecology on the field of urban sociology still is very strong today (see Frisbie and Kasarda, 1988). Contemporary research on European and North American urban patterns often is based on the assumption that spatial arrangements in cities conform to a common, most efficient design (Flanagan, 1995). Some critics have noted, however, that ecological models do not take into account the influence of powerful political and economic elites on the development process in urban areas (Feagin and Parker, 1990).

CONFLICT PERSPECTIVES: POLITICAL ECONOMY MODELS

Conflict theorists argue that cities do not grow or decline by chance. Rather, they are the product of specific decisions made by members of the capitalist class and political elites. These far-reaching decisions regarding land use and urban development benefit the members of some groups at the expense of others (see Castells, 1977/1972). Karl Marx suggested that cities are the arenas in which the intertwined processes of class conflict and capital accumulation take place; class consciousness and worker revolt were more likely to develop when workers were concentrated in urban areas (Flanagan, 1995).

According to sociologists Joe E. Feagin and Robert Parker (1990), three major themes prevail in political economy models of urban growth. First both economic *and* political factors affect patterns of urban growth and decline. Economic factors include capitalistic investments in production, workers, workplaces, land, and buildings. Political factors include governmental protection of the right to own and dispose of privately held property as owners see fit and the role of government officials in promoting the interests of business elites and large corporations.

Second, urban space has both an exchange value and a use value. *Exchange value* refers to the profits industrialists, developers, bankers, and others make from buying, selling, and developing land and buildings. By contrast, *use value* is the utility of space, land, and buildings for everyday life, family life, and neighbourhood life. In other words, land has purposes other than simply that of generating profit—for example, for homes, open spaces, and recreational areas. Today, class conflict exists over usage of urban space, as is evident in battles over rental costs, safety, and development of large-scale projects (see Tabb and Sawers, 1984).

Third, structure and agency are both important in understanding how urban development takes place. *Structure* refers to institutions such as government bureaucracies and capital investment circuits that are involved in the urban development process. *Agency* refers to human actors, including developers, business elites, and activists protesting development, who are involved in decisions about land use.

CAPITALISM AND URBAN GROWTH According to political economy models, urban growth is influenced by capital investment decisions, power and resource inequality, class and class conflict, and government subsidy programs. Members of the capitalist class choose corporate locations, decide on sites for shopping centres and factories, and spread the population that can afford to purchase homes into sprawling suburbs located exactly where the capitalists think they should be located (Feagin and Parker, 1990).

Business involvement in urban development is nothing new. Winnipeg became a major transportation centre because of its location at the junction of the Red and Assiniboine Rivers. However, because of Winnipeg's flooding problems, the small community of Selkirk was originally chosen for the route of the Canadian Pacific Railway (CPR). After several years of intensive lobbying by Winnipeg's political and business leaders, along with promises of subsidies to the CPR, the line was built through Winnipeg in 1881. According to Bellan (1978), Sir Donald Smith, the man who drove the last spike to finish the transcontinental railway, was instrumental in having the route shifted to Winnipeg. A key figure in building the CPR, Smith was also the largest shareholder in the Hudson's Bay Company, which owned a large block of land in the centre of Winnipeg. During the land boom that followed the announcement of the railway's new route, the Hudson's Bay Company made millions of dollars selling this land.

Today, a small number of financial institutions and developers finance and construct most of Canada's major and many of its smaller urban development projects, including skyscrapers, shopping malls, and suburban housing projects, across the country. These decision makers set limits on the individual choices of the ordinary citizen with regard to real estate, just as they do with regard to other choices (Feagin and Parker, 1990). They can make housing more affordable or totally unaffordable for many people. Ultimately, their motivation rests not in benefiting the community, but rather in making a profit; the cities they produce reflect this mindset.

One of the major results of these urban development practices is *uneven development*—the tendency of some neighbourhoods, cities, or regions to grow and prosper while others stagnate and decline (Perry and Watkins, 1977). An example of this is the movement of middle- and upper-class people to the suburbs, which reduces the tax base of the city core. Conflict theorists argue that uneven development reflects inequalities of wealth and power in society. The problem not only affects areas in a state of decline but also produces external costs, even in "boom" areas, that are paid for by the entire community. Among these costs are increased pollution, traffic congestion, and rising rates of crime and violence. According to sociologist Mark Gottdiener (1985:214), these costs are "intrinsic to the very core of capitalism, and those who profit the most from development are not called upon to remedy its side effects."

GENDER REGIMES IN CITIES Feminist perspectives only recently have been incorporated in urban studies (Garber and Turner, 1995). From this perspective, urbanization reflects the workings not only of the political economy but also of patriarchy. According to sociologist Lynn M. Appleton (1995), different kinds of cities have different *gender regimes*—prevailing ideologies of how women and men should think, feel, and act; how access to social positions and control of resources should be managed; and how relationships between men and women should be conducted. The higher density and greater diversity found in central cities serve as a challenge to the patriarchy found in the home and workplace in lower-density, homogeneous areas such as suburbs and rural areas because central cities offer a broader range of lifestyle choices, some of which do not involve traditional patriarchal family structures. For example, cities are more likely than suburbs to support a subculture of economically independent females. Thus the city may be a forum for challenging patriarchy; all residents who differ in marital status, paternity, sexual orientation, class and/or race/ethnicity tend to live in close proximity to one another and may hold and act upon a common belief that both public and private patriarchy should be eliminated (Appleton, 1995).

GLOBAL PATTERNS During the past three decades, urbanization has taken on an increasingly global character. At the global level, nations may be divided into three tiers: core, semiperipheral, and peripheral (Wallerstein, 1979). The United States, Japan, and Germany are ***core nations*—dominant capitalist centres characterized by high levels of industrialization and urbanization**. Most of the African countries and many countries in South America and the Caribbean are ***peripheral nations*—nations that are dependent on core nations for capital, have little or no industrialization (other than what may be brought in by core nations), and have uneven patterns of urbanization**. In peripheral nations, the wealthy benefit from the work of the poor and from their economic relations with capitalists in core countries, whose position they uphold in order to maintain their own wealth and power. ***Semiperipheral nations* are more developed than the peripheral nations but less developed**

than core nations. Theoretically, semiperipheral countries, such as India, Iran, and Mexico, exploit peripheral ones, just as the core nations exploit both.

At a global level, uneven economic growth results from capital investment by core nations; disparity between the rich and the poor within these nations is increased in the process. For example, international capitalism has brought profound changes to Mexico. In northern Mexico, along the U.S./Mexican border, transnational corporations have built plants so that goods intended for sale in the United States, Canada, and elsewhere can be assembled by low-wage workers to keep production costs down.

Because of a demand for a large supply of low-wage workers, thousands of people have moved from the rural regions of Mexico to urban areas along the border in the hope of earning a higher wage; this influx has pushed already overcrowded cities far beyond their capacity. Many people live in *shantytowns* on the edge of town or in low-cost rental housing in central city slums because their wages are low and affordable housing is nonexistent. *Squatters* (persons who occupy land without any legal title to it) are the most rapidly growing segment of the population in many Mexican cities (Flanagan, 1995).

Unlike functionalist explanations that focus on ecological processes, political economy models/conflict perspectives point out that urban patterns result from basic economic processes such as capital accumulation and other manifestations of the class struggle (Flanagan, 1995). Although this approach has been criticized for its deterministic viewpoint that capitalists conspire against others for their own economic gain, it provides important insights into the contemporary development of cities.

INTERACTIONIST PERSPECTIVES: THE EXPERIENCE OF CITY LIFE

Interactionists examine the *experience* of urban life. How does city life affect the people who live in a city? Some analysts answer this question positively; others are cynical about the effect of urban living on the individual.

SIMMEL'S VIEW OF CITY LIFE According to German sociologist Georg Simmel (1950/1905), urban life is highly stimulating and it shapes people's thoughts and actions. Urban residents are influenced by the quick pace of city life and the pervasiveness of economic relations in everyday life. Due to the intensity of urban life, people become somewhat insensitive to events and individuals around them. When city life requires you to interact with hundreds of different people every day, you cannot become personally involved with each of them so most of your contacts will be impersonal. Urbanites are wary of one another because most interactions in the city are economic rather than social. Simmel suggests that attributes such as punctuality and exactness are rewarded but that friendliness and warmth in interpersonal relations are viewed as personal weaknesses. Some people act in a reserved way to cloak deeper feelings of distrust or dislike toward others. However, Simmel did not view city life as completely negative; he also pointed out that urban living could have a liberating effect on people because they had opportunities for individualism and autonomy (Flanagan, 1995).

URBANISM AS A WAY OF LIFE Based on Simmel's observations on social relations in the city, early Chicago School sociologist Louis Wirth (1938) suggested that urbanization is a "way of life." *Urbanism* refers to the distinctive social and psychological patterns of life typically found in the city. According to Wirth, the size, density, and heterogeneity of urban populations typically result in an elaborate division of labour and in spatial segregation of people by race/ethnicity, social class, religion, and/or lifestyle. In the city, primary group ties largely are replaced by secondary relationships; social interaction is fragmented, impersonal, and often superficial ("Hello! Have a nice day"). Even though people gain some degree of freedom and privacy by living in the city, they pay

These photographs represent three of the ways people adapt to city life described by Herbert Gans. Cosmopolites choose to live in the city to enjoy cultural facilities such as Toronto's Roy Thomson Hall. Ethnic villagers live in tightly knit neighbourhood enclaves, such as this Chinese neighbourhood in Richmond, British Columbia. Trapped residents can find no escape from the city, as exemplified by this homeless person in Toronto.

a price for their autonomy, losing the group support and reassurance that comes from primary group ties.

From Wirth's perspective, people who live in urban areas are alienated, powerless, and lonely. A sense of community is obliterated and replaced by "mass society"—a large-scale, highly institutionalized society in which individuality is supplanted by mass messages, faceless bureaucrats, and corporate interest.

Simmel and Wirth share an *environmental determinism* that assumes that the physical environment of the city determines the behaviour of urban dwellers. Their work has contributed to the commonly held view that cities are cold, anonymous, and unfriendly places (Kennedy, 1983). However, other researchers claim that the rural/urban contrast is too simplistic and ignores the wide diversity of lifestyles found in urban areas. This view has led to research into the reasons for the different ways in which urban residents have responded to their environment.

GANS'S URBAN VILLAGERS In contrast to Wirth's gloomy assessment of urban life, sociologist Herbert Gans (1982/1962) suggested that not everyone experiences the city in the same way. Based on research conducted in the west end of Boston, Gans concluded that many residents develop strong loyalties and a sense of community in central city areas that outsiders may view negatively. People make choices about the lifestyle they wish to lead based on their personal characteristics, the most important of which are social class and stage in the life cycle. According to Gans, there are five major categories of adaptation among urban dwellers. *Cosmopolites* are students, artists, writers, musicians, entertainers, and professionals who live in the city because they want to be close to its cultural facilities. *Unmarried people and childless couples* live in the city because they want to be close to work and entertainment. *Ethnic villagers* live in ethnically segregated neighbourhoods; some are recent immigrants who feel most comfortable within their own group. The *deprived* are poor individuals with dim future prospects; they have very limited education and few, if any, other resources. The *trapped* are urban dwellers who can find no escape from the city; this group includes persons left behind by the process of invasion and succession, downwardly mobile individuals who have lost their former position in society, older persons who have nowhere else to go, and individuals addicted to alcohol or other drugs. Transient people in the inner city are most likely to suffer the urban ills described by Wirth, but this is because of residential instability, and not simply an inevitable result of urbanization. Gans concluded that the city is a pleasure and a challenge for some urban dwellers and an urban nightmare for others.

GENDER AND CITY LIFE Do women and men experience city life differently? According to scholar Elizabeth Wilson (1991), some men view the city as *sexual space* in which women are categorized as prostitutes, lesbians, temptresses, or virtuous women in need of protection, based on their sexual desirability and accessibility. Wilson suggests that more affluent, dominant group women are more likely to be viewed as virtuous women in need of protection by their own men or police officers. Cities offer a paradox for women: on the one hand, they offer more freedom than is found in comparatively isolated rural, suburban, and domestic settings; on the other, women may be in greater physical danger in the city. For Wilson, the answer to women's vulnerability in the city is not found in offering protection to them, but rather in changing people's perceptions that they can treat women as sexual objects because of the impersonality of city life (Wilson, 1991).

Michelson (1994) has highlighted another dimension of the vulnerability of women in cities. Women with children are much more likely to be in the paid workforce than they were twenty years ago. When women were more likely to stay home, they spent much of their time in the company of immediate neighbours, and rarely ventured from their neighbourhoods at night without their husbands. Employed women have a much different city experience. Much of their time is now spent with people on the job and they are more often alone outside their immediate neighbourhoods at different hours.

For many women in this situation, travelling to and from work is perceived as dangerous. Michelson cites a Statistics Canada study showing that 80 percent of women fear entering parking garages and 76 percent fear using public transportation after dark. Women feel particularly vulnerable if they have to walk alone after dark because of work or school. Our cities have not yet adapted well to these major social changes in the lives of women.

MICHELSON, FISCHER, AND URBAN CHOICES

Claude Fischer (1976) built on Gans's view of the importance of subgroup values in influencing urban behaviour. Fischer studied the way in which the size of cities and their structural differentiation provided opportunities for the development of urban subcultures. Cities of different sizes and in different locations vary in the kinds of subcultures they support. For example, a city with a large number of manufacturing jobs will support a much more vibrant blue-collar subculture than will a city whose economy is centred on education and financial services. In turn, the latter city will be more likely to have active subcultures focused on the arts, which attract more highly educated people. The diversity of cities creates the opportunity for subgroups to follow a variety of interests which would not be possible in smaller communities. People may be attracted to particular cities because of the subcultural opportunities available to them. The larger and more diverse the city, the broader the range of choices available to its residents. This is one reason large cities continue to attract people. Somali immigrants will feel more at home in Toronto or Ottawa, where there are Somali ethnic subcultures, than they will in Chicoutimi or St. John's where subcultural supports do not exist.

While Fischer demonstrated the importance of urban institutional structures, William Michelson (1976, 1977) argued that the physical environment of cities (buildings, roads, etc.) also has an impact on behaviour. People make residential choices based on factors such as social class, ethnicity, and stage in the life cycle. These choices, in turn, have an impact on their social relationships and their behaviour. For example, in his research on Toronto, Michelson found that different types of physical environment (high-rise downtown apartments, single-family suburban houses, single-family downtown houses, and high-rise suburban apartments) attracted very different types of residents. The chosen environment did have an effect on behaviour. For example, residents who lived near public facilities and conveniences were more socially active than people of the same social characteristics who lived further from these facilities. An Edmonton study by Kennedy (1978) found that the type of residence people chose played a role in the type and nature of contact they had with their neighbours and relatives.

There is, then, a diversity in the life experience of urban dwellers that depends on a wide variety of factors such as age, social class, gender, marital status, and type of residence. The same is likely true of rural residents; the romantic view of rural society held by the early urban sociologists may have been nostalgia for a mythical past. In reality, urban life is not as bad, nor rural life as good, as Wirth and his colleagues assumed.

DIVIDED INTERESTS: CITIES, SUBURBS, AND BEYOND

Since World War II, a dramatic population shift has occurred in North America as thousands of families have moved from cities to suburbs. Even though some people lived in suburban areas prior to the twentieth century, large-scale suburban development began in the 1950s. Postwar suburban growth was fuelled by the large baby boom families, aggressive land developers, inexpensive real estate and construction methods, better transportation, abundant energy, and liberalized mortgage policies (Jackson, 1985; Palen, 1995).

Regardless of its causes, mass suburbanization has created a territorial division of interests between cities and suburban areas (Flanagan,

1995). While many suburbanites rely on urban centres for their employment, entertainment, and other services, they pay their property taxes to suburban governments and school districts. While Canadian cities are very healthy compared with those in the United States and most other countries, they have not been immune to the problems of poverty, homelessness, unemployment, and urban sprawl. During the recession of the early 1990s Canadian cities were faced with cutting services or raising taxes at a time when the tax base already was shrinking because of migration to the suburbs. As services and urban infrastructures deteriorated, even more middle- and upper-class people moved out of cities, with some businesses following suit.

Montreal in particular has suffered from the doughnut effect. As people and industry have moved out of the central island of Montreal to suburban communities, the core has suffered. Urban Montreal has the highest jobless rate of any major North American city, and rates of poverty, homelessness, and infant mortality are all considerably higher than the Canadian average. Despite these very real problems, Montreal is still a vibrant and safe place, and is far more livable than most American central cities. In fact, the Washington-based group Population Action International ranked Montreal first in livability (tied with Melbourne and Seattle) among the world's 100 largest metropolitan areas.

The problems faced by Montreal and several of our other large cities are essentially political. Much of the decline of central cities is caused by a skewed tax system that drives businesses and middle-class residents out to the suburbs. The central cities must provide a wide range of services to their own residents as well as to those who commute downtown from the suburbs. Thus, business and residential property taxes are much higher downtown than in suburban areas. Business taxes in Montreal, for example, are 44 percent higher than in its surrounding municipalities and residential taxes are 30 percent higher (Lalonde, 1996).

The solution to this problem is conceptually simple; develop strong regional governments that would create wider service areas than do existing municipal governments. Regional governments would be responsible for water, sewage, transportation, schools, parks, hospitals, and other public services over a wider area. Revenues would be shared among central cities, affluent suburbs, and suburban municipalities based on the assumption that everyone will benefit if the quality of life is improved throughout the region. Greater Montreal has 102 municipalities ranging in size from Montreal, with 1,017,666 persons in 1991, to Île Cadieux, which had 140 residents in 1991, and only a regional government can avoid the fragmentation this variation produces. London, England, provides an example of how a lack of regional planning and authority can lead to chaos. For example, traffic in that city is extremely congested, at least partly because each of Greater London's 33 boroughs has responsibility for its transportation policy. Once, most of the Thames River bridges were closed at the same time because the local transportation authorities had not coordinated their maintenance schedules (Drohan, 1996).

If the solution is so simple, why has it not been quickly adopted? The reason is politics. Task force reports in Montreal and in Toronto have recommended similar solutions to those described above to the problems of our two major cities. However, the reports have been opposed by politically powerful suburban municipalities whose residents do not want their taxes raised to help the larger community, and neither report is likely to be implemented. Another reason may be that implementation of such changes is the responsibility of the provinces, and provincial governments appear reluctant to establish strong municipal governments in urban areas representing about half of each province's population. Change of this nature is also not likely to occur because many of our provincial governments, including those in Ontario and Quebec, have more support in rural and suburban areas than in the major cities.

POPULATION AND URBANIZATION IN THE TWENTY-FIRST CENTURY

As we move into the twenty-first century, rapid global population growth is inevitable. Although death rates have declined in many developing nations, birth rates have not correspondingly decreased. Between 1985 and 2025, 93 percent of all global population growth will have occurred in Africa, Asia, and Latin America; 83 percent of the world's population will live in those regions by 2025 (Petersen, 1994).

Predicting changes in population is difficult. Natural disasters such as earthquakes, volcanic eruptions, hurricanes, tornados, floods, and so on obviously cannot be predicted. A cure for diseases caused by HIV may be found; however, HIV/AIDS may reach epidemic proportions in more nations and as many as 100 million AIDS cases may exist worldwide by the year 2000. A number of diseases such as tuberculosis, which had been controlled by antibiotics, are now returning in a form that is resistant to the drugs usually used for treatment.

Whatever the impact of disease, developing nations will have an increasing number of poor people. While the world's population will *double*, the urban population will *triple* as people migrate from rural to urban areas in search of food, water, and jobs. Of all developing regions, Latin America is becoming the most urbanized; four megacities—Mexico City (20 million), Buenos Aires (12 million), Lima (7 million), and Santiago (5 million)—already contain more than half of this region's population and continue to grow rapidly. By 2010, Rio de Janeiro and Sao Paulo are expected to have a combined population of about 40 million people living in a 350-mile-long ***megalopolis*—a continuous concentration of two or more cities and their suburbs that have grown until they form an interconnected urban area** (Petersen, 1994).

One of the many effects of urbanization is greater exposure of people to the media. In the twenty-first century, increasing numbers of poor people in less developed nations will see images from the developed world that are beamed globally by new networks such as CNN. As futurist John L. Peterson (1994:119) notes, "For the first time in history, the poor are beginning to understand how relatively poor they are compared to the rich nations. They see, in detail, how the rest of the world lives and feel their increasing disenfranchisement." The impact this will have remains an open question.

The speed of social change means that areas that we currently think of as being relatively free from such problems will be characterized by depletion of natural resources and greater air and water pollution (see Ehrlich and Ehrlich, 1991). At the same time, if social and environmental problems become too great in one nation, members of the capitalist class may simply move to another country. For example, many affluent residents of Hong Kong already have acquired business interests and houses in the United States, Canada, and other countries in anticipation of Hong Kong's reversion to China in the late 1990s. As people become "world citizens," in this way, their lives are not linked to the stability of any one city or nation. However, this option is limited only to the wealthiest of citizens.

In a best-case scenario for the future, the problems brought about by rapid population growth in developing nations will be remedied by new technologies that make goods readily available to people. International trade agreements such as NAFTA (the North American Free Trade Agreement) and GATT (the General Agreement on Trade and Tariffs) will remove trade barriers and make it possible for all nations to engage fully in global trade. People in developing nations will benefit by gaining jobs and opportunities to purchase goods at lower prices. Of course, the opposite also may occur: people may be exploited as inexpensive labour, and their country's natural resources may be depleted as transnational corporations buy up raw materials without contributing to the long-term economic stability of the nation.

With regard to pollution in urban areas, some futurists predict that environmental activism will increase dramatically as people see irreversible changes in the atmosphere and experience first-hand the effects of environmental hazards and pollution on their own health and well-being. These environmental problems will cause a realization that overpopulation is a world problem, a problem that will be most apparent in the world's weakest economies and most fragile ecosystems. Futurists suggest that as we approach the twenty-first century, we must "leave the old ways and invent new ones" (Petersen, 1994:340). What aspects of our "old ways" do you think we should discard? Can you help invent new ways?

CHAPTER REVIEW

Demography is the study of the size, compsition, and distribution of the population. Population growth is the result of fertility (births), mortality (deaths), and migration. The population is growing rapidly in less developed nations, where lower death rates have not been offset by a corresponding decrease in birth rates. By contrast, Canada, the United States, and other developed nations have relatively low fertility and mortality rates.

- Over two hundred years ago, Thomas Malthus warned that overpopulation would result in poverty, starvation, and other major problems that would limit the size of the population. According to Karl Marx, poverty is the result of capitalist greed, not overpopulation. More recently, neo-Malthusians have re-emphasized the dangers of overpopulation and encouraged zero population growth—the point at which no population increase occurs from year to year. Demographic transition theory links population growth to four stages of economic development: (1) the preindustrial stage, with high birth rates and death rates, (2) early industrialization, with relatively high birth rates and a decline in death rates, (3) advanced industrialization and urbanization, with low birth rates and death rates, and (4) postindustrialization, with additional decreases in the birth rate coupled with a stable death rate.
- Because of their limited size, preindustrial cities tend to provide a sense of community and a feeling of belonging. The Industrial Revolution changed the size and nature of the city; people lived in close proximity to factories and to one another, resulting in overcrowding and poor sanitation. In postindustrial cities, some people live and work in suburbs or outlying municipalities.
- Functionalists view urban growth in terms of ecological models. The concentric zone model sees the city as a series of circular areas, each characterized by a different type of land use; the sector model describes urban growth in terms of terrain and transportation routes; and the multiple nuclei model views cities as having numerous centres of development from which growth radiates. According to political economy models/conflict perspectives, urban growth is influenced by capital investment decisions, power and resource inequality, class and class conflict, and government subsidy programs. At the

global level, capitalism also influences the development of cities in core, peripheral, and semiperipheral nations. Interactionist perspectives focus on how people experience urban life. Some analysts view the urban experience positively; others believe that urban dwellers become insensitive to events and people around them.

- During the 1950s, a dramatic population shift occurred in North America as people moved from cities to suburbs. Causes for this movement include the post-World War II baby boom and liberal mortgage loan programs for homeowners. Suburban municipalities develop beyond central cities and suburbs, first with residential areas and then with retail establishments and office parks. These suburban municipalities drain taxes from central cities and older suburbs. Several of our central cities are experiencing fiscal crises that have resulted in cuts in services and a lack of maintenance of the infrastructure.
- Rapid population growth is inevitable in the twenty-first century. The urban population will triple as increasing numbers of people in lesser developed and developing nations migrate from rural areas to megacities that contain a high percentage of a region's population.

KEY TERMS

central city **620**
core nations **626**
crude birth rate **599**
crude death rate **600**
demographic transition **616**
demography **597**
emigration **602**
fertility **598**
gentrification **622**
immigration **602**
infant mortality rate **600**
invasion **622**
megalopolis **632**
metropolis **620**
migration **601**
mortality **600**
peripheral nations **626**
population composition **604**
population pyramid **606**
semiperipheral nations **626**
sex ratio **604**
succession **622**
urban sociology **618**

QUESTIONS FOR ANALYSIS AND UNDERSTANDING

1. What is the significance of fertility and mortality in global population growth? What part does migration play in Canadian population changes?
2. How do the Malthusian and Marxist perspectives on population growth differ? Which perspective best explains contemporary global population trends?
3. What issues divide cities and suburbs? How are these issues related to the fiscal crises in central cities?

QUESTIONS FOR CRITICAL THINKING

1. What impact does a high rate of immigration have on culture and personal identity in Canada?
2. If you were designing a study of growth patterns for the city in which you live (or one you know well), which theoretical model(s) would provide the most useful framework for your analysis?
3. What do you think everyday life in Canadian cities, suburbs, and rural areas will be like in 2020? Where would you prefer to live? What, if anything, does your answer reflect about the future of our cities?
4. What is the role of environmental scarcity as a cause of social conflict? How will this scarcity affect the security of developed countries?

SUGGESTED READINGS

These texts provide in-depth information on the topics in this chapter:

Roderic Beaujot. *Population Change in Canada: The Challenges of Policy Adaptation*. Toronto: McClelland and Stewart, 1991.

Leo Driedger. *The Urban Factor: Sociology of Canadian Cities*. Toronto: Oxford University Press, 1991.

Peter McGahan. *Urban Sociology in Canada (3rd ed.)*. Toronto: Harcourt Brace, 1995.

Wayne W. McVey Jr. and Warren E. Kalbach. *Canadian Population*. Toronto: Nelson Canada, 1995.

The following books discuss global overpopulation and urban growth issues:

Paul Ehrlich and Anne Ehrlich. *The Population Explosion*. London: Hutchinson, 1990.

Thomas Homer-Dixon. *Environmental Scarcity and Global Security*. Foreign Policy Association, Headline Series, Number 300. Ephrata, Penn.: Science Press, 1993.

World Resources Institute. *World Resources 1996–97*. Washington: World Resources Institute, 1996.

Chapter 17

COLLECTIVE BEHAVIOUR AND SOCIAL CHANGE

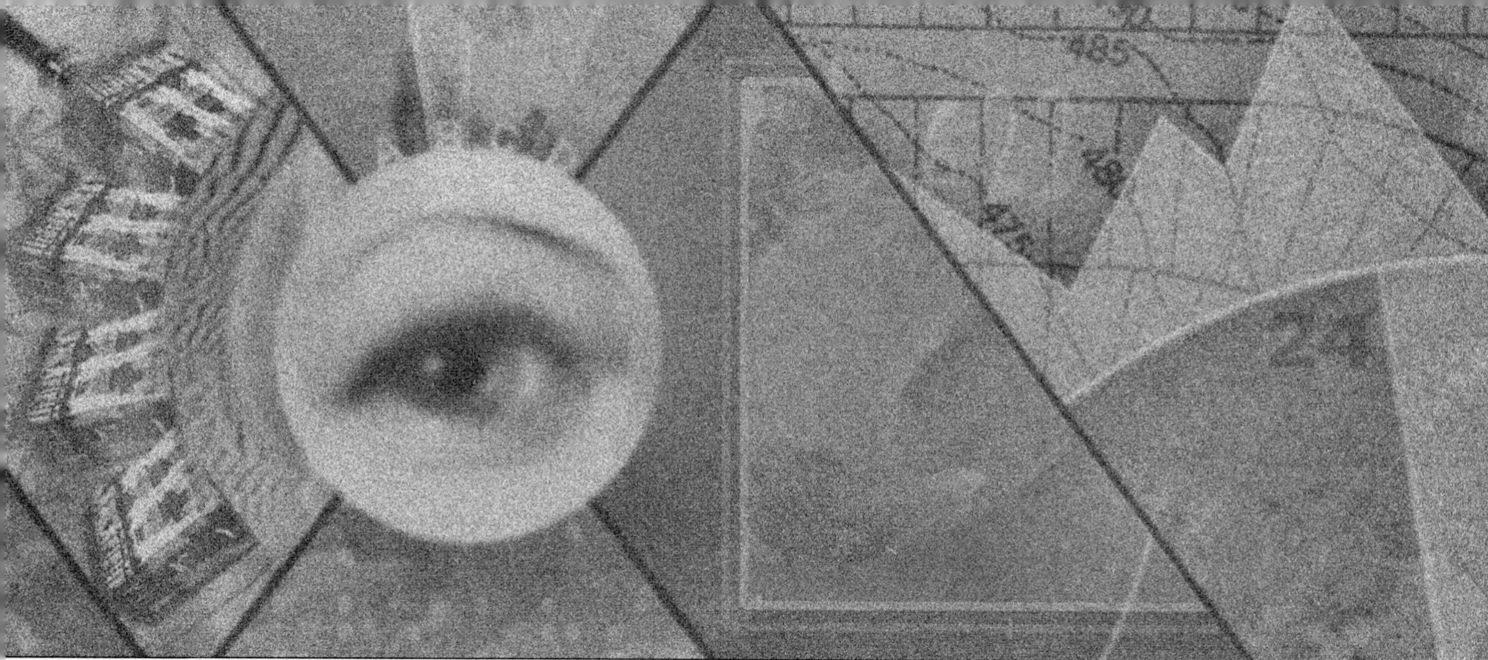

Clayoquot Sound, located on the west coast of Vancouver Island, is one of the world's last original temperate rain forests. Clayoquot Sound was also the site, in the 1990s, of the latest in a series of bitter struggles fought by First Nations peoples and environmental groups to preserve British Columbia's forests. Environmentalists have indicated that the rate at which Canadian firms are clear-cutting forests rivals the devastation in Brazil's Amazon rain forest. Clear-cutting refers to cutting down all the trees in a forested area regardless of their age, size, or species. This practice not only eliminates the trees, but also destroys soil cover, promotes erosion, and eliminates animal habitats. Journalist Peter C. Newman describes his reaction to the clear-cutting in this area—a reaction that provoked him to support the grassroots environmental movement:

A few seasons ago, I sailed with three friends around Vancouver Island, a 600-mile journey along some of the intertidal world's most wondrous coastline. An unforgettable incident during that voyage was gliding, late one Sunday evening, into a tiny cove past Meares Island on Clayoquot Sound ... The four of us felt as if we had drifted into a cloistered cathedral. Until the next morning that is. Dawn revealed that the shores of the cove we had gently entered in darkness the previous evening, had been clear-cut. Our cathedral had been desecrated. We found ourselves anchored in a barren, ugly place that resembled nothing so much as the cone of a burned-out volcano. It is from this highly subjective viewpoint that I judge the current controversy about the forestry companies being permitted to cut trees in Clayoquot Sound. They should on no account be allowed to touch a single tree ... It has always been the land—which really means the forests—that has anchored our sense of who we are and what we want to become. The shape and growth of our landscape has been the most potent influence on formation of the Canadian character. Let's not flatten it. (Newman, 1993:44)

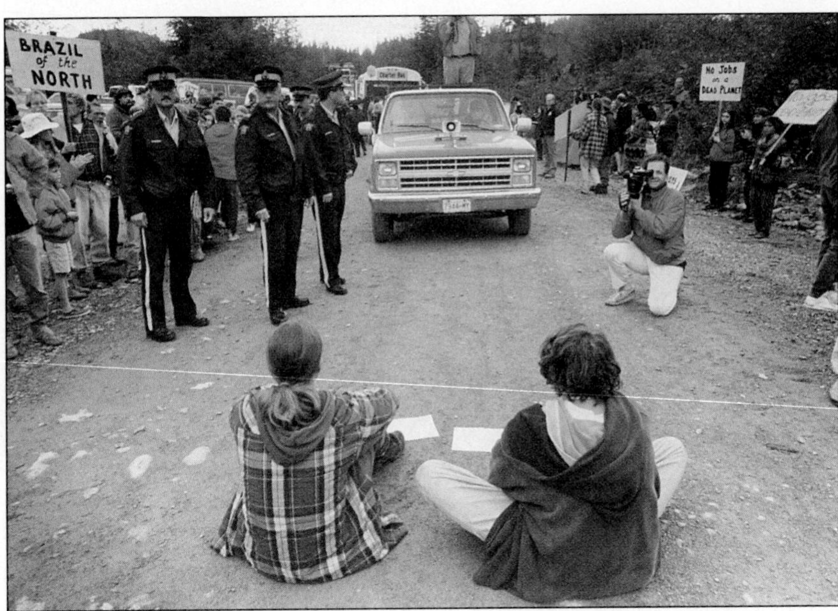

These environmental activists were part of a blockade at Clayoquot Sound, created in protest of the destruction of old-growth rainforest in British Columbia.

Like Newman, many Canadians were sparked out of complacency once they witnessed the devastation of clear-cutting firsthand. In 1993 Clayoquot Sound became a high-profile battleground in which the logging industry was pitted against a coalition of environmental groups including Greenpeace, the Sierra Club, and the Friends of Clayoquot Sound. These environmental activists were seeking social change. ***Social change* is the alteration, modification, or transformation of public policy, culture, or social institutions over time;** such change is often brought about by collective behaviour. In April 1993, the British Columbia government made the decision to allow clear-cut logging in two-thirds of Clayoquot's old-growth forest. This decision precipitated a social movement that received international attention. The pulp and paper firms involved in this dispute assured the government that this tropical rain forest was renewable—environmentalists disagreed. As Newman explains:

> They're wrong for one simple but telling reason. Trees are renewable. Forests are not. It takes literally centuries for bunches of trees to turn themselves into a fully integrated forest. The process involves not just trees, but the quality of the underbrush, natural ponds and the animals that make the forest their habitat. Nature's few original rain forests still remaining on this earth are a precious and highly finite commodity. (1993:44)

In July 1993, to protest the clear-cutting in Clayoquot Sound, demonstrators created a logging-road blockade at the Kennedy River Bridge. Protesters were joined by high-profile environmentalists including MP Svend Robinson, and Robert Kennedy, Jr., in this effort to save the forests. The Clayoquot protest resulted in the largest criminal prosecution of a nonviolent protest in Canadian history: over 800 activists were arrested for blocking the road to logging crews. The environmentalists also successfully lobbied several commercial companies in Canada, Britain, and the United States to cancel their contracts with MacMillan Bloedel to protest the Canadian firm's clear-cut logging practices.

BOX 17.1 SOCIOLOGY IN EVERYDAY LIFE

How Much Do You Know About Collective Behaviour, Social Change and Environmental Issues?

TRUE	FALSE	
T	F	1. The environmental movement in North America started in the 1960s.
T	F	2. People who hold strong attitudes regarding the environment are very likely to be involved in social movements to protect the environment.
T	F	3. Environmental groups may engage in civil disobedience or use symbolic gestures to call attention to their issue.
T	F	4. Most sociologists believe that people act somewhat irrationally when they are in large crowds.
T	F	5. People are most likely to believe rumours when no other information is readily available on a topic.
T	F	6. Influencing public opinion is a very important activity for many social movements.
T	F	7. Social movements are more likely to flourish in democratic societies.
T	F	8. Most social movements in Canada seek to improve society by changing some specific aspect of the social structure.
T	F	9. Sociologists have found that people in a community respond very similarly to natural disasters and to disasters caused by technological failures.
T	F	10. People have the capacity to change the environment for better or for worse.

Answers on page 640

In July 1995, the efforts of the environmental activists paid off: the government of British Columbia accepted a scientific panel's recommendation to ban clear-cutting in Clayoquot Sound.

In this chapter, we will discuss collective behaviour, social movements, and social change. Throughout the chapter, we will use environmental activism as an example of all three topics. Before reading on, test your knowledge about collective behaviour, social change, and environmental issues by taking the quiz in Box 17.1.

QUESTIONS AND ISSUES

How do sociologists distinguish among different types of collective behaviour?

What causes people to engage in collective behaviour?

What are some common forms of collective behaviour?

What draws people into social movements?

What factors contribute to social change?

BOX 17.1 SOCIOLOGY IN EVERYDAY LIFE

Answers to the Sociology Quiz on Collective Behaviour, Social Change, and Environmental Issues

TRUE	FALSE	
T	**F**	1. *False.* The environmental movement in North America is the result of more than one hundred years of collective action. The first environmental organization in North America was the American Forestry Association (now American Forests), which originated in 1875.
T	**F**	2. *False.* Since the 1980s, public opinion polls have shown that the majority of people in Canada have favourable attitudes regarding protection of the environment and banning nuclear weapons; however, far fewer individuals actually are involved in collective action to further these causes.
T	F	3. *True.* Environmental groups have held sit-ins, marches, boycotts, and strikes, which sometimes take the form of civil disobedience.
T	**F**	4. *False.* Although some early social psychological theories were based on the assumption of "crowd psychology" or "mob behaviour," most sociologists believe that individuals act quite rationally when they are part of a crowd.
T	F	5. *True.* Rumuors are most likely to emerge and circulate when people have very little information on a topic that is important to them. For example, rumours abound in times of technological disasters when people are fearful and often willing to believe the worst.
T	F	6. *True.* Many social movements, including grassroots environmental activism, attempt to influence public opinion so that local decision makers will feel obliged to correct a specific problem through changes in public policy.
T	F	7. *True.* Having a democratic process available is important for dissenters. Grassroots movements have utilized the democratic process to bring about change even when elites have sought to discourage such activism.
T	F	8. *True.* Most social movements are reform movements that focus on improving society by changing some specific aspect of the social structure. Examples include environmental movements and the disability rights movement.
T	**F**	9. *False.* Most sociological studies have found that people respond differently to natural disasters, which usually occur very suddenly, and to technological disasters, which may occur gradually. One of the major differences is the communal bonding that tends to occur following natural disasters, as compared with the extreme social conflict that may follow technological disasters.
T	F	10. *True.* One of the goals of most environmental movements is to stress the importance of "thinking globally and acting locally" to protect the environment.

Sources: Based on Worster, 1985; Gamson, 1990; Hynes, 1990; Young, 1990; and Adams, 1991.

COLLECTIVE BEHAVIOUR

***Collective behaviour* is relatively spontaneous, unstructured activity that typically violates established social norms.** Unlike the *organizational behaviour* found in corporations and voluntary associations (such as labour unions and environmental organizations), collective behaviour lacks an official division of labour, hierarchy of authority, and established rules and procedures. Unlike institutional behaviour (in education, religion, or politics, for example), it lacks institutionalized norms to govern behaviour. Collective behaviour can take various forms, including crowds, mobs, riots, panics, fads, fashions, public opinion, and social movements.

CONDITIONS FOR COLLECTIVE BEHAVIOUR

Collective behaviour occurs as a result of some common influence or stimulus that produces a response from a collectivity. A *collectivity* is a relatively large number of people who mutually transcend, bypass, or subvert established institutional patterns and structures. Collectivities in which people are in physical proximity to one another (such as a crowd or riot) are referred to as *localized collectivities;* those in which people are some distance apart from one another (such as with rumours, fashions, and public opinion) are referred to as *dispersed collectivities* (Turner and Killian, 1993).

Three major factors contribute to the likelihood that collective behaviour will occur: (1) structural factors that increase the chances of people responding in a particular way, (2) timing, and (3) a breakdown in social control mechanisms and a corresponding feeling of normlessness (McPhail, 1991; Turner and Killian, 1993). A common stimulus is an important factor. For example, in the case of Clayoquot sound, the issue of clear-cut logging was part of a larger issue of environmental destruction. In the words of one commentator, "Clayoquot is a symbol, a cause, one of those local battles that becomes a flash-point of a larger war" (Fulton and Mather, 1993:20). The clear-cut logging issue came at a time when people were becoming more concerned about social issues and beginning to see that they could empower themselves through grassroots activism.

Timing and a breakdown in social control mechanisms also are important in collective behaviour. Since the 1960s, most urban riots in Canada and the United States have begun in the evenings or on weekends when most people are off work (McPhail, 1971). For example, the 1992 Los Angeles riots erupted in the evening after the verdict in the Rodney King beating trial had been announced. As rioting, looting, and arson began to take a toll on certain areas of Los Angeles, a temporary breakdown in formal social control mechanisms occurred. In some areas of the city, law enforcement was inadequate to quell the illegal actions of rioters, some of whom began to believe that the rules had been suspended. In the aftermath of the Montreal riot following the 1993 Stanley Cup victory, the Montreal Canadiens were protected by hundreds of police officers and a riot squad in an effort to prevent any further breakdown of social control. As discussed in Box 17.2, hundreds of protesters were arrested at Clayoquot Sound in what law enforcement personnel indicated was an effort to prevent any breakdown in social control.

DYNAMICS OF COLLECTIVE BEHAVIOUR

To better understand the dynamics of collective behaviour, let us briefly examine three basic questions. First, how do people come to transcend, bypass, or subvert established institutional patterns and structures? The Friends of Clayoquot Sound initially tried to work within established means through provincial government environment officials. However, they quickly learned that their problems were not being solved through these channels; as the problem appeared to grow worse, organizational responses became more defensive and obscure. Accordingly, some

BOX 17.2 SOCIOLOGY AND LAW

The Legal Response to Civil Disobedience at Clayoquot Sound

At 5:40 a.m., on a logging road near the west coast of Vancouver Island, the sun has begun to tint the sky pink and blue. About 100 demonstrators, mostly under 30 and wearing jeans, sweaters, serapes, and windbreakers, stand in a wide circle before a bridge that spans the Kennedy River. They chant and sing and listen as the blockade coordinator explains what is about to happen., She warns that when an official acting for the Macmillan Bloedel Ltd. forestry company, which is logging in the woods nearby, arrives and reads a court injunction banning protests in Clayoquot Sound, they should remain quiet. "The courts will be tougher if there is noise and disrespect." At 6 a.m., a cavalcade of logging vehicles appears and halts several hundred metres away. Now, the demonstrators form a blockade in front of the bridge, holding up signs that read "We must take care of her—the earth is our mother."

What follows is nonviolent and very Canadian. The vehicles begin moving down the dirt road. As they approach the bridge, a process server informs the protesters that they should be "off the road before this vehicle has stopped." When some stay put, eight RCMP officers approach, politely explain that the protesters are breaking the law and begin arresting them. Many refuse to be escorted away and and have to be carried. "I'm like a tree—you'll have to cut me down," says one woman. She is hauled away by two Mounties. The officers work their way across the bridge and, by 6:30 a.m., the company vehicles—including an explosive truck and four huge logging rigs—rumble across and disappear into the surrounding forest. So goes the almost daily ritual.

The Clayoquot protest resulted in the largest criminal prosecution for nonviolent civil disobedience in Canadian history. Environmentalists and many lawyers have condemned the trials as a government assault on peaceful dissent.

When Janet McIntyre travelled to Clayoquot Sound to see the 1,500-year-old trees in one of the largest temperate rainforests left on earth, she didn't plan to get arrested. What caused her to act was seeing police take a disabled child from its mother's arms to break up a logging-road blockade. She stepped up to the blockade line and was promptly placed under arrest. At a mass trial 3 months later, McIntyre and other first-time offenders were convicted of criminal contempt of court. fined $500 each, and sentenced to 21 days in jail. McIntyre, an unemployed youth worker, could not look for a job during the month-long trial. The jail sentence was "enraging," but the fine was even more stressful. According to McIntyre, "Democracy is at an end if we are not allowed to conscientiously object to wrong-doings in our government and in society" (Goldberg, 1994:13). As the arrests, charges, and criminal convictions of over 800 protesters at Clayoquot Sound demonstrate, civil disobedience has a price—fines for the first 400 arrested ranged from $250 to $3,000; one protester (who was arrested twice on the same offence) received a six-month jail sentence. There is no question that preserving one of the last temperate rain forests in the world is a cause worth fighting for. However, given the severity of the criminal justice system's response, it comes as no surprise that many citizens choose not to participate in social movements. How far do you think you would be prepared to go in support of a social movement that is important to you? Would you risk arrest? detention? criminal conviction?

Source: Adapted from Nichols, 1993; Goldberg, 1994.

activists began acting outside of established norms by holding protests, establishing blockades, and (on one occasion) storming the B.C. legislature and almost breaking into the assembly. Some situations are more conducive to collective behaviour than others. When people can communicate quickly and easily with one another, spontaneous behaviour is more likely (Turner and Killian, 1993). When people are gathered together in one general location (whether lining the streets or assembled in a stadium), they are more likely to respond to a common stimulus.

Second, how do people's actions compare with their attitudes? People's attitudes (as expressed in public opinion surveys, for instance) are not always reflected in their political and social behaviour. Issues pertaining to the environment are no exception. The National Opinion Survey of Canadian Public Opinion on Forestry Issues showed that a majority of Canadians believed that "too many trees are being logged." In fact, 71 percent of Canadians disapproved of clear-cut logging and 61 percent indicated that they "get personally upset" when they see the results of clear-cutting (Harding, 1993:456). However, when the Friends of Clayoqout held their first protest session, only 200 people attended. Nevertheless, they assured the media that 1000 people would gather at Clayoquot on Canada Day. Their confidence was unfounded: only 150 supporters appeared (Brunet, 1993). According to sociologist William A. Gamson (1990), the thousands of people who agreed with the cause but never made it to Clayoquot were *free riders*—people who enjoy the benefits produced by some group even though they have not helped support it.

Third, why do people act collectively rather than singly? Sociologists Ralph H. Turner and Lewis M. Killian (1993:12) say one reason is that "the rhythmic stamping of feet by hundreds of concert-goers in unison is different from isolated, individual cries of 'bravo.'" Likewise, people may act as a collectivity (as was the case for many Clayoquot Sound residents) when they believe it is the only way to fight those with greater power and resources. Collective behaviour is not just the sum of a large number of individuals acting at the same time; rather, it reflects people's joint response to some common influence or stimulus.

DISTINCTIONS REGARDING COLLECTIVE BEHAVIOUR

People engaging in collective behaviour may be divided into crowds and masses. A ***crowd* is a relatively large number of people who are in one another's immediate vicinity** (Lofland, 1993). In contrast, a ***mass* is a number of people who share an interest in a specific idea or issue but who are not in one another's immediate vicinity** (Lofland, 1993). To further distinguish between crowds and masses, think of the difference between a riot and a rumour: people who participate in a riot must be in the same general location; those who spread a rumour may be thousands of miles apart, communicating by telephone or online computer networks.

Collective behaviour also may be distinguished by the dominant emotion expressed. According to sociologist John Lofland (1993:72), the *dominant emotion* refers to the "publicly expressed feeling perceived by participants and observers as the most prominent in an episode of collective behaviour." Lofland suggests that fear, hostility, and joy are three fundamental emotions found in collective behaviour; however, grief, disgust, surprise, or shame also may predominate in some forms of collective behaviour.

TYPES OF CROWD BEHAVIOUR

When we think of a crowd, many of us think of *aggregates*, previously defined as a collection of people who happen to be in the same place at the same time but who have little else in common. However, the presence of a relatively large number of people in the same location does not necessarily produce collective behaviour. Sociologist Herbert Blumer (1946) developed a typology in which crowds are divided into four categories: casual, conventional, expressive, and acting. Other scholars have added a fifth category, protest crowds.

CASUAL AND CONVENTIONAL CROWDS *Casual crowds* are relatively large gatherings of people who happen to be in the same place at the same time; if they interact at all, it is only briefly. People in a shopping mall or a bus are examples of casual crowds. Other than sharing a momentary interest, such as a watching a deer in a park or a fire in a building, a casual crowd has nothing in common.

This crowd is made up of thousands of Canadians from across the country who gathered in Montreal in October 1995 to demonstrate their strong emotions against Quebec separation.

The casual crowd plays no active part in the event—such as a fire that would have occurred whether or not the crowd was present; it simply observes.

Conventional crowds are made up of people who specifically come together for a scheduled event and thus share a common focus. Examples include religious services, graduation ceremonies, concerts, and university lectures. Each of these events has established schedules and norms. Because these events occur regularly, interaction among participants is much more likely; in turn, the events would not occur without the crowd, which is essential to the event.

When some event or stimulus produces strong emotions of fear, hostility, or joy, casual and conventional crowds may participate in collective behaviour. For example, in 1994, a firebomb on a New York City subway car engulfed the car in flames. Passengers who had been part of a casual crowd experienced strong emotions of fear and immediately engaged in collective behaviour. While some fled for their lives, others helped fight the blaze and attempted to assist those who were injured (Barron, 1994).

EXPRESSIVE AND ACTING CROWDS *Expressive crowds* provide opportunities for the expression of some strong emotion (such as joy, excitement, or grief). People release their pent-up emotions in conjunction with other persons experiencing similar emotions. Examples include worshipers at religious revival services; mourners lining the streets when a celebrity, public official, or religious leader has died; and nonrioting crowds at a sporting event.

Acting crowds are collectivities so intensely focused on a specific purpose or object that they may erupt into violent or destructive behaviour. Mobs, riots, and panics are examples of acting crowds, but casual and conventional crowds may become acting crowds under some circumstances. A ***mob*** **is a highly emotional crowd whose members engage in, or are ready to engage in, violence against a specific target—a person, a category of people, or physical property.** Mob behaviour in this country has included fire bombings, effigy hangings, and hate crimes. In the United States mob behaviour has also included lynchings. Mob violence tends to dissipate relatively quickly once a target has been injured,

BOX 17.3 SOCIOLOGY AND MEDIA

Getting Attention for a Cause

We had to keep the media's interest. That was the only way we got anything done. They kept Love Canal in the public consciousness. They educated the public about toxic chemical wastes. One day, we decided we'd take a child's coffin and an adult coffin to the state capital and give it to [New York] Governor Carey. It was a way of keeping us in the news. It would demonstrate our plight ...

Lynn Tolli made the baby coffin. She did an excellent job. It looked real, as if a child were in it. We also got an adult coffin. Mike Nowak carried the coffin over his shoulder up to the capitol. When we got to the front, a police SWAT team checked the caskets. That was really humorous. Did they think we were going to blow up the capitol? Why would we do that? We are law-abiding citizens, not crazies or radicals. (Gibbs, 1982:96–97)

As this description suggests, Love Canal residents worked to keep the media's attention focused on their plight—a plight brought on by the discovery that their properties were contaminated because the land around Love Canal had in the 1930s been used by Hooker Chemical Corporation as a dump site for chemicals and other wastes.

Some scholars believe that the media are a powerful force in arousing public opinion and keeping the spotlight on decision makers who want to look good to voters (see Levine, 1982). While government officials and corporate public relations personnel have access to the media virtually whenever they want it, Love Canal residents had to work to stay in the spotlight. The Hooker Chemical Company and its parent corporation, Occidental Petroleum, maintained a relatively high level of control over what the media said about the corporation. Written statements were distributed by their public relations experts at press conferences. The company purchased full-page advertisements asserting that Hooker was blameless for use of the Love Canal site after their sale of it. The ads emphasized that the corporation had warned the city about the potentially hazardous chemicals when the property was purchased for the token sum of $1.

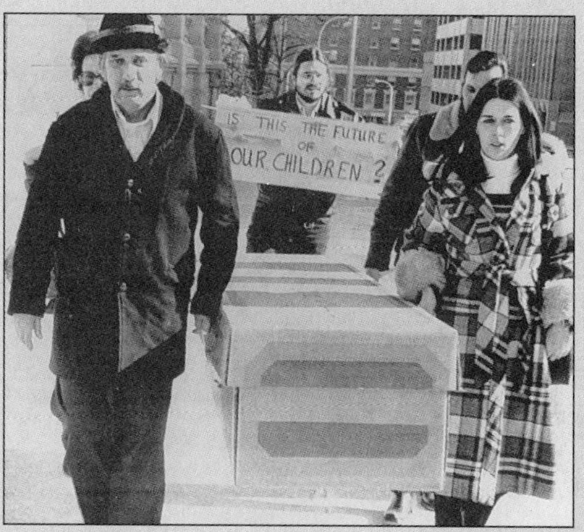

Activists, including these Love Canal residents, often engage in symbolic activity to keep media attention focused on their problem.

In 1994, Love Canal was in the news again. Occidental Chemical Corporation (the corporation's current name) and the state of New York finally reached an out-of-court settlement in a lawsuit filed more than fourteen years earlier. Some homes were renovated, and about 160 buyers immediately came forward. However, they have a highly visible neighbour—a 40-acre grassy landfill, 30 feet high at the centre, with an 8-foot-high chain-link fence surrounding it and more than 21,000 tons of toxic chemical waste and the remains of 239 contaminated houses lying underneath it. Leon Demers, who bought one of the houses, said, "I think there was a problem in the immediate area once, but that's been cleaned up. I have only one lung, so I'm half dead anyway" (quoted in Hoffman, 1994:22). In the future, will the media once again be carrying stories about the health problems experienced by residents of this area?

Sources: Based on Gibbs, 1982; Levine, 1982; and Hoffman, 1994.

killed, or destroyed. Sometimes, actions such as effigy hanging are used symbolically by groups that otherwise are not violent; for example, during the 1990 Oka crisis on the Kanehsatake reserve in Quebec local nonaboriginal residents burned an effigy of a Mohawk to emphasize their displeasure with the blockade of the Mercier Bridge to Montreal. Activities such as these often result in a great deal of media attention, but, as the events described in Box 17.3 illustrate, getting and keeping that attention require effort.

Riots may be of somewhat longer duration than mob actions. **A *riot* is violent crowd behaviour that is fuelled by deep-seated emotions but not directed at one specific target.** Riots often are triggered by fear, anger, and hostility. This was true of the 1992 Los Angeles riots, which, as has been mentioned, resulted from the announcement of the verdict in the Rodney King trial, which was an acquittal of the white police officers involved in the brutal beating of King, a black. These especially destructive riots caused millions of dollars of damage and thousands of injuries, and left more than fifty people dead. They were followed days later by race riots on the streets of Toronto. However, not all riots are caused by deep-seated hostility and hatred; people may be expressing joy and exuberance when rioting occurs. Examples include celebrations after sports victories such as those that occurred in Montreal and Vancouver following wins by their respective teams in the Stanley Cup playoffs.

***Panic* is a form of crowd behaviour that occurs when a large number of people react to a real or perceived threat with strong emotions and self-destructive behaviour.** The most common type of panic, known as *entrapment panic*, occurs when people seek to escape from a perceived danger, fearing that few (if any) of them will be able to get away from that danger. For example, as people sought to flee the burning New York City subway car, many were knocked to the ground by the crush of people (Gonzalez, 1994). Panic sometimes occurs, however, when people attempt to gain access to an event or a location, as was the case at a concert by the British rock group The Who in Cincinnati in 1979. Seating was on a "first come–first served" basis, and when the doors opened, people surged into the arena and began to fall over one another. Unaware of the press of bodies in front of them, those farther back heard the band warming up and began to panic for fear that they would not get a seat. This type of panic is referred to as *exclusion panic.* When people started to realize what was happening, they experienced an overwhelming emotion of fear. Eleven people were killed in the ensuing pile-up.

Panic also can arise in response to events that people believe are beyond their control—such as a major disruption in the economy. Although instances of panic are relatively rare, they receive massive media coverage because they provoke strong feelings of fear in readers and viewers, and the number of casualties may be large.

PROTEST CROWDS Sociologists Clark McPhail and Ronald T. Wohlstein (1983) added protest crowds to the four types of crowds identified by Blumer. *Protest crowds* engage in activities intended to achieve specific political goals. Examples include sit-ins, marches, boycotts, blockades, and strikes. These sometimes take the form of ***civil disobedience*—nonviolent action that seeks to change a policy or law by refusing to comply with it.** Sometimes, acts of civil disobedience become violent, as in a confrontation between protesters and police officers; in this case, a protest crowd becomes an *acting crowd.* Such was the case during the Oka crisis, when a police officer was shot and killed and several persons on both sides of the blockade were injured. Some protests can escalate into violent confrontations even though that is not the intent of the organizers.

At the grassroots level, protests often are seen as the only way to call attention to problems or demand social change. For example, after the B.C. government decided to approve clear-cutting, the residents picketed to halt the loggers, pointing out that reforestation efforts such as replanting were not going to solve the problem of forest devastation.

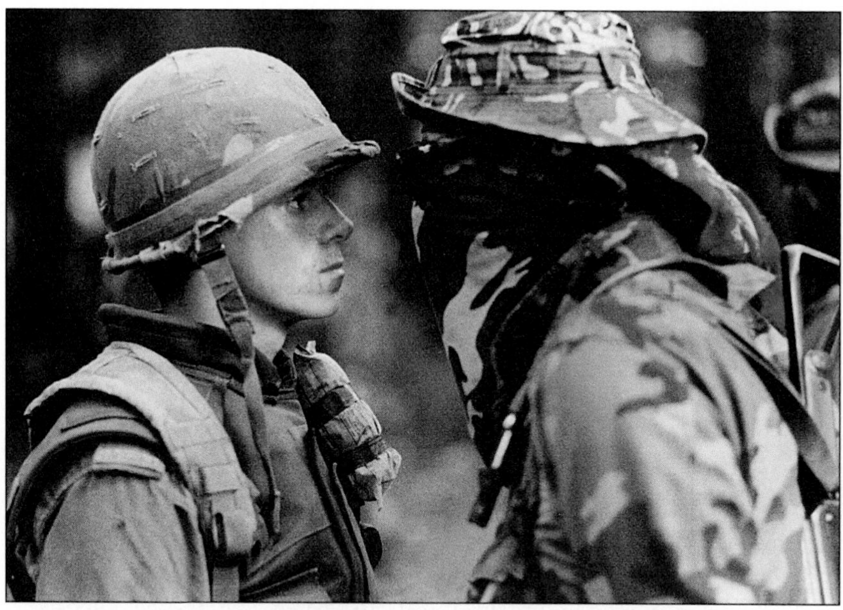

Sometimes acts of civil disobedience become violent even though it is not the intent of the parties involved. During what is referred to as the Oka crisis, a police officer was shot and killed and several people on both sides of the blockade were injured.

As you will recall, collective action often puts individuals in the position of doing things as a group that they would not do on their own. Does this mean that people's actions are produced by some type of "herd mentality"? Some analysts have answered this question affirmatively; however, sociologists typically do not agree with that assessment.

EXPLANATIONS OF CROWD BEHAVIOUR

What causes people to act collectively? How do they determine what types of action to take? One of the earliest theorists to provide an answer to these questions was Gustave Le Bon, a French scholar who focused on crowd psychology in his contagion theory.

CONTAGION THEORY *Contagion theory* focuses on the social-psychological aspects of collective behaviour; it attempts to explain how moods, attitudes, and behaviour are communicated rapidly and why they are accepted by others (Turner and Killian, 1993). Gustave Le Bon (1841–1931) argued that people are more likely to engage in antisocial behaviour in a crowd because they are anonymous and feel invulnerable. Le Bon (1960/1895) suggested that a crowd takes on a life of its own that is larger than the beliefs or actions of any one person. Because of its anonymity, the crowd transforms individuals from rational beings into a single organism with a collective mind. In essence, Le Bon asserted that emotions such as fear and hate are contagious in crowds because people experience a decline in personal responsibility; they will do things as a collectivity that they would never do when acting alone.

The influence of Le Bon's contagion theory is evident in the works of Robert Park and numerous social psychologists. Some social psychologists suggest that people in collectivities may experience *deindividuation*, whereby they are submerged in the group and their identities are lost (see Festinger et al., 1952). Similarly, Philip Zimbardo (1970) noted that novel environments—such as Mardi Gras festivities or riots—may produce a sensory overload that causes people to engage in impulsive, emotional, and sometimes violent behaviour.

Le Bon's theory is still used by many people to explain crowd behaviour. For example, in the aftermath of the panic at The Who concert, psychologists told one reporter that "mob psychology" was operating. *Mob psychology* refers to the "tendency of individuals to be carried away by the excitement of the group, a contagious flow of energy, a situation in which emotion outweighs rational thinking" (Turner and Killian, 1993:6). Critics argue, however, that the "collective mind" has not been documented by systematic studies. Alternative explanations often are offered for behaviour initially attributed to crowd contagion. For example, sociologist Norris Johnson (1987) investigated the aftermath of the panic at The Who concert and found several factors (unrelated to the mentality of the crowd) that contributed to the tragedy. The arena had only two entrance doors, which shared a common lobby, and not enough security personnel were present to handle the crowd. Johnson also noted that many concertgoers actually acted rationally rather than irrationally—they tried to help the fallen by forming a protective ring around them.

SOCIAL UNREST AND CIRCULAR REACTION Robert E. Park, an American sociologist, further developed LeBon's analysis of crowd behaviour. Park believed that Le Bon's analysis of collective behaviour lacked several important elements. Intrigued that people could break away from the powerful hold of culture and their established routines to develop a new social order, Park added the concepts of social unrest and circular reaction to contagion theory. According to Park, social unrest is transmitted by a process of *circular reaction*—the interactive communication between persons such that the discontent of one person is communicated to another who, in turn, reflects the discontent back to the first person (Park and Burgess, 1921). For Park, such reflections of discontent are not the musings of irrational minds; they represent conscious efforts to produce social change in society (Turner and Killian, 1993).

CONVERGENCE THEORY *Convergence theory* focuses on the shared emotions, goals, and beliefs many people bring to crowd behaviour. Because of their individual characteristics, many people have a predisposition to participate in certain types of activities (Turner and Killian, 1993). From this perspective, people with similar attributes find a collectivity of like-minded persons with whom they can express their underlying personal tendencies. For example, the 1996 riots at the National Assembly in Quebec City on St. Jean Baptiste Day were believed to have been started by "professional agitators" who were members of the Northern Hammer Skins, a right-wing extremist organization associated with the neo-Nazi Heritage Front. Such groups are known to publish hate propaganda that glorifies rioting and violence against the government. These individuals may have been present at the St. Jean Baptiste Day celebrations with the intent of participating in violence or instilling a riot. Although people may reveal their "true selves" in crowds, their behaviour is not irrational; it is highly predictable to those who share similar emotions or beliefs.

Convergence theory has been applied to a wide array of conduct, from lynch mobs to environmental movements. In social psychologist Hadley Cantril's (1941) study of one lynching in the United States, he found that the participants shared certain common attributes: they were poor and working-class whites who felt that their own status was threatened by the presence of successful African Americans. Consequently, the characteristics of these individuals made them susceptible to joining a lynch mob even if they did not know the target of the lynching.

Convergence theory adds to our understanding of certain types of collective behaviour by pointing out how individuals may have certain attributes—such as racial hatred or fear of environmental problems that directly threaten them—that initially bring them together. However, this perspective does not explain how the attitudes and characteristics of individuals who take some collective action differ from those who do not. For example, sociologist Clark McPhail (1971) did not find significant attitudinal differences between participants and nonparticipants in early 1970s urban riots in the United States. Likewise, most people remain in control of their behaviour even in lynch mobs, riots, and environmental disasters (for example, a lynch mob must find a tree, obtain a rope, tie a knot, and hoist the body, all of which require rational thought and cooperation) (McPhail, 1991).

EMERGENT NORM THEORY Unlike contagion and convergence theories, *emergent norm theory* emphasizes the importance of social norms in shaping crowd behaviour. Drawing on the interactionist perspective, sociologists Ralph Turner and Lewis Killian (1993:12) asserted that crowds develop their own definition of a situation and establish norms for behaviour that fit the occasion:

> Some shared redefinition of right and wrong in a situation supplies the justification and coordinates the action in collective behaviour. People do what they would not otherwise have done when they panic collectively, when they riot, when they engage in civil disobedience, or when they launch terrorist campaigns, because they find social support for the view that what they are doing is the right thing to do in the situation.

According to Turner and Killian (1993:13), emergent norms occur when people define a new situation as highly unusual or see a long-standing situation in a new light.

Sociologists using the emergent norm approach seek to determine how individuals in a given collectivity develop an understanding of what is going on, how they construe these activities, and what type of norms are involved. For example, in a study of audience participation, sociologist Steven E. Clayman (1993) found that members of an audience listening to a speech applaud promptly and independently but wait to coordinate their booing with other people; they do not wish to "boo" alone.

Some emergent norms are permissive—that is, they give people a shared conviction that they may disregard ordinary rules such as waiting in line, taking turns, or treating a speaker courteously. Collective activity such as mass looting may be defined (by participants) as taking what rightfully belongs to them and punishing those who have been exploitative. For example, following the Los Angeles riots of 1992, some analysts argued that Korean Americans were targets of rioters because they were viewed by Latinos and African Americans as "callous and greedy invaders" who became wealthy at the expense of members of other racial-ethnic groups (Cho, 1993). Thus, rioters who used this rationalization could view looting and burning as a means of "paying back" Korean Americans or of gaining property (such as TV sets and microwave ovens) from those who had already taken from them. Once a crowd reaches some agreement on the norms, the collectivity is supposed to adhere to them. If crowd members develop a norm that condones looting or vandalizing property, they will proceed to cheer for those who conform and ridicule those who are unwilling to abide by the collectivity's new norms.

Emergent norm theory points out that crowds are not irrational. Rather, new norms are developed in a rational way to fit the needs of the immediate situation. However, critics note that proponents of this perspective fail to specify exactly what constitutes a norm, how new ones emerge, and how they are so quickly disseminated and accepted by a wide variety of participants. One variation of this theory suggests that no single dominant norm is accepted by everyone in a crowd; instead, norms are specific to the various categories of actors rather than to the collectivity as a whole (Snow, Zurcher, and Peters, 1981). For example, in a study of football victory celebrations, sociologists David A. Snow, Louis A. Zurcher, and Robert Peters (1981) found that, each week, behavioural patterns were changed in the postgame revelry, with some being modified, some added, and some deleted.

MASS BEHAVIOUR

Not all collective behaviour takes place in face-to-face collectivities. ***Mass behaviour* is collective behaviour that takes place when people (who often are geographically separated from one another) respond to the same event in much the same way.** For people to respond in the same way, they typically have common sources of information, and this information provokes their collective behaviour. The most frequent types of mass behaviour are rumours, gossip, mass hysteria, public opinion, fashions, and fads. Under some circumstances, social movements constitute a form of mass behaviour. However, we will examine social movements separately because they differ in some important ways from other types of dispersed collectivities.

RUMOURS AND GOSSIP ***Rumours* are unsubstantiated reports on an issue or subject** (Rosnow and Fine, 1976). While a rumour may spread through an assembled collectivity, rumours also may be transmitted among people who are dispersed geographically. Although they may initially contain a kernel of truth, as they spread, rumours may be modified to serve the interests of those repeating them. Rumors thrive when tensions are high and little authentic information is available on an issue of great concern.

People are willing to give rumours credence when no offsetting information is available. Once rumours begin to circulate, they seldom stop unless compelling information comes to the forefront that either proves the rumour false or makes it obsolete.

In industrialized societies with sophisticated technology, rumours come from a wide variety of sources and may be difficult to trace. Print media (newspapers and magazines) and electronic media (radio and television), fax machines, cellular networks, satellite systems, and the Internet facilitate the rapid movement of rumours around the globe. In addition, modern communications technology makes anonymity much easier. In a split second, messages (both factual and fictitious) can be disseminated to thousands of people through e-mail, computerized bulletin boards, and newsgroups on the Internet. For example, despite a publication ban imposed on the media regarding the 1993 trial of Karla Homolka in connection with the brutal murders of Leslie Mahaffy and Kristen French in St. Catharines, Ontario, graphic details of the crimes were available on the Internet. A major advertising controversy known as the "Green Card Incident" occurred in 1994 when a couple in the United States placed an announcement on the Internet offering their legal services to help aliens get a green card. In Internet jargon, the couple "spammed" the Net by using a program that placed the ad on nearly every bulletin board in existence. Users were furious, but the couple insisted their ad was a success and threatened to sue their Internet provider when they were cut off. With no official legislation to control the dissemination of information on the World Wide Web, there is also no means to control whether information disseminated on the Net is factually correct. As *Time* magazine reported, "News on the Net may be bogus, error-ridden or just plain wrong" (quoted in Strenski, 1995:33).

Whereas rumours deal with an issue or a subject, ***gossip* refers to rumours about the personal lives of individuals.** Charles Horton Cooley (1962/1909) viewed gossip as something that spread among a small group of individuals who personally knew the person who was the object of the rumour. Today, this often is not the case; many people enjoy gossiping about people they have never met. Tabloid newspapers and magazines such as the *National Enquirer* and *People*, and television "news" programs that purport to provide "inside" information on the lives of celebrities are sources of contemporary gossip, much of which has not been checked for authenticity.

MASS HYSTERIA AND PANIC ***Mass hysteria* is a form of dispersed collective behaviour that occurs when a large number of people react with strong emotions and self-destructive behaviour to a real or perceived threat.** Does mass hysteria actually occur? Although the term has been widely used, many sociologists believe this behaviour is best described as panic with a dispersed audience. You will recall that panic is a form of crowd behaviour that occurs when a large number of people react with strong emotions and self-destructive behaviour to a real or perceived threat.

An example of mass hysteria or panic with a widely dispersed audience was actor Orson Welles's 1938 Halloween evening radio dramatization of H. G. Wells's science fiction classic *The War of the Worlds.* A CBS radio dance music program was interrupted suddenly by a news bulletin informing the audience that Martians had landed in New Jersey and were in the process of conquering the earth. Some listeners became extremely frightened even though an announcer had indicated before, during, and after the performance that the broadcast was a fictitious dramatization. According to some reports, as many as 1 million of the estimated 10 million listeners believed that this astonishing event had occurred. Thousands were reported to have hidden in their storm cellars or to have gotten in their cars so that they could flee from the Martians (see Brown, 1954). In actuality, the program probably did not generate mass hysteria, but rather created panic among gullible listeners. Others switched stations to determine if the same "news" was being broadcast elsewhere. When they discovered that it was not, they merely laughed at the joke being played on listeners by CBS. In 1988, on the fiftieth anniversary of the broadcast, a Portuguese radio station rebroadcast the program and, once again, panic ensued.

Other cases of panic have resulted from people experiencing intense fear. For example, in the aftermath of the New York City subway bomb explosion in 1994, people in the city began to "see bombs everywhere." Police switchboards were flooded with calls reporting suspicious packages (which usually turned out to be holiday presents and unattended luggage). On an average day, about 12 reports of bomb threats or suspicious packages are received by the New York City Police Department; immediately after the bombing, that number rose to 46 per day (Krauss, 1994).

FADS AND FASHIONS A ***fad*** **is a temporary but widely copied activity enthusiastically followed by large numbers of people.** Some examples of fads are pet rocks, Cabbage Patch dolls, Teenage Mutant Ninja Turtles, hula hoops, and mood rings. Can you think of others? A recent fad among college and university students is body piercing, in which the ears, nose, navel, cheeks, nipples, and genitals are pierced and the resulting cavities are usually adorned with jewellery. Many contemporary fads are commercially produced, for example, by toy manufacturers or body-piercing shops, and new ideas and products must be introduced continually because the novelty (and therefore the appeal of the existing fad) rapidly wears off (Hirsch, 1972) Fads can be embraced by widely dispersed collectivities; news networks such as CNN may bring the latest fad to the attention of audiences around the world. North America has witnessed a number of fads. One especially remembered by faculty who have been on university and college campuses for several decades was the 1970s fad of "streaking"—students taking off their clothes and running naked in public. Regardless of how it may sound, this activity was not purely spontaneous. Streakers had to calculate and plan their activity so that an audience (often including members of the media) would be present. Streaking had no meaning if it was not widely publicized; for this reason, some students chose graduation ceremonies and other highly visible occasions for their streaking escapades. Other fads, such as exercise regimes and health practices, tend to be taken more seriously.

Fashion **may be defined as a currently valued style of behaviour, thinking, or appearance that is longer lasting and more widespread than a fad.** Examples of fashion are found in many areas, including child rearing, education, sports, clothing, music, and art. Sociologist John Lofland (1993) found that language is subject to fashion trends. He examined the terms used to express approval during different decades and found: "Neat!" in the 1950s, "Right on!" in the 1960s, "Really!" in the 1970s, "Awesome!" in the 1980s, and of course, "Cool!" in the 1990s. While fashion also applies to art, music, drama, literature, architecture, interior design, automobiles, and many other things, most sociological research on fashion has focused on clothing, especially women's apparel (Davis, 1992).

In preindustrial societies, clothing styles remained relatively unchanged. With the advent of industrialization, however, items of apparel became readily available at low prices because of mass production. Fashion became more important as people embraced the "modern" way of life and advertising encouraged "conspicuous consumption."

Georg Simmel, Thorstein Veblen, and French sociologist Pierre Bourdieu all have viewed fashion as a means of status differentiation among members of different social classes. Simmel (1904) suggested a classic "trickle-down" theory (although he did not use those exact words) to describe the process by which members of the lower classes emulate the fashions of the upper class. As the fashions descend through the status hierarchy, they are watered down and "vulgarized" so that they are no longer recognizable to members of the upper class, who then regard them as unfashionable and in bad taste (Davis, 1992). Veblen (1967/1899) asserted that fashion served mainly to institutionalize conspicuous consumption among the wealthy. Almost eighty years later, Bourdieu (1984) similarly (but most subtly) suggested that "matters of taste," including fashion sensibility, constitute a large share of the "cultural capital" possessed by members of the dominant class.

Herbert Blumer (1969) disagreed with the trickle-down approach, arguing that "collective selection" best explains fashion. Blumer suggested that people in the middle and lower classes follow fashion because it is *fashion*, not because they desire to emulate members of the elite class. Blumer thus shifts the focus on fashion to collective mood, states, and choices: "Tastes are themselves a product of experience ... They are formed in the context of social interaction, responding to the definitions and affirmation given by others. People thrown into areas of common interaction and having similar runs of experience develop common tastes" (quoted in Davis, 1992:116). Perhaps one of the best refutations of the trickle-down approach is the way in which fashion today often originates among people in the lower social classes and is mimicked by the elites. In the mid-1990s, the so-called grunge look is a prime example of this.

PUBLIC OPINION ***Public opinion*** **consists of the political attitudes and beliefs communicated by ordinary citizens to decision makers** (Greenberg and Page, 1993). It is measured through polls and surveys, which utilize research methods such as interviews and questionnaires, as described in Chapter 2. Many people are not interested in all aspects of public policy but are concerned about issues they believe are relevant to themselves. Even on a single topic, public opinion will vary widely based on race/ethnicity, religion, region, social class, education level, gender, age, and so on.

Scholars who examine public opinion are interested in the extent to which the public's attitudes are communicated to decision makers and the effect (if any) that public opinion has on policy making (Turner and Killian, 1993). Some political scientists argue that public opinion has a substantial effect on decisions at all levels of governments (see Greenberg and Page, 1993); others strongly disagree. For example, Dye and Zeigler (1993:158) argue that:

> opinions flow downward from elites to masses. Public opinion rarely affects elite behaviour, but elite behaviour shapes public opinion. Elites are relatively unconstrained by public opinion for several reasons. First, few people among the masses have opinions on most policy questions confronting the nation's decision makers. Second, public opinion is very unstable; it can change in a matter of weeks in response to "news" events precipitated by elites. Third, elites do not

> have a clear perception of mass opinion. Most communications decision makers receive are from other elites—newsmakers, interest-group leaders, influential community leaders—not from ordinary citizens.

From this perspective, polls may create the appearance of public opinion artificially; pollsters may ask questions that those being interviewed had not even considered before the survey.

As the masses attempt to influence elites and vice versa, a two-way process occurs with the dissemination of ***propaganda*****—information provided by individuals or groups that have a vested interest in furthering their own cause or damaging an opposing one.** For example, in the Clayoquot Sound protest, the B.C. government and the logging industry used slogans such as "forest renewal," "world class logging," and "getting greener all the time" (Lam, 1995:24). On the other hand, environmental activists referred to Clayoquot Sound as "the Brazil of the North." Although many of us think of propaganda in negative terms, the information provided can be correct and can have positive effect on decision making.

In recent decades, grassroots environmental activists have attempted to influence public opinion. In a study of public opinion on environmental issues, sociologist Riley E. Dunlap (1992) found that public awareness of the seriousness of environmental problems and support for environmental protection increased dramatically between the late 1960s and the early 1990s. It is less clear, however, that public opinion translates into action by either decision makers in government and industry or individuals (for example, in their willingness to adopt a more ecologically sound lifestyle).

Initially, most grassroots environmental activists attempt to influence public opinion so that local decision makers will feel the necessity of correcting a specific problem through changes in public policy. Although activists usually do not start out seeking broader social change, they often move in that direction when they become aware of how widespread the problem is in the larger society or on a global basis. One of two types of social movements often develops at this point—one focuses on NIMBY ("not in my backyard"), while the other focuses on NIABY ("not in anyone's backyard") (Freudenberg and Steinsapir, 1992). An example of a NIMBY social movement occurred when Metropolitan Toronto proposed the building of a large landfill to handle the city's garbage. Residents of the municipalities identified as possible sites for the landfill protested vigorously and demonstrated the "not in my backyard" approach by counterproposing that the garbage be shipped by rail to abandoned mines in northern Ontario. NIABY movements are prevalent in many parts of the industrial world where it is virtually impossible to dispose of toxic waste because no community will accept construction of such a site on its property. As a result, citizens are at risk because the waste remains.

SOCIAL MOVEMENTS

While collective behaviour is short-lived and relatively unorganized, social movements are longer lasting and more organized and have specific goals or purposes. A ***social movement*** **is an organized group that acts consciously to promote or resist change through collective action** (Goldberg, 1991). Because social movements have not become institutionalized and are outside the political mainstream, they offer "outsiders" an opportunity to have their voices heard.

Social movements are more likely to develop in industrialized societies than in preindustrial societies, where acceptance of traditional beliefs and practices makes such movements unlikely. Diversity and a lack of consensus (hallmarks of industrialized nations) contribute to demands for social change, and people who participate in social movements typically lack power and other resources to bring about change without engaging in collective action. Social movements are most likely to spring up when people come to see their personal troubles as public issues that cannot be solved without a collective response.

Social movements make democracy more available to excluded groups (see Greenberg and Page, 1993). Historically, people in North America have worked at the grassroots level to bring about changes even when elites sought to discourage activism (Adams, 1991). For example, in the United States the civil rights movement brought into its ranks African Americans who had never been allowed to participate in politics (see Killian, 1984). The women's suffrage movement gave voice to women who had been denied the right to vote (Rosenthal et al., 1985). Disability rights advocates brought together a "hidden army" of supporters without disabilities who had friends or family members with a disability (Shapiro, 1993). Similarly, a grassroots environmental movement gave the working-class residents of Clayoquot Sound a way to "fight city hall" and a huge corporation—MacMillan Bloedel.

Most social movements rely on volunteers to carry out the work. Women traditionally have been strongly represented in both membership and leadership of many grass roots movements (Levine, 1982; Freudenberg and Steinsapir, 1992).

The prototype of the grassroots, locally based environmental group is the homeowners' association formed in the 1970s by some of the residents of the Love Canal neighbourhood in Niagara Falls, New York, whose properties, as previously mentioned, had been contaminated by toxic waste buried on it thirty years earlier by a local chemical company (discussed in Box 17.2). The founder of this association was local resident Lois Gibbs. Action taken by the association included protest marches, demonstrations, press conferences, political lobbying, legal injunctions, and a hostage taking. Finally, in 1980, U.S. president Jimmy Carter declared a state of emergency at Love Canal, and 700 families living close to the canal were relocated at government expense (Gibbs, 1982).

The Love Canal activists set the stage for other movements that have grappled with the kind of issues that sociologist Kai Erikson (1994) refers to as a "new species of trouble." Erikson describes the "new species" as environmental problems that "contaminate rather than merely damage ... they pollute, befoul, taint, rather than just create wreckage ... they penetrate human tissue indirectly rather than just wound the surfaces by assaults of a more straightforward kind ... And the evidence is growing that they scare human beings in new and special ways, that they elicit an uncanny fear in us" (Erikson, 1991:15). The chaos Erikson (1994:141) describes is the result of technological disasters—"meaning everything that can go wrong when systems fail, humans err, designs prove faulty, engines misfire, and so on." Examples of such disasters include the toxic chemical pollution at Love Canal and radiation leakage at the Three Mile Island nuclear power plant in the United States, the failure of the nuclear reactor at Chernobyl in the former Soviet Union, the near failure of a reactor in Pickering, Ontario, and the leakage of lethal gases at the pesticide plant in Bhopal, India, which is discussed in Box 17.3.

Social movements provide people who otherwise would not have the resources to enter the game of politics a chance to do so. We are most familiar with those movements that develop around public policy issues considered newsworthy by the media, ranging from abortion and women's rights to gun control and environmental justice. However, a number of other types of social movements exist as well.

TYPES OF SOCIAL MOVEMENTS

Social movements are difficult to classify; however, sociologists distinguish among movements on the basis of their *goals* and the *amount of change* they seek to produce (Aberle, 1966; Blumer, 1974). Some movements seek to change people while others seek to change society.

REFORM MOVEMENTS Grassroots environmental movements are an example of *reform movements,* which seek to improve society by changing

BOX 17.3 SOCIOLOGY IN GLOBAL PERSPECTIVE

Environmental Hazards as a Global Concern

Nothing seems to help.—Ram Singh Thakur

These four words of Thakur sum up the feelings of frustration and resignation felt by many victims of the 1984 chemical disaster at the Bhopal, India, pesticide plant of Union Carbide, a transnational corporation based in the United States. In what to date is the worst chemical disaster in history, over two thousand people died and many others were injured or blinded when the lethal gas methyl isocyanate seeped from the plant.

A decade later, many of the victims still have not received their promised compensation from Union Carbide, and extensive legal wrangling has occurred over whether the ailments people have developed actually were caused by the gas leak. A half-billion dollars has been set aside by the company for compensation; however, only a relatively small percentage has actually reached victims. More than $10 million has been spent in building four hospitals, and another $40 million has been set aside by Union Carbide for building another hospital for medical research and treatment of the victims. Thus far, however, there is no known antidote for exposure to methyl isocyanate.

Disasters like the tragic accident at the Union Carbide pesticide plant in Bhopal, India, spur many people to join social movements and demand changes they hope will prevent future environmental catastrophes.

In the 1990s, life goes on near the plant. Many residents have replaced their wooden huts with brick buildings financed by government grants and loans. Some have been able to buy television sets and motorcycles for the first time. Others have moved to new apartments built on the edge of the city by the government. The only difference is that Union Carbide has sold its interest in the plant to Magor Industries group, an Indian corporation.

Recently, the residents of Charleston, West Virginia, have become acutely aware that environmental disasters do not stop at national borders. Charleston residents were informed by a dozen of the world's largest chemical companies, which have factories in their area, that methyl isocyanate is one of a number of potentially lethal chemicals being produced in their area. The companies appeared to be moving ahead of an Environmental Protection Agency rule that would require companies that make or use hazardous chemicals to disclose to the residents how much of the material they keep on hand and to indicate the potential health risks if it were to escape into the environment through a leak, spill, fire, or explosion. The residents of Charleston now are aware of what a worst-case scenario might look like in their area. However, if they harken back to a journalist's statement in the aftermath of Bhopal, they do not feel a great deal of comfort in their knowledge:

> What truly grips us in these accounts is not so much the numbers as the spectacle of suddenly vanished competence, of men utterly routed by technology, of fail-safe systems failing with a logic as inexorable as it was once—indeed, right up until that very moment—unforeseeable. And the spectacle haunts us because it seems to carry allegorical import, like the whispery omen of a hovering future. (quoted in Erikson, 1994: 155)

Sources: Based on Erikson, 1994; Hazarika, 1994; Holusha, 1994; and Petersen, 1994.

some specific aspect of the social structure. Members of reform movements usually work within the existing system to attempt to change existing public policy so that it more adequately reflects their own value system. Examples of reform movements (in addition to the environmental movement) include labour movements, animal rights movements, antinuclear movements, Mothers Against Drunk Driving, and the disability rights movement.

Sociologist Lory Britt (1993) suggested that some movements arise specifically to alter social responses to and definitions of stigmatized attributes. From this perspective, social movements may bring about changes in societal attitudes and practices while at the same time causing changes in participants' social emotions. For example, the civil rights, gay rights, and aboriginal or native rights movements helped replace shame with pride (Britt, 1993). Consider the comments of Mohawk warrior Mike Myers, who participated in the standoff at Oka:

> For the moment, we have to endure persecution. But, in the long course of history, the face of Canada will be politically, socially, economically, and spiritually changed. Back in favour of our people. At least we will be able to leave the earth knowing that while we were here we did all that we could to set in motion a better future for our great-grandchildren. And so for me that's what Kanehsatake is about. (Obomsawin, 1993)

REVOLUTIONARY MOVEMENTS Movements seeking to bring about a total change in society are referred to as *revolutionary movements.* These movements usually do not attempt to work within the existing system; rather, they aim to remake the system by replacing existing institutions with new ones. Revolutionary movements range from utopian groups seeking to establish an ideal society to radical terrorists who use fear tactics to intimidate those with whom they disagree ideologically (see Alexander and Gill, 1984; Berger, 1988; Vetter and Perlstein, 1991).

***Terrorism* is the calculated unlawful use of physical force or threats of violence against persons or property in order to intimidate or coerce a government, organization, or individual for the purpose of gaining some political, religious, economic or social objective.** Movements based on terrorism often use tactics such as bombings, kidnappings, hostage taking, hijackings, and assassinations (Vetter and Perlstein, 1991). Over the past thirty years, terrorism has become a global phenomenon. For example, the Irish Republican Army has set off dozens of bombs in England; mafia terrorists have targeted judges, prosecutors, and politicians in Italy; and right-wing militia members are suspected in the 1995 bombing of the Alfred P. Murrah Federal Building, a large government office building, in Oklahoma City. In nations such as Lebanon and Jordan, members of revolutionary movements often engage in terrorist activities such as car bombings and assassinations of leading officials. On occasion, they also are the recipients of such actions. In 1994, for example, a car bomb killed one of the officials of the Party of God, a militant Shiite group battling Israeli troops in southern Lebanon. At the time of the killing, the Party of God was suspected in the kidnappings of U.S. citizens (including a newspaper correspondent) who were residing in Lebanon (*New York Times,* 1994). In Jordan, members of a militant Muslim movement were accused of bombing two theatres showing adult films and attempting to bomb a supermarket selling alcohol; pornography and alcohol both represent Western values that the Muslim movement adamantly opposes (*New York Times,* 1994a). In 1995, the Aum Shinri Kyo (Japanese for "sublime truth") religious sect allegedly perpetrated a nerve gas attack on a Tokyo subway that killed ten people, made thousands more ill, and raised the spectre of a new and even deadlier form of terrorism (Wu Dunn, 1995).

Canada is not immune to terrorist activity. In the late 1960s, the Front de Libération du Québec (FLQ), a small group of extremists on the fringe of the separatist movement, carried out 200 bombings. These incidents ranged from mail bombs to

These "pro-lifers" demonstrating outside of the Morgentaler clinic in Toronto are members of a resistance movement. They are seeking to prevent or undo change advocated by another social movement: the "pro-choice" movement.

the bombing of the Montreal Stock Exchange, where 27 people were injured. In addition, Sikh separatists are believed to be responsible for the 1985 bombing of an Air India jet that was travelling to India from Canada. This disaster was the biggest mass killing in Canadian history. Of the 329 people who died, 278 were Canadians.

RELIGIOUS MOVEMENTS Social movements that seek to produce radical change in individuals typically are based on spiritual or supernatural belief systems. Also referred to as *expressive movements*, *religious movements* are concerned with renovating or renewing people through "inner change." Fundamentalist religious groups seeking to convert nonbelievers to their belief system are an example of this type of movement. Some religious movements are *millenarian*—that is, they forecast that "the end is near" and assert that an immediate change in behaviour is imperative. Relatively new religious movements in industrialized Western societies have included Hare Krishnas, the Unification Church, Scientology, and the Divine Light Mission, all of which tend to appeal to the psychological and social needs of young people seeking meaning in life that mainstream religions have not provided for them.

ALTERNATIVE MOVEMENTS Movements that seek limited change in some aspect of people's behaviour are referred to as *alternative movements.* For example, in the early twentieth century, the Women's Christian Temperance Union attempted to get people to abstain from drinking alcoholic beverages. Some analysts place "therapeutic social movements" such as Alcoholics Anonymous in this category; however, others do not, due to their belief that people must change their lives completely in order to overcome alcohol abuse (see Blumberg, 1977). More recently, a variety of "New Age" movements have directed people's behaviour by emphasizing spiritual consciousness combined with a belief in reincarnation and astrology. Such practices as vegetarianism, meditation, and holistic medicine often are included in the self-improvement category. In the 1990s, some alternative movements include the practice of yoga (usually without its traditional background in the Hindu religion) as a means by which the self can be liberated and union can be achieved with the supreme spirit or universal soul.

RESISTANCE MOVEMENTS Also referred to as *regressive movements, resistance movements* seek to prevent change or to undo change that already has occurred. Virtually all of the proactive social movements previously discussed face resistance from one or more reactive movements that hold opposing viewpoints and want to foster public policies that reflect their own viewpoints. Examples of resistance movements are groups organized to oppose free trade, gun control, gay rights, and restrictions on smoking. Perhaps the most widely known resistance movement, however, includes many who label themselves as "pro-life" advocates—such as Operation Rescue, which seeks to close abortion clinics and make abortion illegal under all circumstances (Gray, 1993; Van Biema, 1993a). Protests by some radical anti-abortion groups in Canada and the United States have grown violent, resulting in the deaths of several doctors and clinic workers and creating fear among health professionals and patients seeking abortions (Belkin, 1994).

CAUSES OF SOCIAL MOVEMENTS

What conditions are most likely to produce social movements? Why are people drawn to these movements? Sociologists have developed several theories to answer these questions.

RELATIVE DEPRIVATION THEORY According to relative deprivation theory, people who are satisfied with their present condition are less likely to seek social change. Social movements arise as a response to people's perception that they have been deprived of their "fair share" (Rose, 1982). Thus, people who suffer relative deprivation are more likely to feel that change is necessary and to join a social movement in order to bring about that change. *Relative deprivation* refers to the discontent that people may feel when they compare their achievements with those of similarly situated persons and find that they have less than they think they deserve (Orum and Orum, 1968). Karl Marx captured the idea of relative deprivation in this description: "A house may be large or small; as long as the surrounding houses are small it satisfies all social demands for a dwelling. But let a palace arise beside the little house, and it shrinks from a little house to a hut" (quoted in Ladd, 1966:24). Movements based on relative deprivation are most likely to occur when an upswing in the standard of living is followed by a period of decline, such that people have *unfulfilled rising expectations*—newly raised hopes of a better lifestyle that are not fulfilled as rapidly as they expected or are not realized at all.

Although most of us can relate to relative deprivation theory, it does not fully account for why people experience social discontent but fail to join a social movement. If relative deprivation theory were accurate, many people in Canada and other consumer-oriented societies would be participants in social movements; however, this is not the case. Even though discontent and feelings of deprivation may be necessary to produce certain types of social movements, they are not sufficient to bring movements into existence. In fact, sociologist Anthony Orum (1974) found the best predictor of participation in a social movement to be prior organizational membership and involvement in other political activities.

VALUE-ADDED THEORY The value-added theory developed by sociologist Neal Smelser (1963) is based on the assumption that certain conditions are necessary for the development of a social movement. Smelser called his theory the "value-added" approach, based on the concept (borrowed from the field of economics) that each step in the production process adds something to the finished product. For example, in the process of converting iron ore into automobiles, each stage "adds value" to the final product (Smelser, 1963). Similarly, Smelser asserted, the following six condi-

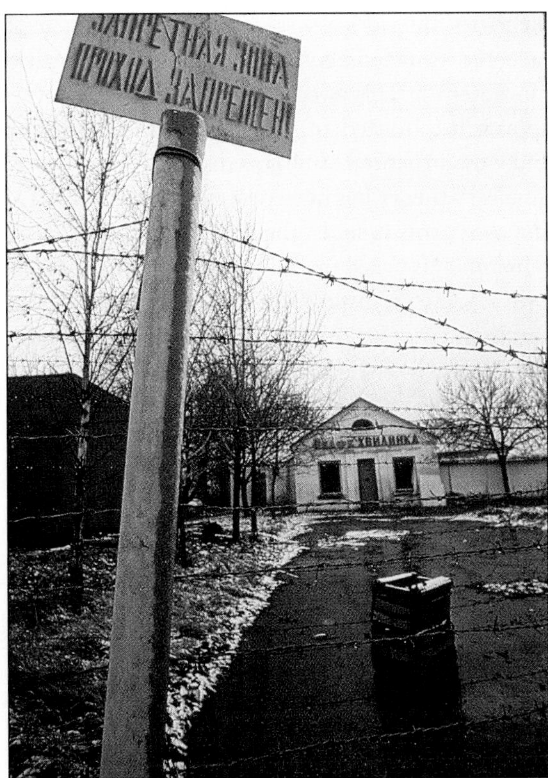

Among the precipitating factors for environmental movements around the world are technological disasters such as the 1986 melt-down and radiation leak at the Chernobyl nuclear power plant in the Ukraine. Dramatic events like these can move people to take action by reinforcing their generalized beliefs about environmental problems.

tions are necessary and sufficient to produce social movements when they combine or interact in a particular situation.

1. *Structural conduciveness.* People must become aware of a significant problem and have the opportunity to engage in collective action. According to Smelser, movements are more likely to occur when a person, class, or agency can be singled out as the source of the problem; when channels for expressing grievances either are not available or fail; and when the aggrieved have a chance to communicate among themselves. At Clayoquot Sound, local residents became aware of the problem when they learned that British Columbia's Ministry of Forests planned to allow extensive clearcutting of B.C.'s rain forests. Vancouver-based MacMillan Bloedel and members of the B.C. government were the immediate targets of their wrath—the logging company for using inadequate reforestation techniques and devastating the forest and the B.C. government for permitting logging in two-thirds of Clayoquot's old-growth forest.
2. *Structural strain.* When a society or community is unable to meet people's expectations that something should be done about a problem, strain occurs in the system. The ensuing tension and conflict contributes to the development of a social movement based on people's belief that the problems would not exist if authorities had done what they were supposed to do. For example, when environmental groups including the Sierra Club, Greenpeace, and the Friends of Clayoquot Sound demanded that logging companies utilize more selective logging techniques, officials were unresponsive. Tensions increased when environmentalists learned that the B.C. government had invested $50 million in MacMillan Bloedel, becoming the firm's largest shareholder.
3. *Spread of a generalized belief.* For a movement to develop, there must be a clear statement of the problem and a shared view of its cause, effects, and possible solution. For example, environmental activists were guided by a shared belief that the environmental degradation in Clayoquot Sound had to be eliminated or controlled. *Environmental degradation* is a disruption of the environment that produces negative consequences for ecosystems (Cable and Cable, 1995)
4. *Precipitating factors.* To reinforce the existing generalized belief, an inciting incident or dramatic event must occur. With regard to technological disasters, some gradually

emerge from a long-standing environmental threat (including the Three Mile Island nuclear power plant), while others involve a suddenly imposed problem. For example, an existing belief regarding the dangers of nuclear power was suddenly and dramatically reinforced by the partial meltdown and subsequent radiation leak at Three Mile Island. The events at Clayoquot occurred more slowly: however, activists were aware that unless clear-cutting was stopped, the Pacific coast's temperate rain forest would disappear by the year 2010 (Harding, 1993).

5. *Mobilization for action.* At this stage, leaders emerge to organize others and give them a sense of direction. In the case of Clayoquot Sound, MP Svend Robinson participated in the blockade at Kennedy River Bridge and informed reporters, "I'm standing here to show my support for people who are here and to join the voices of British Columbians and Canadians who are saying we can't allow this magnificent old-growth forest to be logged" (Brunet, 1993:16). Members of Tla-o-qui-aht First Nations, a 450-member band located at Clayoquot Sound, escorted Robert Kennedy Jr., a member of the renowned political family and an environmental lawyer with the U.S.-based Natural Resources Defense Council, to the protest at Clayoquot. Kennedy met with other citizens to inform them and gain their emotional and financial support, and garnered publicity from national and international media.
6. *Social control factors.* If there is a high level of social control on the part of law enforcement officials, political leaders, and others, it becomes more difficult to develop a social movement or engage in certain types of collective action. As you will recall, 800 protesters were arrested at the blockade at Clayoquot Sound.

Value-added theory takes into account the complexity of social movements, making it possible to use Smelser's assertions to test for the necessary and sufficient conditions that produce such movements. However, critics note that the approach is rooted in the functionalist tradition and view structural strains as disruptive to society. Smelser's theory has been described as a mere variant of convergence theory, which, you will remember, is based on the assumption that people with similar predispositions will be activated by a common event or object (Quarantelli and Hundley, 1993).

RESOURCE MOBILIZATION THEORY Smelser's value-added theory tends to underemphasize the importance of resources in social movements. By contrast, *resource mobilization theory* focuses on the process through which members of a social movement gather, trade, use, and occasionally waste resources as they seek to advance their cause (Oberschall, 1973; McCarthy and Zald, 1977). Resources include money, members' time, access to the media, and material goods such as property and equipment. Assistance from outsiders is essential for social movements. Reform movements, for example, are more likely to succeed when they gain the support of political and economic elites (Oberschall, 1973).

Unlike relative deprivation and structural strain explanations, the resource mobilization approach focuses on the variety of resources that must be mobilized, as well as the linkages of social movements to other groups and their dependence on external support for success. The tactics used by authorities to control or incorporate movements also are important in understanding the success or failure of movements (McCarthy and Zald, 1977).

Resource mobilization theory is based on the belief that participants in social movements are rational people. According to sociologist Charles Tilly (1973, 1978), movements are formed and dissolved, mobilized and deactivated, based on rational decisions about the goals of the group, available resources, and the cost of mobilization and collective action. In other words, social movements do not develop because of widespread discontent but because organizations exist that make it possible to express discontent by concerted social action (Aminzade, 1973; Gamson, 1990). Based on an analysis of fifty-three U.S. social protest groups ranging from labour unions to peace movements between 1800 and 1945, sociologist William Gamson (1990) concluded that the organization and tactics of a movement strongly influence its chances of success.

Unlike perspectives that view persons from deprived populations as the primary participants in social movements, resource mobilization theory asserts that participants must have some degree of economic and political resources to make the movement a success. Critics note, however, that this theory fails to account for social changes brought about by groups with limited resources. Critics also suggest that this theory naively assumes that powerful outsiders will jeopardize their positions in order to help others advocate a change that is unpopular with other community or societal elites. Concept Table 17.A summarizes the three theories of social movements.

EMERGING PERSPECTIVES Scholars continue to modify resource mobilization theory and to develop new approaches for investigating the diversity of movements in the mid-1990s. Emerging perspectives based on resource mobilization theory, for example, emphasize ideology and legitimacy of movements as well as material resources (see Zald and McCarthy, 1987; McAdam et al., 1988).

Recent theories based on an interactionist perspective focus on the importance of the symbolic presentation of a problem to both participants and the general public (see Snow et al., 1986; Capek, 1993). Research based on this perspective is often an investigation of how problems are framed and what names they are given. For example, much of the research on technological disasters points out the ambiguities inherent in "naming" the problems associated with chemical contamination as contrasted with natural disasters. On the basis of studies of Love Canal and their own investigation of a 1981 coal mine fire in Centralia, Pennsylvania, sociologists J. Stephen Kroll-Smith and Stephen Robert Couch (1990:166) concluded, "The more indeterminate the warning and threat stages of an extreme environment and the more they are extended in time, the more residents turn to symbolic activity to ascertain the degree of danger they are facing." As a result of this ambiguity, people attach meanings to clues they receive, hoping to make sense out of their plight. In the process, they seek out others who have similar symbolic interpretations of the warnings and threat signals. However, the groups are not characterized by cooperation. Instead, group members experience conflict because of their different realities, and the conflict results in the demise, not the rebuilding, of a sense of community (Kroll-Smith and Couch, 1990).

Unlike the communal bonding that follows a natural disaster, technological disasters often are followed by extreme social conflict (Raphael, 1986; Kroll-Smith and Couch, 1990). While natural disasters typically strike without regard to the class or race/ethnicity of victims, research suggests that technological disasters often are more class-specific (and sometimes race-specific) issues. Incidents such as the horrible disasters in Bhopal and Chernobyl, which occurred because of lax regulatory standards, are far more likely to victimize residents of underdeveloped countries than residents of Western Europe or North America.

Sociologist Alan Scott (1990) notes that over the past two decades "new social movements" have placed more emphasis on quality-of-life issues than earlier movements that focused primarily on economic issues. In actuality, however, many movements must deal simultaneously with quality-of-life and economic issues.

Examples of already existing "new social movements" include ecofeminism and environmental justice movements. Ecofeminism emerged in the late 1970s and early 1980s out of the feminist, peace, and ecology movements. Triggered by the near-meltdown at the Three Mile Island nuclear power plant in the United States, ecofeminists established World Women in Defense of the

CONCEPT TABLE 17.A

Social Movement Theories

	Key Components
Relative Deprivation	People who are discontented when they compare their achievements with those of others consider themselves relatively deprived and join social movements in order to get what they view is their "fair share," especially when there is an upswing in the economy followed by a decline.
Value-Added	Certain conditions are necessary for a social movement to develop: (1) structural conduciveness, such that people are aware of a problem and have the opportunity to engage in collective action, (2) structural strain, such that society or the community cannot meet people's expectations for taking care of the problem, (3) growth and spread of a generalized belief as to causes and effects of and possible solutions to the problem, (4) precipitating factors, or events that reinforce the beliefs, (5) mobilization of participants for action, and (6) social control factors, such that society comes to allow the movement to take action.
Resource Mobilization	A variety of resources (money, members' time, access to media and material goods such as equipment) are necessary for a social movement; people only participate when they feel the movement has access to these resources.

Environment. *Ecofeminism* is based on the belief that patriarchy is a root cause of environmental problems. According to ecofeminists, patriarchy not only results in the domination of women by men but also contributes to a belief that nature is to be possessed and dominated, rather than treated as a partner (see Ortner, 1974; Merchant, 1983; 1992; Mies and Shiva, 1993).

Another "new social movement" focuses on environmental justice and the intersection of race and class in the environmental struggle. Sociologist Stella M. Capek (1993) investigated a contaminated landfill in the residential community Carver Terrace in Texas. Capek found that residents were able to mobilize for change and win a federal buyout and relocation by symbolically linking their issue to a larger environmental justice framework. Since the 1980s, the emerging environmental justice movement has focused on the issue of environmental racism—the belief that a disproportionate number of hazardous facilities in the United States (including industries such as waste disposal/treatment and chemical plants) are placed in low-income areas populated primarily by people of colour (Bullard and Wright, 1992). These areas have been left out of most of the environmental cleanup that has taken place in the last two decades (Schneider, 1993). Capek concluded that linking Carver Terrace with environmental justice led to it being designated as a cleanup site.

STAGES IN SOCIAL MOVEMENTS

Do all social movements go through similar stages? Not necessarily, but there appear to be identifiable stages in virtually all movements that succeed beyond their initial phase of development.

In the *preliminary* (or incipiency) *stage*, widespread unrest is present as people begin to become aware of a problem. At this stage, leaders emerge to agitate others into taking action. In the *coalescence stage*, people begin to organize and to publicize the problem. At this stage, some movements become formally organized at local and regional levels. In the *institutionalization* (or bureaucratization) *stage*, an organizational structure develops, and a paid staff (rather than volunteers) begin to lead the group. When the movement reaches this stage, the initial zeal and idealism of members may diminish as administrators take over management of the organization. Early grassroots supporters may become disillusioned and drop out; they also may start another movement to address some as yet unsolved aspect of the original problem. For example, some environmental organizations—such as the Sierra Club, the Canadian Nature Federation, and the National Audubon Society—that started as grassroots conservation movements currently are viewed by many people as being unresponsive to local environmental problems (Cable and Cable, 1995). As a result, new movements have arisen.

As we have seen, social movements may be an important source of social change. Throughout this text, we have examined a variety of social problems—including rape, suicide, hate crimes, homelessness, sexual abuse, racial discrimination, sexual harassment, unemployment, and underemployment—that have been the focus of one or more social movements during this century. In the process of bringing about change, most movements initially develop innovative ways to get their ideas across to decision makers and the public. Some have been successful in achieving their goals; others have not. As historian Robert A. Goldberg (1991) has suggested, gains made by social movements may be fragile, acceptance brief, and benefits minimal and easily lost. For this reason, many groups focus on preserving their gains while simultaneously fighting for those they believe they still deserve.

SOCIAL CHANGE: MOVING INTO THE TWENTY-FIRST CENTURY

In this chapter we have focused on collective behaviour and social movements as potential forces for social change in contemporary societies. A number of other factors also contribute to social change, including the physical environment, population trends, technological development, and social institutions.

THE PHYSICAL ENVIRONMENT AND CHANGE

Changes in the physical environment often produce changes in the lives of people; in turn, people can make dramatic changes in the physical environment, over which we have only limited control. Throughout history, natural disasters have taken their toll on individuals and societies. Major natural disasters—including hurricanes, floods, and tornados—can devastate an entire population. Even comparatively "small" natural disasters change the lives of many people. For example, a major forest fire may destroy the resource base of a logging company. In other situations, disasters may become divisive elements that tear communities apart. As sociologist Kai Erikson (1976, 1994) has suggested, the trauma that people experience from disasters may outweigh the actual loss of physical property—memories of such events can haunt people for many years.

Some natural disasters are exacerbated by human decisions. For example, floods are viewed as natural disasters, but excessive development may contribute to a flood's severity. As office buildings, shopping malls, industrial plants,

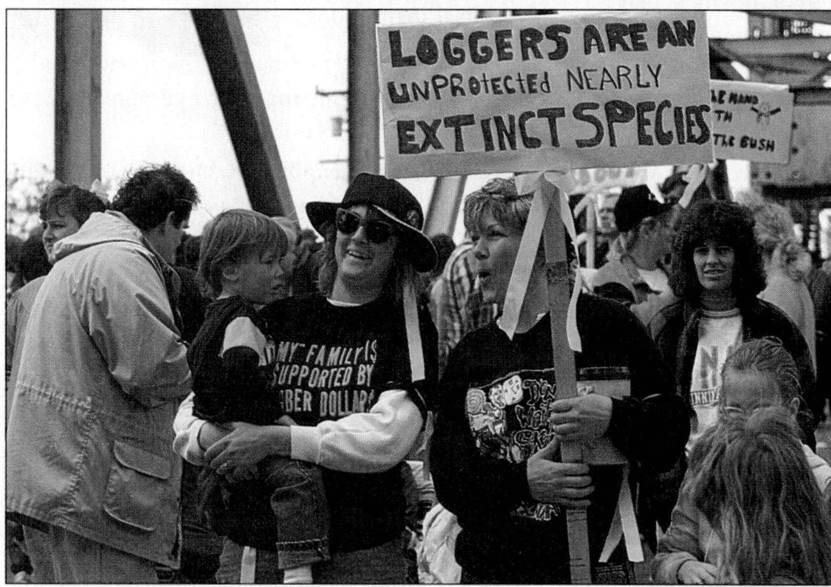

The twenty-first century will continue to see passionate debates over the changes people make to the earth's physical condition. Here, members of EarthFirst protest the clearcutting of trees in hopes of saving the habitat of the endangered spotted owl, while loggers and their families insist that environmental protections threaten their livelihood.

residential areas, and highways are developed, less land remains to absorb rainfall. When heavier-than-usual rains occur, flooding becomes inevitable; some regions in Canada have remained under water for days and even weeks in recent years. Clearly, humans cannot control the rain, but human decisions can worsen the consequences.

People also contribute to changes in the earth's physical condition. Through soil erosion and other degradation of grazing land, often at the hands of people, an estimated 24 billion tons of the earth's topsoil is lost annually. As people clear forests to create farmland and pastures and to acquire lumber and firewood, the earth's tree cover continues to diminish. As hundreds of millions of people drive motor vehicles, the amount of carbon dioxide in the environment continues to rise each year, possibly resulting in global warming. Scientists from a number of nations issued a report in 1990 pointing out that, if the world's economies continue to follow a "business as usual" approach, the average temperature will rise by five degrees Fahrenheit before the end of the century due to increases in carbon dioxide and other trace gasses in the atmosphere (Petersen, 1994).

Just as people contribute to change in the physical environment, human activities also must be adapted to changes in the environment. For example, we are being warned to stay out of the sunlight because of the increased penetrability of the sun's ultraviolet rays, a cause of skin cancer, as a result of the accelerating depletion of the ozone layer. If this prediction is accurate, the change in the physical environment will dramatically affect those who work or spend their leisure time outside.

POPULATION AND CHANGE

Changes in population size, distribution, and composition affect the culture and social structure of a society and change the relationships among nations. As discussed in Chapter 16, the countries experiencing the most rapid increases in population have a less developed infrastructure to deal with those changes. In Canada, increasing urbanization has provided significant changes with respect to housing, environmental issues, employment, and the demand for social programs.

Immigration to Canada has created an increasingly multi-ethnic population. The changing makeup of the Canadian population has resulted in children from more diverse cultural backgrounds entering school, producing a demand for new programs and changes in curricula. An increase in the number of women in the workforce has created a need for more child care; an increase in the older population has created a need for services such as home care and placed increasing demands on programs such as the Canada Pension Plan.

TECHNOLOGY AND CHANGE

Technology is an important force for change; in some ways, technological development has made our lives much easier. Advances in communication and transportation have made instantaneous worldwide communication possible but also have brought old belief systems and the status quo into question as never before. As we approach the twenty-first century, we increasingly are moving information instead of people—and doing it almost instantly (Petersen, 1994). Advances in science and medicine have made significant changes in people's lives. The lightbulb, the automobile, the airplane, the assembly line, and the high-tech developments of the late twentieth century—all have contributed to dramatic changes in people's lives. Individuals in developed nations have benefited from the use of the technology; those in less developed nations may have paid a disproportionate share of the cost of some of these inventions and discoveries.

Scientific advances will continue to affect our lives, from the foods we eat to our reproductive capabilities. Genetically engineered plants have been developed and marketed in recent years, and biochemists are creating potatoes, rice, and cassava with the same protein value as meat (Petersen, 1994). Advances in medicine have made it possible for those formerly unable to have children to procreate; women well beyond menopause now are able to become pregnant with the assistance of medical technology. Advances in medicine also have increased the human lifespan, especially for white and middle- or upper-class individuals in developed nations; they also have contributed to the declining death rate in developing nations, where birth rates have not yet been curbed.

Just as technology has brought about improvements in the quality and length of life for many, it has created the potential for new disasters, ranging from global warfare to localized technological disasters at toxic waste sites. As sociologist William Ogburn (1966) suggested, when a change in the material culture occurs in society, a period

The disastrous floods in Quebec's Saguenay Valley in 1996 following record rainfalls. The flooding may have been magnified by dams that are used to control water flow in the area.

of *cultural lag* follows in which the nonmaterial (ideological) culture has not caught up with material development. As we approach the twenty-first century, the rate of technological advance at the level of material culture is mind-boggling. Many of us can never hope to understand technological advances in the areas of artificial intelligence, holography, virtual reality, biotechnology, and robotics.

One of the ironies of twenty-first-century technology is the increased vulnerability that results from the increasing complexity of such systems. As futurist John L. Petersen (1994: 70) notes, "The more complex a system becomes, the more likely the chance of system failure. There are unknown secondary effects and particularly vulnerable nodes." He also asserts that most of the world's population will not participate in the technological revolution that is occurring in developed nations (Petersen, 1994).

Technological disasters may result in the deaths of tens of thousands of people, especially if we think of modern warfare as a technological disaster. Nuclear energy, which can provide power for millions, also can be the source of a nuclear war that could devastate the planet. As a government study on even limited nuclear war concluded:

> Natural resources would be destroyed; surviving equipment would be designed to use materials and skills that might no longer exist; and indeed some regions might be almost uninhabitable. Furthermore, pre-war patterns of behaviour would surely change, though in unpredictable ways. (U.S. Congress, 1979, quoted in Howard, 1990:320).

Even when lives are not lost in technological disasters, families are uprooted and communities cease to exist as people are relocated. In many cases, the problem is not solved; people simply are moved away from its site.

SOCIAL INSTITUTIONS AND CHANGE

Many changes have occurred in the family, religion, education, the economy, and the political system in the twentieth century. As we saw in Chapter 14, the size and composition of families in Canada have changed with a dramatic increase in the number of single-person and single-parent households. Changes in families have produced changes in the socialization of children, many of whom spend large amounts of time in front of a television set or in child-care facilities. Although some political and religious leaders have advocated a return to "traditional" family life, many scholars have argued that such families never worked quite as well as some might wish to believe.

Public education has changed dramatically in Canada during the twentieth century. This country was one of the first to provide "universal" education for students regardless of their ability to pay. As a result, Canada has had one of most highly educated populations in the world. Today, Canada still has one of the best public education systems in the world for the most students, although it is not meeting the needs of some students, namely, those who are failing to learn to read and write or those who are dropping out. As the nature of the economy changes, schools almost inevitably will have to change, if for no other reason than the demands from leaders in business and industry for an educated work force that allows Canadian companies to compete in a global economic environment.

Political systems have experienced tremendous change and upheaval in some parts of the world during this century. Recent events like the fall of the Berlin Wall and the breakup of the Soviet Union, the growing power of religious fundamentalists in many parts of the world, and the passing of the white-supremacist apartheid regime in South Africa have had a dramatic impact on the world. In the mid-1990s, Canada's government seems unable to determine what its priorities should be, even as the nation faces serious economic and social problems. As the centralized federal government becomes less able to respond to the needs and problems of the country, federal political leaders likely will seek to decentralize services and programs by putting more of the burden onto provincial and municipal governments. Unfortunately, these governments are no better equipped to deal with problems such as poverty and homelessness, environmental pollution, and decaying infrastructures.

Although we have examined changes in the physical environment, population, technology, and social institutions separately, they all operate together in a complex relationship, sometimes producing large, unanticipated consequences. In the twenty-first century, we need new ways of conceptualizing social life at both the macro- and microlevels. The sociological imagination helps us think about how personal troubles—regardless of our race/ethnicity, class, gender, age, sexual orientation, or physical abilities and disabilities—are intertwined with the public issues of our society and the global community of which we are a part.

A FEW FINAL THOUGHTS

In this text, we have covered a substantial amount of material, examined different perspectives on a wide variety of social issues, and have suggested different methods by which to deal with them. The purpose of this text is not to encourage you to take any particular point of view; rather, it is to allow you to understand different viewpoints and ways in which they may be helpful to you and to society in dealing with the issues of the twenty-first century. Possessing that understanding, we can hope that the next century will be something we can all look forward to—producing a better way of life, not only in this country but worldwide.

CHAPTER REVIEW

Social change is the alteration, modification, or transformation of public policy, culture, or social institutions over time; it usually is brought about by collective behaviour, which is relatively spontaneous, unstructured activity that typically violates established social norms.

- Collective behaviour occurs when some common influence or stimulus produces a response from a relatively large number of people. The people engaging in collective behaviour may be categorized as crowds (a relatively large number of people in one another's immediate presence) and masses (a number of people who share an interest in a specific idea or issue but who are not in one another's immediate physical vicinity).
- Sociologist Howard Blumer divided crowds into four categories: (1) casual crowds, (2) conventional crowds, (3) expressive crowds, and (4) acting crowds (including mobs, riots, and panic). A fifth type of crowd is a protest crowd.
- Contagion theory asserts that a crowd takes on a life of its own as people are transformed from rational beings into part of an organism that acts on its own. A variation on this is circular reaction—people express their discontent to others, who communicate back similar feelings, resulting in a conscious effort to engage in the crowd's behaviour. Convergence theory asserts that people with similar attributes find other like-minded persons with whom they can release underlying personal tendencies. Emergent norm theory asserts that, as a crowd develops, it comes up with its own norms that replace more conventional norms of behaviour.
- Mass behaviour is collective behaviour that occurs when people respond to the same event in the same way even if they are not geographically close to one another. Rumours, gossip, mass hysteria, fads and fashions, and public opinion are forms of mass behaviour.
- A social movement is an organized group that acts consciously to promote or resist change through collective action; such movements are most likely to be formed when people see their personal troubles as public issues that cannot be resolved without a collective response. Reform movements seek to improve society by changing some specific aspect of the social structure. Revolutionary movements seek to bring about a total change in society—sometimes by the use of terrorism. Religious movements seek to produce radical change in individuals based on spiritual or supernatural belief systems. Alternative movements seek limited change to some aspect of people's behaviour. Resistance movements seek to prevent change or to undo change that already has occurred.
- Relative deprivation theory asserts that, if people are discontented when they compare their accomplishments with those of others similarly situated, they are more likely to join a social movement than are people who are relatively content with their status. Value-added theory asserts that six conditions must exist in order to produce social movements: (1) a perceived source of a problem, (2) a perception that the authorities are not resolving the problem, (3) a spread of the belief to an adequate number of people, (4) a precipitating incident, (5) mobilization of other people by leaders, and (6) a lack of social control. Resource mobilization theory asserts that successful social movements can occur only when they gain the support of political and economic elites, without whom they do not have access to the resources necessary to maintain the movement.
- Social movements typically go through three stages: (1) a preliminary stage (unrest results

from a perceived problem), (2) coalescence (people begin to organize), and (3) institutionalization (an organization is developed and paid staff replaces volunteers in leadership positions).

KEY TERMS

civil disobedience **646**
collective behaviour **641**
crowd **643**
fad **651**
fashion **651**
gossip **650**
mass **643**
mass behaviour **650**
mass hysteria **650**
mob **644**
panic **646**
propaganda **653**
public opinion **652**
riot **646**
rumours **650**
social change **638**
social movement **653**
terrorism **655**

QUESTIONS FOR ANALYSIS AND UNDERSTANDING

1. How do casual, conventional, expressive, acting, and protest crowds differ?
2. What are the differences between fads and fashions? Can you think of any fads that are turning into fashion?
3. What factors must be present in order for a social movement to have a reasonable chance of success? Why?
4. What factors tend to limit the effectiveness of many social movements?

QUESTIONS FOR CRITICAL THINKING

1. What types of collective behaviour in Canada do you believe are influenced by inequalities based on race/ethnicity, class, gender, age, or disabilities? Why?
2. Which of the four explanations of crowd behaviour (contagion theory, social unrest and circular reaction, convergence theory, and emergent norm theory) do you believe best explains crowd behaviour? Why?
3. In the text, the Clayoquot Sound environmental movement was analyzed in terms of the value-added theory. How would you analyze that movement under the relative deprivation and resource mobilization theories?

4. What types of propaganda influence public opinion at your college or university? In answering this question, keep in mind the various news media, forums available for speakers, and discussions in your classroom. Is this propaganda beneficial or harmful?
5. Using the sociological imagination that you have gained in this course, what are some positive steps that you believe might be taken in Canada to make our society a better place for everyone in the twenty-first century? What types of collective behaviour and/or social movements might be required in order to take those steps?

SUGGESTED READINGS

For more in-depth information on collective behaviour and social movements, both of these texts are excellent:

Russell L. Curtis, Jr., and Benigno E. Aguirre. *Collective Behaviour and Social Movements.* Boston: Allyn & Bacon, 1993.

Ralph H. Turner and Lewis M. Killian. *Collective Behaviour* (4th ed.). Englewood Cliffs, N.J.: Prentice-Hall, 1993.

Sociological and historical perspectives on twentieth-century social movements are found in this interesting text:

Robert A. Goldberg. *Grassroots Resistance: Social Movements in Twentieth-Century America.* Belmont, Cal.: Wadsworth, 1991.

International terrorism is examined in this timely book:

Harold J. Vetter and Gary R. Perlstein. *Perspectives on Terrorism.* Pacific Grove, Cal.: Brooks/Cole, 1991.

This text applies various sociological perspectives to the study of the environment:

Charles L. Harper. *Environment and Society: Social Perspectives on Environmental Issues and Problems.* Englewood Cliffs, N.J.: Prentice-Hall, 1995.

These books provide additional insights on environmental hazards and the social movements that were launched to combat them:

Sherry Cable and Charles Cable. *Environmental Problems, Grassroots Solutions: The Politics of Grassroots Environmental Conflict.* New York: St. Martin's Press, 1995.

Rachel Carson. *Silent Spring.* Boston: Houghton Mifflin, 1962.

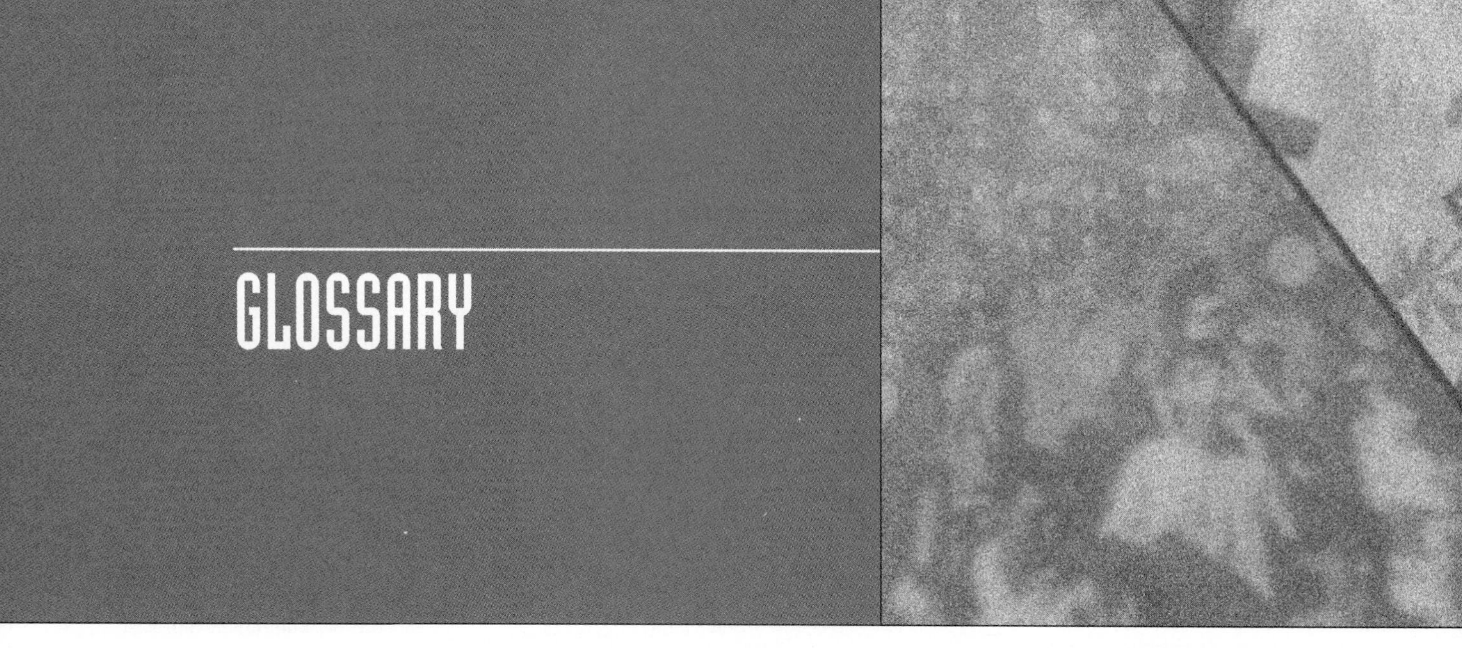

GLOSSARY

absolute poverty A level of economic deprivation in which people do not have the means to secure the most basic necessities of life.

achieved status A social position that a person assumes voluntarily as a result of personal choice, merit, or direct effort.

activity theory The proposition that people tend to shift gears in late middle age and find substitutes for previous statuses, roles, and activities.

age stratification The inequalities, differences, segregation, or conflict between age groups.

ageism Prejudice and discrimination against people on the basis of age, particularly when they are older persons.

agents of socialization Those persons, groups, or institutions that teach people what they need to know in order to participate in society.

aggregate A collection of people who happen to be in the same place at the same time but share little else in common.

aging The physical, psychological, and social processes associated with growing older.

alienation A feeling of powerlessness and estrangement from other people and from oneself.

animism The belief that plants, animals, or other elements of the natural world are endowed with spirits or life forces having an impact on events in society.

anomie Emile Durkheim's designation for a condition in which social control becomes ineffective as a result of the loss of shared values and a sense of purpose in society.

anticipatory socialization The process by which knowledge and skills are learned for future roles.

apartheid The policy of the South African government that required the separation of the races.

ascribed status A social position that is conferred on a person at birth or received involuntarily later in life.

assimilation A process by which members of subordinate racial and ethnic groups become absorbed into the dominant culture.

authoritarian leader A leader who makes all major group decisions and assigns tasks to group members.

authoritarian personality A personality type characterized by excessive conformity, submissiveness to authority, intolerance, insecurity, a high level of superstition, and rigid, stereotypic thinking.

authoritarianism A political system controlled by rulers who deny popular participation in government.

authority Power that people accept as legitimate rather than coercive.

basic class location Positions in the class structure where issues of property ownership and control are relatively clear.

bilateral descent A system of tracing descent through both the mother's and father's sides of the family.

body consciousness How a person perceives and feels about his or her body; it also includes an awareness of social conditions in society that contribute to this self-knowledge.

bourgeoisie (or capitalist class) Karl Marx's term for the class comprised of those who own and control the means of production.

bureaucracy An organizational model characterized by a hierarchy of authority, a clear division of labour, explicit rules and procedures, and impersonality in personnel matters.

bureaucratic personality A psychological construct that describes those workers who are more concerned with following correct procedures than they are with doing the job correctly.

capitalism An economic system characterized by private ownership of the means of production, from which personal profits can be derived through market competition and without government intervention.

caste system A system of social inequality in which people's status is permanently determined at birth based on their parents' ascribed characteristics.

category A number of people who may never have met one another but who share a similar characteristic.

catharsis theory The proposition that televised materialism and violence provide viewers with a vicarious outlet for their own greed or aggressiveness.

central city The densely populated centre of a metropolis.

charismatic authority Power legitimized on the basis of a leader's exceptional personal qualities.

chronological age A person's age based on date of birth.

church A large, bureaucratically organized religious organization that tends to seek accommodation with the larger society in order to maintain some degree of control over it.

civil disobedience Nonviolent action that seeks to change a policy or law by refusing to comply with it.

class The relative location of a person or group within a larger society, based on wealth, power, prestige, or other valued resources.

class conflict Karl Marx's term for the struggle between the capitalist class and the working class.

class system A type of stratification based on the ownership and control of resources and on the kinds of work people do.

cohabitation The sharing of a household by a couple who live to-gether without being legally married.

cohort A category of people who are born within a specified period in time or who share some specified characteristic in common.

collective behaviour Voluntary, often spontaneous, activity that is engaged in by a large number of people and typically violates dominant group norms and values.

commonsense knowledge A form of knowing that guides ordinary conduct in everyday life.

comparable worth (pay equity) The belief that wages ought to reflect the worth of a job, not the gender or race of the worker.

complete observation Research in which the investigator systematically observes a social process but does not take part in it.

conflict perspective The sociological approach that views groups in society as engaged in a continuous power struggle for control of scarce resources.

conformity The process of maintaining or changing behaviour to comply with the norms established by a society, subculture, or other group.

conglomerate A combination of businesses, in different commercial areas, all of which are owned by one holding company.

content analysis The systematic examination of cultural artifacts or various forms of communication to extract thematic data and draw conclusions about social life.

contingent work Part-time work, temporary work, and subcontracted work.

contradictory class location A class position within the productive process that possesses a combination of elements from two different basic class locations (for example, a department head who controls the work of sales personnel but still is accountable to the company's owner).

control group Subjects in an experiment who are not exposed to the independent variable but later are compared to subjects in the experimental group.

conventional (street) crime A term used to denote all violent crime, certain property crimes, and certain moral crimes.

core nation According to world systems theory, a dominant capitalist centre characterized by high levels of industrialization and urbanization and a high degree of control over the world economy.

corporate crime An illegal act committed by corporate employees on behalf of the corporation and with its support.

corporation A large-scale organization that has legal powers (such as the ability to enter into contracts and buy and sell property) separate from its individual owners.

correlation A relationship that exists when two (or more) variables are associated more frequently than could be expected by chance.

counterculture A group that strongly rejects dominant societal values and norms and seeks alternative lifestyles.

credentialism A process of social selection in which class advantage and social status are linked to the possession of academic qualifications.

crime Behaviour that violates criminal law and is punishable with fines, jail terms, and other sanctions.

criminology The systematic study of crime and the criminal justice system, including the police, courts, and prisons.

crowd A relatively large number of people who are in one another's immediate face-to-face presence.

crude birth rate The number of live births per 1000 people in a population in a given year.

crude death rate The number of deaths per 1000 people in a population in a given year.

crude net migration rate The net number of migrants (total in-migrants minus total out-migrants) per 1000 people in a population in a given year.

cult A religious group with practices and teachings outside the dominant cultural and religious traditions of a society.

cultural capital Pierre Bourdieu's term for people's social assets, including their values, beliefs, attitudes, and competencies in language and culture.

cultural imperialism The extensive infusion of one nation's culture into other nations.

cultural lag William Ogburn's term for a gap between the technical development of a society (material culture) and its moral and legal institutions (nonmaterial culture).

cultural relativism The belief that the behaviours and customs of a society must be viewed and analyzed within the context of its own culture.

cultural universals Customs and practices that occur across all societies.

culture The knowledge, language, values, customs, and material objects that are passed from person to person and from one generation to the next in a human group or society.

culture shock The disorientation that people feel when they encounter cultures radically different from their own.

deductive approach Research in which the investigator begins with a theory and then collects information and data to test the theory.

democracy A political system in which people hold the ruling power, either directly or indirectly.

democratic leader A leader who encourages group discussion and decision making through consensus building.

democratic socialism An economic and political system that combines private ownership of some of the means of production, governmental distribution of some essential goods and services, and free elections.

demographic transition The process by which some societies have moved from high birth and death rates to relatively low birth and death rates as a result of technological development.

demography A subfield of sociology that examines population size, composition, and distribution.

denomination A large organized religion characterized by accommodation to society but frequently lacking in ability or intention to dominate society.

dependent variable A variable that is assumed to depend on or be caused by one or more other (independent) variables.

descriptive study Research that attempts to describe social reality or provide detailed facts about some group, practice, or event.

deviance Any behaviour, belief, or condition that violates cultural norms.

differential association theory The proposition that individuals have a greater tendency to deviate from societal norms when they frequently associate with persons who are more favourable toward deviance than conformity.

diffusion The transmission of cultural items or social practices from one group or society to another.

disability A physical or health condition that stigmatizes or causes discrimination.

discovery The process of learning about something previously unknown or unrecognized.

discrimination Actions or practices of dominant group members (or their representatives) that have a harmful impact on members of a subordinate group.

disengagement theory The proposition that older persons make a normal and healthy adjustment to aging when they detach themselves from their social roles and prepare for their eventual death.

domestic partnership A household partnership in which an unmarried couple lives together in a committed, sexually intimate relationship and is granted the same benefits as those accorded to married heterosexual couples.

dramaturgical analysis The study of social interaction that compares everyday life to a theatrical presentation.

dual-earner marriage Marriage in which both spouses are in the labour force.

dyad A group consisting of two members.

dysfunctions A term referring to the undesirable consequences of any element of a society.

ecclesia A religious organization that is so integrated into the dominant culture that it claims as its membership all members of a society.

economy The social institution that ensures the maintenance of society through the production, distribution, and consumption of goods and services.

education The social institution responsible for the systematic transmission of knowledge, skills, and cultural values within a formally organized structure.

egalitarian family A family structure in which both partners share power and authority equally.

ego According to Sigmund Freud, the rational, reality-oriented component of personality that imposes restrictions on the innate pleasure-seeking drives of the id.

elder abuse A term used to describe physical abuse, psychological abuse, financial exploitation, and medical abuse or neglect of people age 65 or older.

elite model A view of society in which power in political systems is concentrated in the hands of a small group of elites and the masses are relatively powerless.

emigration The movement of people out of a geographic area to take up residency elsewhere.

empirical approach Research that attempts to answer questions through a systematic collection and analysis of data.

employment equity A strategy to eliminate the effects of discrimination and to make employment opportunities available to groups who have been excluded.

endogamy Cultural norms prescribing that people marry inside their own social group or category.

ethnic group A collection of people distinguished, by others or by themselves, primarily on the basis of cultural or nationality characteristics.

ethnic pluralism The coexistence of a variety of distinct racial and ethnic groups within one society.

ethnicity The cultural heritage or identity of a group based on factors such as language or country of origin.

ethnocentrism The belief in the superiority of one's own culture compared with that of others.

ethnography A detailed study of the life and activities of a group of people by researchers who may live with that group over a period of years.

ethnomethodology The study of the commonsense knowledge that people use to understand the situations in which they find themselves.

exogamy Cultural norms prescribing that people marry outside their own social group or category.

experiment A research method involving a carefully designed situation in which the researcher studies the impact of certain variables on subjects' attitudes or behaviour.

experimental group Subjects in an experiment who are exposed to the independent variable.

explanatory study Research that attempts to explain cause and effect relationships and to provide information on why certain events do or do not occur.

expressive leadership Group leadership that provides emotional support for members.

extended family A family unit composed of relatives in addition to parents and children who live in the same household.

fad A temporary but widely copied activity followed enthusiastically by large numbers of people.

false consciousness The term used by Karl Marx to indicate that people hold beliefs they think promote their best interests when those beliefs actually are damaging to their interests.

family A relationship in which people live together with commitment, form an economic unit and care for any young, and consider their identity to be significantly attached to the group.

family of orientation The family into which a person is born and in which early socialization usually takes place.

family of procreation The family a person forms by having or adopting children.

fashion A currently valued style of behaviour, thinking, or appearance that is longer lasting and more widespread than a fad.

feminism The belief that all people—both women and men—are equal and that they should be valued equally and have equal rights.

feminization of poverty The trend in which women are disproportionately represented among individuals living in poverty.

fertility The actual level of childbearing for an individual or a population.

folkways Informal norms or everyday customs that may be violated without serious consequences within a particular culture.

formal organization A highly structured group formed for the purpose of completing certain tasks or achieving specific goals.

functional age A term used to describe observable individual attributes such as physical appearance, mobility, strength, coordination, and mental capacity that are used to assign people to age categories.

functional illiteracy The condition in which reading and writing skills are inadequate to carry out everyday activity.

functionalist perspective The sociological approach that views society as a stable, orderly system.

Gemeinschaft (guh-MINE-shoft) A traditional society in which social relationships are based on personal bonds of friendship and kinship and on intergenerational stability.

gender The culturally and socially constructed meanings, beliefs, and practices associated with sex differences.

gender bias Behaviour that shows favouritism toward one gender over the other.

gender identity A person's perception of the self as female or male.

gender role Attitudes, behaviour, and activities that are socially defined as appropriate for each sex and are learned through the socialization process.

gender socialization The aspect of socialization that contains specific messages and practices concerning the nature of being female or male in a specific group or society.

generalized other George Herbert Mead's term for the child's awareness of the demands and expectations of the society as a whole or of the child's subculture.

genocide The deliberate, systematic killing of an entire people or nation.

gentrification The process by which members of the middle and upper-middle classes, especially whites, move into the central-city area and renovate existing properties.

Gesellschaft (guh-ZELL-shoft) A large, urban society, in which social bonds are based on impersonal and specialized relationships, with little long-term commitment to the group or consensus on values.

global interdependence A relationship in which the lives of all people are intertwined closely and any one nation's problems are part of a larger global problem.

goal displacement A process that occurs in organizations when the rules become an end in themselves and organizational survival becomes more important than achievement of goals.

gossip Rumours about the personal lives of individuals.

government The formal organization that has the legal and political authority to regulate the relationships among members within a society and between the society and those outside its borders.

group consciousness An awareness that an individual's problems are shared by others who are similarly situated in regard to race/ethnicity, gender, class, or age.

groupthink The process by which members of a cohesive group arrive at a decision that many individual members privately believe is unwise.

Hawthorne effect A term used in research to describe changes in the subjects' behaviour caused by the researcher's presence or by the subjects' awareness of being studied.

hermaphrodite A person in whom sexual differentiation is ambiguous or incomplete.

hidden curriculum The transmission of cultural values and attitudes, such as conformity and obedience to authority, through implied demands found in rules, routines, and regulations of schools.

homogamy The pattern of individuals marrying those who have similar characteristics, such as race/ethnicity, religious background, age, education, or social class.

hospice A homelike facility that provides supportive care for patients with terminal illnesses.

hypothesis In research studies, a tentative statement of the relationship between two or more concepts or variables.

id Sigmund Freud's term for the component of personality that includes all of the individual's basic biological drives and needs that demand immediate gratification.

ideal culture The values and standards of behaviour that people in a society profess to hold.

ideal type An abstract model that describes the recurring characteristics of some phenomenon.

illegitimate opportunity structures Circumstances that provide an opportunity for people to acquire through illegitimate activities what they cannot achieve through legitimate channels.

immigration The movement of people into a geographic area to take up residency.

independent variable A variable that is presumed to cause or determine a dependent variable.

individual discrimination Behaviour consisting of one-on-one acts by members of the dominant group that harm members of the subordinate group or their property.

inductive approach Research in which the investigator collects information or data (facts or evidence) and then generates theories from the analysis of that data.

industrialization The process by which societies are transformed from dependence on agriculture and handmade products to an emphasis on manufacturing and related industries.

infant mortality rate The number of deaths of infants under 1 year of age per 1000 live births in a given year.

infertility A medical term used to describe one year of attempting to achieve pregnancy without success.

informal structure A term used to describe the aspect of organizational life in which participants' day-to-day activities and interactions ignore, bypass, or do not correspond with the official rules and procedures of the bureaucracy.

ingroup A group to which a person belongs and with which the person feels a sense of identity.

institutional racism A term used to describe the rules, procedures, and practices that directly and deliberately prevent minorities from having full and equal involvement in society.

instrumental leadership Group leadership that is goal or task oriented.

interactionist perspective The sociological approach that views society as the sum of the interactions of individuals and groups.

intergenerational mobility The social movement (upward or downward) experienced by family members from one generation to the next.

interlocking corporate directorates A term used to describe members of the board of directors of one corporation who also sit on the boards of one or more other corporations.

internal colonialism According to conflict theorists, a practice that occurs when members of a racial or ethnic group are conquered or colonized and forcibly placed under the economic and political control of the dominant group.

interview A research method using a data collection encounter in which an interviewer asks the respondent questions and records the answers.

intragenerational mobility The social movement (upward or downward) experienced by individuals within their own lifetime.

invasion The process by which a new category of people or type of land use arrives in an area previously occupied by another group or land use.

invention The process of reshaping existing cultural items into a new form.

invidious distinction A term used to describe wide discrepancies in the income, wealth, life conditions, life chances, and lifestyles between people as a result of systems of stratification.

iron law of oligarchy According to Robert Michels, the tendency of bureaucracies to be ruled by a few people.

job deskilling A reduction in the proficiency needed to perform a specific job that leads to a corresponding reduction in the wages paid for that job.

juvenile delinquency The violation of a law or the commission of a status offence by young people less than a specific age.

kinship A social network of people based on common ancestry, marriage, or adoption.

labelling theory The proposition that deviants are those people who have been successfully labelled as such by others.

labour union An organization of employees who join together to bargain with an employer or a group of employers over wages, benefits, and working conditions.

laissez-faire leader A leader who is only minimally involved in decision making and encourages group members to make their own decisions.

language A system of symbols that express ideas and enable people to think and communicate with one another.

latent functions Hidden, unstated, and sometimes unintended consequences of activities within an organization or institution.

laws Formal, standardized norms that have been enacted by legislatures and are enforced by formal sanctions.

life chances Max Weber's term for the extent to which persons within a particular layer of stratification have access to important scarce resources.

life expectancy The average length of time a group of individuals of the same age will live.

looking-glass self Charles Horton Cooley's term for the way in which a person's sense of self is derived from the perceptions of others.

macrolevel analysis Sociological theory and research that focuses on whole societies, large-scale social structures, and social systems.

majority (dominant) group An advantaged group that has superior resources and rights in a society.

manifest functions Open, stated, and intended goals or consequences of activities within an organization or institution.

marginal job A position that differs from the employment norms of the society in which it is located.

marriage A legally recognized and/or socially approved arrangement between two or more individuals that carries certain rights and obligations and usually involves sexual activity.

mass A large collection of people who share an interest in a specific idea or issue but who are not in another's immediate physical vicinity.

mass behaviour Collective behaviour that takes place when people (who often are geographically separated from one another) respond to the same event in much the same way.

mass hysteria A form of dispersed collective behaviour that occurs when a large number of people react with strong emotions and self-destructive behaviour to a real or perceived threat.

master status A term used to describe the most important status a person occupies.

material culture A component of culture that consists of the physical or tangible creations (such as clothing, shelter, and art) that members of a society make, use, and share.

matriarchal family A family structure in which authority is held by the eldest female (usually the mother).

matriarchy A hierarchical system of social organization in which cultural, political, and economic structures are controlled by women.

matrilineal descent A system of tracing descent through the mother's side of the family.

matrilocal residence The custom of a married couple living in the same household (or community) with the wife's parents.

means of production Karl Marx's term for tools, land, factories, and money for investment that form the economic basis of a society.

mechanical solidarity Emile Durkheim's term for the social cohesion that exists in preindustrial societies, in which there is a minimal division of labour and people feel united by shared values and common social bonds.

medicalization of deviance A term used to describe the transformation of deviance into a medical problem that requires treatment by a physician.

megalopolis A continuous concentration of two or more cities and their suburbs that have grown until they form an interconnected urban area.

meritocracy A social system in which status is assumed to be acquired through individual ability and effort.

metropolis One or more central cities and their surrounding suburbs that dominate the economic and cultural life of a region.

microlevel analysis Sociological theory and research that focuses on small groups rather than large-scale social structures.

migration The movement of people from one geographic area to another for the purpose of changing residency.

minority (subordinate) group A disadvantaged group whose members, because of physical or cultural characteristics, are subjected to unequal treatment by the dominant group and who regard themselves as objects of collective discrimination.

mixed economy An economic system that combines elements of a market economy (capitalism) with elements of a command economy (socialism).

mob A highly emotional crowd whose members engage in, or are ready to engage in, violence against a specific target, which may be a person, a category of people, or physical property.

monarchy A political system in which power resides in one person or family and is passed from generation to generation through lines of inheritance.

monogamy Marriage between two partners, usually a woman and a man.

monotheism Belief in a single, supreme being or god who is responsible for significant events such as the creation of the world.

mores Strongly held norms with moral and ethical connotations that may not be violated without serious consequences in a particular culture.

mortality The incidence of death in a population.

multinational corporations Large companies that are headquartered in one country and have subsidiaries or branches in other countries.

neolocal residence The custom of a married couple living in their own residence apart from both the husband's and the wife's parents.

nonmaterial culture A component of culture that consists of the abstract or intangible human creations of society (such as attitudes, beliefs, and values) that influence people's behaviour.

nonverbal communication The transfer of information between persons without the use of speech.

normative approach The use of religion, custom, habit, tradition, or law to answer important questions.

norms Established rules of behaviour or standards of conduct.

nuclear family A family comprised of one or two parents and their dependent children, all of whom live apart from other relatives.

objective Free from distorted subjective (personal or emotional) bias.

observational learning theory The proposition that we observe the behaviour of another person and repeat the behaviour ourselves.

occupation A category of jobs that involve similar activities at different work sites.

occupational (white-collar) crime A term used to describe illegal activities committed by people in the course of their employment or financial affairs.

oligopoly The situation that exists when several companies overwhelmingly control an entire industry.

operational definition An explanation of an abstract concept in terms of observable features that are specific enough to measure the variable.

organic solidarity Emile Durkheim's term for the social cohesion that exists in industrial societies in which people perform very specialized tasks and feel united by their mutual dependence.

organized crime A business operation that supplies illegal goods and services for profit.

outgroup A term used to describe a group to which a person does not belong and toward which the person may feel a sense of competitiveness or hostility.

panic A form of crowd behaviour that occurs when a large number of people react with strong emotions and self-destructive behaviour to a real or perceived threat.

participant observation A research method in which researchers collect systematic observations while being part of the activities of the group they are studying.

patriarchal family A family structure in which authority is held by the eldest male (usually the father).

patriarchy A hierarchical system of social organization in which cultural, political, and economic structures are controlled by men.

patrilineal descent A system of tracing descent through the father's side of the family.

patrilocal residence The custom of a married couple living in the same household (or community) with the husband's family.

peer group A group of people who are linked by common interests, equal social position, and (usually) similar age.

peripheral nations According to world systems theory, a nation that is dependent on core nations for capital and has little or no industrialization.

personal space The immediate area surrounding a person that the person claims as private.

perspective An overall approach to or viewpoint on some subject.

pink-collar occupation A term used to describe the relatively low-paying, nonmanual, semiskilled positions primarily held by women.

pluralist model An analysis of political systems that views power as widely dispersed throughout many competing interest groups.

polite racism A term used to describe an attempt to disguise a dislike of others through behaviour that appears to be nonprejudicial.

political crime A term used to describe illegal or unethical acts in-volving the usurpation of power by government officials or illegal or un-ethical acts perpetrated against the government by outsiders seeking to make a political statement, undermine the government, or overthrow it.

political party An organization whose purpose is to gain and hold legitimate control of government.

political socialization The process by which people learn political attitudes, values, and behaviour.

political sociology The area of sociology that examines the nature and consequences of power within or between societies.

politics The social institution through which power is acquired and exercised by some people and groups.

polyandry The concurrent marriage of one woman with two or more men.

polygamy The concurrent marriage of a person of one sex with two or more members of the opposite sex.

polygyny The concurrent marriage of one man with two or more women.

polytheism The belief in more than one god.

popular culture The component of culture that consists of activities, products, and services that are assumed to appeal primarily to members of the middle and working classes.

population In a research study, those persons about whom we want to be able to draw conclusions.

population composition In demography, the biological and social characteristics of a population.

population pyramid A graphic representation of the distribution of a population by sex and age.

positivism A belief that the world can best be understood through scientific inquiry.

power According to Max Weber, the ability of people or groups to achieve their goals despite opposition from others.

power elite C. Wright Mills's term for a small clique composed of top corporate, political, and military officials.

prejudice A negative attitude based on faulty generalizations about members of selected racial and ethnic groups.

presentation of self Erving Goffman's term for people's efforts to present themselves to others in ways that are most favourable to their own interests or image.

prestige The respect or regard with which a person or status position is regarded by others.

primary deviance A term used to describe the initial act of rule breaking.

primary group Charles Horton Cooley's term for a small, less specialized group in which members engage in face-to-face, emotion-based interactions over an extended period of time.

primary labour market The sector of the labour market consisting of well-paid jobs with good benefits that have some degree of security and the possibility of future advancement.

primary sector production The sector of the economy that extracts raw materials and natural resources from the environment.

primary sex characteristics The genitalia used in the reproductive process.

profane A term used to describe the everyday, secular or "worldly," aspects of life.

profession A high-status, knowledge-based occupation.

proletariat (working class) Karl Marx's term for those who must sell their labour because they have no other means to earn a livelihood.

propaganda Information provided by individuals or groups that have a vested interest in furthering their own cause or damaging an opposing one.

public opinion The attitudes and beliefs communicated by ordinary citizens to decision makers.

punishment An action designed to deprive a person of things of value (including liberty) because of some offence the person is thought to have committed.

qualitative research Sociological research methods that use interpretive description (words) rather than statistics (numbers) to analyze underlying meanings and patterns of social relationships.

quantitative research Sociological research methods that are based on the goal of scientific objectivity and focus on data that can be measured numerically.

questionnaire A printed research instrument containing a series of items to which subjects respond.

race A category of people who have been singled out as inferior or superior, often on the basis of physical characteristics such as skin colour, hair texture, and eye shape.

racial socialization The aspect of socialization that contains specific messages and practices concerning the nature of one's racial or ethnic status.

racism An organized set of beliefs about the innate inferiority of some racial groups, combined with the power to transform these ideas into practices that can deny or exclude equality of treatment on the basis of race.

random sample A selection in which everyone in the target population has an equal chance of being chosen; in other words, choice occurs by chance.

rationality The process by which traditional methods of social organization, characterized by informality and spontaneity, gradually are replaced by efficiently administered formal rules and procedures (bureaucracy).

rational-legal authority Power legitimized by law or written rules and procedures. Also referred to as bureaucratic authority.

rednecked racism A term used to describe overt racism that may take the form of public statements about the "inferiority" of members of a racial or ethnic group.

real culture The values and standards of behaviour that people actually follow (as contrasted with ideal culture).

reference group A term used to describe a group that strongly influences a person's behaviour and social attitudes, regardless of whether that individual is an actual member.

relative poverty A level of economic deprivation in which people may be able to afford basic necessities but still are unable to maintain an average standard of living.

reliability In sociological research, the extent to which a study or research instrument yields consistent results.

religion A system of beliefs, symbols, and rituals, based on some sacred or supernatural realm, that guides human behaviour, gives meaning to life, and unites believers into a community.

replication In sociological research, the repetition of the investigation in substantially the same way that it originally was conducted.

representative sample A selection from a larger population that has the essential characteristics of the total population.

research method A strategy or technique for systematically conducting research.

resocialization The process of learning a new set of attitudes, values, and behaviours different from those in one's previous background and experiences.

respondent A person who provides data for analysis through an interview or questionnaire.

riot Violent crowd behaviour that is fuelled by deep-seated emotions but is not directed at one specific target.

ritual A symbolic action that represents religious meanings.

role A set of behavioural expectations associated with a given status.

role conflict A situation in which incompatible role demands are placed on a person by two or more statuses held at the same time.

role exit A situation in which people disengage from social roles that have been central to their self-identity.

role expectation A term used to describe a group's or society's definition of the way a specific role ought to be played.

role performance How a person actually plays a role.

role strain The strain experienced by a person when incompatible demands are built into a single status that the person occupies.

role-taking The process by which a person mentally assumes the role of another person in order to understand the world from that person's point of view.

routinization of charisma A term for the process by which charismatic authority is succeeded by a bureaucracy controlled by a rationally established authority or by a combination of traditional and bureaucratic authority.

rumour An unsubstantiated report on an issue or subject.

sacred A term used to describe those aspects of life that are extraordinary or supernatural.

sample The people who are selected from the population to be studied.

sanction A reward for appropriate behaviour or a penalty for inappropriate behaviour.

Sapir-Whorf hypothesis The proposition that language shapes the view of reality of its speakers.

scapegoat A person or group that is incapable of offering resistance to the hostility or aggression of others.

second shift Arlie Hochschild's term for the domestic work that employed women perform at home after they complete their workday on the job.

secondary analysis A research method in which researchers use existing material and analyze data that originally was collected by others.

secondary deviance A term used to describe the process whereby a person who has been labelled as deviant accepts that new identity and continues the deviant behaviour.

secondary group A larger, more specialized group in which the members engage in more impersonal, goal-oriented relationships for a limited period of time.

secondary labour market The sector of the labour market that consists of low-paying jobs with few benefits and very little job security or possibility for future advancement.

secondary sector production The sector of the economy that processes raw materials (from the primary sector) into finished goods.

secondary sex characteristics The physical traits (other than reproductive organs) that identify an individual's sex.

sect A relatively small religious group that has broken away from another religious organization to renew what it views as the original version of the faith.

secularization The process by which religious beliefs, practices, and institutions lose their significance in sectors of society and culture.

segregation A term used to describe the spatial and social separation of categories of people by race/ethnicity, class, gender, and/or religion.

self-concept The totality of our beliefs and feelings about ourselves.

self-fulfilling prophecy A situation in which a false belief or prediction produces behaviour that makes the originally false belief come true.

semiperipheral nation According to world system theory, a nation that is more developed than the peripheral nations but less developed than core nations.

sex A term used to describe the biological and anatomical differences between females and males.

sex ratio A term used by demographers to denote the number of males for every hundred females in a given population.

sexism The subordination of one sex, usually female, based on the assumed superiority of the other sex.

sexual orientation A person's preference for emotional–sexual relationships with members of the opposite sex (heterosexuality), the same sex (homosexuality), or both sexes (bisexuality).

shared monopoly A situation in which four or fewer companies supply 50 percent or more of a particular market.

significant others Those persons whose care, affection, and approval are especially desired and who are most important in the development of the self.

simple supernaturalism The belief that supernatural forces affect people's lives either positively or negatively.

slavery An extreme form of stratification in which some people are owned by others.

small group A collectivity small enough for all members to be acquainted with one another and to interact simultaneously.

social bond theory The proposition that the likelihood of deviant behaviour increases when a person's ties to society are weakened or broken.

social change The alteration, modification, or transformation of public policy, culture, or social institutions over time.

social construction of reality The process by which our perception of reality is shaped largely by the subjective meaning that we give to an experience.

social control Systematic practices developed by social groups to encourage conformity and to discourage deviance.

social Darwinism Herbert Spencer's belief that those species of animals—including human beings—best adapted to the environment survive and prosper while those poorly adapted die out.

social devaluation A situation in which a person or group is considered to have less social value than other individuals or groups.

social disorganization According to functionalist theorists, conditions that undermine the ability of traditional institutions (such as family, church, or school) to govern social behaviour.

social distance A term used to describe the extent to which people are willing to interact and establish relationships with members of racial and ethnic groups other than their own.

social facts Emile Durkheim's term for patterned ways of acting, thinking, and feeling that exist outside any one individual.

social gerontology The study of the social (nonphysical) aspects of aging.

social group A group that consists of two or more people who interact frequently and share a common identity and a feeling of interdependence.

social institution A set of organized beliefs and rules that establish how a society will attempt to meet its basic social needs.

social interaction The process by which people act toward or respond to other people.

social marginality The state of being part insider and part outsider in the social structure.

social mobility The movement of individuals or groups from one level in a stratification system to another.

social movement An organized group that acts consciously to promote or resist change through collective action.

social network A series of social relationships that link an individual to others.

social stratification The hierarchical arrangement of large social groups based on their control over basic resources.

social structure The stable pattern of social relationships that exist within a particular group or society.

socialism An economic system characterized by public ownership of the means of production, the pursuit of collective goals, and centralized decision making.

socialization The lifelong process of social interaction through which individuals acquire a self-identity and the physical, mental, and social skills needed for survival in society.

societal consensus A situation whereby the majority of members share a common set of values, beliefs, and behavioural expectations.

society A large social grouping that shares the same geographical territory and is subject to the same political authority and dominant cultural expectations.

sociobiology The systematic study of how biology affects social behaviour.

socioeconomic status (SES) A combined measure that attempts to classify individuals, families, or households in terms of indicators such as income, occupation, and education.

sociological imagination C. Wright Mills's term for the ability to see the relationship between individual experiences and the larger society.

sociology The systematic study of human society and social interactions.

sociology of family The subdiscipline of sociology that attempts to describe and explain patterns of family life and variations in family structure.

special interest groups Political coalitions comprised of individuals or groups that share a specific interest that they wish to protect or advance with the help of the political system.

split labour market A term used to describe the division of the economy into two areas of employment: a primary sector or upper tier, composed of higher-paid (usually dominant group) workers in more secure jobs; and a secondary sector or lower tier, comprised of lower-paid (often subordinate group) workers in jobs with little security and hazardous working conditions.

state The political entity that possesses a legitimate monopoly over the use of force within its territory to achieve its goals.

status A socially defined position in a group or society characterized by certain expectations, rights, and duties.

status set A term used to describe all the statuses that a person occupies at a given time.

status symbol A material sign that informs others of a person's specific status.

stigma According to Erving Goffman, any physical or social attribute or sign that so devalues a person's social identity that it disqualifies that person from full social acceptance.

strain theory The proposition that people feel strain when they are exposed to cultural goals that they are unable to obtain because they do not have access to culturally approved means of achieving those goals.

subcontracting A form of economic organization in which a larger corporation contracts with other (usually smaller) firms to provide specialized components, products, or services to the larger corporation.

subculture A group of people who share a distinctive set of cultural beliefs and behaviours that differ in some significant way from that of the larger society.

subliminal racism A term used to describe an unconcious criticism of minorities.

succession The process by which a new category of people or type of land use gradually predominates in an area formerly dominated by another group or activity.

superego Sigmund Freud's term for the human conscience, consisting of the moral and ethical aspects of personality.

survey A research method in which a questionnaire or interview is used by researchers to gather facts or determine the relationship between facts.

symbol Anything that meaningfully represents something else.

systemic racism A term used to describe practices that have a harmful impact on subordinate group members even though the organizationally prescribed norms or regulations guiding these actions initially were established with no intent to harm.

taboo A more that is so strong that its violation is considered to be extremely offensive and even unmentionable.

technology The knowledge, techniques, and tools that make it possible for people to transform resources into usable forms, and the knowledge and skills required to use them after they are developed.

terrorism The calculated unlawful use of physical force or threats of violence against persons or property in order to intimidate or coerce a government, organization, or individual for the purpose of gaining some political, religious, economic, or social objective.

tertiary sector production The sector of the economy that is involved in the provision of services rather than goods.

theism A belief in a god or gods.

theory A set of logically interrelated statements that attempts to describe, explain, and (occasionally) predict social events.

total institution Erving Goffman's term for a place where people are isolated from the rest of society for a set period of time and come under the control of the officials who run the institution.

totalitarianism A political system in which the state seeks to regulate all aspects of people's public and private lives.

tracking A term used to describe the assignment of students to specific courses and educational programs based on their test scores, previous grades, or both.

traditional authority Power that is legitimized on the basis of long-standing custom.

transcendent idealism A belief in sacred principles of thought and conduct.

transsexual A person who believes that he or she was born with the body of the wrong sex.

transvestite A male who lives as a woman or a female who lives as a man but does not alter the genitalia.

triad A group comprised of three members.

unemployment rate The percentage of unemployed persons in the labour force actively seeking jobs.

unstructured interview A research method involving an extended, open-ended interaction between an interviewer and an interviewee.

urban sociology A subfield of sociology that examines social relationships and political and economic structures in the city.

urbanization The process by which an increasing proportion of a population lives in cities rather than in rural areas.

validity In sociological research, the extent to which a study or research instrument accurately measures what it is supposed to measure.

value A collective idea about what is right or wrong, good or bad, and desirable or undesirable in a particular culture.

value contradiction A situation in which values conflict with one another or are mutually exclusive.

variable In sociological research, any concept with measurable traits or characteristics that can change or vary from one person, time, situation, or society to another.

visible minority Refers to an official government category of non-white, non-Caucasian individuals.

wage gap A term used to describe the disparity between women's and men's earnings.

wealth The value of all of a person's or family's economic assets, including income, personal property, and income-producing property.

xenocentrism The belief that the products, styles, or ideas of another society are better than those of one's own culture.

zero population growth The point at which no population increase occurs from year to year.

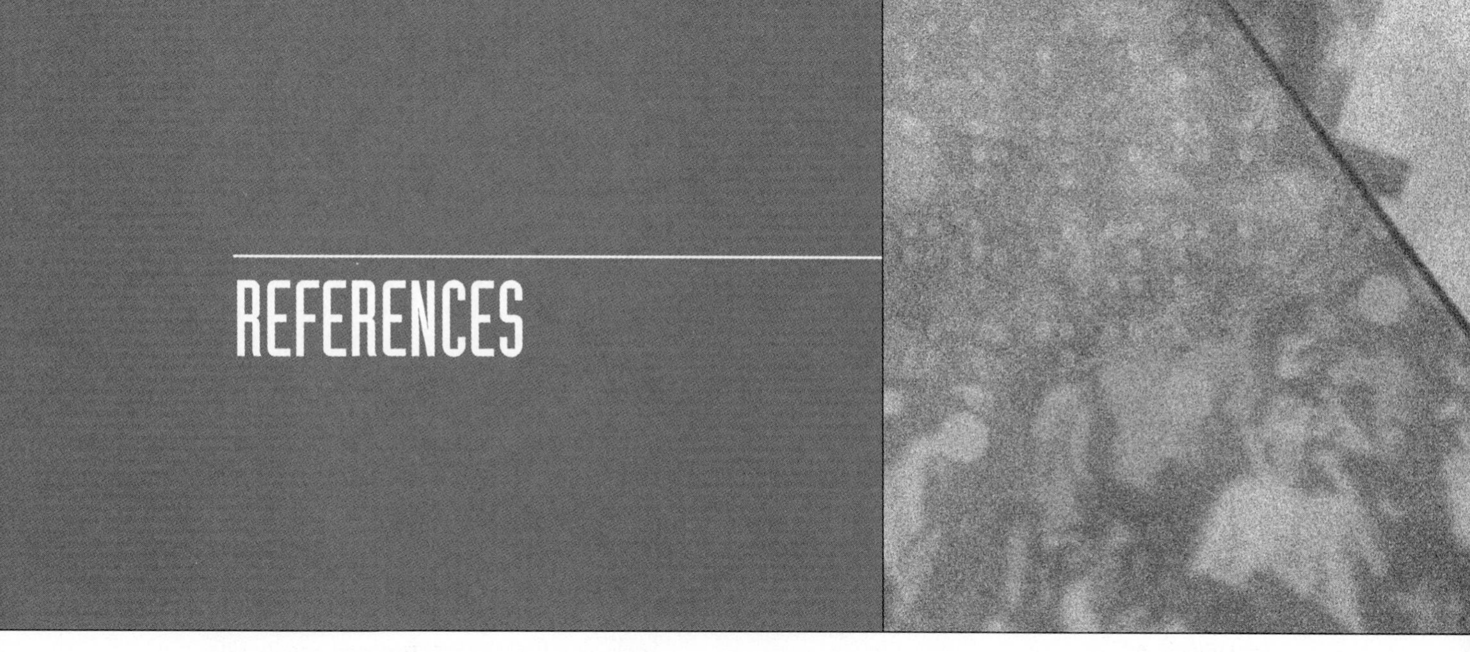

REFERENCES

Abella, Irving. 1974. *On Strike: Six Key Labour Struggles in Canada 1919–1949*. Toronto: James Lewis and Samuel.

Abella, Irving, and Harold Troper. 1982. *None Is Too Many*. Toronto: Lester and Orpen Dennys.

Aberle, David F. 1966. *The Peyote Religion Among the Navaho*. Chicago: Aldine.

Aberle, D. F., A. K. Cohen, A. K. Davis, M. J. Leng, Jr., and F. N. Sutton. 1950. "The Functional Prerequisites of Society." *Ethics*, 60(January):100–111.

Abley, Mark. 1996. "This City Belongs to Us: But It Can Heal or Break Our Hearts." *The Montreal Gazette* (May 4).

Achenbaum, W. Andrew. 1978. *Old Age in the New Land: The American Experience Since 1870*. Baltimore: Johns Hopkins University Press.

Achilles, Rona. 1996. "Assisted Reproduction: The Social Issues." In E.D. Nelson and B.W. Robinson (eds.), *Gender in the 1990s*. Scarborough, Ont.: Nelson Canada, 346–364.

Adams, Owen B. 1990. "Divorce Rates in Canada." In C. McKie and K. Thompson (eds.) *Canadian Social Trends*. Toronto: Thompson Educational Publishing, 146–147.

Adams, Tom. 1991. *Grass Roots: How Ordinary People Are Changing America*. New York: Citadel Press.

Adler, Freda. 1975. *Sisters in Crime: The Rise of the New Female Criminal*. New York: McGraw-Hill.

Adler, Patricia A., and Peter Adler. 1994. *Constructions of Deviance: Social Power, Context, and Interaction*. Belmont, Cal.: Wadsworth.

Adler, Patricia, Steven J. Kless, and Peter Adler. 1995. "Socialization to Gender Roles: Popularity Among Elementary School Boys and Girls." In E.D. Nelson and B.W. Robinson (eds.) *Gender in the 1990s*. Scarborough, Ont.: Nelson, 119–141.

Adorno, Theodor W., Else Frenkel-Brunswick, Daniel J. Levinson, and R. Nevitt Sanford. 1950. *The Authoritarian Personality*. New York: Harper & Row.

Agger, Ben. 1993. *Gender, Culture, and Power: Toward a Feminist Postmodern Critical Theory*. Westport, Conn.: Praeger.

Aiello, John R., and S. E. Jones. 1971. "Field Study of Proxemic Behavior of Young School Children in Three Subcultural Groups." *Journal of Personality and Social Psychology*, 19:351–356.

Albanese, Catherine L. 1992. *America, Religions and Religion*. Belmont, Cal.: Wadsworth.

Albas, Cheryl, and Daniel Albas. 1988. "Emotion Work and Emotion Rules: The Case of Exams." *Qualitative Sociology*, 11(4):259–275.

———. 1989. "Aligning Actions: The Case of Subcultural Proxemics." *Canadian Ethnic Studies*, 21(2):74–81.

Albas, Daniel, and Cheryl Albas. 1988. "Aces and Bombers: The Post-Exam Impression Management Strategies of Students." *Symbolic Interaction*, 11(Fall):289–302.

Albas, Daniel, and Cheryl Mills Albas. 1992. "Love and Marriage." In K. Ishwaran (ed.), *Family and Marriage: Cross-Cultural Perspectives*. Toronto: Thompson Educational Publishing, 127–142.

Albrecht, Gary L. 1992. *The Disability Business: Rehabilitation in America*. Newbury Park, Cal.: Sage.

Alexander, Jeffrey C. 1985. *Neofunctionalism*. Beverly Hills, Cal.: Sage.

Alexander, Peter, and Roger Gill (eds.). 1984. *Utopias*. London: Duckworth.

Alireza, Marianne. 1990. "Lifting the Veil of Tradition." *Austin American-Statesman* (September 23):C1, C7.

Altemeyer, Bob. 1981. *Right-Wing Authoritarianism.* Winnipeg, Manitoba: University of Manitoba Press.

———. 1988. *Enemies of Freedom: Understanding Right-Wing Authoritarianism.* San Francisco: Jossey-Bass.

Altman, Dennis. 1982. *The Homosexualization of America.* Boston: Beacon Press.

Altman, Lawrence K., M.D. 1994. "Infectious Diseases on the Rebound in the U.S., a Report Says." *New York Times* (May 10):B7.

Alwin, Duane, Philip Converse, and Steven Martin. 1985. "Living Arrangements and Social Integration." *Journal of Marriage and the Family,* 47:319–334.

Amdur, Neil. 1994. "Among Female Athletes, Eating Disorders Are on Rise." *New York Times* (August 1):B9.

Aminzade, Ronald. 1973. "Revolution and Collective Political Violence: The Case of the Working Class of Marseille, France, 1830–1871." Working Paper #86, Center for Research on Social Organization. Ann Arbor: University of Michigan, October 1973.

Amott, Teresa. 1993. *Caught in the Crisis: Women and the U.S. Economy Today.* New York: Monthly Review Press.

Amott, Teresa, and Julie Matthaei, 1991. *Race, Gender, and Work: A Multicultural Economic History of Women in the United States.* Boston: South End Press.

Andersen, Margaret L., and Patricia Hill Collins (eds.). 1992. *Race, Class, and Gender: An Anthology.* Belmont, Cal.: Wadsworth.

Anderson, Elijah. 1990. *Streetwise: Race, Class, and Change in an Urban Community.* Chicago: University of Chicago Press.

———. 1994. "The Code of the Streets." *Atlantic Monthly* (May):80–94.

Anderson, Karen. 1996. *Sociology: A Critical Introduction.* Scarborough, Ont.: Nelson Canada.

Angier, Natalie. 1993. "'Stopit!' She Said. 'Nomore!'" *New York Times Book Review* (April 25):12.

Annesi, Nicole. 1993. "Like Mother, Like Daughter." In Leslea Newman (ed.), *Eating Our Hearts Out: Personal Accounts of Women's Relationship to Food.* Freedom, Cal.: Crossing Press, 91–95.

Antonius, Andreas, and Robin Crowley. 1986. "The Ownership Structure of the Largest Canadian Corporations, 1979." *Canadian Journal of Sociology,* 11:253–268.

Applebaum, Eileen R., and Ronald Schettkat. 1989. "Employment and Industrial Restructuring: A Comparison of the U.S. and West Germany." In E. Matzner (ed.), *No Way to Full Employment?* Research Unit Labor Market and Employment, Discussion Paper FSI 89–16 (July):394–448.

Appleton, Lynn M. 1995. "The Gender Regimes in American Cities." In Judith A. Garber and Robyne S. Turner (eds.), *Gender in Urban Research.* Thousand Oaks, Cal.: Sage, 44–59.

Arat-Koc, Sedef. 1995. "The Politics of Family and Immigration in the Subordination of Domestic Workers in Canada." In E.D. Nelson and B.W. Robinson (eds.), *Gender in the 1990s.* Scarborough, Ont.: Nelson, 413–442.

Arendt, Hannah. 1973. *The Origins of Totalitarianism.* New York: Harcourt Brace Jovanovich.

Argyris, Chris. 1960. *Understanding Organizational Behavior.* Homewood, Ill.: Dorsey.

———. 1962. *Interpersonal Competence and Organizational Effectiveness.* Homewood, Ill.: Dorsey.

Armstrong Pat. 1993. "Work and Family Life: Changing Patterns." In G.N. Ramu (ed.), *Marriage and the Family in Canada Today* (2nd ed.). Scarborough, Ont.: Prentice-Hall,127–145.

Armstrong, Pat, and Hugh Armstrong. 1994. *The Double Ghetto: Canadian Women and Their Segregated Work.* Toronto: McClelland and Stewart.

Arnold, Regina A. 1990. "Processes of Victimization and Criminalization of Black Women." *Social Justice,* 17(3):153–166.

Arnup, Katherine. 1995. "We Are Family: Lesbian Mothers in Canada." In E.D. Nelson and B.W. Robinson (eds.), *Gender in the 1990s.* Scarborough, Ont.: Nelson Canada, 330–345.

Asch, Adrienne. 1986. "Will Populism Empower Disabled People?" In Harry G. Boyle and Frank Riessman (eds.), *The New Populism: The Power of Empowerment.* Philadelphia: Temple University Press, 213–228.

Asch, Solomon E. 1955. "Opinions and Social Pressure." *Scientific American,* 193(5):31–35.

———. 1956. "Studies of Independence and Conformity: A Minority of One Against a Unanimous Majority." *Psychological Monographs,* 70(9) (Whole No. 416).

Ashton, Elizabeth. 1982. "Houston's Doctor of Urban Decay." *Texas Business Review* (March):52–53. Quoted in Joe R. Feagin and Robert Parker, Building *American Cities: The Urban Real Estate Game* (2nd ed.). Englewood Cliffs, N.J.: Prentice Hall, 1990, 18-19.

Atchley, Robert C. (ed.). 1994. *Social Forces and Aging.* Belmont, Cal.: Wadsworth.

Aulette, Judy Root. 1994. *Changing Families.* Belmont, Cal.: Wadsworth.

Austin American-Statesman. 1993. "Report: 300 Babies of Rape Victims Abandoned" (January 27):A7.

———. 1994. "River City Currents." (August 13):E1.

———. 1995. "Lawmakers Ask U.S. to Put Cost of Cereals in Check." (March 8):A1, A7.

Axinn, William G., and Arland Thornton. 1992. "The Relationship Between Cohabitation and Divorce: Selectivity or Causal Influence?" *Demography*, 29(3):357–374.

Babbie, Earl. 1992. *The Practice of Social Research* (6th ed.). Belmont, Cal.: Wadsworth.

Backhouse, Constance, Roma Harris, Gillian Mitchell, and Alison Wylie. 1995. "The Chilly Climate for Faculty Women at Western: Postscript to the Backhouse Report." In the Chilly Collective (eds.), *Breaking Anonymity: The Chilly Climate for Women Faculty*. Waterloo, Ont.: Wilfrid Laurier University Press, 118–135.

Baker, Maureen. 1996. "Introduction to Family Studies: Cultural Variations." In M. Baker (ed.), *Families: Changing Trends in Canada*. Toronto: McGraw-Hill Ryerson, 3–32.

Baker, M., and Donna Lero. 1996. "Division of Labour: Paid Work and Family Structure." In Maureen Baker (ed.), *Families: Changing Trends in Canada*. Toronto: McGraw-Hill Ryerson, 78–103.

Baker, Robert. 1993. "'Pricks' and 'Chicks': A Plea for 'Persons.'" In Anne Minas (ed.), *Gender Basics: Feminist Perspectives on Women and Men*. Belmont, Cal.: Wadsworth, 66–68.

Balakrishnan, T.R., K. Vaninadha Rao, Evelyne Lapierre-Adameyk, and Karol J. Krotki. 1987. "A Hazard Model Analysis of the Covariates of Marriage Dissolution in Canada." *Demography*, 24(3): 395–406.

Ballantine, Jeanne H. 1993. *The Sociology of Education: A Systematic Analysis* (3rd ed.). Englewood Cliffs, N.J.: Prentice-Hall.

Baltzell, E. Digby. 1958. *Philadelphia Gentlemen: The Making of a National Upper Class*. New York: Free Press.

———. 1967. "Introduction to the 1967 Edition." In W. E. B. Du Bois, *The Philadelphia Negro: A Social Study*. New York: Schocken Books.

Bandura, Albert. 1973. *Aggression: A Social Learning Analysis*. Englewood Cliffs, N.J.: Prentice-Hall.

———. 1986. *Social Foundations of Thought and Action: A Social Cognition Theory*. Englewood Cliffs, N.J.: Prentice-Hall.

Bane, Mary Jo. 1986. "Household Composition and Poverty: Which Comes First?" In Sheldon H. Danziger and Daniel H. Weinberg (eds.), *Fighting Poverty: What Works and What Doesn't*. Cambridge, Mass.: Harvard University Press.

Banner, Lois W. 1983. *American Beauty*. Chicago: University of Chicago Press.

———. 1993. *In Full Flower: Aging Women, Power, and Sexuality*. New York: Vintage.

Bardwell, Jill R., Samuel W. Cochran, and Sharon Walker. 1986. "Relationship of Parental Education, Race, and Gender to Sex Role Stereotyping in Five-Year-Old Kindergarteners." *Sex Roles*, 15:275–281.

Barer, M.L., R.G. Evans, and C. Hertzman. 1995. *Canadian Journal on Aging*, 14(2):193–224.

Baril, A., and G. Mori. 1991. "Educational Attainment of Linguistic Groups in Canada." *Canadian Social Trends* (Spring) 1991, 17–18.

———. 1993. *In Full Flower: Aging Women, Power, and Sexuality*. New York: Vintage.

Barlow, Hugh D. 1987. *Introduction to Criminology* (4th ed.). Boston: Little, Brown.

Barna, Laray M. 1991. "Stumbling Blocks in Intercultural Communication." In Larry A. Samovar and Richard E. Porter, *Intercultural Communication: A Reader* (6th ed.). Belmont, Cal.: Wadsworth, 345–352.

Barnard, Chester. 1938. *The Functions of the Executive*. Cambridge, Mass.: Harvard University Press.

Baron, Dennis. 1986. *Grammar and Gender*. New Haven, Conn.: Yale University Press.

Baron, Larry, and Murray A. Straus. 1989. *Four Theories of Rape in American Society*. New Haven, Conn.: Yale University Press.

Baron, Stephen. 1994. *Street Youth and Crime: The Role of Labour Market Experiences*. Unpublished Ph.D. diss., University of Alberta.

Barrett, Stanley R. 1987. *Is God a Racist? The Right Wing in Canada*. Toronto: University of Toronto Press.

Barthel, Diane. 1988. *Putting on Appearances: Gender and Advertising*. Philadelphia: Temple University Press.

Basow, Susan A. 1992. *Gender Stereotypes and Roles* (3rd ed.). Pacific Grove, Cal.: Brooks/Cole.

Bates, Stephen. 1994. *Battleground: One Mother's Crusade, the Religious Right, and the Struggle for Our Schools*. New York: Owl/Henry Holt.

Baum, Alice S., and Donald W. Burnes. 1993. *A Nation in Denial: The Truth About Homelessness*. Boulder, Col.: Westview Press.

Baxter, J. 1970. "Interpersonal Spacing in Natural Settings." *Sociology*, 36(3):444–456.

Beaujot, R.P., and Kevin McQuillan. 1982. *Growth and Dualism: The Demographic Development of Canadian Society*. Toronto: Gage.

Beaujot, Roderic. 1991. *Population Change in Canada: The Challenges of Policy Adaptation*. Toronto: McClelland and Stewart.

Beare, Margaret. 1996a. *Criminal Conspiracies: Organized Crime in Canada*. Scarborough, Ont.: Nelson Canada.

———. 1996b. "Organized Crime and Money Laundering." In Robert A. Silverman, James J. Teevan, and Vincent F. Sacco (eds.), *Crime in Canadian Society* (5th ed.). Toronto: Harcourt Brace and Co., 187–245.

Becker, Howard S. 1963. *Outsiders: Studies in the Sociology of Deviance.* New York: Free Press.

Becker, Howard S., Blanche Geer, Everett C. Hughes, and Anselm L. Strauss. 1961. *Boys in White.* Chicago: University of Chicago Press.

Beeghley, Leonard. 1989. *The Structure of Social Stratification in the United States.* Boston: Allyn & Bacon.

———. 1992. *American Stepfamilies.* New Brunswick, N.J.: Transaction.

Beer, William R. 1989. *Strangers in the House: The World of Stepsiblings and Half-Siblings.* New Brunswick, N.J.: Transaction.

Begin, Patricia. 1994. *Child Abuse.* Ottawa: Library of Parliamentary Research.

Belkin, Lisa. 1994. "Kill for Life?" *New York Times Magazine* (October 30):47–51, 62–64, 76, 80.

Bell, Daniel. 1973. *The Coming of Post-Industrial Society: A Venture in Social Forecasting.* New York: Basic Books.

———. 1976. *The Post-Industrial Society: A Venture in Social Forecasting.* New York: Basic Books.

Bell, Inge Powell. 1989. "The Double Standard: Age." In Jo Freeman, *Women: A Feminist Perspective* (4th ed.). Mountain View, Cal.: Mayfield, 236–244.

Bellamy, L., and N. Guppy. 1992. "Opportunities and Obstacles for Women in Canadian Higher Education." In J. Gaskell and A. McLaren (eds.), *Women and Education.* Calgary: Detselig.

Bellan, Ruben. 1978. *Winnipeg First Century: An Economic History.* Winnipeg: Queenston House Publishing.

Belsky, Janet. 1990. *The Psychology of Aging: Theory, Research, and Interventions* (2nd ed.). Pacific Grove, Cal.: Brooks/Cole.

Beneke, Tim. 1982. *Men on Rape.* New York: St. Martin's Press. Quoted in Anna Minas, *Gender Basics: Feminist Perspectives on Women and Men.* Belmont, Cal.: Wadsworth, 1993, 352–358.

Benet, Sula. 1971. "Why They Live to Be 100, or Even Older, in Abkhasia." *The New York Times Magazine* (December 26):3, 28–29, 31–34.

Benokraitis, Nijole V. 1993. *Marriages and Families: Changes, Choices, and Constraints.* Englewood Cliffs, N.J.: Prentice-Hall.

Benokraitis, Nijole V., and Joe R. Feagin. 1986. *Modern Sexism: Blatant, Subtle, and Covert Discrimination.* Englewood Cliffs, N.J.: Prentice-Hall.

Benson, Susan Porter. 1983. "The Customers Ain't God: The Work Culture of Department Store Saleswomen, 1890–1940." In Michael H. Frisch and Daniel J. Walkowitz, *Working Class America: Essays on Labor, Community, and American Society.* Urbana: University of Illinois Press, 185–211.

Berger, Bennett M. 1988. "Utopia and Its Environment." *Society* (January/February):37–41.

Berger, Peter. 1963. *Invitation to Sociology: A Humanistic Perspective.* New York: Anchor.

———. 1967. *The Sacred Canopy: Elements of a Sociological Theory of Religion.* New York: Doubleday.

Berger, Peter, and Hansfried Kellner. 1964. "Marriage and the Construction of Reality." *Diogenes,* 46:1–32.

Berger, Peter, and Thomas Luckmann. 1967. *The Social Construction of Reality: A Treatise in the Sociology of Knowledge.* Garden City, N.Y.: Anchor Books.

Bergmann, Barbara R. 1986. *The Economic Emergence of Women.* New York: Basic Books.

Bernard, Jessie. 1982. *The Future of Marriage.* New Haven, Conn.: Yale University Press (orig. pub. 1973).

———. 1995. "The Good Provider Role: Its Rise and Fall." In E.D. Nelson and B.W. Robinson, *Gender in the 1990s.* Scarborough, Ont.: Nelson Canada, 156–171.

Berry, John W., W. Rudolf Kalin, and Donald M. Taylor. 1977. *Multiculturalism and Ethnic Attitudes in Canada.* Ottawa: Ministry of Supply and Services.

Bettelheim, Bruno. 1959. "Feral Children and Autistic Children." *American Journal of Sociology,* 64:455–467.

Biagi, Shirley. 1994. *Media/Impact: An Introduction to Mass Media* (2nd ed.). Belmont, Cal.: Wadsworth.

Bibby, Reginald W. 1987. *Fragmented Gods: The Poverty and Potential of Religion in Canada.* Toronto: Irwin.

———. 1995. *Mosaic Madness: The Potential and Poverty of Canadian Life.* Toronto: Stoddart.

———. 1996. "Fragmented Gods: Religion in Canada." In R. Brym (ed.), *Sociology in Question: Sociological Readings for the 21st Century.* Toronto: Harcourt Brace, 56–61.

Biblarz, Arturo, R. Michael Brown, Dolores Noonan Biblarz, Mary Pilgrim, and Brent F. Baldree. 1991. "Media Influence on Attitudes Toward Suicide." *Suicide and Life-Threatening Behavior,* 21(4):374–385.

Binder, David. 1993. "As Ethnic Wars Multiply, U.S. Strives for a Policy." *New York Times* (February 7).

———. 1994. "Richard M. Bissell, 84, Is Dead; Helped Plan Bay of Pigs Invasion." *New York Times* (February 10):B10.

Bissoondath, Neil. 1994. *Selling Illusions: The Cult of Multiculturalism in Canada.* Toronto: Penguin.

Bittner, Egon. 1980. *Popular Interests in Psychiatric Remedies: A Study in Social Control.* New York: Ayer.

Blackford, Karen A. 1996. "Families and Parental Disability." In Marion Lynn (ed.), *Voices: Essays on Canadian Families.* Scarborough, Ont.: Nelson Canada, 161–163.

Blau, Judith R. 1984. *Architects and Firms: A Sociological Perspective on Architectural Practice.* Cambridge, Mass.: MIT Press.

Blau, Peter M., and Marshall W. Meyer. 1987. *Bureaucracy in Modern Society* (3rd ed.). New York: Random House.

Blauner, Robert. 1964. *Alienation and Freedom.* Chicago: University of Chicago Press.

———.1972. *Racial Oppression in America.* New York: Harper & Row.

Blinch, Russell. 1995. "Canada Court Upholds Murder Conviction in Mercy Killings." *Reuters* (August 18).

Bluestone, Barry, and Bennett Harrison. 1982. *The Deindustrialization of America.* New York: Basic Books.

Blumberg, Leonard. 1977. "The Ideology of a Therapeutic Social Movement: Alcoholics Anonymous." *Journal of Studies on Alcohol,* 38:2122–2143.

Blumer, Herbert G. 1946. "Collective Behavior." In Alfred McClung Lee (ed.), *A New Outline of the Principles of Sociology.* New York: Barnes & Noble, 167–219.

———. 1969. *Symbolic Interactionism: Perspective and Method.* Englewood Cliffs, N.J.: Prentice-Hall.

———. 1974. "Social Movements." In R. Serge Denisoff (ed.), *The Sociology of Dissent.* New York: Harcourt Brace Jovanovich, 74–90.

Bobet, Ellen. 1994. "Indian Mortality in Canada." In Craig Mckie (ed.), *Social Trends.* Toronto: Thompson Educational Publishing, 57–60.

Bogardus, Emory S. 1925. "Measuring Social Distance." *Journal of Applied Sociology,* 9:299–308.

———. 1968. "Comparing Racial Distance in Ethiopia, South Africa, and the United States." *Sociology and Social Research,* 52(2):149–156.

Bolaria, S. and P. Li. 1988. *Racial Oppression in Canada* (2nd ed.). Toronto: Garamond.

Bolaria, B. Singh, and Rosemary Bolaria. 1994."Inequality and Differential Health Risks of Environmental Degradation." In Bolaria and Bolaria (eds.), *Racial Minorities, Medicine and Health.* Halifax, N.S.: Fernwood, 85–97.

Bologh, Roslyn Wallach. 1992. "The Promise and Failure of Ethnomethodology from a Feminist Perspective: Comment on Rogers." *Gender & Society,* 6(2):199–206.

Bolt, Menno. 1993. *Surviving as Indians: The Challenge of Self-Government.* Toronto: University of Toronto Press.

Bolton, M. Anne. 1995. "Who Can Let You Die?" In Mark Novak (ed.), *Aging in Society: A Canadian Reader.* Scarborough, Ont.: Nelson Canada, 385–392.

Bonacich, Edna. 1972. "A Theory of Ethnic Antagonism: The Split Labor Market." *American Sociological Review,* 37:547–549.

———. 1976. "Advanced Capitalism and Black–White Relations in the United States: A Split Labor Market Interpretation." *American Sociological Review,* 41:34–51.

Bonger, Willem. 1969. *Criminality and Economic Conditions* (abridged ed.). Bloomington: Indiana University Press (orig. pub. 1916).

Bonner, Raymond. 1994. "Ethnic War Lacerates Former Soviet Resort Area." *New York Times* (June 8):A3.

Borchorst, A., and B. Siim. 1987. "Women and the Advanced Welfare State—A New Kind of Patriarchal Power?" In A. Showstack-Sasson (ed.), *Women and the State.* London: Hutchinson, 128–157.

Bordo, Susan. 1993. *Unbearable Weight: Feminism, Western Culture, and the Body.* Berkeley: University of California Press.

Bourdieu, Pierre. 1984. *Distinction: A Social Critique of the Judgement of Taste.* Trans. Richard Nice. Cambridge, Mass.: Harvard University Press.

Bourdieu, Pierre, and Jean-Claude Passeron. 1990. *Reproduction in Education, Society and Culture.* Newbury Park, Cal.: Sage.

Bowker, Lee H. 1980. *Prison Victimization.* New York: Elsevier.

Bowles, Samuel. 1977. "Unequal Education and the Reproduction of the Social Division of Labor." In Jerome Karabel and A. H. Halsey (eds.), *Power and Ideology in Education.* New York: Oxford University Press, 137–153.

Boyd, Monica. 1992. "Gender, Visible Minority Status, and Immigrant Earnings Inequality: Reassessing an Employment Equity Premise." In V. Satzewich (ed.). *Deconstructing a Nation: Immigration, Multiculturalism, and Racism in Canada.* Halifax: Fernwood, 279–322.

———. 1995. "Gender Inequality: Economic and Political Aspects." In Robert J. Brym, *New Sociology: Sociology for the 21st Century.* Toronto, Harcourt Brace and Company.

Boyes, William, and Michael Melvin. 1994. *Economics* (2nd ed.). Boston: Houghton Mifflin.

Bozett, Frederick. 1988. "Gay Fatherhood." In Phyllis Bronstein and Carolyn Pape Cowan (eds.), *Fatherhood Today: Men's Changing Role in the Family.* New York: Wiley, 60–71.

Bradbury, Bettina. 1996. "The Social and Economic Origins of Contemporary Families." In Maureen

Baker (ed.), *Families: Changing Trends in Canada*. Toronto: McGraw-Hill Ryerson, 55–103.

Brand, Dionne. 1991. *No Burden to Carry: Narratives of Black Working Women in Ontario, 1920's to 1950's*. Toronto: Women's Press.

Brand, Pamela A., Esther D. Rothblum, and L. J. Solomon. 1992. "A Comparison of Lesbians, Gay Men, and Heterosexuals on Weight and Restrained Eating." *International Journal of Eating Disorders*, 11:253–259.

Brantingham, Paul J., Shihing Mu, and Aruind Verma. 1995. "Patterns in Canadian Crime." In Margaret A. Jackson and Curt T. Griffiths (eds.), *Canadian Criminology*. Toronto: Harcourt Brace and Company, 187–245.

Braun, Denny. 1991. *The Rich Get Richer: The Rise of Income Inequality in the United States and the World*. Chicago: Nelson-Hall.

Braverman, Harry. 1974. *Labor and Monopoly Capital*. New York: Monthly Review Press.

Breault, K. D. 1986. "Suicide in America: A Test of Durkheim's Theory of Religious and Family Integration, 1933–1980." *American Journal of Sociology*, 92(3): 628–656.

Bridges, Judith S. 1991. "Perceptions of Date and Stranger Rape: A Difference in Sex Role Expectations and Rape-Supportive Beliefs." *Sex Roles*, 24(5/6): 291–308.

Bridges, William. 1994. *Jobshift: How to Prosper in a Workplace Without Jobs*. Reading, Mass.: Addison-Wesley.

Briggs, Sheila. 1987. "Women and Religion." In Beth B. Hess and Myra Marx Ferree (eds.), *Analyzing Gender: A Handbook of Social Science Research*. Newbury Park, Cal.: Sage, 408–441.

Brinson, Susan L. 1992. "The Use and Opposition of Rape Myths in Prime-Time Television Dramas." *Sex Roles*, 27(7/8):359–375.

Brint, Steven. 1994. *In an Age of Experts: The Changing Role of Professionals in Politics and Public Life*. Princeton, N.J.: Princeton University Press.

Brinton, Mary E. 1989. "Gender Stratification in Contemporary Urban Japan." *American Sociological Review*, 54(August):549–564.

Britt, Lory. 1993. "From Shame to Pride: Social Movements and Individual Affect." Paper presented at the 88th Annual Meeting of the American Sociological Association, Miami, August 1993.

Brod, Harry (ed.). 1987. *The Making of Masculinities*. Boston: Allen & Unwin.

Brooke, James. 1993a. "Attack on Brazilian Indians Is Worst Since 1910." *New York Times* (August 21):Y3.

———. 1993b. "Slavery on Rise in Brazil, As Debt Chains Workers." *New York Times* (May 23):3.

Brooks-Gunn, Jeanne. 1986. "The Relationship of Maternal Beliefs About Sex Typing to Maternal and Young Children's Behavior." *Sex Roles*, 14:21–35.

Brown, Robert W. 1954. "Mass Phenomena." In Gardner Lindzey (ed.), *Handbook of Social Psychology*, vol. 2. Reading, Mass.: Addison-Wesley, 833–873.

Brownmiller, Susan. 1975. *Against Our Will: Men, Women and Rape*. New York: Bantam Books.

Brumberg, Joan Jacobs. 1988. *Fasting Girls: The Emergence of Anorexia Nervosa as a Modern Disease*. Cambridge, Mass.: Harvard University Press.

Brunet, Robin. 1993. How to Lose Friends and Influence the Media. *Alberta Report/Western Report* (July, 19):16.

Bryant, Heather. 1990. *The Infertility Dilemma: Reproductive Technologies and Prevention*. Ottawa: Canadian Advisory Council on the Status of Women.

Brym, Robert J. (ed.). 1996. *Society in Question: Sociological Readings for the 21st Century*. Toronto: Harcourt Brace and Company.

Buchignani, Norman. 1991. "Some Comments on the Elimination of Racism in Canada." In Ormond McKague (ed.). *Racism in Canada*. Saskatoon: Fifth House, 199–205.

Buchignani, Norman, Doreen M. Indra, and Ram Srivastiva. 1985. *Continuous Journey: A Social History of South Asians in Canada*. Toronto: McClelland and Stewart.

Bullard, Robert B., and Beverly H. Wright. 1992. "The Quest for Environmental Equity: Mobilizing the African-American Community for Social Change." In Riley E. Dunlap and Angela G. Mertig (eds.), *American Environmentalism: The U.S. Environmental Movement, 1970–1990*. New York: Taylor & Francis, 39–49.

Bumpass, Larry, James E. Sweet, and Andrew J. Cherlin. 1991. "The Role of Cohabitation in Declining Rates of Marriage." *Journal of Marriage and the Family*, 53:913–927.

Bumpass, Larry, James E. Sweet, and Teresa Castro Martin. 1990. "Changing Patterns of Remarriage." *Journal of Marriage and the Family*, 52:747–756.

Burch, Thomas K., and Ashok K. Madan. 1987. *Union Formation and Dissolution: Results from the 1984 Family History Survey*. Ottawa: Statistics Canada.

Burciaga, Jose Antonio. 1993. *Drink Cultura*. Santa Barbara, Cal.: Capra Press.

Burgess, Ernest W. 1925. "The Growth of the City." In Robert E. Park and Ernest W. Burgess (eds.), *The City*. Chicago: University of Chicago Press, 47–62.

Burke, Mary Anne. 1990. "Child Care." In Craig McKie and K. Thompson (eds.) *Canadian Social*

Trends. Toronto: Thompson Educational Publishing Inc.

———, and Susan Crompton, Alison Jones, and Katherine Nessner. 1994. "Caring for Children." In Craig McKie and K. Thompson (eds.), *Canadian Social Trends*, vol. 2. Toronto: Thompson Educational Publishing Inc.

Burnham, Walter Dean. 1983. *Democracy in the Making: American Government and Politics.* Englewood Cliffs, N.J.: Prentice-Hall.

Burns, Tom. 1992. *Erving Goffman.* New York: Routledge.

Burros, Marian. 1994. "Despite Awareness of Risks, More in U.S. Are Getting Fat." *New York Times* (July 17):1, 8.

Busch, Ruth C. 1990. *Family Systems: Comparative Study of the Family.* New York: P. Lang.

Butler, Robert N. 1975. *Why Survive? Being Old in America.* New York: Harper & Row.

———. 1987. "Future Trends." In George L. Maddox, Robert C. Atchley, and Raymond J. Corsini (eds.), *The Encyclopedia of Aging.* New York: Springer, 265–267.

Byrne, John A. 1993. "The Horizontal Corporation: It's About Managing Across, Not Up and Down." *Business Week* (December 20):76–81.

Cable, Sherry, and Charles Cable. 1995. *Environmental Problems, Grassroots Solutions: The Politics of Grassroots Environmental Conflict.* New York: St. Martin's Press.

Cahill, Spencer E. 1986. "Language Practices and Self Definition: The Case of Gender Identity Acquisition." *Sociological Quarterly*, 27(September):295–312.

Calliste, Agnes. 1987. "Sleeping Car Porters in Canada: An Ethically Submerged Split Labour Market." *Canadian Ethnic Studies*, 19:1–20.

———. 1993/94. "Race, Gender, and Canadian Immigration Policy: Blacks from the Carribbean, 1900–1932." *Journal of Canadian Studies*, 28(4):131–148.

Campbell, Anne. 1984. *The Girls in the Gang* (2nd ed.). Cambridge, Mass.: Basil Blackwell.

Canadian Sociology and Anthropology Association. 1994. Statement of Professional Ethics. Canadian Sociology and Anthropology Association.

Cancian, Francesca M. 1987. *Love in America: Gender and Self-Development.* New York: Cambridge University Press.

———. 1990. "The Feminization of Love." In C. Carlson (ed.), *Perspectives on the Family: History, Class, and Feminism.* Belmont, Cal.: Wadsworth, 171–185.

———.1992. "Feminist Science: Methodologies That Challenge Inequality." *Gender & Society*, 6(4):623–642.

Candland, Douglas Keith. 1993. *Feral Children and Clever Animals: Reflections on Human Nature.* New York: Oxford University Press.

Canter, R.J., and S.S. Ageton. 1984. "The Epidemiology of Adolescent Sex-Role Attitudes." *Sex Roles*, 11:657–676.

Cantor, Muriel G. 1980. *Prime-Time Television: Content and Control.* Newbury Park, Cal.: Sage.

———.1987. "Popular Culture and the Portrayal of Women: Content and Control." In Beth B. Hess and Myra Marx Ferree, *Analyzing Gender: A Handbook of Social Science Research.* Newbury Park, Cal.: Sage, 190–214.

Cantor, Muriel G., and Joel M. Cantor. 1992. *Prime-Time Television: Content and Control* (2nd ed.). Newbury Park, Cal.: Sage.

Cantril, Hadley. 1941. *The Psychology of Social Movements.* New York: Wiley.

Capek, Stella M. 1993. "The 'Environmental Justice' Frame: A Conceptual Discussion and Application." *Social Problems*, 40(1):5–23.

Carrier, James G. 1986. *Social Class and the Construction of Inequality in American Education.* New York: Greenwood Press.

Carroll, John B. (ed.). 1956. *Language, Thought, and Reality: Selected Writings of Benjamin Lee Whorf.* Cambridge, Mass.: MIT Press.

Carter, Kevin L. 1993. "Black Women Are Getting a Bad Rap in Popular Culture." *Austin American-Statesman* (October 11):B7.

Cassidy, Margaret L., and Gary R. Lee. 1989. "The Study of Polyandry: A Critique and Synthesis." *Journal of Comparative Family Studies*, 20(1):1–11.

Castles, Stephen. 1995. "Trois Siècles de Dépopulation Amerindienne." In L. Normandeau and V. Piche (eds.), *Les Populations Amerindienne et Inuit du Canada.* Montreal: Presse de l'Université de Montréal.

Castells, Manuel. 1977. *The Urban Question.* London: Edward Arnold (orig. pub. 1972 as *La Question Urbaine*, Paris).

Cavender, Gray. 1995. "Alternative Theory: Labeling and Critical Perspectives." In Joseph F. Sheley (ed.), *Criminology: A Contemporary Handbook* (2nd ed.). Belmont, Cal.: Wadsworth, 349–371.

Celis, William, III. 1993. "Wheelchair Warrior Lays Siege to Schools." *New York Times* (July 28):B7.

———. 1994. "Nations Envied for Schools Share Americans' Worries." *New York Times* (July 13):B4.

Chafetz, Janet Saltzman. 1984. *Sex and Advantage: A Comparative, Macro-Structural Theory of Sex Stratification.* Totowa, N.J.: Rowman & Allanheld.

———. 1989. "Marital Intimacy and Conflict: The Irony of Spousal Equality." In Jo Freeman (ed.), *Women: A Feminist Perspective* (4th ed.). Mountain View, Cal.: Mayfield, 149–156.

Chagnon, Napoleon A. 1988. "Life Histories, Blood Revenge, and Warfare in a Tribal Population." *Science* (February 26):985–992.

———. 1992. *Yanomamo: The Last Days of Eden.* New York: Harcourt Brace Jovanovich (rev. from 4th ed., *Yanomamo: The Fierce People*, by Holt, Rinehart & Winston).

Chalfant, H. Paul, Robert E. Beckley, and C. Eddie Palmer. 1994. *Religion in Contemporary Society* (3rd. ed.). Itasca, Ill.: Peacock.

Chambliss, William J. 1969. *Crime and the Legal Process.* Toronto: McGraw-Hill.

———. 1973. "The Saints and the Roughnecks." *Society*, 11:24–31.

Chandler, Tertius, and Gerald Fox. 1974. *3000 Years of Urban History.* New York: Academic Press.

Chard, Jennifer. 1995. "Factfinder on Crime and the Administration of Justice in Canada." *Juristat*, 15(10). Ottawa: Canadian Centre for Justice Statistics.

Cherlin, Andrew J. 1992. *Marriage, Divorce, Remarriage.* Cambridge, Mass.: Harvard University Press.

Chernin, Kim. 1981. *The Obsession: Reflections on the Tyranny of Slenderness.* New York: Harper & Row.

Chesney-Lind, Meda. 1986. "Women and Crime: The Female Offender." *Signs*, 12:78–96.

———. 1989. "Girls' Crime and Woman's Place: Toward a Feminist Model of Female Delinquency." *Crime and Delinquency*, 35(1):5–29.

Chesney-Lind, Meda, and Noelie Rodriguez. 1983. "Under Lock and Key: A View from the Inside." *The Prison Journal*, 63(2):47–65.

Chidley, Joe. 1995. "Spreading Hate on the Internet." *Maclean's* (May 8):3.

Childe, V. Gordon. 1957. "Civilization, Cities, and Towns." *Antiquity* (March):210–213.

Cho, Sumi K. 1993. "Korean Americans vs. African Americans: Conflict and Construction." In Robert Gooding-Williams (ed.), *Reading Rodney King, Reading Urban Uprising.* New York: Routledge, 196–211.

Chon, Margaret. 1995. "The Truth About Asian Americans." In Russell Jacoby and Naomi Glauberman (eds.), *The Bell Curve Debate: History, Documents, Opinions.* New York: Times Books, 238–240.

Christians, Clifford G.G., Kim B. Rotzoll, and Mark Fackler. 1987. *Media Ethics.* New York: Longman.

Chudacoff, Howard P. 1989. *How Old Are You? Age Consciousness in American Culture.* Princeton, N.J.: Princeton University Press.

Church, Elizabeth. 1996. "Kinship and Stepfamilies." In Marion Lynn (ed.), *Voices: Essays on Canadian Families.* Scarborough, Ont.: Nelson Canada, 81–106.

Church, George J. 1993. "The End Is Near?" *Time* (April 26):32.

Churchill, Ward. 1994. *Indians Are Us? Culture and Genocide in Native North America.* Monroe, Maine: Common Courage Press.

"Citizen's Forum on Canada's Future: Report to the People and Government of Canada." 1991. Ottawa: Privy Council Office.

Clark, L., and D. Lewis. 1977. *Rape: The Price of Coercive Sexuality.* Toronto: The Women's Press.

Clark, S.D. 1942. The Social Development of Canada. New York: AMS Press.

Clarke, Harold D., Jane Jenson, Lawrence LeDuc, John H. Pammett. 1991. *Absent Mandate: The Politics of Discontent in Canada* (2nd ed.). Toronto: Gage.

Clayman, Steven E. 1993. "Booing: The Anatomy of a Disaffiliative Response." *American Sociological Review*, 58(1):110–131.

Clement, Wallace. 1975. *The Canadian Corporate Elite.* Toronto: McClelland and Stewart.

Clines, Francis X. 1993a. "An Unfettered Milken Has Lessons to Teach." *New York Times* (October 16):1, 9.

———. 1993b. "As Gunfire Gets Closer, Fear Comes Home." *New York Times* (December 12):E1, E3.

Cloward, Richard A., and Lloyd E. Ohlin. 1960. *Delinquency and Opportunity: A Theory of Delinquent Gangs.* New York: Free Press.

CNN. 1994. "Both Sides: School Prayer." (November 26).

CNN Headline News. 1993. "United Nations High Commission for Refugees Report" (February 12).

Cock, Jacklyn. 1994. "Women and the Military: Implications for Demilitarization in the 1990s in South Africa." *Gender & Society*, 8(2):152–169.

Cockerham, William C. 1995. *Medical Sociology* (6th ed.). Englewood Cliffs, N.J.: Prentice-Hall.

Cohen, Leah Hager. 1994. *Train Go Sorry: Inside a Deaf World.* Boston: Houghton Mifflin.

Cohen, Marjorie Griffin. 1993. "Capitalist Development, Industrialization, and Women's Work." In Graham S. Lowe and Harvey J. Krahn (eds.), *Work in Canada.* Scarborough, Ont.: Nelson Canada, 142–144.

Colby, David C., and Timothy E. Cook. 1991. "Epidemics and Agendas: The Politics of Nightly News Coverage of AIDS." *Journal of Health Politics, Policy and Law*, 16(2):215–249.

Coleman, Richard P., and Lee Rainwater. 1978. *Social Standing in America: New Dimensions of Class.* New York: Basic Books.

Coles, Gerald. 1987. *The Learning Mystique: A Critical Look at "Learning Disabilities."* New York: Pantheon.

Collier, Peter, and David Horowitz. 1987. *The Fords: An American Epic.* New York: Summit Books.

Collins, Catherine, and Douglas Frantz. 1993. *Teachers: Talking Out of School.* Boston: Little, Brown.

Collins, Patricia Hill. 1989. "The Social Construction of Black Feminist Thought." *Signs,* 14:745–773.

———. 1990. *Black Feminist Thought: Knowledge, Consciousness, and the Politics of Empowerment.* London: HarperCollins Academic.

———. 1991. "The Meaning of Motherhood in Black Culture." In Robert Staples (ed.), *The Black Family: Essays and Studies.* Belmont, Cal.: Wadsworth, 169–178. Orig. pub. in *SAGE: A Scholarly Journal on Black Women,* 4(Fall 1987):3–10.

Collins, Randall. 1971. "A Conflict Theory of Sexual Stratification." *Social Problems,* 19(1):3–21.

———. 1979. *The Credential Society: An Historical Sociology of Education.* New York: Academic Press.

———. 1982. *Sociological Insight: An Introduction to Non-Obvious Sociology.* New York: Oxford University Press.

Collins, Sharon M. 1989. "The Marginalization of Black Executives." *Social Problems,* 36:317–331.

Colombo, John Robert. 1996. *The Canadian Global Almanac: A Book of Facts.* Toronto: Macmillan.

Coltrane, Scott. 1989. "Household Labor and the Routine Production of Gender." *Social Problems,* 36:473–490.

Comack, Elizabeth. 1985. "The Origins of Canadian Drug Legislation: Labelling versus Class Analysis." In Thomas Fleming (ed.), *The New Crinimologies in Canada: State, Crime and Control.* Toronto: Oxford University Press, 65–86.

———. 1996a. "Women and Crime." In R. Linden (ed.), *Criminology: A Canadian Perspective* (3rd ed.). Toronto: Harcourt Brace, 139–175.

———. 1996b. *Women in Trouble.* Halifax: Fernwood Publishing.

Comarow, Murray. 1993. "Are Sociologists Above the Law?" *Chronicle of Higher Education* (December 15):A44.

Comfort, Alex. 1976. "Age Prejudice in America." *Social Policy,* 7(3):3–8.

Condry, Sandra McConnell, John C. Condry, Jr., and Lee Wolfram Pogatshnik. 1983. "Sex Differences: A Study of the Ear of the Beholder." *Sex Roles,* 9:697–704.

Connelly, Patricia M., and Martha MacDonald. 1990. *Women and the Labour Force,* Cat. no. 98-25. Ottawa: Minister of Supply and Services.

Cook, Alice H., Val R. Lorwin, and Arlene Kaplan Daniels. 1992. *The Most Difficult Revolution: Women and Trade Unions.* Ithaca, N.Y.: Cornell University Press.

Cook, Ramsay. 1995. *Canada, Quebec and the Uses of Nationalism* (2nd ed.). Toronto: McClelland and Stewart.

Cook, Sherburn F. 1973. "The Significance of Disease in the Extinction of the New England Indians." *Human Biology,* 45:485–508.

Cook, Shirley J. 1969. "Canadian Narcotics Legislation, 1908–1923. A Conflict Model Interpretation." *Canadian Review of Sociology and Anthropology,* 6(1):36–46.

Cookson, Peter W., Jr., and Caroline Hodges Persell. 1985. *Preparing for Power: America's Elite Boarding Schools.* New York: Basic Books.

Cooley, Charles Horton. 1922. *Human Nature and Social Order.* New York: Scribner (orig. pub. 1902).

———. 1962. *Social Organization.* New York: Schocken Books (orig. pub. 1909).

Coontz, Stephanie. 1992. *The Way We Never Were: American Families and the Nostalgia Trap.* New York: Basic Books.

Copenhaver, Stacey, and Elizabeth Grauerholz. 1991. "Sexual Victimization Among Sorority Women: Exploring the Link Between Sexual Violence and Institutional Practices." *Sex Roles,* 24(1/2):31–41.

Corelli, R. 1996. "Winter of Discontent." *Maclean's* (February 5):46–48.

Corliss, Richard. 1993. "Who's Bad?" *Time* (September 6):54–56.

———. 1995. "Look Who's Talking." *Time* (January 23):22–25.

Corr, Charles A., Clyde M. Nabe, and Donna M. Corr. 1994. *Death and Dying, Life and Living.* Belmont, Cal.: Brooks/Cole.

Corrado, Raymond R. 1996. "Political Crime in Canada." In Rick Linden (ed.), *Criminology: A Canadian Perspective* (3rd ed.). Toronto: Harcourt Brace and Company, 459–493.

Correctional Services of Canada. 1995. *Corrections in Canada: 1994.* Ottawa: Solicitor General of Canada.

Corsaro, William A. 1992. "Interpretive Reproduction in Children's Peer Cultures." *Social Psychology Quarterly,* 55(2):160–177.

Coser, Lewis A. 1956. *The Functions of Social Conflict.* Glencoe, Ill.: Free Press.

Coughlin, Ellen K. 1993. "Author of Noted Study on Black Ghetto Life Returns with a Portrait of Homeless Women." *The Chronicle of Higher Education* (March 31):A7–A8.

Cowgill, Donald O. 1986. *Aging Around the World.* Belmont, Cal.: Wadsworth.

Craig, Steve. 1992. "Considering Men and the Media." In Steve Craig (ed.), *Men, Masculinity, and the Media.* Newbury Park, Cal.: Sage, 1–7.

Crawford, Susan. 1993. "A Wink Here, a Leer There: It's Costly." *New York Times* (March 28):F17.

Crichton, Michael. 1994. *Disclosure*. New York: Knopf.

Crosby, Gary, and Ross Firestone. 1994. *Going My Own Way*. New York: Doubleday. In Jay David (ed.), *The Family Secret: An Anthology*. New York: William Morrow, 229–263.

Cumming, Elaine C., and William E. Henry. 1961. *Growing Old: The Process of Disengagement*. New York: Basic Books.

Currie, Raymond. 1976. "Belonging, Commitment, and Early Socialization in a Western City." In S. Crysdale and L. Wheatcroft (eds.), *Religion in Canadian Society*. Toronto: Macmillan, 462–478.

Currie, Raymond, and John Stackhouse. 1996. "Religious Institutions." In L. Tepperman, J.E. Curtis, and R.J. Richardson (eds.), *Sociology*. Toronto: McGraw-Hill Ryerson, 482–519.

Curtis, Bruce, D.W. Livingston, and Harry Smaller. 1992. *Stacking the Deck: The Streaming of Working Class Kids in Ontario Schools*. Toronto: Our Schools/Our Selves Education Foundation.

Curtis, James E., Edward Grabb, and Neil Guppy (eds.). 1993. *Social Inequality in Canada: Patterns, Problems, Policies* (2nd ed.). Scarborough, Ont.: Prentice Hall.

Curtis, James E., and Ronald D. Lambert. 1994. "Culture." In R. Hagedorn (ed.), *Sociology* (5th ed.). Toronto: Holt Rinehart and Winston, 57–86.

Curtiss, Susan. 1977. *Genie: A Psycholinguistic Study of a Modern Day "Wild Child."* New York: Academic Press.

Cyrus, Virginia. 1993. *Experiencing Race, Class, and Gender in the United States*. Mountain View, Cal.: Mayfield.

Dagg, Alexandra, and Judy Fudge. 1992. "Sewing Pains: Homeworkers in the Garment Trade." *Our Times* (June):22–25.

Dahl, Robert A. 1961. *Who Governs?* New Haven, Conn.: Yale University Press.

Dahrendorf, Ralph. 1959. *Class and Class Conflict in an Industrial Society*. Stanford, Cal.: Stanford University Press.

Daly, Kathleen. 1989. "Neither Conflict nor Labeling nor Paternalism Will Suffice: Intersections of Race, Ethnicity, Gender, and Family in Criminal Court Decisions." *Crime and Delinquency*, 35:136–168.

Daly, Kathleen, and Meda Chesney-Lind. 1988. "Feminism and Criminology." *Justice Quarterly*, 5:497–533.

Daniels, Arlene Kaplan. 1988. *Invisible Careers: Women Civic Leaders from the Volunteer World*. Chicago: University of Chicago Press.

Darley, John M., and Thomas R. Shultz. 1990. "Moral Rules: Their Content and Acquisition." *Annual Review of Psychology*, 41:525–556.

Darnton, John. 1993. "Western Europe Is Ending Its Welcome to Immigrants." *New York Times* (August 10):A1, A6.

Darroch, Gordon. 1995. "Class and Stratification." In Lorne Tepperman, James E. Curtis and R. Richardson (eds.), *The Social World* (3rd ed.). Toronto: McGraw-Hill Ryerson, 267–301.

Das Gupta, Tania. 1995. "Families on Native Peoples, Immigrants, and People of Colour." In Nancy Mandell and Ann Duffy (eds.), *Canadian Families: Diversity, Conflict and Change*. Toronto: Harcourt Brace, 141–174.

David, Jay (ed.). 1994. *The Family Secret: An Anthology*. New York: Morrow.

Davies, James B. 1993. The Distribution of Wealth and Economic Equality. In James E. Curtis et al. (eds.), *Social Inequality in Canada: Patterns, Problems, Policies*. Scarborough, Ont.: Prentice Hall.

Davis, Angela Y. 1981. *Women, Race and Class*. New York: Vintage Books.

Davis, F. James. 1991. *Who Is Black?* University Park: Pennsylvania State University Press.

Davis, Fred. 1992. *Fashion, Culture, and Identity*. Chicago: University of Chicago Press.

Davis, Kingsley. 1940. "Extreme Social Isolation of a Child." *American Journal of Sociology*, 45(4):554–565.

———. 1949. *Human Society*. New York: Macmillan.

———. 1955. "Malthus and the Theory of Population." In Paul Lazarsfeld and M. Rosenberg (eds.), *The Language of Social Research*. New York: Free Press, 540–553.

Davis, Kingsley, and Judith Blake. 1956. "Social Structure and Fertility: An Analytical Framework." *Economic Development and Cultural Change*, 4(April):211–235.

Dean, L.M., F.N. Willis, and J.N. la Rocco. 1976. "Invasion of Personal Space as a Function of Age, Sex and Race." *Psychological Reports*, 38(3) (pt. 1):959–965.

Deaux, Kay, and Mary E. Kite. 1987. "Thinking About Gender." In Beth B. Hess and Myra Marx Ferree (eds.), *Analyzing Gender: A Handbook of Social Science Research*. Newbury Park, Cal.: Sage, 92–117.

Deegan, Mary Jo. 1988. *Jane Addams and the Men of the Chicago School, 1892–1918*. New Brunswick, N.J.: Transaction.

DeKeseredy, Walter S. 1988. *Woman Abuse in Dating Relationships: The Role of Male Peer Support*. Toronto: Canadian Scholar's Press.

———. 1996. "Patterns of Family Violence." In Maureen Baker (ed.), *Families: Changing Trends in Canada*. Whitby, Ont.: McGraw-Hill Ryerson, 249–272.

DeKeseredy, Walter S., and Ronald Hinch. 1991. *Woman Abuse: Sociological Perspectives*. Toronto: Thompson Educational Publishing.

DeKeseredy, Walter S., and Katherine Kelly. 1993a. "Woman Abuse in University and College Dating Relationships: The Contribution of the Ideology of Familial Patriarchy." *Journal of Human Justice*, 4(2): 25–52.

———. 1993b. "The Incidence and Prevalence of Woman Abuse in Canada." *Canadian Journal of Sociology*, 18(2): 137–159.

———. 1995. "Sexual Abuse in Canadian University and College Dating Relationships: The Contribution of Male Peer Support." *Journal of Family Violence*, 10 (1):41–53.

Delmar, Rosalind. 1986. "What Is Feminism?" In Juliet Mitchell and Ann Oakley (eds.), *What Is Feminism?* New York: Pantheon, 8–33.

Denton, Margaret A., and Alfred A. Hunter. 1995. "What Is Sociology?" In Lorne Tepperman and R.J. Richardson (eds.). *The Social World* (3rd ed.). Toronto: McGraw-Hill Ryerson, 1–32.

Denzin, Norman K. 1989. *The Research Act* (3rd ed.). Englewood Cliffs, N.J.: Prentice-Hall.

Derber, Charles. 1983. *The Pursuit of Attention: Power and Individualism in Everyday Life*. New York: Oxford University Press.

Desai, Sabra. 1994. "But You Are Different: In Conversation with a Friend." In Carl E. James and Andrew Shadd (eds.), *Talking About a Difference*. Toronto: Between the Lines, 191–198.

Devereaux, Mary Sue. 1994. "Aging of the Canadian Population." In Craig McKie (ed.), *Canadian Social Trends*. Toronto: Thompson Educational Publishing Company, 3–7.

DeVries, John. 1990. "Language and Ethnicity: Canadian Aspects." In Peter Li, *Race and Ethnic Relations in Canada*. Toronto: Oxford University Press, 231–250.

Dickason, Olive. 1992. *Canada's First Nations*. Toronto: McClelland and Stewart.

Didion, Joan. 1993. "Trouble in Lakewood." *The New Yorker* (July 26):46–65.

DiMaggio, Paul. 1987. "Classification in Art." *American Sociological Review*, 52:440–455.

DiMaggio, Paul, and Michael Useem. 1978. "Social Class and Arts Consumption: The Origins and Consequences of Class Differences in Exposure to the Arts in America." *Theory and Society*, 5(2):141–161.

Dobash, Rebecca Emerson, and Russell Dobash. 1992. *Women, Violence and Social Change*. London: Routledge.

Dollard, John, Neal E. Miller, Leonard W. Doob, O. H. Mowrer, and Robert R. Sears. 1939. *Frustration and Aggression*. New Haven, Conn.: Yale University Press.

Domhoff, G. William. 1970. *The Higher Circles*. New York: Random House.

———. 1978. *The Powers That Be: Processes of Ruling Class Domination in America*. New York: Random House.

———. 1983. *Who Rules America Now? A View for the '80s*. Englewood Cliffs, N.J.: Prentice-Hall.

———. 1990. *The Power Elite and the State: How Policy Is Made in America*. New York: Aldine De Gruyter.

Donovan, Josephine. 1992. *Feminist Theory: The Intellectual Traditions of American Feminism—New Expanded Edition*. New York: Continuum (orig. pub. 1985).

Doob, Anthony, and Julian V. Roberts. 1983. *An Analysis of the Public's View of Sentencing*. Ottawa: Department of Justice Canada.

Dowling, Colette. 1981. *The Cinderella Complex: Women's Hidden Fear of Independence*. New York: Summit Books.

Driedger, Leo. 1977. "Identity and Social Distance: Towards Understanding Simmel's 'The Stranger.'" *Canadian Review of Sociology and Anthropology*, 14:158–73.

———. 1982. "Attitudes of Winnipeg University Students Towards Immigrants of European and Non-European Origin." *Prairie Forum*, vol. 2:213–225.

———. 1994. "Ethnic and Minority Relations." In R. Hagedorn (ed.), *Sociology*, Toronto: Harcourt Brace and Company, 299–332.

———. 1996. *Multi-Ethnic Canada: Identities and Inequalities*. Toronto: Oxford University Press

Driedger, Leo, and Richard A. Mezoff. 1981. "Ethnic Prejudice and Discrimination in Winnipeg High Schools." *Canadian Journal of Sociology*, 6(1):1–17.

Driedger, Leo, and Neena L. Chappell. 1987. *Aging and Ethnicity: Toward an Interface*. Toronto: Butterworths.

Drohan, Madelaine. 1996. "London Traffic Trapped in Carriage Days." *The Globe and Mail* (June 5):A8.

Drozdiak, William. 1993. "Serb Forces Raped 20,000 in Bosnia, Panel Says." *Austin American-Statesman* (January 10):A3.

Du Bois, W.E.B. 1967. *The Philadelphia Negro: A Social Study*. New York: Schocken Books (orig. pub. 1899).

Dubowitz, Howard, Maureen Black, Raymond H. Starr, Jr., and Susan Zuravin. 1993. "A Conceptual Definition of Child Neglect." *Criminal Justice and Behavior*, 20(1):8–26.

Duff, Robert W., and Lawrence K. Hong. 1984. "Self-Images of Women Bodybuilders." *Sociology of Sport Journal*, 2:374–380.

Duffy, Ann, and Nancy Mandell. 1996. "Poverty in Canada." In Robert J. Brym (ed.), *Society in Question: Sociological Readings for the 21st Century.* Toronto: Harcourt Brace and Company, 96–104.

Duffy, Mike. 1992. "How Life Should Be? TV's Families, Then and Now, Reflect the Ideals of a Society." *Austin American-Statesman* (October 25):5.

Dumas, Jean. 1990. *Report on the Demographic Situation in Canada, 1988.* Cat. no. 91-209. Ottawa: Statistics Canada.

Dunlap, Riley E. 1992. "Trends in Public Opinion Toward Environmental Issues: 1965–1990." In Riley E. Dunlap and Angela G. Mertig (eds.), *American Environmentalism: The U.S. Environmental Movement, 1970–1990.* New York: Taylor & Francis, 89–113.

Durkheim, Emile. 1933. *Division of Labor in Society.* Trans. George Simpson. New York: Free Press (orig. pub. 1893).

———. 1947. *The Elementary Forms of the Religious Life.* New York: Free Press (orig. pub. 1912).

———. 1956. *Education and Sociology.* Trans. Sherwood D. Fox. Glencoe, Ill.: Free Press.

———. 1964a. *The Rules of Sociological Method.* Trans. Sarah A. Solovay and John H. Mueller. New York: Free Press (orig. pub. 1895).

———. 1964b. *Suicide.* Trans. John A. Sparkling and George Simpson. New York: Free Press (orig. pub. 1897).

Durrant, Joan, and Linda Rose-Krasnor. 1995. *Corporal Punishment: Research and Policy Recommendations.* Ottawa: Family Violence Prevention Division of Health Canada and the Department of Justice.

Dworkin, Andrea. 1974. *Woman Hating.* New York: Dutton.

Dyck, Rand. 1996. *Canadian Politics: Critical Approaches* (2nd ed.). Scarborough, Ont.: Nelson Canada.

Dye, Thomas R. 1990. *Who's Running America?* (5th ed.). Englewood Cliffs, N.J.: Prentice-Hall.

Dye, Thomas R., and Harmon Zeigler. 1993. *The Irony of Democracy: An Uncommon Introduction to American Politics* (9th ed.). Belmont, Cal.: Wadsworth.

Ebaugh, Helen Rose Fuchs. 1988. *Becoming an EX: The Process of Role Exit.* Chicago: University of Chicago Press.

Eccles, Jacquelynne S., Janis E. Jacobs, and Rena D. Harold. 1990. "Gender Role Stereotypes, Expectancy Effects, and Parents' Socialization of Gender Difference." *Journal of Social Issues,* 46:183–201.

Economic Council of Canada. 1991. *New Faces in the Crowd: Economic and Social Impacts, Immigration.* Ottawa:Economic Council of Canada.

———. 1992. *The New Face of Poverty: Income Security Needs of Canadian Families.* Ottawa: Ministry of Supply and Services.

Eder, Donna. 1985. "The Cycle of Popularity: Interpersonal Relations Among Female Adolescents." *Sociology of Education,* 58(July):154–165.

Eder, Donna, and Stephen Parker. 1987. "The Cultural Production and Reproduction of Gender: The Effect of Extracurricular Activities on Peer Group Culture." *Sociology of Education,* 60:200–213.

Edsall, Thomas Byrne, with Mary D. Edsall. 1992. *Chain Reaction: The Impact of Race, Rights, and Taxes on American Politics.* New York: Norton.

Edwards, Richard. 1979. *Contested Terrain.* New York: Basic Books.

———. 1993. "An Education in Interviewing." In C.M. Renzetti and R.M. Lee (eds.), *Researching Sensitive Topics.* Newbury Park: Sage, 181–196.

Ehrenreich, Barbara. 1989. *Fear of Falling: The Inner Life of the Middle Class.* New York: HarperPerennial.

Ehrenreich, Barbara, and Annette Fuentes. 1981. "Life on the Global Assembly." *Ms.* (January):52–59.

Ehrlich, Paul R. 1971. *The Population Bomb* (2nd ed.). New York: Sierra Club/Ballantine Books.

Ehrlich, Paul R., and Anne H. Ehrlich. 1991. *The Population Explosion.* New York: Touchstone/Simon & Schuster.

Eichler, Margrit. 1988a. *Families in Canada Today* (2nd ed.). Toronto: Gage.

———. 1988b. *Nonsexist Research Methods: A Practical Guide.* Boston: Allen & Unwin.

———. 1996. "The Impact of New Reproductive and Genetic Technologies on Families." In Maureen Baker (ed.), *Familes: Changing Trends in Canada.* Toronto: McGraw-Hill Ryerson, 104–108.

Eichler, Margrit, and Jeanne Lapointe. 1985. *On the Treatment of the Sexes in Research.* Ottawa: Social Sciences and Humanities Research Council of Canada.

Eisenstein, Zillah R. 1994. *The Color of Gender: Reimaging Democracy.* Berkeley: University of California Press.

Eitzen, D. Stanley, and George H. Sage. 1993. *The Sociology of North American Sport* (5th ed.). Dubuque, Iowa: Brown.

Eitzen, D. Stanley, and Maxine Baca Zinn. 1994. *Social Problems* (6th ed.). Boston: Allyn & Bacon.

———. 1995. *In Conflict and Order: Understanding Society* (7th ed.). Boston: Allyn & Bacon.

Elkin, Frederick, and Gerald Handel. 1989. *The Child and Society: The Process of Socialization* (5th ed.). New York: Random House.

Elliot, Jean Leonard, and Augie Fleras. 1990. "Immigration and the Canadian Ethnic Mosaic." In Peter Li (ed.), *Race and Ethnic Relations in Canada.* Toronto: Oxford University Press.

Elliott, Stuart. 1993. "Advertising: The Homeless Give an Anthem New Meaning for the Holidays." *New York Times* (December 24):C14.

Engels, Friedrich. 1972. *The Origins of the Family, Private Property, and the States.* Ed. Eleanor Burke Leacock. New York: International.

Epstein, Cynthia Fuchs. 1988. *Deceptive Distinctions: Sex, Gender, and the Social Order.* New Haven, Conn.: Yale University Press.

Epstein, Ethan B. 1996. "Workers and the World Economy." *Foreign Affairs,* 75(May/June):16–37.

Epstein, Rachel. 1996. "Lesbian Families." In Marion Lynn (ed.), *Voices: Essays on Canadian Families.* Scarborough, Ont.: Nelson Canada, 109–130.

Erikson, Eric H. 1963. *Childhood and Society.* New York: Norton.

———. 1968. *Identity: Youth and Crisis.* New York: Norton.

———. 1980. *Identity and the Life Cycle.* New York: Norton (orig. pub. 1959).

Erikson, Kai T. 1962. "Notes on the Sociology of Deviance." *Social Problems,* 9:307–314.

———. 1976. *Everything in Its Path: Destruction of Community in the Buffalo Creek Flood.* New York: Simon & Schuster.

———. 1991. "A New Species of Trouble." In Stephen Robert Couch and J. Stephen Kroll-Smith (eds.), *Communities at Risk: Collective Responses to Technological Hazards.* New York: Peter Land, 11–29.

———. 1994. *A New Species of Trouble: Explorations in Disaster, Trauma, and Community.* New York: Norton.

Eron, Leonard. 1987. "The Development of Aggressive Behavior from the Perspective of a Developing Behaviorism." *American Psychologist,* 42:435–442.

Esbensen, Finn-Aage, and David Huizinga. 1993. "Gangs, Drugs, and Delinquency in a Survey of Urban Youth." *Criminology,* 31(4):565–589.

Essed, Philomena. 1991. *Understanding Everyday Racism.* Newbury Park, Cal.: Sage.

Etzioni, Amitai. 1975. *A Comparative Analysis of Complex Organizations: On Power, Involvement, and Their Correlates* (rev. ed.). New York: Free Press.

———. 1994. *The Spirit of Community: The Reinvention of American Society.* New York: Touchstone.

Evans, Glen, and Norman L. Farberow. 1988. *The Encyclopedia of Suicide.* New York: Facts on File.

Evans, John, and Alexander Himelfarb. 1996. "Counting Crime." In Rick Linden (ed.), *Criminology: A Canadian Perspective* (3rd ed.). Toronto: Harcourt Brace and Company, 61–94.

Eyre, Linda. 1992. "Gender Relations in the Classroom: A Fresh Look at Coeducation." J. Gaskell and A. McLaren (eds.), *Women and Education.* Calgary: Detselig.

Fabes, Richard A., and Carol L. Martin. 1991. "Gender and Age Stereotypes of Emotionality." *Personality and Social Psychology Bulletin,* 17:532–540.

Fagot, Beverly I. 1984. "Teacher and Peer Reactions to Boys' and Girls' Play Styles." *Sex Roles,* 11:691–702.

Fallon, Patricia, Melanie A. Katzman, and Susan C. Wooley. 1994. *Feminist Perspectives on Eating Disorders.* New York: Guilford Press.

Faludi, Susan. 1991. *Backlash: The Undeclared War Against American Women.* New York: Crown.

Farb, Peter. 1973. *Word Play: What Happens When People Talk.* New York: Knopf.

Faris, Robert E.L. 1967. *Chicago Sociology: 1920–32.* San Francisco: Chandler.

Farley, Christopher John. 1993a. "Today Los Angeles, Tomorrow ... " *Time* (July 26):49.

———. 1993b. "Without a Prayer: The Debate over Religion in Public Schools is Born Again in Mississippi." *Time* (December 20):41.

Fausto-Sterling, Anne. 1985. *Myths of Gender: Biological Theories About Women and Men.* New York: Basic Books.

Feagin, Joe R. 1991. "The Continuing Significance of Race: Antiblack Discrimination in Public Places." *American Sociological Review,* 56(February):101–116.

Feagin, Joe R., and Stella Capek. 1991. "Grassroots Movements in a Class Perspective." *Research in Political Sociology,* 5:27–53.

Feagin, Joe R., and Clairece Booher Feagin. 1978. *Discrimination American Style: Institutional Racism and Sexism.* Englewood Cliffs, N.J.: Prentice-Hall.

———. 1986. *Social Problems: A Critical Power-Conflict Perspective* (3rd ed.). Englewood Cliffs, N.J.: Prentice-Hall.

———. 1993. *Racial and Ethnic Relations* (4th ed.). Englewood Cliffs, N.J.: Prentice-Hall.

———. 1994. *Social Problems: A Critical Power-Conflict Perspective* (4th ed.). Englewood Cliffs, N.J.: Prentice-Hall.

Feagin, Joe R., Anthony M. Orum, and Gideon Sjoberg (eds.). 1991. *A Case for the Case Study.* Chapel Hill: University of North Carolina Press.

Feagin, Joe R., and Robert Parker. 1990. *Building American Cities: The Urban Real Estate Game* (2nd ed.). Englewood Cliffs, N.J.: Prentice-Hall.

Feagin, Joe R., and Melvin P. Sikes. 1994. *Living with Racism: The Black Middle-Class Experience.* Boston: Beacon Press.

Feagin, Joe R., and Hernan Vera. 1995. *White Racism: The Basics.* New York: Routledge.

Featherstone, Mike (ed.). 1990. *Global Culture: Nationalism, Globalization and Modernity.* Newbury Park, Cal.: Sage.

Federal Bureau of Investigation (FBI). 1992. *Crime in the United States, 1991.* Washington, D.C.: U.S. Government Printing Office.

———. 1994. *Crime in the United States, 1992.* Washington, D.C.: U.S. Government Printing Office.

Fedorowycz, Orest. 1996. "Homicide in Canada, 1995." *Juristat*, vol. 16(11). Ottawa: Canadian Centre for Justice Statistics.

Fennell, Tom. 1993. "What's Wrong at School?" *Maclean's* (January 11):28–34.

———. 1995. "The Mercy-Killing Debate." *Maclean's* (January 16):16.

Fennema, Elizabeth, and Gilah C. Leder (eds.). 1990. *Mathematics and Gender.* New York: Teachers College Press.

Ferrante, Joan. 1995. *Sociology: A Global Perspective* (2nd ed.). Belmont, Cal.: Wadsworth.

Ferree, Myra Marx, and Elaine J. Hall. 1990. "Visual Images in American Society: Gender and Race in Introductory Sociology Textbooks." *Gender & Society*, 4(4):500–533.

Festinger, Leon, A. Pepitone, and T. Newcomb. 1952. "Some Consequences of Deindividuation in a Group." *Journal of Abnormal and Social Psychology*, 47:382–389.

Fine, Michelle. 1987. "Silencing and Nurturing Voice in an Improbable Context: Urban Adolescents in Public Schools." In Henry A. Giroux and Peter McLaren (eds.), *Schooling and the Politics of Culture.* Albany: SUNY Press.

———. 1989. "Coping with Rape: Critical Perspectives on Consciousness." In Rhoda Kesler Unger (ed.), *Representations: Social Constructions of Gender.* Amityville, N.Y.: Baywood, 186–200.

Finn Paradis, Lenora, and Scott B. Cummings. 1986. "The Evolution of Hospice in America Toward Organizational Homogeneity." *Journal of Health and Social Behavior*, 27:370–386.

Finnie, R. 1993. "Women, Men and the Economic Consequences of Divorce: Evidence from Canadian Longitudinal Data." *Canadian Review of Sociology and Anthropology*, 30(2):204–241.

Firestone, Shulamith. 1970. *The Dialectic of Sex.* New York: Morrow.

Fischer, Claude S. 1976. *The Urban Experience.* New York: Harcourt Brace Jovanovich.

Fisher, Anne B. 1992. "The New Debate Over the Very Rich." *Fortune* (June 29):42–54.

Fisher, Luke. 1994. "A Holy War Over Holidays." *Maclean's* (August 12):26.

Fisher, Mary. 1993. "Tap Moral Courage to Mold Opinions." *Masthead*, 45(3):27–30.

Fisher-Thompson, Donna. 1990. "Adult Sex-Typing of Children's Toys." *Sex Roles*, 23:291–303.

Fiske, Jo-anne, and Rose Johnny. 1996. "The Nedut'en Family: Yesterday and Today." In Marion Lynn (ed.), *Voices: Essays on Canadian Families.* Scarborough, Ont.: Nelson Canada, 217–224.

Fjellman, Stephen M. 1992. *Vinyl Leaves: Walt Disney World & America.* Boulder, Col.: Westview.

Flanagan, William G. 1995. *Urban Sociology: Images and Structure* (2nd ed.). Needham Heights, Mass.: Allyn & Bacon.

Fleras, Augie, and Jean Leonard Elliot. 1996. *Unequal Relations: An Introduction to Race, Ethnic and Aboriginal Dynamics in Canada* (2nd ed.). Scarborough, Ont.: Prentice Hall.

Fleras, Augie, and Jean Leonard Elliott. 1992. *Multiculturalism in Canada.* Scarborough, Ont.: Nelson.

Florida, Richard, and Martin Kenney. 1991. "Transplanted Organizations: The Transfer of Japanese Industrial Organization to the U.S." *American Sociological Review*, 56(3):381–398.

Fontana, Vincent J. 1991. *Save the Family, Save the Child: Inside Child Abuse Today.* New York: Dutton.

Forbes. 1993. "The Forbes Five Hundred" (April 26):151.

———. 1994. "The Forbes Four Hundred" (October 17): 102–325.

Forcese, Dennis. 1986. *The Canadian Class Structure.* Toronto: McGraw-Hill Ryerson.

Ford, Clyde W. 1994. *We Can All Get Along: 50 Steps You Can Take to Help End Racism.* New York: Dell.

Fox, John, and Michael Ornstein. 1986. "The Canadian State and Corporate Elites in the Post-War Period." *Canadian Review of Sociology and Anthropology*, 23:481–506.

Frankl, Razelle. 1987. *Televangelism: The Marketing of Popular Religion.* Carbondale: Southern Illinois University Press.

Fraser, Sylvia. 1987. *My Father's House: A Memoir of Incest and Healing.* Toronto: Doubleday.

Freedman, Lisa. 1985. "Wife Assault." In Connie Bugerman and Margie Wolfe (eds.), *No Safe Place: Violence Against Women and Children.* Toronto: Women's Press, 41–59.

Freidson, Eliot. 1965. "Disability as Social Deviance." In Marvin B. Sussman (ed.), *Sociology and Rehabilitation.* Washington, D.C.: American Sociological Association, 71–99.

———. 1970. *Profession of Medicine.* New York: Dodd, Mead.

———. 1986. *Professional Powers.* Chicago: University of Chicago Press.

Freudenberg, Nicholas, and Carl Steinsapir. 1992. "Not in Our Backyards: The Grassroots Environmental Movement." In Riley Dunlap and Angela G. Mertig (eds.), *American Environmentalism: The U.S. Environmental Movement, 1970–1990.* New York: Taylor and Francis, 27–37.

Frideres, James S. 1993. *Native Peoples in Canada: Contemporary Conflicts* (4th ed.). Scarborough, Ont.: Prentice Hall.

Friedan, Betty. 1993. *The Fountain of Age.* New York: Simon & Schuster.

Frisbie, W. Parker, and John D. Kasarda. 1988. "Spatial Processes." In Neil Smelser (ed.), *The Handbook of Sociology.* Newbury Park, Cal.: Sage, 629–666.

Fulton, E. Kaye, and Ian Mather. 1993. "A Forest Fable." *Maclean's* (August 16):20.

Gabor, Thomas. 1994. *Everybody Does It: Crime by the Public.* Toronto: University of Toronto Press.

Gailey, Christine Ward. 1987. "Evolutionary Perspectives on Gender Hierarchy." In Beth B. Hess and Myra Marx Ferree (eds.), *Analyzing Gender: A Handbook of Social Science Research.* Newbury Park, Cal.: Sage, 32–67.

Gallagher, John. 1994. "On Shaky Ground." *The Advocate* (November 29):36–38.

Garcia Coll, Cynthia T. 1990. "A Message to a Future Child About the Danger of Gangs." *Austin American-Statesman* (August 17):A6.

Gaskell, Jane. 1994. "Education." In R. Hagedorn (ed.), *Sociology.* Toronto: Harcourt Brace and Company, 469–495.

Gaskell, Jane S., and Arlene Tigar McLaren (eds.). 1987. *Women and Education: A Canadian Perspective.* Calgary: Detselig.

Gaskell, Jane, Arlene McLaren, and Myra Novogrodsky. 1995. "What Is Worth Knowing? Defining the Feminist Curriculum." In E.D. Nelson and B.W. Robinson (eds.), *Gender in the 1990s.* Scarborough, Ont.: Nelson 100–118.

Gamson, William. 1990. *The Strategy of Social Protest* (2nd ed.). Belmont, Cal.: Wadsworth.

Gans, Herbert. 1974. *Popular Culture and High Culture: An Analysis and Evaluation of Tastes.* New York: Basic Books.

———. 1982. *The Urban Villagers: Group and Class in the Life of Italian Americans* (updated and expanded ed.; orig. pub. 1962). New York: Free Press.

Garber, Judith A., and Robyne S. Turner. 1995. "Introduction." In Judith A. Garber and Robyne S. Turner (eds.), *Gender in Urban Research.* Thousand Oaks, Cal.: Sage, x–xxvi.

Gardner, Carol Brooks. 1989. "Analyzing Gender in Public Places: Rethinking Goffman's Vision of Everyday Life." *American Sociologist,* 20(Spring):42–56.

Garfinkel, Harold. 1967. *Studies in Ethnomethodology.* Englewood Cliffs, N.J.: Prentice-Hall.

Garson, Barbara. 1989. *The Electronic Sweatshop: How Computers Are Transforming the Office of the Future into the Factory of the Past.* New York: Penguin.

Gaylin, Willard. 1992. *The Male Ego.* New York: Viking/Penguin.

Gee, Ellen M. 1994. "What Is Family?" In R. Hagedorn (ed.), *Sociology.* Toronto: Harcourt Brace, 369–398.

———. 1995. "Contemporary Diversities." In Nancy Mandell and Ann Duffy (eds.), *Canadian Families: Diversity, Conflict and Change.* Toronto: Harcourt Brace and Company, 79–109.

Geertz, Clifford. 1966. "Religion as a Cultural System." In Michael Banton (ed.), *Anthropological Approaches to the Study of Religion.* London: Tavistock, 1–46.

Gelfand, Donald E. 1994. *Aging and Ethnicity: Knowledge and Services.* New York: Springer.

Gelles, Richard J., and Murray A. Straus. 1988. *Intimate Violence: The Definitive Study of the Causes and Consequences of Abuse in the American Family.* New York: Simon & Schuster.

Gelman, David. 1993. "The Violence in Our Heads." *Newsweek* (August 2):48.

"General Facts on Sweden." 1988. *Fact Sheets on Sweden.* Stockholm: The Swedish Institute.

Gerber, Linda. 1990. "Multiple Jeopardy: A Socio-Economic Comparison of Men and Women Among the Indian, Métis, and Inuit Peoples of Canada." *Canadian Ethnic Studies,* 22(3):22–34.

Gerbner, George, Larry Gross, Michael Morton, and Nancy Signorielli. 1987. "Charting the Mainstream: Television's Contributions to Political Orientations." In Donald Lazere (ed.), *American Media and Mass Culture: Left Perspectives.* Berkeley: University of California Press, 441–464.

Gerson, Kathleen. 1993. *No Man's Land: Men's Changing Commitment to Family and Work.* New York: Basic Books.

Gerstel, Naomi, and Harriet Engel Gross. 1995. "Gender and Families in the United States: The Reality of Economic Dependence." In Jo Freeman (ed.), *Women: A Feminist Perspective* (5th ed.). Mountain View, Cal.: Mayfield, 92–127.

Ghosh, Ratna, and Rabindra Kanungo. 1992. *South Asian Canadians: Current Issues in the Politics of Culture.* Montreal: Shastri Indo-Canadian Institute.

Gibbs, Lois Marie, as told to Murray Levine. 1982. *Love Canal: My Story.* Albany: SUNY Press.

Gibbs, Nancy. 1994. "Home Sweet School." *Time* (October 31):62–63.

Gilbert, Dennis, and Joseph A. Kahl. 1993. *The American Class Structure: A New Synthesis* (4th ed.). Belmont, Cal.: Wadsworth.

Gilbert, S.N. 1989. "The Forgotten Purpose and Future of University Education." *Canadian Journal of Community Mental Health*, 8(2):103–122.

Gilbert, S.N. and B. Orok. 1993. "School Leavers." In *Canadian Social Trends*, Cat no. 11–008E. Ottawa: Statistics Canada, 2–7.

Gilder, George F. 1986. *Men and Marriage.* New York: Pelican.

Gilligan, Carol. 1982. *In a Different Voice: Psychological Theory and Women's Development.* Cambridge, Mass.: Harvard University Press.

Gilligan, Carol, Janie V. Ward, and Jill M. Taylor (eds.). 1988. *Mapping the Moral Domain: A Contribution of Women's Thinking to Psychological Theory and Education.* Cambridge, Mass.: Harvard University Press.

Gillis, A.R. 1995. "Urbanization." In Robert J. Brym (ed.), *New Society: Sociology for the 21st Century.* Toronto: Harcourt Brace and Company, 13.1–13.40.

Gilmore, David D. 1990. *Manhood in the Making: Cultural Concepts of Masculinity.* New Haven, Conn.: Yale University Press.

Gilmour, Glenn A. 1994. *Hate-Motivated Violence* (May). Ottawa: Research Section, Department of Justice.

Glaser, Barney, and Anselm Strauss. 1967. *The Discovery of Grounded Theory.* Chicago: Aldine.

Glastris, Paul. 1990. "The New Way to Get Rich." *U.S. News & World Report* (May 7):26–36.

Glazer, Nona. 1990. "The Home as Workshop: Women as Amateur Nurses and Medical Care Providers." *Gender & Society*, 4:479–499.

Glenn, Norval D. 1991. "The Recent Trend in Marital Success in the United States." *Journal of Marriage and the Family*, 53:261–270.

The Globe and Mail Report on Business Magazine. 1990. (October):B80.

The Globe and Mail. 1992. "Where Immigration Came From." (June 20): A4.

———. 1996. "How the West has Won the Jobs Race." (May 13):A7.

Goffman, Erving. 1956. "The Nature of Deference and Demeanor." *American Anthropologist*, 58:473–502.

———. 1959. *The Presentation of Self in Everyday Life.* Garden City, N.Y.: Doubleday.

———. 1961a. *Asylums: Essays on the Social Situation of Mental Patients and Other Inmates.* Chicago: Aldine.

———. 1961b. *Encounters: Two Studies in the Sociology of Interaction.* Indianapolis, Ind.: Bobbs-Merrill.

———. 1963a. *Behavior in Public Places: Notes on the Social Structure of Gatherings.* New York: Free Press.

———. 1963b. *Stigma: Notes on the Management of Spoiled Identity.* Englewood Cliffs, N.J.: Prentice-Hall.

———. 1967. *Interaction Ritual: Essays on Face to Face Behavior.* Garden City, N.Y.: Anchor Books.

Goldberg, Kim. 1994. "Green Relief for Forest Defenders." *Progressive* (March 1):13.

Goldberg, Robert A. 1991. *Grassroots Resistance: Social Movements in Twentieth Century America.* Belmont, Cal.: Wadsworth.

Golden, Stephanie. 1992. *The Women Outside: Meanings and Myths of Homelessness.* Berkeley: University of California Press.

Gomme, Ian. "Education." In Robert J. Brym (ed.). *New Society: Sociology for the 21st Century.* Toronto: Harcourt Brace and Company, 12.1–12.11.

Gonzales, David. 1994. "Frenzied Passengers, Their Hair and Clothes in Flames, Flee Burning Train." *New York Times* (December 22):A12.

Goode, William J. 1959. "The Theoretical Importance of Love." *American Sociological Review*, 24:39–47.

Goode, William J. 1960. "A Theory of Role Strain." *American Sociological Review*, 25:483–496.

———. 1976. "Family Disorganization." In Robert K. Merton and Robert Nisbet (eds.), *Contemporary Social Problems* (4th ed.). New York: Harcourt Brace Jovanovich, 511–554.

———. 1982. "Why Men Resist." In Barrie Thorne with Marilyn Yalom (ed.), *Rethinking the Family: Some Feminist Questions.* New York: Longman, 131–150.

Goodman, Mary Ellen. 1964. *Race Awareness in Young Children* (rev. ed.). New York: Collier.

Goodman, Walter. 1993. "As TV, Drama in Waco Had a Grim Inevitability." *New York Times* (April 20):B1.

Goold, Douglas. 1996. "Dare to Retire." *The Globe and Mail* (February 24):D1.

Gordon, David. 1973. "Capitalism, Class, and Crime in America." *Crime and Delinquency*, 19:163–186.

Gordon, Milton. 1964. *Assimilation in American Life: The Role of Race, Religion, and National Origins.* New York: Oxford University Press.

Gordon, Robert M., and Jacquelyne Nelson. 1993. *Census '93: The Report of the 1993 Census of Provincial Correctional Centres in British Columbia.* Victoria: Ministry of the Solicitor General.

———. 1996. "Crime, Ethnicity, and Immigration." In Robert A. Silverman, James J. Teevan, and Vincent F. Sacco (eds.), *Crime in Canadian Society* (5th ed.). Toronto: Harcourt Brace and Company, 234–244.

Gorlick, Carolyne A. 1995. "Divorce: Options Available, Constraints Forced, Pathways Taken." In Nancy Mandell and Ann Duffy (eds.), *Canadian Families: Diversity, Conflict and Change*. Toronto: Harcourt Brace and Company, 211–234.

Gorman, Christine. 1993. "Are Some People Immune to AIDS?" *Time* (March 22): 49–51.

Gottdiener, Mark. 1985. *The Social Production of Urban Space*. Austin: University of Texas Press.

Gouldner, Alvin W. 1970. *The Coming Crisis of Western Sociology*. New York: Basic Books.

Gower, David. 1990. "Employment Opportunities of Disabled Canadians." In Craig McKie and Keith Thompson (eds.), *Canadian Social Trends*. Toronto: Thompson Educational Publishers, 218–220.

Grahame, Kamini Maraj. 1985. "Sexual Harassment." In Connie Guberman and Margie Wolfe (eds.), *No Safe Place*. Toronto: Women's Press.

Gratton, Bruce. 1986. "The New History of the Aged." In David Van Tassel and Paul N. Stearns (eds.), *Old Age in a Bureaucratic Society*. Westport, Conn.: Greenwood Press, 3–29.

Gray, Paul. 1993. "Camp for Crusaders." *Time* (April 19):40.

Green, Dan S., and Edwin D. Driver. 1978. "Introduction." In W.E.B. Du Bois, *On Sociology and the Black Community*. Chicago: University of Chicago Press.

Green, Donald E. 1977. *The Politics of Indian Removal: Creek Government and Society in Crisis*. Lincoln: University of Nebraska Press.

Greenberg, Edward S., and Benjamin I. Page. 1993. *The Struggle for Democracy*. New York: HarperCollins.

Greenhouse, Steven. 1994. "State Department Finds Widespread Abuse of World's Women." *New York Times* (February 3):A1.

Greenspan, Edward. 1982. "The Role of the Defence Lawyer in Sentencing." In Craig L. Boydell and Ingrid Connidis (eds.), *The Canadian Criminal Justice System*. Toronto: Holt, Rinehart and Winston, 200–210.

Greenwald, John. 1993. "Japan: How the Miracle Finally Ended." *Time* (December 13): 34–35.

Griffiths, Curt T., and Simon N. Verdun-Jones. 1994. *Canadian Criminal Justice* (2nd ed.). Toronto: Harcourt Brace and Company.

Grindstaff, Carl F., and Frank Trovato. 1994. "Canada's Population in the World Context." In Frank Trovato and Carl F. Grindstaff (eds.), *Perspectives on Canada's Population*. Toronto: Oxford University Press, 5–23.

Gross, Larry. 1993. *Contested Closets: The Politics and Ethics of Outing*. Minneapolis: University of Minnesota Press.

Group of Lisbon, The. 1995. Limits to Competition. Cambridge, Mass. MIT Press.

Grover, K.J., C.S. Russell, W.R. Schumm, and L.A. Paff-Bergen. 1985. "Mate Selection Processes and Marital Satisfaction." *Family Relations*, 34(3):383–386.

Guberman, Connie, and Margre Wolfe (eds.). 1985. *No Safe Place: Violence Against Women and Children*. Toronto: Women's Press.

Gunn, Rita, and Candice Minch. 1988. *Sexual Assault: The Dilemma of Disclosure, the Question of Conviction*. Winnipeg: University of Manitoba Press.

Gunn, R., and R. Linden. 1994. "The Processing of Child Sexual Abuse Cases." In J. Roberts and R.M. Mohr (eds.), *Confronting Sexual Assault: A Decade of Legal and Social Change*. Toronto: University of Toronto Press.

Guppy, Neil. 1984. "Access to Higher Education in Canada." *Canadian Journal of Higher Education*, 14:79–93.

———. 1995. "Education and Schooling." In L. Tepperman, J.E. Curtis, and R.J. Richardson (eds.), *Sociology*. Toronto: McGraw-Hill Ryerson, 450–478.

Guppy, Neil, Sabrina Freeman, and Shari Buchan. 1987. "Representing Canadians: Changes in the Economic Backgrounds of Federal Politicians, 1965–1984." *Canadian Review of Sociology and Anthropology*, 24:417–430.

Haas, J., and W. Shaffir. 1995. "Giving Medical Students a Cloak of Competence." In L. Tepperman and James Curtis (eds.), *Everyday Life*. Toronto: McGraw-Hill Ryerson.

Hackler, James C. 1994. *Crime and Canadian Public Policy*. Scarborough, Ont.: Prentice Hall.

Hadden, Jeffrey K., and Anson Shupe. 1988. *Televangelism: Power and Politics on God's Frontier*. New York: Holt.

Hadden, Jeffrey K., and Charles K. Swann. 1981. *Prime Time Preachers: The Rising Power of Televangelism*. Reading, Mass.: Addison-Wesley.

Hagedorn, Robert. 1983. *Sociology* (2nd ed.). Toronto: Holt Rinehart and Winston.

———. 1994. *Sociology* (5th ed.). Toronto: Harcourt Brace.

Hagan, John, and Bill McCarthy. 1992. "Streetlife and Delinquency." *British Journal of Sociology*, 43(4):533–561.

Hahn, Harlan. 1987. "Civil Rights for Disabled Americans: The Foundation of a Political Agenda." In Alan Gartner and Tom Joe (eds.), *Images of the Disabled, Disabling Images*. New York: Praeger, 181–203.

H.A.L.S. *Health and Activities Limitation Survey*. Cat. no. 82-554. Ottawa: Statistics Canada.

Halberstadt, Amy G., and Martha B. Saitta. 1987. "Gender, Nonverbal Behavior, and Perceived Dominance: A Test of the Theory." *Journal of Personality and Social Psychology*, 53:257–272.

Hall, Edward. 1966. *The Hidden Dimension.* New York: Anchor/ Doubleday.

Halle, David. 1993. *Inside Culture: Art and Class in the American Home.* Chicago: University of Chicago Press.

Hamill, Pete. 1993. "How to Save the Homeless—and Ourselves." *New York* (September 20):34–39.

Hamilton, Allen C. and C. Murray Sinclair. 1991. *Report of the Aboriginal Justice Inquiry of Manitoba*, Winnipeg: Queen's Printer, vol. 1. Winnipeg: Queen's Printer.

Hamper, Ben. 1992. *Rivethead: Tales from the Assembly Line.* New York: Warner Books.

Harding, Jim. 1993. "Ecology and Social Change." In Peter S. Li and B. Singh Bolaria (eds.), Sociology: Critical Perspectives. Toronto: Copp Clark Pitman, 439–466.

Harding, Sandra. 1986. *The Science Question in Feminism.* Ithaca, N.Y.: Cornell University Press.

Hardy, Melissa A., and Lawrence E. Hazelrigg. 1993. "The Gender of Poverty in an Aging Population." *Research on Aging*, 15(3):243–278.

Harlow, Harry F., and Margaret Kuenne Harlow. 1962. "Social Deprivation in Monkeys." *Scientific American*, 207(5):137–146.

———. 1977. "Effects of Various Mother-Infant Relationships on Rhesus Monkey Behaviors." In Brian M. Foss (ed.), *Determinants of Infant Behavior*, vol. 4. London: Methuen, 15–36.

Harman, Lesley. 1989. *When a Hostel Becomes a Home: Experiences of Women.* Toronto: Garamond Press.

———. 1995a. "Family Poverty and Economic Struggles." In Nancy Mandell and Ann Duffy (eds.), *Canadian Families: Diversity, Conflict and Change*. Toronto: Harcourt Brace and Company, 235–269.

———. 1995b. "The Feminization of Poverty: An Old Problem with a New Name." In E.D. Nelson, and B.W. Robinson (eds.), *Gender in the 1990s.* Scarborough, Ont.: Nelson Canada, 405–410.

Harrington Meyer, Madonna. 1990. "Family Status and Poverty Among Older Women: The Gendered Distribution of Retirement Income in the United States." *Social Problems*, 37:551–563.

———. 1994. "Gender, Race, and the Distribution of Social Assistance: Medicaid Use Among the Frail Elderly." *Gender & Society*, 8(1):8–28.

Harris, Anthony R. 1991. "Race, Class, and Crime." In Joseph F. Sheley (ed.), *Criminology: A Contemporary Handbook.* Belmont, Cal.: Wadsworth, 94–119.

Harris, Chauncey D., and Edward L. Ullman. 1945. "The Nature of Cities." *Annals of the Academy of Political and Social Sciences* (November):7–17.

Harris, Debbie. 1991. "Violence Against Women in Universities." *Canadian Women's Studies*, 11(4):35–41.

Harris, Diana K. 1990. *Sociology of Aging* (2nd ed.). New York: Harper & Row.

Harris, Marvin. 1974. *Cows, Pigs, Wars, and Witches.* New York: Random House.

———. 1985. *Good to Eat: Riddles of Food and Culture.* New York: Simon & Schuster.

Harrison, Algea O., Melvin N. Wilson, Charles J. Pine, Samuel Q. Chan, and Raymond Buriel. 1990. "Family Ecologies of Ethnic Minority Children." *Child Development*, 61(2):347–362.

Harrison, Trevor, Bill Johnston, and Harvey Krahn. 1996. "Special Interests and/or New Right Economics? The Ideological Bases of Reform Party Support in Alberta in the 1993 Federal Election." *Canadian Review of Sociology and Anthropology* 33(2):159–179.

Hartmann, Heidi. 1976. "Capitalism, Patriarchy, and Job Segregation by Sex." *Signs: Journal of Women in Culture and Society*, 1(Spring):137–169.

———. 1981. "The Unhappy Marriage of Marxism and Feminism." In Lydia Sargent (ed.), *Women and Revolution.* Boston: South End Press.

Hartnagel, Timothy F., and Harvey Krahn. 1989. "High School Dropouts, Labour Market Success, and Criminal Behaviour." *Youth and Society*, 20(4):416–444.

Hatkoff, T.S., and T.E. Laswell. 1976. "Male–Female Similarities and Differences in Conceptualizing Love." In M. Cook and G. Wilson (eds.), *Love and Attraction: An International Conference.* New York: Pergamon Press.

Hatfield, Elaine. 1995. "What Do Women and Men Want From Love and Sex?" In E.D. Nelson and B.W. Robinson (eds.), *Gender in the 1990s.* Scarborough, Ont.: Nelson Canada, 257–275.

Hauser, Christine. 1996. "Canada Promises Tough Stand Against Child Labour." *Reuters* (January 13).

Hauser, Robert M. 1995. "Symposium: The Bell Curve." *Contemporary Sociology: A Journal of Reviews*, 24(2):149–153.

Hauser, Robert M., and David L. Featherman. 1976. "Equality of Schooling: Trends and Prospects." *Sociology of Education*, 49:99–120.

Havighurst, Robert J., Bernice L. Neugarten, and Sheldon S. Tobin. 1968. "Disengagement and Patterns of Aging." In Bernice L. Neugarten (ed.), *Middle Age and Aging.* Chicago: University of Chicago Press, 161–172.

Haviland, William A. 1993. *Cultural Anthropology* (7th ed.). Orlando, Fla.: Harcourt Brace Jovanovich.

Hawley, Amos. 1950. *Human Ecology.* New York: Ronald Press.

———. 1981. *Urban Society* (2nd ed.). New York: Wiley.

Hazarika, Sanjoy. 1994. "In India's City of Death, Time Has Healed Little." *New York Times* (December 2):A7.

Health Canada. 1994. *Suicide in Canada: Update on the Report of the Task Force on Suicide in Canada.* Ottawa: Health Programs and Services Branch.

Heilbroner, Robert. 1985. *The Nature and Logic of Capitalism.* New York: W.W. Norton and Company.

Heinrichs, Daniel. 1996. *Caring for Norah.* Winnipeg: Daniel Heinricks Publishing.

Hendrick, Dianne. 1996. "Canadian Crime Statistics, 1995." *Juristat*, vol. 16, (10). Ottawa: Canadian Centre for Justice Statistics.

Henley, Nancy. 1977. *Body Politics: Power, Sex, and Nonverbal Communication.* Englewood Cliffs, N.J.: Prentice-Hall.

Henry, Frances, and Effie Ginzberg. 1984. *Who Gets Work: A Test of Racial Discrimination in Employment.* Toronto: Urban Alliance on Race Relations and the Social Planning Council of Toronto.

Henry, Frances, Carol Tator, Winston Mattis, and Tim Rees. 1995. *The Colour of Democracy: Racism in Canadian Society.*. Toronto: Harcourt Brace and Company.

Henry, Frances, Carol Tator, Winston Mattis, and Tim Rees. 1996. "The Victimization of Racial Minorities in Canada. In Robert J. Brym (ed.), *Society in Question: Sociological Readings for the 21st Century*, Toronto: Harcourt Brace and Company, 133–144.

Henslin, James M. 1993. *Sociology: A Down-to-Earth Approach.* Boston: Allyn & Bacon.

Henslin, James M., and Adie Nelson. 1996. *Sociology: A Down to Earth Approach: Canadian Edition.* Scarborough, Ont.: Allyn and Bacon.

Heritage, John. 1984. *Garfinkel and Ethnomethodology.* Cambridge, Mass.: Polity.

Herman, Dianne F. 1989. "The Rape Culture." In Jo Freeman (ed.), *Women: A Feminist Perspective* (4th ed.). Mountain View, Cal.: Mayfield, 20–44.

Heron, Craig. 1993. "The Crisis of the Craftsman: Hamilton's Metal Workers in the Early Twentieth Century." In Graham S. Lowe and Harvey J. Krahn (eds.), *Work in Canada.* Scarborough, Ont.: Nelson Canada, 4–13.

Herzog, David B., K. L. Newman, Christine J. Yeh, and M. Warshaw. 1992. "Body Image Satisfaction in Homosexual and Heterosexual Women." *International Journal of Eating Disorders*, 11:391–396.

Heshka, Stanley, and Yona Nelson. 1972. "Interpersonal Speaking Distances as a Function of Age, Sex, and Relationship." *Sociometry*, 35(4):491–498.

Hesse-Biber, Sharlene. 1989. "Eating Patterns and Disorders in a College Population: Are College Women's Eating Problems a New Phenomenon?" *Sex Roles*, 20:71–89.

Hill, Lawrence. 1994. "Zebra: Growing Up Black and White in Canada." In Carl E. James and Adrienne Shadd (eds.), *Talking About Difference.* Toronto: Between the Lines, 41–47.

Hiller, Harry H. 1986. *Canadian Society: A Macro Analysis.* Scarborough, Ont.: Prentice Hall.

———. 1991. *Canadian Society: A Macro Analysis.* Scarborough, Ont.: Prentice Hall.

———. 1995. "Culture." In L. Tepperman, J.E. Curtis, and R.J. Richardson (eds.), *The Social World* (3rd ed.). Toronto: McGraw-Hill Ryerson, 81–113.

Hindelang, Michael J., Travis Hirschi, and Joseph Weis. 1981. *Measuring Delinquency.* Beverly Hills, Cal.: Sage.

Hirsch, Paul M. 1972. "Processing Fads and Fashions: An Organization-Set Analysis of Cultural Industry Systems." *American Journal of Sociology*, 77:639–659.

Hirschi, Travis. 1969. *Causes of Delinquency.* Berkeley: University of California Press.

Hirschi, Travis, and Michael Gottfredson. 1983. "Age and the Explanation of Crime." *American Journal of Sociology*, 89(3):552–584.

Hochschild, Arlie Russell. 1973. "A Review of Sex Role Research." *American Journal of Sociology*, 78(January):1011–1029.

———. 1983. *The Managed Heart: Commercialization of Human Feeling.* Berkeley: University of California Press.

Hochschild, Arlie Russell, with Ann Machung. 1989. *The Second Shift: Working Parents and the Revolution at Home.* New York: Viking/Penguin.

Hodson, Randy, and Robert E. Parker. 1988. "Work in High Techology Settings: A Review of the Empirical Literature." *Research in the Sociology of Work*, 4:1–29.

Hodson, Randy, and Teresa A. Sullivan. 1990. *The Social Organization of Work.* Belmont, Cal.: Wadsworth.

Hoecker-Drysdale, Susan. 1992. *Harriet Martineau: First Woman Sociologist.* Oxford, England: Berg.

Hoffman, Andrew J. 1994. "Love Canal Lives." *E Magazine* (November/December):19–22.

Hoffnung, Michele. 1995. "Motherhood: Contemporary Conflict for Women." In Jo Freeman (ed.), *Women: A Feminist Perspective* (5th ed.). Mountain View, Cal.: Mayfield, 162–181.

Holland, Dorothy C., and Margaret A. Eisenhart. 1981. *Women's Peer Groups and Choice of Career.* Final report for the National Institute of Education. ERIC ED 199 328. Washington, D.C.

———. 1990. *Educated in Romance: Women, Achievement, and College Culture.* Chicago: University of Chicago Press.

Hollinger, Paul C. 1990. "Suicide and Violent Death: Longitudinal Studies." In David Lester (ed.), *Current Concepts of Suicide.* Philadelphia: Charles Press, 29–39.

———. 1994b. "Child Death Rate for AIDS Expected to Triple by 2010." *New York Times* (April 29):A5.

Holusha, John. 1994. "Bracing for the Worst in Chemicals." *New York Times* (June 4):17, 27.

hooks, bell. 1993. "Violence in Intimate Relationships: A Feminist Perspective." In Anne Minas (ed.), *Gender Basics: Feminist Perspectives on Women and Men.* Belmont, Cal.: Wadsworth, 205–210. Abridged from bell hooks, *Talking Back: Thinking Feminist, Thinking Black.* Boston: South End Press, 1989.

———. 1994. *Outlaw Culture: Resisting Representations.* New York: Routledge.

Homer-Dixon, Thomas. 1993. *Environmental Scarcity and Global Security.* Foreign Policy Association, Headline Series, Number 300. Ephrata, Penn.: Science Press.

Hoover, Kenneth R. 1992. *The Elements of Social Scientific Thinking.* New York: St. Martin's Press.

Horan, Patrick M. 1978. "Is Status Attainment Research Atheoretical?" *American Sociological Review,* 43:534–541.

Hoyt, Homer. 1939. *The Structure and Growth of Residential Neighborhoods in American Cities.* Washington, D.C.: Federal Housing Administration.

Huesmann, L. Rowell, Leonard Eron, Eric Dubow, and E. Seebauer. 1987. "Television Viewing Habits in Childhood and Adult Aggression." *Child Development,* 58:357–367.

Hughes, Colin. 1995. "Child Poverty Campaign 2000 and Child Welfare Practice: Working to End Child Poverty in Canada." *Child Welfare,*74:70–79.

Hughes, Everett C. 1945. "Dilemmas and Contradictions of Status." *American Journal of Sociology,* 50:353–359.

Hull, Jon D. 1993. "A Boy and His Gun." *Time* (August 2):20–27.

Humphrey, Derek. 1991. *Final Exit: The Practicalities of Self-Deliverance and Assisted Suicide for the Dying.* Eugene, Ore.: Hemlock Society.

———. 1993. *Lawful Exit: The Limits of Freedom for Help in Dying.* Junction City, Ore.: Norris Lane Press.

Humphreys, Laud. 1970. *Tearoom Trade: Impersonal Sex in Public Places.* Chicago: Aldine.

Hunter, Floyd. 1953. *Copmmunity Power Structure.* Chapel Hill, N.C.: University of North Carolina Press.

Hurst, Charles E. 1992. *Social Inequality: Forms, Causes, and Consequences.* Boston: Allyn & Bacon.

Huston, Aletha C. 1985. "The Development of Sex Typing: Themes from Recent Research." *Developmental Review,* 5:2–17.

Hyde, Mary, and Carol La Prairie. 1987. "American Police Crime Prevention." Working paper. Ottawa: Solicitor General.

Hynes, H. Patricia. 1990. *Earth Right: Every Citizen's Guide.* Rocklin, Cal.: Prima Publishing and Communications.

Ibrahim, Youseff M. 1990. "Saudi Tradition: Edicts from Koran Produce Curbs on Women." *New York Times* (November 6):A6.

Inciardi, James A., Ruth Horowitz, and Anne E. Pottieger. 1993. *Street Kids, Street Drugs, Street Crime: An Examination of Drug Use and Serious Delinquency in Miami.* Belmont, Cal.: Wadsworth.

Innis, Harold. 1984. *The Fur Trade in Canada.* Toronto: The University of Toronto Press (originally published 1930).

Ip, Greg. 1996. "Shareholders vs. Job Holders." *The Globe and Mail* (March 23):B1.

Ishikawa, Kaoru. 1984. "Quality Control in Japan." In Naoto Sasaki and David Hutchins (eds.), *The Japanese Approach to Product Quality: Its Applicability to the West.* Oxford: Permagon Press, 1–5.

Jackson, Beth E. 1993. "Constructing Adoptive Identities: The Accounts of Adopted Adults." Unpublished masters thesis, University of Manitoba.

Jackson, Kenneth T. 1985. *Crabgrass Frontier: The Suburbanization of the United States.* New York: Oxford University Press.

Jacobs, Gloria. 1994. "Where Do We Go from Here? An Interview with Ann Jones." *Ms.* (September/October):56–63.

Jain, H. 1985. *Anti-discrimination Staffing Policies: Implications of Human Rights Legislation for Employees and Trade Unions.* Ottawa: Secretary of State.

James, Carl E. 1995. Seeing Ourselves: *Exploring Race, Ethnicity and Culture.* Toronto: Thompson Educational Publishing.

James, Carl E., and Adrienne Shadd (eds.). 1994. *Talking About Difference: Encounters in Culture, Language and Identity.* Toronto: Between the Lines.

Janis, Irving. 1972. *Victims of Groupthink.* Boston: Houghton Mifflin.

———. 1989. *Crucial Decisions: Leadership in Policymaking and Crisis Management.* New York: Free Press.

Jankowski, Martin Sanchez. 1991. *Islands in the Street: Gangs and American Urban Society.* Berkeley: University of California Press.

Janofsky, Michael. 1993. "Race and the American Workplace." *New York Times* (June 20):F1, F6.

Jary, David, and Julia Jary. 1991. *The Harper Collins Dictionary of Sociology.* New York: HarperPerennial.

Jenish, D'Ancy. 1992. "Prime Time Violence." *Maclean's*, 105(12–07):40–45.

Jenkinson, Edward B. 1979. *Censors in the Classroom: The Mind Benders.* Carbondale: Southern Illinois University Press.

Jewell, K. Sue. 1993. *From Mammy to Miss America and Beyond: Cultural Images and the Shaping of US Social Policy.* New York: Routledge.

Johnson, Claudia. 1994. *Stifled Laughter: One Woman's Story About Fighting Censorship.* Golden, Col.: Fulcrum.

Johnson, Holly. 1990. "Wife Abuse." In Craig McKie and K. Thompson (eds.), *Canadian Social Trends.* Toronto: Thompson Educational Publishing, 173–176.

———. 1996a. *Dangerous Domains: Violence Against Women in Canada.* Scarborough, Ont.: Nelson Canada.

———. 1996b. "Violence Against Women: A Special Topic Survey." In Robert A. Silveimar, James J. Teevan, and Vincent F. Sacco (eds.), *Crime in Canadian Society* (5th ed.). Toronto: Harcourt Brace and Company, 210–221.

Johnson, Justin M. 1994. "'Flotsam on the Sea of Humanity': A View from the Bench on Class, Race, and Gender." *Social Justice*, 20(1/2):140–149.

Johnson, Norris R. 1987. "Panic at 'The Who Concert Stampede': An Empirical Assessment." *Social Problems*, 34(October):362–373.

Jones, Adele. 1994. "'F' Is for Fired." *NEA Today*, 13(2):23.

Jones, Charisse. 1995. "Family Struggles on Brink of Comfort." *New York Times* (February 18):1, 9.

Joshi, Vijay. 1993. "In Asia, Millions Lose Childhood to Work." *Austin American-Statesman* (September 6):C30.

Juergensmeyer, Mark. 1993. *The New Cold War? Religious Nationalism Confronts the Secular State.* Berkeley: University of California Press.

Jung, John. 1994. *Under the Influence: Alcohol and Human Behavior.* Pacific Grove, Cal.: Brooks/Cole.

Kaihla, Paul. 1991. "Terror in the Streets." *Maclean's* (March 25): 78–21.

———. 1994. "Sex and the Law." *Maclean's* (Oct. 24):30.

Kallen, Evelyn. 1991. "Ethnicity and Human Rights in Canada: Constitutionalizing a Hierarchy of Minority Rights." In Peter Li (ed.), *Race and Ethnic Relations in Canada.* Toronto: Oxford University Press, 77–97.

Kalof, Linda, and Timothy Cargill. 1991. "Fraternity and Sorority Membership and Gender Dominance Attitudes." *Sex Roles*, 25(7/8):417–423.

Kanter, Rosabeth Moss. 1977. *Men and Women of the Corporation.* New York: Basic Books.

———. 1983. *The Change Masters: Innovation and Entrepreneurship in the American Corporation.* New York: Simon & Schuster.

———. 1985. "All That Is Entrepreneurial Is Not Gold." *Wall Street Journal* (July 22):18.

Kaplan, David E., and Alec Dubro. 1987. *Yakuza: The Explosive Account of Japan's Criminal Underworld.* New York: Collier.

Kappeler, Victor E., Mark Blumberg, and Gary W. Potter. 1996. *The Mythology of Crime and Criminal Justice* (2nd ed.). Prospect Heights: Waveland Press.

Karkabi, Barbara. 1993. "Researcher in Houston Surveys Disabled Women About Sexuality." *Austin American-Statesman* (May 26):E8.

Karp, David A., and William C. Yoels. 1976. "The College Classroom: Some Observations on the Meanings of Student Participation." *Sociology and Social Research*, 60:421–439.

Kaspar, Anne S. 1986. "Consciousness Re-evaluated: Interpretive Theory and Feminist Scholarship." *Sociological Inquiry*, 56(1):30–49.

Katz, Michael B. 1989. *The Undeserving Poor: From the War on Poverty to the War on Welfare.* New York: Pantheon.

Katzer, Jeffrey, Kenneth H. Cook, and Wayne W. Crouch. 1991. *Evaluating Information: A Guide for Users of Social Science Research.* New York: McGraw-Hill.

Kauppinen-Toropainen, Kaisa, and Johanna Lammi. 1993. "Men in Female-Dominated Occupations: A Cross-Cultural Comparison." In Christine L. Williams (ed.), *Doing "Women's Work": Men in Nontraditional Occupations.* Newbury Park, Cal.: Sage, pp. 91–112.

Keegan, Victor. 1996. "A World Without Bosses—Or Workers." *The Globe and Mail* (August 24):D4.

Keith, Julie, and Laura Landry. 1994. "Well-being of Older Canadians." In Craig McKie (ed.), *Canadian Social Trends.* Toronto: Thompson Educational Publishing Company, 133–134.

Keller, James. 1994. "I Treasure Each Moment." *Parade Magazine* (September 4):4–5.

Kelly, Gary. 1992. *Sexuality Today: The Human Perspective.* Guilford, Conn.: Dushkin.

Kelly, Liz. 1988. *Surviving Sexual Violence.* Minneapolis: University of Minnesota Press.

Kelman, Steven. 1991. "Sweden Sour? Downsizing the 'Third Way.'" *New Republic* (July 29):19–23.

Kemp, Alice Abel. 1994. *Women's Work: Degraded and Devalued.* Englewood Cliffs, N.J.: Prentice-Hall.

Kendall, Diana, and Joe R. Feagin. 1983. "Blatant and Subtle Patterns of Discrimination: Minority Women in Medical Schools." *Journal of Intergroup Relations* (Summer):21–27.

Kennedy, Leslie W. 1978. "Environmental Opportunity and Social Contact: A True or Spurious Relationship?" *Pacific Sociological Review*, 21:173–186.

———. 1983. *The Urban Kaleidoscope: Canadian Perspectives.* Toronto: McGraw-Hill Ryerson.

Kennedy, Paul. 1987. *The Rise and Fall of the Great Powers.* New York: Random House.

———. 1993. *Preparing for the Twenty-First Century.* New York: Random House.

Kennedy, Randy. 1993. "To Homelessness and Back: A Man's Journey to Respect." *New York Times* (November 28):A15.

Kenyon, Kathleen. 1957. *Digging Up Jericho.* London: Ernest Benn.

Kersten, Joachim. 1993. "Street Youths, *Bosozoku*, and *Yakuza:* Subculture Formation and Societal Reactions in Japan." *Crime & Delinquency*, 39(3):277–295.

Keyfitz, Nathan. 1994. "The Scientific Debate: Is Population Growth a Problem? An Interview with Nathan Keyfitz." *Harvard International Review* (Fall):10–11, 74.

Kilbourne, Jean. 1994. "Still Killing Us Softly: Advertising and the Obsession with Thinness." In Patricia Fallon, Melanie A. Katzman, and Susan C. Wooley (eds.), *Feminist Perspectives on Eating Disorders.* New York: Guilford, 395–454.

Kimmel, Michael S., and Michael A. Messner. 1992. *Men's Lives* (2nd ed.). New York: Macmillan.

Kingsley, Bob. 1996. "Assault." In Leslie W. Kennedy and Vincent F. Sacco (eds.), *Crime Counts: A Criminal Event Analysis.* Scarborough, Ont.: Nelson Canada, 99–113.

Kinsella, Warren. 1994. *Web of Hate: The Far-Right Network in Canada.* Toronto: HarperCollins.

Kirby, Sandra, and Kate McKenna. 1989. *Experience Research Social Change: Methods from the Margins.* Toronto: Garamond.

Kirkpatrick, P. 1994. "Triple Jeopardy: Disability, Race and Poverty in America." *Poverty and Race*, 3:1–8.

Kitano, Harry, and Iris Chi. 1986–87. "Asian Americans and Alcohol Use." *Alcohol Health and Research World*, 11:42–46.

Kitano, Harry, Iris Chi, Siyon Rhee, C. K. Law, and James E. Lubben. 1992. "Norms and Alcohol Consumption: Japanese in Japan, Hawaii, and California." *Journal of Studies on Alcohol*, 53(1):33–39.

Kitcher, Brigitte, Andrew Mitchell, Peter Clutterbuck, and Marvyn Novick. 1991. *Unequal Futures: The Legacies of Child Poverty in Canada.* Toronto: Child Poverty Action Group and the Social Planning Council of Metropolitan Toronto.

Klein, Alan M. 1993. *Little Big Men: Bodybuilding Subculture and Gender Construction.* Albany: SUNY Press.

Klockars, Carl B. 1979. "The Contemporary Crises of Marxist Criminology." *Criminology*, 16:477–515.

Kluckhohn, Clyde. 1961. "The Study of Values." In Donald N. Barrett (ed.), *Values in America.* South Bend, Ind.: University of Notre Dame Press, 17–46.

Knottnerus, J. David. 1993. "The Rise of the Wisconsin School of Status Attainment Research." In Ted R. Vaughan, Gideon Sjoberg, and Larry T. Reynolds (eds.), *A Critique of Contemporary American Sociology.* Dix Hills, N.Y.: General Hall, 252–268.

Knudsen, Dean D. 1992. *Child Maltreatment: Emerging Perspectives.* Dix Hills, N.Y.: General Hall.

Koch, George. 1993. *Soap Sellers Turned Welfare Advocates.* Alberta Report/Western Report, 20(November 22):20.

Kohlberg, Lawrence. 1969. "Stage and Sequence: The Cognitive-Developmental Approach to Socialization." In David A. Goslin, *Handbook of Socialization Theory and Research.* Chicago: Rand McNally, 347–480.

———. 1981. "The Philosophy of Moral Development: Moral Stages and the Idea of Justice." *Essays on Moral Development*, vol. 1. San Francisco: Harper & Row.

Kohn, Melvin L. 1977. *Class and Conformity: A Study in Values* (2nd ed.). Homewood, Ill.: Dorsey Press.

Kohn, Melvin L., Atsushi Naoi, Carrie Schoenbach, Carmi Schooler, and Kazimierz M. Slomczynski. 1990. "Position in the Class Structure and Psychological Functioning in the United States, Japan, and Poland." *American Journal of Sociology*, 95:964–1008.

Kolata, Gina. 1993. "Fear of Fatness: Living Large in a Slimfast World." *Austin American-Statesman* (January 3):C1, C6.

Kopvillem, Peeter. 1996. "Guilty as Charged." *Maclean's* (March 11):24.

Kosmin, Barry A., and Seymour P. Lachman. 1993. *One Nation Under God: Religion in Contemporary American Society.* New York: Crown.

Kotlowitz, Robert. 1994. "From My Wife's Room." *New York Times Magazine* (December 4):84–89.

Kovacs, M., and A.T. Beck. 1977. "The Wish to Live and the Wish to Die in Attempted Suicides." *Journal of Clinical Psychology*, 33:361–365.

Kozol, Jonathan. 1988. *Rachael and Her Children: Homeless Families in America.* New York: Fawcett Columbine.

———. 1991. *Savage Inequalities: Children in America's Schools.* New York: Crown.

Krahn, Harvey J. 1995a. "Non-standard Work on the Rise." *Perspectives on Labour and Income* (Winter).: Ottawa: Statistics Canada 35–42.

———. 1995b. "Social Stratification." In Robert J. Brym, *New Society for the 21st Century*. Toronto: Harcourt Brace and Company, 2.1–2.31.

Krahn, Harvey J., and Graham S. Lowe. 1993. *Work, Industry, and Canadian Society.* Scarborough, Ont.: Nelson Canada.

Krahn, Harvey, and Graham Lowe. 1996. *New Forms of Management and Work in Society in Question: Sociological Readings for the 21st Century.* Toronto: Harcourt Brace and Company.

Krauss, Clifford. 1994. "A Nervous City Sees Bombs Everywhere." *New York Times* (December 24):9.

Kroll-Smith, J. Stephen, and Stephen Robert Couch. 1990. *The Real Disaster Is Above Ground: A Mine Fire and Social Conflict.* Lexington: University Press of Kentucky.

Krotz, Larry. 1980. Urban Indians: The Strangers in Canada's Cities. Edmonton: Hurtig.

Krysan, Maria, and Reynolds Farley. 1993. "Racial Stereotypes: Are They Alive and Well? Do They Continue to Influence Race Relations?" Paper presented at the Annual Meeting of the American Sociological Association, Miami Beach, Florida, August 16.

Kübler-Ross, Elisabeth. 1969. *On Death and Dying.* New York: Macmillan.

Kunen, James S. 1990. "Pop! Goes the Donald," *People* (July 9):29–34.

Kurian, George. 1991. "Socialization in South Asian Immigrant Youth." In S.P. Sharma, A.M. Erwin, and D. Meintel (eds.), *Immigrants and Refugees in Canada.* Saskatoon: University of Saskatchewan.

Labaton, Stephen. 1994. "Denny's Gets a Bill for the Side Orders of Bigotry." *New York Times* (May 29):E4.

Ladd, E.C., Jr. 1966. *Negro Political Leadership in the South.* Ithaca, N.Y.: Cornell University Press.

LaFree, Gary D. 1980. "The Effect of Sexual Stratification by Race on Official Reactions to Rape." *American Sociological Review*, 45:824–854.

———. 1989. *Rape and Criminal Justice: The Social Construction of Sexual Assault.* Belmont, Cal.: Wadsworth.

Lalonde, Michelle. 1996. "The Mayor's Vision." *The Montreal Gazette* (May 4).

Lam, Andrew. 1995. "Beyond Clayoquot Sound." *Earth Island Journal* (June):24.

Lamanna, Marianne, and Agnes Riedmann. 1994. *Marriages and Families: Making Choices and Facing Change* (5th ed.). Belmont, Cal.: Wadsworth.

Langelan, Martha J. 1993. *Back Off! How to Confront and Stop Sexual Harassment and Harassers.* New York: Fireside/Simon & Schuster.

LaNovara, Pina. 1995. "Changes in Family Living." In E.D. Nelson and Augie Fleras (eds.), *Social Problems In Canada.* Scarborough, Ont.: Prentice Hall, 304–317.

Lapchick, Richard E. 1991. *Five Minutes to Midnight: Race and Sport in the 1990s.* Lanham, Md.: Madison Books.

Lapham, Lewis H. 1988. *Money and Class in America: Notes and Observations on Our Civil Religion.* New York: Weidenfeld & Nicolson.

Lapsley, Daniel K. 1990. "Continuity and Discontinuity in Adolescent Social Cognitive Development." In Raymond Montemayor, Gerald R. Adams, and Thomas P. Gullota (eds.), *From Childhood to Adolescence: A Transitional Period?* (*Advances in Adolescent Development*, vol. 2). Newbury Park, Cal.: Sage.

LaRossa, Ralph. 1995. "Fatherhood and "Social Change." In E.D. Nelson and B.W. Robinson (eds.), *Gender in the 1990s.* Scarborough, Ont.: Nelson Canada, 365–379.

Larson, Magali Sarfatti. 1977. *The Rise of Professionalism: A Sociological Analysis.* Berkeley: University of California Press.

Lasch, Christopher. 1977. *Haven in a Heartless World.* New York: Basic Books.

Laumann, Edward O., John H. Gagnon, Robert T. Michael, and Stuart Michaels. 1994. *The Social Organization of Sexuality.* Chicago: University of Chicago Press.

Lavigne, Yves. 1987. *Hell's Angels: Taking Care of Business.* Toronto: Ballantine Books.

Law Reform Commission of Canada. 1974. *The Native Offender and the Law.* Ottawa: Information Canada.

Lee, Alfred McClung. 1986. *Sociology for Whom?* (2nd ed.). Syracuse, N.Y.: Syracuse University Press.

Lee, Sharon M. 1993. "Racial Classifications in the U.S. Census: 1890–1990." *Ethnic and Racial Studies*, 16(1):75–94.

Leenaars, Antoon A. 1988. *Suicide Notes: Predictive Clues and Patterns.* New York: Human Sciences Press.

——— (ed.). 1991. *Life Span Perspectives of Suicide: Time-Lines in the Suicide Process.* New York: Plenum Press.

———. 1992. "Suicide Notes from Canada and the United States." *Perceptual and Motor Skills*, 74:278.

———, and G. Domino. 1993. "A Comparison of Community/Leenaars, Antoon A. Attitudes Toward

Suicide in Windsor and Los Angeles." *Canadian Journal of Behavioural Science*, 25: 253–266.

Lefrançois, Guy R. 1993. *The Lifespan* (4th ed.). Belmont, Cal.: Wadsworth.

Lehmann, Jennifer M. 1994. *Durkheim and Women.* Lincoln: University of Nebraska Press.

Lele, J., G.C. Perlin, and H.G. Thorburn. 1979. "The National Party Convention." In H.G. Thorburn (ed.), *Political Parties in Canada.* Scarborough, Ont.: Prentice Hall, 89–97.

Lemert, Edwin M. 1951. *Social Pathology.* New York: McGraw-Hill.

Lengermann, Patricia Madoo, and Ruth A. Wallace. 1985. *Gender in America: Social Control and Social Change.* Englewood Cliffs, N.J.: Prentice-Hall.

Lenski, Gerhard. 1966. *Power and Privilege: A Theory of Social Stratification.* New York: McGraw-Hill.

Lenski, Gerhard, Jean Lenski, and Patrick Nolan. 1991. *Human Societies: An Introduction to Macrosociology* (6th ed.). New York: McGraw-Hill.

Leonard, Margaret A., and Stacy Randell. 1992. "Policy Shifts in the Massachusetts Response to Family Homelessness." In Padraig O'Malley, *Homelessness: New England and Beyond: New England Journal of Public Policy, Special Issue* (May):483–497.

Lerner, Gerda. 1986. *The Creation of Patriarchy.* New York: Oxford University Press.

LeShan, Eda. 1994. *I Want More of Everything.* New York: New Market Press.

Lester, David. 1988. *Why Women Kill Themselves.* Springfield, Ill.: Thomas.

———. 1992. *Why People Kill Themselves: A 1990s Summary of Research Findings of Suicidal Behavior* (3rd ed.). Springfield, Ill.: Thomas.

Lester, David, and Margot Tallmer (eds.). 1993. *Now I Lay Me Down: Suicide in the Elderly.* Philadelphia: Charles Press.

Letkemann, Peter. 1973. *Crime as Work.* Englewood Cliffs, N.J.: Prentice-Hall.

Leventman, Paula Goldman. 1981. *Professionals Out of Work.* New York: Free Press.

Levin, Jack, and Jack McDevitt. 1993. *Hate Crimes: The Rising Tide of Bigotry and Bloodshed.* New York: Plenum Press.

Levin, William C. 1988. "Age Stereotyping: College Student Evaluations." *Research on Aging,* 10(1):134–148.

Levine, Adeline Gordon. 1982. *Love Canal: Science, Politics, and People.* Lexington, Mass.: Lexington Books.

Levine, Murray. 1982. "Introduction." In Lois Marie Gibbs, *Love Canal: My Story.* Albany: SUNY Press.

Levine, Peter. 1992. *Ellis Island to Ebbets Field: Sport and the American Jewish Experience.* New York: Oxford University Press.

Levitt, Kari. 1970. *Silent Surrender: the Multinational Corporation in Canada.* Toronto: Macmillan of Canada.

Levy, Janice C., and Eva Y. Deykin. 1989. "Suicidality, Depression, and Substance Abuse in Adolescence." *American Journal of Psychiatry,* 146(11):1462–1468.

Lewis, Paul. 1993. "Rape Was Weapon of Serbs, U.N. Says." *New York Times* (October 20):A1, A4.

Leyton, Elliott. 1979. *The Myth of Delinquency: An Anatomy of Juvenile Nihilism.* Toronto: McClelland and Stewart.

Li, Peter S. (ed.). 1990. *Race and Ethnic Relations in Canada.* Toronto: Oxford University Press.

Lichter, S. Robert, Linda S. Lichter, and Stanley Rothman. 1991. *Watching America.* New York: Prentice-Hall.

Liebow, Elliot. 1967. *Tally's Corner: A Study of Negro Streetcorner Men.* Boston: Little, Brown.

———. 1993. *Tell Them Who I Am: The Lives of Homeless Women.* New York: Free Press.

Lightle, Juliana, and Betsy Doucet. 1992. *Sexual Harassment in the Workplace: A Guide to Prevention.* Los Altos, Cal.: Crisp Publications.

Linden, Rick, and Cathy Fillmore. 1981. "A Comparative Study of Delinquency Involvement." *Canadian Review of Sociology and Anthropology* 18:343–361.

———. 1994. "Deviance and Crime." In Lorne Tepperman, James E. Curtis, and R.J. Richardson (eds.), *The Social World* (3rd ed.). Whitby, Ont.: McGraw-Hill Ryerson, 188–226.

Linton, Ralph. 1936. *The Study of Man.* New York: Appleton-Century-Crofts.

Lips, Hilary M. 1989. "Gender-Role Socialization: Lessons in Femininity." In Jo Freeman (ed.), *Women: A Feminist Perspective* (4th ed.). Mountain View, Cal.: Mayfield, 197–216.

———. 1993. *Sex and Gender: An Introduction* (2nd ed.). Mountain View, Cal.: Mayfield.

Lipset, Seymour M. 1986. "Historical Traditions of National Characteristics: A Comparative Analysis of Canada and the United States." *Canadian Journal of Sociology,* 11:113–155.

———. 1990. *The Continental Divide: The Values and Institutions of Canada and the United States.* New York: Routledge.

Livingston, D.W., and Meg Luxton. 1995. "Gender Consciousness at Work: Modification of the Male Breadwinner Norm Among Steelworkers and Their Spouses." In E.D. Nelson and B.W. Robinson (eds.), *Gender in the 1990s.* Scarborough, Ont.: Nelson Canada, 172–200.

Lochhead, Clarence, and Richard Shillington. 1996. *A Statistical Profile of Urban Poverty.* Ottawa: Canadian Council of Social Development.

Lofland, John. 1993. "Collective Behavior: The Elementary Forms." In Russell L. Curtis, Jr., and Benigno E. Aguirre (eds.), *Collective Behavior and Social Movements.* Boston: Allyn & Bacon, 70–75.

Lombardo, William K., Gary A. Cretser, Barbara Lombardo, and Sharon L. Mathis. 1983. "For Cryin' Out Loud—There Is a Sex Difference." *Sex Roles,* 9:987–995.

London, Kathryn A. 1991. "Advance Data Number 194: Cohabitation, Marriage, Marital Dissolution, and Remarriage: United States 1988." U.S. Department of Health and Human Services: Vital and Health Statistics of the National Center, January 4.

London, Kathryn A., and Barbara Foley Wilson. 1988. "Divorce." *American Demographics,* 10(10):23–26.

Lorber, Judith. 1994. *Paradoxes of Gender.* New Haven, Conn.: Yale University Press.

Loseke, Donileen. 1992. *The Battered Woman and Shelters: The Social Construction of Wife Abuse.* Albany: SUNY Press.

Lott, Bernice. 1994. *Women's Lives: Themes and Variations in Gender Learning* (2nd ed.). Pacific Grove, Cal.: Brooks/Cole.

Luffman, Jackie. 1996. "Sexual Assault on Campus: A Contextual and Theoretical Approach." Unpublished Paper presented at Mephistos Conference 1996, University of Toronto.

Lupul, M.R. 1988. "Ukrainians: The Fifth Cultural Wheel in Canada." In Ian H. Angus (ed.), *Ethnicity in a Technological Age.* Edmonton: Canadian Institute of Ukrainian Studies, University of Alberta, 177–192.

Lurie, Alison. 1981. *The Language of Clothes.* New York: Random House.

Luttwak, Eugene. 1996. Quoted in Kenneth Kidd, "Social Contracts." *The Globe and Mail Report on Business Magazine* (September):24.

Luxton, Meg. 1980. More Than a Labour of Love. Toronto: Women's Press.

———. 1995. "Two hands for the Clock: Changing Patterns of Gendered Division of Labour in the Home." In E.D. Nelson and B.W. Robinson (eds.), *Gender in the 1990s.* Scarborough, Ont.: Nelson Canada, 288–301.

Lynd, Robert S., and Helen M. Lynd. 1929. *Middletown.* New York: Harcourt Brace.

———. 1937. *Middletown in Transition.* New York: Harcourt Brace.

Lynn, Marion, and Eimear O'Neill. 1995. "Families, Power and Violence." In Nancy Mandell and Ann Duffy (eds.) *Canadian Families: Diversity, Conflict and Change.* Toronto: Harcourt Brace and Company, 271–305.

Lynn, Marion (ed.). 1996. *Voices: Essays on Canadian Families.* Scarborough, Ont.: Nelson Canada.

Maccoby, Eleanor E., and Carol Nagy Jacklin. 1987. "Gender Segregation in Childhood." *Advances in Child Development and Behavior,* 20:239–287.

MacDonald, Kevin, and Ross D. Parke. 1986. "Parental-Child Physical Play: The Effects of Sex and Age of Children and Parents." *Sex Roles,* 15:367–378.

Macionis, J., Juanne Nancarrow Clarke, and Linda M. Gerber. 1994. *Sociology.* Scarborough, Ont.: Prentice Hall.

Mack, Raymond W., and Calvin P. Bradford. 1979. *Transforming America: Patterns of Social Change* (2nd ed.). New York: Random House.

MacKinnon, Catherine. 1979. *Sexual Harassment of Working Women: A Case of Sex Discrimination.* New Haven, Conn.: Yale University Press.

Mackintosh, Maureen M. 1979. "Domestic Labour and the Household." In Sandra Burman (ed.), *Fit Work for Women.* London: Croom Helm.

Maclean, Michael J., and Rita Bonar. 1995. "The Ethnic Elderly in a Dominant Culture Long-Term Facility." In Mark Novak (ed.), *Aging in Society: A Canadian Perspective.* Scarborough, Ont.: Nelson Canada, 55–78.

MacLeod, Jay. 1988. *Ain't No Makin' It: Leveled Aspirations in a Low-Income Neighborhood.* Boulder, Col.: Westview Press.

MacLeod, Linda. 1980. *Wife Battering in Canada: The Vicious Circle.* Ottawa: Canadian Advisory Council on the Status of Women.

———. 1987. *Battered But NOT Beaten: Preventing Wife Battering in Canada.* Ottawa: Canadian Advisory Council on the Status of Women.

———. 1994. "Wife Battering in Canada." In L. Tepperman, J. Curtis, S.J. Watson, and A. Wain (eds.), *Small World International Readings in Sociology.* Scarborough, Ont.: Prentice Hall, 219–226.

MacSween, Morag. 1993. *Anorexic Bodies: A Feminist and Sociological Perspective on Anorexia Nervosa.* New York: Routledge.

Madigan, Lee, and Nancy C. Gamble. 1991. *The Second Rape.* New York: Lexington Books.

Maguire, Kathleen, and Timothy J. Flanagan (eds.). 1991. *Sourcebook of Criminal Justice Statistics 1990.* Washingtom, D.C.: U.S. Department of Justice, Bureau of Statistics.

Maguire, Kathleen, Ann L. Pastore, and Timothy Flanagan. 1992. *Sourcebook of Criminal Justice Statistics.* Washington, D.C.: 1991. U.S. Department of Justice, Bureau of Justice Statistics.

Malinowski, Bronislaw. 1922. *Argonauts of the Western Pacific.* New York: Dutton.

———. 1964. "The Principle of Legitimacy: Parenthood, the Basis of Social Structure." In Rose Laub Coser (ed.), *The Family: Its Structure and Functions.* New York: St. Martin's Press (orig. pub. 1929).

Malson, Lucien. 1972. *Wolf Children and the Problem of Human Nature.* New York: Monthly Review Press.

Malthus, Thomas R. 1965. *An Essay on Population.* New York: Augustus Kelley, Bookseller (orig. pub. 1798).

Man, Guida. 1996. "The Experience of Middle-Class Women in Recent Hong Kong Chinese Immigrant Families in Canada." In Marion Lynn (ed.), *Voices: Essays on Canadian Families.* Toronto: Nelson Canada, 271–300.

Mann, Patricia S. 1994. *Micro-Politics: Agency in a Postfeminist Era.* Minneapolis: University of Minnesota Press.

Mansfield, Alan, and Barbara McGinn. 1993. "Pumping Irony: The Muscular and the Feminine." In Sue Scott and David Morgan (eds.), *Body Matters: Essays on the Sociology of the Body.* London: Falmer Press, 49–58.

Marble, Michelle. 1995. "Eating Disorders Awareness Week: February 6–12, 1995." *Women's Health Weekly* (February 6):12.

Marchak, Patricia. 1975. *Ideological Perspectives on Canadian Society.* Toronto: McGraw-Hill.

Marcil-Gratton, Nicole. 1993. "Growing Up with a Single Parent, a Transitional Experience? Some Demographic Measurements." In J. Hudson and B. Galaway (eds.), *Single Parent Families with Perspectives on Research and Policy.* Toronto: Thompson Educational Publishing.

Marger, Martin N. 1987. *Elites and Masses: An Introduction to Political Sociology* (2nd ed.). Belmont, Cal.: Wadsworth.

———. 1994. *Race and Ethnic Relations: American and Global Perspectives.* Belmont, Cal.: Wadsworth.

Marks, Peter. 1994. "Buttafuoco Keeps Life in Spotlight." *New York Times* (March 25):A13.

Marriott, Michael. 1993. "Harsh Rap Lyrics Provoke Black Backlash." *New York Times* (August 15):1, 16.

Marsden, Lorna, and Brenda Robertson. 1991. *Children in Poverty: Toward a Better Future.* Ottawa: Standing Committee on Social Affairs, Science, and Technology.

Marshall, Gordon (ed.). 1994. *The Concise Oxford Dictionary of Sociology.* New York: Oxford University Press.

Marshall, Katherine. 1990. "Women in Professional Occupations: Progress in the 1980s." In Craig McKie and Keith Thompson (eds.), *Canadian Social Trends.* Toronto: Thompson Educational Publishers, 109–112.

———. 1995. "Dual Earners: Who's Responsible for Housework?" In E.D. Nelson and B.W. Robinson, *Gender in the 1990s.* Scarborough, Ont.: Nelson Canada, 302–308.

Marshall, Susan E. 1985. "Ladies Against Women: Mobilization Dilemmas of Antifeminist Movements." *Social Problems,* 32:348–362.

———. 1989. "Keep Us on a Pedestal: Women Against Feminism in Twentieth-Century America." In Jo Freedman (ed.), *Women: A Feminist Perspective* (4th ed.). Mountain View, Cal.: Mayfield, 567–580.

———. 1994. "True Women or New Women? Status Maintenance and Antisuffrage Mobilization in the Gilded Age." Paper presented at the American Sociological Association 89th annual meeting, Los Angeles.

Martin, Carol L. 1989. "Children's Use of Gender-Related Information in Making Social Judgments." *Developmental Psychology,* 25:80–88.

Martin, James G., and Clyde W. Franklin. 1983. *Minority Group Relations.* Columbus, Ohio: Charles E. Merrill Publishing.

Martin, Laura. 1992. *A Life Without Fear.* Nashville, Tenn.: Rutledge Hill Press.

Martin, Michael T., and Howard Cohen. 1980. "Race and Class Consciousness: A Critique of the Marxist Concept of Race Relations." *Western Journal of Black Studies,* 4(2):84–91.

Martin, Nick. 1996. "Aboriginal Speech Dying." Winnipeg Free Press (March 29):A8.

Martin, Teresa Castro, and Larry L. Bumpass. 1989. "Recent Trends in Marital Disruption." *Demography,* 26:37–51.

Martineau, Harriet. 1962. *Society in America* (edited, abridged). Garden City, N.Y.: Doubleday (orig. pub. 1837).

———. 1988. *How to Observe Morals and Manners.* Michael R. Hill (ed.). New Brunswick, N.J.: Transaction (orig. pub. 1838).

Marx, Karl. 1967. *Capital: A Critique of Political Economy.* Friedrich Engels (ed.). New York: International Publishers (orig. pub. 1867).

———. 1979. *The Marx-Engels Reader.* Robert C. Tucker (ed.) (2nd ed.). New York: Norton.

Marx, Karl, and Friedrich Engels. 1967. *The Communist Manifesto.* New York: Pantheon (orig. pub. 1848).

Matas, David. 1995. "A Valuable Survey of Canadian Race Controversies." *The Globe and Mail* (July 8):C8.

Matthews, Gwyneth Ferguson. 1983. *Voices from the Shadows: Women with Disabilities Speak Out.* Toronto: Women's Educational Press.

Maynard, Rona. 1987. "How Do You Like Your Job?" *The Globe and Mail Report on Business Magazine* (November):120–25.

McAdam, Doug. 1982. *Political Process and the Development of Black Insurgency*. Chicago: University of Chicago Press.

McAdam, Doug, John D. McCarthy, and Mayer N. Zald. 1988. "Social Movements." In Neil J. Smelser (ed.), *Handbook of Sociology*. Newbury Park, Cal.: Sage, 695–737.

McCall, George J., and Jerry L. Simmons, 1978. *Identities and Interactions: An Explanation of Human Associations in Everyday Life*. New York: Free Press.

McCall, Nathan. 1994. *Makes Me Wanna Holler: A Young Black Man in America*. New York: Random House.

McCarroll, Thomas. 1993. "New Star Over Asia." *Time* (August 9):53.

McCarthy, John D., and Mayer N. Zald. 1977. "Resource Mobilization and Social Movements: A Partial Theory." *American Journal of Sociology*, 82:1212–1241.

McCormick, Chris. 1995. *Constructing Danger: The Misrepresentation of Crime in the News*. Halifax: Fernwood Publishing.

McDaniel, Susan, and Erica Roosmalen. 1985. "Sexual Harassment in Canadian Academe: Explorations of Power and Privilege." *Atlantis* 17(1):3–19.

McDonald, Marci. 1994. "The New Spirituality." *Maclean's* (October 10):44–48.

———. 1996. "Is God a Woman?" *Maclean's* (April 8):46–51.

McEachern, William A. 1994. *Economics: A Contemporary Introduction*. Cincinnati: South-Western.

McElroy, Ann, and Patricia K. Townsend. 1989. *Medical Anthropology in Ecological Perspective* (2nd ed.). Boulder, Col.: Westview Press.

McGee, Reece. 1975. *Points of Departure*. Hinsdale, Ill.: Dryden Press.

McGovern, Celeste. 1995. "Dr. Death Speaks." *Alberta Report/Western Report*, 22(January 9):33.

McGuigan, Cathleen. 1993. "Michael's World." *Newsweek* (September 6):34–39.

McGuire, Meredith B. 1992. *Religion: The Social Context* (2nd ed.). Belmont, Cal.: Wadsworth.

McIntosh, Mary. 1978. "The State and the Oppression of Women." In Annette Kuhn and Ann Marie Wolpe (eds.), *Feminism and Materialism*. London: Routledge and Kegan Paul.

McKague, Ormond (ed.). 1991. *Racial Harassment: Two Individual Reflections*. Saskatoon: Fifth House Publishers, 11–14.

McKenzie, Roderick D. 1925. "The Ecological Approach to the Study of the Human Community." In Robert Park, Ernest Burgess, and Roderick D. McKenzie, *The City*. Chicago: University of Chicago Press.

McKie, Craig. 1994. "Population Aging: Baby Boomers into the 21st Century." *Canadian Social Trends*. Toronto: Thompson Educational Publishing, 3–7.

McLanahan, Sara, and Karen Booth. 1991. "Mother-Only Families." In Alan Booth (ed.), *Contemporary Families: Looking Forward, Looking Backward*. Minneapolis: National Council on Family Relations, 405–428.

McLeod, Jonah. 1994. "Helping China Adopt Free Enterprise." *Electronics* (August 8):15.

McPhail, Clark. 1971. "Civil Disorder Participation: A Critical Examination of Recent Research." *American Sociological Review*, 36:1058–1073.

———. 1991. *The Myth of the Maddening Crowd*. New York: Aldine de Gruyter.

McPhail, Clark, and Ronald T. Wohlstein. 1983. "Individual and Collective Behavior within Gatherings, Demonstrations, and Riots." In Ralph H. Turner and James F. Short, Jr. (eds.), *Annual Review of Sociology*, vol. 9. Palo Alto, Cal.: Annual Reviews, 579–600.

McPherson, J. Miller, and Lynn Smith-Lovin. 1982. "Women and Weak Ties: Differences by Sex in the Size of Voluntary Organizations." *American Journal of Sociology*, 87(January):883–904.

1986. "Sex Segregation in Voluntary Associations." *American Sociological Review*, 51(February):61–79.

McVey, Wayne W., and Warren Kalbach. 1995. *Canadian Population*. Scarborough, Ont.: Nelson Canada.

Mead, George Herbert. 1934. *Mind, Self, and Society*. Chicago: University of Chicago Press.

Medved, Michael. 1992. *Hollywood vs. America: Popular Culture and the War on Traditional Values*. New York: HarperPerennial.

Mental Medicine. 1994. "Wealth, Health, and Status." *Mental Medicine Update*, 3(2):7.

Merchant, Carolyn. 1983. *The Death of Nature: Women, Ecology, and the Scientific Revolution*. San Francisco: Harper & Row.

———. 1992. *Radical Ecology: The Search for a Livable World*. New York: Routledge.

Merton, Robert King. 1938. "Social Structure and Anomie." *American Sociological Review*, 3(6):672–682.

———. 1949. "Discrimination and the American Creed." In Robert M. MacIver (ed.), *Discrimination and National Welfare*. New York: Harper & Row, 99–126.

———. 1968. *Social Theory and Social Structure* (enlarged ed.). New York: Free Press.

Miall, Charlene. 1986. "The Stigma of Involuntary Childlessness." *Social Problems*, 33(4):268–282.

Michael, Robert T., John H. Gagnon, Edward O. Laumann, and Gina Kolata. 1994. *Sex in America.* Boston: Little, Brown.

Michels, Robert. 1949. *Political Parties.* Glencoe, Ill.: Free Press (orig. pub. 1911).

Michelson, William H. 1976. *Man and His Urban Environment: A Sociological Approach with Revisions.* Reading, Mass.: Addison-Wesley.

———. 1977. *Environmental Choice, Human Behavior, and Residential Satisfaction.* New York: Oxford University Press.

———. 1994. "Cities and Urbanization." In Lorne Tepperman, James Curtis, and R.J. Richardson (eds.), *The Social World* (3rd ed.). Toronto: McGraw-Hill, 672–709.

Mies, Maria, and Vandana Shiva. 1993. *Ecofeminism.* Highlands, N.J.: Zed Books.

Milgram, Stanley. 1963. "Behavioral Study of Obedience." *Journal of Abnormal and Social Psychology*, 67:371–378.

———. 1974. *Obedience to Authority.* New York: Harper & Row.

Miliband, Ralph. 1969. The State in Capitalist Society. New York: Basic Books.

Miller, Casey, and Kate Swift. 1991. *Words and Women: New Language in New Times* (updated). New York: HarperCollins.

———. 1993. "Who Is Man?" In Anne Minas, *Gender Basics: Feminist Perspectives on Women and Men.* Belmont, Cal.: Wadsworth, 68–75.

Miller, Dan E. 1986. "Milgram Redux: Obedience and Disobedience in Authority Relations." In Norman K. Denzin (ed.), *Studies in Symbolic Interaction.* Greenwich, Conn.: JAI Press, 77–106.

———. 1956. *White Collar.* New York: Oxford University Press.

Mills, C. Wright. 1959. *The Power Elite.* Fair Lawn, N.J.: Oxford University Press.

———. 1959. *The Sociological Imagination.* London: Oxford University Press.

———. 1976. *The Causes of World War Three.* Westport, Conn.: Greenwood Press.

Minister of Supply and Services Canada. 1991. *Citizen's Forum on Canada's Future: Report to the People and Government of Canada.* Ottawa: Canadian Government Publishing Centre.

Mintz, Laurie B., and Nancy E. Betz. 1986. "Sex Differences in the Nature, Realism, and Correlates of Body Image." *Sex Roles*, 15:185–195.

Misztal, Barbara A. 1993. "Understanding Political Change in Eastern Europe: A Sociological Perspective." *Sociology*, 27(3):451–471.

Mitchell, Catherine. 1995. "Expert Takes a Swipe at Spanking." *Winnipeg Free Press* (November 23).

Mollison, Andrew. 1992. "Study: Sexual Harassment Crosses Global Boundaries." *Austin American-Statesman* (December 1):A2.

Monaghan, Peter. 1993. "Facing Jail, a Sociologist Raises Questions About a Scholar's Right to Protect Sources." *The Chronicle of Higher Education* (April 7):A10.

Money, John, and Anke A. Ehrhardt. 1972. *Man and Woman, Boy and Girl.* Baltimore: Johns Hopkins University Press.

Moody, Harry R. 1994. *Aging: Concepts and Controversy.* Thousand Oaks, Cal.: Pine Forge Press.

Moog, Carol. 1990. *Are They Selling Her Lips? Advertising and Identity.* New York: Morrow.

Moon, R. 1992. "Drawing Lines in a Culture of Prejudice: R. vs. Keegstra and the Restriction of Hate Propaganda." *University of British Columbia Law Review*, 26:99–143.

Moore, Patricia, with C.P. Conn. 1985. *Disguised.* Waco, Tex.: Word Books.

Moore, Robert B. 1992. "Racist Stereotyping in the English Language." In Margaret L. Andersen and Patricia Hill Collins (eds.), *Race, Class, and Gender.* Belmont, Cal.: Wadsworth, 317–329.

Moore, Wilbert E. 1968. "Occupational Socialization." In David A. Goslin (ed.), *Handbook on Socialization Theory and Research.* Chicago: Rand McNally, 861–883.

Moorhead, Caroline (ed.). 1992. *Betrayal: A Report on Violence Toward Children in Today's World.* New York: Doubleday.

Moreau, Joanne. 1994. "Employment Equity." In Craig McKie and Keith Thompson (eds.), *Canadian Social Trends*, vol. 2. Toronto: Thompson Educational Publishers, 147–49.

Morgan, S. Philip, Diane N. Lye, and Gretchen A. Condran. 1988. "Sons, Daughters, and the Risk of Marital Disruption." *American Journal of Sociology*, 94(1):110–129.

Morrow, Lance. 1993. "Unspeakable." *Time* (February 22):48–50.

Mosher, Steven W. 1994. *A Mother's Ordeal: One Woman's Fight Against China's One-Child Policy.* New York: HarperPerennial.

Moss, Kirby. 1990. "Fraternities Condemned at UT Rally." *Austin American-Statesman* (November 29):B1.

Mucciolo, Louis. 1992. *Eightysomething: Interviews with Octogenarians Who Stay Involved.* New York: Birch Lane Press.

Mukerji, Chandra, and Michael Schudson. 1991. *Rethinking Popular Culture: Contemporary Perspectives in Cultural Studies.* Berkeley: University of California Press.

Murdock, George P. 1945. "The Common Denominator of Cultures." In Ralph Linton (ed.), *The Science of Man in the World Crisis.* New York: Columbia University Press, 123–142.

Murphy, Emily F. 1922. *The Black Candle.* Toronto: Thomas Allan.

Murphy, Robert E., Jessica Scheer, Yolanda Murphy, and Richard Mack. 1988. "Physical Disability and Social Liminality: A Study in the Rituals of Adversity." *Social Science and Medicine,* 26:235–242.

Myerhoff, Barbara. 1994. *Number Our Days: Culture and Community Among Elderly Jews in an American Ghetto.* New York: Meridian.

Myles, John. 1991. "Post-Industrialism and the Service Economy." In Daniel Drache and Meric S. Gertler (eds.), *The New Era of Global Competition: State Policy and Market Power.* Montreal and Kingston: McGill-Queen's University Press.

Nader, George A. 1976. *Cities of Canada,* vol. 2. *Profiles of Fifteen Metropolitan Centres.* Toronto: Macmillan of Canada.

Naeyaert, Kathleen. 1990. *Living with Sensory Loss: Vision.* Ottawa: National Advisory Council on Aging.

Nakhaie, M. Reza, and Robert Arnold. 1996. "Class Position, Class Ideology, and Class Voting: Mobilization of Support for the New Democratic Party in the Canadian Election of 1984." *Canadian Review of Sociology and Anthropology,* 33(2):181–212.

Narine, Doug. 1996. "Teen Faces Net Hate Charges." *Winnipeg Free Press* (March 29):A1–A3.

Nason-Clark, Nancy. 1993. "Gender Relations in Contemporary Christian Organizations." In W. E. Hewitt (ed.), *The Sociology of Religion: A Canadian Focus.* Toronto: Butterworths, 215–234.

National Advisory Council on Aging. 1989. *Understanding Seniors' Independence Report #1: The Barriers and Suggestions for Action.* Ottawa: Minister of Supply and Services.

National Council on Crime and Delinquency. 1969. *The Infiltration into Legitimate Business by Organized Crime.* Washington, D.C.: National Council on Crime and Delinquency.

National Council of Welfare. 1992. *Poverty Profile,* Cat no. H67–1/4–1990E. Ottawa: Minister of Supply and Services Canada.

———. 1996. *Poverty Profile 1994.* Ottawa: Minister of Supply and Services Canada.

National Safety Council. 1992. *Accident Facts: 1992 Edition.* Chicago: National Safety Council.

Nelson, Mariah Burton. 1994. *The Stronger Women Get, the More Men Love Football: Sexism and the American Culture of Sports.* New York: Harcourt Brace.

Nemeth, Mary, John Demont, E. Kaye Fulton, John Howse, and Adrienne Webb. 1992. "Chilling the Sexes." *Maclean's* (February 17):42.

Nemeth, Mary, Sharon Doyle Driedger, John DeMont, and Adrienne Webb. 1994. "Body Obsession." *Maclean's* (February 5):44.

Nemeth, Mary, Nora Underwood, and John Howse. 1993. "God Is Alive." *Maclean's* (April 12):32–36.

Nessner, Katherine. 1994. "Profile of Canadians with Disabilities." In Craig McKie (ed.), *Canadian Social Trends.* Toronto: Thompson Educational Publishing Company, 121–124.

Nett, Emily M. 1993. *Canadian Families: Past and Present* (2nd ed.). Toronto: Butterworths.

Nettler, Gwynn. 1984. *Explaining Crime* (3rd ed.). Toronto: McGraw-Hill.

Newman, David M. 1995. *Sociology: Exploring the Architecture of Everyday Life.* Thousand Oaks, Cal.: Pine Forge Press.

Newman, Katherine S. 1988. *Falling from Grace: The Experience of Downward Mobility in the American Middle Class.* New York: Free Press.

———. 1993. *Declining Fortunes: The Withering of the American Dream.* New York: Basic Books.

Newman, Peter C. 1993. "Trees Are Renewable, But Forests Are Not." *Maclean's* (August 16):44.

Nichols, Mark. 1993. "The World Is Watching." *Maclean's* (August 16):22–26.

Ng, Edward. 1994. "Children and Elderly People: Sharing Public Income Resources." In Craig McKie (ed.), *Canadian Social Trends.* Toronto: Thompson Educational Publishing Company, 249–252.

Niebuhr, H. Richard. 1929. *The Social Sources of Denominationalism.* New York: Meridian.

Nielsen, Joyce McCarl. 1990. *Sex and Gender in Society: Perspectives on Stratification* (2nd ed.). Prospects Heights, Ill.: Waveland Press.

Nisbet, Robert. 1979. "Conservativism." In Tom Bottomore and Robert Nisbet (eds.), *A History of Sociological Analysis.* London: Heinemann, 81–117.

Norland, J.A. 1994. *Profile of Canada's Seniors,* Cat. no. 96–312E. Scarborough, Ont.: Statistics Canada and Prentice-Hall.

Norton, Julie. 1993. "Women, Economic Ideology and the Struggle to Build Alternatives." In Eric Shragge (ed.), *Community Economic Development.* Montreal: Black Rose Books, 115–128.

Novak, Mark. 1993. *Aging and Society: A Canadian Perspective.* Scarborough, Ont.: Nelson Canada.

———. 1995. "Successful Aging." In *Aging and Society: A Canadian Reader.* Scarborough, Ont.: Nelson Canada.

Oakes, Jeannie. 1985. *Keeping Track: How High Schools Structure Inequality.* New Haven, Conn.: Yale University Press.

Oberle, Peter. 1993. *The Incidence of Family Poverty on Canadian Indian Reserves.* Ottawa: Indian and Northern Affairs Canada.

Oberschall, Anthony. 1973. *Social Conflict and Social Movements.* Englewood Cliffs, N.J.: Prentice-Hall.

Obomsawin, Alanis. 1993. Kanehsatake: 270 Years of Resistance [motion picture]. Montreal: National Film Board of Canada.

O'Brien, Carol-Anne, and Lorna Weir. 1995. "Lesbians and Gay Men Inside and Outside Families." In Nancy Mandell and Ann Duffy (eds.), *Canadian Families.* Toronto: Harcourt Brace and Company, 111–139.

O'Brien, Jodi. 1995. "Sociology for the Student as Public: A Neglected Genre." *Contemporary Sociology: A Journal of Reviews,* 24(3):307–311.

O'Connell, Helen. 1994. *Women and the Family.* Prepared for the UN-NGO Group on Women and Development. Atlantic Highlands, N.J.: Zed Books.

O'Connor, James. 1973. *The Fiscal Crisis of the State.* New York: St. Martin's Press.

Odendahl, Teresa. 1990. *Charity Begins at Home: Generosity and Self-Interest Among the Philanthropic Elite.* New York: Basic Books.

Oderkirk, Jillian. 1992. "Food Banks." *Canadian Social Trends,* 24(Spring):6–14.

———. 1994. "Parents and Children Living with Low Incomes." In C. McKie (ed.), *Canadian Social Trends,* vol. 2. Toronto: Thompson Education Publishing, 237–242.

Oderkirk, Jillian, and Clarence Lochhead. 1995. "Lone Parenthood: Gender Differences." In E.D. Nelson and B.W. Robinson (eds.), *Gender in the 1990s.* Scarborough, Ont.: Nelson Canada, 397–405.

Ogburn, William F. 1966. *Social Change with Respect to Culture and Original Nature.* New York: Dell (orig. pub. 1922).

Ogmundson, Rick. 1975. "Party Class Images and the Class Vote in Canada." *American Sociological Review,* 40:506–512.

Ogmundson, Rick, and M. Ng. 1982. "On the Inference of Voter Motivation: A Comparison of the Subjective Class Vote in Canada and the United Kingdom." *Canadian Journal of Sociology,* 7:41–59.

Oja, Gail. 1980. "Inequality of Wealth Distributions in Canada, 1970 and 1977." In *Reflections on Canadian Incomes.* Ottawa: Economic Council of Canada, 352.

Oliver, Michael. 1990. *The Politics of Disablement: A Sociological Approach.* New York: St. Martin's Press.

Omi, Michael, and Howard Winant. 1994. *Racial Formation in the United States: From the 1960s to the 1990s.* New York: Routledge.

Ontario Social Assistance Review Committee. 1988. *Transitions.* Ottawa: Queen's Printer for Ontario.

Orbach, Susie. 1978. *Fat Is a Feminist Issue.* New York: Paddington.

O'Reilly-Fleming, Thomas. 1993. *Down and Out in Canada: Homeless Canadians.* Toronto: Canadian Scholar's Press.

Ortner, Sherry B. 1974. "Is Female to Male As Nature Is to Culture?" In Michelle Rosaldo and Louise Lamphere (eds.), *Women, Culture, and Society.* Stanford, Cal.: Stanford University Press.

Ortner, Sherry B., and Harriet Whitehead (eds). 1981. *Sexual Meanings: The Cultural Construction of Gender and Sexuality.* Cambridge, Mass.: Cambridge University Press.

Orum, Anthony M. 1974. "On Participation in Political Protest Movements." *Journal of Applied Behavioral Science,* 10:181–207.

———. 1988. *Introduction to Political Sociology: The Social Anatomy of the Body Politic* (3rd ed.). Englewood Cliffs, N.J.: Prentice-Hall.

Orum, Anthony M., and Amy W. Orum. 1968. "The Class and Status Bases of Negro Student Protest." *Social Science Quarterly,* 49 (December):521–533.

Osterman, Cynthia. 1995. "Rising Child Poverty in World Worries Health Experts." *Reuters* (May 30):2.

Ostrander, Susan A. 1984. *Women of the Upper Class.* Philadelphia: Temple University Press.

O'Sullivan, Chris. 1993. "Fraternities and the Rape Culture." In Emile Buchwald et al. (eds.), *Transforming a Rape Culture.* Minneapolis: Milkweed Ltd.

Owen, Bruce. 1996a. "Former Soldiers Charged in Slaying." *Winnipeg Free Press* (March 2):A1–A3.

Owen, Bruce. 1996b. "Harrassment Ends in Firings." In *Winnipeg Free Press* (March 23).

Page, Charles H. 1946. "Bureaucracy's Other Face." *Social Forces,* 25 (October):89–94.

Palen, J. John. 1995. *The Suburbs.* New York: McGraw-Hill.

Palmore, Erdman. 1981. *Social Patterns in Normal Aging: Findings from the Duke Longitudinal Study.* Durham, N.C.: Duke University Press.

Pammett, Jon H. 1993. "Tracking the Votes." In Alan Frizell et al. (eds.), *The Canadian General Election of 1993.* Ottawa: Carleton University Press.

Panitch, Leo, and Donald Swartz. 1993. *Assault on Trade Union Freedoms* (2nd ed.). Toronto: Garamond.

Parenti, Michael. 1986. *Inventing Reality: The Politics of the Mass Media.* New York: St. Martin's Press.

———. 1988. *Democracy for the Few* (5th ed.). New York: St. Martin's Press.

———. 1994. *Land of Idols: Political Mythology in America.* New York: St. Martin's Press.

Park, Robert E. 1915. "The City: Suggestions for the Investigation of Human Behavior in the City." *American Journal of Sociology*, 20:577–612.

———. 1928. "Human Migration and the Marginal Man." *American Journal of Sociology*, 33.

———. 1936. "Human Ecology." *American Journal of Sociology*, 42:1–15.

Park, Robert E., and Ernest W. Burgess. 1921. *Human Ecology*. Chicago: University of Chicago Press.

Parker, Robert Nash. 1995. "Violent Crime." In Joseph F. Sheley, *Criminology: A Contemporary Handbook* (2nd. ed.). Belmont, Cal.: Wadsworth, 169–185.

Parkinson, C. Northcote. 1957. *Parkinson's Law and Other Studies in Administration*. New York: Ballantine Books.

Parkinson, Gary, and Robert Drislane. 1996. *Exploring Sociology*. Toronto: Harcourt Brace.

Parrish, Dee Anna. 1990. *Abused: A Guide to Recovery for Adult Survivors of Emotional/Physical Child Abuse*. Barrytown, N.Y.: Station Hill Press.

Parsons, Talcott. 1951. *The Social System*. Glencoe, Ill.: Free Press.

———. 1955. "The American Family: Its Relations to Personality and to the Social Structure." In Talcott Parsons and Robert F. Bales (eds.), *Family, Socialization and Interaction Process*. Glencoe, Ill.: Free Press, 3–33.

———. 1960. "Toward a Healthy Maturity." *Journal of Health and Social Behavior*, 1:163–173.

Parsons, Talcott, and Edward A. Shils (eds.). 1951. *Toward a General Theory of Action*. Cambridge, Mass.: Harvard University Press.

Passell, Peter. 1994. "'Bell Curve' Critics Say Early I.Q. Isn't Destiny." *New York Times* (November 9):B10.

Patros, Philip G., and Tonia K. Shamoo. 1989. *Depression and Suicide in Children and Adolescents: Prevention, Intervention, and Postvention*. Boston: Allyn & Bacon.

Patterson, Charlotte J. 1992. "Children of Lesbian and Gay Parents." *Child Development*, 63(5):1025–1043.

Patterson, Christopher, and Elizabeth Podnieks. 1995. "A Guide to the Diagnosis and Treatment of Elder Abuse." In Mark Novak (ed.), *Aging and Society: A Canadian Reader*. Scarborough, Ont.: Nelson Canada.

PBS. 1992a. "The Glory and the Power, Part I."

———. 1992b. "Sex, Power, and the Workplace."

Pearson, Judy C. 1985. *Gender and Communication*. Dubuque, Iowa: Brown.

Pedrick-Cornell, Claire, and Richard J. Gelles. 1982. "Elderly Abuse: The Status of Current Knowledge." *Family Relations*, 31:457–465.

Peritz, I. 1993. "Synagogues Vandalized." *Montreal Gazette* (January 5):A1.

Perrow, Charles. 1986. *Complex Organizations: A Critical Essay* (3rd ed.). New York: Random House.

Perry, David C., and Alfred J. Watkins (eds.). 1977. *The Rise of the Sunbelt Cities*. Beverly Hills, Cal.: Sage.

Perry-Jenkins, Maureen, and Ann C. Crouter. 1990. "Men's Provider Role Attitudes: Implications for Household Work and Marital Satisfaction." *Journal of Family Issues*, 11:136–156.

Peter, Karl A. 1987. *The Dynamics of Hutterite Society*. Edmonton: University of Alberta Press.

Peter, Laurence J., and Raymond Hull. 1969. *The Peter Principle: Why Things Always Go Wrong*. New York: Morrow.

Peters, John F. 1985. "Adolescents as Socialization Agents to Parents." *Adolescence*, 20 (Winter):921–933.

Peters, Linda, and Patricia Fallon. 1994. "The Journey of Recovery: Dimensions of Change." In Patricia Fallon, Melanie A. Katzman, and Susan C. Wooley (eds.), *Feminist Perspectives on Eating Disorders*. New York: Guilford Press, 339–354.

Petersen, John L. 1994. *The Road to 2015: Profiles of the Future*. Corte Madera, Cal.: Waite Group Press.

Peterson, Robert. 1992. *Only the Ball Was White: A History of Legendary Black Players and All-Black Professional Teams*. New York: Oxford University Press (orig. pub. 1970).

Pheasant, Valerie Bedassigae. 1994. "My Mother Used to Dance." In Carl E. James and Adrienne Shadd (eds.), *Talking about Difference*. Toronto: Between the Lines, 35–40.

Piaget, Jean. 1954. *The Construction of Reality in the Child*. Trans. Margaret Cook. New York: Basic Books.

Picard, André. 1992. "Hate Slaying of Gay Men Stuns Montreal: Police Charge Four Neo-Nazi Skinheads." *The Globe and Mail* (December 4):A1–A2.

———. 1996. "Québécois Voices." *The Globe and Mail* (June 13):A21.

Picot, G., and T. Wannell. 1990. "Job displacement." In Craig McKie and Keith Thompson (eds.), *Canadian Social Trends*. Toronto: Thompson Educational Publishers, 271–275.

Pillard, Richard C., and James D. Weinrich. 1986. "Evidence of Familial Nature of Male Homosexuality." *Archives of General Psychiatry*, 43(8):800–812.

Pillemer, Karl A. 1985. "The Dangers of Dependency: New Findings on Domestic Violence Against the Elderly." *Social Problems*, 33 (December):146–158.

Pillemer, Karl A., and David Finkelhor. 1988. "The Prevalence of Elder Abuse: A Random Sample Survey." *The Gerontologist*, 28(1):51–57.

Pinderhughes, Dianne M. 1986. "Political Choices: A Realignment in Partisanship Among Black Voters?" In James D. Williams (ed.), *The State of Black America 1986.* New York: National Urban League, 85–113.

Pineo, Peter C., and John Porter. 1979. "Occupational Prestige in Canada." In James E. Curtis and William G. Scott (eds.), *Social Stratification in Canada* (2nd ed.), 205–220.

Pines, Maya. 1981. "The Civilizing of Genie." *Psychology Today*, 15 (September):28–29, 31–32, 34.

Piturro, Marlene. 1994. "Capitalist China?" *Brandweek*, 35(20):22–27.

Podnieks, Elizabeth. 1989. *A National Survey on Abuse of the Elderly in Canada: Preliminary Findings.* Toronto: Ryerson Polytechnical Institute.

Polakow, Valerie. 1993. *Lives on the Edge: Single Mothers and Their Children in the Other America.* Chicago: University of Chicago Press.

Pomice, Eva. 1990. "Madison Avenue's Blind Spot." In Karin Swisher (ed.), *The Elderly: Opposing Viewpoints.* San Diego: Greenhaven Press, 42–45.

Pope, Carl E. 1995. "Juvenile Justice in the Next Millennium." In John Klofas and Stan Stojkovic (eds.), *Crime and Justice in the Year 2010.* Belmont, Cal.: Wadsworth, 267–280.

Popenoe, David. 1993. "American Family Decline, 1960–1990: A Review and Appraisal." *Journal of Marriage and the Family*, 55(3):527–543.

Popoff, Wilfred. 1996. "One Day You're Family; the Next Day You're Fired." *The Globe and Mail* (March 14):A22.

Porter, John. 1965. *The Vertical Mosaic.* Toronto: University of Toronto Press.

———. 1987. "Education Equality and the Just Society." In J. Porter (ed.), *The Measure of Canadian Society: Education, Equality and Opportunity.* Ottawa: Carleton University Press, 242–280.

Porter, J., M. Porter, and B. Blishen. 1982. *Stations and Callings: Making It Through the School System.* Toronto: Methuen.

Presthus, Robert. 1978. *The Organizational Society.* New York: St. Martin's Press.

Priest, Gordon. 1993. "Living Arrangements of Canada's 'Older Elderly' Population." In Craig McKie, *Canadian Social Trends.* Toronto: Thompson Educational Publishing Company, 183–187.

Prothrow-Stith, Deborah, with Micaele Weissman. 1991. *Deadly Consequences.* New York: HarperCollins.

Quadagno, Jill S. 1984. "Welfare Capitalism and the Social Security Act of 1935." *American Sociological Review*, 49:632–647.

———. 1994. *The Color of Welfare: How Racism Undermined the War on Poverty.* New York: Oxford University Press.

Queen, Stuart A., and David B. Carpenter. 1953. *The American City.* New York: McGraw-Hill.

Quigley, Tim. 1994. "Some Issues in the Sentencing of Aboriginal Offenders." Cited in Royal Commission on Aboriginal Peoples Report: *1996 Bridging the Cultural Divide.* Ottawa: Minister of Supply and Services Canada.

Quinney, Richard. 1974. *Critique of the Legal Order.* Boston: Little, Brown.

———. 1979. *Class, State, and Crime.* New York: McKay.

———. 1980. *Class, State, and Crime* (2nd ed.). New York: Longman.

Rabinowitz, Fredric E., and Sam V. Cochran. 1994. *Man Alive: A Primer of Men's Issues.* Pacific Grove, Cal.: Brooks/Cole.

Raboy, Marc. 1992. "Canadian Broadcasting, Canadian Nationhood: Two Concepts, Two Solitudes, and Great Expectations." In H. Holmes and D. Taras (eds.), *Seeing Ourselves: Media Power and Policy in Canada.* Toronto: Harcourt Brace Jovanovich, 156–187.

Radcliffe-Brown, A.R. 1952. *Structure and Function in Primitive Society.* New York: Free Press.

Raffalli, Mary. 1994. "Why So Few Women Physicists?" *New York Times Supplement* (January):Sect. 4A, 26–28.

Ram, B. 1990. *New Trends in the Family: Demographic Facts and Features.* Ottawa: Statistics Canada.

Ramazanoglu, Caroline. 1989. *Feminisms and the Contradictions of Oppression.* London: Routledge.

Ramu, G.N. 1984. "Family Background and Perceived Marital Happiness: A Comparison of Voluntary Childless Couples and Parents." *Canadian Journal of Sociology*, 9:47–67.

———. 1993. *Marriage and the Family in Canada Today* (2nd ed.). Scarborough, Ont.: Prentice Hall.

Rankin, Robert P., and Jerry S. Maneker. 1985. "The Duration of Marriage in a Divorcing Population: The Impact of Children." *Journal of Marriage and the Family*, 47 (February):43–52.

Raphael, Beverley. 1986. *When Disaster Strikes: How Individuals and Communities Cope with Catastrophe.* New York: Basic Books.

Reckless, Walter C. 1967. *The Crime Problem.* New York: Meredith.

Reich, Robert. 1993. "Why the Rich Are Getting Richer and the Poor Poorer." In Paul J. Baker, Louis E. Anderson, and Dean S. Dorn (eds.), *Social Problems: A Critical Thinking Approach* (2nd ed.).

Belmont, Cal.: Wadsworth, 145–149. Adapted from *The New Republic*, May 1, 1989.

———. 1979. *The Rich Get Richer and the Poor Get Prison: Ideology, Class, and Criminal Justice*. New York: Wiley.

Reiman, Jeffrey H. 1984. *The Rich Get Richer and the Poor Get Prison* (2nd ed.). New York: Wiley.

Reinharz, Shulamit. 1992. *Feminist Methods in Social Research*. New York: Oxford University Press.

Reinisch, June. 1990. *The Kinsey Institute New Report on Sex: What You Must Know to Be Sexually Literate*. New York: St. Martin's Press.

Renzetti, Claire M., and Daniel J. Curran. 1992. *Women, Men, and Society*. Boston: Allyn & Bacon.

———. 1995. *Women, Men, and Society* (3rd ed.). Boston: Allyn & Bacon.

Reskin, Barbara F., and Heidi Hartmann. 1986. *Women's Work, Men's Work: Sex Segregation on the Job*. Washington, D.C.: National Academy Press.

Reskin, Barbara F., and Irene Padavic. 1994. *Women and Men at Work*. Thousand Oaks, Cal.: Pine Forge Press.

Richardson, C. James. 1996. "Divorce and Remarriage in Families." In Maureen Baker (ed.), *Changing Trends in Canada*. Toronto: McGraw-Hill Ryerson, 215–248.

Richardson, John G., and Carl H. Simpson. 1982. "Children, Gender and Social Structure: An Analysis of the Content of Letters to Santa Claus." *Child Development*, 53:429–436.

Richardson, Laurel. 1993. "Inequalities of Power, Property, and Prestige." In Virginia Cyrus (ed.), *Experiencing Race, Class, and Gender in the United States*. Mountain View, Cal.: Mayfield, 229–236.

Richardson, R. Jack. 1992. "Free Trade: Why Did It Happen?" *Canadian Review of Sociology and Anthropology*, 29:307–328.

———. 1994. "Economic Institutions and Power." In Lorne Tepperman, James E. Curtis, and R.J. Richardson (eds.), *The Social World* (3rd ed.). Toronto: McGraw-Hill Ryerson, 558–589.

Richardson, R. Jack. 1990. Economic Concentration and Social Power in Contemporary Canada." In J. Curtis and L. Tepperman (eds.), *Images of Canada: The Sociological Tradition*, 341–351.

Richer, Stephen. 1988. "Equality to Benefit from Schooling: The Issue of Educational Opportunity." In D. Forcese and S. Richer (eds.), *Social Issues: Sociological Views of Canada*. Toronto: Prentice Hall, 262–286.

Richer, Stephen, and Lorne Weir. 1995. *Beyond Political Correctness: Toward the Inclusive University*. Toronto: University of Toronto Press.

Richler, Mordecai. 1991. "A Reporter at Large." *The New Yorker* (September 23):40–92.

———. 1992. *Oh Canada! Oh Quebec!* Toronto and New York: Knopff, p. 1.

Rifkin, Jeremy. 1995. *The End of Work*. New York: G.P. Putnam's Sons.

Riggs, Robert O., Patricia H. Murrell, and JoAnne C. Cutting. 1993. *Sexual Harassment in Higher Education: From Conflict to Community*. ASHE-ERIC Higher Education Reports, Washington, D.C.: George Washington University, 93–2.

Rigler, David. 1993. "Letters: A Psychologist Portrayed in a Book About an Abused Child Speaks Out for the First Time in 22 Years." *New York Times Book Review* (June 13):35.

Riley, Matilda White, and John W. Riley, Jr. 1994. "Age Integration and the Lives of Older People." *The Gerontologist*, 34(1):110–115.

Risman, Barbara J. 1987. "Intimate Relationships from a Microstructural Perspective: Men Who Mother." *Gender & Society*, 1:6–32.

Ristock, Janice L., and Joan Pennell. 1996. *Research as Empowerment: Feminist Links, Postmodern Interruptions*. Don Mills: Oxford University Press.

Ritzer, George. 1993. *The McDonaldization of Society: An Investigation into the Changing Character of Contemporary Social Life*. Thousand Oaks, Cal.: Pine Forge Press.

Roberts, Julian. 1992. *Sexual Abuse in Canada: A Survey of National Data*. Ottawa: Department of Justice.

———. 1995. *Disproportionate Harm: Hate Crime in Canada*. Ottawa: Department of Justice.

Roberts, Lance, and Rodney Clifton. 1990. "Multiculturalism in Canada: A Sociological Perspective." In Peter Li. (ed.), *Race and Ethnic Relations in Canada*. Toronto: Oxford University Press, 120–147.

Robertson, Ian. 1977. *Sociology*. New York: Worth Publishers.

———. 1989. *Sociology: A Brief Introduction*. New York: Worth.

Rockwell, John. 1994. "The New Colossus: American Culture as Power Export." *New York Times* (January 30):Section 2, 1, 30.

Rodgers, Kain, and Rebecca Kong. 1996. "Crimes Against Women and Children in the Family." In Leslie Kennedy and Vincent Sacco (eds.), *Crime Counts: A Criminal Event Analysis*. Scarborough, Ont.: Nelson Canada, 115–132.

Roethlisberger, Fritz J., and William J. Dickson. 1939. *Management and the Worker*. Cambridge, Mass.: Harvard University Press.

Rogers, Harrell R. 1986. *Poor Women, Poor Families: The Economic Plight of America's Female-Headed Households*. Armonk, N.Y.: Sharpe.

Rollins, Judith. 1985. *Between Women: Domestics and Their Employers.* Philadelphia: Temple University Press.

Romaniuc, Anatole. 1994. "Fertility in Canada: Retrospective and Prospective." In Frank Trovato and Carl F. Grindstaff (eds.), *Perspectives on Canada's Population.* Toronto: Oxford University Press, 214–229.

Roof, Wade Clark. 1993. *A Generation of Seekers: The Spiritual Journeys of the Baby Boom Generation.* San Francisco: HarperSanFrancisco.

Roos, Patricia A., and Barbara F. Reskin. 1992. "Occupational Desegregation in the 1970s: Integration and Economic Equity?" *Sociological Perspectives,* 35:69.

Root, Maria P.P. 1990. "Disordered Eating in Women of Color." *Sex Roles,* 22(7/8):525–536.

Ropers, Richard H. 1991. *Persistent Poverty: The American Dream Turned Nightmare.* New York: Plenum.

Rose, Jerry D. 1982. *Outbreaks.* New York: Free Press.

Rosenberg, Howard. 1993. "TV's Peril: Filling Time When There's Nothing More to Say." *Austin American-Statesman* (April 20):A6.

Rosenburg, Michael. 1995. "Ethnic and Race Relations." In L. Tepperman, J.E. Curtis, and R.J. Richardson (eds.), *Sociology.* Toronto: McGraw-Hill Ryerson, 302–344

Rosengarten, Ellen M. 1995. Communication to author.

Rosenthal, Naomi, Meryl Fingrutd, Michele Ethier, Roberta Karant, and David McDonald. 1985. "Social Movements and Network Analysis: A Case Study of Nineteenth-Century Women's Reform in New York State." *American Journal of Sociology,* 90:1022–1054.

Rosenthal, Robert. 1969. "Empirical versus Degreed Validation of Clocks and Tests." *American Educational Research Journal,* 6 (November):689–691.

Rosnow, Ralph L., and Gary Alan Fine. 1976. *Rumor and Gossip: The Social Psychology of Hearsay.* New York: Elsevier.

Ross, Aileen A. 1982. *The Lost and the Lonely: Homeless Women in Montreal.* Montreal: McGill University Printing Service.

Ross, David P., E. Richard Shillington, and Clarence Lochhead. 1994. *The Canadian Fact Book on Poverty.* Ottawa: Canadian Council on Social Development.

Rossi, Alice S. 1973. *The Feminist Papers.* New York: Bantam.

———. 1980. "Life-Span Theories and Women's Lives." *Signs,* 6(1):4–32.

———. 1992. "Transition to Parenthood." In Arlene Skolnick and Jerome Skolnick (eds.), *Family in Transition.* New York: HarperCollins, 453–463.

Rossi, Peter H. 1989. *Down and Out in America: The Origins of Homelessness.* Chicago: University of Chicago Press.

Rossides, Daniel W. 1986. *The American Class System: An Introduction to Social Stratification.* Boston: Houghton Mifflin.

Roth, Guenther. 1988. "Marianne Weber and Her Circle." In Marianne Weber, *Max Weber.* New Burnswick, N.J.: Transaction, vx.

Roth, Nicki. 1993. *Integrating the Shattered Self: Psychotherapy with Adult Incest Survivors.* Northvale, N.J.: Jason Aronson.

Rotheram, Mary Jane, and Jean S. Phinney. 1987. "Introduction: Definitions and Perspectives in the Study of Children's Ethnic Socialization." In Jean S. Phinney and Mary Jane Rotheram (eds.), *Children's Ethnic Socialization.* Newbury Park, Cal.: Sage, 10–28.

Rothman, Robert A. 1993. *Inequality and Stratification: Class, Color, and Gender* (2nd ed.). Englewood Cliffs, N.J.: Prentice-Hall.

Rowe, Patricia. 1992. "Child Abuse Telecast Floods National Hotline." *Children Today,* 21(2):11.

Rowley, Storer H. 1994. "Conference Condemns Mutilation of Female Genitals." *Austin American-Statesman* (September 11):A9.

Royal Commission on Aboriginal Peoples. 1995. *Choosing Life: Special Report on Suicide Among Aboriginal Peoples.* Ottawa: Canada Communications Group Publishing.

Rubin, Lillian B. 1976. *Worlds of Pain: Life in the Working-Class Family.* New York: Basic Books.

———. 1986. "A Feminist Response to Lasch." *Tikkun,* 1(2):89–91.

———. 1994. *Families on the Fault Line.* New York: HarperCollins.

Russell, Diana E.H. 1984. *Sexual Exploitation.* Beverly Hills, Cal.: Sage.

———. 1986. *The Secret Trauma: Incest in the Lives of Girls and Women.* New York: Basic Books.

———. 1990. *Rape in Marriage* (rev. ed.). Bloomington: Indiana University Press.

Rutstein, Nathan. 1993. *Healing in America.* Springfield, Mass.: Whitcomb.

Rymer, Russ. 1993. *Genie: An Abused Child's Flight from Silence.* New York: HarperCollins.

Sacco, Vincent F., and L.W. Kennedy. 1994.*The Criminal Event: An Introduction to Criminology.* Scarborough, Ont.: Nelson Canada.

Sadker, David, and Myra Sadker. 1985. "Is the OK Classroom OK?" *Phi Delta Kappan,* 55:358–367.

———. 1986. "Sexism in the Classroom: From Grade School to Graduate School." *Phi Delta Kappan,* 68:512–515.

———. Updated by Mary Jo Strauss. 1989. "The Report Card #3: The Cost of Sex Bias in Schools and Society." Distributed by the Mid-Atlantic Equity Center, Washington, D.C., and the New England Center for Equity Assistance, Andover, Mass.

Sadker, Myra, and David Sadker. 1982. *Sex Equity Handbook for Schools*. New York: Longman.

———. 1984. *Year 3: Final Report, Promoting Effectiveness in Classroom Instruction*. Washington, D.C.: National Institute of Education.

———. 1994. *Failing at Fairness: How America's Schools Cheat Girls*. New York: Scribner.

Safilios-Rothschild, Constantina. 1969. "Family Sociology or Wives' Family Sociology? A Cross-Cultural Examination of Decision-Making." *Journal of Marriage and the Family*, 31(2):290–301.

Samovar, Larry A., and Richard E. Porter. 1991a. *Communication Between Cultures*. Belmont, Cal.: Wadsworth.

———. 1991b. *Intercultural Communication: A Reader* (6th ed.). Belmont, Cal.: Wadsworth.

Sampson, Robert J. 1986. "Effects of Socioeconomic Context on Official Reaction to Juvenile Delinquency." *American Sociological Review*, 51 (December):876–885.

Samuelson, Paul A., and William D. Nordhaus. 1989. *Economics* (13th ed.). New York: McGraw-Hill.

Sanday, Peggy Reeves. 1981. "The Socio-Cultural Context of Rape." *Journal of Social Issues*, 37:5–27.

———. 1990. *Fraternity Gang Rape: Sex, Brotherhood, and Privilege on Campus*. New York: New York University Press.

Sanger, David E. 1994. "Cutting Itself Down to Size: Japan's Inferiority Complex." *New York Times* (February 6):E5.

Sapir, Edward. 1961. *Culture, Language and Personality*. Berkeley: University of California Press.

Sargent, Margaret. 1987. *Sociology for Australians* (2nd ed.). Melbourne, Australia: Longman Cheshire.

Sass, Robert. 1986. "Workplace Health and Safety: Report from Canada." *International Journal of Health Services*, 16:565–582.

Scarce, Rik. 1990. *Eco-Warriors: Understanding the Radical Environmental Movement*. Chicago: Noble Press.

Schaefer, Richard T. 1993. *Racial and Ethnic Groups*. New York: HarperCollins.

———. 1995. *Race and Ethnicity in the United States*. New York: HarperCollins.

Schiller, Herbert I. 1989. *Culture, Inc. The Corporate Takeover of Public Expression*. New York: Oxford University Press.

Schmetzer, Uli. 1992. "Across Asia, Slave Trade Prospers—Often for Child Labor of Sex." *Austin American-Statesman* (February 22):J1, J7.

Schmidt, William E. 1993. "A Churchill Draws Fire with Remark on Race." *New York Times* (June 1):A2.

Schneider, Beth E., and Meredith Gould. 1987. "Female Sexuality: Looking Back into the Future." In Beth Hess and Myra M. Ferree (eds.), *Analyzing Gender: A Handbook of Social Science Research*. Newbury Park, Cal.: Sage, 120–153.

Schneider, Keith. 1993. "The Regulatory Thickets of Environmental Racism." *New York Times* (December 19):E5.

Schur, Edwin M. 1965. *Crimes Without Victims: Deviant Behavior and Public Policy*. Englewood Cliffs, N.J.: Prentice-Hall.

———. 1983. *Labeling Women Deviant: Gender, Stigma, and Social Control*. Philadelphia: Temple University Press.

Scott, Alan. 1990. *Ideology and the New Social Movements*. Boston: Unwin & Hyman.

Scott, Eugenie C. 1992. "The Evolution of Creationism." In Art Must, Jr. (ed.), *Why We Still Need Public Schools: Church/State Relations, and Visions of Democracy*. Buffalo, N.Y.: Prometheus Books.

Scott, Joan W. 1986. "Gender: A Useful Category of Historical Analysis." *American Historical Review*, 91(December):1053–1075.

Scully, Diana. 1990. *Understanding Sexual Violence: A Study of Convicted Rapists*. Boston: Unwin Hyman.

Searles, Neil. 1995. *Physician Assisted Suicide in Manitoba*. Manitoba Association of Rights and Liberties.

Seegmiller, B.R., B. Suter, and N. Duviant. 1980. *Personal, Socioeconomic, and Sibling Influences on Sex-Role Differentiation*. Urbana: ERIC Clearinghouse of Elementary and Early Childhood Education, ED 176 895, College of Education, University of Illinois.

Seid, Roberta P. 1994. "Too 'Close to the Bone': The Historical Context for Women's Obsession with Slenderness." In Patricia Fallon, Melanie A. Katzman, and Susan C. Wooley (eds.), *Feminist Perspectives on Eating Disorders*. New York: Guilford Press, 3–16.

Sengoku, Tamotsu. 1985. *Willing Workers: The Work Ethic in Japan, England, and the United States*. Westport, Conn.: Quorum Books.

Serbin, Lisa A., Phyllis Zelkowitz, Anna-Beth Doyle, Dolores Gold, and Bill Wheaton. 1990. "The Socialization of Sex-Differentiated Skills and Academic Performance: A Mediational Model." *Sex Roles*, 23:613–628.

Shadd, Adrienne. 1991. "Institutionalized Racism and Canadian History: Notes of a Black Canadian." In Ormond McKague (ed.), *Racism in Canada*. Saskatoon: Fifth House, 1–5.

———. 1994. "Where Are You Really From?" In Carl E. James and Adrienne Shadd (eds.), *Talking About Difference.* Toronto: Between the Lines Press, 9–15.

Shakin, Madeline, Debra Shakin, and Sarah Hall Sternglanz. 1985. "Infant Clothing: Sex Labeling for Strangers." *Sex Roles,* 12:955–964.

Shamai, Shmuel. 1992. "Ethnicity and Educational Achievement: Canada, 1941–1981." *Canadian Ethnic Studies,* 24:43–57.

Shapiro, Joseph P. 1993. *No Pity: People with Disabilities Forging a New Civil Rights Movement.* Toronto: Time Books/Random House.

Shapiro, Susan P. 1990. "Collaring the Crime, Not the Criminal: Reconsidering the Concept of White-collar Crime." *American Sociological Review,* 55:346–365.

Shattuck, Roger. 1980. *The Forbidden Experiment.* New York: Farrar, Straus & Giroux.

Sheff, David. 1995. "If It's Tuesday, It Must Be Dad's House." *New York Times Magazine* (March 26):64–65.

Sheley, Joseph F. 1985. *America's "Crime Problem."* Belmont, Cal.: Wadsworth.

———. 1991. *Criminology: A Contemporary Handbook.* Belmont, Cal.: Wadsworth.

Shenon, Philip. 1994. "China's Mania for Baby Boys Creates Surplus of Bachelors." *New York Times* (August 16):A1, A4.

Sherman, Suzanne (ed.). 1992. "Frances Fuchs and Gayle Remick." In *Lesbian and Gay Marriage: Private Commitments, Public Ceremonies.* Philadelphia: Temple University Press, 189–201.

Shevky, Eshref, and Wendell Bell. 1966. *Social Area Analysis: Theory, Illustrative Application and Computational Procedures.* Westport, Conn.: Greenwood Press.

Shillington, E. Richard. 1991. "Estimates of Native Child Poverty: Census 1986." In *Children in Poverty: Toward a Better Future.* Ottawa: Standing Senate Committee on Social Affairs, Science, and Technology.

Shisslak, Catherine M., and Marjorie Crago. 1992. "Eating Disorders Among Athletes." In Raymond Lemberg (ed.), *Controlling Eating Disorders with Facts, Advice, and Resources.* Phoenix: Oryx Press, 29–36.

———. 1994. "Toward a New Model for the Prevention of Eating Disorders." In Patricia Fallon, Melanie A. Katzman, and Susan C. Wooley (eds.), *Feminist Perspectives on Eating Disorders.* New York: Guilford Press, 419–437.

Shkilynyk, Anastasia M. 1985. *A Poison Stronger Than Love: The Destruction of an Ojibwa Community.* New Haven: Yale University Press.

Shor, Ira. 1986. *Culture Wars: School and Society in the Conservative Restoration 1969–1984.* Boston: Routledge & Kegan Paul.

Shorto, Russell. 1991. "Made-in-Japan Parenting," *Health,* 54 (June):56–57.

Sikorsky, Robert. 1990. "Highway Robbery: Canada's Auto Repair Scandal." *Reader's Digest* (February):55–63.

Silverman, Robert, and Leslie Kennedy. 1993. *Deadly Deeds: Murder in Canada.* Scarborough, Ont.: Nelson Canada

Silverstein, Louise B. 1991. "Transforming the Debate About Child Care and Maternal Employment." *American Psychologist,* 46:1025–1032.

Simmel, Georg. 1904. "Fashion." *American Journal of Sociology,* 62 (May 1957):541–558.

———. 1950. *The Sociology of Georg Simmel.* Trans. Kurt Wolff. Glencoe, Ill.: Free Press (orig. written 1902–1917).

Simon, David R., and D. Stanley Eitzen. 1993. *Elite Deviance* (4th ed.). Boston: Allyn & Bacon.

Simons, Marlise. 1993a. "Homeless Find a Spot in France's Heart." *New York Times* (December 9):A4.

———. 1993b. "Prosecutor Fighting Girl-Mutilation." *New York Times* (November 23):A4.

Simons, Rita James. 1975. *Women and Crime.* Washington, D.C.: U.S. Government Printing Office.

Simpson, George Eaton, and Milton Yinger. 1972. *Racial and Cultural Minorities: An Analysis of Prejudice and Discrimination* (4th ed.). New York: Harper & Row.

Simpson, Sally S. 1989. "Feminist Theory, Crime, and Justice." *Criminology,* 27:605–632.

———. 1990. "Caste, Class, and Violent Crime: Explaining Differences in Female Offending." *Criminology,* 29:115–137.

Singer, Bennett L., and David Deschamps (eds.). 1994. *Gay and Lesbian Stats.* New York: New Press.

Singer, Margaret Thaler, with Janja Lalich. 1995. *Cults in Our Midst.* San Francisco: Jossey-Bass.

Singh, J.A.L., and Robert M. Zingg. 1942. *Wolf-Children and Feral Man.* New York: Harper & Row.

Sjoberg, Gideon. 1965. *The Preindustrial City: Past and Present.* New York: Free Press.

Skocpol, Theda, and Edwin Amenta. 1986. "States and Social Policies." In Ralph H. Turner and James F. Short, Jr. (eds.), *Annual Review of Sociology,* 12:131–157.

Slugoski, B.F., and Ginsburg, G.B. 1989. "Ego Identity and Explanatory Speech." In John Shotter and Kenneth J. Gergen (eds.), *Texts of Identity.* London: Sage, 36–55.

Smandych, Russell. 1985. "Marxism and the Creation of Law: Re-Examining the Origins of Canadian Anti-Combines Legislation." In Thomas Fleming (ed.), *The New Criminologies in Canada: State, Crime and Control.* Toronto: Oxford University Press, 87–99.

Smelser, Neil J. 1963. *Theory of Collective Behavior.* New York: Free Press.

———. 1988. "Social Structure." In Neil J. Smelser (ed.), *Handbook of Sociology.* Newbury Park, Cal.: Sage, 103–129.

Smith, Adam. 1976. *An Inquiry into the Nature and Causes of the Wealth of Nations.* Roy H. Campbell and Andrew S. Skinner (eds.). Oxford, England: Clarendon Press (orig. pub. 1776).

Smith, Allen C., III, and Sheryl Kleinman. 1989. "Managing Emotions in Medical School: Students' Contacts with the Living and the Dead." *Social Science Quarterly,* 52(1):56–69.

Smith, Dorothy. 1985. "Women, Class and Family." In Varda Burstyn and Dorothy Smith (eds.), *Women, Class and the State.* Toronto: Garamond.

———. 1987. *The Everyday World as Problematic: A Feminist Sociology.* Toronto: University of Toronto Press.

Smith, Michael D. 1996. "Patriarchal Ideology and Wife Beating." In Robert J. Brym (ed.), *Society in Question: Sociological Readings for the 21st Century.* Toronto: Harcourt Brace, and Company.

Snider, Laureen. 1988. "Commercial Crime." In Vincent F. Sacco (ed.), *Deviance, Conformity and Control in Canadian Society.* Scarborough, Ont.: Prentice Hall, 231–283.

Snow, David A., and Leon Anderson. 1991. "Researching the Homeless: The Characteristic Features and Virtues of the Case Study." In Joe R. Feagin, Anthony M. Orum, and Gideon Sjoberg (eds.), *A Case for the Case Study.* Chapel Hill: University of North Carolina Press, 148–173.

———. 1993. *Down on Their Luck: A Case Study of Homeless Street People.* Berkeley: University of California Press.

Snow, David A., E. Burke Rochford, Jr., Steven K. Worden, and Robert D. Benford. 1986. "Frame Alignment Processes, Micromobilization, and Movement Participation." *American Sociological Review,* 51:464–481.

Snow, David A., Louis A. Zurcher, and Robert Peters. 1981. "Victory Celebrations as Theater: A Dramaturgical Approach to Crowd Behavior." *Symbolic Interaction,* 4(1):21–41.

Snyder, Benson R. 1971. *The Hidden Curriculum.* New York: Knopf.

Sokoloff, Natalie. 1992. *Black Women and White Women in the Professions.* New York: Routledge.

Soper, Steven Paul. 1985. *Totalitarianism: A Conceptual Approach.* Lanham, Md.: University Press of America.

South, Scott J., Charles M. Bonjean, Judy Corder, and William T. Markham. 1982. "Sex and Power in the Federal Bureaucracy." *Work and Occupations,* 9(2):233–254.

Specter, Michael. 1994a. "Crisis of Bread and Land Afflicts Russian Farming." *New York Times* (September 19):A1, A16.

———. 1994b. "Soaring Unemployment Is Spreading Fear in Russia." *New York Times* (May 8):A6.

Spencer, Metta. 1993. *Foundations of Modern Sociology* (6th ed.). Scarborough, Ont.: Prentice Hall

Spitzer, Steve. 1975. "Toward a Marxian Theory of Deviance." *Social Problems,* 22:638–651.

Stackhouse, John. 1996. "Disenfranchised Asian Youth Rage Against Those in Driver's Seat." *The Globe and Mail* (July 31):A7.

Stamler, Rodney T. 1996. "Organized Crime." In Rick Linden (ed.), *Criminology: A Canadian Perspective* (3rd ed.). Toronto: Harcourt Brace and Company, 423–457.

Stanley, Alessandra. 1994. "Sexual Harassment Thrives in the New Russian Climate." *New York Times* (April 17):1, 7.

Stannard, David E. 1992. *American Holocaust: Columbus and the Conquest of the New World.* New York: Oxford University Press.

Staples, Brent. 1994. "Aunt Jemima Gets a Makeover." *New York Times* (October 19):A14.

Stark, Rodney. 1992. *Sociology* (4th ed.). Belmont, Cal.: Wadsworth.

Stark, Rodney, and William Sims Bainbridge. 1980. "Secularizations, Revival, and Cult Formation." *Annual Review of the Social Sciences of Religion,* 4:85–119.

———. 1981. "American-Born Sects: Initial Findings." *Journal for the Scientific Study of Religion,* 20:130–149.

Starr, Paul. 1982. *The Social Transformation of Medicine: The Rise of a Sovereign Profession and the Making of a Vast Industry.* New York: Basic Books.

———. 1987. "The Sociology of Official Statistics." In William Alonso and Paul Starr (eds.), *The Politics of Numbers.* New York: Russell Sage Foundation.

———. 1992. "Social Categories and Claims in the Liberal State." *Social Research,* 59(2):263–296.

Statham, Anne, Laurel Richardson, and Judith A. Cook. 1991. *Gender and University Teaching: A Negotiated Difference.* Albany: SUNY Press.

Statistics Canada. 1991a. *Health and Activity Limitation Survey: Selected Characteristics of Persons with Disabilities Residing in Households,* Cat. no. 82–555. Ottawa: Minister of Industry, Science, and Technology.

———. 1991b. *1991 Census of Canada, Profile of Census Metropolitan Areas and Census Agglomerations,* Part

A, Cat. no. 93–337. Ottawa: Minister of Industry, Science, and Technology.

———. 1992. Minister of Supply and Services. *Labour Force Annual Averages*. Ottawa: Ministry of Industry, Science, and Technology.

———. 1993a. *Earnings of Men and Women 1990*. Cat. No. 13–217, 1992. Ottawa: Minister of Industry, Science, and Technology.

———. 1993b.*The Labour Force Annual Averages 1991*. Cat. No. 71–220 annual. Ottawa: Minister of Industry, Science and Technology.

———. 1994a. *Women in the Labour Force*. Ottawa: Ministry of Industry, Science, and Technology.

———. 1994b *Juristat: Canadian Crime Statistics*, 15(12) Minister of Supply and Services.

———. 1994c. *Violence Against Women Survey*. Ottawa: Minister of Industry, Science, and Technology.

———. 1995a. *Canada at a Glance*. Ottawa: Minister of Supply and Services.

———. 1995b. *Canada at a Glance*. Ottawa: Minister of Supply and Services.

———. 1996a. *The Daily* (April 24). Ottawa: Minister of Supply and Services.

———. 1996b. *The Daily* (May 9) Ottawa: Minister of Supply and Services.

———. 1996c. "Births and Deaths." The Daily (May 24). Ottawa: Ministry of Supply and Services.

———. 1996d. *Canada at a Glance, Cat. no. 93–319*. Ottawa: Minister of Supply and Services.

Stebbins, Robert A. "Interactionist Theories." In Rick Linden (ed.), *Criminology: A Canadian Perspective* (3rd ed.). Toronto: Harcourt Brace and Company.

Steffensmeier, Darrell, and Cathy Streifel. 1991. "Age, Gender, and Crime Across Three Historical Periods: 1935, 1960, and 1985." *Social Forces*, 69:869–894.

Steffensmeier, Darrell, and Emilie Allan. 1995. "Criminal Behavior: Gender and Age." In Joseph F. Sheley (ed.), *Criminology: A Contemporary Handbook*. Belmont, Cal.: Wadsworth, 83–113.

Steiger, Thomas L., and Mark Wardell. 1995. "Gender and Employment in the Service Sector." *Social Problems*, 42(1): 91–123.

Stein, Peter J. 1976. *Single*. Englewood Cliffs, N.J.: Prentice-Hall.

———. (ed.). 1981. *Single Life: Unmarried Adults in Social Context*. New York: St. Martin's Press.

Steinbacher, Roberta, and Helen Bequaert Holmes. 1987. "Sex Choice: Survival and Sisterhood." In Gena Corea et al. (eds.), *Man-made Women: How New Reproductive Technologies Affect Women*. Bloomington: Indiana University Press, 52–63.

Steinback, Robert L. 1993. "The Melting Pot Is Contrary to American Ideal." *Miami Herald* (August 17):B1.

Steinmetz, Suzanne K. 1987. "Elderly Victims of Domestic Violence." In Carl D. Chambers, John H. Lindquist, O.Z. White, and Michael T. Harter, (eds.), *The Elderly: Victims and Deviants*. Athens: Ohio University Press, 126–141.

Stern, Aimee L. 1993. "Managing by Team Is Not Always as Easy as It Looks." *New York Times* (July 18):F5.

Stevenson, Harold W., and James W. Stigler. 1992. *The Learning Gap: Why Our Schools Are Failing and What We Can Learn from Japanese and Chinese Education*. New York: Summit Books.

Stevenson, Mary Huff. 1988. "Some Economic Approaches to the Persistence of Wage Differences Between Men and Women." In Ann H. Stromberg and Shirley Harkess (eds.), *Women Working: Theories and Facts in Perspective* (2nd ed.). Mountain View, Cal.: Mayfield, 87–100.

Stewart, Abigail J. 1994. "Toward a Feminist Strategy for Studying Women's Lives." In Carol E. Franz and Abigail J. Stewart (eds.), *Women Creating Lives: Identities, Resilience, and Resistance*. Boulder, Col.: Westview, 11–35.

Stiehm, Judith Hicks. 1989. *Arms and the Enlisted Woman*. Philadelphia: Temple University Press.

Stier, Deborah S., and Judith A. Hall. 1984. "Gender Differences in Touch: An Empirical and Theoretical Review." *Journal of Personality and Social Psychology*, 47(2):440–459.

Stolker, Paula B. 1992. "Weigh My Job Performance, Not My Body: Extending Title VII to Weight-Based Discrimination." *New York Law School Journal of Human Rights*, 10(1):223–250.

Stone, Leroy O. 1967. Urban Development in Canada: 1961 Census Monograph. Ottawa: Queen's Printer.

Stout, Cam. 1994. "Common Law: A Growing Alternative." In C. McKie (ed.), *Canadian Social Trends*, vol. 2. Toronto: Thompson Educational Publishing, 179–182.

Strenski, James. 1995. "The Ethics of Manipulated Communication." *Public Relations Quarterly*, vol. 40, 09–011993, 33.

Sumner, William G. 1959. *Folkways*. New York: Dover (orig. pub. 1906).

Sutherland, Edwin H. 1939. *Principles of Criminology*. Philadelphia: Lippincott.

———. 1949. *White Collar Crime*. New York: Dryden.

Swainson, G. 1993. "Hate Crimes on Rise, Police Say." *Toronto Star* (June 16):A7.

Swerdlow, Marian. 1989. "Men's Accommodations to Women Entering a Nontraditional Occupation: A Case of Rapid Transit Operatives." *Gender & Society*, 3:373–387.

Swidler, Ann. 1986. "Culture in Action: Symbols and Strategies." *American Sociological Review*, 51 (April):273–286.

Tabb, William K., and Larry Sawers. 1984. *Marxism and the Metropolis: New Perspectives in Urban Political Economy* (2nd ed.). New York: Oxford University Press.

Takaki, Ronald. 1993. *A Different Mirror: A History of Multicultural America*. Boston: Little, Brown.

Tannen, Deborah. 1990. *You Just Don't Understand: Women and Men in Conversation*. New York: Morrow.

———. 1993. "Commencement Address, State University of New York at Binghamton." Reprinted in *Chronicle of Higher Education* (June 9):B5.

———. 1995. "Wears Jump Suit. Sensible Shoes. Uses Husband's Last Name." In E.D. Nelson, and B.W. Robinson (eds.), *Gender in the 1990s: Images, Realities, and Issues*. Scarborough, Ont.: Nelson Canada, 3–7.

Tavris, Carol. 1993. *The Mismeasure of Woman*. New York: Touchstone.

Taylor, Carl S. 1993. *Girls, Gangs, Women, and Drugs*. East Lansing: Michigan State University Press.

Taylor, Steve. 1982. *Durkheim and the Study of Suicide*. New York: St. Martin's Press.

Tepperman, Lorne. 1994. *Choices and Chances: Sociology for Everyday Life* (2nd ed.). Toronto: Harcourt Brace and Company.

Terkel, Studs. 1990. *Working: People Talk About What They Do All Day and How They Feel About What They Do*. New York: Ballantine (orig. pub. 1972).

The Chilly Collective (eds.). 1995. *Breaking Anonymity: The Chilly Climate for Women Faculty*. Waterloo, Ont.: Wilfrid Laurier University Press.

"The Favored Infants." 1976. *Human Behavior* (June):49–50.

Thiam, Awa. 1986. *Speak Out, Black Sisters: Feminism and Oppression in Black Africa*. Dover, N.H.: Pluto.

Thomas, D. 1992. *Criminality Among the Foreign Born: Analysis of Federal Prison Population*. Ottawa: Immigration and Employment Canada.

Thomas, William I., and Dorothy Swaine Thomas. 1928. *The Child in America*. New York: Knopf.

Thompson, Becky W. 1992. "'A Way Outa No Way': Eating Problems Among African-American, Latina, and White Women." *Gender & Society*, 6(4):546–561. Revised article, "Food, Bodies, and Growing Up Female: Childhood Lessons About Culture, Race, and Class." In Patricia Fallon, Melanie A. Katzman, and Susan C. Wooley (eds.), *Feminist Perspectives on Eating Disorders*. New York: Guilford Press, 1994, 355–378.

———. 1994. *A Hunger So Wide and So Deep: American Women Speak Out on Eating Problems*. Minneapolis: University of Minnesota.

Thompson, Paul. 1983. *The Nature of Work*. London: Macmillan.

Thomson, Elizabeth, and Ugo Colella. 1992. "Cohabitation and Marital Stability: Quality or Commitment?" *Journal of Marriage and the Family*, 54:259–267.

Thorne, Barrie, Cheris Kramarae, and Nancy Henley. 1983. *Language, Gender, and Society*. Rowley, Mass.: Newbury House.

Thornton, Russell. 1984. "Cherokee Population Losses During the Trail of Tears: A New Perspective and a New Estimate." *Ethnohistory*, 31:289–300.

Tidwell, Gary L. 1993. *Anatomy of a Fraud: Inside the Finances of the P.T.L. Ministries*. New York: Wiley.

Tilly, Charles. 1973. "Collective Action and Conflict in Large-Scale Social Change: Research Plans, 1974–78." Center for Research on Social Organization. Ann Arbor: University of Michigan, October.

———. (ed.). 1975. *The Formation of National States in Western Europe*. Princeton, N.J.: Princeton University Press.

———. 1978. *From Mobilization to Revolution*. Reading, Mass.: Addison-Wesley.

Time. 1993. "The Week: Schwarzenegger Body Count." (June 28):22.

Timpson, Joyce. 1995. "Four Decades of Literature on Native Canadian Child Welfare: Changing Themes." *Child Welfare*, 74:525.

Tiryakian, Edward A. 1978. "Emile Durkheim." In Tom Bottomore and Robert Nisbet (eds.), *A History of Sociological Analysis*. New York: Basic Books, 187–236.

Tittle, Charles W., William J. Villemez, and Douglas A. Smith. 1978. "The Myth of Social Class and Criminality." *American Sociological Review* 43(5):643–656.

Toffler, Alvin. 1980. *The Third Wave*. New York: Bantam.

Tomasevski, Katarina. 1993. Prepared on behalf of the UN-NGO Group on Women and Development. *Women and Human Rights*. Atlantic Highlands, N.J.: Zed Books.

Tong, Rosemarie. 1989. *Feminist Thought: A Comprehensive Introduction*. Boulder, Col.: Westview Press.

Tonnies, Ferdinand. 1940. *Fundamental Concepts of Sociology (Gemeinschaft und Gesellschaft)*. Trans. Charles P. Loomis. New York: American Book Company (orig. pub. 1887).

Touraine, Alain. 1971. *Post Industrial Society*. New York: Random House.

Tucker, Robert C. (ed.). 1979. *The Marx-Engels Reader* (2nd ed.). New York: Norton.

Tumin, Melvin. 1953. "Some Principles of Stratification: A Critical Analysis." *American Sociological Review*, 18 (August):387–393.

Turner, Jonathan, Leonard Beeghley, and Charles H. Powers. 1995. *The Emergence of Sociological Theory* (3rd ed.). Belmont, Cal.: Wadsworth.

Turner, Jonathan H., Royce Singleton, Jr., and David Musick. 1984. *Oppression: A Socio-History of Black-White Relations in America*. Chicago: Nelson-Hall (reprinted 1987).

Turner, Ralph H., and Lewis M. Killian. 1993. "The Field of Collective Behavior." In Russell L. Curtis, Jr., and Benigno E. Aguirre (eds.), *Collective Behavior and Social Movements*. Boston: Allyn & Bacon, 5–20.

Twenhofel, Karen. 1993. "Do You Diet?" In Leslea Newman (ed.), *Eating Our Hearts Out: Personal Accounts of Women's Relationship to Food*. Freedom, Cal.: Crossing Press.

Tyler, Patrick E. 1994. "China's Discus Champ: Alone, Disabled, and Barred." *New York Times* (September 8):A3.

United Nations Development Program. 1996. *The Human Development Report*. Cary, North Carolina: Oxford University Press.

Ursel, Jane. 1992. *Private Lives, Public Policy: 100 Years of State Intervention in the Family*. Toronto: Women's Press.

———. 1993. "Family and Social Policies." In G.N. Ramuy (ed.), *Marriage and the Family in Canada Today* (2nd ed.). Scarborough Ont.: Prentice-Hall, 146–165

———. 1996. *Submission to the Commission of Inquiry into the Deaths of Rhonds LaVoie and Roy Lavoie*. Winnipeg.

Vallières, Pierre. 1971. *White Niggers of America*. Toronto: McClelland and Stewart.

Van Biema, David. 1993a. "But Will It End the Abortion Debate?" *Time* (June 14):52–54.

———. 1993b. "When White Makes Right." *Time* (August 9):40–42.

Vanier Institute of the Family. 1994. *Profiling Canadian Families*. Ottawa: Vanier Institute of the Family.

Vaughan, Diane. 1985. "Uncoupling: The Social Construction of Divorce." In James M. Henslin (ed.), *Marriage and Family in a Changing Society* (2nd ed.). New York: Free Press, 429–439.

Vaughan, Ted. R., Gideon Sjoberg, and Larry T. Reynolds, (eds.). 1993. *A Critique of Contemporary American Sociology*. Dix Hills, N.Y.: General Hall.

Veblin, Thorstein. 1967. *The Theory of the Leisure Class*. New York: Viking (orig. pub. 1899).

Veevers, Jean. E. 1980. *Childless by Choice*. Toronto: Butterworths.

Verhovek, Sam Howe. 1993. "Scores Die As Cult Compound Is Set Afire After F.B.I. Sends in Tanks with Tear Gas." *New York Times* (April 20):A1, A12.

———. 1994. "After Tornado, a Slow Recovery but Stronger Ties." *New York Times* (December 27):A1, A7.

Vetter, Harold J., and Gary R. Perlstein. 1991. *Perspectives on Terrorism*. Pacific Grove, Cal.: Brooks/Cole.

Vetter, Harold J., and Ira J. Silverman. 1986. *Criminology and Crime*. New York: Harper & Row.

Vigil, James. 1990. "Cholos and Gangs: Culture Change and Street Youth in Los Angeles." In Ronald C. Huff (ed.), *Gangs in America*. Newbury Park, Cal.: Sage.

Vito, Gennaro F., and Ronald M. Holmes. 1994. *Criminology: Theory, Research and Policy*. Belmont, Cal.: Wadsworth.

Volpe, R. 1989. *Poverty and Child Abuse: A Review of Selected Literature*. Toronto: Institute for the Prevention of Child Abuse.

Wachtel, Andy. 1994. *Child Abuse and Neglect. A Discussion Paper and Overview of Topically Related Projects*. Ottawa: The Circle.

Wagley, Charles, and Marvin Harris. 1958. *Minorities in the New World*. New York: Columbia University Press.

Wagner, Elvin, and Allen E. Stearn. 1945. *The Effects of Smallpox on the Destiny of the American Indian*. Boston: Bruce Humphries.

Walker, Lawrence J. 1989. "A Longitudinal Study of Moral Reasoning." *Child Development*, 60:157–166.

Walker, Lenore. 1979. *The Battered Woman*. New York: Harper & Row.

Wallace, Ruth A. 1991. "Women Administrators of Priestless Parishes: Constraints and Opportunities." *Review of Religious Research*, 32 (June):289–304.

Wallace, Walter L. 1971. *The Logic of Science in Sociology*. New York: Aldine de Gruyter.

Wallerstein, Immanuel. 1979. *The Capitalist World-Economy*. Cambridge, England: Cambridge University Press.

Wannell, Ted, and Nathalie Caron. 1996. The Gender Earnings Gap Among Recent Postsecondary Graduates, 1984–92, Cat. no. 68 #11F0G19MPE. Ottawa: Statistics Canada.

Ward, Mike. 1996. "Firm Fined $6,000 After Man Killed in Unsafe Workplace." *Winnipeg Free Press* (March 7).

Ward, Pamela. 1993. "Rap on Trial." *Austin American-Statesman* (May 30):A1, A10.

Warner, W. Lloyd, and Paul S. Lunt. 1941. *The Social Life of a Modern Community*. New Haven, Conn.: Yale University Press.

Warr, Mark. 1985. "Fear of Rape Among Urban Women." *Social Problems*, 32:238–250.

———. 1993. "Age, Peers, and Delinquency." *Criminology*, 31(1):17–40.

———. 1995. "America's Perceptions of Crime and Punishment." In Joseph F. Sheley, *Criminology: A Contemporary Handbook* (2nd ed.). Belmont, Cal.: Wadsworth, 15–31.

Warshaw, Robin. 1988. *I Never Called It Rape*. New York: Harper & Row.

Watson, Roy E.L., and Peter W. DeMeo. 1987. "Premarital Cohabitation Versus Traditional Courtship and Subsequent Marital Adjustment: A Replication and a Follow-Up." *Family Relations*, 36:193–197.

Webb, Eugene, et al. 1966. *Unobtrusive Measures: Nonreactive Research in the Social Sciences*. Chicago: Rand McNally.

Weber, Max. 1963. *The Sociology of Religion*. Trans. E. Fischoff. Boston: Beacon Press (orig. pub. 1922).

———. 1968. *Economy and Society: An Outline of Interpretive Sociology*. Trans. G. Roth and G. Wittich. New York: Bedminster Press (orig. pub. 1922).

———. 1976. *The Protestant Ethic and the Spirit of Capitalism*. Trans. Talcott Parsons. Introduction by Anthony Giddens. New York: Scribner (orig. pub. 1904–1905).

Weeks, John R. 1992. *Population: An Introduction to Concepts and Issues* (5th ed.). Belmont, Cal.: Wadsworth.

Weigel, Russell H., and P.W. Howes. 1985. "Conceptions of Racial Prejudice: Symbolic Racism Revisited." *Journal of Social Issues*, 41:124–132.

Weinfeld, Morton. 1995. "Ethnic and Race Relations." In R. Brym (ed.), *New Society: Sociology for the 21st Century*. Toronto: Harcourt Brace and Company, 4.1–4.29

Weinraub, Bernard. 1994. "Scarier Than Dinosaurs: The Sexes." *New York Times* (January 5):B1.

Weiskel, Timothy. 1994. "Vicious Circles." *Harvard International Review* 16:12–20.

Weiss, Meira. 1994. *Conditional Love: Parents' Attitudes Toward Handicapped Children*. Westport, Conn.: Bergin & Garvey.

Weitz, Rose. 1993. "Living with the Stigma of AIDS." In Delos H. Kelly (ed.), *Deviant Behavior: A Text-Reader in the Sociology of Deviance* (4th ed.). New York: St. Martin's Press, 222–236.

———. 1995. *A Sociology of Health, Illness, and Health Care*. Belmont, Cal.: Wadsworth.

Weitzman, Lenore J. 1985. *The Divorce Revolution*. New York: Free Press.

Wendell, Susan. 1995. "Toward a Feminist Theory of Disability." In E.D. Nelson and B.W. Robinson (eds.), *Gender in the 1990s*. Scarborough, Ont.: Nelson Canada, 455–465.

Weston, Kath. 1991. *Families We Choose: Lesbians, Gays, Kinship*. New York: Columbia University Press.

Westrum, Ron. 1991. *Technologies and Society: The Shaping of People and Things*. Belmont, Cal.: Wadsworth.

Whitaker, Reg. 1991. *Double Standard: The Secret Story of Canadian Immigration*. Toronto: Lester and Orpen Dennys.

White, James. 1987. "Premarital Cohabitation and Marital Stability in Canada." *Journal of Marriage and the Family*, 49:641–647.

White, Ralph, and Ronald Lippitt. 1953. "Leader Behavior and Member Reaction in Three 'Social Climates.'" In Dorwin Cartwright and Alvin Zander (eds.), *Group Dynamics*. Evanston, Ill.: Row, Peterson, 586–611.

White, Richard W. 1992. *Rude Awakening: What the Homeless Crisis Tells Us*. San Francisco: ICS Press.

Whorf, Benjamin Lee. 1956. *Language, Thought and Reality*. John B. Carroll (ed.). Cambridge, Mass.: MIT Press.

Whyte, William Foote. 1988. *Street Corner Society: Social Structure of an Italian Slum*. Chicago: University of Chicago Press (orig. pub. 1943).

———. 1989. "Advancing Scientific Knowledge Through Participatory Action Research." *Sociological Forum*, 4:367–386.

Whyte, William H., Jr. 1957. *The Organization Man*. Garden City, N.Y.: Anchor.

Wickett, Ann. 1989. *Double Exit: When Aging Couples Commit Suicide Together*. Eugene, Ore.: Hemlock Society.

Wieler, Joseph M. 1986. "The Role of Law in Labour Relations." In Ivan Bernier and Andree Lojoie (eds.), *Labour Law and Urban Law in Canada*. Toronto: University of Toronto Press.

Williams, Christine L. 1989. *Gender Differences at Work*. Berkeley: University of California Press.

———. (ed.). 1993. *Doing "Women's Work": Men in Nontraditional Occupations*. Newbury Park, Cal.: Sage.

Williams, Gregory Howard. 1995. *Life on the Color Line: The True Story of a White Boy Who Discovered He Was Black*. New York: Dutton.

Williams, Robin M., Jr. 1970. *American Society: A Sociological Interpretation* (3rd ed.). New York: Knopf.

Williamson, Robert C., Alice Duffy Rinehart, and Thomas O. Blank. 1992. *Early Retirement: Promises and Pitfalls*. New York: Plenum Press.

Wilson, Edward O. 1975. *Sociobiology: A New Synthesis*. Cambridge, Mass.: Harvard University Press.

Wilson, Elizabeth. 1991. *The Sphinx in the City: Urban Life, the Control of Disorder, and Women.* Berkeley: University of California Press.
Wilson, Everett K., and Hanan Selvin. 1980. *Why Study Sociology? A Note to Undergraduates.* Belmont, Cal.: Wadsworth.
Wilson, William Julius. 1980. *The Declining Significance of Race* (2nd ed.). Chicago: University of Chicago Press.
———. 1981. "Race, Class, and Public Policy." *American Sociologist,* 16:125–134.
———. 1987. *The Truly Disadvantaged: The Inner City, the Underclass, and Public Policy.* Chicago: University of Chicago Press.
Winn, Maria. 1985. *The Plug-in Drug: Television, Children, and the Family.* New York: Viking.
Wirth, Louis. 1938. "Urbanism as a Way of Life." *American Journal of Sociology,* 40:1–24.
———. 1945. "The Problem of Minority Groups." In Ralph Linton (ed.), *The Science of Man in the World Crisis.* New York: Columbia University Press, 38.
Wiseman, Jacqueline. 1970. *Stations of the Lost: The Treatment of Skid Row Alcoholics.* Chicago: University of Chicago Press.
———. 1979. *Stations of the Lost: The Treatment of Skid Row Alcoholics.* Chicago: University of Chicago Press.
Wishart, Cynthia. 1993. "Workplace Harassment." In Graham S. Lowe and Harvey J. Krahn (eds.), *Work in Canada.* Scarborough, Ont.: Nelson Canada.
Wolf, Daniel. 1996. "A Bloody Biker War." *Maclean's* (Jan.15):10–11.
Wolf, Naomi. 1990. *The Beauty Myth: How Images of Beauty Are Used Against Women.* New York: Morrow.
———. 1994. "Hunger." In Patricia Fallon, Melanie A. Katzman, and Susan C. Wooley (eds.), *Feminist Perspectives on Eating Disorders.* New York: Guilford Press, 94–111.
Wolfe, David A. 1987. *Child Abuse: Implications for Child Development and Psychopathology.* Newbury Park, Cal.: Sage.
Wolfe, Jeanne M. 1992. "Canada's Livable Cities." *Social Policy,* 23:56–63.
Women Working Worldwide (eds.). 1991. *Common Interests: Women Organizing in Global Electronics.* London: Women Working Worldwide.
Women's Action Coalition (eds.). 1993. *WAC Stats: The Facts About Women* (2nd ed.). New York: New Press.
Wong, Sandra L. 1991. "Evaluating the Content of Textbooks: Public Interests and Professional Authority." *Sociology of Education,* 64:11–18.
Wood, Chris Caragata. 1994. "The Legacy of Sue Rodriquez." *Maclean's* (February 28): 22.
Wood, Darryl S., and Curt T. Griffiths. 1996. "Patterns of Aboriginal Crime." In Robert A. Silverman, James J. Teevan, and Vincent F. Sacco (eds.), *Crime in Canadian Society* (5th ed.). Toronto: Harcourt Brace and Company, 222–223.
Wood, Julia T. 1994. *Gendered Lives: Communication, Gender, and Culture.* Belmont, Cal.: Wadsworth.
Wooden, Wayne S. 1995. *Renegade Kids, Suburban Outlaws: From Youth Culture to Delinquency.* Belmont, Cal.: Wadsworth.
Woodward, Joe. 1995. "Quality of Life versus Sanctity of Life." *Alberta Report/Western Report,* 22 (March 6):38.
Wooley, Susan C. 1994. "Sexual Abuse and Eating Disorders: The Concealed Debate." In Patricia Fallon, Melanie A. Katzman, and Susan C. Wooley (eds.), *Feminist Perspectives on Eating Disorders.* New York: Guilford Press, 171–211.
Worster, Donald. 1985. *Natures Economy: A History of Ecological Ideas.* New York: Cambridge University Press.
Wouters, Cas. 1989. "The Sociology of Emotions and Flight Attendants: Hochschild's Managed Heart." *Theory, Culture & Society,* 6:95–123.
Wright, Erik Olin, Karen Shire, Shu-Ling Hwang, Maureen Dolan, and Janeen Baxter. 1992. "The Non-Effects of Class on the Gender Division of Labor in the Home: A Comparative Study of Sweden and the U.S." *Gender & Society,* 6(2):252–282.
Wu Dunn, Sheryl. 1995. "Japanese Cult: A Strong Lure and a Danger to Challenge." *New York Times* (March 24):A1.
Wylie, Alison. 1995. "The Contexts of Activism on 'Climate' Issue." In the Chilly Collective (eds.), *Breaking Anonymity: The Chilly Climate for Women Faculty.* Waterloo, Ont.: Wilfrid Laurier University Press, 29–60.
Yelin, Edward H. 1992. *Disability and the Displaced Worker.* New Brunswick, N.J.: Rutgers University Press.
Yinger, J. Milton. 1960. "Contraculture and Subculture." *American Sociological Review,* 25 (October):625–635.
———. 1982. *Countercultures: The Promise and Peril of a World Turned Upside Down.* New York: Free Press.
Young, Anthony. 1990. "Television Viewing." In Craig McKie and K. Thompson (eds.), *Canadian Social Trends.* Toronto: Thompson Educational Publishing, 231–233.
Young, Michael Dunlap. 1994. *The Rise of the Meritocracy.* New Brunswick, N.J.: Transaction (orig. pub. 1958).

Zald, Mayer N., and John D. McCarthy (eds.). 1987. *Social Movements in an Organizational Society.* New Brunswick, N.J.: Transaction.

Zavella, Patricia. 1987. *Women's Work and Chicano Families: Cannery Workers of the Santa Clara Valley.* Ithaca, N.Y.: Cornell University Press.

Zeidenberg, Jerry. 1990. "The Just-in-Time Workforce." *Small Business,* (May):31–34.

Zelizer, Viviana. 1985. *Pricing the Priceless Child: The Changing Social Value of Children.* New Haven, Conn.: Yale University Press.

Zellner, William M. 1978. "Vehicular Suicide: In Search of Incidence." Unpublished M.A. thesis, Western Illinois University, Macomb. Quoted in Richard T. Schaefer and Robert P. Lamm. 1992. *Sociology* (4th ed.). New York: McGraw-Hill, 54–55.

Zimbardo, Philip G. 1970. "The Human Choice: Individuation, Reason, and Order Versus Deindividuation, Impulse, and Chaos." In W.J. Arnold and D. Levine (eds.), *Nebraska Symposium on Motivation, 1969.* Lincoln: University of Nebraska Press.

Zimmerman, Don H. 1992. "They Were All Doing Gender, but They Weren't All Passing: Comment on Rogers." *Gender & Society,* 6(2):192–198.

Zipp, John F. 1985. "Perceived Representativeness and Voting: An Assessment of the Impact of 'Choices' vs. 'Echoes.'" *The American Political Science Review,* 60:3:738–759.

Zuboff, Shoshana. 1988. *In the Age of the Smart Machine.* New York: Basic Books.

Zukewich Ghalam, Nancy. 1994. "Women in the Workplace." In Craig McKie (ed.), *Canadian Social Trends,* vol. 2. Toronto: Thompson Educational Publishing, 141–145.

Zurcher, Louis A. 1983. *Social Roles: Conformity, Conflict, and Creativity.* Beverly Hills, Cal.: Sage.

PHOTO CREDITS

p. 4 © Bob Daemmrich/Stock, Boston; **p. 6** © G. Reekie/Canada Wide; **p. 14** © Al Harvey; **p. 15** © Wide World; **p. 16** (left) The Granger Collection; **p. 16** (right) The Bettmann Archive; **p. 18** The Bettmann Archive; **p. 19** The Granger Collection; **p. 20** The Granger Collection; **p. 21** © Stacy Pick/Stock, Boston; **p. 22** © UPI/ Bettmann; **p. 23** © University of Toronto Archives **p. 26** © T.H./Canapress; **p. 31** © Alex Brandon/Wide World; **p. 40** © Shackman/Monkmeyer Press; **p. 45** © Bob Daemmrich/The Image Works; **p. 46** © Ward Perrin/Canapress; **p. 53** (left) Giraudon/ Art Resource, NY AR 5483/ PEC 7214, E. Degas, At the Cafe (L'Absinthe), Musee d'Orsay, Paris; **p. 53** (right) © Ruben Sprich/Reuters/ Bettmann; **p. 54** (left) © Phyllis Picardi/Stock, Boston; **p. 54** (right) © C. Parry/ The Image Works; **p. 57** © Sestini Agency/Gamma Liaison; **p. 61** © Bob Kalman/ The Image Works; **p. 66** © Peter Arkell/Zuma Images; **p. 86** (top left) © Rob Nelson/Zuma Images; **p. 86** (top right) © Antonio Suarez/Zuma Images; **p. 86** (bottom) © Ira Kirschenbaum/Stock, Boston; **p. 87** (top left) © Nadirsh Naoroji/The Image Works; **p. 87** (top right) © Lee Celano/ SIPA Press; **p. 87** (bottom) © Leggett/Quebec; **p. 89** (left) © Hans Deryk/Canapress; **p. 89** (right) © R.J.G./Canapress; **p. 100** © Lauren Greenfield/Sygma; **p. 104** © Elliott Erwitt/Magnum; **p. 108** © *The Lethbridge Herald*; **p. 109** © Michael Probst/Reuters/ Bettmann; **p. 110** © Victor Englebert/Photo Researchers; **p. 112** © Dave Buston/Canapress; **p. 115** (left) © Moe Doiron/Canapress; **p. 115** (right) © Fred Thornhill/Canada Wide; **p. 116** Karen Kasmauski/Matrix; **p. 124** (left) © James R. Holland/Stock, Boston; **p. 124** (right) © Paul Fusco/ Magnum; **p. 127** © Bachmann/The Image Works; **p. 129** The Granger Collection; **p. 132** © Photo 20-20; **p. 135** (top left) © Bob Daemmrich/ Stock, Boston; **p. 135** (top right) © Richard Hutchings/Photo Researchers; **p. 135** (bottom) © The Image Works; **p. 144** © Al Harvey; **p. 145** © Al Harvey; **p. 152** © Miro Vintoniv/ Stock, Boston; **p. 154** © Canadian Armed Forces; **p. 160** © Gabor Demjen/Stock, Boston; **p. 165** (left) © Andrew Wallace/Canapress; **p. 165** (right) © Frank Gunn/Canapress; **p. 170** © Dick Hemingway; **p. 172** © Le Duc/ Monkmeyer Press; **p. 174** © Rick Browne/Stock, Boston; **p. 177** (left) © Sloan/Gamma Liaison; **p. 177** (right) © Jeff Vinnick/Reuters/ Bettmann; **p. 182** © Paul Chiasson/Canapress; **p. 183** © Nubar Alexanian/Stock, Boston; **p. 185** (left) © Lindsay Hebberd/Woodfin Camp & Associates; **p. 185** (top right) © Eastcott/Momatiuk/Woodfin Camp & Associates; **p. 185** (bottom right) © Misha Erwitt/Magnum; **p. 188** © Bruno Barbey/Magnum; **p. 197** © Mike Cassese/Canapress; **p. 199** © Ted Grant/Canadian Sport Images; **p. 201** © Leonard Freed/ Magnum; **p. 212** (left) © Bob Daemmrich/Stock, Boston; **p. 212** (top right) © Bob Daemmrich/ Stock, Boston; **p. 212** (bottom right) © Ed Lallo/Liaison International; **p. 213** © Bob Daemmrich/The Image Works; **p. 217** © Jean Marc Geloux/Gamma Liaison; **p. 220** (left) © Richard Drew/Wide World; **p. 220** (right) © D. Sorey/Gamma Liaison; **p. 225 (left)** ©, Mark Duncan/Wide World; **p. 225** (right) © Reuters/Bettmann; **p. 234** © K. Faught/Toronto Star; **p. 240** © L. Terry/ Gamma Liaison; **p. 251** © K. Faught/Toronto Star; **p. 261** © Frank Gunn/Canapress; **p. 265** © Mike Cassese/Canada Wide; **p. 269** © Bryan Kelsen/ Gamma Liaison; **p. 281** © Blaise Edwards/Canapress; **p. 284** Moe Doiron/Canapress; **p. 292** © Phil Huber/Black Star; **p. 293** (top left) © Frank Gunn/Canapress; **p. 293** (top right) © Bob Daemmrich/Stock, Boston; **p. 293** (bottom left) © Rob Nelson/Black Star; **p. 293** (bottom right) © Al Harvey; **p. 306** © Gilles-Mingasson/Gamma Liaison; **p. 316** © (left) Mark Masny/ Sipa Press; **p. 316** (right) © Art Seitz/Gamma Liaison; **p. 326** © J. Y. Rabeuf/The Image Works; **p. 331** © Canapress; **p. 336** © Alastair Grant/Canapress; **p. 337** © Warren Toda/Canada Wide; **p. 343** © Lyn Hancock; **p. 346** © Al Harvey; **p. 360** © Thomas Hoepker/Magnum; **p. 361** (left) © Imperial War Museum, London; **p. 361** (right) © Herman Kokojan/Black Star; **p. 366** (top left) © Claus Meyer/Black Star; **p. 366** (top right) © Judah Passow/ JB Pictures; **p. 366** (bottom left) © George Holton/Photo Researchers; **p. 366** (bottom right) © The Bettmann Archive; **p. 371** © Barbara Campbell/ Liaison International; **p. 375** © F. Scott Grant/Canadian Olympic Association **p. 380** (left) © M. Grecco/Stock, Boston; **p. 380** (right) © T. Vogel/ Rapho/ Photo Researchers; **p. 388** © Alan Dorrow/JB Pictures; **p. 389** © David J. Sams/Stock, Boston; **p. 407** © Tony Freeman/ PhotoEdit; **p. 412** (left) © Bob Daemmrich/Stock, Boston; **p. 412** (right) © Ronald Seymour, Inc./Liaison International; **p. 416** © Patrick Guis/ The Gamma Liaison Network; **p. 423** © Tim McKenna/Canada Wide; **p. 427** © Sarah Leen/Matrix; **p. 428** © Chartrand/Canapress; **p. 436** © Sunset Boulevard/Sygma; **p. 441** (left) © The Bettmann Archive; **p. 441** (top right) James Pickerell/The Image Works; **p. 441** (bottom right) © Mulvehill/The Image Works; **p. 454** (top) © Mike Yamashita/Woodfin Camp & Associates; **p. 457** © Louis Psihoyos/ Matrix; **p. 458** © Jim Leynse/Saba; **p. 459** © Leong Kai-Tai/Woodfin Camp & Associates; **p. 474** © Ted Wright; **p. 477** © Shaun Best/Reuters; **p. 480** (top left) © Andy Levin/Photo Researchers; **p. 480** (top right) © Betty Press/Woodfin Camp & Associates; **p. 480** (bottom left) © Cary Wolinsky/Stock, Boston; **p. 486** © Tom Hanson/Canapress; **p. 490** © Tom Hanson/Canapress; **p. 494** © Jacques Boissinot/Canapress; **p. 498** © Fred Chartrand/Canapress; **p. 500** (left) © Fred Chartrand/ Canapress; **p. 500** (right) © Wayne Glowacki/Canapress; **p. 510** © Steve Starr/Stock, Boston; **p. 513** (top) © Shackman/ Monkmeyer; **p. 513** (bottom) © Topham/The Image Works; **p. 523** © courtesy, The Ontario Women's Directorate; **p. 528** © The Bettmann Archive; **p. 534** © Robert Brenner/PhotoEdit; **p. 536** © Dana Schuerholz/Impact Visuals; **p. 538** © Laura Dwight/PhotoEdit; **p. 541** © Haruyoshi Yamaguchi/ Sygma; **p. 554** © Stephen Shames/Matrix; **p. 561** © A. Stawicki/Toronto Star; **p. 566** (left) © Robert McElroy/Woodfin Camp & Associates; **p. 566** (right) © Michele Bartran/JB Pictures; **p. 567** © Jon Burbank/ The Image Works; **p. 574** © Bob Daemmrich/Stock, Boston; **p. 577** © John Zich/Wide World Photos; **p. 578** © Mark O'Neill/Canada Wide; **p. 578** © Peter Bregg/Maclean's; **p. 599** © Betty Press/Woodfin Camp & Associates; **p. 604** (left) © David Guttenfelder/Canapress; **p. 604** (right) © Rikard Larma/Canapress; **p. 614** © (left and right) From Emily F. Murphy, *The Black Candle* © Coles Publishing, 1922; **p. 619** © Dick Hemingway; **p. 624** © P. Power/Toronto Star; **p. 628** (top left) © Gary Crallé/Image Bank; **p. 628** (top right) © Norm Betts/Canada Wide; **p. 628** (bottom) © Bayne Stanley/Canada Wide; **p. 638** © Chuck Stoody/Canapress; **p. 644** © Ryan Remiorz/Canapress; **p. 645** © Guy Noe/ UPI/Bettmann; **p. 647** © Shaney Komulainen/Canapress; **p. 656** © DPA/The Image Works; **p. 657** © Canapress; **p. 659** © Charles Fox/Matrix; **p. 664** (top) © Chuck Nacke/Woodfin Camp & Associates; **p. 664** (bottom) © Dan Lamont/Matrix; **p. 666** © Jacques Boissinot/Canapress.

PERMISSIONS ACKNOWLEDGMENTS

Chapter 1

Quotation, p. 3: from Nemeth, Mary, et al. 1992. "Chilling the Sexes," *Maclean's* (February 17):42. Reprinted by permission.

Table 1.1, p. 29: from DeKeseredy, Walter S., and Katherine Kelly. 1993a. "Woman Abuse in University and College Dating Relationships: The Contribution of the Ideology of Familial Patriarchy." *Journal of Human Justice* 4(2):33. Reprinted by permission.

Chapter 2

Quotation, pp. 39-40: from Shkilnyk, Anastasia. 1985. *A Poison Stronger Than Love: The Destruction of an Ojibwa Community.* New Haven: Yale University Press, p. 17. © 1985 Yale University Press. Reprinted by permission.

Cited on p. 60: from Leenars, Anton, and George Domino. 1993. "A Comparison of Community Attitudes Towards Suicide in Windsor and Los Angeles." *Canadian Journal of Behavioural Science* 25:253-66. © 1993 Canadian Psychological Association. Reprinted with permission.

Chapter 3

Quotation, p. 81: from "Racial Harrassment: Two Individual Reflections."(Author unknown). In *Racism in Canada*, Ormond McKague, general editor (Fifth House Publishers, Saskatoon, 1991). p. 12. Originally published in *The Asianadian.*

Quotation, p. 81: from Picard, Andre. 1992. "Hate Slaying of Gay Men Stuns Montreal: Police Charge Four Neo-Nazi Skinheads." *The Globe and Mail* (December 4):A1-A2. Reprinted with permission from The Globe and Mail.

Quotation, p. 82: from Owen, Bruce. 1996. "Former Soldiers Charged in Slaying." *Winnipeg Free Press* (March 2):A1-A3. Reprinted with permission.

Quotation, p. 93: from Richler, Mordecai. 1992. *Oh Canada! Oh Quebec!* Toronto and New York: Knopf, p. 1. © 1992 Random House Inc. Originally published in *The New Yorker*, September 23, 1991, p. 40.

Cited on pp. 95-96: Excerpts from "The Citizen's Forum on Canada's Future: Report to the People and Government of Canada." 1991. Source: Privy Council Office. Reproduced with the permission of the Minister of Public Works and Government Services Canada, 1996.

Box 3.2, p. 99: from Kopvillem, Peter. 1996. "Guilty as Charged: James Keegstra Reached the End of the Legal Line." *Maclean's* (March 11):24. Reprinted by permission.

Quotation, p. 106: from Shadd, Adrienne. 1994. "Where Are You Really From?" In Carl E. James and Adrienne Shadd (eds.), *Talking About Difference.* Toronto: Between the Lines, p. 11. Reprinted by permission.

Chapter 4

Quotation, p. 123: from Fraser, Sylvia. 1987. *My Father's House: A Memoir of Incest and Healing.* Toronto: Doubleday, pp. 8-11. Copyright © 1987 by Sylvia Fraser. Reprinted with the permission of Doubleday Canada Limited.

Chapter 5

Quotation, p. 159: from O'Reilly-Fleming, Thomas. 1993. *Down and Out in Canada: Homeless Canadians.* Toronto: Canadian Scholar's Press, p. 56. Reprinted by permission.

Quotations, pp. 166, 178: from Lesley Harman, *When a Hostel Becomes a Home: Experiences of Women.* Toronto: Garamond Press, 1989. Reprinted with permission of Garamond Press.

Box 5.2, p. 175: from Chambliss, William J. 1994. *Crime and the Legal Process.* New York: McGraw-Hill. © 1969 McGraw-Hill, New York. Reprinted by permission.

Box 5.2, p. 175: Criminal Code of Canada: 175(1). Source: Justice Canada. Reproduced with the permission of the Minister of Public Works and Government Services Canada, 1996.

Chapter 6

Quotation, pp. 199-200: Owen, Bruce. 1996. "Harrassment Ends in Firings." *Winnipeg Free Press* (March 23). Reprinted by permission.

Box 6.3, p. 223: from Weinraub, Bernard. 1994. "Scarier Than Dinosaurs: The Sexes." *The New York Times* (January 5):B1. © 1994 New York Times Company. Reprinted by permission.

Chapter 7

Quotation, p. 233: from Kaihla, Paul. 1991. "Terror in the Streets." *Maclean's* (March 25):18-21. Reprinted by permission.

Quotation, pp. 240-41: from *The Myth of Delinquency* (pp. 240-241) by Elliott Leyton (1979). Used by permission of McClelland & Stewart Inc., Toronto, The Canadian Publishers.

Quotation, p. 242: from Letkemann, Peter. 1973. *Crime as Work.* Englewood Cliffs, NJ: Prentice Hall, p. 136. Reprinted with the permission of Simon & Schuster. Copyright © 1973 by Prentice Hall, Inc.

Quotation, p. 243: from Wolf, Daniel. 1996. "A Bloody Biker War." *Maclean's* (January 15):10-11. Reprinted by permission.

Quotation, p. 248: from Comack, Elizabeth. 1996. *Women in Trouble.* Halifax: Fernwood Publishing.© 1996 Fernwood Publishing. Reprinted by permission.

Quotation, p. 265: from Quigley, Tim. 1994. "Some Issues in the Sentencing of Aboriginal Offenders." Cited in Royal Commission on Aboriginal Peoples Report. 1996. "Bridging the Cultural Divide," pp. 273-274. Reprinted by permission of the author.

Quotation, p. 266: from Greenspan, Edward. 1982. "The Role of the Defence Lawyer in Sentencing." In Craig Boydell and Ingrid Connidis (eds.), *The Canadian Criminal Justice System.* Toronto: Holt, Rinehart and Winston. Originally cited in *The Trial of Queen Caroline* (1821). Referred to in Freedman. 1975. *Lawyers Ethics in an Adversary System.* New York: Bobbs-Merrill.

Chapter 8

Quotation, p. 277: from O'Reilly-Fleming, Thomas. 1993. *Down and Out in Canada: Homeless Canadians.* Toronto: Canadian Scholar's Press, pp. 147-149. Reprinted by permission.

Cited on pp. 287-289: from Lenski, Gerhard. 1966. *Power and Privilege: A Theory of Social Stratification.* New York: McGraw-Hill.

Box 8.2, p. 295: from Koch, George. 1993. "Soap Sellers Turned Welfare Advocates." *Alberta Report/Western Report* (November 22) 20:20. Reprinted by permission.

Chapter 9

Quotation, p. 315: from Pheasant, Valerie B. 1994. "My Mother Used to Dance." In Carl James and Adrienne Shadd (eds.), *Talking About Difference.* Toronto: Between the Lines, pp. 35-36. Reprinted by permission.

Quotation, pp. 319-20: from Fleras, Augie, and John Leonard Elliott. 1996. *Unequal Relations: An Introduction to Race, Ethnic and Aboriginal Dynamics in Canada,* 2nd ed. Scarborough, ON: Prentice Hall. © Prentice Hall Canada Inc. Used by permission.

Quotation, p. 322: from Desai, Sabra. 1994. "But You Are Different." In Carl James and Adrienne Shadd (eds.), *Talking About Difference.* Toronto: Between the Lines, p. 191. Reprinted by permission.

Quotations, pp. 322, 330: from James, Carl. 1995. *Seeing Ourselves: Exploring Race, Ethnicity and Culture.* Toronto: Thompson Educational Publishing, pp. 60, 107. Reprinted by permission.

Box 9.2, p. 323: from Collins, Doug. Quotations from various articles in *The North Shore News,* North Vancouver, BC. © North Shore News. Reprinted by permission .

Quotation, pp. 327-28: from Labaton, Stephen. 1994. "Denny's Gets a Bill for the Side Order of Bigotry." *New York Times* (May 29):E4. © 1994 New York Times Company. Reprinted by permission.

Box 9.3, p. 334: from Kallen, Evelyn. 1991. "Ethnicity and Human Rights in Canada." In P. Li (ed.), *Race and Ethnic Relations in Canada.* Toronto: Oxford University Press, pp. 77-97. Reprinted by permission of the author.

Quotation, p. 338: from Shadd, Adrienne. 1991. "Institutionalized Racism and Canadian History." In Ormond McKague (ed.), *Racism in Canada.* Saskatoon: Fifth House, p. 1. Reprinted by permission of the author.

Chapter 10

Quotation, p. 355: from Wolf, Naomi. 1990. *The Beauty Myth.* Toronto: Random House of Canada, pp. 202-05. Copyright © 1990. Reprinted by permission of Random House of Canada Limited.

Chapter 11

Quotations, pp. 397, 419: from Wendell, Susan. 1989. "Toward a Feminist Theory of Disability." In E.D. Nelson and B.W. Robinson (eds.). 1995. *Gender in the 1990s.* Scarborough, ON: Nelson. First published in *Hypatia: A Journal of Feminist Philosophy.* 1989. 4(2):104-124. Reprinted by permission of the author.

Box 11.1, p. 400: Answers to the Sociology Quiz on Aging and Disability. Reproduced by authority of the Minister of Industry, 1996, Statistics Canada, from *Adults with Disabilities: Employment Education and Health,* Cat. no. 82-554.

Quotation, p. 406: from Heinrichs, Daniel. 1996. *Caring for Norah.* Winnipeg: Daniel Heinrichs Publishing. Reprinted by permission.

Box 11.4, p. 422: from Tyler, Patrick. 1994. "China's Discus Champ: Alone, Disabled and Barred." *New York Times* (September 8):A3. © 1994 New York Times Company. Reprinted by permission.

Chapter 12

Quotation, p. 435: from Popoff, Wilfred. 1996. "One Day You're Family, the Next Day You're Fired." *The Globe and Mail* (March 14):A22. Reprinted by permission of the author.

Quotation, p. 440: from Heron, Craig. 1993. "The Crisis of the Craftsman." In Graham S. Lowe and Harvey J. Krahn (eds.), *Work in Canada.* Scarborough, ON: Nelson, p. 10. Reprinted by permission of the author.

Chapter 13

Quotation, pp. 473-74: from Vallières, Pierre. 1971. *White Niggers of America.* Toronto: McClelland & Stewart. Used by permission of McClelland & Stewart Inc., Toronto, The Canadian Publishers.

Box 13.4, p. 502: from Cook, Ramsay. 1995. *Canada, Quebec, and the Use of Nationalism* (2nd ed.). Toronto: McClelland & Stewart. Used by permission of McClelland & Stewart Inc., Toronto, The Canadian Publishers.

Chapter 14

Box 14.2, p. 520: The Simpsons. Excerpts of dialogue. Reprinted by permission.

Concept Table 14.B, p. 529: from Hatfield, Elaine. 1995. "What Do Women and Men Want From Love and Sex?" In Elizabeth Allgeier and Naomi McCormick (eds.), 1983. *Changing Boundaries.* Palo Alto, CA: Mayfield Publishing, pp. 106-35. Reprinted by permission of the editors.

Cited on p. 526: Lone-parent families and common-law families (quotations from Statistics Canada data within text). Reproduced by authority of the Minister of Industry, 1996, Statistics Canada, from *General Social Survey,* Cat. no. 11-612, 1995.

Quotation, p. 545: from Church, Elizabeth. 1996. "Kinship and Stepfamilies." In Marion Lynn (ed.), *Voices: Essays on Canadian Families.* Scarborough, ON: Nelson. Reprinted by permission of the author.

Chapter 15

Box 15.2, p. 560: from Fisher, Luke. 1994. "A Holy War Over Holidays." *Maclean's* (August 12):26. Reprinted by permission.

Chapter 17

Quotation, p. 637: from Newman, Peter C. 1993. "Trees Are Renewable, But Forests Are Not." *Maclean's* (August 16):44. Reprinted by permission.

INDEX

To the owner of this book

We hope that you have enjoyed *Sociology In Our Times, First Canadian Edition,* and we would like to know as much about your experiences with this text as you would care to offer. Only through your comments and those of others can we learn how to make this a better text for future readers.

School ________________ Your instructor's name ______________________

Course ___________ Was the text required? _______ Recommended? _____

1. What did you like the most about *Sociology In Our Times?*

____

____

____

2. How useful was this text for your course?

____

____

____

3. Do you have any recommendations for ways to improve the next edition of this text?

____

____

____

4. In the space below or in a separate letter, please write any other comments you have about the book. (For example, please feel free to comment on reading level, writing style, terminology, design features, and learning aids.)

____

____

____

____

Optional

Your name ______________________________ Date _________________

May ITP Nelson quote you, either in promotion for *Sociology In Our Times* or in future publishing ventures?

Yes _______ No _______

Thanks!

You can also send your comments to us via e-mail at **college_arts_hum@nelson.com**

PLEASE TAPE SHUT. DO NOT STAPLE.

TAPE SHUT

TAPE SHUT

FOLD HERE

Canada Post Corporation
Société canadienne des postes

Postage paid	Port payé
if mailed in Canada	si posté au Canada
Business Reply	**Réponse d'affaires**

0066102399 01

Nelson

0066102399-M1K5G4-BR01

TAPE SHUT

TAPE SHUT

ITP NELSON
MARKET AND PRODUCT DEVELOPMENT
PO BOX 60225 STN BRM B
TORONTO ON M7Y 2H1